MW01537261

Annual Unemployment

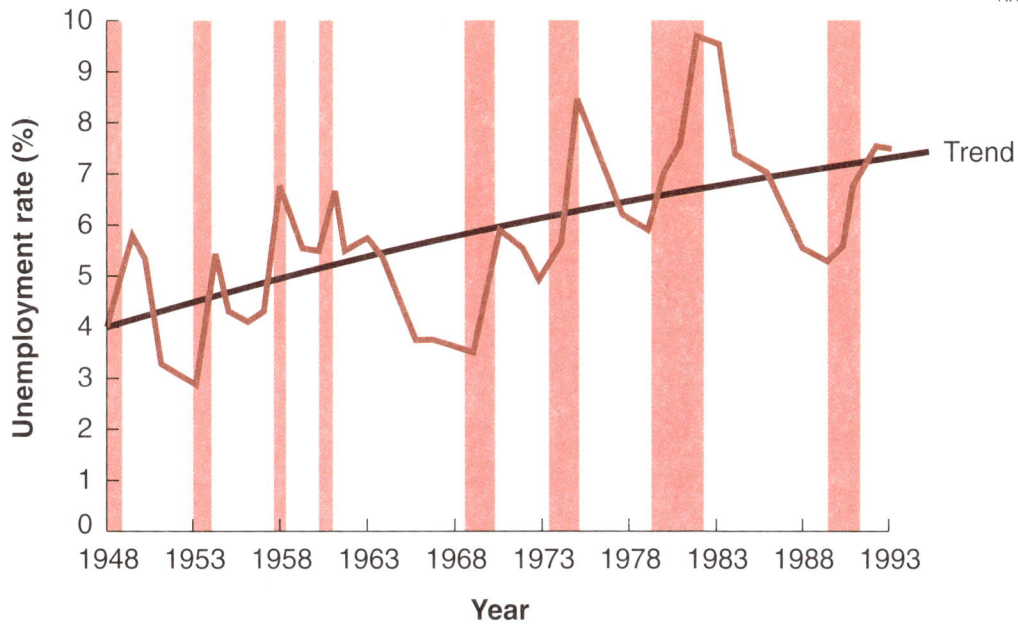

Recent Inflation in the United States

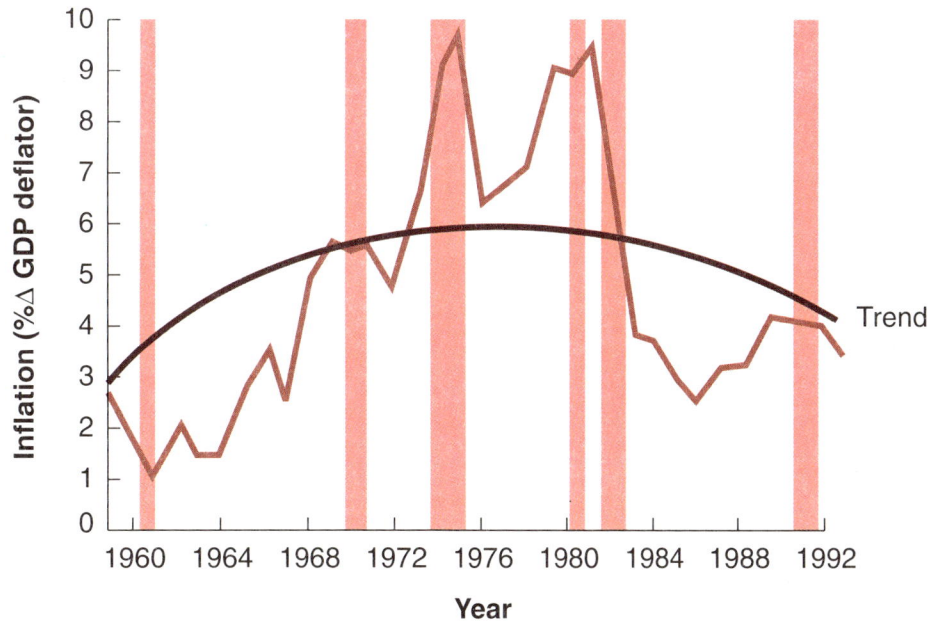

PRINCIPLES
OF
ECONOMICS

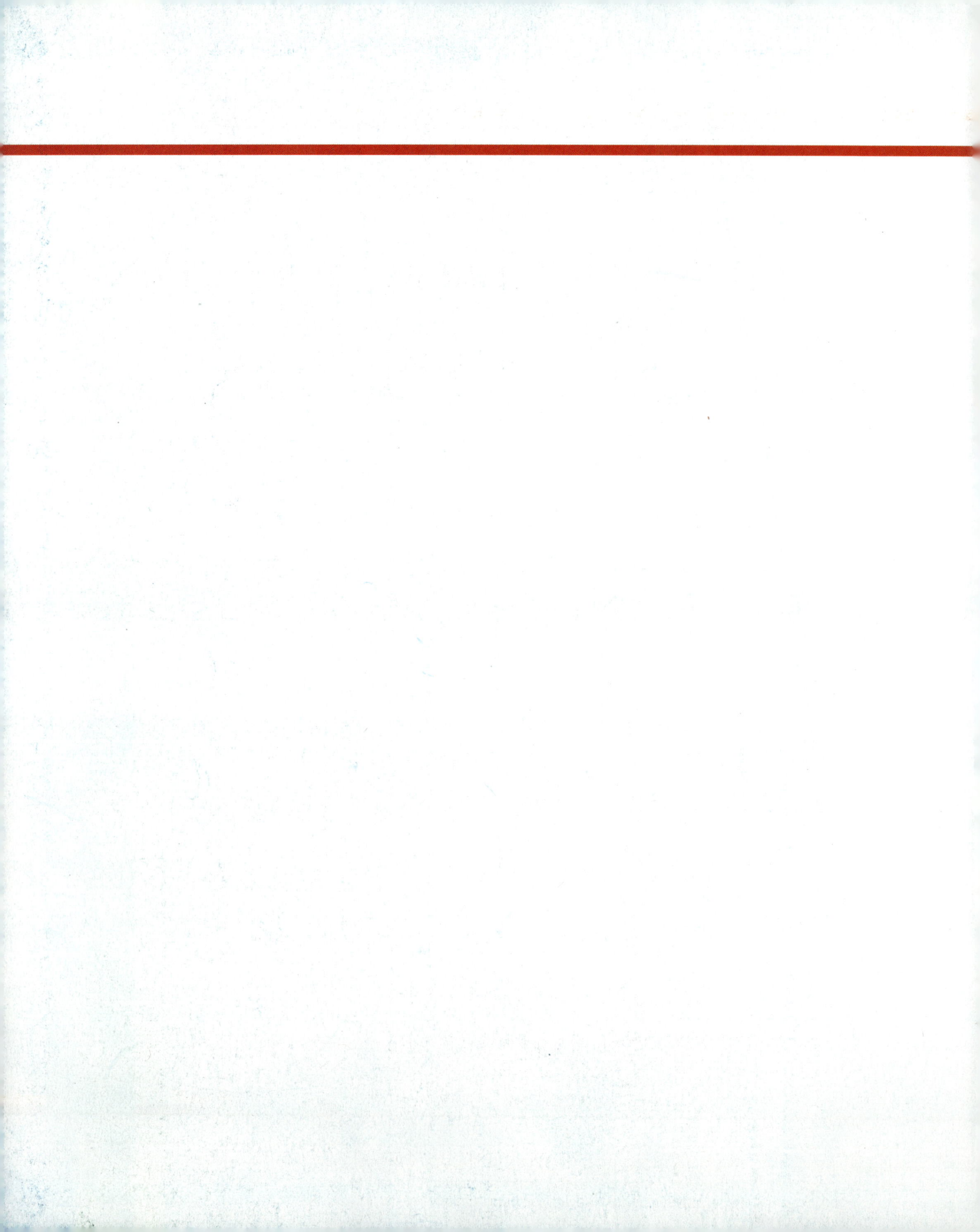

PRINCIPLES OF ECONOMICS

WILLIAM S. BROWN
UNIVERSITY OF ALASKA

WEST PUBLISHING COMPANY

MINNEAPOLIS/ST. PAUL   NEW YORK
LOS ANGELES   SAN FRANCISCO

PRODUCTION CREDITS

Artist: Ed Rose, Visual Graphics Systems
Composition: University Graphics, Inc.
Copyeditor: Pat Lewis
Cover Image: Photograph copyright © Andy Goldsworthy from *A Collaboration with Nature,* Abrams, 1990.
Dummy Artist: Diane Beasley
Cover and Text Design: Diane Beasley
Indexer: Jo-Anne Naples, Naples Editing Services

WEST'S COMMITMENT TO THE ENVIRONMENT

In 1906, West Publishing Company began recycling materials left over from the production of books. This began a tradition of efficient and responsible use of resources. Today, up to 95 percent of our legal books and 70 percent of our college and school texts are printed on recycled, acid-free stock. West also recycles nearly 22 million pounds of scrap paper annually–the equivalent of 181,717 trees. Since the 1960s, West has devised ways to capture and recycle waste inks, solvents, oils, and vapors created in the printing process. We also recycle plastics of all kinds, wood, glass, corrugated cardboard, and batteries, and have eliminated the use of Styrofoam book packaging. We at West are proud of the longevity and the scope of our commitment to the environment.

Production, Prepress, Printing and Binding by West Publishing Company.

PRINTED WITH SOY INK™ ∞ TEXT IS PRINTED ON 10% POST CONSUMER RECYCLED PAPER

British Library Cataloguing-in-Publication Data. A catalogue record for this book is available from the British Library.

COPYRIGHT © 1995 BY
WEST PUBLISHING COMPANY
610 Opperman Drive
P.O. Box 64526
St. Paul, MN 55164-0526

All rights reserved

Printed in the United States of America

02 01 00 99 98 97 96 95   8 7 6 5 4 3 2 1 0

Library of Congress Cataloging-in-Publication Data
Brown, William S. (William Stanley), 1950–
   Principles of economics / William S. Brown.
      p.   cm.
   Includes bibliographical references and index.
   ISBN 0-314-04229-6
   1. Economics.   I. Title.
HB171.5.B722   1995
330--dc20   94-16366
                                 CIP

PHOTO CREDITS

6a Thomas Zimmerman, © Tony Stone Worldwide; **6b** Trevor Wood, © Tony Stone Worldwide; **14** The Bettmann Archive; **52** Hulton Deutsch Collection Limited; **53** Bildarchiv Preussischer Kulturbesitz; **58** The Bettmann Archive; **93** Historical Pictures Collection, Stock Montage; **118** Reprinted by permission of the Wall Street Journal, © 1994 Dow Jones & Co., Inc. All Rights Reserved; **120** Greg Pease, © Tony Stone Worldwide; **138** Charles Krupa, © AP/Wide World Photos; **158** Peter Vandermark, © Stock, Boston; **159** University of Chicago Library; **216** National Portrait Gallery Collection; **251** Steven Barall; **293** Historical Pictures/Stock Montage, Inc.; **299** © Joe McNally, Sygma; **315a** AP/Wide World Photos, Inc.; **315b** Archive Photos/Express Newspapers; **318** © 1982 Bill Gallery, Stock, Boston; **347a** Princeton University Libraries; **347b** The Bettmann Archive; **356** The Bettmann Archive; **363** Columbia University, Columbiana Collection; **375** Wide World Photos, Inc.; **377** Whittle Sports Properties; **380** The Bettmann Archive; **406** The Bettmann Archive; **409** Charles Gupton, Stock, Boston; **414** Andy Sacks, Tony Stone Worldwide; **437** Keith Wood, Tony Stone Worldwide; **461** © Daemmrich, The Image Works; **470** AP/Wide World Photos, Inc.; **485** © P. Gontier, The Image Works; **495** Pete Seaward, Tony Stone Worldwide; **522** © C. Vergara, Photo Researchers, Inc.; **530** Ken Abbott, University of Colorado; **534** © Rod Planck/Tony Stone Worldwide; **547** © Bob Stern/The Image Works; **548** AP/Wide World Photos; **558** © Bob Daemmrich/Stock, Boston; **561** Steven Barall; **572** U.S. Department of Commerce; **591** Courtesy of Dr. Milo Keynes; **596** © Richard Pasley, Liaison International; **679** UPI/Bettmann **698** © Crandall, The Image Works; **705** Courtesy of Century 21 Real Estate Corporation 1994 **725** © Joseph Clauss, Tony Stone Worldwide; **740** John Ficara, Sygma; **742** © 1993 Peter Gridley, FPG International; **745** © Tony Savino, The Image Works; **746** Steven Barall; **791** © Diana Walker, Gamma-Liaison; **792** © Eric Sandler, Gamma-Liaison; **794** © Arthur Grace, Sygma; **812** © Scott Thode, Int'l Stock Photo; **813** Matthew Neal McVay, Tony Stone Worldwide; **816** Courtesy of Northwestern University, Evanston Photo Studios, Inc.; **823** UPI Bettmann; **838a** University of Chicago **838b** The Hoover Institution, Stanford, CA; **845** Federal Reserve Bank of Minneapolis; **850** The Bettmann Archive; **853** © Jane Scherr, University of California, Berkeley; **862** Steven Barall; **877** Springer/Bettmann Film Archive; **889** The Bettmann Archive; **893** © Tass from Sovfoto; **901** Bettmann; **927** Satoru Ohmori, Gamma-Liaison; **931** National Security Agency; **955** McDonald's Corp.; **961** © Jim Pickerell 1991, Stock, Boston; **978** Reuters/Bettmann; **982** Courtesy of MIT

BRIEF CONTENTS

CONTENTS

PART III MICROECONOMICS II: INDUSTRIAL STRUCTURE AND FACTOR MARKETS   257

·······PART IV   MICROECONOMIC POLICIES   443

18 Markets and Government 445

CONTENTS

PART VI MONEY AND MACROECONOMIC POLICIES 719

28 Money, Banking, and the Federal Reserve 721

Functions and Definitions of Money 722
  The Evolution of Money 722
  Functions of Money 723
FOCUS ON: Should We Return to the Gold Standard? 724
  Measures of the Money Supply 726
Fractional Reserve Banking 730
  The Origins of Fractional Reserve Banking 731
  Fractional Reserve Banking Today 735
  The Money Multiplier 736
The Central Bank of the United States: The Federal Reserve System 737
  History of the Federal Reserve 737
  Structure of the Federal Reserve 739
  The Independence of the Fed 739
Tools of the Federal Reserve 739
FOCUS ON: Does the Fed Respond to Political Pressure? 740
  Open Market Operations 741
FOCUS ON: Printing Money, Inflation, and the Deficit 742
  The Required Reserve Ratio 743
  The Discount Rate 743
FOCUS ON: The Savings and Loan Association Crisis 744
FOCUS ON: Reforming the Financial System 746
  The Fed's Minor Tools 746
Summary 748
Key Terms and Concepts 749
Review Questions 749
Problems 750

29 Monetary Theory 751

The Quantity Theory of Money 752
  The Equation of Exchange 752
  The Crude Quantity Theory of Money 752
  A Modern Version of the Quantity Theory of Money 755
  Applying the Modern Quantity Theory 757
Supply and Demand in the Money Market 758
  The Money Supply Curve 759
FOCUS ON: P*: A Modern Application of the Quantity Theory 760
  The Money Demand Curve 760
  Equilibrium in the Money Market 763

FOCUS ON: Interest Rates in the Real World 764
  Shifting the Money Supply Curve 766
  Shifting the Money Demand Curve 767
The Monetary Transmission Mechanism 768
  Interest Rate Linkages 768
FOCUS ON: Forecasting with the Yield Curve 769
  Graphical Analysis 770
  Milton Friedman's Theory of Money Demand 770
Complications: Unstable Money Demand 773
Summary 775
Key Terms and Concepts 775
Review Questions 776
Problems 776

30 Monetary Policy 779

Instruments, Intermediate Targets, and Policy Goals 780
Monetary Policy Complications: Lags, Expectations, and Credibility 781
  Monetary Policy Lags 781
  Expectations and Monetary Policy Effectiveness 782
  The Credibility Effect 784
Nondiscretionary Monetary Policy: The Constant Growth Rate Rule 785
  Assumptions of the Constant Growth Rate Rule 785
  Implementing the Monetary Rule 785
FOCUS ON: An Inflation Game 786
  Problems with the Monetary Rule 788
FOCUS ON: Monetary Policy in the Early 1980s: Volcker's Experiment with a Monetary Rule 790
OUR ECONOMIC HERITAGE: Milton Friedman: The Founder of Monetarism 792
Activist Monetary Policy: Targeting Interest Rates 793
  Assumptions of the Monetary Activists 793
  Implementation 793
FOCUS ON: Interest Rate Targeting in the 1990s 794
  Problems with Interest Rate Targeting 794
  Real Interest Rate Targeting: The Fisher Effect 796
Additional Monetary Targets 798
  Total Credit 798
  Exchange Rates 799
  Nominal Income 800
Foreign Complications 800
Summary 801

PART VII   THE INTERNATIONAL ECONOMY   881

34   Evolving Economic Systems 883

35   International Trade: Comparative Advantage and Gains from Trade 909

36   International Finance: The Balance of Payments and Exchange Rates 939

37   Policy in the Open Economy 971

•••••••PART VIII   THE ECONOMIC DEGREE   995

38   The Economics Degree 997

Glossary of Key Terms and Symbols G-1

Index I-1

PREFACE

"The only reason, the only excuse, for the study of economic theory is to make this world a better place in which to live."

Wesley Clair Mitchell (1874–1948)

The past 20 years have been marked by dramatic economic change, and there is no hint that this trend is about to end. For example:

- There has been a massive shift of labor from manufacturing into the service industries. In 1970, over a third of all workers were employed in goods-producing industries; today, the proportion is barely a fifth. Some service industry jobs are high paying, but many are not.

- The mass-production factory system is becoming a thing of the past as production methods become more specialized. One implication of this change is that most new jobs are being created by small businesses. Another implication is that many large corporations are laying off workers in an effort to become more efficient.

- Few firms can ignore international competition, and some firms have met the challenge of low-cost imported goods by moving their production facilities abroad. One consequence is job loss with downward pressure on wages for many workers. Another consequence is that policymakers must take the threat of industrial relocation seriously: without tax incentives, firms may relocate in a different state or even abroad.

- The collapse of the Soviet Union means that the traditional debate between capitalism and socialism is largely irrelevant. The problem today is to find the best transition path from socialism to capitalism—and the best variety of capitalism.

The pervasiveness of change and evolution means that it is not sufficient to learn a particular body of economic theory and set of economic facts, because the facts are constantly changing. Some economic models that performed well in the past may not work well today or tomorrow. Economists do not and cannot have answers to all of the questions because new questions crop up every day. Students must be aware of this, and they must be ready and able to compare different explanations for economic phenomena. To give students the idea that economics has reached its pinnacle of theoretical development is less than honest. It is also a quick way to assure that students lose interest in economics. Students will find economics more relevant when they are taught that it is evolving with the world around them.

It is this emphasis on economic change and evolution that distinguishes *Principles of Economics* from other principles books on the market. Virtually every idea is presented in historical context and with reference to alternative theories. For example, Adam Smith's *Wealth of Nations* is described in Chapter 1 as a response to the social changes of the 1700s, not merely as the first statement of the allocative power of self-correcting markets. Likewise, the discussion of Keynesian macroeconomics in Chapter 23 sets out the historical context—its relevance to Say's law and the Great Depression—before introducing the multiplier, equilibrium GDP, and so on. Contemporary developments in economic theory are also discussed in evolutionary context. For example, the new industrial economics is developed in Chapter 14 as a response to the failures of the structure-conduct-performance approach; Chapter 27 presents the new growth theory as a consequence of the failure of standard growth models to account for the productivity crisis of the 1970s and 1980s; and Chapter 37 introduces the new international economics as a synthesis between the microeconomics of imperfect competition and standard trade theory.

A FIRM FOUNDATION IN MAINSTREAM ANALYSIS

An understanding of the evolution of economic theory helps develop the ability to think critically, perhaps the most important skill in the economy of tomorrow. The evolutionary perspective means that we must suspend judgment and examine new and alternative views. But this does *not* mean that we can dismiss traditional economics. The law of comparative advantage, discovered early in the nineteenth century, has long been used to show that all countries can gain from the absence of tariffs and other trade restrictions. It is applicable even in this era of tariffs and regional trading blocs because it provides a framework for analysis and a norm for comparison. Without such a framework, it would be difficult to understand who will gain and who will lose from the North American Free Trade Agreement—or the next trading bloc to develop. The world is changing, and economics is changing along with it, but we are a long way from discarding the body of economic knowledge developed over the past two centuries.

It is the existence of a common core of knowledge that distinguishes economics from the other social sciences. This core forms the foundation for economic discussion and debate, and students without a solid understanding of that core are incapable of continuing their studies in economics. Still, scientific debate requires a spirit of pluralism—a point made emphatically in a plea to the economics profession signed by over 40 top economists and published in the May 1992 issue of the *American Economic Review*.[1] *Principles of Economics* provides a solid and rigorous foundation in that core, as well as the pluralism demanded of objective inquiry.

PEDAGOGICAL FEATURES

Like all introductory texts on the market, *Principles of Economics* includes chapter objectives, summaries, key terms, and end-of-chapter questions. Additionally, all graphs are captioned with self-contained explanations to avoid the page-flipping

---

[1]"A Plea for Pluralistic and Rigorous Economics," *American Economic Review* 82 (May 1992): xxv. Among the signers were Moses Abramovitz, Kenneth Boulding, Paul Davidson, Edward Denison, Clive W. J. Granger, and Paul Samuelson.

shuffle that is so frustrating to students, and key formulas are collected at the end of the chapter where they are introduced. Additional pedagogical features of *Principles of Economics* include:

- Periodic *Recap* features to help the student digest material in manageable blocks. Recaps list the key points that students should understand before proceeding to the next section. Most chapters have three to five Recaps.

- Extensive use of real data and real-world examples. Good examples are a key to learning. Too many books use contrived examples with little reference to the real economy. Students often finish the course thinking that economics is all about widgets! *Principles of Economics* contains a wealth of current data and puts it in perspective so that students will know why the numbers are *important*. For example, the poverty data in Chapter 20 are presented both over time and by demographic group, and the actual values of tax credits are used when discussing the earned income tax credit. Most national income data from the period 1930–1993 are included, and the NBER recession dates are marked when appropriate on figures. In the international chapters, students not only see what has happened to the current and capital account over the past decades, but they also discover who the United States' major trading partners are and what products the United States imports and exports. Specific nontariff barriers—for example, on kiwi and automobile imports—are discussed, and the unintended consequences of trade restrictions are illustrated with a case study on computer software export restrictions.

- Discussions of "popular economics" by well-known contemporary economic thinkers. For example, Paul Krugman's *Age of Diminished Expectations* is discussed in Chapters 5 and 33, Labor Secretary Robert Reich's theory of deindustrialization is presented in Chapter 27, and CEA Chair Laura D'Andrea Tyson's work in *Who's Bashing Whom* is analyzed in Chapters 19 and 37. We owe it to our students to provide a careful analysis of the kinds of issues that we believe are so important that we take time away from our research for popular writing. This is also the kind of economics that students are going to be exposed to in the media. Students need to be aware of this information—and be ready to understand the underlying economics.

- Extensive international coverage. Four entire chapters are devoted to international economics, and international issues are discussed in many other chapters as well. For example, cost pressures from international competition are analyzed in Chapter 10; the impact of international competition on wage rates is discussed in Chapters 15 and 16; foreign antitrust laws are contrasted with U.S. antitrust laws in Chapter 19; the 1992 Earth Summit and global environmental policy cooperation are discussed in Chapter 21; the relationship between fiscal and trade deficits is discussed in Chapter 25; and foreign industrial policies are examined in Chapter 33.

- *Focus On* boxes. Most chapters have one or two Focus On boxes that apply or extend chapter concepts to real-world problems. These discussions are set off in boxes to avoid interrupting the flow of the core material. Among the topics included in the Focus On boxes are Reading the Financial Pages (Chapter 5), Cost Competition in High-Technology Industries (Chapter 10), The Value of Brand Names (Chapter 13), Inventory Adjustment and Economic Forecasting (Chapter 23), Can We Have Another Great Depression? (Chapter 26), The

Unemployment Insurance System (Chapter 27), Printing Money, Inflation, and the Deficit (Chapter 28), and The Role of Economists in the Former Soviet Union (Chapter 34).

- *Our Economic Heritage* biographies. Short biographies of 22 famous economists are sprinkled throughout the text. Both historical figures (including Keynes, Marshall, and Veblen) and contemporary greats (including Akerlof, Buchanan, and Tyson) are featured. These biographies not only highlight the economists' important contributions but explain how their personal experiences affected their interest in economics. Students who understand why economics is important to the masters will find it important to their own lives.
- Numerous game theory applications. Most contemporary texts include a chapter on game theory and strategic behavior, but this chapter often stands apart from the rest of the text. *Principles of Economics* includes applications of game theory in several chapters so that students can see the importance of this contemporary approach to economics. Game theory applications include labor/management bargaining (Chapter 16), public goods (Chapter 18), international policy coordination (Chapter 21), inflation policy (Chapter 30), and recessions as coordination failures (Chapter 32).

INNOVATIVE CHAPTERS

Principles of Economics covers the standard material and in a standard order, so most professors will need to make only minor revisions to their course outlines. In addition, several innovative chapters that reflect contemporary developments have been included. Among the more innovative chapters are:

- Chapter 14, "The New Industrial Economics." This chapter covers game theory and strategic decision making, contestable markets, rent-seeking behavior, and asymmetric information. In addition, several chapters throughout the text contain Focus On game theory applications.
- Chapter 21, "Economics and the Environment." An environmental chapter is obligatory today, but most books do little more than mention the Coase theorem and show that the optimal level of pollution is not zero. This chapter also provides discussions of common property resources, biodiversity, population growth, and international policy coordination.
- Chapter 33, "The Long Run: Growth and Productivity." After a brief discussion of Christina Romer's new economic history, this chapter provides a principles-level discussion of the neoclassical growth model, the social model of Bowles, et al., and Paul Romer's new growth theory. It then examines policies designed to stimulate productivity growth, including Aschauer's work on public infrastructure and the pros and cons of industrial policies.
- Chapter 34, "Evolving Economic Systems." This chapter breaks away from the standard "capitalism versus socialism" approach to comparative systems to focus on the contemporary issue of economic transition in the former socialist states, eurosclerosis, and the varieties of capitalism.
- Chapter 37, "Policy in the Open Economy." Most books treat tariffs in the inter-

national trade chapter and look at the advantages of fixed versus flexible exchange rates in the international finance chapter, but then say little more about international economic policies. This chapter explores the important issues of exchange rate target zones, regional trading blocs (including NAFTA and the European Union), policy coordination, and strategic trade policies.

- Chapter 38, "The Economics Degree." Students often end the principles course asking, "So what?" This chapter supplies an answer: it provides the student with information on additional economics courses, career paths, and graduate school. It serves both as a capstone chapter and as an aid in the advising process.

COURSE OUTLINES

Principles of Economics is meant to be used in a two-semester course for students with little or no previous exposure to economics. It is available both as a single, two-semester hardback and as two, one-semester paperbacks. The paperbacks are designed so that either micro or macro can be taught first in the course sequence. The macro split does not assume that the student has previously worked through the micro chapters. Both paperback splits include the introductory chapters (1–6), the international chapters (34–37), and the final chapter (38). Students planning to take the two-semester sequence can save a little money by buying the two-semester hardback, but they may find it easier to carry the paperbacks with them to class.

ANCILLARIES

The following ancillaries are available for use with *Principles of Economics:*

- *Study Guide.* Written by Melissa Thomasson, University of Arizona, and Daniel Lee, Shippensburg University. This supplement is available in micro/macro splits as well as a combined volume.

  Scrupulously coordinated with the text, each chapter of the manual presents overviews as well as a review of key concepts, graphs and equations. Essay, completion, multiple-choice and true/false questions are included with complete answers given. Each chapter affords extensive practice in graphical analysis and construction. "Beyond the Basics" problems refer to a current article or reading which challenges the students' skills in applying economic theory.
- *Instructor's Manual.* Written by the author, William Brown, and Liz Hagen, University of Montana. This supplement offers chapter overviews, teaching suggestions and alternative examples. Complete answers to all end-of-chapter questions and problems are provided as well as additional essay and discussion questions.
- *Test Bank.* Written by William Shingleton of Indiana University Northwest and available as a manual and on WESTEST 3.0, a computerized testing program for DOS, Windows and Macintosh. The test bank contains over 4,000 multiple-choice and true/false items, all classified according to one of six categories: definition, theory, application, history/institutions, policy and table/calculation.
- *Transparency Acetates and Masters.* All of the graphs and art from the text are available

as masters. Over 150 4-color acetates of key graphs and art from the text are also available to adopters.

- *Astound Presentation Software.* Astound presentation software is an electronic transparency package that enables an instructor to create and manipulate images for classroom display. A package of slides which consists of significant graphs and key figures from *Principles of Economics* accompany the software. The instructor may edit these slides or add to them as desirable.

- *West's Video Library for Economics.* Critical thinking and thematic videos are available for classroom use that apply the concepts in this text. The videos, in particular, stress the global economy as well as other select topics such as the deficit and the natural environment. An instructor's manual for the video library includes lecture notes on the videos.

- *Limited English Proficiency (LEP) Manual.* Written by Elaine Kirn, Language Arts Chair and ESL Specialist, West Los Angeles College, this manual is designed to help ESL/developmental students succeed in the course. Tied specifically to the foundational chapters (1–6), the LEP manual aids students in recognizing parts of speech, deriving meaning from context, as well as offering a number of techniques and exercises for analyzing the textbook.

- *West Graphing Software.* Interactive tutorial software is available to students which is specifically tied to the core micro and macro chapters of *Principles of Economics.* The package which works within Windows requires the student to create, modify and interact with key graphs.

- *The Writer's Guide to College Economics.* Written by Thomas L. Wyrick of Southwest Missouri State University. This title is a paperback research and writing guide designed to help students in preparing term papers and reports. More than just a style and reference manual, the *Writer's Guide to College Economics* also seeks to improve the students' ability to think like an economist.

TO THE STUDENT

Principles of economics is one of the most popular college courses in the United States—over a million students enroll in introductory economics courses every year. Many of these students take economics as a requirement. It is required for business degrees and most social science degrees, and it also serves as a liberal arts core requirement at many schools. If you are one of those students who is required to take this course, take heart: thousands of students actually choose economics as an elective. They take economics for a simple reason: economics is important. It is indispensable for understanding the world around us. It is a way to think. It will help you understand the evening news. It will help you vote intelligently. It will help you make important career decisions. And if you do go into business when you graduate, you will find that economic reasoning is mandatory every day.

Now back up a moment and re-read the previous paragraph. It said that many college students take economics classes. It said that economics would help you vote and solve problems—*but it said nothing about the factual content of economics*. This isn't an oversight; the factual content of economics changes! You do need to know some economic facts, but the most important thing to learn from an economics class is how to *think* like an economist. Thinking like an economist will help you see why economic issues are important—how they affect your job prospects, the value of your savings, and your future. It will teach you that everything valuable involves a choice and that alternative decisions always have costs and benefits. It will teach you how to think logically and how to use economic reasoning on a daily basis.

AND FINALLY . . .

Writing a textbook isn't as difficult as it is demanding. It requires three or four years of intense discipline: put it down for just a week, and you'll inevitably discover that you'll spend another week just finding out where you were. That said, writing *Principles of Economics* was a pleasure in one important sense: it was a joy to know that it will provide students with their first exposure to something as exciting—and important—as economics.

My debts are many. I could not have written this book without the help and encouragement of my editor, Bob Horan. Bob had the faith that I could write a successful book, and he kept pushing me to write the best book that I could. Bob and I worked closely with the developmental editor, Janine Wilson, and the production editor, Stacy Lenzen. Janine and Stacy turned an unruly manuscript into the stunningly beautiful book you are holding.

Principles of Economics has been class tested for three years at the University of Alaska, and I thank my students who put up with far too many typos and other problems inherent in working from a living document. I listened to and learned from all of my students' comments and suggestions, but want to single out two for their special contributions, Marco Castaneda and Larry Hurlock. Finally, West Publishing is to be commended for finding the resources to subject the first edition of this book to nearly 100 reviewers, many of whom looked at several portions of the manuscript as it went through three complete drafts. I incorporated as many of the reviewers' ideas as possible and was amazed at the diligence that most reviewers put into their reviews. The reviewers were:

Christine Amsler
Michigan State University

Glen Atkinson
University of Nevada—Reno

Moshen Bahmani-Oskooee
University of Wisconsin—Milwaukee

Bill Ballard
College of Charleston

A. Paul Baroutsis
Slippery Rock University

Raymond G. Batina
Washington State University

Randall W. Bennett
Gonzaga University

Basudeb Biswas
Utah State University

John P. Blair
Wright State University

Bob Blewett
St. Lawrence University

Scott Bloom
North Dakota State University

Laura A. Boyd
Denison University

W. David Bradford
University of New Hampshire

Kathleen Brook
New Mexico State University

Paul Burkett
Indiana State University

Michael J. Carter
University of Massachusetts—Lowell

David L. Cleeton
Oberlin College

Addington Coppin
Oakland University

Allin Cottrell
Wake Forest University

Sarah Culver
University of Alabama—Birmingham

Susan Dadres
Texas Christian University

Jamshid Damooei
California Lutheran University

Gregg Davis
Marshall University

David Denslow
University of Florida

Smile Dube
California State University—Sacramento

Mary E. Edwards
St. Cloud State University

Beth Ehresman
Northern Illinois University

David Emery
St. Olaf College

Brendan P. Finucane
Shippensburg State University

Robert P. Gilles
Virginia Polytechnic Institute

Bob Gillette
Texas A&M University

Arunee C. Grow
Mesa Community College

Liz Hagen
University of Montana

Simon Hakim
Temple University

Craig Heinicke
Baldwin-Wallace College

Gregory D. Hess
University of Kansas

Dennis K. Hoover
AT&T Economic Analysis Division

Lee Huskey
University of Alaska—Anchorage

Adam Kessler
Fairleigh Dickinson—Rutherford

Pauline W. Kopecky
Oklahoma State University

Michael Kupilik
University of Montana

J. David Lages
Southwest Missouri State University

Daniel Y. Lee
Shippensburg University

Anu Luther
Santa Clara University

Henry N. McCarl
University of Alabama—Birmingham

J. Harold McClure, Jr.
Villanova University

Amy L. McCormick
William and Mary University

Margaret Malixi
California State University—Bakersfield

Michael L. Marlow
*California Polytechnic State University—
San Luis Obispo*

Ann Mari May
University of Nebraska—Lincoln

Charles Michalopoulos
Virginia Polytechnic University

Elliott Middleton
Metropolitan State University

Janet Miller
New Mexico State University

Gary Mongiovi
St. Johns University

Paul L. Morgan
Westmont College

Noelwah R. Netusil
Reed College

Nicholas R. Noble
Miami University

Anthony Patrick O'Brien
Lehigh University

Dennis M. O'Toole
Virginia Commonwealth University

Jan Palmer
Ohio University

Maurice Pfannestiel
Wichita State University

Keith E. Phillips
University of Tennessee—Knoxville

Ronnie J. Phillips
Colorado State University

Kathleen Possai
Wayne State University

Thomas Potiowsky
Portland State University

James J. Rakowski
University of Notre Dame

Jean Hart Sandver
Capital University

Sue Lynn Sasser
University of South Dakota

George A. Schieren
Appalachian State University

Richard C. Schiming
Mankato State University

Mehrdad Setayesh
University of Texas at Arlington

Edwin A. Sexton
Virginia Military Institute

Virginia Shingleton
Valparaiso University

William Shingleton
Indiana University, Northwest

Ben Shippen, Jr.
Florida State University

David E. Sisk
San Francisco State University

Charles L. Skoro
Boise State University

Robert Sorenson
University of Missouri—St. Louis

George A. Spiva
University of Tennessee

Frederick R. Strobel
Kalamazoo College

Ellen Szarleta
Canisius College

Paul M. Taube
University of Texas—Pan American

Robert W. Thomas
Iowa State University

Melissa Thomasson
University of Arizona

Ashish Vaidya
California State University, Los Angeles

Edward Vedder
Seattle, Washington

John Wade
Western Carolina University

C. Richard Waits
Texas Christian University

Fred Wallace
Appalachian State University

Arthur L. Welsh
Pennsylvania State University

Mark Wheeler
Eastern Michigan University

David Whitaker
University of Richmond

Charles K. Wilbur
University of Notre Dame

Dewey R. Woodall
Illinois State University

Jeffrey T. Young
St. Lawrence University

The real cost of any project of this magnitude is time. Not only time away from friends and family as I hibernated upstairs in front of my computer, but the times when my economic ruminations made it impossible for me to stop thinking economics even while I made the pretense of socializing. My wife Rhonda incurred every bit as much of these costs as I did. This book is dedicated to her.

William S. Brown
jfwsb@acad1.alaska.edu
Juneau, Alaska
September 1994

ABOUT THE AUTHOR

WILLIAM S. BROWN received his undergraduate degree from Texas Christian University in 1971 and his Ph.D. from the University of Colorado in 1977. His main research interests are policy issues, macroeconomics, and the economic transition of the former socialist economies. He is the author of numerous journal articles and two previous texts, *Macroeconomics* (Prentice-Hall, 1988) and *Introducing Econometrics* (West, 1991). Professor Brown has taught at several universities and has twice been cited for his teaching excellence. In his spare time, Bill enjoys salmon fishing, backpacking, and gourmet cooking. He lives in Juneau, Alaska, with his wife Rhonda and their Siamese cat Max. Their home, surrounded by 200-foot-high trees, is within jogging distance of the Mendenhall Glacier. Only occasionally do bears wander into the backyard.

PART I

INTRODUCTION

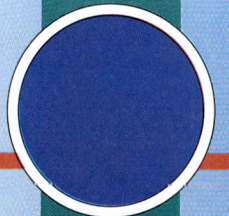

CHAPTER 1

What Is Economics?

Everyone needs to understand economics. It is indispensable in everyday life. Should you worry about the government deficit? Is now the right time for your business to expand? Will your savings be enough to put your children through college? Can the United States compete with foreign producers in Japan? In Taiwan? The answers to each of these questions—and more—lie in an understanding of economics.

Economics is the study of the ways societies and individuals produce, distribute, and use goods and services. The resources needed to make goods and services are not available in unlimited quantities, so a main focus of economic analysis centers on the questions of scarcity and the choices we make every day. At the most basic level, economics is a way to think, a technique for making sense of seemingly unrelated facts. More than anything else, the purpose of this course is to teach you how to think like an economist. The economists you see on television predicting recessions or forecasting interest rates rely on complex mathematical and computer models, but their careers inevitably started with a course quite similar to the one you have just begun. Some of you will go on to major in economics, but whether you do or not, the material you learn in this course will help you understand economic reports in the media and apply them in your work or your daily life. It will also help you know how and when it is necessary to discount those economic forecasts.

THINKING ECONOMICS

You already have some idea of what economics is about just from watching the evening news. To the newscaster, economics is about inflation, unemployment, the stock market, interest rates, and so on. Economics means much more than that to an economist. It is a way to think about not only these issues but other important issues of the day as well. For example, the horrible oil spill that occurred in Valdez, Alaska in 1989 made the nightly news for months. When you heard about the millions of dollars Exxon spent to clean up the mess and the number of jobs lost by the Alaskan fisheries, you might have thought, "This is what economics is about." It is, but the economist would immediately think beyond the numbers and consider the choices and *tradeoffs* that society made to allow the problem to happen and the choices that will have to be made to solve it.

When the tanker terminal at Valdez was built, society was making several tradeoffs including a tradeoff between increased availability of oil and the potential risk of damaging the environment. Assessing the tradeoff was exceedingly difficult—even for economists—because the value of oil is easy to determine but the probability of a disaster and the value of a healthy environment are not. The government regulations and safeguards that were placed on the terminal and tanker operations are an indication of the value assigned to the environment. Had regulators valued the environment more highly, even more stringent regulations would have been implemented. For example, each ship might have been required to have two captains and a double hull. Under these conditions, the damage from an accident would have been less severe—but the cost would have been higher oil prices rather than a contaminated environment.

Economists would also consider the tradeoff between fish and oil. At the time of the oil spill, the price of a barrel of oil was about $20, and millions of barrels were shipped annually. But oil is not the only use of the harbor at Valdez. A large fishing fleet is also based there. When oil was selling for $20, the wholesale price for the average-sized king salmon was about the same—and tons of salmon were harvested every year. The oil spill killed thousands of young salmon—no one knows how many—and may affect the salmon harvest for years to come. Furthermore, the amount of Alaskan oil is fixed—production may be exhausted by the end of this century—but if managed properly, the Alaskan salmon industry might last indefinitely. Is a fixed amount of oil important enough to our economy to have risked the environment and long-run supply of salmon? It certainly might be; that is an issue for the public and policymakers to decide. But before making this decision, they need to consult with economists. Economists are trained to look at and evaluate these kinds of tradeoffs.

This is the kind of analysis that economists do. In later chapters we will find out that choices and tradeoffs are often made automatically in the marketplace by the interaction of buyers and sellers. By studying these cases, economists often gain insight into the kinds of policies to propose when the usual outcome of market processes is undesirable.

In this chapter you will learn basic economic terminology and be exposed to the economic way of thinking. This chapter covers quite a bit of ground, but almost all of it will be discussed in more detail later, so don't let the volume of material overwhelm you. Our main aim is to introduce some terms and put the course in perspective.

AFTER READING AND STUDYING THIS CHAPTER, YOU SHOULD BE ABLE TO:
· · · Define economics and state the economic problem
· · · Discuss the three fundamental economic questions
· · · Briefly outline the history of economics
· · · Explain the role of scientific methodology in economic analysis
· · · Use the circular flow diagram to illustrate the relationship between households and firms

SCARCITY: THE ECONOMIC PROBLEM

Why are *tradeoffs* so important to economic analysis? The reason is that most economic problems involve **scarcity,** and scarcity forces us to choose between alternatives. Scarcity exists because human wants are seemingly unlimited, but the resources available to satisfy those wants are limited. A main focus of economics is the analysis of how individuals and societies respond to scarcity. In some societies—for example, a society of Buddhist monks—the scarcity problem is solved with an ethic that preaches the advantage of a simple lifestyle with few material possessions. In most modern societies, however, people desire ever increasing amounts of material possessions so a mechanism is necessary to handle scarcity.

Economic activities are the choices we make to deal with scarcity. When you decided to attend college, you were making an economic choice. For most students, the choice is to attend college or work full-time. There is not enough time to do both because time is scarce. What is the cost of attending college? It is probably much more than you think. Tuition and books represent only a small part of the cost of college. The real cost is what economists refer to as **opportunity cost**—the value of the best forgone alternative sacrificed when making a choice. The $15,000 job you turned down to attend college is part of the opportunity cost of attending college. The energy and effort you spend studying are a cost of attending college. And if you find that your studies leave you with less time to socialize, this is an opportunity cost of attending college as well. Scarcity means that we must make choices, and every choice involves an opportunity cost.

Scarcity The fundamental economic problem because wants are insatiable and resources are finite.

Opportunity cost The value of the best forgone alternative.

The Three Economic Questions

Economic systems have evolved in order to deal with scarcity. All economic systems must answer three fundamental questions.

FOCUS ON

SCARCITY AND THE MARKET FOR HORSE MANURE

The concept of scarcity is important enough for a rather detailed example. Economic theory says that something is scarce if and only if it is scarce relative to the uses society has for it; that using it one way means that some other use must be sacrificed. In the 1970s and early 1980s, New Jersey racetrack owners were able to sell horse manure to local mushroom farmers. Horse manure had value because it was scarce relative to the use society had for it. When cheaper Chinese mushrooms became available, however, New Jersey mushroom farmers were pushed out of the market, and the demand for New Jersey horse manure collapsed. The price of horse manure went to zero because it was no longer scarce relative to the wants of society.

And now, the rest of the story: With the collapse of the New Jersey mushroom industry, racetrack owners had to figure out a way to dispose of the manure. In 1985 the cost was close to $400,000 for Meadowlands Racetrack: $150,000 to dispose of the manure plus a loss of $250,000 the track had been earning from selling manure to the mushroom farmers. Facing similar losses, Saratoga Racetrack began test marketing a fertilizer for home gardeners, "Saratoga Organic."

SOURCE: Paul Vellely, "Horses Efforts Go to Waste," *London Times*, July 23, 1986, p 13.

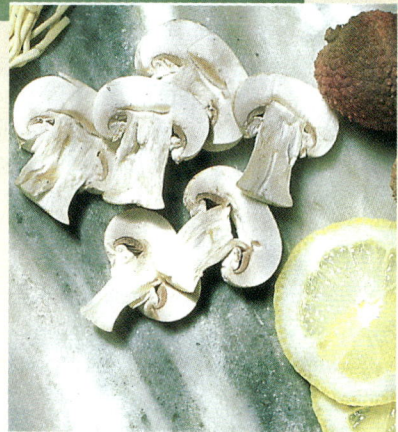

What to Produce? We cannot have everything. There are not enough economic resources—machines, workers, energy, and so on—to make this possible. Society must somehow decide which goods and services to produce.

How to Produce? This question has two major elements. First, society must choose a production technology. For example, should producers use lots of unskilled workers and a few machines, or a few skilled workers and lots of machines? This decision may be more complicated today than ever before because technology and alternative production methods are evolving so rapidly. Second, society must make institutional decisions regarding the ownership of the production facilities. Should production facilities be owned by private individuals, the government, or the workers?

Who Receives the Production? Should everyone get the same amount of goods and services? Should people be paid according to need or deed? This is not just a question of fairness. We will find out later that the chance of becoming rich may act as an *incentive* to make people work harder—and thus increase the amount of work that gets done.

. . . .

Economic Systems

Societies have used many kinds of economic systems to deal with the three economic questions, but it is convenient to classify economic systems into four groups.

Tradition. The fundamental economic questions are frequently answered according to tradition. This has been especially true in less-developed countries. For example, in many peasant societies, children normally follow the profession of their parents. This was the case under feudalism, the socioeconomic system that existed in Europe in the Middle Ages. If your parents were serfs, you would be a serf; if your parents were nobles, you would be a member of nobility as well. This system gave people a sense of identity. The problem with traditional economic systems is that they resist change to a fault. Children who are encouraged to follow the footsteps of their parents have little incentive for advancement.

Command. A command system exists when the ruling authority answers the economic questions by issuing decrees. Until its collapse in 1991, the economic system of the Soviet Union was, to a large extent, a command economy. The central planning authority answered the three economic questions according to its perception of the greater good for the state. To accomplish this end, factories and most farms were state owned, and workers were paid what often appeared to be arbitrary wages. Among other things, this meant that workers did not have an incentive to work hard, and too often the goods that were produced were not what consumers wanted. Cuba adopted a command system patterned after the Soviets in the 1960s and still maintains one today; North Korea can be classified as a command economy as well.

Market. **Market** economies answer the three economic questions by the interaction of individual choices, a process we discuss in the next section. To an economist, "markets" are not necessarily places; they are processes whereby buyers and sellers transact business. Most economists believe that market economies are more efficient than other economic systems, though this idea is not without its critics by any means. We will look at a brief example of the market process momentarily.

Although much economic analysis focuses on the behavior of "pure" market processes, it is important to realize that the market is a social institution and the product of culture and history. Even a "pure" market economy requires rules on

Market economy An economic system where decisions about resource allocations are made by voluntary interactions between buyers and sellers.

ownership and property rights. Without culturally or governmentally sanctioned property rights, transactions would be of the "might makes right" variety—hardly what economists think of when they speak of markets. The historical influence on markets is apparent with just a brief look at different cultures: price haggling is encouraged in the streets of Tijuana but not in your local Safeway.

Mixed Economies. All economic systems have elements of tradition, command, and the market. For example, though most economic decisions in the United States are made in the market, the U.S. economy also has elements of both command and tradition, so it is best classified as a **mixed economy.** The government decides how many resources to devote to the military or highways, regulates the number of captains on ships, and so on. Traditional elements persist in several aspects of American society. For example, despite the feminist revolution of the 1960s and 1970s, some jobs are widely perceived as "men's jobs" and others as "women's jobs." (How many men do you find employed as office receptionists? How many women are CEOs of large corporations? And it is still illegal for American women to serve on the front lines during war.) The existence of command and traditional elements in the economy explains why the U.S. economy and the economies of the Western democracies are classified as mixed economies.

Mixed economy An economic system that combines elements of different economic systems.

MARKET INCENTIVES: AN EXAMPLE

Why do so many economists believe that the market system is more efficient than other economic systems? There are several reasons, but the main one is that markets provide incentives that encourage people to work and innovate. The incentives come in the form of profits and income. The following example will illustrate how markets work.

Suppose that, as finals approach, you perceive the need for the availability of blue books for sale outside the lecture hall. Thinking you can make a few dollars in the process, you buy 100 blue books at the bookstore for 5¢ each and decide to sell them for 25¢ to those unfortunate souls who forgot to buy them. As people start arriving for the exam, you make several sales, but some students, noting your rather exorbitant markup, make a last-minute dash to the bookstore and buy their blue books. You have two responses: If you think you can still sell all 100 books at 25¢, you should hold firm on your price. But if you are afraid that you will have many blue books left over when the exam begins, you should lower the selling price. People who would not pay 25¢ might pay 20¢. If sales are still slow, you can always drop the price even more. On the other hand, if you are really lucky—say, the bookstore burns down immediately after you buy your stock of blue books—you may be able to charge a dollar per book. This is how the market works: an enterprising individual perceives a need and attempts to fill it, making profits in the process. Prices adjust to assure that the quantity offered *(quantity supplied)* is equal to the quantity purchased *(quantity demanded)*.

Four comments about the market mechanism are necessary before going on. First, *price flexibility* has reduced the chance that there will be a shortage or glut in the marketplace. You raised and lowered the price of your blue books based upon the quantity demanded. Price inflexibility is one of the chief criticisms of command systems. The planners have no way of really knowing what or how much to produce unless they know what is happening to the selling price. The shortages that were so common in stores in the former Soviet Union were one result of price inflexibility. We will use graphical analysis in Chapter 3 to show the theory behind shortages.

Second, the market mechanism does not involve force. No one was forced to buy your blue books; they had the opportunity to buy them beforehand or run to the bookstore at the last minute. They only bought your books if they felt that the book was worth at least as much as the price you charged. That is, there was a **voluntary exchange.** Since both parties—the buyer and the seller—voluntarily agreed to the exchange, they both expected to be better off after the exchange. You would rather have money than the blue books; your customers would rather have the blue books than money, or they would not have made the purchase.

Voluntary exchange Trade between two parties that is not mandated by government decree.

Third, notice that the free market has helped allocate resources into the production process. You, the enterprising economics major, noted the need for last-minute blue books and responded accordingly and profitably. Other people had the same opportunity, but you saw it first and jumped in. If your enterprise is successful, however, you should expect other people to enter the last-minute blue books industry next semester. The increased availability of blue books—competition—will tend to lower the price of blue books and reduce your profits but benefit the consumers.

Finally, while most economists agree that profit incentives cause people to provide goods and services, whether the market always generates the "best" outcome is another question. In this example, it is possible that someone without a quarter or a blue book would not be able to take the exam and would fail the course. A traditional system that provided blue books to everyone might prevent this from occurring; a command system with distribution based on need might be able to do the same thing. Which solution would be "best" is certainly debatable, but the problem does explain why most societies choose to intervene in certain markets.

DEFINING ECONOMICS

These brief examples of economic thinking give a glimpse of what economics is about, but they do not really define the subject. Now it is time to define economics a bit more formally. We will look at five definitions. At first glance, these definitions may appear to be quite different, but a little thinking shows that they are really quite similar.

1. *Economics is the study of mankind in the everyday business of life.* This definition, suggested by Alfred Marshall (1842–1924), the great English economist of the nineteenth century, conveys the importance of economics.[1] Think for a

---

[1]Clearly, this definition is not quite politically correct; the politically correct wording today would be something along the lines of "The study of people in the everyday business of life," but we can excuse Marshall for this intransigence because of the times in which he lived. We might note, however, that some scholars believe that Marshall's greatest book, *Principles of Economics* (1890), was actually written by his wife Harriet, but the times, again, prevented her from taking credit for its authorship.

moment: What do you do that does not have an economic element? When are you not making a choice or tradeoff?

2. *Economics is the study of material provisioning.* This definition comes from Kenneth Boulding (1910–1993), an Englishman who did most of his work in the United States. Boulding's definition stresses that economics is not just about scarcity, but also about the distribution of material goods and services. Much of Boulding's work was an attempt to look at the ethical foundations of economic analysis.

3. *Economics is the science of choice.* This too comes from an English economist, Lionel Robbins (1898–1984). All economic decisions involve choices; if no choice is involved, you are not making a decision (it has been made for you). The term "science" is important as well. Economics is a science in the sense that it follows scientific methodology. It is perhaps significant that of all the social sciences, the Nobel Prize Committee recognizes only economics as being scientific enough to warrant the annual award.[2] This is partially because economics has a widely accepted theoretical core that permits statistical study and some experimental replication.

4. *Economics is what economists do.* No one can dispute this definition, attributed to the Canadian economist Jacob Viner (1892–1970), but whether it provides much insight into the subject is another matter. Does it? Perhaps. Because it does not list a category of things done by economists, it suggests that economists do several things and, more importantly, that the interests of economists change over time. Some economists today are using laboratory animals to test theories of economic behavior. Economists of the past have studied sun spots to assess their effect on the business cycle. Economists tomorrow may be studying the feasibility of asteroid mining—or cost-effective ways to decontaminate after nuclear war.

5. *Economics is the study of the allocation of scarce resources to alternative ends.* This definition, also from Lionel Robbins, may be the most informative definition, and it is important enough for some elaboration. A *resource* is an input into the productive process. We have already defined scarcity and emphasized its importance. If a good is not scarce, there is no need to determine how to allocate it to alternative ends because there is enough to go around. Goods that are not scarce are said to be *noneconomic goods* and do not have a price. Note too that the term "alternative ends" implies choice—a key economic concept.

· · · · · · · ·

Microeconomics and Macroeconomics

Microeconomics The branch of economic theory that deals with "small" economic issues such as the behavior of individual households.

Macroeconomics The branch of economic theory that deals with "large" economic issues such as inflation and unemployment.

Economic theory has been divided into two main branches, **microeconomics** and **macroeconomics,** since about the middle of the twentieth century. Microeconomics deals with the small view—the economic choices of individual households and firms. Macroeconomics, on the other hand, takes the large view—the choices of society as a whole. For example, a microeconomist might study the pricing strategy a particular

[2]Not all economists consider economics a "science." Gunnar Myrdal, winner of the Nobel Prize, certainly does not. He has said he would have rejected the prize for this reason, but the call came so early in the morning he was asleep!

firm takes in order to maximize profits, while the macroeconomist looks at the average price level in the entire economy. Another example is employment. Microeconomists examine the factors that determine why one person has a job; macroeconomists study the national unemployment rate. The distinction between micro- and macroeconomics is so well entrenched that the vast majority of schools offer a two-course introduction to economics with one course focusing on macro and another on micro. It should be pointed out, however, that the two fields are not nearly as distinct as this dichotomy seems to indicate. Contemporary macroeconomics has roots in microeconomics, and macroeconomic events—recessions and inflation—frequently have microeconomic implications. You are not well versed in economics until you understand both micro- and macroeconomics.

A SHORT HISTORY OF ECONOMICS

Scholars of the history of economic thought have traced the roots of economics back beyond the ancient Greeks, but a reasonable starting place for modern economic thought is eighteenth-century Scotland and the person of **Adam Smith** (1723–1790). As the Economic Heritage box on page 14 reveals, Adam Smith's field of study, moral philosophy, led him to address the key issues of the day.[3]

European society was undergoing dramatic changes in the eighteenth century. The last vestiges of feudalism were ending and the church and nobility no longer exerted the stabilizing influence they once did. The philosophical question of the day was how social order could come from the chaos of individualistic behavior. Smith's masterpiece, *An Inquiry into the Nature and Causes of the Wealth of Nations* (1776), provided an answer and marked the beginning of modern economics.

Adam Smith (1723-1790) Scottish economist often called the father of modern economics.

Classical Economics

The discovery of the laws of gravity by Isaac Newton (1643–1727) had changed the emphasis of eighteenth-century scientific inquiry. Scientists used this discovery to predict the motion of the planets, and it appeared that nature had a grand plan for the universe. Instead of studying things in isolation, scientists began to look for order in the universe. In the social sciences, the quest for order became an analysis of the processes that generated social stability. But did such order exist in the social universe? Smith believed it did. He argued that the interplay of self-interest and competition resulted in the best of all possible worlds: people made profits by providing useful goods, while price flexibility and the process of competition kept prices close to the cost of production. Workers were paid a "just" wage in accordance with their productive contribution.

---

[3]This introduction to the history of economic thought is extremely short. Biographies of famous economists are scattered throughout this book, but there are several excellent introductions to the history of economic thought that you might want to read. Two of the most popular are Daniel R. Fusfeld, *The Age of the Economist* (Harper-Collins, 1994), and Robert L. Heilbroner, *The Worldly Philosophers* (Simon and Schuster, 1990.) Both books are well written and have gone through several editions.

Specialization of labor Dividing job tasks into small components so that workers can become proficient; increases worker productivity.

Invisible hand Metaphor used by Adam Smith to describe the workings of market economies. If each person were free to pursue his or her own self-interest, nature would guide the economy as if it had an invisible hand.

Classical school School of economic thought founded by Adam Smith that dominated economics in the eighteenth and nineteenth centuries.

Laissez faire French phrase meaning "leave us alone." Used by economists to express the view that markets work best in the absence of government intervention.

The times had a great influence upon Smith's work. Europe was beginning the *Industrial Revolution*, and production was moving from small shops to the factory system. Smith noticed that, over the long run, progress would result from new technology and the **specialization of labor**—the division of production tasks into smaller, more specialized tasks. Such a division was possible only in factories and only if the market was large enough to permit long production runs. To Smith, all these developments fit together and spelled out progress. It was as if nature had a grand plan and an **invisible hand** to guide society. Smith's ideas were extended by other economists and resulted in the first school of modern economic thought, the **classical school.**

It is not too much of an exaggeration to say that two centuries of economic research have been directed at little more than an elaboration of Smith's work. Smith's vision of a self-correcting market economy signaled the beginning of modern economic analysis. A simple policy prescription resulted from Smith's insights: Leave the economy alone. Since competition and the market resulted in the best of both worlds, government intervention was ill-advised. Today this policy is captured in the phrase *laissez faire,* from the French for "leave us alone."[4]

In the middle of the nineteenth century, the German social philosopher *Karl Marx (1818–1883)* moved to London and began writing about the same system that Smith had praised. Marx's most important work, *Das Kapital* (1867), argued that the market system was prone to crisis. Marxian theory held that an inherent class conflict existed between the workers and the factory owners or capitalists. Marx's work was the basis for the communist revolution in Russia, although recent reforms in the Soviet Union and Eastern Europe have relegated Marxian economic theory to a less important role. It would be wrong, however, to suggest that Marxism is dead; some economists still find the Marxist approach a good tool for studying the evolution of modern capitalism.

• • • • • • • •

Neoclassical Economics

Neoclassical economics Orthodox school of economic thought whose proponents generally espouse *laissez faire.*

General equilibrium Condition where all markets within the economy are in simultaneous equilibrium and there is no tendency for change.

While Marx and his followers found faults with Smith's view of market capitalism, another group of economists extended Smith's work, and by the late nineteenth century, the idea of a self-correcting economy had been formalized into a school of thought, **neoclassical economics.** According to the neoclassical school, the market mechanism is strong enough to overcome most external shocks and quickly move the economy to **general equilibrium,** a position of rest where there is no tendency for change. The neoclassical vision implied that society had a social order much like the natural order of the physical world. Neoclassical theory became a cohesive body

---

[4]There is an interesting story as to how *laissez faire* came to be used in economics. In the eighteenth century, French industrialists were having a difficult time exporting goods to the New World. As a result, France was importing more goods than it was exporting. In an attempt to remedy the situation, the king of France met with his finance minister and asked what could be done. The response was to simply *laissez faire*—stop regulating business and let the industrialists produce what they wanted to produce however they wanted to produce it. Despite this episode, France's proclivity for regulation remains to this day. Virtually everything written on a French wine bottle label or cheese package is the result of regulation.

of knowledge used to explain prices, income distribution, interest rates—virtually everything that economists found interesting. The neoclassical school has persisted, and many economists call themselves neoclassicals today.

The elegance of the neoclassical vision captured nearly the whole of the economics profession, at least until the 1930s when the world economy fell into the most serious depression in modern times. Economists could not explain the *Great Depression* of the 1930s because self-correcting forces were supposed to prevent severe recession from ever occurring. And since economists did not understand the cause, they were not able to offer corrective policies. For a decade, the world economy floundered. Unemployment reached 25 percent of the workforce in the United States, and most factories operated at less than capacity for nearly a decade.

There had been other depressions, of course, but the Great Depression was different. In the past, depressions had usually been caused by an obvious external event—a drought or war was frequently the culprit. The 1930s depression did not seem to have an obvious cause, and as the depression dragged on, many began to think that something systemic had gone wrong with the world economy. Even today many economists believe that the Great Depression was worsened by inept economic policies, but there is still no general agreement as to the initiating cause.

The Keynesian Critique

It may have been obvious to noneconomists in the 1930s that the economy did not always self-correct, but neoclassical economists were a bit baffled. Economic actors were supposed to interrelate in such a way as to generate equilibrium. Why had the Roaring Twenties suddenly become the Depressed Thirties? An answer came from an Englishman, **John Maynard Keynes** (1833–1946). Keynes's book, *The General Theory of Employment, Interest and Money* (1936), provided a revolutionary theory of the depression and offered a policy prescription. Keynes's economic vision contrasted completely with that of the neoclassicals: self-correcting market forces were weak, the economy was prone to wide fluctuations, and government intervention was necessary. Keynes was especially concerned with the ability of the economy to establish full employment. By the 1950s, a hybrid version of **Keynesian** economics had become the standard approach to economics in the United States, and most textbooks had a decidedly Keynesian slant. The apparent success of this "Keynesian Revolution" affected not only textbooks but the main thrust of economic research. Economists began to focus their research more and more on policy questions: How should government policies be designed to fight inflation and unemployment?

Modern Schools of Thought

In the 1970s, inflation appeared to be uncontrollable, and the recessions of 1973–1975 and 1981–1982 caused many economists to question whether Keynesian policies had any effect on the economy at all. Economic debate, especially about the effectiveness of macroeconomic policies, continues on many fronts, but it is possible to classify the debaters into two main groups. Like Adam Smith and his followers, one group of economists feels that the modern mixed economy is generally self-regulating. These economists are hesitant to intervene with government policies,

John Maynard Keynes (1883–1946) British economist whose book *The General Theory* (1936) presented the framework for much modern macroeconomics.

Keynesian Generic label often applied to economists who are willing to use activist government policies to guide the economy.

OUR ECONOMIC HERITAGE

ADAM SMITH, THE FATHER OF MODERN ECONOMICS

The world would not be the same had Adam Smith not published *An Inquiry into the Nature and Causes of the Wealth of Nations* in 1776. The *Wealth of Nations* has influenced prominent thinkers and governments more than any other economics book ever written—some people say it is the most important *book* ever written. It not only explained how markets worked, but it offered a compelling argument that natural law applied to the social and economic world as much as to the physical world.

Smith was born in Kirkcaldy, Scotland, in 1723. He was brilliant and highly gifted, but also absentminded. Stories about the latter trait are legion. Once while walking in his garden, dressed only in a nightshirt, he wandered 15 miles before he realized what he had done. When signing official documents, he occasionally meticulously copied the signature of another signer instead of writing his own name. He enjoyed society and conversation though, and was a member of numerous social clubs.

Smith may have been absentminded, but he was also the preeminent scholar of his era. After studying classics at Oxford, he returned to the University of Glasgow to take up moral philosophy—a subject that combined theology, ethics, law, and politics. He stayed at Glasgow from 1751 to 1764. His first book, *The Theory of Moral Sentiments* (1759), was an immediate success. *Moral Sentiments* focused on human motivation and sympathy—something of a contrast to his focus on self-interest in his next book, *Wealth of Nations*. The success of *Moral Sentiments* led to Smith's appointment as the tutor to a nobleman, the duke of Buccleuch. This position paid more than the university and allowed Smith time to travel and begin work on *Wealth of Nations*.

Wealth of Nations covers so much ground that summarizing even the most important ideas in a paragraph or two is difficult, but at least a few concepts must be mentioned. Above all, it was an appeal to free trade. Smith presented a coherent model arguing that natural law and the "invisible hand" could guide the economy better than government intervention. This idea was heretical, but it was also welcome news at a time when the church and nobility were weakening substantially. The wealth of nations, said Smith, came from economic growth; it was a product of labor specialization, the pursuit of self-interest, and frugality.

If Smith's analysis has a weakness, it is probably his theory of price and value determination, which was unclear and confusing. At times he appeared to advocate the *labor theory of value,* which holds that goods exchange according to how much labor is embodied in the productive process. For example, if a worker can make one table or four chairs in one day, then the price of a table should be four times the price of a chair. While some Marxist economists espouse a modern version of this theory, most orthodox economists have rejected it because it does not take the preferences of the consumer into account.

Like *The Theory of Moral Sentiments, Wealth of Nations* was a smashing success. Not only did it become mandatory reading for the educated classes on the British Isles and the Continent, but it had an immediate influence on politics and economic policies. Britain began to eliminate restrictive policies and practice free trade. Some people have even argued that Smith's arguments for free trade influenced the revolutionaries of the French Revolution. In fact, the French authorities were so convinced that political economy fostered "dangerous" and radical thoughts that they allowed very few tracts on political economy to be published in France for the remainder of the eighteenth century.

thinking that the government often does more harm than good. The other group feels that the economy is prone to crisis and that government intervention is frequently necessary. The key question, of course, is *why* this disagreement exists. If we can answer that question, we will have gone a long way toward understanding economics.

THE METHODOLOGY OF ECONOMICS

If one concept can be said to unite all scientific inquiry, it is that the real world is complex. It is so complex, in fact, that abstractions are necessary before we can make any sense out of it. Can you look out the window and understand why inflation tends to decelerate as the economy enters recession? Hardly. Inflation is too complex a process—and the things you actually observe outside the window probably have little to do with inflation under any circumstance. To understand inflation, unemployment, or any economic process, it is necessary to isolate the factors that are most important and then try to discover a cause and effect relationship.

Much economic research is a search for an abstraction—also called a **theory**—that can explain and/or predict phenomena in the real world. All scientific theories have four components: variables, assumptions, hypotheses, and predictions. Once a theory has been formulated, it is usually tested with a *model*. Economic models are often statistical or graphical.

> **Theory** A framework used for testing hypotheses.

Variables

Economic theories are expressed in terms of variables. Variables are often numerical measures that change between observations. For example, the unemployment rate is a variable. When it changed from 5.5 percent of the workforce in 1990 to 7 percent of the workforce in 1991, economists tried to explain why with their theories.

Assumptions

All theories must rest upon **assumptions.** Assumptions are necessary to isolate the variables that the theorist feels are most important in explaining the phenomenon in question. For example, an important theory we will discuss in Chapter 3 is the theory of demand. In its simplest terms, this theory states that people will tend to buy less of a product at higher prices and more of a product at lower prices. While this theory has exceptions, it generally holds true.[5] However, several assumptions are necessary for it to hold. For example, you would probably agree that you would tend to buy fewer compact disks if the price went from $14 to $25. But what if you won the state lottery on the same day a compact disk price hike was announced? You might

> **Assumption** A postulate or premise used as a starting place for the development of a theory in order to isolate the issue of interest.

---

[5]If there were no exceptions, we would be dealing with a *law* not a theory. There are very few laws in economics, perhaps only two, the law of diminishing returns and the law of comparative advantage, both of which will be discussed in later chapters.

go out and buy *lots* of compact disks despite the price hike. The point is that all theories require assumptions. In this case, the theory of demand requires the assumption that your income is fixed. Does this mean that the theory of demand is rendered useless when your income changes? Not at all. Many assumptions are made even though the investigator realizes that they are not true or that they can change. The purpose of most assumptions is to isolate the key variables under investigation. This allows the theorist to see what happens if they hold and thus what might happen when they do not hold. In this case, we are concerned with buying behavior as prices change *assuming* your income is constant; nothing in the theory says that you will not buy more CDs if you do get lucky.

A key assumption made in all economic theories is the **ceteris paribus** assumption. *"Ceteris paribus"* is Latin for "everything else held constant." Stating the theory of demand as "An increase in price will result in a decrease in the quantity demanded, *ceteris paribus"* allows the theory to hold even if you win the lottery. We will discover in Chapter 3 the factors that are held constant with the *ceteris paribus* assumption.

Ceteris paribus Latin phrase meaning "everything else held constant." Frequently applied to economic models to isolate the variable of interest.

. . . .

Hypotheses

Once the key variables are isolated and the assumptions are stated, the theorist then forms a **hypothesis.** This is usually a cause and effect statement. For example, the theory of demand hypothesizes an inverse relationship between the selling price and the quantity demanded. The relationship is said to be *inverse* because price and quantity move in opposite directions; as price increases, the quantity demanded decreases and vice versa. A *direct* relationship exists when the two variables move in the same direction. Notice that the hypothesis implies a direction of causality—from price to quantity, not the reverse. In this case, we would call price the **independent variable** and the quantity demanded the **dependent variable.** The value of the dependent variable is determined or *caused* by the independent variable; the value of the independent variable is taken as given or determined by external factors.

Hypothesis Guess or conjecture to be tested by scientific analysis.

Independent variable The cause variable in a multivariable relationship.

Dependent variable The "effect" variable; if *x* causes *y*, then *y* is the dependent variable.

It is important to recognize the distinction between *correlation* and a *causal relationship.* Correlation is a statistical relationship; it does not imply any sort of causality. Causality refers to a dependent relationship between two or more variables. The concepts are often confused, and as a result, statistics are sometimes claimed to prove a hypothesis that in fact need not be true! Consider the following story. While watching sunsets one summer, a sociology major noticed that the rate of cricket chirping seemed to increase on warm evenings and decrease on cooler evenings. This suggested a hypothesis: An increase in the rate of cricket chirping *causes* the temperature to rise. To test the hypothesis, our sociology major collected the following data on six consecutive evenings:

| Temperature: | 73 | 86 | 77 | 81 | 92 | 88 |
| Cricket chirps per hour: | 21 | 33 | 32 | 33 | 41 | 35 |

A quick glance seems to indicate the hypothesis is verified—higher temperatures are *correlated* with increased chirping. However, it is not possible to use these data to determine whether the cricket chirps are caused by the higher temperature or whether cricket chirping raises the temperature! Most of us would agree that, if anything, temperature is the causal factor, but it is also possible that an unobserved factor is causing the rate of chirping.[6] In many cases, causality is not obvious, and it is almost never possible to determine causality with data alone.

Try another example. Every January some commentators note that the outcome of the Super Bowl is a predictor of stock market performance. When a National Conference team wins, the stock market advances; when an American Conference team wins, the market declines. If this were a cause and effect relationship, your route to wealth would be simple: Take a cellular phone to the Super Bowl and call your stockbroker the moment the outcome is clear. The fact that this relationship is cited repeatedly in the news suggests that there is some sort of correlation—but there is little chance that any cause and effect relationship is involved. This is an example of the methodological error of assigning causality just because two events follow each other in time. The Latin phrase *post hoc, ergo propter hoc,* which translates loosely to ''after this, therefore because of this,'' is used to describe this common logical fallacy.

· · · · · · · ·

Prediction

Once a hypothesis has been formulated, the final task is to test it empirically. This often involves prediction. For example, it is possible to use the theory of demand to predict the response to price changes: *Ceteris paribus*, an increase in the price of oil will result in energy conservation. Good theories should be able to explain and predict economic phenomena—but economic predictions are notorious for their errors. Does this mean that there are few good economic theories? No. Whenever an economist makes a prediction, it is based upon theory, and theories rest on assumptions. Good economists always qualify their predictions by making important assumptions clear and recognize that their predictions will be incorrect if their assumptions do not hold. For example, when the Organization of Petroleum Exporting Countries (OPEC) quadrupled oil prices in 1973–1974, nearly everyone was surprised. Economists whose inflation forecasts for those years turned out to be correct should have been embarrassed—because without the unforeseen oil shock, their forecasts would have been wildly incorrect.

· · · · · · · ·

Some Methodological Pitfalls

Even though economists use the scientific method, economics differs significantly from laboratory sciences in that it is usually impossible to conduct *controlled experiments*. In a controlled experiment, the investigator is able to control all causal variables except one in order to determine the effect of one independent variable on the dependent variable. While there have been some recent attempts at experimental economics, most economic events take place in society, so it is impossible to hold everything else constant. Partly because of the difficulty of making controlled experiments, economic theorists must rely on logic and data more than explicit experimentation, and unfortunately, this can lead to certain problems.

---

[6]Crickets ''chirp'' by rubbing their back legs together. Given the friction involved, this probably does raise the temperature in the backyard a *tiny* amount, but please drop the class now if you really believe that cricket chirping is a major factor affecting temperature.

Fallacy of composition Methodological error holding that what is correct for one is correct for all.

The **fallacy of composition** is an error made frequently by beginning economists. The error here is in thinking that what is true for the individual is true for the group. This is not always the case. For example, if you stand up at a Garth Brooks concert, you will be able to see over the person wearing the cowboy hat sitting in front of you. But if everyone stands up, no one will be able to see any better than they do sitting down. What is good for you to do in isolation may not be good if everyone else does the same thing.

How does this idea relate to economics? Let's consider two quick examples. First, suppose you decided to save more of your weekly paycheck, say, 20 percent instead of 10 percent. You would be able to buy that BMW a little sooner. But if everyone in the economy decided to save more, the amount of saving in the economy might actually fall! Why? If everyone saved more, everyone would spend less. If people bought fewer products, the number of jobs needed to produce goods would fall and fewer people would have any money to save. This idea is known as the *paradox of thrift* and will be discussed in more detail in Chapter 24. For another example, suppose that several cattle ranchers are allowed to graze their cattle on public land for free. If one rancher decides to increase the number of cattle on the land, he will probably be better off. But if all the ranchers do the same thing, the land will be depleted more quickly making everybody worse off. This is known as the *tragedy of the commons* and will be analyzed in more detail in Chapter 21.

A very difficult methodological problem exists simply because economics is a social science. Economic theories are vitally important to everyone because they are used as the basis for social policy. Policies affect our well-being and standard of living, so almost everyone has a vested interest in economic theory and policy. Most economists believe that a clear distinction must be made between *positive economics* and *normative economics*. Positive economics deals with questions of "what is"; normative economics deals with questions of "what ought to be." Most positive questions can be tested empirically; this is not true of normative economic questions. For example, the questions "What causes unemployment?" and "What policies can be used to reduce unemployment?" are positive economic questions. Both questions could be examined with a statistical model. On the other hand, "Should we reduce unemployment?" is a question of normative economics, and a very difficult one at that. One economic theory holds that there is a tradeoff between inflation and unemployment—lower unemployment tends to increase inflation while higher unemployment tends to reduce inflation. Further, unemployment tends to hurt the poor while inflation tends to hurt the rich. We may know *how* to reduce unemployment (positive economics), but whether we *should* (normative economics) is another question.

But as a practical matter, it is often difficult to separate positive from normative economic analysis. Our values determine the questions we ask in the first place, what data we use, and how we conceive the problem. If we believe that unemployment is a serious social problem (a normative judgment), we are more inclined to study how to get rid of it (a positive inquiry); if we feel that unemployment is not a serious social problem (a normative judgment), we will focus attention on other economic problems. We should keep in mind that the role of economists—in business, government, and the classroom!—is to provide information about tradeoffs and let the manager, politician, or society decide how to use it. *We* can tell if and how much unemployment will be required to reduce the rate of inflation; *they* can decide whether the tradeoff is worthwhile.

ECONOMIC POLICY

The government has three main kinds of economic policies at its disposal: fiscal policy, monetary policy, and regulation. **Fiscal policies** entail changing taxes or the level of government spending to affect economic performance. Many economists believe that lower taxes and higher government spending can help the economy recover from a recession. **Monetary policy** is conducted by the Federal Reserve, the central bank of the United States. The Federal Reserve has the power to influence the money supply and, indirectly, the level of interest rates. A slow growth rate in the money supply usually reduces inflation, though it may also cause the unemployment rate to rise. A faster growth rate of the money supply can stimulate economic growth, but may also accelerate inflation. Finally, the government has the power to regulate business and consumer behavior. Some regulations are designed to prevent firms from producing pollution; others are aimed at ensuring that the workplace is safe or that food is produced in a sanitary environment. All government regulations are designed to benefit society, but they also incur compliance costs that business may not like. Whether government regulations provide more benefits than costs is frequently difficult to determine—which is one reason why there are frequent debates over the role of government in the economy.

Economic policies should be adopted and can be evaluated only in the context of stated economic objectives. As we will find out in later chapters, there can be considerable disagreement over the effectiveness of any particular policy, but there is a wide agreement with respect to at least four broad objectives. The problem is that these policy objectives often conflict with one another.

Fiscal policy Tax and spending policies of the government.

Monetary policy Actions by the Federal Reserve to influence the amount of money and credit in circulation.

Efficiency

Economists use the term **efficiency** in several different contexts. One common usage refers to resource allocation. A policy is efficient if a reallocation of resources can make no one better off without making someone else worse off. As an example, suppose that a firm is unaware of modern technology and is thus wasting energy in its production process. A policy that provided technological information would permit the firm to lower the cost of production and the selling price of its output. Such a policy would increase allocative efficiency—consumers are better off with lower prices and producers are no worse off.[7] In a later chapter we will discuss a method of determining whether firms are operating efficiently or not, but we must point out here that it is often very difficult to determine whether people are better off or not after the implementation of policy. This does not mean that the efficiency objective should be dismissed, just that it must be regarded with care.

Efficiency Important welfare criterion. Exists when output is maximized for a given amount of input.

Equity

A second policy objective is **equity,** or fairness. Unfortunately, though everyone

Equity Fairness; a normative judgment. Many economic policies must trade off efficiency and equity.

---

[7]The cost of providing the information must be insignificant for this result to hold. If it is costly to provide the information, it is not clear that the benefits from conservation and lower selling prices exceed the costs.

agrees that equity is important, no one quite knows how to define it. Does equity mean that everyone should have an equal amount? Or does it mean that everyone should have what they need? Perhaps it means that everyone should get what they earn for themselves. We will spend more time on equity when we discuss poverty and income distribution in Chapter 20.

Growth

Gross domestic product (GDP)
Final market value of all goods and services produced in a year.

Efficiency and equity are usually thought of as microeconomic objectives; economic growth is primarily a macroeconomic objective. Economic growth is usually measured in terms of the growth of **gross domestic product (GDP).** We will define GDP more carefully later, but as a first approximation, it can be thought of as the total value of all final goods and services produced in the domestic economy in a year. Rising GDP typically means falling unemployment, but it can also lead to an undesirable by-product—inflation. The nature of the tradeoff between inflation and unemployment is a key concern of macroeconomic theory.

Stability

A fourth economic goal is macroeconomic stability. By this we mean the absence of wide swings in the overall level of economic activity—depression, inflation, and so on. Why is stability so important? Most economists believe that economic stability is necessary before firms will invest in machinery and new technology. Investment is necessary for at least two reasons. First, investment is the key to economic growth. Second, the United States can remain competitive in the international economy only with modern factories and quality products.

Conflicting Goals

The real problem with these goals is that they can conflict quite seriously. We have already mentioned that excessive economic growth can lead to inflation. Another potential conflict is between the efficiency and equity goals. Some economists argue that the most efficient economic system would have no welfare system or unemployment compensation because these programs can reduce the incentive to work and allow people to "live off the dole." But, many welfare recipients are people who are too old or too young to work. Would it be equitable to these people to eliminate welfare?

Another example of conflicting goals concerns income taxes. In the United States and most industrial countries, the federal income tax system is somewhat *progressive*, meaning that people pay a higher tax rate as their income increases. Many people would argue that this is "fair" or "equitable" because the rich can afford to contribute more to the common needs of national defense, education, social welfare, and so on. However, it is frequently argued that a progressive tax system reduces economic growth because people are less inclined to work hard if they know that their next dollar will be taxed at a high rate.

THE CIRCULAR FLOW DIAGRAM

One more concept, the circular flow diagram, will complete this chapter and our introduction to the topics covered in this book. The circular flow diagram is useful for illustrating several of the concepts we have just described, but it does more than that: it emphasizes that the economy is always moving as goods, services, and money change hands. The circular flow diagram is a model, and as such, it is a simplification of economic reality. The circular flow diagram divides the economy into two components: decision makers and coordination mechanisms.

The simplified circular flow model in Figure 1.1 shows two kinds of decision makers in the economy, households and firms. *Households* consist of individuals or

•••• FIGURE 1.1 THE CIRCULAR FLOW DIAGRAM

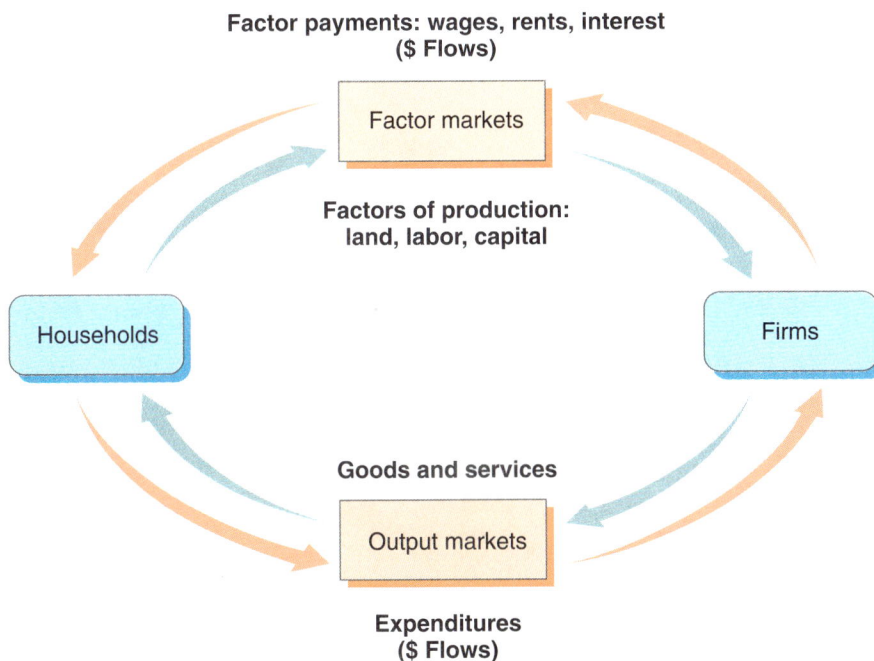

The circular flow diagram illustrates the flow of income and expenditures in the economy. Households own the factors of production (land, labor, and capital) and sell them to firms to earn income (in the form of rents, wages, and interest). This income is then used to buy goods and services in the output market. Factor payments are determined by the interaction of supply and demand in the factor market. Firms buy factors of production and combine them with production technology to produce goods and services for sale in the output market. The prices of goods and services are determined by the interaction of supply and demand in the output market.

groups of people living together. Households work to earn income, which they save or spend on goods and services. Every person in the economy is considered a member of a household, even if he or she lives alone. *Firms* are organizations involved in the production of goods and services. For most of the analysis in this book, we will assume that the goal of firms is to maximize profits. It is important to recognize that most people are members of more than one group. For example, when you go to work, you are acting on behalf of a firm, but when you return home, you are behaving as a householder.

Society could not exist without mechanisms to coordinate the activities of different decision makers. For example, households have only limited incomes, so they benefit from low prices. But firms want to maximize profits, which means that they benefit from high prices. How to reconcile these conflicting goals is one of the key questions in economics. The circular flow diagram shows the links between different groups. Markets are important coordinating mechanisms in most modern economies and a central focus of most economic analysis.

Factor market The market for inputs—land, labor, and capital.

Output market The market for goods and services.

Entrepreneur Person who takes risks and combines the various factors of production into a business enterprise.

Factor payment Payments to labor, land, and capital—wages, rent, and interest.

There are two basic kinds of markets in the economy: **factor** or **input markets** and **output** or **goods markets.** Inputs into the production process are traded in the factor markets. These inputs include *land, labor,* and *capital.* To an economist, the term "land" represents all valuable natural resources—not only real estate, but also crude oil, iron ore, and so on. Labor refers to the physical and mental skills of workers. Capital refers to machinery and factories used by firms.[8] Some economists add a fourth factor of production, *entrepreneurship.* An **entrepreneur** is a manager who combines the factors of production and takes risks to make profits. Although this four-part classification offers certain advantages, we can stick with just three factors because we have included mental skills in our definition of labor.

Households own the factors of production and sell them to earn the income necessary to buy goods and services. Each factor of production receives a **factor payment.** *Wages* are the payment to labor, *rent* is the payment to land, and *interest* is the payment to capital. Firms buy factors and apply production technologies to convert them into goods and services for sale in the output market. Factor payments and the prices of goods and services sold in the output market are influenced by the interplay of supply and demand, a topic we begin in Chapter 3.

At first glance, the circular flow diagram seems to indicate that the flow of income and expenditures in the economy is a smooth, coordinated operation. It often is, but not always. In fact, one of the key concerns of economics is to investigate the reasons why the circular flow gets interrupted. For example, what happens if households do not spend all of the money they earn? Firms could find that they were not able to sell all of their production. The result could be business losses and layoffs—unemployment. We will explore the causes and consequences of unemployment in later chapters.

---

[8]Notice that we are *not* using the term "capital" to refer to "money." When economists mean money, they will say "money" or, occasionally, "financial capital." This is probably different terminology than your finance and accounting teachers use.

• • • • • • •

Extensions to the Circular Flow Model

You probably detected that the diagram in Figure 1.1 is extremely simplified. We covered enough to define some important terms, but we omitted three important elements that would be part of a more complete circular flow diagram.

Financial Institutions. Few people spend all of the income they earn; most save a little. In modern societies, this typically means putting money in the bank or buying some sort of financial asset that you hope will turn a profit. Banks and other financial institutions accept deposits because they intend to lend the money out to investors. We will discover later that the financial linkage between savers and investors has an important impact on economic activity.

Government. The government sector taxes both firms and households and uses the tax revenue for two things. First, governments provide goods and services (defense, education, housing, health care, and so on) that cannot be produced efficiently or in sufficient quantities by the private sector. Second, governments provide *transfer payments* and *subsidies*. Transfer payments include welfare and other programs that are designed to aid certain groups. Subsidies are payments intended to increase various kinds of activities. For example, in recent years, subsidies have been given to firms engaged in alternative energy programs, the argument being that without the government subsidies, the research would be too costly or risky to undertake.

Foreign Sector. Finally, goods, services, and incomes flow between the United States and the rest of the world, so a more complete circular flow diagram would include a foreign sector. The foreign sector is more important in today's economy than ever before in history. Many domestic workers are paid by foreign firms, many domestically produced goods are sold abroad, and many goods bought at home were produced in foreign nations.

• • • • • • • **SUMMARY**

This chapter has covered quite a bit of ground, but almost all of it will be discussed in more detail later. Still, it is important that you understand these ideas and definitions. That will make the rest of the course much easier.

1. A fundamental economic problem is scarcity. Scarcity arises when human wants are unlimited and the resources available to satisfy those wants are limited. Goods that are scarce have a price; goods that are not scarce are free. Scarcity implies choice and opportunity cost.
2. The three fundamental economic questions are: What to produce? How to produce? Who receives the production? These questions have been answered with traditional, command, and market economies. The United States is best described as a mixed economy.

3. Economics is a way to think. A good working definition is: Economics is the study of the allocation of scarce resources among alternative uses.

4. Modern economic analysis is often dated from Adam Smith's *Wealth of Nations* (1776). One of Smith's most important ideas is the invisible hand, a metaphor for the automatic working of the market system.

5. There are many modern schools of economic thought. Like Smith, some economists think that the market system is best left alone. Others feel that government intervention is necessary because the market is prone to crisis and may not result in socially desirable outcomes.

6. Economics is based upon scientific methodology. Economic theories are abstractions developed to explain and predict economic phenomena. All theories are based upon assumptions. The *ceteris paribus* assumption is used to indicate that everything else is held constant.

7. The main goals of economic policy are efficiency, equity, growth, and stability. Policy objectives are subject to frequent conflicts.

8. The circular flow diagram illustrates the flow of income and spending in the economy. The main decision makers in the circular flow diagram are households, firms, and governments. The primary coordinating mechanisms are output markets and factor markets.

•••••••KEY TERMS AND CONCEPTS

tradeoff	theory
scarcity	variable model
opportunity cost	assumption
tradition	*ceteris paribus*
command	hypothesis
market	independent variable
mixed economy	dependent variable
price flexibility	*post hoc, ergo propter hoc*
voluntary exchange	fallacy of composition
microeconomics	fiscal policy
macroeconomics	monetary policy
Adam Smith	efficiency
specialization of labor	equity
invisible hand	gross domestic product (GDP)
classical school	household
laissez faire	firm
Karl Marx	factor market
neoclassical economics	output market
general equilibrium	entrepreneur
John Maynard Keynes	factor payments
Keynesian	transfer payments

······ REVIEW QUESTIONS

1. List and explain the three economic questions all societies must resolve.
2. What are some of the traditional elements in the U.S. economy? Do you think they hinder economic progress?
3. How do economists define the term scarcity? Do you think scarcity will ever be abolished?
4. What are the two main branches of economic theory? Give examples of the kinds of questions that are the focus of each branch.
5. Outline the main attributes of classical, neoclassical, and Keynesian economic theory.
6. Define positive and normative economics and give examples of each.
7. Why are assumptions a necessary component of all economic theories?
8. What are the four main goals of economic policy? Why is it so difficult to achieve all four goals simultaneously?

······ PROBLEMS

1. Suppose your friend tells you that going to the game tonight is too costly, even though you have free tickets. Is she confused, or has she just done a bit of economic thinking?
2. Buddhist monks speak of Nirvana as being a state of freedom from wants. What would be the role of an economist in Nirvana?
3. Theory A says that inflation can be eliminated if unemployment is allowed to rise to 15 percent. Theory B says that unemployment can be eliminated at a cost of 20 percent annual inflation. Is it possible for both theories to be correct? How would policymakers choose between the two theories?
4. One of the definitions in the text stated that economics is what economists do. The author of your textbook spends a considerable amount of time fishing for salmon (as a recreation, not commercially). In what ways is recreational fishing an economic activity for the author?
5. Is air an economic good? (*Hint:* It is, but it is also free. Isn't it?)
6. Being as precise as possible, calculate the opportunity cost of a college education. Are books a high percentage of that cost? Is tuition?
7. Adam Smith felt that one of the keys to economic growth was specialization of labor. Let study be input and grades be output. Suppose that your goal is straight A's next semester. How could you use specialization of labor to increase the output of your studies?
8. The text example of the theory of demand said that you would buy fewer compact disks at high prices than at low prices; however, if you won the lottery, you might buy more compact disks even at the higher price. What other factors do you think would cause you to buy more compact disks even if the price went up? (This question should help you determine how much economic intuition you have. After you answer it, you might want to read ahead in Chapter 3.)

9. State whether each of the following is a positive or normative statement. Explain your answer.
   a. Democrats believe unemployment is a more serious problem than do Republicans.
   b. Unemployment is a more serious social problem than inflation.
   c. The United States is capable of putting a person on Mars.
   d. The United States spends too much on the space program.
   e. The government deficit will be ruinous for our posterity.
   f. The government deficit causes high interest rates.
10. In terms of the circular flow diagram, every person in society is a member of a household. Is every person also a member of a firm or the government?
11. Draw a circular flow diagram for a command economy that has no markets. Explain why and how it differs from the circular flow diagram in Figure 1.1.

CHAPTER 2

Cost, Choice, and a Review of Graphical Analysis

You can't have everything. If you go to school, you can't party all the time. There are only so many hours in a day, and at least a few must be set aside for study. If you take that trip to Europe when you graduate, you will have a tough time paying for a new car the same year. You (or your parents) face limited funds—scarce resources in the jargon of the economist. Life, inevitably, involves choices. And every choice, by definition, involves costs—if nothing else, the cost of not having the other choice. The concepts of cost and choice are behind virtually every idea we will learn in economics. People must deal with costs and choices, and so must societies.

In this chapter, the production possibilities curve (PPC) will be developed to illustrate two of the most important concepts in economics, cost and choice. Like many concepts in economics, the PPC can best be illustrated graphically. But before we do that, it is probably a good idea to review some basic concepts of graphical analysis.

AFTER READING AND STUDYING THIS CHAPTER, YOU SHOULD BE ABLE TO:
• • • Write the general form of a linear function, and calculate the slope and intercept
• • • Understand the relationship between tangency, slope, and extreme values of nonlinear functions
• • • Know the assumptions behind the production possibilities curve, and use it to illustrate scarcity, choice, and the law of increasing opportunity cost
• • • Explain why and how changes in technology, resources, and opportunity costs affect the production possibilities curve

SOME REVIEW: GRAPHS AND FUNCTIONS

Many of the concepts that economists deal with are quantitative. How many people are unemployed? How much did prices rise last year? How much will they rise next year? Will interest rates rise or fall? Individuals may be satisfied with a single number when they ask these questions, but economists invariably want more. They want to know the trends and patterns in the data. Is unemployment higher this year than last year? Forecasting unemployment without knowing the unemployment rate from last year would be difficult. No one would try to predict how much prices will rise this year without knowing what happened last year.

As we will find out in later chapters, economists analyze data in many ways, but they usually begin their analysis with a picture—a graph—of the data to help them visualize trends and other important characteristics of the data. After graphing the data, economists are then ready to proceed with the more elaborate analysis necessary to compute forecasts, guide policy, and so on.

Line Graphs

Line graphs can be a quick and effective way to illustrate data. For example, you have to look at the data in Table 2.1 pretty closely to notice that new home mortgage rates rose, then fell over the period 1970–1993, but just a quick glance at the line graph in Figure 2.1 shows the same thing.

Graphing is often a useful way to convey ideas and data, but some cautions must be kept in mind when reading graphs. First, graphs are not as precise as numerical data. For example, Figure 2.1 shows us that mortgage rates rose slightly between 1981 and 1982, but it is not easy to tell from the graph that the mortgage rate rose to 15.14 percent in 1982. More importantly, the scale used on the axis determines the shape of the graph and may influence the inferences we draw from the data. For example, Figure 2.2 also plots the data from Table 2.1, but with a different scale on

• • • • TABLE 2.1 NEW HOME MORTGAGE RATES

Year	Mortgage	Year	Mortgage
1970	8.45%	1982	15.14
1971	7.74	1983	12.57
1972	7.60	1984	12.38
1973	7.96	1985	11.55
1974	8.92	1986	10.17
1975	9.00	1987	9.31
1976	9.00	1988	9.19
1977	9.02	1989	10.13
1978	9.56	1990	10.05
1979	10.78	1991	9.32
1980	12.66	1992	8.24
1981	14.70	1993	7.20

SOURCE: 1994 *Economic Report of the President*, Table B-72.

···· **FIGURE 2.1** NEW HOME MORTGAGE RATES, 1970–1993

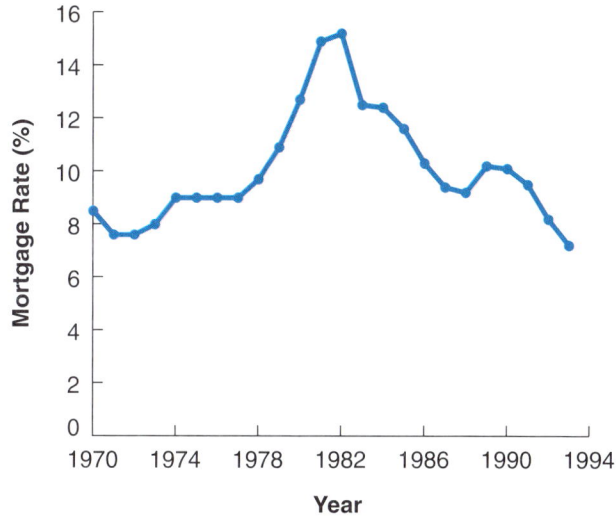

SOURCE: 1994 *Economic Report of the President,* Table B-72

···· **FIGURE 2.2** NEW HOME MORTGAGE RATES, 1970–1993

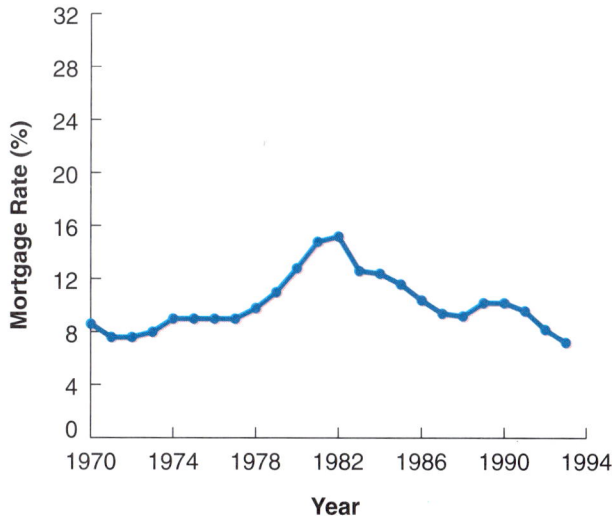

SOURCE: 1994 *Economic Report of the President,* Table B-72

the vertical axis so that a one percentage point increase in the mortgage rate corresponds to only half as much vertical distance as in Figure 2.1. The effect is significant: what used to look like a significant "spike" in interest rates in the early 1980s now looks like only a shallow peak.

We will not focus our attention on interest rates until later in the book, but these data are worth a brief comment while we are here. Since most people finance their homes over 30 years, interest charges are usually the largest part of the cost of buying a home. For example, for a 30-year, $100,000 mortgage, a 12 percent mortgage rate results in a monthly payment of more than $1,030, but an 8 percent mortgage rate lowers the monthly payment to about $733. A lot more people can afford to buy homes with 8 percent mortgages than 12 percent mortgages. This is one reason why the housing market was devastated in the early 1980s when mortgage rates rose above 10 percent. It also explains why the housing market boomed later in the decade when mortgage rates dropped below 10 percent.

Other Kinds of Graphs

Line graphs are not the only way to visualize data. We will occasionally use pie charts and bar charts. Pie charts are most useful for showing how data break down into groups. Figure 2.3 is a pie chart of the data in Table 2.2, federal government outlays for the fiscal year 1992. A quick glance shows that defense and Social Security were the largest components of government spending, followed by interest on the national debt, income security, and the ubiquitous "other" category.

Pie charts are most useful when there are only a few categories because it is difficult to tell the relative importance of more than five or six groups. In this case, a very close inspection is needed to tell whether defense spending or Social Security pay-

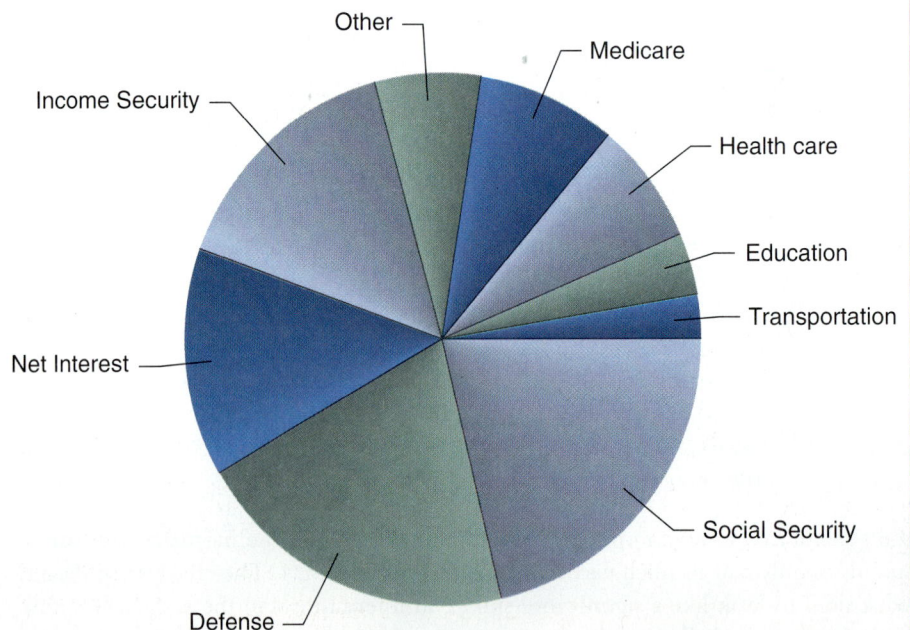

FIGURE 2.3 FEDERAL GOVERNMENT OUTLAYS, 1992: PIE CHART

SOURCE: 1994 *Economic Report of the President,* Table B-78. Data are in billions of dollars.

TABLE 2.2 FEDERAL GOVERNMENT OUTLAYS,

Social Security	$ 304.6	Health care	$ 99.4
Defense	291.1	Other	91.5
Income security	207.3	Education	50.0
Net interest	198.8	Transportation	35.0
Medicare	130.5	Total	$1,408.2

SOURCE: 1994 *Economic Report of the President,* Table B-78. Data are in billions of dollars.

ments was the largest component of government outlays in 1993, and it is hard to rank the sizes of several other components of spending. When the data to be illustrated fall into a number of categories, a bar chart like the one in Figure 2.4 is usually a better way to convey information. Notice that ordering the categories by size makes it much easier to convey relative magnitudes than in the pie chart.

Scattergrams

Economists often want to show the relationship between two or more sets of data. This allows them to hypothesize whether there is an underlying cause and effect or *functional* relationship among the variables. Generally, the *independent* or causal vari-

FIGURE 2.4 FEDERAL GOVERNMENT OUTLAYS, 1993: BAR GRAPH

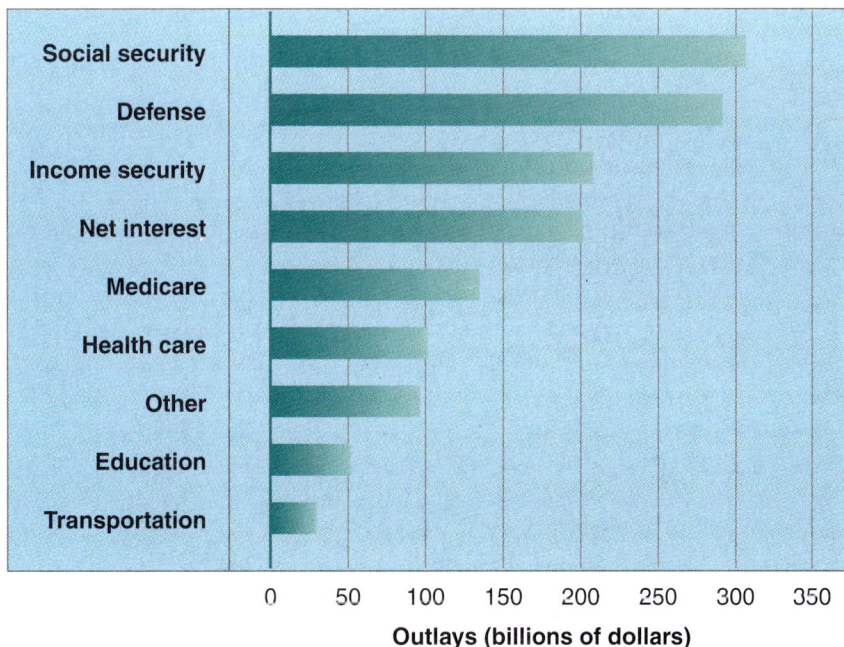

SOURCE: 1994 *Economic Report of the President,* Table B-78. Data are in billions of dollars.

····FIGURE 2.5 SCATTERGRAM

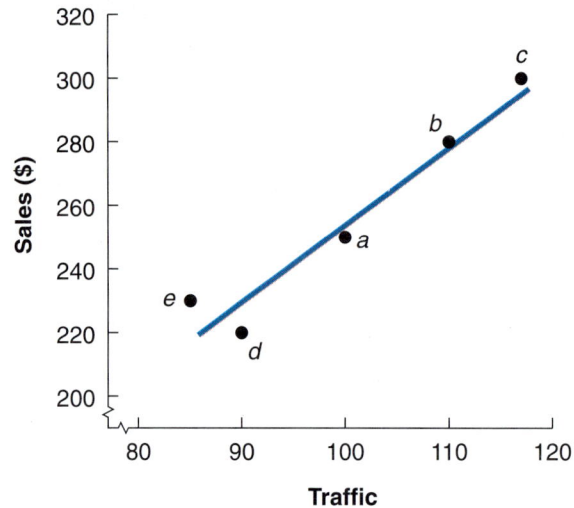

····TABLE 2.3

Point	a	b	c	d	e
Traffic	100	110	117	90	85
Sales	$250	$280	$300	$220	$230

Scattergram Statistical plot of two sets of data; often an economic series against time.

Direct relationship If y increases (decreases) when x increases (decreases), then the relationship between x and y is direct.

Inverse relationship If y increases when x decreases, then x and y have an inverse relationship.

able is drawn on the horizontal axis, and the *dependent* or effect variable is measured on the vertical axis.[1] As an example, consider Figure 2.5; it is a **scattergram** of the hypothetical data in Table 2.3, which plots the number of people traveling through a shopping mall and the daily sales of a department store.

Notice that the data points in Figure 2.5 are generally upward sloping, an indication that higher traffic values usually correspond to higher sales and vice versa. This is known as a **direct relationship** between the two variables. If sales fell when traffic increased, the relationship would be said to be **inverse.** A common inverse relationship in economics is the relationship between the quantity of a good that people will buy and the selling price. Other things being equal, people tend to buy less of a product at higher prices than at lower prices.

One of the most important tasks for economists is to analyze data like these and develop forecasts. For example, notice the straight line drawn in Figure 2.5. If that line "fits" the data well, knowledge of mall traffic next year would help the forecaster predict department store sales. Several statistical techniques are used to develop this kind of forecast. The most common one is called *regression analysis,* a topic you will

---

[1] One glaring exception to this rule is supply and demand analysis, the topic of the next two chapters. Economists place price (usually considered the independent variable) on the vertical axis and quantity (the dependent variable) on the horizontal axis.

undoubtedly talk about in your statistics class. The branch of economics devoted primarily to applying statistical methods to economics is called *econometrics,* and economists who focus their attention on econometric models are called *econometricians.*

Linear Functions

Graphs that can be drawn as straight lines are called **linear functions;** curved functions are called **nonlinear functions.** Generally speaking, linear functions are easier to work with and have many applications in economic analysis.

The general form of a linear function is:

$$y = a + bx \qquad [1]$$

Where:

y = the dependent variable
x = the independent variable
a = the vertical or y-intercept
b = the slope, defined as $\Delta y/\Delta x$
Δ = change; i.e., $x_1 - x_2$

As an example, look at the numbers in Table 2.4.

The numbers from Table 2.4 are plotted in Figure 2.6. Several things are important

Linear function A function that, when graphed, is a straight line.

Nonlinear function A mathematical relationship that, when plotted, is not a straight line.

TABLE 2.4

Dependent variable (y)	50	130	210	290	370	850
Independent variable (x)	0	100	200	300	400	1,000

FIGURE 2.6 A LINEAR FUNCTION

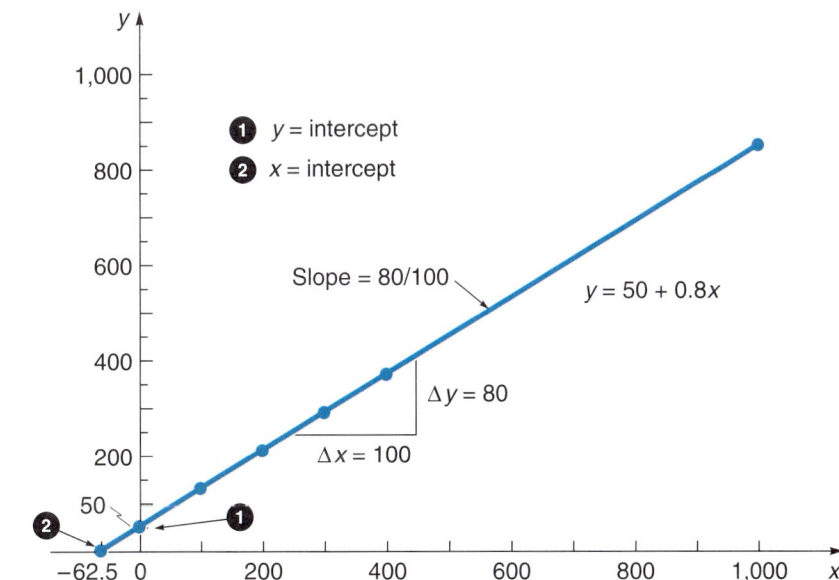

Slope In a graphical analysis, the ratio of the vertical change of a function to the horizontal change.

Intercept In graphical analysis, the point where the function (line) crosses an axis.

about Figure 2.6. First, notice that each time x changes by $+100$ units, y changes by $+80$ units. Thus, the **slope** of the line, $\Delta y/\Delta x$, is $0.8 = 80/100$. The slope is often the most important piece of information we need from a linear relationship because it tells how much the dependent variable changes for a one-unit change in the independent variable. Slope also tells whether the two variables are inversely or directly related: A positive slope indicates a direct relationship; a negative slope indicates an inverse relationship. Second, notice that when $x = 0$, $y = 50$. The value of y when $x = 0$ is the vertical or y-**intercept.**

The slope and intercept are all that you need to know to write the equation of any linear function. Using the notation in Equation 1, $a = 50$ and $b = 0.8$, so the equation can be written as $y = 50 + 0.8x$. Once we know the equation, we can find any point on the linear function. For example, the table does not provide the horizontal or x-intercept—the point where the line would cross the x-axis. To find this value, just substitute $y = 0$ into the equation and solve. That is:

$$y = 50 + 0.8x$$

Let $y = 0$:

$$0 = 50 + 0.8x$$

Subtract 50 from each side:

$$-50 = 0.8x$$

Then divide by 0.8 to get the horizontal intercept:

$$x = -50/0.8 = -62.5$$

Nonlinear Functions

Unlike linear functions, nonlinear functions do not have a constant slope. There are many examples of nonlinear relations in economics so we will use them frequently. Unfortunately, no general equation will work for all nonlinear functions, and finding the slope can require calculus, so we will work primarily with their graphs, not their equations. To illustrate some important points about nonlinear functions, look at the values in Table 2.5, which have been plotted on Figure 2.7.

Two concepts that will be especially important when dealing with nonlinear relationships are *extreme values* and *tangency*. Consider the nonlinear graph in Figure 2.7. Notice that the U-shaped curve, A, is touched at two points, m and n. At these points, the dashed lines B and C are said to be **tangent** to the curve A. Two curves are said to be tangent if they touch at a single point but do not intersect. Why is tangency so important? Without calculus, it is difficult to find the slope of a nonlinear function, but one can prove that two curves have the same slope where they are tangent. For example, look at point m where line B is tangent to line A. Both lines are upward sloping. At points to the left of point m, A is flatter than B; thus, the slope of A is less than the slope of B. At points to the right of m, A is steeper than B; thus, the slope of A is greater than the slope of B. At only one point m, do the two curves have the same slope. At this point, the functions A and B are tangent. The result can be generalized: The slope at any point on a nonlinear function can be found by calculating the slope of a straight line that is tangent to the function at that point.

Tangent In graphical analysis, one curve is tangent to another if they touch but do not intersect.

•••••TABLE 2.5

Dependent variable (y)	9	6	5	6	9	14	21
Independent variable (x)	−3	−2	−1	0	+1	+2	+3

•••••FIGURE 2.7 A NONLINEAR FUNCTION

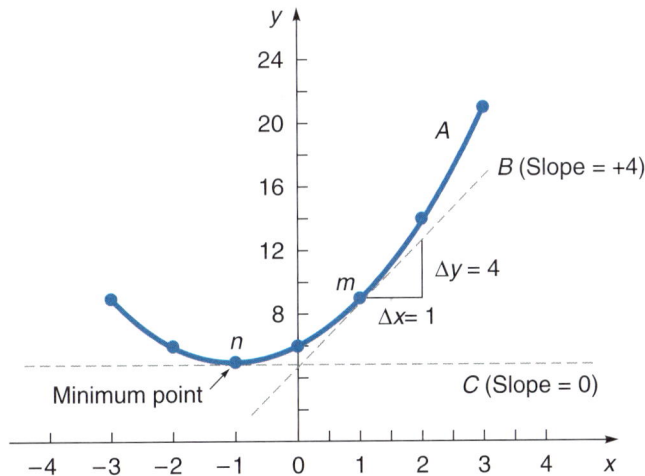

Nonlinear functions do not have a constant slope as do linear functions. Notice that the curved line A is downward sloping over the range −3 to −1 and then becomes upward sloping. However, the slope at any point can be found by computing the slope of a straight line that is tangent at the point of tangency. The slope at point m is 4 since the dashed line B has a slope of +4. A horizontal line can be tangent only at a point of relative maxima or minima. This occurs at point n where line C is tangent to line A.

Line C is a horizontal line so it has a zero slope, $\Delta y/\Delta x = 0$. Notice that to the left of point n, A has a negative slope, $\Delta y/\Delta x < 0$, and to the right of point n, it has a positive slope, $\Delta y/\Delta x > 0$. Tangency at point n assures that C and A have the same slope at the point of tangency. Point n is of special interest: Given the U-shape of A, a horizontal line can be tangent only at the minimum point, a result people with calculus are sure to recognize. If A had an upside down U-shape, the only point where a horizontal line could be tangent would be at its maximum. Maximum and minimum points are two kinds of **extreme values.** We will find out later that extreme values are often of special interest to economists.

This important result can be generalized for all nonlinear functions. *If a tangent line has a zero slope, the point of tangency must occur at an extreme value of the function.* The function A in Figure 2.7 has only one minimum point, but it is possible to have a "wavy" function with many extreme values. At each of these extreme values, however, the function will "reverse direction" just as curve A does at point n: to the left of n, curve A is downward sloping; to the right of point n, it is upward sloping.

Extreme value In graphical analysis, the maximum or minimum point on a curve.

Production possibilities curve (PPC) Curve showing production combinations available to an economy given finite factor inputs and technology.

········ # THE PRODUCTION POSSIBILITIES CURVE

One of the simplest and most useful economic models is the **production possibilities curve (PPC).** This model is used to illustrate some of the most important concepts in economics, including scarcity, choice, and opportunity cost. It can also be used to give us practice at reading and using graphs—skills that are invaluable in analyzing real-world problems. We will begin our development of the PPC with a simple linear example and then develop a more realistic nonlinear version of the PPC.

········

Linear Opportunity Costs

Say you are having a hard time finding a summer job when you read about Student Painters, a company that employs college students to paint houses in the summer. You apply, and since you show an aptitude for management, you are hired as a crew chief. Your job is to find houses that need painting. You then bid on the jobs and, if successful, buy paint and make sure your work team does a good job. By midsummer, your reputation for managing a quality painting crew has spread far and wide, and you have more than enough jobs to finish the summer. In fact, you have so many potential jobs lined up that you can choose between painting several small houses, a few large ones, or some of each.

Large houses usually take twice as much time to paint as small houses. Given the size of your crew and the time left before you have to return to school, you calculate that you could paint 20 small houses or 10 large houses. You could also paint different combinations of the two—10 small houses and 5 large houses, 18 small houses and 1 large house, and so on. In economists' jargon, the **opportunity cost** of painting a large house is two small houses because every large house you paint means that you have to forgo painting two small houses. Alternatively, it means the same thing to say that the opportunity cost of every small house is one-half of a large house. (Notice that one-half is just the reciprocal of two.) A few calculations result in the information in Table 2.6 and the graph in Figure 2.8.

Several things about Figure 2.8 are worth remembering:

Opportunity cost The value of the best forgone alternative.

- The intercepts of a PPC show the maximum amount of production of each product. In this case, the horizontal intercept gives the number of small houses that can be painted (20) if no large houses are painted. The vertical intercept gives the number of large houses (10) that can be painted if no small houses are painted.
- The slope of a PPC represents the opportunity cost of choosing one option over the other. In this case, the slope is -0.5 because every small house (S) you paint means giving up the opportunity to paint one-half of a large house (L). This can be calculated as $\Delta L / \Delta S = -1/+2 = -0.5$. If the PPC were drawn with small houses on the vertical axis, the slope would be -2.0. Notice that -2.0 is the reciprocal of -0.5.
- Points on the PPC are said to be *efficient* because they represent the maximum amount of houses that can be painted with available resources and technology. By resources we mean the number of workers, technology, time, and so on that are available. You could decide to paint any combination of houses on or inside the

•••• **TABLE 2.6** HOUSE PAINTING POSSIBILITIES

Small houses	20	18	16	14	12	10	8	6	4	2	0
Large houses	0	1	2	3	4	5	6	7	8	9	10

•••• **FIGURE 2.8** HOUSE PAINTING PRODUCTION
POSSIBILITIES CURVE

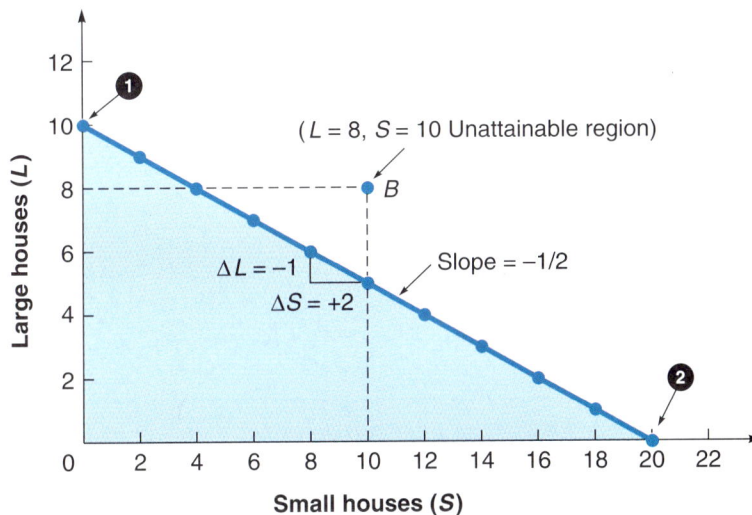

❶ If no small houses are painted, 10 large houses can be painted.

❷ If no large houses are painted, 20 small houses can be painted.

The intercepts of the PPC show the maximum number of each product that can be produced if all resources are devoted to the production of that item. In this case, a maximum of 10 houses or 20 small houses can be painted. Since painting a large house means that two small houses cannot be painted, the opportunity cost of each large house is two small houses, and the slope of the PPC is −0.5.

PPC, but operating inside the PPC would indicate that you are not working up to your capabilities—due perhaps to a sudden case of laziness or some other kind of inefficiency. All points inside the PPC are attainable but inefficient.

- Points on and inside the PPC comprise the **feasible region.** Points outside the PPC—for example, the point representing 8 large houses and 10 small houses— are in the **unattainable region.** The only way to operate at these points is to increase the resource base—hiring more workers or achieving a technological breakthrough that speeds up the painting process.

The data and PPC show the painting opportunities available, but they do not reveal which combination of large and small houses should be selected. How do you

Feasible region The area of attainable outcomes.

Unattainable region The area of outcome that cannot be achieved due to lack of resources.

make this choice? That depends on your *preferences*. Obviously, if you can make more profits from painting large houses than small houses, you would select the large houses. If you like variety, you might select some of each if you make the same profits from painting two small houses as you make from painting one large house. But without further information, the PPC does not help you decide what choice to make. It only illustrates the "menu" of available choices and the fact that every choice involves opportunity costs. We will find out later that one of the most important choices that society can make is deciding where to operate on the national PPC.

Changing the Slope of the PPC. The PPC in Figure 2.8 was based on hypothetical data that supposed that you could paint two small houses for every large house. Suppose that, upon further reflection, you conclude that you could actually paint 30 small houses this summer if you spent all of your time painting small houses. If you could still paint only 10 large houses this summer, the horizontal intercept would change from 20 to 30, and the PPC would look like the one in Figure 2.9.

Two things should be apparent from comparing the PPC in Figure 2.9 to the one in Figure 2.8. First, the opportunity cost of one large house has increased from two small houses to three small houses. As a result, the slope of the PPC has changed from -0.5 to -0.33. Second, the feasible region has expanded and it is now possible to paint more houses. For example the point $(S = 6, L = 8)$ is on the new PPC but was previously unattainable.

FIGURE 2.9 PRODUCTION POSSIBILITIES CURVE

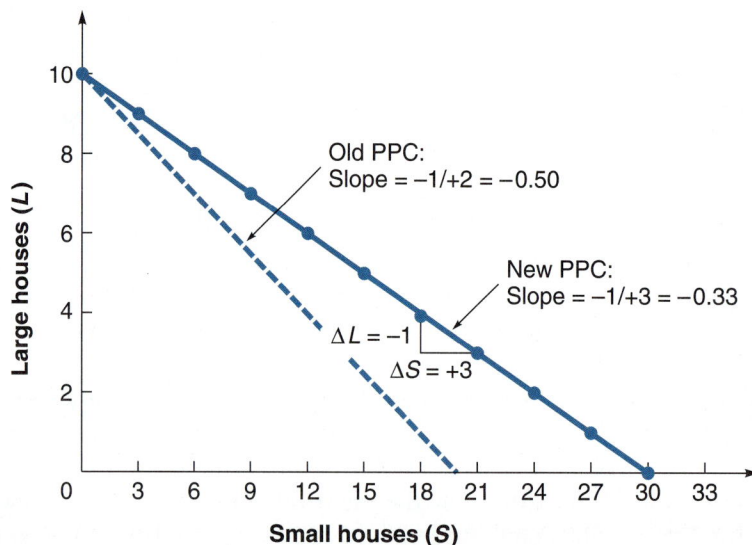

The slope of the PPC will change if the intercept of one of the axes changes. In this case, it is assumed that if all resources are devoted to painting small houses, 30 houses could be painted. If it is still possible to paint a maximum of 10 large houses, the slope of the PPC will change from -0.5 to -0.33 so the new PPC is less steep than the old PPC.

Shifting the PPC. Several things can shift the entire PPC. Two of the most important shift factors are the amount of available resources and changes in technology. For example, suppose that after seeing how many houses need painting, you decided to hire another work crew. This would increase the number of both large and small houses you could paint and would shift the entire PPC outward. The same thing would happen if a technological advance occurred—say, you were able to get hold of a new kind of paint that required only one coat instead of the customary two or perhaps a spray gun to use instead of brushes. Both events would result in a parallel outward shift in the PPC and an increase in the attainable region. Notice, however, that neither event would change the slope of the PPC. The effect of an increase in available resources or technology is shown in Figure 2.10.

FIGURE 2.10 SHIFTING THE PRODUCTION POSSIBILITIES CURVE

An increase in technology or available resources will expand production possibilities and result in a parallel outward shift in the PPC. In this case, available resources have increased by 50 percent so it is possible to paint 15 large houses, 45 small houses, or any combination on the PPC that passes through these points. A decrease in available resources would cause the PPC to shift inward.

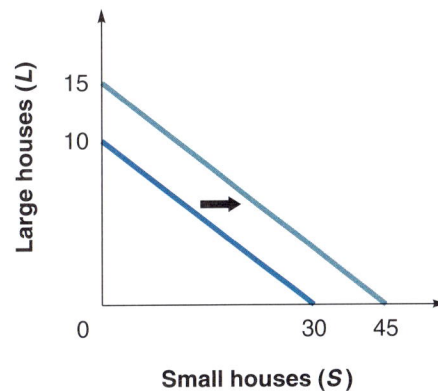

Nonlinear Opportunity Costs

Our story about Student Painters was a bit contrived. It was meant only to introduce some of the key points behind PPC analysis—opportunity cost, choice, and scarcity. In the real world, the PPC is most often nonlinear because of an important economic law, the **law of increasing opportunity costs.** Stated simply, the law of increasing opportunity costs says that as any production process proceeds, the cost of producing subsequent units of a paticular product must eventually rise. This occurs because *resources are finite, and some factors are better suited for producing some goods than other goods.* The classic illustration of the law of increasing costs is the guns and butter example.

Suppose that society can produce only two kinds of goods, defense goods (guns = G) and consumer goods (butter = B). Suppose, further, that if all available resources and technology are fully employed, 150 units of butter or 50 units of guns can be produced. Other combinations of guns and butter are possible; if the law of increasing costs holds, however, the resulting PPC is bowed out from the origin or *concave* with respect to the origin as shown in Figure 2.11.

The hypothetical data in Table 2.7 and Figure 2.11 reflect increasing opportunity costs. More important than the actual numbers, however, is the reasoning behind

Law of increasing opportunity costs As the production of anything rises, the opportunity cost of forgone production will eventually increase.

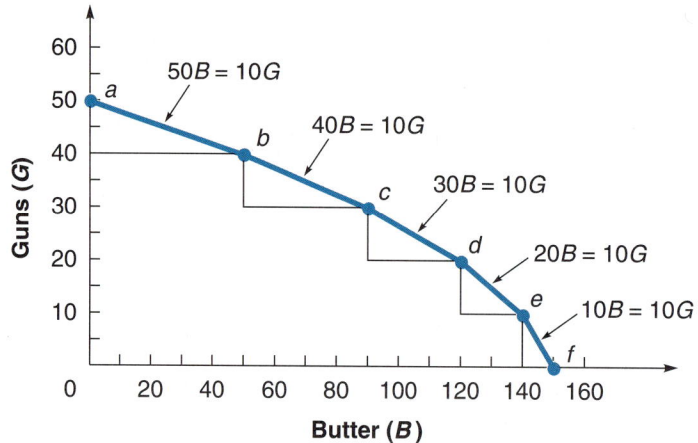

FIGURE 2.11 THE LAW OF INCREASING COSTS: GUNS AND BUTTER PPC

The concave shape of the nonlinear PPC illustrates the law of increasing opportunity costs. Moving from point *a* to point *b* represents a reduction in gun production by 10 units and a 50-unit increase in butter production. Thus, the opportunity cost of the first 50 units of butter is 10 guns, or $50B = 10G$, which can be written as $1B = 0.2G$. As butter production increases, however, the opportunity cost of butter rises. Moving from point *b* to point *c* again represents a sacrifice of 10 units of guns, but results in only 40 additional units of butter. Thus, the opportunity cost of butter has risen to $1B = 0.25G$.

TABLE 2.7 GUNS AND BUTTER PPC

				Point		
	a	b	c	d	e	f
Guns (G)	50	40	30	20	10	0
Butter (B)	0	50	90	120	140	150
Opportunity cost of one unit of butter in terms of guns		0.20	0.25	0.33	0.50	1.00
Opportunity cost of one unit of guns in terms of butter		5	4	3	2	1

the numbers. It goes something like this. Begin at point *a* where production is 50 guns and no butter ($G = 50$, $B = 0$). Chances are, we would all starve at point *a*, so let's take resources out of gun production and put them into the butter industry. According to our table, cutting gun production by just 10 units will free enough resources to enable the production of 50 units of butter. Thus, the opportunity cost of the first 50 units of butter (50*B*) is 10 units of guns (10*G*). On average, then, the opportunity cost of each of the first 50 units of butter is 0.2 units of guns, or $1B = 0.2G$.

Now suppose that society decides that 50 units of butter are not enough to feed everyone so the decision is made to reduce gun production by 10 more units. How much more butter can be produced? The table shows point *c* with 30*G* and 90*B*. This means that the opportunity cost of the next 40 units of *B* is 10*G*, or 40*B* = 10*G*, which means that 1*B* = 0.25*G*. We have just illustrated increasing opportunity costs: As the production of something rises, the opportunity cost of forgone production will eventually increase. In this case, the opportunity cost of butter production rose from 0.20*G* for each of the first 50 units of butter to 0.25*G* for each of the next 40 units. The question is *why* this is likely to occur. The answer is a key aspect of economic reasoning.

When the first few workers are taken from gun production and sent to the farm, they will have the entire resource base with which to make butter. Thus, each worker will have a large amount of farmland, tractors, and so on to use in butter production. Well-equipped workers are productive workers. The first few workers will also work on the very best farmland. As more workers are taken from gun production, however, they will have to use land that is less well-suited to butter production, so the butter production per worker will begin to decline. Consequently, the same amount of lost guns results in fewer units of butter; that is, the cost of butter production increases. The law of increasing costs applies to all production processes.

Changing the Slope and Intercepts of the PPC. As with the linear PPC in Figure 2.8, the intercepts of the nonlinear PPC in Figure 2.11 show how much can be produced if all resources are devoted to the production of only one of the goods, and the slope shows the opportunity cost of production. The PPC will shift if there is a change in technology or available resources. As shown in Figure 2.12a, additional resources or an improvement in technology that has an equal effect on the production

FIGURE 2.12 CHANGING THE SLOPE AND SHIFTING THE PPC

The PPC will shift when there is an increase in resources or technology. Panel (a) illustrates what happens when an increase in resources or technology affects the production of both guns and butter: there is a parallel outward shift and an expansion of the feasible region. An increase in resources or technology that affects only gun production raises the intercept on the gun axis and changes the slope of the PPC, as shown in panel (b). The opportunity cost of butter production is now greater because more guns are lost for each unit of butter that is produced.

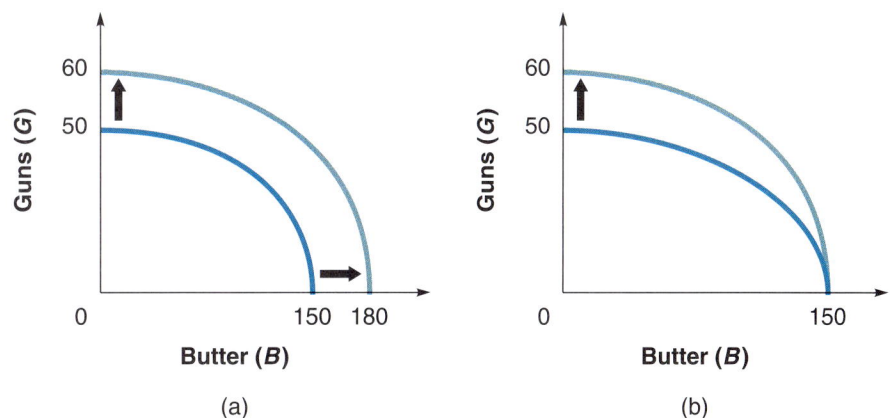

of both goods will result in a parallel outward shift of the PPC. This expands the feasible region and means that society can have more of both goods.

Figure 2.12b shows what happens when a technological change or an increase in resources affects the production of only one good, guns in this case: the guns intercept increases, but there is no change in the butter intercept. In this case, the guns intercept rises from 50 to 60 so the PPC becomes steeper over its entire range. As a result, the opportunity cost of butter production rises because more guns must be given up for every unit of butter that is produced. Had butter technology improved or the number of cows increased, the intercept on the butter axis would have expanded, and the opportunity cost of guns would have increased.

Choice and the PPC. We still haven't figured out how society decides where on the PPC to operate. The PPC gives us choices, but the best choice is determined by society's values at a particular point in time. In a market society, the most important criterion is relative consumer demand. For example, if society can make either good A or good B, but consumers want more of good A, more A and less B will be produced. How do producers know which good to produce? By looking at the price consumers are willing to pay and the number of goods left on the shelf. If consumers are willing to pay a high price for good A, producers are more likely to make a profit and will produce that good. We will look more at how the market provides and responds to price signals throughout the course.

In a command economy, the decision about what to produce is centralized. For example, for many years after World War II, Soviet economic planners devoted many resources to producing defense goods at the expense of consumer goods.[2] The result was an impressive military—but disgruntled consumers. Since prices were often set by central planners, they did not reflect consumers' wants. This is one reason why there were so often long lines at stores. It is also one of the major reasons why the Soviet system collapsed.

Economic Growth. An interesting application of the PPC is to economic growth. **Economic growth** occurs when the total output of the economy increases over time. To see how this issue can be analyzed with the PPC, consider Figure 2.13 where capital goods (K) have been placed on the vertical axis and consumption goods (C) are on the horizontal axis.[3] Society can presumably choose between any point on the initial PPC through (K_0,C_0), but the choice can have important implications for the future. For example, if point a is chosen, relatively many capital goods and relatively few consumption goods will be produced. This will increase the prospects for future economic growth and movement to the higher PPC passing through (K_a,C_a). Why? An increase in capital goods means that workers have more machinery to work with and are thus more productive. Additionally, new capital is technologically sophisticated capital. On the other hand, if point b is selected, future growth

Economic growth Typically refers to the GDP; rising GDP over time due to additional resources or more efficient production methods.

---

[2] Of course, the United States did the same thing, though to a lesser degree: U.S. consumers could have enjoyed more consumer goods had it not been for the Cold War.
[3] Remember the definition of capital from Chapter 1: A capital good is a machine used by a firm. Firms acquire capital in order to expand production or replace worn-out machines.

••••• **FIGURE 2.13 ECONOMIC GROWTH AND THE PPC**

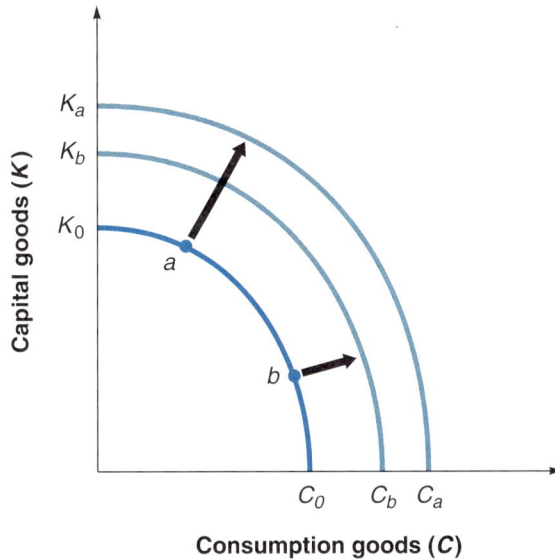

One factor that influences economic growth is how current production is split between capital goods (K) and consumption goods (C). If the current PPC passes through (K_0, C_0) and society chooses to produce at point a, the future generation will enjoy the PPC passing through (K_a, C_a); if current production is at point b, the future generation will have less production possibilities as illustrated by the PPC passing through (K_b, C_b). This is because point a represents more capital goods than point b. At point a, the current generation is sacrificing more current consumption, whereas at point b, the current generation is better off, but future economic growth will be slower.

will probably be slower—the economy will move only to the PPC passing through (K_b, C_b)—but consumers would be better off today.

Economic growth is a complicated issue that we will address in some detail in later chapters, but we can make a few comments here. First, many observers believe sluggish capital accumulation in the United States for the past 20 years or so is a major reason why economic growth has been slower than previously. This may be part of the reason why the U.S. standard of living has been increasing more slowly in the 1970s and 1980s than it did in the 1960s. It may also be part of the reason why the United States is finding it increasingly difficult to compete on international markets. Many of our trading partners have higher rates of capital accumulation, and many have invested more in **human capital** (education) as well. What could or should be done to increase capital investment remains a difficult issue for economists and policymakers. Finally, while economic growth is an important indication of economic progress, what is most important is whether the economy is growing faster than the population. That is, economists are concerned with the growth in *per capita* output, or total output in the economy divided by the population. This is important because the rise in our standard of living is closely related to the rise in per capita income and production.

Human capital The sum total of all knowledge, skills, and education of the individual.

SUMMARY

This chapter is important for two main reasons. First, it has provided a review of mathematical and graphical concepts that we will be using throughout the course. Second, it has developed an economic model, the production possibilities curve, to illustrate the important concepts of scarcity, choice, and opportunity cost.

1. Much economic analysis involves the use of graphical or mathematical models. Linear functions appear as a straight line on a graph; nonlinear functions are generally graphed as a curve. The slope of a function shows how much the dependent variable is affected by a one-unit change in the independent variable.

2. The production possibilities curve shows how much can be produced with given resources and technology assuming that all factors of production are employed. It is concave to the origin because of the law of increasing opportunity costs. The slope of the PPC shows the opportunity cost of producing one good in terms of another.

3. The intercepts of the PPC show how much of either good can be produced if all resources are devoted to a single product. Points on the PPC are efficient and attainable; points inside the PPC are attainable but inefficient; points outside the PPC are unattainable. The PPC will shift outward if there are more resources or technological advances. An outward shift in the PPC represents economic growth.

KEY TERMS AND CONCEPTS

scattergram
direct relationship
inverse relationship
linear function
nonlinear function
slope
intercept
tangent

extreme value
production possibilities curve (PPC)
feasible region
unattainable region
law of increasing opportunity costs
economic growth
human capital
opportunity cost

REVIEW QUESTIONS

1. Changing the scale on a graph's axis does not affect the *slope* of a function, but it does affect whether the graph is relatively steep or relatively flat. Explain.
2. Explain how to calculate the slope of a linear function and a nonlinear function. Draw graphs to illustrate your answer.
3. What are the assumptions behind the PPC model?
4. Explain how the PPC model illustrates scarcity, choice, opportunity cost, and economic efficiency.
5. What would cause a parallel shift in the PPC? What would change the slope of the PPC?

·······PROBLEMS

1. a. Plot the following data and determine the equation of the linear function:

X: 1   3   5   7   9   11   13   15
Y: 22 19 16 13 10 7   4   1

b. Now suppose that X is price and Y is quantity. Do you think these data better fit the behavior of producers or buyers? Why?

2. Refer back to Figure 2.13. If society were allowed to vote between point *a* and point *b*, how do you think the age distribution of the population would affect the outcome of the vote?

3. The line through Figure 2.5 has the equation $S = 11.3 + 2.4T$, where S = sales and T = traffic. What would you forecast sales to be if traffic were 150?

4. Refer back to Figure 2.9.

a. Suppose you developed a method to double your painting productivity. How would this affect the PPC? Draw a graph to illustrate your answer.

b. Now suppose that you find a new kind of ladder that allows you to paint large houses twice as quickly, but does not affect your painting speed on small, single-story houses. How would this affect the PPC? Draw a graph to illustrate your result.

5. Suppose that the PPCs for Country *A* and Country *B* are as shown below. In which country is the opportunity cost of gun production lower? In which country is the opportunity cost of butter production lower? Why? *Be careful; the answer may not be as obvious as you think!*

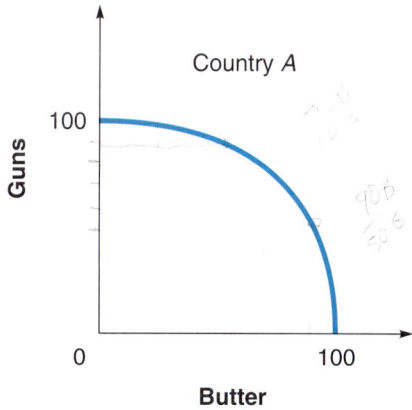

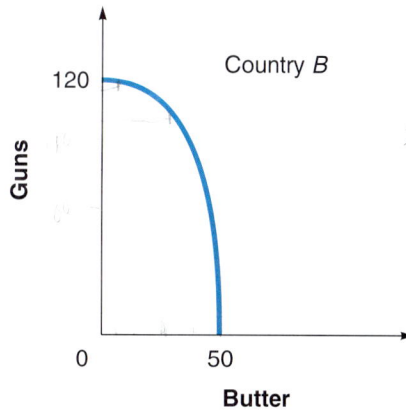

6. Under what conditions might a PPC look like the one below?

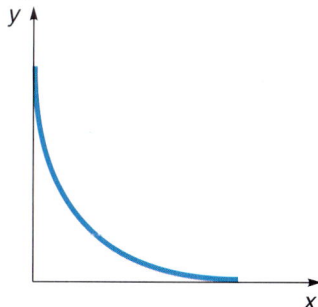

7. **a.** Plot the function $C = 2 + Q^2$ over the range $Q = \{0, 1, 2, 3, 4\}$.
   b. Now suppppose that Q = quantity produced and C = cost of production. Provide an economic interpretation of your graph.
   c. What is the slope of your function at $Q = 0$? (*Hint:* Plug in the value $Q = -1$.)
8. Answer the following questions based on the graph below:

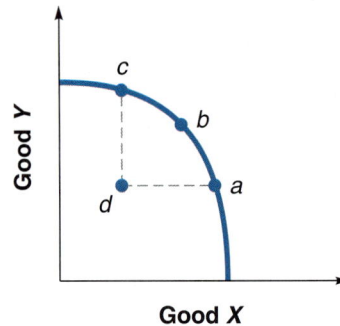

Good X

   a. At which point, *a* or *c*, is the opportunity cost of good X higher? Why?
   b. What is the opportunity cost of moving from point *d* to point *a*?
   c. Suppose that X represents capital goods and Y represents consumption goods. Which point is more *efficient,* point *c* or point *a*?
   d. Suppose that X-production technology increased. Would this raise or lower the opportunity cost of good X? Of good Y? Show how this would look on the graph.
9. Do you think that a PPC that traded off wheat and soybeans would be more or less concave than a PPC that traded off guns and butter? Why?

CHAPTER 3

Supply, Demand, and the Role of Markets

Most people have an intuitive grasp of the workings of markets. You know that when there are just a few sellers and lots of buyers, the sellers are likely to ask a higher price than if the situation were reversed. Some of the buyers will pay the high price, and others will try to find substitute goods. You also know that if one producer is making high profits, other firms will enter that business to try to make the same high profits. The market process is really little more than this; the market merely elicits and digests the actions of rational people. In some situations, however, your intuition may not be enough to determine how the market will respond. For example, do you understand how rent controls can reduce the availability of rental apartments? Why the minimum wage may actually increase the unemployment rate for young people and new entrants into the labor force? To evaluate these propositions requires an understanding of supply and demand analysis, the topic of this and the next chapter.

Supply and demand determine prices, and prices are signals that determine the allocation of resources in a market economy. It is vitally important that you understand the ideas presented in this chapter before proceeding any further in the text.

AFTER READING AND STUDYING THIS CHAPTER, YOU SHOULD BE ABLE TO:
- • • Explain how the price mechanism works to allocate resources, goods, and services
- • • Understand the theoretical underpinnings of the supply and demand curves
- • • Know the difference between a *movement along* and a *shift* in the supply and demand curves
- • • List several factors that shift supply and demand curves
- • • Explain how market forces establish the equilibrium price and quantity

CONSUMER BEHAVIOR AND THE DEMAND CURVE

We already know that a market is a process for buyers and sellers to transact business. Just as importantly, it is a device for providing information to those market participants. The most important information the market provides is *price*. In a market economy, prices convey information about both the costs of production and the wants of consumers. As costs or wants change, so do prices. The task at hand is to analyze the factors that affect costs and wants and thus see how they will affect prices. We will first look at consumer behavior and the demand side of the market.

Diminishing Marginal Utility

Think for a minute: After a workout at the gymnasium, a glass of lemonade sure hits the spot. You may even need a second glass. And if you're really thirsty, you might opt for a third glass. But at some point, even if the lemonade is free, you will stop drinking. There is a simple reason why: Other things being equal, the added satisfaction you receive from consuming successive units of a good declines as additional units are consumed. If we substitute the word "utility" for satisfaction and recognize that the added utility from consuming the next or the *marginal* unit is less than from the previous unit, we have a statement of the *principle of diminishing marginal utility*. This principle dates back to the late nineteenth century when it was developed separately but simultaneously by W. Stanley Jevons, Carl Menger, and Léon Walras (see Our Economic Heritage on page 52). Jevons, Menger, and Walras used the principle of diminishing marginal utility as the basis for the theory of demand.

Contemporary economists use a slightly different line of logic to develop the theory of demand, but marginal utility theory is still useful for a first introduction. Suppose that you have just finished a workout and really do need to quench your thirst. Suppose further that drinking that first glass of lemonade gives you 30 units— called "utils"—of satisfaction. It is reasonable to think that a second glass of lemonade would give you less additional satisfaction, perhaps only 20 utils, while the third glass would provide just 10 utils more. In the terminology of the utility theorists, the **marginal utility** of successive glasses of lemonade *diminishes,* as shown in Figure 3.1. The term "marginal" is especially important in economic analysis; it refers to the next or incremental unit. Notice that diminishing marginal utility does not mean that *total* utility decreases as you drink additional glasses of lemonade; it means only that the satisfaction from the next unit is less than the satisfaction from the previous unit.[1] In this case, the *total* utility of drinking three glasses of lemonade is 60 utils; the *marginal* utility of the third glass is just 10 utils.

The Law of Demand

The most important use of marginal utility theory today is in introducing a far more important concept, the **law of demand:**

Marginal utility The change in satisfaction (utility) associated with consumption of one additional unit of a good.

Law of demand The quantity demanded varies inversely with price, *centeris paribus.*

[1]What if you drank so much lemonade that you got sick? Then that last glass would actually provide negative utility—but that would indicate that you were behaving irrationally or with incomplete information regarding the consequences of lemonade overindulgence.

····**FIGURE 3.1** DIMINISHING MARGINAL UTILITY

The principle of diminishing marginal utility states that the satisfaction ("utility") from the consumption of successive units of a good diminishes. In this case, the first glass of lemonade delivers 30 utils, the second glass delivers 20 utils, and the third glass provides just 10 utils. The *total utility* of consuming all three glasses is 60 utils.

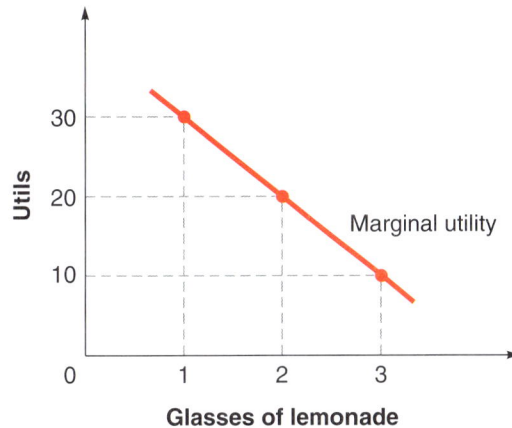

DEFINITION: The Law of Demand. The quantity of a good demanded varies inversely with price, *ceteris paribus*.

In other words, people will tend to buy less of a product at high prices, and more at low prices, if all other factors influencing demand are held constant. The law of demand follows directly from the principle of diminishing marginal utility: if you get lots of satisfaction from the first unit, you should be willing to pay a high price; if you get less satisfaction from subsequent units, you will buy them only at lower prices.

Another explanation for the inverse relationship between price and quantity demanded is the existence of *substitution* and *income effects*. Consumers typically choose among several products, and when the price of one good falls relative to another good, they tend to substitute the cheaper good for the more expensive good. This process is known as the **substitution effect:** A rise in price will cause people to substitute other goods and thus decrease their purchases of the good whose price has risen. The **income effect** is also brought about by a change in prices. It refers to the fact that as the price of a good rises, the purchasing power of your income falls because you can purchase fewer goods. Analysis of income and substitution effects is important in many areas of economics and will be discussed in more detail in later chapters.

The law of demand is illustrated in Figure 3.2. The *demand schedule* gives hypothetical data showing how many glasses of lemonade would be purchased at alternative prices in a given interval of time. In this case we are supposing that a particular consumer would purchase one glass when the price is $1.00, two glasses at a price of $0.75, and so on. The **demand curve** is a graphical representation of the demand schedule. Its downward slope is consistent with the law of demand: More tends to be bought at low prices than at high prices. A more precise definition of the demand curve is this:

Substitution effect An effect of a price change. A rise (fall) in the price of good X raises (lowers) the relative price of good X with respect to good Y and reduces (increases) the quantity demanded of good X.

Income effect An effect of a price change. A rise (fall) in prices lowers (raises) real income and reduces (increases) the amount that can be purchased.

Demand curve A graphical representation of the relationship between the price and the quantity that will be purchased.

FIGURE 3.2 THE DEMAND CURVE

Demand Schedule	
Price	Quantity
$1.00	1
0.75	2
0.50	3
0.25	4

The demand curve represents the different quantities that will be purchased at alternative prices over a given interval of time, *ceteris paribus*. The downward slope of the demand curve is consistent with the principle of diminishing marginal utility.

> **DEFINITION: The Demand Curve for a particular good gives the different quantities that will be purchased at various prices over a given interval of time, *ceteris paribus*.**

Shifting Versus Moving Along the Demand Curve. When we defined the demand curve, the ubiquitous *ceteris paribus* showed up at the end of the definition. The reason, of course, is that several things affect the demand curve other than price. What if you had no money? You would not have been able to buy even the first glass of lemonade. Or what if you were allergic to lemons? These and other factors will obviously have an effect on your decision to purchase a glass of lemonade.

An almost infinite number of elements can affect buying decisions, but before we explore some of these things, we need to get the graphical terminology down carefully. When we derived the demand curve for lemonade, we were talking about movements *along* a given demand curve. A change in the price of the good under discussion is the only factor that can result in movement along a demand curve. A change in price results in a **change in the quantity demanded.** For instance, if the price of lemonade were to fall from $1.00 to $0.50 in Figure 3.2, the quantity demanded would rise from 1 to 3 glasses of lemonade. Everything else that affects demand results in a shift in the entire demand curve. A shift in the entire demand curve is called a **change in demand.** A rightward shift of the demand curve (away from the price axis) is called an *increase in demand* because buyers are willing to purchase more lemonade at all prices. Similarly, a leftward shift of the demand curve (toward the price axis) is called a *decrease in demand*. The distinction between a change

Change in quantity demanded An increase or decrease in the quantity demanded, represented graphically by movement along the demand curve.

Change in demand An increase or decrease in demand, represented graphically by a shift in the demand curve.

in demand and a change in the quantity demanded is very important—and often confusing. Figure 3.3 illustrates the difference between a change in demand and a change in the quantity demanded.

Factors that Shift the Demand Curve. The number of things that can shift the demand curve is literally infinite, so it is impossible to memorize them all. The solution is to *understand* why the demand curve shifts, and apply your reasoning to specific situations. To cement our understanding of demand curve shifts, we will look at some of the specific factors that might affect the demand for espresso coffee. However, the real task for you is to be able to generalize from these examples.

Here's the story: Yours truly, an espresso aficionado, has been buying espresso coffee at the local Heritage Coffee House for nearly four years now. In the past, espresso usually sold for $2, and I generally dropped by Heritage House twice a week. When the price rose to $3, I would stop at the coffee house only once a week. And when espresso went on special for only $1 a cup, I drank at least three espressos a week. And I will continue this pattern as long as the *ceteris paribus* assumption holds.

· · · · **FIGURE 3.3** MOVING ALONG VERSUS SHIFTING THE
        DEMAND CURVE

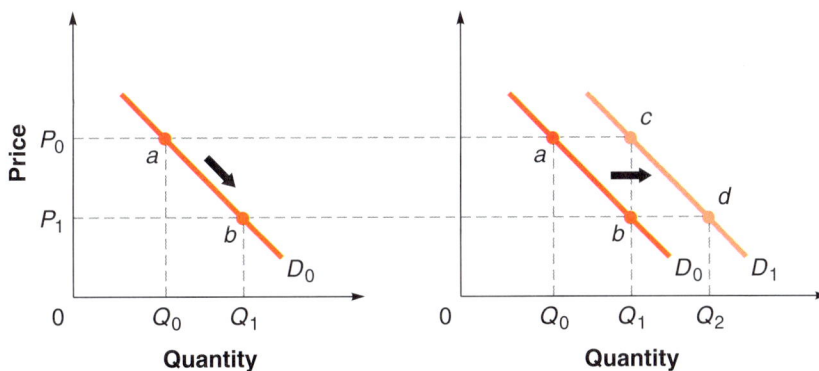

(a) A change in the *quantity demanded*   (b) A *change in demand*

Panel (a) illustrates movement along a given demand curve. A decrease in price from P_0 to P_1 results in an increase in the quantity demanded from Q_0 to Q_1. A change in price is the *only* thing that can cause a change in the quantity demanded. Panel (b) illustrates a change in demand. Beginning with the initial demand curve, D_0, a factor other than price causes an increase in demand. This shifts the entire demand curve out to D_1. The difference between the two effects can be seen by comparing the movement from *a* to *b* with the movement from *a* to *c*. In the first case, the lower price, P_1, elicits an increase in the quantity purchased. In the second case, more is purchased even at the initial price, P_0. This can only occur if an external event—perhaps an increase in the consumer's income—causes the demand curve to shift outward.

OUR ECONOMIC HERITAGE

THE MARGINAL UTILITY SCHOOL

Philosophers and economists had been talking about utility and marginalism since the late eighteenth century, but the application of utility theory to economics did not take off until the almost simultaneous publication in the 1870s of works by an Englishman, W. Stanley Jevons (1835–1882), a Frenchman, Léon Walras (1834–1910), and an Austrian, Carl Menger (1840–1921). Their remarkably similar views did not gain an audience immediately, but did make more headway than earlier works on similar topics. Why the ideas of these authors became popular when others did not is a matter of conjecture. Some have argued that the authors had immediate credibility because they were all academic economists. Others note that Menger, in particular, was able to attract talented students who spread his ideas. Others have argued that the

mathematical arguments of Jevons and Walras added an air of scientific rigor that previous presentations had lacked.

What were the key insights of the members of the marginal utility school? Three things might be mentioned. First, drawing on the work of the English philosopher Jeremy Bentham (1748–1832),[1] Jevons was able to construct a vision of economics as a "hedonistic calculus of pleasure and pain," and he noted that people made decisions on the margin—views that are still at the heart of modern economics. Jevons's skill as an engineer and mathematician influenced his methodology. He used calculus and anticipated modern econometrics and even helped develop a "logical machine," a distant ancestor of the modern computer.

Walras is best remembered for his work in the area of *general equilibrium*. A talented mathematician, Walras was able to conceive of the entire economy as a system of simultaneous equations that show the complex interconnection among all the markets in the economic system. Most modern eco-

Income. As I pick up my mail on the way to the coffee shop, I notice a letter from my aunt. I open it and find that Aunt Mabel has decided to give me $10,000 each year until she dies. Because that represents a significant increase in my annual income, I begin thinking how to spend it. One way, of course, is to celebrate with a double espresso. I do so—even though espresso carries the usual $2 price. My espresso demand curve has undergone an outward and parallel shift. The graphical story of the effects of Aunt Mabel's gift is shown in Figure 3.4. Had I received a notice from the IRS that I owed back taxes, my espresso demand curve would have shifted in the opposite direction, toward the price axis because I would have less income to spend on espresso.

Inferior good A good people use less of at a lower price.

There is an important exception to the foregoing: **inferior goods.** An inferior good is one that is purchased only because a superior substitute is unavailable or too expensive for the consumer's budget. For example, coffee drinkers generally prefer coffee house espresso to fast-food restaurant coffee even though espresso prices are

nomic models begin with the concept of general equilibrium.

Menger and the Austrian branch of the marginal utility school are perhaps best remembered for using marginal utility theory as an attack on Marxian economics. By the 1870s, the labor theory of value had become a cornerstone of the Marxian theory of exploitation. Workers, it was argued, were exploited because they were paid a wage less than the value of their labor effort. But if goods were priced according to the labor embodied in the productive process, there would not be enough purchasing power to buy everything that was produced. The result: Capitalism was prone to crisis. Menger and his followers countered this argument by noting that price and value are determined by utility and scarcity, not by labor alone. They concluded that workers were not exploited and that capitalism was not prone to crisis. Marginal utility theory thus became ammunition against Marxism.

The seeds planted by the marginal utility school continue to grow. The dominant school of economic thought today, *neoclassical economics,* is a direct descendant of the marginal utility school. Just as important, today's use of mathematics can be traced in part to the pioneering work of Jevons and Walras. Finally, an offshoot of the Menger branch of the marginal utility school, the Austrians, is still at work criticizing Marxian and radical economics. In 1974, a contemporary Austrian economist, Friedrich von Hayek, won the Nobel Prize in economics.

[1] Bentham's work in utility theory is enough to classify him as an economist in many people's eyes, which makes it appropriate to relay one rather interesting (or perhaps disturbing) anecdote about him. Bentham was a quite successful investor, and when he died, he left all of his money to his university, University College of London, with one provision—that he oversee the annual meeting of the Board of Trustees forever. That was made possible by a taxidermist who embalmed Bentham, fitted him with a wax replica of his head, and placed him in a glass display case. Bentham still resides at University College—really.

four or five times as high. Both goods have downward-sloping demand curves, but income affects them differently. The reasoning goes like this. Suppose that as a semi-starving student, you survive on coffee from the local McDonald's for most of your four years in college. When you complete your economics degree and get your first real job, your income triples. Does this mean that you will drink more McDonald's coffee? Probably not. Most likely, you will drink *less* McDonald's coffee and *more* espresso. Your demand curve for fast-food coffee will have shifted toward the left, just the opposite of what occurs for normal goods. We need to emphasize that most goods are not inferior goods, so an increase in income typically does cause the demand curve to shift to the right.

Tastes. Changes in taste can shift the demand curve in much the same way as a change in income. Some people do not like espresso and will not drink it regardless of its price or their income. I have always liked espresso, but began drinking more

•···· FIGURE 3.4 SHIFTING THE DEMAND CURVE

An increase in income will shift the demand curve away from the price axis so that a higher quantity is purchased at every price. Along D_0, two espressos are purchased at $P = \$2$; along D_1, three espressos are purchased at $P = \$2$. A decrease in income will shift the demand curve toward the price axis, and fewer goods will be bought at every price. Inferior goods are an exception to this analysis: An increase in income will reduce the demand for an inferior good; a decrease in income will increase the demand for an inferior good.

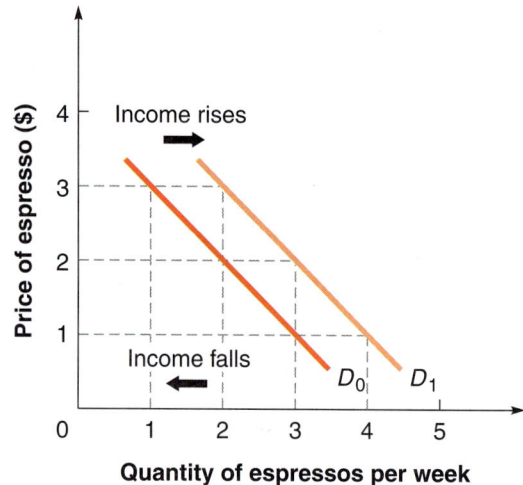

of it when I realized that coffee shops were good places to meet interesting people. If I could just convince myself that there was nothing wrong with the caffeine, my espresso demand would shift outward—just as it did with an increase in income—and I would buy more espressos at every price. On the other hand, if I heard on the radio that espresso can cause ulcers, my demand curve would shift to the left.

Substitute good A good that can be used in place of another.

Prices of substitutes and complements. **Substitute goods** are goods that satisfy the same general need or want. For example, tea may be a reasonable substitute for espresso. In fact, I occasionally opt for a cup of hot Earl Grey at the Heritage House, and when there is a special price on tea, I often drink it instead of espresso. On the other hand, when the price of tea is high, I do not even consider buying it and stick with my standard cup of espresso. The result: When the price of a substitute good like tea falls, the demand for espresso decreases, and the demand curve shifts to the left; when the price of a substitute good rises, the demand for the good under consideration increases, and the demand curve shifts to the right. This is shown in Figure 3.5.

Complementary good A good that is used in conjunction with another.

A **complementary good** is one that is used with the good in question. For example, Heritage House makes a great cinnamon roll that goes well with espresso. On those rare occasions when cinnamon rolls go on sale, I am even more inclined to stop by for an espresso—and a cinnamon roll, of course. And when they raise the price of cinnamon rolls, I might forgo the espresso completely. The result: If the price of a complementary good rises, espresso demand falls, and the demand curve shifts to the left; if the price of a complementary good falls, the demand for espresso rises, and the demand curve shifts out. This is also shown in Figure 3.5. Notice that a change in the price of a complementary good has the opposite effect as a change in the price of a substitute good: An increase in the price of a substitute good increases demand for the good under consideration; an increase in the price of a complementary good decreases the demand for the good under consideration.

···· **FIGURE 3.5 CHANGES IN THE PRICE OF SUBSTITUTE AND COMPLEMENTARY GOODS**

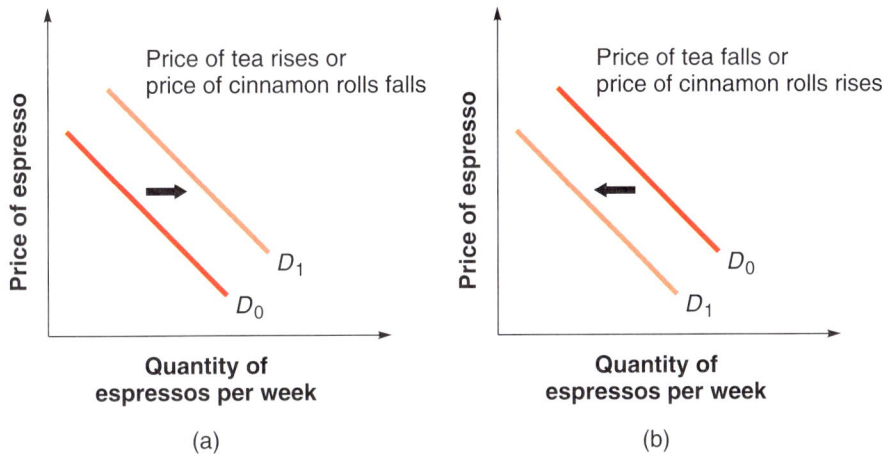

Changes in the price of substitutes and complements shift the demand curve. If the price of a substitute like tea rises or the price of a complement like cinnamon rolls falls, the demand curve for espresso will shift out as shown in panel (a). If the price of a substitute falls or the price of a complement rises, the demand curve will shift inward as in panel (b).

Expected Prices. The Heritage House is not the only place I drink espresso. I also drink it at home. Suppose that I hear on the radio that a drought in Colombia has decimated the coffee crop and the price of coffee beans is expected to rise in the near future. The reasonable thing to do would be to run to the store today and stock up on coffee *before* the price rises. The result would be an outward shift in my coffee bean demand curve. On the other hand, if I expect coffee prices to fall—perhaps due to a relaxation of coffee import restrictions—I might drink tea until the price comes down. This would shift the espresso demand curve inward.

Of course, buying in anticipation of price increases or waiting for the price to drop can be constrained by several factors. For example, if you are buying espresso beans for home consumption, you need to realize that coffee only keeps a few weeks. And if you *really* like espresso coffee, you may not want to settle for tea while you wait for the price to drop. Finally, if coffee drinking is an important social ritual—perhaps you are "expected" to offer coffee to guests at dinner parties—anticipated price changes may have little to do with your behavior.

The number of buyers. So far, all of the discussion has concerned the demand curve of a single individual. It is also possible to construct *market demand curves*. A market demand curve is found by adding together individual demand curves. For example, suppose there are three people in the espresso market, Bill, Max, and Rhonda. To find the market demand curve, it is only necessary to find and sum the different quantities that each market participant will purchase at various prices. This technique

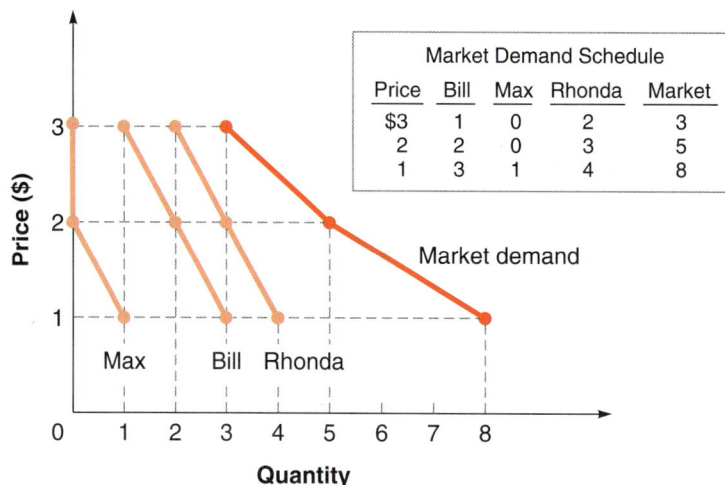

•••• FIGURE 3.6 MARKET DEMAND CURVE

Market Demand Schedule				
Price	Bill	Max	Rhonda	Market
$3	1	0	2	3
2	2	0	3	5
1	3	1	4	8

The market demand curve is found by adding together individual demand curves. For example, when price is $2, $Q_{Max} = 0$, $Q_{Bill} = 2$, and $Q_{Rhonda} = 3$ so $Q_{market} = 5$; when price is $1, $Q_{Max} = 1$, $Q_{Bill} = 3$, and $Q_{Rhonda} = 4$ so $Q_{market} = 8$. The market demand curve is flatter than the individual demand curves and farther from the price axis.

is sometimes called horizontal addition. The demand schedules and resulting demand curves are shown in Figure 3.6.

Three important points should be noted about the relationship between individual and market demand curves. First, the market demand schedule will always be farther from the price axis than any individual demand curve. Second, as more people enter the market, the demand curve will shift to the right. Finally, the market demand curve will always be flatter than individual demand curves. We will find out later that the steepness of a demand curve can be especially important.

Other factors. The five shift factors we have just discussed—income, tastes, the prices of substitutes and complements, expected prices, and the number of buyers—are not the only things that can cause the demand curve to shift. Depending on the particular good under consideration, almost anything can cause the demand curve to shift. For example, the demand for coffee beans would decrease (a tiny amount) if electricity prices rose dramatically because it would be too expensive to operate home coffee bean grinders. Even war could cause the demand for espresso to change if returning soldiers had fond memories of the excellent espresso they enjoyed while overseas. The point is that you cannot simply memorize the various shift factors. You need to understand *why* these—and other—events cause the demand curve to shift. The exercises at the end of this chapter will help you with some examples.

Exceptions to the law of demand. Although these examples are useful for understanding consumer behavior regarding most goods, certain exceptions should be noted before we leave our discussion of demand.

One of the foundations of modern economic analysis is the idea that people are *rational.* Rational behavior means that people prefer more to less and are goal seeking. Although this assumption is generally true, there are cases when it might not be. For example, Thorstein Veblen (1857–1929), an early critic of conventional economics and a founder of the institutionalist school of thought (see Our Economic Heritage on page 58), argued that people in modern societies are often afflicted with what he called **conspicuous consumption.** Conspicuous consumption occurs when people buy things because they are expensive in an effort to impress their friends. Is a BMW 325 really worth $8,000 more than a Honda Accord? Perhaps, but it is also possible that many people buy BMWs primarily to show off. If people truly believe that BMWs are worth the extra money, then they are not engaged in conspicuous consumption, but if they are trying to show off their ability to buy expensive cars, they certainly are. The demand curve for a product purchased by a conspicuous consumer is upward sloping because more of it is bought at a higher price.

> **Conspicuous consumption** The idea that people will sometimes choose to consume expensive goods to impress their neighbors.

The opposite of conspicuous consumption is what might be called the *blue jeans effect.* Some people buy products because they are inexpensive; that is, their satisfaction comes not from the product itself, but because they got a special deal on it. People who spend their weekends at garage sales and then brag about their purchases at the office might fall into this category. Why is this behavior an exception to the law of demand? The law of demand refers to the utility associated with *using* the product, not *buying* it. It is rational to look for bargains, but to buy products solely because they are sold at a discount is to fall prey to the act of shopping.

We should not make too much of these exceptions to the law of demand. Cases of conspicuous consumption and the blue jeans effect are probably rare, so unless you have very good reason to suspect otherwise, it is best to accept the law of demand as a reasonable description of behavior.

BUSINESS BEHAVIOR AND THE SUPPLY CURVE

The demand curve gives only one side of the market, the side of the consumer. But products are available to consumers only if sellers make them available. Businesses offer or *supply* products if they think they can make a profit. Profits are essentially the difference between the selling price and the costs of production, so firms must consider production costs carefully in their quest for profits.

Supply and Time

Virtually everything we have just said about demand has an analogue in supply. For example, the **law of supply** states:

> **Law of supply** The quantity supplied varies directly with price, *ceteris paribus.*

> **DEFINITION: The Law of Supply. The quantity of a product supplied varies directly with price, *ceteris paribus.***

The corresponding supply curve is defined as:

> **DEFINITION: The Supply Curve gives the different quantities of a good that will be offered at various prices during an interval of time, *ceteris paribus.***

OUR ECONOMIC HERITAGE

THORSTEIN B. VEBLEN

There may be no more curious figure in the history of economics than Thorstein B. Veblen (1857–1929). Born in Wisconsin to Norwegian immigrants, Veblen attended Carleton College where he took courses from J. B. Clark, one of the leading economists of the day. (Clark is the subject of an Economic Heritage in Chapter 15.) After graduation, Veblen spent a year teaching elementary school before he enrolled at Yale to study philosophy. He earned his doctorate in 1884. Despite excellent recommendations from his professors, Veblen was unable to find a university teaching position so he returned to the family farm. In 1891 he enrolled at Cornell University to continue his study of economics. A year later he joined the economics faculty at the University of Chicago.

Chicago was only the first of several stops in Veblen's academic career; he also taught at Stanford, the University of Missouri, and New York University. Why did Veblen move so much? Part of the reason is that he was rather deficient in social skills, and while he was undoubtedly brilliant, his lectures were less than inspiring, to say the least. But the main reason may have been that his work was so critical of orthodox economics that his colleagues were uncomfortable having him around.

Veblen published his first book, *The Theory of the Leisure Class,* in 1899. In this biting and witty social satire, Veblen first advocated the study of economic institutions and argued that economics must be an evolutionary science concerned with the processes of economic change. Unlike many of his contemporaries, Veblen drew upon anthropology, psychology, history, and the physical sciences for his inspiration. Veblen argued that orthodox neoclassical economics was more concerned with classification than with understanding real economic processes; he believed that orthodox economists deliberately ignored the "disturbing factors" that did not fit into their mathematical models. He was critical of the economists' conception of economic man as a "lightning calculator of pleasure and pain"; his theory of conspicuous consumption was offered as an example of the often irrational nature of economic behavior. Veblen was also critical of the economists' conception that the "captains of industry" were motivated to produce goods and services. He argued that their primary motivation was financial ("pecuniary" as he put it) and that they obtained their economic rewards by financial manipulation and monopoly power. Such an argument left open the possibility that government intervention in the economy might be necessary—not the sort of thing that *laissez faire*–minded neoclassical economists wanted to hear. Veblen also felt that equilibrium analysis was an inappropriate tool for studying an evolving economy.

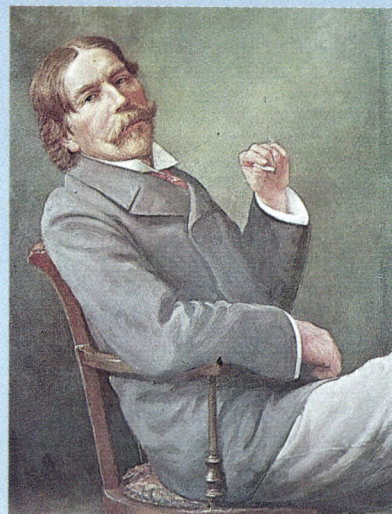

Veblen's criticism of orthodox economics developed into a a school of economics that is still alive today, *institutionalism.* Though institutionalism has never seriously challenged the prevailing neoclassical orthodoxy, there are still pockets of institutionalists at several universities. Like Veblen, institutionalists reject overly abstract economic theorizing and prefer instead to focus on real-world factors that affect economic evolution. In particular, institutional economists focus on the interaction between institutions and technology and on how this interaction affects the evolution of the economy. Contemporary economists associated with institutionalism include John Kenenth Galbraith of Harvard, Lester Thurow of MIT, and the Swedish economist and Nobel laureate, Gunnar Myrdal (1898–1987).

Before we develop the reasoning behind the law of supply and the supply curve, we need to say a few words about time. Firms can supply goods and services only if they have them, and this usually means that the goods and services must be produced. Because production takes time, it is important to distinguish between different periods of time.

Economists generally speak about **analytical time** as opposed to **historical time**. Historical time is just the time of everyday usage—days, weeks, hours, and the like. In contrast, analytical time does not refer to specific units of time. Instead, it is divided into periods that are useful for the specific analysis at hand. Three periods of analytical time are useful for analyzing the firm's supply decision: the market period, the short run, and the long run. These situations are shown in Figure 3.7.

- The **market period** is defined as a period of time when all production has taken place so the firm has a fixed quantity it is trying to sell. An example of the market period is the moment a fisher brings fish to the dock. When the catch is large, the fish usually sell at a low price; when the catch is poor, the price of fish is high. The important point to notice is that production has already taken place, so the selling price has no influence on the amount that is supplied in the market period. This is why the supply curve in Figure 3.7a is vertical.
- The **short run** is a period of time when at least one factor of production is fixed but the firm can vary output by increasing or decreasing other factors of production. For example, if production takes place in a single factory, the firm can increase output by hiring more workers. This means that the quantity the firm is able to supply can vary in the short run. However, as long as at least one factor of production is fixed, the costs of production will eventually rise as output

Analytical time Economists often divide time into periods useful for analysis; for example, the short run and the long run.

Historical time Time as measured by clocks and history.

Market period The period of analytical time when all production has taken place and goods are brought to the market.

Short run The period of analytical time when something is fixed and/or complete adjustment is not possible.

FIGURE 3.7 TIME AND PRODUCTION

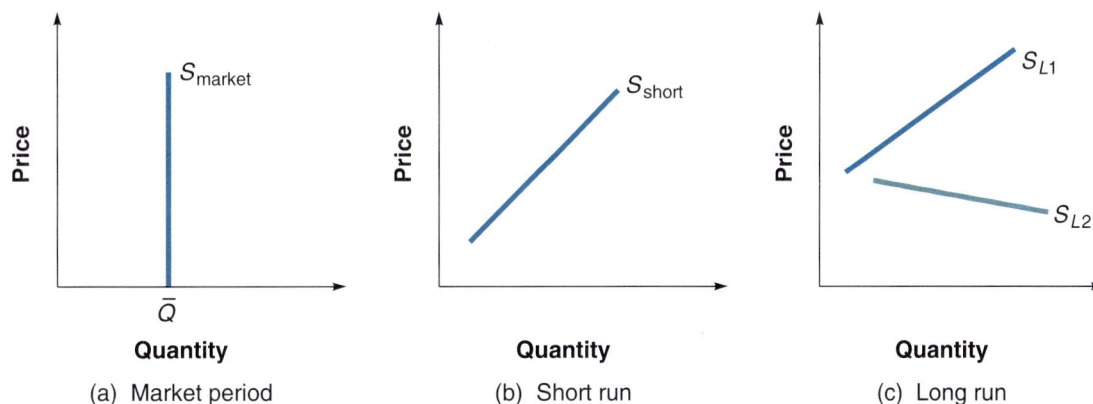

(a) Market period   (b) Short run   (c) Long run

Panel (a) presents the conditions that prevail in the market period. All production has taken place, so the firm offers a quantity, $\overline{Q}$, on the market regardless of price. The price that can be charged depends on demand. In the short run, panel (b), at least one factor of production is fixed, so costs rise as more goods are produced. Firms need higher prices to cover the costs of producing a greater quantity. The long-run supply curve, panel (c), will slope downward (S_{L2}) if increasing specialization lowers costs or upward if costs rise (S_{L1}), perhaps due to a shrinking natural resource base.

Long run The period of analytical time when there are no constants; everything can change.

increases. Here is the reason: as more workers are added to a fixed amount of machinery, there will be less machinery per worker, and thus workers will be less productive. If the new workers are paid the same wage as the old workers, the costs per unit of output will rise. Higher production costs mean that the firm must raise its selling price in order to remain profitable. This is why the short-run supply curve in Figure 3.7b slopes upward.

• The **long run** is defined as a period of time when no factors of production are fixed. In the long run, the firm cannot only hire more workers, but also build new factories, adopt new technologies, and so on. Technology, the resource base, and other factors affect the costs of production and thus the shape of the long-run supply curve. For example, the long-run supply curve for personal computers is downward sloping because of increasing specialization: as the volume of personal computer production has expanded, computer firms have been able to adopt more specialized equipment and lower the cost of production. On the other hand, dwindling oil reserves are causing the long-run cost of gasoline production to increase because firms are having to drill deeper and in more remote areas to find oil. This is why Figure 3.7c shows both an upward-sloping and a downward-sloping long-run supply curve.

· · · · · · · ·

The Short-Run Supply Curve

We will focus most of our attention in this and the next few chapters on the short run so the supply curves we will be dealing with will typically be upward sloping. In other words, as price increases, the quantity supplied increases, *ceteris paribus*. Remember that this result holds in the short run, but not in the market period. It may or may not hold in the long run.

Shifting the Short-Run Supply Curve. As you probably suspect, changes in price result in movement along a given supply curve. When other factors change, there is a change in supply, and the entire supply curve shifts. The factors that shift supply curves are different from those that shift demand curves. In fact, supply and demand curves are generally thought of as being independent; if something shifts the demand curve, it rarely has an effect on the supply curve. Nevertheless, it is important to realize that although the factors that shift the supply curve usually do not shift the demand curve, a shift in the supply curve does cause movement along the demand curve and vice versa. This will be apparent momentarily.

Before we discuss the variables that shift the supply curve, however, we need to make sure we know what is meant by an increase or decrease in supply. The phrase an "increase in supply" means that the firm is willing to offer a higher quantity at every price. Likewise, the phrase a "decrease in supply" indicates that the firm is willing to offer a lower quantity at every price. Figure 3.8 illustrates both an increase and a decrease in supply. Begin on the initial supply curve, S_0, and notice that the firm is willing to offer the quantity Q_0 on the market if the price is $\bar{P}$. Now look at the supply curve S_1. The same price, $\bar{P}$, results in a greater quantity supplied, Q_1; this is an increase in supply. The opposite occurs along supply curve S_2. The price $\bar{P}$ results in a smaller quantity, Q_2, being offered; this is a decrease in supply. These results can be generalized: An increase in supply causes the supply curve to shift to

•••••**FIGURE 3.8** SHIFTING THE SUPPLY CURVE

An increase in supply shifts the supply curve away from the price axis. A decrease in supply shifts the supply curve toward the price axis. To see this, consider a fixed price, $\bar{P}$, and notice that along the initial supply curve, S_0, the quantity supplied is Q_0. Along S_1 a larger quantity, Q_1, is supplied at the same price. This indicates an increase in supply. Along S_2 the same price results in a lower quantity, Q_2, being supplied. This indicates a decrease in supply.

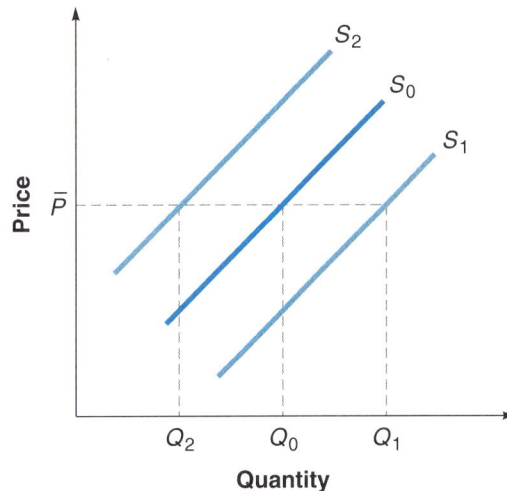

the right and away from the price axis; a decrease in supply causes the supply curve to shift to the left and toward the price axis. This is sometimes confusing, because as we will see momentarily, *an increase in supply is often the same thing as a decrease in cost and a decrease in supply is often the same thing as an increase in cost.*

Factors That Shift the Short-Run Supply Curve. Several things can shift the supply curve. Among the most important are factor costs, technology, price expectations, and the number of sellers:

• *Factor costs.* Along a given supply curve, wages, interest, rent, and the other factor costs are assumed to be fixed. If the cost of production increases, the selling price will have to rise to cover these higher costs. For example, suppose that the wholesale cost of coffee beans were to double. Heritage House and other retail coffee shops would be forced to raise the price of espresso to cover their higher production costs. Graphically, an increase in costs will shift the supply curve to the left, toward the price axis. This is illustrated as a shift from S_0 to S_2 in Figure 3.9. A decrease in costs—say, due to falling wholesale coffee prices, lower wages, or reduced utility bills—would cause the supply curve to shift outward and away from the price axis. This is illustrated as the shift from S_0 to S_1 in Figure 3.9.

• *Technology and regulations.* Firms typically adopt new production technology only if it lowers the cost of production. This means that an improvement in production technology will cause the supply curve to shift away from the price axis—an increase in supply. Does technology ever work in reverse? Not really, but government regulations can affect firms as if technology reversed itself. For example, when the government imposes regulations on firms requiring them to reduce pollution or adhere to certain safety specifications, costs rise and the supply curve shifts toward the price axis. This is not to say that such regulations are necessarily

FIGURE 3.9 FACTOR COSTS SHIFT THE SUPPLY CURVE

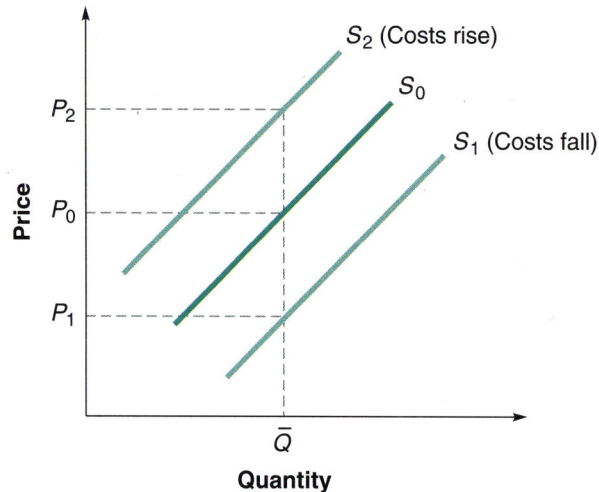

The supply curve indicates the different quantities that will be offered at various prices, *ceteris paribus*. Here the quantity, $\overline{Q}$, will be offered at price P_0 along supply curve S_0. An increase in costs will force the firm to raise the selling price to cover the higher costs. This is illustrated by the shift from S_0 to S_2. Notice that the firm is able to offer $\overline{Q}$ only at the higher price, P_2. A decrease in costs would allow the firm to offer the same quantity but at a lower selling price. This is represented by the shift from S_0 to S_1. This means that the same quantity is being offered at the lower price of P_1.

bad—the regulators clearly believe that society is better off without pollution and with safer products—but they do involve definite costs. We will examine government regulations and related issues in more detail in later chapters.

- *Expectations*. Expectations can shift the supply curve as well as the demand curve. For example, suppose that Compaq Computer fears that IBM is on the verge of introducing a new personal computer model that will take away sales. One strategy would be for Compaq to lower its price and increase supply today to forestall the IBM advance. This would cause the supply curve to shift to the right. On the other hand, if the news is that the new IBM models will be delayed, Compaq might withhold its current production and raise the selling price. This would shift the supply curve to the left.
- *The number of firms*. A market supply curve can be constructed the same way we constructed the market demand curve—with horizontal addition. When firms enter the industry, more of the good can be offered at all prices. The result is an increase in supply, so the supply curve shifts away from the price axis. The market supply curve is also flatter than individual supply curves. Why would firms enter the industry? One reason would be that existing firms are making high profits and others want to emulate them. Firms exit the industry when they are experiencing losses.
- *Other factors can shift the supply curve as well*. These examples should help you put your thoughts in order, but we did not—and could not—include all factors that

can potentially affect supply. Several other things can be important. For example, the weather can have an important effect on the supply of many goods, and not just agricultural products. Construction, transportation, and many other activities slow appreciably in the winter, at least in northern climates. The point is that it is not enough to memorize the supply curve shifts, you need to understand *how* and *why* it shifts.

> **RECAP**   Working with Supply and Demand Curves
>
> We need to recap what we have just learned before we put the supply and demand curves together.
>
> 1. A change in demand (supply) shifts the entire demand (supply) curve; a change in the quantity demanded (supplied) causes movement along a given curve. A change in price is the only thing that can cause movement along a given demand or supply curve.
> 2. Important factors that shift the demand curve include income, tastes, other prices, the number of buyers, and price expectations.
> 3. An increase in demand is represented by a shift away from the price axis; a decrease in demand is represented by a shift toward the price axis.
> 4. Important factors that shift the supply curve include costs, technology, the number of sellers, and expectations.
> 5. An increase in supply is represented by a shift away from the price axis; a decrease in supply is represented by a shift toward the price axis.

SUPPLY AND DEMAND TOGETHER: THE DETERMINATION OF MARKET PRICE

By themselves, neither the supply nor the demand curve is of much use. When put together, however, they can be used to determine market prices. Prices are exceedingly important in market economies because they provide information to market participants. If people are willing to pay a higher price, producers will increase production in the hope of making more profits, and other firms may enter the industry. When consumers see that the goods they want to buy carry a higher price, they look for substitutes. The interaction between buyers and sellers causes prices to change, so that prices generally reflect the costs of production and consumer preferences. This section explains how supply and demand interact to determine price.

Flexible Prices and Equilibrium

The supply curve and the demand curve give several price/quantity combinations, but only one price/quantity combination can satisfy both the buyer and the seller. This is the **equilibrium** point. Economists borrowed the term "equilibrium" from the physical sciences and use it to refer to a position of rest. In the context of supply and demand, equilibrium exists when there is no tendency for change. This occurs

Equilibrium A state of balance. A market is in equilibrium if the quantity supplied is equal to the quantity demanded.

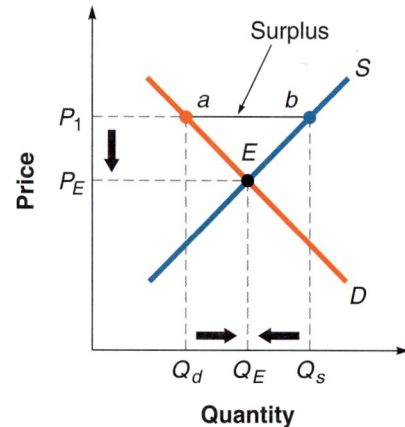

FIGURE 3.10 SURPLUSES AND ADJUSTMENT TO EQUILIBRIUM

A price greater than the equilibrium price ($P_1 > P_E$) results in an excess supply because the quantity supplied (Q_s) is greater than the quantity demanded (Q_d). If there are no restrictions on the market, competition among sellers will result in price declines, and the market will move to equilibrium where quantity supplied equals quantity demanded, $Q_s = Q_d$, and the price, P_E, is at the intersection of the demand and supply curves.

at the intersection of a supply and demand curve. It is the single point where the quantity demanded is equal to the quantity supplied. Of course, if something shifts the supply or demand curve, the equilibrium price and quantity will change.

Figure 3.10 illustrates how the market moves to equilibrium. Suppose, initially, that price P_1 prevails. The demand curve gives the different quantities that will be demanded at alternative prices, so people would try to buy the quantity Q_d. This occurs where P_1 crosses the demand curve at point a. Likewise, P_1 means that producers would try to supply Q_s at point b. Because the quantity supplied is greater than the quantity demanded, there is an *excess supply*. This situation cannot exist indefinitely. Without coercion, consumers will not buy more than they want to, and producers will incur serious losses if they keep producing more than they can sell. The market response to an excess supply is competition among sellers: sellers will hold "sales" to get rid of excess supplies and prices will decline. Consumers will respond to lower prices with an increase in the quantity demanded. Producers will respond to lower prices by decreasing the quantity supplied. These adjustments will continue until equilibrium is reached; that is, until $Q_d = Q_s$ and $P = P_E$.

Just the opposite occurs when price is less than the equilibrium price. The low price is an indication that consumers want more than firms are willing to offer; that is, $Q_d > Q_s$. The firms respond by increasing production. To do so, they must raise the selling price. As prices rise, the quantity demanded falls. This process continues until $Q_d = Q_s$ and $P = P_E$. The market response to shortages is shown in Figure 3.11.

Speed of Adjustment. How long does it take for adjustment to equilibrium? There isn't a simple answer. The adjustment time depends upon the particular industry and the kinds of products. For example, when the Mazda Miata sports car was introduced in 1989, Mazda was unable to meet the initial demand at the list price. As a result, buyers typically paid several thousand dollars above the list price. In this case, the market responded rather quickly—dealers boldly added a "market adjustment factor"

•••• FIGURE 3.11 SHORTAGES AND ADJUSTMENT TO EQUILIBRIUM

A price less than the equilibrium price ($P_2 < P_E$) results in a shortage because the quantity demanded (Q_d) is greater than the quantity supplied (Q_s). If there are no restrictions on the market, competition among buyers will result in price increases, and the market will move to equilibrium where quantity supplied equals quantity demanded, $Q_s = Q_d$, and the price, P_E, is at the intersection between the demand and supply curves.

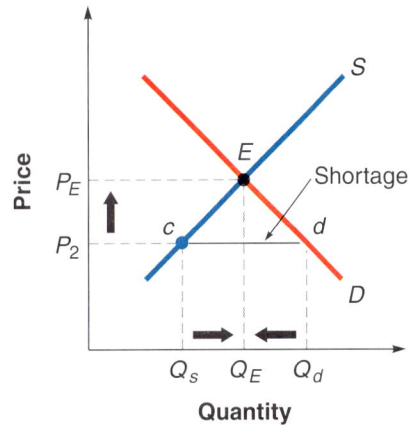

to window stickers—and the price rose enough to equate the quantity demanded with the short supply. The high price that consumers were willing to pay was a signal to Mazda to increase production in subsequent years, but it took two years before the actual selling price of a Miata approached the manufacturer's list price.

The Miata story is instructive. Most importantly, it illustrates that prices and quantities can adjust at different speeds. In this case, price adjusted more quickly than quantity. Dealers were quick to add a few thousand dollars to the price of a new Miata, but it took years for Mazda to gear up its factories to increase Miata production. In some markets quantities adjust faster than prices. This is often true in the labor market. When firms find that their sales are falling, they often lay off workers (a quantity adjustment) before they lower wages (a price adjustment). We will discuss why this might occur in Chapter 16. Movie tickets are another example where quantity often adjusts faster than price: your local theater is much more likely to put in an extra showing of a hit movie than to raise the price of tickets. The point is that market pressures can affect both price and quantity, and in most cases both price and quantity adjust, but how much and how quickly each adjusts depends on the particular market under consideration.

•••••••

Supply and Demand Shocks

Equilibrium will exist only as long as the supply and demand curves are stationary. If either curve shifts, the equilibrium price and quantity will change. It is important to be able to analyze how changes in supply and demand affect equilibrium.

An Increase in Demand Raises Equilibrium Price and Quantity. Suppose that the market begins in equilibrium at the intersection of D_0 and S_0 as shown in Figure 3.12. As long as the supply and demand curves are fixed, the market will remain in equilibrium with price P_0 and quantity Q_0. Suppose, however, that consumer preferences change and demand increases. The result would be an outward shift in the

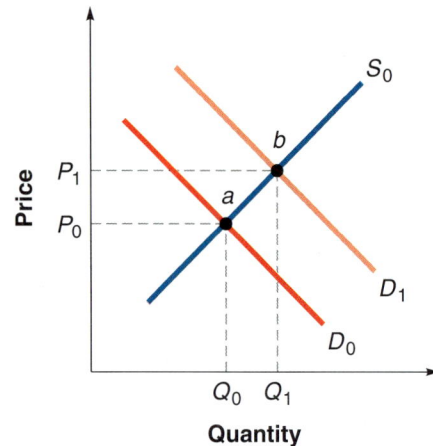

•••• FIGURE 3.12 AN INCREASE IN DEMAND

An increase in demand will shift the demand curve outward from D_0 to D_1. If the supply curve is upward sloping, the result will be an increase in equilibrium price and equilibrium quantity.

demand curve from D_0 to D_1. If the price stays at P_0, there will be a shortage. However, if the supply curve is upward sloping—as it usually is in the short run—both the equilibrium price and the equilibrium quantity will rise, and the market will move from point *a* to point *b*. Notice that the higher price elicits a greater amount of output—an increase in the quantity supplied—but it does not cause the supply curve to shift. Remember: With few exceptions, the factors that shift the demand curve do not shift the supply curve.

A Decrease in Demand Lowers Equilibrium Price and Quantity. A decrease in demand will have the opposite effect: Both the equilibrium price and the equilibrium quantity will fall. For example, suppose that massive layoffs in the local community reduce consumer income. This would cause the demand curve for many products to shift inward. As Figure 3.13 shows, the result would be a decline in both equilibrium price and equilibrium quantity. As before, the quantity supplied changes, but the supply curve does not shift.

An Increase in Supply Lowers Equilibrium Price and Increases Equilibrium Quantity. Suppose that new firms enter the industry. As Figure 3.14 shows, the result will be an increase in supply as the supply curve shifts out from S_0 to S_1. The increase in supply results in a lower selling price and a larger quantity available on the market. The quantity demanded increases because of the lower selling price, but the demand curve does not shift.

A Decrease in Supply Raises Equilibrium Price and Lowers Equilibrium Quantity. Wages are one of the biggest costs of production. Suppose workers form a union and negotiate a large wage increase. This would cause the cost of production to increase. An increase in factor costs causes a decrease in supply, so the supply curve will shift toward the price axis. As shown in Figure 3.15, the result will be an increase in equilibrium price and a decrease in equilibrium quantity.

····· FIGURE 3.13 A DECREASE IN DEMAND

A decrease in demand will shift
the demand curve inward from D_0
to D_2. If the supply curve is
upward sloping, the result will be
a decrease in equilibrium price and
equilibrium quantity.

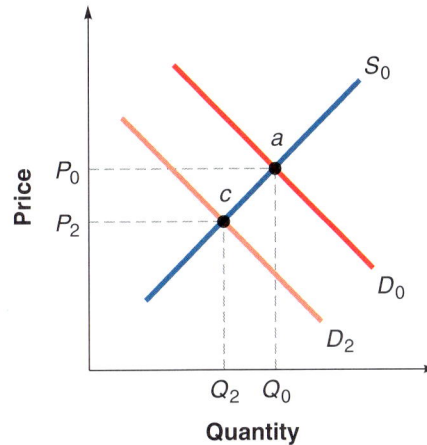

····· FIGURE 3.14 AN INCREASE IN SUPPLY

If the supply curve shifts out along
a downward-sloping demand
curve, the result will be an
increase in equilibrium quantity
and a decrease in equilibrium
price. When the market goes from
point a to point d, price falls from
P_0 to P_3 and quantity rises from Q_0
to Q_3.

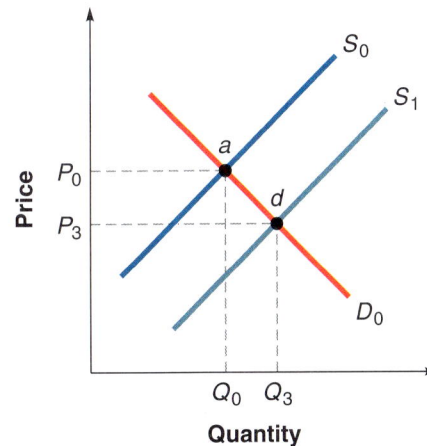

If Both Curves Shift, the Result Depends Upon Their Relative Magnitudes. Of
course, it is possible for an event to affect both supply and demand or for several
events to affect the market at the same time. For example, consider what would
happen if industry leaders decided to initiate a nationwide advertising program. If
successful, such a program would shift the demand curve outward and thus tend to
increase both equilibrium price and quantity. Advertising is not free, however.
Increased spending on advertising would mean higher costs of production and thus
an inward shift in the supply curve. This would increase price but lower the quantity.

•••••FIGURE 3.15 A DECREASE IN SUPPLY

A decrease in supply will result in a higher price and a decline in the equilibrium quantity demanded. The market goes from point a to point e, price rises from P_0 to P_4, and quantity falls from Q_0 to Q_4.

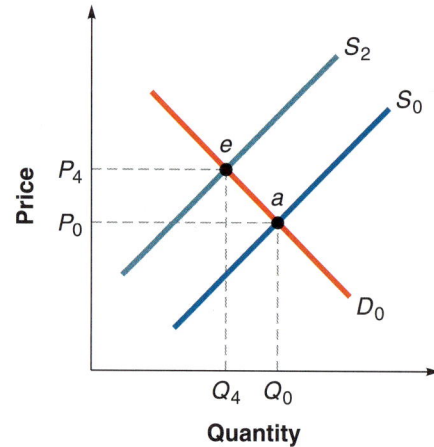

•••••FIGURE 3.16 SHIFTS IN BOTH SUPPLY AND DEMAND

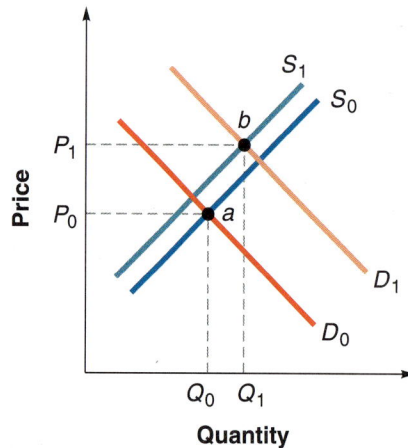

(a)

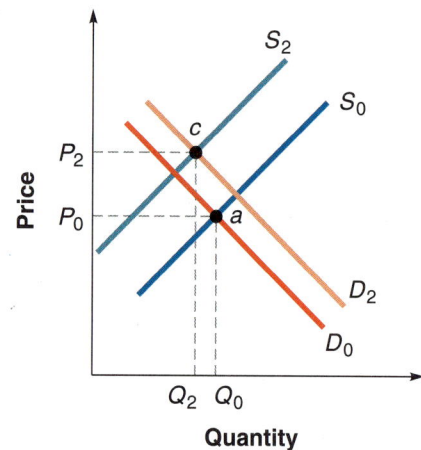

(b)

If both the demand and supply curves shift, the effect on price and quantity depends on the relative magnitudes of the shifts. In both instances here, supply has decreased and demand has increased. In panel (a) the demand shift is larger so both price and quantity rise as the market moves from point a to point b. In panel (b) the supply curve shifts more than the demand curve. The result is a decline in quantity coupled with an increase in price (point c).

The overall effect of these two shifts depends on their relative magnitudes. Figure 3.16 illustrates these cases.

Extreme Cases: Vertical and Horizontal Supply and Demand. The principle of diminishing marginal utility holds that the demand curve is downward sloping, and we know that the short-run supply curve is typically upward sloping. However, it is possible for either curve to be vertical or horizontal. We will have more to say about the implications of the shape of the supply and demand curves later, but it is important to see some of the consequences of different slopes before we go on.

The demand curve could be vertical if the good in question had no substitutes so that people were willing to buy the product regardless of price. Diabetics might consider insulin such a good. If the demand curve is vertical, a change in supply will affect only price, not the quantity demanded. A product with many possible substitutes would have a demand curve that approached horizontal because a small increase in price would cause people to buy substitutes rather than this product, so quantity demanded would approach zero. Figure 3.17 illustrates vertical and horizontal demand curves.

Supply curves are vertical when technical or natural constraints limit the quantity that can be produced. We know that this occurs, by definition, in the market period, but it can also occur in the short run in some cases. For example, if the number of firms in an industry is fixed, output can increase until factories are working 24 hours a day. A new factory could be built—but only in the long run. It is also possible for the short-run supply curve to be horizontal. In fact, this is fairly common. Recall that the short-run supply curve is usually upward sloping; as more workers are added to a fixed amount of machinery, the amount of machinery per worker declines, and

FIGURE 3.17 VERTICAL AND HORIZONTAL DEMAND CURVES

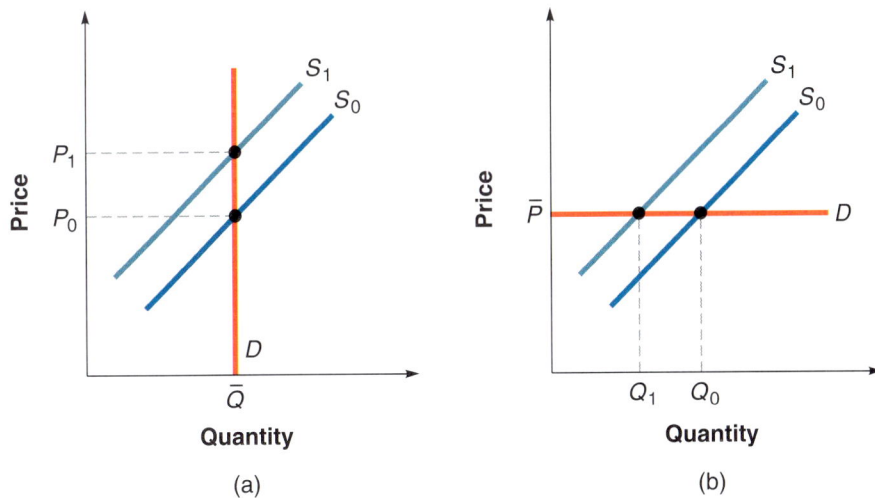

Panel (a) illustrates a vertical demand curve for a good with no substitutes. A change in supply will affect only price, not quantity. Panel (b) illustrates the horizontal demand curve for a good with many substitutes. A change in supply will affect quantity, not price.

FIGURE 3.18 VERTICAL AND HORIZONTAL SUPPLY CURVES

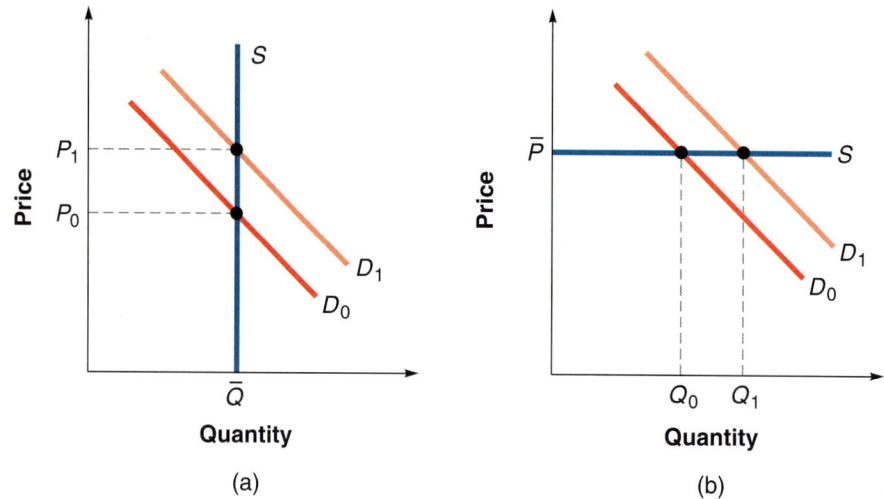

Panel (a) illustrates a vertical supply curve, possibly the result of a technical or natural constraint on production. A change in demand will affect only price, not quantity. Panel (b) illustrates a horizontal supply curve, possibly the result of excess plant capacity. A change in demand will affect quantity, not price.

the output per worker decreases. If the factory starts with unused capacity, however, it can add workers without causing output per worker to decline. In this case, the costs of production would not rise as output increases. The result: The short-run supply curve is flat until plant capacity is approached when it begins to slope upward. Figure 3.18 illustrates vertical and horizontal supply curves.

RECAP   The Effect of Slope on Price and Quantity Responses

The extreme cases illustrated in Figures 3.17 and 3.18 occur only occasionally in the real world, but slope is a very important variable in supply and demand analysis. It is worth pausing for a generalization:

1. When the demand curve is relatively steep, most of the effect of a change in supply will be on price; there will be little quantity response.
2. When the supply is relatively steep, most of the effect of a change in demand will be on price; there will be little quantity response.
3. When the demand curve is relatively flat, most of the effect of a change in supply will be on quantity; there will be little price response.
4. When the supply curve is relatively flat, most of the effect of a change in demand will be on quantity; there will be little price response.

SUMMARY

This chapter has been exceedingly important. Thumb through the next 800 pages or so and you will find supply and demand graphs in almost every chapter—supply and demand for labor to determine wage rates, supply and demand for money to determine interest rates, supply and demand for foreign currencies to determine exchange rates, and so on. The importance of understanding supply and demand analysis cannot be overstated. Supply and demand determine prices, and prices are the signals that allocate resources in market economies. The key points to remember from this chapter are:

1. The law of demand states that people will buy less of a product at higher prices and more at lower prices, *ceteris paribus*. The demand curve slopes downward.

2. A change in price results in movement along a demand curve; a change in any other relevant factors will cause the demand curve to shift. The main factors that shift the demand curve are income, tastes, price expectations, the prices of substitutes and complements, and the number of buyers. An increase in demand will tend to raise price and the quantity supplied; a decrease in demand will tend to lower price and the quantity supplied.

3. The law of supply states that, in the short run, firms will offer more of a product at higher prices and less at lower prices, *ceteris paribus*. The short-run supply curve slopes upward.

4. A change in price results in movement along a given supply curve; a change in other relevant factors will cause the supply curve to shift. The main factors that shift the supply curve are costs, technology, expectations, and the number of sellers. An increase in supply will tend to decrease price and raise the equilibrium quantity demanded; a decrease in supply will tend to raise price and lower the equilibrium quantity demanded.

5. The intersection of the supply and demand curves is the point of equilibrium. The market will stay in equilibrium until disturbed by an outside influence.

KEY TERMS AND CONCEPTS

marginal utility
law of demand
substitution effect
income effect
demand curve
change in quantity demanded
change in demand
inferior good
substitute good
complementary good
conspicuous consumption
law of supply

analytical time
historical time
market period
short run
long run
equilibrium

REVIEW QUESTIONS

1. Why do demand curves slope downward? Answer with reference to the principle of diminishing marginal utility, as well as the income effect and the substitution effect.
2. Carefully distinguish between a change in demand and a change in the quantity demanded. What factors can cause a change in demand? What factors can cause a change in the quantity demanded?
3. Under what conditions are supply curves upward sloping? Vertical? Horizontal?
4. Carefully distinguish between a change in supply and a change in the quantity supplied. What factors can cause a change in supply? A change in the quantity supplied?
5. What conditions hold when the market is in equilibrium? What will cause a market to move toward a new equilibrium?
6. Explain how the slopes of the supply and demand curves affect how market price and quantity respond to external shocks. Draw graphs to illustrate your answer.

PROBLEMS

1. Does money have diminishing marginal utility?
2. The text noted that market demand curves are flatter than any individual demand curves that make up the market. What would the market demand curve look like for a market with an infinite number of buyers? Draw a graph to illustrate the implications of your answer.
3. Suppose that the market for home computers is in equilibrium. Determine how the following shocks will affect the equilibrium price and quantity. Draw a graph to illustrate each answer.
   a. Computers become easier to use.
   b. The price of DRAM memory chips falls.
   c. Software prices fall.
   d. All college students are required to own personal computers.
   e. The price of electricity rises substantially.
   f. Doctors warn of health risks from radiation from video terminals.
4. Suppose that the market for wooden number 2 lead pencils is in equilibrium. Determine how the following shocks will affect the equilibrium price and quantity. Draw a graph to illustrate each answer.
   a. Professors require ink on all exams.
   b. The price of lead increases.
   c. School attendance falls.
   d. Environmental legislation restricts lumber harvests.
   e. Pencil makers receive a large wage increase.
   f. The price of ballpoint pens falls.
5. Would the demand curves for the following goods be relatively flat or relatively steep? Why?
   a. Gasoline
   b. Airline tickets
   c. Wool blankets

    d. Coca–Cola Classic

    e. Bic ballpoint pens

6. Would the supply curves for the following goods be relatively flat or relatively steep? Why?

    a. Crude oil

    b. Feed corn

    c. Apple Macintosh computers

    d. IBM–clone computers

    e. Studio apartments near campus

7. Two exceptions to the law of demand are conspicuous consumption and the blue jeans effect. Draw demand curves illustrating both concepts and explain why you drew your graphs as you did.

CHAPTER 4

Applications of Supply and Demand: Ceilings, Floors, Taxes, Externalities, and Elasticity

The real beauty of economic models is not that they can help us understand simple things, but that they can help us understand more complicated things. For example, many of you probably worked for the minimum wage while in high school, but did you know that the minimum wage law may actually have made it more difficult for you to find that job? And some of you may appreciate the fact that you live in rent-controlled apartments. But did you know that rent control may be responsible for the apartment shortage? This does not mean that all kinds of intervention are bad: If the market does not recognize all costs and benefits, government intervention in the market is appropriate— but supply and demand analysis can help us understand how and when to intervene. This chapter will present several applications of the supply and demand model. This material is valuable in its own right, but it also provides a useful test of your understanding of the basics of supply and demand from the previous chapter. As you are about to find out, supply and demand is the single most important concept in economics.

AFTER READING AND STUDYING THIS CHAPTER, YOU SHOULD BE ABLE TO:

- • • Explain why price floors can cause surpluses, and apply this analysis to minimum wages
- • • Explain why rent controls and other price ceilings can cause shortages
- • • Explain why the selling price does not usually rise as much as a sales tax
- • • Explain why government intervention may be necessary in the presence of externalities
- • • Illustrate producer and consumer surplus, and explain why taxes result in deadweight losses
- • • Define, calculate, and use price elasticity of demand

PRICE CEILINGS AND FLOORS

All of the analysis to this point has assumed that prices are flexible and respond to excess supply and excess demand. This is not always the case, however. For example, the wage rate, the price of labor, is sometimes subject to a **price floor,** the minimum wage. And some apartments are subject to **price ceilings**—rent controls—that make it illegal for landlords to raise rents. As we are about to find out, price floors can cause surpluses and price ceilings can cause shortages.

Before proceeding, we need to stress that the terms "shortage" and "surplus" have very specific definitions to economists. Both are defined only in relation to price, and neither can persist if prices are flexible. A **shortage** occurs if the price is kept artificially low and people cannot buy all they want to buy at this price. If the price were allowed to rise, the "shortage" would vanish because the quantity demanded would equal the quantity supplied. Notice, however, that some people could still be priced out of the market. To these people there is still a "shortage," but this is not what economists mean by the term. A **surplus** occurs only when prices are kept artificially high and the quantity supplied is greater than the quantity demanded. If prices are allowed to fluctuate freely, seller competition will cause prices to fall, the quantity demanded will increase, the quantity supplied will decrease, and the surplus will be eliminated.

Price floor A government regulation that prevents prices from falling below a certain level; can cause surpluses.

Price ceiling A government regulation that prevents prices from rising above a certain level; can cause shortages.

Shortage A situation where the quantity demanded is greater than the quantity supplied.

Surplus A situation where the quantity supplied is greater than the quantity demanded.

Minimum Wages

The *minimum wage* law is certainly well motivated. It *seems* only right that people who work should make enough to live on. Unfortunately, economists have long argued that minimum wages can cause unemployment, especially among low-skilled and young workers, so it is not clear whether we are better off with or without minimum wages.

Figure 4.1 uses a supply and demand diagram to analyze the effects of minimum wages. The vertical axis measures the wage rate (W), which is the price of labor. The horizontal axis measures the quantity of labor (N). (The letter N is used for labor to represent "input" because much of our analysis will focus on labor as an input into the production process; the letter L will be reserved for land.) The labor demand curve, D_N, shows the quantity of workers that will be offered jobs at various wage rates. Like most demand curves, it slopes downward. When wages are high, firms can afford to hire only a few workers; when wages are low, they will want to hire more workers. The labor supply curve, S_N, shows the quantity of labor that will be offered at various wage rates. When wages are high, more people will look for jobs; when wages are low, fewer people will be in the labor force.

In the absence of a minimum wage, the wage rate would be W_0 and the quantity of labor would be N_0. Notice what happens when a minimum wage is set at W_{min} above the equilibrium wage rate: the minimum wage acts as a wage floor and prevents the wage from falling to its equilibrium level. As a result, only N_d workers are demanded but N_s labor is offered. Because $N_d < N_s$, there is a *surplus* of people looking for jobs—unemployment by any other name.

••••FIGURE 4.1 MINIMUM WAGES AND UNEMPLOYMENT

Minimum wages prevent wages from falling to the market level and cause unemployment. In this example, the minimum wage, W_{min}, is set above the market wage, W_0. The high wage causes more people to offer their job services than firms are willing to hire, that is, $N_s > N_d$. In the absence of the minimum wage, the quantity of labor supplied would equal the quantity of labor demanded at N_0.

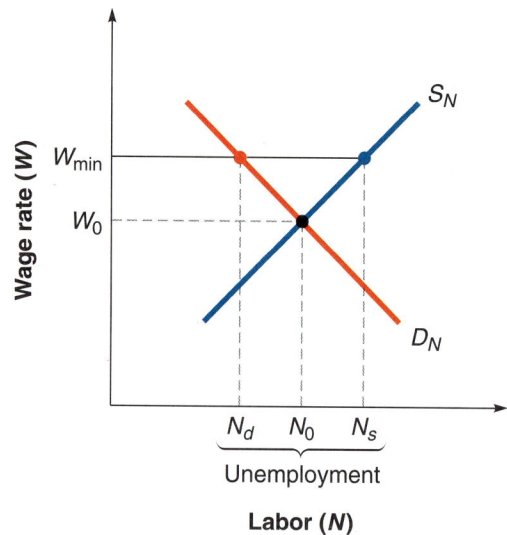

We will have more to say about minimum wage laws in Chapter 16, but a couple brief comments should be made here. First, economists generally agree that minimum wages do cause some unemployment, especially among low-skilled workers and new entrants into the labor force—one estimate is that teen unemployment rises by about 1.5 percentage points when the minimum wage increases by 10 percent. However, some economists—including a few in the Clinton administration—believe that a higher minimum wage would be beneficial to the economy even if it did cause a small increase in umemployment because expensive labor forces firms to invest in productivity enhancing capital. A higher minimum wage may also encourage workers to look harder for jobs.[1]

••••••••

Price Supports for Agriculture

Agricultural price supports are another example of price floors. The United States and most other industrialized nations have a long history of policies designed to prop up farm prices. Figure 4.2 illustrates the basic problem. Advances in agricultural technology have resulted in a rapid outward movement of the supply curve for food, which has resulted in declining agricultural prices over time and caused problems for farmers. To deal with this problem, farmers have lobbied Congress for a series of measures designed to keep prices high. Unfortunately, price supports generate crop surpluses just as minimum wages cause labor surpluses. What can be done with the surplus food? Unfortunately, there is no simple answer. Giving the food away to less-

[1]A summary of the new arguments on the minimum wage can be found in Aaron Bernstein, et al., "A Higher Minimum Wage: Minimal Damage?" *Business Week* (March 22, 1993): 92–93.

····· **FIGURE 4.2** AGRICULTURAL PRICE SUPPORTS

Agricultural price supports result in surplus farm products. Beginning at point a, suppose that technological advances shift the supply curve from S_0 to S_1. To maintain the previous price, price supports are enacted so that the price cannot fall below P_{min}. The result is a surplus. At P_{min}, the quantity supplied is Q_s, which is greater than the quantity demanded, Q_d. To eliminate such surpluses, governments frequently enact quantity restrictions along with price floors.

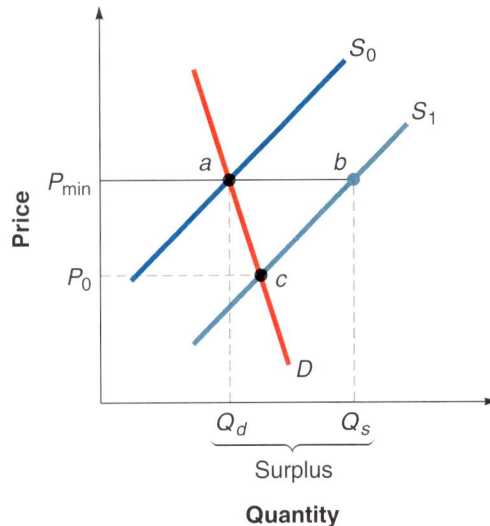

developed countries (LDCs) may seem like the humane thing to do—but that just lowers food prices in the LDCs and makes it difficult for LDC farmers to stay in business.

Figure 4.2 illustrates the effects of price supports. Let the market begin at point a, and suppose that technology shifts the supply curve from S_0 to S_1. Farm output expands and prices fall. Concerned that the market price is too low for farmers to stay in business, the government enacts price supports to maintain the price at P_{min}. The result is a surplus because the quantity supplied, Q_s, is greater than the quantity demanded, Q_d. In the past, the government has responded to such surpluses by buying excess production or enacting crop restrictions.

Generally, agricultural price supports have been coupled with quantity restrictions. Congress has actually paid farmers *not* to plant crops. Needless to say, this sort of thing was not especially popular with the voters. Nor was it very effective; farmers removed the least productive acreage from cultivation, so the surpluses often persisted despite quantity restrictions. The Reagan administration came up with an innovative program to help farmers and solve the agricultural surplus problem at the same time, the Payment-In-Kind or PIK program. Under this scheme, farmers who agreed to take acreage out of cultivation were paid not in dollars but in surplus corn that the government had purchased in previous years. The farmers then had the right to sell the corn on the open market. Sounds good, right? Not quite. Poor forecasts by government economists resulted in the government running out of surplus corn. The only solution was for the government to buy corn on the open market and give it to the farmers, who then turned around and sold it on the market.

We cannot go on without a comment on the source of the agricultural "problem." A major reason why the U.S. government was forced to use agricultural price supports was the "Green Revolution," which expanded agricultural output dramatically. But this revolution was not exactly the product of blind market forces. Much of the technology that increased farm output was developed as a result of government intervention in the guise of sponsored research and land grant colleges. Had the government not devoted so many resources to these programs, the farm "problem" might have been averted, but there would have been less food on our tables. The message is clear: intervention in the market is not nearly as simple as it may appear at first. If intervention is necessary—and it certainly is at times—we must be ready to enact secondary measures. And tertiary measures.

· · · · · · · ·

Price Ceilings
Other Price Controls

You can probably think of several examples where prices are set arbitrarily by authority rather than by the market. During World War II and again in the first half of the 1970s, the United States imposed wage and price controls in an attempt to reduce inflation. Price controls frequently result in shortages and black markets because artificially low prices mean that the quantity demanded is greater than the quantity supplied.

As an example of the effects of price controls, consider what happens at many sporting events.[2] The price for a good seat to a World Series game is about $100. Every year more people want to attend the World Series than there are seats, so this price must be below the market price. The only way to get tickets legally is to wait in line at the ticket office over night—quite an opportunity cost. (Is the price of a ticket *really* $100?) If you do not want to wait in line, you can always buy a ticket on the black market from a scalper. How much should you be willing to pay a scalper? The answer is $100 plus something less than the value of the time you would have spent waiting in line to buy tickets legally.

This situation can be illustrated quite easily with supply and demand diagrams. Because the supply of tickets is fixed, the supply curve is vertical like the one in Figure 4.3. Now, because thousands of people are willing to camp out all night to buy tickets, we can be fairly certain that there is an excess demand for tickets, at least at the price of $100. This means that the demand curve must intersect the supply curve at a price higher than $100, let's say $200. The distance between Q_d and Q_s represents the shortage caused by the artificially low price. Had the baseball authorities set the price at $200, the market would have been in equilibrium, and there would have been no shortage. You could have taken a leisurely trip to the ticket office to select your box seats—if you had the $200.

· · · · · · · ·

The Role of Speculators

Ticket scalping is one kind of *speculation*. You know who speculators are—those wheeler-dealer types who make a living by buying low and selling high. As a consumer, it probably rankles you to know that the speculator paid only $100 for those

---

[2]Ticket prices for World Series games are not controlled by the government, but they are set by Major League Baseball authorities. Economists know that the prices are set too low because there is always a shortage of seats.

• • • • **FIGURE 4.3** PRICE CONTROLS AND SHORTAGES

If the price ceiling is set below the equilibrium price, there will be a shortage. In this case, the market price of $100 is below the equilibrium price of $200. The distance $b - a = Q_d - Q_s$ represents the shortage. Shortages often cause waiting lines and black markets.

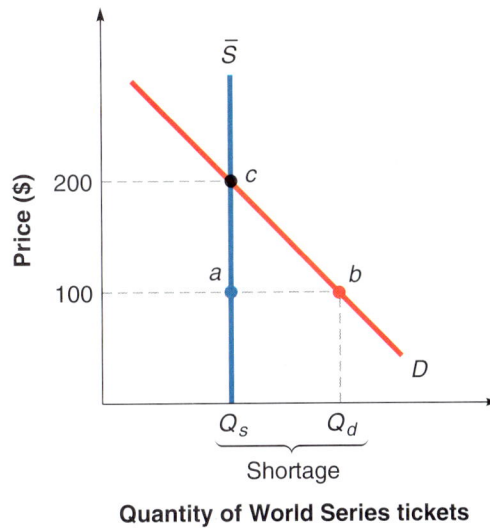

tickets and sold them to you for $200. Of course, you would not pay the $200 unless you felt that the tickets were worth at least that much, but you would rather pay only $100. That is only normal. But does it mean that speculation is the *cause* of the ticket shortage or high prices? Almost certainly not. When the speculators waited in line to buy the tickets, they were taking a risk that the game would not sell out. If the game does sell out, they can scalp the tickets for whatever price the market will bear. In so doing, the speculators have supplied a service—providing tickets to people willing to pay $200. Further, when the speculators bought their $100 tickets, they reduced the risk that the baseball teams would fail to sell enough tickets to turn a profit. Both producers and consumers can benefit from the presence of speculators.

• • • • • • • •

Rent Controls

There is only so much land in a city, and as the population grows, the demand for living space increases. Over time, the result has been an astronomical increase in the price of housing. To prevent people from being priced out of urban housing, many communities—including New York City and Berkeley, California—have enacted rent controls, or ceilings on the amount of rent that can be charged.

Unfortunately, rent controls can lead to a shortage of housing. To see why, look at Figure 4.4. Rent controls prevent the price from rising to the market level, so $P_{RC} < P_0$, and there is excess demand for rental housing, $Q_d > Q_s$.

Rent controls also have other negative consequences. If landlords cannot earn the rent they think their rental units are worth, they frequently fail to maintain the units— which may explain why it is so hard to find good rental properties. Also, low rents act as a disincentive to further construction in the rent-controlled area. Builders prefer to construct new units outside rent-controlled districts. But housing prices are too

•••• FIGURE 4.4 RENT CONTROLS

Rent controls can lead to short-ages. At a rental of P_{RC}, quantity demanded is greater than quantity supplied, $Q_d > Q_s$, the definition of a shortage. Additionally, rent controls have been blamed for landlords' failure to maintain their rental units properly.

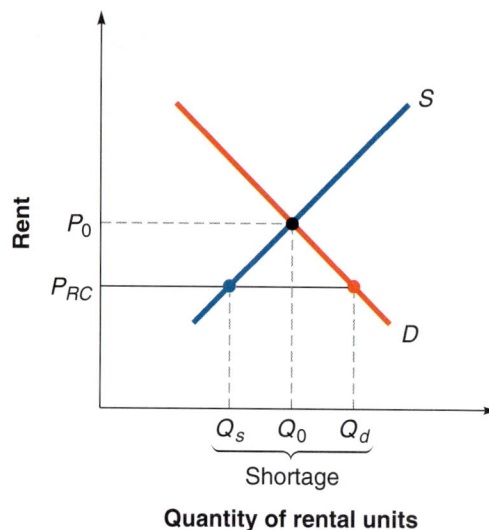

high for many people to afford. Does this mean that rent controls are necessary and humane even though they cause some problems? Not necessarily. If society believes that some people need help paying for housing, a better solution might be to provide vouchers or subsidies for low-income people. Doing this would allow the price mechanism to allocate resources and avoid the negative consequences of rent controls. Of course, income subsidies may be less popular politically because they *appear* to cost the taxpayer more than rent controls. Do they?

RECAP   The Effect of Price Ceilings and Floors

Price ceilings and floors may prevent markets from operating. Price ceilings prevent prices from rising to the equilibrium level and can result in shortages because the quantity demanded exceeds the quantity supplied. Black markets are a common response to shortages. Price floors may cause surpluses because the quantity supplied exceeds the quantity demanded.

••••• SUPPLY AND DEMAND ANALYSIS OF SALES TAXES

Tax incidence Who actually pays the tax to the government.

One issue of concern to economists is **tax incidence;** that is, who really pays the tax. For example, business is legally required to submit sales tax receipts to the government, but businesses try to collect these taxes from consumers by raising prices. When the businesses are successful, the *legal incidence* of the tax (who is required to give the tax to the government) differs from the *economic incidence* (who really pays the tax). In general, the price does not rise by the full amount of the sales tax, so some of the tax is paid by the buyer and some is paid by the seller. Supply and demand analysis can show us why this occurs.

There are two kinds of sales taxes: **unit sales taxes** and **ad valorem sales taxes.** A unit sales tax is levied on a per unit basis, such as per carton or gallon. Gasoline, liquor, and some other goods are subject to unit sales taxes. An ad valorem sales tax is levied as a percentage of price; most state sales taxes are ad valorem taxes. This section willl analyze only unit sales taxes, but the results for ad valorem sales taxes are quite similar.

Unit sales tax A tax levied as a fixed amount for each unit sold.

Ad valorem sales tax A tax levied as a percentage of the price.

. . . .

Incidence of a Unit Sales Tax

Suppose that a tax (T) of $1.00 is imposed on each unit that is sold. Because the seller will experience this as an increase in the cost of doing business, the effect will be to shift the supply curve upward just like any cost increase. This is shown in Figure 4.5. The vertical distance between S and $S + T$ is the amount of the unit tax, $1.00. As always, the selling price is where the supply and demand curves intersect. In this case, price went from $10.00 to $10.50. But notice what happened: *Price rose less than the amount of the sales tax.* The graphical explanation is clear enough: given the slope of the demand curve, the intersection of the new supply curve, $S + T$, occurs at a point such that the price change ($\Delta P = 0.50) is less than the unit tax; that is, $\Delta P < T$. But what is the economic explanation? The slope of the demand curve indicates that people will buy less of a product at higher prices. Thus, when the tax raises the selling price, people respond by buying less, and as a result, quantity supplied falls. As quantity supplied falls, the nontax costs to the firm fall, and price does not rise as much as the tax. In this case, the firm receives $9.50 per unit sold and consumers pay $10.50. How much revenue does the government collect from this tax? It collects

· · · · · **FIGURE 4.5** **INCIDENCE OF A UNIT SALES TAX**

If the demand curve is down-ward sloping, a unit sales tax will raise selling price less than the amount of the tax. In this case, the supply curve shifts up from S to $S + T$. This is the amount of the tax, $1.00. However, price rises only from $10.00 to $10.50, less than the amount of the tax. The government will collect $100 in tax revenues because 100 units are sold after the tax is imposed.

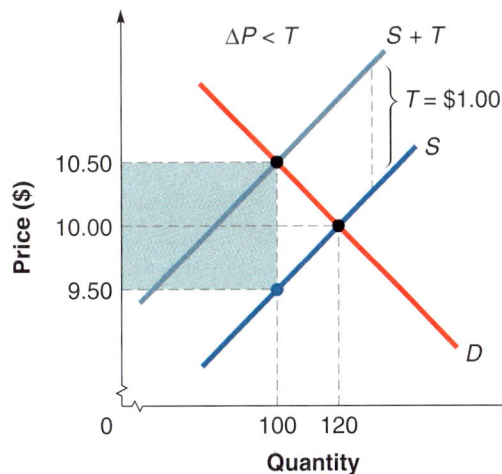

••••FIGURE 4.6 TAX INCIDENCE AND THE SLOPE OF THE DEMAND CURVE

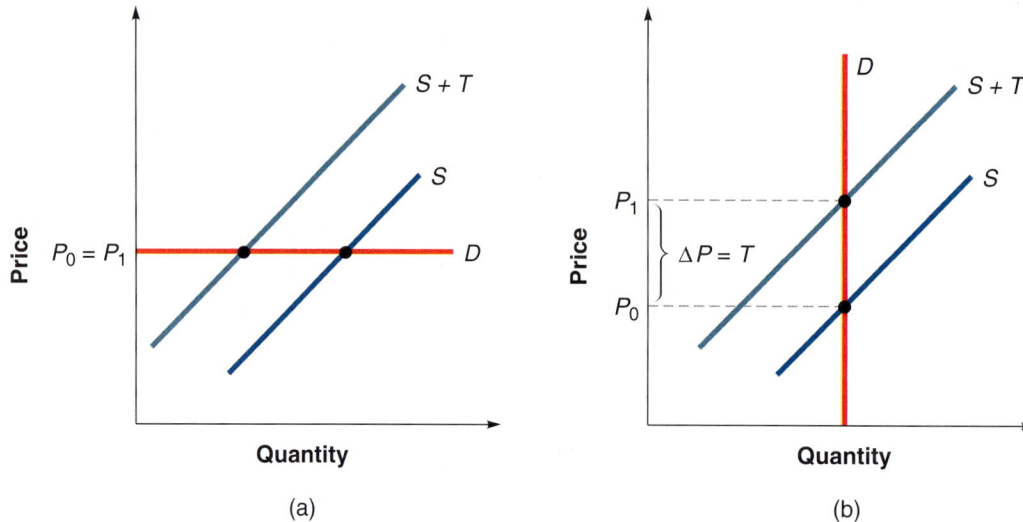

(a)   (b)

The shape of the demand curve determines how much of a unit sales tax can be passed on to the consumer. Panel (a) shows what happens if the demand curve is perfectly flat: All of the tax is paid by the seller and price does not change. Panel (b) shows that if the demand curve is vertical, the seller can pass all of the tax on to the consumer.

$1.00 on each unit sold and 100 units are sold. The shaded area on the graph represents the government's share: ($10.50 − 9.50)(100) = $100.

In the example in Figure 4.5, half of the tax is paid by business and half is paid by consumers, but this is not always the case. A little thought should make it clear that the slopes of the demand and supply curves determine who pays the tax. The effect of the demand curve on tax incidence is illustrated in Figure 4.6. As panel (a) illustrates, when the demand curve is perfectly horizontal, all of the tax is paid by the seller. This is because buyers can find good substitutes and are thus unwilling to pay a higher price for the product. Panel (b) shows the opposite: if the demand curve is perfectly vertical, all of the tax is paid by the buyer. In this case, buyers can find no substitutes for the product and are forced to pay the higher price or do without. In the real world, of course, demand curves are rarely perfectly flat or horizontal, but the point should be clear: Other things being equal, the steeper the demand curve, the greater the proportion of the tax paid by the buyer.

The slope of the supply curve also affects tax incidence as illustrated in Figure 4.7. This time we have drawn a single downward-sloping demand curve and two sets of supply curves on the same diagram. Sales taxes of equal sizes are imposed on the two supply curves. Notice that when the supply curve is perfectly horizontal (S_1), the entire sales tax can be passed on to the buyer, but when the supply curve is upward sloping, only some of the tax is passed on to the buyer. Also, sales taxes reduce quantity more when the supply curve is flat than when it is steep.

In fact, tax incidence depends on the slopes of both the demand and supply curves or, more precisely, on the relative slopes of the two curves. *Ceteris paribus,* when the

FIGURE 4.7 TAX INCIDENCE AND THE SLOPE OF THE SUPPLY CURVE

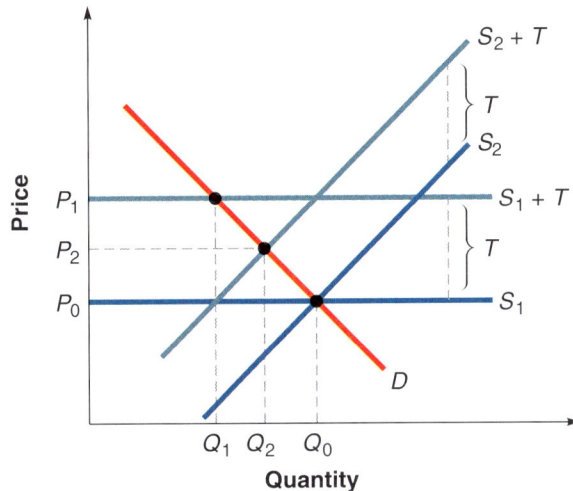

The slope of the supply curve also affects tax incidence. When the supply curve is perfectly horizontal as is S_1, a unit sales tax will be paid entirely by the buyer. Additionally, the quantity produced and sold will fall significantly, from Q_0 to Q_1. If the supply curve is relatively steep, the seller will pay some of the tax, so price will rise less than the amount of the tax. Quantity will fall less (to Q_2) than when the supply curve is flat.

demand curve is steep relative to the supply curve, more of the tax will be paid by the buyer; when the demand is flat relative to the supply curve, more of the tax will be paid by the seller.

RECAP   Supply and Demand Analysis of Taxes

Unit sales taxes shift the supply curve vertically the amount of the tax, but the selling price typically rises less than the amount of the tax. The slopes of the demand and supply curves determine how much of the sales tax will be paid by the buyer and how much will be paid by the seller: *Ceteris paribus,* when the demand curve is steep relative to the supply curve, more of the tax will be paid by the buyer; when the demand curve is flat relative to the supply curve, more of the tax will be paid by the seller.

CONSUMER AND PRODUCER SURPLUS

Taxes have another effect on the economy: they can cause an efficiency loss, or what economists call a loss in *economic welfare*. Remember that when consumers buy a product, they must conclude that they would rather have the product than the

Consumer surplus The difference between what people are willing to pay for a product and the market price; represented graphically by the area below the demand curve but above the market price.

Producer surplus The difference between the price a firm would be willing to sell a product for and the price received; represented graphically by the area above the supply curve but below the market price.

Deadweight loss Efficiency loss due to government intervention.

money they must spend to buy it. In fact, the downward slope of the demand curve indicates that people might be willing to pay an ever higher price for the first few units purchased, but they do not have to because of the single price that prevails in the market. When people value a product higher than the price they have to pay, they are said to be receiving **consumer surplus.** Likewise, the upward slope of the supply curve indicates that producers would be willing to sell the first few units of their products at a price lower than the market price. This means that they are earning a **producer surplus** on their sales. Economic theory reveals that private markets maximize the amount of producer plus consumer surplus. Consumer and producer surplus are illustrated in Figure 4.8.

Intervention in the market can reduce the amount of producer and consumer surplus and result in economic inefficiency. This is shown in Figure 4.9, which illustrates the effect of a unit sales tax. Before the tax is imposed, consumer surplus was equal to the triangle P_0cf, and producer surplus was equal to P_0ca. When the tax is imposed, the supply curve shifts up from S to $S + T$, and price rises from P_0 to P_1. This causes both producer and consumer surplus to fall. Consumer surplus is now equal to the area P_1ef, and producer surplus is equal to the area abg. The government collects tax revenues equal to the rectangle $gbeP_1$. The government can presumably use this revenue to provide goods that society needs. What happened to the triangle bce? It vanishes in the form of lost efficiency or what economists call **deadweight loss.** It represents a reduction in consumer and producer surplus that does not go to the government in the form of tax revenue.

As with tax incidence, the slopes of the demand and supply curves determine the amount of consumer and producer surplus as well as the deadweight loss from taxes. If the demand curve is relatively flat, both consumer surplus and deadweight loss are

FIGURE 4.8 CONSUMER AND PRODUCER SURPLUS

Consumer surplus is the difference between what people are willing to pay for a product and the market price. Graphically, it is the shaded area under the demand curve and above the market price. Producer surplus is the difference between the market price and the price at which producers are willing to sell. It is the area below the market price and above the supply curve. Left alone, competitive private markets maximize producer and consumer surplus.

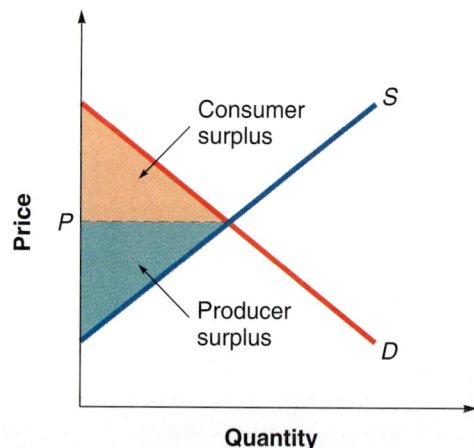

···· **FIGURE 4.9** THE DEADWEIGHT LOSS FROM TAXES

Taxes impose efficiency costs on private markets. In this case, before the unit sales tax is imposed, consumer plus producer surplus is represented by the area *acf*. Implementation of the tax reduces consumer surplus to the area P_1ef, and producer surplus falls to *abg*. Government collects revenue in the amount $gbeP_1$. The efficiency or deadweight loss is the triangle *bce*.

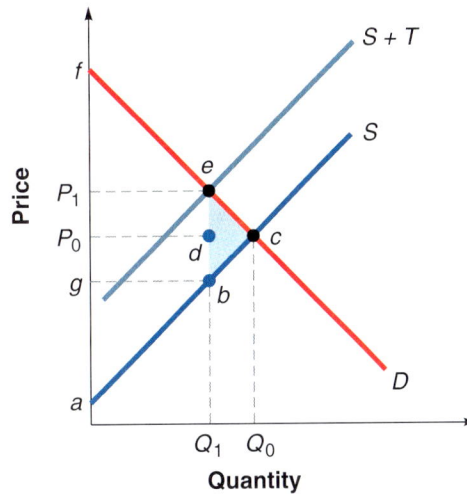

likely to be small; when the demand curve is relatively steep, consumer surplus and deadweight loss are larger. The same can be said of the supply curve and producer surplus: a flat supply curve indicates little producer surplus and thus little deadweight loss; a steep supply curve indicates the opposite. Although these statements are certainly true, it should be emphasized that consumer and producer surplus are theoretical concepts and actually measuring them in the real world can be difficult. The reason why is that we usually observe only the single market price that prevails, not the entire demand and supply curves. Unless we know the entire curves, we have no way of measuring the area under them. The difficulty of finding empirical estimates of deadweight loss and consumer surplus does not mean that the concepts are useless, however. On the contrary, not only is the theory impeccable, but because we *know* that taxes impose welfare costs on society, we must be careful about their implementation and continue to look for more efficient ways to raise the money needed by the government. We will return to the concept of deadweight loss again when we look at the relationship between government and the economy in detail in Chapter 18.

RECAP   Producer and Consumer Surplus

If people are willing to pay a higher price than they have to pay, they are receiving a consumer surplus; if producers are receiving a higher price that they would be willing to sell for, they are receiving producer surplus. Private markets maximize the amount of producer and consumer surplus. Taxes reduce producer and consumer surplus and result in deadweight loss.

Negative externality The cost to
society from a private action that
is not included in price or cost
calculations.

Positive externality A benefit to
society from a private action that is
not included in private cost or price
calculations.

EXTERNALITIES

Our discussion of price regulation should not lead you to believe that economists are always opposed to interference in the market. In fact, in numerous situations economists generally agree that government intervention is appropriate. One such situation is when market prices do not reflect all of the costs or benefits. This is the case of externalities.

Externalities can come in two varieties. A **negative externality** occurs when the production or consumption of a good imposes a cost on a party not involved in the market transaction. For example, if a paper mill emits smoke or fouls the river when it produces paper, it has imposed a cost on society that is not reflected in the cost of producing paper. The other kind of externality is a **positive externality.** Consider the benefits associated with the college degree you are about to earn. You benefit because you will be able to qualify for a higher-paying and more rewarding job. But society undoubtedly benefits more than you do. Not only will you be more productive once you receive your degree, but there is a much smaller chance that you will resort to a life of crime or end up on welfare.

Pollution Taxes

Externalities can be illustrated with supply and demand analysis, and doing so can give a hint at the appropriate policy response of the government. Let's look at the case of negative externalities first. Figure 4.10 shows the market for paper where D is the market demand curve and S_p is the supply curve. As usual, the supply curve gives the different quantities that would be offered at various prices. This supply curve includes all of the *private* costs of production—wages, electricity, lumber, and so on. In the absence of government intervention, the selling price is $10 per ream of paper, and the quantity is 500 reams.

The supply curve S_s is the *social* supply curve. This curve represents all of the private costs of production plus the additional social costs of producing paper—the loss of clean air and water due to pollution. In this example, the extra social costs of producing paper are estimated to be $5 per ream of paper. The social supply curve intersects the demand curve at a higher price and lower quantity—$12 and 375 reams of paper. Notice that even though the extra social cost of producing paper is $5 per ream, the price of paper rises only $2 because the demand curve is downward sloping. As we found out in our discussion of unit sales taxes, this result depends on the relative slopes of the supply and demand curves.

Economists consider the $12 price and 375 quantity to be "optimal" in the sense that they reflect all benefits and costs of paper production. The market will not establish this price and quantity automatically, however, because the firm is not required to pay the social costs of pollution. This is where government intervention comes in. If the government were to impose a pollution tax equal to $5 per ream of paper, the firm would be forced to charge a higher price for its output. Graphically, a $5 tax would result in an upward shift of the supply curve so that it would be equivalent to the social supply curve. Consumers would pay $12 per

····**FIGURE 4.10** TAXING NEGATIVE EXTERNALITIES

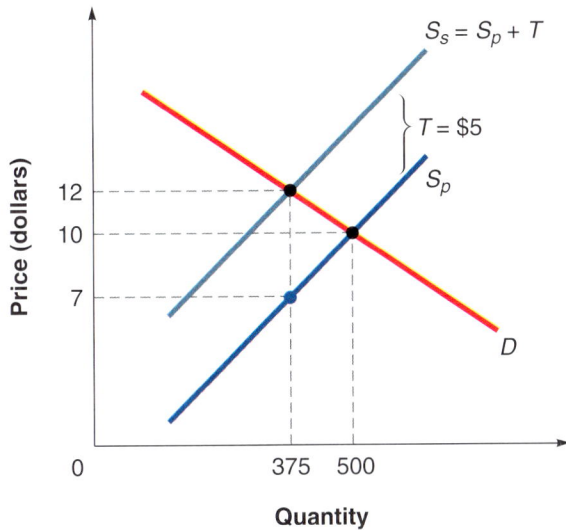

The government can force firms to internalize their externalities by levying a pollution tax equal to the external cost. In this case, the private supply curve, S_p, represents only the firm's costs, and the social supply curve, S_s, represents the firm's costs plus the pollution costs to society. If the government imposed a $5 pollution tax, the selling price would rise, less would be produced and sold, and there would be less pollution. In general, the selling price will rise less than the amount of the tax. In this case, the firm receives an after-tax price of $7 per ream of paper, buyers pay $12 per ream, and the government collects $5(375) = $1,875 in pollution tax revenues.

ream of paper, and the firm would receive only $7 after paying the $5 tax to the government.

In the terminology of the economist, the pollution tax has caused the firm to "internalize its externalities." The pollution tax has also reduced the amount of pollution because less paper is produced and purchased at the higher price. Notice, however, that the pollution tax has *not* eliminated pollution entirely. To do so would almost certainly entail costs that exceed the benefits, a point we will develop in more detail in later chapters.

········

Subsidies

Positive externalities call for government subsidies instead of taxes. This is shown in Figure 4.11, which presents the market for years of college. The supply curve for college, S, is upward sloping to reflect the fact that the cost of providing college education increases as more is offered. The private demand curve for college, D_p, is downward sloping and reflects the fact that people receive fewer benefits from additional years of college. The social demand curve D_s, includes private benefits plus the positive externalities from education—reduced chance for a life of crime and so on. Graphically, the extra social benefit of a year of college is the vertical distance

···· **FIGURE 4.11 SUBSIDIZING POSITIVE EXTERNALITIES**

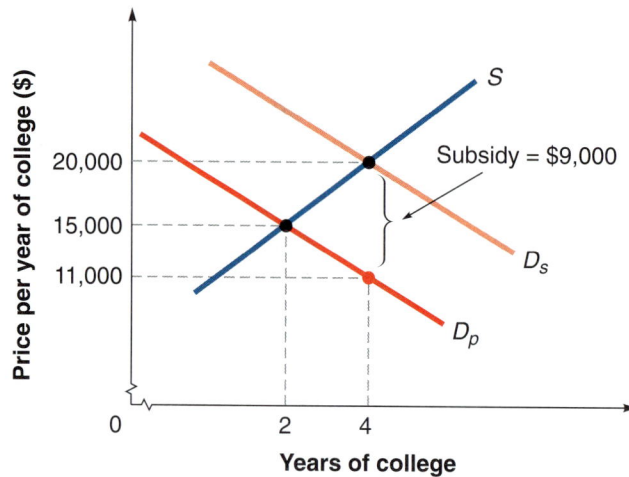

When social benefits exceed private benefits, it is necessary to subsidize consumption to achieve optimality. In this case, the social benefits of college exceed the private benefits by $9,000 per year. In the absence of a subsidy, most people would attend college for only two years because the cost of another year of college would exceed the private benefits. If the government subsidizes college, people will attend college longer. In this case, a $9,000 per year subsidy is necessary.

between the private demand curve and the social demand curve. In this case, that distance is assumed to be $9,000.

Now, in the absence of government subsidies, people will go to college only as long as the cost of an additional year of college is equal to the (private) benefit of that year. In this case, people will attend college for only two years and pay a price of $15,000 per year. If society wants to encourage people to attend four years of college, it will be necessary to subsidize college tuition. In this case, a subsidy of $9,000 per year would be required to get people to spend four years in college.

········

Some Caveats

This section has only touched the surface of the analysis of externalities; we will have to postpone a more detailed examination until later. Still, we need to add one very important qualification. Although taxes and subsidies can indeed be used to internalize externalities, it is quite another thing to find the *correct* taxes and subsidies. The fact that pollution is external to the costs of the firm means that actually measuring its true social cost is very difficult. The same can be said for college: How much does society really benefit from your going to school? (How much do you benefit?) Without knowing the answers to these questions, it is impossible to determine the correct taxes or subsidies. We can only hope to come to a reasonable approximation.

> **RECAP**   **Supply and Demand Analysis of Externalities**
>
> Externalities exist when the market does not recognize all costs and benefits. Negative externalities can be internalized with taxes; positive externalities can be internalized with subsidies.

A GLIMPSE AT ELASTICITY

Supply and demand analysis can almost always tell us the *direction* of a price or quantity change.[3] For example, we know that an increase in the price of gasoline will cause people to use less gasoline. Without additional information, however, supply and demand analysis cannot tell us how much less gasoline people will buy when the price rises. Nevertheless, our intuition can help us guess at an answer: Because there are so few good substitutes for gasoline, most people will use about the same amount unless the price increases considerably. On the other hand, suppose that the price of imported French wine rises. Many people would suddenly find that California wines are good substitutes. Economists use the concept of **elasticity** to help them understand the quantitative relationship between a relative change in price and the corresponding change in quantity demanded.

Elasticity The responsiveness of one variable to a change in another variable.

Elasticity is used in several contexts in economics, but the most common usage is probably the price elasticity of demand. This section will provide the rudiments of price elasticity to help us through the next few chapters. Elasticity is examined in more detail in Chapter 8.

Determinants of Price Elasticity of Demand

The price elasticity of demand tells how much quantity demanded changes relative to a change in price. Several factors determine price elasticity of demand, but perhaps the most important is the availability of good substitutes. For example, most cars run on gasoline and nothing else, so gasoline has few good substitutes. This suggests that the demand for gasoline is **inelastic** or relatively insensitive to changes in price. On the other hand, California wines compete favorably with even the best French wines, so a rise in the price of French wines will probably cause many people to switch to California wines. In other words, the demand for French wines is **elastic** or relatively sensitive to changes in the price of French wine.

Inelastic Being relatively insensitive to a change in another variable.

Elastic Being relatively sensitive to a change in another variable.

In addition to the availability of good substitutes, several other factors can also influence the price elasticity of demand:

• Necessities are usually price-inelastic; people may grumble at a price hike, but there is little they can do except pay the price if the good is truly a necessity. What can you do about the rising price of medicine? Either pay the price or go without. On the other hand, luxury goods are usually price-elastic. You may want to treat

---

[3]Students in microeconomics courses may want to skip this section and wait for the complete discussion of elasticity in Chapter 8.

your partner to a special lobster dinner, but if the price of lobster rises, a simpler meal will have to do.

• The price of the good relative to the consumer's budget can also affect elasticity. For example, most of the time you would not even notice if the price of ballpoint pens were to rise from 25¢ to 50¢. But if you have only a dollar and need to buy both a pen and a cup of coffee before the exam, you might think about using a pencil instead of a pen.

• Finally, elasticity also varies over time. People can usually find better substitutes in the long run than in the short run. For example, when gasoline prices doubled in the 1970s, many people just bit the bullet and paid higher prices, but when it was time to buy a new car, they looked for cars with better fuel economy.

Before going on, we need to qualify much of the foregoing. We just said that the demand for gasoline is inelastic because there are few good substitutes for gasoline. A 15 percent increase in the price of gasoline from $1.00 to $1.15 a gallon would have very little effect on most people's demand for gasoline. But what if the 15 percent rise was from $10.00 to $11.50 per gallon? Most people would find substitutes rather quickly—car pooling would become more popular, as would walking and bicycles—and reduce the quantity demanded of gasoline. This has an important implication: In general, demand is more elastic at high prices than at low prices. Just how high is "high" and how low is "low"? There is no single answer, which is why we need to learn how to calculate elasticity coefficients.

· · · · · · · · ·

Elasticity Formulas

The price elasticity of demand. E_p, is defined as the percentage change in quantity demanded divided by the percentage change in price, or:

$$E_p = \frac{\text{percentage change in quantity}}{\text{percentage change in price}} \qquad [1]$$

Equation 1 is of little use if you do not remember how to calculate percentage changes, but that is simple enough to do. The percentage change in a variable is computed as the change in the variable divided by the variable itself. This means we could write Equation 1 as:

$$\text{Price elasticity of demand: } E_p = \left| \frac{\dfrac{\Delta Q}{\overline{Q}}}{\dfrac{\Delta P}{\overline{P}}} \right| \qquad [2]$$

Where:

ΔQ = change in quantity; i.e., $Q_1 - Q_2$

$\overline{Q}$ = the midpoint between Q_1 and Q_2, i.e., $(Q_1 + Q_2)/2$

ΔP = change in price; i.e., $P_1 - P_2$

$\overline{P}$ = the midpoint between P_1 and P_2, i.e., $(P_1 + P_2)/2$

We need to make some comments about the formula in Equation 2 before we are ready to apply it. First, the two vertical bars indicate to take the *absolute value* of the fraction inside the bars. The absolute value of a negative number eliminates the minus sign, but has no effect on a positive number. For example, $|-5| = 5; |+5| = 5$. This means that the price elasticity of demand is always a positive number. Second, we are using the midpoints of P and Q because elasticity changes over the demand curve. The elasticity coefficient will depend on whether the low or high values of P and Q are used in the computation.[4] The quantity and price midpoints are found by adding the two points together and dividing by 2: $\overline{Q} = (Q_1 + Q_2)/2$ and $\overline{P} = (P_1 + P_2)/2$.

Some calculations based on the demand curve in Figure 4.12 will show how to use the price elasticity of demand formula. First, let's calculate elasticity as price rises from \$6 to \$8. When price rises over this region, the quantity demanded falls from 2 to 1 units. Substituting these values into Equation 2 gives:

[4]This formula finds the *arc* elasticity over the region between P_1 and P_2. This is a good first approximation, but for more precise analysis, the elasticity at a single point can be calculated with calculus.

The formula is $E_p = \left(\dfrac{dQ}{dP}\right)\left(\dfrac{P}{Q}\right)$.

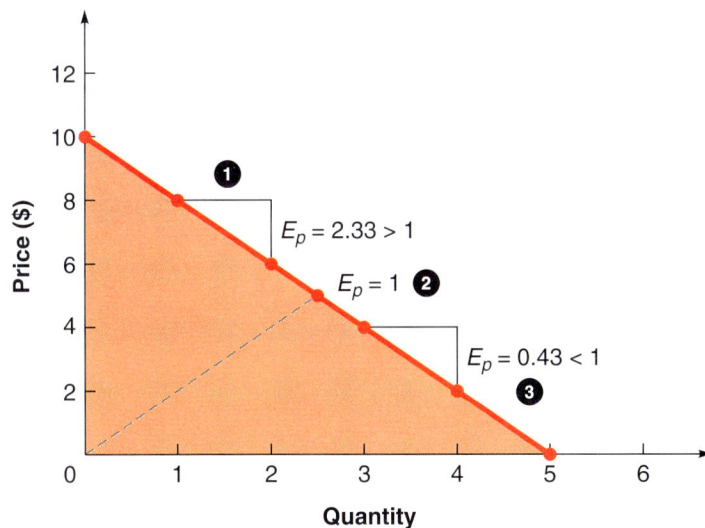

FIGURE 4.12 DEMAND AND ELASTICITY

❶ "High" prices = Elastic demand
❷ Midpoint = Unitary elasticity
❸ "Low" prices = Inelastic demand

Every linear demand curve has regions of elastic, inelastic, and unitary demand. At high prices, people can always find a substitute; this is the region of elastic demand, $E_p > 1$. At low prices, people may not even look for substitutes; this is the region of inelastic demand, $E_p < 1$. The midpoint of the demand curve has unitary elasticity, $E_p = 1$.

$$E_p = \left|\frac{\frac{\Delta Q}{\overline{Q}}}{\frac{\Delta P}{\overline{P}}}\right| = \left|\frac{\frac{Q_1 - Q_2}{(Q_1 + Q_2)/2}}{\frac{P_1 - P_2}{(P_1 + P_2)/2}}\right| = \left|\frac{\frac{2 - 1}{(2 + 1)/2}}{\frac{6 - 8}{(6 + 8)/2}}\right| = \left|\frac{\frac{1}{3/2}}{\frac{-2}{7}}\right| = \left|\frac{2}{3}\left(\frac{7}{-2}\right)\right|$$

$$= \frac{14}{6} = 2.33 > 1 \rightarrow \text{elastic demand}$$

What does this answer mean? As price rises from $6 to $8, the percentage change in quantity is 2.33 times as large as the percentage change in price. When the elasticity coefficient is greater than 1, the percentage change in quantity is greater than the percentage change in price, and demand is said to be *elastic*. This means that the quantity demanded is highly responsive to price changes.

Look what happens when we calculate the elasticity over a different price range, say, as the price rises from $2 to $4. In this case, the quantity demanded falls from 4 to 3 units, so the calculations are:

$$E_p = \left|\frac{\frac{4 - 3}{(4 + 3)/2}}{\frac{2 - 4}{(2 + 4)/2}}\right| = \left|\frac{\frac{1}{7/2}}{\frac{-2}{3}}\right| = \left|\frac{2}{7}\left(\frac{3}{-2}\right)\right| = \frac{6}{14} = 0.43 < 1 \rightarrow \text{inelastic demand}$$

In other words, as price rises from $2 to $4, the percentage change in the quantity demanded is less than half as large as the percentage change in price. When the elasticity coefficient is less than 1, demand is said to be *inelastic*. This means that the quantity demanded is relatively unresponsive to price changes.

Finally, the midpoint of a linear demand curve always has an elasticity coefficient equal to 1; this is the point of **unitary elasticity.** This can be verified by calculating the elasticity coefficient as the price rises from $4 to $6:

$$E_p = \left|\frac{\frac{3 - 2}{2.5}}{\frac{4 - 6}{5}}\right| = 1 \rightarrow \text{unitary elasticity}$$

A unitary elastic coefficient means that the percentage change in quantity is equal to the percentage change in price.

Unitary elasticity A percentage change in quantity is equal to the percentage change in price.

. . . .

A Look Ahead

Elasticity is a general concept that will be used in several contexts throughout the book. For example, the "interest rate elasticity of investment" is a measure of the relative responsiveness of investment to a change in the interest rate. This will be important when we develop a basic macroeconomic model in later chapters. You may have already guessed that it is possible to calculate supply elasticity coefficients. Supply elasticity is the relative change in the quantity supplied in response to a change in price. Economists also calculate income elasticities (the percentage change in the

OUR ECONOMIC HERITAGE

ALFRED MARSHALL, THE FATHER OF SUPPLY AND DEMAND ANALYSIS

We cannot end our discussion of supply and demand analysis without mentioning the great English economist, Alfred Marshall (1842–1924). Marshall was one of the truly stellar economists of all time. He came from a strict evangelical Protestant background, which may explain his sincere desire to use economics for the betterment of humanity. Although trained as a mathematician, he used mathematics more sparingly and cautiously than some of his predecessors. He was probably most influenced by the marginal utility school, though he had wide respect for Adam Smith and other classical economists.

Like most economists of his time, Marshall believed that economic laws were natural laws, and yet his famous book, *Principles of Economics,* was not nearly as mechanistic as one might expect. Marshall saw economics as more analogous to the biological sciences than to physics. The quotation that opened *Principles, "natura non facit saltum"* (Latin for "nature does not make leaps"), established his view that economic evolution was a smooth process. Unlike many of his followers, he included a discussion of the historical

evolution of economic systems alongside his more technical analysis.

Marshall's great conceptual breakthrough was to combine the theory of production developed by the classical economists with the marginalists' theory of demand. The result was his "Marshallian Cross"—which we know today as the supply and demand diagram. Marshall used this analysis to show that supply and demand determine price much "like the blades of a pair of scissors." He also made important contributions in the analysis of costs, producer and consumer surplus, and other areas.

Marshall is regarded as one of the fathers of neoclassical economics, still the dominant school of economic thought today. His text, though originally published in 1890, was still being used as a college text in the 1950s and later. Undoubtedly, his most famous student was John Maynard Keynes (1883–1946), the founder of modern macroeconomics, but his favorite student was reputedly A. C. Pigou (1877–1959), who made important contributions in both micro- and macroeconomics.

The "Marshallian Cross" and *Prin-*

ciples laid the groundwork for generations of economists, but many of Marshall's followers have made what some regard as unfortunate breaks from the founding father. Some modern economists concentrate so much on technique that they ignore the social and evolutionary aspects of the economy that Marshall thought were so important. It is perhaps significant that in Marshall's *Principles,* all graphs are relegated to footnotes and equations appear only in appendixes.

quantity demanded relative to the percentage change in income) and cross elasticities (the percentage change in the quantity demanded of good *X* relative to the percentage change in the price of good *Y*). Those elasticities will be important later on, but for the time being, the general concept that elasticity measures the relative responsiveness of one variable to another is all that is necessary.

> **RECAP** Elasticity
>
> Elasticity is a measure of the relative responsiveness of one variable to another. It is used in several contexts in economics. The price elasticity of demand is the ratio of the percentage change in quantity demanded to the percentage change in price. Important determinants of price elasticity of demand are the number of available substitutes, whether the good is a luxury or a necessity, and time. Demand is said to be "elastic" if the percentage change in quantity demanded is larger than the percentage change in price. Demand is said to be inelastic if the percentage change in quantity demanded is less than the percentage change in price.

SUMMARY

This chapter has only begun to touch on the power of supply and demand analysis. Be sure that you understand the *whys* of the analysis because you will be extending much of it in the coming chapters. To be certain that you understand the material, be sure that you can draw as well as read supply and demand graphs. The key points to remember from this chapter are:

1. Price ceilings can cause shortages and often result in black markets.
2. Price floors can create surpluses and may necessitate quantity restrictions.
3. Tax incidence depends on the relative slopes of the supply and demand curves. Other things being equal, the steeper the demand curve, the greater the proportion of the tax paid by the buyers; the steeper the supply curve, the greater the proportion of the tax paid by the sellers.
4. Externalities prevent private markets from achieving optimality. Negative externalities can be internalized with taxes; positive externalities can be internalized with subsidies.
5. The price elasticity of demand is a measure of the relative responsiveness of quantity demanded to a change in price. Elasticity depends on the number of available substitutes, whether the good is a necessity or a luxury, and time. The formula for calculating price elasticity of demand is $E_p = (\Delta Q/\overline{Q})/(\Delta P/\overline{P})$. When the elasticity coefficient is greater than 1, demand is said to be elastic; when it is less than 1, demand is inelastic; when it is equal to 1, it is unitary.

KEY TERMS AND CONCEPTS

price floor	consumer surplus
price ceiling	producer surplus
shortage	dead weight loss
surplus	externality
minimum wage	negative externality
rent control	positive externality
tax incidence	elasticity

unit sales tax   elastic
ad valorem sales tax   unitary elasticity
inelastic

·······REVIEW QUESTIONS

1. Using graphs and words, explain why price ceilings may result in shortages and price floors may result in surpluses.
2. List several kinds of positive and negative externalities, and draw graphs to illustrate how government policies can be used to internalize externalities.
3. Using graphs, explain how the slopes of the demand and supply curves affect the incidence of a unit sales tax.
4. What are the determinants of price elasticity of demand? Why are all linear demand curves elastic at high prices? Why are they inelastic at low prices?

·······PROBLEMS

1. Indicate whether and how the following shocks would shift the demand or supply curves in the market for mechanical pencils. Assume that no firms can enter or exit the industry.
   a. The price of ink increases.
   b. The price of paper increases.
   c. School attendance falls.
   d. Teachers require ink on all exams.
   e. The Mechanical Pencil Makers Union goes on strike.
   f. Apple introduces a cheap, friendly notebook computer.
   g. The government freezes all wages and prices for 90 days.
2. Price controls were imposed in 1971 and lasted until 1974. During that period, there were shortages of several products including paper. One night, talk show host Johnny Carson joked about the impending toilet paper shortage. As a result, many people stocked up on toilet paper in anticipation of the shortage. Draw a supply and demand diagram to illustrate the initial shortage caused by the price controls and show why the shortage became even more severe after people began hoarding toilet paper.
3. Why do so many goods cost more at the local convenience store than they do at the grocery store? Can you illustrate your answer with supply and demand graphs?
4. Suppose that the government concludes that solar energy is the wave of the future and decides to subsidize all solar energy producers. Draw a supply and demand diagram of the solar energy industry before and after the subsidy has been implemented. Interpret your results.
5. One proposed modification of the minimum wage law is a special subminimum wage for teenagers. Would this be a good idea? How do you think it would affect teenage unemployment?
6. Many communities in the United States face a shortage of high school math teachers. Using supply and demand analysis, explain why this shortage exists. Also, why do you think there is a shortage of math teachers but not a shortage of English

teachers? You can assume that high school teachers earn the same salaries regardless of the subjects they teach.

7. There were long lines at gas stations following the Arab oil embargo in 1973, largely because price controls prevented the price of gasoline from rising. Using a supply and demand diagram, show the combined effect of the reduced supply of gasoline and price controls. Also, do you think people were better off waiting in line at gas stations than they would have been had the price of gasoline risen to market levels?

8. Given the following linear demand schedule:

P	0	2	4	6	8	10
Q	20	16	12	8	4	0

a. Graph the demand curve.

b. Find the price elasticity of demand coefficient in an elastic region of the demand curve.

c. Find the price elasticity of demand coefficient in an inelastic region of the demand curve.

d. Now suppose that the numbers in the schedule represent the private demand curve, but that there are negative externalities in consumption; that is, the data could represent liquor, which, if consumed in excess, can result in traffic accidents and other problems. Illustrate the social demand curve under such circumstances.

APPENDIX 4A

The Algebra of Supply and Demand

Graphs are useful for a great deal of economic analysis, but algebra is more precise. Also, when developing computer models for economic forecasting, it is necessary to express relationships in equation form. This appendix presents an algebraic analysis of supply, demand, and market equilibrium. We also use algebra to illustrate the incidence of a sales tax on market equilibrium.

SUPPLY AND DEMAND EQUATIONS

Table 4A.1 presents hypothetical data for the computer chip market. Column 1 shows alternative prices while Columns 2 and 3 show the quantities that would be demanded and supplied at these prices. (We will be using Column 4 in just a moment.) Plotting these data would generate the demand and supply curves, but without a very carefully drawn graph, it would be difficult to determine the precise equilibrium price and quantity. If the data are converted into equation form, however, it is possible to solve the equation system simultaneously and determine the exact equilibrium price and quantity.

Finding the Supply and Demand Equations

All linear equations are defined by their slope and intercept. The general form of the

TABLE 4A.1 SUPPLY AND DEMAND DATA

Price	Quantity Demanded	Quantity Supplied	Quantity Supplied if Tax = $2
$ 1	40	3	−3
2	36	6	0
3	32	9	3
4	28	12	6
5	24	15	9
6	20	18	12
7	16	21	15
8	12	24	18
9	8	27	21
10	4	30	24

demand equation is shown in Equation A.1:[1]

$$P = a - bQ \qquad \text{[A.1]}$$

Where:
  $a > 0$ is the vertical intercept
  b is the slope, $\dfrac{\Delta P}{\Delta Q}$

Likewise, the equation for a linear supply curve is Equation A.2:

$$P = c + dQ \qquad \text{[A.2]}$$

Where:
  c is the vertical intercept
  d is the slope, $\dfrac{\Delta P}{\Delta Q}$

To find either equation, all that is necessary is to find the intercept and slope. For the demand curve, notice that each positive one-unit change in price is associated with a negative four-unit change in quantity. Because the slope of the demand curve is defined as $\Delta P/\Delta Q$, this gives a slope of $+1/-4$ or -0.25. The vertical intercept is the point where the demand curve crosses the price axis; that is, it is the price that would result in zero quantity demanded. In this case, a price increase from $10 to $11 would decrease the quantity demanded from 4 units to 0 units. Thus, the vertical intercept is $11. Substituting these values into Equation A.1 gives:

$$P = 11 - 0.25Q$$

To find the equation of the supply curve, notice that when $P = \$1$, $Q_s = 3$ and when $P = \$2$, $Q_s = 6$. Thus, the slope of the supply curve is $(2 - 1)/(6 - 3) = +0.33$. When $P = 0$, $Q_s = 0$ so the vertical intercept of the supply curve is zero. This means that the equation of the supply curve is:

$$P = 0 + 0.33Q = 0.33Q$$

· · · · · · · ·

Solving for Equilibrium

To find equilibrium, it is necessary to solve the two equations simultaneously. First, set the supply function equal to the demand function:

$$0.33Q = 11 - 0.25Q$$

Now, add $0.25Q$ to each side of the equation:

$$0.58Q = 11$$

and divide each side by 0.58:

[1]Math students will notice that economists do things a little differently. Instead of following the usual practice of putting the dependent variable, Q, on the vertical axis, economists have put the independent variable on the vertical axis. This does confuse things a bit, but it does not change the results in any way.

• • • • FIGURE 4.A1 SUPPLY AND DEMAND EQUILIBRIUM

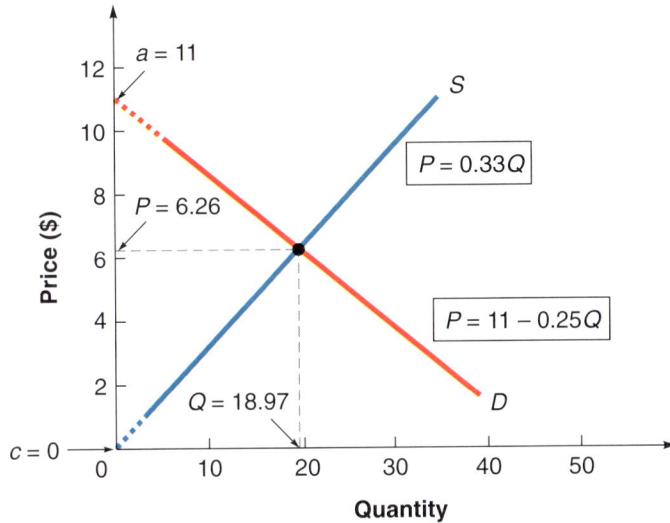

The solution to the supply and demand equation system is $P = \$6.26$ and $Q = 18.97$.

$$Q = \frac{11}{0.58} = 18.97$$

which is the equilibrium quantity.

To find the equilibrium price, substitute the equilibrium quantity into either the demand or supply equation and solve. Using the supply equation gives:

$$P = 0.33(18.97) = 6.26$$

These results are illustrated in Figure 4A.1.

• • • • • • • IMPACT OF A UNIT SALES TAX

As we found out in Chapter 4, in general, price will not rise by the full amount of a unit sales tax. To show this with algebra, suppose that a $2 per unit sales tax is implemented. How do we know that the tax is $2? Look back at Columns 3 and 4 of Table 4A.1, which represent the different quantities that will be offered by the firm before and after the $2 per unit sales tax has been imposed. The firm, of course, will treat the tax as an additional cost and will try to pass it on to the buyer. Notice that with no tax (Column 3) the firm would offer 9 units at a price of $3. Once the tax is imposed, the firm will offer 9 units only at a price of $5.

We know that the selling price will not rise by the entire amount of the tax, but how much will it rise? To find out, construct the equation of the new supply curve, and use it to solve for equilibrium with the fixed demand curve. The slope of the new supply curve is still 0.33, but the intercept is now +2. Thus, we need to solve the equations:

$$P = 2 + 0.33Q$$

and

$$P = 11 - 0.25Q$$

Set the supply function equal to the demand function to get:

$$2 + 0.33Q = 11 - 0.25Q$$

subtract 2 and add 0.25Q to each side:

$$0.58Q = 9$$

and divide by 0.58 to get equilibrium Q:

$$Q = 15.52$$

Now, substitute the equilibrium quantity into either of the equations:

$$P = 11 - 0.25(15.52)$$

and solve to get:

$$P = 7.12$$

Before the tax was imposed, the price was $6.26. This means that the $2 tax raised prices by only $0.86—less than the amount of the tax. This is shown in Figure 4A.2.

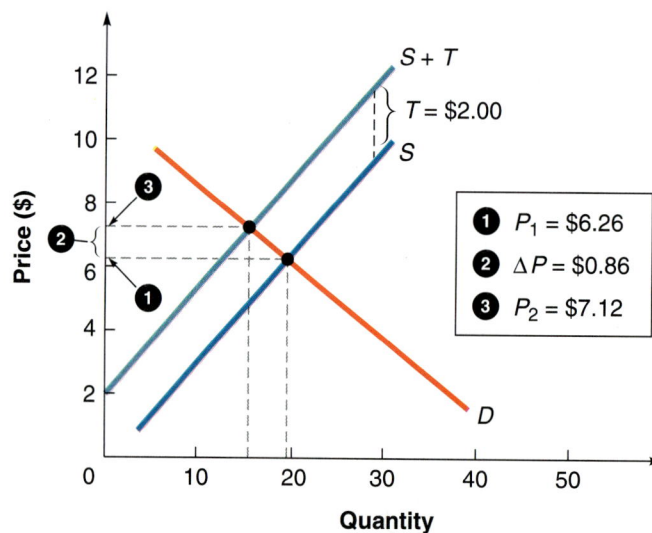

•••• FIGURE 4.A2 IMPACT OF A UNIT SALES TAX

If the demand curve is downward sloping and the supply curve is upward sloping, a unit sales tax will raise price less than the amount of the tax increase. In this case, the tax is $2 per unit. This shifts the supply curve up by $2 from S to $S + T$. However, price increases by only $0.86, from $6.26 to $7.12. The steeper the demand curve, the more the tax can be passed on to buyers.

PROBLEMS

1. Using the data in the table below:
   a. Find the equations of the supply and demand curves and graph your results.
   b. Now suppose that a \$1 per unit sales tax is imposed. Find the $S + T$ equation and determine how much equilibrium price rises. Graph your results.

Price	Quantity Demanded	Quantity Supplied
1	20	2
2	16	6
3	12	10
4	8	14
5	4	18

2. Suppose that the demand curve is given by the equation $P = 10 - 0.5Q$ and that the supply curve is a horizontal line through the price 6.
   a. Graph your equation system and solve for equilibrium price and quantity with algebra.
   b. Now suppose that the demand curve is fixed at $Q = 5$ and the supply curve is given by the equation $P = 2 + 0.5Q$. Graph this equation and solve for equilibrium price and quantity.
   c. Under what conditions would you expect a vertical demand curve? When would you expect to find a horizontal supply curve?

3. Refer back to Figure 4A.2.
   a. What is the after-tax price received by the firm? (You will need to use the corresponding equations to answer this question.)
   b. How much tax revenue does the government raise from this tax?

4. As noted in footnote 1, mathematicians would prefer that the supply and demand curves be drawn with Q on the vertical axis and P on the horizontal axis. Show how this would change your answers from the previous question.

CHAPTER 5

The Institutional
Framework I:
The Private Sector

The 1970s and 1980s were not kind to the American people. The drug problem and AIDS crisis reached epidemic proportions. The school dropout rate approached 25 percent nationwide and was much higher in many areas. Homelessness became a national concern, and the nuclear family seemed a thing of the past. Racism began to rear its ugly head once again, and this time even showed up on college campuses. Two-income couples postponed families, and more couples than ever chose to remain childless. A generation of people who had grown up believing that they could have everything—or at least more than their parents—realized that the world was changing. The American dream of home ownership slipped away from most young couples. And problems were not confined to the household. The banking system seemed on the verge of collapse. American business seemed to be losing its ability to compete in international markets. The trade deficit grew to unheard-of proportions. It appeared that many Americans actually preferred foreign products, even though they had to pay a higher price for them. The era came to be known as the Age of Diminished Expectations after a best-selling book by MIT economist Paul Krugman.[1]

Things seem to be improving so far in the 1990s: income growth is advancing, many American firms now compete quite successfully in international markets, and the banking crisis has been averted, if only temporarily. But serious social problems remain: the school dropout rate is still intolerably high, almost 750,000 people are homeless, and nearly one in five children is officially classified as living in poverty. Economists believe that many—perhaps

[1]Paul Krugman, *The Age of Diminished Expectations*. Cambridge, Mass.: MIT Press, 1990.

most—of these social problems are caused by a weak economy. If we want to deal with social problems, then, we must first deal with the economy. But before we can do that, we need to look at some of the numbers and details that describe the economy. This chapter presents some of the facts and details that will help us understand the past and, we hope, the future.

AFTER READING AND STUDYING THIS CHAPTER, YOU SHOULD BE ABLE TO:
- • • Convert nominal data into real data
- • • Know some of the basic demographic facts about the U.S. population
- • • Identify the sources and uses of household income
- • • List the advantages and disadvantages of the three functional forms of business
- • • Discuss the roles and functions of financial intermediaries
- • • Explain why modern business must pay special attention to international issues

REAL AND NOMINAL DATA: USING PRICE INDICES

Before we look at household income, we need to take an important detour to examine the difference between real and nominal data. This detour is necessary so that we can discuss changes in living standards and economic well-being over time. *Real* data have been adjusted for changes in the price level; *nominal* or *current* data have not. For example, if your income rises by 10 percent, but prices also rise by 10 percent, you have not gained because you will need those extra dollars just to pay the higher prices. If prices rise 10 percent and you get only a 5 percent raise, you are actually worse off even though you take home more dollars than before.

The procedure for converting nominal values into real values involves the use of **price indices.** A price index is calculated by constructing a typical market basket that reflects the prices and quantities of goods and services bought in an initial or *base year,* and then comparing the base year price with the price of the same market basket in subsequent years to see how much prices have changed. You have probably heard about two of the most important price indices, the **consumer price index (CPI)** and the **producer price index (PPI).** As you might suspect, the CPI is the best measure to use when studying changes in the retail prices paid by consumers, while the PPI is best for analyzing price changes at the wholesale level. Another price index is the *GDP (gross domestic product) deflator.* The GDP deflator is the most comprehensive measure because it includes the prices of more goods and services than either of the other two.

Price index A single number used to provide a measure of aggregate price level.

Consumer price index (CPI) A price index based on a standard market basket of goods and services purchased by a typical urban consumer.

Producer price index (PPI) A price index that reflects changes in prices at the wholesale level.

Constructing a Price Index

As an example, assume that the typical market basket consists of just three goods, apples (good *a*), bananas (good *b*), and cherries (good *c*), and that 2 pounds of apples,

3 pounds of bananas, and 4 pounds of cherries are bought every time period. Suppose further that in Year 1, apples are priced at $1 per pound, bananas are priced at $2 per pound, and cherries are priced at $3 per pound. The total expenditure necessary to buy a typical market basket in Year 1 is found by multiplying price times quantity for each good in the basket and then summing the totals:

$$Q_a = 2, P_a = \$1 \Rightarrow P \times Q = \$ \ 2$$
$$Q_b = 3, P_b = \$2 \Rightarrow P \times Q = \ \ \ 6$$
$$Q_c = 4, P_c = \$3 \Rightarrow P \times Q = \ \underline{\ 12}$$
$$\$20$$

The price of the market basket in Year 1 is $20.

Now, suppose that by Year 2, the prices have changed as follows:

$$Q_a = 2, P_a = \$2 \Rightarrow 2 \times 2 = \$ \ 4$$
$$Q_b = 3, P_b = \$2 \Rightarrow 2 \times 3 = \ \ \ 6$$
$$Q_c = 4, P_c = \$4 \Rightarrow 4 \times 4 = \ \underline{\ 16}$$
$$\$26$$

Thus, it will cost $26 to buy the same market basket in Year 2 as it did in Year 1; note that we have assumed that the same quantities are bought in both years. To construct a price index, P, take the ratio of the price of the market basket in Year 2 (P_2) to the price in Year 1 (P_1):

$$\frac{P_2}{P_1} = P = \frac{\text{price of market basket in current year}}{\text{price of market basket in base year}} = \frac{26}{20} = 1.3$$

Frequently, price indices are multiplied by 100. This would convert the 1.3 to 130.

The base year of a price index is always assigned a value of 1.0 or 100. This permits easy comparison between the initial year and subsequent years. A price index of 1.3 or 130 means that the market basket costs 30 percent more in Year 2 than it did in the base year. Notice that no single price rose 30 percent—apples doubled in price, the price of bananas did not change, and cherries rose 33 percent. But if consumers want to buy the same basket in Year 2 as in the base year, they will have to pay 30 percent more.

Inflation A continuing rise in the price index.

The price index is not the same thing as the *inflation rate*. **Inflation** is defined as a continuing rise in the price index. The inflation rate (p) can be calculated from the price index by computing the percentage change in the price index:

$$p = \frac{P_2 - P_1}{P_1} = \frac{\Delta P}{P_1} \qquad [1]$$

For example, if the price index in Year 1 is $P_1 = 120$ and the price index in Year 2 is $P_2 = 135$, the inflation rate would be:

$$p = \frac{135 - 120}{120} = \frac{15}{120} = 0.125 = 12.5\%$$

However, most economists would not define this 12.5 percent change in the price index as inflation unless it continued for several time periods. A one-period change in the price index is just that—a one-period change in the price index—whereas inflation is a *continuing* rise in the price index. Notice that we are using an uppercase *P* for the price index and a lowercase *p* to indicate inflation. This convention will be followed throughout the text.

. . . .

Converting Nominal Values to Real Values

For the time being, our main use of price indices will be to convert nominal values into real values. A nominal value is expressed in current or "money" terms; a real value has been adjusted for price changes. For example if you made $10 per hour in 1990 and $20 per hour in 1995, your nominal wage rate doubled. But if all prices also doubled, your real wage did not change because it took twice as many dollars to buy the same goods in 1995 as it did in 1990.

When the base year is assigned a value of 1.0, nominal values can be converted to real values by dividing the nominal value by the price index. For example, nominal income (Y) can be converted to real income (Q) with the formula in Equation 2:

$$\text{Real income} = \frac{\text{nominal income}}{\text{price index}} = \frac{Y}{P} = Q \qquad [2]$$

When the base year has a value of 100, the formula in Equation 2 must be modified by multiplying by 100. The formula for real income in this case is:

$$\text{Real income} = \frac{Y}{P}(100) = Q \qquad [3]$$

The formula in Equation 3 is probably more common because most published price indices have a base value of 100.

As an example, in 1993, nominal GDP was $6,374.0 billion. What was this in real terms? The GDP price deflator, using 1987 as the base year, was 124.2 in 1993. Substituting these values into Equation 3 shows that real GDP in 1993 was:

$$\frac{\$6,374.0}{124.2}(100) = \$5,132.0 \text{ billion}$$

Since real GDP was $4,539.9 billion in 1987, real GDP grew about 13 percent over the six-year period: ($5,132.0 − 4,539.9)/$4,539.9 = 0.13. Nominal GDP, however, grew considerably more: ($6,374.0 − $4,539.9)/$4,539.9 = 40 percent.[2] The difference was due entirely to price changes. With very few exceptions, data reported in this text will be in real values.[3]

---

[2]Notice that real GDP and nominal GDP were equal in 1987. This is always true in the base year:

$$Q = \frac{Y}{P} = \frac{Y}{1.0} = Y$$

[3]The technique we have just developed *cannot* be used to convert nominal interest rates to real interest rates. As we will find out later, the real interest rate is (essentially) equal to the nominal interest rate minus the inflation rate.

·······HOUSEHOLD DEMOGRAPHICS

A household is defined as a group of one or more people living in the same dwelling. In 1990, there were about 92 million households in the United States. An understanding of the makeup and behavior of households is crucial for an understanding of the economy. Household spending comprises almost two-thirds of the spending in the entire economy. If we can understand household economic behavior, we have a first step toward understanding much of the economy. In this section, we will look at the age and income distribution of the American household in the 1990s.

········

Age Distribution

How people earn and spend their incomes depends partially upon their age. Young people often go into debt to buy new homes and cars, middle-aged people save for retirement, and the elderly live off their accumulated savings.

During the period 1960–2000, the population of the United States will have grown almost 50 percent—from about 180 million to almost 270 million. More important, perhaps, is the significant change in the age distribution of the population, which is illustrated in Figure 5.1. Three trends might be mentioned. First, the percentage of the population in the 18–44 age group has grown substantially over this period. This occurred because of the baby boom: When soldiers returned from World War II, married, and started families, the birthrate jumped and stayed high until about 1960. Census projections are that this group will begin to diminish as a percentage of the population by the turn of the century—because the baby boomers chose to

····FIGURE 5.1 U.S. POPULATION AND AGE DISTRIBUTION, 1960–2000

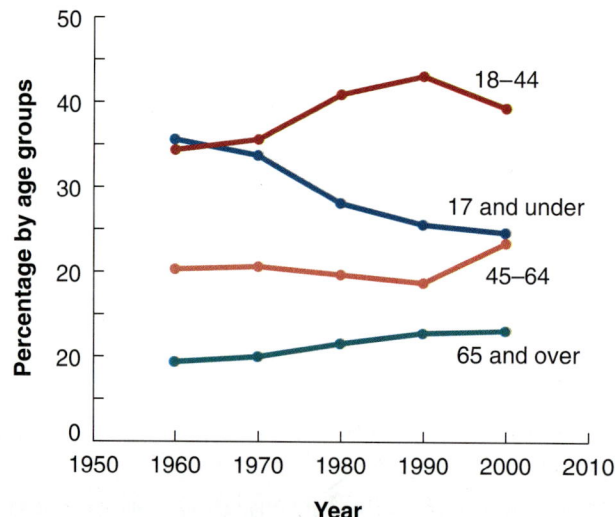

SOURCE: *Statistical Abstract of the United States*, various issues.

have smaller families than their parents—but it will still be a much larger percentage of the population than in the 1960s or earlier. The second significant feature is the steady increase in the size of the 65 and over age group, which has occurred because people are living longer than ever before. Third, the percentage of the population in the 17 and under group has shown a steady decline due to birth control and the popularity of smaller families.

Why are these changes so important? When the baby boomers entered the work-force in the 1970s, they found the competition for jobs especially stiff because so many of them were looking for new jobs at the same time. This was one reason why real wages did not grow very much in the 1970s and 1980s—the large supply of workers meant that firms did not have to pay high wages to fill their slots. Students who graduate in the mid-to-late 1990s may find less competition for entry-level jobs, but will almost certainly find more competition as they move up the corporate ladder. Many middle management positions are still filled with now-aging baby boomers.

The increasing size of the over-65 group has different but no less important implications. The rapid growth in the number of retirement-age people means that the working-age population will have more people to support because many retirees do not have enough personal savings. For the baby boomers, the increase in the number of retirement-age people was more than offset by a decline in the number of people age 17 and below; however, this will not be the case for post–baby boomers. The number of elderly people continues to grow, and a "baby boom echo" is making the 17 and under group grow as a percentage of the population as well. How society (read people aged 18–64 who have jobs) will support an ever larger group that does not or cannot work will become an ever more serious problem in the future.

· · · · · · · ·

Median Income

There are several measures of "average" income. The most useful measure is probably **median income,** which is the income level such that half of all families have higher incomes and half have lower incomes. Why is the median preferred to the **mean** or arithmetic average income? Mean income is found by summing all family incomes and dividing by the number of families, so a few extreme values can distort the meaning of "average." For example, suppose that there are only five families in the population and they have incomes of $10,000, $12,000, $14,000, $16,000, and $200,000. The median income is $14,000—two families make less than $14,000 and two make more than $14,000. This figure provides a reasonable description of family incomes. The mean income, however, is $50,400 (= $252,000/5), a figure that gives a distorted picture of the population.

Several things are worth noting about the data in Table 5.1. First, real median family income has grown quite slowly—under 0.5 percent per year—since 1970. This slow growth stands in stark contrast to the growth rate of almost 3 percent per year in the 1960s. This figure is especially disconcerting because most of the increase was due to the sharp rise in two-income families, not higher wages or production. Second, notice that the real median income of females working full-time grew slightly over the same period while the real median income of males who worked full-time fell. What caused this change is not clear, but part of the reason is that demand

Median income The income level such that half of all families have higher incomes and half have lower incomes.

Mean income The arithmetic average income.

TABLE 5.1 REAL MEDIAN INCOME

Year	Number of Families (Millions)	Family Income	Full-Time Male Income	Full-Time Female Income	Total Percentage below Poverty
1971	53.3	$33,480	$31,351	$18,558	12.5%
1975	56.2	34,249	32,289	19,270	12.3
1980	60.3	35,839	32,685	19,760	13.0
1985	63.6	36,164	32,596	21,191	14.0
1990	66.3	37,950	31,108	22,103	13.5
1991	67.2	37,021	31,244	21,885	14.2
1992	68.1	36,812	31,012	22,167	14.5

NOTE: A "family" refers to a group of two or more persons related by blood, marriage, or adoption and residing together. This differs slightly from the concept of "household."

SOURCE: 1994 *Economic Report of the President,* Table B-31. Data are in constant 1992 dollars.

increased for service workers, many of whom are women, and decreased for manufacturing workers, most of who have been males in the past.

Finally, the last column of the table gives the percentage of persons below the poverty level. The official poverty level is defined by the U.S. Bureau of the Census and is calculated for family size and adjusted for inflation. Official poverty levels are updated each year to reflect changes in the CPI. In 1992, the official poverty level for a family of four was about $14,300 and $7,100 for a single individual. It is interesting to note that there is little apparent relationship between the growth in median income and poverty in the United States. Rapid median income growth in the 1960s may have been partially responsible for the decline in poverty from 22.2 percent in 1960 to 12.6 percent in 1970, but the period also saw significant government spending on programs to combat poverty. Stagnating median income growth in the 1970s and 1980s did not seem to cause the poverty rate to increase dramatically.

SOURCES AND USES OF HOUSEHOLD INCOME

Our glance at income data raises some immediate questions: Where does the income come from? What do people do with their income? These questions are more difficult than they might appear at first, but we can get some insight by looking at the sources and uses of household income.

Sources of Income

By definition, households are the owners of the factors of production and earn income by selling or renting these factors to business. The total income earned from production is called *national income.* The main components of national income are presented in Table 5.2 and defined as follows:

- *Compensation for employees* is the return to labor and includes wages, salaries, bonuses, and fringe benefits. It is the largest component of national income—

•••••**TABLE 5.2** SOURCES OF INCOME AS A PERCENTAGE OF TOTAL

Year	Employee Compensation	Proprietor's Income	Rental Income of Persons	Corporate Profits	Net Interest
1940	65.6%	15.8%	3.4%	11.1%	4.1%
1950	64.8	16.2	3.2	14.6	1.3
1960	69.8	12.3	3.6	11.6	2.7
1970	74.3	9.6	2.2	9.0	4.9
1980	74.3	8.2	0.3	8.0	9.1
1990	73.4	8.6	0	6.7	10.6
1991	75.6	8.1	0	7.6	9.9
1992	74.0	8.6	0	8.4	9.1

SOURCE: 1994 *Economic Report of the President,* Table B-25.

about three-fourths—and has been growing as a percentage of national income in recent years.

- *Proprietor's income* is the profit that goes to the owners of businesses. Because it is often difficult to separate employee income from the proprietor's income, part of this category may actually belong in the compensation for employees category. Due in part to the declining role of small business in the United States, proprietor's income has declined almost 50 percent as a fraction of national income since 1940 and is now under 10 percent. We should point out, however, that this trend appears to be reversing. Small business has been responsible for the bulk of the employment gains in the United States over the past decade.
- *Rental income of persons* represents income earned from renting property. It is the smallest source of income and currently represents less than 1 percent of national income.
- *Corporate profits* have declined from about 11 percent of national income in 1940 to about 8 percent in 1992. However, corporate profits are especially volatile and vary over the business cycle, so these numbers could change in the future.
- *Net interest* represents the interest people earn on financial assets. Net interest increased substantially in the 1980s. The reason for this increase was the substantial rise in indebtedness in both the private and public sector. The federal government went into debt to finance its deficit spending, and both consumers and businesses increased their borrowing. Net interest now represents about 9 percent of national income.

The fact that the largest source of income is employee compensation highlights the obvious: Most people have to work to earn income! Indeed, one of the key factors affecting the U.S. economy over the past 30 years has been changes in **civilian labor force participation rates.** The civilian labor force participation rate is the percentage of people over age 16 who are working or actively looking for work. As shown in Table 5.3, a decline in the adult male labor force participation rate has been more than offset by increases in the labor force participation rates of women.

There are several explanations for the change in labor force participation rates.

Civilian labor force participation rate The percentage of the noninstitutional population over age 16 who are working or actively looking for work.

••••• TABLE 5.3 LABOR FORCE PARTICIPATION RATES

Year	Total	Adult Men	Adult Women	Both Sexes, Age 16–19	Black and Other
1950	59.2%	86.4%	33.9%	51.8%	NA
1960	59.4	83.3	37.7	47.5	64.5%
1970	60.4	79.7	43.3	49.9	61.8
1980	63.8	77.4	51.5	56.7	61.7
1990	66.4	76.1	57.5	53.7	63.7
1992	66.3	75.6	57.8	51.3	63.8
1993	66.2	75.2	57.9	51.5	63.1

SOURCE: 1994 *Economic Report of the President,* Table B-37.

Sociological factors are clearly important. The women's movement and birth control partially explain why so many women are now part of the labor force. Likewise, the rise in working wives may partially explain why the male labor force participation rate has declined. But much of the reason is simple economics. Many women went to work in the 1970s because their husbands were no longer earning enough income to support the lifestyle they wanted and expected. Finally, the emphasis of the industrial structure shifted from manufacturing to services, and women workers are traditionally concentrated in the service sector.

Labor force participation is not the only thing that determines income. Other factors matter as well, with education probably being the single most important. In 1990, people with four years of college had a real median annual income that was nearly $15,000 higher than people with only a high school degree. (Stay in school! That adds up to perhaps $600,000 more in a working lifetime.) Marital status also appears to matter: married men earn more than unmarried men. Skills and luck are also significant.

•••••••••

Uses of Income

How do households spend their income? As Table 5.4 shows, the bulk is spent on personal consumption, next comes taxes and nontax payments, followed by saving and interest. These data are important for several reasons:

- *Consumption spending is the largest use of personal income.* Consumption spending accounts for about 80 percent of total income. This is important because it suggests that if we can understand the factors that influence consumption, we will be a long way toward understanding the macroeconomy.
- *U.S. households save very little.* U.S. citizens have saved only about 5 percent of their income in recent years, a smaller fraction than people in any other advanced industrial nation. Japanese consumers, for example, save nearly 15 percent of their after-tax income. Many economists believe that a low *savings rate* influences the level of investment. A high level of savings produces a large pool of money that firms can borrow for investment. Households are not the only source of savings available to borrowers, of course; businesses also save. Finally, government deficits

• • • • TABLE 5.4 USES OF INCOME, BY PERCENTAGE

Year	Consumption	Personal Taxes	Personal Saving	Interest Payments
1950	84.2%	9.0%	5.5%	1.0%
1960	80.8	12.3	5.1	1.7
1970	76.9	14.0	6.9	2.0
1980	76.7	15.1	6.1	2.1
1990	74.3	15.1	3.9	2.3
1991	80.5	12.8	4.1	2.3
1992	80.5	12.5	4.6	2.3
1993p	81.5	12.7	3.5	2.1

SOURCE: 1994 *Economic Report of the President,* Table B-27. 1993 data are preliminary.

are considered *negative* saving because they mean that the government is borrowing from the pool of savings. This can reduce the supply of savings available to borrowers in the private sector.

• *Households pay low taxes in the United States.* Despite what the tax protesters would have you believe, the United States is a very low tax nation. In 1983, for example, total taxation as a percentage of GDP was about 31 percent in the United States, quite close to the 29.9 percent rate in Japan. However, it was 44 percent in Great Britain, 46.1 percent in West Germany, and over 50 percent in France and Sweden.[4] The perception of high taxes may be due to the increase in personal income taxes from 9 percent of personal income to 15 percent in just 20 years.

• • • • • • THE CHANGING NATURE OF MODERN BUSINESS

The business sector of the U.S. economy has undergone changes no less significant than the household sector. Gone are the days of giant factories employing hundreds of unskilled workers simply "tightening bolts." Gone are the days when U.S. corporations could ignore foreign competition. And gone, to some extent, are the days when management had to deal with powerful labor unions. These changes took place at almost lightning speed and can be traced to main two factors: technological progress and increased foreign competition.

• • • • • • • •

The Evolving Factory System

The mass production factory system that characterizes so many production facilities has not existed forever. It was a product of the Industrial Revolution of the nineteenth century when the development of steam and electrical power permitted long assembly lines and huge factories. Cities grew up around the factories to meet the need for workers. Too often this meant that children worked from dawn to dark without

[4]From Edward Nell, *Prosperity and Public Spending* (Boston: Unwin-Hyman, 1988), p. 256.

ever seeing the light of day—one of the main reasons for the simultaneous rise of the labor movement and child labor laws. Long assembly lines were capable of turning out enormous quantities of identical products. The main job for workers was to apply physical labor and make sure the machines kept running. To succeed, the new mass production factory system required two things: (1) market demand had to be large enough to absorb the rapidly expanding output, and (2) the number of people with the technical and financial abilities to set up competing factories had to be limited. Both of these conditions began to change by the middle of the twentieth century.

International trade grew slowly, then rapidly in the years following World War II. At first, trade opened markets for the output of U.S. firms, but technological transfers inevitably accompanied trade. By the mid-1970s, the mass production factory system of the United States and many developed nations was clearly in trouble. Most of the "talent" in the factories was tied up in machines, so even unskilled workers could work in the steel, auto, and other industries. But shipping machines across borders is easy, and U.S. business found that it was suddenly facing competition not only from Europe and Japan, but from less-developed countries as well. How could U.S. businesses compete with foreign firms using the same technology but paying their workers only a fraction of U.S. wage rates?

Something had to happen, and it did. Many businesses were forced to "downsize" to a smaller, more manageable size. Too often the displaced workers found jobs with lower wages than they were accustomed to earning. But significant changes in the way of doing business were also set in motion. Many firms began to produce specialized products with short production runs instead of long runs of identical products. For example, successful steel companies began turning out specialty steels instead of rolled sheet steel. The shift toward specialty steels meant, among other things, that production runs had to be shortened. Specialty steels are produced for particular production processes; rolled sheet steel has a wider market. The computer industry may be the best example of the post–mass production industry: technology advances so quickly and international competition is so severe that significant model changes occur every six months.

Perhaps the most important consequence of this modern industrial evolution was that the roles of labor and capital changed. No longer do workers simply "tighten bolts"; now they must be skilled enough to read blueprints and adjust to the shorter, specialized production runs. Capital cannot be massive and single purpose; it must be adaptable and flexible. The role of the entrepreneur has changed as well. Today's successful entrepreneur must have technological expertise; money alone is rarely enough.

Something else happened in the 1980s. More than Japan and most other countries, managers in the United States are rated on their ability to turn quarterly profits. But it is difficult to design, produce, market, and sell a new product in a year, much less a quarter, so managers had to make quarterly profits in other ways. The popular way in the 1980s was financial investment, or *paper entrepreneurialism* as it came to be called. Financial traders bought low, sold high, and earned millions. Unfortunately, such paper entrepreneurial activities may do little to increase international competitiveness. They also detracted from the problem at hand: because many large corporations were making high profits in their financial divisions, they had less incentive to revamp their production strategies and adopt new technologies.

Not everyone fell for the allure of paper entrepreneurialism, of course. The 1980s and 1990s have already seen an impressive number of technological advances and innovations, but many of these advances have come from small firms with nonconformist managers. Steve Jobs, one of the cofounders of Apple Computer, spent a year in India, not business school, before he helped make the original Apple computer in a friend's garage. And Bill Gates, the founder of Microsoft, the largest software company in the world, dropped out of Harvard before developing the system software for MS-DOS computers. Business is changing and it looks like a new kind of person will lead the charge.

Plants, Firms, and Industries

We have already used several terms related to business structure. We should take time now to define them carefully before we analyze them in some detail.

A *plant* is an establishment that produces or distributes goods and services. It can be a factory, a warehouse, or a retail or wholesale store. A *firm* may own one or more plants. Multiplant firms can be organized in one of three ways. A **horizontal combination** consists of two or more plants engaged in the same kind of operation. For example, a grocery store chain with stores in several locations is a horizontal combination. A **vertical combination** is a firm that owns plants operating at different stages of the production process. A grocery store that also owns a farm and canning operation would be a vertical combination. Most of the large steel companies in the United States—Bethlehem, USX, Republic—are vertical combinations because they own coal and iron ore mines, blast furnaces, and fabricating shops. A third type of organization is the **conglomerate.** A conglomerate firm is engaged in several unrelated businesses. The acquisition of Marathon Oil by U.S. Steel (now USX) was a conglomerate combination.

An *industry* is a collection of firms producing the same, similar, or related products.[5] While apparently simple, the concept is actually much more complex. For example, do mobile home producers belong in the housing industry? Are truck producers part of the automobile industry? The answer depends on the context of the question. To someone in a low-income bracket, mobile homes may represent an affordable housing solution; to other people, they do not.

The Legal Forms of Business

There are many different kinds of businesses—from the Mom and Pop grocery store earning only a hundred dollars a day to AT&T with worldwide operations and nearly a million employees. Because the business population is so diverse, we need to use a classification system for analysis. One useful scheme is to classify businesses according to their legal structure. The government recognizes three legal forms of business organization, the sole proprietorship, the partnership, and the corporation.

A **sole proprietorship** is a business owned by single person. The sole proprietor is ultimately responsible for all aspects of the operation, from obtaining financing to

Horizontal combination A multiplant firm with two or more plants engaged in similar operations.

Vertical combination A multiplant firm with two or more plants that have a producer/supplier, producer/distributor, or similar relationship.

Conglomerate A large firm with many subsidiaries producing unrelated products.

Sole proprietorship A business organization owned and operated by a single individual.

[5]Occasionally, industries are defined by their primary inputs. The leather industry is one such industry.

production and distribution, but most sole proprietorships hire people to share some of the work.

The sole proprietorship form of business offers three main advantages. First, establishing a sole proprietorship is easy and involves very little governmental red tape. Second, there is a strong incentive to do well because the firm's profits are the proprietor's income. Finally, managerial decision making is simplified because no consensus building is necessary.

The sole proprietorship also has three disadvantages. First, rarely does an individual have sufficient resources for long-term growth, and raising funds for expansion. Second, there may be little opportunity for specialization. For example, the sole proprietor may have started the company after inventing the better mousetrap, but whether she is also good at marketing or financial management is not clear. Finally, the sole proprietor is subject to *unlimited liability;* that is, proprietors risk not only the firm's assets but their personal assets as well. If the better mousetrap snags a few of the customers' family pets instead of mice, the proprietor may be subject to a lawsuit and incur losses in excess of the value of the Better Mousetrap Company. Given the high rate of failure among sole proprietorships, unlimited liability can be a very significant drawback.

Partnership A business organization owned and operated by two or more individuals.

A **partnership** is a business organization owned and operated by two or more individuals. The partnership is a logical outgrowth of sole proprietorships because it overcomes some of their disadvantages. Partners can make managerial decisions almost as easily as proprietors, can enjoy some specialization, and can pool their financial resources as necessary. However, they are still subject to unlimited liability, and disagreement among partners can be frequent. Finally, the continuity of the partnership can be a problem. If one of the partners dies or withdraws from the partnership, the firm must dissolve or completely reorganize.

Corporation A form of business characterized by limited liability, separation of ownership from control, and relatively easy access to financial markets.

The third legal form of business is the **corporation.** A corporation is considered a legal entity separate from the people who own it in the eyes of the law and the Internal Revenue Service. Corporations can own assets, incur debt, and engage in lawsuits, as well as produce and distribute products.

Stock A share in the ownership of a corporation.

Bond A debt instrument or promissory note.

Corporations offer three main advantages. First, the corporation is the most effective business organization for raising money. Corporations have the ability to issue shares or ownership, **stock,** and can borrow by issuing **bonds.** As a result, corporations have access to vast amounts of household and business saving. Organized exchanges facilitate trading of stock and bonds. Ready access to financial markets is especially significant becuse it allows corporations to grow large enough to achieve the advantages of specialization. The chief financial officer of the corporation is involved only with financial decisions, the engineers engage only in product design, and so on. A second advantage of the corporation is its **limited liability.** The owners of the corporation, the stockholders, can share in the corporation's profits—called stock dividends—but can lose only the amount they have invested in stock. The corporation can be sued, but the stockholders cannot. Finally, unlike sole proprietorships and partnerships, the corporation can outlive its owners and any individual corporate officers. This gives corporations a measure of permanence that other business forms lack.

Limited liability The liability of the owners of the firm—the stockholders—is limited to the amount of money they have invested in stock.

But the corporate structure also has significant disadvantages. First, setting up a corporation is time-consuming and costly because many government regulations and legal expenses are involved in securing a corporate charter. Also, corporations are subject to what is commonly called *double taxation*. Double taxation exists because the corporation's profits are taxed before dividends are paid out to the shareholders, who are then taxed on their dividend income. Finally, corporations differ from proprietorships and partnerships because there is a *separation of ownership from control*. The owners of the corporation—the stockholders—do not manage the corporation. Separation of ownership from control gives rise to potential conflicts of interest because the goals of the managers may be different from the goals of the owners. The stockholders obviously want high stock prices and dividends, but the managers may want high salaries and long vacations. Managers may even try to drive down stock prices to make it easier for them to buy stock and take over the company. Firms try to reduce the conflict of interest with incentive-based pay schemes—bonuses for high profits and the like—and paying managers with shares of stock instead of cash.

RECAP   Advantages and Disadvantages of the Three Forms of Business

	Sole Proprietorship	Partnership	Corporation
Ease of formation	Very easy	Easy	Difficult; government regulations are extensive
Management incentives	Profit = income	Profit = income	Separation of ownership from control can create difficulties
Specialization	Very limited	Limited	Extensive
Access to capital	Limited	Limited	Extensive; can issue stock and bonds
Liability	Unlimited	Unlimited	Limited to value of stock
Continuity	Ends with death of proprietor	Problem if death of one partner	Permanent

Data on the Legal Forms of Business

Table 5.5 presents data on the number, receipts, and net income of the three legal forms of business for 1988. Over 70 percent of the firms in the United States are sole proprietorships, but these companies generate only 6 percent of business receipts.

TABLE 5.5 THE LEGAL FORMS OF BUSINESS

Form	Number of Firms	Percentage of All Firms	Business Receipts	Percentage of Business Receipts	Net Income	Percentage of Net Income
Sole proprietor	13,679,000	72.4%	$ 672	6.1%	$126	22.8%
Partnership	1,654,000	8.8	464	4.2	14	2.6
Corporation	3,563,000	18.9	9,804	89.6	413	74.6

NOTE: "Net income" is defined differently for each form of organization, but is essentially total taxable receipts less deductions, including cost of sales. Net receipts are closely related to the firm's profits.

SOURCE: 1993 *Statistical Abstract of the United States,* Table 848. Data are for 1988 and in billions of current dollars.

Corporations account for under 20 percent of all firms and almost 90 percent of total business receipts. Some economists believe this concentration of power has negative social consequences; others believe that large corporations are necessary to amass the financial resources necessary for modern research and development. Finally, notice that sole proprietorships accounted for over 22 percent of all business net income, even though they generated only 6 percent of business receipts. This indicates that sole proprietorships, though small, are relatively profitable.

....

The Rise of the Corporation

What the data in Table 5.5 do not show is that the corporation has not always been as prominent as it is today. Although large and powerful corporations have existed for two hundred years, corporations now dominate business more than ever before. Corporate earnings now account for almost 90 percent of total business receipts—a significant increase over the 66 percent rate as recently as 1945.

What has brought about the increased prominence of the corporation? At least three factors can be cited. First, the technological changes that made the mass production factory system possible meant that large amounts of financial capital were necessary to build factories as large as a city block. An efficient way to raise that money was by selling corporate stock. Second, expanding markets created in the nineteenth century by westward expansion and later by international trade meant that large companies could be profitable.

Merger The consolidation of two or more firms into a single larger firm.

Mergers are a third reason for the rise of the corporation. A merger is the combination of two or more firms into a single larger firm. The nineteenth century saw a wave of *horizontal mergers* as firms acquired other firms in the same industry. Horizontal mergers reduce the number of firms in the industry and can thus reduce the amount of competition. Because of this, antitrust legislation was passed to restrict horizontal mergers. A recent wave of mergers occurred in the 1980s when the Reagan administration adopted a permissive attitude toward horizontal mergers. Why the change? Part of the reason was the administration's fundamental belief in *laissez faire* and resistance to government intervention. Another reason was that many economists felt that mergers might make it easier for U.S. firms to compete with increasing foreign competition. We will look at mergers and antitrust policies in detail in Chapter 19.

FINANCIAL INSTITUTIONS

One of the advantages of corporations is that they have better access to the financial markets than partnerships and proprietorships. In fact, all businesses—and households—need access to financial institutions and financial markets. The main role of the financial institutions is to provide a link between savers and borrowers, a process known as *financial intermediation*. Like all businesses, financial institutions are in business to make a profit. They do this by paying a lower interest rate on deposits than they charge on loans. This section provides institutional details and discusses the role of financial institutions. Although recent legislation has blurred the distinctions among the various kinds of financial institutions, enough differences remain to make a listing worthwhile. The most important kinds of financial institutions in the United States are commercial banks, savings and loan institutions, insurance companies, and securities markets.

Commercial Banks

Commercial banks are institutions that advertise as being "full-service banks" in the media. Commercial banks accept deposits and make loans. Until recently, only commercial banks were allowed to offer checking accounts and were prohibited by law from paying interest on checking accounts. When these regulations were relaxed in the 1970s and 1980s, many of the differences between banks and other financial institutions were eliminated. Commercial banks hold more assets than any other financial intermediaries. In 1992, for example, commercial banks' total assets amounted to $3.6 trillion, or about 60 percent of the size of GDP.[6]

Savings and Loan Associations

Savings and loan associations (S&Ls) were established primarily to provide low-interest loans to home buyers. Regulations kept the interest rate on S&L deposits low and required S&Ls to invest primarily in housing loans. In the 1970s, however, when high interest rates caused people to take their deposits out of S&Ls, the interest rate ceilings were removed. Since then, S&Ls have also been permitted to offer checking accounts and invest outside the housing market. As a result, the distinction between commercial banks and S&Ls is largely superficial today. Many S&Ls went out of business during the financial turmoil of the 1980s, but they are still the third largest financial intermediary. In 1992 their total assets were $832 billion, a little less than a quarter of commercial bank assets.

Insurance Companies

In terms of assets, *insurance companies* are the second largest financial intermediaries in the United States. People buy insurance to cover themselves in case of an unlikely event—death, auto accident, fire, and so on. Insurance companies then invest the premiums in the stock market, real estate, and elsewhere. Life insurance companies held $1.6 trillion in assets in 1992; casualty insurance companies—auto, fire, and the like—held $629 billion. Because there are ample opportunities for fraud—imagine paying premiums for 20 years and then finding that the company has no assets when you need to collect it!—insurance companies are highly regulated at both the state and federal level.

Securities Markets

The *securities markets* allow people to buy and sell stocks and bonds. Stocks are shares of ownership in a corporation. Bonds represent loans to a government or a

[6]Data for this section are from the 1993 *Statistical Abstract of the United States,* Table 784.

The Dow Jones Industrial Average

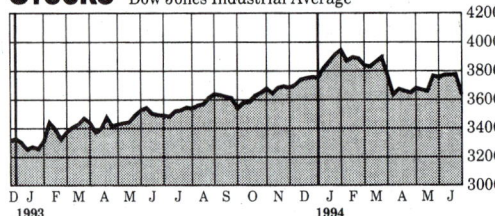

You need to understand the Dow Jones Average for at least two reasons. First, if we count the stock holdings in pension funds, life insurance, and so on, almost 50 percent of the public owns corporate stock, so even if you now keep your life savings in your back pocket, you are likely to find yourself owning stock someday. Second, the stock market is a leading indicator of economic activity. An increase in the stock market often precedes an upturn in economic activity. The most popular stock market index is the *Dow Jones Industrial Average (DJIA),* named after the 1882 cofounders of Dow Jones and Company, the publisher of the *Wall Street Journal.*

MARKETS DIARY — 6/24/94

STOCKS Dow Jones Industrial Average

3636.94 −62.15

INDEX	CLOSE	NET CHNG	PCT CHNG	12-MO HIGH	12-MO LOW	12-MO CHNG	PCT	FROM 12/31	PCT
DJIA	3636.94 −	62.15 −	1.68	3978.36	3449.93 +	146.05 +	4.18	− 117.15 −	3.12
DJ Equity	418.67 −	6.24 −	1.47	456.27	416.31 −	5.76 −	1.36	− 23.52 −	5.32
S&P 500	442.80 −	6.83 −	1.52	482.00	438.92 −	4.80 −	1.07	− 23.65 −	5.07
Nasdaq Comp.	693.79 −	7.06 −	1.01	803.93	693.79 −	1.02 −	0.15	− 83.01 −	10.69
DJ World Index	113.69 −	0.73 −	0.64	119.04	105.29 +	8.40 +	7.97	+ 2.61 +	2.35
London (FT 100)	2876.6 −	65.8 −	2.24	3520.3	2814.1 −	10.9 −	0.38	− 541.8 −	15.85
Tokyo (Nikkei 225)	20766.75 −	273.46 −	1.30	21552.81	16078.71 +	1107.18 +	5.63	+ 3349.51 +	19.23

Reprinted by permission of *The Wall Street Journal,* © 1994 Dow Jones & Company, Inc. All Rights Reserved Worldwide.

Selecting stocks for the index

The 30 stocks in the DJIA are selected to represent a broad spectrum of American industry. The combined assets of these companies constitute almost 20 percent of the over $1 trillion market value of the New York Stock Exchange. The stocks that make up the DJIA occasionally change when conditions warrant. For example, Johns-Manville Corporation was deleted from the index in 1982 following a suit from people harmed by asbestos. In the spring of 1991, several changes were made to reflect the increased importance of the service sector in the U.S. economy. Though broad based, the DJIA is often criticized because it includes only large, well-known corporations, the so-called blue chip companies. With much of the dynamism of the modern economy coming from smaller companies, the DJIA may be less representative than it was in the past. Another index, the *Standard and Poor's Stock Market Index,* includes 500 stocks and is often considered a better gauge of financial markets.

Originally, the DJIA was computed by simply adding together the prices of 12 stocks and dividing by 12; when the index was later changed to include 20 stocks, the divisor was 20. Today, however, the divisor is not 30. The reason for the change is to reflect historical changes. For example, if management believes that a stock price is getting too high, they may announce a *stock split* and convert each outstanding share of stock into two or more shares. A 2-for-1 split can cause the price of the stock to fall immediately, even though the company is just as valuable as before the split. To take account of these events, the divisor on the DJIA must be adjusted periodically. The current divisor is published daily in the *Wall Street Journal.*

The following 30 companies made up the DJIA as of late 1991:

Allied-Signal
AT&T
Caterpillar
Disney
Exxon
Goodyear
McDonalds
J. P. Morgan
Sears & Roebuck
United Technologies

Alcoa
Bethlehem Steel
Chevron
Dupont
General Electric
IBM
Merck
Philip Morris
Texaco
Westinghouse Electric

American Express
Boeing
Coca-Cola
Eastman Kodak
General Motors
International Paper
Minnesota M & M
Procter & Gamble
Union Carbide
Woolworth

firm. People can earn income from stock in two ways: dividends and capital gains. A **dividend** is a share of the corporation's profits that is passed on to the stockholder. A capital gain occurs when the stockholder buys stock at a low price and sells it for a high price. Stock prices rise and fall depending on the profit expectations of the firm and the state of the economy, but no one can forecast stock prices with very much precision. People gain from holding bonds in two ways as well. Bonds pay interest—called **coupon payments**—and can be sold for a capital gain when interest rates fall.[7]

There are both primary and secondary securities markets. In the primary market, new issues are sold, and the money used to buy stocks and bonds actually goes to the corporation. In the secondary market, existing stocks and bonds are bought and sold; none of the money that changes hands in the secondary market goes to the company that issued the stock or bond. The existence of the secondary market is important: Not only is it the source of potential capital gains (and losses!), but it increases the **liquidity** of stocks and bonds. A liquid investment is one that can be easily and safely converted into cash. Real estate is not a very liquid investment; it often takes months to find a buyer. Stocks and bonds can usually be sold at a moment's notice—though a forced sale may mean selling when the market is down—and are thus better short-term investments than real estate and some other investments. The vast majority of stock market transactions are secondary transactions, so most stock market transactions have no effect on the corporation's finances. Money flows to the corporation only when the stock is first issued. The stock market is discussed in more depth in the Focus boxes on pages 118 and 120.

Dividend The stockholder's share of corporate profits.

Coupon payment Annual or biannual return on a bond.

Liquidity The ability to convert assets from one form to another.

Other Financial Institutions

There are several other types of financial institutions as well. Credit unions, investment banks, and pension funds, are probably the most important. Credit unions are typically small institutions affiliated with a place of employment. They usually make small, low-interest loans to their members. The main role of investment banks is to underwrite new stock issues and assist in corporate mergers. Because these activities are considered risky, commercial banks have been prohibited from such activities in the United States. Pension funds, which are regulated much like life insurance companies, invest retirement funds deposited by workers and their employers.

BUSINESS IN THE GLOBAL ECONOMY

It is a rare firm these days that can afford to ignore international markets or international competition. Nearly a seventh of all goods and services consumed in the United States are produced abroad, and in the 1980s and 1990s, the fastest-growing U.S. corporations were expanding into international markets. This trend will undoubtedly continue in the future.

---

[7]The relationship between bond prices and interest rates is examined in more closely in Chapter 29.

FOCUS ON

READING THE FINANCIAL PAGES

Reading the financial pages is not difficult, but you do need to know the language. The inset is a mock-up of one stock quotation from the financial section of the *Wall Street Journal*. All of the information is useful for the investor.

THE WALL STREET JOURNAL   TUESDAY, MAY 24, 1994   C3

NEW YORK STOCK EXHANGE COMPOSITE TRANSACTIONS

| 52 Weeks | | | | | Yld | | Vol | | | | Net |
Hi	Lo	Stock	Sym	Div	%	PE	100s	Hi	Lo	Close	Chg
48 5/8	36	Disney	DIS	.30f	.7	29	5799	43	42 3/8	42 7/8	−1/4

1. *52-week hi-lo range.* This gives the trading range for the stock over the past year. It does not include the latest trading day. Notice that stock prices are listed as common fractions: 48⅝ stands for $48.63. This tradition dates back to the days when prices were posted by hand and will likely be changed in the future.

2. *Stock.* Tells what stock is being reported. Occasionally, the company name is followed by a suffix to indicate a special kind of stock.

3. *Ticker symbol.* Identifies the stock for the exchange's ticker and electronic information systems.

4. *Dividend payment.* Indicates the annual dividend. For common stock, dividend payments fluctuate over the business cycle. The annual dividend was $0.30 in this case.

5. *Percent yield.* This is calculated as the ratio of the dividend of each share to current market price. The .7 percent figure is calculated by taking the ratio of $0.30 to the closing price of $42.88: (.3/42.88 = 0.007).

6. *Price-earnings ratio (PE).* The ratio of the current market price to the company's per share earnings for the most recent four quarters. Generally, high PE ratios indicate that investors are optimistic about the company, but low PE ratios often indicate good buys—or that the company is in trouble.

7. *Trading volume.* Lists the number of shares traded in hundreds.

8. *Hi/lo.* The trading range for the most recent day.

9. *Close.* The last price recorded on the most recent trading day.

10. *Net change.* The difference between the closing price and the price at the close of the previous trading day.

Now, a caution is in order: You are not ready to invest your life savings just yet! But you do know enough to start reading stock quotations and follow companies you may have an interest in. And if you find this stuff interesting, look into a finance course next semester!

The Growing Role of International Trade

Between 1960 and 1990, real GDP rose almost two and a half times, from $1,971 billion to $4,878 billion, but U.S. merchandise exports rose almost sixfold, from $88 billion to $510 billion in constant 1987 dollars. These data are shown in Figure 5.2. Two things should be apparent from these data. First, the ratio of merchandise trade to GDP has more than doubled since 1960—from about 4 percent to around 10 percent—with most of the increase coming since 1970. Second, the United States has been running a merchandise trade deficit—imports exceeded exports—since the 1970s.

The information in Figure 5.2 is important to U.S. firms for several reasons. First, the high volume of imports means that domestic firms are facing increasing competition from foreign firms. By some estimates, fully 70 percent of all products bought in the United States face direct or potential competition from foreign products. This means that if U.S. firms want to maintain their domestic market share, they must be ready to counter the actions—product innovations, price cuts, and so on—of potential foreign rivals. Second, the increasing volume of trade is one indication that domestic firms face increased competition in foreign markets. Finally, because the volume of world trade is growing faster than world income, successful firms must be ready and able to enter new international markets.

FIGURE 5.2 THE INCREASING ROLE OF INTERNATIONAL TRADE

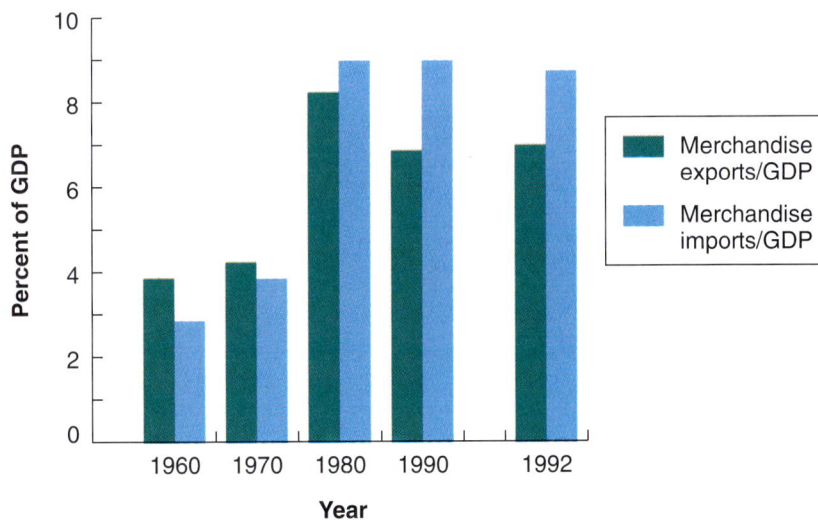

The foreign sector has become increasingly important to U.S. business in recent years, with merchandise trade approaching 10 percent of the size of GDP. Until the mid-1970s, merchandise exports exceeded merchandise imports; since then, imports have exceeded exports.

SOURCE: 1994 *Economic Report of the President,* Tables B-2 and B-103.

Foreign Investment and Capital Flows. One result of the large balance of trade deficits over the past 20 years is that foreigners have been able to use their export earnings to invest in the U.S. economy. The numbers are impressive: Foreign investment in the United States increased in real terms almost 22-fold between 1960 and 1989. Two concerns have been expressed about foreign investment in the United States. First, some people fear that if foreigners were to withdraw their money from U.S. stock and bond markets, these markets would collapse. Most economists dismiss this as very unlikely because there is no reason to think that foreign investors would unite and decide to sell U.S. securities in mass. In fact, most economists believe that foreign participation in U.S. financial markets is beneficial to the United States because the foreigners represent an additonal supply of financial capital that borrowers need.

The second concern is that we are "selling America" to foreigners. Japanese investors, in particular, have been the subject of scathing editorials: Do they have the right to buy farmland in the heartland? Is it right that the Japanese own so many large banks in California? Should we have allowed Sony to buy Paramount Studios? Most of these concerns stem from cultural and sociological issues more than economics per se.[8] When foreigners buy an American asset, they are making a business decision and hope to make profits. To do this, they often have to expand production and create more jobs—exactly the kind of things any economy needs. But some observers are concerned—perhaps rightly—that foreign ownership will change the way the newly acquired companies do business. Will Sony direct Paramount Pictures to produce only action-adventure films? Will the Japanese-owned banks in California show a preference for giving loans to multinational corporations instead of farmers and home owners? To date, there is little evidence that this sort of change is taking place, but the concerns will likely remain for quite some time. Any such concerns should be tempered with recognition that American business has had a dominant economic and cultural presence in the global economy for nearly a century.

SUMMARY

The purpose of this chapter was to give you an overview of the changing nature of American households and businesses. Try to keep this material in mind as we develop models in the remaining chapters that will help you put these facts in context. The main points to remember from this chapter are:

1. U.S. population demographics still reflect the baby boom generation. The group of people aged 18–44 occupies a larger fraction of the total population than it has in past decades.

2. Real median family income, about $36,000 in 1992, has grown slowly in the past two decades. About three-fourths of household income comes from employee compensation.

3. The labor force participation rate for adult men has been declining since 1950 and is now about 75 percent. Women's labor force participation rate has risen steadily over the same time period and is now about 60 percent.

[8]Michael Crichton's best-selling novel (also a movie by the same name) *Rising Sun* (New York: Ballentine Books, 1992) is indicative of the social and cultural fears of Japanese domination of American business.

4. American business is undergoing a transition from the mass production factory system to specialized production methods. This transition has been brought about by technological change and increased foreign competition.

5. Businesses with a corporate structure have easy access to financial markets, but must deal with extensive regulations. Proprietorships and partnerships are easy to set up but often find it difficult to raise money for expansion. Corporations earn about 75 percent of all net business income in the United States.

6. Financial institutions link borrowers and savers. Major financial institutions include commercial banks, insurance companies, savings and loan associations, and the securities markets.

7. International competition has become more intense in the past 20 years. Successful firms must be ready to enter and adapt to international markets.

KEY TERMS AND CONCEPTS

price index
consumer price index (CPI)
producer price index (PPI)
inflation
median income
mean income
civilian labor force participation rate
savings rate
paper entrepreneurialism
plant
horizontal combination
vertical combination
conglomerate
industry
sole proprietorship

partnership
corporation
stock
bond
limited liability
separation of ownership from control
merger
financial intermediation
commercial bank
savings and loan association (S&L)
insurance company
securities market
dividend
coupon payment
liquidity

REVIEW QUESTIONS

1. What is the difference between nominal income and real income? What is a price index? Explain how to use a price index to convert nominal values to real values.

2. Define median and mean income. Explain why most economists believe that median income is a better measure for describing income distribution.

3. What have been the major changes in the labor force participation rate over the past 30 years? Why have these changes occurred? How has it affected family income?

4. What are the main sources of household income? How do U.S. households spend their money?

5. What are the main characteristics of the mass production factory system? How has it evolved in the past 50 years?

6. Define the three legal forms of business, and list the advantages and disadvantages of each.

7. How has the relationship between the U.S. economy and the global economy changed in the past 30 years?

PROBLEMS

1. In what ways has the baby boom affected the demographic profile of the United States? How has it affected median income?
2. Nominal GDP was $2,708 billion in 1980 and rose to $5,522 billion in 1990. The GDP deflator was 71.7 in 1980 and 113.2 in 1990.
   a. How much did real GDP increase between 1980 and 1990?
   b. Suppose your wage rate was $10 per hour in 1980 and rose to $15 per hour in 1990. Were you better off in 1980 or 1990?
3. The rise in median income in the United States has been accompanied by an increase in the proportion of income spent on services. Do you think this is just coincidence or is there a causal relationship?
4. Would you benefit from mandatory retirement for people age 65 and over? Would society as a whole?
5. Suppose General Motors, Ford, and Chrysler were allowed to merge into a single giant auto firm, AmerAuto. How do you think this would affect the price of automobiles in the United States? The world? Would consumer choices be expanded, contracted, or hardly changed?
6. Many business firms in the United States have shifted away from the mass production factory system because they found it difficult to compete with low-wage foreign producers. However, some firms and labor unions have argued that a better solution would be to pass legislation to keep out imports from low-wage countries. Would you approve or disapprove of such legislation? Why or why not?
7. Suppose your investment time horizon is long term, say, 10 years. Would you prefer to invest in the stock of companies that did business entirely in the United States or those whose income was earned largely abroad? Why?
8. The Japanese may have been the most prominent people buying U.S. assets in the 1980s and 1990s, but the Dutch, British, and Canadians have long invested in the United States, and, as a group, hold more U.S. assets than do the Japanese. Why do you think the Japanese have been singled out as the ''villains'' while so little is said about the purchase of U.S. assets by other nationalities?

CHAPTER 6

The Institutional Framework II: The Public Sector

These are difficult times for the government. Ballooning deficits make it appear that government spending is out of control. Political posturing makes voters wonder just what kind of people they voted into office. Political gridlock makes us wonder whether we will ever get out of "this mess." The situation is so bad that billionaire businessmen with no political experience become legitimate presidential contenders. All rhetoric aside, the government does play an important role in modern mixed economies: it protects property rights, provides national defense, funds schools and health care, helps the less fortunate, and more. These are important functions, but they are not without their costs. Not only are taxes required to provide these services, but government involvement in the economy can cause inflation, affect the efficiency of the private sector, and limit individual choices.

This chapter will provide a first look at the role of the government in the economy. We cannot settle the debates you hear about on the evening news, but we will be able to put those debates in context and help you better understand some of the issues involved.

AFTER READING AND STUDYING THIS CHAPTER, YOU SHOULD BE ABLE TO:
- • • Understand the main economic functions of the government sector
- • • Discuss the sources and uses of funds for the federal, state, and local governments
- • • Define different kinds of taxes and tax progressivity
- • • Explain the difference between the government deficit and the national debt, and indicate why some economists are concerned about them

THE ECONOMIC ROLE OF GOVERNMENT

With so many negative things being said about the government these days, one might think that the government does nothing but waste taxpayers' money. There is undoubtedly some waste, but the government also performs legitimate functions. At the very least, the government must protect property rights, provide for national defense and other goods that cannot be produced in the private sector, and overcome market failures. In most nations, the government also aids the educational system. Many economists would add at least one other function for the government—the maintenance of economic stability. This section outlines some of the key roles the government plays in most modern mixed economies. Later chapters will expand on the topics we introduce in this chapter.

Protection of Property Rights

The main difference between capitalism and socialism is that the ownership of private property is encouraged under capitalism and discouraged under socialism. Unfortunately, given human nature, simply stating that private ownership of property is legal may not be enough. There must be legal institutions—the courts and police—to prevent theft and crime; otherwise, the institution of private property means little.

The government also acts, via the legal system, to ensure that contracts are enforced. Contract enforcement reduces the risks associated with market transactions and makes the economy more efficient. For example, if your customers know you can take them to court if the check bounces, you can expect most of them will take care to make sure that their checks are good, and you will not have to spend as much time and money researching credit history. This reduces the cost of doing business and expands the volume of trade.

Provision of Public Goods

Public good A good that everyone in society can consume freely and that no one can be excluded from consuming; cannot be allocated efficiently by the market.

Private good A good that is consumed only by its buyer who must pay to enjoy its benefits; can be efficiently allocated by market processes.

Law enforcement is just one example of a **public good**. A **private good** is consumed only by the buyer and must be paid for before one can enjoy the benefits. In contrast, a public good is free to be consumed by everyone in society, and no one can be excluded from consuming it. The classic example of a public good is national defense. All citizens receive benefits from national defense whether they pay for it or not. If a national defense system protects me, it also protects my neighbor.

Consumers use their "dollar votes" to tell the market which and how many private goods to produce. If people are willing to pay high prices for cotton but only low prices for polyester, producers will produce more cotton and less polyester. The situation is different with public goods. People obtain benefits from public goods whether they pay for them or not, so there is no market process to provide price signals. For example, suppose national defense was funded with voluntary taxes. Some people would be honest and send a check, but others would recognize that those nuclear missiles would protect them whether they sent their checks or not. These people—called **free riders**—would benefit from the public good without paying for it. This explains why taxes are mandatory and why the government must decide

Free rider People who receive benefits from public goods without paying for them.

which and how many public goods to produce. Unfortunately, politicians have no way to determine precisely how many public goods to produce, so political debates over issues like defense spending are inevitable.

Market Failures

Public goods are an example of **market failure**—a situation where the private market is incapable of efficient resource allocation. The market also fails when there are externalities—a situation we covered briefly in Chapter 4. There we discovered that when a factory belches smoke, an external cost—pollution—is imposed on society, but forcing the producer to pay for that smoke is difficult without government intervention. We also learned in Chapter 4 that government subsidies are appropriate when there are external benefits—which explains why public education is subsidized.

Market failure The situation where market outcomes are not optimal.

Another kind of market failure occurs when information is imperfect or incomplete. For example, consumers may not know that a particular pesticide is unsafe when used around small children or pets. Without this knowledge, people may buy the pesticide and use it in an unsafe manner. Government warning labels can make this information available to consumers and thus reduce the demand for this product.

Economic Stabilization

One of the most significant pieces of legislation of the twentieth century is the **Employment Act of 1946**. This act stated that it was the responsibility of Congress to achieve "maximum employment, production, and purchasing power." Few people today would quibble with those goals; however, the act did not mention *how* the government was to go about achieving them. Should high taxes be used to combat inflation? What about wage and price controls? Or is the proper role of government an extreme version of noninterventionist *laissez faire*? None of these issues were spelled out in the Employment Act. Nor did the act define what was meant by the phrase "maximum employment, production, and purchasing power." Is it necessary to have zero inflation to maintain maximum purchasing? Does "maximum employment" mean "full employment"? And if so, what is the definition of full employment? These issues may never be resolved.

Employment Act of 1946 Law that established the Council of Economic Advisers and required Congress to pursue policies for high employment, economic growth, and price stability.

The Employment Act did establish the government as an active maker of economic policy. Tax policy decisions today are based at least as much on their perceived impact on economic activity as on the need for public goods or the desire for a balanced budget. For example, one of the main arguments against the defense spending cuts and base closings of the 1990s was the effect they would have on employment in the local communities; little was said about the cuts making the world unsafe for democracy.

Other Functions of Government

The functions of government we've just described are by no means exhaustive. The government also provides or subsidizes the production of certain goods that are deemed to provide important social benefits. Health care and Social Security are but two examples. The government also enacts tax and spending policies to redistribute income. Finally, the government regulates business to assure safe working conditions, product quality, and so on. Certain kinds of businesses are outlawed (illegal drugs, prostitution, and the like), zoning laws specify where businesses can be located, and some businesses, primarily utilities, are owned and operated by the government.

SIZE AND SCOPE OF THE GOVERNMENT SECTOR

In 1978, the state of California passed Proposition 13, a law that rolled back property taxes and limited the ability of the state government to raise taxes. Proposition 13 became the rallying cry of a tax revolt that culminated with the election of Ronald Reagan in 1980. No one likes taxes. But why did things come to a head when they did? Didn't the voters recognize that tax revenues are needed to pay for the goods that the government provides? It may be hard to understand the mind of the voter—especially one voting on pocketbook issues—but a glance at the numbers tells much of the story.

Federal Government

Figure 6.1 shows the rise in real federal government spending from 1940 until 1993 in billions of 1987 dollars.[1] Over this period, real government spending rose from under $100 billion to about $1,135 billion, an increase of about 5.0 percent per year.[2] Tax revenues increased from about $50 billion to about $900 billion over the same period. Because real GDP grew at only 3.5 percent per year, federal government spending became a higher fraction of total spending, rising from just 10 percent of GDP in 1940 to over 23 percent in 1990. The increasing relative size of the government is clearly one reason why people began to question the role of government.

A second reason people began to question the role of government was the rising fiscal deficit. The fiscal **deficit** is defined as the difference between government spending and tax revenues. Between 1946 and 1970, the government deficit was relatively small; journalists talked about it occasionally, but few economists expressed serious concern. In the early 1980s, however, the deficit started to grow at previously unheard-of rates, and perceptions began to change. Whether government deficits actually harm the economy was not really the question. The public began to see the government deficit as an indication of political incompetence. The only other time the United States has experienced comparable deficits was during World War II, but the expenses of the war provided a reason for the deficit, so there was little public outcry. This point is significant: The public is apparently more willing to tolerate deficits when they can see tangible results and legitimate needs. Unfortunately, few people understood *why* the deficits existed in the 1980s and 1990s and why it was so difficult to do anything about them. In fact, as we will see momentarily, these deficits were only partly a result of deliberate fiscal policies; they were also a product of the 1981–1982 recession and sluggish economic growth.

Deficit (fiscal) The difference between government spending and tax revenues.

---

[1]The phrase "billions of 1987 dollars" means that the base year is 1987 and that the data are real.

[2]In nominal terms, things look even more extreme: spending rose from $9.5 billion to $1,408 billion, and the $3 billion surplus became a $220 billion deficit!

···· **FIGURE 6.1** REAL FEDERAL GOVERNMENT SPENDING AND REVENUES, 1940–1993

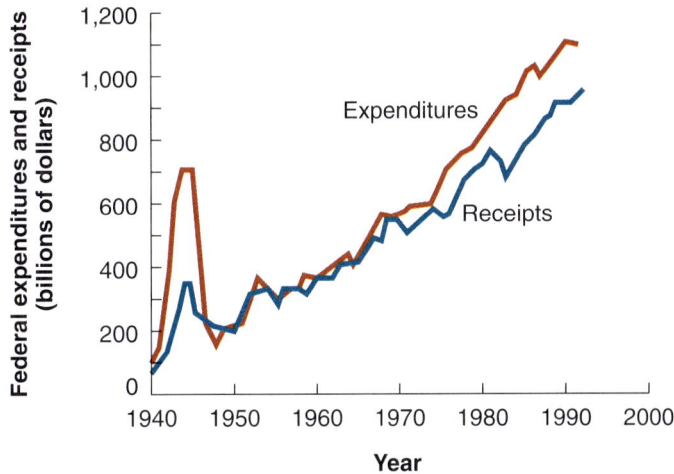

Between 1940 and 1993, real government spending increased at a rate of about 5.0 percent per year. Revenues did not increase as rapidly, so the fiscal deficit became a significant factor in policy discussions in the 1980s. The deficit that existed in the 1940s was brought about by the increased spending necessary to fight World War II. Data are in billions of 1987 dollars.

SOURCE: 1994 *Economic Report of the President,* Table B-77 and B-3.

·······

Should We Be Concerned about the Deficit?

Whether the deficit is really a problem is far from clear and is an issue we will have to come back to in later chapters. For the time being, we should note that the effect of deficits depends largely on the state of the economy. Deficits that occur during recessions may help the economy. When the economy goes into a recession, people lose their jobs and thus pay less in taxes; many qualify for unemployment compensation, food stamps, or welfare. As a result, government spending automatically rises, revenues fall—and the deficit increases. Recession-induced deficits help the economy recover: less taxes taken from the private sector means that more is available to be spent by the private sector; welfare and unemployment compensation provide another stimulus to the economy.

Deficits that occur during periods of full employment may be another story. When the government borrows money to pay for the deficit, interest rates may tend to rise. At any time, only so much saving is available to borrowers, and if the government wants to borrow a large portion of this money, it must be willing to pay high interest rates. If the government is paying high interest rates to borrow money, so must corporations and households. High interest rates tend to reduce business and household spending because they raise the price of any good bought on time. This is less of a problem when the economy is in a recession because few corporations engage in capital expansion projects during recessions.

We will have more to say about deficits in later chapters, but you should note one additional point here: *We said nothing about the deficit causing the government to go bankrupt!* The federal government will never go bankrupt because it has the ability to tax and print money. Deficits are not necessarily bad. It depends on when they are incurred, what the deficit money is being used for, and how they are financed.

· · · · · · · ·

The Annual Deficit versus the National Debt

National debt The total of all annual fiscal deficits since the United States became a sovereign state.

The terms "national debt" and "government deficit" are often incorrectly interchanged. They are not the same thing. The deficit is an annual figure; the **national debt** is the total of all past annual deficits and surpluses. As Figure 6.2 shows, the real national debt has risen rather dramatically since World War II, with most of the increase coming since 1980. Is the national debt something we should be worried about? Most economists feel that the debt is not a big problem except under two conditions: if it is growing faster than GDP or if an increasing portion of it is held by foreign citizens. Both of these conditions did exist in the 1980s, but this has changed in the 1990s.

· · · · · · · ·

State and Local Government

When economists talk about the "government sector," they are usually referring to the federal government, but not always. State and local governments exert consid-

· · · · · **FIGURE 6.2 THE NATIONAL DEBT, 1940–1993**

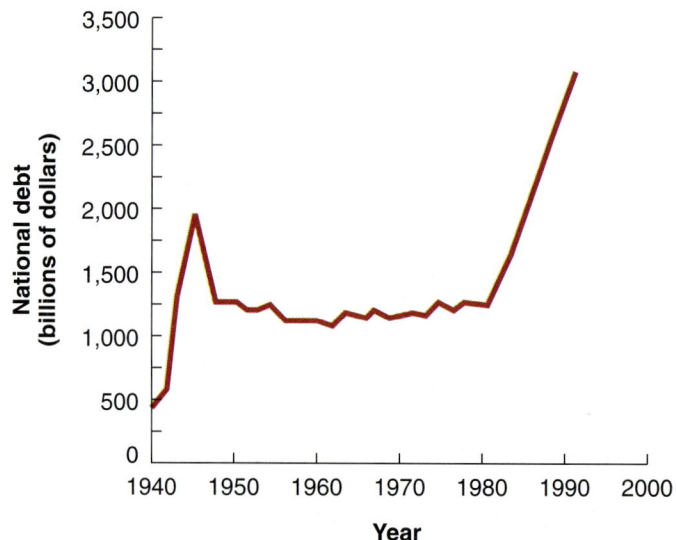

The national debt has risen significantly since World War II, with most of the increase coming since 1980. Between 1980 and 1985, the real national debt increased from $908 billion to $1,817 billion. Data are in billions of 1987 dollars. In current dollars, the national debt topped $4.3 trillion in 1993.

SOURCE: 1994 *Economic Report of the President,* Tables B-78 and B-3.

FIGURE 6.3 REAL STATE AND LOCAL GOVERNMENT
EXPENDITURES AND REVENUES, 1960–1993

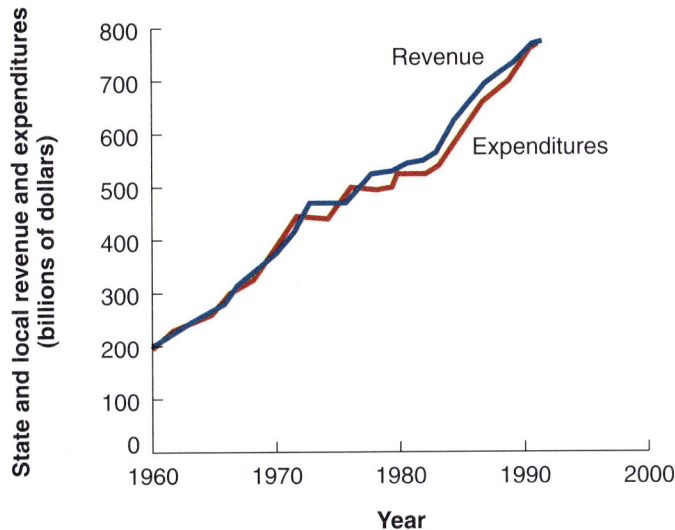

Real state and local government spending has grown at about 4.4 percent per year over the past 30 years. Unlike the federal government, most state and local governments must, by law, maintain balanced budgets. This explains why spending and revenue lines generally overlap. Data are in billions of 1987 dollars.

SOURCE: 1994 *Economic Report of the President,* Tables B-83 and B-3.

erable influence on the economy as well. Figure 6.3 shows the growth in state and local spending and revenues over the period 1960–1993 in real 1987 dollars.

Three things are important about state and local government spending over this period. First, state and local governments spend and tax about two-thirds as much as the federal government. In 1993, real state and local government spending was just over $713 billion compared to about $1,135 billion for the federal government. Together, federal and state and local government spending account for about one-third of GDP. Second, state and local government deficits are quite small compared to federal government deficits. One reason for this is that most state and local governments must, by law, run a balanced budget annually.[3] When state and local governments discover that they do not have enough funds to finance current or planned spending, they raise taxes or cut back on services. Finally, real state and local government spending has risen more slowly than federal government spending, about 4.4 percent per year compared to about 5.0 percent. However, this trend may change in the future as more responsibilities are shifted from the federal to the state and local levels.

[3]It should be pointed out that the accounting practices used by state and local governments make deficits easier to avoid. State and local governments distinguish between current operating expenses and capital expenses; the federal government does not. Most state and local capital expenses are financed by bonds and are not considered "deficits." The federal government does not distinguish between current and capital expenditures, and all bond financing is considered a deficit.

······ SOURCES OF FUNDS

How do governments raise the money they spend? They raise it through taxes and borrowing. This section looks at the general and specific kinds of taxes used by government. We also look briefly at some of the implications of government borrowing.

········

Proportional, Regressive, and Progressive Taxes

Not all taxes are alike. Some taxes affect the poor more than the rich and vice versa. Some taxes are relatively easy to collect, others are not. And some taxes affect the incentive to work or to save more than others.

Proportional tax A tax that takes the same fraction of income at all income levels.

   Proportional taxes take the same fraction of income from every person, regardless of income level. For example, a 5 percent flat rate income tax is a proportional tax. The person making $10,000 per year is taxed $500, and the person making $30,000 per year is taxed $1,500, so both pay 5 percent of their income in taxes. Many state income taxes are close to being proportional taxes. It is important to recognize that under a proportional tax scheme high-income people do pay more taxes than lower-income people because the upper-income people have a higher tax base. Table 6.1 illustrates how to calculate taxes from a proportional income tax.

Regressive tax A tax that takes a higher percentage of income from low-income people than from high-income people.

   Regressive taxes take a higher percentage of income from people in low income brackets than from people in high income brackets. Sales taxes are typically regressive. Why? Sales taxes are typically set at a constant fraction—say, 8 percent—of the value of the sale, but people in low income brackets typically spend a higher fraction of their income than do rich people. Rich people have enough money to save, the poor do not. Therefore, a higher fraction of poor people's income is subject to the sales tax. Table 6.2 illustrates a regressive sales tax.

Progressive tax A tax that takes a higher percentage of income from rich people than from poor people.

   Progressive taxes take a higher fraction of income as income increases. The federal income tax is progressive. Income under about $22,000 is taxed at a 15 percent rate, and income between $22,000 and $53,000 is taxed at 28 percent.[4] Thus, low-income people pay a lower tax rate than upper-income people. Don't get confused:

[4]We have simplified the example considerably here: Tax liability is based on *taxable income,* which is income after adjustments for exemptions and deductions. These adjustments make the tax system more progressive.

····· TABLE 6.1 PROPORTIONAL TAX CALCULATIONS

Tax rate on income = 5%

Income	Tax Liability	Average Tax Rate
$10,000	$ 500	500/10,000 = 5%
30,000	1,500	1,500/30,000 = 5%

A proportional tax is levied as a constant fraction of income for all income brackets. Many state income taxes are approximately proportional taxes.

•••••**TABLE 6.2 REGRESSIVE TAX CALCULATIONS**

Tax rate on spending = 8%

Income	Spending	Saving	Tax Liability	Average Tax Rate
$10,000	$ 9,000	$1,000	$ 720	720/10,000 = 7.2%
30,000	25,000	5,000	2,000	2,000/30,000 = 6.7%

A regressive tax takes a higher fraction of income from low income brackets than high income brackets. A sales tax is regressive since lower-income people typically spend a higher fraction of their income than do upper-income people. Therefore, more of their income is subject to the sales tax. In this example, the low-income individual spends $9,000 dollars so 90 percent of income is taxed. The upper-income person spends $25,000, but this is only 83 percent of income so less income is subject to the sales tax.

•••••**TABLE 6.3 PROGRESSIVE TAX CALCULATIONS**

Income	Total Tax	Average Tax Rate
$10,000	0.15(10,000) = 1,500	1,500/10,000 = 15%
30,000	0.15(22,000) = 3,300	5,540/30,000 = 18.5%
	0.28(8,000) = 2,240	
50,000	0.15(22,000) = 3,300	11,140/50,000 = 22%
	0.28(28,000) = 7,840	

A progressive tax takes a higher fraction of income from high income brackets than from low income brackets. The federal income tax is progressive. In this example, the low-income person ($10,000 income) pays 15 percent of total income of $10,000. The middle-income person ($30,000 income) pays 15 percent of the first $22,000 and 28 percent of the remaining $8,000 for an average tax rate of 18 percent. The upper-income person pays the same marginal tax rate as the middle-income person (28 percent on income over $22,000) but a higher average tax rate because a larger portion of income is taxed at the 28 percent rate.

under a progressive tax scheme, the tax rates are higher on the next or *marginal* unit of income, not on all income earned. Upper-income individuals pay the same tax rate on their first dollars as do lower-income individuals. The example in Table 6.3 is similar to the current federal income tax.

••••••••

Incentive Effects

One of the criteria economists use when assessing alternative taxes is their effect on incentives. What is the best way to (legally) avoid income taxes? Don't work! If you do not work, you will not have to pay income taxes. Few of us would choose the abject poverty of unemployment to avoid having to pay income taxes, but there is some evidence that people may choose not to work overtime, take a second job, or work outside the home because of high income tax rates. Work disincentives are one reason some economists are opposed to income taxes. Few economists dismiss the idea that income taxes cause work disincentives, but most studies show that work disincentives are rather small. Some evidence also indicates that low-income people respond to higher income taxes by working more because they need to put in more hours to make ends meet.

What is the best way to avoid sales tax? Don't spend your money. In other words, sales taxes act as an incentive to save. Some economists advocate reducing income taxes and replacing lost revenue with a national sales tax. One disadvantage of this approach is that sales taxes tend to be regressive, though regressivity might be reduced by exempting food, clothing, and other essentials from the tax. Income taxes are an established element of the total tax structure, so there is little chance that they will be eliminated in the near future. However, the tax system is frequently changed, and sometimes quite significantly. The possibility of a national sales tax as an addition to the current income tax cannot be dismissed.

· · · · · · · ·

Federal Revenue Sources

In recent years, the federal government has obtained about half of its revenues from personal income taxes, just over a third from Social Security contributions, and just over a tenth from the corporate income tax.[5] The data for 1993 are shown in Table 6.4.

The distributional impact of federal taxation is not easy to assess. As just mentioned, the personal income tax is progressive, but when combined with the various deductions and loopholes, it appears to be approximately proportional over most income brackets. Tax changes enacted in 1993 increased the progressivity somewhat. There is considerable debate over the incidence of the corporate income tax. Some economists believe that corporate taxes are "passed forward" into higher selling prices. If correct, this would suggest that corporate income taxes are regressive. Other investigators believe that most of the corporate income tax burden falls on the stockholders, who tend to be wealthier than the public as a whole. If this view is correct, the corporate income tax is progressive. Economists generally agree that Social Security contributions are regressive. Under current law, 1993 Social Security contribu-

---

[5]Technically, Social Security contributions are earmarked for the Social Security payments; in recent years, however, much of this money—$50 billion per year—has been transferred to general revenues.

· · · · TABLE 6.4 FEDERAL GOVERNMENT SOURCES OF FUNDS, 1993

Source	Amount	Percent of Total
Total	$1,153.6	100%
Individual income taxes	509.7	44
Social insurance	428.3	37
Corporate income tax	117.5	10
All others	98.1	9

SOURCE: 1994 *Economic Report of the President,* Table B-78. Data are in billions of current dollars.

tions were set at about 7.65 percent of income up to about $57,600; no Social Security taxes are levied on incomes over $57,600. Thus, Social Security taxes are proportional for incomes up to $57,600, but regressive over the entire population.

Debt Financing

As Figure 6.1 makes painfully obvious, the federal government has been running large deficits for the past several years. How can the government spend money that it does not have? The answer is borrowing. The federal government borrows money by selling government securities—primarily savings bonds and treasury notes—to the public and financial institutions. Because much of the borrowing during the 1980s occurred when the economy was close to full employment, many economists worried that the deficits raised interest rates and made it expensive for firms to borrow money needed for investment. Another concern was that much of the debt was being purchased by foreign investors.

For the individual investor, government securities are considered an extremely safe investment because there is almost no chance that the government will default. There are two main kinds of government securities, **savings bonds** and **treasury debt** of various denominations and maturities. Savings bonds are small-denomination certificates sold to individuals. People buy savings bonds at a discount, then redeem them for face value in the future. For example, a 10-year, $50 savings bond that pays 5 percent would be sold for $30.70; it could be redeemed for $50 in 10 years. Savings bonds pay relatively low interest rates, but they are safe and offer some tax advantages to small savers. Treasury debt comes in larger denominations—$1,000 and above— and has maturities as short as 90 days and as long as 30 years. Treasury debt generally pays higher interest rates than savings bonds as well. There is an active secondary market for treasury debt. This means that many people sell treasury notes to other individuals before those notes mature and are redeemed by the Treasury.

Savings bond A small-denomination financial instrument issued by the federal government to finance government debt.

Treasury debt Larger-denomination financial instruments (bonds, bills, and notes) issued by the federal government to finance government debt.

State and Local Revenue Sources

State and local governments have different funding sources than the federal government. State governments receive much of their revenues from sales and income taxes. Local governments obtain most of their revenues from sales and property taxes. Table 6.5 gives a breakdown of revenue sources for fiscal year 1990–1991.

As with federal taxes, it is hard to determine the incidence of state and local taxes. Sales taxes are clearly regressive, and most state income taxes are proportional or slightly progressive, but the combined effect of the two taxes is not clear. Economists debate whether property taxes are progressive or regressive. If they fall on the property owner, they are probably progressive since rich people tend to own more property than poor people. If they are passed on to renters as higher rents, they may be regressive. This issue is even more complicated when we consider that many states fund school districts from property taxes. This means that relatively high tax neighborhoods also have the most funds for schools. Under these circumstances, the combined effect of property taxes and school funding is probably regressive. This may explain why the courts have required many states to equalize school expenditures between rich and poor school districts.

TABLE 6.5 STATE AND LOCAL GOVERNMENT SOURCES OF FUNDS, 1990–91

Source	Amount	Percent of Total
Total	$902,207	100.0%
Sales taxes	185,570	20.6
Property taxes	167,999	18.6
Revenue from federal government	154,099	17.1
Personal income taxes	109,341	12.1
Corporate income taxes	22,242	2.5
All other	262,956	29.1

SOURCE: 1994 *Economic Report of the President*, Table B-84. Data are in billions of current dollars.

Finally, we should add that the data in Table 6.5 are aggregate data so they tell us nothing about individual states. For example, while personal income taxes account for 12 percent of state and local government revenues in the aggregate, four states do not have a personal income tax. We should note too that property taxes account for only 18 percent of total state and local revenues, but they make up almost 75 percent of local revenues.

Debt Financing

State and local governments also use debt financing; however, state and local government debt is almost always issued to finance a particular project, not to cover current general spending. State and local governments issue municipal bonds to finance long-term capital projects that cannot be covered with tax dollars. The interest on municipal bonds is tax-free, so state and local governments can often raise money at interest rates below prevailing market rates.

USES OF FUNDS

No debates are probably more heated than those about how the government should spend its money. What should be purchased? From whom? And where should the spending take place? Economists contribute to these discussions, but most often the decision is based more on political criteria than economic criteria.

Federal Government Spending

The pattern of federal government spending changes slightly from year to year, but in recent years, the biggest components have been national defense, Social Security, interest on the national debt, and income security, which represents expenditures to help the aged, disabled, unemployed, and other people with little or no income. Table 6.6 shows how the government spent its money in 1993.

•••••**TABLE 6.6** FEDERAL GOVERNMENT SPENDING, 1993

Category	Amount	Percentage of Total
Total	$1,408.2	100.0%
Social Security	304.6	21.6
National defense	291.1	20.7
Income security	207.3	14.7
Net interest	198.8	14.1
Medicare	130.6	9.3
Health	99.4	7.1
All others	176.4	12.5

SOURCE: 1994 *Economic Report of the President,* Table B-78. Data are in billions of current dollars.

It is interesting to note that these percentages have remained roughly constant over the past decade; only interest on the national debt grew significantly, from 10.1 percent of total federal government spending to the present level of more than 14 percent. Over the past 30 years, however, the spending priorities of the national government have changed significantly. For example, in 1960 national defense accounted for almost 60 percent of the federal government budget.[6] What caused defense spending to fall so much as a percentage of federal government spending? The answer is not so much that defense became less important, but that social spending became more important. The "all other" category of the 1960 budget—space research, health, education, welfare, labor, commerce, and transportation spending—accounted for only 15 percent of the total budget. Spending priorities changed dramatically in the 1960s with the passage of numerous programs aimed at the elimination of poverty and other social ills. How successful these programs have been is difficult to assess, but from a strictly fiscal standpoint, they have complicated the job of government budget planners considerably. Many of these programs have become **entitlements** in the sense that people are "entitled" by law to certain government benefits—welfare, Social Security, food stamps, and so on. The growth of entitlement programs fueled much of the rise in government spending between 1960 and 1980. After 1980, interest on the growing national debt became a contributing factor in the growth of government spending.

Entitlement program Programs such as welfare, Social Security, and Medicare to which people are "entitled" by law.

••••••••

State and Local Government Spending

As Table 6.7 shows, the largest categories of state and local government spending are education, highways, and public welfare. Additionally, there is a rather substantial "all other" category. This category includes spending for libraries, hospitals, police and fire protection, sewage, and other items. One of the consequences of the federal

[6]In 1960, total federal government spending, in current dollars, was $76.5 billion, of which $45.7 billion was spent on national defense. 1964 *Economic Report of the President,* Table C-57.

THE CRISIS IN HEALTH CARE

The data in Table 6.6 show what appears to be only a small amount of money being spent on health by the federal government—about 6 percent of total federal spending—but that figure is misleading. When Medicare is added, the total exceeds 15 percent. More importantly, private citizens and state and local governments also spend money for health. In fact, the United States spends more on health care than any other nation in the world: fully 14 percent of GDP was spent on health care in 1993, up from only 6 percent 30 years earlier. In the absence of substantial reform, health care expenditures are projected to account for 19 percent of GDP by the year 2000.

The amount spent on health care would not be such an issue if U.S. citizens were the healthiest people in the world. We are not. Infant mortality rates are higher than in most developed nations, and the people of several countries live longer. What is the problem? What should we do about it? Can economic analysis add anything to the discussion?

The health care crisis has several economic elements. First, in 1993 the United States was one of only two industrialized nations in the world without nationalized health insurance. (The other country is South Africa.) As a result, a sizable portion of the population—perhaps 20 percent— cannot afford medical care. Second, the explosion of medical technology allows people to live today who would have died just a few years ago. Unfortunately, this technology is *extremely* expensive, and many of the people

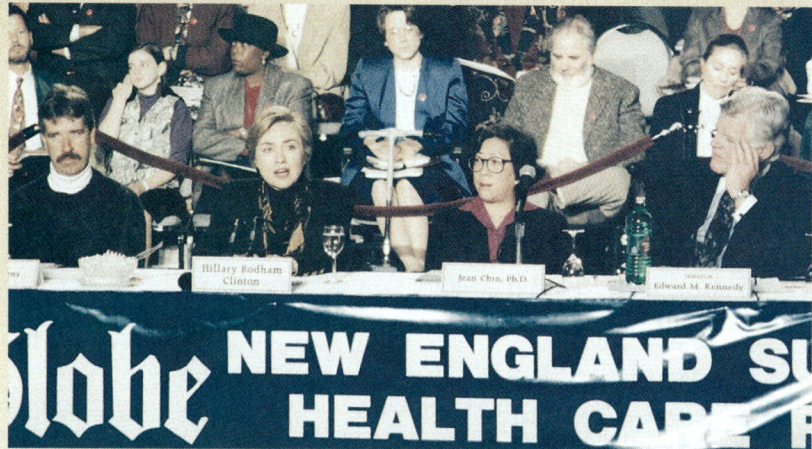

First Lady, Hillary Rodham Clinton, presiding at the New England Summit on Health Care Reform, one of several forums the Clinton Administration used to promote their health plan.

who receive miracle technology—organ transplants, for example—require very expensive follow-up care. Third, strange as it may seem, competition among hospitals may also contribute to rising health care costs. In many cities, hospitals compete for patients by purchasing state-of-the-art machinery. As a result, these cities often have redundant services, and hospital patients end up paying the costs of excess medical equipment.

The health care crisis was one of the main issues in the 1992 presidential campaign, with candidate Bill Clinton promising a program of universal health insurance. Soon after his election, President Clinton appointed his wife, Hillary Rodham Clinton, to head a task force to design the health care program. At this writing, the Clinton health care program has yet to be implemented, but the administration plans to guarantee all American citizens universal, cradle-to-grave health care and a choice of provider. The cost of the program is to be paid

by savings in the current Medicare budget, increased taxes (on alcohol, cigarettes, and other items), and reduced administrative costs due to the elimination of overlapping programs. All employers will be required to contribute for their employees. Quality care will be assured with explicit health care standards and increased funding for research and development.

From the outset, two major criticisms have been levied at the Clinton proposal. First, many argue that it will cost too much and that the American people will not tolerate the tax increases necessary to pay for it. Second, many people argue that small businesses cannot afford to contribute to the health care of their workers. Both criticisms clearly contain some truth, but whether they are enough to negate the social value of national health care will not be clear for years.

SOURCE: The White House Domestic Policy Council, *The President's Health Security Plan: The Clinton Blueprint* (New York: Times Books, 1993).

PART II

MICROECONOMICS I:
CONSUMER
BEHAVIOR AND
THE PRODUCTION
PROCESS

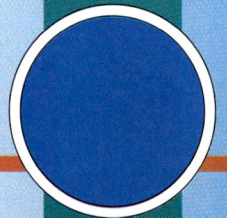

CHAPTER 7

The Theory of Consumer Behavior

Most of the time you go to the store with a pretty good idea of what you want to buy. You may buy on impulse occasionally, but most people shop to find the best prices and buy only goods that deliver the desired benefits. What kind of mental calculations do you conduct before you decide what to buy or even whether to buy anything? Do you compare the costs and benefits of your prospective purchases? Do you try to get the most satisfaction out of each dollar spent? Perhaps not consciously, but you almost certainly go through some sort of calculation. Otherwise, you would end up with a bunch of things you do not want or need! Consumers express their preferences with dollar votes; firms are successful only if they offer products that meet consumer demands. By studying consumer behavior, economists can gain important insights into how markets operate and how different policies can be used to affect market behavior.

We talked about consumer behavior when we developed the demand curve in Chapter 3. The theory we used to develop these ideas—marginal utility theory—is more elaborate than you might think: it can be used to derive the conditions for consumer equilibrium and show how and why people respond to changes in income and prices. Additionally, the theory of consumer behavior can be used to explain a wide variety of consumer choices, including the choice between spending and saving, and the work disincentives of income taxes.

AFTER READING AND STUDYING THIS CHAPTER, YOU SHOULD BE ABLE TO:

- • • Present the conditions for consumer equilibrium and explain how consumers behave to maximize utility subject to a budget constraint
- • • Explain the relationship between consumer equilibrium and the law of demand

••• Understand the roles of income and substitution effects in the law of demand

••• Use consumer theory to analyze the work/leisure and save/spend decision

UTILITY THEORY AND CONSUMER EQUILIBRIUM

We already know that the satisfaction or "utility" derived from an additional unit of an item declines as the consumption of that item increases. This idea—the theory of diminishing marginal utility—is helpful in understanding consumer behavior and the law of demand. Unfortunately, marginal utility theory has a major defect: there is no way to measure utility. People may be able to state that they like one good more than another, or that satisfaction declines as they increase consumption of a particular good, but no one has been able to come up with a scale for measuring utility. For this reason, early twentieth-century economists developed a new model of consumer behavior based on **ordinal** instead of **cardinal** measurement of utility.

What is the difference between cardinal and ordinal measurement? The first three cardinal numbers are one, two, three; the first three ordinal rankings are first, second, third. For example, the *New York Times* best-seller list is an ordinal ranking. It tells you which book was the best-seller last week and which book was the second-best seller—but it does not give a cardinal measure of how many copies of each book were sold. Cardinal utility theory assumed that utility could be measured on a numerical scale. Early economists even spoke of fictitious units of utility called "utils" and tried to determine precisely how many utils were associated with various consumption behaviors. An ordinal scale does not assign specific values, it only ranks different levels. Ordinal utility analysis thus removed the need to develop theories in terms of those fictitious utils. It was only necessary to assume that consumers could determine whether a particular consumption bundle provided more or less satisfaction than another. The new approach is more methodologically sound, but more technically demanding than the earlier cardinal utility theory—which is why this material is confined to the appendix to this chapter. Fortunately, the results of the two models turned out to be identical, so for many purposes, an understanding of cardinal theory is adequate.

Ordinal utility Theory that assumes that consumers are only able to rank consumption bundles, not to measure the quantity of utility with cardinal numbers.

Cardinal utility The idea that consumer satisfaction can be measured in countable units called "utils."

Marginal Utility Theory

The theory of marginal utility says that as the consumption of any item increases, the additional satisfaction (utility) derived from that item declines at some point, *ceteris paribus*. To develop this idea, the marginal utility theorists of the late nineteenth century assumed that utility could be measured on a cardinal scale. For example, if you buy a new sweater, you might get a great deal of satisfaction from it, say, 100 "utils." If you buy a second sweater, you will probably get less satisfaction, perhaps only 90 utils; a third sweater will give even less satisfaction, and so on. That seems clear enough—it might be nice to have several fashionable sweaters, but you can probably get by with only one or two to keep out the cold. The real question is how many sweaters you should buy given your limited budget. In the terminology of marginal utility theory, the answer is that you should buy the number of sweaters that maximizes your utility subject to your budget constraint.

The marginal utility theorists discovered that consumer satisfaction is maximized if consumers buy the quantity such that the **marginal utility** of the last product purchased is equal to the price, $MU = P$. To reach this conclusion, the theorists had to recognize that spending money always incurs an opportunity cost because you cannot spend that same money on something else. If you spend $50 to buy the sweater, you cannot spend that same $50 on anything else, say, for dinner at a nice restaurant. Should you buy the sweater? Only if you believe that it will give you at least as much satisfaction as dinner at the nice restaurant—or anything else you could buy for $50. Suppose you do buy the sweater. Should you buy a second sweater? Perhaps—but remember the principle of diminishing marginal utility: The second sweater will give you less satisfaction than the first one. If it too is priced at $50, you might get more satisfaction by going out to dinner. Consumers will continue buying as long as the marginal utility of the next unit is at least as great as the price.

> **Marginal utility** The additional utility a person receives from consuming an additional unit of a particular good.

• • • • • • • •

The Budget Constraint

The only problem with the $P = MU$ decision rule is that it does not say anything about the consumer's budget constraint. When we go shopping, we must decide how best to spend our scarce money to maximize utility. Consumers are said to be in equilibrium when utility is maximized for a given budget. We are about to find out that consumer equilibrium exists when the marginal utility of the last penny spent on each item is equal. This exceedingly important result needs to be examined in detail.

Suppose that you have allocated $50 for entertainment each month, and that you decide to spend it on only two items, video rentals and compact discs. The price of video rentals is $5 and the price of compact discs is $10. Given your budget, you could buy 10 videos, or 5 compact discs, or some combination of the two every month. (We are using a 2-good example to keep things simple, but the same technique could be used for as many goods as you might purchase.)

Your income and the prices of the goods define your **budget constraint**. The budget constraint is written as:

> **Budget constraint** The amount of purchasing power available to the consumer.

$$\text{Budget constraint: } B = P_1X_1 + P_2X_2 + \cdots + P_nX_n \qquad [1]$$

Where:
   B = budget constraint
   X_i = different goods in the "consumption bundle"
   P_i = prices of goods in the consumption bundle

The budget constraint for our 2-good example is:

$$50 = 10c + 5v$$

Where:
   c = compact disc
   v = video rentals

•••• **FIGURE 7.1 FEASIBLE CONSUMPTION**

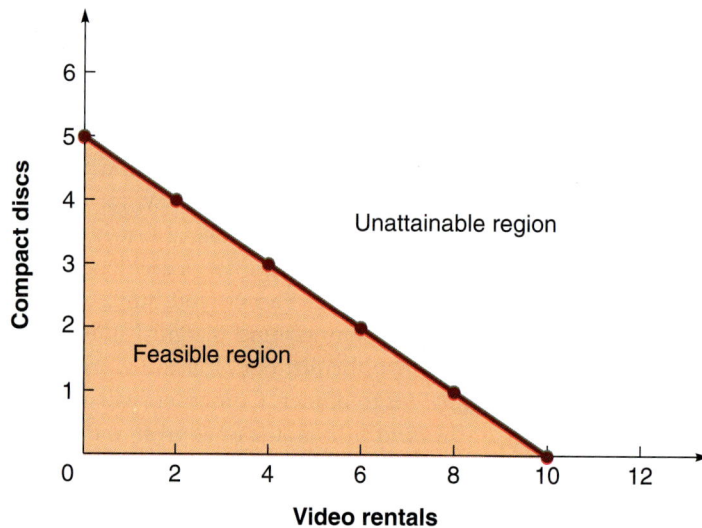

The budget constraint gives the different combinations of goods that can be purchased with a given budget. The intercepts of the budget constraint are equal to the budget divided by the price of the good measured on that axis. The slope of the budget constraint is the ratio of the two prices, $-(P_v/P_c)$, where P_v is the price of the good measured on the horizontal axis (video rentals) and P_c is the price of the good measured on the vertical axis (compact discs). In this example, the slope is:

$$-\frac{P_v}{P_c} = -\frac{5}{10} = -\frac{1}{2}$$

This budget constraint indicates that you have allocated $50 for entertainment, the price of compact discs is $10, and the price of video rentals is $5.

The budget constraint is shown as a straight line in Figure 7.1. The intercepts of the budget constraint are found by dividing the budget by the price of the goods on each axis:

Intercept of budget constraint: $\frac{\text{Budget}}{\text{Price}}$ [2]

If we place compact discs on the vertical axis, the vertical intercept of the budget constraint is the point where all money is spent on compact discs. It is found by dividing the budget by the price of compact discs:

$$\frac{\$50}{\$10} = 5$$

The intercept of the horizontal axis shows how many videos could be rented if the entire budget were spent on videos. It is found by dividing the budget by the price of videos:

$$\frac{\$50}{\$5} = 10$$

The budget constraint defines the **feasible region**—those combinations of compact discs and video rentals that are attainable given the budget. Points on the budget constraint indicate that the consumer is spending the entire budget. Points inside the budget constraint indicate that not all of the budget is being spent. For example, if you rented 2 videos and bought 2 compact discs, you would be spending only 2(5) + 2(10) = $30. Points outside the feasible region are unattainable; the set of all unattainable points is called the **unattainable region**.

Feasible region On a graph, the combination of goods that are attainable given the budget constraint.

Unattainable region On a graph, the combinations of goods that cannot be attained given the budget constraint.

Slope of the Budget Constraint. We will need to use the slope of the budget constraint shortly, so we might as well compute it now. The slope of a straight line can be calculated if we know any two points on the line. We already know two points on the line, the two intercepts. Remembering that the slope is defined as the rise over the run and that the two intercepts are (0, 5) and (10, 0), we have:

$$\text{Slope} = \frac{\text{rise}}{\text{run}} = \frac{\text{change in compact discs}}{\text{change in video rentals}} = \frac{\Delta c}{\Delta v} = \frac{5 - 0}{0 - 10} = -\frac{1}{2}$$

which means that for every compact disc you decide to buy, you have to give up two video rentals. In other words, the opportunity cost of a compact disc is two video rentals. To put it another way, the opportunity cost of one video rental is one-half of a compact disc. This is important: The slope of the budget constraint gives the opportunity cost of buying one good in terms of the other.

Another way to find the slope of the budget constraint is to take the negative ratio of the prices of the two goods, with the price of the good measured on the horizontal axis in the numerator:

Slope of budget constraint: $-\dfrac{P_{\text{horizontal axis}}}{P_{\text{vertical axis}}}$ [3]

Substituting $5, the price of video rentals, in the numerator, and $10, the price of compact discs, in the denominator gives the same slope we found before:

$$\text{Slope} = -\frac{P_{\text{horizontal}}}{P_{\text{vertical}}} = -\frac{\$5}{\$10} = -\frac{1}{2}$$

Why does this formula work? It can be derived with a little algebra, but the intuition is more important.[1] Remember that the slope of the budget constraint measures the opportunity cost of buying one good as opposed to the other. In this case it is the opportunity cost of buying compact discs instead of video rentals. For every compact disc you are willing to give up, you can rent two videos, because the price of video rentals ($5) is one-half the price of compact discs ($10). Therefore, the slope of the budget constraint, $\Delta c/\Delta v$, is the relative price ratio, $-(5/10) = -(1/2)$.[2]

Changing the Slope of the Budget Constraint. The slope of the budget constraint measures opportunity cost, and as opportunity costs change, so will consumption decisions. A rise in the price of compact discs increases the opportunity cost of buying a compact disc because more video rentals will have to be sacrificed to buy another compact disc. For example, if the price of compact discs rises from $10.00 to $12.50, the vertical intercept of the budget constraint will fall from 5 to 4 (=$50.00/$12.50), and the budget constraint will become flatter. The slope of the new budget constraint is:

$$-\frac{P_v}{P_c} = -\frac{\$5.00}{\$12.50} = -0.4$$

This is shown in panel (a) of Figure 7.2. Notice too that the feasible region has shrunk because the higher price has reduced the purchasing power of your budget. Panel (b) shows what happens if the price of video rentals falls from $5 to $3. This reduces the opportunity cost of renting a video because a video rental is now only 30 percent as expensive as a $10 compact disc. As a result, the budget constraint becomes flatter and its slope is -0.3. The price reduction has also expanded the feasible region so it is now possible to buy more goods. In general, price decreases will reduce the opportunity cost of buying a good and expand the feasible region while price increases will raise the opportunity cost and reduce the feasible region.

Shifting the Budget Constraint. Two things can cause a parallel shift in the budget constraint: (1) income changes and (2) proportional changes in both prices. Suppose your income increases so much that you can afford to allocate $100 instead of $50 per month to entertainment. The budget constraint would shift out and expand the feasible region. The new intercepts would be $100/$10 = 10 on the compact disc axis and $100/$5 = 20 on the video rental axis. If you decide to allocate less money to entertainment, the opposite would happen: the budget constraint would shift inward, and the feasible region would shrink. Notice that a shift in the budget constraint does not change its slope so there is no change in the opportunity cost of buying one good or the other. A parallel shift in the budget constraint would also result if both prices fell or rise by the same proportion. For example, if both prices fell by half, the original

[1]The algebra is straightforward. The budget constraint is $B = P_X X + P_Y Y$, which can be written as:

$$Y = \frac{B}{P_Y} - \frac{P_X}{P_Y}X$$

This is just the form of a linear equation with intercept B/P_Y and slope $-(P_X/P_Y)$.

[2]We defined relative prices in Chapter 3. The relative price is a price ratio—the price of one good compared to another. In contrast, an absolute price is the actual dollar price of a good.

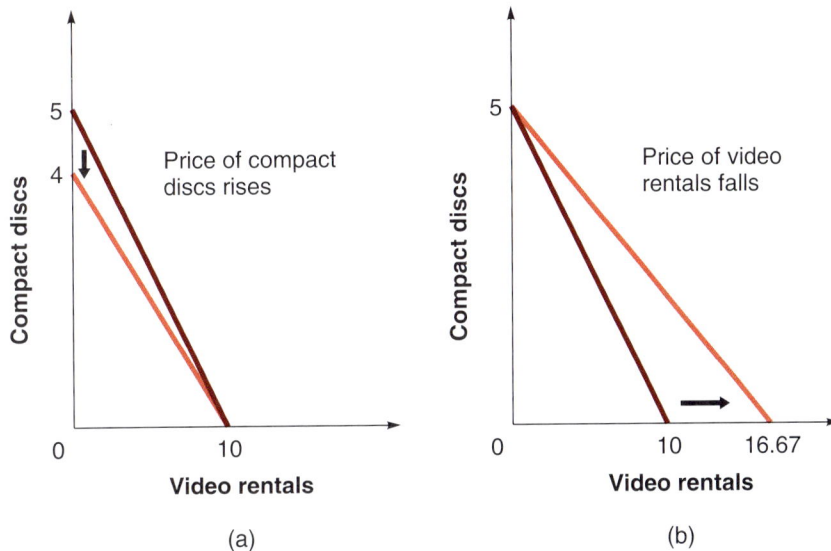

•••• FIGURE 7.2 CHANGING THE SLOPE OF THE BUDGET
CONSTRAINT

Changes in price will change opportunity costs and the slope of the budget constraint.
Panel (a) indicates what will happen if the price of compact discs rises from $10.00 to
$12.50. This raises the opportunity cost of compact discs, shrinks the feasible region, and
makes the budget constraint flatter. The vertical intercept falls to 4 because $50.00/
$12.50 = 4. Panel (b) illustrates the effects of a decline in the price of video rentals from
$5 to $3. This will reduce the opportunity cost of video rentals and expand the feasible
region. The horizontal intercept rises to 16.67 because $50/$3 = 16.67. In general,
price decreases reduce opportunity costs and expand the feasible region while price
increases raise opportunity costs and contract the feasible region.

$50 budget would buy the same amount as $100 would have bought at the old prices.
Parallel shifts of the budget constraint are shown in Figure 7.3.

••••••••

Consumer Equilibrium

It is possible to pick any point on or inside the budget constraint, but only one point
maximizes **total utility** given the budget constraint, prices, and consumer preferences.
This is the point of **consumer equilibrium**. Table 7.1 shows how to find consumer
equilibrium. Columns 1 and 2 give the quantity of video rentals and marginal utility
(measured in "utils" of satisfaction) of an additional video rental. Two things are
important about Column 2. First, notice that the marginal utility of video rentals
declines as the quantity rented increases. This is a result of the principle of diminishing
marginal utility—as you rent more videos, the satisfaction of additional rentals diminishes. Second, the entries in Column 2 are placed between the entries in Column 1
because marginal utility represents the change in utility as additional units are consumed. Columns 4 and 5 provide the same information for compact discs. Columns
3 and 6 give the ratio of the marginal utility to price.

Total utility The total satisfaction a
person receives from consuming a
particular good; equal to the sum of
the satisfaction received from consuming separate units of the good.

Consumer equilibrium Consumers
are in equilibrium when their spending yields maximum satisfaction.

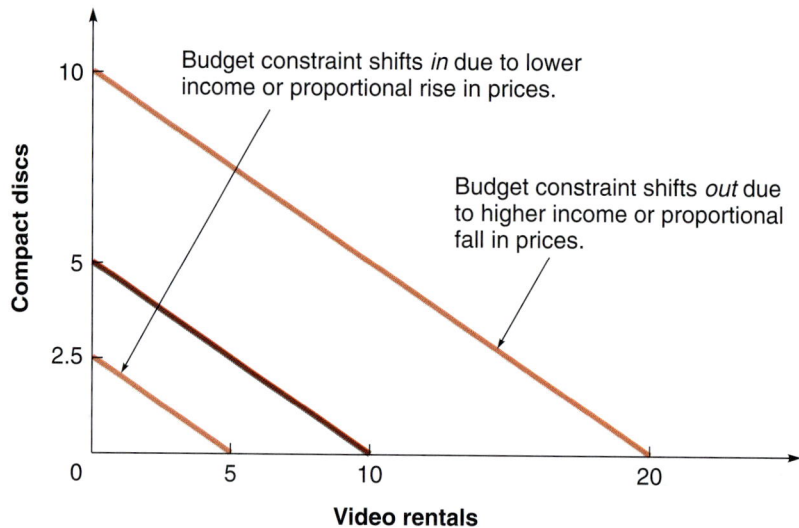

FIGURE 7.3 PARALLEL SHIFTS OF THE BUDGET CONSTRAINT

A change in the budget or a proportional change in both prices will result in a parallel shift of the budget constraint but will not change its slope. If the budget rises from $50 to $100 or both prices fall by half, the budget constraint will shift out. If the budget falls to $25 or both prices double, the budget constraint will shift in.

TABLE 7.1 SOLVING FOR CONSUMER EQUILIBRIUM

(1) Q_v		(2) MU_v	(3) MU_v/P_v	(4) Q_c		(5) MU_c	(6) MU_c/P_c
0				0			
	→	20	4.0		→	30	3.0
1				1			
	→	17	3.4		→	26	2.6
2				2			
	→	14	2.8		→	22	2.2
3				3			
	→	11	2.2		→	18	1.8
4				4			
	→	8	1.6				
5							
	→	5	1.0				
6							
	→	2	0.4				
7							

Key: Q = quantity, v = video rentals; MU = marginal utility; P = price; c = compact disc. Utility is measured in "utils" of satisfaction.

To find the point of consumer equilibrium, we need to find a consumption bundle that (1) is feasible and (2) maximizes total utility. One feasible consumption bundle consists of 4 compact discs and 2 videos. We know this combination is feasible because $4 \times \$10 + 2 \times \$5 = \$50$. To find the total utility of this combination, we sum the marginal utilities of the first 4 compact discs ($30 + 26 + 22 + 18 = 96$) and the marginal utilities of the first two video rentals ($20 + 17 = 37$):

Total utility of 4 compact discs: $30 + 26 + 22 + 18 =$	96 utils
Total utility of 2 video rentals:	$20 + 17 =$ 37 utils
Total utility of consumption bundle 1:	$96 + 37 = 133$ utils

This is not a point of consumer equilibrium because there is another way to spend the same $50 that yields higher total utility: 3 compact discs and 4 video rentals. The total utility of this consumption bundle is:

Total utility of 3 compact discs:	$30 + 26 + 22 =$ 78 utils
Total utility of 4 video rentals:	$20 + 17 + 14 + 11 =$ 62 utils
Total utility of consumption bundle 2:	$78 + 62 = 140$ utils

The rational consumer will choose the second combination because it yields the most satisfaction for a given amount of expenditure.

There is a quicker and much simpler way to find the point of consumer equilibrium: *Find the consumption bundle where the ratio of marginal utility to price is equal for all goods.* Look down Columns 3 and 6 and notice that:

$$\frac{MU_v}{P_v} = \frac{\$11}{\$5} = 2.2 = \frac{MU_c}{P_c} = \frac{\$22}{\$10}$$

You can verify that this combination maximizes utility by inspecting every other feasible bundle. For example, if one more compact disc were purchased, you would have to rent two fewer videos. What would happen to utility? The extra compact disc would increase utility by 18 units, but the lost videos would reduce utility by $11 + 14 = 25$. More utility is lost than gained, so this combination is inferior.

If you went through the trouble of checking every feasible combination in the table, you would still find that the consumer maximizes utility by purchasing 3 compact discs and renting 4 videos, but that still doesn't answer the real question: *Why is utility maximized when the consumer equates the **marginal utility/price ratios**?* A little thought should explain why. The basic idea is that consumer equilibrium exists when the last penny spent on each good gives equal satisfaction; if you could have spent a penny on something else that would give you more satisfaction, you are not in equilibrium. The following rather contrived example will explain why.

Suppose that you go to the store and buy some apples and bananas, which both happen to be priced at $1. While standing in the checkout line, you begin trying to calculate your marginal utility/price ratios—after all, you've just finished reading your economics text! To your dismay, you discover that you are not in equilibrium because you estimate that the last apple would give you 20 utils of satisfaction while the last banana would give you only 15. This means that your marginal utility/price ratios are not in equilibrium:

Marginal utility/price ratios Consumer equilibrium exists when the ratio of marginal utility to price is equal for all goods.

$$\frac{MU_{apple}}{P_{apple}} > \frac{MU_{banana}}{P_{banana}}$$

or:

$$\frac{20}{1} > \frac{15}{1}$$

This starts you thinking: These apples look *really* great, much better than the rather mediocre bananas, so you leave the checkout line and return to the produce section. If you put back a banana, you can afford to buy one more apple. Look what happens when you do: Apples are now more abundant in your shopping cart, so the marginal utility of the next apple must be below 20 utils; let's say 18 utils. You now have fewer bananas, so they are scarcer in your shopping cart. This means that your last banana will provide more than 15 utils of satisfaction. In other words, your marginal utility/price ratios change as you buy more apples and fewer bananas:

$$\left(\frac{MU_{apple} \downarrow}{P_{apple}}\right) \text{ and } \left(\frac{MU_{banana} \uparrow}{P_{banana}}\right)$$

But look what happened in the process: You became better off by 3 utils. You lost 15 utils of satisfaction by putting back the banana, and you gained 18 utils from picking up another apple. You should keep replacing bananas with apples until the last penny spent on apples give you the same amount of utility as the last penny spent on bananas.

The point of the story is that a consumer buying two goods is in equilibrium when the marginal utility/price ratios are equal for both goods:

$$\text{Consumer equilibrium: } \frac{MU_1}{P_1} = \frac{MU_2}{P_2} \qquad [4]$$

When applied to the *n*-goods case, consumer equilibrium exists when the marginal utility/price ratios are equal for all goods:

$$\text{Consumer equilibrium: } \frac{MU_1}{P_1} = \frac{MU_2}{P_2} = \cdots = \frac{MU_n}{P_n} \qquad [5]$$

In words, these conditions mean that the consumer is maximizing utility from a given budget when the marginal utility of the last penny spent on each good is equal.

It is sometimes useful to look at consumer equilibrium from a slightly different perspective. If we multiply each side of Equation 4 by P_1 and then divide by MU_2, we get:

$$\text{Consumer equilibrium: } \frac{P_1}{P_2} = \frac{MU_1}{MU_2} \qquad [6]$$

Equation 6 means that the consumer is in equilibrium when the price ratio of the two goods is equal to the marginal utility ratio for the two goods. In other words, if good 1 costs twice as much as good 2, then the marginal utility of good 1 must be twice that of good 2. This result will be important shortly.

> **RECAP**   Consumer Equilibrium
>
> 1. The principle of diminishing marginal utility says that the satisfaction from consuming additional units of a good at a point in time declines. In the case of buying only one good, people will buy the good until price is equal to the marginal utility of the last unit purchased.
> 2. The consumer's budget constraint gives the feasible combinations of goods that can be purchased with a given budget. The intercepts of the budget constraint are found by dividing the budget by the price of the goods; the slope is the negative of the price ratio. The slope measures the opportunity cost of buying one good in terms of the other.
> 3. The consumer is in equilibrium when the marginal utility/price ratio is equal for all goods:
>
> $$\frac{MU_1}{P_1} = \frac{MU_2}{P_2} \cdots$$
>
> This means that the consumer is in equilibrium when the marginal utility of the last penny spent on each item is equal.
> 4. An alternative expression for consumer equilibrium is:
>
> $$\frac{P_1}{P_2} = \frac{MU_1}{MU_2}$$
>
> which indicates that the ratio of marginal utilities should be equal to the relative price ratio for all goods.

INCOME AND SUBSTITUTION EFFECTS

Two effects are responsible for most changes in consumer equilibrium, the income effect and the substitution effect. The **income effect** is caused by a change in real income or purchasing power that shifts the budget constraint. The **substitution effect** is caused by a change in the price of one good relative to another that results from a change in the slope of the budget constraint.

Income effect Results from a change in real income or purchasing power; shifts the budget constraint, thereby changing the feasible region.

Substitution effect Results from a change in relative prices; changes the slope of the budget constraint.

Income Effects

Income effects are caused by a shift of the budget constraint due to a change in income or prices. We already know that if you get a raise, your budget will expand and you will be able to buy more of all goods. We talked about this situation when we shifted the budget constraint in Figure 7.3. Income effects can also be caused by price changes. If your pay does not change but the price of apples fall from 50¢ to 25¢, your purchasing power increases as though you had gotten a raise because you can buy more apples. In fact, you may be able to buy more bananas (or other goods) as well, even though their prices haven't changed, because you are saving money on the inexpensive apples.

In general, larger budgets and lower prices allow consumers to buy more of both goods; that is, the budget constraint shifts outward and expands the feasible region.

A smaller budget or higher prices do just the opposite; fewer goods are purchased as the feasible region shrinks. However, higher budgets and lower prices do not always cause the consumer to buy more goods. As we discovered in Chapter 3, people may choose inferior goods when their incomes are low, but as their incomes rise, they may shift into more desirable normal goods. For example, many people consider hamburger an inferior good relative to steak and reduce their consumption of hamburger when their incomes rise.

· · · · · · · ·

Substitution Effects

When people decide which goods to buy, they look at *absolute* prices as well as *relative* prices. Absolute prices are the actual dollar prices of goods: the absolute price of an apple is 50¢; the absolute price of a banana is 25¢. A relative price is the price of one good in terms of another. The price of an apple is twice as high as a banana, so the relative price of an apple is 2 = 50¢/25¢. If the absolute price of apples fell to 40¢, the relative price would fall from 2 to 1.6 = 40¢/25¢. The lower relative price of apples would cause you to buy more apples because apples would be a "better buy" relative to bananas. The lower relative price of apples could cause you to buy fewer bananas even though the absolute price of bananas has not changed. Bananas used to cost only half as much as an apple (25/50); now they cost 62 percent as much (25/40).

How do relative price changes affect consumer equilibrium? Look back at Equation 6. The left side is the relative price ratio. As this ratio changes, consumption must change in order for the consumer to stay in equilibrium. The consumption adjustment in response to a relative price change is called the substitution effect. For example, if you are in equilibrium when apples cost 50¢ and bananas cost 25¢, the marginal utility/price ratios would be:

$$\frac{MU_{apple}}{MU_{banana}} = \frac{50¢}{25¢}$$

When the price of apples falls to 40¢, the ratios would no longer be equal:

$$\frac{MU_{apple}}{MU_{banana}} > \frac{40¢}{25¢}$$

To maximize utility, you would have to change your consumption bundle. If you bought more apples, the marginal utility of apples would decline, and the ratios would move toward equality. The substitution effect is always negative because relative prices and quantity demanded always change in the opposite direction: an increase in the relative price of apples will cause a decrease in the quantity of apples demanded; a decrease in the relative price of apples will cause an increase in the quantity of apples demanded.

In fact, price changes usually result in *both* income and substitution effects, and it is their combined effect that determines how demand changes in response to price changes. Look what happens if the price of apples falls from 50¢ to 40¢ while the price of bananas stays at 25¢: The lower price of apples causes an income effect because your budget goes further. There is also a substitution effect because the price of apples has fallen relative to bananas. This means that you have two reasons to buy more apples—greater purchasing power and lower relative price. Whether you will buy more or fewer bananas is not clear. Your real income has increased but the relative price of bananas has risen. If the income effect is stronger than the substitution effect, you will buy more bananas; if the substitution effect is stronger, you will buy fewer bananas.

RECAP   **Income and Substitution Effects**

1. Price changes affect consumption decisions through the operation of income and substitution effects.
2. The income effect is caused by a change in real income or purchasing power. Higher income causes people to buy more normal goods but fewer inferior goods.
3. The substitution effect is caused by a change in relative prices. A higher relative price acts as a signal for people to buy less of a good; a lower relative price acts as a signal for people to buy more.

THE DEMAND CURVE AND CONSUMER EQUILIBRIUM

The ideas we have just developed can be used to provide a better derivation of the demand curve than the one we used in Chapter 3. Working through this derivation should be good practice to make sure you understand the theory of consumer behavior and consumer equilibrium.

Suppose that you plan to buy goods X and Y, priced at \$3 and \$2, respectively. Given your budget and preferences, you initially decide to buy 10 units of X and 20 units of Y. Also, imagine that some quick mental calculations reveal that you receive 30 utils of satisfaction from the tenth unit of X and 20 utils of satisfaction from the twentieth unit of Y. This means that you are in equilibrium because marginal utility/price ratios are equal:

$$\frac{MU_X}{P_X} = \frac{30}{\$3} = \frac{20}{\$2} = \frac{MU_Y}{P_Y}$$

Now, suppose that the price of X increases to \$4. Even if your budget allowed you to continue to buy 10 units of X, you should not do so because you would not be in equilibrium. The marginal utility/price ratios are no longer equal:

$$\frac{MU_X}{P_X} = \frac{30}{\$4} < \frac{20}{\$2} = \frac{MU_Y}{P_Y}$$

To maximize total utility, you should buy less X, and you may want to buy more Y. According to the principle of diminishing marginal utility, buying less X will increase the marginal utility of the last unit of X, and buying more Y will decrease the marginal utility of the last unit of Y. How much less of X and more of Y should you buy? That depends on your preference structure, but to keep the example simple, let's suppose that you receive 36 utils from the ninth unit of X and 18 utils from the twenty-first unit of Y. If you buy 9 units of X and 21 units of Y, the marginal utility/

FOCUS ON

CONSUMER SOVEREIGNTY AND THE DEPENDENCY EFFECT

We have just said quite a bit about how people act to maximize utility, and earlier we talked about consumers using their "dollar votes" to express their preferences. The question arises: Do consumer wants originate with the consumer, or are they created by advertising executives? Traditional economic theory holds that wants do come from within the consumer; that is, that *consumer sovereignty* ("consumer is king") prevails. Others believe that consumers can be swayed by advertisers to buy things they do not really want. The implications are important.

When you go to the store, you probably have a good idea about what you want to buy—but where did you get that idea? Would you have decided, on your own, that you wanted lights and pumps on your tennis shoes? That you wanted a salad shooter to chop, dice, and spray lettuce, cucumbers, and radishes into the bowl? If advertising induced you to buy something that you would not

have bought otherwise, it is not clear that you—or society—actually benefited from the transaction. As a result, your "voluntary" transaction did not result in mutual benefit. The seller gained, but you just bought something you were made to believe you really wanted.

Critics of modern business frequently argue that advertising expenditures are wasteful and that too much that consumers purchase is the product of Madison Avenue hype. They conclude therefore that the amount of spending in the economy is only distantly related to consumers' well-being. There is some truth to this argument, but also at least two problems. First, advertising can be informative. When the consumer has literally millions of products to choose from, someone must provide information on the choices available. Second, to say that the consumer can be conned into buying unwanted products is to say that consumers are stupid.

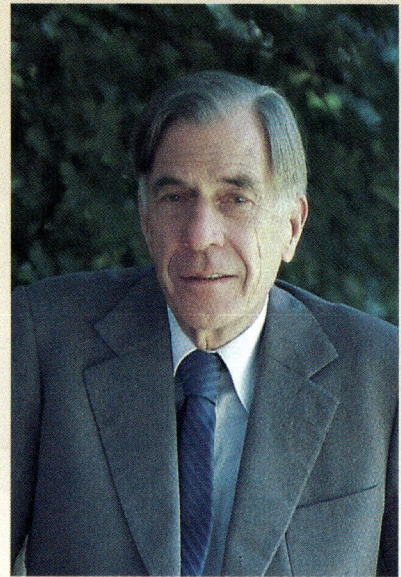

John Kenneth Galbraith

Are they? You can decide as well as anyone.

These issues were eloquently addressed by John Kenneth Galbraith in

price ratios will be equal:

$$\frac{MU_X}{P_X} = \frac{36}{\$4} = \frac{18}{\$2} = \frac{MU_Y}{P_Y}$$

This discussion has a direct relationship to the demand curve: Changes in the price of good X result in movement along the demand curve and, if X and Y are substitute goods, will cause the demand curve for good Y to shift. This is shown in Figure 7.4. Initially, the consumer is at point a on both graphs. The increase in the price of X from \$3 to \$4 results in movement along the demand curve for X and a decrease in the quantity of X demanded. This movement is brought about by *both* the income and the substitution effects that were caused by the price increase. If we were con-

Friedrich Von Hayek

his important and widely read book, *The Affluent Society* (Boston: Houghton-Mifflin, 1958). Galbraith argued that most important private desires are already satisfied in modern society, so big business must create new wants it can satisfy with additional sales. Galbraith called this process the *revised sequence*—instead of consumers expressing preferences and firms responding to them, consumer preferences are formed by mass advertising. The revised sequence, said Galbraith, means that consumer wants "come to depend on output"—a process he called the *dependency effect*. To Galbraith, the revised sequence and the dependency effect are enough to conclude that much production is wasteful.

Like everything Galbraith has ever done, his theories of the revised sequence and the dependency effect are not without their critics. One of the most vocal early critics was the Nobel Prize winner Friedrich A. von Hayek who asserted that the dependency effect was a *non sequitur* (Latin for "does not follow").[1] One telling example from Hayek is enough to make his point: the demand for literature. The demand for literature does not originate within the individual; it is the product of culture. Our culture determines whether a given work is a great book or a trashy novel. Does this mean that the production and consumption of great books do not generate social utility? Certainly not. To Hayek, many of our wants are culturally induced—so many that to attempt to criticize the market economy by stating that wants depend on the production process is nonsense. Galbraithians counter that "culture" and "corporate power" are far from synonymous. It is one thing to say that great books are the product of culture and also generate social benefits. Can the same argument really be applied to salad shooters and toasters that burn one's initials into the bread?

[1] Hayek's criticism is found in "The *Non Sequitur* of the 'Dependence Effect,'" *Southern Economic Journal* (1961).

sidering the market for good X in isolation, that would be the end of the story. If goods X and Y are substitutes, however, a change in the price of X will spill over into the market for Y. When consumers find that the price of X has risen, they will increase their purchases of good Y. As a result, the demand curve for Y will shift out so that more is demanded.

SOME EXAMPLES OF CONSUMER CHOICES

The kind of analysis that consumers make when deciding whether to buy one good or another applies to other economic choices as well. For example, you

•••••• **FIGURE 7.4 CONSUMER EQUILIBRIUM AND THE DEMAND CURVE**

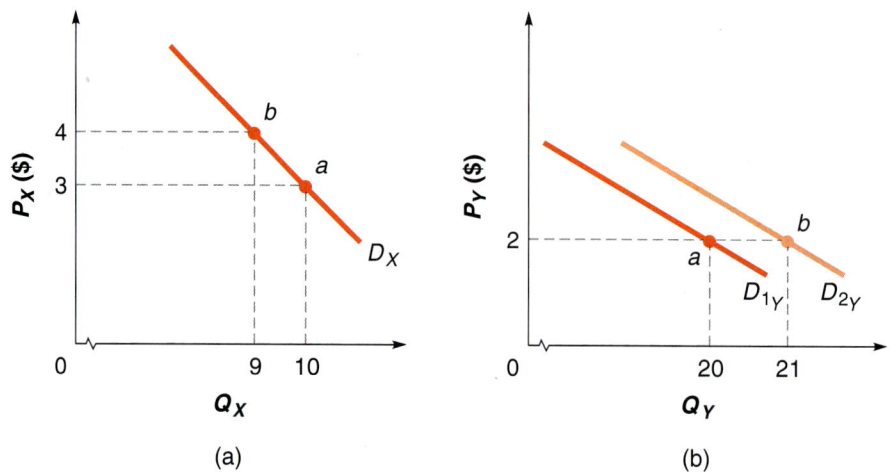

(a)   (b)

An increase in the price of good X from $3 to $4 results in movement *along* the demand curve for X, D_X, because of the combined effects of the income and substitution effects. If good X and good Y are substitutes, an increase in the price of X may cause an outward *shift* in the demand curve for Y, D_Y. By decreasing purchases of X and increasing purchases of Y, the consumer raises the marginal utility of X and lowers the marginal utility of Y. This moves the ratio of marginal utilities toward equality with the ratio of prices.

must decide whether to spend your money today or save it to spend tomorrow. The decision to work involves a tradeoff between income and leisure; the more you work, the greater your income, but the less time you have to enjoy it. These and other decisions can be studied with the same kind of analysis that we used to analyze consumer equilibrium.

••••••••

The Spend/Save Decision

Most middle- and upper-income families have discretionary income—an amount beyond what is needed to pay the bills. What should they do with this money? They could spend it on nonessentials, or they could save it for the future. In fact, most of us do a little of each, but how much depends on economic factors and can be analyzed with utility analysis. Most consumers apply the same sort of decision rule as was developed in Equation 5; that is, they will equate the marginal utility/price ratios of the different spending options. The only catch is to calculate the appropriate marginal utilities and relative prices.

As an illustration, suppose that you have just earned a $1,000 bonus and you are trying to determine how much of the money to spend and how much to save. You could spend it all on a new stereo. You could do as your parents recommend and

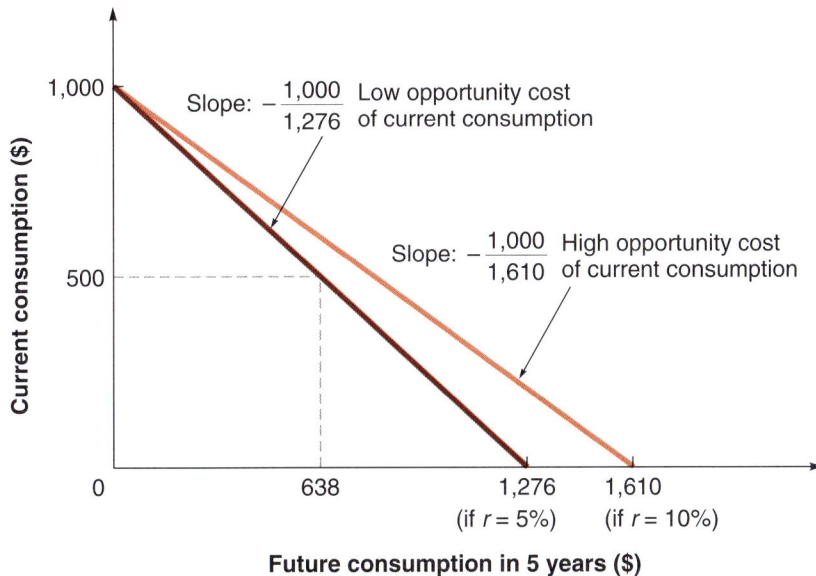

•••• **FIGURE 7.5 THE SPEND/SAVE DECISION**

The decision to spend or save is actually the decision to spend today or spend tomorrow, and the interest rate is an important variable in this decision. If the interest rate is 5 percent, a $1,000 deposit will be worth $1,276 in five years; this is the opportunity cost of spending $1,000 today. This is represented by the budget constraint passing through $1,276. If $500 is spent today, the remaining $500 can be placed in the bank and will be worth $638 after five years. If the interest rate is 10 percent, a $1,000 deposit will be worth $1,610 in five years. This is represented by the outer budget line. The higher interest rate increases the opportunity cost of current consumption and may result in increased savings.

put all of the money in the bank. Or you could get a new pair of speakers for $500 and save the remaining $500. (You could also spend different fractions of the $1,000, but we'll omit those options to simplify the example.) What should you do? It depends, of course, on what you *want* to do—as determined by the marginal utility/ price ratios—but before making that decision, you should examine the feasible consumption set carefully.

Figure 7.5 presents the budget constraint and feasible region to help you decide how to spend your $1,000 bonus. The vertical axis measures money spent on current consumption. The horizontal axis measures future consumption, the outcome of current saving. The amount of consumption you will be able to enjoy in the future depends not only on how much you save today, but also on the interest rate you can earn on your savings. The higher the interest rate, the higher the future potential consumption. For example, if the interest rate is 5 percent, and you save all of the $1,000, after 5 years you will have $1,276.28; if the interest rate is 10 percent, you will have $1,610.51 after five years.[3] These two values are indicated by the horizontal intercepts of the two budget constraints drawn in the figure.

What you should do depends on how you value future consumption relative to current consumption. Without a marginal utility schedule, we cannot determine what choice will be made. However, we can get a hint at the solution by looking at the slope of the budget constraint. The slope of the budget constraint in Figure 7.5 shows the opportunity cost of current consumption in terms of lost future consumption. For example, the slope of the low interest rate budget constraint is $-(1,000/1,276.28)$. This means that spending $1,000 to buy the new stereo today would cost you $1,276.28 in future income. Spending $500 for the new speakers would cost $638.14 in future income, and it would provide you with a savings account worth $638.14 that you could use for consumption five years in the future. When interest rates are higher, the budget constraint becomes flatter. This indicates that the opportunity cost of current consumption is higher. The slope of the budget constraint when the interest rate is 10 percent is $-(1,000/1,610.51)$, so spending the $1,000 for the new stereo would mean giving up $1,610.51 in future savings.

But we still do not know whether people will tend to save more at higher interest rates than at lower interest rates because the income and the substitution effects are operating in opposite directions. According to the substitution effect, when interest rates are high, each dollar spent today costs more in terms of forgone future consumption than when they are low. This implies less current consumption at higher interest rates. The income effect implies the opposite: higher interest rates mean that each dollar saved earns more, so people may not have to save as much. This would tend to increase current spending and decrease current saving. Economists settle these questions with statistical studies—studies that are formulated in the context of the model we have just developed.

· · · · · · · ·

Taxes, Work, and Leisure

Another consumer choice is the work/leisure decision. Most jobs require that you work a fixed number of hours—you either work full-time or do not work—but there are often opportunities to put in overtime or take a second job. How do you decide whether to work overtime or not? Sometimes it is a simple matter of whether you "need" the money, but not always. The most interesting cases to study are when you have to decide whether you want to earn a little extra money. This is especially interesting in the context of income taxes.

Consider the worker who earns $10 per hour and has the opportunity to work 12 hours per day, six days a week. (The factory is closed on Sunday.) If she works as much as is allowed, she makes $720 per week. If she does not work, she enjoys

---

[3]These figures were calculated on a financial calculator but can be done by hand in a pinch. The formula for computing the future value (FV) of an initial deposit (PV) is $FV_i = PV(1 + r)^i$ where r is the interest rate and i is the number of years the money is on deposit. If you deposit $1,000 in an account that earns 5 percent per year, compounded annually, your deposit will grow as follows: $1,000, $1,050, $1,102.50, $1,157.63, $1,215.51, and $1,276.28. If the interest rate is 10 percent, compounded annually, the values would be $1,000, $1,100, $1,210.00, $1,331.00, $1,464.10, and $1,610.51.

72 hours of leisure per week. Is that leisure time free? Not at all. Taking time off incurs an opportunity cost of forgone income at $10 per hour. Let us suppose that she initially decides to work 40 hours per week—8 hours a day for five days—and thus earns $400 and has 32 hours of leisure. This choice is shown as point *a* in Figure 7.6.

An interesting situation occurs when we allow for taxes. If the worker is subject to a 20 percent income tax, her maximum weekly income falls to $576 ($8 per hour times 72 hours), and the budget constraint rotates in as shown in the figure. How she responds to the tax depends on her preferences and the relative magnitudes of the income and substitution effects. If she still wants to earn $400 per week, she will have to put in extra hours—working 10 hours on Saturday would be enough to maintain $400 per week, but she would lose 10 hours of leisure. This choice is shown as point *b*. At point *b*, the income effect dominates: the tax increase has reduced the "purchasing power" of the worker's work effort, so more work is expended to "buy" income and less leisure is "purchased" with time off. On the other hand, the tax increase also reduces the opportunity cost of leisure from $10 to $8 of forgone income an hour. This means that the relative price of leisure has fallen so there should be a

---

· · · · FIGURE 7.6 WORK/LEISURE TRADEOFFS

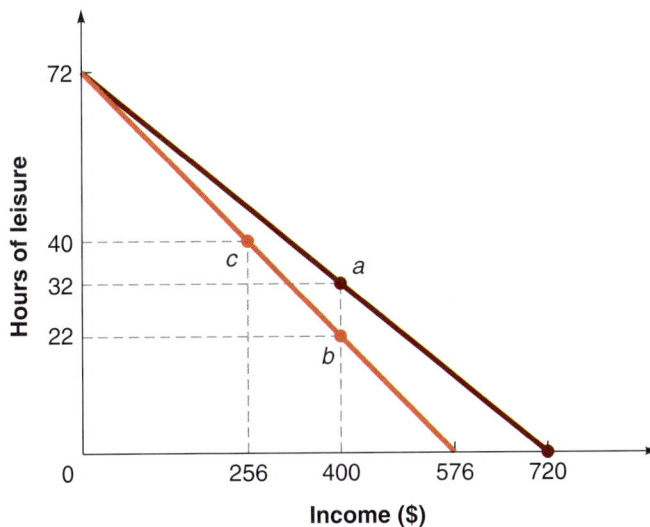

The decision to work involves a tradeoff between income and leisure. Each hour of leisure incurs the opportunity cost of forgone income. At point *a*, the worker is working 40 hours per week at $10 per hour and enjoying 32 hours of leisure per week. A 20 percent income tax will reduce maximum income from $720 to $576. To maintain pretax income, the worker must put in more hours; this is represented by point *b*, 50 hours per week. Point *b* represents an income effect: the "purchasing power" of the worker's effort has fallen from $10 to $8 per hour, so she must work additional hours to "buy" as much income as before. The tax also reduces the opportunity cost of leisure and may result in fewer hours being worked. Point *c* represents this choice.

substitution effect. Our worker might opt for a 32-hour week and three-day weekends. This choice is shown as point *c*.

Can we tell whether tax increases will increase or decrease work effort? Not yet—but the analysis we have just been through is important nevertheless because it provides a framework for statistical studies to answer this and related questions. Statistical studies are always subject to specific qualifications, but most economists believe that income taxes do generate small **work disincentives**. Further, many empirical studies indicate that most of the work disincentive from income taxes falls on families with two wage earners—such families tend to have enough discretionary income to allow them to adjust work hours as taxes change.

Work disincentive Something that reduces the opportunity cost of leisure, thereby deterring individuals from working more; may be generated by income taxes.

• • • • • • SUMMARY

Wait a minute—do consumers *really* behave this way? Do they *really* go through marginal utility calculations every time they run to the store? Probably not. What they do is much more complex—as any psychologist who has studied personality theory will tell you. People have hunches and intuition. They respond to cultural factors. They make mistakes. They demand adventure and variety. They are motivated by sexual desires. But with all due respect for the psychology profession, it will probably be quite some time before psychologists develop a comprehensive theory of personality and behavior—or even a theory that addresses something as simple as why people buy material goods. The theory of consumer behavior is not a theory of personality; it has a much less lofty goal. It is merely a *simple* model used to describe and predict the consumer's response to changing economic variables like prices and incomes. And it does this fairly well: You may not go through marginal utility calculations at the store, but don't you usually buy less at higher prices and more at lower prices? Don't you look for substitutes when the relative price of a good increases? Think for a minute: Is there *anything* about the theory of consumer behavior that is blatantly inconsistent with your actual behavior? Probably not.

You may think that the analysis we have just completed is akin to using an elephant gun to kill a mouse. There may be some truth to that, though you will probably begin to dismiss that idea as you become comfortable with the basic terminology and concepts of consumer theory. More importantly, the theory we have developed in this chapter is extremely powerful because it can be applied to situations that are difficult to understand without it—the tradeoffs between income and leisure and between current and future consumption are but two examples. Consumer theory also provides a framework for empirical models to assess the impact of taxes, price changes, and other events in the real world.

The key points to remember from this chapter are:

1. The consumer maximizes utility when the marginal utility/price ratio is equal for all goods.
2. Substitution effects are the result of relative price changes. The substitution effect is always negative: As the relative price increases (decreases), the quantity demanded decreases (increases).

3. Changes in real income result in income effects. Income effects are usually positive: As real income increases (decreases), the quantity demanded increases (decreases). Inferior goods are the exception to this rule.

4. People decide whether to spend or save their money by examining the tradeoff between current and future consumption. Higher interest rates raise the opportunity cost of current consumption because they increase the value of saving.

5. Income taxes drive a wedge between income and take-home pay. An increase in income taxes lowers the opportunity cost of leisure and thus generates a work disincentive.

KEY TERMS AND CONCEPTS

ordinal utility   total utility
cardinal utility   consumer equilibrium
marginal utility   marginal utility/price ratio
budget constraint   income effect
feasible region   substitution effect
unattainable region   work disincentive

IMPORTANT FORMULAS

Budget constraint: $B = P_1X_1 + P_2X_2 + \cdots + P_nX_n$

Intercept of budget constraint: $\dfrac{\text{Budget}}{\text{Price}}$

Slope of budget constraint: $-\dfrac{P_X}{P_Y}$ (X is on the horizontal axis)

Consumer equilibrium: $\dfrac{MU_1}{P_1} = \dfrac{MU_2}{P_2}$ (for 2 goods)

Consumer equilibrium: $\dfrac{MU_1}{P_1} = \dfrac{MU_2}{P_2} = \cdots = \dfrac{MU_n}{P_n}$ (for n goods)

Consumer equilibrium: $\dfrac{P_1}{P_2} = \dfrac{MU_1}{MU_2}$ (for 2 goods)

REVIEW QUESTIONS

1. What condition holds when a consumer is maximizing utility for a given budget? Explain what adjustments would be made as the consumer moves from disequilibrium to equilibrium.

2. What factors will cause a parallel shift in the budget constraint? What factors will change the slope of the budget constraint?

3. Explain how income and substitution effects are related to movement along and shifts in demand curves.

4. Explain how income and substitution effects influence the decisions to save and work. What are the incentive effects of income taxes?

PROBLEMS

1. Refer back to Figure 7.1 and illustrate how the budget constraint would change if:
   a. the budget rises to $100.
   b. the price of compact discs rises to $12.
   c. the price of video rentals falls to $2.50.
2. Refer back to Table 7.1.
   a. Let the price of video rentals rise to $6 and the price of compact discs rise to $12. How many videos and compact discs would you purchase?
   b. Let the price of video rentals fall to $4 and the price of compact discs fall to $8. How many videos and compact discs would you purchase?
3. Refer back to Figure 7.3. What price changes would cause the budget line to shift out the same amount as if the budget rose from $50 to $100?
4. Suppose the price of a gallon of gasoline rose from $1.25 to $1.50 per gallon. Would both an income and a substitution effect occur? Why or why not?
5. Suppose the consumer is initially in equilibrium, $MU_a/P_a = MU_b/P_b$, but that the price of good b rises. Using graphs, illustrate how this will affect the demand for both goods assuming:
   a. both goods are normal goods.
   b. good a is a normal good, and good b is an inferior good.
   c. good a is an inferior good, and good b is a normal good.
   d. both goods are inferior goods.
6. The policymakers who designed the Economic Recovery Tax Act of 1981 hoped that the tax cuts of 1981, 1982, and 1983 would result in a balanced budget. What assumptions must the policymakers have made about the income and substitution effects of the tax cut?
7. Suppose that you meet the person of your dreams and decide to get married next month. As is usually the case with marriages, you decide to send wedding invitations to your 200 nearest and dearest friends. Your spouse to be, a budding young economist, recommends that you include a note on the wedding invitation asking for money instead of gifts. You counter that this is tacky; your fiancée counters that your utility will be higher. Granted, it *is* tacky, but would the money or gifts generate more utility? Why?
8. Most economists feel that the consumer is sovereign and that honest advertising should be permitted because it provides information. In general, do you agree or disagree? Would you change your answer if the question involved only advertising on Saturday morning children's television?
9. Some goods—caviar, sushi, and Brie cheese come to mind—have what is called an "acquired taste"; that is, most people do not like them until they have eaten them a few times. Draw the marginal utility curve for a good that has an acquired taste. Do these goods contradict the principle of diminishing marginal utility? Why or why not?

APPENDIX 7A

Indifference Curve Analysis

The theory of consumer behavior developed in Chapter 7 has a rather worrisome defect: it was derived from the unrealistic assumption that utility can be represented on a cardinal scale. Fortunately, we are about to find out that the results we developed do not depend upon the assumption of cardinal measurement. To illustrate this point, we need to develop a new analytical device, the indifference curve. When economists developed indifference curve analysis, one of their main motivations was to replace the cardinal utility assumption with something more realistic, specifically, the assumption of ordinal utility. As we mentioned in the first section of Chapter 7, the ordinal numbers are "first, second, third . . ."; the cardinal numbers are "one, two, three. . . ." The ordinal utility assumption holds that people rank their preferences—consumption bundle A is preferred to consumption bundle B—but does not contain the fiction that people can actually measure the amount of satisfaction they derive from either bundle.

INDIFFERENCE CURVES

Indifference curve analysis begins with two assumptions. The first assumption is the **diminishing marginal rate of substitution**. Diminishing marginal rate of substitution means that in order for utility to stay constant, people will be willing to give up only diminishing amounts of one good to obtain additional units of another good per time period. This assumption follows from the idea of diminishing marginal utility, but it does not require us to measure how much utility declines, only to ascertain that the decline takes place. We will give an example to illustrate diminishing marginal rate of substitution momentarily. Second, we assume that people are rational and can rank their preferences on an ordinal scale. This means that people know when they prefer one consumption bundle to another, or whether they have no preference between consumption bundles. When consumers consider consumption bundles to be equally desirable, they are said to be "indifferent." Again, this assumption does not imply that people know *how much* they prefer one bundle to another, only that when faced with the choice between two bundles, consumers know which and whether one bundle is preferred to another.

Diminishing marginal rate of substitution To keep utility constant, people will be willing to give up only diminishing amounts of one good to obtain additional units of another good per time period.

Diminishing Marginal Rate of Substitution

The table in Figure 7A.1 presents hypothetical combinations of goods X and Y that are assumed to yield equal utility to the consumer. While the numbers are hypo-

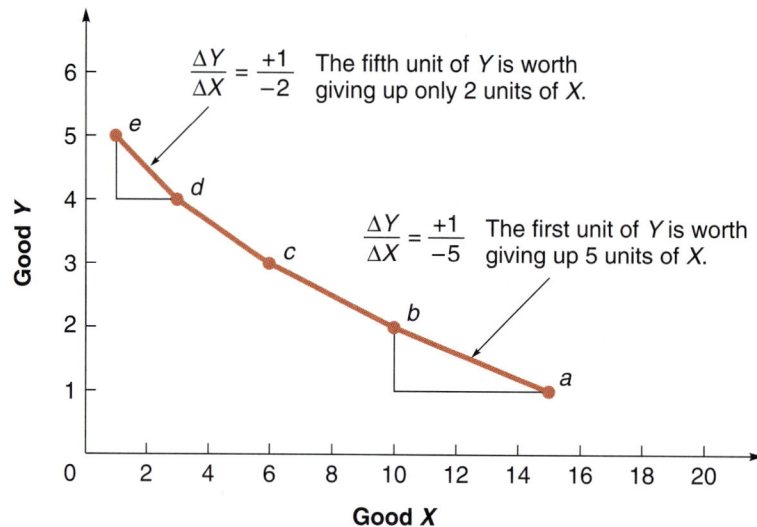

•••• FIGURE 7A.1 INDIFFERENCE CURVE

Point	Good Y	Good X	ΔY	ΔX	Slope
a	1	15	—	—	—
b	2	10	1	−5	−0.20
c	3	6	1	−4	−0.25
d	4	3	1	−3	−0.33
e	5	1	1	−2	−0.50

Indifference curves are convex to the origin because of the diminishing marginal rate of substitution. Between points *a* and *b*, the consumer is willing to give up 5 units of good *X* for just 1 unit of good *Y*. This is indicated by the −(1/5) slope between points *a* and *b*. As more *X* is exchanged for *Y*, *X* becomes scarcer, and the marginal utility of the next unit of *X* increases. Therefore, less *X* is offered in exchange for each *Y*; that is, there is a diminishing marginal rate of substitution of *X* for *Y*.

thetical, they were selected to illustrate diminishing marginal rate of substitution, one of the key ideas behind indifference curve analysis.

Indifference curves are plots of different combinations of goods that yield equal satisfaction. At point *a* on the graph in Figure 7A.1, the consumer is holding 15 units of good *X* and 1 unit of good *Y*. This gives a certain amount of utility, say, U_0. At point *b*, the consumer holds 2 units of *Y* and 10 units of *X*. This point is also on the indifference curve, so it must yield the same amount of satisfaction as point *a*. For point *b* to have the same amount of satisfaction as point *a*, the 1 additional unit of good *Y* must provide the same amount of satisfaction as was lost by giving up 5 units of good *X*. Now look what happens as we move from point *b* to point *c*: To get 1 more unit of *Y*, the consumer is willing to give up only 4 units of *X*. Why? At point *a*, the consumer had 15 units of *X* and 1 unit of *Y*. This meant that good *Y* was very

Indifference curves Graphical device used to depict consumer theory; they plot different combinations of goods that yield equal levels of satisfaction.

scarce and good X was quite abundant, so the consumer was willing to trade 5 units of X for 1 unit of Y. At point b, good X is less abundant and good Y is less scarce; therefore, the consumer is willing to trade only 4 units of X for 1 unit of Y. Continuing up the curve through points c, d, and e, notice that as each additional unit of good Y is acquired, fewer units of good X are substituted.

. . . .

Finding the Slope of Indifference Curves

All indifference curves exhibit diminishing marginal rate of substitution so fewer and fewer units of one good will be sacrificed for additional units of another good along a given indifference curve. As a result, indifference curves are bowed in toward the origin, or *convex* in the terminology of mathematicians.[1] It is difficult to calculate the exact slope of nonlinear curves without calculus, but we do not really need a numerical value of the slope anyway. What we do need to determine is the conceptual basis for the slope. This will help us derive the conditions for consumer equilibrium momentarily.

Figure 7A.2 illustrates an indifference curve, which, like all indifference curves, is convex to the origin. The slope over any region is the ratio $\Delta Y/\Delta X$, so if we wanted to find the slope between points a and b, all we would need to do is calculate that ratio. Fortunately, we know something extra about the slope of an indifference curve: when the consumer gives up a unit of good Y, the lost satisfaction must equal the gain in utility from acquiring extra units of good X; otherwise, utility would not be constant along the indifference curve. This means that the marginal utility lost from consuming one less unit of good Y, MU_Y, may be measured in terms of the marginal utility obtained from consuming extra units of good X, MU_X. This is why the slope of an indifference curve is the ratio of the marginal utilities.

$$\text{Slope of an indifference curve: } \frac{\Delta Y}{\Delta X} = -\frac{MU_X}{MU_Y} \qquad \text{[A.1]}$$

Indifference curves have a negative slope because as the consumer gives up one good for another, the satisfaction lost from one $(-MU_Y)$ must be offset by the satisfaction gained from the other $(+MU_X)$. The slope of an indifference curve gives the marginal rate of substitution of one good for another.

An alternative derivation of the slope of an indifference curve can be found with simple algebra. First, remember that utility is constant along a given indifference curve. Now, as the consumption changes along a given indifference curve, the extra utility from a change in good X plus the extra utility from a change in good Y must equal 0—otherwise utility would not be constant. In equation form, this means:

$$MU_X \Delta X + MU_Y \Delta Y = 0$$

If we subtract $MU_X \Delta X$ from each side, we have:

$$MU_Y \Delta Y = -MU_X \Delta X.$$

Finally, if we divide both sides by MU_Y and ΔX, we are left with Equation A.1.

[1]In contrast, remember that production possibilities curves were *concave* to the origin because of the law of increasing costs.

···· **FIGURE 7A.2 FINDING THE SLOPE OF AN INDIFFERENCE CURVE**

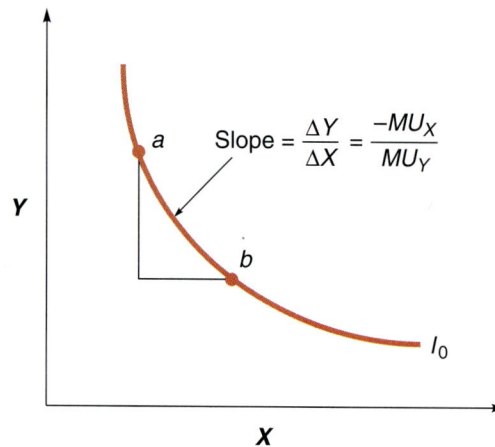

The slope of any line is the ratio of the rise to the run or $\Delta Y/\Delta X$. For movements along an indifference curve to yield equal utility, the loss in utility of one good must be compensated with a gain in utility from the other good. Between points a and b, lost satisfaction from good Y, $-MU_Y$, is offset by gained utility from good X, MU_X. This gives a slope of $-MU_X/MU_Y$. The slope of an indifference curve is called the marginal rate of substitution.

········

Characteristics of the Indifference Curve Map

Before solving for consumer equilibrium, we need to make two more comments about indifference curves. First, every consumer actually has an infinite number of indifference curves, one for each possible level of utility, which increases as you move away from the origin. This is known as the **indifference map**. An indifference map is shown in Figure 7A.3. In addition, only indifference curves within the feasible region of the budget constraint are attainable.

The second point is that indifference curves are infinitely close to each other, but do not touch and cannot cross. To see why indifference curves cannot cross, look at Figure 7A.4, which shows two indifference curves crossing. Suppose the consumer is asked to choose between points a and b. The obvious choice is point b because it provides more of both goods. This would suggest that indifference curve I_1 is preferred to I_0. However, when the choice is between points c and d, the best choice is point d—which is on indifference curve I_0. This cannot be. If utility is constant along a given indifference curve, it is impossible for an indifference curve to be preferred in one region and inferior in another region.

Indifference map The hypothetical plot of all possible indifference curves.

FIGURE 7A.3 THE INDIFFERENCE MAP

Consumers have an indifference curve map consisting of an infinite number of indifference curves. Indifference curves away from the origin represent higher utility.

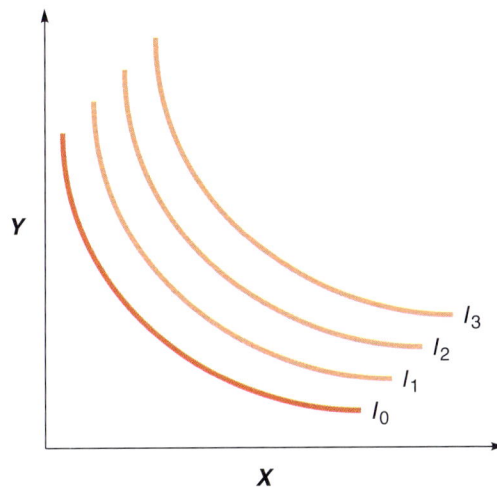

FIGURE 7A.4 INDIFFERENCE CURVES CANNOT CROSS

Indifference curves cannot cross. When points *a* and *b* are compared, the consumer would choose point *b* because it provides more of both goods X and Y. Point *b* is on indifference curve I_1. When comparing points *c* and *d*, however, the preferred choice, point *d*, is on indifference curve I_0. This violates the assumption of constant utility along a given indifference curve.

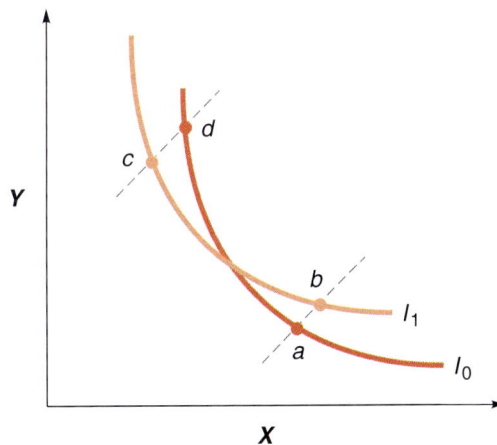

CONSUMER EQUILIBRIUM

We just went through that rather detailed development of indifference curves to set the stage to solve for consumer equilibrium in a more elegant way than we did with marginal utility analysis. Although the result will be identical—the consumer is in equilibrium when the marginal utility/price ratios are equal—the method we are using is much more powerful and can be extended to other cases of analysis.

···· **FIGURE 7A.5 CONSUMER EQUILIBRIUM**

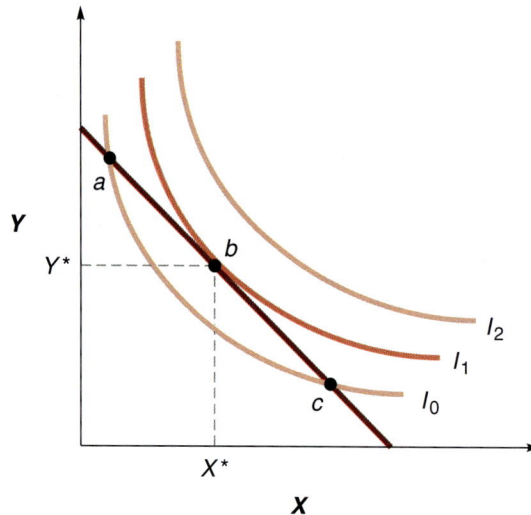

The consumer is in equilibrium when the budget constraint is tangent to the highest possible indifference curve. This occurs at point b where the consumer buys the bundle $(Y^\star/X^\star)$. The slope of the budget constraint is $-(P_X/P_Y)$, and the slope of the indifference curve is $-(MU_X/MU_Y)$. The slope of a curve is equal to the slope of a straight line tangent to the curve so:

$$-\frac{P_X}{P_Y} = -\frac{MU_X}{MU_Y} \quad \text{or} \quad \frac{MU_X}{P_X} = \frac{MU_Y}{P_Y}$$

The essential problem for the consumer is to maximize utility subject to a budget constraint. In terms of indifference curve analysis, this translates to attaining the highest possible indifference curve. This situation is pictured in Figure 7A.5 where three indifference curves are drawn along with the consumer's budget constraint. The consumer would prefer to be on the indifference curve I_2 because it represents the highest amount of utility, but this is impossible because it lies outside the feasible region. Both indifference curves I_0 and I_1 lie, at least partially, in the feasible region so the consumer could choose either. Three possible choices are points a, b, and c. Which point should be chosen? Points a and c give the same amount of utility and would require spending the entire budget, but point b is preferable to either because it lies on the highest indifference curve.

The interesting fact about point b is that it occurs where the budget constraint is tangent to the indifference curve so the two curves have the same slope.[2] We found out in Chapter 7 that the slope of the budget constraint is the relative price ratio, and we just found out that the slope of the indifference curve is the marginal utility ratio, so it follows that:

---

[2]Remember from Chapter 2 that two curves are tangent if they touch but do not intersect. The two curves have the same slope at the point of tangency.

$$\text{Slope of indifference curve} = -\frac{MU_X}{MU_Y} = -\frac{P_X}{P_Y} = \text{slope of budget constraint} \qquad [\text{A.2}]$$

This result is very important. If we multiply each side of the equation by MU_Y and then divide each side by P_X, we have:

$$\text{Consumer equilibrium: } \frac{MU_X}{P_X} = \frac{MU_Y}{P_Y} \qquad [\text{A.3}]$$

which is identical to Equation 4, the condition we found for consumer equilibrium in Chapter 7.

RECAP   **Indifference Curves**

1. Indifference curves plot different combinations of goods that yield the same amount of satisfaction.
2. Indifference curves are convex to the origin because of the diminishing marginal rate of substitution.
3. Every consumer has an indifference map consisting of an infinite number of convex indifference curves.
4. Indifference curves cannot cross.
5. The slope of an indifference curve at any point is the ratio of the marginal utilities, $-(MU_X/MU_Y)$.
6. The consumer is in equilibrium when the budget constraint is tangent to the highest possible indifference curve. Only at this point is the slope of the budget constraint equal to the slope of the indifference curve, so

$$\frac{MU_X}{P_X} = \frac{MU_Y}{P_Y}$$

7. The chief advantage of indifference curve analysis is that it does not assume cardinal utility measurement. Additionally, indifference curve analysis has been shown to be helpful in understanding a wide variety of economic situations.

COMPARATIVE STATIC ANALYSIS

One of the most important kinds of economic analysis is **comparative static analysis**. Comparative static analysis is the study of how equilibrium changes in response to external shocks. Much of the supply and demand analysis we did in Chapters 3 and 4 was comparative static analysis. For example, when we explored what happened if income increased—the demand curve shifted out and both price and quantity demanded increased—we were conducting a comparative statics experiment. Indifference curve analysis is well suited to comparative statics analysis because

Comparative static analysis Economic methodology that involves analysis of different points of static equilibrium; the study of how equilibrium changes in response to external shocks.

it can be used to help understand why and how behavior changes in response to prices, income, and other factors.

· · · · · · · ·

Income Effects

We already know that an increase in income will, *ceteris paribus*, cause the demand curve to shift outward and increase demand (assuming that the good in question is a "normal" good). This can be illustrated quite simply with indifference curves. In Figure 7A.6 the initial budget is $100, and the price of good X is $4 while the price of good Y is $5. Equation 2 in Chapter 7 tells us that the intercepts of the budget constraint are $Y:\$100/\$5 = 20$ and $X:\$100/\$4 = 25$. Given the consumer's indifference map, utility is maximized on indifference curve I_0 so that 10 units of good X and 12 units of good Y are purchased.

Now, to see how a change in income affects consumption, let income increase to $150. This will change the intercepts of the budget constraint to $Y = 30$ and $X = 37.5$ and result in an outward and parallel shift of the budget constraint. The consumer is now able to move to a higher indifference curve, I_1, with a corresponding higher level of utility. This occurs at point b where consumption is $X = 20$ and $Y = 14$. Notice that the consumption of goods X and Y increased by different proportions than the change in income. (The budget increased by 50 percent, consumption of good X increased by 100 percent, and consumption of good Y increased by about 17 percent.) Should consumption increase by the same proportion as income? Not

FIGURE 7A.6 INCOME EFFECTS

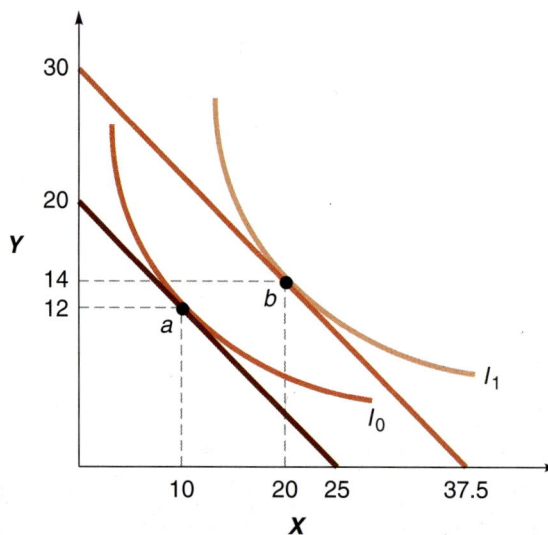

An increase in income causes a parallel shift in the budget constraint. Higher income allows the consumer to move to a higher indifference curve and thus to a higher level of utility. The movement from a to b is the income effect.

necessarily because buying plans can change as income changes. Suppose the two goods were food and clothing. As income increases, the demand for food increases only a little, but many people find that they "need" more clothes as they enter higher income brackets. All we know is that as the budget increases, people will increase their purchases (of normal goods), and if they are to maximize utility, they will buy until the marginal utility/price ratios are equal.

Substitution Effects

The movement between points a and b in Figure 7A.6 was called an income effect because it was brought about solely by an increase in purchasing power; nothing happened to the relative prices of the goods. When relative prices change, both income and substitution effects affect the consumption decision.

Figure 7A.7 illustrates a substitution effect. Suppose the consumer begins in equilibrium at point r where the initial budget constraint, X_0Y_0, is tangent to the highest possible indifference curve, I_0. Now, let the price of good X rise so that the budget constraint rotates from X_0Y_0 to X_1Y_0. This reduces the feasible region so the consumer must move to a lower indifference curve, I_1, where tangency occurs at point

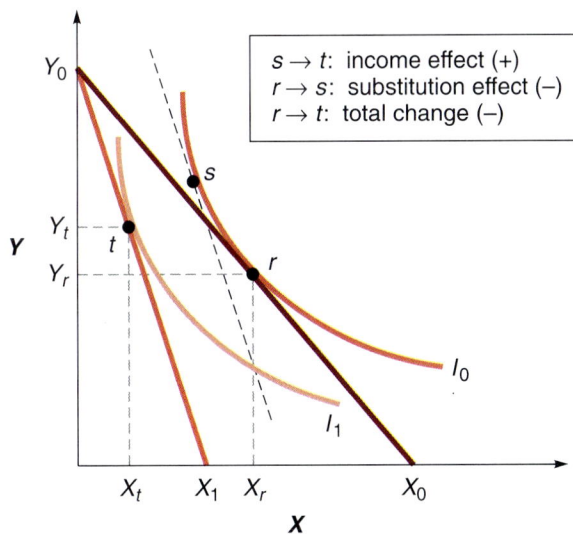

•••••FIGURE 7A.7 INCOME AND SUBSTITUTION EFFECTS

$s \rightarrow t$: income effect (+)
$r \rightarrow s$: substitution effect (−)
$r \rightarrow t$: total change (−)

From an initial position of equilibrium, point r, an increase in the price of good X swivels the budget constraint from X_0Y_0 to X_1Y_0 and moves the consumer to point t and a lower level of utility on indifference curve I_1. This change is brought about by both an income and a substitution effect. To separate the income and substitution effects, a hypothetical budget constraint is drawn parallel to the new budget constraint and tangent to the old indifference curve. The income effect is illustrated by the movement from s to t; the substitution effect is the movement from r to s.

t. The movement from *r* to *t* is brought about by both an income and a substitution effect. An income effect occurs because the higher price of good *X* reduces the purchasing power of the budget. The substitution effect occurs because the relative price of good *X* has risen. Our task is to separate the two effects.

Remember that an income effect causes a parallel shift in the budget constraint. To separate the income effect from the substitution effect, we draw a hypothetical budget constraint parallel to the new budget constraint and tangent to the old indifference curve. By drawing the hypothetical budget constraint in this way, we accomplish two things. First, because it is parallel to the new budget constraint, it illustrates a pure income effect. Second, by being tangent to the old indifference curve, it shows how a pure income effect would result in the same level of utility as the relative price change. It is then a simple matter to separate the income from the substitution effect: the movement *between* indifference curves, from *s* to *t*, is the income effect. In this case, the income effect is positive because the change in purchases and the change in income have the same sign—both decrease. It is rare but possible for the income effect to be negative, a situation we explore in the next section. The movement *along* the old indifference curve, from *r* to *s*, is the substitution effect. The substitution effect is always negative: the change in relative price and the change in the quantity demanded always have the opposite sign. The total effect, however, is often ambiguous, as we will see in the next example.

• • • • • • • •

Inferior Goods

The situation pictured in Figure 7A.7 is not the only possible scenario. Look what happens in Figure 7A.8. The price of good *X* again increases, the budget constraint again shifts from X_0Y_0 to X_1Y_0, and the consumption of both goods declines. Look at the income effect, however. When the hypothetical budget constraint is constructed, the tangency occurs at point *s*, an indication that *more*, not less of good *X* would be consumed because of the income effect. This is an indication that good *X* is an inferior good because more is consumed at low income than at high income. In this case the substitution effect dominates the income effect so consumption falls. If *X* were an extremely inferior good, the income effect would dominate the substitution effect and cause consumption of *X* to increase despite the price rise. Such a good is called a *Giffen good*.

• • • • • • • • **SUMMARY**

Indifference curve analysis is a powerful tool that is used in many areas of economic analysis. Students planning to take additional economic courses are strongly encouraged to cover this material carefully. The main points to remember are:

1. Indifference curves plot different combinations of goods that yield equal satisfaction to the consumer. They are convex to the origin because of the diminishing marginal rate of substitution. Every person has an indifference map consisting of an infinite number of convex indifference curves, one for each possible level of utility. Indifference curves cannot cross.

····**FIGURE 7A.8** INDIFFERENCE CURVE ANALYSIS OF AN
INFERIOR GOOD

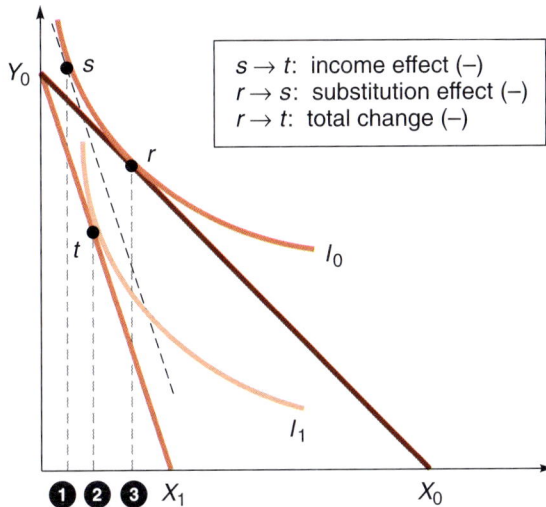

Inferior goods are characterized by a negative income effect: As income increases (decreases), demand decreases (increases). In this case, an increase in the price of good X lowers real income. When the income effect is isolated by constructing the hypothetical budget constraint tangent at point s, it shows an increase in the demand for good X. This is an indication that good X is an inferior good. Notice, however, that when both the income and substitution effects are considered, the quantity demanded of good X decreases.

2. The consumer is in equilibrium when the budget constraint is tangent to the highest possible indifference curve. At this point:

$$-\frac{MU_X}{MU_Y} = -\frac{P_X}{P_Y} \quad \text{and} \quad \frac{MU_X}{P_X} = \frac{MU_Y}{P_Y}$$

3. As prices and incomes change, income and substitution effects occur. The substitution effect is illustrated by movement along a given indifference curve. It is caused by changes in relative prices. Substitution effects are always negative; consumers always substitute away from the relatively more expensive good. The income effect is illustrated by movement between indifference curves with parallel budget constraints. Income effects are positive for normal goods and negative for inferior goods.

KEY TERMS AND CONCEPTS

ordinal utility
diminishing marginal rate of substitution
indifference curve
convex
slope of indifference curve
indifference map
consumer equilibrium

slope of budget constraint
comparative static analysis
income effect
normal good
substitution effect
inferior good
Giffen good

REVIEW QUESTIONS

1. List and explain the meaning of the main assumptions behind indifference curve analysis. Why is indifference curve analysis superior to marginal utility analysis?
2. Can indifference curves ever intersect? Use graphs to illustrate your answer.
3. State the conditions that hold in consumer equilibrium, and illustrate these conditions with indifference curves. Now, assume a price change and use the diagram to illustrate the income and substitution effects.

PROBLEMS

1. Explain the relationship between good A and good B if the indifference curves looked like the ones in the accompanying graphs.

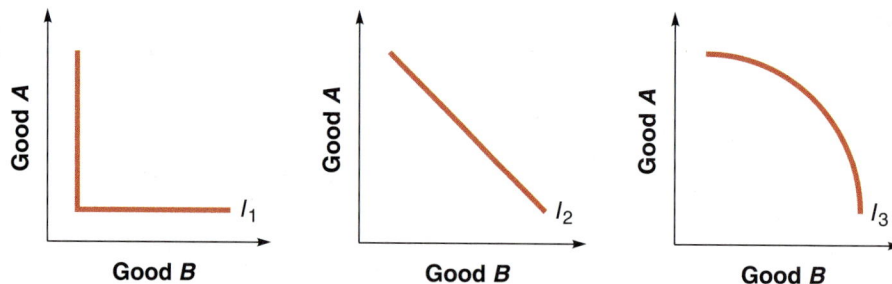

2. A Giffen good is an extremely inferior good. The classic example is the potato to Irish peasants. The standard diet of Irish peasants was potatoes and mutton. During the potato famine of the nineteenth century, potato prices increased dramatically, but Irish peasants ate more potatoes and less mutton. Illustrate this situation with indifference curve analysis.
3. Use indifference curve analysis to illustrate the choice between current consumption and future consumption. Let the interest rate rise and draw situations depicting current consumption as both an inferior good and a normal good.
4. Can indifference curves ever intersect the axis? Why or why not?
5. Ray likes to consume both Guns n' Roses compact discs and Beavis and Butthead T-shirts. Citizens Opposed to Violence on the Entertainment Networks (COVEN) has advocated a tax on Beavis and Butthead T-shirts. Using indifference curve analysis, analyze how such a tax would affect Ray's consumption choices.

CHAPTER 8

Elasticity

One of the consequences of the Arab-Israeli War of 1973 was an oil embargo. The Organization of Petroleum Exporting Countries (OPEC) punished countries that supported Israel in the war by refusing to export oil to them. The immediate result, as you might expect, was a dramatic increase in the world price of oil from under $2 to over $5 per barrel. Perhaps because of the price increase, the oil embargo only lasted a few months—by which time the OPEC nations had agreed to restrict oil exports to keep the price high. The oil-importing nations grumbled, but still imported millions of barrels of oil. That grumbling had hardly died down when the Shah of Iran talked his OPEC colleagues into a price hike to almost $11 per barrel in early 1974. As expected, the oil-importing nations protested, but did little else. We wanted oil and they had it. If they raised the price, we would have to pay it, at least until we found other sources.

The decision by OPEC to raise prices was not popular in the West, but it should have been expected even without the pretext of the Arab-Israeli War. Oil is an exhaustible resource, and once it is gone, the OPEC nations will have lost their most valuable resource. By raising the price of oil, the OPEC nations were able to bring in more money for national development. It is no coincidence that the OPEC nations began to spend billions on education, desalination plants, medical care, and other projects in the late 1970s.

A second reason for raising the price of oil brings us to the topic of this chapter. In the short run, there are few, if any, good substitutes for oil, so even a substantial increase in price resulted in only a small change in the quantity demanded of imported oil. Economists describe this situation by saying that the demand for oil is *inelastic*. If the change in the quantity of oil demanded was large relative to the change in price, demand would be said to be *elastic*. How to calculate and use elasticity is the main topic of this chapter.

AFTER READING AND STUDYING THIS CHAPTER, YOU SHOULD BE ABLE TO:
- • • Define price elasticity of demand, know the factors that determine elasticity, and calculate elasticity coefficients
- • • Show the relationship between price elasticity and total revenue
- • • Calculate and use cross-price, income, and supply elasticities
- • • Explain how supply and demand elasticity affect tax incidence

ELASTICITY: BASIC CONCEPTS AND COMPUTATIONS

Suppose that you are elected treasurer of your sorority, and as your first task, you must decide what price to charge for tickets to the annual charity raffle. Last year, tickets sold for $5 and 1,000 tickets were sold, bringing in $5,000 in revenues. The hope is to raise more money this year. One strategy might be to raise ticket prices. If you charge $10 per ticket, you will almost certainly sell fewer tickets, but how many? As long as more than 500 tickets are sold, revenues will exceed what the sorority made last year, but if sales fall below 500 tickets, revenues will fall below $5,000. An alternative strategy would be to lower ticket prices and hope that sales increase significantly. At a ticket price of $1, more people will buy tickets and some people will buy several. But again, whether this is a good strategy depends on how many more tickets are sold. You will need to sell 5,000 tickets to do as well as last year. Is it reasonable to expect sales to be that high? This is a difficult question because many things could have changed over the past year. The first step to answering it is to compute the relative responsiveness of the change in quantity demanded to the change in price—the price elasticity of demand. Much of this chapter will focus on how to calculate, use, and interpret elasticity.

Elasticity is used in several contexts in economics, but the most common usage is the price elasticity of demand. Knowledge of price elasticity can be useful in several ways. For example, firms know that when they raise their selling price, the quantity they sell usually falls. The question is how much: if a 10 percent price increase results in only a 1 percent decline in sales, the price increase is probably the right thing to do. But if the same 10 percent price increase causes sales to fall by 20 percent, the firm may have to reconsider the price hike. Policymakers often need to compute elasticity as well. For example, a gasoline tax increase may be intended as a conservation measure to reduce gasoline usage, but without knowing how much quantity demanded will fall as price increases, it will be impossible to determine how much to raise taxes. What information is necessary to determine how much sales and quantity demanded respond to price changes? Only one thing is needed: the elasticity coefficient.

The price elasticity of demand tells how much quantity demanded responds relative to a change in "own-price." In this chapter, we will frequently need to distinguish between the price of the good under consideration and the prices of related goods, so we will use the term "own-price" when appropriate to avoid confusion. We can get some idea how elasticity works by seeing what happens to the two demand curves in Figure 8.1 when own-price falls from $6 to $5. On the relatively

• • • • **FIGURE 8.1** ELASTIC AND INELASTIC DEMAND CURVES

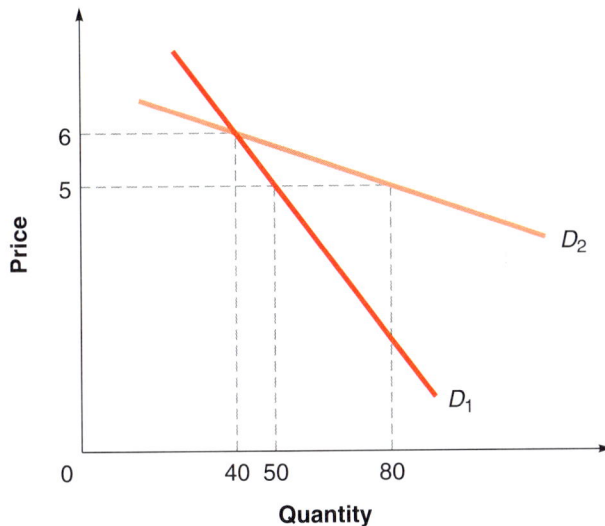

As price falls from \$6 to \$5, the quantity demanded along demand curve D_1 rises from 40 to 50 units; along demand curve D_2, quantity demanded rises a larger amount, from 40 to 80 units. This means that D_1 is inelastic relative to demand curve D_2 over this region.

steep demand curve D_1, the quantity demanded rises by only 10 units, from 40 to 50 units. On the relatively flat demand curve D_2, the quantity demanded doubles from 40 to 80 units. Economists would say that demand curve D_1 is *inelastic* relative to demand curve D_2. The term "inelastic" indicates that a price change results in a relatively small quantity response. It means the same thing to say that demand curve D_2 is *elastic* relative to demand curve D_1—because there is a larger quantity response for a given price change along D_2 than along D_1.

Before we go on, we need to dispel a common confusion: Elasticity is not slope! It is true that the quantity demanded changes less along D_1 than along D_2, so it is correct to say that D_1 is inelastic relative to D_2, at least over the region illustrated in the figure. As we are about to find out, however, unlike slope, the elasticity of a straight demand curve changes everywhere along the curve. This is why we must actually be able to compute elasticity coefficients.

• • • • • • • •

Determinants of Price Elasticity of Demand

Price elasticity of demand is defined as the percentage change in quantity demanded divided by the percentage change in own-price. Several factors determine price elasticity of demand, but perhaps the most important is the *availability of good substitutes*. For example, most cars run on gasoline and nothing else, so gasoline has few good substitutes. This suggests that the demand for gasoline is probably *inelastic* because a

Price elasticity of demand The relative responsiveness of a change in quantity demanded to a change in price; calculated as the percentage change in quantity demanded divided by the percentage change in own-price.

change in the price of gasoline ordinarily has only a small effect on the quantity of gasoline demanded, at least in the short run. In contrast, the demand for fast-food hamburgers is relatively *elastic*. McDonald's Big Mac, Burger King's Whopper, and Wendy's Dave's Deluxe are comparable products to most people, so if McDonald's raised the price of a Big Mac, many people would just go across the street for a Whopper.

Other factors influence the elasticity of demand as well. The demand for goods that are considered necessities is usually inelastic; people may grumble at a price hike, but if the good is truly a necessity, they generally have to pay the price. What can you do about rising textbook prices? If your professor requires the book, you will have to pay the price or drop the course. Insulin is another good with very inelastic demand; most diabetics would buy insulin even if the price were to double or quadruple. On the other hand, luxury goods often exhibit elastic demand. Häagen-Dazs ice cream is great stuff—but if they raise the price too much, you might make do with Ben and Jerry's.

The price of the good relative to the size of the consumer's budget can also influence elasticity. For example, an increase in the price of chewing gum from 25¢ a pack to 50¢ a pack would go unnoticed by most people because an extra 25¢ does not mean much if your grocery store bill is $50 per week. But to the 8 year old on a dollar-a-week allowance, the same price hike would definitely be cause for alarm—and probably a lower quantity demanded.

Finally, elasticity varies over time because people can usually find better substitutes in the long run than in the short run. If the price of heating oil rises, the quantity of heating oil demanded will decline only a little in the short run, but over the long run, people will find sweaters more fashionable, insulate their homes, switch to electric heating or natural gas, or even move to smaller houses. The same thing happened following the OPEC oil price hikes of the 1970s: in the short run, people had to bite the bullet and feed expensive gasoline into their gas-guzzling cars, but it was not long before automakers began turning out smaller cars and more fuel-efficient engines.

Before going on, we need to add some qualifications. We just said that the demand for gasoline is inelastic because there are few good substitutes for gasoline. An increase in the price of gasoline from $1.00 to $1.15 a gallon would have very little effect on the quantity demanded of gasoline. But what if the price of gasoline were to suddenly increase to $10 a gallon? Those same people would find substitutes rather quickly—car pooling would become more popular, as would walking and bicycles. What does this mean? In general, demand is more elastic at high prices than at low prices. Just how high is "high" and how low is "low"? There is no single answer—which is why we need to learn how to calculate elasticity coefficients.

Elasticity Formulas. The coefficient of price elasticity of demand, E_p, is measured as the percentage change in quantity demanded divided by the percentage change in own-price, where price is assumed to be the causal variable.[1] The formula for the coefficient of price elasticity of demand is:

[1]Remember that the causal or independent variable determines the value of the effect or dependent variable; that is, changes in price *cause* changes in quantity demanded.

$$E_p = \frac{\text{percentage change in quantity demanded}}{\text{percentage change in price}} \qquad [1]$$

Equation 1 is of little use if you do not remember how to calculate percentage changes, but that is simple enough to do. The percentage change in a variable is computed as the change in the variable divided by the variable itself:

$$\text{Price elasticity of demand: } E_p = \left| \frac{\frac{\Delta Q}{\overline{Q}}}{\frac{\Delta P}{\overline{P}}} \right| \qquad [2]$$

Where:

ΔQ = change in quantity; i.e., $Q_1 - Q_2$
$\overline{Q}$ = the midpoint between Q_1 and Q_2
ΔP = change in price; i.e., $P_1 - P_2$
$\overline{P}$ = the midpoint between P_1 and P_2

We need to make some comments about the formula in Equation 2 before we apply it. First, the two vertical bars indicate that we need to take the *absolute value* of the fraction inside the bars. The absolute value of a negative number eliminates the minus sign, but has no effect on a positive number. For example, $|-5| = 5; |+5| = 5$. This means that the price elasticity of demand is always a positive number. Second, we are using the midpoints of P and Q because elasticity changes over the demand curve. The elasticity coefficient will depend on whether the low or high values of P and Q are used in the computation.[2] As we will show below, the quantity and price midpoints are found by adding the two points together and dividing by 2: $\overline{Q} = (Q_1 + Q_2)/2$ and $\overline{P} = (P_1 + P_2)/2$.

Some calculations based on the demand curve in Figure 8.2 will show how to use the price elasticity of demand formula. First, let's calculate elasticity as price rises from \$6 to \$8. When price rises over this region, the quantity demanded falls from 2 to 1 units. Substituting these values into Equation 2 gives:

$$E_p = \left| \frac{\frac{\Delta Q}{\overline{Q}}}{\frac{\Delta P}{\overline{P}}} \right| = \left| \frac{\frac{Q_1 - Q_2}{(Q_1 + Q_2)/2}}{\frac{P_1 - P_2}{(P_1 + P_2)/2}} \right| = \left| \frac{\frac{2 - 1}{(2 + 1)/2}}{\frac{6 - 8}{(6 + 8)/2}} \right| = \left| \frac{\frac{1}{3/2}}{\frac{-2}{7}} \right| = \left| \left(\frac{2}{3}\right)\left(\frac{7}{2}\right) \right|$$

$$= 2.33 > 1 \rightarrow \text{elastic demand}$$

What does this answer mean? As price rises from \$6 to \$8, the percentage change in the quantity demanded is 2.33 times as large as the percentage change in price. When

---

[2]This formula finds the *arc* elasticity over the region between P_1 and P_2. This is a good first approximation, but for more precise analysis, the elasticity at a single point can be calculated with calculus. The formula is:

$$E_p = \left(\frac{\partial Q}{\partial P}\right)\left(\frac{P}{Q}\right) = \left(\frac{1}{\text{slope of demand curve}}\right)\left(\frac{P}{Q}\right)$$

FIGURE 8.2 DEMAND AND ELASTICITY

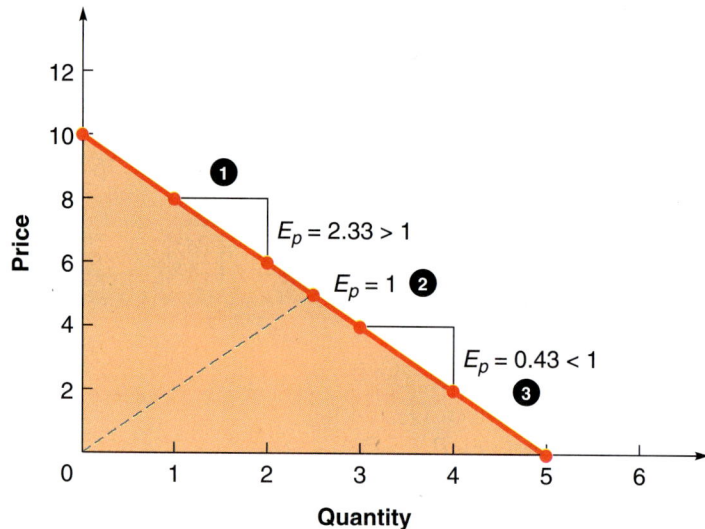

① "High" prices = Elastic demand
② Midpoint = Unitary elasticity
③ "Low" prices = Inelastic demand

Every linear demand curve has regions of elastic, inelastic, and unitary demand. At "high" prices, people can almost always find a substitute; this is the region of elastic demand, $E_p > 1$. At "low" prices, people may not even look for substitutes; this is the region of inelastic demand, $E_p < 1$. The midpoint of the demand curve has unitary elasticity, $E_p = 1$.

Elastic demand The percentage change in quantity demanded is greater than the percentage change in price. Quantity demanded changes proportionately more than own-price changes, and the elasticity coefficient is greater than 1.

the elasticity coefficient is greater than 1, the percentage change in quantity demanded is greater than the percentage change in price, and demand is said to be **elastic**. This means that the quantity demanded is highly responsive to price changes.

Look what happens when we calculate the elasticity over a different price range, say, as the price rises from \$2 to \$4. In this case, the quantity demanded falls from 4 to 3 units, so the calculations are:

$$E_p = \left| \frac{\frac{4-3}{(4+3)/2}}{\frac{2-4}{(2+4)/2}} \right| = \left| \frac{\frac{1}{7/2}}{\frac{-2}{3}} \right| = \left| \left(\frac{2}{7}\right)\left(\frac{3}{-2}\right) \right|$$

$$= \frac{6}{14} = 0.43 < 1 \rightarrow \text{inelastic demand}$$

Inelastic demand The percentage change in quantity demanded is less than the percentage change in price. Quantity demanded changes proportionately less than own-price changes, and the elasticity coefficient is less than 1.

In other words, as price rises from \$2 to \$4, the percentage change in the quantity demanded is less than half as large as the percentage change in price. When the elasticity coefficient is less than 1, demand is said to be **inelastic**. This means that the quantity demanded is relatively unresponsive to price changes.

Finally, the midpoint of a linear demand curve always has an elasticity coefficient equal to 1; this is the point of **unitary elasticity**. This can be verified by calculating the elasticity coefficient as price changes from $4 to $6. As price rises from $4 to $6, the quantity demanded falls from 3 to 2, so the elasticity coefficient is:

$$E_p = \left| \frac{\frac{3-2}{2.5}}{\frac{4-6}{5}} \right| = 1 \rightarrow \text{unitary elasticity}$$

Unitary elastic demand The percentage change in quantity demanded is equal to the percentage change in price, and the elasticity coefficient is 1.

A unitary elasticity coefficient means that the percentage change in quantity demanded is equal to the percentage change in price.

· · · · · · · ·

Special Cases

We also need to examine three special cases: vertical and horizontal demand curves, and nonlinear demand curves.

Vertical Demand Curves. A vertical demand curve means that there is no quantity response regardless of the change in price. Few goods exhibit this characteristic in the real world, but a good with no substitutes at all might have a demand curve that is almost vertical. The demand curve for a diabetic's insulin may be almost vertical. A vertical demand curve is perfectly inelastic and has a zero elasticity coefficient because the ΔQ in the numerator of Equation 2 equals zero. A perfectly inelastic demand curve is shown in Figure 8.3a.

Horizontal Demand Curves. An all-purpose good might have a horizontal demand curve. Why? If the good is truly all-purpose, it can be used as a substitute for every other good. In this situation, even a tiny decline in price would cause people to purchase more of the good to be used as a substitute for some other good. Are there any examples of all-purpose goods? Perhaps not, but there are goods that are perfect substitutes for *some* other goods. For example, you should not care whether the wheat you buy is from Farmer Brown or Farmer Smith; Smith's wheat is a perfect substitute for Brown's wheat. Thus, if Farmer Smith raised the price of wheat by even a penny, you'd give your business to Farmer Brown, When the demand curve is perfectly horizontal, it is said to be perfectly elastic, and the elasticity coefficient approaches infinity. A perfectly elastic demand curve is shown in Figure 8.3b.

Nonlinear Demand Curves. Demand curves are often nonlinear, and in such cases it is difficult to calculate elasticity coefficients without calculus. Nevertheless, the general results we have just developed still apply. At relatively high prices, the elasticity coefficient tends to be high; at relatively low prices, the elasticity coefficient tends to be low; and there may be a region of unitary elasticity in between. However, it is possible for nonlinear demand curves to have a constant elasticity over the entire curve; this occurs when the demand curve is a rectangular hyperbola. A rectangular hyperbola is shown in Figure 8.3c.

····· FIGURE 8.3 SPECIAL CASES OF DEMAND ELASTICITY

The demand curve is vertical if there are no substitutes; this results in an elasticity coefficient of 0, as shown in panel (a). The demand curve is horizontal if the good is an all-purpose good or if there are perfect substitutes; this results in an elasticity coefficient that is undefined, but approaches infinity. This is shown in panel (b). No set rule governs the elasticity coefficient of a nonlinear demand curve. One possibility is a rectangular hyperbola that has constant unitary elasticity, as shown in panel (c).

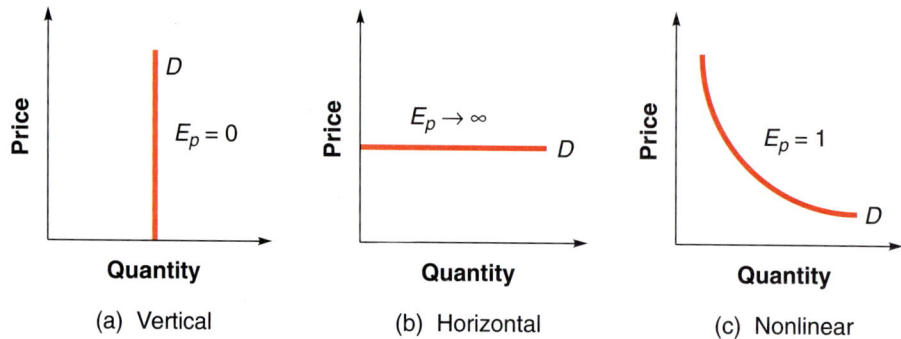

(a) Vertical $E_p = 0$ (b) Horizontal $E_p \to \infty$ (c) Nonlinear $E_p = 1$

······· ELASTICITY AND TOTAL REVENUE

One of the most important applications of elasticity concerns the concept of **total revenue**. Total revenue is the entire amount of money that a firm receives from selling a product. It is calculated as the selling price times the quantity sold, or:

Total revenue The total amount that a firm receives for its product; calculated as selling price times quantity sold.

$$\text{Total revenue: } TR = \text{price} \times \text{quantity} = PQ \qquad [3]$$

Firms are vitally interested in their total revenue. If total revenue exceeds the total costs of production, the firm has profits that can be used for expansion; if total revenue is less than production costs, the firm has losses and may face bankruptcy. As prices change, the quantity sold changes, and total revenue usually changes as a result. To understand how much total revenue changes, and whether it rises or falls in response to a price change, the firm needs to understand price elasticity of demand.

········

The Geometry of Total Revenue

As shown in panel (a) of Figure 8.4, total revenue is the rectangular area with dimensions of price and quantity. For example, if $P = \$10$ and $Q = 6$, the total revenue received by the firm is $TR = PQ = \$10(6) = \$60$. This is represented by the orange area with dimensions 0–6–a–10. However, look what happens if the firm decides to raise its price to $12 as it does in panel (b). Quantity falls to 3 units, and total revenue is now equal to $PQ = \$12(3) = \$36$. This is represented by the area with dimensions 0–3–b–12. By raising price from $10 to $12, the firm's total revenue has declined by the orange area 3–6–a–c but increased by the dark green area 10–c–b–12. The dark green area $(3 \times 2 = 6)$ is smaller than the orange area $(10 \times 3 = 30)$, so total revenue has declined.

· · · · FIGURE 8.4 TOTAL REVENUE

Total revenue is found by multi-plying price times quantity. In panel (a), total revenue is represented by the orange rectangle bounded by the selling price and quantity, 0–6–*a*–10. Panel (b) shows that total revenue falls if the firm raises price in an elastic region of the demand curve. The firm loses the revenue in the large orange rectangle 3–6–*a*–*c*, but gains only the revenue in the smaller dark green rectangle 10–*c*–*b*–12.

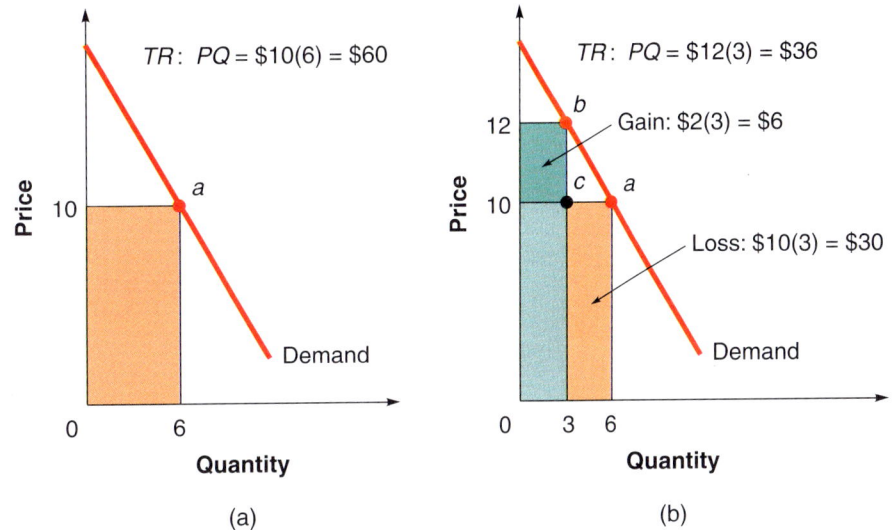

$TR: PQ = \$10(6) = \$60$

$TR: PQ = \$12(3) = \$36$

Gain: $2(3) = $6

Loss: $10(3) = $30

(a)

(b)

The result that we have just illustrated—that total revenue falls if price is increased—holds only when demand is elastic. Why? When demand is elastic, the relative change in quantity demanded is greater than the relative change in price, so their product, *PQ*, declines. A price cut will increase total revenue when demand is elastic because the increase in quantity demanded is enough to offset the losses from a lower price.

The reverse happens when demand is inelastic. The relative change in quantity demanded is less than the relative change in price, so price hikes increase total revenue and price cuts decrease total revenue. This is shown in Figure 8.5. Panel (a) shows total revenue to be $45 when price is $5 and quantity is 9 units. Panel (b) shows that a price increase to $8 raises total revenue to $56 as quantity falls to 7 units. A quick check shows that demand is inelastic over this price range:

$$E_p = \left| \frac{\dfrac{7-9}{(7+9)/2}}{\dfrac{8-5}{(8+5)/2}} \right| = \frac{13}{24} = 0.54 < 1$$

· · · · · · · ·

Elasticity and Total Revenue: An Application

The farming industry is one of the most highly subsidized industries in the United States. Farmers receive a variety of price supports and subsidies from the government. Part of the reason for this treatment is the special role farmers have played in U.S. history; Thomas Jefferson and many of our founding fathers considered a nation of small farmers to be the ideal state. But there are economic reasons that might also

**·····FIGURE 8.5 PRICE INCREASES RAISE TOTAL REVENUE
IF DEMAND IS INELASTIC**

When demand is inelastic, price increases raise total revenue. In this case, if price is $5, the quantity demanded is 9 units so total revenue is $45. An increase in price to $8 will reduce the quantity demanded to 7 units, but total revenue will rise to $56 because the relative decline in quantity is less than the relative increase in price. A price cut causes total revenue to decline when demand is inelastic.

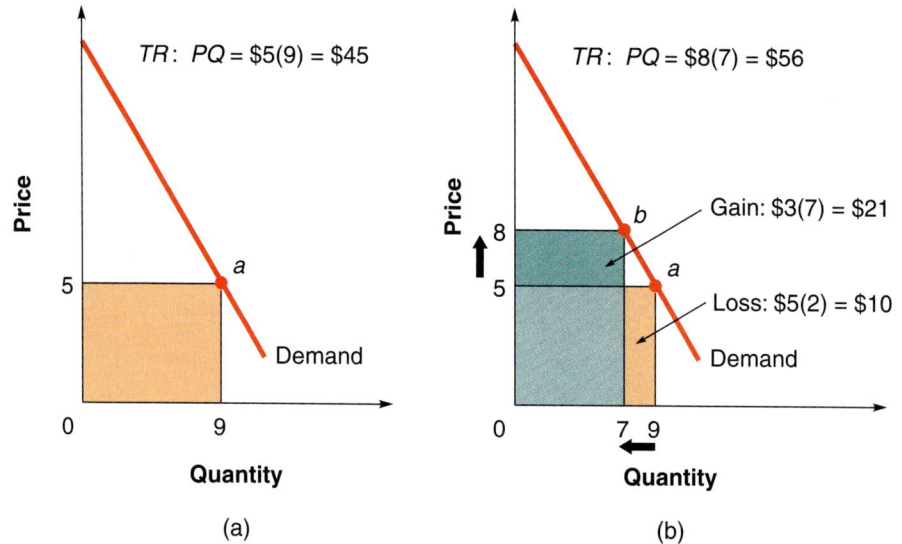

TR: PQ = $5(9) = $45

a

Demand

0   9

Quantity

Price

5

(a)

TR: PQ = $8(7) = $56

b   Gain: $3(7) = $21

a

Loss: $5(2) = $10

Demand

0   7 9

Quantity

Price

8

5

(b)

justify special aid for farmers. We can understand one of these reasons by looking at the relationship between elasticity and total revenue.

The roots of the farm problem can be traced to three facts. First, the demand for food is price inelastic because there are few good substitutes for food.[3] Thus, the demand curve for food can be thought of as being relatively steep, at least over the usual price range; consequently, the percentage change in quantity demanded will be less than the percentage change in price. Second, the agricultural supply curve has shifted out rapidly since the 1920s and 1930s with the advance of technology. This has caused farm prices to fall, and because demand is inelastic, so has farmers' total revenue. Finally, farmers have also had to face the problem of price volatility. With a steep demand curve, fluctuating crop yields cause large fluctuations in price because relatively small shifts in the supply curve result in large changes in price. This is illustrated in Figure 8.6. Notice that the increase in supply caused price to fall and resulted in a net loss in total revenue: farmers gained the small rectangle *dgfh* but lost the larger rectangle *ehcb*.

Several solutions to the farm problem have been proposed, but none have been completely successful. A variety of price support programs have been instituted to prevent prices from falling to market levels, but these have often resulted in market gluts as farmers increased production in response to the higher prices. Price supports

[3]We need to be careful what we mean by the word "substitute" in this context. There is no substitute for food in the sense that you must eat it or you will die, but there is a good substitute for domestically produced food—imported food. However, strict regulations on the kinds and amounts of food that can be imported limit their role as substitutes. For example, sugar prices in the United States are almost five times the world price—largely because sugar import quotas exist to help domestic sugar farmers.

····FIGURE 8.6 TOTAL REVENUE AND THE FARM PROBLEM

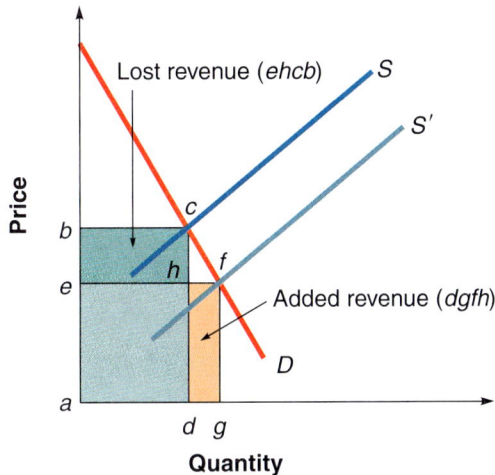

The demand for food is inelastic, so an increase in supply reduces total revenue. The technological advances of the twentieth century have shifted the supply curve outward from *S* to *S′* and caused total revenue to fall from the area *adcb* to *agfe*. Notice that lost revenue, *ehcb*, is greater than gained revenue, *dgfh*, so total revenue declines as price falls.

were often accompanied by crop restriction programs that paid farmers to take land out of cultivation. These were only partially successful because, as you might guess, only the least productive land was removed from production. Attempts to increase exports have been only partially successful as well.[4]

One of the more recent programs designed to aid farmers was the Payment-in-Kind or PIK program. Under this program, farmers who took acreage out of cultivation were paid with grain the government had purchased in earlier years as a means of supporting farm prices. Unfortunately, so many farmers signed up for the PIK program that the government had to *buy* grain on the market in order to have enough grain to *give* away to PIK participants.

The farm problem is far from settled. It is true that farmers must deal with volatile and often very low prices; however, it is not true that farmers are an economically disadvantaged group. In 1988, the average income of farm operator households was $33,535, less than $500 below the U.S. average.[5] However, farm income is concen-

[4]Most countries provide special protection for their farmers, but Japan may have the most extreme policies. Japan bans almost all rice imports alleging the need to maintain self-sufficiency; others argue that the real reason is the political power of Japanese farmers. As a result, the price of rice is many times the world price. In March 1991, American officials at a Tokyo food exhibition were threatened with arrest unless they removed a 10-pound bag of American rice. Japanese tourists returning from the United States often take home bags of rice. Quite a souvenir! Japan began to relax rice import restrictions in 1993.

[5]This figure comes from *Agricultural Income and Finance: Situation and Outlook Report* (Washington, D.C.: U.S. Department of Agriculture Economic Research Service, 1990).

trated in the hands of a few large farmers: in 1989, barely a quarter of all farmers had sales exceeding $40,000.[6] Given the problems caused by interference with the market and continuing government budget deficits, we can probably expect to see fewer price controls and quantity restrictions in the future.

RECAP   Price Elasticity of Demand

1. Elasticity measures the relative responsiveness of one variable to changes in another. The most important factors that influence the price elasticity of demand are the number of available substitutes, whether the product is a necessity, the significance of the product in the consumer's budget, and time.

2. The formula for calculating price elasticity of demand is:

$$E_p = \left| \frac{\Delta Q / \overline{Q}}{\Delta P / \overline{P}} \right|$$

3. If the percentage change in quantity is greater than the percentage change in price, the price elasticity coefficient is greater than 1, $E_p > 1$, and demand is said to be elastic.

4. If the percentage change in quantity is less than the percentage change in price, the price elasticity coefficient is less than 1, $E_p < 1$, and demand is said to be inelastic.

5. If the percentage change in quantity is equal to the percentage change in price, the elasticity coefficient is equal to 1, $E_p = 1$, and demand is said to be unitary.

6. All downward-sloping linear demand curves have elastic, inelastic, and unitary elastic portions. Demand is elastic at high prices, inelastic at low prices, and unitary at the midpoint. Vertical demand curves are perfectly inelastic; horizontal demand curves are perfectly elastic.

7. When demand is elastic, an increase in price reduces total revenue, and a decrease in price raises total revenue. When demand is inelastic, an increase in price increases total revenue, and a decrease in price decreases total revenue. When demand is unitary elastic, a change in price will not change total revenue.

OTHER KINDS OF ELASTICITY

So far we have discussed only one kind of elasticity, the price elasticity of demand. This may be the most important kind of elasticity, but it is not the only application of the elasticity concept that economists find useful. Other applications include income elasticity, cross-price elasticity, and the elasticity of supply.

---

[6]Bruce L. Gardner, "Changing Economic Perspectives on the Farm Problem," *Journal of Economic Literature* 30 (March 1992): 62–101. This article gives a good overview of recent farm policy in the United States.

Income Elasticity

Income elasticity of demand measures the relative responsiveness of a change in demand to a change in income.[7] It is defined as the percentage change in demand divided by the percentage change in income, or:

Income elasticity A measure of the relative responsiveness of a change in demand to changes in income; the percentage change in demand divided by the percentage change in income.

$$\text{Income elasticity: } E_y = \frac{\dfrac{\Delta Q}{\overline{Q}}}{\dfrac{\Delta Y}{\overline{Y}}} \qquad [4]$$

where Y stands for income and Q is the quantity that will be purchased at different income levels. For example, if your income rose from \$1,000 to \$1,100 per month and you increased your trips to the movie from once a month to twice a month, your income elasticity of demand coefficient would be:

$$E_y = \frac{\dfrac{\Delta Q}{\overline{Q}}}{\dfrac{\Delta Y}{\overline{Y}}} = \frac{\dfrac{2-1}{1.5}}{\dfrac{1,100-1,000}{1,050}} = 7$$

We need to make a few comments about the formula in Equation 4. First, unlike the formula in Equation 2, there are no absolute value bars. This is because we need to know the sign of the income elasticity coefficient. For example, an increase in income will result in an increase in demand for *normal* goods, but it will cause a decrease in the demand for *inferior* goods. As we found out in Chapter 3, inferior goods—hamburgers as opposed to steak—are goods that people would prefer not to consume and do so only because of their low income. As income rises, the quantity demanded of inferior goods falls.

For normal goods, the income elasticity coefficient is positive, but what determines whether it is "large" or "small"? One of the main factors is whether the good is considered a luxury or a necessity. For example, the income elasticity of demand for automobiles has been estimated to be about 1.2; it is almost 6 for airline travel.[8] High income elasticity is one reason why the airline industry offers huge fare discounts during recessions; when people's incomes fall, they cut back on luxuries like vacation air travel. The income elasticity of demand for restaurant meals (almost 2) is considerably higher than the income elasticity of demand for grocery store food, which is under 1. This is probably because most people consider restaurant meals to be luxuries. Interestingly, the income elasticity of demand for alcoholic beverages is less than 1, an apparent indication that people's consumption of alcoholic beverages

[7]Notice that we have used "demand" instead of "quantity demanded." This is because, by definition, a change in quantity demanded is brought about only by a change in own-price. To actually calculate an income elasticity of demand coefficient, it is necessary to find the particular quantities that are demanded at various income levels, but we assume that the own-price is fixed.

[8]The elasticity estimates in this paragraph are from H. S. Houthakker and Lester D. Taylor, *Consumer Demand in the United States* (Cambridge, Mass.: Harvard University Press, 1970).

remains relatively stable despite relatively large changes in income. This suggests that many drinkers consider alcohol essential, or that there are no good substitutes for alcoholic beverages.

· · · · · · · ·

Cross-Price Elasticity

Cross-price elasticity Measures the relative responsiveness of the demand for one good to the relative price change of another good.

It is also possible to compute cross-price elasticities of demand. **Cross-price elasticity** measures the relative responsiveness of the demand for one good to the relative price change of another good. The formula for cross-price elasticity is:

$$\text{Cross-price elasticity: } E_{x,y} = \frac{\dfrac{\Delta Q_y}{\overline{Q}_y}}{\dfrac{\Delta P_x}{\overline{P}_x}} \qquad [5]$$

As with income elasticity, the formula for cross-price elasticity has no absolute value bars. This is to distinguish between complementary and substitute goods: if the price of a complementary good increases, the demand for the good under consideration will decrease; if the price of a substitute good increases, demand will increase. The numerical value of the cross-price elasticity coefficient determines the degree of complementarity or substitutability between the goods. For example, suppose the price of video rentals rose from $5 to $6. This would probably have an effect on your demand for movie tickets because video rentals and movies are substitute goods. If you decide to go to the movies three times a month instead of only twice, the cross-price elasticity of demand would be:

$$E_{x,y} = \frac{\dfrac{\Delta Q_y}{\overline{Q}_y}}{\dfrac{\Delta P_x}{\overline{P}_x}} = \frac{\dfrac{3-2}{2.5}}{\dfrac{6-5}{5.5}} = 2.2$$

The positive value indicates that video rentals and movie tickets are substitute goods; had the cross-price elasticity coefficient been negative, we would have concluded that video rentals and movie tickets were complementary. The high value of the cross-price elasticity coefficient (2.2 > 1.0) indicates that the two goods are good substitutes for each other; a value close to zero would indicate that the price of videos had little effect on the demand for movie tickets. A cross-price elasticity coefficient of zero would indicate that the two goods were unrelated.

Although we can often guess whether two goods are complements or substitutes, sometimes the relationship is more complex. For example, at first glance you might think that personal computers and personal computer software are complementary goods. However, if the new software increases the capability of your existing computer so much that you decide you do not have to buy a new computer, then the new software is a substitute for a computer.[9]

---

[9]Probably the best example of computer software as a substitute for hardware is a file compression program. Programs like Stacker, DiskDoubler, and StuffIt increase disk capacity by as much as 100 percent and therefore reduce the need to buy a larger hard disk.

Elasticity of Supply

It is also possible to compute the price elasticity of supply. The price **elasticity of supply** measures the relative responsiveness of the quantity supplied to the change in price. The formula for supply elasticity is shown in Equation 6:

$$\text{Elasticity of supply: } E^{\sigma} = \frac{\text{percentage change in quantity supplied}}{\text{percentage change in price}} = \frac{\dfrac{\Delta Q^{s}}{\overline{Q^{s}}}}{\dfrac{\Delta P}{\overline{P}}} \quad [6]$$

Elasticity of supply Measures the relative responsiveness of the quantity supplied to changes in price; calculated as the percentage change in the quantity supplied divided by the percentage change in price.

where Q^{s} is the quantity supplied.

Supply elasticity depends on several factors, but time and technological constraints are probably the most important. As we found out in Chapter 3, the supply curve is vertical in the market period because all production has already taken place. This means that supply is perfectly price inelastic in the market period. In the short run, the supply curve is upward sloping because firms respond to price increases by raising output. When production approaches plant capacity, production costs become exorbitant, and the supply curve becomes very steep. Elasticity is higher in the long run because firms have the ability to build new plants or expand existing facilities.

Figure 8.7 illustrates supply elasticity in the market period and the short run. Quantity is fixed on the vertical market period supply curve so the ΔQ in the numerator of Equation 6 equals zero; this gives an elasticity coefficient of zero as well. The short-run supply curve in panel (b) shows that supply elasticity depends on plant

····FIGURE 8.7 SUPPLY ELASTICITY

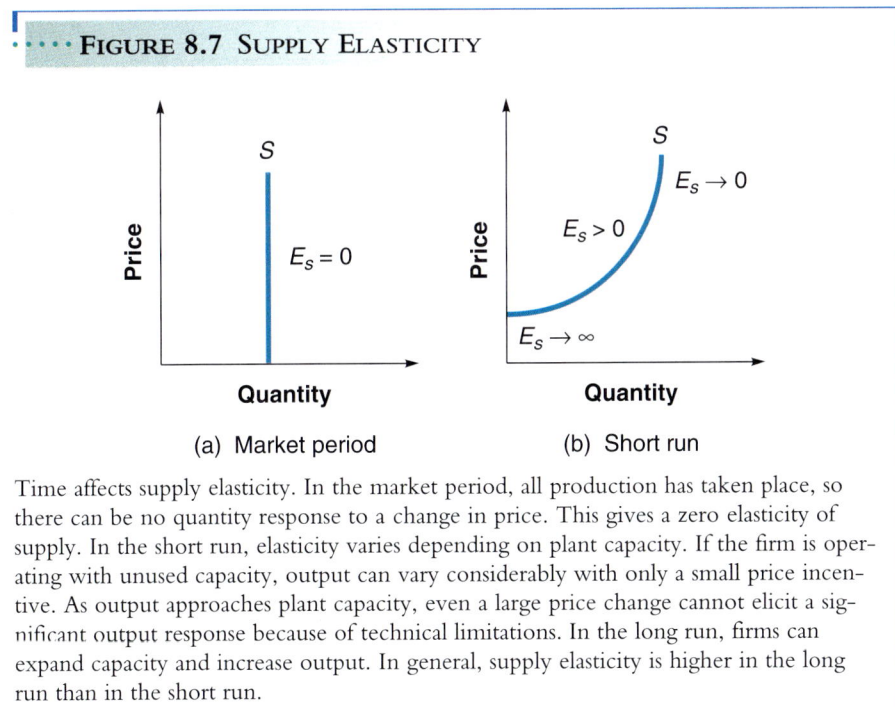

(a) Market period   (b) Short run

Time affects supply elasticity. In the market period, all production has taken place, so there can be no quantity response to a change in price. This gives a zero elasticity of supply. In the short run, elasticity varies depending on plant capacity. If the firm is operating with unused capacity, output can vary considerably with only a small price incentive. As output approaches plant capacity, even a large price change cannot elicit a significant output response because of technical limitations. In the long run, firms can expand capacity and increase output. In general, supply elasticity is higher in the long run than in the short run.

capacity. When output is considerably less than capacity, the supply curve is relatively flat, so supply elasticity is very high. As output expands, the supply curve gets steeper, and the elasticity coefficient declines until the firm is faced with technical constraints on production. At this point, output cannot expand (in the short run) regardless of the change in price, so the elasticity coefficient approaches zero.

What about a diagram of the long run? Remember the distinction between the short run and the long run that was introduced in Chapter 3: at least one factor is fixed in the short run, but everything can change in the long run. This means that the long-run supply curve—and hence the elasticity coefficient for long-run supply— can look like just about anything. It is possible for the long-run supply curve to be flat ($E_s \rightarrow \infty$), vertical ($E_s = 0$), or even downward sloping ($E_s < 0$).

Computing Supply Elasticity Coefficients. The formula in Equation 6 can be used to calculate supply elasticity coefficients, but an easier method is available for linear supply curves: If the supply curve intersects the price axis at a positive price, the elasticity coefficient is greater than 1 everywhere along the supply curve; if it passes through the origin, the coefficient is equal to 1; if it intersects the price axis at a negative price, the elasticity coefficient is less than 1 everywhere along the curve. Figure 8.8 illustrates the relationship between intercept and elasticity and includes the calculations for the elasticities at one point along each supply curve.

Does the analysis in Figure 8.8 mean that all we need to do is find the intercept of the supply curve in order to determine supply elasticity? No. The intercept of the supply curve determines whether the supply elasticity coefficient is less than, equal to, or greater than 1, but the supply elasticity coefficient is not constant everywhere along a linear supply curve. For example, the calculations in the figure show that as price changes from $15 to $18 along S_3, the supply elasticity coefficient is 1.43; however, as price changes from $5 to $15, quantity supplied rises from 0 to 20, and the supply elasticity coefficient is 2.0. The only time an upward-sloping linear supply curve has a constant elasticity is when it passes through the origin. Another problem is that most real-world supply curves—and demand curves, for that matter—are nonlinear. Consequently, we need to calculate the elasticity at the point we are interested in; this is usually the prevailing or expected price. Unfortunately, precisely because supply curves are nonlinear and change over time, it is often difficult to arrive at an unambiguous supply elasticity estimate. Finally, supply curves in the real world rarely intersect the price axis at or below zero, so the elasticity coefficient is usually greater than 1. Firms need a positive price before they are willing to offer anything on the market and then will offer several units of the product or nothing at all.

RECAP   Nonprice Elasticities

Elasticity is used in many contexts in economics. In addition to price elasticity of demand, other important elasticities include the following:

1. Income elasticity is the ratio of the percentage change in demand to the percentage change in income. Income elasticity is positive for normal goods and negative for inferior goods.
2. Cross-price elasticity is the ratio of the percentage change in the demand for

good Y to the percentage change in the price of good X. Cross–price elasticity is positive for substitute goods and negative for complementary goods.

3. The price elasticity of supply is the ratio of the percentage change in the quantity supplied to the percentage change in price. Supply is usually more elastic at low levels of output than at high levels of output.

FIGURE 8.8 CALCULATING SUPPLY ELASTICITY COEFFICIENTS

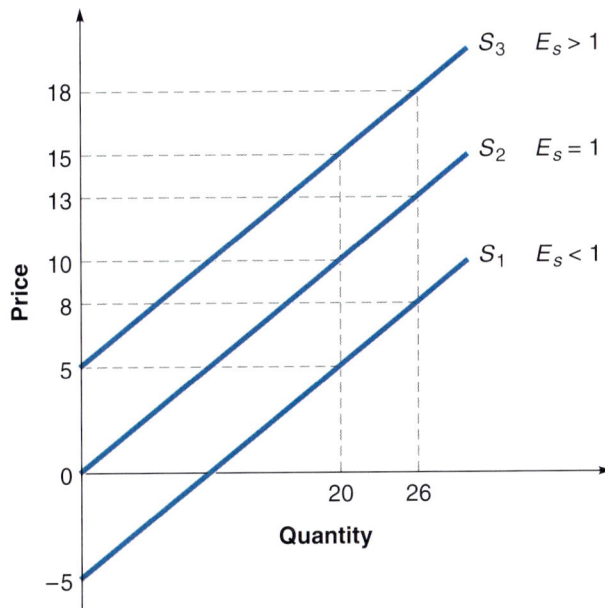

For upward-sloping, linear supply curves, whether the elasticity coefficient is greater than, equal to, or less than 1 is determined by the vertical intercept:

• S_1: If the supply curve intersects the price axis at a negative price, its coefficient is less than 1:

$$E_s = \frac{(26 - 20)/23}{(8 - 5)/6.5} = 0.57$$

This situation is very unlikely because it implies that the firm would supply goods at zero or negative prices.

• S_2: If the supply curve passes through the origin, the elasticity coefficient is equal to 1:

$$E_s = \frac{(26 - 20)/23}{(13 - 10)/11.5} = 1.00$$

• S_3: If the supply curve intersects the price axis at a positive price, the elasticity coefficient is greater than 1:

$$E_s = \frac{(26 - 20)/23}{(18 - 15)/16.5} = 1.43$$

Legal tax incidence Where the responsibility for paying a tax falls by law.

Economic tax incidence Where the burden of paying a tax actually falls; often differs from the legal tax incidence.

Sales tax An indirect business tax levied on final sales; typically a percentage of the value of the sale.

········ APPLICATION: TAX INCIDENCE AND ELASTICITY

Elasticity also helps us understand who really pays a given tax. The **legal incidence** of a tax refers to the person who is responsible for paying the money to the government. If that money actually comes from someone else, then the **economic incidence** of the tax differs from the legal incidence. For example, businesses are required to pay sales taxes to the government, but they try to collect these taxes from customers. This means that the legal incidence of a sales tax is on business, but the economic incidence may rest on the customer. We can often distinguish between legal and economic incidence by looking at the elasticity of demand and supply. This section will show how elasticity can help us understand tax incidence, but we need to recognize at the outset that the study of tax incidence is complex and requires more in-depth analysis. The study of tax incidence is a major topic of courses in public finance.

········

Sales Taxes

Sales taxes, often called excise taxes, come in two basic varieties: unit taxes and *ad valorem* taxes. As we found out in Chapter 4, unit taxes shift the supply curve up by the amount of the tax. An *ad valorem* tax is levied on the value of the goods that are sold. For example, a 6 percent sales tax is an *ad valorem* tax. The two taxes affect the supply and demand diagrams a little differently, but their effect on tax incidence is not substantially different: If the demand curve is more elastic than the supply curve, more of the tax is borne by the seller; if the demand curve is less elastic than the supply curve, more of the tax is borne by the consumer.

Figure 8.9 shows the tax incidence of a unit sales tax. In panel (a), the steep demand curve indicates that demand is relatively inelastic compared to supply. Before the tax, the equilibrium price is $4.00 and 12 units are sold. When a unit sales tax of the amount $T = \$1.00$ is imposed on the sellers, the supply curve shifts vertically by the amount of the tax. This results in movement along the fixed demand curve, and price rises to $4.90 while quantity sold falls to 10 units. In this case, most of the sales tax is "shifted forward" to the consumer so there is a divergence between the legal and economic incidence of the tax. Why does the consumer pay most of the tax? An inelastic demand curve indicates that there are few good substitutes for the product in question so consumers have no easy way to avoid the tax.

In panel (b), the demand curve is more elastic than the supply curve. Before the tax, the equilibrium price and quantity are again $4.00 and 12 units. The $1.00 unit sales tax again shifts the supply curve up by $1.00, but price rises to only $4.40 while quantity sold falls to 6 units. Why does the difference occur? The elastic demand curve indicates that good substitutes are available so consumers switch to a different product. Price rises only a small amount because the quantity sold decreases significantly when demand is elastic relative to supply. When demand is relatively elastic, it is also possible for the sales tax to be "backward shifted" to workers in the form of lower wages—rather than cutting production, the firm might pay lower wages and try to maintain sales.

The story told by Figure 8.9 has many applications in the real world. For example,

····· **FIGURE 8.9** THE TAX INCIDENCE OF UNIT SALES TAXES

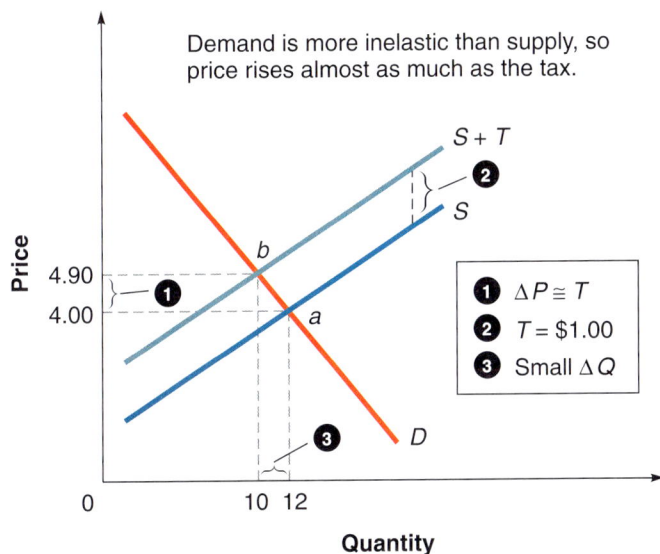

Demand is more inelastic than supply, so price rises almost as much as the tax.

(a)

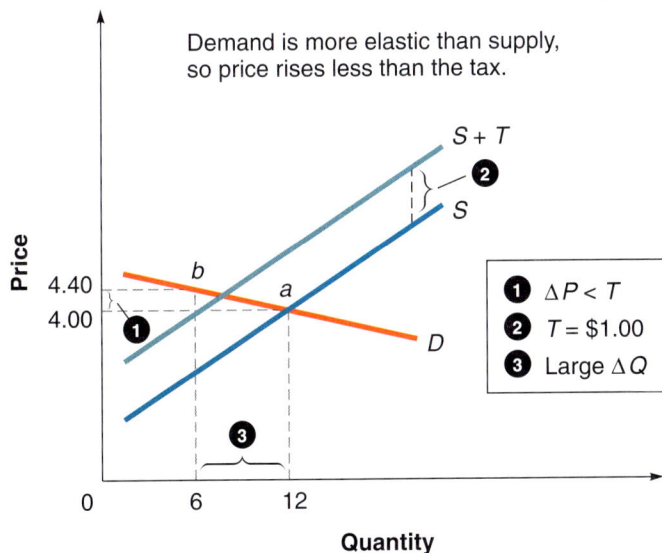

Demand is more elastic than supply, so price rises less than the tax.

(b)

When the demand curve is more inelastic than the supply curve, more of the tax is borne by the buyer than by the seller. This is shown in panel (a) where the change in price is almost as much as the tax ($\Delta P = \$0.90 \approx T = \$1.00$) and the quantity demanded declines only a little. When the demand curve is more elastic than the supply curve, more of the tax is borne by the seller than the buyer. This is shown in panel (b) where the change in price is considerably less than the tax ($\Delta P = \$0.40 < T = \$1.00$) and quantity demanded falls by a large amount.

when the Bush administration imposed an excise tax on pleasure boats, the response was just what we would expect: pleasure boats are a luxury so many people simply chose not to buy pleasure boats. The quantity demanded for pleasure boats fell, and the boating industry saw sales plummet so drastically that the tax was repealed a few years later. In contrast, taxes on "necessities" like cigarettes have long been a good source of revenue for the government. Smokers complain about high cigarette taxes—more than $1 a pack in many states and over $4 in Canada—but because there are no good substitutes for cigarettes, smokers continue to smoke and pay taxes.[10]

• • • • • • • •

Gasoline Taxes

The federal government and most states have unit taxes on gasoline. Gas taxes may seem high, but they are much lower in the United States than in most of the rest of the world. For example, gasoline costs over $4 per gallon in most European nations, even though the price of a barrel of crude oil is the same in Europe as in the United States. The price differential is caused almost entirely by higher taxes.

In the United States, many states designate their gas tax revenues to be spent on highway and road construction. Federal gas tax revenues are used for highway construction, oil and gas exploration, and other uses. At current prices, the demand for gasoline is relatively inelastic, so gasoline taxes do not change behavior very much. Precisely because the demand for gasoline is so inelastic—most estimates are around 0.1—gas taxes make a good source of revenue. Low price elasticity coefficients mean that most gasoline taxes are borne by the consumer. When the Clinton administration enacted a 4.6¢ per gallon tax increase in 1993, gas prices rose about a nickel a gallon— or almost the exact same amount as the tax.

In the short run, people can conserve on gasoline only so much. In the long run, however, gas taxes reduce the demand for oil as people respond to higher prices by purchasing fuel-efficient cars, making better use of mass transit, and the like. This is one reason why many economists and politicians have advocated higher taxes on gas and oil.

• • • • • • • •

"Sin" Taxes

Sin tax A tax on cigarettes, alcohol, and other items people consider "sinful."

Tobacco and alcohol also have high federal and state excise taxes. The revenue from these taxes is frequently earmarked for particular purposes, often education. Tobacco and alcohol are ripe targets for excise taxes because many people consider these products "sinful"; thus, such taxes are often known as **"sin taxes."**

Do sin taxes change behavior? Perhaps. A recent study by the National Bureau of Economic Research estimated that tying beer taxes to the inflation rate since 1951

---

[10]It is perhaps ironic that when the Clinton administration considered raising taxes to help pay for its health care program, the initial thought was to raise taxes even more than they finally proposed. The lower tax plan was suggested because the administration feared that any higher tax would reduce tax revenue—because it would curtail smoking too much!

would have resulted in 1,600 fewer high-school-age children being killed by drunk driving each year between 1982 and 1988.[11] The point is that price signals may be a stronger deterrent to underage drinking than legal sanctions alone. Many investigators have made similar arguments in reference to cigarette taxes: high cigarette taxes may not have much of an effect on current smokers, but they do appear to deter kids from lighting that first cigarette.

·······SUMMARY

Elasticity is important in many areas of economics, so important that many statistics programs used by economists automatically compute elasticity coefficients. Firms need to understand price elasticity in order to compute total revenue; policymakers need to understand elasticity to predict the response to tax changes; and we will find many other uses of the elasticity concept in later chapters. It is important that you have a firm understanding of elasticity and know how to compute elasticity coefficients. The central ideas from this chapter are:

1. The price elasticity of demand is a measure of relative responsiveness of the quantity demanded to a change in own-price. Factors that influence price elasticity of demand are the availability of substitutes, whether the good is a luxury or a necessity, and the price of the good relative to the consumer's income.
2. If the percentage change in price is less than the percentage change in quantity demanded, price elasticity of demand is greater than 1 and is said to be elastic. If the percentage change in price is more than the percentage change in quantity demanded, price elasticity of demand is less than 1 and is said to be inelastic. If the percentage change in price is equal to the percentage change in quantity demanded, price elasticity of demand is equal to 1 and is said to be unitary elastic.
3. All linear demand curves have all three regions of elasticity. Demand is elastic at "high" prices because people will find substitutes. Demand is inelastic at "low" prices because there is little incentive to look for substitutes.
4. Income elasticity is a measure of the percentage change in demand relative to the percentage change in income. Cross-price elasticity measures the responsiveness of demand for one good relative to the change in price of a related good. Supply elasticity is a measure of the relative change in quantity supplied to the change in price. Supply is usually more elastic in the long run than in the short run.
5. Elasticity affects tax incidence. If demand is inelastic relative to supply, the burden of sales taxes falls largely on the consumer. If demand is elastic relative to supply, most of the burden falls on the producer.

[11]Michael Grossman, "Effects of Alcohol Price Policy on Youth," NBER Working Paper 4385, 1993. Cited in "Beer, Taxes, and Death," *The Economist,* September 18, 1993, p. 33. The federal tax on beer in the United States is $2 per liter of pure alcohol; it is $18.20 in Britain.

KEY TERMS AND CONCEPTS

price elasticity of demand (E_p)

elastic demand ($E_p > 1$)

inelastic demand ($E_p < 1$)

unitary elastic demand ($E_p = 1$)

total revenue ($TR = PQ$)

income elasticity (E_y)

cross-price elasticity ($E_{x,y}$)

elasticity of supply (E_s)

legal tax incidence

economic tax incidence

sales tax

"sin" tax

IMPORTANT FORMULAS

Price elasticity of demand: $E_p = \left| \dfrac{\dfrac{\Delta Q}{\overline{Q}}}{\dfrac{\Delta P}{\overline{P}}} \right| = \begin{cases} > 1, \text{ elastic} \\ = 1, \text{ unitary} \\ < 1, \text{ inelastic} \end{cases}$

Total revenue: $TR = \text{price} \times \text{quantity} = PQ$

Income elasticity: $E_y = \dfrac{\dfrac{\Delta Q}{\overline{Q}}}{\dfrac{\Delta Y}{\overline{Y}}} \begin{cases} > 0, \text{ normal goods} \\ < 0, \text{ inferior goods} \end{cases}$

Cross-price elasticity: $E_{x,y} = \dfrac{\dfrac{\Delta Q_y}{\overline{Q}_y}}{\dfrac{\Delta P_x}{\overline{P}_x}} \begin{cases} > 0, \text{ substitutes} \\ = 0, \text{ not related} \\ < 0, \text{ complements} \end{cases}$

Elasticity of supply: $E_s = \dfrac{\dfrac{\Delta Q^s}{\overline{Q}^s}}{\dfrac{\Delta P}{\overline{P}}}$

REVIEW QUESTIONS

1. What are the main determinants of price elasticity? Explain why all downward-sloping linear demand curves have elastic, inelastic, and unitary elastic regions. What is the difference between elasticity and slope?

2. How are total revenue and price elasticity of demand related? Would a firm planning a price increase be better off if the demand for its product was elastic or inelastic? Why?

3. Define and give examples of each of the following: income elasticity, cross-price elasticity, and supply elasticity.

4. Explain how elasticity affects the incidence of sales taxes.

PROBLEMS

1. Examine the following pairs and discuss which component of each has a higher price and income elasticity:
   a. movies / taxicabs   b. tobacco / gasoline   c. electricity / water
   d. telephone service / clothing   e. inter-city buses / doctor's services
2. Refer back to the discussion of the farm problem and elasticity. Using supply and demand graphs, illustrate:
   a. why price supports have often led to quantity restrictions.
   b. how the PIK program affected production and price.
3. The text stated that the long-run supply curve can be flat, vertical, or even downward sloping. Give one example of each situation and explain why the long-run supply curve would be shaped as you describe.
4. Figure 8.8 illustrated three linear supply curves with different intercepts. Do you think supply curves in the real world typically have positive, negative, or zero intercepts. Why?
5. A "gas guzzler" tax was passed in the late 1970s that imposed a tax of several hundred dollars on automobiles that did not meet federal gas mileage guidelines. What do you think were the short-run effects of this tax? The long-run effects?
6. Suppose that the demand schedule is given as:

Q	20	22	24	26	28	30	32	34
P	$70	60	50	40	30	20	10	0

   a. Graph these data and find the vertical intercept. Assume the demand curve is everywhere linear.
   b. Calculate an elasticity coefficient in the inelastic range of the demand curve.
   c. Calculate an elasticity coefficient in the elastic range of the demand curve.
   d. Find the point of unitary elasticity.
   e. Find the point of maximum total revenue.
7. Suppose that a supply curve is given as:

Q	30	28	26	24	22	20
P	$60	50	40	30	20	10

   a. Graph these data.
   b. Calculate an elasticity of supply coefficient.
   c. Suppose that a unit sales tax of $10 is implemented. Show how this affects the elasticity of supply.
8. Draw the initial supply curve from part (a) of Problem 7 and the demand curve from Problem 6 on the same diagram.
   a. Solve for equilibrium price and quantity.
   b. Determine whether most of the tax from part (c) of Problem 7 falls on the consumer or the producer.
   c. Show how the tax affects the producer's total revenue.
9. Calculate each of the following:
   a. Find the cross-price elasticity coefficient and determine whether the two goods are complements or substitutes: $Q_{X1} = 20$, $Q_{X2} = 25$; $P_{Y1} = \$100$, $P_{Y2} = \$120$.

    b. Find the income elasticity coefficient and determine whether the good is a normal or an inferior good: $Q_1 = 50$, $Q_2 = 55$; $Y_1 = \$1,000$, $Y_2 = \$900$.

10. The price of an out-of-state fishing license in Alaska is currently $50, but there is a proposal to increase the price to $100 or even $150. How do you think this increase will affect the quantity of out-of-state fishing licenses demanded? Why?

11. As manager of the Eagle Crest Ski Resort and Lodge, you announce an increase in the price of lift tickets from $30 to $35. The number of skiers falls, but your total revenue increases.

    a. What does this say about the elasticity of demand for lift tickets? Should you raise ticket prices even more?

    b. Your sorority sister, an avid skier and economics major—but in no way affiliated with the ski lodge—says she is actually *happy* that you raised the ticket prices. How could she think such a thing?

12. Charitable giving has an income elasticity coefficient less than 1. Does this mean that people consider charitable giving to be a necessity? Explain.

CHAPTER 9

The Production Process

When Henry Ford first started producing automobiles, most of his employees were skilled crafts people. He could not hire workers to just "tighten bolts" on the assembly line because the parts that went into the early Fords were not standardized. It took skill—and time and money—to shape individual parts so that everything fit together. As you might guess, those early automobiles were expensive. But Ford was an innovator, and when he convinced his engineers to find a way to produce standardized parts, the wildly successful—and inexpensive—Model T was born. Almost a century in development, the mass-production factory system had come of age.

Ford's mass-production factory system was to transform the face of society and the structure of business. He changed the production process from one that employed skilled workers using inexpensive tools and machines to one that combined unskilled workers with expensive and specialized machines. His engineers saw that this was possible; he saw that it would be profitable. As other firms and industries adopted Ford's methods, the U.S. economy boomed and export markets grew.

The mass-production factory system could not last forever, however. Capital was expensive, but it could move across international boundaries. And with much of the work being done by uneducated, unskilled workers, there was no reason for corporations to locate their factories in a high-wage country like the United States. As production moved abroad, both managers and labor realized that only two things could be done: take wage cuts, or change the productive process. The competitiveness of the American economy and our standard of living and that of our children will depend on how this issue is resolved.

The main questions we will explore in this chapter are why and how firms choose their production methods. Answering these questions will require an investigation of one of the most important laws in economics, the law of diminishing returns, and an analysis of the relationship between the different factors of production.

AFTER READING AND STUDYING THIS CHAPTER, YOU SHOULD BE ABLE TO:

• • • State the assumptions and implications of the law of diminishing returns
• • • Explain the relationship between average, total, and marginal product
• • • Define the capital/labor ratio, and explain how firms choose the optimal production technique
• • • Explain the difference between product and process technologies and relate these concepts to industrial evolution in the United States

THE LAW OF DIMINISHING RETURNS AND THE PRODUCTION PROCESS

One of the few laws in economics is the law of diminishing returns. Discovered by the English economist David Ricardo (1772–1823),[1] the law of diminishing returns explains why we cannot grow the world's food supply in a flowerpot. In itself, this idea is not especially profound, but by explaining why we cannot grow the world's food supply in a flowerpot, we can better understand the relationship between factor inputs and production. Firms need to know the relationship between inputs and output in order to decide how many workers or machines to employ and how to produce output at the lowest possible cost.

The Production Function

A production function gives the connection between the factors of production and output. We already know that there are three factors of production—land, labor, and capital.[2] The factors of production are inputs into the production process, so a production function is just a statement of the relationship between these three inputs and output:

$$\text{Production function: } Q = f(L, N, K) \qquad [1]$$

Where:
  Q = total production
  L = land and natural resources
  N = labor
  K = capital (machinery)

[1]Ricardo is the topic of the Our Economic Heritage box on page 216.
[2]As we pointed out in Chapter 1, some economists designate four factors of production—land, labor, capital, and entrepreneurship. Adding a fourth factor to the law of diminishing returns does not change the results.

The law of diminishing returns applies to a short-run production function. As we found out in Chapter 3, the **short run** is a period of time when something is fixed, so a short-run production function implies that at least one factor of production is held fixed. In most of the examples that follow, we will be assuming that two factors of production—capital and land—are fixed. This means that the firm can increase output only by hiring additional workers.

Now we are ready to state the law of diminishing returns. The law of diminishing returns is a statement of how output changes as additional factor inputs are added in the short run:

DEFINITION: The Law of Diminishing Returns: *If at least one input is fixed, output will eventually increase at a diminishing rate as additional units of variable inputs are added.*

The law of diminishing returns is exceedingly important because it applies to *all* production processes. It is also the basis for production and cost theory, the main topics of this and the next chapter.

Does production always exhibit diminishing returns? Not quite—notice the word "eventually" in the statement of the law of diminishing returns. All production processes will *eventually* go through a stage of diminishing returns, but most production processes actually go through three stages, with diminishing returns occurring in only one stage. The three stages of production are:

DEFINITION: The Three Stages of Production: *If at least one factor of production is fixed, as additional units of variable factors are added, output will go through three stages: (1) increasing marginal returns, (2) diminishing marginal returns, and (3) negative marginal returns.*

Before we go through a numerical example to illustrate the three stages of production, we need to make sure we are clear on the definition of the word "marginal." As we found out in Chapter 7, economists use the word "marginal" to indicate the incremental effect of the next unit. In the context of the production function, "marginal returns" refers to the additional output associated with the next unit of input. For example, if a 10th worker is hired and output rises from 1,000 to 1,050 units, the marginal return associated with the 10th worker is 50. The *total* return from all 10 workers is 1,050.

Here's the example. Suppose we have an orchard of orange trees that is ready for harvesting. Unfortunately, the only tools we have are a fixed number of empty bushel baskets. The task is to hire workers to pick the oranges. Table 9.1 shows how output changes as we hire additional workers. Column 1 lists the number of variable inputs (labor in this example) that is added to the production process. The symbol for labor is N (the letter L is reserved for land). Column 2 measures **total product**. Total product is the quantity that is produced, so the symbol for total product will be Q.

The third column is the **marginal product of labor**. Marginal product is the extra output associated with adding one additional unit of the variable input—one more worker in this case. The notation for marginal product of labor is MP_N. The formula for marginal product of labor is:

Short run The period of time in which at least one input is fixed.

Total product The entire output from a production process.

Marginal product of labor The output associated with adding one additional worker.

···· **TABLE 9.1 THE LAW OF DIMINISHING RETURNS**

N	Q	MP_N	AP_N
0	0		—
		→ 40	
1	40		40.00
		→ 50	
2	90		45.00
		→ 60	
3	150		50.00
		→ 50	
4	200		50.00
		→ 40	
5	240		48.00
		→ 30	
6	270		45.00
		→ 20	
7	290		41.43
		→ 10	
8	300		37.50
		→ 0	
9	300		33.33
		→ −10	
10	290		29.00
		→ −20	
11	270		24.55

Definitions and Formulas:

N = variable labor inputs
MP_N = marginal product = $\dfrac{\Delta Q}{\Delta N}$

Q = total product
AP_N = average product = $\dfrac{Q}{N}$

$$\text{Marginal product of labor} = MP_N = \frac{\Delta Q}{\Delta N} \qquad [2]$$

where, as always, the Greek letter delta (Δ) stands for "change in." Notice that the entries in the marginal product column are aligned between the entries in the first two columns. This is to indicate that marginal product represents the output associated with the change in labor inputs. In this case, one worker is added in each line of the table, so the marginal product is just the change in total product. For example, when the fifth worker is added, production rises from 200 to 240. This means that the marginal product of the fifth worker is:

$$MP_5 = \frac{\Delta Q}{\Delta N} = \frac{Q_5 - Q_4}{1} = \frac{240 - 200}{1} = 40$$

Average product Total product divided by the number of units of a variable input.

The fourth column shows the **average product** per worker. Average product is calculated by dividing total product by the number of variable inputs, labor in this case:

$$\text{Average product of labor} = AP_N = \frac{Q}{N} \qquad [3]$$

For example, when there are 5 workers, output is 240. The average product of 5 workers then is:

$$AP_5 = \frac{240}{5} = 48$$

A key to understanding the production function and the law of diminishing returns is the relationship between inputs and total, average, and marginal product. Line 1 of the table reveals the obvious: if we do not hire anyone, the oranges go to waste and there is no production. The second line says that if we hire one worker, total output will be 40 bushels of oranges per day. The first worker raised total product from 0 to 40, so the marginal product of the first worker is 40:

$$MP_1 = \frac{\Delta Q}{\Delta N} = \frac{40 - 0}{1 - 0} = 40$$

The average product of the first worker is also 40:

$$AP_1 = \frac{Q}{N} = \frac{40}{1} = 40$$

It gets more interesting as we hire additional workers.

Line 3 shows what happens if we add a second worker. Total product increases from 40 to 90 bushels of oranges per day. This gives a marginal product of 50 bushels and an average product of 45:

$$MP_2 = \frac{\Delta Q}{\Delta N} = \frac{90 - 40}{1 - 0} = 50 \qquad AP_2 = \frac{Q}{N} = \frac{90}{2} = 45$$

Why did both the AP and the MP rise when the second worker was added? The two workers combined their skills and *specialized* in production. Worker specialization is the process of dividing jobs into simple components so that workers can do single tasks more efficiently. In this case, specialization was accomplished when Worker 2 climbed on the back of Worker 1 to shake the oranges concentrated at the top of the tree.

Specialization continues with the addition of the third worker. Total product rises from 90 to 150, so marginal product increases to 60 bushels per day and average product rises to 50 bushels. (Maybe Worker 3 scurried about gathering the oranges that rolled away from the trees being shaken by Worker 2.) When marginal product increases as additional variable inputs are added, the production process is in Stage I, the stage of **increasing marginal returns**. Firms never operate in Stage I: Why limit inputs if the next worker will always be more productive than the previous worker?

As Workers 4 through 8 are added, total product continues to increase but at a diminishing rate—50, 40, 30, and so on. Why? At some point it is no longer possible to achieve gains from specialization—how many workers can climb on your back?—but for a while at least, adding workers will increase output, though by smaller and smaller amounts. This is Stage II of the production process, the stage of **diminishing**

Increasing marginal returns First stage of the production function; if the capital stock is fixed, adding additional workers will result in more output per worker because of specialization. Firms never operate in this stage.

Diminishing marginal returns Production stage when additional inputs cause output to increase, but at a diminishing rate.

Negative marginal returns Production stage when additional inputs cause output to decline.

marginal returns. Stage II is characterized by positive but declining marginal product. Firms typically operate in Stage II of the production function.[3]

Marginal product becomes negative when more than nine workers are added, so total product begins to fall. What causes this to happen? There are too many workers for the size of the orchard; apparently, the workers get in each other's way and hinder production. This is Stage III of the production process, the stage of **negative marginal returns**. Stage III is rarely if ever observed in the real world because it never pays to operate in this stage of production—why hire more workers if output is going to fall?—but some traditional societies may occasionally reach this point.[4]

· · · · · · · ·

Graphical Analysis

The numbers from Table 9.1 are shown graphically in Figure 9.1. The upper curve in the graph is the production function or the total product curve. As labor inputs rise from 0 to 2.5, it becomes steeper; this is Stage I of the production function. (The 2.5 on the labor input axis indicates that we are plotting marginal product as the number of workers rises from 2 to 3.) Notice that the marginal product curve is upward sloping in Stage I. When the marginal product curve begins to slope downward, the total product curve becomes less steep, and production enters Stage II. Stage II continues as long as total product rises and marginal product is positive. This occurs when between 2.5 and 8.5 workers are hired. If more than 8.5 workers are employed, marginal product becomes negative and total product begins to fall. This is Stage III of the production function.

· · · · · · · ·

The Relationship between Total, Average, and Marginal Product

Figure 9.1 also plots the average and marginal product curves. Marginal product represents the output of the next input. This means that as long as the marginal product is positive, total output will be increasing. This occurs in Stages I and II of the production function. If marginal product is negative, total product will be decreasing. This occurs in Stage III of the production function. This relationship can be summarized by writing:

$$
\begin{aligned}
&\text{If } MP > 0 \Rightarrow Q \uparrow \\
&\text{If } MP < 0 \Rightarrow Q \downarrow
\end{aligned}
\qquad [4]
$$

There is also an important relationship between marginal product and average product—marginals "pull" averages. For example, suppose that your cumulative grade point average after two years in college is 3.0. This is the average product of your study effort. The grade point average you get next semester will be your mar-

---

[3]Actually, firms will not operate at the very beginning of Stage II when the marginal product is greater than average product because hiring an additional worker would increase the average output per worker. This is why many books designate Stage I as the region with increasing average product and Stage II as the region with decreasing average product but positive marginal product.

[4]For example, in some agrarian societies, a family plot of land is worked ever more intensely as more and more children are born.

·····FIGURE 9.1 THE THREE STAGES OF PRODUCTION

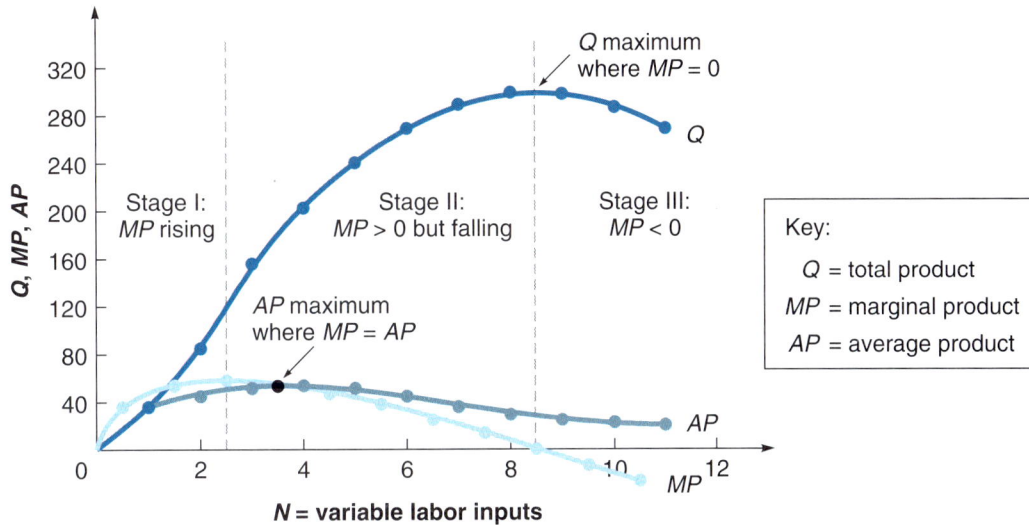

As a variable factor (labor) is added to a fixed factor (capital and land in this example), output will typically go through three stages: (1) increasing marginal returns, (2) diminishing marginal returns, and (3) negative marginal returns. These three stages are determined by the shape of the marginal product curve. When the marginal product curve is rising, production is in Stage I, and the total product curve is getting steeper. When the marginal product curve is positive but declining, total product is increasing but at a diminishing rate, so the total product curve is upward sloping but getting less steep. This is Stage II of the production function. When marginal product becomes negative, additional inputs cause output to decline, so the total product curve begins to slope downward. This is Stage III of the production function.

ginal product. If you get a 3.5 next semester, your cumulative grade point average will rise above 3.0. But if you get a 2.5 next semester, your cumulative grade point average will fall below 3.0. The same thing will happen if the marginal product of labor is greater than the average product of labor—the average product of labor will rise. On the other hand, if the output of the next worker (marginal product) is less than the output of the average worker (average product), then the average will fall. This explains why the marginal product curve intersects the average product curve at the maximum of the average product curve. When the marginal product curve is above the average product curve, the average product is rising; when the marginal product curve is below the average product curve, the average product is falling.

$$\text{If } MP > AP \Rightarrow AP \uparrow$$
$$\text{If } MP < AP \Rightarrow AP \downarrow \qquad [5]$$
$$MP = AP \text{ at maximum } AP$$

Equation 5 gives a hint of the most desirable position for society to operate on the production function —at the point of maximum average product. At this point, the output per unit of input is maximized, so we are getting the most possible out of our scarce resources. Is this also the position where the firm should operate? Perhaps, but probably not. The firm is interested in maximizing profits—the difference between revenues and costs—but Equation 5 says nothing about either revenues or costs, only physical output. To determine revenue, we need to know the selling price of output, and to determine costs, we need to know the wage rate, price of capital, and so on. We will bring that information into the analysis in the next few chapters.

· · · · · · · ·

Shifting the Production Function

If either of the fixed factors of production (capital or land in this example) increases, or if there is an improvement in technology, worker productivity will increase, and the entire production function will shift upward. For example, if the orchard owner bought an additional acre of land, workers would have more trees to harvest and would be more productive because they would pick more oranges. Or if the owner bought a ladder—a capital good—for each worker, they would not have to climb on each other's backs, and productivity would again increase. The new ladders would also represent an increase in technology because ladder technology was not previously used in the orchard. These events—more land, more capital, or technological advance—will shift the production function upward and increase the output per

· · · · ·**FIGURE 9.2 SHIFTING THE PRODUCTION FUNCTION**

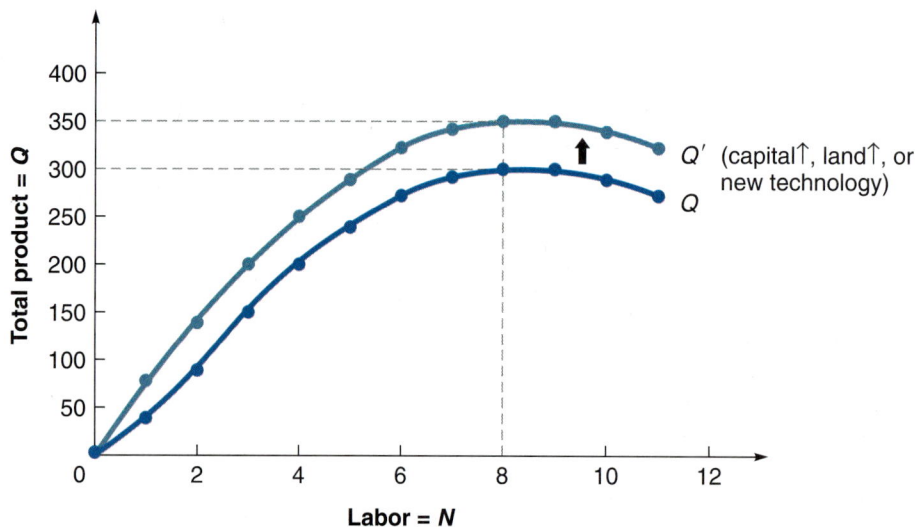

An increase in the stock of capital or land or a technological advance will increase the output per worker and cause the entire production function to shift upward from Q to Q'. In this case, the production function has shifted so that eight workers can produce 350 instead of 300 units of output. A decrease in capital, land, or technology would shift the production function downward.

worker. This is shown in Figure 9.2. A decrease in any of these factors would shift the production function downward and reduce the output per worker. This would be represented as a shift from Q' to Q in the figure.

. . . .

The Long Run: Allowing All Factors to Vary

In the **long run**, the firm can vary all inputs—the amount of capital and land as well as the number of workers—and the law of diminishing returns no longer applies. Economists use the term *returns to scale* or **economies of scale** to refer to long-run changes that occur when the firm proportionally increases all factors of production. Three situations can arise if all factors are increased: (1) constant returns to scale, (2) decreasing returns to scale, and (3) increasing returns to scale:

- **Constant returns to scale** may be the most common situation. This situation occurs if output increases by the same proportion as all inputs. For example, if doubling all inputs causes output to double, the production process exhibits constant returns to scale. A firm that builds an identical factory next door to an existing factory might experience constant returns to scale.

- **Decreasing returns to scale** occur when output increases by less than inputs—doubling input causes output to increase by only 80 percent, for example. Decreasing returns to scale might occur if expansion results in the firm becoming so large that management is inefficient. Concern over decreasing returns to scale may be one explanation for the "downsizing" that has characterized American business in the past decade. For example, some people believe that the Big Three U.S. automobile companies are too large—that they have expanded to the point where returns to scale begin to decrease. In deciding to make its Saturn automobile plant in Tennessee virtually autonomous from Detroit headquarters, General Motors may have recognized the disadvantages of size. Minnesota Mining and Manufacturing Co. (3M) recognized the disadvantages of large size in the 1970s: the company now has almost 90,000 employees, but its average production facility employs under 300 workers. This permits management flexibility and may be responsible for 3M's continuing innovation and successful development of new products.[5]

- **Increasing returns to scale** exist when output increases proportionally more than inputs; that is, doubling inputs causes output to increase threefold. How can this occur? One possibility would be for new workers to create *synergy* with existing workers. Synergy is defined as the interaction between two or more forces so that their combined effect is greater than the sum of their individual effects. For example, suppose that a firm hires new workers for the product design division. If the new workers come from different backgrounds or schools of thought, their ideas could provide new insights to help the existing workers come up with new products or novel ways of doing things. As a result, output would expand by a higher proportion than inputs—increasing return to scale.

Long run The period of time in which all inputs can vary. None are fixed.

Economies of scale Long-run changes in output that occur when the firm proportionally increases all factors of production.

Constant returns to scale When output increases by the same proportion as all inputs.

Decreasing returns to scale When output increases proportionately less than inputs.

Increasing returns to scale When output increases proportionately more than inputs.

---

[5]Some of the advantages of small production facilities were explored in a fascinating collection of essays by E. F. Schumacher entitled *Small Is Beautiful: Economics as if People Mattered* (New York: Harper and Row, 1973). These essays explore, among other things, the link between economics and ecology, the possibility of Buddhist economics, and unemployment problems in less-developed nations.

> **RECAP**   Production and the Law of Diminishing Returns
>
> 1. A production function is a statement of the relationship between inputs and output. At least one factor of production is fixed on a short-run production function.
> 2. Most production processes go through three stages: increasing marginal returns, diminishing marginal returns, and negative marginal returns.
> 3. The law of diminishing returns states that if at least one factor of production is fixed, marginal returns must eventually diminish.
> 4. When marginal product is greater than average product, average product will rise; when marginal product is less than average product, average product will fall; marginal product equals average product at the maximum of average product.
> 5. All factors can vary in the long run. An increase in a fixed factor of production will shift the entire production function upward. Production processes can exhibit constant, increasing, or decreasing returns to scale.

CHOOSING THE PRODUCTION TECHNIQUE: FACTOR SUBSTITUTION

Capital/labor ratio The ratio of the amount of machinery used in a production process to the number of workers.

Our discussion of the production function and the law of diminishing returns sidestepped an important issue: As more workers are added to a fixed stock of capital, the number of machines per worker, or the **capital/labor ratio** changes. In other words, each worker has less machinery to work with as more workers are added to the production process. When alternative capital/labor ratios can be used, managers must choose the optimal capital/labor ratio to operate efficiently. Choosing the optimal production technique is a long-run decision because the firm must find the right amount of fixed and variable inputs to employ.[6] In contrast, in the short run, the firm must only decide the right amounts of variable inputs to employ because the quantity of fixed inputs has already been decided.

Choice of Technique

Suppose the manager of Max's Salmon Cannery must decide how best to produce canned salmon. The first step is to ask the marketing division to do a study on the demand for salmon. Let's suppose the marketing team reports back that there is demand for 1,000 cases of canned salmon per week. This becomes the production target. Next, the manager commissions an engineer to find alternative production techniques—combinations of labor and capital—that can be used to produce canned salmon. This information is then turned over to the economist to determine which production technique is least costly. Finding the production technique that minimizes costs is important because lower costs increase the firm's profits.

[6]Appendix 9A discusses this topic in a more precise and rigorous manner.

•••••**TABLE 9.2** CHOICE OF TECHNIQUE: PRODUCTION = 1,000

(1)	(2) Q_N	(3) Q_K	(4) TC	(5) P_N / P_K	(6) MP_N / MP_K
A	1	7	$750	0.5	
					→ 3.00
B	2	4	500	0.5	
					→ 1.00
C	4	2	*400*	0.5	
					→ 0.33
D	7	1	450	0.5	

Key: Q_N = number of workers; Q_K = number of machines; TC = total cost, P_N = price
of labor = $50; P_K = price of capital = $100; MP_N = marginal product of labor;
MP_K = marginal product of capital.

Table 9.2 gives the information needed to provide an approximate solution to the problem of choosing the optimal production technique. Columns 2 and 3 give the various quantities of labor and capital necessary to produce the desired 1,000 cases of canned salmon. The numbers in these columns illustrate the **diminishing marginal rate of factor substitution**. As more of one factor (labor) is used, less of the other factor (capital) is necessary to maintain the production level. Notice that the tradeoff between labor and capital is not constant: to produce the same amount of output at factor combinations A and B, only 1 additional worker must be added to offset the lost output from 3 machines. In contrast, to produce the same output at combinations B and C, 2 additional workers are needed to offset the lost output from just 2 machines. Changing capital/labor tradeoffs are the result of diminishing returns: As more workers are hired, the marginal product of labor diminishes; further, as fewer machines are used, the marginal product of capital increases. Therefore, a larger number of workers is needed to replace the output from machines as more workers are hired and fewer machines are used.

Column 4 gives the total cost (TC) of production assuming that labor (N) and capital (K) are the only factors of production and factor prices are fixed at $P_N = \$50$ and $P_K = \$100$. Which production technique should be chosen? The best choice is combination C because this production technique represents the least-cost combination consistent with the production goal.

Diminishing marginal rate of factor substitution Combining additional units of one factor with a fixed amount of another factor causes the marginal product of the first factor to decline; therefore, to maintain fixed output, fewer units of the second factor are substituted for the first factor.

••••••••

Optimal Production Technique

In the real world, the choice of techniques can sometimes be limited much as we did with the four choices in Table 9.2; in that case, finding the *optimal production technique* may not be too complicated. But when there are many possible techniques, the optimal solution can be found using a decision rule quite similar to the one we used for consumer equilibrium in Chapter 7. In that chapter, we found that the consumer was maximizing utility for a given budget constraint when the relative price ratio was equal to the ratio of marginal utilities:

$$\text{Consumer equilibrium: } \frac{P_a}{P_b} = \frac{MU_a}{MU_b} \qquad [6]$$

We are about to discover that the firm is in equilibrium when the relative factor price ratio is equal to the marginal product ratio for each of the factors of production. Demonstration of this rule is left to the appendix to this chapter, but we can get an idea of it from looking at Columns 5 and 6 of Table 9.2.

Column 5 gives the relative factor price ratio, $P_N/P_K = \$50/\$100 = 0.5$. It is constant because both factor prices are assumed to be fixed. Column 6 gives the ratio of the marginal product of labor to the marginal product of capital. To calculate these ratios, note what happens when moving from factor combination A to factor combination B: one unit of labor was added and three units of capital were given up. Combinations A and B produce the same amount of output, so one unit of labor must be three times as productive as one unit of capital. Thus, the ratio of marginal products is 3/1 or 3. Likewise, between combinations B and C, two units of labor are added and two units of capital are removed, so the marginal product ratio is 1/1 or 1 because each new machine produces exactly as much output as each displaced worker.

We cannot calculate the marginal product ratio at point C precisely because we only know the marginal product between points as input combinations change, not the marginal product of a specific input. However, look what happens as the production technique moves between points B and D: The marginal product ratio falls from 1.0 to 0.33. This means that the marginal product ratio must equal 0.5 somewhere between points B and D—and 0.5 just happens to be the relative price ratio. This should be enough information to enable you to use your economic intuition to guess the optimal production technique decision rule:

Optimal Production Technique: *The optimal production technique requires that the relative factor price ratio be equal to the ratio of the marginal products. Alternatively, the ratio of marginal product to factor price must be equal for all factors of production.*

This can be written as:

$$\frac{P_N}{P_K} = \frac{MP_N}{MP_K} \qquad [7]$$

In words, Equation 7 means that if Factor N costs twice as much as Factor K, the marginal product of Factor N must be at least twice as high as the marginal product of Factor K, or it does not pay to buy the last few units of Factor N.

The alternative expression for the optimal production technique involving all three factors of production is:

$$\frac{MP_K}{P_K} = \frac{MP_N}{P_N} = \frac{MP_L}{P_L} \qquad [8]$$

Equation 8 means that the extra output per dollar spent on each factor must be equal. If not, the firm should buy additional units of the factor that is producing more output per dollar spent. For example, if:

$$\frac{MP_N}{P_N} > \frac{MP_K}{P_K}$$

then the firm should hire more workers and/or employ fewer machines. This will lower the marginal product of labor and/or raise the marginal product of capital—and move the expression closer to equality.

- - - - - - - - -

Changing Input Prices

A quick review of the discussion surrounding Equations 4 and 5 in Chapter 7 should be enough to convince you that the decision rule for choosing the optimal production technique is similar to the one used to find consumer equilibrium. Just as price changes affect consumption choices, factor prices affect choices in production technique. An increase in the price of labor will cause the firm to substitute capital for labor. For example, one result of paying higher wages to migrant farm workers was the displacement of some workers by mechanical harvesters. Likewise, Labor Secretary Robert Reich's 1993 call for an increase in the minimum wage was based only partially on the desire to raise the hourly wages of low-income workers. He also thought that higher wages would act as an incentive for firms to train workers and acquire productivity-enhancing capital. The reverse happens when the price of capital rises relative to the price of labor. For example, the high interest rates that prevailed in the United States during much of the 1980s meant that the cost of financing new capital acquisitions was prohibitively high. As a result, much of that decade was characterized by large increases in employment, but little capital formation.

RECAP   **Optimal Production Technique**

1. The optimal production technique requires that the relative factor price ratios be equal to the marginal product ratios. This is equivalent to saying that the marginal product/factor price ratios must be equal for all factors of production.
2. Changes in factor prices result in changes in the optimal production technique. For example, if the price of labor rises, firms will substitute capital or land for labor; if the price of capital rises, firms will substitute labor or land for capital.

DYNAMIC ELEMENTS IN THE PRODUCTION PROCESS

We have just been through the economist's rather technical discussion of the production process. Although this is an important prelude to our analysis of costs in the next chapter, it may elicit a "So what?" from the business executive. Knowing that all production processes obey the law of diminishing returns is of little solace if you have just lost your market to foreign imports. Business executives know they cannot stand still. The techniques and products that are successful today may not be

OUR ECONOMIC HERITAGE

DAVID RICARDO: THE FIRST "MODERN" ECONOMIST

It would be hard to find an economist who has had more influence on modern economics than the Englishman David Ricardo (1772–1823). Not only did Ricardo discover the laws of comparative advantage and diminishing returns, but he adopted the same kind of abstract, deductive methods used by most economists today. Ricardo received only a meager formal education and was not exposed to economics until he read *The Wealth of Nations* at age 27. Economics became his passion almost immediately, but he did not publish anything in economics for a decade. Ricardo's most important work, *Principles of Political Economy and Taxation* (1821), is still considered a path-breaking contribution to theoretical economics.

Ricardo was the third child in a Jewish family of 17 children. At the age of 14, he began to work in the stock market with his father. He quickly made a reputation for himself, but when he married a Quaker at age 21, his father banished him from the family business. Fortunately, Ricardo's reputation was enough for him to obtain financial backing from a bank to set up his own stock brokerage house. His success continued and he soon became quite wealthy. He left a huge estate when he died.

Ricardo saw the economy as a logical system. He reduced the economy to a few important variables and de-duced conclusions from simplifying assumptions. He was more theoretical than most of his contemporaries and forerunners. Ricardo's abstract view of the economy and economic theorizing may be his most important legacy to modern economics. By the time he was elected to the House of Commons in 1819, Ricardo was a leading authority on economics. In most matters he sided with reformers—he favored the secret ballot, the extension of voting rights, and free and open discussion of religious matters. Some of his policy proposals—like his plan to tax capital to pay off the national debt—were unpopular, but his views were always considered important and worthy of discussion.

Perhaps his most controversial proposal was his plan to repeal the "Corn Laws," which limited the importation of grain ("corn") into England. The Corn Laws were an obvious boon to farmers because they kept food prices high. Ricardo, however, felt that wages would automatically move to the "subsistence level," so high food prices meant high wages. High wages, said Ricardo, would reduce business profits and make it difficult for the business sector to expand. Ricardo's views on the Corn Laws were challenged most vehemently by Robert Malthus who felt that cheap food would result in a population explosion. In the end, Ricardo's position won out and the Corn Laws were repealed.[1] The influx of cheap food imports from the Continent hurt the English agricultural sector, but also freed workers for the factories in the cities. These workers formed the labor pool that helped fuel England's shift from an agricultural economy to an industrial economy.

David Ricardo. A savvy speculator and political reformist with a passion for abstract economic theory.

[1] Recent scholarship in the history of economic thought suggests that Malthus changed his views on the Corn Laws and came out in favor of free trade in 1824. See Samuel Hollander, "Malthus's Abandonment of Agricultural Protectionism: A Discovery in the History of Economic Thought," *American Economic Review* 82 (June 1992): 650–59.

successful tomorrow.[7] And as production changes, managers must be constantly aware of the concepts we have just developed—the possibility of decreasing returns to scale, minimizing costs for a given output target, and so on.

. . . .

Product and Process Technologies

The **mass-production** factory system that Henry Ford set up to produce the Model T used relatively expensive capital and relatively inexpensive, unskilled labor. The capital used in most mass-production processes is task-specific; that is, it can be used for only one kind of production. The advantage of using task-specific capital is that it is possible to employ relatively unskilled workers because workers must be trained to use the machinery only once. As Ford was to find out, mass production can be an efficient production technique if the market is large enough to pay for the long production runs necessitated by the large capital expenditures.

Mass production Production in quantity using standardized parts, task-specific capital, and unskilled labor.

The Model T represented an innovation in both **product** and **process technology**. The product technology was the car itself—a hugely successful product. Process technology is the method of producing products. The process technology of the Model T was the mass-production factory system. The Model T dominated the automobile market for several years, but not forever. As soon as competitors copied the Model T and introduced mass-production factories of their own, Ford's share of the automobile market began to shrink. Ford responded with another product innovation—a new automobile model. This set the pattern for competition in the automobile industry for the next 50 years: consumers expected and companies offered new cars and new features almost every year.

Product technology Technology for creating new products.

Process technology Technology necessary for producing goods and services efficiently.

The Model T story is instructive because it can help explain the evolution of U.S. business in the last half of the twentieth century. The early implementation of mass-production techniques was not the only reason the United States vaulted to the lead in the world economic race by the middle of the twentieth century. Three other advantages also contributed: (1) abundant and inexpensive natural resources, (2) a highly educated workforce, the product of a longer history of compulsory high school than any other industrialized nation, and (3) the good fortune to survive World War II without a bomb having been dropped on its manufacturing base. As a result, the United States had a competitive advantage over most other nations in the world until the 1960s or 1970s.[8]

. . . .

Import Competition

Unfortunately, this competitive advantage could not last forever. The successful competitive strategy that the automobile industry used—the introduction of new product technologies to keep ahead of the competition—became a model for corporate

---

[7]This section is based on Chapter 2 of Lester Thurow, *Head to Head* (New York: William Morrow and Company: 1992).

[8]You can find more about the evolution of the mass-production factory system in Michael J. Piore and Charles F. Sabel, *The Second Industrial Divide* (New York: Basic Books, 1984) and Robert Reich, *The Work of Nations* (New York: Knopf, 1991). Neither book is without its critics, but both address important issues and make you think.

behavior in much of the economy. Research and development was directed toward the development of new products. Unfortunately, the profits from new product technology can last only temporarily in today's world because information and technology can move across international boundaries with astonishing speed. Our trading partners adopted the competitive strategy of copying products developed in the United States, but producing them at lower cost. Copying goods produced by mass-production factory methods was especially easy because only unskilled workers were needed. All that was necessary was to build factories similar to those in the United States and staff them with lower-paid workers. About the only way U.S. products can compete with these imports—in the absence of tariffs or other import restrictions—is by lowering U.S. wages, not an enticing thought.

The competitive strategy adopted by Japanese and German firms was somewhat different and has significant implications for the U.S. economy in the years ahead. The Japanese and Germans devoted most of their R&D effort to process technology and more efficient ways of producing products. Instead of building factories similar to those in the United States and staffing them with low-wage workers, they found ways to produce products using high-skill—and thus high-wage—workers. The success of Japanese process technology has been nothing short of amazing—at least until Japan fell into a recession in the early 1990s. For example, the technology for the video camera and recorder was invented in the United States, but the Japanese were able to develop a low-cost production process. There has never been a commercial VCR manufactured in the United States. Almost the same thing can be said about fax machines; some fax machines are produced in the United States, but the market is overwhelmingly dominated by the Japanese. The United States is not the only country with this problem: much of the technology for compact discs was invented by the Dutch, but the industry is, for all intents and purposes, a Japanese industry today.

. . . .

Policy Implications

That U.S. producers have lost markets to foreign producers is not necessarily bad. There is an ebb and flow to economic relations, and it is possible that we will regain these markets. For example, the United States appears to be regaining some of the automobile market lost to the Japanese in the 1970s and 1980s. But some analysts are not so sure whether we will or even want to regain lost markets. The mass-production techniques that the United States used so successfully early in the century cannot be the model for the future. Capital will always move to the nation with the lowest labor costs. If we want to compete in these industries, it will be necessary to reduce labor costs to the level of the competitors in these industries—or develop new process technologies.[9]

Many economists argue that the best way to compete against low labor costs is to develop process technologies that are not based on the mass production of standardized products. Instead of producing long runs of standardized products, firms should

---

[9]An alternative would be to reach international cooperation on the protection of intellectual property rights so that foreign firms could not copy domestic products. Protection of intellectual property rights was one of the key issues of the 1993 Uruguay Round of GATT (General Agreement on Tariffs and Trade) negotiations. GATT is discussed in Chapter 37.

be flexible enough to do short runs of specialized products. This requires a different labor/capital mix. Instead of using task-specific capital and low-skill labor, production must be organized to employ general capital and skilled labor. This is already being done in the computer industry. Computer models are often produced for less than six months and then replaced by more powerful—and usually less costly—new models.

For this shift to be effective, the labor force must be upgraded. Skilled professional workers in the United States—perhaps the highest paid 20 percent of the work-force—are as good as any in the world. But the next 50 percent of the workforce—the middle class, blue-collar workers—have fewer skills than the same workers in Japan, Germany, and many other industrial countries. These are the workers who must operate the assembly lines of the future. They must be able to read blueprints and conduct statistical tests to assure that new products and processes meet exacting technical standards. Unfortunately, too many U.S. workers are deficient in basic literacy and mathematics skills.[10] Finally, upgrading the workers on the assembly line may not be sufficient. It will also be necessary to upgrade management styles: "smart" managers will be needed to manage "smart" blue-collar workers. Until these deficiencies are corrected, we are liable to see continuing downward pressure on wages.[11]

Does this mean that managers can ignore the kind of technical analysis in the first part of this chapter? Not at all. Production processes and technologies are dynamic, but at any point in time, the successful firm will adopt techniques that correspond to the criteria developed earlier: Combine the factors of production such that the marginal product/factor price ratios are equal for all factors of production. The successful firm must also use production techniques that are flexible enough to allow quick responses to the ever changing competitive environment.

RECAP   Dynamic Elements in Production

The mass-production factory system relies upon expensive, single-purpose capital and unskilled labor. The United States lost its competitive advantage in many of these industries as firms located abroad in search of low wages. For the United States to remain competitive in these industries, there will either have to be wage reductions or new process technologies that employ high-skill, high-wage workers. This will require upgrading the labor force and finding new approaches to management.

[10]The deficiency in mathematics ability is especially acute. Standardized test scores in math are *twice* as high in Japan and Europe as in the United States. Some economists believe that math ability is a critical factor in explaining productivity growth. For example, see Louis Ferleger and Jay R. Mandle, "Co-Signs and Deviations of America's Two-Score Decline: Poor Math Skills, Poor Productivity Growth," *Challenge* (May–June 1992): 48–50.

[11]In his *Scale and Scope: The Dynamics of Industrial Capitalism* (Cambridge, Mass.: Harvard University Press, 1990), Alfred Chandler presents the thesis that firms and markets evolve together to shape industrial outcomes. Chandler contends that the strategic and organizational choices of managers are critical in this evolution and that these choices are not necessarily dictated by markets and technology. This is consistent with the view that managers must be "smart," because it suggests that different managerial decisions will result in alternative industrial evolutions. An extensive review of Chandler's book is found in David J. Teece, "The Dynamics of Industrial Capitalism: Perspectives on Alfred Chandler's *Scale and Scope*," *Journal of Economic Literature* 31 (March 1993): 199–225.

·······SUMMARY

This chapter has presented the facts about the production process—the relationship between inputs and outputs, the law of diminishing returns, and how firms choose the optimal production technique. We have also examined some of the complexities involved in the dynamics of production—how firms must constantly adjust their products and processes in response to competitive pressures. The next chapter will use this information as a basis for the analysis of costs and supply.

The main points to remember from this chapter are:

1. The law of diminishing returns states that as more units of a variable factor are added to a fixed factor, output will go through three stages: increasing marginal returns, diminishing marginal returns, and negative marginal returns.
2. Total product is at its maximum where marginal product is zero; average product is at its maximum at the quantity where it equals marginal product. When marginal product is greater than zero, total product is rising; when marginal product is less than zero, total product is falling. When marginal product is greater than average product, average product is rising; when marginal product is less than average product, average product is falling.
3. All factors of production can change in the long run. Production processes can exhibit constant, decreasing, or increasing returns to scale in the long run.
4. The optimal production technique results in the most output for a given expenditure on inputs. Firms find the optimal production technique by equating the marginal product/price ratios for all factors of production.
5. Mass-production factory systems use task-specific capital and unskilled labor. The United States has been losing its market share for mass-produced products to countries with lower wage rates. The future of the U.S. economy may lie in process technologies that use skilled, high-wage workers and produce specialized products on short production runs. To do so will require a commitment to upgrading the skills of the U.S. workforce and new management styles.

·······KEY TERMS AND CONCEPTS

short run
law of diminishing returns
total product (Q)
marginal product (MP)
average product (AP)
increasing marginal returns
diminishing marginal returns
negative marginal returns
long run
economies of scale

constant returns to scale
decreasing returns to scale
increasing returns to scale
capital/labor ratio
diminishing marginal rate of factor
    substitution
optimal production technique
mass production
product technology
process technology

.... IMPORTANT FORMULAS

Marginal product $= \dfrac{\text{change in total product}}{\text{change in factor input}}$; $MP_N = \dfrac{\Delta Q}{\Delta N}$

Average product $= \dfrac{\text{total product}}{\text{total factor input}}$; $AP_N = \dfrac{Q}{N}$

Relationship between marginal and total product:

   If $MP > 0 \Rightarrow Q \uparrow$

   If $MP < 0 \Rightarrow Q \downarrow$

Relationship between average and marginal product:

   If $MP > AP \Rightarrow AP \uparrow$

   If $MP < AP \Rightarrow AP \downarrow$

   $MP = AP$ at maximum AP

Optimal production technique: $\dfrac{MP_K}{P_K} = \dfrac{MP_N}{P_N} = \dfrac{MP_L}{P_L}$

Optimal production technique: $\dfrac{P_N}{P_K} = \dfrac{MP_N}{MP_K}$

.... REVIEW QUESTIONS

1. State the law of diminishing returns. What assumptions must hold for the law to apply? What are the three stages of production?
2. Carefully explain the relationship between marginal product, average product, and total product.
3. How do firms pick the optimal production technique? What conditions apply when factor proportions are optimal?
4. What is the difference between product technology and process technology? Why is this distinction so important in the contemporary economy?

.... PROBLEMS

1. Indicate whether the following statement is true or false, and explain why: No firm would ever knowingly operate in Stage I of the production function.
2. a. Use the formulas for total, marginal, and average product to fill in the blanks in the following table:

N	Q	MP	AP
3	100		33.33
		$\rightarrow$ a	
4	140		b
		$\rightarrow$ 30	
5	170		34.00
		$\rightarrow$ 20	
6	c		31.67

    b. Graph your data and determine which stage of the production function these data fit.

    c. Now, illustrate how an increase in the stock of capital would affect your graph. Explain why you drew what you did.

3. Refer back to Table 9.2.

    a. Let $P_N = \$100$ and $P_K = \$100$. What is the optimal production technique?

    b. Let $P_N = \$100$ and $P_K = \$200$. What is the optimal production technique? Is this result sensible?

4. Indicate whether the following are true or false, and why:

    a. If $MP_K/P_K > MP_N/P_N$, the firm should buy more machines.

    b. $MP = AP$ where TP is maximum.

    c. If $MP > AP$, production is in Stage I.

    d. Firms should expand only if production is Constant Returns to Scale (CRS) or Increasing Returns to Scale (IRS).

    e. If the wage rate falls, firms should hire more workers.

    f. MP is the slope of the Q curve.

5. a. The text notes that a possible reason for decreasing returns to scale is management inefficiency. List and comment on other possible explanations for decreasing returns to scale.

    b. The text notes that a possible reason for increasing returns to scale is synergy. List and comment on other possible explanations for increasing returns to scale.

6. In the past 20 years, most U.S. jobs have been created by small business. What does this say about the existence of decreasing returns to scale? Anything?

7. IBM, the computer giant, has lost a great deal of its market share to the "clone" manufacturers—smaller companies that produce IBM compatible machines and sell them at substantially lower prices. Explain this situation, and relate it to the concepts of process and product technology.

8. It is possible to conceive of a production function for college education. Some of the important inputs would be classroom buildings, professors, staff, and so on. One of the outputs would be the increased salaries of college graduates. Elaborate on the college education production function. Discuss the three stages of the production function, factors that cause the function to shift, and the like.

9. The production function illustrated in Figure 9.1 is correct; however, many economists draw the production function like the one below. Explain and comment.

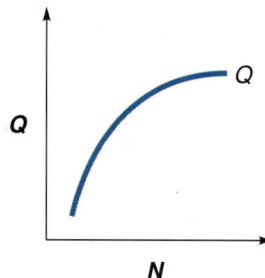

10. Are there diminishing returns to years of education? To knowledge in general?
11. Refer back to Table 9.2 and assume that workers cost $80 and machines cost $40.
    Calculate the data for the total cost, price ratio, and marginal product ratio
    columns, and determine the optimal factor combination given these factor prices.

Isoquant-Isocost Analysis

This appendix is an elaboration of our discussion of the choice of technique in production. Our analysis here involves the use of isoquant and isocost curves. Isoquant and isocost curves are quite similar to indifference curves and budget constraints, and the main result—the conditions that prevail in the optimal production technique—appears to be almost identical. Also, like indifference curve analysis, a main advantage of isoquant-isocost analysis is that it can be extended to the analysis of more interesting situations. In this appendix we will develop the isoquant-isocost model, use it to derive the conditions for optimal production, and then use it to illustrate fixed coefficient production.

ISOQUANT AND ISOCOST CURVES: THE MECHANICS

The production decision boils down to one of two things: producing the maximum amount for a given level of input costs, or minimizing the cost of inputs necessary to produce a desired level of output. In either case, the criteria for achieving these goals are identical: equate the marginal product/factor price ratios for all inputs. This can be illustrated quite easily with isoquant-isocost analysis.

Isocost Lines

Isocost A line representing the various combinations of factor inputs that can be acquired for a given cost.

Suppose that a firm has exactly $1,000,000 to spend on a production process and is searching for the best combination of labor and capital to use. The manager knows that workers cost $20,000 and that machines cost $100,000. This information is used to define the firm's cost equation in the same way the consumer's budget line was constructed in Chapter 7:

$$C = P_N N + P_K K \qquad \text{[A.1]}$$

Where:
  C = the firm's cost constraint
  P_N = the price of labor; i.e., a worker's annual salary
  N = the number of workers
  P_K = the price of capital
  K = the amount of capital

Substituting C = $1,000,000, P_N = $20,000, and P_K = $100,000, gives the isocost line:

$$\$1,000,000 = \$20,000N + \$100,000K$$

The equation of the isocost line is found by solving the budget constraint for the good on the vertical axis of the graph. In this case, we will put labor (N) on the vertical axis, so if we subtract $P_K K$ from each side of Equation A.1 and then divide by P_N, we have the equation of the isocost curve:

$$N = -\frac{P_K}{P_N} K + \frac{C}{P_N} \qquad \text{[A.2]}$$

The isocost line is graphed in Figure 9A.1. Equation A.2 is a linear equation of the standard form $y = mx + b$, where m is the slope, so we know that the slope of the isocost curve is the negative of the ratio of the two factor prices:

$$\text{Slope of isocost curve: } -\frac{P_K}{P_N} \qquad \text{[A.3]}$$

where labor (N) is measured on the vertical axis. The slope of the isocost line in this example is:

$$-\frac{P_K}{P_N} = -\frac{\$100,000}{\$20,000} = -5.0$$

FIGURE 9A.1 ISOCOST LINE

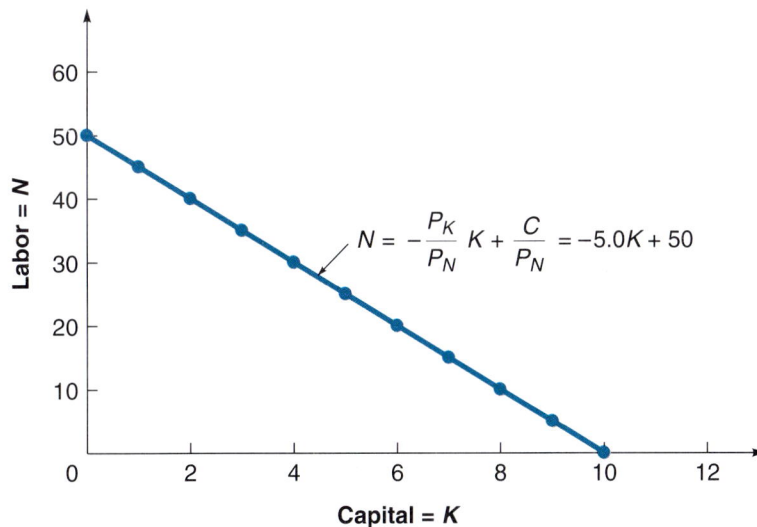

The isocost line plots the feasible combinations of factors that can be purchased with a given expenditure. The slope of the isocost curve is the negative of the relative factor price ratio, $-(P_K/P_N)$, which is equal to -5.0 in this example.

The intercepts of the isocost line are found by dividing the cost constraint by the price of the factors:

$$\text{Intercept: } \frac{C}{P_f} \qquad \text{[A.4]}$$

In this case the intercepts are:

$$\frac{C}{P_N} = \frac{\$1,000,000}{\$20,000} = 50 \quad \text{and} \quad \frac{C}{P_K} = \frac{\$1,000,000}{\$100,000} = 10$$

· · · · · · · ·

Isoquant Curves

Suppose that an engineering study reveals there are several ways to combine labor and capital to produce the desired level of output, say, 1,000 units. Five of the plausible methods are shown in Table 9A.1. These data are plotted in the **isoquant** graph in Figure 9A.2. An isoquant is the graph of different factor combinations that produce the same level of output.

Isoquants are convex to the origin because of the *diminishing marginal rate of factor substitution*. To see why there is a diminishing marginal rate of factor substitution, compare points *a*, *b*, and *c*. At point *a*, 1 machine and 53 workers can produce 1,000 units of output. At point *b*, the same output is produced with 2 machines and 41 workers. This means that the rate of factor substitution is 12 workers per machine ($53N - 41N = 12N$; $2K - 1K = 1K$). Now, at point *c*, the factor proportion is 3 machines and 35 workers, so the rate of substitution of labor for capital has diminished to 6 to 1 ($41N - 35N = 6N$; $3K - 2K = 1K$). The diminishing marginal rate of factor substitution exists because of the law of diminishing returns: As more capital is used, the marginal product of capital falls; as less labor is employed, the marginal product of labor rises. The diminishing marginal rate of substitution of labor for capital is illustrated by the movement between points *a* and *e* because each new machine is less and less productive while forgone workers are more and more productive.

Figure 9A.2 shows, I_0, the isoquant for 1,000 units of output derived from the

Isoquant A plot of different factor combinations that give equal output.

· · · · · **TABLE 9A.1 ISOQUANT DATA: N, K COMBINATIONS NEEDED TO PRODUCE 1,000 UNITS OF OUTPUT**

Point	Machines (K)	Workers (N)		MP_N/MP_K
a	1	53		
			→	12:1
b	2	41		
			→	6:1
c	3	35		
			→	3:1
d	4	32		
			→	1:1
e	5	31		

FIGURE 9A.2 ISOQUANTS

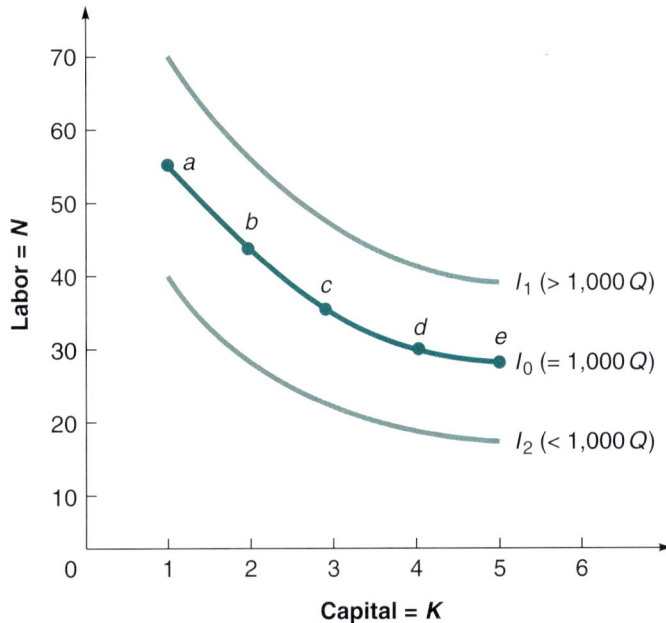

Isoquants plot different input combinations that can be used to produce the same level of output. Isoquants are convex to the origin because of the diminishing marginal rate of factor substitution. Isoquant I_0 plots the data from Table 9A.1 and shows the various (K, N) combinations that can be used to produce 1,000 units of output. Isoquant I_1 represents a higher level of output than I_0 because it is farther from the origin and thus uses more inputs for any given capital labor ratio; isoquant I_2 represents a lower level of output because it is closer to the origin and uses fewer inputs.

data in Table 9A.1 as well as two other isoquants, I_1 and I_2. Actually, the number of theoretical isoquants is infinite with each representing a different level of output. Isoquants farther from the origin like I_1 represent more inputs of both factors and thus a higher level of output, and isoquants closer to the origin like I_2 indicate fewer inputs and lower levels of output. All isoquants are convex to the origin and no two isoquants can cross.[1] The problem for the firm is to get on the highest possible isoquant given its cost constraint.

The slope of an isoquant is the negative of the ratio of the marginal productivities of the two factors of production. This can be demonstrated in much the same way we showed that the slope of an indifference curve is the negative ratio of marginal utilities. First, note that in order for output to be fixed along a given isoquant, it must be true that the marginal product of capital times the change in capital plus the marginal product or labor times the change in labor is equal to zero:

$$MP_K(\Delta K) + MP_N(\Delta N) = 0 \qquad \text{[A.5]}$$

[1]The proof to this statement is identical to the proof that indifference curves cannot cross. See the appendix to Chapter 7.

Then, if we subtract $MP_K(\Delta K)$ from each side of the equation and divide by ΔK, we have the slope of an isoquant:

$$\text{Slope of isoquant: } \frac{\Delta N}{\Delta K} = -\frac{MP_K}{MP_N} \qquad \text{[A.6]}$$

THE OPTIMAL PRODUCTION TECHNIQUE

All that is necessary now is to put the isocost and isoquant curves together and find the optimal production technique. Optimality occurs where the isoquant curve is tangent to the lowest possible isocost curve. To see why, look at Figure 9A.3. The isoquant curve consistent with 1,000 units of output has been drawn along with three possible isocost curves. The isocost curve TC_1 passing through the points $N = 45$ and $K = 9$ indicates a total cost of $900,000: labor costs $20,000 and capital costs $100,000, so $45(\$20,000) = 9(\$100,000) = \$900,000$. Unfortunately, $900,000 is not enough money to produce 1,000 units of output because TC_1 does not meet the isoquant curve for 1,000 units of output. Now look at isocost curve TC_3 passing through the points $N = 55$ and $K = 11$. This represents a total cost of $1,100,000, and it would be possible to produce 1,000 units of output by spending this amount of money. Either of the factor combinations indicated by the intersection of the

FIGURE 9A.3 OPTIMAL PRODUCTION TECHNIQUE

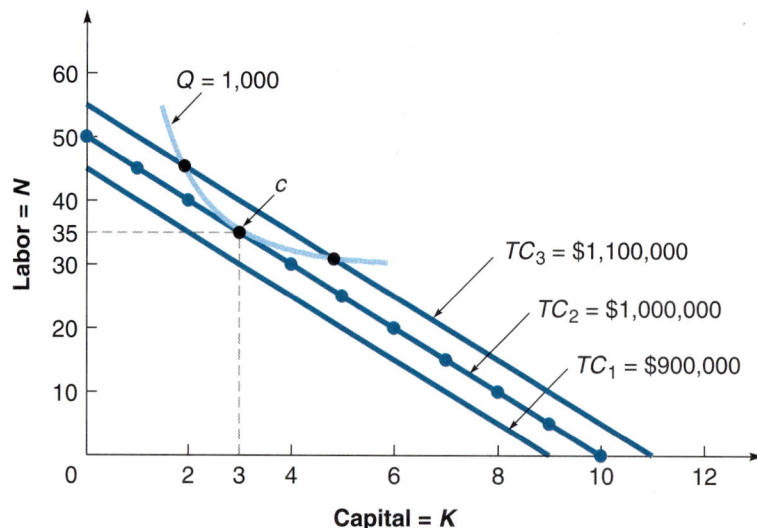

The optimal production technique is found where the isoquant curve is tangent to the lowest possible isocost curve. This occurs at point c, where $K = 3$ and $N = 35$. At point c, the slopes of the isoquant and isocost are equal so that the ratio of factor prices is equal to the ratio of marginal productivities.

isoquant curve and TC_3 could be used to produce 1,000 units of output, but neither of these factor combinations would be efficient because the same level of output could be produced at a lower cost. Finally, look at isocost line TC_2 passing through the points $N = 50$ and $K = 10$. This isocost curve indicates a total cost of $1,000,000. Isocost TC_2 is tangent to the isoquant curve, so it is possible to produce 1,000 units of output at the factor combination $N = 35$, $K = 3$. This is the most efficient factor combination because it represents the least cost for a given level of output. Our conclusion: The firm should produce where the isocost curve is tangent to the isoquant curve.

We know that curves have the same slope when tangent, so the slope of the isocost curve is equal to the slope of the isoquant curve at point c, the point of tangency. Table 9A.1 does not provide the exact slope of the isoquant curve at point c; it only gives the slope at either side of point c. Between points b and c, the slope is -6; between points c and d, the slope is -3. We can deduce that the slope is -5 at point c, which just happens to be the slope of the isocost curve. Our conclusion, then, is that the optimal production technique occurs when:

Optimal production technique:

$$\text{slope of isocost curve} = -\frac{P_K}{P_N} = -\frac{MP_K}{MP_N} = \text{slope of isoquant} \quad \text{[A.7]}$$

Where:
 MP = marginal product
 K, N = factors of production
 P = factor price

If we multiply each side of Equation A.7 by MP_N and then divide by P_K, we arrive at an alternative statement for the optimal production technique:

$$\text{Optimal production technique: } \frac{MP_K}{P_K} = \frac{MP_N}{P_N} \quad \text{[A.8]}$$

Equation A.8 indicates that the firm is using the optimal factor combination when the marginal products of the last dollar spent on each factor are equal. If the marginal product/factor price ratios are not equal, then the factor combinations should be changed. For example, if it happened that:

$$\frac{MP_K}{P_K} > \frac{MP_N}{P_N}$$

it would mean that the firm could increase output without raising costs by using more capital and less labor. As more capital was employed, the marginal product of capital would fall, while using less labor would raise the marginal product of labor. This would move the marginal product/price ratios toward equality.

Changing Factor Prices

As prices or marginal productivities change, the optimal production technique will also change. For example, an increase in the price of capital makes the isocost curve

···· **FIGURE 9A.4 CHANGING FACTOR COMBINATIONS**

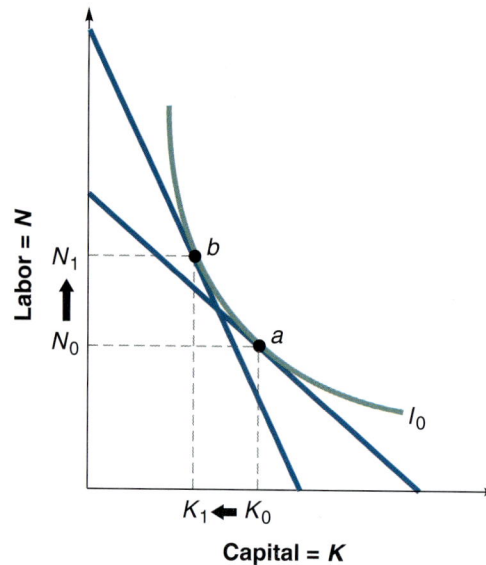

An increase in the price of either factor will cause the isocost line to swivel as relative factor prices change. In this example, the price of capital has increased. If the producer wants to continue to produce the level of output indicated by the isoquant I_0, more will have to be spent on factor inputs. In this case, the optimal factor combination will change from (K_0, N_0) at point a to (K_1, N_1) at point b. The new factor combination has more labor and less capital than the original factor combination because the relative price of capital has increased.

steeper and causes the firm to substitute labor for capital—and if the firm still has a 1,000-production target, the total costs must increase. This is shown in Figure 9A.4. A decrease in the price of capital would do the opposite: the isocost curve becomes flatter and machines are substituted for labor. When the price of labor changes, the vertical intercept shifts. An increase in the wage rate lowers the vertical intercept and results in the substitution of machines for workers; a decrease in the price of labor raises the vertical intercept and causes the firm to hire more workers.

········

Duality

Production managers can usually think about the production decision in two equivalent ways: (1) find the maximum output that can be produced for a given cost of inputs, or (2) minimize the input costs for a given production target. These two approaches to the production decision can be written as:

1. Maximize Q subject to $C = \overline{C}$.
2. Minimize C subject to $Q = \overline{Q}$.   [A.9]

Where:

C = cost
$\overline{C}$ = cost constraint
Q = output
$\overline{Q}$ = output target

In either situation, the optimal production technique is the one that obeys the decision rule in Equation A.7. In Case I, the firm sets its product goal (isoquant) and then finds the isocost curve that is exactly tangent. In Case II, the firm looks at factor prices and cost limitations (the isocost curve) and then finds the production technology (isoquant) that is tangent.

Economists refer to the analogous relationship between output maximization and cost minimization as **duality**. Case I is the dual of Case II and Case II is the dual of Case I. Depending on the particular problem at hand, it is sometimes more useful to speak in terms of cost minimization rather than output maximization or vice versa. The important point to remember is that it does not make any difference which case is studied; they will result in the same solution.

> **Duality** The idea that maximizing output subject to a cost constraint is equivalent to minimizing cost subject to an output constraint.

FIXED COEFFICIENT PRODUCTION

Isocost-isoquant analysis is based on the assumption that firms can change the capital/labor ratio without too much difficulty. This is not always the case. Some production processes—called **fixed coefficient production**—allow only one capital/labor ratio, and others permit only a small range of ratios. Under these circumstances, it is not always possible to change the capital/labor ratio in response to changes in factor prices. If the wage rate changes and the firm cannot substitute capital for labor, the only options are to cut production or raise prices.

> **Fixed coefficient production** Production process that is possible with only one capital/labor ratio.

Fixed coefficient production results in L-shaped isoquants like those shown in Figure 9A.5. Why are these isoquants L-shaped? Suppose a particular process requires exactly 10 workers per machine. This is illustrated by point a on the diagram. If there are 9 workers and 1 machine (point b), the job cannot be completed, so this point is off the isoquant. If there are 11 workers and 1 machine (point c), one worker will sit idle, but the same amount of production will take place as at point a so point c is on the isoquant. Similarly, a second or third machine would make no contribution to output if there are only 10 workers.

The complications imposed by fixed coefficient production are illustrated in Figure 9A.6 where various isocost curves have been added to a given L-shaped isoquant. Suppose that the production process is initially at point a, where the L-shaped isoquant touches the initial isocost curve K_0N_0. Does this production technology meet the optimality condition in Equation A.7? It is impossible to say because we cannot determine the slope at the corner of the isoquant. The slope of the isoquant changes from infinity in the vertical segment to zero in the horizontal segment—but that leaves quite a few values in between! There is no way to determine whether the technique implied by the isoquant is optimal or not. The fact that many isocost curves—for example, K_1N_1 as well as K_0N_0—touch the corner of I_0 suggests that relative factor prices play a less important role in the production decision. Another situation is illustrated with the isocost curve through points K_0 and N_2. In this case,

FIGURE 9A.5 FIXED COEFFICIENT PRODUCTION: L-SHAPED ISOQUANTS

When the production technology exhibits fixed coefficients, the corresponding isoquants are L-shaped. In this case, capital and labor must be combined in a fixed ratio of $K = 1$ and $N = 10$. If there are only 9 workers and 1 machine, point b, no output can be produced. If there are 11 workers and only 1 machine, point c, the same amount of output is produced as if there are 10 workers and 1 machine. If there are 2 machines, exactly 20 workers are needed. This is indicated by point d.

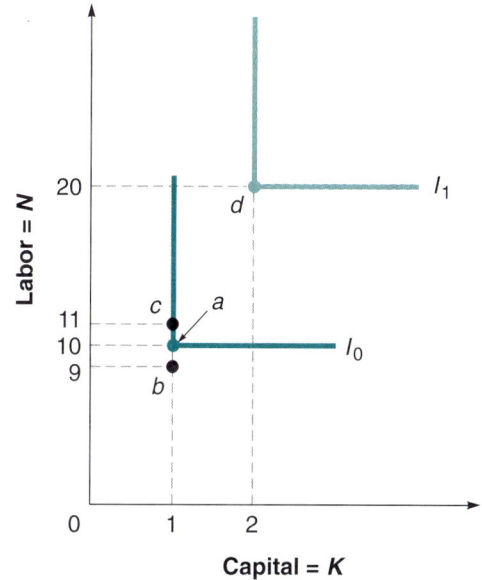

FIGURE 9A.6 CHANGING FACTOR PRICES AND FIXED COEFFICIENT PRODUCTION

When production is fixed coefficient, changing relative factor prices may not affect the production technique or factor combination. For example, the two isocost lines, (K_0, N_0) and (K_1, N_1), touch the isoquant curve at its corner. This means that two factor price ratios may result in the same factor combination. The isocost curve through (K_0, N_2) indicates that a decrease in the price of labor has no effect on the number of workers hired; unless the firm can afford to acquire more machines, the additional workers will not be hired.

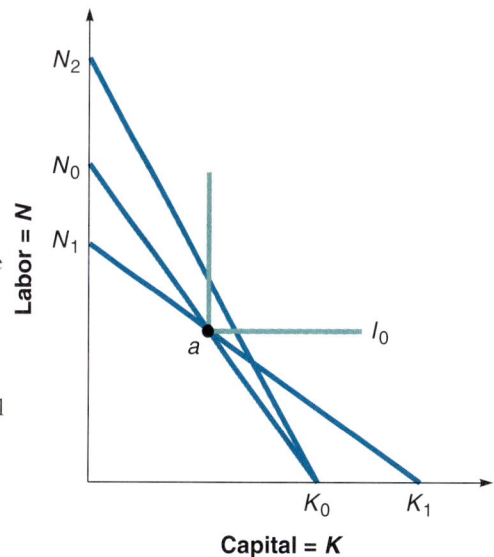

the wage rate has fallen, but there is no change in the factor combination; workers took a wage cut, but the level of employment did not change.

How important is fixed coefficient production in the real world? There is not a definitive answer. Most economists would agree that fixed coefficients are more important in the short run than the long run, but little else can be said with certainty. What we can say is this: the existence of fixed coefficient production processes tends to weaken the ability of the price mechanism to allocate resources efficiently.

SUMMARY

Actual business firms do not draw isoquants and isocost curves when they make their production decisions, but if their decisions are optimal, they will combine factors of production so that the marginal product/price ratios are equal. More important for our purposes, however, is the fact that isocost-isoquant analysis sheds important light on the relationships between factor prices and production decisions and resource allocation. These are key issues in understanding how market processes operate. The main points to remember from this appendix are:

1. Isocost curves plot different factor combinations that can be purchased with a given level of expenditure. Isoquant curves plot different factor combinations that result in a fixed amount of output. The slope of an isocost curve is the negative of the factor price ratio. The slope of an isoquant curve is the negative ratio of marginal products. Isoquant curves are convex to the origin because of the diminishing marginal rate of factor substitution.

2. The production technique is optimal when the isocost curve is tangent to the highest possible isoquant curve. At this point:

$$\frac{MP_K}{MP_N} = \frac{P_K}{P_N} \quad \text{and} \quad \frac{MP_K}{P_K} = \frac{MP_N}{P_N}$$

This condition means that if one factor of production costs twice as much as another factor of production, its marginal product must be twice as high.

3. Changes in relative factor prices change the slope of the isocost curve and the optimal input combination. Lower labor (capital) prices decrease (increase) the capital/labor ratio; higher labor (capital) prices increase (decrease) the capital/labor ratio.

4. If the production process is fixed coefficient, factor price changes may not affect the optimal factor proportion.

KEY TERMS AND CONCEPTS

isocost
slope of isocost
isoquant
convex
diminishing marginal rate of factor
  substitution

slope of isoquant curve
duality
optimal production technique
fixed coefficient production

REVIEW QUESTIONS

1. What is the slope of an isocost curve? Of an isoquant curve? What factors would cause the slope of an isocost to change? What factors would change the slope of an isoquant curve? What conditions hold at the point where the isoquant is tangent to the isocost curve?
2. Draw and carefully label an isoquant graph to illustrate the conditions that must hold when a firm is using the optimal production technique.
3. How does the duality concept relate to isoquant analysis?
4. What does the isoquant look like when production exhibits fixed coefficients? How do firms respond to changes in factor prices when production is fixed coefficient?

PROBLEMS

1. Illustrate each of the following with an isocost–isoquant diagram:
   a. an increase in the price of labor
   b. an increase in the budget for capital expenditures
   c. an increase in labor productivity
   d. a decrease in the price of capital
   e. a production process possible with an infinite number of capital/labor ratios
   f. a production process possible with only one capital/labor ratio
   g. a production process where machinery must be purchased in whole units
   h. a production process with a constant rate of factor substitution
2. Refer back to Figure 9A.5. What is the slope of a line between points *a* and *d*? What is the economic meaning of your answer?
3. Refer back to the Appendix of Chapter 7, Problem 2. Is it ever possible to have inferior or "Giffen" factors of production? Why or why not?
4. Refer back to Figure 9A.3 and Table 9A.1. What factor prices and cost constraints would have to exist for the optimal production technique to be 41 workers and 2 machines? 32 workers and 4 machines?
5. Use separate isoquant-isocost diagrams to illustrate constant returns to scale, increasing returns to scale, and decreasing returns to scale.

CHAPTER 10

The Costs of Production

Try this thought experiment: Suppose you are told that you can make a product using either of two processes, a labor-intensive technique that employs 100 workers using simple hand tools or a capital-intensive technique that employs 10 workers in an automated factory. Which technique would you pick?

If you picked *either*, you earn demerits—unless you first asked about the costs of production. Engineers can tell us the feasible production methods, but economists are needed to find the least-cost and most efficient methods. If labor is cheap relative to capital, the labor-intensive technique is better; if capital is cheap relative to labor, the capital-intensive technique is better.

In this chapter we will examine the costs of production. Our goal is to convert the information from the last chapter on production theory into a theory of cost. We will find that almost all of the important concepts from that chapter—marginal product, the stages of production, and so on—have direct analogies in the analysis of cost. Cost analysis is critical to firm behavior. Most firms seek to maximize profit, and economic profit is the difference between revenue and cost.

AFTER READING AND STUDYING THIS CHAPTER, YOU SHOULD BE ABLE TO:
- • • Define and graph fixed, variable, average, and marginal costs
- • • Explain the relationship between the costs of production and the law of diminishing returns
- • • Understand the difference between long-run and short-run costs
- • • Explain the relationship between cost and capacity utilization rates

SHORT-RUN COSTS
AND THE PRODUCTION FUNCTION

Costs are directly related to the production function and the law of diminishing returns in the short run. The decision of how much to produce also affects the costs of production. If too little is produced, the ability of workers to specialize is limited. As a result, worker productivity is low and the cost of production is high. On the other hand, if the firm tries to produce too much in the short run, it will enter Stage III of the production function, and output will decline. To make the correct production decision, the firm needs to understand the relationship between costs and production.

•••••••••

Fixed, Variable, and Total Costs

Table 10.1 replicates the production function data from Table 9.1 of Chapter 9 and adds seven new columns containing cost data. The first three measures of cost are fixed, variable, and total costs. The presence of fixed costs indicates that this analysis relates to the short run. In the long run, everything—including all costs—can vary so there are no fixed costs.

Fixed cost Cost that does not vary with output.

Fixed costs *(FC)* do not vary with output. One example of a fixed cost is a fire insurance premium on real property owned by the firm. Even if the firm closes down and produces nothing, the fire insurance premium must be paid. Other examples of fixed costs include security guard services and existing debt payments. In Table 10.1, fixed costs are assumed to be $300 for all levels of production.

Fixed costs are represented by the horizontal line in Figure 10.1. The intercept of the fixed cost curve is the amount of fixed costs; the slope of the fixed costs curve

•••••**FIGURE 10.1** TOTAL, VARIABLE, AND FIXED COSTS

The three kinds of costs are fixed, variable, and total costs. Fixed costs do not vary as output changes and are represented by a horizontal line. The variable cost curve gets its **S**-shape from the law of diminishing returns. The total cost curve is the vertical summation of the fixed and variable cost curves. Its intercept is equal to fixed costs; it is shaped like the variable cost curve.

In this figure, the dots on the curves represent the contributions of additional workers. For example, the first worker produced 40 units of output, which is represented by the dots at $Q = 40$. The first two workers produced 90 units of output, which is represented by the dots at $Q = 90$.

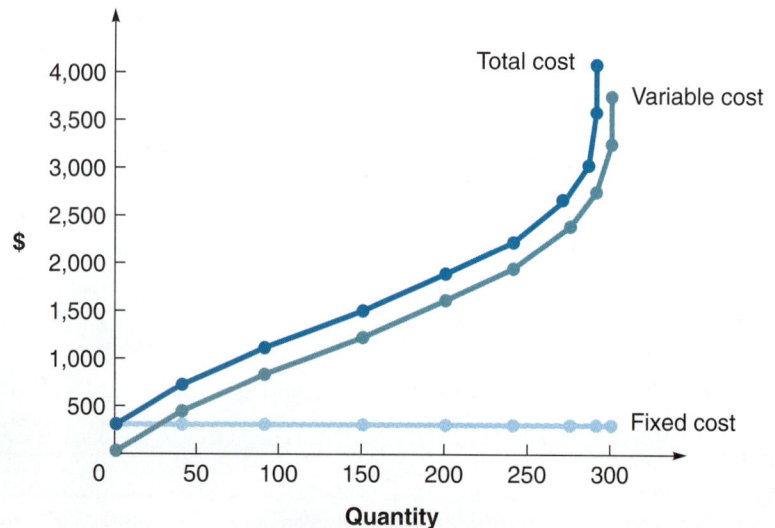

•••• **TABLE 10.1 COSTS AND PRODUCTION**

(1) N	(2) Q	(3) MP	(4) AP	(5) FC	(6) VC	(7) TC	(8) MC	(9) AFC	(10) AVC	(11) ATC
0	0	—	—	$ 300	0	$ 300		—	—	—
		→ 40					→ $10.00			
1	40		40.00	300	400	700		$7.50	$10.00	$17.50
		→ 50					→ 8.00			
2	90		45.00	300	800	1,100		3.33	8.89	12.22
		→ 60					→ 6.67			
3	150		50.00	300	1,200	1,500		2.00	8.00	10.00
		→ 50					→ 8.00			
4	200		50.00	300	1,600	1,900		1.50	8.00	9.50
		→ 40					→ 10.00			
5	240		48.00	300	2,000	2,300		1.25	8.33	9.58
		→ 30					→ 13.33			
6	270		45.00	300	2,400	2,700		1.11	8.89	10.00
		→ 20					→ 20.00			
7	290		41.43	300	2,800	3,100		1.03	9.66	10.69
		→ 10					→ 40.00			
8	300		37.50	300	3,200	3,500		1.00	10.67	11.67
		→ 0					→ ⇒ ∞			
9	300		33.33	300	3,600	3,900		1.00	12.00	13.00

Definitions and Formulas:

N = variable inputs (labor)

Q = total product

P_N = price of labor = $400

MP = marginal product = $\dfrac{\Delta Q}{\Delta N}$

AP = average product (of labor) = $\dfrac{Q}{N}$

FC = fixed cost

VC = variable cost

TC = total cost

MC = marginal cost = $\dfrac{\Delta TC}{\Delta Q} = \dfrac{\Delta VC}{\Delta Q}$

AFC = average fixed cost = $\dfrac{FC}{Q}$

AVC = average variable cost = $\dfrac{VC}{Q}$

ATC = average total cost = $\dfrac{TC}{Q}$

is zero to reflect the fact that fixed costs do not change as output changes; i.e., $\Delta FC/\Delta Q = 0$.

Variable costs *(VC)* are costs that do change with the level of output. For many firms, the most important variable cost is labor. Labor costs increase as production increases because more workers must be hired. Other variable costs include the cost of energy, raw materials, and intermediate goods that are used in the production process.

Variable cost Cost that changes as output changes.

To keep our example simple, labor is treated as the only variable cost of production. The cost per worker is $400, so the entries in the *VC* column are found by multiplying the number of workers (*N*) by $400. The zero in the first row of Table 10.1 indicates that there are no variable costs when no workers are employed.

The **S**-shape of the variable cost curve in Figure 10.1 is a result of the three stages of production and the law of diminishing returns. The intercept of the variable cost curve is zero because there are no variable costs when no workers are hired. As the first few workers are hired, the variable cost per unit of output changes. This may not make sense at first because each worker is paid the same wage, $400. However, even though the variable cost *per worker* is always $400, each worker produces a different amount of output than the previous worker, so the variable cost *per unit of output* changes. The variable cost curve has three stages just like a typical production function:

- *Increasing marginal returns: variable costs rise at a decreasing rate.* At very low levels of output, the variable cost curve is relatively steep, but as output expands, it becomes flatter as worker specialization begins to take place. This corresponds to Stage I of the production function, the stage of increasing marginal product. The production function gets steeper in Stage I as more workers are hired; the variable cost curve gets flatter in Stage I as more workers are hired. This should make sense to you: if the next worker is more productive than the previous worker, then the variable cost per unit of output will decline.
- *Diminishing marginal returns: variable costs rise at an increasing rate.* As more workers are hired and production increases, the point is reached when each additional worker still increases output, but less than the previous worker. This is Stage II of the production function, the stage of diminishing marginal returns. The variable cost curve begins getting steeper in Stage II: the cost per worker is still assumed to be constant, but each worker produces less than the previous worker, so the variable cost per unit of output begins to increase.
- *Negative marginal returns.* If the firm continues hiring workers, it will reach the point when additional workers actually decrease total product. This is Stage III of the production function, the stage of negative marginal product. What happens to the variable cost curve in Stage III? If the firm actually did hire enough workers to move into Stage III, the variable cost curve would bend backward—an indication that output is falling while variable costs continue to rise. A real-world firm is unlikely to do this, so the variable cost curve is usually drawn vertical at the maximum level of output.

Total cost Fixed plus variable costs.

Total cost (*TC*) is found by adding together fixed and variable costs. That is:

$$TC = FC + VC \quad\quad [1]$$

The total cost curve has the same shape as the variable cost curve and the same intercept as the fixed cost curve.

Explicit and Implicit Costs. We need to emphasize that total costs include *all* costs of production, not only explicit costs like wages, but also implicit costs like the opportunity cost of forgone alternatives. One important implicit cost is the lost interest from using internal funds to acquire new machinery. For example, if you have $1,000,000 in retained profits and decide to use it to build a new plant, you cannot use the $1,000,000 to buy interest-earning financial assets. If the interest rate is 10 percent, this means that the new plant will cost you $1,000,000 plus the lost $100,000 per year that you could have earned from putting your money in an interest-earning financial asset.

Normal and Economic Profits. A **normal profit** for the owner is also included in total cost. What is a "normal" profit? Like so many concepts in economics, the answer must be "it depends" because we cannot say something like 5 percent or $500. Many economists define normal profits as the minimum profit necessary for the firm to stay in business at its current scale of operation. Another definition of normal profit is the opportunity cost of investment; that is, the rate of return on the best forgone investment alternative. For example, if your firm is making a 5 percent profit, but you could have made 10 percent by investing in another operation, you are making less than normal profits—and you should probably invest your money elsewhere.

Profits above and beyond normal profits are called **economic** or **abnormal profits**. Economic profits consist of the surplus of the firm's revenues over the costs of production, including opportunity costs. Some economists define economic profit as profits great enough to allow the firm to expand; however, the existence of economic profits does not necessarily mean that the firm *will* expand, so this definition must be used carefully.

Normal profit Profit just sufficient for the firm to stay in business but not expand.

Economic (abnormal) profit Profit greater than the rate necessary to maintain the established level of production.

· · · · · · · · ·

Average and Marginal Costs

Firms are also concerned about the costs of producing individual units. Four cost measures are important in this context.

Marginal cost (MC) is the incremental cost of producing the next unit of output. It represents the direct change in total cost associated with producing one more unit of output. It is important to remember that marginal cost is unrelated to fixed costs. Fixed costs do not change in the short run and thus have no influence on the cost of producing the next unit—marginal cost. This means that the change in total cost is equal to the change in variable cost. The formula for marginal cost is:

Marginal cost The change in total cost associated with the production of one additional unit of output.

$$\text{Marginal cost: } MC = \frac{\Delta TC}{\Delta Q} = \frac{\Delta VC}{\Delta Q} \qquad [2]$$

The marginal cost curve gives the slope of the total and variable cost curves.

Marginal cost is shown in Column 8 of Table 10.1 as well as in Figure 10.2. Like marginal product, the marginal cost data are set between the rows of total cost to show that they represent the change in total cost. Note that the marginal cost curve is U-shaped like an upside-down marginal product curve. A quick inspection of Columns 3 and 8 reveals that marginal cost starts high, then declines before it rises again. This is the opposite of what happens to marginal product: the marginal product of labor increases as the first three workers are added, then begins to decrease.

When the first worker is added, output rises from 0 to 40, and total cost rises from $300 to $700. Substituting these values into Equation 2 shows that marginal cost is $10:[1]

---

[1]Actually, the value $10 is really the average marginal cost of each of the first 40 units that are produced. Strictly speaking, marginal cost typically refers to the cost of producing *one* more unit, not 40 more units as in these calculations. We cannot compute the marginal cost of one more unit because of the limitations of Table 10.1.

···· **FIGURE 10.2 AVERAGE AND MARGINAL COST CURVES**

The average total cost, average variable cost, and marginal cost curves are **U**-shaped, a consequence of the three stages of production and the law of diminishing returns. The average fixed cost curve is downward sloping but declines at a diminishing rate over its entire range because higher output reduces the fixed cost per unit. The marginal cost curve intersects the average total cost curve and the average variable cost curve at their minimum points. The difference between average total cost and average variable cost is average fixed cost. For example, when $Q = 40$, $AFC = \$7.50$. This is equal to the difference between $ATC = \$17.50$ and $AVC = \$10.00$.

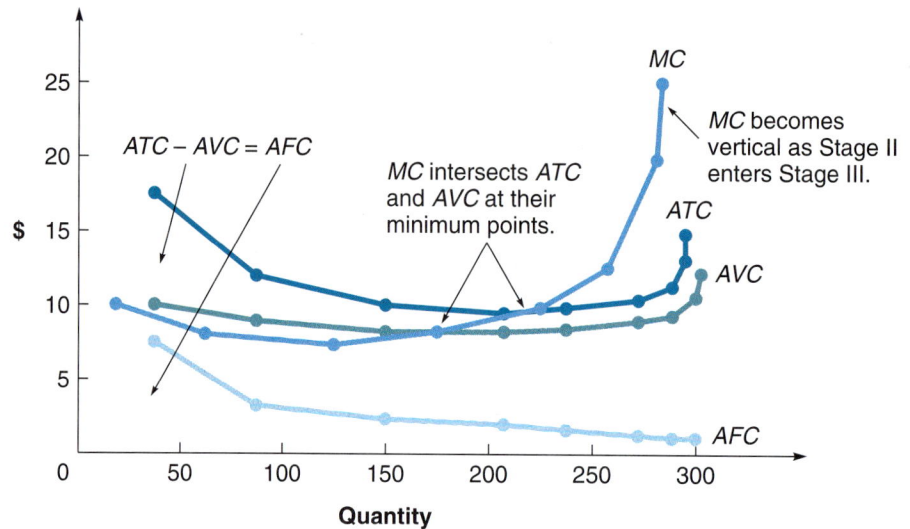

$$MC = \frac{\Delta TC}{\Delta Q} = \frac{\$700 - \$300}{40 - 0} = \$10$$

But when output increases from 40 to 90, marginal cost falls to $8 because of worker specialization:

$$MC = \frac{\Delta TC}{\Delta Q} = \frac{\$1,100 - \$700}{90 - 40} = \$8$$

Table 10.1 shows that marginal cost falls to $6.67 when the third worker is added and then begins to rise as production moves into Stage II. Marginal cost rises at an increasing rate as more and more workers are added in this stage. Finally, in Stage III of the production function, marginal cost will approach infinity if the firm continues to hire and pay additional workers as marginal product approaches zero.

Average fixed cost Total fixed cost divided by quantity.

Average fixed cost (AFC) is found by dividing fixed costs by total product:

$$\text{Average fixed cost: } AFC = \frac{FC}{Q} \qquad [3]$$

Fixed costs do not vary with output, but average fixed costs do: the more the firm produces, the more fixed costs can be "spread out." As a result, the average fixed cost curve declines steadily and by progressively smaller amounts as output increases. For example, if insurance costs $1,000 per year and the firm is able to sell only 10 units of output, average fixed costs are $100 per unit, but if sales increase to 20 units per year, average fixed costs are only $50 per unit, and if sales rise to 30 units, average fixed costs are $33.33 per unit. Figure 10.2 illustrates how fixed costs are spread out as output increases.

Average variable cost *(AVC)* is found by dividing variable costs by total product:

Average variable cost Variable cost divided by quantity.

$$\text{Average variable cost: } AVC = \frac{VC}{Q} \qquad \text{[4]}$$

The average variable cost curve is U-shaped as shown in Figure 10.2. At low levels of output, average variable costs are high, but as output increases, worker specialization lowers the variable cost per unit. The average variable cost curve will eventually begin to slope upward after diminishing returns have set in and the marginal cost of the next unit is higher than the average variable cost.

There is an important relationship between average and marginal costs—one you may have guessed given our discussion of average and marginal in the last chapter. In fact, the relationship between average and marginal holds regardless of the quantities being measured. For example, if the average height of the first 10 people in a room is 5 feet 9 inches and a person who is 6 feet 6 inches tall enters the room, the average height of the people in the room will rise; if the next person who enters is only 5 feet 5 inches tall, the average height will fall. This relationship has a direct application to cost theory. Marginal cost represents the cost of producing the next unit, so if marginal cost is less than average variable cost, average variable costs must be declining; if marginal cost is greater than average variable cost, average variable costs will rise. Finally, the marginal cost curve intersects the average variable cost curve at its minimum point. The importance of this relationship will be apparent in the next chapter when we analyze competitive firms.

Average total cost *(ATC)* is found by dividing total cost by total output; because total cost is equal to fixed cost plus variable cost, the formula for average total cost can be written in different ways:

Average total cost Total cost divided by quantity.

$$\text{Average total cost: } ATC = \frac{TC}{Q} = \frac{FC + VC}{Q} = AFC + AVC \qquad \text{[5]}$$

The average total cost curve is U-shaped like the average variable cost curve. The average total cost curve is not quite parallel to the average variable cost curve, however, because total costs include fixed costs as well as variable costs. As output increases from low levels of output, average total costs fall for two reasons: spreading fixed costs and increasing marginal productivity. The minimum point of the average total cost curve occurs at a higher level of output than the minimum point of the average variable cost curve because falling average fixed costs offset the initial rise in variable costs. Eventually, however, the rise in average variable costs will overpower the continuing, but progressively smaller decline in average fixed costs, so the average total curve will begin to rise. The marginal cost curve intersects the average total cost curve at its minimum point.

We will be using diagrams like Figure 10.2 quite a bit in the next few chapters, so a few comments are in order. First, we will rarely need to draw the average fixed cost curve. Average fixed cost is the difference between average total cost and average variable cost, so we can get that information—and a less cluttered diagram—by just noting the distance between *AVC* and *ATC*. Second, we can calculate total cost and variable cost from their respective average cost curves. For example, consider point *a* on the average total cost curve in Figure 10.3. This corresponds to quantity 90 and

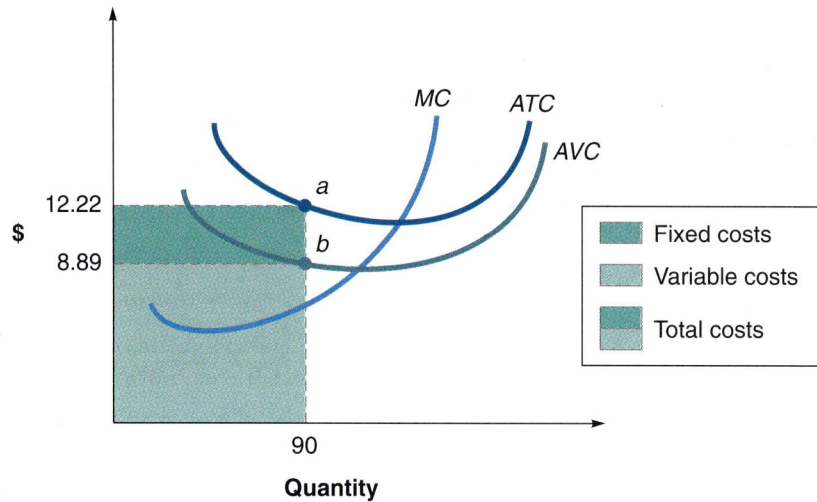

•••••FIGURE 10.3 FINDING TOTAL COSTS FROM AVERAGE COSTS

The total cost of producing any quantity can be found by multiplying quantity times average total cost. In this figure, the total cost of producing 90 units of output is 90($12.22) = $1,099.80. This is the entire rectangle 0–90–a–$12.22. Variable costs can be found by multiplying average variable cost by quantity. In this case, the variable cost of producing 90 units is 90($8.89) = $800.10. It is usually unnecessary to draw the AFC curve because fixed costs can be found as the difference between total costs and variable costs. Here fixed costs are represented by the dark green rectangle, $8.89–b–a–$12.22, which is equal to $1,099.80 − $800.10 = $299.70 ≈ $300.

average total cost $12.22 from Table 10.1. To find the total cost of producing 90 units of output, all that is necessary is to multiply quantity by the average total cost of production. That is:

$$TC = ATC \times Q \qquad [6]$$

In this case, total costs are 90($12.22) = $1,099.80.

Likewise, to find variable costs, multiply average variable costs by quantity:

$$VC = AVC \times Q \qquad [7]$$

We know from Table 10.1 that the average variable costs at quantity 90 are $8.89, so variable costs are 90($8.89) = $800.10.

Finally, fixed costs are the difference between total costs and variable costs, so fixed costs—indicated by the dark green rectangle—are $1,099.80 − $800.10 = $299.70 (which differs from the table value of $300 because of rounding).

• • • • • • • •

Factors That Shift Cost Curves

The two most important factors that shift short-run cost curves are (1) changes in technical knowledge that shift the production function and (2) factor prices. An

• • • • • **FIGURE 10.4 FACTOR PRICES AND MARGINAL COST**

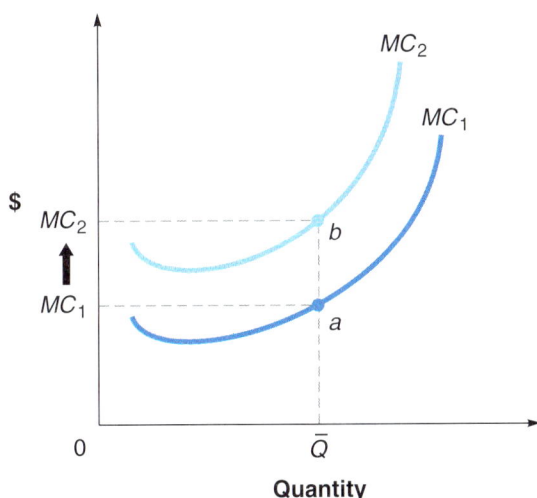

Higher factor prices will shift the marginal cost, average variable cost, and average total cost curves upward. Lower factor prices or advancing technology will shift them downward. This diagram illustrates the effect of higher factor costs on only the marginal cost curve. Notice that higher marginal costs are illustrated by a shift toward the vertical axis. This is because the same quantity, $\overline{Q}$, can be produced only at a higher cost, MC_2 versus MC_1, if factor costs have risen.

advance in technology will increase the amount of production from a given amount of inputs and thus lower the costs of production. For example, the development of automated assembly plants has reduced the cost of producing personal computers dramatically. As a result, the average total, average variable, and marginal cost curves have shifted downward—as has the price of personal computers. Lower factor prices—wages, interest, or rent—will also cause a downward shift in the average and marginal cost curves; higher factor prices shift them upward. Figure 10.4 illustrates the effect of higher costs on the marginal cost curve; the average cost curves have been omitted to simplify the diagram. Notice that higher costs shift the marginal cost curve vertically and *toward* the vertical axis, not away from it.

What shifts the fixed cost curve? Nothing in the short run because, by assumption, fixed costs are fixed with respect to output. When fixed costs do change, we enter the long run, the subject of the next section.

RECAP   **Costs in the Short Run**

The terms and concepts we have just discussed will be used extensively over the next several chapters, so it will help to pause and make sure they are clear.

1. The costs of production depend on the production function and the law of diminishing returns. In the short run, some costs do not vary with output;

these are called fixed costs. Variable costs do vary with output. Total costs are fixed costs plus variable costs. Total costs include all costs including a normal profit for the owner. Marginal cost is the cost of producing the next unit of output.

2. Average fixed costs decline steadily and become less and less important as output increases. The average total cost, average variable cost, and marginal cost curves are all U-shaped. The marginal cost curve intersects the average variable cost and average total cost curves at their minimum points.

3. The marginal cost, average total cost, and average variable cost curves will shift when factor prices or technology changes. Fixed costs can change only in the long run.

COSTS IN THE LONG RUN

Thus far, all of our discussions have dealt with the short run because we have assumed that there were fixed costs. In the long run, there are no fixed costs and everything can change. How do costs vary in the long run? There is no counterpart to the law of diminishing returns for the long run, so each situation must be analyzed separately.

The factors that we were assuming were fixed in the short run were land and the size of the plant—the capital stock. The stock of capital affects the productivity of labor and therefore both variable and marginal costs. Suppose that the owners of the firm estimate sales to be a certain level and then build a plant hoping to produce at the minimum point on the average total cost curve. If demand is greater than anticipated, the firm will be able to sell more. It may be able to meet the higher demand temporarily by drawing down inventories, but if demand stays high, it will have to hire more workers and increase production. This would cause average costs to rise as production moved beyond the minimum point on the average total cost curve. To remain profitable, the firm would have to raise prices, but this could cut into sales. The alternative would be to build a larger and more efficient plant—which would move the firm to a different set of cost curves. The *long-run average cost curve (LRAC)* is an "envelope" that contains all of the short-run cost curves representing different plant sizes. The **optimal plant size** is the plant that minimizes average total costs in the long run.

Figure 10.5 shows the relationship between short-run and long-run costs. Each of the small ATC curves represents the short-run average costs associated with a different plant size. Notice that as the size of the plant increases from ATC_1 to ATC_2, the average cost of production falls. Why is this the case? As the market expands, the firm may be able to use more sophisticated technology and lower the average cost of production. However, if production expands beyond quantity $\overline{Q}$ and the plant size indicated by ATC_3, average costs begin to rise. Why? One possibility—there are others as well—is that the firm has become so large that management is inefficient.

The long-run average cost curve is constructed by drawing a line tangent to the short-run average cost curves corresponding to different plant sizes. Notice that the long-run average cost curve is *not* tangent to the minimum points of the short-run

Optimal plant size Plant size that minimizes average total costs in the long run.

···· FIGURE 10.5 LONG-RUN COSTS: THE ENVELOPE CURVE

The long-run average cost curve, *LRAC*, is an "envelope" that holds all of the short-run cost curves representing different plant sizes. The optimal plant size corresponds to the minimum point on the *LRAC*, $\bar{Q}$. As output expands from zero toward $\bar{Q}$, costs fall because the firm can become more efficient by acquiring more capital. Over this region, the firm is called a decreasing-cost firm. After $\bar{Q}$, average costs begin to rise, and the firm becomes an increasing-cost firm.

average cost curves, except at the minimum point of the LRAC. The minimum points have a slope of zero, so connecting these points would result in a series of horizontal lines. The tangency occurs on the downward-sloping portion in the decreasing-cost region and the upward-sloping portion of the increasing-cost region.

The long-run average total cost curve calls attention to **economies of scale**, the idea that long-run average total costs depend on the size or scale of the plant. Where the firm is operating on the long-run average cost curve is important. If production is on the downward-sloping portion (the region between ATC_1 and ATC_3 in Figure 10.5), it is called a **decreasing-cost firm** because average costs fall as plant size increases. If the firm is operating on the upward-sloping portion (plant size greater than ATC_3), it is an **increasing-cost firm** because average costs will rise if the scale of operation is expanded. The plant size that results in ATC_3 is the optimal plant size. The long-run average cost curve is tangent to the minimum point of this short-run average total cost curve.

An interesting situation arises at points like Q_2 on Figure 10.5. This level of production can be produced with the plant indicated by ATC_1, the larger plant suggested by ATC_2, or even an intermediate-size plant with an average total cost curve between ATC_1 and ATC_2. Which plant should the firm choose? That depends on its forecast of future sales. If the firm expects sales to grow beyond Q_2 in the future, the larger plant is indicated; if Q_2 is expected to be temporary, the smaller

Economies of scale The idea that long-run average total costs depend on the size of the plant.

Decreasing-cost firm If long run average total costs fall as output expands, the firm is a decreasing-cost firm and is operating on the downward-sloping portion of the long run average total cost curve.

Increasing-cost firm If long run average total costs rise as output expands, the firm is an increasing-cost firm and is operating beyond optimal capacity on the upward-sloping portion of the long run average total cost curve.

plant is probably preferable. Certain complications make this kind of decision especially difficult, however. If costs fall as output increases, the firm might do best to opt for the larger plant to grab market share before a competitor enters the market and undercuts its costs of production. But if the firm's forecast is wrong and it builds a plant that is too large, it will have made a costly mistake because finding buyers for used factories and machinery can be difficult.

Figure 10.5 also shows the *long-run marginal cost curve (LRMC)*. As you might suspect, long-run marginal cost represents the incremental cost of producing one more unit of output in the long run. The shape of the *LRMC* curve occurs because it has essentially the same relationship with the *LRAC* curve as the short-run *MC* curve has with the *ATC* curve. When the *LRMC* is below *LRAC, LRAC* must be falling; when *LRMC* is above *LRAC, LRAC* must be rising. The *LRMC* intersects the *LRAC* at its minimum point.

Figure 10.6 distills the most important information from Figure 10.5. The short-run cost curves have been eliminated to reduce the clutter. This makes the long-run cost diagram look very much like the short run, but with one noticeable difference: there is only one average cost curve, not two. The reason is that there are no fixed costs in the long run so average variable cost is the same as average total cost. The *LRAC* will be especially important in the next few chapters when we compare different market structures.

Shifting Long-Run Cost Curves

The same factors that shift short-run cost curves—production technology and factor prices—also shift long-run cost curves. An advance in technology or lower factor prices will lower the long-run average and marginal cost curves; higher factor costs

FIGURE 10.6 LONG-RUN COSTS

The diagram for long-run costs looks like the diagram for short-run costs with one important difference: there is only one average cost curve. This is because all costs can vary in the long run, so there is no difference between average variable cost and average total cost.

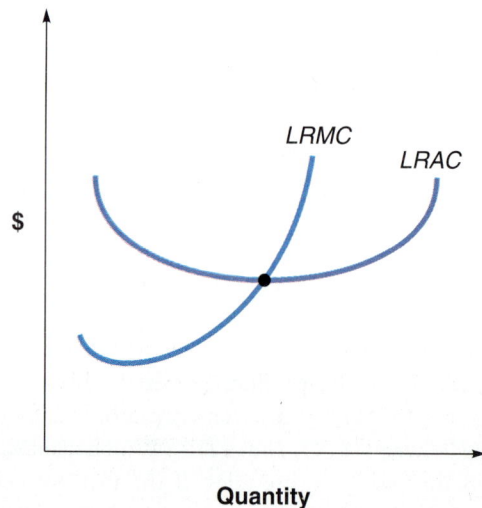

····FIGURE 10.7 CHANGING LONG-RUN COSTS

A decline in long-run costs or a technological advance will cause both the long-run marginal cost curve and the long-run average total cost curve to shift downward. The new marginal cost curve will intersect the new long-run average total cost curve at a higher level of output, indicating that average total costs are minimized with a larger plant size.

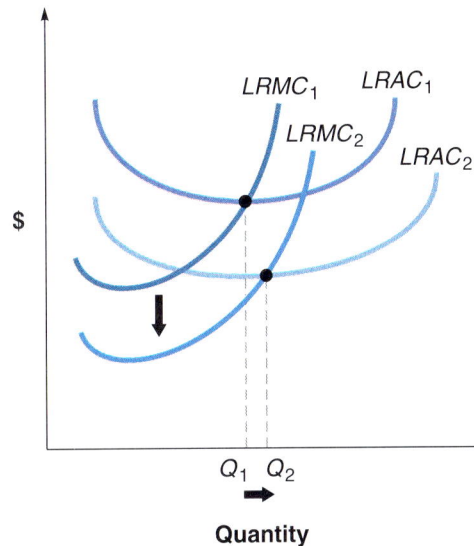

will shift them upward. Changing technology can also affect costs and optimal plant size. For example, Figure 10.7 illustrates the situation where a technological advance reduces costs and results in a larger optimal plant size because the new long-run marginal cost curve intersects the long-run average total cost curve at a higher level of output. It is also possible for a technological advance to decrease the optimal plant size. For example, personal computers using desktop publishing software can now produce printed documents much more cheaply than was possible with old-fashioned typesetting equipment. Small print shops like Kinko's Copy Centers represent serious competition for printing companies using traditional methods.

RECAP   Costs in the Long Run

The difference between the short run and the long run is the existence of fixed costs: There are fixed costs in the short run but not in the long run.

1. The long-run average cost curve is an envelope that contains short-run cost curves for every plant size. The minimum point on the long-run average cost curve gives the optimal plant size.
2. Firms operating on the downward-sloping portion of the long-run average cost curve are called decreasing-cost firms because costs would fall if plant size were increased. Firms operating on the upward-sloping portion of the long-run average cost curve are called increasing-cost firms because costs would rise if plant size were increased.
3. Factors that shift long-run average cost curves and long-run marginal cost curves include factor prices and technology.

COSTS IN THE REAL WORLD

Our discussion of U-shaped cost curves requires one important qualification: it is most applicable to situations when firms are operating very close to optimal capacity—the minimum point on the average total cost curve. When firms have a large amount of unused capacity, average and marginal costs are either roughly constant over or declining over a wide range of output. Firms often deliberately build plants with excess capacity, so we need to look at the relationship between costs and plant capacity closely.

Costs and Capacity

Sales fluctuate as the economy goes through cycles, and it is difficult or impossible to forecast sales precisely. One strategy for dealing with sales fluctuations is to produce more than is needed for current sales during slack times, store the excess in inventory, and then sell out of inventory when sales pick up. The problem with this strategy is that inventories are costly. Money tied up in inventory incurs an opportunity cost of forgone interest.

Another strategy is to build a plant large enough to meet expected peak sales demand. Firms that do this can keep smaller and less costly inventories and still be confident they will be able to meet sales demand during peak periods. The only extra cost they incur is the initial fixed cost of building a plant larger than the optimal size. This strategy is apparently quite common among larger business firms. Nationwide, the **capacity utilization rate** is typically under 85 percent even during business cycle expansions. If firms did not build in excess capacity, we would expect capacity utilization rates to be higher.[2]

When factories have excess capacity, the short-run average and marginal cost curves appear to have a different shape than those drawn in Figure 10.2. Both are essentially flat over the typical range of production and slope upward only as plant capacity is reached. Figure 10.8 illustrates the marginal and average total cost curves under these conditions. Does this negate everything we have said about production theory and the law of diminishing returns? Not at all. The average and marginal cost curves in Figure 10.8 obey the law of diminishing returns just as well as the curves in Figure 10.2—it is just that the minimum points of the curves have been stretched out a bit. Both curves have a downward-sloping portion representing increasing marginal product and an upward-sloping portion that indicates diminishing marginal product. The reason these cost curves are roughly horizontal is that unused capital goods are available for new workers, so the marginal product of labor does not show a significant decline as employment and output increase. When the plant is operating close to capacity, any new workers that are hired must be added to the existing stock of capital, so the marginal product of labor declines and the cost of production rises.

Building a plant that exhibits costs like those pictured in Figure 10.8 may offer an additional advantage. Because costs are roughly constant over a large region, the firm

Capacity utilization rate The rate at which plant capacity is being used. By examining changes in this rate, economists can get an idea of the state of the economy.

---

[2]Capacity utilization rates are collected by the Federal Reserve and published in the *Economic Report of the President* and elsewhere. The average capacity utilization rate during the 1980s was 80.4 percent.

·····**FIGURE 10.8** COSTS AND CAPACITY

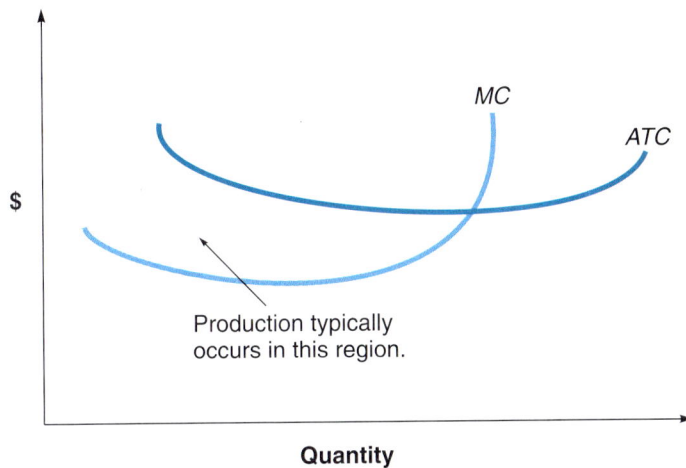

If the factory is built with planned excess capacity, short-run marginal and average costs are roughly constant over a wide range of output. This allows the firm to maintain fixed prices in the face of changing demand.

does not have to change prices as output goes through normal fluctuations. Thus, the firm has little reason to continually change prices or issue new price lists.[3] Not only is the act of changing prices costly in itself, but it can alienate customers. How would you like it if the price changed every time you shopped at your favorite store?

········

Costs and Competitiveness

Costs and competitiveness are intimately related. The firm that can produce at the lowest cost will gain market share at the expense of less-efficient firms. In today's world, information and technology move between firms and across international boundaries at literally the speed of light. The firm that has a cost advantage today almost certainly will not have it tomorrow unless it is willing and able to make a change. Some of the factors that influence the dynamics of cost advantages are product and process technology and inventory practices.

Product and Process Technology. As we found out in the last chapter, *product technology* refers to the production of a new good; *process technology* is a way of producing goods. Both can affect costs and competitiveness. Firms that spend research and development (R&D) dollars to develop new product technologies may come up with the next hot item—but they will enjoy profits only until competitors figure out how to make similar products at lower cost. Perhaps the best recent example is the personal com-

[3]The costs associated with changing prices and issuing new price lists are called *menu costs*. The effects of menu costs are discussed in Chapter 32.

250

FOCUS ON

COST COMPETITION IN HIGH-TECHNOLOGY INDUSTRIES

When the Apple Macintosh computer was introduced in January 1984, it came with 0.128 megabytes of random access memory (RAM), a single 0.4 megabyte floppy disk drive, and a $2,495 price tag. Several iterations later, in 1992, the Macintosh Classic II came out with 2 megabytes of RAM, a 1.4 megabyte floppy disk drive, a 40 megabyte hard disk, and a $1,995 price tag. It was also roughly four times as fast. Apple has been an innovator in the computer industry, but no more so than many other computer manufacturers. A rule of thumb in the computer industry is that prices decrease 10 percent per year and capability increases by 10 percent per year. How can firms compete in a world of such intense price and cost competition? It is not always easy. Just look at the graveyard of failed high-tech companies. With new models coming out every six months and small, start-up firms offering high-quality products at ever lower prices, the only way for firms to remain profitable is to keep constant pressure on the costs of production. Successful companies have used a variety of strategies to compete in this intense marketplace.

- *Motorola* makes cellular telephones and other high-tech consumer electronic goods as well as the microprocessor chips that power Apple Macintoshes. Most of Motorola's products are protected by patent laws, but competitors are constantly trying to take away market share, so Motorola must keep on its toes. Foremost in Motorola's strategy is maintenance of high quality. It accomplishes this in several ways. Perhaps the most important is a continuing effort to reduce manufacturing defects. Not only do defects require costly service and repairs, but short product cycles make it doubly important that customers be satisfied. Who will buy the next generation product if they had problems with the last generation? Motorola has also attempted to reduce the learning cycle so that new products can be produced with lower start-up costs. Among other things, this requires a commitment to hiring talented and educated workers. Finally, the 1993 Motorola flagship microprocessor—the 68040—contained 1.2 million transistors, but within a decade, computer chips will have as many as 10 billion transistors. To assure quality, Motorola engineers are working on built-in redundancy so that the chips will work even if a number of their transistors have failed. This increases manufacturing costs—but reduces defects and lowers support costs even more. It also increases quality, the main aim of Motorola's long-term competitive strategy.

- *Microsoft* stock was valued at some $22 billion in mid-1992, about the same as the value of General Motors stock. Not bad for a company that employs only about 10,000 people and had sales of only $1.8 billion in 1991. In contrast, General Motors employs more than 750,000 people and had sales in excess of $124 billion in 1991. Headed by the Harvard dropout turned billionaire, Bill Gates, Microsoft dominates the world software industry as few other firms have ever dominated an industry. How does Microsoft do it? First, it had the luck to be picked by IBM to write the system software for the original IBM personal computer. When that platform became the worldwide standard, Microsoft's success was assured: today, over 90 percent of all IBM-compatible computers run Microsoft system software. But Microsoft had to take additional steps to become the giant that it is today.

   The most important component of any knowledge-based company is its workforce, and Microsoft has done everything in its power to attract the best and the brightest. Neither Gates nor his recruiters are interested in haircuts, fashion, even

Plummeting retail prices for computer products are evidence of intense cost competition in the industry. High technology firms are forced to employ a wide variety of strategies to remain profitable.

work experience; they care only about raw talent and commitment. In 1991, Microsoft recruiters visited 137 college campuses, looked at 120,000 résumés, interviewed 7,400 candidates—and hired only 2,000 people. Many of the people who were hired accepted lower salaries than they were offered elsewhere. This obviously keeps costs low, but Microsoft has something else working for it: an *esprit de corps* that most firms can only envy. Microsoft workers are expected to put in 60- to 80-hour weeks; most do so gladly, or they are out the door. Employee turnover is under 6 percent, and productivity is booming. Microsoft is a major player in not only system software (MS-DOS and Windows), but also word processing (Word) and spreadsheets (Excel). Database and networking publishers fear Microsoft's recent entries into those markets.

- *Hewlett-Packard* turned 55 in 1994, making it one of the oldest high-tech companies in the world. How has it managed to keep up with the competition? Good products and low production costs are the answer. Between 1989 and 1992, the workforce was cut by almost 6 percent, but sales per worker increased by over 60 percent. HP also streamlined its management style to make it easier to design and bring out new models. In 1991, all 21 of HP's personal computers and work stations were replaced with new models. HP is the world leader in laser and ink-jet printers. It has about 60 percent of the domestic market for desktop laser printers, but the less costly ink-jet printers are more profitable. Why? The reason is that HP makes more of the parts for its ink-jets; many of the parts for its laser printers are imported.

HP's management style may be its most important competitive attribute. When it announced a new work station in 1991, analysts said that the $7,500 price was too high. The result: HP repriced the machine to $4,990 before it was even introduced and found it had a winner on its hands. Few analysts believe that HP can continue the cost-reducing moves of 1990 and 1991 so the company's future will be with new products and new markets. Portable printers and new palm-size computers are under development at HP.

(continued on next page)

(continued)

Apple Computer enjoyed a monopoly advantage with its easy-to-use Macintosh computer for several years, but the introduction of a new version of Microsoft Windows in 1990 eliminated much of that advantage. The long-heard complaint that Macintoshes were too expensive finally caught up with Apple. It responded by bringing out much lower priced models and slashing profit margins. Workers were laid off and more production facilities were moved overseas. Sales of the low-cost models boomed and Apple gained market share, but profits were down. It was clear that if Apple was to survive into the twenty-first century, more changes were necessary.

In 1993, Apple introduced the Newton, a handheld personal computer that understands handwriting. Apple also decided to put more resources into software and to write applications for other platforms including Windows and IBM-compatible machines. Why? The profit margin on computer hardware is typically under 40 percent; the margin on software can be as high as 80 percent.

Apple also formed strategic alliances with IBM, Sony, Sharp, and other high-tech companies. Each alliance was designed to reduce the costs of production. The alliance with IBM was a trade of sorts: Apple traded its system software technology for IBM's RISC (reduced instruction set computing) hardware technology. This decreased the need for Apple to spend R&D dollars on the development of its own RISC technology. The Sony alliance allowed Apple to bring out its wildly successful PowerBook laptop computers on schedule. Sony had experience making laptops, Apple did not. Similarly, the alliance with Sharp was necessary for the production of Newton because Sharp already had factories set up for producing hand-size personal computers.

The pace of technological change will continue to accelerate in the future, and the pressure for both product and process technology innovations will accelerate as well. The computer of the future will not only be faster and easier to use, but it will also have capabilities we only dream of today. A dominant force behind these changes will be cost competition and the quest for profits.

SOURCES: "Microsoft," *Business Week,* February 24, 1992, pp. 60–65; "Suddenly, Hewlett-Packard Is Doing Everything Right," *Business Week,* March 23, 1992, pp. 88–90; "Apple's Daring Leap into the All-Digital Future," *Business Week,* May 25, 1992, pp. 120–122; "Japan's Less-than-Invincible Computer Makers," *The Economist,* January 11, 1992, p. 61.

puter market. When IBM introduced its original personal computer in 1981, the computer was an immediate success—and, almost immediately, came under intense competition from low-cost clones. How could the clone makers offer computers at half the price of IBM machines? Most were produced abroad by low-wage workers, and the clone makers benefited from IBM's R&D without having to pay for it, but these were not the only reasons for the cost advantage. Many of the production facilities in Japan, Korea, and Taiwan used more sophisticated and efficient process technologies than did IBM. Despite a reputation for quality and service, IBM's share of the personal computer market fell steadily throughout the 1980s.[4] The message is

---

[4]Not until late in the decade did IBM begin to treat competition from low-cost clones seriously. Then it adopted more efficient process technologies so that it could slash costs (and prices) to regain market share.

clear: unless you can produce the product at lowest cost, you will lose your market. And the way to produce at lowest cost is to develop efficient process technologies—or pay your workers lower wages. The Focus box on page 250 highlights some of the cost-saving strategies used by high-tech firms.

Inventory Practices. Firms keep two kinds of inventories: an inventory of final products ready for sale, and an inventory of intermediate products ready to be used as inputs. Unfortunately, U.S. firms are only now catching up with the Japanese in efficient inventory practice. This has been particularly noticeable in the automobile industry. Japanese firms practice what is called "just-in-time" inventory management—intermediate parts are in stock for less than 20 minutes compared to two weeks or more for the Big Three U.S. automobile manufacturers. Combine better inventory practices with more advanced robot production techniques, and you have much of the explanation for the $1,500 cost advantage that the Japanese auto manufacturers enjoyed through much of the 1980s.[5]

• • • • • • • •

Dynamic Considerations

Many modern production processes follow a similar pattern. The firm invests in a cost-reducing innovation in Period I. Lower production costs allow the firm to reap profits in Period II. In Period III, the cost-reducing innovation becomes available to competitors, and profits fall. This story has several important implications, both for individual firms and for the economy as a whole.

The individual firm clearly has an incentive to devote resources to cost-reducing technologies—but less of an incentive than if these innovations could not be copied. But what if the cost-producing innovation exhibits decreasing costs? That is, what if costs fall even more as production increases? In this situation, the firm has an incentive to expand market share—perhaps by opening up overseas markets—and thus keep forcing down the costs of production. Doing this would keep competitors out of the market and allow the innovating firm to maintain its high profits.

Firms know this—and so do nations. This is why many nations have sought to subsidize investment and research and development in particular industries. If the domestic industry can enter the world market first and gain enough market share, it will be difficult for other firms or nations to enter that market—at least until a new cost-reducing innovation can be found. This is why Japan subsidized its steel and shipbuilding industries in the 1950s and 1960s. These subsidies appear to have been successful, but similar government subsidies for fax and copy machines enacted in the 1980s were less successful.[6]

---

[5]This advantage has been shrinking and may have vanished by the 1990s. Not only have the U.S. automakers adopted many Japanese manufacturing practices—partly as a result of joint production agreements—but the depreciation of the dollar has reduced U.S. auto worker wages to below Japanese auto worker wages.

[6]The debate over the effectiveness of government subsidies and international competitiveness is ongoing and will continue. In *The Competitive Advantage of Nations* (New York: Free Press, 1990), Michael Porter argued that government subsidies generally have little effect when he said, "Government is indeed an actor in international competition, but rarely does it have a starring role" (p. 4). Other writers, including Laura Tyson, chair of the Council of Economic Advisers under President Clinton, disagree. We will look at this issue in more detail in Chapter 37.

SUMMARY

This chapter has examined the costs of production. We will find it necessary to refer to the concepts developed here continually in the next several chapters. The most important concepts to remember from this chapter are:

1. In the short run, firms have both fixed and variable costs. Fixed costs do not vary with output; variable costs do. Total cost is defined as fixed cost plus variable cost. Marginal cost is the cost of producing one more unit of output. It is computed as the change in variable costs divided by the change in output. In the long run, all costs can vary so there are no fixed costs.

2. The marginal cost curve intersects both the average variable cost curve and the average total cost curve at their minimum points. When marginal cost is less than average cost, average costs are falling; when marginal cost is greater than average cost, average costs are rising. The average fixed cost curve declines as output increases.

3. The long-run average cost curve is U-shaped. When production takes place on the downward-sloping portion of the average cost curve, the firm is said to exhibit decreasing costs; if production takes place on the upward-sloping portion, the firm is experiencing increasing costs. The minimum point on the average cost curve defines the optimal plant size.

4. If firms operate with excess capacity, both the marginal cost curve and the average cost curve tend to be flat. This suggests that the firm can increase output without experiencing substantially higher costs.

5. Cost considerations are a vitally important component of competitiveness. Successful firms manage inventory effectively and are continually looking for low-cost production technologies.

KEY TERMS AND CONCEPTS

fixed cost (FC)

variable cost (VC)

total cost (TC)

normal profit

economic (abnormal) profit

marginal cost (MC)

average fixed cost (AFC)

average variable cost (AVC)

average total cost (ATC)

optimal plant size

economies of scale

decreasing-cost firm

increasing-cost firm

capacity utilization rate

IMPORTANT FORMULAS

Total cost: $TC = FC + VC$

Marginal cost: $MC = \dfrac{\Delta TC}{\Delta Q} = \dfrac{\Delta FC + \Delta VC}{\Delta Q} = \dfrac{\Delta VC}{\Delta Q}$

Average fixed cost: $AFC = \dfrac{FC}{Q}$

Average variable cost: $AVC = \dfrac{VC}{Q}$

Average total cost: $ATC = \dfrac{TC}{Q} = \dfrac{FC + VC}{Q} = AFC + AVC$

Total cost: $TC = ATC \times Q$

Total variable cost: $VC = AVC \times Q$

REVIEW QUESTIONS

1. Define and give examples of fixed, variable, total, marginal, and average costs. Draw graphs to illustrate these costs.
2. What is the difference between the long run and the short run? How does time frame affect cost graphs? Draw graphs to illustrate your answer.
3. What is the difference between normal and economic profits? Where do profits appear in the costs of production?
4. When is the plant size optimal? Draw a graph to illustrate your answer.
5. Why do average and marginal cost curves often appear to be approximately flat in the real world? Does this violate the law of diminishing returns?

PROBLEMS

1. Table 9.1 in Chapter 9 had 12 rows of data, but Table 10.1 in this chapter has only 9 rows. The 3 rows were omitted because firms would not operate in Stage III of the production function. However, suppose that one did. Calculate the average, total, and marginal costs for those rows of the table. Explain the meaning of your answers.
2. The text lists three examples of fixed costs—fire insurance premiums, security guard services, and existing debt payments. List and discuss three other fixed costs for a manufacturing firm.
3. Fill in the blanks (indicated by the letters) to complete the following table:

N	Q	MP	AP	FC	VC	TC	MC	AFC	AVC	ATC
0	0		—	$500	e	$500		—	—	—
		→ a					→ $4.00			
1	50		50.00		c	200	f	$10.00	4.00	k
		→ 40						→ h		
2	90		b		d	400	g		j	4.44	l
		→ 60						→ i		

4. Suppose that you fear competition from a low-cost foreign rival. Recognizing that labor costs are your largest cost of production, you decide to announce a 10 percent across-the-board wage reduction. Do you think this would affect the productivity of labor? Why or why not? How does your answer relate to the data in the first four columns of Table 10.1?

5. Is a decreasing-cost firm necessarily experiencing increasing marginal returns? Why or why not?

6. Explain whether and how each of the following would affect short-run marginal, variable, fixed, and total costs:
   a. The wage rate paid to assembly line workers increases.
   b. The salary paid to upper management increases.
   c. The firm is required to implement new environmental controls.
   d. The price of oil decreases.
   e. Demand falls so the firm cuts back on production.
   f. Property taxes rise.
   g. Demand increases so the firm pays workers overtime.

7. Find the areas that correspond to short-run total cost, short-run total variable cost, and total fixed costs on the following diagram:

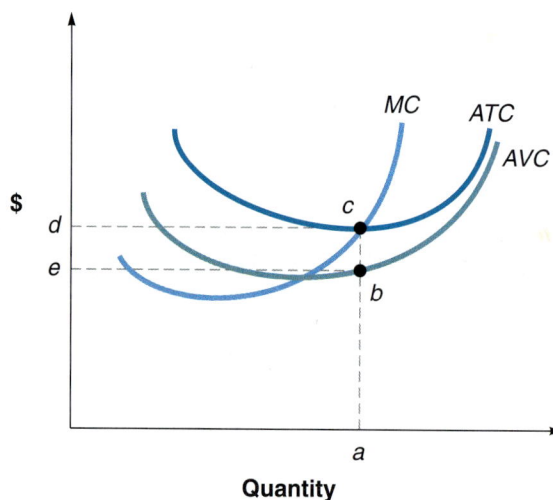

Quantity

8. Indicate whether each of the following is true, false, or uncertain and why:
   a. $AVC = ATC$ as $Q \to \infty$.
   b. $AFC + AVC + MC = ATC$.
   c. AFC falls as production proceeds through Stages I and II; it begins to rise in Stage III.
   d. MC intersects the minimum point of AFC.
   e. $ATC = AVC = AFC$ at $Q = 0$.
   f. In the short run, an increase in factor prices causes the MC to intersect ATC at a higher level of output.
   g. In the long run, advancing technology makes the optimal plant size smaller.
   h. The $LRAC$ envelope curve is tangent to the minimum points of the short-run average total cost curves.

PART III

MICROECONOMICS II: INDUSTRIAL STRUCTURE AND FACTOR MARKETS

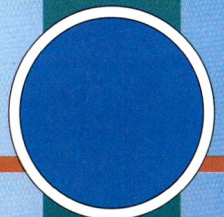

CHAPTER 11

Pure Competition: The Competitive Ideal

The word "competition" is part of our everyday vocabulary. We talk about competition between baseball teams, competition in the classroom, and competition between siblings. And we even talk about economic competition. Actually, there are several kinds of economic competition—which is why confusion often arises when economists use the term. In everyday language, "economic competition" usually means the process of sellers struggling to attract buyers. This conception of competition is not wrong, but it is rarely precise enough for our needs. Economists must distinguish between the *process* of competition and various *competitive market structures*. To help do this, they usually combine the word "competition" with a descriptor—*pure* competition, *monopolistic* competition, or something else.

Why are we making so much about semantics? The reason is that we need to be very careful about how we define *pure competition,* the main topic of this chapter. We will find that pure competition generates efficiency, something that cannot be said of any other market structure. Unfortunately, the economist's conception of pure competition does not exist in the real world. So why do we devote an entire chapter to it? There are two reasons: First, although few markets fit the pure competition model exactly, many markets do exhibit most of the characteristics of pure competition, so if we can understand the model, we may better understand many markets in the real world. Second, pure competition is an ideal state we will use for evaluating real-world markets. Without a definition of the ideal, we cannot assess the advantages and disadvantages of real, but less-than-ideal markets.

AFTER READING AND STUDYING THIS CHAPTER, YOU SHOULD BE ABLE TO:

• • • Define the four main market structures and give examples of each
• • • Explain why the demand curve facing a purely competitive firm is horizontal and how this relates to economic efficiency
• • • Discuss the conditions that must hold for firms to maximize profits
• • • Explain how the process of entry and exit eliminates economic profits in the long run

VARIETIES OF MARKET STRUCTURE

Alaska Power and Light sells electricity in Juneau, Alaska. Delta Airlines sells airline tickets. Arthur Andersen, Inc., prepares income tax reports. Bob Warren sells live dungeness crabs. What do these firms have in common? They all combine inputs and produce outputs, and they all strive to make profits. But after that they are rather different. The utility company has no direct competitors; if you live in Juneau and want electricity, you either buy it from AP&L or you run a generator. If you want to fly from Seattle to Juneau, Alaska, you fly on Delta—or one of only two other carriers that fly the route. If you need someone to do your income taxes, you can talk to a CPA at Arthur Andersen—or look in the Yellow Pages for the phone number of dozens of other CPAs and tax preparers in town. All of these firms claim to do a credible job and get you all of the legal deductions, but they charge different fees. Which should you select? Do you get better services for a higher price? If you want a live dungeness crab, go to the fish market. Bob's cost $5 apiece, weigh about three pounds, and were caught in the bay. So were Alan's, Barb's, and the crabs of every other person selling crabs at the market. How do you choose whose crabs to buy? There is no difference at all in price or quality.

The four firms we just mentioned are examples of different kinds of firms. Alaska Power and Light is a monopoly, Delta is an oligopoly firm, Arthur Andersen is a monopolistically competitive firm, and Bob Warren is a pure competitor. Each of these firms faces a different kind of competition, and each has a different effect on the economy. In the next four chapters, we will analyze these market structures in some detail, but it will help if we first define each market structure.

• • • • • • • •

Pure Competition

Pure competition A market structure characterized by many sellers of homogeneous products and free entry and exit.

A **purely competitive** market has three main attributes. First, there is a very large number of buyers and sellers. How large is "large"? There are so many sellers that no one seller is large enough to influence price. If Bob has a bad day and brings only half of his usual number of crabs to the dock, he will be hard-pressed to raise the price of his crabs because Alan, Barb, and the other crabbers will undercut him with their normal $5 price. This is why competitive firms are said to be **price takers**. Purely competitive firms cannot set their selling price; they can only charge the price determined by supply and demand in the entire market.

Price taker A firm that does not have the ability to control the price of the product it sells; it can only charge the price determined in the market.

The second main attribute of purely competitive firms is that their products are identical or *homogeneous* in the economist's lexicon. It makes no difference whether you buy from Bob, Alan, or Barb; their crabs came from the same water and are the same size and quality. Given that the crabs are identical, would you pay even a penny more for a crab from Bob than from Alan or Barb? You would not.

Finally, purely competitive markets are characterized by *free entry and exit* from the industry. This means that anyone can become a crabber and any crabber can decide to quit and do something else. Free entry and exit does not mean that it is costless to enter or exit a market, only that no restrictions are placed on doing so. What would cause firms to enter or exit the market? In a word: profits. If crabbers start making lots of profit, more people will enter the industry. And as they do, the additional supply of crabs on the market will tend to lower prices. This will bring profits down to a more normal level. On the other hand, if crabbers are experiencing losses, some people will leave the industry. As the supply of crabs on the market shrinks, the price will rise and restore profits for the remaining crabbers.

There are few good examples of firms that fit these criteria exactly, but farmers, some small retail stores, and stockbrokers come fairly close. Farmers produce identical crops—#12 red winter wheat is the same whether Farmer Brown or Farmer Garcia produces it—but the existence of numerous government regulations and subsidies means that farming deviates somewhat from the model of pure competition. For example, price subsidies and crop controls make it less attractive for farmers to exit the industry than it would be in their absence. Small retail stores are quite competitive, but do not precisely fit the model of pure competition because they are in different locations. This means that they are not quite identical to the consumer. You would not consider a store on the other side of town identical to the one down the street, would you? Stockbrokers all trade identical stocks for their customers, but some brokers offer financial counseling and "hot tips" while others do little more than execute their clients' wishes. As a result, stockbrokers offer similar but not quite identical products, so the market does not fit the model of pure competition exactly.

Monopolistic Competition

There is only one significant difference between a **monopolistically competitive** firm and a purely competitive firm: the products produced in a monopolistically competitive industry are not homogeneous. Any of the CPA firms you find in the Yellow Pages can do your taxes, but you may believe that one firm will do a better job than another. Arthur Andersen is one of the prestigious Big 6 accounting firms. It will be years before the recent college graduate who just hung up a shingle in the mall has the same kind of prestige or client list as Arthur Andersen. Even a slight product difference is enough to let monopolistically competitive firms develop brand loyalty—and charge different prices. Unlike firms under pure competition, monopolistically competitive firms frequently use advertising to convince buyers that their products have no good substitutes. That new CPA might attract customers by advertising same-day service or computer tax filing, but how can a farmer gain by advertising #12 red winter wheat that is sold at the same price as everyone else's?

Many firms can be classified as monopolistic competitors. Ice cream producers are a good example: there are many producers (Häagen Dazs, Ben and Jerry's, Breyers, Dreyers, and local brands); entry is relatively inexpensive and easy; and there are many product variations and price ranges. Other examples include clothing manu-

Monopolistic competition A market structure characterized by many sellers with differentiated products and free entry and exit.

facturers, IBM-compatible computer manufactures, cigarettes, and principles of economics textbook publishers.

. . . .

Oligopoly

Oligopoly A market structure in which there are only a few sellers and entry and exit is restricted.

An **oligopoly** industry is characterized by a few firms in a market with restricted entry. How many is "few"? There are so few that each firm must pay careful attention to the actions of its rivals. If Delta Airlines raises the price of its Seattle-Juneau tickets but Alaska Air lowers the price of its tickets, Delta stands to lose considerable market share. But if Alaska Air also raises its price, Delta's sales will not fall nearly as much. The need to react and anticipate the actions of rivals is the key characteristic that distinguishes oligopoly from other market structures.

Oligopoly firms can produce either homogeneous or differentiated products. The airline industry is a differentiated oligopoly; some airlines advertise great food, others offer better frequent flier discounts. The steel and aluminum industries are homogeneous oligopolies. It makes little difference whether you buy your next steel girder from USX or Bethlehem; both girders meet the exact same specifications and may have the same price.

. . . .

Monopoly

Monopoly A market structure in which there is only one firm that sells a product for which there are no close substitutes; barriers to entering the industry are high.

Price maker A seller that has the ability to control to some degree the price it receives for its product.

A **monopoly** not only produces a product for which there are no good substitutes, but it is the only firm in the industry. Most towns have only one utility company, and since there are few good substitutes for public utilities, the utility industry is a monopoly. Cable television is another industry with monopoly status in many communities.

In contrast to competitive firms, monopolists, oligopolists, and monopolistically competitive firms are **price makers**, not price takers. Price makers can set the price they want to charge because their competitors do not sell identical products. Does this mean that they should charge as high a price as possible? Almost certainly not. There may be no *good* substitutes for monopoly products, but if the price is set too high, people will find some sort of substitute. People may not even look for substitutes at low prices, but they probably will at high prices. For example, at a price of $15 per month, there may be no "good" substitute for local telephone service, but if the price were $100 a month, many people would suddenly find that letter writing is not so bad after all! Still, monopolists may be able to set the price quite high before people turn to inferior substitutes—which is why monopolists are usually regulated by the government.

. . . .

A Caveat

Before proceeding, we need to qualify much of the forgoing as well as the examples in Table 11.1. Though economists generally agree on the theoretical characteristics of the different market structures, it is virtually impossible to find examples that fit the categories exactly. As a result, there is often considerable disagreement as to where to place particular firms. For example, many economists would argue that the Arthur

• • • • TABLE 11.1 VARIETIES OF MARKETS

	Pure Competition	Monopolistic Competition	Oligopoly	Monopoly
Number of firms	Many	Many	Few	One
Products	Identical	Differentiated	Differentiated or identical	No good substitutes
Entry and exit	Unrestricted	Unrestricted	Significant barriers	None
Examples	Farmers, stockbrokers	Retail sales, soft drinks	Airlines (differentiated), steel (homogeneous)	Public utilities, professional sports teams

Andersen CPA firm is more of an oligopoly than a monopolistically competitive firm because it is so large and wields market power; others would contend that even Arthur Andersen faces real potential competition from small CPA firms. The same argument can be made about the soft drink industry: some economists would contend that the prominence of Coke and Pepsi makes the soft drink industry an oligopoly; others would say that increasing competition from private label brands has eroded the power of Coke and Pepsi. These issues are interesting, but outside our primary focus just now. The purpose of the classification scheme is to provide a framework for analysis. After we develop that framework, we can *try* to classify particular industries.

PROFIT MAXIMIZATION: THE GOAL OF COMPETITIVE FIRMS

The main aim of purely competitive firms is to maximize profits. To understand how this is accomplished, we need to recall some definitions and then develop the revenue and sales curves facing the purely competitive firm.

Profits, Costs, and Revenue

The owner of a purely competitive firm is often also the manager, so the owner's income is the firm's profits. You should have a good idea of what constitutes profits: **profit** is what is left after the firm pays all costs of production. In other words, the firm's profit (π) is equal to its total revenue (TR) minus total costs (TC):

Profit The difference between total revenue and total cost.

$$\text{Profit: } \pi = TR - TC \qquad [1]$$

We already know about total costs from the last chapter. Total costs consist of fixed plus variable costs. We know too that the total cost curve is **S**-shaped because of the three stages of production and the law of diminishing returns. We will need to combine this information with the total revenue function momentarily, but first we need to review the definition of total costs. Two points are especially important:

1. The total cost curve includes a *normal profit* paid to the owner; this is the owner's wage. This means that the definition of profit in Equation 1 actually refers to what we called *economic profits* in the last chapter. In this chapter the word "profit" will usually be used to refer to the concept of profit as defined in Equation 1. When it is important to distinguish between normal and economic profits, we will use those terms explicitly.

2. We also found out in the last chapter that total costs include explicit as well as implicit costs. Explicit costs are measurable costs like wages, rent on land, and so on. Implicit costs are opportunity costs of forgone earnings. For example, if you must spend weekends at the shop to keep your small business out of bankruptcy, lost weekend leisure time is an implicit cost of running your own business. Implicit costs increase total costs so profits fall—at least in the eyes of an economist. Accountants measure only explicit costs when they calculate profit, so they would ignore the lost weekend leisure time. For tax purposes, you would use the accountant's definitions of profit and cost, but if you are trying to decide whether to open your own business, the economist's definitions are more appropriate. Unless stated otherwise, we will always use the economist's definitions of profit and cost in this book.

· · · · · · · · ·

The Demand Curve Facing a Firm under Pure Competition

Do you think that the price of wheat would fall if Farmer Jones doubled or even tripled the acreage devoted to wheat production? It almost certainly would not in

· · · · **FIGURE 11.1 THE DEMAND CURVE FACING A FIRM UNDER PURE COMPETITION**

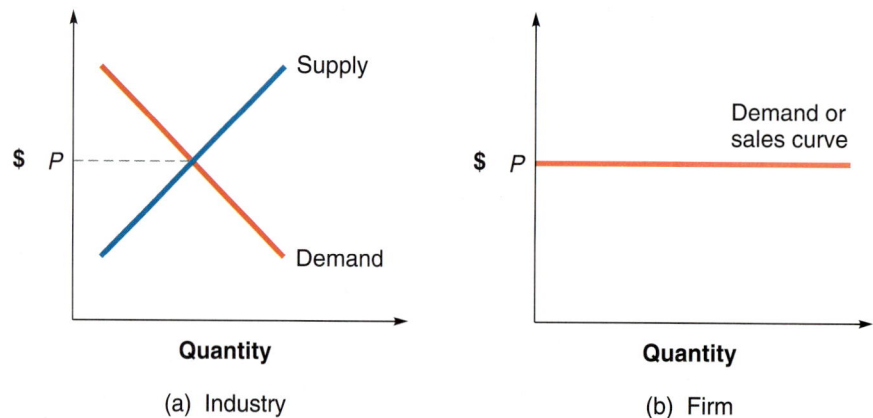

(a) Industry

(b) Firm

The demand curve facing a competitive *industry* is downward sloping because if all firms offer more on the market, price must fall or consumers will not buy the increased quantity that is offered. The demand (sales) curve facing a single firm under pure competition is perfectly horizontal because each firm produces such a small portion of industry output that it perceives that it can sell an unlimited quantity at the prevailing market price.

the real world—and definitely not in the textbook world! Remember that purely competitive firms are price takers because there are so many firms in the industry that no single firm can influence the market price. This means that a competitive firm like a wheat farmer faces a perfectly horizontal demand curve like the one shown in Figure 11.1b. The demand curve facing the firm is often called the **sales curve** because it represents the different quantities that the firm can sell at the market price. Panel (a) shows the industry supply and demand curves. Notice that the industry demand curve is downward sloping like most demand curves—an indication that if *all* wheat farmers decided to double or triple their production, there most certainly would be a change in the price of wheat. The interplay of industry supply and demand determines the market price that all firms within the competitive industry charge. As industry conditions change, the price that individual firms can charge will change, but a single firm cannot affect the industry price so individual demand curves are horizontal. Before we go on, we need to emphasize that sales curves are perfectly horizontal only when the market is pure competition; in all other market structures, the sales curve is downward sloping. We will explore those cases in the next two chapters.

Sales curve The demand curve facing a firm; equivalent to the average revenue curve.

· · · · · · · ·

Total Revenue

The receipts the firm earns from selling goods and services are its total revenue. For every good (Q) that is sold, the firm receives the selling price (P) of that good. This means that **total revenue** is computed by multiplying price times quantity:

$$\text{Total revenue: } TR = P \times Q = PQ \qquad [2]$$

Total revenue The receipts a firm receives from selling its product; equals price times quantity.

Table 11.2 replicates the total cost information from Table 10.1 in Columns 1 and 2 and adds four new columns. Column 3, TR = total revenue, is calculated by multiplying the quantities in Column 1 by \$6, the (assumed) fixed market price. Notice that the firm's total revenue keeps rising as more is produced and sold. Column 4, π = profit, is calculated by subtracting total cost from total revenue. A glance down Column 4 shows that profits rise from −\$300 to +\$140 as output and sales rise from zero to 240 units. Why doesn't the firm increase production and sell more than 240 units? After all, it is a competitive firm so it can sell as much as it wants at the fixed market price of \$6. The reason is found in Column 2: a higher level of output would cause costs to rise faster than revenues so profits would fall.

The information in Table 11.2 has been plotted on Figure 11.2. As in Chapter 10, the total cost curve is **S**-shaped because of the three stages of production and the law of diminishing returns. The intercept is equal to fixed costs of \$300. The total revenue curve for a purely competitive firm is a straight line because revenue increases by the same amount (\$6, the fixed market price) for every unit of output that is sold. Profit is equal to the vertical distance between the total revenue and total cost curves. When output is less than 150 or greater than 290 units, the total cost curve is above the total revenue curve. This indicates that the firm is incurring losses or making negative profits. The horizontal distance of the shaded area—output between 150 and 290 units—is the range of production that results in positive profits. The maximum profit is where the vertical distance between total revenue and total cost is greatest.

•••• **TABLE 11.2 PROFIT, TOTAL COST, AND TOTAL REVENUE**

(1) Q	(2) TC	(3) TR	(4) π	(5) AR	(6) MR
0	$300	$ 0	$−300	$—	
					→ 6
40	500	240	−260	6	
					→ 6
90	700	540	−160	6	
					→ 6
150	900	900	0	6	
					→ 6
200	1,100	1,200	100	6	
					→ 6
240•	1,300	1,440	140•	6	
					→ 6
270	1,500	1,620	120	6	
					→ 6
290	1,700	1,740	+40	6	
					→ 6
300	1,900	1,800	−100	6	

Definitions and Formulas:

Q = total product

TR = total revenue = PQ

AR = average revenue = $\dfrac{TR}{Q}$ = P

TC = total cost

π = profit = $TR - TC$

MR = marginal revenue = $\dfrac{\Delta TR}{\Delta Q}$ = P

NOTE: $P = \$6$ for all sales levels.

Marginal Revenue and Marginal Cost

Students who have taken a calculus course may have already suspected an important fact about profit maximization from looking at Figure 11.2 closely: The profit-maximizing level of output occurs at the point where the slopes of the total revenue curve and the total cost curve are equal. This is shown in Figure 11.3, which replicates the total cost and total revenue curves from Figure 11.2, but has been labeled to illustrate the slopes of the total revenue and total cost curves. Let's explore why profit is maximum where the slopes of the total revenue curve and total cost curve are equal.

The slope of the total revenue curve is called **marginal revenue**. Marginal revenue is calculated as the change in total revenue divided by the change in quantity or:

Marginal revenue The change in revenue from selling one more unit of output.

$$\text{Marginal revenue: } MR = \frac{\text{change in total revenue}}{\text{change in quantity}} = \frac{\Delta TR}{\Delta Q} \qquad [3]$$

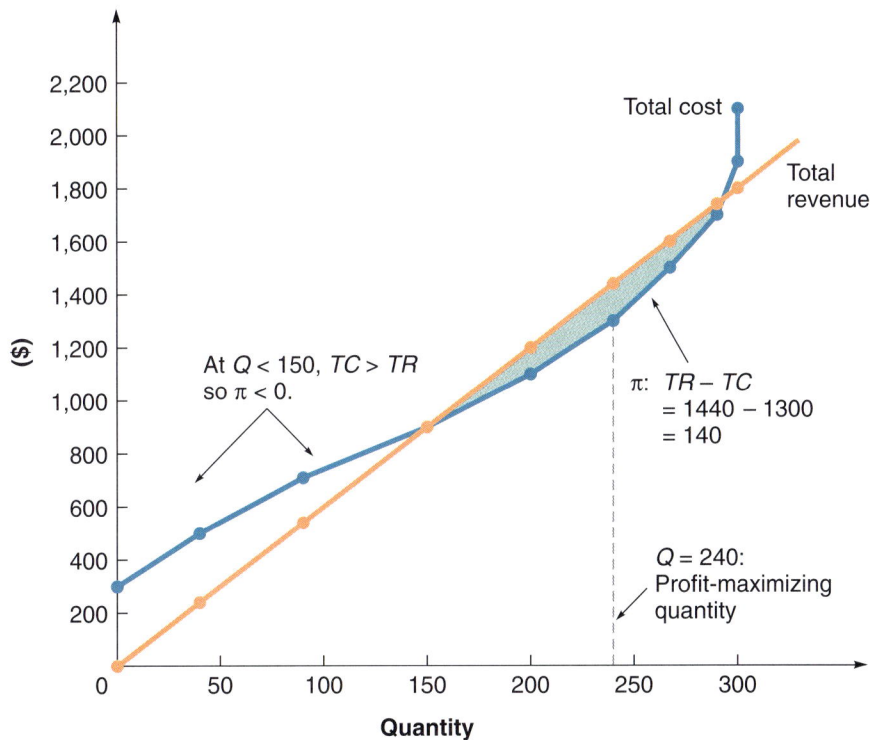

····FIGURE 11.2 TOTAL COST, TOTAL REVENUE, AND PROFIT MAXIMIZATION

The shape of the total cost curve is determined by the three stages of production and the law of diminishing returns. The total revenue curve for a purely competitive firm is a straight line because the selling price is fixed ($6 in this example). Profit maximization occurs where the vertical distance between the total revenue curve and total cost curve is greatest. This occurs when output is 240.

The total revenue curve for a firm under pure competition is a straight line, so its slope, marginal revenue, is constant. Marginal revenue is calculated between quantity 40 and 90 on Figure 11.3. When quantity sold rises from 40 to 90, total revenue rises from $240 to $540, so marginal revenue is:

$$MR = \frac{\$540 - \$240}{90 - 40} = \$6$$

This is important: for a pure competitive firm, marginal revenue is equal to selling price.

The slope of the total cost curve is marginal cost. As we found out in the last chapter, marginal cost is the change in cost associated with producing another unit of output or:

•••••**FIGURE 11.3** $MR = MC$ **AT THE PROFIT-MAXIMIZING OUTPUT**

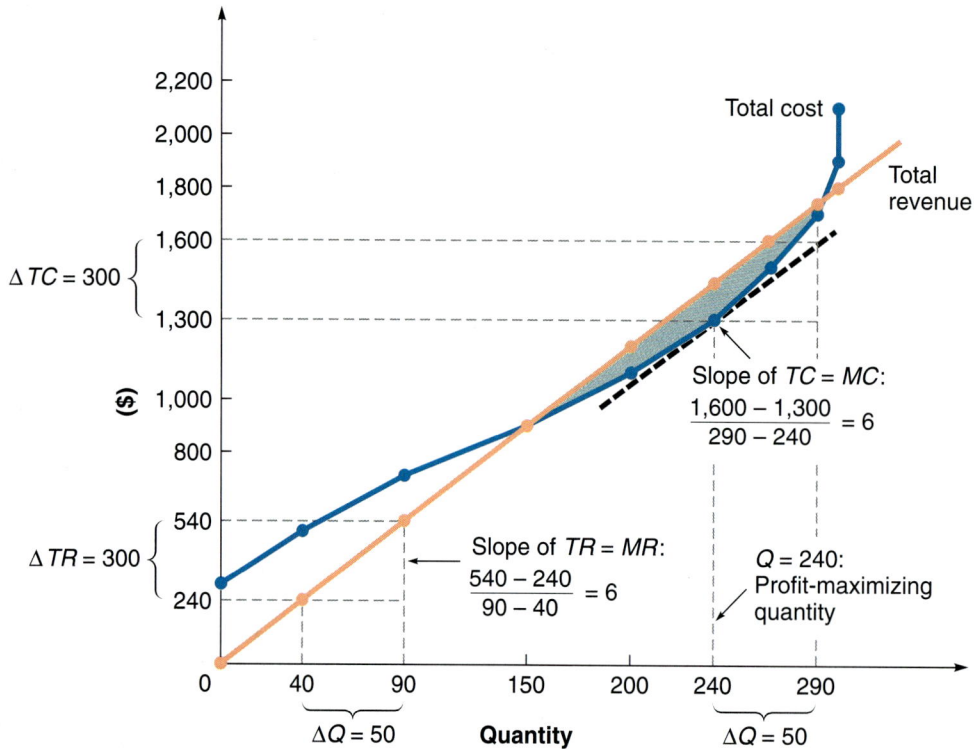

The slope of the total cost curve is equal to the slope of the total revenue curve at the profit-maximizing level of output. In this case, the slope of the total revenue curve, marginal revenue, is $6 because each good sold earns the selling price of $6. The slope of the total cost curve, marginal cost, varies depending on the level of output. When output is 240 units, marginal cost is $6 because the slope of a line drawn tangent to the total cost curve at $Q = 240$ has a slope of $6.

$$\text{Marginal cost: } MC = \frac{\text{change in total cost}}{\text{change in quantity}} = \frac{\Delta TC}{\Delta Q} \qquad [4]$$

The total cost curve is not linear, so its slope and thus marginal cost vary as output changes. We can find marginal cost at the profit-maximizing quantity by drawing a line tangent to the total cost curve at the profit-maximizing quantity and finding the slope of that line. This is done graphically in Figure 11.3. The marginal cost of producing the 240th unit of output is:

$$MC = \frac{\$1,600 - \$1,300}{290 - 240} = \$6$$

This is the result we were looking for: The slope of the total revenue curve (marginal revenue) is equal to the slope of the total cost (marginal cost) at the profit-maximizing level of production.

Average Revenue = Marginal Revenue = Demand = Price

Average revenue is defined as total revenue divided by quantity, and because total revenue is defined as price times quantity, average revenue is just the selling price:

Average revenue Total revenue divided by quantity.

$$\text{Average revenue: } AR = \frac{TR}{Q} = \frac{PQ}{Q} = P \qquad [5]$$

The average revenue for $Q = 240$ in Table 11.1 is:

$$AR = \frac{TR}{Q} = \frac{\$1{,}440}{240} = \$6$$

Average revenue is constant for all levels of output because the selling price is assumed to be fixed at $6.

The average revenue curve is a plot of the different quantities the firm can sell at different prices; in other words, it is what we called the sales curve or the demand curve facing the firm in Figure 11.1. In the case of a purely competitive firm, only one price can be charged—the market price—so the next unit sold always brings in as much revenue as the previous unit that was sold. As a result, the average revenue curve is the same as the marginal revenue curve, but we need to emphasize that this is true only for a firm under pure competition.

THE FUNDAMENTAL RULE FOR PROFIT MAXIMIZATION

The profit-maximizing condition we developed in Figure 11.3 is especially important because it applies to all market structures, not just pure competition. In fact, it is so important that it is sometimes referred to as the Fundamental Rule for Profit Maximization and bears repeating:

FUNDAMENTAL RULE FOR PROFIT MAXIMIZATION: *Profit maximization occurs at the level of output where marginal cost is equal to marginal revenue*

The Fundamental Rule can best be illustrated by combining the demand curve with the marginal cost curve we developed in the last chapter. This is done in Figure 11.4. First, look what happens when the firm produces 50 units of output. At this point, the marginal cost of production is $1 and the marginal revenue is $3. The firm is making profits on the 50th unit because it is earning more revenue than it costs to produce that unit of output. The profit on the 50th unit is $2. Now look at a higher quantity, say, 100 units of output. The marginal cost of the 100th unit has risen to $2, but it is still less than marginal revenue of $3. This means that the profit on the 100th unit is only $1, but it is still positive, so at least 100 units should be produced. Production should continue up to 120 units of output, the point where the Fundamental Rule applies; that is, where marginal cost is equal to marginal revenue. The

PART III   MICROECONOMICS II: INDUSTRIAL STRUCTURE AND FACTOR MARKETS

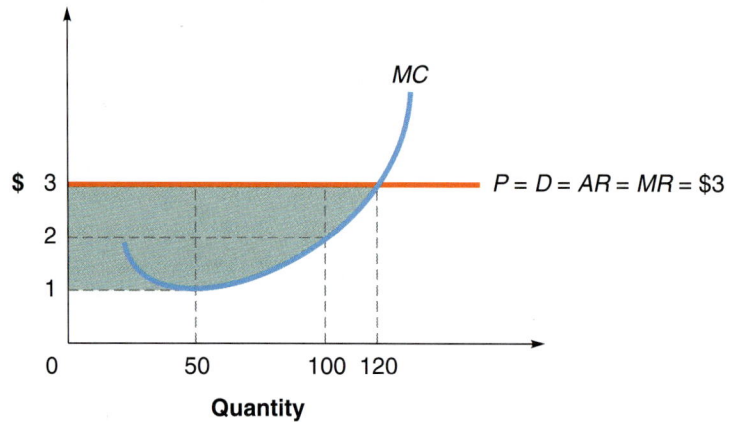

FIGURE 11.4 MARGINAL COST AND MARGINAL REVENUE UNDER PURE COMPETITION

The firm finds the profit-maximizing quantity by equating marginal cost and marginal revenue. If 50 units are produced, the marginal revenue, $3, is greater than the marginal cost of production, $1, so the firm is making profits. If 100 units are produced, the profit per unit on the last unit is only $1, but this is still positive, so the firm should continue producing. To maximize profits, production should continue to the point where marginal revenue equals marginal cost, $Q = 120$. The profit on the last unit produced is tiny—but positive. At this point the firm is maximizing total profits, even though the profit on the last unit produced approaches zero. If more than 120 units are produced, the firm will incur losses because the marginal cost of production is greater than marginal revenue.

profit on the last unit approaches zero, but producing at this level assures that total profits have been maximized. Finally, consider what would happen if production moved beyond 120 units of output: marginal revenue would remain at $3, but the marginal cost would rise above $3. Thus, the firm would incur losses on every additional unit that it produced.

The only problem with the analysis in Figure 11.4 is that we mentioned only marginal costs. Marginal costs may be the most important cost to consider, but they are not the only important cost. Firms must look at variable and fixed costs as well when making their output decisions. To see why, look at the three panels of Figure 11.5. All of the relevant short-run cost curves—average total cost, average variable cost, and marginal cost—have been drawn along with a different marginal revenue curve in each panel.

Normal Profits

First, look at panel (a) of Figure 11.5 where the price line is at $5 ($P = MR = \$5$). To maximize profits, the firm should produce 100 units of output because this is where marginal cost equals marginal revenue, at point a. Notice that in this case, the price line is exactly tangent to the minimum point of the average total cost curve,

····FIGURE 11.5 PROFITS AND LOSSES IN THE SHORT RUN

Profit maximization occurs at point *a* because $MC = MR$. In this case, the selling price is equal to the average total cost of production so the firm is making *normal profits*.

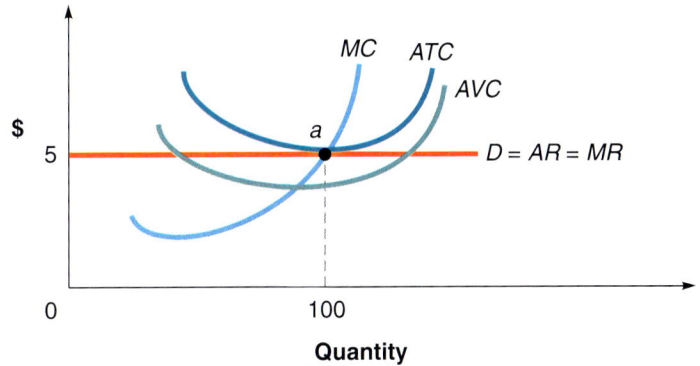

(a) Normal profits

If the selling price is greater than average total cost, the firm is making *economic profits*. The economic profit per unit of output is the difference between the selling price and the average cost, $8 − $6 = $2. The total amount of economic profits is given by the shaded area, 120 × $2 = $240.

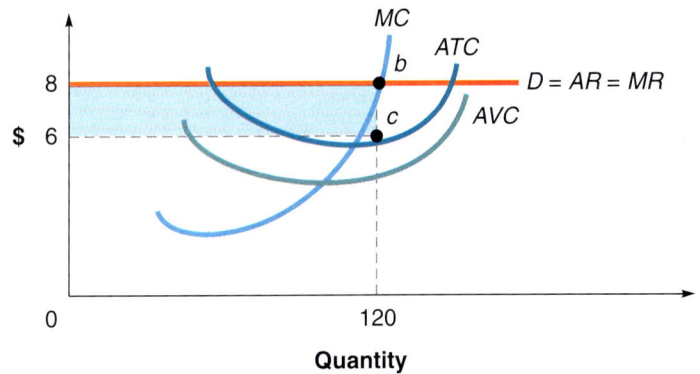

(b) Economic profits

If the selling price is less than average total cost, the firm is incurring losses. The loss per unit of output is equal to $2. This is the distance between the average cost of production, $6, and the selling price, $4. The total loss is $180 and is equal to the shaded area. In the short run, the firm should remain in operation as long as the price is at least as high as the minimum point on the average variable cost curve. At this point, all variable costs are being covered, and some fixed costs are being covered. The firm should *shut down* if price falls below the minimum point on the AVC curve, point *e*.

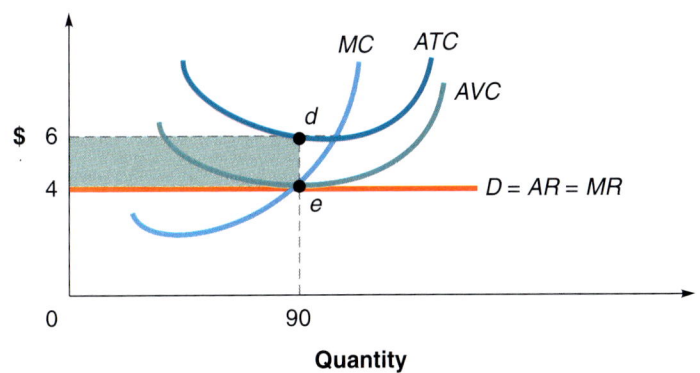

(c) Loss minimization and the shutdown point

the point where the marginal cost curve intersects the average total cost curve. When price is equal to the average total cost of production, the firm is making only normal profits—just enough profit to stay in business.

· · · · · · · ·

Economic Profits

In panel (b), the market price of $8 intersects the marginal cost curve above the minimum point of the average total cost curve. To maximize profits, the firm again equates marginal cost and marginal revenue. This occurs when production is set at 120 units of output. At this point, the firm is making economic profits. How do we know? The selling price, $8, is greater than the average cost of production, $6. The difference between price and cost ($8 − $6 = $2) is the profit per unit of output. The total amount of economic profits is the shaded area in the diagram, 120 × $2 = $240. Notice that the average cost of production is higher at $Q = 120$ than at $Q = 100$. This means that the firm is producing more than the optimal level based on its plant size, but as long as marginal revenue is greater than marginal cost, the firm is making additional profits on additional units, so it pays to produce at this level.

· · · · · · · ·

Minimizing Losses and the Shutdown Point

Panel (c) shows what happens if the selling price is less than the average total cost: the firm incurs losses. However, this does *not* necessarily mean that the firm should shut down. In the short run, if price is at least as high as the minimum point of the average variable cost curve, the firm should continue to operate. Why stay in business if you are experiencing losses? If you shut down, you will reduce costs because your variable costs will go to zero—but you will still have to pay your fixed costs. If your selling price covers your variable costs, you might as well stay in business and hope things improve in the future enough to cover your fixed costs. For example, suppose you start up a term paper–typing business. The initial costs are $4,000 for a computer and laser printer, which you buy and finance with monthly payments. You then place a series of weekly advertisements in the school newspaper and buy paper and toner cartridges for the printer. If you find that you do not have enough customers to cover all of your expenses, you might consider shutting down. However, it would make more sense to continue operating as long as you earn enough to cover your variable expenses—the advertisements, paper, toner cartridges for the laser printer, the value of your time, and so on. If you shut down, you will be able to avoid these variable expenses, but you will still have to make the monthly payments on your computer and laser printer. If you stick it out, sales may increase enough to cover both your fixed costs (monthly computer payments) as well as your variable costs (paper, toner, and the like).

In the long run, of course, even losing a penny per job will spell bankruptcy, but if you weather the short-run losses, things might improve in the future—say, next semester when your reputation for quick, quality work gets around campus. If business is really bad, however, and the price you can charge falls below average variable cost, you should shut down because you are covering neither variable costs nor fixed

···· **FIGURE 11.6** DERIVATION OF THE COMPETITIVE FIRM'S SHORT-RUN SUPPLY CURVE

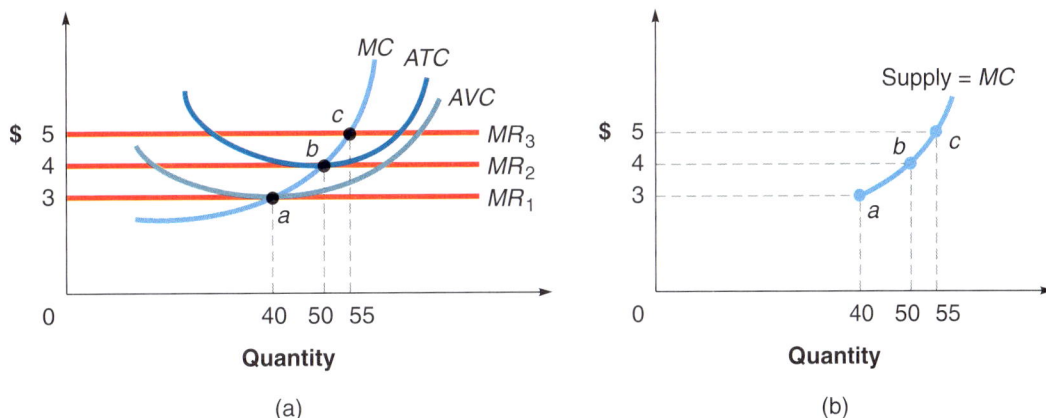

A supply curve gives the different quantities that will be offered at various prices. The supply curve of a competitive firm is the marginal cost curve above the shutdown point (the minimum point on the average variable cost curve). It can be constructed by noting the intersection between various marginal revenue curves—MR_1 = \$3, MR_2 = \$4, and MR_3 = \$5—and a fixed marginal cost curve, MC. The points a, b, and c on the marginal cost curve in panel (a) become three points on the supply curve in panel (b). Therefore, the marginal cost curve above the minimum point of the average variable cost curve is the firm's supply curve.

costs. When price is below average variable cost, you have higher losses by staying open than by shutting down. This is why the minimum point on the average variable cost curve is called the **shutdown point**. The shutdown point is point e in panel (c) of Figure 11.5.

The shutdown point illustrates an important fact: fixed costs do not affect production decisions because these costs must be paid regardless of what you do. You signed a contract when you took the loan for the computer system, and if you renege on the loan, your credit record will be ruined. Successful businesses must earn enough revenue to cover fixed costs, but day-to-day decisions are always based on the relationship between marginal revenue and marginal cost. And because marginal cost is not dependent upon fixed costs, fixed costs do not influence the production decision.

Shutdown point The point at which price falls below average variable cost where the firm should cease operations.

········

The Competitive Firm's Supply Curve

The information in Figure 11.5 is the basis for another important result: the marginal cost curve above the shutdown point is a competitive firm's supply curve. To see this, first recall the definition of a supply curve: it gives the different quantities that will be offered at various prices. Figure 11.6 combines the price lines from the three panels in Figure 11.5 on one diagram. Notice that as the price rises from \$3 to \$4 to \$5, the profit-maximizing quantity rises from 40 to 50 to 55. In other words, as price rises, the quantity that the firm offers also rises—a supply curve by any other name.

> **RECAP**   Key Ideas on Profit Maximization
>
> We have just covered the main ideas on profit maximization, so it might help to collect our results:
>
> 1. Profit maximization occurs at the quantity where the difference between total revenue and total cost is greatest. To find this point, firms equate marginal revenue and marginal cost.
> 2. The average revenue curve is the same as the firm's sales or demand curve. For a purely competitive firm, this curve is horizontal, because the firm perceives that it can sell an unlimited quantity at the going market price.
> 3. When price is equal to average total cost, the firm is making normal profits. When price is below average total cost, the firm is incurring losses. When price is greater than average total cost, the firm is making economic profits.
> 4. In the short run, firms should continue to operate as long as price is above the shutdown point, the minimum point on the average variable cost curve. This indicates that price covers all variable costs and some fixed costs.
> 5. A competitive firm's supply curve is its marginal cost curve above the minimum point on the average variable cost curve.

PROFITS AS SIGNALS: ENTRY AND EXIT UNDER PURE COMPETITION

Everything we have said so far relates to a single firm in a purely competitive market. Individual firms in a purely competitive industry cannot influence the market, but if all firms act together, they will have noticeable effects. For example, if all firms decide to produce more, industry supply will increase and the market price will fall. More importantly, industry profits or losses act as signals that cause firms to enter and exit the industry in the long run. This changes industry supply and thus the market price.

Industry Supply and Demand Curves

In the short run, the graph of a purely competitive industry looks just like the supply and demand graphs we developed in Chapters 3 and 4. The supply curve is the horizontal summation of the marginal cost curves above the shutdown point for all the firms in the industry. The short-run individual marginal cost curves are upward sloping, so the short-run industry supply curve is upward sloping.

The industry demand curve is found by horizontal summation of the individual consumer demand curves, and like most market and demand curves, it is downward sloping. But wait: How can the industry demand curve be downward sloping when the demand curves facing each firm in the industry are perfectly horizontal? In fact, the industry demand curve would not be downward sloping if the individual demand curves were *perfectly* horizontal, but they are not. The demand curves for the individual firms are almost horizontal even when the industry demand curve is relatively

···· **FIGURE 11.7** PROFITS AS SIGNALS: ENTRY

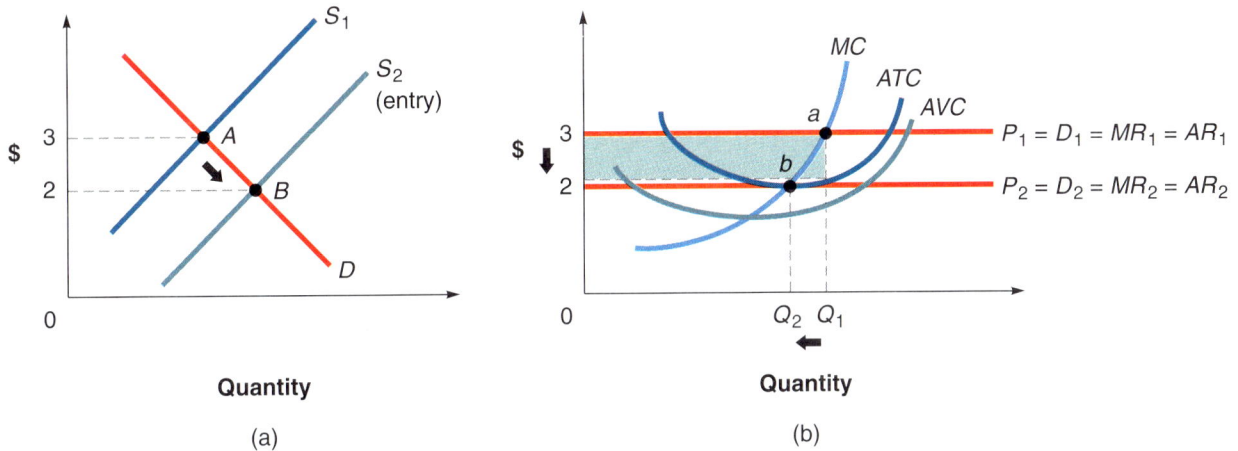

The intersection between industry demand and industry supply determines the price for all firms in the competitive industry. When price is greater than average total cost, firms are making economic profits. This attracts other firms to the industry. In this case, industry demand and supply intersect at point A, which establishes P_1 for all firms in the industry. P_1 is greater than average total cost, so the typical firm makes economic profits in the amount of the shaded area. Positive economic profits invite entry into the industry. As new firms enter, the industry supply curve shifts from S_1 to S_2, and price falls for every firm in the industry. Entry will continue until economic profits are eliminated and only normal profits remain.

inelastic.[1] To see this, suppose that there are 1,000 identical firms in an industry and one firm doubles output. This would cause industry output to increase by 0.1 percent. Now, if industry elasticity of demand is 0.5, price would fall by only 0.2 percent.[2] From the standpoint of the individual firm, this change is so small that it may go unnoticed. This is why economists treat the individual demand curves as horizontal.

Figure 11.7 shows the industry response to profit signals, specifically, positive economic profits. The market price is always set by the intersection of the industry supply and demand curves, and individual firms must price at this level. For example, suppose that currently 10 students are offering term paper–typing services on campus, and given the substantial writing requirements of the new Writing Across the Curriculum program, demand is such that the market price is $3 per typed page. This is shown in Figure 11.7a where the initial supply curve, S_1, intersects with the industry demand curve, D. Panel (b) shows that the $3-per-page price translates into economic profits of an amount equal to the shaded area for the typical term paper–typing firm.

---

[1] As we found out in Chapter 8, price elasticity of demand is the percentage change in quantity demanded divided by the percentage change in price. The demand for a good with few substitutes is typically inelastic with a price elasticity coefficient less than 1. Elasticity is *not* slope, but it is sometimes convenient to think of an inelastic demand curve as being relatively steep and an elastic demand curve as being relatively flat.

[2] To see why price falls by only 0.2 percent, substitute $E_p = 0.5$ and $\%\Delta Q = 0.1$ into the formula for price elasticity of demand, $E_p = \%\Delta Q / \%\Delta P$ and solve for $\%\Delta P = 0.05$.

Now, because there are no restrictions on entry and exit, the economic profits act as an incentive for entry into the competitive term paper–typing industry. When more people invest in computers and laser printers and begin typing term papers, the industry supply curve will shift from S_1 to S_2, and the price will fall. Entry will continue until the price has fallen so much that economic profits are eliminated and there is nothing to attract additional entry. In this case, entry will continue until price falls to $2 per page.

The reverse will happen if the demand for term paper typing falls: the price will fall and firms will lose money. As firms shut down and exit the industry, the industry supply curve will shift toward the left, and the industry price will rise. This will restore normal profits for the remaining firms in the industry.

Finally, firms will also be forced to exit a competitive industry if they are poorly managed. The fact that firms in a purely competitive industry make only normal profits means that there is little leeway for mistakes or management errors. Competition forces firms to stay on their toes and assures that only the fittest will survive.

• • • • • • • •

Industry Equilibrium

There are no restrictions on entry and exit under pure competition so whenever the profit rate differs from the normal profit rate, firms will enter or exit the industry. Entry and exit will continue until profit returns to the normal rate. This fact allows us to state the conditions for **industry equilibrium**:

> **INDUSTRY EQUILIBRIUM:** *A purely competitive industry is in equilibrium when profits are normal. This occurs where the sales curve is tangent to the minimum point on the average total cost curve.*

WELFARE CONDITIONS: THE EFFICIENCY OF COMPETITIVE MARKETS

When economists use the word "welfare," they are usually not speaking about aid to the homeless or downtrodden. They are usually referring to how well the economy or a particular market operates. The two most important welfare conditions are allocative efficiency and technical efficiency. A main reason for studying purely competitive markets is that they automatically generate allocative and technical efficiency in the long run. This is not true of any other market structure.

• • • • • • • •

Allocative Efficiency: $P = MC$

Allocative efficiency Welfare condition holding that the marginal benefit of a good must equal the opportunity cost of producing that good; exists when price equals marginal cost.

Economists say that **allocative efficiency** exists when the selling price is equal to the marginal cost of production. Why is this defined as allocative efficiency? Think back to the discussion of utility theory in Chapter 7. There we demonstrated that people will buy goods only if the marginal benefit ("utility") they receive from a product is at least as high as the opportunity cost of the goods that must be given up by spending money. And as more goods are purchased, the marginal benefit received from additional units declines. Rational consumers will buy products until the marginal benefit of the last unit purchased is just equal to the price of the product. This means that price is equal to marginal benefit when the consumer is in equilibrium.

Now, if allocative efficiency exists when price is equal to marginal cost, and consumer equilibrium exists when price is equal to marginal benefit, then we can write the allocative efficiency condition as:

$$\text{Allocative efficiency condition: } P = MB = MC \qquad [6]$$

This situation is considered efficient because the benefit that consumers get from the last unit is exactly equal to the marginal cost of producing that last unit. Resources have been allocated efficiently because the cost of using up resources is equal to the marginal benefits consumers receive. Look what happens when price is greater than marginal cost. The value (marginal benefit) of the product is greater than the marginal cost of producing the product, so more should be produced because society benefits more from the goods than it costs to produce them. As production increases, marginal cost rises and marginal benefit falls, so price and marginal cost move closer together. The reverse will occur when price is less than marginal cost: the benefit is less than cost, so less should be produced.

• • • • • • • •

Technical Efficiency: P = Minimum ATC

Economists define **technical efficiency** as the absence of waste, or the situation when the maximum amount of output is generated from a given amount of resources. If a production process is technically efficient, any change in resource utilization will result in less output. For example, if a firm's costs fall when it builds a new plant, the old plant was not technically efficient. If it is not possible to build a new plant that will have lower production costs, then the current plant is technically efficient.

Technical efficiency Welfare condition that exists when maximum output can be produced at minimum cost; exists when price equals minimum average total cost.

Competitive firms make only normal profits in the long run, so any firm that chooses the wrong technology or builds the wrong-size plant will go out of business because profits will fall below the normal level. This means that, in the long run, purely competitive firms must choose the optimal—and technically efficient—plant size. Further, the absence of economic profits means that the selling price must be equal to average total costs. Finally, because the competitive firm's demand curve is horizontal, it will equal average total costs at the minimum point. Therefore, the technical efficiency condition can be written as:

$$\text{Technical efficiency condition: } P = \text{minimum } ATC \qquad [7]$$

• • • • • • • •

$P = MC = AC$ in the Long Run under Pure Competition

Graphical analysis is especially useful when describing the welfare conditions for a competitive firm. This is done in Figure 11.8 where the long-run marginal and average total cost curves are combined with a demand curve. Competitive pressures put production at point a in the long run. At this point, both allocative and technical efficiency exist. To understand why the firm will automatically end up at point a, we need to combine much of the material from the chapter.

FIGURE 11.8 EFFICIENCY UNDER PURE COMPETITION IN THE LONG RUN

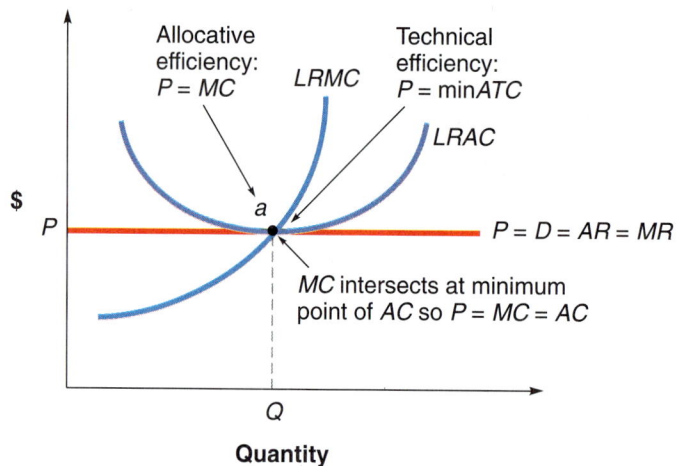

In the long run, pure competition establishes both allocative and technical efficiency. To maximize profits, firms equate marginal cost and marginal revenue. The marginal revenue curve is horizontal under pure competition and equal to the selling price. Price must equal average total cost because of unrestricted entry and exit. The only place where marginal cost, marginal revenue, and average total cost can all be equal is at the minimum point of the average total cost curve. At this point, both the allocative efficiency condition ($P = MC$) and the technical efficiency condition ($P = \min AC$) are satisfied.

First, remember that firms maximize profits by producing the quantity where marginal revenue equals marginal cost. For a purely competitive firm, the marginal revenue curve is equal to price. Thus, the quantity that is produced must correspond to the intersection between MC and price. Second, unrestricted entry and exit means that there can be no economic profits or losses in the long run. This means that the selling price must equal the average cost of production. Finally, note that price (equals marginal revenue) can equal marginal cost and average cost at only one place: point a, the minimum point of the average cost curve. At this point $P = MC$ and $P = \min ATC$, so both allocative and technical efficiency are established.

The situation pictured in Figure 11.8 is one of the main reasons why economists spend so much time studying pure competition. As we examine different market structures in the next few chapters, we will need to refer to diagrams like Figure 11.8 constantly. No other market structure can achieve both of the welfare criteria: Without easy entry and exit, there is no mechanism to assure that $P = \min ATC$, so firms can make economic profits. Neither oligopoly nor monopoly has easy entry and exit, so both violate the technical efficiency condition. And we will find out in the next chapter that unless the firm's demand curve is perfectly horizontal, price and marginal revenue will differ. This means that only pure competition can automatically achieve allocative efficiency.

Some Qualifications

The beauty of competitive markets is their automatic ability to generate both technical and allocative efficiency. This explains why economists are fascinated by pure competition and why regulations aimed at noncompetitive markets are often designed to make them behave as if they were competitive. Nevertheless, we need to make some important qualifications.

Externalities. First, when we said that allocative efficiency exists when price is equal to marginal cost, we should have said that efficiency exists when price is equal to marginal *social* cost. Marginal social cost is the incremental cost to society of producing that last unit of output. Thus, marginal social cost includes both the costs paid by the firm—wages, rent, interest, and so on—and any **externalities** or **external costs** that may exist. Externalities are costs or benefits that are not reflected in market prices. Pollution is an example of a negative externality. When a factory produces goods, it often produces pollution as well. Pollution represents a cost to society, but in the absence of government intervention, it is not a cost to the firm. This means that marginal *private* cost is less than marginal *social* cost. When marginal private cost is less than marginal social cost, the market price is lower than it should be, and consumers buy too much. Allocative efficiency does not prevail.

Externalities can also be positive. If a beekeeper locates next to an apple orchard, apple production will be enhanced from the bees' pollination. The apple farmer benefits from the activities of the beekeeper, but pays nothing to the beekeeper. If the apple farmer did pay a "pollination fee" to the beekeeper, honey prices might fall, and the market would be closer to achieving allocative efficiency. Government intervention can sometimes be used to generate a more efficient outcome. We will look at externalities and related problems in Chapters 18 and 21.

Imperfect Information. The second qualification relates to the information and knowledge of the consumer. We say allocative efficiency exists when price is equal to marginal cost because we assume that people will pay a price equal to the marginal benefits they get from the product. But what if people have imperfect information? What if they do not know that their food contains carcinogenic ingredients? What if they are misled by advertising into thinking they need a product when they really do not? In either of these cases, price will diverge from marginal benefit, and the market outcome will not meet the allocative efficiency condition. In recognition of this problem, some economists add the assumption of perfect information to the model of pure competition and call the resulting model **perfect competition**.

Income Distribution. Finally, we should mention that both technical and allocative efficiency depend on the distribution of income in society. For example, if the society includes a large segment of rich people, the demand for yachts will be high. This would be a signal to boat manufacturers to build large plants that take advantage of economies of scale. The interaction of demand and supply will determine the price of yachts, and as long as the price equals the marginal and average cost of making a yacht, both allocative and technical efficiency will prevail. If, however, there are few rich people and thus little demand for yachts, boat builders will build smaller plants

Externalities Costs or benefits that are not reflected in market prices.

Perfect competition Term occasionally used to refer to a market structure that is pure competition plus perfect information.

that do not have the benefits of economies of scale. The result will be fewer yachts sold at higher prices, but as long as this price equals the marginal cost of producing yachts, this outcome will be efficient as well. It is impossible to say which outcome is "better," but we can say that they are both efficient in the economist's sense.

······ SUMMARY

This chapter is exceedingly important, not because pure competition is prominent in the real world, but because we need a framework and a norm for comparison. The real economy is simply too complex to understand without some sort of framework; the model of pure competition provides much of that framework. The graphical analysis from this chapter is especially important. When we compare competition with monopoly, oligopoly, and monopolistic competition in the next few chapters, many of our arguments will rely on graphical analysis. Make sure you can *draw* as well as understand the graphs.

The main points from this chapter are:

1. Pure competition is an idealized market structure characterized by many buyers and sellers, a homogeneous product, and free entry and exit. Few good examples of pure competition exist in the real world, but economists study this idealization as a norm for comparison to the real world.
2. The main goal of firms under pure competition is profit maximization. Profits are defined as the difference between total revenue and total cost. To maximize profits, firms produce the quantity where marginal cost equals marginal revenue.
3. The demand curve facing a purely competitive firm is horizontal because every firm in the industry produces identical products. The demand curve, sales curve, average revenue curve, marginal revenue curve, and price line are equivalent for firms under pure competition; they are *not* equivalent for other market structures.
4. In the long run, free entry and exit assures that there will be no economic profits or losses under pure competition. Economic profits or losses will encourage entry or exit. Free entry and exit assures equality between market price and average total cost.
5. The firm's supply curve is its marginal cost curve above the shutdown point, the minimum point on the average variable cost curve. In the short run, firms should operate as long as price is above the shutdown point. Under these conditions, the firm is covering all of its variable costs and some of its fixed costs.
6. Pure competition generates both allocative and technical efficiency in the long run. Allocative efficiency holds when price is equal to marginal cost. Technical efficiency holds when price is equal to the minimum point on the average cost curve. Graphically, this occurs at the minimum point of the average cost curve. At this point, the sales curve is tangent and the marginal cost curve intersects. Allocative and technical efficiency can be achieved simultaneously only in a purely competitive market.
7. Externalities and imperfect information can prevent competitive markets from achieving allocative and technical efficiency. Further, both efficiency criteria depend on the distribution of income.

···· KEY TERMS AND CONCEPTS

pure competition
price taker
homogeneous products
free entry and exit
monopolistic competition
oligopoly
differentiated products
monopoly
price maker
profit (π)
normal profit
economic profit

sales curve
total revenue (TR)
marginal revenue (MR)
average revenue (AR)
profit maximization
shutdown point
industry equilibrium
allocative efficiency
technical efficiency
externalities
perfect competition

···· IMPORTANT FORMULAS

Profit: $\pi = TR - TC$

Total revenue: $TR = P \times Q = PQ$

Marginal revenue: $MR = \dfrac{\Delta TR}{\Delta Q}$ (= slope of total revenue)

Marginal cost: $MC = \dfrac{\Delta TC}{\Delta Q}$ (= slope of total cost)

Average revenue: $AR = \dfrac{TR}{Q} = P$

Profit maximization: $MR = MC$

Normal profits: $P = AC$

Economic profits: $P > AC$

Allocative efficiency: $P = MC$

Technical efficiency: $P = \text{minimum } ATC$

···· REVIEW QUESTIONS

1. Define and give examples of each of the four kinds of firms.
2. What rule must firms follow in order to maximize profits? Illustrate this rule with two different graphs.
3. Under what conditions should a firm stay in business even if it is incurring losses? When should it shut down? Illustrate your answers with graphs.
4. Explain how profits act as signals for entry and exit in competitive industries.
5. Explain how competitive industries automatically achieve allocative and technical efficiency in the long run. Use graphs to illustrate your answer.

PROBLEMS

1. Explain why each of the following is or is not a good example of pure competition:

Jack's Handyman Repair Service	7-11 Convenience Stores
a state university	your local public library
USA Today	McDonald's (fast-food restaurant)
Wall Street Journal	a roadside vegetable stand

2. Fill in the blanks (indicated by the letters) and indicate the profit-maximizing level of output:

Q	P	TR	AR	MR	TC	MC	π
10	$20	$200	$20		$185		$g
				→ c		→ e	
11	20	220	20		195		h
				→ d		→ f	
12	20	a	b		215		i

3. a. Redraw Figure 11.7 assuming that the typical firm is making short-run losses.
   b. If the "typical" firm is making losses, which firms will exit the industry? Does this suggest that all firms in a purely competitive industry are not identical?

4. We noted that the sales curve for a competitive firm has a very slight downward slope. How does this affect the ability of a competitive market to achieve allocative and technical efficiency?

5. Indicate whether the following are true or false and explain why:
   a. Perfectly competitive firms never advertise.
   b. If $P > MC$, the firm should always increase output.
   c. If $P > AC$, neither of the efficiency conditions can hold.
   d. To maximize profits, purely competitive firms find the price such that the marginal cost of the quantity produced is equal to marginal revenue.
   e. If $MR = MC$, the firm is making profits.
   f. There is only one point where $MR = MC$.
   g. $\pi = AR(Q) - ATC(Q)$.

6. Suppose that price is *exactly* equal to average variable cost. Under what conditions should the firm shut down? When should it stay in operation?

7. Economic profits can exist under pure competition only in the short run; however, they also act as a signal to invite entry into the industry. As a prospective entrant into a competitive industry, would you be concerned that the economic profits would cease before you entered? Would this deter you from entering the industry? Why or why not?

8. In Chapter 10, we noted that in the real world, average and marginal cost curves are frequently fairly flat. Can this condition exist under pure competition? Why or why not?

9. Suppose that there are 100 identical firms in a competitive industry, that the industry price elasticity of demand is 0.8, and that the initial price is $10. Show what will happen to price under the following conditions and draw graphs to illustrate your analysis:
   a. Each firm increases output by 10 percent.

   b. One firm doubles output.

   c. Two firms exit the industry.

10. Suppose that a purely competitive firm is producing 100 units of output and that $P = \$10$ and $MC = \$8$ at this level of output.

   a. Is the firm maximizing profits? How do you know?

   b. Suppose you discover that average fixed costs are $2 and average variable costs are $7. Draw a picture of this situation and indicate what the firm should do.

   c. Calculate the economic profits (if any) assuming the cost conditions in part (b) hold and price stays at $10 and quantity remains at 100.

CHAPTER 12

Monopoly

Photography is becoming more popular all the time. Novices can take great snapshots, thanks to high-quality but inexpensive automatic cameras. The price of 35-millimeter, single-lens reflex cameras—the professional's choice—has come down so much that professional-quality photographs are within everyone's reach. And new camera technology is appearing every day. Video recorders make home movies almost *too* easy; you do not really want to watch your neighbor's vacation movies again, do you? Some cameras take "pictures" on 3.5-inch disks to be replayed on a television set. Disposable cameras sell for little more than the price of a roll of film—and take good pictures! Environmentalists may dislike the waste, but the public apparently does not mind; these cameras have been a smashing success.

But one kind of photography differs significantly from all others: instant pictures. If you want to take a picture and see it a minute later, you have only one choice: buy a Polaroid camera. Polaroid has a complete monopoly in the production of instant cameras. It produces a product that has no close substitutes. Polaroid has *monopoly power* and is a price maker. How high should Polaroid set its price? As high as possible? Almost certainly not—at least not if it wants to maximize profits.

The history of Polaroid is revealing. Edwin Land, Polaroid's founder and CEO until 1980, dropped out of Harvard in the 1930s because he needed more time to study light and the polarization process. By 1942 he had patented a method for making instant cameras, and he was soon able to produce a commercially successful product, a black and white camera. Instant color pictures, higher-quality and more environmentally sound film, and even an instant movie camera system eventually followed. As you might suspect, Polaroid was extremely profitable. Not only did it make good products, but patent laws protected it from competition. And under the leadership of Land—an inventor with vision—these monopoly profits were used to turn out a stream of high-quality products. This is a major advantage of monopolies: long-run profits provide a pool of resources that can be used for research and development.

Polaroid's success was the envy of camera and film makers worldwide, not the least of which was Kodak. In the late 1970s, Kodak brought out its own line of instant cameras. Consumers benefited from the lower prices and wider selection of instant camera models, but only briefly. Polaroid immediately sued for patent infringement, and Kodak was ordered to cease production of its instant cameras. It was also ordered to give rebates to customers who requested them and pay millions of dollars in damages to Polaroid. The ability to suppress competition is one of the chief disadvantages of monopoly power. Polaroid remains the only producer of instant cameras in the world.

In this chapter we will look at the reasons for the existence of monopolies, see how they affect the economy, and explain why most monopolies are regulated by the government.

AFTER READING AND STUDYING THIS CHAPTER, YOU SHOULD BE ABLE TO:
- Cite the reasons for the existence of monopolies
- Explain why the monopolist's demand and marginal revenue curves are shaped as they are, and how monopolists behave to maximize profits
- Explain how the allocative and technical efficiency criteria relate to the monopoly firm
- Show how firms with monopoly power can use price discrimination to increase profits
- Explain how monopolists can be regulated to establish efficiency and equity

REASONS FOR MONOPOLY

Why do **monopolies** exist? There are several reasons. The source of Polaroid's monopoly power is its patent on instant camera technology. No firm can copy Polaroid's process for making instant pictures. Patent laws are one kind of legal **barrier to entry** that prevent other firms from entering the industry. Other barriers that prevent firms from entering a monopoly industry include economies of scale, government licensing, and exclusive control over an important resource.

Monopoly An industry composed of one firm selling a product for which there is no good substitute; barriers to entry prevent other firms from entering the industry.

Barrier to entry A condition that precludes firms from entering an industry to compete for profits.

Economies of Scale

We talked about economies of scale briefly in Chapter 10. There we noted that as the firm expands, it may be able to acquire more sophisticated technology or specialize the production process and reduce the average cost of production. How do economies of scale relate to the existence of monopolies? Suppose that five firms currently share a market and that each sells 100 units of output at a break-even price of $10 per unit. If technology exists that would enable a single firm to produce 500 units of output at a price of $5, one of the existing firms would inevitably use it and put the other four firms out of business. Monopolies that arise from economies of scale are often called *natural monopolies*.

There are several examples of natural monopolies in the real world. Perhaps the most common examples are public utilities. Most communities have only one electric company; a second utility would have to lay duplicate power lines and so forth, so the scale economies achievable with a single public utility would no longer be possible. In some communities, public utility companies are privately owned but tightly regulated; in others they are publicly owned and managed. Cable television can also be classified as a natural monopoly. Many communities have only one cable television supplier, typically a private company that is tightly regulated at both the federal and state levels. Technological changes may be eroding the natural monopoly aspects of cable television, however. The ability to transmit television signals on demand through the phone lines may provide competition in this industry.

· · · · · · · ·

Government Licensing and Patents

Government licenses constitute legal barriers to entry. The U.S. Postal Service owes its monopoly status to the government-sanctioned exclusive right to deliver first-class mail. The U.S. Postal Service is classified as a *pure monopoly* because it is the single firm allowed to deliver first-class mail. However, most legal barriers limit the number of competitors, but do not result in a single pure monopoly firm. For example, many states require hospitals and nursing homes to file a Certificate of Need to obtain permission to expand. Such laws are designed to prevent unnecessary duplication of services, but they also result in a reduction in the number of hospitals. Many state governments require licenses for liquor stores, barbershops, funeral parlors, and other establishments. Why do legal barriers to entry exist in these industries? Ostensibly, these barriers exist to protect the public—you would not want your hair cut by anyone but a trained professional, would you?—but barriers to entry often serve business more than the public. Requiring licenses reduces the number of competitors and increases the *monopoly power* of firms within the industry. Monopoly power is defined as the ability to influence market price.

Patents are another kind of government license. Most countries have patent laws, and international agreements protect patents in many countries in the world. In the United States, patents grant the owner exclusive production rights—pure monopoly status—for 17 years. Once a patent is granted, the owner has the exclusive right to use a process or manufacture a product; other people must apply for permission. Patents entail both costs and benefits. The benefit to the inventor is 17 years of monopoly profits to recover the investment. Society as a whole also benefits to the extent that patent laws encourage innovation. The cost to consumers is that without competition, the monopolist is likely to charge a higher price and produce a lower quantity.

Many other kinds of government actions can also result in monopoly power. For example, tariffs—taxes on imports—can raise the price of imported goods so much

Government license Government authorization to engage in business. To obtain a license, various requirements must be met, and the number of licenses granted is often restricted.

Patent The exclusive right to use a process or manufacture and sell a product; granted to the inventor for a term of years.

that foreign competition is eliminated. This obviously benefits domestic producers, but generally hurts the consumer. Government regulations can also give rise to monopolies. For example, the Food and Drug Administration applies what some people believe to be excessively stringent quality-control standards on pharmaceutical firms. These regulations can be quite costly—so costly that they prevent some firms from ever entering the market. Existing firms have less competition and a measure of monopoly power. This may be one reason for high pharmaceutical prices in the United States.

Control over an Important Resource

Finally, a monopoly can arise if a single firm has exclusive control over a resource needed by the industry. For example, before World War II, the Aluminum Company of America (ALCOA) had almost complete control over the known world supply of bauxite, the most important ingredient in aluminum. How long can this sort of monopoly last? Certainly not forever. ALCOA is still a major player in the world aluminum market, but new bauxite finds after World War II shifted the world market from a monopoly to an oligopoly. Today, competition in the aluminum industry comes from another source—recycling—and even ALCOA is involved in aluminum recycling. Another company with monopoly power due to its control over an important resource is DeBeers, the South African–based diamond company. For many years DeBeers was virtually able to set the world price of diamonds, but the discovery of large deposits of diamonds in Australia in the 1970s has weakened this power.

PROFIT MAXIMIZATION UNDER MONOPOLY

Should we be concerned about monopolies? To many people, the term "monopoly" has negative connotations, but governments have long encouraged monopolies, so perhaps they have some positive features as well. Before we can analyze monopolies, however, we need to rid ourselves of the excess ideological baggage. We need an objective method of analysis. The economist's graphical model of monopoly is a good starting place.

The Monopolist's Demand and Revenue Curves

There is only one firm in a monopoly industry, so the demand curve facing a monopoly firm is the industry demand curve. It is downward sloping, which means that the monopolist must lower the selling price to sell a higher quantity. Table 12.1 presents some hypothetical data to illustrate the monopolist's demand and revenue curves. The first two columns of the table give the demand curve facing the monopolist: as price falls from $10 to $0, the quantity sold rises from 0 to 5 units. These values are plotted in Figure 12.1. Column 3 gives the total revenue for different points along the monopolist's demand curve. If we recall the definition of total revenue—price times quantity—the entries in Column 3 can be computed by simple multiplication.

Column 4 presents the marginal revenue from selling different quantities. As always, marginal revenue represents the change in revenue associated with selling

TABLE 12.1 MONOPOLY SALES AND REVENUE DATA

P	Q	TR		MR
$10	0	$ 0		
			→	+8
8	1	8		
			→	+4
6	2	12		
			→	0
4	3	12		
			→	−4
2	4	8		
			→	−8
0	5	0		

Definitions and Formulas:

P = price Q = total product TR = total revenue = PQ

MR = marginal revenue = $\dfrac{\Delta TR}{\Delta Q}$

one more unit of output, so the entries in this column are placed between the entries in the first three columns. Inspection of the marginal revenue column shows one of the main differences between pure competition and monopoly: under pure competition, the demand and marginal revenue curves were identical; under monopoly they are different. The marginal revenue curve slopes down twice as fast as the demand curve.[1] Notice that every time the monopolist lowers price by $2, marginal revenue falls by twice as much, $4. What causes this to happen? When the monopolist lowers price to sell a higher quantity, it has to lower the price of *all* units it sells, not just the extra ones it will sell by lowering price. For example, to increase sales from 3 to 4 units, price falls from $4 to $2. Thus, the slope of the demand curve is $\Delta P/\Delta Q = -2/1 = -2$. The same price change causes total revenue to fall from $12 to $8, so the slope of the marginal revenue curve is $\Delta TR/\Delta Q = -4/1 = -4$.

Figure 12.1 is a plot of the information from Table 12.1. Panel (a) shows the demand (= sales = average revenue) curve and the associated marginal revenue curve. Two things should be noted about this figure. First, the horizontal intercept of the marginal revenue curve ($Q = 2.5$) is exactly half of the intercept of the demand curve ($Q = 5$). This relationship occurs because the marginal revenue curve slopes down twice as fast as the demand curve. Second, notice the relationship between the price elasticity of demand (E_p) of the demand curve and marginal revenue. As we learned in Chapter 8, the midpoint of a linear demand curve always has a price elasticity of demand coefficient of 1. This occurs at the same quantity where marginal revenue is zero. Demand is price-elastic ($E_p > 1$) at high prices—you can usually find a substitute if the price is high enough—and price-inelastic ($E_p < 1$) at low prices.

---

[1] This is always true only for *linear* demand curves.

•••• FIGURE 12.1 MONOPOLY SALES AND REVENUE

Panel (a) shows the demand curve for a monopoly firm, which is also the industry demand curve. It slopes downward because lower prices are necessary to attract more buyers. The marginal revenue curve slopes down twice as fast as the demand curve because the price of all goods must be lowered in order to sell more. The marginal revenue curve intersects the horizontal axis at a quantity exactly half the value of the horizontal intercept of the demand curve. The demand curve is elastic at high prices, inelastic at low prices, and has unitary elasticity at the midpoint. The total revenue curve in panel (b) is nonlinear because price changes as quantity changes. At high prices, price cuts raise total revenue; at low prices, price cuts lower total revenue. This occurs because the price elasticity of demand coefficient changes over the demand curve.

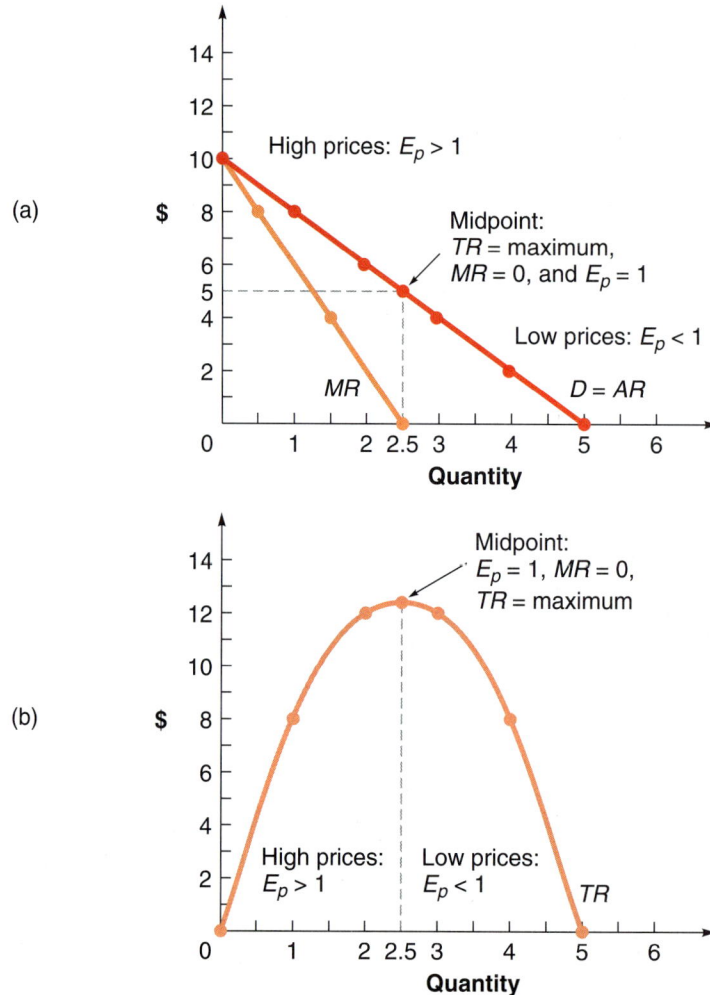

Panel (b) plots the total revenue data from Table 12.1. To make it easy to see the relationship between total revenue, marginal revenue, and demand, the same scale is used for the horizontal axis in both panels. Notice that, in contrast to pure competition, the total revenue curve is nonlinear. In the inelastic region of the demand curve, price increases raise total revenue; in the elastic portion of the demand curve, price increases decrease total revenue. Note too that total revenue is at maximum when the price elasticity coefficient is equal to 1. This occurs where marginal revenue is zero, which is at the midpoint of the demand curve.

• • • • • • • •

Monopoly Profit Maximization: The TR, TC Approach

The demand and revenue curves for the monopolist look quite different from those for a pure competitor, but the cost curves look exactly the same because in both cases

FIGURE 12.2 PROFIT MAXIMIZATION UNDER MONOPOLY

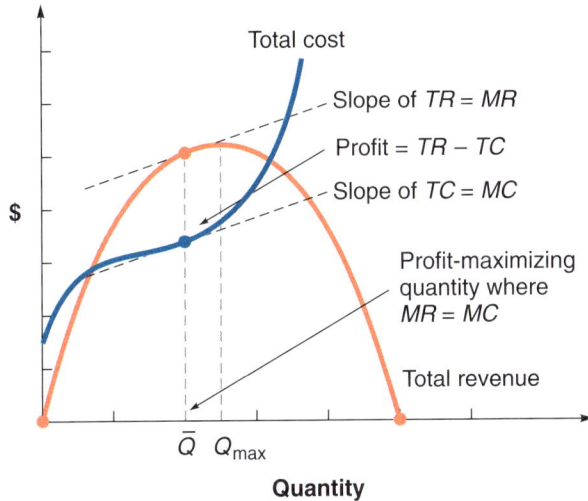

Monopolists maximize profits in the same way as all firms—by maximizing the difference between total revenue and total cost. Profit maximization occurs where the total revenue (TR) and total cost (TC) curves are parallel, at quantity $\overline{Q}$ in this figure. Notice that $\overline{Q}$ is *not* the point of maximum total revenue; total revenue is maximized by producing quantity Q_{max}. The slope of the total revenue curve is marginal revenue (MR), and the slope of the total cost curve is marginal cost (MC). It follows that profits are maximized at the quantity where marginal revenue equals marginal cost.

the curves are based on the law of diminishing returns and the three stages of production.

Figure 12.2 shows the total cost and total revenue curves for a typical monopolist. We know that the total cost curve has a smoothed **S**-shape, and we have just found out that the total revenue curve has an inverted **U**-shape. Profits are maximized where the distance between total revenue and total cost is greatest. This occurs at quantity $\overline{Q}$. Just as we found in the last chapter, the total revenue and total cost curves have the same slope at the point of profit maximization. The slope of the total revenue curve is marginal revenue, and the slope of the total cost curve is marginal cost. This verifies our Fundamental Rule for Profit Maximization: Produce the quantity where marginal revenue equals marginal cost.

· · · · · · · ·

Profit Maximization: The $MR = MC$ Approach

Monopoly behavior can also be analyzed in terms of the relationship between marginal cost and marginal revenue. This is done in Figure 12.3. The demand and marginal revenue curves represent the same kind of reasoning we used in Figure 12.1, and the average total cost (ATC), the average variable cost (AVC), and marginal cost (MC) curves are identical to those in Figure 11.5 from Chapter 11. As before, profits are maximized by producing quantity $\overline{Q}$ and charging price $\overline{P}$. At this point the revenue from the last unit sold is exactly equal to the incremental cost of producing that unit.

FIGURE 12.3 PROFIT MAXIMIZATION: THE $MR = MC$ APPROACH

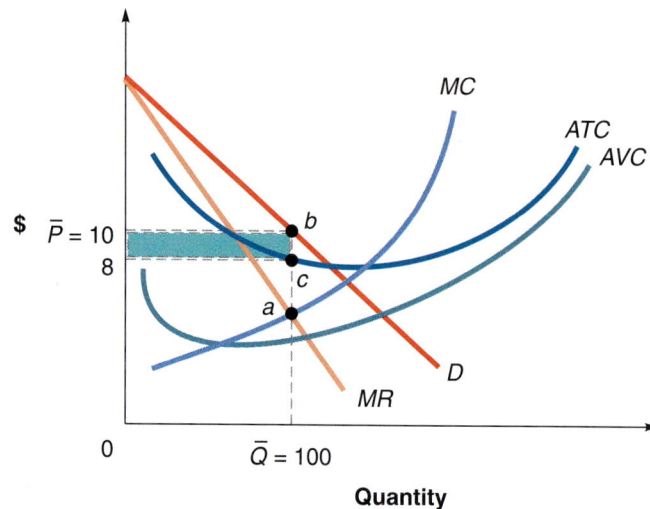

Monopolists maximize profit by producing the quantity where $MR = MC$. To find this position, note where the marginal revenue and marginal cost curves cross (point a), and extend a line to the quantity axis at $\overline{Q} = 100$. This is the quantity that maximizes profit. Now, extend a line vertically from $\overline{Q}$ to the demand curve (point b), and draw a horizontal line from b to the price axis. This gives $\overline{P} = \$10$, the profit-maximizing price. The average cost per unit is found by extending a line from $\overline{Q}$ to the average cost curve at point c, which shows the average cost of production to be $8. The monopolist is making a $2 economic profit on each of the 100 units sold because selling price exceeds average cost. Total economic profits are shown by the shaded area and are equal to $200.

Finding the profit-maximizing price and quantity may seem complicated at first glance, but it is really just a simple application of the Fundamental Rule for Profit Maximization we introduced in the last chapter. First, find point a, the intersection of marginal revenue and marginal cost, and draw a vertical line from point a to the horizontal axis. This gives the profit-maximizing quantity, $\overline{Q}$, which is equal to 100 in this example. Price always comes off the demand curve, so the next step is to extend a vertical line from the profit-maximizing quantity to the demand curve at point b. Finally, draw a horizontal line from point b to the vertical axis to get the profit-maximizing price, $\overline{P} = \$10$. Notice that the monopoly price, $10 in this example, is a market-clearing price in the sense that everything offered for sale is purchased. The monopolist has no competitors, so it could charge a higher price, but there would be no reason to because profits are maximized at $\overline{P} = \$10$.

The firm in Figure 12.3 is making economic profits. How do we know? The selling price ($10) is greater than the average cost of production ($8), so the firm is making an economic profit of $2 (=$10 − $8) on each unit that it sells. The total amount of economic profit is the shaded area in the diagram ($200 = 100 \times \$2$). Unlike competitive firms, monopolies can make long-run economic profits because firms do not enter the industry and drive down prices. However, monopolies do not always make economic profits. If the demand curve is below the average cost curve, the monopoly will experience long-run losses. When this occurs, government sub-

OUR ECONOMIC HERITAGE

ANTOINE AUGUSTIN COURNOT

Like the ideas of too many remarkable thinkers, the work of the Frenchman Augustin Cournot (1801–1877) went almost unnoticed until his death. Trained in mathematics and philosophy, Cournot was responsible for path-breaking work in the theory of the firm and mathematical economics. Perhaps his most important contribution was the discovery of what we have called the Fundamental Rule of Profit Maximization—the marginal revenue = marginal cost condition. He also made important contributions to probability theory and philosophy. During his career, Cournot worked as a civil servant, professor, and college president.

Cournot's work failed to receive the acclaim that it deserved for perhaps two reasons. First, his research methodology was based on the French rationalist school of philosophy. Cournot believed that reasoning and introspection were the best ways to

discover how the economy worked. This approach was in sharp contrast to the empirical approach of most of his contemporaries. Second, Cournot's work was highly mathematical—far too mathematical for most readers of his time. While it may have limited his audience, Cournot's mathematical approach made it easier for other economists to extend his analysis. For example, Léon Walras's work in general equilibrium theory used Cournot's equations as a starting place.

This mathematical approach did not attract a wide audience in Cournot's era, but it became the methodology of modern mainstream economics, and much of Cournot's work is now a standard part of contemporary economics. Cournot gave precise interpretations of demand and supply and was the first to develop the concepts of marginal revenue and marginal cost. He also developed the first systematic theory of monopoly and, by adding

firms to the industry, showed how monopoly and pure competition differed. One of Cournot's most celebrated models was his duopoly model—a two-firm industry. This model illustrated how each duopolist would respond to the behavior of the other, an approach that preceded the game theory approach to oligopoly by over 100 years. Game theory is a main topic of Chapter 14.

sidies are necessary if the monopolist is to survive. We will have more to say about this issue shortly.

EFFICIENCY CRITERIA: MONOPOLY VERSUS PURE COMPETITION

We just found out that monopolies differ from purely competitive firms in two ways: Monopolies' demand and marginal revenue curves are downward sloping, and they can make economic profits in the long run. Though these differences are important, more important may be the fact that monopolies produce less and charge higher prices than do comparable competitive firms. Further, the monopolist's production decision results in neither allocative nor technical efficiency.

· · · · · · · ·

Price and Output Comparisons

Figure 12.4 compares the profit-maximizing price and output levels for a monopolist and pure competitor. To facilitate price and output comparisons, the two firms are assumed to have identical cost curves. As always, the demand and marginal revenue curves for the monopolist are downward sloping to reflect the fact that monopolists must reduce price to sell additional units of output. Profit is maximized by producing the quantity where marginal revenue is equal to marginal cost (Q_m) and finding the selling price (P_m) from the demand curve. Notice that the monopolist is making economic profits because the selling price is greater than the average cost of production.

The demand curve for the competitive firm is the dashed horizontal line, an indication that it can sell an unlimited amount at the fixed market price (P_c). The demand curve and the marginal revenue curve are identical, so this firm maximizes profit by producing the quantity (Q_c) where demand (= marginal revenue) crosses the marginal cost curve. Entry and exit assures that there will be no economic profits in the long run, so price must equal average cost. A comparison of the price and output decisions of the two firms gives the result we are looking for: *Other things being equal, monopolists produce less and charge higher prices than purely competitive firms.*

Diagrams like Figure 12.4 are instructive, but only if used and interpreted very carefully. To make the diagram serviceable, we needed to assume that the two firms

· · · · **FIGURE 12.4 COMPETITION VERSUS MONOPOLY IN THE LONG RUN**

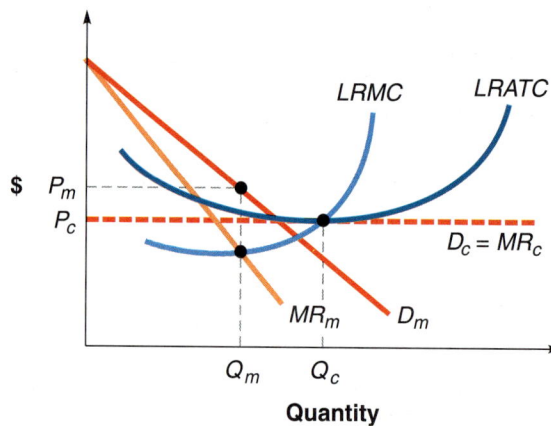

Monopolists charge higher prices and produce less than do competitive firms. In this case, both firms are assumed to have the same cost curves. The monopolist's demand curve is D_m, and its marginal revenue curve is MR_m. To maximize profits, it will produce Q_m and sell at price P_m. This price results in long-run economic profits because it is greater than the average total cost of production. The competitor's demand curve is the horizontal dotted line, $D_c = MR_c$. The competitor will produce Q_c and sell at price P_c. The competitive firm makes no long-run economic profits. The fact that $Q_m < Q_c$ and $P_m > P_c$ is an indication of the welfare loss due to monopoly.

have identical cost structures. It is hard to imagine that this would occur in the real world. For example, suppose that technology and the market result in an optimal plant size so small that there is room for many competitive firms in a particular industry. By definition, this would rule out the existence of a monopoly in the same industry, so a comparison between monopoly and competition would become moot. And if technology increased the optimal plant size so much that the market could support only a single natural monopoly firm, then all of the competitive firms would be put out of business by the single, low-cost monopolist. Again the comparison would be moot. So why did we go through the exercise of comparing pure monopoly and pure competition? We did it for two reasons. First, the mental gymnastics should help you understand the theoretical differences between the two market structures, and this will be helpful in understanding the more realistic models in the next chapter. Second, there are very few unregulated monopolists in the real world. When policymakers attempt to devise measures to assure that monopolies act in the best interest of the public, they often try to force the monopolist to behave as if it were a purely competitive firm. Requiring it to increase output and charge lower prices is one step in that direction.

········

Allocative Efficiency under Monopoly

Monopoly firms do not generate allocative efficiency. As we learned in the last chapter, allocative efficiency exists when the selling price is equal to the marginal cost of production. This condition is considered allocative efficiency because the marginal benefit people receive from buying a good is at least as high as the opportunity cost of spending their money, and if this marginal benefit is equal to the marginal cost of producing the good, then resources have been allocated efficiently. This does not occur under monopoly because price does not equal marginal cost.

How much allocative inefficiency results from monopoly pricing? It is impossible to give an exact answer, but we can get an idea by returning to three ideas we developed in earlier chapters—producer surplus, consumer surplus, and elasticity. Panels (a) and (b) of Figure 12.5 illustrate the welfare conditions under pure competition and pure monopoly assuming that the demand curve is relatively elastic. Panel (a) shows consumer and producer surplus assuming that the industry is competitive. Panel (b) shows what happens under monopoly. Now, we already know that the monopoly price is higher and the monopoly quantity is lower, but monopoly also results in an efficiency loss called *deadweight loss*. As can be seen by comparing panels (a) and (b), high monopoly prices shift some consumer surplus to the monopolist and increase the monopolist's producer surplus. This makes the monopolist better off at the expense of the consumer. However, social welfare declines because the consumer's losses exceed the monopolist's gain by an amount equal to the triangle *ecd*. This is the deadweight loss of monopoly. The existence of deadweight loss means that welfare is less than it would be in the absence of monopoly power. Notice in panel (b) that marginal benefit is greater than the marginal cost at the monopolist's output level, Q. This indicates that welfare would increase if production were increased to Q*—as it would be under pure competition.

The effect of price elasticity of demand on allocative efficiency under monopoly can be seen by comparing panels (b) and (d). The steeper demand curve in panel (d)

···· **FIGURE 12.5** WELFARE LOSSES UNDER MONOPOLY

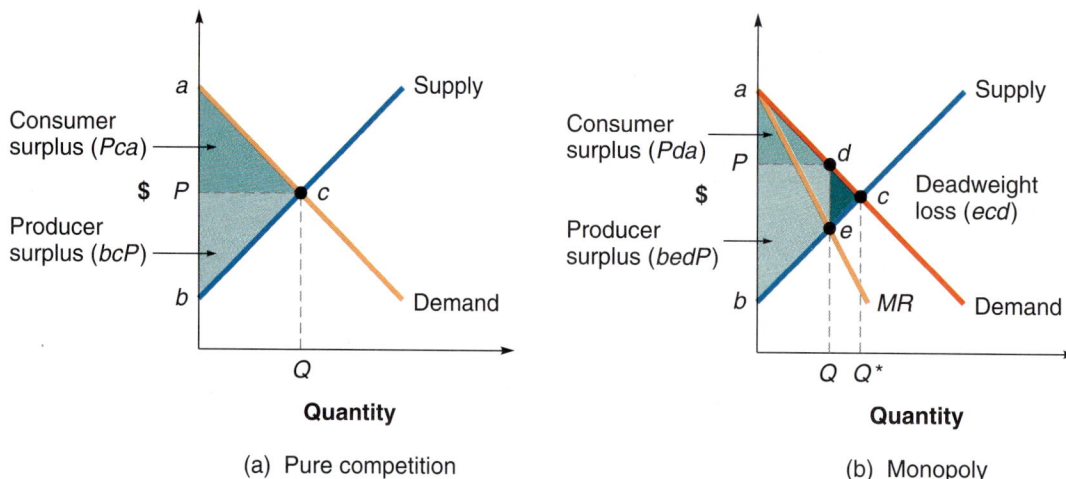

(a) Pure competition

(b) Monopoly

Elastic demand

Monopoly results in allocative inefficiency because the monopoly price is not equal to marginal cost. Panel (a) shows consumer and producer surplus under pure competition. Panel (b) shows what happens under monopoly: not only is price higher and quantity lower, but consumer surplus shrinks and producer surplus expands. There is also a deadweight loss—the difference between the reduction in consumer surplus and the increase in producer surplus that no one gets.

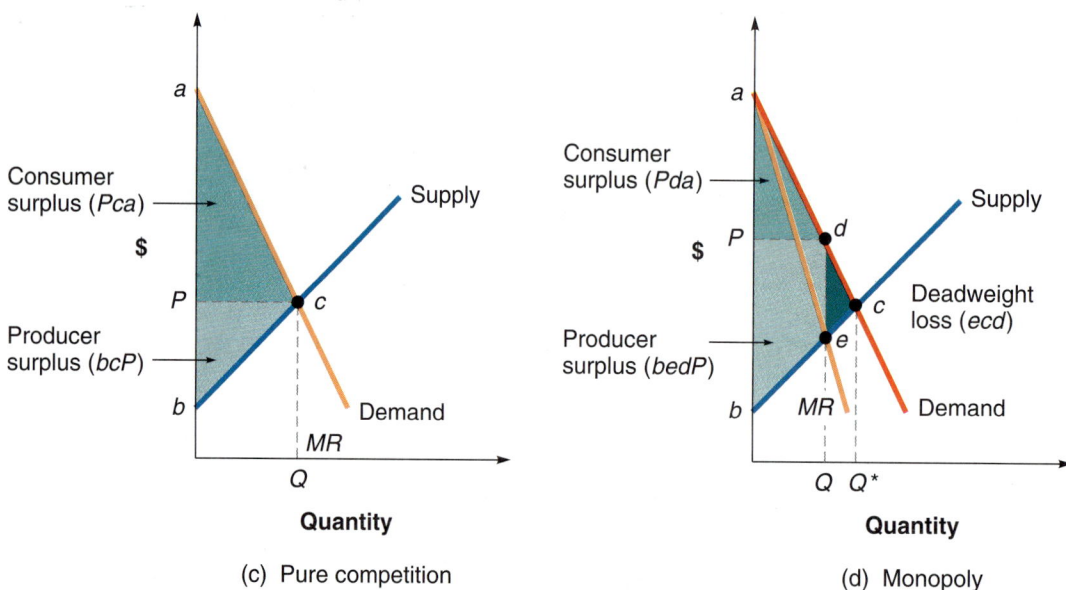

(c) Pure competition

(d) Monopoly

Inelastic demand

How much monopoly power reduces consumer surplus depends on the elasticity of demand. The demand curves in panels (c) and (d) are steeper than those in panels (a) and (b), an indication that demand is more inelastic over the relevant price range. The monopoly price exceeds the competitive price by a greater amount when demand is inelastic. There is also a larger reduction in consumer surplus.

is an indication that price elasticity is lower (at the initial price) than in panel (b). Lower price elasticity means that consumers have fewer substitutes to choose from, so the monopolist can raise price with less fear of losing sales. As a result, monopoly prices reduce consumer surplus more when the price elasticity of demand is low than when it is high.

Technical Efficiency under Monopoly

Whether monopolies increase or decrease technical efficiency depends on how the concept is defined. Barriers to entry keep the monopolist's price above the average cost of production, so the formal definition of technical efficiency we used in the last chapter—price equal to the minimum of average total cost—does not hold. If technical efficiency is defined in a more general way, however, we might get another answer. Think of it this way: Which would you prefer, a large number of small competitive firms using labor-intensive production methods and making zero economic profits, or a single monopolist that makes economic profits in a highly efficient modern factory? If the large monopolist enjoyed scale economies and was able to charge lower prices than the competitive firms, you would be better off—even if the monopoly was making substantial economic profits and not producing at the minimum point on the average total cost curve. Consequently, we must look carefully at the specific details of any industry before we decide that concentration and monopoly power are necessarily bad. Other things being equal, competition is clearly preferred to monopoly, but the advantages of competition may not be sufficient to offset the technical advantages of large production facilities.

We have at least one reason to suspect that monopolies do not achieve technical efficiency despite any economy of scale advantages they may have. Monopolies can make long-run economic profits, so there is little competitive pressure to force monopolists to minimize costs.[2] Thus, monopoly workers (and managers) have some leeway in how hard they must work. If monopoly workers want to maximize profits, they will work hard, but if they are satisfied with less than maximum profits, they will put in only minimal effort on the job. In contrast, workers in competitive industries are forced to put in maximum effort out of fear that a competitor will undercut their costs and drive them out of business. The efficiency associated with work effort was named **x-efficiency** by Harvey Leibenstein who developed the idea.[3] Leibenstein recognized that any industry characterized by economic profits could be subject to x-*in*efficiency.

X-efficiency The efficiency associated with work effort. The idea that workers in competitive industries work harder than people in monopolies because their firms could be threatened by more efficient competitors.

Rent Seeking and Other Welfare Losses

Economists have recently begun studying other kinds of welfare losses due to monopoly. One of the most important is known as **rent seeking.** What is the economist's definition of "rent"? It is not what you pay your landlord every month. Economic

Rent seeking Actions designed to limit competition and make economic profits.

[2]When we develop the theory of contestable markets in Chapter 14, however, we will discover that the threat of potential entry into a monopoly industry can act as an incentive for monopoly firms to behave like competitive firms.
[3]Harvey Leibenstein, *Beyond Economic Man* (Cambridge, Mass.: Harvard University Press, 1976).

rent refers to a factor payment over and above the amount necessary to bring a factor into production. For example, movie star Julia Roberts makes as much as $10 million per movie—but would probably accept a role for a mere $1 million if that was all she could get. That extra $9 million represents her economic rent. Why does she earn it? The explanation is simple—there is only one Julia Roberts.

In the context of monopoly, rent refers to the economic profits that monopolists earn by keeping competitors out of the industry, and rent seeking is the act of trying to keep out the competition. These efforts might include lobbying to prevent imports or lawsuits to enjoin other firms from producing similar products. The point is that rent-seeking behavior is costly, and any resources the monopolist spends rent seeking are unavailable for productive uses.

Another welfare loss of monopoly is the lack of incentives to develop new products or new ways of doing things. For example, one reason most economists oppose tariffs and other restrictions on imports is that they reduce the need for domestic firms to produce world-class, competitive products. Without tariffs, firms would either design and produce competitive products or exit the industry. The counter to this argument is that the existence of economic profits provides a source of funds for research and development. Of course, monopoly profits can be used both to eliminate competition and for investment in research and development, a point suggested by the Microsoft Corporation Focus on page 299.

RECAP   Monopoly versus Pure Competition

There are few good examples of pure monopoly or pure competition in the real world, but the models of these market structures provide good norms for comparing the real with the ideal. The main differences between pure competition and monopoly are:

1. Monopolists are price makers; pure competitors are price takers.
2. The monopolist's demand curve is downward sloping because it must lower price to sell more output. The pure competitor's demand curve is horizontal because it can sell an unlimited amount at the market-determined price. The monopoly marginal revenue curve slopes down twice as fast as the demand curve. Under pure competition, marginal revenue is equal to the selling price and equivalent to the demand curve.
3. Other things being equal, monopolists produce less and charge higher prices than purely competitive firms.
4. In the long run, both allocative efficiency ($P = MC$) and technical efficiency ($P = $ minimum ATC) are established under pure competition. Neither condition holds under pure monopoly.

PRICE DISCRIMINATION

The analysis so far has dealt with a single-price monopoly, a monopoly that charges the same price to all of its customers. In many instances, however, it is to the monopolist's benefit to charge different prices. For example, if the monopolist

MONOPOLY IN THE SOFTWARE INDUSTRY: THE CASE OF MICROSOFT

Other than public utility firms, there are few good examples of pure monopolies in the real world. In some cases, though, a single firm so dominates an industry that it can act like a virtual monopolist. Except in very rare instances, however, these quasi monopolists face competitive threats and must act accordingly.

One of the best examples of this kind of "monopoly" is Microsoft Corporation. As we found out in the Focus in Chapter 10, Microsoft dominates the computer software industry with a nearly 85 percent share of the personal computer system software market. This position has given Microsoft a huge advantage in the development of application software. Microsoft software engineers know about future modifications to the basic system software, so it is easier for them to design and update applications to take advantage of system modifications. Some have accused Microsoft of using this advantage unfairly. Software developers have told the Federal Trade Commission that Microsoft purposely misled the industry into thinking that OS/2—an operating system Microsoft helped IBM develop—would replace MS-DOS while it was developing a strategy to market Windows, its own competing product. Others have accused Microsoft of purposely making Windows incompatible with Lotus 123, the most popular spreadsheet in the world. Why? To make customers

buy Excel, a competing spreadsheet published by Microsoft.

No one can deny that Microsoft's growth has been phenomenal since it was founded in 1977, and few would deny that some of that growth has been the result of the company's monopoly advantage. Still, Microsoft has always been aware that it needed to innovate and change quickly if it was to maintain its dominant role. It has done this by hiring committed, hardworking people with high "bandwidth"—the Microsoft term for intelligence. Founder and CEO Bill Gates has been accused of running his company like a slave driver, but he has also managed to achieve extremely rapid growth. All tasks are organized around small groups, none larger than 200 people, and every Microsoft employee has access to Gates through an inhouse electronic mail system.

What would happen to Microsoft's "monopoly" position if it sat still and tried to reap monopoly profits? Other vendors would bring out competing products and take away market share. In short, Microsoft would suffer the same fate as IBM. IBM began the 1980s with a dominant presence in the mainframe and personal computer industries. Unfortunately, its centralized management style made rapid change difficult—so difficult that its share in the world computer market fell from 36 percent to barely 20 percent over the decade. A long overdue restruc-

William Gates, founder and chairman of Microsoft.

turing in 1992 and 1993 did not come cheap: over 40,000 of IBM's 350,000 employees were laid off or were asked to retire early, and the company was organized around smaller divisions with less centralized authority. IBM also formed strategic alliances with Apple and other companies. Whether these changes will prove successful will not be known for some time, but few are ready to write off IBM just yet. IBM's size and revenues are enough to fund a world-class research division. If it can just learn to turn research into product—and quickly—it could once again command the lead in the computer industry.

SOURCES: "The New IBM," *Business Week,* December 16, 1991, pp. 112–118; "Microsoft," *Business Week,* February 24, 1992, pp. 60–65.

Price discrimination The ability to charge different prices to different customers.

could charge high prices to high-income people and low prices to low-income people, monopoly profits would increase. Such a practice is called **price discrimination**. Strictly speaking, price discrimination is not limited to pure monopolies—any firm with some monopoly power can price-discriminate—but price discrimination is easiest for pure monopolies. Economists distinguish among three types of price discrimination:

- Under *first-degree price discrimination,* the monopolist finds the highest possible price that each person is willing to pay and then charges that price. This is the best situation from the monopolist's standpoint because all consumer surplus has been extracted from the buyer. First-degree price discrimination is rare in the real world, but several examples do come to mind. One example is an auction sale. The bidding may start at a very low price, but as people begin bidding against one another, the price can go as high—but not higher than—the maximum price the winning buyer is willing to pay. Another example is the small-town doctor who bases fees on the patient's ability to pay.

- The most common form of *second-degree price discrimination* is the quantity discount. The monopolist charges the same price to everyone, but gives discounts to people who buy in large quantities. Like all forms of price discrimination, firms give quantity discounts for a simple reason—to maximize profits. In the case of second-degree price discrimination, profits are maximized by spreading fixed costs over a wider range of output. Many utility companies practice second-degree price discrimination with bloc rate pricing schemes. Customers who use large amounts of electricity are given a lower price per kilowatt-hour than customers who use smaller amounts. Because the large-use customers are typically businesses, home users sometimes complain about bloc rate pricing. However, bloc rate pricing may enable the utility to better plan plant capacity and may be an important factor in luring new business to the community.

- Under *third-degree price discrimination,* the monopolist charges different prices to different groups or categories of customers, but every unit sold to each person within a particular group carries the same price. Movie theaters do this all the time. Senior citizens and students get discounts because these groups typically have lower incomes than other moviegoers. Airlines also practice third-degree price discrimination when they offer cut-rate tickets for vacationers who are able to make advance purchases. This practice allows the airline to fill up the plane, but still charge higher prices to business travelers and others who must make last-minute travel plans.

The consequences of first- and third-degree price discrimination are most interesting, so we will analyze them more closely.

· · · · · · · ·

First-Degree Price Discrimination

First-degree price discrimination is illustrated in Figure 12.6. To simplify the analysis, marginal and average costs are assumed to be constant—a reasonable assumption if the firm is operating with excess capacity.

To compare price discrimination with a single-price monopolist, first assume that the monopolist cannot price-discriminate. As a result, the marginal revenue curve

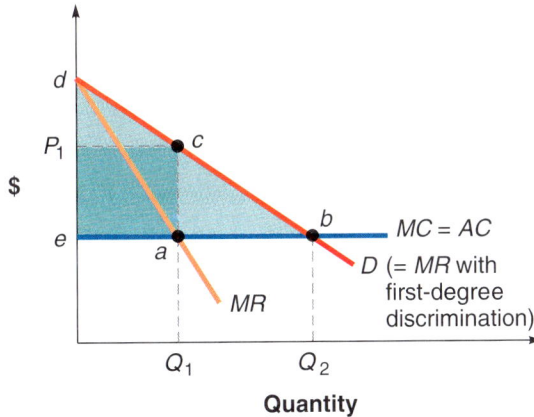

FIGURE 12.6 FIRST-DEGREE PRICE DISCRIMINATION

First-degree price discrimination can increase profits considerably. Without price discrimination, the monopolist must lower the price of all goods in order to sell more. This causes the marginal revenue curve to slope down faster than the demand curve. The output decision is made by equating marginal revenue to marginal cost, point a, and finding selling price from the demand curve, P_1. The resulting economic profit is equal to the green rectangle $eacP_1$. If the firm can practice first-degree price discrimination, it will charge the highest possible price to each of its customers and sell as many units as possible as long as price exceeds average cost. This is quantity Q_2. Customers will be charged a price anywhere between e and d, depending upon how they value the product. The demand curve and the marginal revenue curve are equivalent under first-degree price discrimination because to sell additional units, only the price of those additional units has to be lowered, not the price of all goods. The economic profits will be equal to the triangle ebd.

slopes down twice as fast as the demand curve. To maximize profits, quantity Q_1 will be produced and the price will be set at P_1. Economic profits will be equal to the green area, $eacP_1$. Now look what happens if the monopolist can price-discriminate: The demand curve and the marginal revenue curve are equivalent because the firm lowers the price only on the additional units it wants to sell, not all units. This means that the marginal revenue curve on the diagram is no longer relevant, and the firm will produce and sell Q_2. This is the maximum amount that can be sold at a price that covers average costs. Selling price will be anywhere from e to d, depending on the valuation placed on the product by the customer. Profit will be the area of the green triangle, ebd.

In essence, what first-degree price discrimination does is to eliminate consumer surplus. Instead of consumers thinking they got a "bargain" by paying less than they think the product is worth, the monopolist charges prices exactly equal to the value that consumers receive. Consumer surplus is maximized under pure competition; there is *no* consumer surplus under first-degree price discrimination. Consumer surplus would be the area ebd under pure competition. It would be P_1cd if the monopolist did not price-discriminate, and it would fall to zero under first-degree price discrimination.

• • • • • • • •

Third-Degree Price Discrimination

Third-degree price discrimination is shown in Figure 12.7. As before, marginal and average costs are assumed to be constant. Two conditions are necessary for third-degree price discrimination. First, the seller must be able to distinguish between different segments of the market. In this case, we are assuming that the market is composed of two groups, say, senior citizens and all other customers. The second necessary condition is the ability to separate the different segments of the market to prevent **arbitrage**. Arbitrage is defined as the purchase and sale of an item with the expectation of profit. For example, if a senior citizen bought a cheap movie ticket and immediately turned around and sold it to the next person in line, the theater would lose money. This is why you must show your student ID to get a student discount and why airline tickets inevitably say NOT TRANSFERABLE.

The two demand curves in Figure 12.7, D_{ns} and D_s, are the demand curves for nonsenior citizens and senior citizens, respectively, and each demand curve has its corresponding marginal revenue curve, MR_{ns} and MR_s. To maximize profits, the seller will produce the quantity such that marginal revenue equals marginal cost in all markets and charge the corresponding price from each of the demand curves. This means that there will be two prices, P_{ns} for nonsenior citizens and P_s for senior citizens, with quantities Q_{ns} and Q_s. Economic profit will be the area $eabP_{ns}$ plus $ecdP_s$.

Arbitrage The purchase and sale of an item with the expectation of profit.

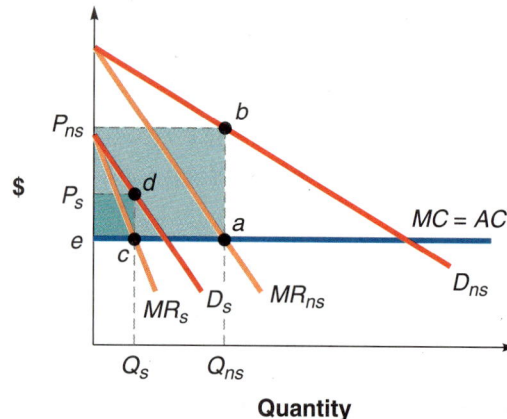

•••• FIGURE 12.7 THIRD-DEGREE PRICE DISCRIMINATION

Third-degree price discrimination requires that the monopolist separate the different segments of the market and prevent arbitrage. In this example, D_{ns} is the demand from nonsenior citizens, and D_s is the demand from senior citizens. Each demand curve has its corresponding marginal revenue curve, MR_{ns} and MR_s. To maximize profits, marginal revenue is set to equal marginal cost for each segment of the market, and price is charged accordingly. Senior citizens pay price P_s and buy quantity Q_s; others pay price P_{ns} and buy quantity Q_{ns}. Economic profits are equal to the area $eabP_{ns}$ plus $ecdP_s$.

Third-degree price discrimination results in higher profits for the monopolist and appears to benefit senior citizens as well. Does it? Certainly—but price discrimination is possible only when the firm is making economic profits to begin with. If the market were competitive, free entry and exit would lower price to average cost, and all customers would enjoy lower prices.

REGULATING MONOPOLIES

Consumers do not like to pay high monopoly prices, and the thought of monopoly inefficiency is unsettling, at least to economists. This is why most real-world monopolies are regulated by the government. The theory of regulation is long and complex, so we can only touch on the main issues here; we will have more to say about the topic in Chapter 19. One approach to **monopoly regulation** is to try to make the monopolist behave as much as possible like a competitive firm. In some cases, this involves trying to establish competition in the industry—perhaps by subsidizing the entry of other firms into the industry. But most often monopoly regulation includes policies designed to force the monopolist to make output and price decisions consistent with the regulatory body's concept of the public interest. In this section we will take a brief look at one of the key issues surrounding government regulation of monopolies—whether regulations should be designed to make monopolies more efficient or more "equitable."

Monopoly regulation Government rules and policies designed to make a monopoly behave more like a purely competitive firm or to make it conform to the regulator's idea of the public interest.

Regulating Monopoly Profits: $P = AC$

Government regulations are often designed to force monopolists to charge "fair" prices, and this frequently means setting price equal to the average cost of production. Setting price equal to average cost eliminates economic profits. Figure 12.8 illustrates a regulated monopoly that has been required to set its price equal to average cost. As always, the selling price must come off the demand curve, and to ensure that the monopolist makes only normal profits, price and quantity are determined by the intersection between demand and average cost. This occurs at point a. The regulated price and quantity are P_{ac} and Q_{ac}. Comparing these values with the unregulated, profit-maximizing price and quantity ($\overline{P}$ and $\overline{Q}$ on the diagram) shows that regulation lowers price and increases output.

Regulating Allocative Efficiency: $P = MC$

The alternative regulatory strategy—and the one generally preferred by many economists—is to establish the allocative efficiency criterion by requiring the monopolist to set price equal to marginal cost. Unfortunately, under some circumstances, this can mean forcing the firm to lose money and thus necessitate government subsidies.

Figure 12.9 illustrates two cases of efficiency regulation. Panel (a) shows a decreasing-cost firm, and panel (b) shows an increasing-cost firm. As we discovered in Chapter 10, a decreasing-cost firm produces on the downward-sloping portion of the average cost curve, while an increasing-cost firm produces on the upward-sloping portion of the average cost curve. Now, to assure efficiency, the selling price must

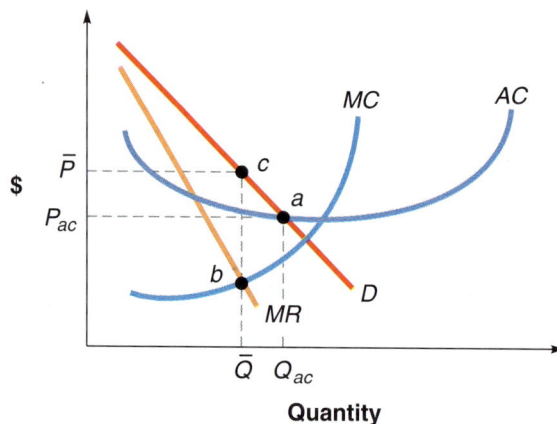

•••• FIGURE 12.8 REGULATING MONOPOLY PROFITS

If the regulator wants to eliminate economic profits, it will require the monopolist to set price equal to average cost. This occurs at point *a*, at the intersection of the demand and average cost curves. The resulting selling price is P_{ac}, and the output is Q_{ac}. If the monopolist is unregulated, the selling price would be found by producing the quantity where marginal cost equals marginal revenue, point *b*, and selling at the corresponding price along the demand curve, point *c*. Price is higher and output is lower without regulation.

be equal to the marginal cost of production. This occurs where the demand curve crosses the marginal cost curve, point *a* in both panels. Notice that in panel (a), setting price equal to marginal cost causes the monopolist to incur losses because the regulated price is less than the average cost of production, $P_{mc} < AC$. Thus, a subsidy would be required to prevent bankruptcy. Consumers would benefit, however, because the regulated price is less than the profit-maximizing price, $\overline{P}$, and more is produced and offered on the market.

Panel (b) shows what happens when an increasing-cost firm is regulated to achieve efficiency. The firm is still making economic profits, though not as much as it would if it were not regulated. We know this because the monopolist no longer produces the profit-maximizing output where marginal cost equals marginal revenue.

Is it appropriate for regulated increasing-cost firms to continue to make economic profits? Perhaps, but there is a tempting and somewhat appealing reason to tax these profits away: Use these tax revenues to subsidize decreasing-cost firms. In fact, this is just what Alfred Marshall suggested over a hundred years ago. (Alfred Marshall was the subject of an Economic Heritage box in Chapter 4.) Marshall hinted that it might be possible to raise enough tax revenue from increasing-cost firms to subsidize the losses of regulated decreasing-cost firms. There is little reason to believe that the taxes and subsidies would cancel out exactly, but the idea has merit. Production by increasing-cost firms should be discouraged because they are operating beyond the optimal plant size. Likewise, production by decreasing-cost firms should be encouraged to move them toward optimal use of the plant. Marshall's suggestion of a system of taxes and subsidies is a step in that direction, albeit a small one.

····· FIGURE 12.9 REGULATING MONOPOLY FOR ALLOCATIVE EFFICIENCY

····· **FIGURE 12.9 REGULATING MONOPOLY FOR ALLOCATIVE EFFICIENCY**

Forcing a decreasing-cost firm to set price equal to marginal cost will result in losses to the firm. To set price equal to marginal cost, find the intersection between the demand curve and marginal cost, point *a*, set price equal to P_{mc}, and produce quantity Q_{mc}. Point *b* shows that average cost is greater than P_{mc}, so the firm is losing money and will need to be subsidized. The shaded area represents the firm's losses from regulation. If the monopolist is unregulated, it will produce the quantity where marginal cost equals marginal revenue, point *c*. The unregulated, profit-maximizing price, $\bar{P}$, is greater than the regulated price.

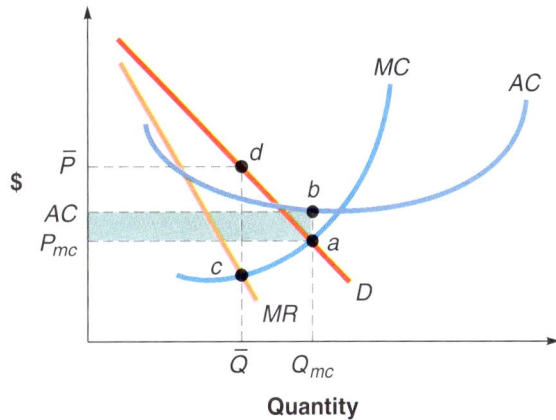

(a) Decreasing-cost monopoly

If an increasing-cost firm is regulated to set price equal to marginal cost, price will be lower, but the firm may still make economic profits. The regulated price is found by locating the intersection between the demand curve and marginal cost, point *a*, setting price equal to P_{mc}, and producing quantity Q_{mc}. Point *b* shows that the average cost, *AC*, is less than the regulated price, P_{mc}, so the firm is making economic profits. The shaded area represents the economic profits with regulation. If the monopolist is unregulated, it will produce the quantity where marginal cost equals marginal revenue, point *c*. The profits of regulated increasing-cost firms could be taxed away and used as subsidies for regulated decreasing-cost firms.

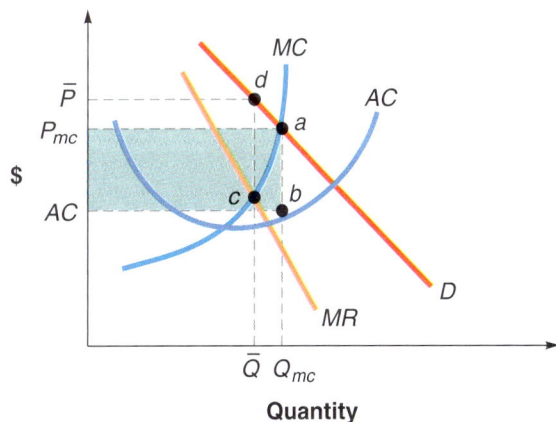

(b) Increasing-cost monopoly

········

The Advantages of Marginal Cost Pricing

When given a choice between setting price equal to average cost or marginal cost, economists almost inevitably opt for marginal cost. Marginal cost pricing results in better use of resources and plants that are closer to the optimal size.

One kind of marginal cost pricing is **peak load pricing**, which involves setting different prices depending upon the usage rate. Many public utility firms practice peak load pricing. One of the best examples is the French electricity pricing system. French electricity prices are set according to the marginal cost of production by time of day. When demand is high in the morning and early evening, production increases

Peak load pricing Firms raise prices during periods of maximum use to reduce demand and thus reduce the optimal size of the plant.

and moves up the marginal cost curve; when demand falls back at midday and late at night, marginal costs fall as production moves down the marginal cost curve.

Electricity prices are set higher in the morning and early evening and lower at midday and late at night to reflect the marginal costs of production. The high prices encourage energy conservation during the times of highest use; the low prices allow more energy use when demand is less likely to tax generation capacity. The main benefit of peak load pricing is that it reduces the optimal size of the plant because peak demand is less.

The Costs of Regulation: A Glimpse

Regulation is *far* more complex than we have just implied. It can also be far more costly. It is impossible to simply tell a firm to set price equal to average or marginal cost. Before any regulation can take place, a regulatory agency must be set up, and the costs of running this agency may outweigh the benefits gained from regulation. Regulation also presents a political problem: Who will be the regulators? The people with the most information about the industry are inevitably current or former employees. One has to wonder how objective they can be. Complete outsiders may be more objective, but do they know enough to do a good job? The existence of regulatory bodies also acts as a powerful incentive for firms to engage in rent-seeking behavior designed to influence the regulators.

Another problem is trying to calculate costs. For example, one component of average total cost is average fixed cost, but unless the level of output is known precisely, there is no way to compute average fixed cost. Another problem is capacity utilization. If the firm is operating with excess capacity, the marginal cost curve is flat. This makes marginal cost relatively easy to calculate. But if the firm is operating close to capacity, marginal cost might change significantly over a small region. Where do you set the price?

SUMMARY

It is easy to get upset about monopolies. Why is the electricity bill so high? Why is automobile service so much more expensive at the one Volvo dealership in town than at Joe's Foreign Auto Service? Other things being equal, monopolies do charge higher prices and produce less output than do competitive firms, but this does not *necessarily* mean that all monopolies are bad. Do we really want to have a dozen or so electricity companies in town? We would have something that looks like competition, but we would also have 12 sets of electricity wires and power poles running down the block with higher costs and prices. In some cases, it just makes more sense to leave production to a single firm; public utilities are an obvious example. When monopolies do exist, it is usually necessary to regulate them, but this brings up the difficult issue of government intervention.

The main points from this chapter are:

1. A monopoly is a firm that produces a product that has no close substitutes. Monopolies can only exist if there are substantial barriers to entry. Important

barriers to entry include economies of scale, government licenses and patents, and control over important resources.

2. The monopolist's marginal revenue curve slopes down faster than the demand curve because the firm must lower the price of all goods to sell more output. The result is an inverted U-shaped total revenue curve. Profit is maximized by producing the quantity where marginal revenue is equal to marginal cost.

3. Other things being equal, monopolists produce less and charge higher prices than do purely competitive firms. In the real world, however, it would be impossible to find a purely competitive firm and a monopoly with the same or even similar costs of production.

4. Profit-maximizing monopolists set price greater than marginal cost and greater than average cost. Monopolies do not result in allocative efficiency because price is greater than marginal cost; however, monopolies may be technically efficient if they are large enough to enjoy economies of scale. Monopoly firms devote resources to rent seeking and may be x-inefficient.

5. Monopolies that are able to price-discriminate can increase their economic profits. Several types of price discrimination are possible, but all require that the monopolist separate the market into different segments and charge multiple prices.

6. Monopoly regulations are typically designed to establish allocative efficiency or to reduce economic profits. Economic profits can be eliminated by requiring the regulated monopolist to set price equal to the average cost of production. Allocative efficiency can be established by requiring the monopolist to set price equal to the marginal cost of production. This generates allocative efficiency, but decreasing-cost industries incur losses and increasing-cost industries still make economic profits.

KEY TERMS AND CONCEPTS

monopoly
barrier to entry
economies of scale
government license
patent
marginal revenue
demand elasticity
economic profit

welfare criteria
x-efficiency
rent seeking
price discrimination
arbitrage
monopoly regulation
peak load pricing

REVIEW QUESTIONS

1. What are the three main reasons for the existence of monopolies? Does the existence of a monopoly require the simultaneous occurrence of all three criteria?

2. Using *words,* not numbers, carefully explain why a monopolist's marginal revenue curve slopes down faster than its demand curve.

3. Explain why monopoly pricing meets neither the allocative or technical efficiency criterion in the long run. Explain why it is so difficult for government regulation to establish both welfare criteria simultaneously.

4. Define and give examples of first-, second-, and third-degree price discrimination.
5. The examples of third-degree price discrimination used in the text were movie theaters and airlines. Are these monopolists? To what extent?
6. What kind of rent-seeking behavior does the professional baseball player Ken Griffey Jr. engage in?

PROBLEMS

1. Many communities have so many hospitals that most beds are unused at any point in time. Do you think that the government should limit the number of hospitals that can be built in such communities? Why or why not?
2. Public utility officials are elected in some states and appointed in others. Assuming that the only two approaches to utility regulation are marginal cost pricing and average cost pricing, which approach do you think elected officials would be most likely to advocate? Which approach would be advocated by appointed officials? Why?
3. Suppose that the average and marginal cost curves for a particular monopolist are flat over the relevant region of production. How would this affect the regulated average cost price? The regulated marginal cost price?
4. Some communities charge a flat monthly fee for residential water while others charge by the gallon. Which rate structure do you think economists would favor? Why? Which rate structure do you think most consumers would favor? Why? Which rate structure do *you* favor?
5. Indicate whether the following are true, false, or uncertain and explain why:
   a. Demand is price elastic over the region where total revenue rises as price increases.
   b. Profit is maximum where total revenue is maximum.
   c. Monopoly firms produce less than competitive firms.
   d. It is impossible for a monopolist's profit-maximizing price to generate zero economic profits.
   e. It is impossible for a monopolist's profit-maximizing price to meet the efficiency criterion.
   f. The marginal revenue curve for a monopolist always slopes down twice as fast as the demand curve.
6. Movie theaters have long given price breaks to senior citizens and students. Suppose they started giving breaks to families with small children and charging a "Yuppie Tax" on dating couples.
   a. What would be the economic rationale for this pricing strategy?
   b. How do you think such a pricing policy would affect the behavior of young couples? Of families with small children?
   c. Finally, ignore for the moment how such a policy would affect you personally. Do you think it would be a good idea? Why or why not?
7. The text noted that the monopolist must be making economic profits before it can engage in first- or third-degree price discrimination. Is this requirement also necessary before it can engage in second-degree price discrimination? Why or why not?

CHAPTER 13

Intermediate Competition: Monopolistic Competition and Oligopoly

Over 80 percent of the industrial output of the United States is produced and sold by only 200 large firms. None of these firms are price takers like pure competitors, but few are pure monopolies either. These firms—and the overwhelming majority of the firms in the United States—are best classified as either oligopolies or monopolistically competitive firms.

Oligopolies like Exxon and the other giants of the petroleum industry seem to make huge profits every year. Why doesn't rivalry among Exxon, Shell, Mobil, and the other oil companies bring profits down to the normal level? Like Compaq Computer, Hewlett Packard, and other personal computer manufacturers, most monopolistically competitive firms have substantial advertising budgets. How can they afford the cost of advertising in the face of stiff competition? Won't the low-price clone makers—Dell, Leading Edge, and others—be able to undercut their costs and sell for lower prices? This chapter will help us understand these and other kinds of behavior.

Theories of oligopoly and monopolistic competition are much closer to the real world than the theories of pure competition and pure monopoly. This should offer solace to people worried that the models in the last two chapters have been unrealistic. Unfortunately, the real world is complex, and the models we are about to develop reflect that fact: they are not as neat and tidy as the models of pure competition and pure monopoly. In fact, economists have yet to agree on a single model of oligopoly.

AFTER READING AND STUDYING THIS CHAPTER, YOU SHOULD BE ABLE TO:

• • • Know the basic facts and data on the size and economic power of large corporations in the United States

• • • Explain why monopolistically competitive firms typically resort to advertising and operate with excess capacity

• • • Know the economic reasons for the existence of oligopolies, and explain how oligopolists make price and output decisions

DEFINITIONS AND DATA

The line of demarcation between oligopoly and monopolistic competition is not as well defined as the line between pure competition and pure monopoly. The definitions we used in Chapter 11 remain valid, but fitting a particular firm into a precise definition is often difficult. Before we develop models to help understand the behavior of oligopoly and monopolistic competition, we need to recall definitions and look at data on market concentration.

Monopolistically competitive industries consist of many firms selling differentiated products. The barriers to entry are small or insignificant, so high profits generally attract other firms to enter the industry. Monopolistically competitive firms often use advertising to generate brand loyalty, which may allow them to set prices slightly higher than under pure competition. The automobile industry, once considered an oligopoly, is now classified as a monopolistically competitive industry by some economists. The Big Three U.S. producers now compete with numerous foreign auto producers, and a booming U.S. economy is all that is necessary to attract new foreign imports.

Oligopoly industries are dominated by a few large firms, so few that each firm must pay careful attention to the actions of its rivals. Mutual interdependence between firms is the key characteristic that distinguishes oligopoly from other market structures. There are substantial barriers to entry under oligopoly, so firms can make long-run economic profits. Both pure and differentiated oligopolies exist. A pure oligopoly produces a homogeneous product; the steel and oil industries are examples. A differentiated oligopoly has a small number of producers making differentiated products. The airline industry is an example.

Monopolistic competition A market structure characterized by many firms selling differentiated products and by low or insignificant barriers to entry.

Oligopoly A market structure characterized by a small number of firms that must pay close attention to each other's actions; barriers to entry are high.

• • • • • • • •

Measures of Concentration

How prevalent are oligopoly and monopolistic competition in the United States? This question can be answered in several ways, but none is definitive. In 1991, 88 percent of all manufacturing assets were held by the 200 largest firms in the United States.[1] Clearly, many of these firms were large enough to have a measure of market power. Firms desire market power so that they can ". . . ensure, as far as may be possible, that there is no alternative at a lower price."[2] However, mere size does not necessarily mean market power. For example, the Big Three automakers are huge,

---

[1]Data are from the 1992 *Statistical Abstract of the United States*, Table 868.
[2]The quotation is from John Kenneth Galbraith, *The Anatomy of Power* (Boston: Houghton Mifflin, 1983), p. 137. Market power is a difficult concept and can involve more than pricing discretion. *Anatomy of Power* explores power in social, corporate, political, and other contexts. Like everything Galbraith writes, it is both well written and controversial.

· · · · **TABLE 13.1 CONCENTRATION RATIOS IN MANUFACTURING, 1982**

Industry	Number of Companies	4-Firm Ratio	8-Firm Ratio	20-Firm Ratio
Petroleum refining	282	28%	48%	76%
Motor vehicles and car bodies	284	92	97	99
Electronic computing equipment	1,520	42	64	82
Radio and TV equipment	2,083	22	35	57
Aircraft	139	64	81	98
Newspapers	7,520	22	34	49
Pharmaceutical preparations	584	26	42	60
Cigarettes	8	x★	x★	NA

★Information withheld to avoid disclosure. Estimates put the 4-firm concentration ratio as high as 85.
SOURCE: 1989 *Statistical Abstract of the United States*, Table 1266.

but they face such severe competition from foreign producers that the domestic auto industry is perhaps better classified as monopolistically competitive than as oligopolistic.

One method used to gauge the extent of market power is the **concentration ratio**. Concentration ratios give the portion of industry sales held by the 4, 8, or 20 largest firms in the industry. Table 13.1 presents the 4-, 8-, and 20-firm concentration ratios for selected domestic industries for 1982, the latest data available at this writing. Concentration ratios give some idea about market concentration, but they say little about the extent of competition or geographical factors. For example, even though the 4-firm concentration ratio for newspapers is only 22 percent, many towns have only one newspaper, so many local newspapers have virtual monopoly status. Another problem with concentration ratios is that they say nothing about potential competition. Some industries with very high concentration ratios behave much like competitive industries because of the threat of entry into the industry—prices are kept low to discourage entry.[3] Finally, remember that the data in Table 13.1 represent only domestic production. This explains why the 4-firm concentration ratio in motor vehicles is 92 percent even though imported automobiles make up about 30 percent of domestic sales.

A more serious problem with concentration ratios is that they do not distinguish between an industry in which one firm dominates and one where a small number of large firms share the market. For example, if one firm had 57 percent of the market and the other 43 firms in the industry each had 1 percent, the 4-firm concentration ratio would be 60. This is the same concentration ratio as an industry with 4 firms having 15 percent of the market apiece and 40 firms with 1 percent shares. Industry behavior might be similar in both cases, but it is also possible that the large firm would dominate the industry in the first case, while the four firms in the second case would resort to cutthroat competition.

Concentration ratio A common measure of industrial concentration. The higher the concentration ratio, the greater the degree of monopoly power.

[3]The threat of competition from potential entrants is the point of departure for the theory of contestable markets discussed in the next chapter.

Herfindahl index Index of industrial concentration calculated by squaring the percentage shares of each firm.

This problem can be eliminated by using a different measure of market concentration, the **Herfindahl index**. The Herfindahl index is calculated by squaring the percentage share of each firm. This puts extra weight on firms with a larger market share. The formula for computing a Herfindahl index is:

$$\text{Herfindahl index: } H = s_1^2 + s_2^2 + \cdots s_i^2 \cdots + s_n^2 \qquad [1]$$

where s_i is the market share of the ith firm. The Herfindahl index can run from 100 for an industry composed of identically sized firms to 10,000 for a pure monopoly. For the two examples above, the index would be:

$$H = 57^2 + 1^2 + 1^2 + \cdots + 1^2 = 3,249 + 43 = 3,292$$

$$H = 15^2 + 15^2 + 15^2 + 15^2 + 1^2 + \cdots + 1^2 = 4(225) + 40 = 940$$

The Herfindahl index is widely considered to be a superior measure of market concentration because it can isolate the presence of a single or few dominant firms. The Justice Department has used it since 1982 to determine the effect of mergers on competition.[4] However, the interpretation of Herfindahl indices is not as intuitive as concentration ratios, so concentration ratios are still useful. Further, the Herfindahl index suffers from some of the same problems as concentration ratios: it says nothing about potential competition or geographical concentration.

. . . .

A Caveat: The Structure-Conduct-Performance Approach

The main reason economists calculate Herfindahl indices and concentration ratios is the belief that there is a relationship between market structure, conduct, and performance—an approach to the study of industrial economics known by its acronym SCP. According to the **SCP model**, concentrated industries with significant barriers to entry will behave more like a monopoly than industries that are less concentrated and have few barriers to entry. This is true in general; however, there are enough exceptions that many economists have begun to question the SCP model. For example, if oligopoly firms fear entry into their industry, they will tend to charge lower prices to make entry less attractive. In this situation, there is a divergence between structure and performance: the oligopolistic structure is performing more like a competitive structure by setting price close to average cost.

SCP model An approach to industrial economics that holds that market structure, conduct, and performance are related.

Analysis of the relationship between industry structure and performance is the starting place for contemporary research into what is called the *new industrial economics*. Advocates of the new industrial economics believe that the SCP approach omits several important aspects of business strategy. In particular, it says little about the quantity or quality of information that various market participants have, and it ignores specific factors in different competitive settings. For the time being, we will overlook the new industrial economics and concentrate on the more traditional SCP approach. The standard SCP approach provides important terminology and concepts that are necessary before we are ready for the new industrial economics in the next chapter.

---

[4]The Justice Department uses the Herfindahl index when deciding whether to allow mergers. In general, if the Herfindahl index would exceed 1,000 after the merger and the merger would add 100 points or more to the index, then the merger is likely to be challenged. Antitrust law is a main topic of Chapter 19.

MONOPOLISTIC COMPETITION

Firms in a monopolistically competitive industry differ from purely competitive firms in only one significant way: monopolistically competitive firms produce differentiated products. Often these product variations give each firm enough market power to allow it to be a price maker. Because there is free entry into the industry, however, monopolistically competitive firms cannot make economic profits in the long run. If they set their prices too high, new firms will enter the industry and customers will buy from competitors.

The theory of monopolistic competition dates back to the 1930s when it was simultaneously but independently described by E. H. Chamberlin and Joan Robinson. The Economic Heritage box on page 315 provides some background on Chamberlin and Robinson and tells how their codiscovery, sadly, turned into something of a battle over intellectual originality.

Demand and Revenue under Monopolistic Competition

Figure 13.1 presents a monopolistically competitive firm in both short-run and long-run equilibrium. As under monopoly, the demand curve is downward sloping to reflect the fact that the monopolistically competitive firm has the ability to set prices because of product differentiation. Note too that the marginal revenue curve slopes down twice as fast as the demand curve. To maximize profits, the firm produces the quantity where marginal cost is equal to marginal revenue, point a. The selling price is then derived from the demand curve at point b.

To this point, the graphs in the figure look just like those of a monopoly firm. However, notice that in panel (b), the demand curve is tangent to the average total cost curve directly above the intersection of marginal revenue and marginal cost. Why is the demand curve tangent to the average total cost curve? Economic profits cause firms to enter the industry, and this reduces the demand for existing firms. Firms will continue to enter the industry until economic profits go to zero. The only way to have zero economic profits—and also to have the firm be producing the profit-maximizing quantity where marginal cost equals marginal revenue—is for the demand curve to be exactly tangent to the average total cost curve above the intersection of marginal revenue and marginal cost. This is not the case under pure monopoly because substantial barriers to entry permit long-run economic profits.

Panel (b) also shows that price is higher and output is lower under monopolistic competition than under pure competition. The monopolistic competitor's price (P_{mc}) is higher than the pure competitor's price (P_{pc}) because production takes place on the downward-sloping portion of the long-run average total cost curve; under pure competition, production takes place at the minimum point on the long-run average total cost curve. This also explains why output is lower under monopolistic competition (Q_{mc})—production occurs at less than optimal plant capacity.

The Inefficiency of Monopolistic Competition

Price is greater than marginal cost so monopolistic competition does not meet the allocative efficiency criterion. How serious is allocative inefficiency under monop-

FIGURE 13.1 EQUILIBRIUM UNDER MONOPOLISTIC COMPETITION

The demand curve under monopolistic competition is downward sloping to reflect product differentiation. To maximize profits, the firm produces the quantity where marginal cost is equal to marginal revenue, point *a*, and sets price from the demand curve, point *b*. In the short run, monopolistically competitive firms can make economic profits or losses. In this case, the firm is making economic profits. The average cost per unit is *d*, so the firm is making economic profits in the amount *dcbP*.

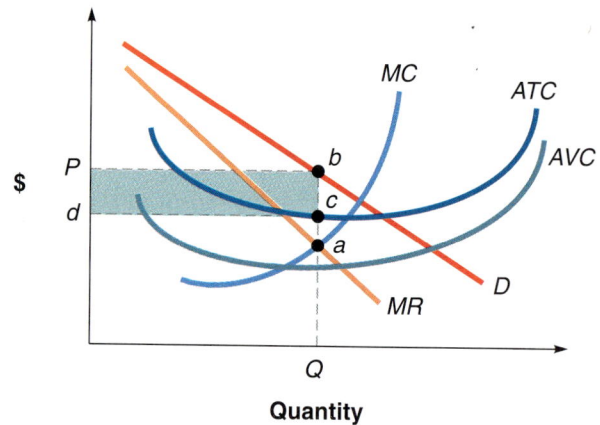

(a) Short-run equilibrium

The absence of barriers to entry allows firms to enter the industry in response to short-run profit signals. Entry causes the demand curve facing each firm in the industry to shift in, causes price to fall to long-run average cost, and eliminates long-run economic profits. Long-run equilibrium is established when there are no economic profits and the demand curve is tangent to the *LRAC* curve at the point directly above the intersection of marginal revenue and marginal cost. This occurs at point *d* with price P_{mc} equal to average total cost.

Monopolistic competition results in higher prices and lower output than pure competition. In the long run under pure competition, price and output will move to the minimum point of the *LRAC* so that $P_{pc} < P_{mc}$ and $Q_{pc} > Q_{mc}$.

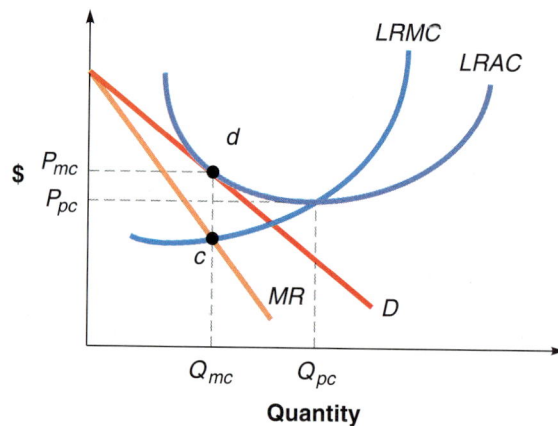

(b) Long-run equilibrium

Excess capacity theorem The tangency between the average revenue curve must occur on the downward-sloping portion of the average total cost curve, so monopolistically competitive firms never operate at the minimum point on their average cost curves.

olistic competition? It is impossible to say, but we can identify what that inefficiency "buys"—variety. If there were no product differentiation, the demand curve would be horizontal, and price would equal both average cost and marginal cost in the long run. That would be more efficient, but consumers might not be better off: think how you would feel if the government mandated that, in the interest of efficiency, only one kind of ice cream could be produced. Price would fall and economic efficiency would increase, but you could not buy Cherry Garcia.

Another result of monopolistic competition is the **excess capacity theorem**. Given the shape of the demand and average total cost curves, tangency must occur on the downward-sloping portion of the average total cost curve. This means that the technical efficiency criterion—P = minimum ATC—cannot be achieved in the

When Edward Hastings Chamberlin (1899–1967) revised his Harvard Ph.D. thesis and published *The Theory of Monopolistic Competition* in 1933, he knew that he had something important. He just did not know how important. Seven years earlier, an Italian economist, Piero Sraffa at Cambridge, England, had published an article, "The Laws of Return under Competitive Conditions," which addressed many of the same ideas. Chamberlin would later claim that he had never read Sraffa's piece, though scholars today note that Chamberlin's professors at Harvard in Cambridge, Massachusetts, did have contact with economists at the "other Cambridge" in England. Whatever the case, it was not Sraffa's work that stole some of the limelight from Chamberlin, it was *The Economics of Imperfect Competition* published by the English economist Joan Robinson (1903–1983) in the same year that Chamberlin's work appeared. The two books were remarkably similar—enough so that today the terms "imperfect competition" and "monopolistic competition" are used interchangeably. Unfortunately, Chamberlin devoted too much of his energy to pointing out the differences between his and Robinson's work instead of extending his ideas or researching other areas. Robinson went on to make important critical and helpful contributions in Keynesian and Marxian economics.

In fact, there were some differences between the economics of Chamber-

Edward Chamberlin

Joan Robinson

lin and Robinson, though not as many as Chamberlin seemed to believe. Both spoke of the "tangency solution" under monopolistic competition. Both focused their attention on individual firms as opposed to the entire industry. And both used downward-sloping demand and marginal revenue curves, though only Robinson used the term "marginal revenue." The differences that did exist were more in emphasis than content. Robinson credited the genesis of her work to Sraffa when she argued that under conditions of decreasing costs, the main obstacle preventing a firm from increasing sales is not the threat of rising costs, but the ability of the market to absorb additional output. This was to be a critical element in Robinson's plea for increased aggregate demand as a solution to unemployment—the standard Keynesian remedy. Chamberlin stressed that

downward-sloping demand curves would lead to advertising or "nonprice competition" as he called it. Robinson saw the waste from excess capacity and called for government intervention. Chamberlin underlined the variety and choice made possible by monopolistic competition.

The work of Robinson and Chamberlin was truly revolutionary. It changed the focus of twentieth-century microeconomics by shifting the emphasis from the industry to the firm and by providing a framework that allowed economists to study the intermediate cases between pure monopoly and pure competition. Only a small group of economists—primarily those affiliated with the conservative Chicago school—rejected this work, and today, even these economists are doing work in monopolistic competition and oligopoly.

long run. Consequently, firms could lower average total costs by increasing production because the typical plant is larger than necessary for technical efficiency. This is certainly true of many retailers who contend that they could lower unit costs if they could only increase sales.

. . . .

Advertising

Finally, because product differentiation plays such a critical role in monopolistic competition, advertising plays an important role in the activities of the firm. Firms try to establish brand loyalty to convince customers that there are no good substitutes for their products. Advertising has several effects on the market: First, advertising is a cost of production so it shifts the average and marginal cost curves upward. Second, if advertising is successful, it will also shift the demand and marginal revenue curves outward. The result is that advertising raises production costs and selling price.[5]

Do higher production costs mean that advertising is wasteful? Not necessarily. There are two kinds of advertising. **Informative advertising** provides information to potential buyers. If an advertisement provides you with important product information, that information is valuable—and potentially worth the cost. Informative advertising reduces the cost of acquiring information. The other kind of advertising is **persuasive advertising**. Persuasive advertising uses jingles and slogans to convince people to purchase things they might not otherwise buy.

How often advertisers persuade people to buy things they otherwise would not is a matter of debate—consumers do have minds of their own, do they not?—but in numerous cases, the consuming public has been convinced that one product was superior to another when, in fact, there was no difference. One case was Bayer Aspirin. Until the company was forced to abandon it, Bayer's advertising slogan was "All aspirin are not alike." Consumers inferred that Bayer was sufficiently superior to justify paying a premium price. When a study discovered that all aspirin *were* alike, Bayer was forced to drop its advertising campaign. Bayer remains the best-selling aspirin in the country and still charges a premium price. Another example is Clorox bleach. All bleaches contain the same active ingredients, 5 percent sodium hydrochloride, yet many consumers remain convinced that Clorox is superior to other brands and are willing to pay a premium price. Or consider what Russian president Boris Yeltsin said when he had his first sip of Russian-bottled Coke: It tastes just like Pepsi! Apparently, Yeltsin did not understand the importance of brand names—and he *certainly* did not understand what the new Coke bottlers wanted him to say. Cases like these are apparently having an impact. As discussed in the Focus box on page 318, consumers appear to be turning away from name brands in favor of low-price generic goods.

Informative advertising Advertising that increases consumer knowledge about products and thus allows more informed choices.

Persuasive advertising Advertising designed to convince people to buy things they might not otherwise buy.

---

[5]But not necessarily. Firms operating on the downward portion of their average cost curves may realize lower costs if they can successfully increase sales through advertising. But it is also possible that more advertising by competitors will make demand curves more elastic, thereby lowering price despite higher average total costs.

RECAP   Monopolistic Competition

1. Monopolistic competition exists when there are many firms producing differ-entiated products in an industry with no substantial barriers to entry.
2. Price is higher and output is lower under monopolistic competition than under pure competition. However, monopolistic competition provides more variety and consumer choice than pure competition.
3. Price is greater than marginal cost, so monopolistic competition does not achieve allocative efficiency. Further, although unrestricted entry and exit eliminate long-run economic profits, firms under monopolistic competition will typically be producing on the downward-sloping portion of their average cost curves, so the technical efficiency criterion is violated as well.
4. Monopolistically competitive firms use advertising to generate brand loyalty and provide information about product differences. Advertising can be infor-mative or persuasive.

OLIGOPOLY

The key distinction between oligopoly and other market structures is that oligopolies must pay careful attention to the actions of their rivals. Perfectly com-petitive firms could not care less what other firms in the industry do; every firm can sell as much as it wants at the market price but nothing at a higher price. By definition, pure monopolists *have* no competitors; however, if they raise their prices too high, people will find substitute goods. And if monopolistically competitive firms use advertising effectively, they can establish brand loyalty and carve out their particular niche in the market. But oligopolists are different. There are so few firms in the industry that each has to look over its shoulder. If your rival brings out a new model, your market share might shrink—unless you counter with a new model or lower prices on your current model. Should you bring out a new model first? Maybe—but you might end up wasting your money if your rival brings out one at the same time. It might be better to wait to see what your rival does and then respond with lower prices, style changes, or whatever.

The point is that decision making under oligopoly involves strategies, and it is this strategy-making process that oligopoly theory must capture. Unfortunately, trying to capture the strategic interaction in a simple model is difficult because strategies depend very much on circumstance—and circumstances can differ considerably from market to market. As a result, economists have yet to settle on a single oligopoly model. The remainder of this chapter outlines the reasons oligopolies exist, presents two classic oligopoly models, and looks at the efficiency of oligopoly. We will have to wait until Chapter 14 before we look at game theory and more modern views on oligopoly strategy.

Like monopolies, oligopolies can exist only if there are sufficient barriers to prevent firms from entering the industry. Both technical and strategic barriers can exist. Many oligopolies are also the result of mergers and acquisitions.

FOCUS ON

THE VALUE OF BRAND NAMES

The 1980s saw a number of important economic events, but none made more headlines than the mega-mergers and acquisitions: Kohlberg, Kravis, and Roberts bought out RJR Nabisco for $25 billion, Philip Morris bought Kraft for $12.9 billion, and Nestlé paid $4.5 billion for Rowntree. What was so amazing about these acquisitions was not just the huge sums of money involved, but that the buyers were willing to pay sums that were significantly higher than the book value of the firms' stock. Nestlé paid five times the book value for Rowntree; Philip Morris and Kohlberg, Kravis paid similarly high multiples of book value. Why were these companies worth so much money? One explanation was that the acquirers were buying not just a company, but well-known brand names.

Brand recognition can be a valuable commodity because consumers are

Own-label products now account for almost 15% of grocery sales in the United States and for over 20% in Europe.

willing to pay higher prices for name-brand products. However, the importance of brand recognition appears to have changed in the 1990s. Part of the reason was the recession and the increased focus on price, but at least

. . . .

Technical Barriers to Entry

MES (minimum efficient scale)
The smallest plant size that can use the most modern and technologically advanced production methods.

The main technical barriers to entry are economies of scale and a related concept, the **minimum efficient scale (MES)** of operation. As we discovered in Chapter 10, long-run average total costs depend on the size or scale of the plant: a firm that is too small is not able to use the most efficient technology so its costs will be high, but a firm that has grown too large may also have high average total costs because of management inefficiency. Economies of scale result in oligopoly when the costs of production are minimized with a small number of firms, each of which is large relative to the overall size of the market. For example, suppose that total market demand is 1,000 units per year and that this quantity could be produced with 20 small firms each selling 50 units or with 4 large firms each selling 250 units. If the average cost

three other factors were at work as well:

- *Perceived product parity*. A recent study showed that nearly two-thirds of consumers worldwide believe that there are "no relevant or discernible differences" between rival brands in a wide variety of products. They are probably right in many instances because modern manufacturing techniques have made it easier for competitors to copy.
- *Special promotions*. With so many products on the market, retailers often auction off shelf space to the highest bidder. In 1992 alone, over 16,800 new products were introduced in the United States. This gives retailers more pricing discretion, and they often set price below cost. As a result, consumers can frequently find bargains in new products that compete with established brand names.
- *Own-label products*. Many stores—expecially supermarkets—began experimenting with products sold under their own labels in the 1980s. Today, own-label products account for over 20 percent of supermarket sales in Europe and almost 15 percent in the United States. These products are considerably cheaper than brand-name products and frequently are just as good—because they are often made by the same firms that make the brand-name products! Heinz, Ralston-Purina, and Campbell Soup are among the companies that produce own-label products for supermarkets.

What are companies doing about lost brand loyalty? One example is Philip Morris Co., the maker of Marlboro cigarettes. After years of battering from both generic cigarettes and the declining popularity of smoking, Philip Morris lowered the price of Marlboros by 40¢ a pack in April 1993. It also began a special Marlboro products campaign, the Marlboro Country Store, which enables Marlboro smokers to trade in empty cigarette packs for Marlboro-labeled western wear. Philip Morris's strategy seems to be working, but how long it will work and whether generic brands will counter with still lower prices remain to be seen.

The decline of brand names does not mean that the theory of monopolistic competition is a thing of the past. As long as consumers perceive any product differentiation at all, the model of monopolistic competition is a better tool than the model of pure competition. To the extent that perceived product variations are lessening, however, demand curves will tend to flatten and firms will operate with less excess capacity. In other words, the decline of brand loyalty could be a step toward increased economic efficiency.

SOURCES: "Shoot Out at the Check-out," *Economist*, June 5–11, 1993, pp. 69–72; Laura Zinn, "The Smoke Clears at Marlboro," *Business Week*, January 31, 1994, pp. 76–77.

of production falls as output increases to 250 units, then the large firms could undercut the prices of the small firms. The result: Cost incentives will cause the industry to evolve into an oligopoly with at most four firms. Why wouldn't it evolve into a monopoly? It will if costs continue to fall as output expands beyond 250 units. If costs begin to rise after 250 units of output are produced, however, the industry will stabilize with four firms.

Figure 13.2 illustrates the long-run average total cost curve and minimum efficient scale. As usual, the long-run average total cost curve (*LRAC*) is U-shaped. The downward-sloping portion indicates that average costs fall as output expands; this is the region of economies of scale. The upward-sloping region shows that costs rise if

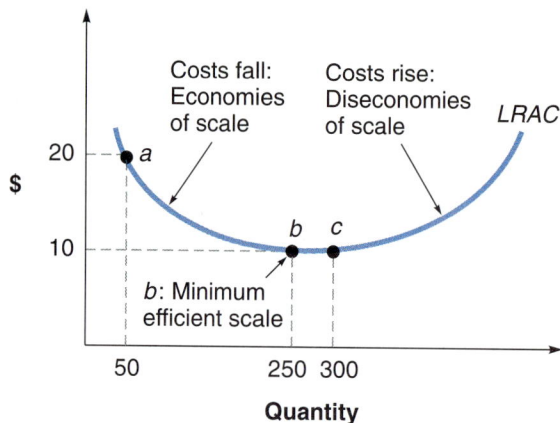

FIGURE 13.2 LONG-RUN AVERAGE TOTAL COSTS AND THE MINIMUM EFFICIENT SCALE

The minimum efficient scale (MES) is the point where long-run average costs reach their minimum. If the industry is shared by several small firms each producing 50 units of output apiece, the average cost of production will be $20. If costs fall to $10 as output expands to 250 units, these small firms will have an incentive to expand production and lower prices. If the market is saturated with 1,000 units of output, the industry will evolve toward a four-firm oligopoly.

production is carried very far beyond 250 units; this is the region of diseconomies of scale. Now, if 20 small firms share the market and each produces 50 units of output, their average cost would be $20, as indicated by point *a* on the *LRAC* curve. The MES is at point *b*, the point where the *LRAC* reaches its minimum at a cost of $10 per unit. Notice that the *LRAC* was drawn with constant average costs between points *b* and *c*. As we found out in Chapter 10, constant costs are common in the real world and generally result from excess capacity. Firms producing any quantity between 250 and 300 units of output could charge a price as low as $10 and still make normal profits. A more likely outcome, however, would be for the oligopolists to charge a price higher than $10. As long as this price is lower than $20, consumers will benefit despite the market concentration.

How prevalent are these situations? Several economists have tried to calculate the MES for various industries. Measurement problems and changing technology make any estimate suspect, but interestingly, few industries have an MES as large as the observed market concentration seems to imply. For example, the 4-firm concentration ratio in tobacco products is as high as 85 percent, yet the MES is closer to about 7 percent of market share. Likewise the MES for oil refining is only 3 percent, yet a 4-firm concentration ratio of 28 percent implies a scale of operation more than twice this amount.[6] These data suggest that clearly something else is going on that deter-

[6]These and other MES estimates can be found in F. M. Scherer and D. Ross, *Industrial Market Structure and Economic Performance* (Boston: Houghton Mifflin, 1990).

mines firm size. One factor is that the MES refers to *plant* size, not *firm* size. A firm composed of several plants operating at the MES might be just as efficient as a firm with one MES plant. Second, some economists argue that the success of any particular firm depends as much or more on luck and managerial skill as on technical cost advantages. This may explain why plant size often differs considerably from the MES. Clearly, however, some industries are dominated by plants larger than the MES. Hospitals may be one example. Studies have indicated that the MES for hospitals is between 200 and 400 beds—considerably smaller than the hospitals in many big cities. This may be one (of many) reasons why medical costs are so high.

Finally, technological change can complicate the picture enormously. Just one example will show why. Suppose that just moments after a four-firm oligopoly invested millions to achieve the MES, a technological innovation made the old technology obsolete. Small firms without the excess baggage of the old technology might find it easier to get loans for the new technology. Very quickly the concentration ratio and the MES would change drastically.

Strategic Barriers to Entry

By setting profit-maximizing prices, oligopolists risk the possibility of entry into the industry. For example, suppose that the profit-maximizing price is $10 above average cost at the MES. A new firm could enter the industry, set up a plant at the MES, and set its price $5 above average cost, take market share from the existing firms, and still earn economic profits. To avoid this possibility, oligopolists can adopt a strategy of **limit pricing**. When a firm uses limit pricing, it sets its price at less than the profit-maximizing price and thus makes entry into the industry less enticing. Does limit pricing mean that the goal of firms is to not maximize profits? Not at all. Limit pricing may be the best way to maximize long-run profits; the marginal cost/marginal revenue approach could result in only short-run profit maximization.

> **Limit pricing** An oligopoly pricing strategy of charging low prices to deter entry into the industry.

The topic of limit pricing raises several important issues regarding oligopoly strategy. For example, mere knowledge that existing firms *might* lower prices could be enough to deter potential entrants. Further, if the threat of price reductions does deter entry, existing firms can charge profit-maximizing prices; that is, set marginal cost equal to marginal revenue. For example, in 1992 Mark Air began offering passenger service between Seattle, Washington, and Juneau, Alaska, a route previously served only by Alaska Airlines. (A third carrier, Delta Airlines, offers only summer service.) Alaska Airlines responded by cutting its round-trip fares by almost $200. This move accomplished two things: First, it forced upstart Mark Air out of the Juneau-Seattle passenger transport business; Alaska Airlines then raised prices to the previous level. Second, and perhaps more importantly, this episode established the credible threat that Alaska Airlines would lower prices if other air carriers entered the Juneau-Seattle market. Limit pricing and similar pricing strategies are still under study. We will look at these issues again in the next chapter.

Mergers and Acquisitions

Many oligopolies are the result of mergers or acquisitions. A merger occurs when two firms decide to combine into one firm; an acquisition occurs when one firm

Synergy The interaction between two or more forces so that their combined effect is greater than the sum of their individual effects. Synergy effects make the value of merged company greater than the sum of the value of the two individual companies.

Economies of scope A reduction in average cost resulting from the joint production of two or more products.

Horizontal merger A merger between firms in the same industry.

Vertical merger A merger between firms at different stages of the production process.

Conglomerate merger A merger between unrelated firms that leads to a conglomerate.

Congeneric merger A merger between related firms that do not produce the same product or have a producer-supplier relationship.

buys out another firm. There are at least three possible reasons why mergers and acquisitions occur. First, successful mergers and acquisitions often result in **synergy**. As we learned in Chapter 9, synergy is the interaction between two or more forces such that their combined effect is greater than the sum of their individual effects. In the case of mergers and acquisitions, synergy can make the new company more valuable than the two individual companies were. Synergy can come from several sources including economies of scale, improved managerial efficiency, and increased market power. Computer software companies frequently merge in a quest for market power. For example, when Symantec acquired Norton Computing in 1991, it was able to combine the best features of Symantec Utilities for the Macintosh with the features of its chief competitor, Norton Utilities for the Macintosh. Symantec continued this process in 1993 by acquiring Fifth Generation Systems, the publisher of Public Utilities for the Macintosh, another competitor in the Macintosh utility market.

A second reason for mergers is to generate **economies of scope**. Economies of scope refer to the reduction in average cost that occurs when two or more products are produced by a single firm. For example, a merger between two airline companies, one a passenger carrier and the other a freight carrier, would result in economies of scope because much of the same fixed capital—aircraft, baggage-handling equipment, and so on   could be used for both operations. The acquisition of Kraft Foods by Philip Morris in 1988 may have generated economies of scope because many of the same distribution channels and advertising techniques are used for both cigarettes and food. Finally, mergers can also offer tax and financial advantages—topics that are perhaps better treated in your accounting or finance class.[7]

There are four types of mergers:

1. A **horizontal** merger is between two firms in the same industry. The 1988 merger between Shearson Lehman and E. F. Hutton, two brokerage houses, was a horizontal merger. Horizontal mergers can be beneficial because the new firm may enjoy economies of scale.

2. A **vertical** merger happens when a firm acquires one of its suppliers or distributors. Vertical mergers occur when firms at different stages of production unite. For example, if a steel producer wanted better control over the supply of iron ore, it might consider a merger with an iron mining company; if it wanted better control over distribution, it might acquire a trucking company.

3. A **conglomerate** merger is between unrelated firms. A firm might want to acquire a firm in an unrelated industry for diversification purposes. For example, when U.S. Steel (now USX) bought Marathon Oil in the late 1970s, the hope was that profits in the oil industry could offset losses in the steel industry.

4. A **congeneric** merger is between related firms that do not produce the same product or have a producer-supplier relationship. Congeneric mergers often result in economies of scope. The acquisitions of General Foods in 1986 and Kraft in 1988 by tobacco maker Philip Morris would be considered congeneric mergers. Congeneric mergers allow a degree of diversification and may be somewhat safer than conglomerate mergers because management may better

---

[7]For a more in-depth discussion of the advantages of and reasons for corporate mergers, see Chapter 15 of Eugene F. Brigham, *Fundamentals of Financial Management*, 5th ed. (Chicago: Dryden Press, 1989). This section draws upon Brigham.

understand the ins and outs of the acquired firm's industry. In this case, Philip Morris's knowledge of the marketing and distribution of consumer products was helpful when it expanded from the tobacco industry into food.

There have been four waves of mergers in U.S. history. Many firms in the basic industries merged in the late 1800s, the booming stock market of the 1920s provided firms with ready cash to finance acquisitions, conglomerates became popular in the 1960s, and "merger mania" struck in the 1980s. Mergers became so popular in the 1980s for several reasons. The depressed dollar made it easy for foreign firms to buy American firms. Also, the Reagan administration made it clear that "bigness was not necessarily badness" and argued that large U.S. firms could better compete with foreign competition. Many of the mergers and acquisitions of the 1980s were financed by the sale of **junk bonds**—high-risk, high-return bonds—and sought to improve short-term profits with little attention on the long term.

Junk bonds High-risk, high-return bonds, often used to finance mergers.

The 1990s may mark the beginning of a fifth merger movement. In contrast to many of the mergers of the 1980s, most of the mergers in the 1990s have been driven by long-term strategic concerns and have been between firms in related industries. For example, AT&T's $12.6 billion acquisition of McCaw Cellular Communications was a strategic move to improve AT&T's position in the important cellular phone market. Likewise, Mattel paid $1 billion for Fisher-Price to increase its market share in the infant toy market. Mattel, now the nation's largest toy company, hopes to use its marketing and distribution clout to increase its market share even further.

Efficiency Considerations

As you might suspect, oligopolies do not necessarily achieve either allocative efficiency or technical efficiency in the long run. Barriers to entry prevent competition from forcing price down to average costs, and the divergence between demand and marginal revenue means that price cannot equal marginal cost if the firm is to be a profit maximizer. However, analyzing the effect of oligopoly in terms of the economist's formal efficiency conditions ignores several important aspects of oligopoly behavior.

The sheer size of oligopolies brings with it both benefits and costs. The benefits are not only the size that may be necessary to achieve the minimum efficient scale, but also the financial resources necessary to do expensive research and development. The advantages of size are one reason why so many high-tech firms are now forming production and research consortiums. What are the costs of oligopolies? Firms as large as AT&T and General Motors wield not only economic power, but also political power. They have the resources to lobby Congress for protectionist legislation, and states and municipalities frequently offer special property tax concessions to oligopolies that are not offered to smaller firms.

DECISION MAKING UNDER OLIGOPOLY I: THE CARTEL MODEL

Oligopoly firms are price makers so they decide the price to charge and quantity to produce. As we hinted in the section on strategic barriers, the price that

Cartel An association of producers who agree to limit output and fix prices.

Joint profit maximization A strategy used by cartels to maximize profits for all firms within the industry; typically involves output constraint.

an oligopoly firm charges is important not only because it affects profits, but because it will influence how other firms set their prices and whether new firms will enter the industry. The best strategy from the oligopolists' standpoint is to set up a **cartel** and practice **joint profit maximization**. Under a cartel arrangement, each participant is given a specific share of the market and asked to restrict output to the assigned amount. These restrictions are necessary to keep the selling price high. In essence, cartels amount to oligopolists uniting and behaving like a single profit-maximizing monopolist. Cartels are illegal in the United States and most other industrial countries, but several international cartels are operating in the world today. The Organization of Petroleum Exporting Countries (OPEC) is the best-known cartel, but there are also diamond, coffee, and other cartels.

To be successful, a cartel must meet three main requirements. First, the cartel must have almost complete control over the supply of the product. Second, it must have a method of monitoring its members' production quotas. Among other things, this means that the cartel cannot include very many firms because monitoring becomes increasingly difficult as the number of members increases. Finally, all successful cartels in the past have had the force of government sanction behind them.

There have been several cartels in history, but all have eventually failed for the same reason—cheating. As Figure 13.3 shows, the incentive to cheat on a cartel is quite strong. Suppose that the market demand (*D*) and marginal revenue (*MR*) curves are as shown and that the industry experiences constant marginal and average costs

FIGURE 13.3 CHEATING ON THE CARTEL

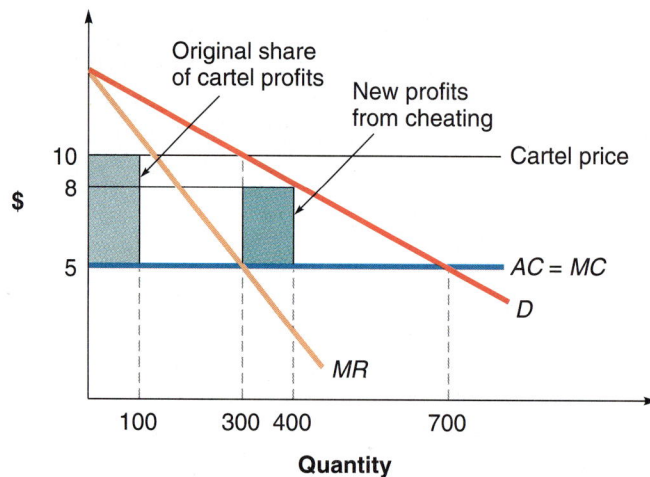

The incentive to cheat is so strong that cartels almost inevitably fail. In this case, the cartel sets the price at $10 and assigns quotas based on a quantity of 300 units. If we follow the cartel's recommendations, we will produce 100 units and make $500 in economic profits. However, if we cheat and lower price to $8, we can attract additional buyers. Economic profits will increase by $300, the amount in the blue area. For this strategy to work, the cheater must prevent its old customers and fellow cartel members from learning about the lower prices being offered to new customers.

at the level $AC = MC = \$5$. If the cartel members agree to a joint profit maximization strategy, they will set price at \$10 and produce 300 units of output. To enforce the cartel price, each member is assigned a production quota. Suppose that our quota is set at 100 units. If we produce that quantity and sell at the cartel price, our economic profits will be equal to the green area, \$500. Not bad, but members have a strong incentive to cheat on the cartel because higher sales would be possible at a lower price. For example, if we can avoid letting our current customers or the other cartel members know about it, we could make an additional \$300 in economic profits by offering to sell an extra 100 units at a price of \$8. This is shown as the blue area between $Q = 300$ and $Q = 400$ on the diagram. Cheating is such an obvious way to increase profits that it inevitably happens. In the late 1950s, several large U.S. electric equipment companies conspired in an attempt to fix prices, but in the words of one executive, "Everyone would come to the meeting, the figures would be settled, and they were only as good as the distance to the closest telephone before they were broken."[8] The same thing happened to OPEC between 1980 and 1986 when prices fell from almost \$30 per barrel to \$10. It has happened to the International Coffee Organization on several occasions. And it has happened to copper, diamond, and other cartels.

Tacit Collusion

Collusion that leads to cartels is illegal in the United States and most other industrial countries for the same reason most monopolies are regulated: successful cartels behave just like monopolies so production is inefficient and firms make long-run economic profits. The consumer has nowhere to turn but the government. While it is relatively easy to detect overt collusion, it is much more difficult to determine whether oligopoly firms are engaged in **tacit collusion**. Tacit collusion is the result of "winks and nods" between firms in an oligopolistic industry. For example, a classic case of tacit collusion occurred in the famous Gary dinners. In the early 1900s, the chair of U.S. Steel, Judge E. H. Gary, held monthly dinner meetings with the heads of competing steel companies. These dinners may have been just a gathering of friends who happened to be in the same business—but talk of price stabilization always came up, and the steel companies always seemed to adopt similar pricing strategies. The Gary dinners became the object of investigation by the Justice Department, an issue we will explore more in Chapter 19.

Often what appears to be tacit collusion is not collusion at all, however. For example, two St. Louis dairies were accused of collusion in the Pevely Dairy case of 1949.[9] The two firms had a combined market share of about 65 percent and behaved similarly in many ways. When one raised its price, the other inevitably followed, usually within two days, and they had nearly identical delivery schedules. But a court

Tacit collusion Unwritten complicity between firms to divide the market, fix prices, or otherwise act as a cartel.

---

[8]Hearings on Administered Prices by the U.S. Senate Committee on the Judiciary, Subcommittee on Antitrust and Monopoly, *Price Fixing and Bid-Rigging in the Electrical Manufacturing Industry*, Parts 27–28, 87th Congress, 1st Session (1961): 16,884. Many of the conspirators went to jail. Cited in Stephen J. K. Walters, *Enterprise, Government, and the Public* (New York: McGraw-Hill, 1993), p. 179.
[9]*Pevely Dairy Co. v. United States*, 178 F.2d 363 (8th Cir. 1949).

ruled that they were not guilty of collusion because the two firms paid the same (government-supported) price for milk and the same union wage rates, so it was reasonable that their price changes would coincide.

DECISION MAKING UNDER OLIGOPOLY II: THE KINK DEMAND CURVE MODEL

Kink demand curve Oligopoly model with the following key assumption: rivals will match price cuts, but not price hikes.

One of the classic models of oligopoly is the **kink demand curve** model. This model was developed in the 1930s by Paul Sweezy to explain why oligopoly prices tended to be rigid. This was important to Sweezy, a Marxist, because it implied that rising labor costs were not responsible for inflation in oligopoly industries. Given that most unions are associated with concentrated industries, this amounted to an argument that unions could not be held liable for inflation. Sweezy's model has been criticized on several grounds, but it is still useful for illustrating several important aspects of oligopoly behavior.

The kink demand curve model is interesting because of its assumptions about pricing behavior. It assumes that if one oligopolist raises its price, other firms will not follow by raising their prices; if one firm lowers its price, however, other firms will follow with lower prices. As a result, the demand curve facing the oligopolist is relatively flat above the initial price and relatively steep below the initial price. Why? If you raise your price, you will lose sales not only because of the price hike, but because some of your customers will buy from your rivals. If you lower your price, however, you will gain sales, but not at the expense of your rivals because they will have lowered their prices as well.

The kink in the demand curve results in a discontinuity in the marginal revenue curve directly below the kink. To see why, the two parts of the demand curve have been extended to create two separate demand curves in Figure 13.4. Their corresponding marginal revenue curves slope down twice as fast, as always, but instead of having a kink, they have a blank space directly below the kink.[10] Sweezy used the presence of this blank space in the marginal revenue curve to show that prices would tend to be rigid in oligopolies. For example, suppose that the initial marginal cost curve is MC_1 so that price and quantity are set at $\overline{P}$ and $\overline{Q}$ to maximize profits. An increase in marginal cost from MC_1 to MC_2—say, because of higher union wages— should have no effect on price because it still intersects the blank portion of the marginal revenue curve.

Criticisms of the Kink Demand Curve Model

Though interesting, the kink demand curve model has been criticized on several grounds. One problem is that oligopoly prices do not tend to be any more rigid than

---

[10]The presence of the blank spot can also be detected with simple calculus. First, recognize that marginal revenue is the first derivative of total revenue with respect to quantity. Now, because the demand is also average revenue, multiplying demand by Q will give total revenue. This means that the total revenue curve will have a kink just like the kink demand curve. The blank space exists because the derivative is undefined at the kink.

•••• **FIGURE 13.4 THE KINK DEMAND CURVE**

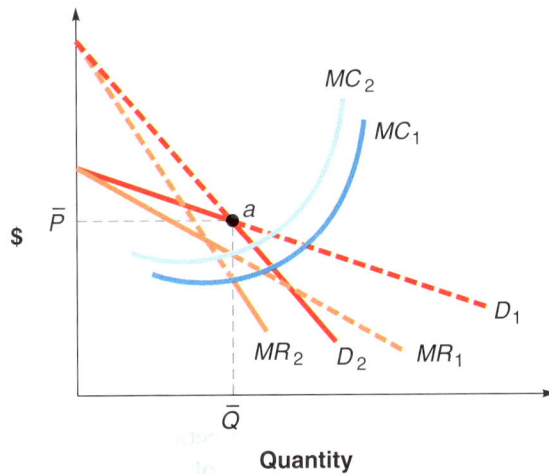

The kink demand curve is the result of assumptions about oligopoly pricing behavior. Suppose the price begins at $\bar{P}$ and the firm decides to raise its price. If other firms do not follow with price hikes, sales will fall significantly; this is indicated by D_1, the relatively flat demand curve above point *a*. On the other hand, if rivals do follow with price reductions, sales will increase, but not at the expense of other firms, so demand curve D_2 is relatively steep below point *a*. The two demand curves have different marginal revenue curves, MR_1 and MR_2, respectively. When the two segments are put together, there is a blank spot below the kink in the demand curve. Paul Sweezy used this blank spot to argue that unions could not cause inflation. If wages rise, the marginal cost curve will shift from MC_1 to MC_2. However, it will still "intersect" the marginal revenue curve in the same spot, so profit-maximizing firms should not raise prices.

prices in other industries. Oligopoly prices do change, but this model does not explain why; it only *assumes* a specific kind of price leadership. Second, it does not explain where the initial price comes from. The initial price is often assumed to be the "traditional" price, but such an assumption is far short of an explanation. Finally, the model does not explain some of the key aspects of oligopoly behavior—why and how entry occurs, whether limit pricing occurs, and so on.

RECAP   Oligopoly

1. Oligopoly exists when there are a few firms producing identical or differentiated products in an industry with significant barriers to entry. Oligopoly firms must pay explicit attention to the actions of their rivals.
2. An oligopoly industry will evolve from a competitive industry if the minimum efficient scale of operation is such that the entire market can be served by a smaller number of firms. Oligopolists are price makers, but they may use limit pricing to deter entry into the industry.

3. When oligopolies form a cartel, the market is divided up and each participant is given a production quota. This results in joint profit maximization and behavior identical to a monopolist. Cartel members have strong incentives to cheat.

4. The kink demand curve model assumes that other firms will follow price cuts, but not price hikes. The result is a demand curve with a kink at the initial price and a marginal revenue curve with a blank space. This model implies that prices will tend to be rigid under oligopoly, but it has been criticized by many economists.

SUMMARY

Though very few real-world firms fit any economic model precisely, most have attributes that put them somewhere between oligopoly and monopolistic competition. Both oligopolies and monopolistically competitive firms are price makers, but only oligopolies can make long-run economic profits.

The main points from this chapter are:

1. Market concentration can be measured with concentration ratios and the Herfindahl index. These measures are useful, but say nothing about potential competition or the extent of competition between the firms in the industry.

2. Monopolistically competitive industries are characterized by many sellers of slightly differentiated products with no barriers to entry or exit. Production does not meet the allocative efficiency criterion because price is greater than marginal cost. Firms are characterized by chronic excess capacity and do not make long-run economic profits.

3. Oligopolies are characterized by a few sellers of homogeneous or differentiated products with substantial barriers to entry. Mergers and technical and strategic barriers to entry can give rise to oligopolies. When oligopoly firms collude to form a cartel, they behave like a single monopoly and maximize profits. However, the incentive to cheat is strong so most cartels are short-lived.

KEY TERMS AND CONCEPTS

monopolistic competition
product differentiation
oligopoly
concentration ratio
Herfindahl index
SCP model
excess capacity theorem
informative advertising
persuasive advertising
economies of scale
MES (minimum efficient scale)
limit pricing

synergy
economies of scope
horizontal merger
vertical merger
conglomerate merger
congeneric merger
junk bonds
cartel
joint profit maximization
tacit collusion
kink demand curve

REVIEW QUESTIONS

1. Give examples of each of the four kinds of markets. Use examples other than those in the text!
2. Compare and contrast the price and quantity decisions for the four kinds of markets, and determine whether each of the four kinds of firms achieves allocative and technical efficiency.
3. Why is advertising so important under monopolistic competition but unimportant under perfect competition? Who benefits from advertising?
4. Why do oligopolies exist? How do economists measure industrial concentration?
5. Why do firms merge? Does society benefit?
6. Why do economists believe that cartels are inherently unstable?
7. What are the assumptions behind the kink demand curve model? How has the model been criticized?

PROBLEMS

1. Determine whether each of the following is a horizontal, vertical, conglomerate, or congeneric merger:

   - Purchase of EDS Data Systems by General Motors
   - Purchase of U.S. Steel coal reserves by Standard Oil
   - Purchase of Getty Oil by Texaco
   - Purchase of Conoco Oil by Du Pont Chemical
   - Purchase of RCA by General Electric

2. **a.** Calculate the 4-firm concentration ratio and Herfindahl index for the following industries:

Industry I	Industry II
Firm A: 20% share	Firm A: 60% share
Firm B: 25% share	Firm B: 15% share
Firm C: 5% share	Firm C: 10% share
Firm D: 30% share	Firm D: 5% share
Firm E: 20% share	Firm E: 10% share

   b. Explain why both measures give reasonable descriptions of Industry I, but the Herfindahl index gives a much better description of Industry II.

3. Could an oligopoly industry exist if there were no barriers to entry? Why or why not?
4. The OPEC cartel has 13 members. Do you think the cartel would have had better success if there were only 7 members? Would it matter which 7 countries were members? Would it have to be the largest members?
5. What would it mean if the demand curve facing an oligopolist looked like the one to the right?
6. Some economists classify the automobile industry as an oligopoly, and others classify it as monopolistically competitive. Explain why either classification may be correct.

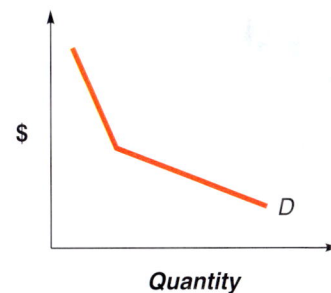

7. Refer back to Figure 13.3. What is the maximum amount of economic profits that you could make by cheating on the cartel? Assume that other members maintain their quotas and the cartel price.

8. Draw a diagram showing long-run equilibrium output and price for an oligopoly firm in an industry with no price leader. In what ways does this firm differ from a monopolist?

9. Define both persuasive advertising and informative advertising, and give examples of each. Do you think that persuasive advertising should be limited by the government? Why or why not?

CHAPTER 14

The New Industrial Economics: Contestable Markets and Game Theory

When Joan Robinson and Edward Chamberlin developed their theories of imperfect competition in the 1930s, they also provided what appeared to be a tight classification scheme for the analysis of industrial economics. Economists had long recognized pure competition and pure monopoly, and with the addition of two kinds of intermediate competition—oligopoly and monopolistic competition—they seemed to have all of the bases covered. For much of the next 40 years, economists used this framework to study the industrial economy. Research often involved case studies. Economists would analyze a specific firm or industry and see how well it fit into the classification scheme. Classification was an important first step in economic analysis because most economists practiced the *structure-conduct-performance* (SCP) methodology. According to this approach, firm and industry behavior depended on industrial structure, so once industrial structure was classified, conduct and performance could be readily deduced.

Beginning in the 1960s, industrial economists began to rely increasingly upon elaborate statistical models. Most of these econometric models were attempts to verify important hypotheses of the SCP methodology. One of the most important hypotheses was the notion that profits should be higher in concentrated industries than in competitive industries. Most studies generated results consistent with this hypothesis, but some did not—enough, in fact, that a number of economists began to question the traditional SCP approach to industrial economics. The result was a revolution of sorts and what is known today as the new industrial economics. This chapter will cover some of the main ideas of the new industrial economics.

AFTER READING AND STUDYING THIS CHAPTER, YOU SHOULD BE ABLE TO:

• • • Explain why many economists are replacing the structure-conduct-performance approach with the new industrial economics

• • • Understand the concepts and criticisms of contestable markets theory

• • • Explain the basic concepts of game theory and apply it to strategic behavior

• • • Explain how asymmetric information and rent-seeking behavior can interfere with the ability of the market to achieve optimality

NEW INDUSTRIAL ECONOMICS AND THE SCP MODEL

Since the 1930s and 1940s, the traditional approach to industrial economics has been the structure-conduct-performance (SCP) model that we used in the last three chapters. The benefit of this approach is that it provides a classification scheme for different kinds of firms and a way to compare and contrast the different market structures. In the 1960s and 1970s, however, a number of economists began to find problems with the SCP approach and started looking for new ways to study industrial economics, and the new industrial economics was born. But before we look at the new industrial economics, we should summarize the SCP methodology.

The SCP Approach

As the name implies, the SCP approach holds that there is an important relationship between structure, conduct, and performance:

• *Structure*. The key components of an industrial structure are the (1) number of firms in an industry, (2) entry and exit conditions, and (3) degree of product differentiation. Other important aspects are the extent of vertical integration, the amount and quality of information available to firms, and the amount of risk.

• *Conduct*. The structure of the industry determines whether firms are price takers (pure competition) or price makers (all other market structures), whether they engage in advertising (firms in pure competition markets do not), whether there is competition or cooperation among different firms and so on. The important point is that conduct is associated with structure.

• *Performance*. Finally, conduct determines performance. Three of the most important elements of performance are profitability, economic efficiency, and consumer welfare. The various market structures are assumed to perform differently. For example, there are no long-run economic profits under pure competition and monopolistic competition, efficiency exists only under pure competition, and so on. The key insight of the new industrial economics is that these performance criteria may not automatically follow from structure.

Endogeneity question Whether industrial performance is completely determined by industrial structure as the SCP approach holds.

The Endogeneity Question. The most serious problem with the SCP approach is what has been referred to as the **endogeneity question**. Economists use the word "endogenous" and its opposite, "exogenous," in many contexts. *Endogenous* means determined within the system; *exogenous* means predetermined or determined outside the system. In the context of the SCP approach, the endogeneity question concerns whether industrial performance is completely determined by industrial structure.

The basic premise of the SCP approach is that performance depends on conduct and structure. However, conduct is assumed to be dependent on structure. This implies that performance is determined by structure alone. If correct, this premise would mean that once industry structure is classified, industry performance will be known. For example, an industry characterized by "many" firms, no barriers to entry, and homogeneous products would tend to perform like a competitive industry; an industry with only a few firms and substantial barriers to entry would perform like an oligopoly.

What is wrong with the premise that industry structure determines industry performance? First, it implies that industry structure is predetermined ("exogenous") and that managers and entrepreneurs only passively respond to the industrial environment. This is inconsistent with what we know about businesspeople: they are constantly trying to shape the industrial environment to fit their needs. For example, large firms may try to drive rivals out of business by offering goods for abnormally low prices, a strategy known as **predatory pricing**. Another example is **limit pricing**: if a monopoly firm keeps its prices low to deter entry, the industry will remain a monopoly; if it charges higher prices, firms will enter, and the monopoly will evolve into an oligopoly. How much predatory or limit pricing actually takes place is a matter of debate. To the extent that this kind of strategic behavior does exist, however, industrial structure is a function of the activities of the firms and should not be treated as being exogenous.

Predatory pricing Pricing strategy in which prices are set abnormally low; used by large firms to drive competitors out of the market.

Limit pricing Oligopoly pricing strategy of charging low prices to deter entry into the industry.

Many traditional SCP economists recognize the impact of conduct and performance on structure, but their emphasis is usually on the effect of structure on performance. In contrast, the new industrial economists begin their analysis with the premise that structure, conduct, and performance are endogenous; that is, jointly determined by the interaction of many factors including technology, demand conditions, and information as well as the strategic decisions of firms. This makes the analysis a bit messier because there is no longer a simple, deterministic classification scheme that fits all firms and industries. However, it also means that industrial economics is a lot closer to the real world.

Another problem with the SCP approach is that it does not say very much about the evolution of industrial markets. This is a key problem because competition is an evolutionary and historic process. Firms are profitable one year, file for bankruptcy the next, and merge with a rival in the third year. By treating industrial structure as given, SCP analysis cannot take into account strategy and the multiple interactions among firms. To capture the dynamic interactions between firms, new industrial economists often use *game theory*, a mathematical technique useful for analyzing strategic interaction. Game theory makes it possible to study strategic behavior and eliminates the need to assume an exogenous industrial structure. Unfortunately, game theory comes at a cost: only rarely does it depict a simple relationship between structure, conduct, and performance. Instead it offers an often bewildering array of possible permutations—including the possibility of an indeterminate solution.

The Philosophical Debate

Perhaps the key difference between SCP and the new industrial economics is the focus on strategy versus determinism. Traditional industrial economists believe that existing firms, markets, and production methods are a reasonable approximation of the most efficient adaptation to the existing technology that could be imposed by an external order. The important point is that this approximation comes about *automatically* without any intervention from policymakers, so there is little role for strategic behavior by businesspeople. New industrial economists hold a much different worldview: instead of being driven by a deterministic force, the market economy evolves through the interplay of firms and policymakers, who try to control economic evolution—they innovate rather than yield to the industrial environment.

The importance of this point cannot be overstated. If you believe that the natural economic outcome is almost always efficient, policy has little role other than to enforce antitrust legislation to prevent the buildup of monopoly power. On the other hand, if business strategy and policy do affect the evolution of the economy, then the course the economy has taken is not necessarily correct, and possibly, policy intervention can make things better. Market processes are so complex, however, that determining the outcome of policy intervention can be exceedingly difficult.

CONTESTABLE MARKETS

One of the first theories to offer an alternative to the SCP methodology was the theory of **contestable markets** developed by William Baumol and others.[1] The key insight of contestable markets theory is that the existence of *potential* entrants into a market could be enough to make an industry behave as if it were competitive. In essence, the theory of contestable markets replaces the notion of price competition with the possibility of rapid entry and exit.

Four conditions must hold for the theory of contestable markets to apply. First, the potential entrant(s) must be able to serve the same market demand as the existing firms in the industry. Second, the same production techniques used by existing firms must be available to the potential entrants. Third, potential entrants must incur zero **sunk costs**. Sunk costs are costs that cannot be recovered even if a firm exits an industry. The assumption of zero sunk costs means that the potential entrants must be able to recover all costs associated with entry.[2] Finally, the potential entrants must

Contestable markets Theory that even monopoly firms may act like competitive firms if they fear the potential entry of other firms.

Sunk costs Costs that cannot be recovered even after liquidation.

[1]William Baumol, J. Panzar, and Robert Willig, *Contestable Markets and the Theory of Industrial Structure* (San Diego: Harcourt Brace, 1982), and William Baumol, "Contestable Markets: An Uprising in the Theory of Industrial Structure," *American Economic Review* 72 (March 1982): 1–15. Harold Demsetz's paper, "Barriers to Entry," *American Economic Review* 72 (March 1982): 47–57, raised many of the same points. An early collection of papers that anticipated the new industrial economics and contestable markets was Harvey J. Goldschmid et al., eds., *Industrial Concentration: The New Learning* (Boston, Mass.: Little, Brown, 1974).
[2]Notice that we are *not* assuming that incumbent firms have zero sunk costs. In fact, the typical incumbent firm will have incurred sunk costs—perhaps by investing in capital goods that have no scrap value. If the potential entrants cannot enter the industry without similar sunk costs, entry may not occur, and contestable markets theory does not apply.

estimate profits based on existing industry prices; that is, their entry into the industry cannot depress prices and eliminate profits.

What happens if all four of these conditions hold? The potential entrants will enter the industry if firms are making economic profits and consequently will drive down prices and profits. This is the same situation that would occur under pure competition. If the incumbent firms are not making economic profits, the potential entrants will not enter—again the same thing that would occur under pure competition. In the terminology of contestable markets theory, an industrial configuration is **sustainable** when there is no incentive for entry; that is, when firms are not making economic profits.

One example of a contestable market offered by proponents of the theory is the airline industry. Suppose two towns can support only one flight between them per day and thus only one airline company. This is a classic natural monopoly, but the key requirements for contestable markets are met so the incumbent firm must watch for entry: (1) The new airline company would serve the existing market. (2) Potential entrants—airline companies not currently serving this market—have the same available technology. Further, airline capital—airplanes—is quite mobile so it is easy to move airplanes to new markets. (3) The sunk costs of entering the market would be negligible for airline companies that do not yet serve this market. The biggest sunk cost would be the cost of moving a few key employees from the home office; most remaining expenses—landing fees, hangar and airport counter rental fees, and the like—would be recoverable if entry did not work out. (4) Finally, if the potential entrant believes that airfares will remain at the level currently charged by the incumbent firm, entry will take place.

If all of these conditions hold, and the incumbent firm behaves like a monopolist and sets a profit-maximizing price that ignores the possibility of entry, entry will take place. This means that the industrial configuration is not sustainable if the incumbent firm behaves like a monopolist. According to the theory of contestable markets, however, the incumbent firm is likely to set price equal to average cost and prevent entry. The industry will still have only one firm, but that firm will behave as if it faced competition.

The theory of contestable markets is not without its critics.[3] The most common criticism is that the theory assumes away barriers to entry, and if barriers to entry do exist, the theory is rendered useless. As we found out in Chapters 12 and 13, barriers to entry can be the result of technical, legal, or other elements. In the case of airlines, for example, the potential for contestable markets is reduced by route regulations, the availability of airport space, and other factors. One of the key insights of the new industrial economists is that barriers to entry can also be the result of deliberate strategies on the part of existing firms in the industry. For example, suppose that an incumbent firm builds a large, specialized factory that results in significant economies of scale. If the machines in this factory are custom-designed and capable of producing only a single good, then they would have little value on a secondary market. In other words, the expenditure on these machines is a sunk cost to the incumbent firm

Sustainable industrial configuration An industrial configuration is sustainable when no firm is making economic profits and thus there is no incentive for entry.

[3]Among the critics is William Shepherd, "Contestability vs. Competition," *American Economic Review* 74 (September 1984): 572–87.

because they could not be sold if the firm shut down. However, such sunk costs may serve as a strategic barrier to entry. If the only way a potential entrant could match the incumbent's production costs was to incur sunk costs and build the same special-purpose capital, then it would think twice before entering. But if economic strategy does result in barriers to entry, then the structure of the industry cannot be considered a given—precisely the issue addressed by the endogeneity question.

> **RECAP**   Contestable Markets Theory
>
> One of the first theories to question the SCP approach was the theory of contestable markets developed by William Baumol and others. This theory holds that the potential for entry into an industry acts as an incentive for firms to behave as if they are in a competitive market. Four conditions are necessary for the theory to apply: (1) potential entrants must be able to serve the same markets as incumbent firms; (2) potential entrants must have access to the same production techniques; (3) potential entrants must have zero sunk costs; and (4) profit estimates must be based on prices that prevail before entry. The main criticism of the theory is that it downplays the role of barriers to entry. If there are substantial barriers to entry, the theory does not apply.

GAME THEORY

Game theory A mathematical technique used to analyze the strategic interactions of a small number of participants.

The key methodology of the new industrial economics is **game theory**, a mathematical technique that can be used to study strategic behavior. Game theory was developed in the 1940s by John von Neumann, a mathematician, economist, and computer scientist, and Oskar Morgenstern, an economist, but has been popular in economics only since the 1970s. Like so much modern economics, game theoretic models can be quite mathematical; however, even very simple applications of game theory can shed light on many kinds of strategic behavior. The examples we will be discussing in this section are meant as much to illustrate basic concepts of game theory as to illustrate the new industrial economics. Contemporary economists have applied game theory to many areas of economic analysis. In this book game theory is applied to collective bargaining (Chapter 16), public goods (Chapter 18), environmental economics (Chapter 21), monetary policy (Chapter 30), and recession (Chapter 32).

Terms and Definitions

The term "game theory" does not mean that we are really going to be playing games, but it is appropriate because each "game" involves players, strategies, and payoffs. To "play" a game, each player—different firms, labor unions, management, or policymakers—must consider the costs and benefits of alternative strategies as well as the possible strategies that might be adopted by other players. The purpose of each game is to win the payoff—market share, wages, profits, achievement of policy goals, or whatever. To be successful, a player must adopt a strategy that correctly anticipates the response of its opponent. For example, if a firm in an oligopoly industry is considering the introduction of a new product, it must consider not only the costs of product development and the likely response of consumers, but also whether its rival firms will also introduce new products. If only one firm introduces a new product, it may be able to capture a large market share and pay for development costs, but if all firms introduce new products, the development costs may exceed the increased sales revenue.

There are both **zero-sum games** and **non-zero-sum games**. In a zero-sum game, the winners' gains exactly offset the losers' losses. Poker is an example of a zero-sum game. If I win the hand, you lose it, and my winnings equal your losses. In non-zero-sum games, gains and losses do not cancel out. Gains exceed losses in a positive-sum game. A voluntary exchange is an example of a positive-sum game. When you pay $2.25 for a Big Mac, you are better off because you would rather have the Big Mac than the $2.25 (otherwise you would not have bought the burger); when McDonald's sells you the Big Mac for $2.25, it would rather have the money than the burger, so it is better off. War is an example of a negative-sum game: one country wins and the other loses, but people from both countries die.

Finally, game theory can involve both *cooperative* and *noncooperative games*. In a cooperative game, the players are allowed to make binding agreements. For example, when oligopolists agree to divide the market into segments and practice joint profit maximization, they are playing a cooperative game. Noncooperative games do not allow binding agreements or coalitions. From the standpoint of economics, cooperative games are less interesting so we will focus primarily on noncooperative games. The prisoner's dilemma is one example of a noncooperative game.

Zero-sum game Game in which the winner's gains exactly offset the losses of the loser.

Non-zero-sum game Game in which the winner's gain is not equal to the loser's loss.

The Prisoner's Dilemma

One of the simplest games is the **prisoner's dilemma**. Suppose that two criminals, call them Art and Betty, are held as suspects in a bank robbery. The evidence is convincing, but without a confession, the most that the police can pin on each of them is a one-year jail term for a known previous petty crime. If they both confess, each will get a five-year term. The best strategy for both suspects is to hold out and spend only a year in jail—but the police want a confession to the bank robbery. To coax a confession out of the prisoners, the police can use a simple application of game theory. Put Art and Betty in separate rooms so they cannot communicate, and offer each a suspended sentence (zero years) for confessing and naming the other as an accomplice. The accomplice then goes to jail for 10 years. This offer is made to each suspect. Betty knows that if she and Art both clam up, they get only a year in jail, but if Art squeals and she does not confess, she will go to jail for 10 years. Art knows the same thing. What should the suspects do?

The payoff matrix in Table 14.1 illustrates the dilemma faced by the two prisoners. Art's strategies—hold out or confess—are shown along the top, and Betty's strategies are shown at the left. The matrix cells show their respective payoffs; Art's payoffs are in the upper quadrants and Betty's are in the lower quadrants. Interpreting the payoff matrix is straightforward. The entry (A:1, B:1) in the northwest corner shows what happens if both Art and Betty hold out—both go to jail for one year. The entry (A:0, B:10) in the northeast corner shows what happens if Art confesses and Betty

Prisoner's dilemma A classic situation from game theory; has dominant strategy for both prisoners to confess to crime.

···· TABLE 14.1 PAYOFF MATRIX FOR THE PRISONER'S DILEMMA

Art

	Actions →	Hold Out	Confess
Betty	Hold Out	A:1 / B:1	A:0 / B:10
	Confess	A:10 / B:0	A:5 / B:5

The payoff matrix shows the outcomes—years in jail—for each player depending on whether they confess or hold out. This is a noncooperative game because the players cannot communicate and make a binding agreement. The dominant strategy is to confess. If Art confesses, Betty will spend 10 years in jail if she holds out but only 5 years if she confesses. If Art holds out, Betty will spend 1 year in jail if she also holds out but 0 years if she confesses. Art faces the same choices. The dominant strategy equilibrium is in the southeast corner.

holds out—Art gets the suspended sentence and Betty goes to jail for 10 years. The payoff in the southeast corner (A:5, B:5) shows what happens if they both confess to the robbery and name the other as an accomplice—they each get 5 years in jail.

What is the most likely outcome of the game? To make the most advantageous decision, each player needs to consider the action of the other. Consider the situation from Art's standpoint first. Suppose that Betty confesses. If Art also confesses, he gets 5 years; if he holds out, he gets 10 years. The best strategy is to confess. But what if Betty holds out? If Art also holds out, he will get 1 year. If he confesses, he will get a suspended sentence. Again, the right choice is to confess. You get the same solution if you look at it from Betty's standpoint: If Art confesses, Betty should confess; if Art holds out, Betty should still confess. Unless Art and Betty have made a binding agreement not to confess, the game will end up in the southeast corner with both Betty and Art confessing and spending 5 years in jail.

Confessing is the *dominant strategy* because it gives each player the best payoff regardless of the strategy chosen by the other player. Regardless of what Art does, Betty should confess, and regardless of what Betty does, Art should confess. A dominant strategy is the only likely outcome of a prisoner's dilemma game. When both players adopt their dominant strategies, the game rests in **dominant strategy equilibrium**. Finally, we should note that the outcome of the prisoner's dilemma game is not the best payoff for the two players. If the prisoners were able to reach a binding agreement to hold out, both would be better off since each would spend only one year in jail. In the absence of such an agreement, however, this game will end up in dominant strategy equilibrium.

········

Cartel Behavior

The prisoner's dilemma game has been applied to several areas in economics, most notably, oligopoly behavior. We can apply it to the classic case of cartel cheating.

Dominant strategy equilibrium
The outcome when both players choose the strategy that yields the best result regardless of what the other player does.

····· TABLE 14.2 CHEATING ON THE CARTEL

		Firm A	
	Actions →	Low Output	High Output
Firm B Low Output		A:6 B:6	A:9 B:2
High Output		A:2 B:9	A:3 B:3

The incentive to cheat is so strong that cartels almost inevitably fail. If the two firms form a cartel and agree to limit output, they can charge high prices, maximize profits, and earn $6 million each. However, the dominant strategy is to cheat on the cartel. If Firm A cheats, Firm B must respond by cheating to keep its profits from falling to $2 million. If Firm A does not cheat, Firm B can increase its profits from $6 to $9 million by cheating. Thus, "cheat–cheat" is the dominant strategy, so the game ends up in the southeast corner.

Suppose that two firms share a market and must decide whether to produce high quantity (*H*) or low quantity (*L*).[4] If the firms form a cartel and agree to restrict production, they can charge high prices and earn $6 million in profits each. This is represented by the (A:6, B:6) entry in the northwest corner of Table 14.2. If there is no cartel agreement and both firms produce high output, price will fall and bring profits down to $3 million per firm. This is represented by the (A:3, B:3) entry in the southeast corner of the table. The other entries in the table show what happens if one firm cheats on the cartel while the other maintains low production. The cheater will increase sales at the expense of the rival, and profits rise to $9 million for the cheater and fall to $2 million for the rival.

Again, we need to determine the most likely outcome to this game. Look at the situation from the perspective of Firm A. If Firm B keeps to the cartel agreement, then Firm A can increase its profits from $6 million to $9 million by cheating. And if Firm B cheats, Firm A should still cheat; otherwise its profits will fall to $2 million. Firm B faces the same choices, so the dominant strategy for both firms is to cheat on the cartel. This is another explanation for why cartels almost inevitably fail, a point we made in Chapter 13.

Nash Equilibrium

You may have guessed that the payoffs illustrated in Table 14.2 are not the only possible outcomes. Suppose that the same two firms are faced with the payoff matrix in Table 14.3. If they stick to their cartel agreement, they each make $6 million in

[4]An oligopoly composed of exactly two firms is called a *duopoly*.

•••• **TABLE 14.3 NASH EQUILIBRIUM**

Firm A

		Low Output	High Output
	Actions →		
Firm B	Low Output	A:6 B:6	A:8 B:3
	High Output	A:3 B:8	A:0 B:0

In this game, there is no dominant strategy because the game has more than one plausible outcome. If Firm A knows that Firm B will maintain the cartel agreement, then Firm A should cheat to increase its profits from $6 to $8 million. The same can be said of Firm B: if it knows that Firm A will maintain the cartel agreement, then it should cheat on the agreement. The outcome in such games depends on timing and information.

economic profits, and if both firms cheat on the cartel and increase output, price will fall to average cost, and economic profits will be eliminated. But if only one firm cheats, it stands to make $8 million in profits while the other makes only $3 million. This is a reasonable outcome if the combined output is still low enough to keep price above average cost. In this situation, there is no dominant strategy.

The outcome of this game depends on timing, information, or other factors. For example, suppose that Firm A "knows" that Firm B will maintain cartel discipline. The best strategy for Firm A is to cheat and thereby increase its profits from $6 million to $8 million. This play would result in equilibrium in the northeast cell. Firm B may not like the fact that its profits have been eroded because of Firm A's cheating, but if Firm B abandons cartel discipline, its profits will fall even more. Look what happens if Firm B "knows" that Firm A will maintain cartel discipline. Firm B should cheat, raise its profits to $8 million, and the game will end up in the southwest cell. Both outcomes are equally plausible so there is no dominant strategy in this game. Once the game gets to either cell, there is no incentive to change strategies. This situation is known as **Nash equilibrium**. All dominant strategy equilibria are also Nash equilibria, but not all Nash equilibria are dominant strategy equilibria.

In this game, it obviously pays to be the first to move. If Firm A cheats first, it wins; if Firm B cheats first, it wins. In some cases, it pays to be second. For example, some employers ask job candidates what salary they are expecting. Candidates who give a high figure do not get the job, but if they offer to work for an extremely low salary, the employer smiles (inwardly) and offers the job. This strategy is sometimes called a *grim strategy*.

Nash equilibrium Exists when there is no tendency for change once an equilibrium is reached, but there may be no dominant strategy.

Repeated Games

The examples we have just discussed assume that the game is played only once. In fact, in many cases a game is played over and over through time. For example, the big three television networks have a tacit agreement to show reruns over the summer and begin their new seasons in the fall. What do you think would happen if NBC started its new season in the summer and showed reruns in the fall? NBC might gain audience at the expense of ABC and CBS over the summer. This would change the rules of the game, however, so NBC would not know how the other networks would respond.[5] Would ABC and CBS respond by changing the timing of their new seasons? Or would they ignore NBC and maintain the previous schedule? And what if NBC discovered that its audience share fell? Would it return to the old schedule in the following year? Or would it begin its new season in the spring? These are the kinds of issues that can be analyzed with game theory models of repeated games. There are many different strategies for repeated games.

Tit-for-Tat Strategy. Players in repeated games sometimes use the **tit-for-tat strategy**. In this strategy, one player cooperates if the other player cooperated in the previous period, but does not cooperate if the other player broke the agreement in the previous period. For example, suppose that the OPEC nations agreed to limit production to keep the price of oil at $20 per barrel. If one member nation—say, Iran—breaks the agreement and produces more than its quota, the price of oil will fall a few dollars per barrel. Iran might gain in the short run by increasing market share, but things may be different in the long run. If the other OPEC members adopt a tit-for-tat strategy, they will increase production in the following period. The result: The price of oil will fall even more and cause everyone to lose profits. If Iran learns its lesson, it will cut back on production in the third period. If other cartel members follow, the price of oil will rise to the cartel price. If Iran does not learn its lesson, oil production will stay high and the cartel will dissolve.

Tit-for-tat strategy Players cooperate or not, depending on the actions of the other players in the previous period; results in a mild form of retaliation.

The diamond cartel provides an example of tit-for-tat behavior. Until the early 1980s, the South African company DeBeers had almost complete control of the world diamond market. However, the opening of a huge mine in Australia and cheating by Zaire threatened the cartel. DeBeers responded with a tit-for-tat strategy—increased diamond production, which caused diamond prices to fall temporarily. DeBeers's behavior was enough to restore cartel discipline and gain cooperation from the Australians and other producers. DeBeers did accept a reduction in its own production quota, however.

Trigger Strategy. Another repeated game strategy is the **trigger strategy**. Under this strategy, one player cooperates if the other cooperates, but adopts the most extreme form of punishment possible if the other breaks the agreement: it too reneges on the agreement and does so indefinitely. In the OPEC example, this would mean that

Trigger strategy Results in the strongest form of punishment; if one player breaks the agreement, the other punishes forever.

[5]In an attempt to take market share from the established networks, the fledgling Fox Network began showing first-run shows in the summer. The big three networks *said* they would ignore Fox programming—but they did seem to schedule more specials and summer replacements when it appeared that the Fox strategy might be working.

FOCUS ON

PRICING TO DETER ENTRY: AN EXAMPLE OF GAME THEORY IN EXTENSIVE FORM

All of the game theory examples we have discussed so far have been in what is called *strategic form*. Strategic form entails the use of payoff matrices, decision rules, and so on. Game theory models can also be presented in *extensive form*. A game in extensive form consists of a decision tree describing how the game is played. The tree presents the possible events, their probabilities of occurrence, and the strategic actions the players can take. In general, game theory models can be presented in either strategic or extensive form, so the choice of approach depends on the particular game under study. As an example of an extensive-form game, consider the classic case of pricing to deter entry.

Suppose that an established monopolist perceives growing demand for its product and is considering a price hike to increase profits. The firm fears, however, that a higher price may attract entry into the industry. From the monopolist's standpoint, assume that there are four possible results: (1) Raise price without attracting entry. This will result in $12 million in profits. (2) Raise price and attract entry. This will reduce market share and lower profits to only $3 million. (3) Maintain price and no entry. The monopolist will make $10 million. (4) Maintain price but entry occurs anyway. The potential for market growth might attract entry even if the monopolist keeps its price low. In this case,

so many goods will be offered that price will fall and each firm will lose $5 million. The question game theory attempts to answer is which strategy will be followed by the two firms, the existing monopolist and the potential entrant.

To help answer this question, an extensive-form game theory model is shown in the accompanying figure. To determine the most likely outcome, we apply the same kind of reasoning that we used in the other game theory exercises. One possible strategy is the *maximin strategy*—both players will attempt to *maximize* their *minimum* payoffs. (Another possible strategy, *maximax*, is illustrated in Problem 10 at the end of this chapter.) First

once Iran broke the agreement, all of the other OPEC members would abandon their production quotas and increase output as much as they wanted. The price of oil would fall, and economic profits would be eliminated.

Intermediate Cases and Uncertainty. Several other strategies can also be used in repeated games. For example, if one player cheats, the other might punish for three periods—more than once as in the tit-for-tat strategy, but not indefinitely as in the trigger strategy. Another strategy is **reputation building**—players can cultivate a reputation for cooperation or tough bargaining by establishing consistent behavior for several rounds of the game. In the case of the prisoner's dilemma, the only way for the two prisoners to win is for them both to remain silent—and the only way Art can be sure that Betty will remain silent is if she has a reputation of silence while under police interrogation. Reputation building is also important in oligopoly models. For example, a firm that has repeatedly lowered its price to deter entry in the past may not have to do so in the future.

Reputation building Players cultivate a reputation for cooperation or tough bargaining with consistent behavior for several rounds of the game.

look at the situation from the stand-point of the monopolist: If it raises price, it will make $12 million if there is no entry, but only $3 million if there is entry. If it does not raise price, it will make $10 million if there is no entry, but lose $5 million if there is entry. The minimums being compared are therefore $3 million and −$5 million. Under the maximin strategy, the incumbent firm should raise price (and hope that there is no entry) because this strategy maximizes the minimum gain. The circled $3 on the diagram indicates this choice.

From the perspective of the potential entrant, entry will result in a $3 million profit, but only if the monopolist raises its price. If the monopolist maintains low prices, the new firm will lose $5 million by entering. If the potential entrant follows the maximin

Possible Strategies of Monopolist	Possible Reactions of Entrant	Profits Monopolist	Entrant
Maintain price	Enter	−$5	−$5
	Don't enter	+$10	0
Raise price	Enter	+$3	+$3
	Don't enter	+$12	0

If firms follow the maximin strategy, they will attempt to act in a way that maximizes their minimum payoff. For the existing monopolist, the high-price strategy will earn at least $3 million, and the low-price strategy could result in a $5 million loss; the best strategy is high prices. For the potential entrant, entry could mean a loss of $5 million while staying out means a loss of $0. It should stay out of the industry.

strategy, it will not enter, so its profits will be zero as indicated by the circled zeros on the diagram. The result: If maximin is followed by both parties, the monopolist will raise price—and entry will not take place.

Repeated games are often complicated by uncertainty because players do not have perfect information about the actions or intentions of their rivals. For example, suppose that the demand for oil declines and the price of oil falls. OPEC members, remembering Iran's past behavior, may think that the price decline is due to more cheating by Iran. If OPEC adopts a trigger strategy, the cartel would dissolve.

Case Study: Game Theory in the Business World

Game theory is a relatively new approach to economic analysis, but it is already showing up in real-world applications. One recent application of game theory occurred in 1994 when the Federal Communications Commission (FCC) was deciding how to allocate licenses for wireless phone systems.[6] In the past FCC licenses had

[6]This section comes from Mark Lewyn, "What Price Air?" *Business Week*, March 14, 1994, pp. 48–54.

been awarded through hearings or lotteries. This time, the FCC wanted to auction off the rights and generate revenue. The problem was to determine the best kind of auction. Should it be a standard "English auction" where an auctioneer keeps raising the price until a single bidder remains? The problem with English auctions is that they can invite collusion, especially when there are only a few bidders, as would be the case in this situation. Another option is a sealed bid auction where bidders write down their bids, and the highest sealed bid wins the license. A problem with sealed bids is that they tend to generate less revenue than open bidding. A third kind of auction is the "Dutch auction." In this type of auction, the auctioneer starts high and lowers the price until someone bids. Bidders tend to be cautious in Dutch auctions, so the FCC would stand to make less money—but the winning bidder might have more money left over to set up a good communications system.

To determine the best approach, the FCC sought advice from John McMillan of the University of California at San Diego, an economist who specializes in applications of game theory. Not to be outdone, the potential bidders, including Pacific Bell, Bell Atlantic, and MCI, also hired economists specializing in game theory as consultants. At this writing, the format of the FCC auction has yet to be decided, but one thing is certain: this will not be the last time that auctions are used to allocate licenses and other properties. Economists trained in game theory will undoubtedly be in demand by both business and the government in the future.

RECAP   The Fundamentals of Game Theory

Game theory models have become increasingly important in all areas of economics, not just the new industrial economics. The main use of game theory is to model strategic behavior when the number of participants is small. Unlike most models we have examined so far, game theory models do not always generate unique solutions. This characteristic is a strength, not a weakness: it suggests that the methodology is flexible enough to be applied to many situations. The central concepts of game theory are:

1. A game consists of players, strategies, and payoffs. Game theory has been applied to help understand oligopolies, cartels, collective bargaining, and many other areas in economics. In zero-sum games, the gains and losses cancel out; in non-zero-sum games, the gains and losses do not cancel out.

2. The prisoner's dilemma is a classic type of game. Prisoner's dilemma games have a dominant strategy equilibrium because the best strategy for each player is independent of the strategy of the other player, and the outcome is the same for each player. A dominant strategy equilibrium is unique.

3. Some games result in a Nash equilibrium, an outcome where neither player has an incentive to change once the game arrives at equilibrium. All dominant strategy equilibria are Nash equilibria, but Nash equilibria are not necessarily dominant strategy equilibria. There can be more than one Nash equilibrium in a game.

4. Many games are repeated. In the tit-for-tat strategy, players respond to the actions of the other players in the previous period only. With this strategy, a mild form of punishment is imposed for breaking the rules of the game. The

trigger strategy results in the strongest form of punishment. If one player breaks the agreement, the other punishes indefinitely.

5. Uncertainty can complicate strategies and game theory analysis. When uncertainty exists, it is not clear whether a particular event is the result of cheating on an agreement or is due to external factors. Players may try to build reputations to reduce the amount of uncertainty.

OTHER ELEMENTS IN THE NEW INDUSTRIAL ECONOMICS

We will end this chapter with glimpses of three more topics, asymmetric information, the agency problem, and rent-seeking behavior. All of them show up in many areas of economic analysis and are not strictly confined to what we have been calling the new industrial economics. They are included here because they illustrate the importance of strategy in economic behavior.

Asymmetric Information

Have you heard that you lose $1,000 the moment you drive your new car off the showroom floor? This is generally true. You might have gotten a great deal on that new Chevy, but once you sign the note and take the car for a spin around the block, it is a used car, and you will not be able to sell it for anything close to what you paid for it. Why? The reason is asymmetric information. *You* may know that the car is in tip-top shape, but prospective used car buyers do not. They cannot tell whether you are an honest seller or not.[7] Should prospective buyers simply trust your honest face? Perhaps (you *are* honest, aren't you?), but a little thought will reveal why they probably should not. Not only is it difficult for them to tell whether a complex piece of machinery is defective, but many used cars on the market are "lemons"—and lemons just happen to be the cars most likely to appear on the used car lot. Good used cars may not be traded at all. The problem is that there is **asymmetric information** in the market for used cars. The seller may know whether or not the car is a lemon, but in most cases the buyer does not. Even honest sellers are penalized because the buyer cannot distinguish between good and bad used cars. Asymmetric information causes market failure because market prices do not reflect quality.

Asymmetric information Differences in information held by parties in a market transaction.

What can be done about the "lemon" problem? Some used car dealers offer guarantees to shift the risk from the buyer to the seller, but this does little to help private parties trying to buy or sell used cars. To help solve the problem, some states have passed Lemon Laws to protect used car buyers from unscrupulous sellers, and the federal Consumer Products Safety Commission provides product information and

[7]This idea was first discussed by George Akerlof in his classic paper, "The Market for Lemons: Quality Uncertainty and the Market Mechanism," *The Quarterly Journal of Economics*, 84 (August 1970): 488–500. Reprinted in George A. Akerlof, *An Economic Theorist's Book of Tales* (New York: Cambridge University Press, 1984). This section draws on that article. A biography of George Akerlof appears in an Economic Heritage box Chapter 32.

OUR ECONOMIC HERITAGE

JOHN VON NEUMANN AND OSKAR MORGENSTERN, FOUNDERS OF GAME THEORY

The development of game theory is usually credited to the mathematician John von Neumann (1903–1957) who published a paper on game theory in 1928 when he was only 25. Sixteen years later, von Neumann collaborated with Oskar Morgenstern (1902–1977) to produce *The Theory of Games and Economic Behavior*, still considered a standard reference in the subject. Scholars today recognize several important early contributors to game theory including Augustin Cournot, who introduced a concept related to Nash equilibrium in 1838; J. Bertrand, who showed the importance of specific choice strategies in 1883; and Francis Edgeworth, who suggested the possibility of nonexistence of equilibrium in 1897.

Born in Hungary, John von Neumann moved to the United States in 1931 where he became a professor of physics and mathematics at Princeton. Von Neumann made important con-

tributions in cybernetics—he made important contributions to the development of the first modern computer—and was a leading figure in the creation of the atom bomb. Von Neumann was one of the first pure mathematicians to take an interest in economics. He did so with the expectation that his knowledge of mathematics would provide important insights into economics, but also with the hope that his study of the social sciences would improve his understanding of mathematics. His focus on game theory differed from earlier mathematical work on games. Previously, most mathematicians had looked at games of *chance*; von Neumann was concerned with games of *strategy*. It was this focus on strategy that made game theory an indispensable tool of economic analysis. Von Neumann's legacy went beyond his important work in economics, mathematics, and physics: his daughter,

Marina von Neumann Whitman, a first-rate economist in her own right, served on the Council of Economic Advisers under President Nixon and later became the chief economist for General Motors.

Oskar Morgenstern was born in Silesia in Germany and was educated at the University of Vienna where he did important work in business cycle theory in the 1930s. In 1938, after the Nazis occupied Austria, he was dismissed from the university and emigrated to the United States. He took a position at Princeton, where he was known as an outstanding teacher. Morgenstern's task was to translate the high mathematics of game theory into practical applications for the student and researcher. Morgenstern later did important work on economic forecasting and the economics of defense.

Few economists today would deny the importance of game theory to ec-

---

investigates consumer complaints. Buyers can also find information in publications like *Consumer Reports*, which provides quality, safety, and other information on a wide variety of products.

Adverse Selection in Insurance Markets. Asymmetric information characterizes many insurance markets, particularly health insurance. Elderly people often have a difficult time buying health insurance. Why? The risks to the insurer increase with age so the insurance premiums (the price paid for insurance coverage) must also be increased. As premiums increase, however, only those people who stand to gain the most from medical insurance—people who feel they have a high probability of needing medical

onomics, but this view did not become widespread until the 1970s. Why did game theory take so long to catch on? We can only guess. One possibility is that the perfect competition model so dominated economic theory that oligopoly models—the first useful applications of game theory—took a back seat. Another possibility is that most early work in game theory was so technical that few economists could read the literature. By the 1970s, these problems had been resolved, and game theory began showing up in many areas of economic analysis. The importance of game theory was recognized when the 1994 Nobel Prize in Economics was awarded to three economists for their contributions in game theory: John Nash (of Nash equilibrium fame), and John Harsanyi and Reinhard Selten who introduced uncertainty and time to game theory models.

John von Neumann

Oskar Morgenstern

care—will be willing to pay the higher premium. The result is a phenomenon known as **adverse selection**: The insurance company does not know whether or not a person is at risk, so it charges the same premium regardless of risk. The problem is that higher premiums discourage "healthy" people from buying insurance, so the people who tend to buy insurance are those who are most at risk. The insurance company ends up "selecting" the least healthy people to insure.

The task for health insurance companies is to provide incentives for people to reveal how healthy they really are. One technique is to require a medical examination, but this may put off applicants who only fear that they might not be healthy. Another strategy is to offer insurance with the lure that no one will be turned down—

Adverse selection A transaction that is biased in favor of one party due to asymmetric information in insurance, the population taking out insurance is likely to have less favorable characteristics than the entire population.

but such policies inevitably contain a clause (in fine print) saying that benefits are greatly reduced in the first few years of coverage. In this case the insurance company is betting that if people have reason to believe that they are going to die soon, they will die quickly.

What should be done about adverse selection in health insurance? Some economists believe it provides a rationale for Medicare or some other national health insurance program that spreads the risk of illness among a larger group. This was one of the main arguments behind President Clinton's proposal for universal health care coverage.

Job Signaling. A final example of asymmetric information is job signaling.[8] Asymmetric information exists on the job market because workers know how talented they are, but employers do not. For example, suppose that there are two types of workers, those with low innate ability and those with high innate ability. Employers want to hire the high-ability workers, but determining ability from a short interview or an application is difficult so the employers must resort to other means. One method is to screen applicants based on years and quality of education. Workers recognize that schooling will help their job prospects, but school is more "costly" for low-ability workers because they may fail some classes and will have to study more hours than high-ability workers. As a consequence, high-ability workers tend to go to school longer than low-ability workers. How does this relate to hiring practices? Simple: The employer's hiring strategy is to treat years of education as the signal for employee ability and to base job and salary offers on the amount of education. Further, when numerous applicants have the same amount of education, candidates are ranked according to the reputation of their schools.

Using years of education as a job market signal may seem reasonable from the employer's standpoint, but this practice has potentially significant social implications. For example, some people have argued that the educational system discovers talent instead of developing talent. This view is hotly debated, but it is consistent with the job market signaling model: the longer you go to school, the more talented you must be, and the more useful you will be once the *firm* trains you to do the job. Perhaps more significant is the implication of the importance of school reputation and quality. If perceived quality of school has an important effect on the hiring decision, then applicants from schools in low-income neighborhoods—often perceived as being inferior to schools in high-income neighborhoods—will find it especially difficult to find jobs.

If employers do use years and quality of education as a job market signal, and if this practice does tend to discriminate against people from schools in low-income neighborhoods, then the case for affirmative action programs is strengthened significantly. Employers frequently complain that the paperwork necessitated by affirmative action programs is costly, but discrimination—for any reason—is costly to society as well. We will have more to say about the job market in Chapters 15 and 16.

---

[8]This example is based on Michael Spence, *Market Signalling* (Cambridge, Mass.: Harvard University Press, 1974).

The Agency Problem

One of the most important applications of asymmetric information has been to the **principal-agent** or **agency problem**. Agency problems arise whenever one group delegates authority to another group. When corporate stockholders (the principals) delegate authority to managers (the agents), they presumably assume that the managers will act in the best interest of the stockholders. Another example is union membership: workers (principals) delegate authority to union leadership (agents) with the hope that the leaders will be able to negotiate a good contract on their behalf. How does the principal-agent problem relate to asymmetric information? Principals have only imperfect information about the behavior of their agents. Corporate managers have been known to grant themselves pay raises instead of paying out stockholder dividends; union leaders have been known to abscond with union funds.

> **Agency (principal-agent) problem** Exists when an "agent" acts on behalf of a principal and the motivations of the agent differ from those of the principal.

A particularly interesting agency problem is the potential conflict between stockholders and debt holders. When creditors lend funds to the firm, they charge interest rates based on the riskiness of the firm's existing assets, capital structure,[9] and other factors. Now suppose that management, in the interest of the stockholders, takes on a new and especially risky project. If the project is a failure, the stockholders and bondholders will share in the losses, but if the project is successful, only the stockholders will gain. High profits benefit stockholders through higher dividends, but the return on debt capital is fixed, so bond holders will receive none of these benefits.

What can be done about agency problems? To solve stockholder/creditor conflicts, creditors often protect themselves with agreements that restrict the actions of the firm. The manager/stockholder agency problem can be solved by paying managers with stock dividends and other performance incentives; this makes the goals of managers and stockholders more consistent. Many firms also take actions to monitor management behavior or design organizational structures that place limits on managerial actions. The problem is that such solutions inevitably impose *agency costs*— costs associated with monitoring the actions of agents to assure that they act in the best interest of the principals. How significant are agency costs? It is difficult to arrive at a precise figure. For example, restricting the actions of management to protect the stockholders could make it hard for management to make quick decisions. Accurately measuring the costs of this restriction is difficult, but we do know this: if stockholders could just trust the managers, then managers would be free to devote all their energy to management instead of compliance with agency rules.

Rent-Seeking Behavior

Suppose that your company, CableView, has just lost a bid to the only other bidder, VisionCable, which was awarded a contract to set up a monopoly TV cable system in your home town of Walnut Grove. Suspecting (hoping?) that city officials may

---

[9]The capital structure of a firm refers to the ratio of debt (bond) to equity (stock) financing. The advantage of debt capital is that interest payments are tax deductible; the advantage of equity finance is that dividends do not have to be paid in lean years. The disadvantage of debt finance is that the firm goes bankrupt if it cannot make interest payments; the disadvantage of equity finance is that it is not tax deductible. Financial analysts assess the riskiness of firms by looking at, among other things, the debt/equity ratio.

DUP (directly unproductive activities) Rent-seeking behavior. Often refers to the act of acquiring a monopoly license so the firm can earn lucrative monopoly returns.

have failed to comply with all of the regulations regarding contract bidding, you instruct your legal department to sue Walnut Grove for the job. You allow the legal department to spend as much as a million dollars on the suit. Why do you do this? Simple: To get the lucrative job, but more importantly, to extract *economic rent*. As we found out in Chapter 12, economic rent is a factor payment over and above the payment necessary to bring that factor into production. In the case of a monopoly cable franchise, the prospects for gain can be enormous—much higher than the cost of building a system and delivering cable TV to the customers. Earning that economic rent is worth the considerable legal expenditures you allocate. But whether you actually earn economic rents depends on how well you anticipate and understand the actions of your rivals; in other words, rent-seeking behavior is strategic behavior.

Rent-seeking behavior is sometimes known by another name: **DUP** for *directly unproductive activities*. The name comes from the fact that the act of acquiring a monopoly license—a license to extract economic rents—is unproductive, at least from society's standpoint. To the firm, the license represents monopoly power and lucrative returns, but the process of acquiring the license is competitive and often quite costly. How much unproductive effort and money will be spent by firms trying to acquire the license? We can get a hint from our analysis of pure competition in Chapter 11: in the long run, economic profits go to zero, so firms will spend an amount approximately equal to their estimate of the economic rents they would expect to gain from the license. The important point to remember is that the money spent by the firms bidding for the contract does not result in any production for society.

Cases of rent-seeking behavior abound. Suppose a union fears foreign competition in the domestic market. Such entry would mean additional competition, lower demand for products, and thus lower demand for union workers. Ultimately, union wages would decline. To keep wages high—that is, to maintain economic rent from the absence of competition—union leaders spend large sums lobbying Congress to keep out foreign products. Consumers may not like paying higher prices and having choices limited to domestically produced goods, but no one can blame unions for trying to extract their economic rents—or for allocating a lobbying budget almost as high as the rents they are currently earning.

▪▪▪▪▪▪ SUMMARY

The new industrial economics has come to dominate research in applied microeconomics in recent years and looks to become even more important in the future. Economists are continually finding new applications of strategic behavior and game theory, and you will want to keep the methodology as well as the specific ideas from this chapter in mind as you read the rest of the book. The main points to remember from this chapter are:

1. The SCP approach to industrial economics holds that economic structure determines economic conduct and performance. The theory has been criticized for its assumption of an exogenous economic structure.

2. The theory of contestable markets holds that monopolies will behave like competitive firms if there are potential entrants into the market. This theory has been criticized because it downplays the role of barriers to entry.

3. Game theory is a technique used to model strategic behavior. A game consists of players, rules, strategies, and payoffs. There can be zero-sum and non-zero-sum games. In zero-sum games, the gains exactly match the losses; in non-zero-sum games, gains and losses do not cancel out.

4. A well-known game is the prisoner's dilemma. One example of the prisoner's dilemma is cartel behavior: all parties gain if they can agree to hold an established price, but the gains from cheating are so strong that cheating is almost inevitable.

5. The prisoner's dilemma results in a dominant strategy equilibrium. If both players adopt their dominant strategies, the result is a dominant strategy equilibrium. In contrast, a Nash equilibrium exists when no player has an incentive to change behavior once the game arrives at equilibrium. The outcome depends on timing and other factors.

6. Several strategies are possible for repeated games. With the tit-for-tat strategy, one player punishes the other for cheating on an agreement, but then returns to the agreement once the violator "learns its lesson." Under a trigger strategy, players cooperate until one violates the agreement; then the other breaks the agreement indefinitely. The trigger strategy is an extreme form of punishment. Uncertainty and information problems can complicate any strategy.

7. Asymmetric information complicates market processes and can result in prices that are not "correct" in the sense that they do not reflect quality. The markets for secondhand goods, insurance, and hiring are three examples of asymmetric information. Asymmetric information can result in adverse selection.

8. The agency problem refers to the situation where principals employ agents to carry out actions on their behalf. Principals do not have complete control over their agents, so agency costs are often incurred to assure that agents behave in the best interest of the principals. Agency costs represent wasted resources from society's point of view.

9. Market imperfections and limited supplies can result in economic rents and rent-seeking behavior as people try to obtain those economic rents. Rent-seeking behavior represents directly unproductive activity and wasted resources.

·········· KEY TERMS AND CONCEPTS

SCP

endogeneity question

predatory pricing

limit pricing

contestable markets

sunk costs

sustainable industrial configuration

game theory

zero-sum game

non-zero-sum game

cooperative game

noncooperative game

prisoner's dilemma

dominant strategy equilibrium

Nash equilibrium

grim strategy

tit-for-tat strategy

trigger strategy

reputation building

maximin

asymmetric information

adverse selection

agency (principal-agent) problem

rent-seeking behavior

DUP (directly unproductive activities)

REVIEW QUESTIONS

1. What are the main assumptions and predictions of the SCP methodology? In what key ways does it differ from the new industrial economics?

2. What conditions must hold for contestable markets theory to be applicable? What are the main criticisms of contestable markets theory?

3. Give examples of the kinds of behavior that are best modeled with game theory. Also, explain why game theory problems often have indeterminate solutions.

4. Most games are played in several "rounds." Discuss alternative strategies for repeated games.

5. Explain and provide examples to show why the existence of asymmetric information can provide a rationale for government regulation.

6. What is the agency problem? Give examples and explain how agency problems can be costly.

7. Explain whether and how each of the following is related to rent seeking: occupational licenses, tariffs on imported goods, high admission standards to medical schools, quotas for commercial salmon fishers.

PROBLEMS

1. In the 1980s, the Department of Justice eased its restrictions on horizontal mergers and allowed many more firms to merge than would have been allowed in previous years. Coincidentally, this was also a time when contestable markets theory was becoming popular. How might contestable markets theory be used in support of allowing horizontal mergers?

2. Explain whether each of the following is a zero-sum or a non-zero-sum game:
   a. a baseball game
   b. a boxing match
   c. international trade between two developed nations
   d. international trade between a developed nation and an underdeveloped nation
   e. collective bargaining between labor and management

3. Refer back to the prisoner's dilemma payoff matrix in Table 14.1. Suppose that Art and Betty have been caught before and neither has ever confessed. How would this affect the outcome to the game? What if Betty had confessed in a previous arrest but Art had not? What if Betty and Art were both members of organized crime?

4. Some foreign automobiles—for example, Volvos and Mercedes—traditionally have had extremely high resale values. Unfortunately, some American cars have low resale values. Do you think that Lemon Laws would favor foreign or American automobile producers? Would they favor the owners of foreign or American automobiles? Why?

5. The discussion of extensive-form game theory discussion in the chapter Focus box defined the maximin strategy. Apply this strategy to the game theory examples in Tables 14.1, 14.2, and 14.3. Do you get the same outcomes? Does this make sense? Why or why not?

6. The payoff matrix on page 353 represents the after-tax profits for two duopoly firms considering the introduction of a new model. If the two firms do not

introduce the new product, they will continue to make $5 million. If Firm A introduces the new product but Firm B does not, Firm A will earn $9 million in after-tax profits while Firm B will earn only $1 million because of lost market share. The same payoff would go to Firm B if it introduced the new product but Firm A did not. If both firms introduce new products, profits will fall to $2 million because the costs of introducing the new products can barely be covered by expanded sales. Determine the most likely outcome to this game. Is there a dominant strategy equilibrium? A Nash equilibrium? Does it depend on which firm acts first?

Firm A

	Actions →	Old	New
Firm B	Old	A:5 / B:5	A:9 / B:1
	New	A:1 / B:9	A:2 / B:2

7. The theory of contestable markets holds that under many circumstances, monopoly firms will behave as if they are competitive if a potential entrant is present. The discussion of extensive-form game theory in the chapter Focus came to a different conclusion. Explain and comment.

8. The SCP approach to industrial economics makes the assumption that industry structure is exogenous. Do you think this assumption is more realistic in competitive markets or oligopoly markets? Why?

9. Draw a payoff matrix illustrating the OPEC tit-for-tat repeated game strategy example discussed in the text. Is this game a prisoner's dilemma? Why or why not?

10. The extensive-form game theory example in the Focus box assumed that the participants were following a maximin strategy. This was only one of several possible strategies, and other strategies can generate different outcomes.
   a. Suppose instead that both firms followed a maximax strategy; that is, they adopted strategies to maximize the maximum return. What is the likely outcome in this case?
   b. Suppose that the incumbent firm follows a maximin strategy but the potential entrant follows a maximax strategy. What is the likely outcome in this case?
   c. Suppose that the potential entrant follows a maximin strategy but the incumbent follows a maximax strategy. What is the likely outcome in this case?

CHAPTER 15

Factor Pricing and Income Distribution: Marginal Productivity Theory

The main thesis of *Time on the Cross*, a very controversial book published in 1974, was that slaves were better off materially under slavery than after emancipation.[1] You can probably guess why the book was so controversial: How could anyone be better off in chattel than in freedom, regardless of the working conditions? Robert Fogel and Stanley Engerman, the authors of *Time on the Cross*, replied that most of their critics were missing the point. Freedom is better than slavery, but because slaves were valuable "property," the plantation owners had a strong incentive to take good care of them. The result was that slaves were fed, clothed, and housed reasonably well—and, in many cases, received better care than they did immediately following emancipation. The fact that some slaves chose to remain on the plantation after emancipation suggests that there may be some truth to this argument. Just as important, the former slave owners wanted the former slaves to continue as paid workers, an indication that what the slave owners wanted was the output of the slaves, not the slaves themselves.

The point here is not to rehash the *Time on the Cross* debate. No one would deny that freedom is precious or that it is an inalienable right in all just societies. Our point is that so long as the slaves were valuable to their owners, the owners had an incentive to take care of their "property." The slaves provided labor, a factor input, and because all inputs are valuable, they command a price. Our primary task in this and the next two chapters is to explain the determinants of factor prices.

[1]Robert W. Fogel and Stanley L. Engerman, *Time on the Cross* (Boston: Little, Brown, 1974). Fogel shared the 1994 Nobel Prize in economics with Douglas North for their contributions to the study of economic history.

Traditionally, economists have used marginal productivity theory to explain factor prices and income distribution. This chapter presents the basic concepts of marginal productivity theory. The next two chapters extend marginal productivity theory and discuss other factor-pricing theories.

AFTER READING AND STUDYING THIS CHAPTER, YOU SHOULD BE ABLE TO:

• • • Discuss the determinants of the factor demand and factor supply curves
• • • Explain the relationship between factor prices and factor productivity
• • • Use marginal productivity theory to explain the prices of labor, capital, and natural resources
• • • Explain how marginal productivity theory relates to income distribution

• • • • • • • THE DEMAND FOR THE FACTORS OF PRODUCTION

Even under slavery, the southern plantation owners did not really want the slaves per se, they wanted the money they could earn from selling the output that the slaves helped produce. This is why the demand for factor inputs—all factor inputs, not just labor—is called **derived demand**. The demand for input factors is derived from the demand for goods sold in the output market. A key proposition of marginal productivity theory is that the demand for the factors of production depends on the value of the output produced by the factors of production.

Marginal productivity theory was developed simultaneously by several economists, but John Bates Clark (1847–1938) and Eugen von Böhm-Bawerk (1851–1914) were

Derived demand In marginal productivity theory of factor pricing, the demand for the factors of production is "derived" from the output of the factors.

Slave labor was a factor input in 19th Century America.

two of the most important contributors. (J. B. Clark is profiled in the Economic Heritage box on page 363.) Marginal productivity theory holds that factor payments—wages, interest, rents, and profits—depend on the productivity of the factor. Workers who are more productive receive higher wages than workers who are less productive, fertile land commands a higher rent than barren land, and so on. An important implication of this theory was that the payments to the factors of production were "just" in the sense that factor owners "deserve" what they are paid. This idea was crucial to Clark and the other nineteenth-century economists as they developed theories to refute the exploitation arguments of Karl Marx. Marginal productivity theory also seemed to provide a "scientific" argument in support of the existing income distribution because people were being paid in accordance with their productive contributions to society.

Marginal Revenue Product

Table 15.1 provides a numerical example to show how the demand for labor inputs is related to productivity and prices in the output market. Columns 1, 2, and 3 are repeated from Table 9.1 where we developed the law of diminishing returns. As before, N stands for labor inputs and Q is total product. The third column shows the marginal product of labor, but in this table it is labeled MPP instead of MP to emphasize that it is the marginal *physical* product of labor. The **marginal physical product** of labor is a measure of the output of labor in terms of goods and services; it is *not*

Marginal physical product The output, measured in physical units, not dollar values, of the next factor input.

•••• TABLE 15.1 MARGINAL REVENUE PRODUCT AND DERIVED DEMAND

(1) N	(2) Q	(3) MPP	(4) P	(5) TR	(6) MRP
3	150		$3	$450	
		→ 50			→ $150
4	200		3	600	
		→ 40			→ 120
5	240		3	720	
		→ 30			→ 90
6	270		3	810	
		→ 20			→ 60
7	290		3	870	
		→ 10			→ 30
8	300		3	900	

Definitions and Formulas:

N = input (labor)

Q = total product

TR = total revenue = PQ

MPP = marginal physical product = $\dfrac{\Delta Q}{\Delta N}$

MRP = marginal revenue product = $\dfrac{\Delta TR}{\Delta N} = P(MPP)$

P = selling price (fixed under pure competition)

Marginal revenue product The additional revenue associated with employing one additional factor of production; marginal physical product times marginal revenue (selling price under pure competition).

the monetary value of these goods and services. Column 4 gives the selling price of output, assumed to be $3 regardless of how much is sold. A fixed selling price means we are assuming that the firm is operating under pure competition in the output market—an assumption that we will be making throughout this entire chapter.[2] Column 5 shows the total revenue (TR) from selling output. Total revenue is found by multiplying total product (Q) times the selling price. Column 6 shows the monetary value of marginal physical product, the **marginal revenue product (MRP)**. Marginal revenue product is the additional revenue earned from hiring one more worker. Firms are more concerned with marginal revenue product than with marginal physical product because their goal is to earn profit from the sale of output. Marginal revenue product is found by finding the change in total revenue associated with one more unit of labor. An equivalent definition of marginal revenue product is marginal revenue times the marginal physical product. The formula for marginal revenue product is:

$$\text{Marginal revenue product: } MRP = \frac{\Delta TR}{\Delta N} = \frac{\Delta (PQ)}{\Delta N} = MR\,(MPP) \quad [1]$$

We found out in Chapter 11 that under pure competition marginal revenue is just the selling price, so marginal revenue product can be found by multiplying marginal physical product by the (assumed constant) selling price in the output market. We are assuming pure competition throughout this chapter, so it will be easiest to calculate marginal revenue product as:

$$MRP = \text{Marginal revenue product under pure competition:}$$
$$MRP = \frac{\Delta TR}{\Delta N} = P\,(MPP) \quad [2]$$

Slope of the **MRP** *Curve.* The marginal revenue product figures from Table 15.1 are graphed in Figure 15.1. The marginal revenue product curve is downward sloping over its whole region because we are using information only from Stage II of the production function, the region of diminishing marginal product.[3] The downward slope indicates that the incremental contribution from additional workers declines as more workers are added. Two things determine whether the marginal revenue product curve is relatively steep or relatively flat. First, the slope of the marginal revenue product curve depends on the slope of the marginal physical product curve: if the marginal physical product curve is steep—an indication that marginal product falls significantly each time a worker is added—the marginal revenue product curve will be steep as well. Second, the higher the selling price of output, the steeper the marginal revenue product curve for a given marginal physical product will be. For example, in Table 15.1, the selling price is assumed to be $3. The slope of the marginal revenue product curve is −30/1 because marginal revenue falls by $30 every time one worker is added. With a selling price of $5, the total revenue associated with 4,

---

[2] In other markets, the selling price will fall as output increases. This will make the *MRP* curve steeper, a point we illustrate in the next chapter.

[3] Recall from Chapter 9 that most production processes have three stages: increasing marginal product (Stage I), diminishing marginal product (Stage II), and negative marginal product (Stage III).

•••• **FIGURE 15.1** MARGINAL REVENUE PRODUCT

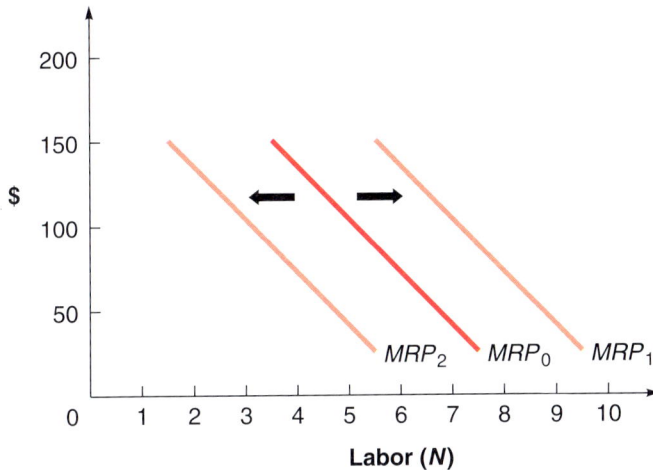

When there is pure competition in the output market, the marginal revenue product (*MRP*) curve is found by multiplying marginal physical product by the selling price of output. The downward slope is due to diminishing returns. As additional workers are added to a fixed stock of capital, output per worker declines when production is in Stage II of the production function. The curve MRP_0 is a plot of the information in Column 6 of Table 15.1.

The marginal revenue product curve will shift whenever the marginal physical product curve shifts or the selling price of output changes. An increase in marginal physical product or a rise in the output selling price will shift the marginal revenue product curve to the right from MRP_0 to MRP_1. A decrease in marginal physical product or a decline in the output selling price will shift the marginal revenue product curve to the left from MRP_0 to MRP_2.

5, and 6 workers would be \$1,000, \$1,200, and \$1,350, respectively. The marginal revenue of adding the fifth worker is \$200 (= \$1,200 − \$1,000), and when the sixth worker is added, it is \$150 (= \$1,350 − \$1,200). Each worker adds \$50 less revenue than the previous worker, so the slope of the marginal revenue curve is −50/1.

Shifting the **MRP** *Curve.* Several things can shift the marginal revenue product curve. An increase in the selling price of output will shift the marginal revenue product curve outward to the right because the contribution of each worker would increase; a decrease in selling price will shift the curve inward to the left. The marginal revenue product curve will also shift any time the marginal physical product curve shifts due to, say, increased worker effort, additional capital to work with, or improved technology.

•••••••
Profit Maximization and the Input Decision

The problem for the firm is to determine the profit-maximizing number of workers to hire. The decision rule for hiring the optimal number of workers (or any variable input) is an application of what we called the Fundamental Rule for Profit Maximization in Chapter 11: hire workers until the marginal revenue product of labor is equal to the *marginal factor cost* of labor. That is, the firm should hire workers until:

$$MRP_N = MFC_N \qquad [3]$$

where the N subscripts indicate that the variable input under consideration is labor. This rule holds for all factors of production, so Equation 3 can be generalized as:

$$MRP_i = MFC_i \qquad [4]$$

where i represents the ith factor of production.

Marginal factor cost is the change in total costs associated with hiring one more unit of the variable factor. Marginal factor cost depends on the state of competition in the input market. In this chapter we will be assuming that there is pure competition in the input market as well as in the output market. (Imperfect competition in the input market is explored in the next chapter.) This means that the firm is so small relative to the labor market that it can hire as many workers as needed without having to raise the wage rate. Under these circumstances, the marginal factor cost of labor is the wage rate so Equation 3 can be written as:

$$MRP_N = W \qquad [5]$$

Why does Equation 5 result in the profit-maximizing level of employment? To answer this question, we first need to define the concept **net marginal revenue product**. Net marginal revenue product is the difference between the marginal revenue product of hiring the next worker and the cost of hiring that worker. In this example, we are assuming that the only cost associated with hiring the next worker is the wage, so the area between the marginal revenue product curve and the wage line in Figure 15.2 might be called "accumulated net marginal revenue product." We need to point out that accumulated net marginal revenue is not the same thing as profit; it is only revenue derived from the employment of labor in excess of the amount necessary to pay the workers. Some of this revenue represents profit, but some must also be used to pay for capital and the other factors of production. We will elaborate on this idea shortly.

Figure 15.3 uses the information from Table 15.1 to show what happens if the firm does not follow the profit-maximizing strategy of Equation 5. Suppose that the wage rate is $75 and the firm chooses to hire a number of workers such that $MRP \neq W$, say, $N = 5$. If only 5 workers are hired, the marginal revenue product of the fifth worker is greater than the wage rate, $105 > 75. (The MRP of the fifth worker is found by taking the midpoint between $120 and $90; this is the MRP of moving between 4 and 6 workers.) The net marginal revenue product of the fifth worker is positive, so the fifth worker should be employed. However, the firm is forfeiting the net marginal revenue it could get from hiring the sixth worker. This is the area of the shaded triangle above the wage line. On the other hand, if the firm chooses to hire 7 workers, the marginal revenue product of the seventh worker is less than the wage rate ($45 < $75), so the firm loses net marginal revenue product equal to the area of the shaded triangle below the wage line. The rule is clear: The firm should employ factors until the marginal revenue product of the last unit is just equal to the marginal cost of that unit.

Marginal factor cost Change in total costs from hiring one more unit of a variable factor.

Net marginal revenue product The difference between marginal revenue product and marginal factor cost.

····· **FIGURE 15.2** NET MARGINAL REVENUE PRODUCT

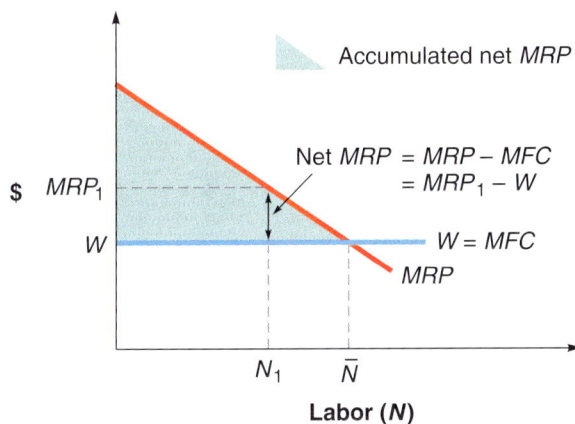

The marginal factor cost of labor is equal to the wage rate if all workers can be hired at the same wage rate. Net marginal revenue product is the difference between marginal revenue product and the marginal factor cost of an individual worker; the net marginal revenue product of the N_1 worker is $MRP_1 - W$. Accumulated net marginal product is the entire area between the marginal revenue product curve and the marginal factor cost line. To maximize profits, firms should hire workers until $MRP = W$, or until the net marginal revenue product of the last factor employed is zero.

····· **FIGURE 15.3** THE OPTIMAL QUANTITY OF LABOR

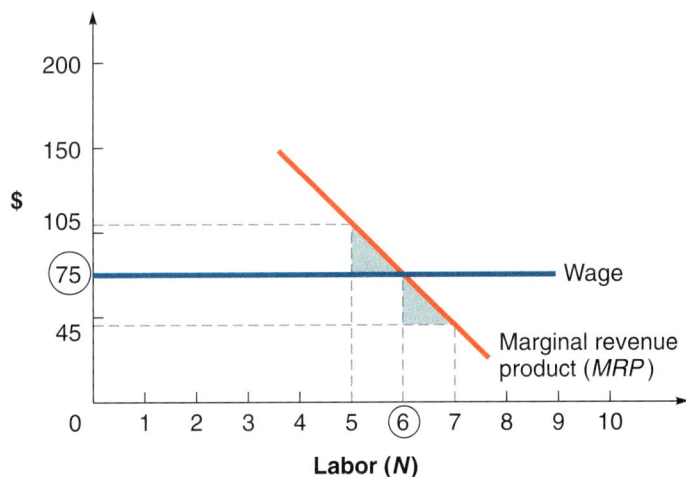

Firms should hire factors until the marginal factor cost (the wage in this example) is equal to the marginal revenue product. In this example, the marginal revenue product of the sixth worker is equal to the wage rate, $75, so 6 workers should be hired. If only 5 workers were hired, the marginal revenue product would be greater than the wage rate, $105 > $75, and the firm would be forfeiting net marginal revenue product equal to the shaded triangle above the wage line. If 7 workers were hired, the marginal revenue product would be less than the wage rate, $45 < $75, so net marginal revenue product would fall by the amount in the shaded area below the wage line.

FIGURE 15.4 MARGINAL REVENUE PRODUCT OF LABOR = DEMAND CURVE FOR LABOR

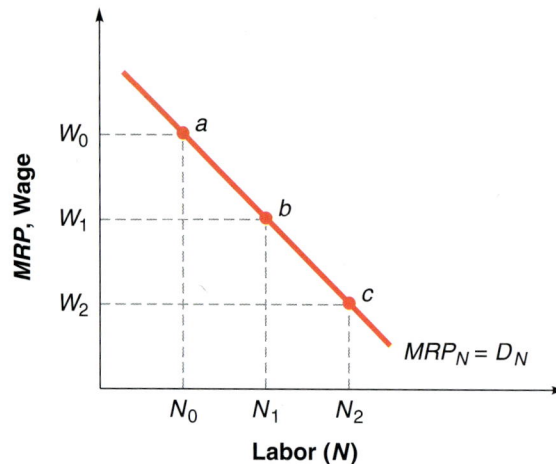

The marginal revenue product curve is the factor demand curve. As factor prices (wages) fall from W_0 to W_2, the number of workers demanded (hired) rises from N_0 to N_2.

The Factor Demand Curve

Like all demand curves, the firm's factor demand curve shows the different quantities of a factor that will be demanded at various prices. It turns out that the marginal revenue product curve is the firm's factor demand curve. This is illustrated in Figure 15.4. Assume that the wage rate falls from W_0 to W_2 along a fixed marginal revenue product curve. As wages fall, the optimal number of workers to hire increases. In other words, the marginal revenue product curve gives the quantity of workers that are hired at various wage rates—which is the definition of the firm's labor demand curve.

The marginal revenue product curve is the firm's labor demand curve, so the same variables that shift the marginal revenue product curve also shift the labor demand curve—selling prices in the output market, technology, and productivity are among the most important. The only thing that results in movement along a factor demand curve is a change in the price of the factor.

THE LABOR MARKET

There is very little difference in the analysis of the demand curves for labor, land, and capital. All depend on marginal revenue product, and the optimal quantity to be employed is always found with the decision rule $MRP_i = MFC_i$. Unfortunately, the same cannot be said for factor supply curves. The conditions that affect the supply

OUR ECONOMIC HERITAGE

JOHN BATES CLARK AND MARGINAL PRODUCTIVITY THEORY

Several economists have made important contributions to marginal productivity theory, but no one was more important than the American economist John Bates Clark (1847–1938). Clark was educated at Amherst, Brown, and the University of Heidelberg and spent most of his professional career teaching at Columbia University. As a youth, he was torn between the clergy and economics. Economics eventually won out, but there are religious overtones in much of Clark's work. They are particularly apparent in his analysis of the marginal productivity theory of income distribution, which he considered a manifestation of justice on earth.

Clark's most important book is undoubtedly *The Distribution of Wealth: A Theory of Wages, Interest, and Profits* (1899). Here Clark developed what many people consider to be the most comprehensive and detailed statement of marginal productivity theory ever written. Technically elegant, it was to become the basis for many of the theoretical advances in the theory of income distribution over the next century. More than a few economists questioned Clark's assertion that nineteenth-century capitalism was oper-

ating by the rule "to each what he creates," but this view was largely responsible for the relegation of Marxian theories of labor exploitation to the backwaters of economic analysis.

Clark was writing at a time when many others were working in the same areas so it is hard to say that he was an innovator. Still, much of what he did added to or made important extensions to the work of others. For example, Clark was the first to note the distinction between "capital" and "capital goods," a point missed by the leading capital theorist of the era, Eugen von Böhm-Bawerk. The difference between the two concepts remains the subject of debate today, but one of the key points made by Clark was that capital goods differ from many other factors in that they are often useful for only a single purpose: most workers can do a variety of jobs, but a wood lathe is useful only as a lathe. This has important implications on how the price of capital is determined. Perhaps his most innovative work appeared in *Essentials of Economic Theory* (1907). Here Clark laid the foundations for the theory of economic dynamics, a chief concern of many economists even today.

Another legacy of Clark was his son, John Maurice Clark. Though J. B. and J. M. did do some work together, J. M. took a much different approach to economics and is often associated with the institutionalist school. J. M. Clark is probably best known for his contributions to the theory of investment, but he also did work in business pricing and developed a theory of effective competition that he proposed as a standard for socially acceptable business behavior.

of labor are quite different from those that affect the supply of capital or land, so we need to look at each factor supply curve separately before we can determine factor prices.

• • • • • • • •

The Supply Curve for Labor

What affects your decision to offer time and effort to an employer? Income is probably the most important condition for most people—you need income to survive, and most of us would not have enough unless we worked. Unfortunately, the time we spend at work gives us less time to enjoy the income we earn; that is, the decision to work involves a tradeoff between income and leisure. This is the key concept behind the labor supply curve.

According to traditional marginal productivity theory, leisure is a "good" and work is a "bad." The only reason people work is to earn money to enjoy their leisure. Rational behavior involves a tradeoff between work and leisure. The opportunity cost of working is forgone leisure; the opportunity cost of leisure is forgone income. As the wage rate rises, the opportunity cost of leisure increases because each hour of leisure incurs additional lost income. As leisure becomes more expensive, people "buy" less of it—and thus work more hours. As the wage rate falls, leisure gets less expensive, so people "buy" more of it and work fewer hours. And if the wage rate is too low, people will not work at all.

As shown in Figure 15.5, the labor supply curve is drawn with the wage rate on the vertical axis and the quantity of labor on the horizontal axis. The tradeoff between work and leisure means that the labor supply curve is generally upward sloping, like most supply curves. At very high wages, however, the labor supply curve may exhibit a backward-bending portion. Why? Suppose your wage rate increased a phenomenal amount, say, to $1,000 per hour. Would you continue to work 40 hours per week,

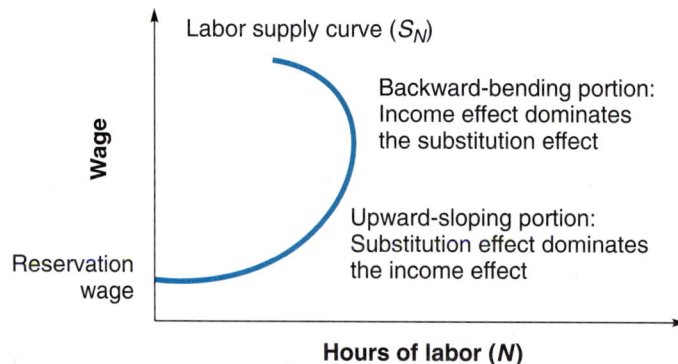

···· **FIGURE 15.5   THE LABOR SUPPLY CURVE**

The labor supply curve, S_N, shows the number of hours of work that will be offered at various wage rates. Workers decide how many hours to work by trading off work and leisure. At relatively low wages, the labor supply curve is upward sloping because the substitution effect is more powerful than the income effect. At some very high wage rate, the labor supply curve may bend backward because the income effect is stronger than the substitution effect. The vertical intercept of the labor supply curve is the minimum wage necessary to attract people into the labor market. Our analysis will focus on the upward-sloping portion of the labor supply curve.

or would you work fewer hours and spend some of your hard-earned wages on much needed leisure? Many people would choose to work fewer hours and enjoy more leisure—which would cause the labor supply curve to bend backward at very high wages. In general, the backward-bending portion of the labor supply curve is probably not very important, though there may be one notable exception: between 1960 and 1990, the percentage of adult males who held jobs fell from 86 to 76 percent even though the real wage was rising. This suggests a backward-bending labor supply curve for adult males. Over the same period, however, the percentage of adult women with jobs rose from 38 percent to 58 percent, so men were probably responding to cultural factors as well as to their wage rate. Most economists believe that backward-bending labor supply curves are rare in the real world, so we will draw the labor supply curve upward sloping in this and the next chapter.[4] We will also simplify the diagrams a bit by using linear labor supply and demand curves throughout the rest of the chapter. This doesn't change the results in any significant way, and it will make it easier for you to draw the diagrams in your notes as you read along, which, by the way, is strongly advised.

Income and Substitution Effects. A more elegant way to analyze the tradeoff between work and leisure is in terms of the income and substitution effects. The combined effect of the income and substitution effects determines whether the labor supply curve is upward sloping or backward bending.

The substitution effect in the labor supply response is caused by a change in the relative price of work and leisure. An increase in the wage rate raises the relative price of leisure because each hour of leisure now represents more forgone income. This tends to reduce the amount of leisure. For example, an increase in the wage rate from $6 to $9 might cause you to work more than 40 hours per week—which is exactly why many jobs pay "time and a half" for overtime. A decrease in the wage rate does just the opposite: the relative price of leisure is lower, so more is "purchased" with forgone income. Have you ever wondered why people working in fast-food restaurants call in "sick" so often?

The income effect measures the effect of a change in the wage rate on the purchasing power of the worker. Other things being equal, a higher income will cause people to buy more goods—including leisure. The income effect implies that higher wages will tend to reduce the number of hours worked. Does this fly in the face of the upward-sloping labor supply curve? No. It only means that the substitution effect is more powerful than the income effect in the upward-sloping portion of the labor supply curve. The opposite is true in the backward-bending portion: there the income effect is stronger than the substitution effect.

---

[4]One example of a backward-bending labor supply curve involves native workers in the diamond mines of South Africa in the nineteenth and early twentieth century. Though the workers were exploited with low wages and harsh working conditions, the wages they were paid were so high *relative to what they were used to making* that many chose to work only a few months; then they would use their earnings to buy a few needed goods and return home. White owners used this behavior to make racist remarks about the laziness of natives; economists would say it illustrated rational behavior. In the 1960s, newspaper editorials made similar remarks about Hispanic workers from south Texas who moved to the Dallas–Fort Worth area to work in the aerospace industry. After working just a few months, many workers took their money and returned home.

Shifting the Labor Supply Curve. Several factors can cause the labor supply curve to shift. The motivation to work, income taxes, and unemployment compensation are three of the most important. Changes in work effort shift individual labor supply curves. For example, if you are suddenly struck with ambition, you may decide to work more hours even though your wage rate has not changed. This would cause your labor supply curve to shift to the right and away from the wage axis. Income taxes can also affect work effort. If you know that your next hour of labor will be subject to a 50 percent tax, you may think twice about putting in overtime. If the tax rate is only 20 percent, the extra time at the office is more enticing. Income tax increases tend to shift the labor supply curve to the left; income tax cuts tend to shift the labor supply curve to the right.

Unemployment compensation reduces the pain of being unemployed and may influence how hard people look for a job. If unemployment compensation is universal and covers 100 percent of lost wages, some people may be inclined to sit at home and watch Oprah instead of looking for a new job; this would shift the labor supply curve to the left. On the other hand, the existence of unemployment compensation may provide a cushion for people as they search for a new job that uses their skills. You would not want to be forced to take a job flipping burgers the day after you were laid off from your Big 6 public accounting firm, would you?

Few economists question that these factors shift the labor supply curve, but they do not agree on the magnitude of the shifts. Perhaps the most important debate concerns the labor supply response to income taxes. This is potentially very important: if income taxes have a significant effect on work effort, then policymakers must be very careful before raising taxes. If there is a consensus on this issue, it is probably that changes in income taxes have only a small effect on labor supply, and most of that effect is on the decision to work overtime. If this view is correct, income tax changes probably have more effect on the demand side of the economy than on the supply side because taxes affect the buying power of consumers.

· · · · · · · ·

The Market Labor Supply Curve

A single firm under pure competition is able to hire as many workers as it needs at the going wage rate, so the wage lines in Figures 15.2 and 15.3 can be considered the supply of labor facing a single firm. However, if all firms in the entire industry wanted to hire more workers, the wage rate would normally have to rise to induce people to give up leisure in exchange for work. The market labor supply curve is found by adding together the individual labor supply curves for everyone in the particular labor market. Anything that causes an individual labor supply curve to shift will also shift the market labor supply curve. Additionally, the market labor supply curve will shift due to population growth and changes in the labor force participation rate. As we found out in Chapter 5, the labor force participation rate is the ratio of the labor force to the working age population. The labor force participation rate can change for several reasons. Over the past 30 years, the biggest change has been the large increase in women in the workforce, as we observed earlier. Population growth affects the labor supply curve much like increases in the labor force participation rate.

Figure 15.6 illustrates shifts in the labor supply curve. Anything that increases work effort, the number of workers in a particular market, or the labor force participation

···· **FIGURE 15.6** **SHIFTING THE LABOR SUPPLY CURVE**

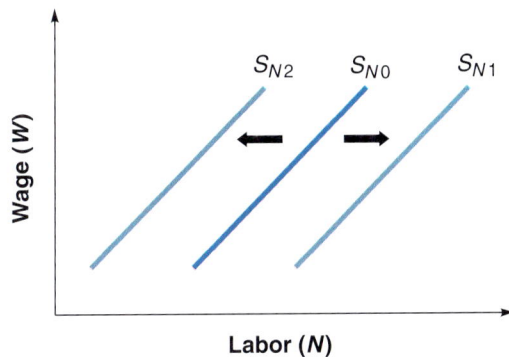

The labor supply curve shifts in response to changes in work effort, population, and the labor force participation rate. An increase in work effort, population growth, or a higher labor force participation rate will shift the labor supply curve from S_{N0} to S_{N1}. This represents additional hours being offered at every wage rate. If work incentives decrease (perhaps due to higher income taxes), or if the labor force participation rate declines, the labor supply curve will shift from S_{N0} to S_{N2}.

rate will shift the labor supply curve away from the vertical axis, from S_{N0} to S_{N1} on the diagram. Factors that do the opposite—a decrease in work effort, a decline in population, or a reduction in the labor force participation rate—will shift the labor supply curve toward the vertical axis, from S_{N0} to S_{N2}.

········

The Equilibrium Wage Rate

We can find the wage rate that clears the labor market—the equilibrium wage rate—by combining the labor demand curve and the labor supply curve. This is done in Figure 15.7. The **equilibrium wage rate** is the rate at which the quantity of labor demanded is equal to the quantity of labor supplied. The equilibrium wage rate is equal to the marginal revenue product of the last worker hired.

Figure 15.7 also illustrates the effects of shifts in the demand and supply for labor. Suppose the labor market begins at the intersection of D_{N0} and S_{N0} so that the equilibrium wage rate is W_0. An increase in the demand for labor will shift the labor demand curve outward from D_{N0} to D_{N1} and cause the equilibrium wage rate to rise to W_2, assuming that all other factors are held constant. If the labor supply curve shifts outward (S_{N0} to S_{N1}), the wage rate will fall to W_1, assuming again that all other factors are held constant, and the demand curve is D_{N0}.

Over the long run, the labor supply has grown because of population growth, and we know that labor force participation rates have increased over the past 40 years as well. Does this mean that wages have fallen over the same period? Not necessarily. In some markets, the demand for labor has increased faster than the supply of labor, causing wages to rise. This has been true in many markets for skilled labor. On the other hand, when the demand for labor falls relative to supply, the wage rate will

Equilibrium wage rate The rate at which the quantity of labor demanded is equal to the quantity of labor supplied; equals the marginal revenue product of the last worker hired.

···· **FIGURE 15.7** EQUILIBRIUM WAGES

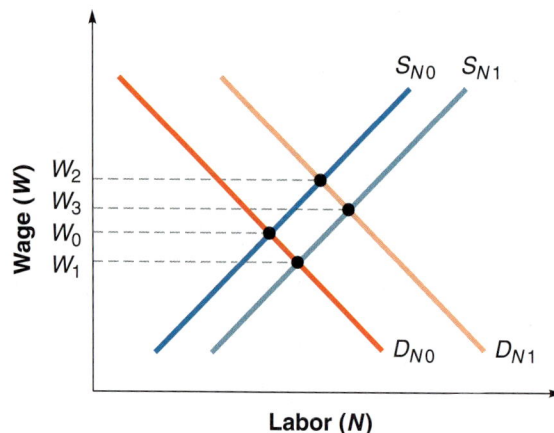

The equilibrium wage rate exists where the quantity of labor demanded is equal to the quantity of labor supplied. If labor demand is initially D_{N0} and the labor supply is initially S_{N0}, the equilibrium wage will be W_0. Other things being equal, an increase in the supply of labor will cause the wage rate to fall. This is represented by the shift from S_{N0} to S_{N1} and the wage decline from W_0 to W_1. An increase in the demand for labor will raise the equilibrium wage rate. This is illustrated by the shift from D_{N0} to D_{N1} and the wage hike from W_0 to W_2. When both labor supply and labor demand increase, the effect on wages will depend on the relative magnitudes of the shifts. For example, an increase in the wage rate from W_0 to W_3 indicates that labor demand has increased more than labor supply.

fall. Many people believe that this is why the wage rate for many unskilled workers has fallen in the past decade.

Does the existence of an ''equilibrium wage rate'' imply that there is no unemployment? Perhaps—but it depends on which economist you ask. Some economists contend that as long as wages and prices are free to fluctuate, any people who are unable to find a job must be **voluntarily unemployed** because they are unwilling to accept a wage rate that is consistent with their productivity. In this view, any unemployment that exists is caused by union or government policies that prevent wages from moving to the equilibrium level. Other economists, however, contend that the labor market does not operate quite as efficiently as this model implies and that workers may be unable to find a job even if wages and prices are perfectly flexible. We will explore this view in more detail in the next chapter.

Voluntary unemployment Unemployment caused by workers refusing to work at the market wage.

········

Marginal Productivity and Wage Differentials

Why do garbage collectors make lower salaries than game show hosts? Why do teachers make lower salaries than accountants? Different occupations earn different wages because there are many different labor markets. The skills (?) that it takes to be a game show host are not directly applicable to the garbage collection profession, so it is not clear that an unemployed game show host could easily find a job in the promising field of urban sanitation. Marginal productivity theory can be a powerful tool for explaining wage differentials when we take account of four additional factors: job attractiveness, human capital, labor mobility, and discrimination.

Job Attractiveness. Jobs that involve danger, tedium, or significant physical labor often carry a wage somewhat higher than jobs with otherwise comparable characteristics. For example, offshore oil workers earn more than onshore oil workers, and the "graveyard" shift typically carries a 10 percent wage premium. More recently, people who worked to disarm the millions of bombs and land mines left after the Gulf War earned salaries starting at $100,000—for six months of work. Such wage differentials are called **compensating differentials**. Do compensating differentials violate marginal productivity theory? Not at all—because such jobs attract few people, the supply of labor for these jobs is low, and that increases the wage rate. Problem 10 at the end of this chapter asks you to use diagrams to illustrate the effects of job attractiveness as well as human capital, labor mobility, and discrimination on wages and employment.

Compensating differentials Pay differences based on job attractiveness, danger, or similar factors.

Human Capital. Why do college graduates typically earn $300,000 more over their lifetime than high school graduates? Why do workers in the United States earn 25 times as much as workers in India? One reason is that U.S. workers have more physical capital (machinery) to work with, but another reason is that U.S. workers typically have more **human capital** than workers in India. Human capital is the education, training and experience that increases worker productivity and income. College graduates earn more income than high school graduates because they possess more skills; the same can be said of workers in the United States relative to workers in India. Workers with more human capital are more productive than workers with less human capital. Human capital shifts the labor demand curve for skilled workers to the right and increases the wage rate.

Human capital The experience, education, and training that increase worker productivity and income.

Labor Mobility. Workers in Alaska receive, on average, incomes that are about 25 percent higher than comparable workers in the lower 48 states. Part of the reason for this differential may be that many people consider jobs in Alaska to be unattractive and thus require a compensating wage differential. But another reason may be that Alaska is so isolated that Alaskan workers do not face competition from lower-paid workers Down South. With perfect **labor mobility**, both between regions and between jobs, wage differentials would not exist. For example, if moving to Alaska were cost-free, the 25 percent wage differential would cause people to emigrate from the lower 48 states to Alaska. The increase in the labor supply in Alaska would cause wages to decline, while wages in the lower 48 states would rise because the labor supply had been reduced. Emigration would stop when the wages were equal.

Labor mobility The ability of workers to move from one area to another area.

Discrimination. It is a sad fact of life, but **discrimination** against women and ethnic minorities exists in most countries. In the United States, for example, women earn only about 70 percent as much as men. Ethnic and racial minorities suffer similar discrimination; minority males earn only about 60 percent as much as white males in the United States. Does this mean that women are less productive than men or that ethnic minorities are less productive than whites? The answer could be affir-

Discrimination Treating people differently on a basis other than individual merit (e.g., on the basis of race, sex, or ethnic group).

mative, but only if there was no discrimination. Discrimination is one reason why women and minorities earn less than men and why cultural minorities earn less than cultural majorities.[5]

There are several kinds of discrimination, and all are costly to society. If all employers suddenly decided (irrationally) that women or minorities could not do the job as well as white males, then the labor supply curve—which would then be comprised exclusively of white males—would shift to the left. This would cause the wages paid to white males to rise and, because wages are a cost of production, would result in lower profits for the firms. The effect of discrimination does not stop here. The wages paid to women and minorities will decline because now fewer employers are willing to hire women and minorities. Further, the lower wages paid to women and minorities are one reason why these groups historically change jobs more frequently than white males; it is much easier to quit a crummy job than a good one. Frequent job changes are a reason why women and minorities have such a difficult time building up seniority and moving into upper management. A different kind of discrimination may provide another reason why women and minorities are rarely seen in upper management: corporate executives—overwhelmingly white and male—seem resistant to promote women and minorities, a phenomenon known as the "glass ceiling."

One of the main sources of discrimination against women is the cultural attitude that designates "**women's jobs**" and "men's jobs." Nursing, child care, and hair styling are considered "women's work" in our society; over 80 percent of the workers in these professions were women in the 1980s. Sales agents, stockbrokers, and engineers are predominantly men; less than 20 percent of these jobs were filled with women in the 1980s. The effect on male/female wage differentials is obvious: "women's jobs" are among the lowest-paid occupations; "men's jobs" are among the highest-paid occupations. Until these stereotypes can be eliminated, the task of eliminating male/female wage differentials will be difficult.[6]

> **"Women's" jobs** Jobs that have been traditionally held by women.

RECAP   Supply and Demand in the Labor Market

We will have much more to say about the labor market in the next chapter, but we should recap the main ideas before going on. Many of the ideas we have just developed have direct relevance to capital and land.

1. The demand for labor is derived from the productivity of labor and the demand for final products. As more workers are added to a fixed stock of capital, the marginal product of labor declines. The marginal revenue product is the demand curve for labor. When there is competition in the output market, marginal revenue product is found by multiplying the marginal physical product of labor by the selling price of output. Firms hire workers until the

---

[5]An excellent collection of essays on discrimination against women and minorities is Susan F. Feiner, *Race and Gender in the American Economy* (Englewood Cliffs, N.J.: Prentice-Hall, 1994). We look at some other reasons why women and ethnic minorities earn lower wages in Chapters 20 and 27.
[6]For more data on the extent and changing nature of discrimination against women and ethnic minorities, see Lawrence Mishel and Jared Bernstein, *The State of Working America*, 1992–93 (M. E. Sharpe, 1993). *The State of Working America* is published in alternate years.

marginal revenue product of the last worker hired is equal to the marginal factor cost.

2. The main factors that shift the labor demand curve are worker productivity and the selling price of output. Other things being equal, an increase in the demand for labor will increase the number of workers that are hired and raise the wage rate.

3. The supply curve of labor depends on the tradeoff between work and leisure and is usually upward sloping. As the wage rate increases, the opportunity cost of leisure increases, so people typically offer more hours of labor. At very high wage rates, however, the labor supply curve may be backward bending. The slope of the labor supply curve depends on the relative magnitudes of the income and substitution effects. If the substitution effect is stronger, the labor supply curve is upward sloping. If the income effect is stronger, the labor supply curve is backward bending.

4. The labor supply curve will shift when there are changes in work effort, the labor force participation rate, and population. Other things being equal, an increase in the supply of labor will increase the number of workers that are hired and lower the wage rate.

5. Wage differentials can often be explained by factors that shift the labor supply or labor demand curve. Compensating differentials exist in jobs that are unattractive, dangerous, or difficult. Human capital increases worker productivity and the wage rate. Discrimination accounts for some wage differentials. Firms that discriminate face a reduced supply of available workers and thus raise the wage rate for eligible workers.

THE MARKET FOR CAPITAL

The rationale behind the demand curve for capital goods is the same as the rationale behind the demand curve for labor: firms acquire *capital goods* because they need them in the production process and will keep buying capital goods as long as the marginal revenue product exceeds the marginal factor cost of capital goods. The supply curve for *capital* is quite different from the supply curve for labor however. Instead of a tradeoff between work and leisure, there is a tradeoff between saving and consumption. This is important because firms need financial capital before they can buy physical capital, and the source of financial capital is saving. Savings can come from many sources including households (personal saving), business (retained earnings), and the foreign sector (financial capital inflows).[7]

We italicized "capital" and "capital goods" in the preceding paragraph because we need to make a careful distinction between the two concepts. A capital good is a piece of machinery that the firm uses in the production process. The supply of capital goods depends on the price of capital goods and the production capacity of

---

[7]The government can also save, but to do so, it must run a surplus. Government deficits represent dissaving—more money is spent than is received in taxes—and the federal government has run deficits in all but four years since 1960. In contrast, state and local governments typically run small surpluses. Unlike households and businesses, however, government saving is not a function of the interest rate.

the capital goods industry. However, before a firm can acquire a capital good, it must have financial capital, so the supply of financial capital puts a constraint on the stock of capital goods. In this sense, saving represents the supply of (financial) capital, but not necessarily the supply of capital goods. Financial capital becomes capital goods only if the firm believes that the expected return on the capital goods is greater than the cost of using the financial capital, the interest rate.

• • • • • • • •

Interest Rates, Saving, and the Capital Stock

Other things being equal, higher interest rates increase saving while lower interest rates decrease saving. Why is the interest rate an important determinant of saving? People need an incentive to postpone current consumption. Collecting interest on savings means that more can be consumed in the future, but unless the interest rate is high enough, people will choose to save very little today. How high does the interest rate have to be to induce saving? That depends on the individual, but it must be high enough to cover two factors: **time preference** and *risk*. Time preference refers to how people rank current versus future consumption. If they value current consumption more than future consumption, then a high interest rate will be necessary to induce people to save. If they value future consumption highly relative to current consumption, then saving will take place at relatively low interest rates.

Risk affects the saving decision because the future is unknown. If you are afraid that your savings will not be there when you want to withdraw them, you will need a very high interest rate to overcome the risk of loss. On the other hand, if you are confident that your savings will be there in the future, you may be willing to save at a low interest rate. Risk explains why the interest rate on government bonds is usually lower than the interest rate on corporate securities. The chances of the government declaring bankruptcy are exceedingly small, so people are willing to buy government debt at a low interest rate. On the other hand, even Blue Chip companies might go bankrupt so people need a *risk premium* to cover the chance of loss; that risk premium takes the form of an interest rate point or two. But wait: Aren't treasury bills and corporate securities investments? No. To economists, "investment" is the acquisition of plants and machinery and can be undertaken only by firms. When households "invest" in the stock market or buy bonds, they are actually saving. This money does end up as investment if the financial institution or firm uses the funds for capital acquisition, but the household decision to save is separate from the firm's decision to invest. Households trade off current and future consumption when they decide to save; the firm's investment decision depends on other factors including the expectation of profits.

One more preliminary point is necessary before we can draw the supply and demand curves for capital. We need to recall the distinction between investment and capital. Investment is a flow; capital is a stock. The process of acquiring capital is investment; once investment has taken place, the firm has a stock of capital goods. This is an important distinction because the process of investment is often spread out over several years. At any point in time, the capital stock is fixed. In the long run, however, the supply of capital can be considered infinite because capital goods producers can produce as much capital as industry demands—if they have the right price signals.

Time preference The choice between consuming today or in the future.

The Supply Curves for Capital

The interest rate is the price of capital. Why? When a firm buys a capital good, it ties up money for several years, so it only makes sense to buy a capital good if the return is at least as high as the interest rate that could be earned if the money were spent on a financial asset instead. The return on capital is expressed as a percentage— the ratio of additional profits to the cost of capital. This allows firms to compare the return on capital to the interest rate on financial assets. The firm should buy capital as long as the expected return on capital is at least as high as the interest rate.

The long gestation period for capital means that we can think of there being two capital supply curves at any point in time: a perfectly inelastic short-run supply curve and a perfectly elastic long-run supply curve. These are shown in Figure 15.8. The **short-run supply curve for capital** goods, SS_K, is a vertical line above the current stock of capital goods, K_0. This curve will shift with changes in the stock of capital goods. An increase in the stock of capital goods will shift the curve to the right, a decrease will shift it to the left.

The **long-run supply curve for capital** goods, LS_K, is horizontal to reflect the assumption of a perfectly elastic supply of *financial* capital in the long run. The vertical intercept of the LS_K is the interest rate, $r^\star$, just high enough to overcome perceptions of risk and time preference and induce saving. At interest rates above $r^\star$, savers will be willing to supply additional savings, so the financial capital necessary to acquire capital goods will be available to firms. At interest rates below $r^\star$, no additional saving

Short-run supply curve of capital
Fixed amount of capital goods available in the short run; perfectly inelastic.

Long-run supply curve of capital
Perfectly elastic supply curve for financial capital.

FIGURE 15.8 THE SHORT-RUN AND LONG-RUN SUPPLY CURVES FOR CAPITAL

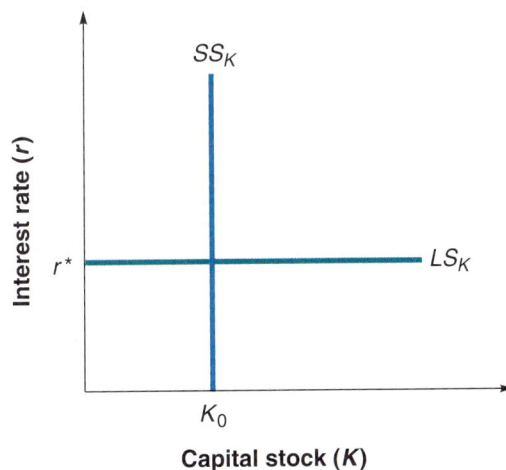

The short-run supply curve for capital, SS_K, is perfectly inelastic because the stock of capital is fixed in the short run. The horizontal intercept of SS_K is the existing stock of capital, K_0. The long-run supply curve for capital, LS_K, is perfectly elastic because households are willing to supply financial capital (savings) at interest rates at or above $r^\star$.

and thus no financial capital will be forthcoming, so firms will not be able to increase the stock of capital goods.

• • • • • • • •

The Equilibrium Capital Stock

The capital stock is in equilibrium when the marginal revenue product of capital is equal to the marginal factor cost of capital. The marginal factor cost of capital is the interest rate whether firms borrow or use retained earnings. Firms that borrow to acquire financial capital must pay the interest rate, and firms that use retained earnings incur the opportunity cost of forgone interest they could have earned on an interest-earning financial asset.

When the capital stock is not in equilibrium, adjustments will move it toward equilibrium. This is shown in Figure 15.9, which combines the two capital supply curves from Figure 15.8 with a single capital demand curve. Assume initially that the capital demand curve, D_K, intersects the short-run capital supply curve, SS_{K0} at r_0, an interest rate above $r^\star$. This means that the return on capital is greater than the interest rate required for additional saving. Thus, firms will be willing to offer rates above $r^\star$ to borrow money. This will increase the amount of saving. When this money is lent to firms, the short-run capital stock will increase, and the short-run

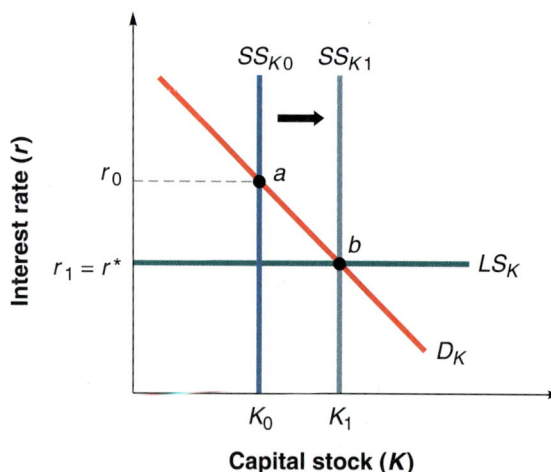

FIGURE 15.9 THE EQUILIBRIUM CAPITAL STOCK

Long-run equilibrium occurs when the long-run capital supply curve (LS_K), the short-run capital supply curve (SS_K), and capital demand curve (D_K) intersect. In the short run, the capital market operates at the intersection between the short-run capital supply curve and the capital demand curve. If the market begins at point a with the interest rate r_0 above $r^\star$, households will increase saving because the interest rate is higher than the minimum rate necessary to overcome time preferences. This causes the capital stock to increase and the short-run capital supply curve to move out from SS_{K0} toward SS_{K1}. Capital accumulation will continue until the interest rate reaches $r^\star$. This occurs at point b with capital stock K_1 and the simultaneous intersection of SS_{K1}, LS_K, and D_K.

OUR ECONOMIC HERITAGE

GARY BECKER: HUMAN CAPITAL AND RATIONAL BEHAVIOR— VERY RATIONAL BEHAVIOR

Few economists were surprised when the 1992 Nobel Prize in economics went to Gary Becker of the University of Chicago. Professor Becker is known for work in two main areas: the application of economic analysis to kinds of behavior that were previously thought to be irrational—marriage, discrimination, suicide, and others—and for his development of human capital theory. Perhaps the biggest compliment that can be paid to Becker is to point out that his once-heretical ideas are now mainstream. The public gets a steady diet of Becker economics in his monthly columns for *Business Week.*

Becker was born in 1930 and educated at Princeton and Chicago. He taught at Columbia from 1960 until 1970, when he took a position at the University of Chicago. In 1964, Becker published *Human Capital,* a book that many consider to be his most important work. Becker argued that education should be considered an investment and that people expect to receive a return over time. Though the concept of human capital seems obvious today, it revolutionized the way economists studied labor economics. Human capital is also critical in macroeconomic growth models.

In the early 1980s, most of Becker's work focused on the application of supply and demand analysis to family and social issues. For example, in his book *A Treatise on the Family,* Becker argued that the cost of having children falls if the children are put to work at an early age—a plausible explanation of why agricultural societies typically have large families. Becker also argued that the number of children falls as women get better jobs because the opportunity cost of raising children rises. Why do people marry? They get more pleasure from being married than being single and searching for a mate. Why do they divorce? They are no longer better off married than single. Also, when a woman's income rises relative to her husband's, the couple is more likely to get divorced because the woman's gain from remaining married is lowered. Needless to say, not everyone agrees with Becker's superrational view of human behavior, but few can say that his work did not cause them to think. And very few economists would argue that Becker's view of human behavior does not contain at least a shred of truth.

When he won the Nobel Prize, Becker said that he was surprised because University of Chicago economists had won the award the previous two years. (The 1991 award was won by Ronald Coase, and the 1990 award was shared by Merton Miller and two other financial economists.) He did note that he would resist the temptation to use the honor as a ". . . pulpit to launch sermons against political candidates . . ." and hoped that the prize would not ". . . delude me into thinking I have all the answers. . . ." He also noted that he would have no trouble finding a use for the $1.2 million in prize money because "wants always take advantage of new opportunities."

SOURCE: The quotations are from Gary Becker, "When the Wake-up Call Is from the Nobel Committee," *Business Week,* November 2, 1992, p. 20.

FOCUS ON

COMPARABLE WORTH LAWS: THE CANADIAN EXPERIENCE

Most people would agree that there should be "equal pay for equal work." For example, two firefighters with the same skills, experience, and job assignments should receive the same wage. Similarly, two nurses working the same shift with the same education and experience would expect the same wage. But should nurses receive the same wage as firefighters? In general they do not: firefighters often earn considerably more than nurses, even though it would be hard to argue that nurses have fewer skills, are less productive, or are less valuable to society than firefighters. Supply and demand in the labor market certainly explain some of the wage differential, but social and cultural discrimination may also be occurring. Nursing has long been considered a "woman's job"; fire fighting is considered a "man's job." Situations like these abound in modern economies and are the main source of reasoning behind the call for comparable worth legislation.

The premise behind comparable worth is that jobs of equal worth should be paid equal wages. Assigning precise values to different occupations can be extremely difficult, however. Most economists would say that the market can best determine the worth of different jobs. The problem with the economists' view, say comparable worth advocates, is that wages are not always set entirely by market forces. This may be especially true in the case of "women's jobs," given the history of male domination in Western society.

Comparable worth laws have been enacted in Iowa, Washington, Michigan, Minnesota, and a few other states, but the provinces of Canada have gone further in this direction than any state in the United States. The Canadian debate over comparable worth has gone beyond the issue of whether it is appropriate. The aim now is to design the most effective program for achieving "pay equity," the term used in Canada for comparable worth. An understanding of the Canadian experience may give insights into the viability of comparable worth laws in the United States.

The Canadian program is based on three key ideas. First, comparable worth legislation is intended to be proactive. This means that firms must implement comparable worth policies whether a complaint has been filed or not. Second, comparable worth initiatives are applied through the collective bargaining process between labor and management. Finally, flexibility is important. For example, large firms typically have job evaluation procedures in place—Clerk Typists I earn less than Clerk Typists II, and so on—so they have a mechanism that can be modified to restructure wage differentials. Most smaller firms do not have such mechanisms, so requiring them to implement comparable worth immediately could result in layoffs, hardly the aim of comparable worth advocates.

The Canadian comparable worth experiment is ongoing, but it seems to have had some positive effects since its inception in the mid-1980s. Between

capital supply curve will shift to the right. This will continue until the short-run supply curve, SS_{K1}, crosses the capital demand curve at its intersection with the long-run supply curve LS_K. If the situation were reversed and the market interest rate began below $r^\star$, the capital stock would shrink—firms will not replace worn-out machinery—and the short-run supply curve would shift left until long-run equilibrium is restored. Our conclusion: The capital stock is in equilibrium only when the return on capital is equal to $r^\star$.

The Coors Silver Bullet professional women's baseball team: Should they receive salaries comparable to male professional baseball players?

That, of course, depends upon whom you ask. People who feel that they are being discriminated against would probably say yes. But market-oriented economists would counter that any interference with the market is likely to cause problems. If the wage rates paid for "women's jobs" are increased, too many people will apply for those jobs and too few people will apply for other jobs. On the other hand, a recent *Business Week* survey of women managers revealed that fully 70 percent felt that male domination and the glass ceiling are obstacles to advancement. The fact that only 3 percent of all senior executive positions are occupied by women provides evidence for this position. Until women have the same job opportunities as men, we will continue to face the difficult issue of comparable worth.

1967 and 1989, women's average wages rose from 58.4 percent to 65.8 percent of male wages, and because women work fewer hours than men, the ratio probably increased even more. Advocates believe that the key behind the program's success was its proactive approach. Unfortunately, it is very difficult to isolate how much of this change was brought about by comparable worth and how much was brought about by other factors. For example, one study showed that the male/female wage differential shrank by about 6 percentage points between 1979 and 1988 even without nationwide comparable worth laws.

Should the United States implement a comparable worth program modeled after the Canadian program?

SOURCES: Morley Gunderson and W. Craig Riddell, "Comparable Worth: Canada's Experience," *Contemporary Policy Issues* 10 (July 1992): 85–94; "Corporate Women: Progress? Sure. But the Playing Field Is Far from Level," *Business Week*, June 8, 1992, pp. 74–83; and John Bound and George Johnson, "Changes in the Structure of Wages in the 1980s: An Evaluation of Alternative Explanations," *American Economic Review* 82 (June 1992): pp. 371–92.

· · · · · · · ·

Some Caveats

Like our discussion of the labor market, this section is meant to be only a brief introduction to marginal productivity theory of capital—Chapter 17 goes into more detail—but we still need to mention a couple of issues here before proceeding. First, when we drew the demand and supply curves for capital, we were implicitly stating that it was possible to buy capital goods in infinitesimal units. That is only rarely the case. Most often, capital goods are available only in "lumpy" units—you either buy a whole machine or you do not. This means, among other things, that changes in the demand for capital or interest rates may not always result in a change in the amount of capital that is actually purchased. A second problem is that new capital goods are often different from old capital goods. In fact, technological evolution may mean that it is impossible to buy capital goods like your old ones. The new ones may be technologically superior, but they may also be more expensive or require different kinds of labor inputs. Even cheap and highly productive capital goods may not be a good deal if you have to retrain the entire workforce. These and other problems with the marginal productivity theory of capital do not mean that we should reject the analysis entirely, only that we must use it cautiously.

RECAP   Marginal Productivity Theory of Capital

The acquisition of capital is complex and time-consuming, but firms follow the same kind of optimization rules as they do for any other factor of production.

1. The supply of financial capital depends on the supply of household savings. Households will save if the interest rate is above $r\star$, the rate necessary to cover risk and time preference. Firms must acquire financial capital before they can purchase capital goods.
2. In the short run, the stock of capital goods is fixed so the supply curve for capital goods is perfectly inelastic. The long-run supply curve for capital is perfectly elastic because financial capital is available if interest rates exceed $r\star$.
3. The return on capital is the ratio of the change in profits attributable to the new capital good to the cost of the capital good. Firms acquire capital goods as long as the return on new capital goods is equal to or greater than $r\star$.
4. If the return on capital is greater than $r\star$, the short-run capital supply curve will shift out and increase the capital stock; if the return on capital is less than $r\star$, the short-run capital supply curve will shift in and decrease the capital stock.

THE MARKET FOR LAND AND NATURAL RESOURCES

When economists use the term *land*, only rarely are they actually referring to the ground we walk on. Most often they are referring to undeveloped land or natural resources. The markets for undeveloped land and natural resources differ from the markets for labor and capital in an important way: they are in fixed supply. The analysis of both resources is similar, so we will use the term "land" when we are referring to either except where a distinction is necessary.

Goods that are in fixed supply are represented by vertical supply curves like the one shown in Figure 15.10. The vertical axis measures the amount of **economic rent** that landowners charge for use of their land. Economic rent is a factor payment over and above the payment necessary to bring that factor into production. Unde-

Economic rent A factor payment exceeding the payment necessary to bring that factor into production.

···· **Figure 15.10 The Price of Unimproved Land**

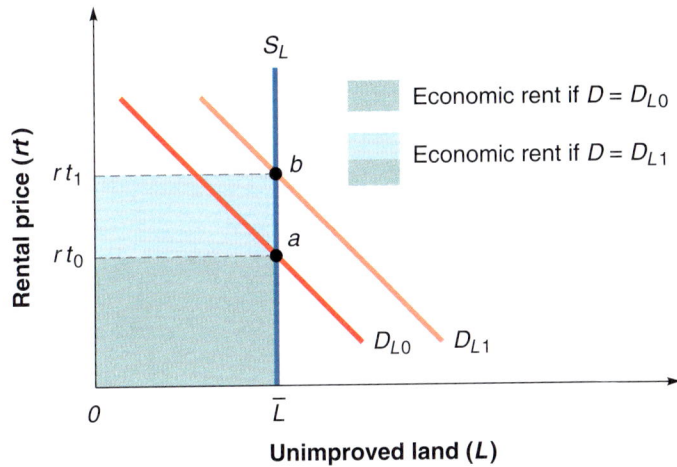

The supply of unimproved land (and natural resources) is fixed, so it can be represented by a vertical supply curve. The demand for land determines the rental price that can be charged. When demand is D_{L0}, the landowner receives economic rent equal to the green area. An increase in population will increase the demand for land and shift the demand curve out from D_{L0} to D_{L1}. This will cause the rental price to rise from rt_0 to rt_1. All of this rent is called economic rent because the same quantity of land, $\bar{L}$, would be available whether any rent was paid or not.

veloped land is there for the taking, so no payment is needed to use it—unless landowners charge for it. If there is no demand for land, the landowner receives no payment. As demand for land increases, the landowner can charge a higher price, even though the quantity of unimproved land has not changed.[8]

The earnings of the landowner depend strictly on the level of demand. This is shown in Figure 15.10 where the initial level of demand is D_{L0}. The demand curve intersects the fixed supply curve at point a and results in a rental price of rt_0. The landowner receives rent equal to the crosshatched area $0\bar{L}art_0$. If the population grows and the demand curve shifts out to D_{L1}, the rental price will rise to rt_1, and the landowner will gain the shaded area rt_0abrt_1. The key point is that the landowner did nothing to earn this extra income; the rent increased solely because of population growth. This was the basis for Henry George's proposal to tax landowner income. This proposal led to the *single tax movement* of the nineteenth century, which is discussed in the Economic Heritage box on page 380.

It is important to distinguish between improved and unimproved land. Land in its natural state is in fixed supply, so the payment to the landowner represents pure

---

[8]As we discovered in Chapter 12, the term "economic rent" is more general than this paragraph may seem to indicate. Economists say that a factor of production earns an economic rent whenever the factor payment is greater than the amount necessary to bring that factor into production. For example, celebrity movie stars earning millions of dollars per performance are earning economic rents if they would be willing to do the same work for a lower fee.

OUR ECONOMIC HERITAGE

HENRY GEORGE AND THE SINGLE TAX MOVEMENT

Is it right that landowners should earn economic rents even though they are not really contributing anything to society? Absolutely not! At least that was the opinion of the nineteenth-century American economist and politician Henry George (1839–1897). George felt that much of the inequality of the nineteenth century was due to the economic rents paid to landowners. He expressed his views in *Progress and Poverty* (1879), which argued that all government revenues could and should be raised from a single tax on land. George's basic argument was simple: social factors—primarily the population expansion to the American West—were the source of gains to landowners, so society should reap the benefits of those gains.

George was one of the most widely read American economists of his time, both in America and Europe. He was born in Philadelphia but spent most of his life in San Francisco as a newspaper writer. He dabbled in politics, and although he was never elected to office, he did make a strong run for mayor of New York. George's popularity probably stemmed from the simplicity of his ideas: landowners became rich not through hard work but through fortuitous events. This would not be so bad, thought George, except that the wealth of the landowners came at the expense of the public at large. Said George:

So long as all the increased wealth which modern progress brings but to build up great fortunes, to increase luxury and make sharper the contrast between the House of Have and the House of Want, progress is not real and cannot be permanent.

George has never enjoyed the popularity with economists that he did with the public. Most economists argued that rising land values were not the only fortuitous reason people became rich; there have always been passive investors who become rich investing in the stock market. To single out landowners is a bit capricious— and would have little effect on income distribution under any circumstances. Still, George must have hit something right: the perimeter of public land around Stockholm was established to deny landowners the unearned income from population growth, and a London Greenbelt serves much the same purpose. Various Henry George Institutes around the world are devoted to study of the single tax. Today, however, few conventional economists put much credence in George's ideas. If income distribution is a problem, most economists believe that it can be tackled with progressive income taxes and transfer programs.

Marginal productivity rent Rent on improved land; it depends on the productivity of the improvements and is determined by supply and demand.

economic rent. On the other hand, the supply of improved land is not fixed, and higher rents will induce the landowner to increase the quantity supplied of improved land. The rent on improved land depends on both supply and demand and is called **marginal productivity rent**, not economic rent.

Finally, even though economists use the term "land" to refer to both land and natural resources, at times it is necessary to make a distinction between the two. An example is the question of how much of a particular natural resource exists. Geologists tell us that there is a fixed amount of oil in the ground, but economists know that much of that oil is too expensive to extract. As the price of oil rises, however, the quantity of available oil will rise. For example, only after OPEC raised the price of oil to $30 per barrel did it make economic sense to search for oil in the Arctic and the Bering Sea. Consequently, the supply curve for many natural resources is only vertical at *very* high prices or when available technology allows all the resource to be extracted. Until that point, the supply curve for natural resources is upward sloping.

PROFITS AND THE ADDING UP PROBLEM

Are labor, land, and capital the only three factors of production? Certainly—if you define the categories broadly enough. For example, technology can be included in capital, and human skills—human capital—serve to distinguish between different classifications of labor. Still, economists do not agree on how to categorize the work of the manager or *entrepreneur*. Many economists recognize that there are different kinds of labor and simply lump management into labor. But others believe that entrepreneurial behavior is fundamentally different from other kinds of labor. Not only must entrepreneurs determine how to combine the factors of production in the most efficient manner, but they also take risks when they set up a new business. As payment, these risk-taking entrepreneurs receive profit—not a trivial concept if you believe that the quest for profit is the most important incentive in market economies.

Defining profit is not as easy as you might think. The simplest definition is probably the residual left over after all other costs of production have been paid. This definition corresponds to the formula we used in Chapter 11: Profit equals total revenue minus total costs. Unfortunately, when we actually try to measure profits in the real world, all sorts of complications arise. For example, suppose that total cost is $1 million and total revenue is $1.2 million. This means the firm has earned $200,000 in profits, right? Not necessarily. If the entrepreneur decides to plow that $200,000 back into the firm, profits—at least from the tax accountant's standpoint—go to zero because the "profit" has just become a production expense. Defining profit from a regulatory standpoint is even more difficult. Utility regulations often permit utility firms to make a "fair return on a fair valuation of capital." But just what is a "fair return"? If we knew that, many of the utility rate battles of the past would never have occurred. The point is that profit is a nebulous concept.

Marginal productivity theory treats profit as another factor payment, the reward to the entrepreneur. However, it is also considered a residual and calculated after the fact by appealing to an important theorem known as **Euler's theorem**. ("Euler" is pronounced "oiler.") The essential result of Euler's theorem is that factor payments must "add up" to exhaust the value of output. In other words, if output sells for $1 million, the payments to the factors of production must also be equal to $1 million. This will always be true because the payment to the entrepreneur is the residual left over after all other factors have been paid.

Euler's theorem Holds that factor payments will exhaust the selling price of output.

•••• FIGURE 15.11 THE ADDING UP PROBLEM

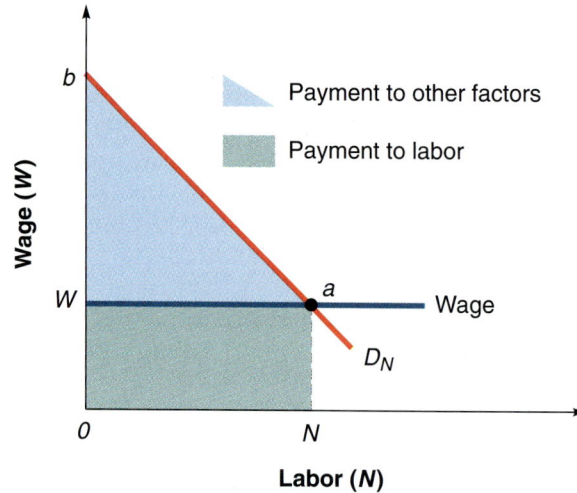

According to Euler's theorem, total factor payments exhaust the revenue earned from selling the product. In this diagram, the wage bill for labor is equal to the area $0NaW$. Labor contributes more to the production process only because it has capital and land to work with. The triangle Wab represents the contributions of other factors to the productivity of labor. This revenue is needed to pay the other factors of production.

We can see the importance of Euler's theorem by looking at Figure 15.11, which shows the market for labor. As usual, competitive firms hire workers until the marginal revenue product ($MRP = D_N$) of the last worker hired is equal to the wage rate. This means that the total payment is equal to the wage rate, W, times the number of workers hired, N. This is the area $0NaW$ in the diagram. Because of diminishing returns, however, labor's contribution to the production process is greater than $0NaW$. Only the last worker hired had a contribution equal to the wage rate; the marginal revenue product of all other workers was higher than the wage rate. Does this mean that those workers have been "exploited"?[9] No, at least not according to marginal productivity theory. Workers are productive only if they have land and capital to work with, so some of the workers' contribution must be set aside to pay for the other factors of production. The triangle Wab represents that payment. The same arguments apply to the other factors of production. According to Euler's theorem, the area in the triangle Wab is exactly equal to the contribution of all factors of production except labor.

What makes this result interesting (or questionable, depending upon your point of view) is that whatever payment is left for the entrepreneur after paying wages,

[9]As we will find out in Chapter 34, one of the early socialist arguments was that workers were exploited by the capitalists. Some analysts believe that marginal productivity theory was developed in part to refute these arguments.

interest, and marginal productivity rents is assumed to be a payment for risk taking, efficient management, and so on. Thus, an entrepreneur who makes $100,000 "deserves" $100,000 because of efficient management; an entrepreneur who loses $100,000 "deserves" to lose $100,000 because of ineptitude. As we will see in the next chapter, not everyone agrees with this view.

SUMMARY

Not all economists believe that marginal productivity theory is the best or even a reasonable first approximation for explaining factor prices. The demand and supply of labor may depend on social factors as much as or more than economic calculations. Do you always consider work a "bad"? Or do you make friends and define your self-worth on the job? If so, the basis for the labor supply curve—the tradeoff between work and leisure—must be called into question. The market for capital has just as many problems. When a decision that you make today has such long-term consequences, hunches and guesses may enter the calculations alongside your risk and return computations. Still, most economists believe that marginal productivity theory is a good starting place for understanding factor prices and income distribution. It is also pretty straightforward, as long as you remember how to apply supply and demand analysis.

The main topics covered in this chapter were:

1. The demand for factors of production is derived from factor productivity and the demand for final output. The factor demand curve is the marginal revenue product curve.

2. The labor supply curve depends on a tradeoff between work and leisure. It is generally upward sloping because higher wages increase the opportunity cost of leisure. Under rare circumstances, it may be backward bending. The equilibrium wage rate occurs where the labor supply curve crosses the marginal revenue product curve.

3. In the short run, the stock of capital is fixed; in the long run, the stock of capital is perfectly elastic. The capital stock will grow if the rate of return on capital is greater than $r^\star$, the interest rate high enough to induce household saving. The capital stock will shrink when the rate of return is less than $r^\star$ because saving will contract.

4. When factors of production are in fixed supply, they command economic rents. This may be the case with undeveloped land: landowners receive higher rents if the demand for unimproved land increases even though the supply of unimproved land is fixed.

5. Profit is the residual that is paid to the entrepreneur after all factors of production have received their payments. According to marginal productivity theory, profit is the reward entrepreneurs receive for taking risks. Total income is completely exhausted by total factor payments.

KEY TERMS AND CONCEPTS

derived demand
marginal physical product
marginal revenue product
profit maximization
optimal factor inputs
net marginal revenue product
equilibrium wage rate
voluntary unemployment
compensating differentials
human capital
labor mobility
discrimination
women's jobs
comparable worth

marginal factor cost
time preference
capital stock
short-run supply of capital
long-run supply of capital
economic rent
single tax movement
marginal productivity rent
entrepreneur
profit
residual
Euler's theorem
adding up problem

REVIEW QUESTIONS

1. Why is the demand for the factors of production called derived demand?
2. Why is the *MRP* curve downward sloping? What factors cause it to shift? Answer with respect to the *MRP* for each of the factors of production.
3. Explain the rationale behind the optimal input rule; that is, that firms should hire factors until $MRP = MFC$. Draw a diagram to illustrate your answer.
4. Under what conditions is the labor supply curve upward sloping? When is it backward bending? What factors cause the labor supply curve to shift?
5. How can marginal productivity theory be used to explain wage differentials? Give specific examples.
6. What conditions must hold for the capital market to be in equilibrium? What will happen if the return on capital is less than the rate necessary to overcome risk and time preference? Draw a diagram to illustrate your result.
7. Carefully distinguish between marginal productivity rent and economic rent. When does land command economic rent? Marginal productivity rent? Draw a diagram to illustrate your answer.
8. Do entrepreneurs "deserve" the money they make? Answer according to marginal productivity theory.

PROBLEMS

1. *Ceteris paribus*, which of the following would tend to cause the wage rate to increase? Draw diagrams to explain your answers.
   a. an increase in the labor force participation rate
   b. technological advance
   c. higher selling prices for output
   d. additional education
   e. an increase in the work effort

2. What would it mean if the labor demand curve were vertical? If it were horizontal? Do you think either of these cases could apply to the real world?

3. When we constructed the *MRP* curve in the chapter, we assumed that the selling price in the output market was fixed. This means that the output market must be one of pure competition. Suppose that the output market is monopolistically competitive. How would this affect the marginal revenue product curve? (*Hint:* After you think about this question, you might peek ahead into the next chapter.)

4. In the 1970s, the U.S. steel industry contracted severely; workers were laid off and factories were closed. Can you illustrate and explain this using supply and demand for capital and labor diagrams?

5. The assumption behind the labor supply curve is that people trade off work and leisure. Work is assumed to be a "bad" but necessary for earning income while leisure is assumed to be a "good." What if people actually enjoy work? In other words, what if work is a "good"? How would this affect the shape of the labor supply curve?

6. Suppose that the marginal revenue product of capital is greater than $r^\star$, the interest rate necessary to induce saving. Instead of buying more capital, however, the firm hires more labor. Would this tend to increase or decrease profits? Why?

7. Economic rents can be earned on all factors of production, not just unimproved land. Explain whether and why each of the following may command economic rent:
   a. a Beatles reunion concert
   b. Harvard University
   c. a burger flipper at McDonald's
   d. your college economics professor
   e. your high school history teacher

8. Suppose you bought 100 acres of farmland, installed an irrigation system, and built a farmhouse. You then rented the property for $5,000 per month. Five years later you have made no improvements on the land, but you raise the rent to $7,000 per month. Does the rent increase represent pure economic rent? Why or why not?

9. Indicate whether the following is true or false and explain your answer. Higher labor force participation rates by women have lowered the wage rates for men.

10. Using diagrams, illustrate:
   a. why offshore oil workers have higher wages than onshore oil workers.
   b. how human capital raises a worker's wage.
   c. why Alaskan workers have higher wages than workers in the lower 48 states.
   d. why discrimination raises the wage rate for workers who are not discriminated against.

CHAPTER 16

Labor Markets under Imperfect Competition

Marginal productivity theory is a widely accepted tool for long-run analysis, but few economists would use it to explain day-to-day and short-run movements in wages and employment. Too many cultural and noneconomic factors influence what we are paid and where we work.

FOR EXAMPLE:

• • • In markets dominated by unions or monopolies, wages and employment can depend on power and the collective bargaining process as much as on marginal productivity. We can analyze some of these situations with modifications of the basic marginal productivity model, but other situations are better suited to analysis with game theory or other methods.

• • • In many job markets, college graduates typically have a better chance of being hired than do high school graduates, even though the job does not require college skills. This is hard to explain with marginal productivity theory: Why would any employers hire an overqualified individual and pay a premium wage if they do not have to?

• • • The unemployment rate is typically higher for low-skilled workers than high-skilled workers. According to marginal productivity theory, this should not happen: as long as low-skilled workers do not ask for wages higher than their productivity, they should be able to find a job. How can we explain this empirical fact?

This chapter will explore these and other phenomena first by extending marginal productivity theory and then by looking at alternative theories of the labor market. Our first task is to modify marginal productivity theory to account for noncompetitive conditions in both the input and the output markets. We then survey the role and impact of labor unions. Finally, we will look at different theories of the labor market that offer alternative explanations for wages and employment in modern economies.

AFTER READING AND STUDYING THIS CHAPTER, YOU SHOULD BE ABLE TO:

• • • Explain how monopoly in the output market and monopsony in the input market affect employment and wages

• • • Discuss the strategies and effects of unions and trace their evolution in the American economy

• • • Outline alternative theories of the labor market, and compare them to marginal productivity theory

MARGINAL PRODUCTIVITY THEORY OF NONCOMPETITIVE LABOR MARKETS

You may remember that we made two assumptions when we developed the theory of the labor market in the last chapter. First, we assumed that there was pure competition in the output market and that firms could sell as much as they desired at a fixed market price. This is only rarely the case in the real world. In markets with less than pure competition in the output market, firms must lower the selling price in order to sell more. This has an important effect on the demand for labor. As we are about to discover, the need to reduce selling prices in order to increase sales gives the marginal revenue product curve a steeper slope than it would have otherwise. The second assumption we made in Chapter 15 related to competition in the input market. There we assumed that there were many employers and workers in the labor market. This is often the case, but not always. Labor markets with only one employer differ considerably from markets with many employers. In general, when there is less than pure competition in the input market, both the wage rate and the level of employment will be lower than when there is competition.

The Labor Market with Monopoly in the Output Market

As we learned in Chapter 12, monopoly firms must lower their selling prices in order to increase sales. This means that as additional workers are hired, the marginal revenue product of labor declines for two reasons: (1) each additional worker produces less output than the previous worker because production always takes place in Stage II of the production function, and (2) the revenue from each additional unit sold is less than the revenue from the previous unit because the selling price must be reduced as additional output is placed on the market.

Table 16.1 provides an example to show how a declining selling price affects the demand curve for labor. The first three columns are repeated from Table 15.1. Column 4 shows the average physical product (*APP*). Average physical product is the same thing we called average product in Chapter 9. It is found by dividing total product by the number of labor inputs. Column 5 shows the selling price of output (*P*). In this example, a price of $5.50 will result in 150 units of sales, and price must

TABLE 16.1 MONOPOLY AND MARGINAL REVENUE PRODUCT

(1) N	(2) Q	(3) MPP	(4) APP	(5) P	(6) TR	(7) MR	(8) MRP	(9) ARP
3	150		50.00	$5.50	$ 825			$275.00
		→ 50		5.25		→ $3.50	$175	
4	200		50.00	5.00	1,000			250.00
		→ 40		4.75		→ 2.00	80	
5	240		48.00	4.50	1,080			216.00
		→ 30		4.25		→ 0	0	
6	270		45.00	4.00	1,080			180.00
		→ 20		3.75		→ −3.25	−65	
7	290		41.43	3.50	1,015			145.00
		→ 10		3.25		→ −11.50	−115	
8	300		37.50	3.00	900			112.50

Definitions and Formulas:

N = input

MPP = marginal physical product = $\dfrac{\Delta Q}{\Delta N}$

TR = total revenue = PQ

MRP = marginal revenue product = $\dfrac{\Delta TR}{\Delta N}$ = $MR(MPP)$

Q = total product

P = selling price

MR = marginal revenue = $\dfrac{\Delta TR}{\Delta Q}$

ARP = average revenue product = $\dfrac{TR}{N}$ = $P(APP)$

be lowered to $3.00 in order to sell 300 units of output. Columns 6 and 7 show total revenue (*TR*) and marginal revenue (*MR*).

Column 8 shows marginal revenue product (*MRP*), the additional revenue associated with hiring additional workers. Marginal revenue product can be found in two ways: by dividing the change in total revenue by the change in the number of workers, or by multiplying marginal revenue by the marginal physical product of the next worker:

$$\text{Marginal revenue product} = MRP = \frac{\Delta TR}{\Delta N} = MR(MPP) \qquad [1]$$

Notice that the last term in Equation 1 differs slightly from the formula for marginal revenue product we used in the last chapter. There we were able to find marginal revenue product by multiplying the marginal physical product by the selling price. Why the change? When there is pure competition in the output market, price and marginal revenue are equivalent and assumed constant. When there is less than pure competition in the output market, price must be lowered in order to sell more, so price does not equal marginal revenue. The key is that the firm must lower the selling price of *all* goods sold, not just the additional units, so marginal revenue product falls faster than price.

Figure 16.1 plots both the marginal revenue product information from Table 16.1 and the marginal revenue product curve from Chapter 15 when selling price was

···· **FIGURE 16.1 MARGINAL REVENUE PRODUCT IS STEEPER**
IF PRICE FALLS AS SALES INCREASE

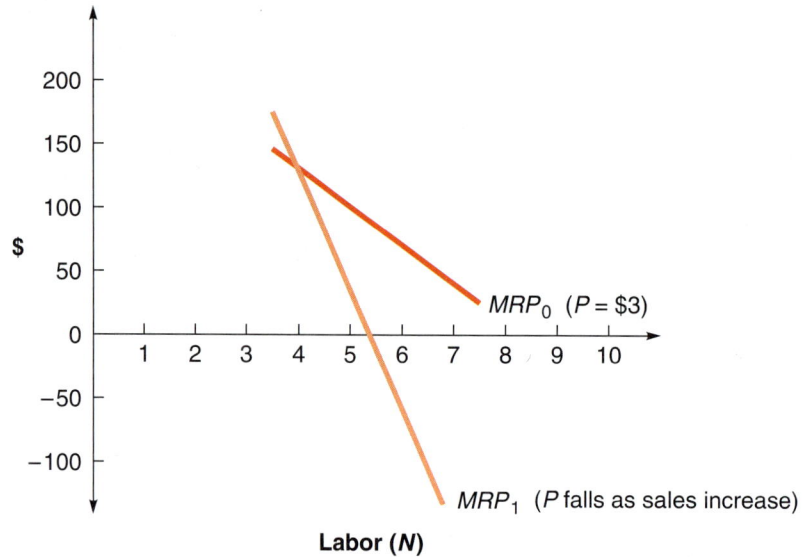

The marginal revenue product curve under monopoly (MRP_1) is steeper than the marginal revenue product curve under pure competition (MRP_0). As additional workers are hired, the selling price must be lowered so the revenue from hiring additional workers declines for two reasons—diminishing marginal product and lower selling price.

assumed fixed at $3. Notice that lowering the selling price causes the resulting marginal revenue product curve, MRP_1, to be steeper than if the selling price is fixed as it is assumed to be along MRP_0.

The ninth column in Table 16.1 shows the **average revenue product (ARP)**. The average revenue product of labor is found by either dividing total revenue by the number of workers or by multiplying average physical product by selling price:

Average revenue product (ARP)
Total revenue divided by the number of workers, or average physical product times selling price.

$$\text{Average revenue product} = ARP = \frac{TR}{N} = P(APP) \qquad [2]$$

As shown in Figure 16.2, average revenue product is always greater than marginal revenue product. It is not hard to understand why: the next worker always contributes less to total revenue than the previous worker. Look what happens when a fourth worker is added in Table 16.1: the total revenue of the first three workers is $825, so the average revenue product of the first three workers is $825/3 = $275. The marginal revenue product of the fourth worker is only $175, so the total revenue of four workers is $1,000 (= $825 + $175) and the average revenue product is $250 (= $1,000/4). Our conclusion: marginal revenue product falls faster than average revenue product.

Once the firm has computed marginal revenue product, it uses this information to determine the profit-maximizing number of workers to hire. As always, the firm

· · · · · **FIGURE 16.2** AVERAGE AND MARGINAL REVENUE PRODUCT
UNDER MONOPOLY

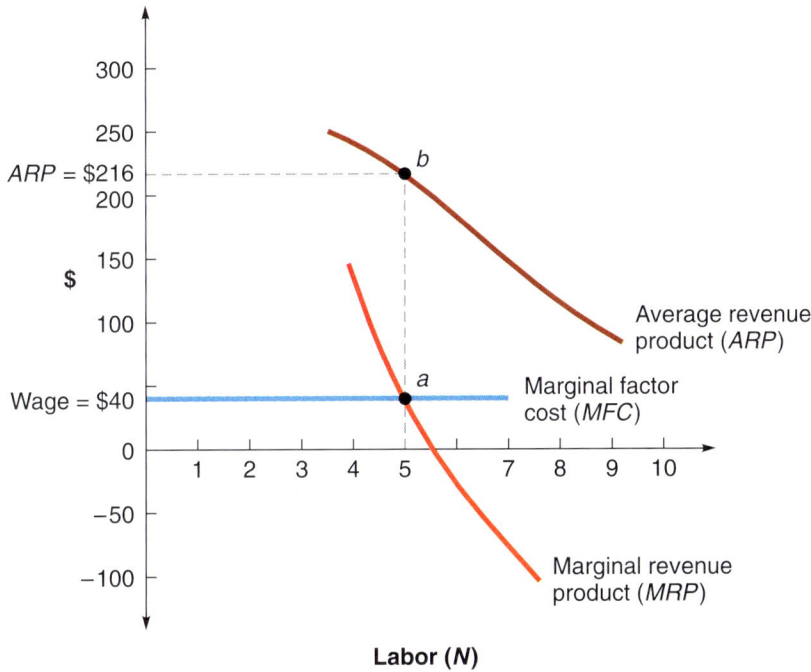

When firms operate in less than perfectly competitive output markets, the marginal revenue product curve (*MRP*) slopes down for two reasons: diminishing returns and lower selling prices as additional output is sold. The marginal revenue product curve slopes down faster than the average revenue product curve (*ARP*) because the contribution to revenue from the next worker is less than from the last worker.

Firms maximize profits by hiring workers until the marginal revenue product of labor is equal to the marginal factor cost of the last worker hired. This occurs at point *a*, the intersection of the *MRP* and marginal factor cost (*MFC*) lines. The average revenue product of labor is greater than the marginal revenue product of labor (point *b*); some people say that this constitutes labor exploitation.

should hire workers until the marginal revenue product of the last worker hired is equal to the marginal factor cost (*MFC*) of hiring that worker. If the firm can hire as many workers as needed at a given wage, say, $40 per day,[1] then the profit-maximizing number of workers would be 5. This is shown in Figure 16.2.

Notice that the average revenue product (= $216) is greater than the marginal revenue product and wage rate (= $40) when the firm is hiring the optimal number of workers. This means that the typical worker is producing output with a value

[1]The wage rate $40 is the midpoint between $80 and $0 in Column 8 of Table 16.1; $80 is the *MRP* of between 4 and 5 workers, and $0 is the *MRP* between 5 and 6 workers. The *MRP* of the fifth worker will be exactly $40 only if the *MRP* curve is linear. It is not, so this value must be taken as an approximation.

greater than the wage rate. Does this mean that workers are being treated unfairly or "exploited"? Not necessarily—and this is certainly not the kind of exploitation that Marxist economists talked about in the nineteenth century.[2] Without government or other nonmarket intervention, the firm has no reason to pay a higher wage or employ more workers. Paying the workers $216 would make wages equal to average revenue product, but the firm has no reason to do this because we have assumed that there are enough workers willing and able to work at the going wage of $40 per day. If a sixth worker were hired, average revenue product would be closer to the wage rate, but this would not be the profit-maximizing level of employment because the contribution of the last worker to total revenue would be less than the cost of hiring that worker; that is, $MRP < MFC$. No firm would employ that sixth worker, at least not without some kind of coercion.

Finally, we should note that the level of employment is lower when there is monopoly rather than pure competition in the output market. Under pure competition, the selling price does not fall as additional goods are put on the market, so the marginal revenue product curve would be less steep than the one pictured in Figure 16.2. Given the same wage rate and horizontal MFC curve, the MRP and MFC curves would intersect at a higher level of employment.

. . . .

Imperfect Competition in the Input Market: Monopsony

Monopsony A market in which there is only one buyer.

A mono*poly* is a market characterized by one seller; a mono*psony* is a market with only one buyer.[3] While **monopsonies** are not very common in the United States today, several examples do come to mind. For example, the Defense Department is the only buyer of certain top-secret military goods, and the Forest Service is the only buyer of tools specially designed for fighting forest fires. When there is only buyer, the bargaining process between buyer and seller changes considerably. In the case of the Defense Department or Forest Service, bargaining entails contract bidding between different potential sellers. Once the contract is awarded, the process is complete—assuming, of course, that (seemingly inevitable) cost overruns do not exceed those allowed for in the contract.

When only one firm is hiring labor, the situation is also complex. Consider a town with only one employer, a so-called company town.[4] Unless there is massive unemployment—so much that people are willing to work at almost any wage—the monopsonist can hire additional workers only by offering a higher wage. This is a simple consequence of our assumption that the labor market supply curve is upward sloping. But the upward slope of the labor market supply curve does not mean that the employer can hire some workers at low wages and raise the wage rate only for the

---

[2]We discuss Marx and his concept of labor exploitation in more detail in Chapter 34.
[3]Likewise, an oligo*poly* is a market with a few sellers, and an oligop*sony* is a market with just a few buyers. The results we develop for monopsonies can be easily extended to most oligopsonies.
[4]There are few true company towns in the United States today, but several have existed in the past. Many of these towns sprang up in the Old West to support huge ranches; Kingsville, Texas, home of the largest ranch in the world, the King Ranch, was once a reasonable example of a company town. Bartlesville, Oklahoma, home of Phillips Petroleum, also had many of the attributes of a company town in the early twentieth century; the same could be said of coal mining towns in Appalachia in the same era. Many college towns represent good examples as well.

additional workers that it hires. The monopsonist employer must offer a higher wage to *all* workers if it wants to hire more workers; rarely is it possible to "wage-discriminate" by paying low wages to the first few workers hired and increasing wage offers only to attract additional workers. As a consequence of having to raise the wage of all workers to attract additional workers, the marginal factor cost of additional workers is higher than the wage rate or the **average factor cost (AFC)** of all workers. Average factor cost is defined as total factor cost divided by the number of units of a factor that are employed. In this case, the total factor cost of labor is the wage bill—the number of workers times their wage. Dividing the wage bill by the number of workers gives the average factor cost.

Table 16.2 and the accompanying Figure 16.3 illustrate the divergence between marginal factor cost and average factor cost under monopsony. Column 1 shows the number of workers (N) that are hired. Column 2 shows the wage rate (W) paid to all workers. The wage rate is also equal to the average factor cost (AFC). Column 3 shows the wage bill to the firm. It is found by multiplying the number of workers in Column 1 by the wage rate in Column 2. Column 4 presents the marginal factor cost (MFC). The **marginal factor cost** is the increase in factor costs incurred from employing an additional unit of a factor of production. In the case of labor, the marginal factor cost is the change in the wage bill caused by hiring one more worker. The key is that the monopsonist must raise the wage of all workers when any new workers are hired, so the wage bill increases by more than the wage rate. The formula for the marginal factor cost of labor is:

$$\text{Marginal factor cost} = MFC = \frac{\Delta\text{wage bill}}{\Delta N} \qquad [3]$$

Average factor cost (AFC) Total factor cost divided by the number of units of a factor employed.

Marginal factor cost (MFC) The increase in factor costs incurred from employing an additional unit of a factor of production.

•••• **TABLE 16.2 MONOPSONY IN THE INPUT MARKET**

(1) N	(2) AFC = W	(3) Wage Bill	(4) MFC
0	—	$ 0	
			→ $ 5
1	$5	5	
			→ 7
2	6	12	
			→ 9
3	7	21	
			→ 11
4	8	32	
			→ 13
5	9	45	

Definitions and Formulas:

N = labor inputs AFC = average factor cost = wage

Wage bill = $W(N)$ MFC = marginal factor cost = $\dfrac{\Delta\text{wage bill}}{\Delta N}$

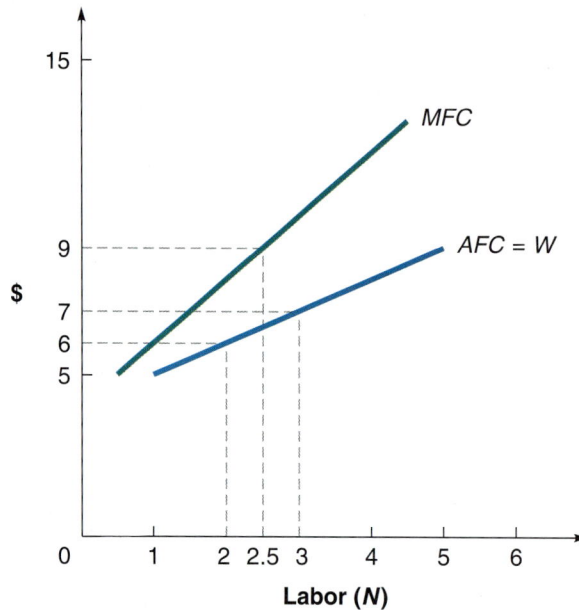

•••• **FIGURE 16.3** FACTOR COSTS UNDER MONOPSONY

Under monopsony, the employer must raise the wage rate for all workers in order to attract additional workers. As a result, the marginal factor cost rises faster than the wage rate or average factor cost. Based on the information in Table 16.2, the firm can attract two workers at a wage rate of $6, but to attract a third worker, it will have to raise the wage to $7. Under most circumstances, the firm will have to raise the wage rate of all workers to $7; thus, the marginal cost of hiring the third worker is $7 plus the $1 wage increase given to the first two workers or $9. This $9 figure is between $N = 2$ and $N = 3$ because marginal factor cost represents the change in cost that occurs when the monopsonist expands the labor force from two to three workers.

••••••••

Wage Determination under Monopsony

Other things being equal, firms will pay lower wages and hire fewer workers under monopsony than under pure competition. This is shown in Figure 16.4 where there is monopsony in the input market and pure competition in the output market. When there is pure competition in the output market, firms can sell as much output as they wish at the going market price so the labor demand curve ($=MRP$) slopes down for only one reason—diminishing marginal product. To maximize profits, the firm hires N_{mc}, the number of workers such that marginal revenue product equals marginal factor cost. (The subscript m indicates monopsony in the input market; the subscript c indicates competition in the output market.) This occurs at point a on Figure 16.4. The wage rate W_{mc}, is then read from the average factor cost curve directly below at point b. The average factor cost curve gives the various amounts of workers that will be available at different wage rates, so it is really just the labor supply curve for the industry. The labor supply curve facing the monopsonist is the labor supply curve

···· **FIGURE 16.4 WAGES AND EMPLOYMENT UNDER MONOPSONY**

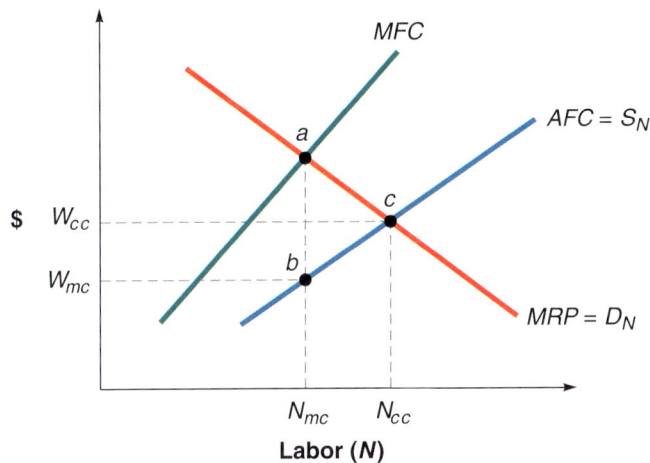

When the input market is characterized by monopsony (one buyer), and the firm raises its wage offer to attract additional workers, it will typically have to raise the wage for all workers. As a result, the marginal factor cost of labor (*MFC*) curve rises faster than the average factor cost (*AFC*) curve. To maximize profits, the firm hires the number of workers, N_{mc}, such that marginal revenue product equals marginal factor cost, point *a*. The wage rate, W_{mc}, is then read off the average factor cost curve, point *b*. The average factor cost curve is also the labor supply curve because it gives the number of workers that would be willing to work at various wage rates.

Other things being equal, both employment and wages are lower under monopsony than under pure competition. If there is competition in both the input and the output markets, new firms can attract workers by paying the going wage and do not have to raise the wage rate of existing workers. If *all* firms want to attract additional workers, however, the wage rate will have to increase. Under these conditions, the upward-sloping *AFC* curve is also the industry labor supply curve. Employment will be at N_{cc}, and the wage rate will be W_{cc}, point *c*.

for the entire industry because a monopsonist is the only employer in a particular labor market.

Figure 16.4 can also be used to show the wage rate and level of employment when there is competition in both markets. We know from the last chapter that a single firm in a purely competitive industry is able to hire additional workers without raising the wage rate, so the marginal factor cost of hiring one more worker is equal to the average factor cost, the wage rate. This means that the average factor cost curve is equivalent to the marginal factor cost curve under pure competition. If *all* firms in a competitive industry tried to hire more workers, however, the wage rate would have to rise to induce more people to enter the labor market. Consequently, the market labor supply curve is upward sloping, even under pure competition. In terms of the figure, this means that the $AFC = S_N$ curve is also the *MFC* curve for a competitive industry and profits are maximized by hiring N_{cc} and paying the wage rate W_{cc}. The general result: Both employment and wages are higher under pure competition than under monopsony.

· · · · · · · ·

Imperfect Competition in Both Markets: Monopsony and Monopoly

What happens when there is monopsony in the input market and monopoly in the output market? In general, both the wage rate and employment will be lower than if there were competition in either or both markets. A diagram of a monopoly/monopsony market would be similar to Figure 16.4, although the MRP curve would be somewhat steeper to indicate that the monopoly firm must lower its selling price to sell additional output.

RECAP   **Wages and Employment under Different Market Structures**

We have just shown how wages and employment are determined under monopsony in the input market and monopoly in the output market. The accompanying diagram summarizes these results and contrasts the outcomes under four situations: competition in both markets (point a), competition in the input market but monopoly in the output market (point b), monopsony in the input market but competition in the output market (point c), and monopoly in the output market with monopsony in the input market (point d). Notice that this diagram is just illustrative; it would be impossible to have all four markets on one graph!

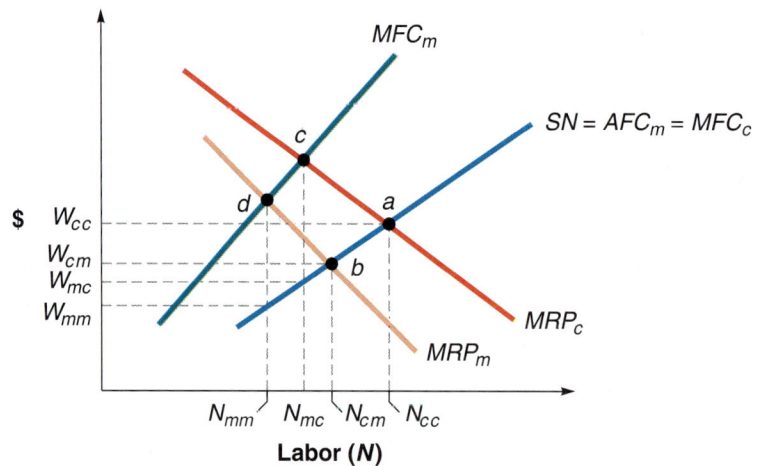

- Point a: Competition in both the input and the output markets. Marginal revenue product declines only because of diminishing marginal physical product (MRP_c), and firms raise wages only to attract new workers (MFC_c).

- Point b: Competition in the input market, monopoly in the output market. Marginal revenue product (MRP_m) declines faster because the firm must lower the selling price to sell additional units of output.

- Point c: Monopsony in the input market, competition in the output market. Marginal factor cost (MFC_m) rises faster than the wage rate (= average factor cost) because the single firm must raise the wage of current as well as new workers to attract more job applicants.

- Point *d*: Monopoly in the output market, monopsony in the input market.
- *Note*: Whether W_{cm} is greater or less then W_{mc} depends on the slope of the monopolist's marginal revenue product curve relative to the monopsonist's marginal factor cost curve. If the marginal revenue product curve is steep relative to the marginal factor cost curve, then $W_{mc} > W_{cm}$; if the marginal factor cost curve is steep relative to the marginal revenue product curve, then $W_{mc} < W_{cm}$.

LABOR UNIONS

You do not have to take this class to know what labor unions want: they want higher wages, better working conditions, job security, and expanded benefits. Unions have also pressed for grievance procedures, quality control, and better arbitration rules. You may also know that unions have had a long and checkered history in the United States. The first attempts at unionization came in the nineteenth century but were largely unsuccessful. The union movement strengthened through the 1930s and 1940s, and in 1955, the most powerful and important federation of unions, the **AFL/CIO**, was established as a merger between the powerful American Federation of Labor and the Congress of Industrial Organizations. Nearly 85 percent of all union members today are affiliated with the AFL/CIO. Throughout much of this history, unions and management have been at odds—a rather peculiarly American phenomenon given that union-management cooperation has been the norm rather than the exception in most Western democracies. Some key events in the history of organized labor in the United States are discussed in the Focus box on page 406.

AFL/CIO Umbrella organization for most organized labor in the United States.

Some government and service workers have begun to unionize in recent years, but unions are most prominent in concentrated oligopolistic industries for at least three reasons. First, industrial concentration makes it easier for union leaders to bargain with management; union representatives would have difficulty negotiating with the thousands of managers in a competitive industry. Second, concentrated industries have the potential for labor exploitation—as we just discovered when we examined the labor market when there is monopoly in the output market. Finally, as we found out in Chapters 12 and 13, industrial concentration can lead to economic profits. These profits are a target of unions, which want a larger share of the economic pie.

What effects do unions have on the economy? That depends upon whom and what you ask, but at least three issues need to be addressed. One issue is the union/nonunion wage differential. Some studies show that union wages are about 10 to 15 percent higher than nonunion wages, but this differential can vary significantly. Unionized hotel workers receive only a tiny bit more than nonunion hotel workers; unionized construction workers earn 30 percent more than nonunionized construction workers. A second issue is whether union gains come at the expense of shareholders or other workers. This is a tougher question, but few economists believe that unions are able to redistribute income from capital to labor. In other words, most union gains seem to come at the expense of nonunion, low-wage, low-skilled workers. Finally, with union membership at its lowest in over 50 years—just 16 percent of the workforce was unionized in 1990—should we even bother to study unions at all? The answer to this question is an unequivocal yes. Union wages often influence nonunion wages, and some of our most important industries are heavily unionized. It is possible too that we are entering a new "pro-union" phase in the United States. After American Airlines flight attendants had been on strike for just five days, President Bill Clinton intervened on November 22, 1993, and appointed an arbitrator to bring the two parties together. Many observers interpreted this as a pro-union move.[5]

Union Wages and Employment

In the past the main goal of unions was often higher wages. Excessive union wage demands can result in declining union employment, but not necessarily. To see this, look at Figure 16.5, which illustrates a competitive labor market. Suppose that initially the labor market is in equilibrium and that the wage rate is $10 per hour. If the union demands and receives a higher wage rate, $12, the number of workers demanded will decline from 60 to 40. At the same time, the higher union wages will attract more job applicants, 80 instead of the previous 60. In other words, the higher union wage will lead to unemployment, much as a minimum wage will. What will happen to the unemployed workers? They may just wait around hoping to get one of those

· · · · FIGURE 16.5 UNION WAGES AND EMPLOYMENT

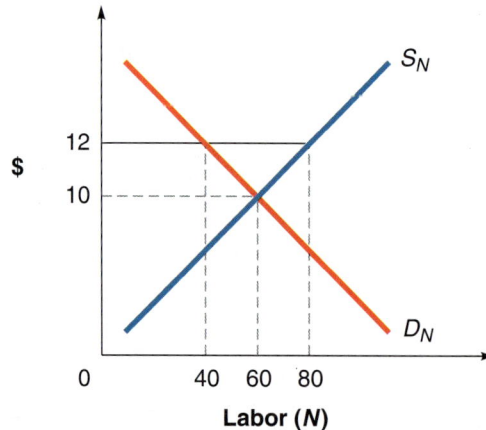

When unions demand higher wages, they are risking unemployment. If the market wage is $10 and unions demand and receive a wage increase to $12, the consequences will be a reduction in the number of workers demanded by the firm to 40 and a simultaneous increase in the number of people seeking union employment to 80.

[5]The flight attendants threatened an 11-day strike during the busy Thanksgiving holiday travel season. Had the strike lasted that long, American Airlines would have lost an estimated $200 million. Why Clinton intervened may never be known, but at the time, some people suggested he had made this very public pro-labor stance to appease labor for the recently passed North American Free Trade Agreement. See Wendy Zeller, Mike McNamee, and Seth Payne, "Did Clinton Scramble American's Profit Picture?" *Business Week*, December 6, 1993, p. 44.

high-paying union jobs, or perhaps they will get discouraged and look for a lower-paying job outside the union sector. In the meantime, the unemployed workers will exert downward pressure on wages. This explains why unions have often combined wage demands with restrictions on entry into the labor market.

The only problem with Figure 16.5 is that unions are most likely to be present in concentrated industries, not competitive industries, and it is not clear that union wage demands will always lead to layoffs in concentrated industries. This is shown in Figure 16.6, which is drawn to illustrate the effects of union wage demands in an industry characterized by concentration in both the input and the output markets. As always, we know that the firm will maximize profits by hiring the number of workers such that the marginal revenue product of the last worker hired is just equal to the marginal factor cost of hiring that worker. This occurs at point a where 75 workers are hired at a wage rate of $16 per hour. Now suppose that the union demands and receives a wage rate of $20. The monopolist could hire as many as 85 workers and still make profits because this point ($W = \$20$, $N = 85$) is on the firm's labor demand curve. In other words, union wage demands do not *necessarily* lead to layoffs in concentrated industries. Of course, if wages went above $20, the firm would have to lay off workers—and any wage above $16 would cut into the firm's profits and could lead to less expansion in the future. In this sense, union wage demands could lead to layoffs and unemployment even in a concentrated industry.

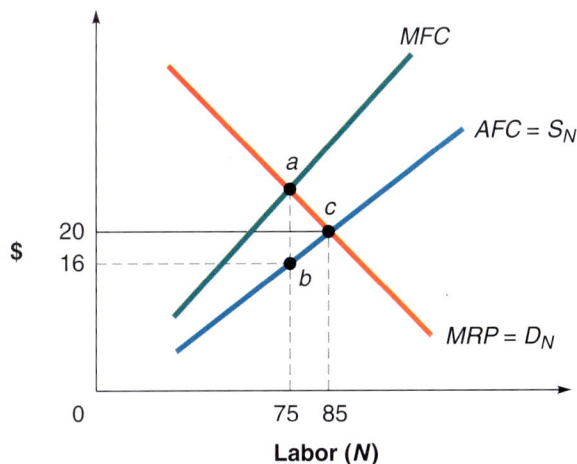

FIGURE 16.6 UNION WAGE DEMANDS IN CONCENTRATED INDUSTRIES

The profit-maximizing level of employment is found by equating marginal factor cost to marginal revenue product. This occurs at point a, and the monopoly firm hires 75 workers and pays a wage rate of $16 per hour. A union wage demand as high as $20 would not necessarily lead to union layoffs because point c with 85 workers and a wage rate of $20 is on the firm's labor demand curve. Such a wage increase would represent a transfer of income from the firm to the workers and a decline in the firm's profits.

The analysis in Figures 16.5 and 16.6 indicates that union wage demands are less likely to lead to layoffs in concentrated industries than in competitive industries. Unions are rare in competitive industries, but it would be a mistake to conclude that union wage demands never lead to layoffs. Just because a firm in a concentrated industry *can* make economic profits does not mean that it necessarily *does* so, and if the firm is not making economic profits, wage increases may necessitate price increases that will reduce sales and lead to layoffs. Productivity growth also affects the relationship between wage demands and employment. Most wage bargains struck in the real world are related to productivity growth. Only when output per worker increases less than the wage rate do wage demands necessarily lead to higher prices and the potential for job losses. For example, a 5 percent wage increase coupled with a labor productivity increase of 7 percent would result in lower production costs, lower selling prices, increased sales—and higher employment.

Finally, the timing and dynamic nature of labor contracts are often important in determining whether union wages affect employment levels. In the United States, some contracts are written for as long as three years and often contain various kinds of **cost of living** or **COLA clauses**. These clauses call for automatic wage adjustments equal to a fraction of the inflation rate. For example, if inflation is 10 percent, wages might increase 8 percent without additional negotiation between labor and management. Workers like COLA clauses because they reduce the erosion of real wages by inflation, but policymakers do not because the clauses make inflation especially difficult to eliminate. If wages automatically rise when inflation accelerates, the connection between wages and productivity disappears, and inflation can develop a momentum of its own. This is especially true when the economy is hit by external supply shocks—increases in the price of imported oil, agricultural prices, or similar events. The susceptibility of the economy to external supply shocks is one reason why COLA clauses are illegal in many countries, including Germany and Japan. The Focus box on page 408 examines union behavior in these and other nations. Many U.S. unions traded COLA clauses for job security assurances in the low-inflation years of the 1980s.

COLA (cost of living) clause A clause in union contracts that indexes wages to inflation.

· · · · · · · ·

Union Strategies to Increase the Demand for Labor

Higher wages have not been the unions' only demand. In the 1930s and 1940s, unions often negotiated contracts that artificially increased the demand for union workers, a practice known as **featherbedding**. For example, when diesel locomotives replaced steam locomotives, union contracts called for the railroads to continue to employ workers who had previously loaded coal into the steam engines, even though loading coal was no longer necessary. When recorded music began to replace live music on radio shows, some musicians' unions were able to get contracts that required radio stations to hire musicians even though the stations played only recorded music. Perhaps the most extreme example of featherbedding today concerns the dock workers of New York. Since 1966, senior dock workers have received a guaranteed income whether they work or not. Some senior dock workers simply punch the clock and go home—all to the tune of some $35,000 per year.

Featherbedding A labor union tactic designed to increase the demand for union labor by requiring management to use more workers than are needed for production.

Featherbedding as extreme as the cases just mentioned is uncommon, but unions do frequently try to negotiate measures to increase the demand for union labor. For

····**FIGURE 16.7** UNIONS AND THE DEMAND FOR LABOR

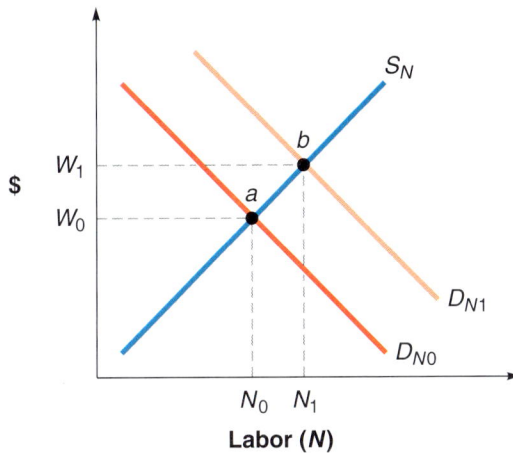

If unions are able to increase the demand for union labor, the wage rate will rise. In this case, the labor market is initially at point *a*, and the wage is W_0. A union contract that increases the demand for labor will shift the labor demand curve out to D_{N1} and raise the wage rate to W_1.

example, airline pilots contend that safety mandates three pilots in the cockpit of commercial airlines while the airline companies counter that only two pilots are needed.[6] The effect of these and similar measures to increase the demand for labor is illustrated in Figure 16.7. If the market is initially at point *a*, the intersection of D_{N0} and S_N, an increase in the demand for labor will shift the labor demand curve out to D_{N1}. The result is an increase in the wage rate from W_0 to W_1 per hour. Such a strategy could be used to reduce the layoffs from a labor-saving technological advance or to reduce the unemployment caused by the kind of wage demands illustrated in Figure 16.5.

········

Union Strategies to Decrease the Supply of Labor

Alternatively, unions can work to reduce competition from nonunion labor. For example, unions have frequently supported measures to restrict immigration into the United States to reduce competition for union jobs. Unions have also been active supporters of child labor laws—laws making it illegal for children under a certain age to work—and not simply for altruistic reasons. By making it illegal for children to work, the supply of labor is reduced and wages tend to rise.

Unions have occasionally been able to influence legislation that restricted the conditions of employment. For example, in the past, some states allowed **closed shops**—firms that required job applicants to join the union before they could begin working—but most closed shops were declared illegal by the **Taft-Hartley Act** in

Closed shop Arrangement between union and management that restricts hiring to members of the union.

Taft-Hartley Act Federal statute enacted in 1947 that makes most closed shops illegal.

[6]Strictly speaking, if safety is improved by having three pilots, then this is not a case of featherbedding.

FOCUS ON

GAME THEORY AND COLLECTIVE BARGAINING: INDETERMINATE SOLUTIONS

The renegotiation of big labor contracts is often front-page news. Part of the reason for this, of course, is that many people are affected by the outcome. If the talks break down and the union goes on strike, consumers—not just labor and management—can be hurt. If the talks proceed amicably, the resulting contract often forms the basis for wage negotiations in other industries. But union negotiations are also newsworthy because the outcome is often indeterminate. No one really knows how they will come out. Regardless of what we know going into the negotiations—that the union received a high wage last time, that the firm is experiencing high profits, that management has announced they will take a tough negotiating stance, or whatever—the nature of the negotiation process often results in surprises. This can be shown with an application of game theory, a technique of analysis introduced in Chapter 14.

As an example, suppose that labor sits down with management to renegotiate their three-year contract. In this case, two main issues are on the table, wages and job security. Labor wants high wages and complete job security; management wants low wages and the freedom to dismiss workers as conditions warrant. Neither party expects to get everything, but both hope they can. The first issue on the table is wages.

- *Labor's strategy:* Labor's reasoning goes like this: if we win a high wage, there is less chance that we will get the job security guarantees we want. The correct strategy might be to stress job security with moderate wages and hope that management comes to the table with a high-wage offer. That will get us a reasonable wage increase plus job security. On the other hand, the collective bargaining process involves give and take, so if

we ask for a high wage, we will have room to trade wages for job security. The downside to that strategy is that if our wage demand is too high, management might refuse to bargain, call a lockout, and hire nonunion workers. We will do almost anything to avoid a strike—but we can't tell management that we feel this way.

- *Management's strategy:* Management's strategy is as follows: if we offer a low wage, we can counter the likely union demand for high wages with some job security provisions and settle for only a moderate wage increase. If we go to the table with a high-wage offer, labor will perceive us as weak and counter with demands for even higher wages and lifetime employment guarantees, and our profits will fall appreciably. This is the worst possible outcome. We will do almost anything to avoid having

---

Union shop A shop that requires new employees to join a union within a specified period of time.

Open shop A firm that hires both union and nonunion workers.

Right-to-work state A state in which no one can be required to join a union as a prerequisite for employment.

1947. The effect of a closed shop is to prevent the firm from hiring low-paid workers to replace higher-paid union workers. A less extreme version is the **union shop**, where new employees are required to join the union within a specified time after beginning employment. In an **open shop**, workers are not required to join the union. States that prohibit provisions requiring union membership are called **right-to-work states**. Currently, there are 21 right-to-work states, most of them in the South.

Closed and union shops reduce the supply of labor as illustrated in Figure 16.8. If the labor supply is initially at point *a*, a reduction in the supply of labor will shift the labor supply curve from S_{N0} to S_{N1}. As a result, the wage rate increases from W_0 to

		Labor	
	Offer →	Low Wage	High Wage
Management	Low Wage	L:− / M:+	L:0 / M:0
	High Wage	L:0 / M:0	L:+ / M:−

to call a lockout—but we can't let labor know we feel this way.

- *Payoff matrix:* The payoff matrix represents the different outcomes. The best outcome from labor's standpoint (L:+) is in the southeast corner. Management's initial high-wage offer is accepted, and some job security is thrown in as the negotiations proceed. This is the worst outcome for management (M:−). The worst outcome for labor is in the northwest quadrant (L:−). Management agrees to a low-wage demand but does not counter with acceptable job security concessions. This is the best outcome for management (M:+)—unless there is a strike.

The off-diagonal cells represent the outcome of compromise—moderate wages, because one party asked for high wages and the other countered with low wages, and some job security provisions tossed in to seal the deal. The entries in the off-diagonal cells are all 0's to indicate that neither side is a clear winner or loser.

What is the most likely solution to this game? The off-diagonal payoffs may seem most likely: if labor asks for high wages, management counters with a low-wage offer, and compromise takes place. If labor asks for low wages but complete job security, management offers a higher wage and less than complete job security. Unfortu-

nately, the solution is not that simple. It depends on bargaining power, bluffing, and the perceived or actual strength of the opponents. For example, if labor believes that management cannot afford a strike or lockout, they will demand high wages and refuse to budge; the game will end in the southeast corner—but only if labor's belief is correct. If management is confident they can hire strike breakers to replace union workers, they will offer tiny wage concessions, and the game will end in the northwest corner.

In short, the solution to this collective bargaining game is indeterminate. Does this mean that our game theory exercise has been useless? No, because formulating the problem in this fashion makes it easier to see the possible outcomes. It is also useful to the players as they form their strategies. Finally, it may help explain why experience is so important in labor-management bargaining: experienced negotiators are better able to anticipate the response of their opposition and better able to avoid undesirable outcomes.

W_1. Notice that this strategy does not increase unemployment—at least not in the economist's sense of the quantity supplied exceeding the quantity demanded at the given price (wage). The intersection of the labor supply and demand curves determines the wage rate and employment, so there is no "shortage"—remember that economists define shortages as situations that can exist only when price is held artificially low. The strategy does reduce the number of jobs, however, so not everyone benefits from reducing the supply of labor. In fact, union negotiating strategies are always complicated because the union can never be certain how management will respond. This issue is highlighted in the focus box on page 402.

····**FIGURE 16.8 UNIONS AND THE SUPPLY OF LABOR**

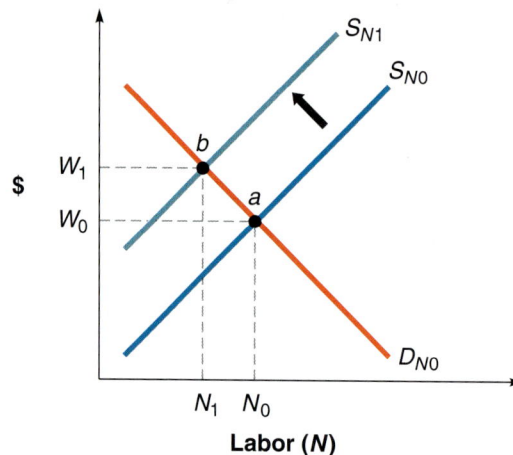

Union support for measures to reduce the supply of labor—including child labor laws, immigration quotas, and other policies—can result in higher wages. If the market is initially at point *a*, a decrease in the supply of labor will shift the labor supply curve from S_{N0} to S_{N1} and raise the wage rate from W_0 to W_1.

········

Recent Union Trends

Several important trends can be identified in the contemporary union movement. Most important perhaps is that the fraction of the workforce that belongs to unions continues to show a steady decline: a third of the workforce was unionized in the 1950s, a quarter held union cards in 1975, and less than a fifth belonged to unions in 1990. There are several explanations for this decline. For one thing, employment in the manufacturing sector of the economy—where unions have typically been concentrated—has declined significantly as the economy has shifted toward an information and service economy. Another explanation is that more manufacturing firms are locating in right to work states to avoid what they regard as "union problems."[7] It is possible too that fewer workers see the benefits of union membership. Other explanations for the decline in union membership are suggested in the Focus box on page 406.

The goals of unions may be changing in the 1990s. Many union workers, fearing massive layoffs, have made job security their major collective bargaining goal instead of wages. Job guarantees may win more public sympathy than wage demands, but

[7]It is perhaps significant that when Nissan and Toyota decided to open plants in the United States, they located in the South, with lower wages and no unions. Not all Japanese automobile makers have followed this pattern. Mazda built a plant in Detroit and employed union workers. When the plant opened for business, it was besieged with 100,000 applicants for only 3,500 positions. Mazda is partly owned by Ford. Honda's main production facility is in Ohio and remains nonunion, despite strong pressure from the United Autoworkers.

they create just as many problems for the firm. Being contractually obligated to keep workers—even during recessions—represents a cost just like wages. In exchange, some unions have agreed to accept cuts in benefits packages (health, retirement, vacation, and the like); some firms have put early retirement programs in effect; and many bargaining agreements have made explicit reference to productivity goals.[8] Finally, unions were vocal opponents of the North American Free Trade Agreement (NAFTA). Passed in 1993, this treaty will phase out most tariffs between Canada, Mexico, and the United States over the next decade. Most union opposition to NAFTA stemmed from the fear that union workers would lose their jobs to low-paid Mexican workers.[9] NAFTA is discussed in more detail in Chapter 37.

RECAP   Union Strategies

Traditionally, the main goals of unions have been higher wages and job security. Unfortunately, these two goals can be incompatible: higher wages often mean fewer jobs. Several techniques have been used to bring about these goals.

1. Unions can negotiate to raise their wages directly, but this can lead to union layoffs, especially if the industry is competitive. Union wage increases in concentrated industries do not necessarily lead to price increases and layoffs. Wage increases that are less than the rate of productivity growth should not lead to price increases and layoffs.
2. Unions have sought to increase the demand for union labor. This will increase wages without causing unemployment to rise. Featherbedding is one technique that has been used to increase labor demand.
3. Several measures have been used to reduce the supply of labor. Immigration quotas and child labor laws are two examples. Shop rules that require workers to join unions also reduce competition from nonunion workers and help keep wages high.

·····• ALTERNATIVE THEORIES OF THE LABOR MARKET

Can the labor supply decision really be described as a tradeoff between work and leisure? Is labor productivity determined solely by worker skills and the stock of capital? Many economists would answer "no" to these questions. They argue that at least one member of the family has to work regardless of the wage rate, so the concept

---

[8]For a classic analysis of union behavior in the United States, see Richard Freeman and James Medoff, *What Do Unions Do?* (New York: Basic Books, 1984).

[9]Unions were concerned too that Mexican workers would not be allowed to organize to move their wages in line with U.S. wages. For example, unions filed complaints in early 1994 arguing that both General Electric and Honeywell had fired Mexican workers who had attempted to organize unions. See Robert L. Rose, "Labor Unions File First Tests of Nafta Office," *Wall Street Journal*, February 15, 1994, p. A2. For a commentary that discusses the union anti-NAFTA stance and the political fallout, see Susan B. Garland, "The Unions vs. Pro-Nafta Democrats: Get Over It," *Business Week*, December 6, 1993, p. 45.

FOCUS ON

THE LABOR MOVEMENT IN THE UNITED STATES: KEY EVENTS AND IDEAS

The first national labor organization in the United States, the Knights of Labor, was founded in the middle of the nineteenth century. Originally a secret organization open to all workers except "lawyers, bankers, gamblers, liquor dealers and Pinkerton detectives," the Knights of Labor sought to form one great union for the entire nation. The Knights were as interested in social and political reform as in strictly economic issues, and confusion over goals was to be instrumental in their demise. Another factor was rising antilabor sentiment generated by the Haymarket Riot of 1886. The riot, which took place after a labor rally in support of the eight-hour day grew violent, and led to the death of 11 people including a number of Chicago police officers.

The present-day labor movement began in 1881 with the formation of the American Federation of Labor (AFL). The leader of the AFL until his death in 1924 was Samuel Gompers. The AFL was a federation of *craft unions*. Craft unions are organized on the basis of specific work skills—a separate union for carpenters, another for printers, and so on. The craft union structure of the AFL did not fit the mass-production factory system that began to dominate American industry in the early twentieth century. Under

Samuel Gompers (1850–1924), President of the American Federation of Labor, at a meeting with its executive council, 1924.

the factory system, labor's voice could be better heard with *industrial unions*—unions composed of all workers in an industry instead of a particular craft. For example, everyone working in an automobile plant qualifies for membership in the present-day UAW—the United Auto Workers union. The formation of the Congress of Industrial Organizations (CIO) in 1935 signified recognition of the changing role of unions in the American economy and provided for competition with the

AFL. In 1955 the AFL and CIO merged into the AFL/CIO.

The U.S. Congress has passed several important pieces of legislation affecting unions and labor relations:

- The *Clayton Act* (1914) was intended as an extension of the Sherman Antitrust Act of 1890, (discussed in Chapter 19). This act removed organized labor from antitrust prosecution.
- The *Railway Labor Act* (1926) for-

mally established the legality of collective bargaining.

- The *Norris–La Guardia Act* (1932) severely limited the ability of the federal government to interfere in labor disputes.
- The *National Labor Relations (Wagner) Act* (1935) may be the most important piece of pro-labor legislation in U.S. history. This act established the National Labor Relations Board (NLRB) to assure that employers do not engage in unfair labor practices and gave all workers the legal right to organize.
- The *Fair Labor Standards Act* (1938) barred child labor, established time-and-a-half pay for overtime, and set the minimum wage for most nonfarm workers.
- The *Taft-Hartley Act* (1947) was passed because many people thought that legislation had become too pro-labor. This act gave the government the right to impose an 80-day "cooling off" period to halt strikes that interfere with public health or safety. Taft-Hartley also made closed shops illegal and gave states the right to pass right-to-work legislation.

Union membership in the United States has fallen significantly since its high in the 1950s. There are several reasons for this. First, more and more firms have decided to resist union strike threats. One important and very visible case occurred in 1981 when President Ronald Reagan fired 11,400 striking members of the Professional Air Traffic Controllers (PATCO). The strike was illegal—the PATCO contract did not permit strikes—but the president's decision to fire that many people in such an important profession seemed to set the tone for labor relations for the next decade.

Another reason for the decline in union membership is foreign competition. Without the threat of foreign competition, American workers could demand high wages and expect their firms to pass on the costs as higher prices. But with the threat of cheap foreign imports, union demands for high wages often led to layoffs. In response, many unions reopened their wage contracts and offered to take wage cuts. Even the steelworkers took their first wage cuts in modern history, and the Teamsters voluntarily froze the wages of truck drivers. Such behavior may have saved a few jobs, but it also provided a strong signal that union membership did not mean as much as it had in the past.

The deregulation of the late 1970s and 1980s also hurt the union movement. For example, when the airline industry was deregulated, several new airlines entered the industry. These new airlines paid their pilots, flight attendants, and other workers roughly half of what the unionized workers were making at the established airlines. The new airlines then proceeded to offer cut-rate fares. As a result, many of the established, unionized airlines went out of business or forced their workers to take pay cuts—or both. When workers realized that their union could not save their jobs, many stopped paying dues and quit the union.

Finally, the changing structure of the economy is having an effect on union membership. In the past, union organizers were most successful in manufacturing industries, in part, because it is easier for union leaders to negotiate with management in a concentrated industry. However, the U.S. economy is evolving into a service and information-based economy, and the number of workers in manufacturing industries is declining. Some service and information workers are unionized, but a much smaller percentage than manufacturing workers.

Are we to conclude that unions are a thing of the past? No, at least not yet. Even though union membership is down, union workers are still a very vocal group in politics as well as business, as the recent NAFTA debate made clear. Perhaps most importantly, when union wages change, so do many nonunion wages. We will certainly see changes in the relationship between unions and management, just as we have seen a shift in demands from higher wages to increased job security. But unions of one sort or another are likely to be around as long as capitalism is around.

FOCUS ON

LABOR RELATIONS IN OTHER COUNTRIES

The major difference between U.S. labor relations and those in most other industrialized nations is that the labor-management relationship in the United States is adversarial, whereas in other countries it is cooperative. But wait: Isn't there *supposed* to be conflict between labor and management? Don't higher wages mean lower profits? Not necessarily. A profitable company has productive employees and little turnover. High wages may instill employee loyalty and increased effort to achieve this end.

About 16 percent of the U.S. workforce belongs to unions; this compares to an average of about 40 percent in other industrialized nations. Does higher union membership lead to more "labor problems"? Not necessarily. In fact, strong union movements are typically associated with fewer strikes and moderate wage demands. Strikes are less prevalent in the United States than is commonly thought—fewer days are lost to strikes than to the common cold!—but they are much less common in other industrial countries than in the United States. Strikes indicate a breakdown in the collective bargaining process.

Many countries in continental Europe have strong centralized union movements. These unions are usually identified with a political party, so labor negotiations are often conducted through the political process rather than collective bargaining between individual firms and unions. There are generally fewer strikes. This is not to say strikes are unheard of: a nationwide truck strike in the spring of 1992 made things difficult for the grand opening of the Euro-Disneyland theme park outside Paris, and a strike by French farmers following the European Community's decision to lower tariffs on agricultural imports from the United States in late 1992 was front-page news. But the fact remains that strikes are *less* common in economies with stronger union movements and more union-management cooperation. Even Sweden, where over 80 percent of the nonagricultural workforce is unionized, lost fewer days to strikes than the United States—by a factor of nearly 20. The counterexample is Italy where both union membership and strike incidence are high, but Italy appears to be an exception.

The question is *why* there are so many fewer strikes in other countries. One explanation is that wage negotiations are often conducted on the national level, so there is less concern over relative wages. For example, in the United States, if steelworkers are accustomed to making 10 percent more than glass workers, an increase in the wage rate paid to glass workers can set in motion a demand by the steelworkers for a comparable wage increase.

The situation is different in Japan, which does not have a strong national labor movement. Instead, there are many autonomous company unions much like in the United States. However, all wage contracts last one year, and all negotiations take place in the annual "Spring Offensive." When unions ask for wage increases, they are made aware of the effect of their demands on corporate profits and prices and whether price increases will result in a decline in exports. When wage negotiations take place, all parties are aware of the consequences of their actions. One result of this awareness is a trivially low level of strikes—only 20 percent as many strikes as in the

of a tradeoff between work and leisure is often meaningless. Further, since many people find self-worth and friendship in the workplace, work is not always a "bad" that must be traded for a paycheck. If working conditions and the perception of fairness influence worker effort and productivity, firms will find it difficult to measure

Japanese management and employees enjoying the arrival of Spring in Ueno Park, Tokyo.

United States though Japanese union membership is almost 50 percent higher. It is worth noting too that the incidence of strikes in Japan was much higher until cooperative labor-management relations developed in the 1960s.

Two other factors distinguish Japanese labor-management relations. Few firms provide special perks for management—executive bathrooms, assigned parking spaces, and so on—and the wage differential between labor and management is typically much less than in the United States. These factors may be responsible for better worker morale and productivity growth—factors that may partially explain why Japanese wages have grown significantly faster than U.S. wages over the past 20 years.

Such differences have not gone unnoticed in corporate America. The economic problems of the 1970s and 1980s resulted in some serious soul-searching by workers and managers, as well as policymakers. While policymakers were discovering that they did not have a magic bullet to solve what was appearing to be a long-run competitiveness problem of the U.S. economy, labor and management realized that cooperation was better than conflict. Many firms reduced executive perks and began to give more responsibility to workers. Labor representatives began to show up in corporate boardrooms, and the attitudes that both labor and management brought to wage negotiations began to change. In short, U.S. labor-management relations are starting to resemble those in Germany, Japan, and our other trading partners. Finally, as international treaties expand the volume of trade and reduce trade barriers, both unions and management are finding that they must pay more attention to foreign competition. The future of the union movement in the United States—and the world—will depend on how well union workers can adapt to increasing foreign competition.

the productivity of labor, much less equate it to the wage. In fact, some economists find so little value in the labor supply and demand framework that they refuse even to use the term "labor market." They offer instead a variety of theories based on nonmarket, sociological, and institutional factors. This section briefly explores some of these theories.[10] Though clearly distinct, the theories discussed in this section all share an important commonality: they are all based on the assumption that the labor market is not perfectly competitive.

Wage Contours

Wage contour The intra- and inter-firm wage structure. Wage contours affect workers' perception of fairness and labor productivity because the labor market allocates hours, not effort.

Except when wages are very low, workers are likely to be just as concerned about their relative wages as their real wages. The intra- and inter-firm array of wage differentials has been called the wage structure or the **wage contour**.[11] Related to the wage contour are the concepts of the *key job* and the corresponding *key wage*. The key job may be the top of a promotion ladder or the job with the most workers; it is always a very visible job within the firm and industry. The key wage is the wage rate paid to workers holding the key job. Other wages are set in relation to the key wage. Once the wage contour is established, workers tend to adapt to the historical structure of wages and accept it as fair.

Wage differentials are influenced by several factors. Custom frequently has a strong influence, but market conditions matter as well. Newer and expanding industries often have to pay higher wages to attract workers. If the demand for output is price-inelastic and wages are a small portion of total costs, wages can be higher because the firm can pass on higher wage costs without a significant decline in sales. In the long run, wage and skill differences respond to the pattern of industrialization and labor scarcity—but this theory suggests that wages can be divorced from market conditions in the short run.

The wage contour affects workers' perceptions of fairness and labor productivity because the labor market allocates hours, not effort.[12] If workers feel they are earning a fair wage, they work harder than if they feel they are being treated unfairly. Workers will certainly feel they are being treated unfairly if they are forced to take a wage cut; this is nothing new. What is new is the idea that the perception of fairness can depend on wages paid to workers in an unrelated industry. For example, if the aluminum workers receive a 10 percent increase, the construction workers are likely to ask for a similar raise. Why is this important? If wages are based on "fairness" instead of productivity or market conditions, then any wage increase—even if it is noninflationary and warranted by productivity growth—can set in motion inflationary wage growth in other industries.

Dual Labor Markets

Dual economy The conception of the economy as being composed of large firms in the core and small firms in the periphery.

Many economists believe that the labor markets in competitive industries differ so much from the markets in concentrated industries that it is best to speak of a **dual**

---

[10]We have space to touch on only some of the issues. For a very readable nontechnical paper that includes a good bibliography, see Dell Champlin, "Structural Change in U.S. Labor Markets," *Review of Social Economy* 51 (Spring 1993): 40–61.

[11]The classic reference on wage contours is a 1957 article by John Dunlop, "Wage Contours," which was reprinted in Michael J. Piore, ed., *Unemployment and Inflation* (White Plains, N.Y.: M. E. Sharpe, 1979), pp. 63–74.

[12]This idea is similar to the "wage gifts" paid to workers under efficiency wage theory, a topic that will be covered in Chapter 32.

economy.[13] The dual economy has technologically advanced, oligopolistic industries at its *core*, and smaller, less technologically sophisticated firms on its *periphery*. Core firms account for approximately two-thirds of all manufacturing production in the United States. A key to understanding the dual economy is to note that core firms generally make higher profits than firms on the periphery. Higher profits allow some leeway in firm behavior.

The dual economy implies a segmented labor market with different wages, working conditions, and opportunities for advancement. Jobs in the core sector are typically characterized by high wages, good fringe benefits, and stability—although the structural changes of the 1980s and 1990s have undermined job stability even for many workers in the core sector. Unions are frequently prominent in the core sector, and there is often industrial concentration. In the periphery, turnover is high and wages are low—so low, in fact, that many workers on the periphery work full-time but still qualify for welfare. There is little industrial concentration in the periphery. In the 1980s, nearly three-quarters of the new jobs created were in the periphery. Some of these were high-paying jobs in high-tech industries, but many were low-paying jobs in the service sector. One reason so many jobs were created by smaller firms is that it is easier for smaller firms to adjust to changing economic conditions. Another reason is that smaller firms are less encumbered by the need to pay employee benefits.

The dual economy is a product of historical evolution. As oligopoly industries became more prominent in the late nineteenth century, a skilled, stable workforce was needed to make use of the large amounts of capital employed in mass production. The high capital/labor ratios employed by core firms allowed them to pay high wages—workers are more productive if they have more machinery to work with—and helped ensure a stable workforce. Labor concentration was instrumental in the rise of unions, which sought to countervail some of the power of big business. Though unions influenced wage rates, they also enhanced worker stability since managers could negotiate more easily with a few union leaders than with hundreds of individual workers.

More recently, core firms have made worker stability a major selection requirement for employment. Since it is difficult and costly to accurately test for worker stability, many firms resort to superficial screening devices to reduce the number of applicants and lower the costs of hiring and recruitment. A common screening device is discrimination against groups with a history of unstable work patterns—minorities, women, and teenagers. This practice may be "rational" from the firm's perspective, but it also means that these groups will maintain high overall unemployment rates. And since many work skills are acquired through on-the-job training, these groups will always be at a disadvantage. Firms on the periphery cannot afford this kind of discrimination for a simple reason: it is costly because it limits the size of the labor pool the firm can draw from and thus forces the firm to pay higher wages. Profits in

---

[13]The dual economy is a key idea of post-Keynesian and institutional economics. A good introduction to this model can be found in Eileen Applebaum, "The Labor Market in Post-Keynesian Theory," *Challenge* (January/February 1979): 39–47. This paper is reprinted in Alfred Eichner, ed., *A Guide to Post Keynesian Economics* (White Plains, N.Y.: M. E. Sharpe, 1979), and the Piore reader cited in note 11.

CHANGING WAGE DIFFERENTIALS IN THE 1980S: ALTERNATIVE EXPLANATIONS

A recent paper by two economists at the University of Michigan, John Bound and George Johnson, examined changes in the wage structure that occurred in the 1980s.★ Bound and Johnson were interested in explaining three changes: (1) why the average wage of college-educated workers increased by 15 percent over non-college-educated workers; (2) why the earnings of older workers without college increased relative to the earnings of younger workers without college; and (3) why the male/female wage differential shrank by about 6 percentage points between 1979 and 1988.

Bound and Johnson explored four possible explanations for these changes. The first possibility was the decline in manufacturing employment. This was plausible because manufacturing jobs have typically paid well but required little education. The second explanation centered on the decline of union power in manufacturing. These two explanations are related because union power is concentrated in manufacturing. The third explanation looked at the role of computers and changes in technology. Increases in technology require more educated workers and thus increase the relative demand for college graduates. The final hypothesis examined the decline in the number of college-educated workers entering the labor force in the 1980s. Fewer college graduates in the face of increasing demand will tend to raise the wage of college graduates.

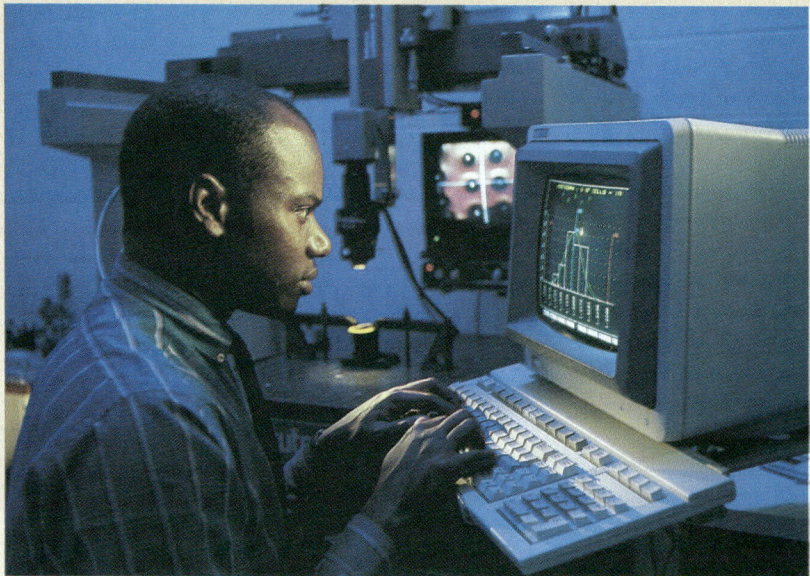

To test these hypotheses, the authors constructed a series of elaborate econometric models and looked at data spanning the 1970s and 1980s. They found it difficult to account for the large relative wage decrease of young workers, but they were able to reach the conclusion:

Our analysis points strongly to the conclusion that the principal reason for the increases in wage differentials by educational attainment and the decrease in the gender differential is a combination of skilled-labor-biased technical change and changes in unmeasured labor quality.

"Unmeasured labor quality" refers to increasing productivity of women that cannot be associated directly with increased education or technology; it may be associated with increasing work experience. But simply put, Bound and Johnson contend that technical change has tended to favor those with the skills to use new technology. The authors speculate that these trends will almost certainly increase in the future unless there is a sharp rise in college attendance and completion rates.

★"Changes in the Structure of Wages in the 1980s: An Evaluation of Alternative Explanations," *American Economic Review* 82 (June 1992): 371–92.

the periphery are typically low, so firms have to take what they can get—which often means workers with little education and unstable work histories.

Credentials are also used as a screening device. By considering only applicants with advanced degrees from prestigious institutions, a firm can reduce the cost of hiring significantly. Note, however, that while credentials screens can reduce the cost of hiring, they can also lead to higher wages for the workers who are employed because the firm has a smaller candidate pool to draw from. A change in credential requirements also serves as a market-like device to help clear the labor market. When the supply of skilled workers exceeds demand, credentials inflation, not wage deflation, is the result. Evidence of such credentials inflation seems to be everywhere: How many fast-food management trainees have college degrees? Nevertheless, the increase in the demand for and wages of college graduates relative to workers without college degrees does not necessarily support the credentials inflation argument. This point is developed in the Focus box on page 412.

An extension of dual labor market theory is the **job competition** model developed by Lester Thurow. Thurow believes wages are tied to specific jobs, not individual productivity. Job applicants are ranked according to background credentials—college degree, grades, extracurricular activities, and the like. Background credentials are used to help estimate the training costs necessary to make the worker productive; training an unskilled, uneducated person will be more costly than training a skilled, educated one. Job opportunities and income depend on a worker's position in the job queue. Easily trainable people are at the top of the queue and find jobs associated with higher productivity and higher wages. Easily trainable people are also the most profitable people for the firm to hire because it incurs lower costs in training them.

Job competition Wages are tied to specific jobs, not individual productivity, and job applicants are ranked according to background credentials.

The Vita Theory. The fact that workers are not homogeneous is the basis of another theory of the labor market, the **vita theory** developed by E. Ray Canterbery. According to this theory, workers should be classified by location, skill, and skill level. When there is a discrepancy between skills supplied and skills demanded, short-run disequilibrium will prevail. Long-run disequilibrium will exist when a particular skill and skill level are in chronic excess supply.

Figure 16.9 illustrates the vita theory. The labor market has been divided into four skill levels and three geographic regions. The entries in the cells represent excess supply (XS), excess demand (XD), and equilibrium (0). Disequilibrium in the labor market causes people to try to move between cells. A move upward is possible only if workers somehow acquire the additional job skills needed through on-the-job training or formal education. Downward moves are accepted only reluctantly, but are generally easier than upward moves. Downward moves can result in "bumping" people in less-skilled cells. By assumption, workers can move only one cell in the short run and can skip cells only by exiting the labor force to acquire new skills.

In the example illustrated, there is excess demand for highly skilled, blue-collar workers in Region 1. This excess demand can be met by low-skilled, blue-collar workers in Region 1 moving up or by highly skilled, blue-collar workers in Region 2 moving over. Which move occurs depends on several factors—primarily the cost of a geographic move relative to the cost of training—but one thing is apparent: there is nothing to assure that the excess demands and supplies will cancel out, at

Vita theory Theory of the labor market that holds that workers are not homogeneous and should be classified by location, skill, and skill level. Disequilibrium results when there is a discrepancy between skills supplied and skills demanded.

• • • • FIGURE 16.9 THE VITA THEORY

	Regions		
	(1)	(2)	(3)
Executive	0	0	XS
Highly skilled blue-collar	XD	XS	0
Low-skilled blue-collar	XS	0	XD
Unskilled	XS	0	XS

KEY: XS = excess supply of labor; XD = excess demand for labor; 0 = labor market equilibrium.
SOURCE: Adapted from Figure 1 of H. Peter Gray, "Employment Arguments for Protection and the Vita Theory," *Eastern Economic Journal* 10 (January/March 1984): 1–13.

least not in the short run. Supply and demand may cancel out in the long run—but just how long this will take is anybody's guess. And in the meantime, there can be unemployment in some markets and labor shortages in other markets.

The vita theory offers an explanation for chronic unemployment of unskilled workers. For example, the executives in Region 3 could bump highly skilled, blue-collar workers, who could then find jobs as low-skilled blue-collar workers. If some of these workers accept jobs as unskilled laborers, this would increase the unemployment of unskilled workers—but these people in the bottom cells have no one to bump. Studies have shown that unemployment among the unskilled typically averages between 12 and 20 percent, more than double the overall rate in the economy. If job markets were competitive, there would be no reason for unemployment to be higher in one skill level than another.

• • • • • • • SUMMARY

This chapter has built on the material from the last chapter to consider some real-world factors—unions, imperfectly competitive markets, and the perception of fairness among others—that affect labor markets and employment. Still, some people would say that we have overlooked the essential issues: Even if workers have jobs today, will they have them tomorrow? Will the products they produce have a market, or will those products be undercut by better or cheaper products produced elsewhere? Can you count on a job when you finish school? No one can answer these questions definitively, because the one certainty of the economy of the 1990s and beyond is that the nature of work and the labor market will change and evolve. Still, our discussion does contribute to an understanding of these issues because it provides a framework for analysis. Such a framework should help as you try to make sense of the changing workplace.

The main points covered in this chapter include:

1. The marginal revenue product curve is steeper when there is monopoly in the output market than when there is pure competition because the firm must lower its selling price to sell additional units of output. The wage rate is less than the average revenue product.

2. Monopsony in the input market requires that the firm raise the wage rate to hire additional workers. This causes the marginal factor cost to rise faster than the wage rate.

3. Other things being equal, both employment and the wage rate are highest when there is competition in both the input and output markets; both employment and the wage rate are lowest when there is monopsony in the input market and monopoly in the output market.

4. Union strength seems to have diminished in the past 20 years, but the union/nonunion wage differential is still significant. Labor unions can employ several strategies to increase wages and job security. If they increase the wage directly, employment may fall, so wage demands are often coupled with measures designed to increase the demand for labor. Reducing the supply of labor, or limiting the number of people eligible to hold union jobs, will also increase the wage rate.

5. Some economists hold that the labor market is not a "market" at all because the wage rate does not act as a market-clearing mechanism. These economists have developed alternative theories to explain wages and employment. The wage contour thesis focuses on the importance of relative wages and the perception of fairness; the dual labor market and vita theories stress that workers are not homogeneous and that credentials and factors other than marginal productivity determine employment and wages.

KEY TERMS AND CONCEPTS

marginal revenue product (*MRP*)

average revenue product (*ARP*)

monopsony

average factor cost (*AFC*)

marginal factor cost (*MFC*)

labor union

AFL/CIO

COLA (cost of living) clause

featherbedding

closed shop

Taft-Hartley Act

union shop

open shop

right-to-work state

Wagner Act

wage contour

key job

key wage

dual economy

core

periphery

job credentials

job competition

vita theory

REVIEW QUESTIONS

1. Why does the *MRP* curve slope down faster under monopoly than under pure competition? How does this affect the wage rate and the number of workers that are hired? Draw a diagram to illustrate your answer.
2. Why is the *MFC* curve steeper than the *AFC* curve under monopsony? How does this affect the number of workers that are hired and the wage rate? Draw a diagram to illustrate your answer.
3. What strategies do unions use to raise union wages? What strategies do unions use to increase the demand for union employment? Are there any conflicts between these two demands?
4. What have been the main effects of unions in the United States? How do U.S. unions differ from unions in other countries?
5. Explain how the perception of fairness, the structure of labor markets, and the fact that workers are not homogeneous affect wages and employment.

PROBLEMS

1. In the 1980s, nearly a quarter of all college graduates took jobs that did not require a college degree. Explain this fact with reference to several of the labor market theories in the chapter.
2. There are six large public accounting firms in the United States, the so-called Big Six. Do you think that these firms behave like oligopsonies? Why or why not? (*Hint:* You may want to ask a friend who is a senior accounting major about Big Six hiring practices before answering this question.)
3. Do you think that featherbedding should be outlawed? Why or why not?
4. Some countries outlaw COLA clauses. Do you think they should be illegal in the United States? Why or why not?
5. a. Fill in the blanks and graph the resulting *ARP* and *MRP* curves:

N	Q	MPP	P	TR	MRP	ARP
3	30		$10	$300		$100
		→ ?			→ $60	
4	40		9	?		?
		→ ?			?	
5	48		8	?		?
		→ ?			?	
6	?		7	378		?

   b. Fill in the blanks and graph the resulting *AFC* and *MFC* curves:

N	AFC = W	Wage Bill	MFC
3	$20	$60	
			→ $28
4	?	88	
			→ ?
5	24	?	
			→ ?
6	26	?	

    c. Graphically solve for the equilibrium wage and number of workers that are hired assuming monopsony in the input market and monopoly in the output market. (You will not get round numbers.)

    d. Use your graph to illustrate how the wage and employment levels would change with monopoly only in the output market and competition in the input market, and with monopsony in the input market and competition in the output market.

6. Unions can achieve wage increases by bargaining for measures to change labor demand, labor supply, or the wage rate directly. Use supply and demand diagrams to show how this is done, and explain why there are usually adverse consequences for unions when they achieve their bargaining goals.

7. What policies would you recommend if unemployment was caused by:

    a. excessive union wage demands

    b. credentials inflation

    c. discrimination against women and minorities

    d. inadequate demand for goods and services

    e. geographical dislocation

8. Some economists believe that almost all unemployment is "voluntary" in the sense that the wage the unemployed worker is asking for is too high. How do you think advocates of the alternative theories of the labor market would respond to this assertion?

9. Affirmative action laws are designed to prevent discrimination. Do you think that affirmative action laws would be more necessary under a system of pure competition or monopsony? Which of the alternative theories of the labor market indicate a need for affirmative action laws?

10. The cost of a college education has risen dramatically over the past decade—much faster than the cost of living. Part of the reason for this is that professors' salaries have risen (almost) as fast as the cost of living but professor productivity has hardly changed. Do you think that colleges should require professors to show that their productivity has increased before granting wage increases? Why or why not?

11. Why would a firm ever agree to a contract that called for featherbedding? Would it depend on the nature of competition in the input and/or output market? Explain.

CHAPTER 17

The Markets for Capital and Natural Resources

The most difficult—and often the most important—decision a manager can make is whether to expand production capacity. Should you build a new plant in Little Rock? What about a new assembly line for the Scranton facility? These decisions are so difficult because they have such long-term consequences: whether building the new plant is a good decision will not be known for several years—and the future cannot be known with certainty. How can the manager hope to arrive at the right decision? At least two factors are critical: recognition that there are alternative uses for the funds that would go into the new project, and understanding that income earned in the future is less valuable than income earned today. Combine this with a bit of entrepreneurial intuition, and it might be possible to come to the right conclusion.

Society faces a similar dilemma when it uses natural resources. Many resources are nonrenewable; once they are used, they are gone. If we decide to use resources today, they will not be available for our children. That seems unethical. Or maybe not—it is possible that these resources are more valuable to us than they would be to posterity. We may be able to provide our children with technologies that substitute for the resources we have used up.

This chapter will look at the markets for capital and nonrenewable natural resources. These two markets are similar because both have important time dimensions—capital goods wear out, and nonrenewable natural resources can be exhausted—but there are also important differences between the two markets.

AFTER READING AND STUDYING THIS CHAPTER, YOU SHOULD BE ABLE TO:

••• Explain the relationship between time preference, the rate of return on capital, and the price of capital goods

• • • Understand the discounting process and show how it relates to the investment decision
• • • Distinguish between different concepts of rent, and explain how rent and taxes are capitalized into factor prices
• • • Explain why it is so important for natural resource prices to reflect all costs

ROUNDABOUT PRODUCTION AND THE RATE OF RETURN ON CAPITAL

Handwoven sweaters can be beautiful works of art. They can also be quite expensive, even when they are made in low-wage nations. There is a simple reason why: their price must reflect the time that it takes the craftsperson to knit the sweater. Most sweaters bought in the developed countries are machine-made. They may not have as much character as handwoven sweaters, but they certainly are cheaper. Low price is the main reason why the market for machine-made sweaters is also much larger than the market for handwoven sweaters.

Why don't all sweater makers convert to capital-intensive, mass-production methods? Some sweater makers have artistic reasons: they take great pride in their product and would rather work with their hands than with a machine. But for many sweater makers, art has nothing to do with how they produce sweaters. They make sweaters by hand because they cannot afford to buy mechanical looms and the other capital goods necessary to set up a modern sweater factory. Just as importantly, they cannot afford the *time* it would take to change their production methods. The time spent making and installing mechanical looms is unproductive in the sense that it does not earn anything directly for the sweater producer. When would it make sense to postpone production and buy the looms? How many looms should be bought? These are the questions we deal with in this section.

• • • • • • • •

Roundabout Production and the Optimal Capital Stock

Roundabout production Production process that uses capital; called roundabout because it is first necessary to make the machines.

Economists say that production methods using capital are **roundabout** because capital goods must be produced before the final products can be produced and sold. Building an irrigation ditch is a roundabout method of growing crops; it is possible to carry water in buckets, but an irrigation ditch makes things much easier. Cutting wood with a chain saw is roundabout production; it is much quicker than using a hand ax, but you first have to get the money to buy the chain saw. In modern economies virtually all production processes involve some capital goods, so the interesting question is usually whether a firm should acquire more or fewer capital goods. Economic analysis can help make this decision.

Figure 17.1 shows how the handmade-sweater producer can analyze the problem of whether to invest in mechanical looms. To simplify the problem, we have assumed that there are only two periods in the analysis, the current period and the future. (We will look at the more realistic many-period case in the next section.) The horizontal axis measures the quantity of capital goods, the number of looms the sweater producer is considering purchasing. The vertical axis measures the marginal physical

····· **FIGURE 17.1 THE RATE OF RETURN ON CAPITAL**

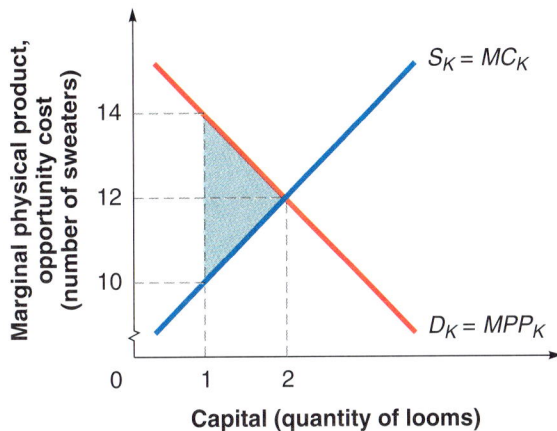

Firms should acquire additional capital as long as the marginal physical product of capital is greater than the opportunity cost of forgone current production. In this two-period example, if the firm buys one loom, the marginal physical product is 14 sweaters, and forgone current production is only 10 sweaters. If the second loom is purchased, 12 sweaters will be produced in the second period while 12 sweaters will be given up in the current period. The second machine should be purchased only if the firm values future production the same amount as current production. If future production is valued less than current production, the second machine should not be bought.

product of the looms and the opportunity cost of future sweaters in terms of lost current sweater production.

The marginal physical product curve is the demand curve for capital, MPP_K. As always, the marginal physical product curve is downward sloping because of the law of diminishing returns: as more units of a capital good are added to a fixed stock of labor and land, the output per unit of capital declines. The capital goods supply curve is the upward-sloping marginal opportunity cost of capital, MC_K. The upward slope of the MC_K curve is also based on the law of diminishing returns: to acquire additional units of capital, resources must be removed from current production, and each additional resource that is removed reduces current production by larger and larger amounts. This means that each new unit of capital produces less than the previous unit and costs more in terms of forgone current production.

As is usually the case in economics, things happen when marginal curves cross. In this case, the intersection between the demand and supply curves determines the optimal stock of capital goods. If the sweater maker buys two mechanical looms, the marginal physical product of capital equals the marginal opportunity cost of capital at 12 sweaters. To see why two looms should be purchased, look what happens if only one loom is bought instead. The marginal physical product of the first machine is 14 sweaters while the marginal opportunity cost is only 10 sweaters. In other words, 4 fewer sweaters are lost in the present period than are gained in the future. It looks like the first machine is a good deal. Should the second loom be bought as well?

Perhaps. The shaded area represents the net gains—$MPP_K > MC_K$—that would be missed if only one loom were bought. If future production is valued less highly than current production, however, it may not be appropriate to buy that second loom. We will say more about this momentarily.

• • • • • • • •

Rate of Return, Time Preference and Loanable Funds

Rate of return The ratio of profits to the cost of an investment good.

Roundabout production means that you have to wait a while before you can produce goods for sale. That's fine—but only if your new roundabout production methods allow you to produce more in the future than you can today. How much more you can produce depends on the **rate of return** on capital. In the two-period case we are using as an example, the rate of return is just the increase in future output divided by lost current output. [The rate of return on the first loom would be $(14 - 10)/10 = 40\%$.] In the more general t-period case, the rate of return on capital is a percentage figure calculated as the ratio of the increase in output attributable to the new capital goods to their price. For example, if you spent \$1,000 on a new machine and output increased by \$100 per year forever, the rate of return would be $100/1,000 = 10\%$.

Time preference A preference for earlier availability of goods over later availability of goods; expressed as a percentage.

Is a 10 percent return high enough for you to forgo current production? That depends on your rate of **time preference**. Time preference is expressed as a percentage: if you require 11 sweaters tomorrow to give up 10 today, your rate of time preference is 10 percent $[(11 - 10)/10 = 10\%]$ per day. If you require 12 sweaters next year to give up 10 sweaters this year, your rate of time preference is 20 percent $[(12 - 10)/10 = 20\%]$ per year. Everyone has a different rate of time preference. Someone with a great deal of patience might have a rate of 3 percent; a child who cannot wait to open her Christmas presents might have a 100 percent rate (meaning that she would need twice as many presents to postpone her whining!). All we know for certain is that the rate of time preference must be positive. A negative rate of time preference would mean that you valued future goods more than current goods and were thus willing to have less goods in the future than you have today. Few people seem to behave that way. Besides, what would a negative time preference indicate about the maxim "A bird in the hand is worth two in the bush"?

Loanable funds Money that savers are willing to lend to borrowers.

In equilibrium, the rate of return on capital must equal the rate of time preference, and both are equal to the interest rate that prevails in the market for **loanable funds**. Here is the reason. Suppose that Alan, a patient sort, has a low rate of time preference, say, 5 percent. He will lend money if the interest rate is above 5 percent, and the higher the interest rate, the more he is willing to lend. On the other hand, youthful Barb wants everything today. She wants to increase her current consumption and is willing to borrow to do so. Her preference is to pay a low interest rate, but she is willing to pay as much as 15 percent to buy a new machine for her business. The two strike a deal, and Alan agrees to lend money to Barb at, say, 10 percent. The market they have created, the market for loanable funds, is shown in Figure 17.2.[1]

The demand for loanable funds, D_{lf}, represents borrowers' demand for funds to be used for current consumption or investment. It is downward sloping because less will be desired at high interest rates than at low interest rates. The supply of loanable

---

[1] A slightly different version of the loanable funds theory will be presented in Chapter 30.

···· **FIGURE 17.2 THE LOANABLE FUNDS MARKET**

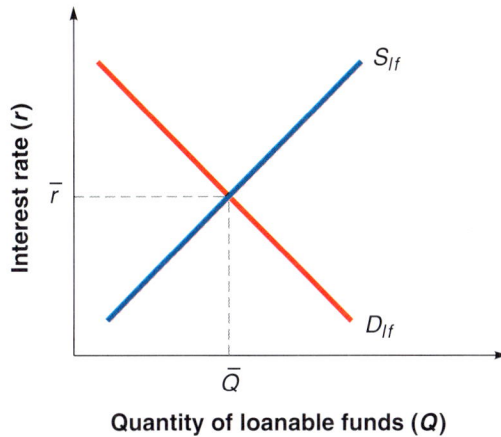

Quantity of loanable funds (Q)

The interest rate is determined in the market for loanable funds. People are willing to lend money at rates that exceed their rate of time preference. Because higher interest rates will induce more people to lend money, the loanable funds supply curve, S_{lf}, is upward sloping. The loanable funds demand curve, D_{lf}, is downward sloping because people want to borrow more at low interest rates than at high interest rates. The intersection of D_{lf} and S_{lf} determines the equilibrium interest rate.

funds, S_{lf}, is upward sloping because people will be more willing to lend at high interest rates than at low interest rates. The intersection of the curves determines the interest rate, r, that will prevail in the market.

Lending takes place whenever there are different rates of time preference, and market pressures move the interest rate to equate the quantity demanded of loanable funds to the quantity supplied. Further, this interest rate will equal the rate of return on capital. How do we know? Simple: Barb, the borrower, will borrow as long as the rate of return on capital is at least as high as the cost of borrowing—the interest rate determined in the market for loanable funds. As she continues borrowing and adding to her stock of capital goods, however, the rate of return on capital will fall because of diminishing returns. When the rate of return falls to the interest rate, she will stop borrowing because additional capital will yield less than it costs.

RECAP   The Market for Capital: The Two-Period Case

1. Production processes that use capital are said to be roundabout because the capital goods must be produced before the final products can be produced.
2. Firms will acquire additional capital if the marginal product of capital exceeds the opportunity cost of lost current production.
3. The interest rate is determined in the market for loanable funds. People will lend when the interest rate exceeds their rate of time preference; people will borrow when the interest rate is less than their rate of time preference.

4. In the long run, the rate of return on capital is equal to the interest rate and the rate of time preference.

RISK AND THE DISCOUNTING PROCESS

The foregoing discussion was simplified in two important ways. First, our example dealt only with the unrealistic two-period case. Virtually all investment decisions are based on a much longer payout period. Second, we said nothing explicit about risk. Incorporating these factors makes analysis of the capital market much more realistic.

Present Value Analysis

Suppose your long-lost Uncle Stan has an unexpected streak of generosity and sends you a Christmas present of $10,000. The only constraint Uncle Stan puts on the gift is that you cannot spend it for 10 years. That's not all bad because if you buy a 10-year certificate of deposit (CD), you can earn quite a bit of interest. After visiting your friendly bankers, you discover that the best interest rate you can get is 10 percent, compounded annually. How much money will you have in 10 years? Your first thought might be that you will have $20,000: 10 percent of $10,000 is $1,000, and you get that for 10 years. In fact, you will have considerably more than $20,000 because of the compounding process. Here is how it works.

After one year, the initial deposit will be equal to $11,000:

$$\$10,000(1 + 0.1) = \$11,000$$

where the interest rate is 0.1. In the second year, the 10 percent interest rate is applied to the $11,000, not just to the original $10,000 deposit:

$$\$11,000(1 + 0.1) = \$10,000(1 + 0.1)(1 + 0.1) = \$10,000(1 + 0.1)^2 = \$12,100$$

After three years, the initial $10,000 will be worth:

$$\$12,100(1 + 0.1) = \$10,000(1 + 0.1)^3 = \$13,310$$

And 10 years later when you finally take your money out, you will have:

$$\$10,000(1 + 0.1)^{10} = \$25,937.42$$

Or, in general, the future value at year t of your initial deposit will be equal to:

$$\text{Future value: } FV_t = PV(1 + r)^t \quad [1]$$

Where:
FV_t = future value of initial deposit after t years
PV = present value of initial deposit
r = interest rate

Present value The current value of having a stream of income over time.

Sometimes, Equation 1 is written slightly differently. If we divide each side by $(1 + r)^t$, we would have an expression of the **present value** of the initial deposit:

$$\text{Present value: } PV = \frac{FV_t}{(1 + r)^t} \qquad [2]$$

Capital Budgeting and the Discounting Process

While you may think of your CD as an "investment," economists would call it saving; the term "investment" refers only to the acquisition of capital goods by firms. However, the reasoning we used to determine how much you will earn on the CD is quite similar to the reasoning firms use when they decide whether or not to budget funds for capital goods.

Suppose you are considering an expansion project with expected after-tax returns of $100,000 each year for the next three years.[2] The expansion would cost $250,000 today. Should you expand? That depends on several factors. One factor to consider is that future income must be *discounted* because it is less valuable than current income. Current income can be reinvested to earn additional income; this is not possible with income that will not be earned for several years. How much should future income be discounted? That too depends on several factors. The minimum **discount rate** is the interest rate that could be earned on alternative uses of the money used to buy the capital goods. If you cannot earn at least as much on your investment as you could make by putting your money in an interest-earning account, you should definitely not expand. But even that rate may not be enough for you to expand if your rate of time preference exceeds the return on the investment. If you are quite impatient, your rate of time preference may be 20 percent—meaning that you would need 20 percent more in the future than you could have today to postpone current consumption.

Discount rate The rate at which future returns are discounted because of time preference; the interest rate that could be earned on alternative uses of money.

Back to the problem at hand: Should you spend $250,000 to earn $100,000 per year each year for three years? The answer depends on how we choose to discount the future income. The formula for discounting three years of future income is:

$$PV = \frac{R_1}{(1 + r)^1} + \frac{R_2}{(1 + r)^2} + \frac{R_3}{(1 + r)^3} \qquad [3]$$

where the R_t's represent the return in year t. While it is beyond our scope to derive Equation 3, it should make a certain amount of sense if you refer back to Equation 2, where we calculated the present value of a future value t years in the future. Equation 3 is a generalization of Equation 2 where the future values are indicated as annual returns, the R_t's, and each annual return is divided by the *discount factor*, $(1 + r)^t$. In this case, each annual return is a future value and is divided by the discount factor. If you choose 5 percent as your discount rate and the income is $100,000 per year for three years, this becomes:

$$PV = \frac{\$100,000}{(1 + 0.05)^1} + \frac{\$100,000}{(1 + 0.05)^2} + \frac{\$100,000}{(1 + 0.05)^3} = \$272,324.80$$

[2]Accounting students will know that this example is simplified substantially. In the real world, scrap value, depreciation, and other factors would go into the calculations.

Another way to interpret this expression is to say that if the interest rate is 5 percent and you want to earn $100,000 per year for three years, you would need to deposit $272,324.80 in the bank today.

The general formula for the present value after T periods is:

$$\text{Present value: } PV = \sum_{t=1}^{T} \frac{FV_t}{(1 + r)^t} \qquad [4]$$

Because r appears in the denominator of the fraction, Equation 4 makes it apparent that an increase in the interest rate lowers present value. This should make sense: the higher the interest rate, the more you can earn from depositing your money in the bank today. That means a given future value could be obtained from a lower initial deposit—that is, a lower present value.

Now we can answer the question we asked at the beginning: Should you invest $250,000 in the project? The answer is only if the interest rate is low enough. With an interest rate of 5 percent, the present value of receiving $100,000 per year for the next three years is $272,324.80—considerably more than the $250,000 it would cost to fund the project. When the present value of the project is greater than the cost of the project, the **net present value (NPV)** is positive:

Net present value The difference between present value and cost.

$$\text{Net present value: } NPV = PV - C_0 \qquad [5]$$

where C_0 is the initial cost of the project ($250,000 in this example). Investment projects should be undertaken when the net present value is greater than zero.

Net present value depends on the interest rate, not just future payments and the cost of the project. For example, if an interest rate of 10 percent is used instead of 5 percent in the discounting formula, present value falls significantly:

$$PV = \frac{\$100,000}{(1 + 0.10)^1} + \frac{\$100,000}{(1 + 0.10)^2} + \frac{\$100,000}{(1 + 0.10)^3} = \$248,685.20$$

and net present value is negative:

$$NPV = PV - C_0 = \$248,685.20 - \$250,000 = -\$1,314.80$$

You should not invest in this project if the discount rate is 10 percent because you could earn more by depositing the $250,000 in the bank.

· · · · · · · ·

Risk and the Investment Decision

Financial economists have developed elaborate discounting techniques, and financial calculators can carry out the calculations in an instant. Still, many investment projects lose money for a simple reason: almost all of the information used in the discounting and present value formulas is based on estimates. No one can *know* the level of future income. The $100,000 figure we used is just an estimate. It could be on the mark, but if a competitor introduces a better product, you will lose your shirt. Even the cost of the project may be incorrectly estimated. A labor strike could increase the cost of construction, or import controls might increase the cost of necessary intermediate products.

Financial economists adjust their calculations to take account of these and other kinds of **risk**. There are several ways to do this, but the most common method is to add a few percentage points to the discount rate. Why does this make sense? Suppose you have the $250,000 and can either put it in an insured bank account that earns 5 percent or expand your business. *All* investment projects carry some risk, so reason dictates that you will need a higher expected return on your project than you could earn at the bank. The question, of course, is just how high. For example, if the interest rate is 5 percent and your estimate of risk indicates a 5 percent risk factor, the discount rate is 10 percent, and the investment project we have been considering should be forgotten. But if you assign a 4 percent risk factor, the discount rate is only 9 percent, and the net present value is positive:

> **Risk** The chance of an event not occurring with a known probability.

$$PV = \frac{\$100,000}{(1 + 0.09)^1} + \frac{\$100,000}{(1 + 0.09)^2} + \frac{\$100,000}{(1 + 0.09)^3} = \$253,129.47 > \$250,000$$

Unfortunately, there is no good way to decide how much risk to assign to individual projects, and in this case, a single percentage point error makes a significant difference. Most firms use rules based on industry experience, trade journals, and other factors when they estimate risk factors.

RECAP   The Demand for Capital: The *T*-Period Case

Most capital goods have a long lifetime so firms must discount future return and calculate the net present value before deciding whether to invest. These decisions are difficult because the future is risky.

1. The future value at year t of a deposit earning compound interest is found with the following formula:

$$FV_t = PV(1 + r)^t$$

Before deciding to invest in a capital good, a firm must determine that it will earn more from the investment than from depositing the money in an interest-earning account.

2. The present value of a project earning income for T years is found with the following formula:

$$PV = \sum_{t=1}^{T} \frac{FV_t}{(1 + r)^t}$$

For a given stream of future returns, the higher the interest rate, the lower the present value.

3. Investment should take place when net present value is positive. Net present value is defined as the difference between present value and cost, $NPV = PV - C_0$.

4. All investment decisions are risky. To adjust for risk, many firms add a few percentage points to their present value calculations. This reduces net present value.

LAND, RENT, AND CAPITALIZATION

In Chapter 15 we noted that in many contexts, economists use the terms "land" and "natural resources" interchangeably. We are not about to recant that statement, but now is the time to study the situation when the two concepts are not identical. The main difference is that at least when properly managed, "land" is permanent and inexhaustible. The continents have been here a long time and will be here for some time to come! Many natural resources, on the other hand, can be exhausted and are nonrenewable. There are only so many prehistoric swamps out there, and when we run out, we will have to shift away from reliance upon fossil fuels as our major source of energy. This section will concentrate on land; the next section will look at nonrenewable natural resources.

Kinds of Rent

Pure economic rent A factor payment in excess of the amount necessary to bring that factor into production.

Economists distinguish between different kinds of rent. As we learned in Chapter 15, **pure economic rent** is paid on any factor of production that is fixed in supply. The classic example of pure economic rent is the payment for unimproved land, but there are actually many other cases. Economic rent arises any time a factor of production is paid more than necessary to bring that factor into production. There is a fixed supply of Shaquille O'Neil in the world, so he can command a salary considerably greater than what he really needs to play basketball. That extra salary he earns is pure economic rent. Figure 17.3 illustrates pure economic rent.

••••FIGURE 17.3 PURE ECONOMIC RENT

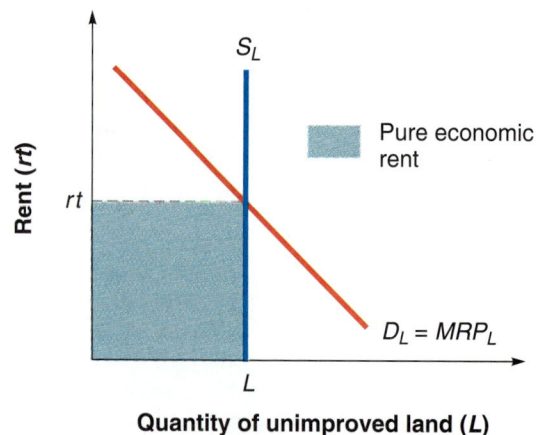

Pure economic rent requires factors to be fixed in supply. The classic case is unimproved land. The rent paid on the land depends on the demand (= marginal revenue product) for land. The landowner receives the rental payment, *rt*, by virtue of the fact that he or she owns the land. An increase in demand—brought on by population growth or whatever—will increase economic rent but bring no more land into production.

Not all land earns the same rent in a competitive market, of course. Different plots of land have different climates, fertility, location, or other advantages. Farms (or firms) located on better land will be more productive than farms located on inferior land. However, this does not mean that the farmers will earn higher profits—at least not in a competitive market. Competition for the best land will bid up rents paid to the landowners and exhaust the economic profits that would have gone to the farmers working the better land. As a result, rent differentials reflect the productivity of land, and landowners, not farmers, reap the gains from better land. **Differential rent** is illustrated in Figure 17.4.

Inframarginal rents arise when suppliers differ in their willingness to offer their services. As shown in Figure 17.5, some factors earn some inframarginal rents in most markets. For example, your professor's love of teaching is probably so high that he or she would be willing to work for the minimum wage, but market conditions result in a considerably higher salary. The difference between the factor payment and the minimum payment necessary to bring the factor into production is inframarginal rent. Inframarginal rent is also called *producer surplus*, a concept we introduced in Chapter 4.

Differential rent Rent on land that depends on marginal productivity.

Inframarginal rent Rent that exists when suppliers differ in their willingness to offer their services; the difference between the factor payment and the minimum payment necessary to bring the factor into production.

. . . .

Capitalization of Land Values

An important characteristic of land is that its market value is the *capitalized* value of rent. Further, the capitalized value of economic rent is captured entirely by the original property owner, not the second or third owners who later buy and sell it. This has important consequences for income distribution and tax incidence.

· · · · · **FIGURE 17.4 DIFFERENTIAL RENT**

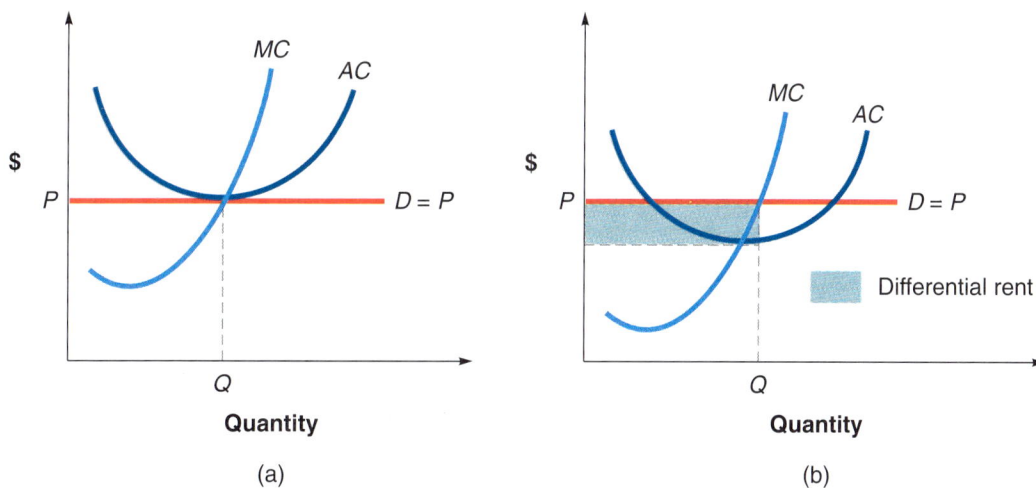

Differential rents exist because not all land is equally productive. The graph in panel (a) represents a perfectly competitive firm renting land of average productivity. The graph in panel (b) represents a perfectly competitive firm renting land of above-average productivity. The firm in panel (b) earns economic profits because of the highly productive land. In a competitive market, however, this profit would be eliminated by higher rent payments to the landowner.

FIGURE 17.5 INFRAMARGINAL RENTS

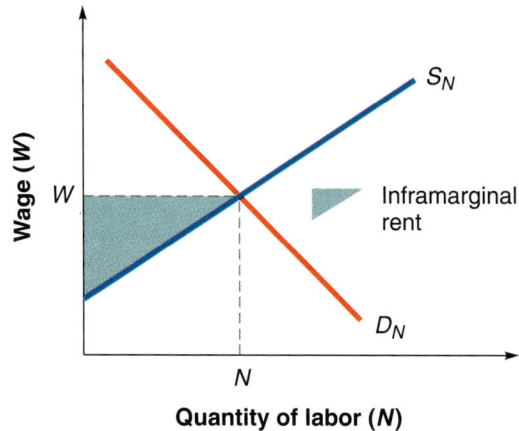

In many markets the willingness to supply factors of production differs considerably. When factor payments exceed the amount necessary to bring that factor into production, factors earn inframarginal rents. Inframarginal rents may be most common in labor markets because some people would be willing to work for lower salaries than they are paid.

Suppose that you lay claim as the original owner to an unimproved plot of land and determine that it has an annual rental income of $1,000. If we assume that the land will earn rent forever and that the appropriate discount rate is 10 percent, the present value of your land is equal to $1,000/0.10 = $10,000.[3] The process of calculating the selling price of an asset as the present value of future rents is called **capitalization**. What price would you be willing to take for the land? The answer is not a cent less than $10,000. This is also the maximum price that a buyer should be willing to pay.

How does land price capitalization relate to income distribution? The only person who receives pure economic rent from land is the original landowner. You were bright (or lucky) enough to lay claim to the land before anyone else did. Your selling price of $10,000 is pure economic rent. But to the second owner, that same $10,000 is a cost of acquiring an asset that will return $1,000 per year. The second buyer receives no economic rent at all!

Capitalization The process of calculating the value of an asset from its return stream; the capitalized value of land is the annual rent divided by the interest rate.

. . . .

Tax Incidence

Land price capitalization also has an important implication for tax incidence. This is shown in Figure 17.6a. Before taxes, the annual rent on the land is $1,000, determined

[3]This is a special case of the present value formula in Equation 1. Equation 1 applies when future payments last for only a finite number of years; this formula applies when $T \to \infty$ and the annual payments are fixed. The general formula for the capitalized value of an asset that pays forever is $PV = \text{rent}/r$, where r is the appropriate discount rate and rent is the annual payment. This is an appropriate formula because we are assuming that the land is not exhausted.

• • • • FIGURE 17.6 LAND TAXES

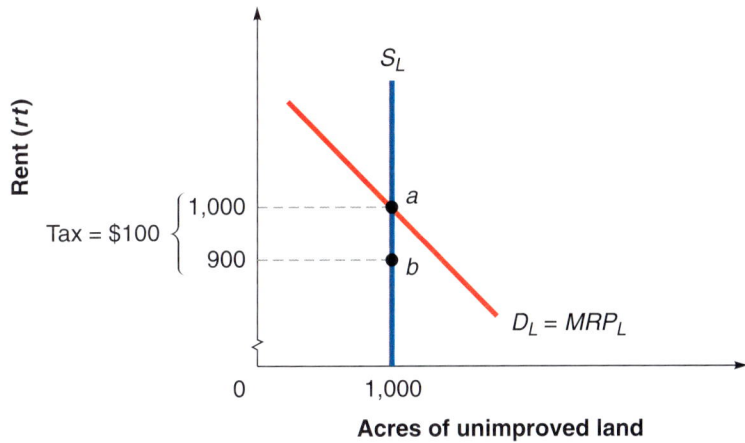

(a)

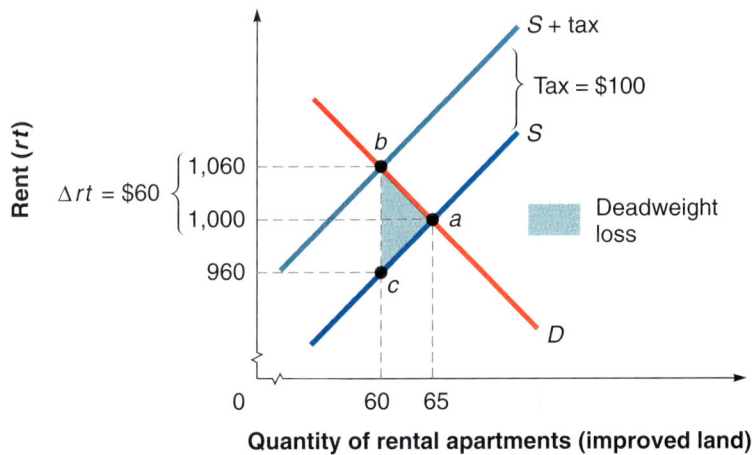

(b)

An advantage of taxes on unimproved land is that there are no efficiency losses. In panel (a), a $100 tax on land reduces the after-tax payment to the landowner from $1,000 to $900, but the supply of land on the market does not change. In panel (b), a tax shifts the supply curve for improved land upward by the amount of the tax. Given the shape of the demand curve, however, rent rises by less than the amount of the tax. The shaded triangle represents the efficiency or deadweight loss due to the tax. In essence, the tax means that people are not using resources in the ways they would without government intervention.

by the intersection of the vertical supply curve, S_L, and the downward-sloping demand curve, D_L. Now, let the government impose a tax on the landowner of $100 per year. The landowner still charges tenants $1,000 per year, but the after-tax rent is now only $900. Assuming a discount rate of 10 percent, the tax lowers the present value of the land to $9,000. The tax has *permanently* reduced the income of the landowner.

But can't the landowner pass on the tax to the tenants? Not in this case. If panel (a) correctly describes the market, tenants will pay no more than $1,000 to rent the land. This differs from the usual situation for *improved* land, say, apartments, where the supply curve is upward sloping as shown in panel (b). Landlords can pass on some of the tax, but when they do, they end up with fewer tenants. In this situation, the tax falls on both the landowner and the tenant. For example, suppose the market begins at point *a* in panel (b) where the monthly rent is $1,000. A $100 per month tax will shift the supply curve up by that amount, but price (monthly rent) will rise less than the tax. In this case, the rent rises by only $60 to $1,060. The after-tax rental income to the landowner falls to $960, so the consumer pays $60 of the tax and the landowner pays $40 in lost monthly rents. Further, the higher rent may reduce the number of apartments that the landowner can rent out. The decline in the monthly rental income reduces the present value of the rental property—but just for the owner who is unlucky enough to hold the property when the tax is imposed.

From an efficiency standpoint, the tax on unimproved land is superior to the tax on improved land because there is no resource misallocation or deadweight loss. Notice that in panel (a), the tax does not affect the quantity of land utilized. It does not generate a work disincentive either because the landowner is doing just as much work before the tax is implemented as after. (Remember that this is *unimproved* land.) This is one reason for the single tax movement we discussed in the Economic Heritage box on Henry George in Chapter 15. When the tax is imposed on improved land in panel (b), rent rises to $1,060 so the landowner is able to pass on part of the tax. The after-tax rent is only $960, however, so the tax falls on both the renter and the landowner. The government collects $6,000 in tax ($100 for each of the 60 apartments that are rented out). The shaded triangle *cab* is a deadweight loss caused by resource misallocation: more apartments would be offered and rented without the tax than with the tax, so preferences are being frustrated.

THE MARKET FOR NONRENEWABLE NATURAL RESOURCES

In the past 20 years or so, natural resource economics has become quite popular. The reason for this is simple: the oil crises of the 1970s. The OPEC oil embargo, subsequent price controls, and gasoline shortages caused gas lines to wrap around the block. Many people began to wonder whether we were in for massive shortages—not only for oil but for other important resources as well. Economic reasoning was the obvious place to look for an answer.

It may come as a surprise, however, that economists generally do *not* believe that we are on the brink of widespread resource shortages. This is not to say that there are no problems on the horizon. There are, but there are also obvious economic solutions—though whether the political will exists to implement these solutions is another matter. The most common policy recommendation is deceptively simple:

Make sure that prices accurately reflect the costs—*all* costs—of extracting and using resources. If this is done, say many economists, the market mechanism will generate efficient resource utilization, and firms and households will automatically switch from one resource to another as prices change. This section will explain why pricing natural resources is so important and, sometimes, so difficult. Before doing so, we need to define a few terms.

. . . .

Terms and Definitions

When economists say they do not expect resource *shortages*, they are not saying they expect the end of *scarcity*. This argument is not just semantics; the two concepts are quite different. All goods that have value and carry a positive price are scarce; shortages exist only when the selling price is below the equilibrium price.[4] The simplest way to have eliminated the gas lines caused by the OPEC embargo would have been to raise the price of gasoline. Had there been no price controls, the price of a gallon of gasoline would have risen from the then-current price of about 40¢ per gallon to perhaps $1.50 per gallon. More people would have carpooled, taken mass transit, or stayed at home, and the lines at gas stations would have vanished immediately. Few consumers would have liked the higher prices, but many would have preferred higher prices to having to wait in line or to having no gas at all.

The difference between shortage and scarcity has an important consequence for the analysis of natural resources: many economists argue that we will *never* run out of most natural resources. To understand why, we need to distinguish between three measures of the stock of resources:

- *Current reserves* are the amount of a resource that is available with current technology and that can be extracted profitably at current prices.
- *Potential reserves* are the amount of a resource that is available with current technology if we are willing to pay the cost of extraction.
- The *resource endowment* is the total amount of the resource available in the earth's crust.

To see why this taxonomy is important, consider what happened when the oil shock hit in the 1970s and the price of crude oil rose from under $5 to over $30 per barrel. Nothing happened to the earth's resource endowment, but reserves in the North Sea and the North Slope of Alaska became commercially feasible; that is, they became part of our potential reserve base. As soon as the new oil drilling platforms became operational, those potential reserves became part of the current stock of reserves. If the price of oil rises to $50 per barrel, current reserves will jump again because it will be profitable to extract oil from shale deposits in Colorado and Utah. There is an important message here: resource prices affect resource availability. This is the main reason why economists are emphatic that market prices should reflect all costs of extraction and production.

Natural resources can be classified according to use, technology, and physical conditions:

---

[4]Shortages were analyzed in detail in Chapter 4.

• Oil is a *depletable and nonrenewable* resource. The earth's crust contains only so much oil, and it cannot be renewed. Optimal use means determining the correct speed of exhaustion: How much should this generation use? How much should be available for the next generation?

• Aluminum is an example of a *depletable but recyclable* resource. Again, there is a fixed quantity of bauxite (the main ore used to manufacture aluminum) in the earth, but recycling aluminum from most uses is technologically feasible. However, 100 percent recycling is impossible, so the available supply of aluminum will diminish over time.

This chapter will focus only on nonrenewable resources, but we should list two other classifications of resources just for comparison. Both of these classifications will be discussed in Chapter 21.

• Water is perhaps the most important *replenishable but depletable* resource. If it is used wisely, the prospect of shortages is remote; if it is used unwisely, fights over water rights will become commonplace. Unlike oil and aluminum, much water is naturally replenishable through rainfall. Unfortunately, groundwater replenishes so slowly that many economists consider it to be nonrenewable.

• Finally, there is a class of resources called *common property resources*. These resources are "owned" by everyone, not individuals. The fish in public waterways are an example. Chronic overuse is a typical consequence of common property resources, a point we develop in Chapter 21.

········

Transition between Depletable and Renewable Resources

California is a leader in the development and use of solar and wind power. One reason for this, of course, is that the sun shines and the wind blows in California. But another reason is just as important: California power plants must meet stricter antipollution standards than power plants in many other states. As a result, energy prices can be quite high and thus provide an incentive to develop alternative energy sources. This can be shown with a model of *intertemporal allocation*—resource allocation over time. We need to define a few more terms before we are ready to analyze this model in Figure 17.7.

Marginal extraction cost The cost of extracting one additional unit of a natural resource.

Marginal user cost Use of finite resources today means that less will be available tomorrow, so future prices will be higher.

Total marginal cost The sum of marginal extraction cost plus marginal user cost.

The incremental cost of extracting the next unit of a resource from the earth is called the **marginal extraction cost**. For simplicity, we are assuming that the marginal extraction cost of the nonrenewable resource (oil) is constant, but the results we are about to develop hold with either constant or increasing marginal extraction costs.[5] If a resource is in fixed supply, current use imposes a cost on future generations because less is available in the future. As resources become scarcer, their prices tend to rise, so current use imposes a cost on future generations in terms of higher future resource prices. This cost is called the **marginal user cost**. Marginal user cost increases over time because of increasing scarcity. Finally, **total marginal cost** is the sum of marginal extraction cost plus marginal user cost.

[5]This is not as unrealistic an assumption as you might think. Technological advances have reduced the extraction costs for many resources.

FIGURE 17.7 INTERTEMPORAL RESOURCE ALLOCATION

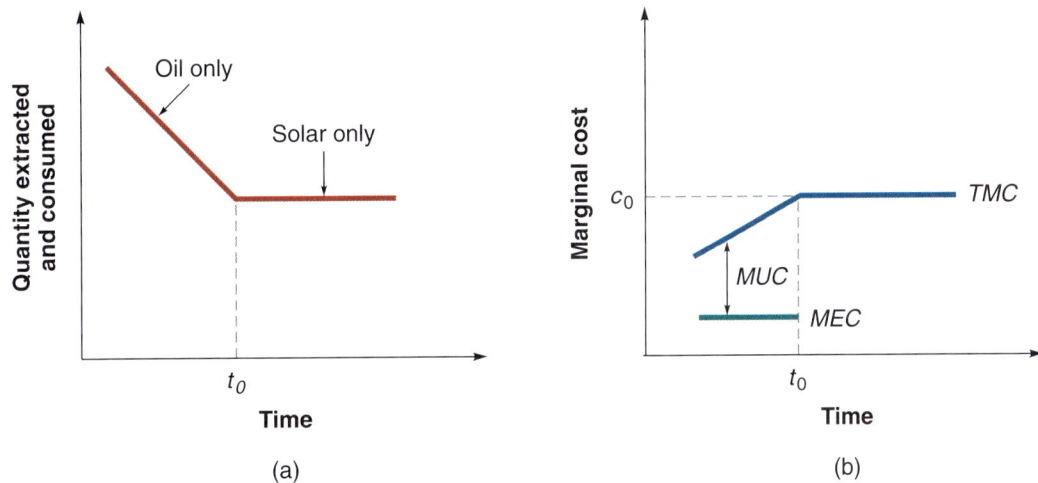

(a)

(b)

If market prices reflect all costs, the economy will undergo a transition from one resource to another. The quantity of oil extracted and consumed will decline over time even if the marginal extraction cost (MEC) is constant. This occurs because the marginal user cost (MUC) of oil rises: current use imposes a cost on future generations because it reduces the amount available in the future. When the total marginal cost ($TMC = MEC + MUC$) of oil reaches the total marginal cost of solar energy, a transition from oil to solar energy takes place. This transition occurs at time t_0, the switch point. Assuming the marginal cost of solar energy is constant, society will use a constant amount of solar energy in the future.

Figure 17.7a shows the extraction and consumption of two energy resources, oil, a nonrenewable resource, and solar power, a renewable resource.[6] The current price of oil is initially low relative to the price of solar energy because solar technology is still under development. As oil consumption increases, however, marginal user cost and price will rise. The rising price of oil acts as an incentive for the development of technology necessary for solar power. We are also assuming that the marginal cost of solar power is constant. This is reflected by the horizontal portion of the total marginal cost curve in panel (b). It is reasonable to assume that no marginal user cost is associated with solar power because just as much solar power will be available to our great-grandchildren as is available today. Notice that the *vertical* axis of panel (a) measures quantity extracted and consumed, and the horizontal axis measures time. The downward-sloping curve shows that the extraction and consumption of oil decrease over time. This occurs because the total marginal cost (and hence the selling price) increases over time and people will buy less of a good at higher prices, *ceteris paribus*. Total marginal cost increases because of rising marginal user costs, shown as the difference between total marginal costs and the (assumed) constant marginal extraction costs.

[6]This figure is a simplification of Figure 6.3 from Tom Tietenberg, *Environmental and Natural Resource Economics*, 3d ed. (New York: Harper-Collins, 1992).

FOCUS ON

COUNTERPRODUCTIVE ENERGY POLICIES: THE CASE OF THE DOMESTIC OIL INDUSTRY

The oil industry in the United States presents a good example of what happens when policymakers try to interfere with resource prices. Problems in the oil industry date back to the 1930s when the first elements of federal regulation of the industry were put into effect.

Oil prices fluctuated dramatically in the first part of the twentieth century. When they bottomed out following the discovery of the huge oil fields in east Texas in the 1930s, the oil-producing states instituted a series of measures designed to prop up and stabilize oil prices. Texas and other states instituted *prorationing*—laws that were designed to control output at the wellhead and maintain high prices. In 1935, the federal government enacted legislation making interstate transportation of nonregulated oil illegal.

In the 1950s, President Eisenhower signed into law import quotas on foreign oil. Eisenhower's argument was that cheap foreign oil was a risk to na-

tional security because it could put the domestic industry out of business. The foreign import quota was set at 12.5 percent of domestic production. Import licenses were given to domestic oil producers who could buy foreign oil for about $1.25 per barrel and then sell it for over $2.50 per barrel—a rather substantial guaranteed profit courtesy of the U.S. government.

At the same time the government was restricting oil imports, it was also subsidizing oil exploration—again based on the national security argument. Several "innovative" subsidies were given to the oil companies. First, the companies were allowed to deduct their *intangible drilling expenses* in the year they were incurred. These expenses—including materials, labor, depreciation on drilling equipment, and other expenses—were often more than half of the cost of drilling. Allowing the deduction of intangible drilling expenses meant, in essence, that firms could deduct more than half of the

cost of drilling a well in the first year. This dramatically increased profits. Second, firms were given *foreign tax credits*; that is, U.S. companies with foreign subsidiaries were allowed to deduct foreign taxes from their U.S. tax liability. This seems to make sense—except that it had the effect of encouraging foreign governments to raise their taxes until they equaled the U.S. tax level. In this case, U.S. corporations would pay no taxes to the U.S. government. The third subsidy for oil companies, the *oil depletion allowance*, was the most controversial. The idea behind the depletion allowance was similar to depreciation. As firms pump oil, they are using up their assets, so they need a tax break, or so went the argument. Congress initially gave the oil companies a 27.5 percent depletion allowance. This meant that if profits were less than 27.5 percent of gross sales, taxes would be zero.

Taken together, these programs certainly helped the oil companies, but

---

Switch point The point where the transition from one resource to another is complete; occurs when the total marginal cost of one resource equals the total marginal cost of the other.

The story told by Figure 17.7 is that the transition from oil to solar power can be brought about automatically by market forces. As the extraction and consumption of oil increase, rising prices cause people to look for substitute energy sources. When the cost of oil rises to the cost of solar power, the **switch point** is reached, and the transition is complete. Notice that this switch occurs before we have completely exhausted the supply of oil; there is still oil in the ground, but it is not worth the cost of extraction because an alternative energy source is available.

they probably did more harm than good to the nation as a whole. Prorationing limited the output from individual wells, so the only way for firms to increase profits was to drill more wells—which was encouraged by the depletion allowance and the deductibility of intangible drilling expenses. By the mid-1960s, the United States had more than enough operational oil wells to meet domestic needs and *far* more than would have been needed had an unrestricted amount of imports been allowed.

The net result of these policies was that American oil was used first, leaving the United States vulnerable to interruptions in foreign oil imports in the future. It took the oil shocks of the 1970s to reveal how shortsighted U.S. energy policies had been. The depletion allowance, prorationing, and import quotas were all eliminated. Had the United States allowed unrestricted imports in the 1950s and 1960s, it would not have been necessary to search for oil in the North Slope of Alaska or the Bering Sea because the "cheap" Texas oil would still have been in the ground. And had U.S. oil prices been comparable to world oil prices—gas was 35¢ a gallon in the United States when it was $2 per gallon in Europe—the economy would have responded to the higher prices with more fuel-efficient cars, smaller and better insulated homes, and so on. The oil shocks of the 1970s would have been little more than a minor inconvenience.

The oil industry today still receives subsidies for exploration, but the real incentive for exploration was OPEC's artificially high price of oil. It is perhaps ironic that many economists—and even a few politicians—now advocate substantial tax increases on oil and gas. Such tax increases could encourage conservation, speed up the transition to alternative fuels—and maybe even put a dent in the federal deficit. And with today's (April 1994) inflation-adjusted price of oil actually *less* than the price of oil in 1970, the argument for higher gas taxes is even stronger.

Of course, knowing that the transition will eventually take place does not mean that it will be as smooth as this model may seem to imply. For example, when electric and oil heat reduced the demand for coal, thousands of coal miners discovered they had no other marketable skills, and numerous coal mining towns were devastated. A shift from oil to solar energy could have a similar impact on the petroleum industry and oil-producing states.

It is important to recognize that the transition from one resource to another will take place only if prices are allowed to rise and reflect increasing scarcity. Policies designed to keep prices artificially low will postpone the inevitable transition. Further, most economists believe that if price controls are used even temporarily, their inevitable removal will result in an abrupt and destabilizing transition phase. The Focus box on page 436 examines this situation. Policies designed to keep the price of resources artificially *high*—as is done in many countries around the world—will result in conservation and act as an incentive to find alternative fuels.

. . . .

Other Resource Transitions

The oil–solar energy example is just one application of the general model of intertemporal resource allocation. Several other applications are possible. For example, a similar diagram could be used to show how the economy shifts between two depletable resources. As the cost of the first depletable resource increases, a switch point will be reached where it is more economical to use the second depletable resource. The shift between firewood and coal might be one example. Geometrically, this case would differ from Figure 17.7 because no portion of the consumption line or the *TMC* curve would be perfectly flat. Another application is the transition from virgin resources to recycled resources. Virgin resources will be used until the total marginal cost exceeds the cost of recycling; at that point, recycling will become economically feasible. Policies designed to encourage recycling could be used to speed up this transition.

SUMMARY

The markets for capital and natural resources differ from other factor markets because of the important role of time. Capital takes time to build and pays out over several years; nonrenewable natural resources are fixed in supply so it is important to use them optimally over time. The main points from this chapter included:

1. Production methods that use capital are said to be roundabout because production of the final products is delayed until the capital goods can be built. In the simplified two-period case, firms should acquire capital as long as the marginal revenue product of the capital good is greater than the opportunity cost of forgone current production. In the *T*-period case, capital should be acquired if the rate of return on capital exceeds the rate of time preference.

2. A market for loanable funds will develop when rates of time preference differ. Patient people have low rates of time preference; they are willing to lend to people with higher rates of time preference. In the long run, the rate of return on capital equals the rate of time preference and the interest rate on loanable funds.

3. The present value of an asset is the sum of future returns discounted by the appropriate discount rate. The net present value of an asset is the present value minus the cost of acquiring the asset. Firms should invest when the net present value is positive. Risk can be incorporated into investment decisions by increasing the discount rate. The higher the discount rate, the lower the net present value of an asset.

4. Factors that are in fixed supply command pure economic rent; unimproved land is an example of a factor that receives pure economic rent. Land is not of uniform quality, so differential rents are often charged on land. Inframarginal rents are paid when owners of some units of a factor are more willing to offer their services than other factor owners.

5. Rent and taxes are capitalized into the value of land. This means that only the original landowner receives the economic rents or pays the land tax.

6. Most economists believe that there would be few natural resource shortages if market prices reflected all costs of production. This includes extraction costs as well as user costs. Further, as the price of natural resources increases to reflect increasing user costs, market processes will generate a transition from one resource to another.

KEY TERMS AND CONCEPTS

roundabout production	shortage, scarcity
rate of return	current reserves
time preference	potential reserves
loanable funds	resource endowment
present value	depletable resources
discount rate	nonrenewable resource
net present value	recyclable resource
risk	common property resources
pure economic rent	intertemporal allocation
differential rent	marginal extraction cost
inframarginal rent	marginal user cost
capitalization	total marginal cost
land tax incidence	switch point

IMPORTANT FORMULAS

Future value of a single payment: $FV_t = PV(1 + r)^t$

Present value of an income flow: $PV = \dfrac{FV_1}{(1 + r)^1} + \dfrac{FV_2}{(1 + r)^2} + \dfrac{FV_3}{(1 + r)^3} + \cdots$

Present value of an income flow: $PV = \sum\limits_{t=1}^{T} \dfrac{FV_t}{(1 + r)^t}$

Net present value: $NPV = PV - C_0$

REVIEW QUESTIONS

1. Why is production involving capital goods called "roundabout production"? What criteria should firms use before they decide to buy additional capital?

2. Explain how interest rates are determined in the market for loanable funds. Draw a

diagram to illustrate your answer. Why is the interest rate equal to the rate of time preference and the rate of return on capital in the long run?

3. What is the discount rate? How is it related to the present value of a flow of income from a capital project?

4. Explain how firms account for risk when they make investment decisions.

5. Define, give examples of, and use diagrams to illustrate the three kinds of rent.

6. Explain how economic rent and taxes are capitalized into the price of land.

7. Why do economists believe it is so important that the price of natural resources accurately reflect all costs?

8. Explain how the market can automatically bring about the transition from one resource to another. Draw a diagram to illustrate your answer.

PROBLEMS

1. Many computer programs allow users to write *macros*—small programs that simplify repetitive tasks. For example, instead of having to tell the computer to (1) sum a column of data, (2) divide by n to compute the average, and then (3) form a ratio of the last entry in the column to the average computed in step 2, a macro allows you simply to hit a function key and get the desired result. Unfortunately, writing macros can be time-consuming. Is macro writing roundabout production? Where is capital involved?

2. Suppose you believe you can earn $500 per year for three years on an investment project that would cost you $1,000. (These problems are much easier on a financial calculator, but working them by hand is not too tough.)
   a. Assume the interest rate is zero. Should you invest?
   b. Assume the interest rate is 10 percent. What is the *NPV*?
   c. How high would the interest rate have to be before you decided not to invest?
   d. Suppose you can get the $500 per year return and the current interest rate is 15 percent. How much would you be willing to pay for that return stream?

3. Interest rates are typically much higher in developing countries than they are in developed nations. Can you explain why?

4. Differential rents are paid on unimproved land of different qualities. Does this mean that landowners "deserve" their rental income because they correctly assess the productivity of their land? Or does Henry George's argument that economic rent represents unearned income still hold? Explain and comment.

5. Both the demand for and the use of petroleum products increased tremendously in the early twentieth century, yet both the current and the potential reserves of petroleum were higher by the middle of the twentieth century than in the nineteenth century. Explain and comment.

6. Figure 17.6 shows that taxes on unimproved land are more efficient than taxes on improved land. A generalization of this statement is that taxes on factors with inelastic supply curves are more efficient than taxes on factors with elastic supply curves. Use this concept to explain which of the following pairs would be a more efficient tax:
   a. sales tax on food, income tax
   b. liquor tax, driver's license fee
   c. toll roads, bus fares
   d. higher electricity bills, higher tuition rates at public universities

7. Figure 17.7 illustrated the transition from oil to solar energy. Redraw the diagram to illustrate the transition from heating oil to natural gas. You should suppose that initially the total marginal cost of heating oil is greater than that of natural gas.

8. Can you think of any cases when the rate of time preference would be negative? (*Hint:* Would it be nice if your parents' rate of time preference was negative?)

9. In 1993 the Clinton administration proposed a broad BTU tax to generate revenue and increase energy conservation. (BTU stands for British thermal unit and is the measurement unit for power that comes from any energy source.) Had it been passed, the BTU tax would have raised the price of all kinds of energy. Do you think a broad-based energy tax like the BTU tax would be preferable to taxes targeted on only certain kinds of energy, say, gasoline? Does your answer depend on your income level? Where you live? On the purpose of the tax?

PART IV

MICROECONOMIC
POLICIES

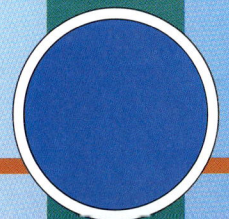

CHAPTER 18

Markets and Government

Adam Smith celebrated free-market capitalism in his *Wealth of Nations*, but he also noted that the government has several important roles in market economies: to provide national defense, maintain justice, and engage in certain public works. Smith also spoke of the need for measures to maintain competition and combat monopoly power. Today, the governments of most industrialized nations play a much more prominent role than Smith would probably think they should. Modern governments provide public education, welfare, subsidies for research and development, health care, and a host of other goods and services. Most nations also have a variety of policies designed to help certain industries thought to be critical for international trade, national defense, or other reasons.

   In the United States, nearly one dollar in three flows through the government sector. This may seem like a large amount, but it is smaller than in most industrialized nations. Is such a large government sector necessary? Are those bureaucrats just taking advantage of the public? Few would answer an unqualified "yes" to these questions, but fewer still would answer with an unqualified "no." How do we determine the proper role of the government in the economy? How does the government make decisions? And why does there seem to be so much government waste? These are the questions we will explore in this chapter.

AFTER READING AND STUDYING THIS CHAPTER, YOU SHOULD BE ABLE TO:
• • • Distinguish between private and public goods, and explain why government allocation of public goods is necessary

• • • Show how government policies are used to deal with external costs and benefits
• • • Understand the principles of taxation
• • • Discuss the main elements of public choice theory, and use economic analysis to better understand the actions and motives of voters and elected officials

• • • • • • • MARKET FAILURE AND THE GOVERNMENT

After all we have said about market efficiency, it might seem a bit strange that we are about to set out criteria for government involvement in the economy. If markets always worked like those we described in Chapter 11, this chapter would be unnecessary because there would be no economic need for government involvement in the economy. Unfortunately, markets do not always achieve the efficient and equitable outcomes described in the textbook. Markets automatically result in optimal outcomes—allocative and technical efficiency—only under the very specific set of conditions that define perfect competition. As we noted at the end of Chapter 11, pure competition exists when there are many sellers, product homogeneity, and easy entry and exit. Perfect competition requires these three conditions plus perfect information. When any of these conditions are absent, a **market failure** occurs, and the door is opened for government intervention.

Markets characterized by imperfect competition—monopolistic competition, oligopoly, and monopoly—represent one kind of market failure. These markets may require government regulation or antitrust policies, the main topics of the next chapter. Incomplete information can also lead to market failure. For example, if consumers were not aware that a Häagen Dazs ice cream bar contains 30 grams of fat or that excessive consumption of high-fat food can lead to heart disease and cancer, they might eat more ice cream than is good for them. A market failure of this type might be resolved by government-mandated package labeling to warn ice cream lovers of the health risk of fat. This issue is also addressed in Chapter 19. Finally, some economists consider macroeconomic fluctuations a form of market failure and call for government policies to control inflation and the output losses that occur during recessions. This is a main subject of macroeconomics, the topic of Chapters 22—33. This chapter will focus primarily on two other sources of market failure, public goods and externalities.

Market failure Situation where market outcomes are not optimal; may be due to imperfect information, public goods, or externalities.

Public Goods

A private good differs from a **public good** in two important ways: (1) Private goods are subject to the **exclusion principle**; public goods are not. I must pay for a cup of espresso before I can drink it; if I do not pay for it, the coffee shop owner will exclude me from drinking it. You may not have to pay for national defense to receive the benefits. Some of my taxes will be used to pay for defense, but even though you are a starving student earning no income and paying no taxes, you cannot be excluded from receiving the benefits of national defense. National defense is a public good;

Public good A good that is not subject to the exclusion principle or rival consumption. Such goods cannot be allocated efficiently by the market.

Exclusion principle A person using a private good can exclude others from using it; a person using a public good cannot exclude others from using the same good.

espresso is a private good. (2) The consumption of public goods is **nonrival** in the sense that if I consume a public good, my consuming it does not diminish your ability to consume it as well. National defense is again a good example: my benefit in no way reduces the amount of benefits you receive. On the other hand, once I drink that espresso, it is not available to you.

Public goods result in a market failure because there is no way to get people to voluntarily reveal their preferences or pay for public goods. For example, if you want an espresso, you have to pay $1.50. And if many people pay $1.50 for a cup of espresso, the espresso coffee industry will expand, and espresso kiosks will appear on every street corner. Public goods like national defense are different. People understand that they will receive the benefits from national defense whether they pay for it or not, so the market has no way to determine just how much or what kind of national defense people want. People may vote for candidates who favor strong national defense, but elections are an imprecise way to determine which or how many military goods the people want. As a result, military spending decisions are left to the political process. The theory of public choice developed later in this chapter will give us some insight into how these decisions are made.

Externalities

Externalities can also interfere with market efficiency. An externality exists whenever the market does not recognize all of the costs or benefits of production or consumption. Externalities can be either negative or positive. Pollution is an example of a **negative externality** in production. When a paper mill emits foul odors, it is imposing a cost on the people in nearby communities, yet without government intervention, these people are not compensated. Furthermore, the firm's cost of making paper does not include this cost, so a divergence occurs between the private costs and social costs. Private costs include only those costs that must be paid by the firm; social costs include private costs as well as external costs like pollution. When negative externalities exist, the private market produces too much, and selling prices are too low. A wide variety of government regulations and taxes are used to reduce or eliminate negative externalities, a point we mentioned when externalities were first introduced in Chapter 4.

Positive externalities in production occur when one production process provides an external benefit to another process or individual. For example, suppose that Farmer Jones spends the time and money to track down the fox that has been raiding all of the chicken farms in the area. Not only does Jones benefit, but so do all of his neighboring farmers. The benefit to the neighboring farmers is a positive externality that results from Farmer Jones's fox hunting efforts. The neighboring farmers receive these benefits for free—unless Farmer Jones is able to get them to subsidize the cost of his hunt. Positive externalities often indicate the need for subsidies.

There can also be externalities in consumption. For example, if you get a little carried away at the big game and drink too much, your obnoxious behavior will make the game less enjoyable for other fans. It will also make driving home more dangerous to you and the other people on the road. This is a negative externality in consumption. A liquor tax might raise the price of alcohol, reduce alcohol consumption, and reduce these negative externalities. On the other hand, if you play

Rival consumption Consumption is rival if my consumption makes it impossible for you to consume the good as well.

Negative externality The cost to society from a private action that is not included in market price or cost calculations.

Positive externality A benefit to society from private action that is not included in market cost or price calculations.

your stereo so loud that the entire dorm is able to rock along with you, you have provided a positive externality—but only if they like your taste in music! If the Dorm Council agrees that your music benefits everyone, it would be appropriate for them to subsidize your music collection: other students have benefited, so they should help pay the cost of the music.

PRINCIPLES OF TAXATION: EFFICIENCY VERSUS EQUITY

But just recognizing that market failures may require government intervention does not solve the problem. We also need to determine the extent of government involvement and the best way to raise tax revenues to pay for any needed government spending. Both issues are difficult. Politicians, policymakers, and the public are forever trying to decide how many public goods are needed, how to measure externalities, and how to collect tax revenues to finance these programs. This section will look at the criteria that can be used to design tax programs. The next sections will develop the criteria for determining the optimal quantity of a public good and methods for dealing with externalities.

Tax Efficiency

Once a given level of government involvement is decided upon, the next step is to determine how to raise the funds to finance that spending. This decision involves more than merely determining whether to use progressive, regressive, or proportional taxes;[1] it is also important to use efficient tax collection methods. Two criteria can be used to assess the efficiency of the tax collection system. First, the tax should have a minimum effect on economic incentives and activity. For example, many economists believe that income taxes adversely affect the incentive to work because they reduce take-home pay. These economists believe that income taxes are less efficient than sales taxes because sales taxes have little effect on work incentives: you pay sales taxes only when you buy things, not when you work, so there is no disincentive to work longer hours.[2] Second, the cost of collecting the tax revenues should be low. In other words, a tax that requires a large team of tax collectors is inefficient; a tax that is paid voluntarily with 100 percent compliance would be efficient. Many econ-

---

[1]These terms were defined in Chapter 6. Recall that a progressive tax takes a higher fraction of income as income rises; a regressive tax takes a lower fraction of income as income rises; and a proportional tax takes a constant fraction of income as income rises. The federal income tax is somewhat progressive; sales taxes are regressive; and many state income taxes are approximately proportional.

[2]An important qualification should be added: taxes designed to deal with externalities should affect incentives. For example, a tax designed to reduce pollution would be efficient if it did generate a strong disincentive to pollute. A pollution tax that did not reduce pollution would be considered inefficient.

omists believe that income taxes are inferior to most sales taxes according to this criterion as well.

. . . .

Tax Equity

A shortcoming of these efficiency criteria is that politicians and the public are just as concerned with equity as efficiency. Sales taxes may be efficient, but they are regressive. Is it "fair" for a rich person to pay a lower portion of his or her income in taxes than a poor person? What if the poor person is lazy and the rich person is hardworking? Many economists believe that taxes should be based on one of two tax-equity principles, ability to pay or benefits received. According to the **ability-to-pay** principle, rich people should pay more taxes than poor people because they can afford to. Taxes on luxury goods fit this criterion; equal taxes on every citizen would not, because poor people would find it harder to pay the tax than rich people would. According to the **benefits-received** principle, people should pay higher taxes if they receive greater benefits from government programs. For example, a person with a great deal of property would pay higher taxes to support the police (who presumably would protect the property) than a person with little or no personal property. For another example, in the fall of 1993, the U.S. Forest Service announced that it would begin charging people who needed its rescue services. This policy is clearly in line with benefits received, but whether it is equitable is another matter entirely. The tradeoff between efficiency and equity is one of the most important issues surrounding the government's role in the economy. It is also one of the most difficult: equity is exceedingly difficult to measure, but many economists would agree that the most efficient taxes—sales taxes and uniform head taxes—tend to be the least equitable.

Ability to pay Criterion for determining fairness of taxes; progressive income taxes fit this criterion because people in higher income brackets pay a higher portion of their income in taxes.

Benefits received Criterion for determining fairness of taxes; property taxes may meet this criterion because people with more property may stand to benefit more from public services like police protection.

. . . .

Earmarked Taxes

Should taxes be tied to specific goods or services? For example, should the revenues from the sale of fishing licenses be used for restocking rivers? Should gasoline taxes be used for highway construction and maintenance? The answer to this question—like so many in economics!—can only be, "It depends." Most states do tie fishing and hunting license proceeds to wildlife programs, and most gasoline taxes are used for highway construction. That seems "fair," right? Perhaps. What about property tax revenues? Should they be used to fund projects that benefit only property owners? In many states, property taxes are the main source of revenues for public education, but it would be hard to argue that education benefits property owners more than people who do not own property. And what about income taxes? If income tax revenues were used to provide goods that benefited only income tax payers, it would be impossible to fund income redistribution and welfare programs.

Earmarking every tax would be impossible, but it might be appropriate to tie specific taxes to specific benefits in those cases where it is possible. Earmarking reduces the apparent capriciousness of taxes and may increase taxpayer compliance. This may explain why people seem to complain most bitterly about income, sales, and property taxes; none are directly tied to specific benefits. The fact that most federal, state, and local taxes are not earmarked may be one reason there are so many citizen complaints about tax fairness.[3]

· · · · · · · ·

A Prologue

Even before we get into the details, you should be able to anticipate much of what follows. Many of the issues in public economics are subject to rather heated debate. Accurately measuring the impact of externalities or determining the right quantity of a public good to provide is almost always difficult, and there are numerous conflicting criteria for determining the best ways to collect tax revenues. These disagreements probably lie at the core of those jokes so often heard about economists, but they actually should be considered a strength of economics, not a weakness. The role of economists is to provide policymakers with alternative policies—and to understand the consequences of those alternatives. The economists' principles of public finance and taxation serve their intended roles quite well: they are useful for developing alternative policy proposals and for illustrating their consequences to policymakers. The policymakers must decide which policy to implement.

· · · · · · · · PUBLIC GOODS

Try this thought experiment: Suppose that in a desperate bid to win reelection, the new president allows people to voluntarily contribute funds for national defense. The average contribution, she argues, should be about $1,350 per person— the $350 billion defense budget divided by the population of 260 million—but you are free to contribute as much or as little as you like. How much would you contribute? Out of a sense of civic duty, you might send in the recommended $1,350. But if you are a **free rider**, you will recognize that you will receive the benefits of the national defense whether you send in any money or not. National defense is a public good so no one can exclude you from enjoying its benefits. Unsettling as this may be, the self-serving approach might be to decline to contribute to national defense because you will receive the benefits anyway. Public goods cannot be allocated in the market because people have no incentive to voluntarily reveal their preferences or pay even if they do.

Free rider A person who receives benefits from public goods without paying for them.

· · · · · · · ·

Efficient Allocation of Public Goods

We learned in Chapter 11 that allocative efficiency for a private good requires that the marginal benefit of the last unit consumed be equal to the marginal cost of

---

[3]In early 1993, the Clinton administration proposed a BTU tax to raise revenue to reduce the deficit. BTU stands for "British thermal unit," a measure of energy. One reason for the BTU tax was equity. For example, an oil tax would hurt people in the Northeast who rely heavily on home heating oil; a gas tax would hurt the western states where driving distances are long. But another reason for the BTU tax was that it was more easily hidden than, say, a per-gallon tax on gasoline; many people would not know they were paying higher taxes. This is the antithesis of an earmarked tax, but perhaps it is politically expedient. The BTU tax proposal did not survive as part of Clinton's 1993 tax package. It was replaced by a 4.6¢ per gallon tax on gasoline.

production. Rational consumers are willing to pay a price equal to the marginal benefit they receive from the private good, so the *allocative efficiency criterion* can be stated as:

Allocative efficiency criterion for a private good: $P = MB = MC$

Two complications arise when we try to apply this criterion to public goods. First, it is not clear that people will reveal their preferences, but we will have to skirt this issue for a moment and assume that people do reveal their preferences. The second problem is that everyone receives the same amount of the public good, so the total demand curve for a public good is constructed differently than the market demand curve for private goods.

Efficient allocation of a public good is shown in Figure 18.1. For simplicity, we are assuming that only two people use the public good, person a and person b. Their individual demand curves are illustrated as D_a and D_b. The total demand curve for the public good, D_{a+b}, is found by determining the total price that society would pay for each quantity of a public good, perhaps hours of public radio broadcasts. D_{a+b} is found by vertical addition: add the price person a would pay for each quantity

FIGURE 18.1 EFFICIENT ALLOCATION OF A PUBLIC GOOD

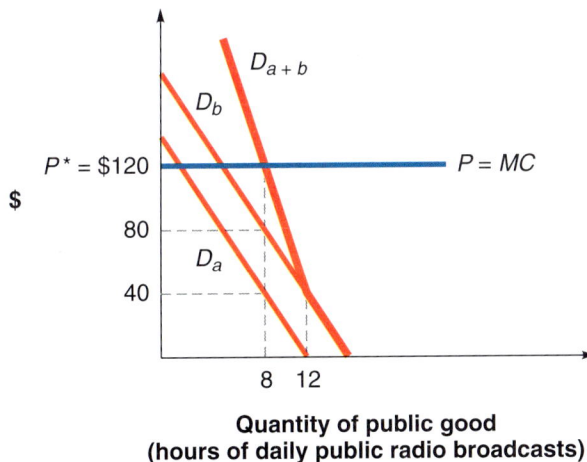

**Quantity of public good
(hours of daily public radio broadcasts)**

The total demand for a public good is found by vertical addition because each person consumes the same quantity. For every possible quantity, the prices that each individual is willing to pay are added together. The public good in this case is hours of public radio broadcasts. Person a is willing to pay an annual fee of $40 for 8 hours of daily broadcasts, and person b is willing to pay $80 for the same 8 hours of daily broadcasts. This means that the total demand curve, D_{a+b}, passes through the point ($120, 8).

Allocative efficiency exists when price equals marginal cost. This occurs at the intersection between the total demand curve, D_{a+b}, and the supply curve, $P = MC = 120. The social price of the good, $P\star$, is the total price that all consumers would pay for the fixed quantity. Once the optimal quantity of the public good is found, it is necessary to determine how to finance it. This may entail charging each consumer a different price.

to the price person *b* would pay for the same quantity to find the total price that society would pay for every quantity. In this example, person *a* and person *b* are willing to pay annual fees of $40 and $80, respectively, for 8 hours of daily public radio broadcasts. If *a* and *b* are the only people in society, then the total price that society would be willing to pay for 8 hours of daily public radio is $120. The same technique is used to find all points of the total demand curve, D_{a+b}. Two things are worth noting about the resulting total demand curve. First, person *a* would not voluntarily pay for more than 12 hours of radio broadcasts at any price. This means that for quantities greater than 12 hours, the total demand curve is identical to person *b*'s demand curve. Second, the upper portion of the total demand curve is steeper than either of the individual demand curves because the change in price is larger relative to the quantity on the total demand curve than it is on either of the individual demand curves.

The optimal quantity of the public good is found where the supply curve intersects the total demand curve. If we assume that the marginal cost of providing public radio is constant, then the supply curve is just the price line, $P = MC$, which is equal to $120 in this example.[4] The optimal number of public radio broadcast hours is 8. Once the optimal quantity of the public good is calculated, it is necessary to determine how to raise the $120 to pay for it. One option is to charge each person a different price based on the individual demand curves. In this case, person *a* would pay $40 and person *b* would pay $80. This may seem reasonable because people would be paying a price equal to their marginal benefit of consuming the public good, but implementing such a program might be politically difficult. Precisely because people are reluctant to reveal their preferences for a public good, it is often necessary to use other criteria—ability to pay, for example—to fund public goods.

Some Real-World Complications

The scenario we have just laid out has a few problems. First, people have incentives to hide their preferences and become free riders. As a result, it is virtually impossible to draw true individual demand curves as we did in Figure 18.1. Second, even if we could determine the actual preferences of everyone who benefits from a public good, rather severe political problems could develop when we tried to charge different prices (taxes) to people who received the same quantity of the public good. This means, of course, that the politicians must decide how much of a public good to provide as well as how to tax people to pay for it. How close the outcome approximates the economist's definition of efficiency is difficult to determine.

Another problem arises when the public good can be provided with a very low or zero marginal cost. For example, once a public radio station is operational, the marginal cost of providing the service to one more listener is zero, so the efficient tax price of listening to the radio should be zero as well. Great—but how do you pay to build the radio station in the first place? If people were required to pay to listen to the radio (perhaps via the purchase of a special box to decode scrambled

[4]The intersection between the total demand curve found by vertical addition and the supply curve for the public good is called a *Lindahl equilibrium*, after the Swedish economist Erik Lindahl (1891–1960) who first developed the conditions for efficient allocation of a public good.

radio waves), some people would not listen, and the level of radio listening would fall below the optimal level. In this case, the radio station would no longer be a public good because exclusion would be possible. An alternative financing scheme is to use general tax revenues to build and operate the station, but this would eliminate the connection between the people who pay the taxes and those who receive the benefits. Another method, which is used with varying success by public radio stations around the nation, is to rely on voluntary contributions. Those annual fund drives may not be fun to listen to, but they often do work.

Finally, the examples we have used so far were chosen to make the distinction between public and private goods as clear as possible, but in the real world the distinction is often not so clear. Some goods are best classified as *quasi-public goods*. Two examples of quasi-public goods are parks and education. The private sector could provide both goods because (1) people could be excluded from using them without payment and would therefore be forced to reveal their preferences, and (2) consumption is rival in that if too many people enroll in school or use the park, the benefits will decline. At the same time, these goods also have attributes like public goods. Consumption is, within limits, nonrival because a few more people in the park or classroom would not detract from the benefits enjoyed by others. Most quasi-public goods also have significant externalities. The quasi-public nature of schools and parks explains why they are sometimes provided by the public sector and sometimes by the private sector. The private allocation of pure public goods inevitably entails consequences, however, a point that is demonstrated in the Focus box on page 454.

RECAP   **The Provision of Public Goods**

The fundamental difference between private and public goods can be summarized as follows: everyone pays the same price for a private good, but buys different quantities; everyone consumes the same quantity of a public good but is willing to pay a different price. Additionally:

1. The consumption of public goods is neither rival nor exclusive.
2. No one can be excluded from the consumption of public goods, so people have an incentive to be free riders; that is, to consume the product without paying for it. This is why the market cannot provide public goods efficiently.
3. The optimal quantity of public goods is the quantity such that the marginal benefit of the good is equal to the marginal cost for all taxpayers. Graphically, the demand curve for a public good is found by vertical addition of individual demands for the public good.

EXTERNAL COSTS AND BENEFITS

Free markets result in efficiency only when all costs and benefits are reflected in the selling price. Costs that are not reflected in price are called *negative*

FOCUS ON

PRIVATELY PROVIDED PUBLIC GOODS: A GAME-THEORETIC APPROACH

When Vice-President Bush ran for president in 1988, he offered an innovative program to reduce government spending on social programs, the Thousand Points of Light program. The aim of this program was to use private volunteers instead of paid government workers to solve pressing social problems like homelessness and poverty. When the program was announced, it received popular support, but some economists were leery from the outset. In essence, this program was an effort to provide a public good (the elimination of social problems) by the private sector. A simple example using game theory can show why this is so difficult.

Suppose that there are two people in a neighborhood that needs a streetlight. The people calculate that the benefits from the streetlight amount to $100 per person. The streetlight costs $150 to buy and install, and each person has the choice of contributing to the streetlight or not. If they both contribute, they will split the cost evenly and each will pay $75; this will result in a net gain of $25 (= $100 − $75) for each person. If only one person contributes, the cost will be $150 to that person. The gains to the contributor will be −$50 (= $100 − $150) while the person who does not contribute (the free rider) will gain $100

	Person A	
Actions →	Contribute	Don't Contribute
Person B Contribute	A:25 B:25	A:100 B:−50
Don't Contribute	A:−50 B:100	A:0 B:0

in benefits while paying nothing. This information has been placed in the above payoff matrix.

What is the most likely outcome of this game? Like all game theory problems, the solution is found by looking at the situation from each player's perspective and determining how they would act based on possible actions of the other player. Think of the situation from Person A's perspective: if Person B contributes, A should be a free rider (not contribute) and make a $100 gain; if B does not contribute, A should do the same and make zero gain. B would reach the same conclusions: if A contributes, don't contribute; if A does not contribute, don't contribute. Our conclusion: The streetlight will not be installed by private initiative.

This example is extremely simplified, and it is possible that in a repeated

game the streetlight would be built. As we mentioned in our discussion of the public radio station, voluntary contributions do sometimes work. This may be especially true in cases where there is a history of cooperation and voluntary contribution.[1] Wearing a pin that says you contributed to the public radio station may be very chic in some circles—chic enough to foster a spirit of voluntary contribution to a public good. The situation was apparently different in the case of President Bush's Thousand Points of Light program: it made news for the first few months of the Bush administration, but volunteerism did not have a significant impact on social policy over the next four years.

[1]Some of the issues concerning voluntary cooperation are discussed in Pranab Bardhan, "Symposium on Management of Local Commons," *Journal of Economic Perspectives* 7 (Fall 1993): 87–92.

externalities; benefits that are not reflected in price are called *positive externalities*.[5] Governments are frequently called upon to enact measures so that market prices reflect all costs and benefits. Two ways to solve the problem of externalities are covered in this section: the use of taxes or subsidies to internalize externalities, and the assignment of property rights and the development of a market for the right to pollute.

. . . .

Negative Externalities

When managers calculate least-cost production methods, they consider both explicit and implicit costs of production. Explicit costs include wages, interest expenses, rents, and so on. Implicit costs are primarily the opportunity costs of time and forgone alternatives: if the decision is made to produce product *a*, it may not be possible to produce product *b*, take a vacation, or whatever. Both explicit and implicit costs are considered private or internal costs because they are borne by business and counted when setting the selling price of output. However, many production processes also generate costs that do not need to be paid by the firm or the consumer, and someone has to bear that cost. These are external costs. One common external cost is pollution. Unless required to do so by the government, neither firms nor consumers pay for preventing or cleaning up pollution even though pollution represents a real cost to society. When external costs like pollution are not included in the firm's cost calculations, the private cost of production is less than the social cost of production. As a result, from society's perspective, the selling price is too low and output is too high.

Figure 18.2 shows the market for a product with an external cost. The industry supply curve is the marginal *private* cost curve. If the industry is unregulated, the market price ($10) and quantity (100) will be determined by the intersection between demand and supply. The supply curve does not include the external costs of pollution, however, so this price is too low and consumption is too high. The vertical distance between the marginal social cost curve and the marginal private cost curve represents the social costs of the externality. The solution to this sort of problem was first suggested by the English economist A. C. Pigou (1877–1959).[6] Pigou showed that efficient resource allocation would be achieved if policymakers imposed a tax equal to the vertical distance between marginal social cost and marginal private cost ($4 in this case) on each unit that is produced. This makes the industry supply curve equal to the marginal social cost curve. The tax would have three effects: (1) the selling price would rise to $12, (2) producers would receive a lower after-tax price, $8, and (3) the quantity demanded would fall to 80 units. Resource allocation would be

---

[5]A number of terms are sometimes used instead of externality. Some authors prefer the term *neighborhood effects* or *spillover effects*. Others refer to negative externalities as *external diseconomies* and positive externalities as *external economies*. We will stick with positive and negative externality throughout this chapter.

[6]Pigou developed these ideas in his classic *Wealth and Welfare* (1912), which was revised and transformed into *The Economics of Welfare* (1920). Pollution taxes are sometimes called *Pigouvian taxes* in recognition of Pigou's contribution in this area.

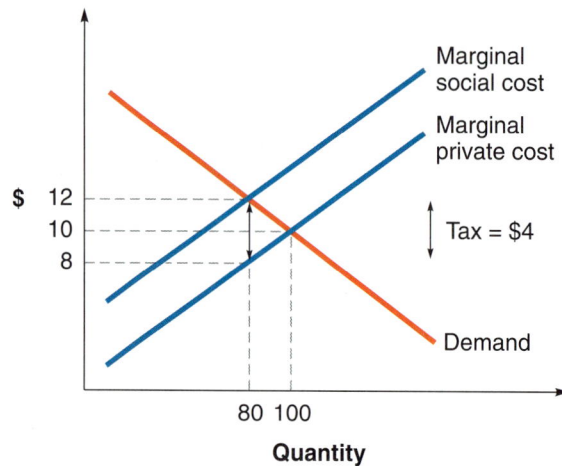

····· **FIGURE 18.2 NEGATIVE EXTERNALITIES**

When the production process involves external costs, marginal social costs are greater than marginal private costs. If the market is unregulated, output will be higher than the optimal level, and the selling price will be lower than optimal. The optimal level of production can be established by imposing a tax equal to the amount of the external cost. In this case, a tax of $4 per unit is levied on each unit sold. As a result, the selling price rises from $10 to $12, and the quantity sold falls from 100 to 80 units. The firm must pay the $4 to the government so it receives only $8 per unit sold.

efficient because marginal social costs would equal marginal social benefit at 80 units of output.

Why don't we just pass a law making it illegal to use production methods or manufacture products that pollute? We will say more about this in Chapter 21, but the simple explanation is that the *optimal level of pollution is almost never zero*. The cost of getting rid of that last iota of pollution is almost certainly greater than the benefit society receives. Then why don't we pass a law restricting pollution to a certain level? In fact, this is often done, but economists generally believe that taxes are preferable to quantity restrictions. The reason is that an emissions tax provides firms with an incentive to avoid the tax by developing production methods that reduce pollution; quantity restrictions provide no such incentives. If the tax is implemented correctly, firms will design and use nonpolluting production methods whenever the cost of new technology is less than the tax. The issue of taxes versus direct controls is explored in more detail in Chapter 21.

Finally, we need to make two additional comments before we go on. First, though marginal social costs often are clearly higher than marginal private costs, determining just how much higher can be difficult. This is important when designing a pollution tax policy. Second, we need to recognize that pollution taxes have some unpleasant side effects, even though they may result in allocative efficiency. Not only do pollution taxes cause prices to rise, but they could force some firms out of the industry and cause unemployment.

Positive Externalities

Not all externalities are negative. In fact, there are many positive externalities. For example, when you go to college, both you and society benefit. You stand to earn a higher income because you are more productive. Society benefits from your higher productivity as well and receives the additional benefit that you are less likely to resort to a life of crime. You should be willing to pay a price equal to the marginal private benefit you get from the school. And if society receives additional benefits, it should subsidize some of the costs of your schooling. This is one reason why most industrialized nations subsidize public education.

Many other examples of products with positive externalities can be cited. When Intel or Motorola develops the next-generation computer chip many computer firms benefit, and so do job seekers who find new job openings in companies that manufacture computers with the new chips. Further, the production techniques used to make the new computer chips will have spinoffs for production methods in the next generation of high-technology products. Recognition of these externalities is the main reason why most nations provide huge subsidies for their high-technology industries. In fact, *all* nations that have semiconductor industries aid their semiconductor producers.[7] A Focus box in Chapter 19 looks at this issue in more depth.

The effect of positive externalities is shown in Figure 18.3, which illustrates the market for schooling. The marginal private benefit curve is the demand curve for education by individuals. The marginal social benefit curve is society's demand curve for education. It is the sum of the marginal private benefit curve plus the positive externalities of education. In the absence of government intervention, the price of education would be $\overline{P}$, and people would attend school for $\overline{Q}$ years. This is suboptimal because the marginal social benefit of education is greater than the marginal cost (= supply price) of education. To achieve optimality, education should be subsidized by an amount equal to the vertical distance between the two marginal benefit curves. This effectively shifts the marginal private benefit curve to the marginal social benefit curve. People would then pay only P_s for education but would attend school for the optimal number of years, $Q\star$.

Most economists agree that education should be subsidized, but it is never clear how large the subsidy should be because it is so difficult to measure the external benefits of education accurately. There is also ongoing debate among economists as to whether the subsidy should be given to the school district or directly to the students. This issue is addressed in the Focus box on page 460.

Property Rights and the Coase Theorem

There is another deceptively simple solution to the problem of externalities: have the government assign and enforce property rights to internalize the external costs or

---

[7]Semiconductors are the basic building blocks of computers; logic boards, power supplies, and memory chips all use semiconductors. The name semiconductors comes from the fact that they have electrical conductivity properties greater than insulators but less than good conductors.

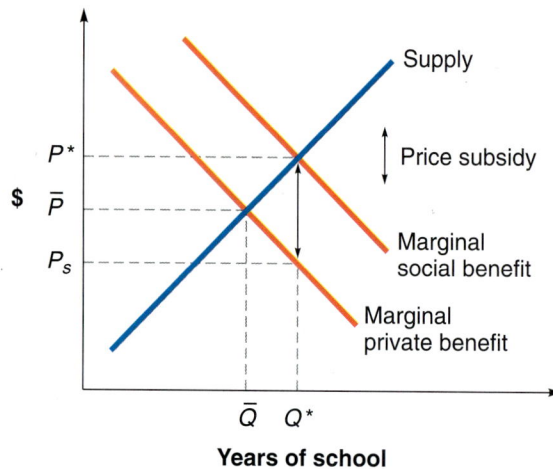

••••FIGURE 18.3 POSITIVE EXTERNALITIES

When there are positive externalities in consumption, efficient resource allocation requires that prices be subsidized. In this case, the marginal social benefit of education is greater than the marginal private benefit of education because of the positive externality. A subsidy in an amount equal to the distance between the two marginal benefit curves would lower the price paid for education from $\bar{P}$ to P_s while the price received by the school would rise to $P^\star$. At $Q^\star$, the marginal social benefit of education is equal to the marginal cost of education so resource allocation is efficient.

Coase theorem Externalities do not lead to resource misallocation as long as there is a system of well-defined property rights.

benefits, and then allow private individuals to bargain among themselves. This is the major result of the **Coase theorem**, named after the 1991 Nobel laureate in economics, Ronald Coase. Here is how the Coase theorem would be applied.

Suppose two different groups use the water in a river: the citizens downstream who use it for drinking and bathing, and the producers upstream who use it for paper processing. If the government assigns the citizens the right to drink clean water, then the effluents from the paper mill would infringe on the citizens' right to clean water. The paper company will have to stop polluting—or buy the right to pollute from the people downstream who are harmed by the pollution. People do not like dirty water, but most would be willing to put up with it if they were paid enough money. How much money would the citizens require? Just enough so that the marginal benefit of the payment is equal to the marginal discomfort and harm of dirty water.

The interesting thing about the Coase theorem is that it does not matter who is assigned the property rights as long as the rights are well-defined and voluntary market transactions are allowed to take place. For example, if the government gave the right to pollute to the paper mill, consumers could buy cleaner water by paying the paper mill to pollute less. Such a transaction would make the firm recognize that destroying clean water involves an opportunity cost. Clean water can be sold to consumers downstream; dirty water cannot. Further, it can be shown that the payment will be the same regardless of which party is assigned the property rights. Does this mean that it does not matter whether the firm is given the right to pollute or the consumer is given the right to clean water? Not necessarily. The initial assignment of property rights affects income distribution. If consumers are assigned the right to clean water, then the firm will lose income when it is forced to pay for the right to pollute; the reverse will happen if the firm is given the right to pollute.

As we will see in the next section, some economists believe that government intervention is so inherently inefficient that measures designed to ensure efficient operation of market processes are almost always preferable to direct government involvement. This is one reason for the broad appeal of the Coase theorem; however, its practical applicability in the real world has been limited by *transactions costs*. The transactions costs associated with the Coase theorem include the difficulty of setting up a mechanism for the two (or more) parties to bargain. For example, suppose that the downstream consumers had previously enjoyed swimming in the clean river for free. Would they be willing to sacrifice free swimming in clean water for $5 per person? For $10? At some price, the paper mill would be forced to close down, but there may be an efficient price that will enable the downstream consumers to build a swimming pool (or tolerate a little pollution) and the paper mill to continue operating—and providing jobs. But finding that efficient price can be quite difficult. In these cases, it may be more efficient to resort to pollution taxes or direct controls. Programs to assign property rights and create markets for pollution have been instituted in California, New Jersey, and some other states, a topic we will explore in Chapter 21.

RECAP   Government Policies for Externalities

Externalities exist whenever there are ill-defined property rights and costs or benefits that are not included in the market price. Pollution is a common external cost; education has external benefits because the benefits to society are greater than the benefits to the individual student. When externalities are present, the free-market outcome is inefficient.

1. External costs result in prices that are too low and quantities that are too high. One way to internalize external costs is to impose a tax. This will raise the selling price and reduce the quantity that is produced and sold. Calculating the correct tax is often difficult, however.
2. External benefits cause the selling price to be too high and quantity to be too low. One way to internalize external benefits is to give subsidies. This will lower the selling price and increase production and consumption of the good. Calculating the correct subsidy is often difficult, however.
3. According to the Coase theorem, well-defined property rights are all that is necessary to overcome the problems of externalities. Once property rights are well-defined, parties can engage in voluntary bargaining to pay for any external costs or benefits. The practical applicability of the Coase theorem may be limited by the presence of significant transactions costs.

FOCUS ON

SCHOOL VOUCHERS

One frequently cited reason for the rapid rise of the United States to economic dominance in the nineteenth and twentieth centuries was our system of public education. The United States was the first nation in the world to have free, compulsory schooling. Mandatory schooling was difficult to implement and expensive, but it paid off in the most highly educated and productive workforce in the world. At least that was the case until very recently. By some accounts, the U.S. pre-college education system is now among the weakest in the industrialized world. Our children go to school fewer weeks and shorter days than the children of our economic competitors. We consistently score among the lowest in the important math and science reasoning categories.

Why and how our school system went from the top to near the bottom is a matter of rather heated debate. Some attribute the problems to a generalized decay of the family, urban violence, and crime or the difficulties of educating a population that is becoming more ethnically diverse. Others believe that the school system has deteriorated simply because society no longer values education highly and thus does not demand quality education. Many economists provide a market-based explanation: teachers in the United States earn such low salaries that it is difficult to attract the "best and the brightest." This may be especially true of science and math graduates who often have considerably higher offers from business. As a result, students are being taught math and science by well-

meaning but inappropriately trained history and English majors.

One recommended solution to the problems of our schools is a system of *vouchers* that would generate competition in the school system. All parents would be given vouchers equivalent to the state's cost of educating their children in a public school. If the parents wanted to send their kids to public school, they would turn over the voucher to the public school system, and the child would receive a public education. If the parents felt that their children could get a better education from a private school, they could use the voucher as partial payment for private school tuition. This would reduce the cost of attending private school. Advocates of the system believe that the resulting competition for students

THE THEORY OF PUBLIC CHOICE

We have just established that government has important roles in market economies, but we still have not considered how government decisions are actually made. We know that markets respond to "dollar votes": when Americans "voted" for fuel-efficient cars by buying Japanese cars, Detroit responded by increasing the fuel efficiency of American automobiles. When health-conscious consumers started eating less red meat, restaurant menus were quick to offer more fish and chicken.

We vote for politicians and political initiatives as well, but it is far too simplistic to say that government decisions are the result of the democratic voting process. Most modern democratic governments are really republics—representative democracies—and the decisions are made by elected officials. A **public choice** is defined as a

Public choice A method for applying economic reasoning to the government decision-making process, voting, and collective choice.

Children of transcendental meditation practitioners attending an alternative school. Under a voucher system, this school might be eligible for tax dollars.

would force public schools to improve. Critics argue that a voucher system would hurt the public schools because it would make it easier for middle- and upper-income families to send their kids to private schools. Only the poorest children would go to public schools. And as public school enrollment dropped, so would funding.

Some cities have used school vouchers on a small experimental basis with mixed results. One interesting application was in Chicago where private businesses provided qualifying families with school vouchers. In 1992, Colorado voters turned down an initiative that would have implemented a voucher system for the state. Voters turned down a similar bill in California in 1993, even though a survey conducted before the vote showed that nearly two-thirds of the voters were so concerned about the public education system that they were willing to try almost anything, even the use of public money to fund private schools. The current Clinton administration takes a cool view toward school vouchers, but many Republicans feel that school vouchers are the best solution to our educational problems. We will undoubtedly hear more about voucher systems in the years to come.

decision made through the political process according to established rules. The theory of public choice is an application of economic principles to government decision making and the political process.

The theory of public choice is a relatively new branch of economics. Some of the groundwork was laid in Joseph Schumpeter's *Capitalism, Socialism, and Democracy* (1942) and Kenneth Arrow's *Social Choice and Individual Values* (1951), but most contemporary work probably stems from a 1957 book by Anthony Downs, *An Economic Theory of Democracy*. Downs argued that the main motivation of politicians is reelection and presented a framework for analyzing political behavior in this context. Downs also made two other points that remain at the center of public choice theory: (1) politicians have strong incentives to move to the center of the political spectrum,

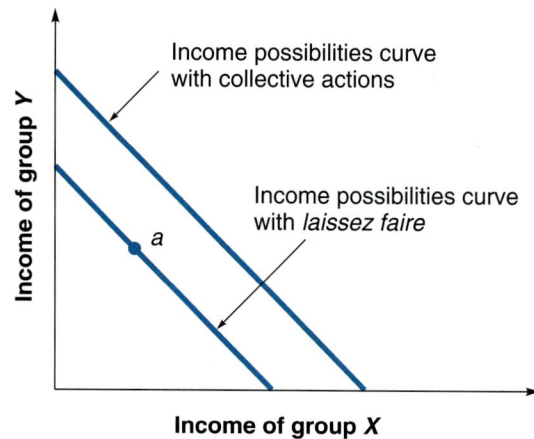

FIGURE 18.4 THE LOGIC OF COLLECTIVE ACTION

Collective goods can increase the efficiency of private markets and thus expand the income possibilities for all groups in society. In the absence of collective action, the income possibilities of the *laissez faire* economy are constrained to pass through point *a*. Collective actions that make the economy more efficient—for example, improved social infrastructure—could shift the *IPC* outward and make all groups in society potentially better off.

and (2) the act of voting must provide utility to the voter because the probability that an individual vote will affect the outcome of the election is extremely small.

Another landmark in the development of public choice theory was the publication of *The Calculus of Consent* by James Buchanan and Gordon Tullock in 1962. Buchanan and Tullock provided an economic rationale for constitutional rules. A more controversial point was their advocacy of unanimous votes on political decisions. They argued that anything short of unanimity involves coercion of groups in society who do not support the policy. It does not take a rocket scientist to realize that if all political decisions had to win the unanimous support of the voters, the government sector would be rather small. Buchanan received the Nobel Prize in economics in 1986 for his work in public choice theory and other areas. He is featured in the Economic Heritage box on page 470.

The Logic of Collective Action

One of the key insights of public sector economics is that public spending can expand the income possibilities of all groups in society.[8] For example, if the government

[8]The title of this section is taken from the book of the same name by Mancur Olson (Cambridge, Mass.: Harvard University Press, 1965, 1971). Olson has done considerable work in the theory of public finance and public choice. His book *The Rise and Decline of Nations* (New Haven: Yale University Press, 1982) argues that special interest groups sway political decisions and may account for economic stagnation. The influence of special interest groups on politicians is discussed briefly in the next section.

•••••FIGURE 18.5 EFFICIENT AND INEFFICIENT COLLECTIVE

ACTIONS

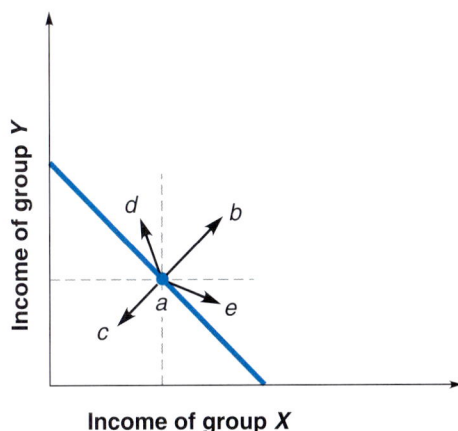

Collective action may or may not make both groups better off. If the economy begins at point *a*, a collective action that moves the economy toward point *b* would make both groups better off. The gains might result from the production of social infrastructure, public education, or other goods with substantial positive externalities. Movement to point *c* is unlikely, but not impossible: government production could be inefficient or irrational and produce goods that hurt both groups. Movement to either point *d* or *e* indicates that one group has gained at the expense of the other. These outcomes are possible under systems of majority rule; the majority votes for measures that hurt the minority. Concern over such tyranny of the majority is why some public choice theorists favor unanimity voting rules.

were to build a highway system, private businesses could expand because they could more easily serve distant markets. This point is illustrated in Figure 18.4. Suppose there are two groups in society, group *X* and group *Y*, and that in the absence of government spending, their income possibilities are constrained to the *laissez faire* income possibilities curve (*IPC*) that passes through point *a*. If the two groups form a government and vote for taxes to pay for public ("collective") goods, the *IPC* will shift out and make both groups potentially better off. The possibility that government actions can make all groups better off is known as the logic of collective action.

•••••••

Special Interest Groups

But the fact that collective action *can* make both groups better off does not mean that it necessarily *will* make both groups better off. To see this, look at Figure 18.5. If the *laissez faire* economy begins at point *a*, collective actions could move in any direction. Point *b* is clearly preferred because both groups have higher incomes. This would be a universally beneficial outcome from a collective action. In contrast, both groups are worse off at point *c*. This outcome is unlikely, but not impossible. If the collective action consisted entirely of the production of defense goods that were never used, both groups would end up worse off.

Tyranny of the majority A simple majority rule can result in actions that help the majority at the expense of the minority.

The more interesting scenarios are movements toward points *d* and *e*. Notice that in each case one group is better off and the other group is worse off. These outcomes are possible whenever the voting rules allow nonunanimous elections. For example, suppose that group *X* is the "majority" and group *Y* is the "minority." If everyone in the majority votes for high taxes on the minority and additional spending on parks and schools in majority neighborhoods, the economy would move toward point *e*. The majority gains at the expense of the minority. Such an outcome is called **tyranny of the majority**.[9]

Is tyranny of the majority a common outcome of election processes? Perhaps—but we also find what may be called "tyranny of the minority." For example, tariff laws often help a small group at the expense of a much larger group. The small group consists of the workers and companies hurt by import competition. The large group consists of the consuming public who must pay higher prices because of the tariff. Why do elected officials enact programs that help the minority at the expense of the majority? Tariffs have different impacts on the two groups. They help the minority a great deal—so much so that labor unions and industry leaders are willing to contribute substantial sums to political campaigns—while consumers may hardly notice that prices have risen. Union members also vote in very high numbers; the same cannot be said of the public at large.

Which outcome is more likely? That depends on several factors, but we can get some insight from work by Gary Becker[10] and others on the economics of special interest groups. Special interest groups like the Moral Majority and the Sierra Club seek to influence taxes, government regulations, and spending plans to raise the well-being of their members. Becker's key point is that special interest groups that are small relative to the population as a whole are more likely to be successful than large special interest groups. This may seem odd at first, but it really shouldn't. Suppose there are 1,000 members in society and two special interest groups, one comprised of 10 members and one comprised of 100 members. If each special interest group asks society for a $50 per person training voucher, it would cost each member of society only 50¢ to support the small group but $5 to support the large group. The power of small special interest groups is consistent with empirical observation: in countries like the United States and Japan where agriculture is a small industry, farmers receive substantial subsidies; in nations like Poland where agriculture is a large industry, farmers receive relatively few subsidies.

Why Do People Vote?

We are told from grade school on that voting is a privilege and a patriotic duty. But think for a minute: Do you *really* believe that your vote matters in the least? Even in small local elections, only very rarely does a single vote decide the outcome. Why

[9]This definition is similar, but not identical to the definition of tyranny of the majority used by Lani Guinier, President Clinton's unsuccessful nominee for assistant attorney general, Civil Rights Division, in 1993. The Guinier nomination created intense controversy. For Professor Guinier's views on her nomination, see Lani Guinier, "Who's Afraid of Lani Guinier?" *New York Times Magazine*, February 6, 1994, p. 38–.
[10]Gary S. Becker, "A Theory of Competition among Pressure Groups for Political Influence," *Quarterly Journal of Economics* 98 (August 1983): 371–400.

should you even bother to vote? The answer may be that people consider voting a consumer good and that it makes them feel good because they are being patriotic. This does not mean that political involvement is futile. If you become actively involved, you may be able to convince others that your views are correct. In essence, this means that you will have more than one vote—the beginning of political power.

When we vote, we assume that the candidates we are voting for will act in our best interest. Will they? Perhaps, but experience with broken campaign promises makes many people cynical. Why do elected officials act as they do? Public choice theorists assume that politicians are motivated more than anything else by the desire to be reelected. In other words, elected officials' main motivation is to maximize their votes in the next election. This may seem crass, but it really should not: by behaving as their constituents want, elected officials enhance their chances for reelection.

What should politicians do to maximize votes? One strategy is to "move to the center" in their political views. To see why a move to the center is important, look at Figure 18.6. Suppose that Candidate Smith begins the campaign as a conservative

FIGURE 18.6 THE CENTRIST VIEWS OF POLITICIANS

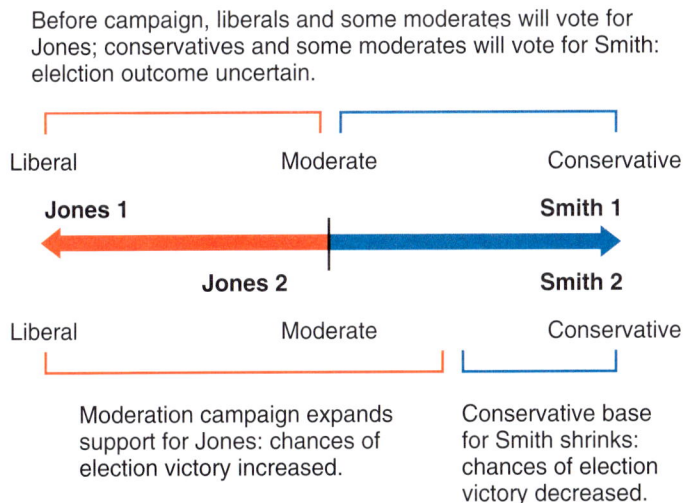

Before campaign, liberals and some moderates will vote for Jones; conservatives and some moderates will vote for Smith: elelction outcome uncertain.

Liberal   Moderate   Conservative

Jones 1   **Smith 1**

Jones 2   **Smith 2**

Liberal   Moderate   Conservative

Moderation campaign expands support for Jones: chances of election victory increased.

Conservative base for Smith shrinks: chances of election victory decreased.

Politicians can maximize their receipt of votes by moving toward the center of the political spectrum. Suppose that Jones begins the campaign as a liberal (Jones 1) and Smith begins as a conservative (Smith 1). If voters are distributed equally along the political spectrum, the outcome of the election is uncertain—liberals and moderate liberals will vote for Jones while conservatives and conservative moderates will vote for Smith. But, if Jones can convince voters that she is not quite so liberal (Jones 2), she will move toward the center of the political spectrum. She will still capture liberal voters as well as some of the more liberal conservatives. If Smith continues to campaign as a conservative, his prospects of victory will decline considerably. His best strategy would also be to move toward the center. If the process continues throughout the campaign, the two candidates will end up with quite similar positions—in the center of the political spectrum.

opposing change while Candidate Jones, a liberal, really wants to shake up the system.[11] Their views would place them at the right (conservative) and left (liberal) of the political spectrum. If voters are equally distributed along the political spectrum and if neither candidate changes during the course of the campaign, the election outcome will be up for grabs: liberals and moderate liberals will support Jones while conservatives and moderate conservatives will support Smith. But suppose that Candidate Jones begins to make more moderate speeches so that the voters begin to perceive her as a moderate. This will move her toward the center of the political spectrum and closer to the views of more voters. Candidate Jones stands to win the election as long as Smith sticks to his hard-line conservative agenda. But if Smith also moves toward the center, a Jones victory will be less certain. Political candidates are not stupid; over a long campaign, the fight becomes a battle for the center, and speeches and proposals become more alike than different.[12]

In the terminology of public choice theory, political campaigns are often a battle for the *median voter*, the voter whose most-preferred outcome is the median of the most-preferred outcomes of all those voting. As we learned in Chapter 5, the median of a population is the value such that half of all values are higher and half are lower. In the context of voting, the median voter is a centrist with as many people on the left as on the right. Political candidates who can capture the median voter generally win elections.

Finally, what about those politicians who advertise themselves as being altruistic? You know, the ones who say they are acting in the public interest regardless of the political consequences? It is hard to imagine that politicians would make such statements if they did not believe that doing so would increase their chances for reelection. Besides, there is no way to determine whether politicians *really* are acting in the public interest regardless of the political consequences or are simply saying that they are acting in the public interest while *thinking* that this strategy is the best way to maximize votes. If acting in the public interest does not maximize votes, that politician will not be reelected—so we will only have to study this kind of behavior for one term.

· · · · · · · ·

Voting Rules

Unanimity rule A voting rule that requires 100 percent approval before passage of any legislation.

The possibility of tyranny by the majority is one reason why some early public choice theorists favored **unanimity rules**, meaning that legislation passes only if it receives

---

[11]The terms "liberal" and "conservative" have many meanings in politics and economics today. No definition appeals to everyone, but most people would probably agree on one point: conservatives generally stand for the status quo and are reluctant to change; liberals are usually much more willing to make changes. But after this, the distinction between the two groups depends on context. As used in our discussion of public choice theory, a conservative is someone who wants as little government involvement in the economy as possible; a liberal is someone who sees an important role for government intervention. A main reason for this disagreement is that conservatives tend to have more faith in the market than do liberals. Part of the reason for the confusion may be that many conservatives today are activists in the sense that they want to change the system—they want to reduce government involvement.

[12]This view may have been captured best by Alabama governor and independent party presidential candidate George Wallace in 1968 when he remarked that there was ". . . not a dime's worth of difference" between the two major-party presidential candidates.

100 percent approval. As we mentioned earlier, the problem with the unanimity rule is that nothing would ever get done. There is always a curmudgeon who opposes everything! A compromise voting rule is the **supermajority rule**. Under this rule, legislation passes only if it receives substantially more than 50 percent of the votes. The rule that Congress must have a two-thirds majority to override a presidential veto is an example of a supermajority rule.

Voting processes can present other potential problems as well. One problem is that people usually vote for a bundle of attributes. For example, suppose you like Smith's stand on crime control and aid to the cities, but you prefer Jones's stand on defense spending. How should you vote? If you vote for Smith, you are voting against your preferences on national defense, but if you vote for Jones, you do not get the crime control or urban aid you want. Voting differs considerably from market behavior, where you use dollar votes to buy what you like. Occasionally, you are forced to buy a bundle of attributes—you may not want air conditioning but it comes standard in the car you otherwise want to buy—but the market usually provides so many choices that these cases are typically rare.

> **Supermajority rule**   A compromise voting rule that requires a less than unanimous but more than 50 percent vote for passage.

• • • • • • • •

Arrow's Impossibility Theorem

Another potential problem with voting is that voting outcomes can be *intransitive*. In other words, the voting process can result in what can only be called nonsensical results. A transitive relationship works like this: if *a* is preferred to *b*, and *b* is preferred to *c*, then *a* is preferred to *c*. The relationship would be intransitive if *a* is preferred to *b*, and *b* to *c*, but *c* is preferred to *a*. The possibility of intransitive outcomes is one of the major results of 1972 Nobel laureate Kenneth Arrow's famous **impossibility theorem** and the related **voting paradox**.[13]

As a simple example of the impossibility theorem, suppose that there are only three voters and they must vote on the size of the school budget. The preferences of the three voters are shown in the table below where *p* means "prefers." Jones, the liberal, prefers the highest school budget possible. He would prefer the high budget, *H*, to the moderate budget, *M*, to the low budget, *L*. Garcia is a moderate. She prefers the moderate budget to the low budget. Her last choice would be the high budget. Lee wants the low budget so that taxes will be low and she can send her kids to private school. If she cannot have the low budget, she will opt for the high budget, presumably better public education, and forgo private school. Her last choice is the moderate budget. These individual choices differ, but they are all reasonable.

> **Impossibility theorem**   Majority rule can lead to nonsensical (intransitive) results.
>
> **Voting paradox**   There is no voting rule that can assure consistent and reasonable outcomes; all election outcomes are suspect.

Voter	Preference Ranking
Jones	H *p* M *p* L
Garcia	M *p* L *p* H
Lee	L *p* H *p* M

---

[13]Arrow presented his views on the impossibility theorem and the voting paradox in *Social Choice and Individual Values* (1951). This is a classic work, but not something beginning students will want to attack. Arrow's ideas were anticipated some 200 years earlier by the Frenchman Marquis de Condorcet (1743–1794).

Now, suppose that the voters first vote on reducing the budget from the current moderate budget to a low budget. Both Jones and Garcia would vote *M*, while only Lee would vote *L*, so the moderate budget is the winner. Now a second vote is taken: Do voters prefer the moderate or a high budget? Only Garcia would say moderate; both Jones and Lee would say high, so the high budget proposal wins. But look what would happen if a third vote were taken between the apparent winner, high, and the initial loser, low: Lee and Garcia opt for the low budget while only Jones votes for the high budget; the low budget proposal wins. This does not make sense: the first two votes led us to conclude that high is preferred to moderate and moderate is preferred to low:

$$H \; p \; M \; p \; L$$

but from the last vote we know that low is preferred to high:

$$H \; p \; M \; p \; L \; p \; H$$

which is nonsense. When rational behavior results in irrational outcomes, we have a voting paradox.

Kenneth Arrow went further to show that, short of granting dictatorial powers, no voting rule—including majority rule—can assure consistent and reasonable outcomes; all election outcomes are suspect. This little example also shows the importance of setting the political agenda. Notice that the outcome of our election depends on the order in which the votes are taken: if the choices are (*M* versus *L*) then (*M* versus *H*), the high budget will be the winner. But if the vote is between (*M* versus *H*) then (*H* versus *L*), the low budget is the winner.

• • • • • • • •

The Inherent Inefficiency of Government

Government failure Governments are just as likely to make mistakes as markets; therefore, the smaller the role of government, the better.

Although most economists believe that government can play an important role in correcting market failures, many public choice theorists believe that **government failures** are just as likely as market failures. A government failure occurs whenever the government provides the wrong kind or amount of public services, or uses too many inputs to provide the right kind and amount of public services. At least three arguments can be made to suggest that government is inefficient.

First, government projects rarely face competitive pressures to keep costs low. For example, public schools face little real competition from private schools, so they have little incentive to improve the quality of education. In fact, government agencies have incentives to increase their operating budgets. The civil service rating of many government officials is determined partially by the size of their budgets, and in some cases, government workers can receive raises or promotions only if they can make a case for hiring additional employees. This is exactly the opposite of how private markets work in theory—the private sector manager who is able to reduce costs gets the promotion. This kind of inefficiency is a major reason why some economists are calling for school voucher systems and other programs to put competitive pressures on government programs and agencies.

A second reason for government inefficiency is based on supply and demand analysis. The level of public services is determined by demand as expressed by voters and the voting rules of the constitution. The supply of public services, however, is determined by government politicians who seek to maximize their votes and budgets. Bureaucrats are supposedly constrained by the political process, but William Niskanen[14] and others have argued that these constraints are rarely sufficient. As a result, public budgets are often larger than necessary to provide the public services demanded by the voters. This is the main reason Niskanen, Buchanan, and others have argued for constitutional restrictions on the size of the government budget.

A third reason for government failures is a lack of well-defined property rights. Recall that, according to the Coase theorem, market failures can be eliminated by establishing a system of well-defined property rights and allowing voluntary market transactions. The converse is also true. If property rights are not well-defined and voluntary transactions are not allowed, market failures can occur. This is the case with government. Government resources are not freely transferable, so there is no way to determine their "correct" price and value. The implication is that government involvement in the economy is likely to be the source of "market" failure.

As you might suspect, not everyone agrees with the view that government failures are as common as public choice theory seems to imply. Kenneth Arrow and Mancur Olson, for example, contend that empirical tests do not show government to be consistently less efficient than private markets. This is not to say that government provision of public goods is always efficient, only that it is not necessarily less efficient than private markets. Further, most economists believe that some public goods are necessary and that they must be provided by the government. The real issue, then, is how to make government involvement in the economy as efficient as possible.

RECAP   Public Choice Theory

Public choice theory has provided important insights into the behavior of politicians and voters, as well as into the efficiency of government activity. Public choice theory involves much more than this rather abbreviated and selective introduction has provided.

1. Public choice theory is the application of economic reasoning to public decision making. Many public choice theorists believe that governments are inherently inefficient.
2. The provision of public goods depends on the voting rules of the constitution. Unless voting is unanimous, it is possible for one group to gain at the expense of another.
3. Individual votes have such an insignificant effect on electoral outcomes that many economists believe people vote only because voting is a consumption good.
4. Political candidates attempt to maximize votes. To do so, they often move their platforms to the political center.
5. Voting outcomes can often yield unintended results. When there are more than two choices, it is possible to get intransitive outcomes. Kenneth Arrow

---

[14]William Niskanen, *Bureaucracy and Representative Government* (Chicago: Aldine, 1971). Niskanen was an economic adviser to President Reagan.

Very few economists can say that their work was so influential that it started a school of economic thought. James Buchanan is one such economist. As the seminal figure in the public choice school, Buchanan has influenced a generation of students. Not everyone agrees with his views—he has been criticized, sometimes severely, by both liberals and conservatives—but few can deny Buchanan's main accomplishment: the application of economic analysis to the workings of governments.

Buchanan grew up in the rural South in the 1920s surrounded by poverty, but he had a middle-class upbringing. He hoped to attend expensive Vanderbilt University to study law. The Great Depression made that financially impossible, so he wound up at Middle Tennessee State Teachers College. When he later enrolled in the economics graduate program at the University of Chicago, like most of his classmates, he considered himself a socialist. It took less than a semester of work with Frank Knight to convince him of the advantages of *laissez faire* capitalism.

Buchanan credits two people along with Knight for having the most influence on his work in public choice theory. One was the Swedish economist Knut Wicksell (1861–1926). In 1896, Wicksell had argued that the best test of government efficiency is unanimity, a view that Buchanan was to make one of the pillars of public choice theory. Buchanan has often said that he never again felt the intellectual excitement he experienced when he discovered Wicksell and that he could never have developed many of his views without Wicksell's earlier studies. The second great influence was Gordon Tullock, one of Buchanan's graduate students at the University of Virginia. It was Tullock who convinced Buchanan that all economic agents—even government bureaucrats—are out to pursue their own interest.

Unlike so many contemporary economists, Buchanan is impressed with neither mathematics nor empirical arguments. Instead, he relies upon logic and an occasional graph. This may be one reason why his most important work, *The Calculus of Consent* (coauthored with Tullock), was not an immediate success. Today, it is undoubtedly a classic. In *The Calculus of Consent*, Buchanan and Tullock argued that government intervention in the economy is only rarely appropriate—even when markets fail—because governments are inherently inefficient. This view is frequently used as an argument against government intervention. Still, while Buchanan is extremely critical of most government involvement in the economy, he does advocate public schools and measures designed to ensure equal opportunity for all. Buchanan is occasionally accused of being an anarchist. His response is that constitutional systems are necessary to maintain private property. He has frequently called for more positive economic analysis of alternative constitutional systems.

Buchanan has expressed surprise that the majority of the economics profession has not come to agree with him on the inherent inefficiency of government intervention. His views have certainly received more attention since he was awarded the Nobel Prize in 1986, and several of Reagan and Bush's economic advisers seemed sympathetic to Buchanan's ideas, but Buchanan remains controversial. He is extremely critical of Keynesian economists whom he believes have torpedoed the social contract against deficit spending. Likewise, he was a harsh critic of the Reagan and Bush administrations for eroding the "moral consensus" against burdening future generations with current deficits. He has been a long-time critic of mainstream economics for its emphasis on technique instead of substance.

SOURCES: James M. Buchanan, "The Economic Theory of Politics Reborn," *Challenge* (March/April 1988): 4–10; James M. Buchanan, "The Constitution as Economic Policy," *American Economic Review* 77 (June 1987): 243–51; Gregory B. Christainsen, "James Buchanan and the Revival of Classical Political Economy," *Challenge* (March/April 1988): 11–15; and Thomas Romer, "On James Buchanan's Contributions to Public Economics," *Journal of Economic Perspectives* 2 (Fall 1988): 165–79.

demonstrated that there is no method of social choice that avoids these problems. Also, people often vote for positions they do not favor because candidates represent a bundle of attributes.

6. Critics contend that public choice theory is a rationalization of the view that the best government is the smallest government and that the theory's empirical foundation is weak.

SUMMARY

Economists laud the beauty of the market system, but most also recognize that in some situations government can play important roles. Unfortunately, though we know that these situations exist, it is exceedingly difficult to determine the optimal extent of government involvement in the real world. Further, many public choice theorists argue that government involvement is inherently inefficient. Not only are there no competitive pressures on government bureaucrats, but the aim to maximize votes can often result in politicians pandering to special interest groups at the expense of the rest of society. The main ideas from this chapter are:

1. Public goods cannot be efficiently allocated by private markets because there is no mechanism to force people to reveal their preferences. People receive the benefits of public goods whether they pay or not because the consumption of public goods is nonrival and nonexclusive.

2. External costs and benefits are not included in market prices, so many economists believe the government should enact measures to internalize externalities. Pollution is an example of an external cost; technological spillover from research and development is an example of an external benefit. External costs should be taxed; external benefits should be subsidized.

3. According to the Coase theorem, market failures can be eliminated by establishing a system of well-defined property rights and allowing voluntary trades to take place. High transactions costs may make it difficult to apply the Coase theorem.

4. The theory of public choice seeks to apply economic reasoning to the political process and government decision making. Many public choice theorists believe that government is inherently inefficient and prone to failure. Most public choice theorists believe that the smallest government is the best government.

5. Collective actions can expand the income and production possibilities of a society. However, whether they do so or not depends on the outcome of the voting process. It is possible for majority rule to benefit one group at the expense of another.

6. Vote maximization is a primary goal of politicians. Politicians may support programs favoring small special interest groups at the expense of larger groups if the benefits to the interest group are concentrated and known, while the costs to the larger group are small per person. Political platforms tend to move to the center to broaden their appeal.

7. Voting can often result in less than optimal outcomes. The impossibility theorem shows that votes can be intransitive. When people vote for a candidate, they are voting for a bundle of attributes and may not agree with many of them.

KEY TERMS AND CONCEPTS

market failure   efficiency criterion
public good   Coase theorem
exclusion principle   voucher system
rival consumption   public choice
negative externality   tyranny of the majority
positive externality   unanimity rule
efficiency vs. equity   supermajority rule
ability to pay   impossibility theorem
benefits received   voting paradox
free rider   government failure

REVIEW QUESTIONS

1. What is a market failure? Explain how externalities and public goods can lead to market failures. Give examples of each and draw diagrams to illustrate your answers.
2. Define the benefits-received and the ability-to-pay principles of taxation. How do these principles relate to tax efficiency and tax equity? What are earmarked taxes?
3. What are the two main attributes that distinguish public goods from private goods? What conditions must hold for optimal allocation of public goods?
4. What policies can be used to internalize externalities? Draw diagrams to illustrate your answer. Explain how application of the Coase theorem would make pollution taxes unnecessary.
5. How is it possible for the public sector to expand the income possibilities for society? Does public sector involvement always expand everyone's income possibilities? How does this issue relate to voting rules?
6. Why do people vote? Why do voting outcomes sometimes appear to be irrational? Why do politicians take the stands that they do?
7. Why do some economists believe that government failures are just as likely as market failures?

PROBLEMS

1. Suppose that a beach has enough customers to support exactly two lemonade stands. The people are distributed equally along the beach. Where should the two lemonade stands be located to minimize the distance customers must travel to buy lemonade? Where will they be located if both lemonade stand owners are profit maximizers?
2. Identify the public good attributes of each of the following. Also, explain how (and if) goods could be efficiently provided by the private sector.
   a. a lighthouse   b. an income redistribution plan
   c. universal health care   d. snow removal service
   e. cable television   f. broadcast television

3. Suppose that a factory currently dumps waste into the river. Explain how taxes and property rights could be used to solve this problem.

4. The demand curve for a public good is constructed by vertical addition and is steeper than any of the individual public good demand curves from which it is constructed. What does this imply about the "social elasticity of demand" for a public good? How much quantity response would you expect from an increase in the price of the public good, *ceteris paribus*, if "many" people benefited from the public good?

5. Suppose that congestion in the city gets so bad that the city council asks for a $5 per person commuter tax to be levied on everyone driving during the rush hour. As the city economist, you are concerned that the cost of collecting such a tax would be prohibitively high—the city would have to build toll booths, for example. Suggest another program that could be used to reduce the external costs of driving during rush hour.

6. Public choice theorists like the unanimity rule because it eliminates the chance of coercion by government. However, it also makes it very difficult to enact income redistribution measures, such as progressive taxes and welfare. Explain. Recommend a voting scheme that would make it easier to enact income redistribution measures.

7. Why do you think so many public choice theorists favor a constitutional amendment requiring a balanced federal budget?

8. Suppose that the school budget voting preferences for Smith, Garcia, and Lee are as follows:

Voter	Preference Ranking
Jones	H p M p L
Garcia	M p H p L
Lee	L p H p M

Let the vote proceed as in the text example—(M versus L) then the winner against H—and determine whether the outcome is transitive or intransitive. Compare your result to the text example and explain.

9. a. In many states, property taxes are earmarked for public schools. A perennial argument is that property owners who do not have children should pay less or even be exempt from property taxes. Explain why this argument may be fallacious.

   b. Many states have policies that set tuition at public universities at a fixed fraction—often 20 or 25 percent—of the state's cost of providing the education. Is this a reasonable policy? Why or why not?

10. Footnote 3 noted that the Clinton administration proposed a BTU tax as part of its tax program in 1993. The BTU tax was ultimately defeated. Discuss the BTU tax versus a tax on imported oil. Who wins and loses under each tax? Which tax would be more efficient?

11. The national parks receive millions of visitors annually, and the roads through the parks are often clogged with bumper-to-bumper traffic. Do you think this would be true if the national parks were sold to private business? Would you favor such a sale? Why or why not? Can you think of an alternative solution to the crowding problem in the national parks?

12. Early in the chapter, we suggested that a market failure occurs if ice cream consumers are not aware of the high-fat content of ice cream. Suppose that the

government does require all ice cream producers to include the fat content on the label along with a stern warning that high-fat diets can lead to heart disease. Some people (notably your author) would ignore the warnings and continue to consume mass quantities of both Ben and Jerry's Cherry Garcia and Häagen Dazs macadamia nut ice cream on a regular basis. Does this mean that the labeling did not eliminate the market failure? Why or why not?

CHAPTER 19

Regulation and Antitrust

Until it shut down in the spring of 1993, the Greens Creek mine on Admiralty Island in southeast Alaska was the largest silver mine in the United States. The mine closure meant layoffs for almost 300 people—not an insignificant number of jobs for Juneau, a town of barely 30,000, where most of the miners lived. Several factors led to the closure of Greens Creek. The collapse of the silver market was certainly one of them. With silver selling for barely $3 per ounce, profits were hard to come by, so it made more sense to leave ore in the ground until prices rose in the future. Nevertheless, the mine might have been able to turn a profit had it not been for extensive government regulations. Greens Creek management had long complained that regulations were killing them: waste water had to be specially treated; mine tailings had to be disposed of properly; strict safety precautions were mandated; chemical disposal had to follow prescribed methods, and so on. By some accounts, regulatory compliance represented fully half of the total operating cost of the mine. The question, of course, is whether the benefits from these regulations—a clean environment and safe working conditions—are worth their cost. This is the question that must be addressed in analyzing all government regulations.

Stated simply, the power to regulate is the power to coerce. All government regulations represent an attempt to force people to behave in ways they otherwise would not. For example, in the case of Greens Creek, regulations coerced the mining company to dispose of mine tailings in an environmentally sensitive manner; without the regulations, the mine would have disposed of the tailings in the most cost-efficient manner. That the benefits of regulation come at a cost is why it is so important to analyze them carefully.

This chapter will examine how and why the government regulates the behavior of business. Our first task will be to look at the theory of government regulation and highlight some important examples. We will then look at a particular kind of government regulation, antitrust. In this section we will look at important pieces of antitrust legislation, but the focus will be on the contemporary—and changing—theories of antitrust policy.

AFTER READING AND STUDYING THIS CHAPTER, YOU SHOULD BE ABLE TO:

• • • Relate the theory of government regulation to market and government failure
• • • Outline the attributes of efficient regulation, and discuss recent examples of regulation and deregulation
• • • Discuss major pieces of antitrust legislation, and explain how they have sought to curtail monopoly power
• • • Explain how the court interpretation of antitrust statutes has changed over time

• • • • • • • THE THEORY OF GOVERNMENT REGULATION

You may not be aware of the extent of government regulation. Our food is regulated, children's toys are regulated, the workplace is regulated; virtually every aspect of the modern economy must deal with some sort of regulation. Just a few examples will illustrate the kind of problems regulators face.

The U.S. Department of Agriculture regulates and inspects meat to assure that it is free of contamination. And to make doubly sure we are safe, federal standards require restaurants to cook meat to a temperature of 140 degrees to kill any bacteria missed by the inspectors.[1] Toy manufacturers are required to use nontoxic paint so that toddlers will not be injured when they inevitably chew (rather than play with) their new toys. Seat belts and safety glass are required in all automobiles; soon all new automobiles will be equipped with dual air bags. All of us want healthy food, safe toys for our children, and safe automobiles—but at what cost? Meat inspection is not free; neither are nontoxic paint and air bags.

Financial institutions have been heavily regulated since the 1930s. The Federal Reserve has long required that banks adhere to legal reserve requirements, and beginning in the 1980s, it established capital requirements as well.[2] Further, banks have

---

[1] Despite these regulations, there are occasional deaths due to contaminated meat. In the winter of 1992–1993, several Jack-in-the-Box fast-food restaurants on the West Coast served hamburgers that were tainted by the *E. coli* bacteria. At least two young children died. The legal costs to Jack-in-the-Box exceeded $2 million, and it also lost clientele. Jack-in-the-Box was covered with a $100 million insurance policy to pay for just such emergencies.

[2] As we will find out in Chapter 28, the required reserve ratio is the fraction of demand deposits (essentially checking accounts) that banks must hold on deposit at the Federal Reserve or as vault cash. The reserve requirement on most standard checking accounts is about 10 percent; it is only 3 percent or less for most other accounts. The bank capital requirement is the ratio of bank capital—stockholder equity and other bank assets—to outstanding loans. The current ratio is about 7 percent.

only recently been allowed to pay interest on checking deposits. Such restrictions are designed to instill confidence and ensure the safety of financial institutions, but they are also costly to those institutions: Required reserves do not earn interest, and the inability to pay interest on checking account deposits often made it difficult for banks to attract funds. The U.S. financial system has been undergoing deregulation since the late 1970s. The result has been a period of rather severe adjustment—more banks and savings and loan institutions went bankrupt in the 1980s than in the 1930s—but many economists feel that even more bank deregulation is necessary to help U.S. banks compete effectively in the global economy.

The Regulatory Process

When a federal regulatory agency decides that regulation is necessary, it prepares a Regulatory Impact Analysis to examine the costs and benefits of the regulation. This study is then submitted to the Office of Management and Budget (OMB) for review. If the OMB approves the regulation, a notice is published in the *Federal Register*, and public comment is invited, usually for a period of 30 to 90 days. The OMB then has 30 days to analyze any comments made by interested parties. Congress has the right to review the regulation, but most regulations are enacted if they get to this stage. Congress also occasionally initiates regulatory reform itself. One recent example occurred in late 1993 and early 1994 when Congress required cable television companies to roll back their prices.

Though it sounds simple, the actual process of making a new regulation can stretch out for some time. For example, licensing proceedings for the Interstate Commerce Commission and Civil Aeronautics Board average 19 months, and rate-making cases by these two agencies typically take 21 months.[3] The time lag involved with enacting new regulations or changing old regulations can lead to a problem known as **regulatory lag**. For example, suppose that regulators decide that the "fair" rate of profit is 10 percent and that this results in a price of P_R. Now, suppose that the regulated firm invests in a new production process that reduces costs so that the current regulated price, P_R, now results in a profit rate of 15 percent. During the time that it takes the regulatory commission to review and adjust prices to the new level of costs, the firm will make excess profits. The converse is also true. If poor management or higher input costs reduce profits to only 5 percent, several months will pass before a new regulated price can be established. At first glance, regulatory lag seems like the competitive process in that efficient firms are rewarded while inefficient firms are penalized. In this case, however, the reward system is established by the regulatory commission, and it is difficult to determine whether these rewards provide the correct incentives or not.

Regulatory lag The time lag involved with enacting new regulations or changing old regulations.

Principles of Government Regulation

Regulation is appropriate only when its benefits exceed its costs. Unfortunately, measuring the costs and benefits of regulation is not always easy, so the regulatory

---

[3]"Delay in the Regulatory Process," *Study on Federal Regulation*, vol. 4, U.S. Senate, Committee on Governmental Affairs, July 1977. Cited in W. Kip Viscusi, John M. Vernon, and Joseph E. Harrington, Jr., *Economics of Regulation and Antitrust* (Lexington, Mass.: D. C. Heath, 1992), p. 308. Much of the material in this chapter is drawn from this book.

Cost-benefit analysis The costs are compared to the benefits; if benefits exceed costs, the policy is implemented.

process is typically characterized by debate and disagreement. Further, the costs and benefits are often measured in different units: Is an increase in workplace safety worth the cost of higher prices and fewer jobs? The answer may rely as much on value judgments as on objective **cost-benefit analysis**.

Since 1981, all new federal regulations must be subjected to cost-benefit analysis. This policy was instituted by the Reagan administration in an effort to stem the growth of new regulations. Cost-benefit analysis of federal government regulations involves (1) estimating the costs and benefits of the proposal in dollar terms and then (2) discounting future net benefits.[4] A government proposal is enacted only if the net present value of the program is positive. Unfortunately, determining the costs and benefits of government programs can be difficult because the output of government projects is rarely sold on the market. For example, we may know that requiring seat belts on automobiles costs X per car and even that it saves Y lives per year, but unless we are ready to estimate the value of a life, it is difficult to actually calculate the costs and benefits of seat belt requirements. Further, a regulation frequently involves indirect as well as direct costs and benefits. For example, a regulation to outlaw cigarette advertising might increase public health, but if it also puts thousands of tobacco farmers out of business, it will increase the need for unemployment compensation and will entail other costs as well. These and other complications explain why government cost-benefit analysis is best reserved for advanced courses.[5]

There are at least three additional reasons to be cautious of the regulatory process. First, even when regulators are motivated solely by public interest—as they are according to the **public interest theory** of regulation—no one can predict all of the consequences of a particular initiative. For example, mandates increasing average fuel economy may have been partially responsible for the production of lighter and less safe automobiles—and, consequently, additional highway deaths.

Public interest theory of regulation Government regulations provide public benefits; assumes regulators are motivated solely by public interest.

Second, according to George Stigler's **capture theory** of regulation, the regulatory agency can be "captured" by the specific groups that it seeks to regulate.[6] For example, before 1975, stock brokerage commissions were fixed by the Securities and Exchange Commission (SEC), ostensibly to assure that only honest and qualified people were selling stocks. Consumers may have benefited from SEC regulations that prevented fraud, but the brokers also liked the high fees they were required to charge by law. In the context of capture theory, the high brokerage fees could be an indication that brokers had "captured" their regulators. When fixed commissions were eliminated, stock brokerage fees fell dramatically, and customers were able to choose between "discount" brokers and full-service brokers—but the chances of having an incompetent or unscrupulous broker increased.[7] A similar argument can be made about regulated airfares. Airline regulations were designed to assure that most communities were served by safe air transportation, but they also served to keep airfares

Capture theory of regulation The regulators will be "captured" by the regulatees and thus will enact regulations that benefit the regulatees more than the public.

[4]The discounting process was discussed in Chapter 17.

[5]You can find a good introductory discussion of government cost-benefit analysis in most public finance textbooks. See, for example, Chapter 6 of David Hyman, *Public Finance* (Fort Worth: Dryden Press, 1993).

[6]George J. Stigler, *The Citizen and the State* (Chicago: University of Chicago Press, 1975).

[7]Discount brokers typically do little more than execute transactions at the customer's request; full-service brokers give investment advice in addition to executing transactions.

high and assure high profits for the airline companies; the regulated high airfares could be an indication that the airline industry had captured the airline regulators. After the airline industry was deregulated in the late 1970s, airfares between most large cities fell, as expected. However, fares between many smaller communities rose because many were now served by only a single carrier that charged monopoly prices.

Why would a regulatory agency allow itself to be captured by the industry it seeks to regulate? One explanation is based on the special interest group theory developed in the last chapter. Recall that small special interest groups lobby the government for special subsidies to benefit their groups. Interest groups seek to influence ("capture") regulations for their benefit just as they seek to lobby the government for any other purpose. Interest groups have an almost automatic entry into regulatory bodies because regulatory agencies need regulators with industry-specific expertise and therefore often hire employees from regulated industries.

The third reason to be cautious about the regulatory process is that regulation does not accommodate change very well, especially technological change. Consider the telephone industry. Until its breakup in 1984, American Telegraph and Telephone (AT&T) had a virtual monopoly over the telephone industry. AT&T was tightly regulated to prevent it from abusing its monopoly power. The government-sanctioned telecommunications monopoly may have been appropriate in the past when it could be argued that telecommunications was a natural monopoly. By the 1980s, however, it seemed to serve primarily to restrict competition. For example, the development of cheap and efficient microwave transmission technologies meant that competition in the telephone industry was technically possible, but it was not legal as long as entry into the industry was restricted by regulations. The breakup of AT&T has not been without some costs—local rates are higher in many communities—but few would deny that the pace of technological innovation has accelerated in the communications industry. Further, had government regulations not prevented entry into the telephone industry, consumers might have enjoyed these benefits earlier.

It was this sort of reasoning that led to the deregulation movement of the 1970s and 1980s. Not only were the securities and telecommunications industries deregulated, but so were the banks, airlines, trucking, and other industries. Additionally, many of the rules on safety in the workplace and pollution were relaxed. Still, this does *not* mean that government regulation will have no rule in the future. In fact, the Republican Reagan and Bush administrations—generally regarded as having a "hands-off" approach to regulation—developed a set of criteria for future government regulation. The main difference between these criteria and those used in the past is the reliance upon market incentives whenever possible. The Bush administration's criteria for efficient government regulations were spelled out as follows:[8]

- Regulations should rely upon market incentives whenever possible.
- Regulations should be implemented at the lowest possible cost.
- Regulations should provide clarity and certainty to the regulated community.
- Regulations should be designed to minimize the potential for litigation.

---

[8]These criteria and much of this section are taken from Chapter 5, "Markets and Regulatory Reform," in the *Economic Report of the President*, 1993.

These criteria were applied in the development of several regulatory programs including the Clean Air Act of 1990 and the Energy Policy Act of 1990. The Clinton administration has also emphasized the role of market incentives in the regulatory process, but seems to be more willing to use government regulations when necessary.

. . . .

Price Regulation Formulas

Oligopolies and monopolies are often subject to government price regulations. As we found out in Chapters 12 and 13, oligopolies and monopolies typically charge prices that are inefficient in the sense that they exceed marginal cost. Further, price may exceed average total cost so oligopolies and monopolies make long-run economic profits. Government price regulations are designed to reduce excess profits and bring price in line with marginal costs. Price regulations are rarely rigid; they are typically based on a formula that allows some price adjustment as conditions warrant. Unfortunately, even the most flexible price regulation formulas can create problems as market conditions change. Three approaches to price regulation are the cost-of-service formula, the price-cap formula, and yardstick competition.

Cost-of-service formula Companies provide the regulatory agency with cost information, and the agency sets a regulated price based on a "fair profit."

Under the **cost-of-service formula**, companies provide the regulatory agency with cost information, and the agency sets a regulated price based on a "fair profit." The problem with this approach is that it gives firms little incentive to reduce costs because there may be no profit reward for a cost reduction. As costs fall, so do regulated prices. This can reduce the firm's total revenue and, potentially, its profits.

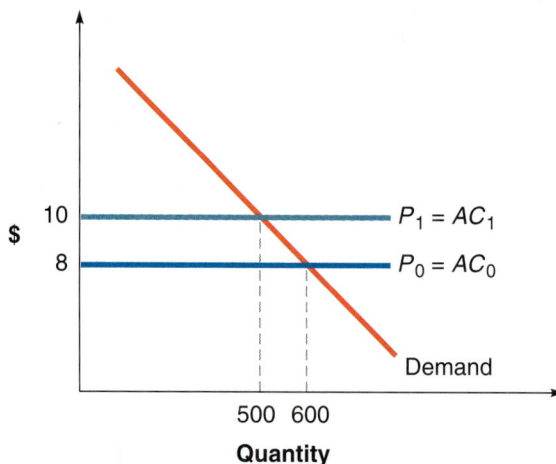

· · · · FIGURE 19.1 THE COST-OF-SERVICE FORMULA

The cost-of-service formula can provide an incentive to maximize costs. Suppose that the regulatory agency requires that price be set equal to average costs and, further, that the normal profit rate (included in average costs) is equal to 2 percent of total revenue. If the average costs are initially $8, the firm will sell 600 units and earn $4,800 in total revenue. This will result in profits of $96 = 0.02($4,800)$. If costs rise to $10, sales will fall to 500 units, but total revenue will rise to $5,000. Profits will be $100.

The converse is also true: as costs rise, prices rise, and under some circumstances, so do profits. As a result, the cost-of-service formula can act as an incentive for firms to maximize costs, not quite the paragon of economic efficiency! The cost-of-service model is currently used to regulate the price of natural gas in interstate natural gas pipelines. The cost-of-service formula is illustrated in Figure 19.1. In this example, an increase in average costs from $8 to $10 reduces sales from 600 to 500 units, but both total revenue and total profits increase.

Another regulation strategy is the **price-cap formula**. Under this approach, the regulatory body establishes an initial level of prices and then links the regulated company's future price increases to an aggregate price index minus expected industry productivity increases. The problem with the price-cap model is that it uses current prices as its base rate. As costs change over the long run, firms may earn economic profits or incur losses. The price-cap formula is illustrated in Figure 19.2. Suppose the initial regulated price is set equal to average total costs at $10, and that the aggregate price index minus aggregate productivity increases by 20 percent. The regulated firm would be allowed to raise its price as high as $12. If costs have not changed, the firm will make economic profits equal to the green area in the diagram. On the other hand, if the regulated firm's average costs rose by more than 10 per-

Price-cap formula The regulatory body establishes an initial level of prices and links the regulated company's future price increases to an aggregate price index minus expected productivity increases.

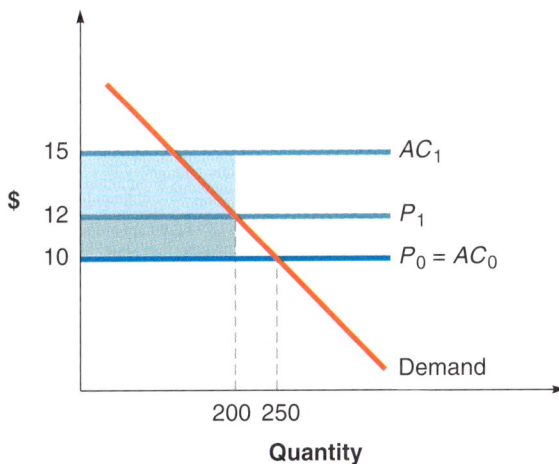

•••• **FIGURE 19.2** THE PRICE-CAP FORMULA

The price-cap formula can result in economic profits or losses as the regulated firm's costs change. Suppose the initial regulated price is $10, which is set equal to the firm's average costs; remember that average costs include a normal profit. Future price increases are based on the aggregate price index adjusted for expected productivity changes. If the regulated firm's costs remain at $10 but aggregate prices rise so that the regulated price can be raised to $12, the regulated firm will make economic profits equal to the green area, $2(200) = $400. On the other hand, if the regulated firm's average costs rise more than the aggregate price index, it will incur economic losses because it will not be able to raise prices enough to cover costs. If average costs rise to $15, economic losses will equal the blue area, $3(200) = $600.

cent—say, 50 percent because of a shortage of an important input—the price regulations would cause the firm to lose money because average cost ($15) is higher than the regulated price.

A modern alternative to the price-cap model is **yardstick competition**. Under this approach, the regulated company is allowed price changes comparable to price changes in similar industries. The advantage to this approach is that it provides an incentive for firms to find ways to lower costs and thus increase profits; the disadvantage is that it is frequently difficult to find "similar" industries.

Yardstick competition The regulated company is allowed price changes comparable to price changes in similar industries.

LANDMARK GOVERNMENT REGULATIONS

The regulatory process in the United States has gone through several distinct stages. From the 1870s until the 1920s, most regulations were aimed at public utilities and the railroads. The depression years of the 1930s saw regulations being applied to the communications and banking industries. Regulation expanded into other areas before the trend shifted toward deregulation in the late 1970s and 1980s.

1877–1930: The Early Years

Government regulation in the United States began in the late nineteenth century when the Supreme Court issued several decisions regarding the regulation of monopolies. In *Munn v. Illinois (1877)*, the Court ruled that the state of Illinois could regulate prices at grain elevators—an act deemed necessary because grain elevator operators had colluded to keep their selling prices artificially high. This ruling was important because it broadened the range of industries that was subject to regulation. In the words of Justice Watt, property becomes "clothed in the public interest when used in a manner to make it of public consequences. . . ." A decade later, the railroad industry came under regulation. Not only had aggressive price wars damaged the industry, but railroads were discriminating against isolated rural customers who often paid higher rates for short hauls than city customers did for long hauls. The result was the Interstate Commerce Act and the Interstate Commerce Commission (ICC), which was given the right to regulate rail prices.

An important extension of *Munn v. Illinois* came in *Nebbia v. New York (1934)*. Until *Nebbia*, it was not clear whether it was constitutional to regulate all industries or only public utilities like grain elevators and the railroads. The Supreme Court's decision in *Nebbia* settled this issue by ruling that the state of New York could legally regulate the price of milk. The majority opinion said that ". . . a state is free to adopt whatever economic policy may reasonably be deemed to promote public welfare." In other words, government regulations could be applied to *any* industry if it could be shown that the regulations benefited the public.

The 1930s: Spreading Regulations

The Great Depression and the regulatory latitude supplied by *Nebbia* created a favorable environment for the expansion of government regulation. The power of the

ICC was expanded considerably. All surface transportation—trucks, barges, even oil pipelines—now came under the purview of the ICC. The one exception, ocean shipping, was regulated by the new Federal Maritime Commission, which was established in 1936. The ICC was also expanded to augment existing state and local regulations of electricity (1935) and natural gas (1938). In 1934, the Federal Communications Commission (FCC) was established to regulate broadcasting and the telecommunications industry.

The stock market crash of 1929 and four years of bank failures led to a number of regulations for the banking and securities industries. The Banking Acts of 1933 and 1935 created the Federal Deposit Insurance Corporation (FDIC) and made it illegal for banks to pay interest on checking accounts. The Glass–Steagall Act drew a legal distinction between commercial banks and investment banks: commercial banks could accept checking deposits but were restricted from underwriting businesses; investment banks had few restrictions on the use of their funds but could not accept checking account deposits. The reasoning behind the Glass–Steagall Act was that restrictions on commercial banks would increase depositor safety. Massive losses on the stock market—due in part to fraud—led to the Securities Act of 1933, which mandated that securities dealers must disclose full information to their clients. In 1934, the Securities and Exchange Commission (SEC) was created to monitor the securities industry.

········

1940–1970s: Continuing Regulatory Growth

The number of government regulations increased steadily between 1940 and the 1970s. The energy and communications industries probably came under the heaviest regulation. Until 1954, federal regulation of oil and natural gas was restricted to interstate pipelines, but an SEC decision in that year let the federal government regulate the wellhead price of natural gas. In 1971, the wellhead price of oil also came under regulation. Cable television, regulated at the local and state level almost since its inception, came under the jurisdiction of the federal government in 1968. In 1969, in a portent of things to come, MCI was allowed to enter the telecommunications market. Previously, the natural monopoly argument had been used to prohibit entry into the telecommunications industry. But, with the development of inexpensive fiber optics and other technologies, competition in the industry became possible.

Toward the end of this period, several agencies were established to regulate health, safety, and the environment. The Consumer Products Safety Commission, the Occupational Safety and Health Administration (OSHA), and the Nuclear Regulatory Agency were among the most important. All of these agencies had worthy purposes, but none was to escape criticism. OSHA made work safer for many, but was the object of more than a little ridicule when it saw fit to establish legal standards for the shape of toilet seats. The safety record of the nuclear power industry is a commendation for the Nuclear Regulatory Agency, but this agency has been accused of having been "captured" by the industry almost since its inception. There have also been occasional disputes over regulatory jurisdiction. For example, the Food and Drug Administration wants sausage makers to keep clean floors, but OSHA is concerned that wet floors are unsafe.

SETTING REGULATIONS AND STANDARDS FOR HIGH-DEFINITION TELEVISION

According to many futurists, the next innovation in broadcast technology will be high-definition television, or HDTV as it is usually called. HDTV provides better picture quality by sending television signals that have higher resolution because there are more lines per inch. HDTV broadcast signals and the television receivers will have to be compatible. The Federal Communications Commission (FCC) is currently investigating the best way to establish and regulate the new industry.

Until quite recently, Japan and Europe seemed to have a leg up in the HDTV revolution. The Japanese began experimental HDTV transmissions in 1979 and, armed with government subsidies, were able to start regular "HiVision" television broadcasts in 1989. Traditional television sets cannot receive Japanese HiVision broadcasts, but new sets have converters that allow them to receive both traditional and HiVision broadcasts. Almost $200 million in funding from the European Community served as seed money for European research into HDTV that began in 1986. HDTV has not caught on very well in Europe, in part because broadcasters contend that HDTV offers little advantage over traditional television. The European standard, "D2-MAC," differs from the Japanese HiVision system.

To understand why the HDTV revolution poses difficult regulatory problems in the United States, we need to look at two issues: the physics of broadcasting and the relationship between broadcasters and the regulatory process. The physics part is straightforward. Radio and television signals are broadcast in the electromagnetic spectrum, where there is only so much room for broadcasts. The FCC assigns space on the spectrum to different broadcasters to assure that only one station broadcasts on each frequency. The problem is that the bandwidth specified by current FCC regulations is too narrow for HDTV broadcasts. Until the FCC regulations are changed, it will not be possible to make land-based HDTV broadcasts from the United States; only satellite-based broadcasts are legal. Changing the FCC bandwidth regulations is proving difficult because broadcasters do not see significant revenue gains from HDTV. The broadcasting industry has resisted efforts to establish the regulations necessary for HDTV because it does not want to use scarce space on the electromagnetic spectrum for HDTV broadcasts.

Though slow, some progress has been made toward implementation of

• • • • • • • •

1970s–1990: Deregulation

The regulatory climate changed in the 1970s as economists and policymakers began to focus on the costs of government regulation. Just how significant are the costs of government regulation? The estimates vary widely, but one recent study concluded that in 1992 alone, government regulations resulted in between $413 and $533 billion in lost real GDP due to higher production costs and related factors.[9] This sort of analysis has led to the **deregulation** of a number of industries:[10]

Deregulation Any number of measures designed to reduce government interference with business.

[9]Michael T. Belongia, "Have Regulatory Burdens Slowed the Growth in Real GDP?" *National Economic Trends*, Federal Reserve Bank of St. Louis (March 1993): 1. The data are in 1988 dollars.
[10]An excellent and nontechnical survey of recent deregulation initiatives can be found in Clifford Winston, "Economic Deregulation: Days of Reckoning for Microeconomists," *Journal of Economic Literature* 31 (September 1993): 1263–89.

High-definition television at the David Sarnoff Research Lab in New Jersey, a work group for NBC and RCA.

HDTV standards and regulations. The FCC's current policy differs from the policies used in Japan and Europe. Instead of adopting a centralized HDTV standard and then implementing a set of regulations, the FCC is trying a market approach. Different developers are encouraged to explore alternative HDTV systems, and market rivalry will determine which system is best. This is much like the market test that was conducted on VHS and Beta formats for video tapes; consumers chose VHS, and the Beta format was discontinued. After the HDTV market test, the FCC will then choose the HDTV system for the United States.

The FCC's market test has the advantage of allowing market forces to help determine the best technology, but a few qualifications are in order before declaring victory for the market. First, the market solution is costly in the sense that the investment in losing alternative technologies is simply lost. Second, market forces are still restrained by bandwidth and other FCC regulations, so it is not clear that the "winner" will be the optimal system. Despite these qualifications, at this writing (April 1994) it does appear that the U.S. HDTV standard will win out. The Japanese government has recently reduced funding for HDTV research and has hinted that U.S. HDTV systems are superior.

SOURCES: Joseph Farrell and Carl Shapiro, "Standard Setting in High-Definition Television," *Brookings Papers on Economic Activity: Microeconomics* (1992): 1–94; Peter Coy and Neil Gross, "This Reception Is Great But . . .", *Business Week*, March 7, 1994, p. 50.

- *Transportation*. The Airline Deregulation Act of 1978 made entry into the airline industry easier and removed most regulated airfares. It also eliminated requirements that airlines serve particular destinations. The result—after a bit of havoc and the bankruptcy of several air carriers—was lower airfares for many well-traveled routes but higher airfares for less well-traveled routes. The Staggers Act of 1980 deregulated the railroads; trucking was deregulated with the Motor Carrier Act of 1982; and the Bus Regulatory Reform Act of 1982 deregulated bus transportation.
- *Telecommunications*. Perhaps the most widely studied case of deregulation was the 1984 breakup of AT&T, which had previously been regarded by some as a textbook case of natural monopoly. But by the 1980s, technological innovations had made competition in telecommunications possible. Today, AT&T competes with MCI, Sprint, and numerous other companies for long-distance service.

• *Financial markets.* The banking regulations established in the 1930s may have been desirable in a period of stable prices and low interest rates, but neither case held in the 1970s. When market interest rates rose above the regulated interest rates that banks and savings and loans were allowed to pay on deposits, depositors took their money out of these financial institutions and put them in assets that offered higher returns. This process—known as *disintermediation*—was a major factor in the passage of two important laws calling for financial deregulation: the Depository Institutions Deregulation and Monetary Control Act (DIDMCA) of 1980 and the Garn–St. Germain Act of 1982. Among other things, these acts removed most interest rate ceilings and allowed banks and savings and loans to invest in a wider variety of assets. These deregulations may have proceeded too quickly, and bad luck may have played a role as well, because the 1980s saw a record number of bank and savings and loan failures.[11]

Estimating the Benefits of Deregulation. Several economists have attempted to quantify the social benefits of deregulation. This is ongoing work, but a typical estimate is that society benefited on the order of $36 to $46 billion annually from deregulation.[12] Most of these benefits went to consumers in the form of lower prices. The benefits have not been distributed equally throughout society, however. Some firms have suffered because they are no longer able to charge monopoly prices and earn economic rents, and some workers now earn lower wages.

RECAP   **Regulation and Deregulation**

Government regulations may be necessary when private markets do not automatically result in socially desirable outcomes. Both costs and benefits are associated with regulation, so it is important to determine whether the benefits outweigh the costs.

1. Regulations are designed to serve the public interest; the regulatory process can be "captured" by the firms that are being regulated, however, and result in regulations that serve special interests more than the public.
2. Good regulations produce benefits that exceed costs. The costs of regulations may include higher prices, bureaucratic "red tape," lower profits, and less production. The benefits depend on the specific regulation. It is often difficult to measure costs and benefits accurately.
3. Current regulatory policy calls for regulations that rely on market incentives, are implemented at least cost, and minimize the prospect for litigation. Price regulation formulas should be flexible and permit adjustments in response to market changes.
4. Regulations have been applied to many areas of the economy. Public utility regulation dates back to the nineteenth century; financial markets became subject to regulation in the 1930s, and since that time, health, safety, consumer products, telecommunications, transportation, and many other industries have been regulated.

---

[11]This subject is explored in more detail in Chapter 28.
[12]Winston (1993): 1284. Data are in constant 1990 dollars.

5. The trend since the late 1970s has been toward deregulation. Regulations have been removed or relaxed on transportation, banking, telecommunications, and many other industries.

ANTITRUST LEGISLATION: THE SHERMAN ACT AND ITS AFTERMATH

The U.S. economy went through several adjustments following the Civil War. By some accounts, the 1873–1878 recession is still the most severe in U.S. history. But for our purposes, the most significant thing about the economy in the 20 years or so after the Civil War is that prices fell by nearly half.[13] Just why prices fell is a matter of debate—one popular explanation is that the withdrawal of "greenbacks" from circulation reduced the money supply—but this is beside the point just now. We need to examine what firms thought about falling prices and what they then did about the decline.

In the 1870s, firms competed by cutting prices below the level of their competitors. The problem was that price cutting became so widespread that many firms ended up selling their goods at a loss and going out of business. The term coined at the time to describe the practice, **cutthroat competition**, was fitting. As the economy began to recover in the late 1870s, businesses evolved and developed strategies to avoid another outbreak of cutthroat competition. Some firms reached agreements to keep prices high and divide up the market. Other firms, led by the so-called robber barons, appeared to use low prices to drive competitors out of the market and then raised prices once the competitors were gone. John D. Rockefeller was the most celebrated robber baron. In 1879, his Standard Oil Company refined nearly 90 percent of the nation's oil and managed its entire pipeline capacity.

Cutthroat competition Pricing strategy designed to drive competitors out of the market; typically involves setting prices very low.

The Sherman Act

To prevent ruinous competition, some competing firms formed *trusts*. A trust is much like a cartel—an association of firms within the same industry that attempt to divide the market and practice joint profit maximization. Trusts may have stabilized the market a bit, but from the public's standpoint, they served exactly one function: they kept prices high. As a result, the first federal antitrust law, the **Sherman Act**, was passed in 1890. The Sherman Act remains the core of antitrust policy today, and much contemporary antitrust legislation can be interpreted as modifications of the Sherman Act. It has two main sections: Section 1 prohibits "contracts, combinations, and conspiracies in the restraint of trade." The intent of this section is to prevent price fixing. Section 2 of the act is aimed at market dominance. It "prohibits monopolization, attempts to monopolize, and combinations or conspiracies to monopolize any part of the trade or commerce among several states, or with foreign nations." The Sherman Act was also used to prevent unionization until passage of the Norris–

Sherman Act (1890) Key antitrust law. Prohibits monopolies and conspiracies to restrain trade.

[13]The National Bureau of Economic Research cycle dates for the period are December 1867 peak, June 1869 trough, October 1870 trough, October 1873 peak, March 1879 trough, March 1882 peak. Real GDP growth averaged 3 percent over the period.

La Guardia Act in 1932. A major problem with the Sherman Act was that it did not define anticompetitive behavior precisely enough. As a result, there were numerous court battles, and the act was largely ineffective for many years. For example, the Standard Oil case (discussed later in the chapter) went to court in 1890 but was not decided until 1911.

. . . .

The Clayton Act

Clayton Act (1914) Important amendment to the Sherman Act. Forbade price discrimination, tying arrangements, and exclusive dealing.

The **Clayton Act** was passed in 1914 to augment the Sherman Act and define anticompetitive acts more precisely. The Clayton Act outlawed several specific kinds of anticompetitive behavior including price discrimination and mergers between competitors. It also prohibited tying clauses, exclusive dealing agreements, and interlocking directorates. Tying clauses require customers to buy one good in order to get another; this allows the seller to get rid of unpopular products. Tying clauses can be effective only when monopoly power prevents customers from buying from other suppliers. An exclusive dealing arrangement works like this: Firm A agrees to supply goods to the buyer, but only if the buyer promises not to do business with Firm B. Obviously, this arrangement hurts Firm B, and if Firm B goes out of business, Firm A is then free to raise prices and hurt the customer. An interlocking directorate exists when the same directors sit on the boards of different companies. The Sherman Act had made it illegal for two firms in the same business to merge, but nothing prevented the firms from sharing the same directors. And since the "competing firms" had the same people on their boards of directors, the firms were likely to share the same management goals, pricing strategies, and so on.

. . . .

Other Important Antitrust Legislation

The Clayton Act provided more precise definitions of anticompetitive acts, but several problems still remained. First, the law stated that prosecution was warranted only if anticompetitive behavior "substantially" lessened competition or tended to create a monopoly. In practice, this meant that prosecution and enforcement of antitrust still wound up in the courts because the word "substantially" had not been defined. Two laws were passed in an attempt to remedy this problem. In 1936, the Robinson-Patman Act was passed to improve the Clayton Act's section on price discrimination. Not everyone believes that the Robinson-Patman Act was an improvement. Among other things, it made it illegal for large food chains to pay lower prices for produce than small grocery stores unless they could demonstrate that costs fell because of large bulk sales. In 1950, the Celler-Kefauver Act was passed to close a loophole in the merger section. The Celler-Kefauver Act was necessary because the Supreme Court had interpreted the Sherman Act as prohibiting mergers between firms via the sale of stock but not prohibiting mergers accomplished by the sale of physical assets.

The Federal Trade Commission (FTC) Act was also passed in 1914. Its main aim was to create a special agency to investigate alleged infractions and reach judgments; previously, the Antitrust Division of the Justice Department had carried out these duties. The FTC Act also included a section that outlawed "unfair" methods of competition. An important amendment to the FTC Act was the Wheeler-Lea Act passed in 1938. Prior to the passage of this act, numerous court decisions had weakened the FTC to the point that the courts were hesitant to rule against deceptive advertising and other unfair business practices. The Wheeler-Lea Act extended the power of the FTC and made prosecution for unfair business practices easier.

COURT CASES AND INTERPRETATIONS

Much of the wording in antitrust legislation is so ambiguous that its interpretation is often left to the courts. The courts have used two main philosophical rules in applying antitrust legislation, the **per se rule** and the **rule of reason**. The per se rule works like this: certain practices—say, price fixing by a cartel—can have only harmful effects, so price fixing by the cartel is considered a "per se" offense or an offense "in itself" and must be outlawed. The rule of reason gives more latitude in enforcement. Suppose that two firms in different industries decide to merge into a conglomerate. Such a merger would not necessarily be harmful, so the courts would have to look into the "evident purpose" or reason for the merger to decide whether it should be allowed. As you might guess, per se rule antitrust cases tend to be resolved much faster than cases based on rule of reason arguments.

Per se rule Antitrust philosophy that holds that the mere existence of monopoly is enough to warrant antitrust action.

Rule of reason Antitrust philosophy that holds that trusts should be broken up only if there was intent to restrain trade.

The Rule of Reason

The rule of reason was established with a series of court cases beginning with the famous Standard Oil case of 1911. In less than 40 years, however, the rule of reason was supplanted by the per se rule. Two of the more important cases settled according to the rule of reason were the Standard Oil case and the U.S. Steel case.

Standard Oil (1911). The first major application of the Sherman Act occurred in 1911 when the U.S. Supreme Court used the rule of reason to require the breakup of Standard Oil Company. Two weeks after Standard Oil was broken up, the American Tobacco Company was also broken up under the rule of reason.

The Rockefeller family had built Standard Oil by acquiring more than 120 competitors in the oil industry and buying pipelines to cut off supplies to rivals. The company was also charged with conducting business espionage and other acts. One of its main techniques was to set prices so low that it drove competitors from the market, a practice known as **predatory pricing**. Why is charging low prices bad? The Court ruled that it is not necessarily harmful, unless the prices are set so low that they drive out firms that are "as efficient or more efficient" than the firm charging predatory prices. According to their opponents, the Rockefellers were able to engage in predatory pricing because their immense wealth enabled them to sustain losses longer than their competitors. Once the competitors were out of business, the Rockefellers raised their prices.[14]

Predatory pricing Practice used by large firms to drive competitors out of the market; involves setting prices so low that less well financed firms fold first.

---

[14]We need to add that some contemporary economists do not believe firms ever practice predatory pricing. The reasoning behind this argument is deceptively simple: If a firm is currently maximizing profits, how could it pay to enter a new market and lower prices? There is more to this argument, and the interested student is referred to an excellent introduction to this and other issues in the contemporary debate over antitrust economics in Walter Adams and James Brock, *Antitrust Economics on Trial* (Princeton, N.J.: Princeton University Press, 1991). *Antitrust Economics on Trial* is written as a play with three characters, the judge, an attorney, and the expert witness, who is an economist. It is humorous as well as informative.

After several years of litigation, the Supreme Court handed down its ruling in the Standard Oil case. The Court ruled that monopolization requires two elements: First, the firm must have a monopoly position; Standard Oil's 90 percent market share met this requirement. Second, there must be evidence of *intent* to acquire the monopoly position; Standard Oil's predatory pricing met this requirement. This second point was to become the basis for the rule of reason.

United States Steel (1920). The Justice Department brought a suit against U.S. Steel in 1911, but the case was not resolved until 1920. Beginning in the late nineteenth century, U.S. Steel was built with a series of steel mergers, and by 1901, the company controlled almost 75 percent of the domestic iron and steel industry. In 1907, Judge E. H. Gary, the chair of U.S. Steel, began having monthly dinner meetings with the heads of competing firms. These dinners—which came to be called the Gary Dinners—were intended to stabilize prices and generate friendship among industry leaders. The friendship was important: when U.S. Steel was taken to court, no one testified against it. This silence was in stark contrast to the Standard Oil case, where competing firms lined up to accuse Standard Oil of using unfair pricing practices. As a result, the Supreme Court deemed U.S. Steel a "good citizen" and ruled that it was not guilty of monopolization. The U.S. Steel decision was to have important implications for the future of antitrust: it is not *size* that invites court action, but *performance*. This decision reiterated the rule of reason approach first used in the Standard Oil case.

· · · · · · · ·

The Per Se Rule

A series of cases led to the replacement of the rule of reason with the per se rule in 1940. The per se rule toward price fixing seemed to have been established in 1927 when the Supreme Court ruled against an association of 23 toiletry pottery manufacturers in *United States v. Trenton Potteries Co.* These manufacturers controlled over 80 percent of the market and sought to fix prices. Six years later, however, the Supreme Court seemed to reverse itself in *Appalachian Coals, Inc. v. United States.* In this case, 137 companies had joined together to form a selling agency to market coal at fixed prices. The Supreme Court ruled that ". . . a close and objective scrutiny of particular conditions . . ." is required in each case. The Great Depression and depressed industry conditions were significant factors in this decision.

Socony-Vacuum (1940). The per se rule was again invoked in 1940 in an important ruling against Socony-Vacuum in *United States v. Sacony-Vacuum Oil Co.* In 1935 and 1936, several major oil refiners, including Socony-Vacuum (now Mobil Oil Company), had a purchasing arrangement designed to keep prices high. Each of the major refiners picked an independent refiner and agreed to purchase its surplus gasoline and keep it off the market. The Supreme Court ruled that any combination formed for the purpose of price fixing was illegal, and that no consideration of "reasonableness" was necessary. The per se rule against price fixing has remained the least ambiguous part of antitrust law since *Socony*.

ALCOA (1945). The rule of reason was put to rest for good with the ALCOA case in 1945. In 1940, there was only one aluminum producer in the United States, the Aluminum Company of America (ALCOA).[15] In *United States v. Aluminum Company of America*, Circuit Judge Learned Hand ruled that ALCOA was guilty of illegal monopolization because of its size alone. Said Judge Hand: "ALCOA did not have to seize every opportunity . . ." to be guilty of monopoly behavior. It is important to note that ALCOA had *not* used any of the aggressive or predatory practices that had been the basis for antitrust litigation in the past.

ALCOA owed its monopoly status to four main factors. First, it owned exclusive patents for converting aluminum oxide into aluminum. Second, it was protected from foreign competition by high tariffs on imported aluminum. Third, it owned extensive deposits of bauxite and several sources of cheap electric power. Finally, it practiced *limit pricing*, the strategy of keeping prices low to deter entry. This last point is especially important: the fact that ALCOA kept prices low would seem to indicate that, despite its size, ALCOA was acting as a "good citizen" and thus not subject to prosecution.

Judge Hand ruled otherwise. He noted that ALCOA's sales plus its own internal use of aluminum constituted fully 90 percent of the total production plus imports, the correct share to constitute a monopoly.[16] Interestingly, the solution was not to dissolve ALCOA. Instead, the federal government subsidized the entry of Reynolds and Kaiser Aluminum into the aluminum industry by selling them war plants at bargain prices. Later, three more entrants into the aluminum industry were given subsidies.

· · · · · · · ·

Penalties and Enforcement

When firms lose antitrust suits, they are typically required to cease and desist. In the case of price fixing, this means abolition of the association or structure that was used to keep prices high; in the case of monopolization, it usually results in the dissolution of the monopoly. Further, beginning with the landmark 1962 case, *United States v. General Electric et al.*, the executives involved with antitrust violations have also been subject to prison sentences and/or fines.

The *Antitrust Procedures and Penalties Act of 1974* increased the criminal penalty for antitrust violations from a misdemeanor to a felony. The argument, of course, was that the possibility of stiffer penalties would deter crime. This measure appears to have been successful. Though the total number of cases filed by the Antitrust Division of the Justice Department has increased since 1974, the number of "significant" cases has declined.[17] This finding is important for at least two reasons: First, it suggests that stiffer fines do have an impact on antitrust behavior. Second, it may be evidence that

---

[15]Actually, ALCOA was the only producer of aluminum from virgin ore; several companies were producing aluminum from scrap.

[16]It must be noted that the 90 percent rule that Judge Hand applied is not universal in all industries. For example, in *United States v. Von's Grocery Co.* in 1965, the courts ruled that the merger of two supermarkets in the Los Angeles area would restrain competition, even though the merged firm would have had only 7.5 percent of the market.

[17]Edward A. Snyder, "New Insights into the Decline of Antitrust Enforcement," *Contemporary Policy Issues* 7 (October 1989): 1–18. Snyder qualifies his argument by noting that his results depend on the assumption that recent budget cuts in the Antitrust Division have not reduced its effectiveness.

recent antitrust enforcement has not only been just as tough as previously, but that it has been more successful.

At least one caveat must be added here. The U.S. legal system gives judges considerable sentencing discretion in most antitrust cases. One recent—and controversial—study has concluded that (1) Republican judges tend to give harsher penalties than Democratic judges, and (2) sentencing can be influenced by the judge's prospect of promotion to a higher court position.[18] This finding may suggest a need for more rigid sentencing guidelines.

ANTITRUST AND THE INTERNATIONAL ECONOMY

Antitrust philosophy has changed significantly over the past century. Early antitrust legislation was aimed at the domestic economy with little attention given to international competitiveness. Increasing international competition has led some economists to call for relaxation of antitrust rules to allow firms to merge and form cooperative ventures to better compete in the international arena. Others disagree and argue that most jobs and innovations are created by small firms, so strong enforcement of antitrust rules is as necessary today as ever.

As we mentioned in Chapter 13, there have been four major merger waves in U.S. history. The most recent wave occurred in the 1980s during the Reagan administration. The Reagan administration felt that the less government interference the better and sought to revise much antitrust legislation. This effort was largely unsuccessful, so the administration did what it considered the next best thing: it used executive authority to establish a policy of "blatant non-enforcement of the antitrust statutes" and ". . . aggressively [pursued] the appointment of federal judges sympathetic to its *anti*-antitrust agenda."[19] The magnitude of mergers and acquisitions during the Reagan years was staggering: The total value of acquisitions rose from $50 billion in 1983 to over $200 billion in 1988. Included in these mergers were some of the largest in history, including the "deal of the century," a $25 billion buyout of RJR-Nabisco by Kohlberg, Kravis, Roberts, & Company.[20]

The key to understanding the change in antitrust attitudes lies in understanding the original intent of antitrust. From the very beginning, antitrust legislation focused almost exclusively on price competition, not consumer welfare or economic efficiency. For example, mergers were ruled illegal when the resulting entity would gain enough power to charge monopoly prices, even if there would have been significant efficiency gains. In other words, economic efficiency was not important. In the eyes

---

[18]Mark A. Cohen, "The Role of Criminal Sanctions in Antitrust Enforcement," *Contemporary Policy Issues* 7 (October 1989): 36–46.

[19]Patrick M. Boarman, "Antitrust Laws in a Global Market," *Challenge* (January/February 1993): 31. Much of this section is based on the Boarman article.

[20]The "deal of the century" did not work out quite as well as the investors hoped. According to Randall Smith, " 'Deal of the Century'? Not for RJR Investors," *Wall Street Journal*, March 4, 1993: p. C1, the investors would have been better off to have put their $25 billion in a common stock index fund.

of Robert Bork, disregarding efficiency means that ". . . consumer welfare is not important, and that in turn means that the primary reason for preserving competition is to be disregarded."[21] Which situation would you prefer—a competitive price of $10 with zero economic profits for the firms, or a monopoly price of $8 with the firm making significant economic profits? Under traditional antitrust law, you would pay the $10. Judge Bork—and many economists—feel that consumers would be better off (and thus prefer) paying $8.

Most consumers would prefer to pay $8 even if it meant the monopolist was making economic profits, but that may not be the real issue. The real issue is whether you will continue to pay $8 over the long run—and thus reap the benefits of the monopolist's scale economies—or whether the monopolist will limit production and raise prices once it is certain it faces no competition. The answer to this question may come down to your assessment of the theory of contestable markets. If the threat of potential entry into a market is sufficient to force a monopoly to keep its price low, then it is probably best not to enforce the antitrust law and break up large firms. But, as we found out in Chapter 14, the theory of contestable markets is not without its critics. This issue will be the subject of continuing debate for years to come.

· · · · · · · ·

Japanese Antitrust Policies

Antitrust policies in Japan allow for the existence of cartel-like structures called *keiretsu*. In these company groups, producers, customers, suppliers, banks, and government agencies are linked together to share in the knowledge base and generate efficiency gains. It is important to note that a *keiretsu* is not a single conglomerate firm; the companies retain their individual identities. A *keiretsu* composed of firms within the same industry—a horizontal *keiretsu*—could help maintain industry stability and engage in long-term investment planning, but would almost certainly run afoul of antitrust laws in the United States. There is also some evidence that the *keiretsu* structure may be able to bring new products to market faster than individual firms. *Keiretsu*-like structures are not confined to Japan. In 1990, the two biggest business groups in the world—Mitsubishi of Japan and Daimler-Benz-Deutsche Bank of Germany—met in Singapore to discuss a global alliance. Such a meeting would have been clearly illegal in the United States, but it did not violate antitrust laws in Japan or Germany.[22]

U.S. firms have begun to emulate the *keiretsu* approach, at least within the confines of existing antitrust legislation. The 1991 alliance of IBM, Motorola, and Apple Computer to jointly develop personal computers and software is one example; the General Motors/Toyota joint venture producing automobiles in California is another. Nevertheless, it is clear that without wholesale changes to the antitrust laws, U.S. firms will be restricted in their ability to engage in *keiretsu*-like arrangements.

---

[21]Robert Bork, *The Antitrust Paradox* (New York: Basic Books, 1978). Quoted in Boarman. Bork was nominated to the Supreme Court by Reagan but rejected by the Senate.

[22]This point comes from Lester Thurow, *Head to Head* (New York: William Morrow, 1992). *Head to Head* suggests that antitrust policy in the United States is simply out of tune with antitrust as it is practiced in the rest of the world. *Head to Head* is quite readable—and opinionated!

FOCUS ON

ANTITRUST AND THE SEMICONDUCTOR INDUSTRY

The U.S. semiconductor industry provides a good case study of the evolution of antitrust policies over the past 30 years. In the 1960s and 1970s, the industry was dominated by small "merchant" firms—firms that produced semiconductors for sale to other companies. Venture capital was available for bright engineers willing to take a risk, and the military's pockets were deep enough to buy state-of-the-art products even at high prices. There was also a good flow of information from universities to business. Finally, the risk of antitrust prosecution made it difficult for large, vertically integrated firms—AT&T and IBM, for example—to enter the market and produce semiconductors for their own use.

Much of this changed with the entry of the Japanese into the semiconductor market in the mid-1970s. The Japanese successfully used a system of tariffs and quotas to get their infant semiconductor industry off the ground, and by the mid-1980s, Japan was a dominant force in the world semiconductor market. Japanese companies were outperforming U.S. companies in many areas of the semiconductor market. A study conducted in 1986 by the National Science Foundation and the National Materials Advisory Board showed the Japanese were ahead in several areas. By 1988, certain types of semiconductors could only be bought in Japan.

Business and government concern over declining market share and competitiveness of the U.S. semiconductor industry led to the formation of Sematech in 1988. Sematech is an association of several high-tech firms engaged in cooperative research. Funding consists of some $200 million per year, with about half coming from industry and the remainder from the federal government as well as state and local governments. Much of the federal money is channeled through the Defense Department. This point is significant: the Defense Department has always supported semiconductor research, but previously its funding was for "hardened chips" capable of withstanding nuclear hits. The new aid for civilian semiconductor research is recognition of the fact that many important defense-related technology advances are the result of civilian research.

Why should the government fund a particular industry? And won't cooperative research lead to *de facto* monopolization? Neither question has a simple answer. Economists who support aid to the semiconductor industry argue that the social benefits of semiconductor research and development are significantly higher than the private benefits. In particular, jobs in the semiconductor industry are typically high-wage, high-productivity jobs. High-tech firms often provide training for their workers so the skill level of the general workforce increases. Further, there is evidence that high-tech industries like semiconductors have important geographical spinoffs. This explains why so many computer firms are located in the Silicon Valley of California or along the Miracle Mile outside Boston.

· · · · · · · ·

Issues for the Future

Industrial cooperation along *keiretsu*-like lines is not the only issue that must be addressed as antitrust laws adapt to competition in the 1990s and beyond. Perhaps the key issue is simply that the increasing internationalization of the economy has made it difficult to define monopoly and monopoly power. Other important issues that must be debated as the antitrust environment evolves include the following:

Electronic diagram to be reduced and put on silicon chip.

Still, the kind of cooperative research and development allowed at Sematech seems to run smack in the face of antitrust. Sematech supporters deny this criticism for two reasons. First, by fostering the development and dissemination of frontier process technology, cooperative ventures like Sematech increase the likelihood that U.S. companies will survive. Even supporters doubt whether it will permit U.S. companies to recapture market share, but without cooperative ventures like Sematech, the semiconductor market would soon be dominated completely by Japanese companies. Cooperative research and development is legal in Japan.

Second, Sematech supporters note that generic research benefits all participating firms but does not determine market outcomes. In other words, Sematech technology will be available to all firms, but it will be up to the firms to figure out how to bring that technology to market.

Has Sematech been successful? It has certainly improved communication between the semiconductor industry and the semiconductor equipment industry, and U.S. computer manufacturers are beginning to shift away from Asian suppliers to U.S. suppliers. After falling for several years, the U.S. share of the world semiconductor market has begun to rise appreciably; it reached 47 percent in 1991. Still, the debate over the effectiveness of Sematech and the desirability of cooperative research will continue because it is impossible to state with certainty what caused the apparent revival of the U.S. semiconductor industry. It is possible that the same events would have transpired in the absence of Sematech.

SOURCE: Laura D'Andrea Tyson, *Who's Bashing Whom? Trade Conflict in High-Technology Industries* (Washington, D.C.: Institute for International Economics, 1992).

- Continuing work will be needed to separate the positive and negative effects of cartels. The positive effects include efficiency gains and economies of scale; the negative effects include market power and price fixing. Recent work on the theory of contestable markets may provide insights here, but it is also important to recognize that political power increases along with economic power.

- Production flexibility and innovation must be examined carefully. Large merged firms often have higher break-even points and less production flexibility than small firms. This may suggest that it is best not to change current merger laws. On the other hand, Japanese *keiretsus* seem to be able to bring new products to market quickly.

- Some studies have suggested that the merger wave of the 1980s was so costly that merger firms were forced to cut back on spending for research and development in order to pay off the debt incurred in the buyout process. Such mergers may generate short-term profits but yield few long-term social benefits. This suggests that it may be necessary to develop the financial and tax policy components of antitrust legislation.

- Finally, Laura D'Andrea Tyson, chair of the Council of Economic Advisers under President Clinton, argues that some industries provide important external benefits to society over and above the benefits they provide for the firms. This is especially true of the high-tech industries where the social return for private research and development is often much higher than the private return. She advocates "easing antitrust restrictions on cooperative production projects, and increased support for engineering education."[23] Tyson's views seem to suggest that antitrust policies should be applied differently depending on the industry under consideration. Tyson's ideas are not without their critics, but policies will certainly be influenced by this view, at least for a few years. The Sematech Focus box describes a cooperative research and development effort by the semiconductor industry.

RECAP   Antitrust Policy

Antitrust policy in the United States dates back to 1890 when the Sherman Act was passed to break up Standard Oil. Since that time, numerous additional acts and court interpretations have changed our views on antitrust.

1. The two most important antitrust laws are the Sherman Act (1890), which prohibited trusts and combinations, and the Clayton Act (1914), which defined anticompetitive behavior more precisely.

2. The Standard Oil case established the rule of reason—the idea that trusts should be broken up only if there was intent to restrain trade.

3. The rule of reason was replaced with the per se rule in 1940 with the *Socony-Vacuum* case. According to the per se rule, the mere existence of monopoly power is enough to invoke antitrust.

4. Many contemporary economists believe that antitrust policies should be revised to take account of international competition. Some economists believe that the government should actively encourage cooperative research and development, especially in high-tech industries.

[23]Laura D'Andrea Tyson, *Who's Bashing Whom? Trade Conflict in High Technology Industries* (Washington, D.C.: Institute for International Economics, 1992), p. 152.

SUMMARY

In few areas in economics is there more disagreement than surrounds the topic of regulation and antitrust. All regulations and antitrust policies represent government interference with business activity and restrictions on private behavior—not exactly what the phrase *laissez faire* brings to mind. Still, regulations and antitrust policies are appropriate if it can be shown that the benefits of the regulations outweigh the costs. Unfortunately, it is frequently difficult to measure the costs and benefits accurately. The main points from this chapter are:

1. Government regulations are designed to serve the public interest; however, it is possible for the regulatory process to be "captured" by the groups that are being regulated. Good regulations rely on market incentives and are implemented at minimum cost.

2. Regulations have been applied to many industries in the United States. In the nineteenth century, most regulations were aimed at monopolies like public utilities and the railroad industry to prevent price gouging. Today, regulations are designed to ensure public safety, protect the environment, and control monopoly power. Several industries have been deregulated since the late 1970s.

3. The first important antitrust act passed in the United States was the Sherman Act of 1890. This act outlawed monopolies and restraint of trade. Its language was imprecise, so the Clayton Act was passed in 1914 to better define specific anticompetitive acts. A number of other important antitrust laws have been passed since then.

4. The courts have used two main philosophies in interpreting antitrust law. Under the rule of reason, monopolies were subject to prosecution only if they acted in an anticompetitive manner. In 1940, this rule was replaced with the per se rule, which states that the mere existence of monopoly power is enough to warrant antitrust prosecution.

5. Today, many economists feel that there should be more latitude toward antitrust because cooperative ventures may allow firms to compete better internationally. Some economists believe that the government should subsidize cooperative research and development, especially in the high-tech industries.

KEY TERMS AND CONCEPTS

regulatory lag
cost-benefit analysis
public interest theory of regulation
capture theory of regulation
Securities and Exchange Commission
    (SEC)
cost-of-service formula
price-cap formula
yardstick competition
Munn v. Illinois

Interstate Commerce Commission (ICC)
Nebbia v. New York
Federal Deposit Insurance Corporation
    (FDIC)
Glass-Steagall Act
Occupational Safety and Health
    Administration (OSHA)
deregulation
DIDMCA
cutthroat competition

Sherman Act   rule of reason
Clayton Act   predatory pricing
per se rule   *Socony-Vacuum*

REVIEW QUESTIONS

1. What are the basic principles of government regulation? How do the two main theories of government regulation fit these principles?
2. Compare and contrast the price-cap, cost-of-service, and yardstick competition models of price regulation. Use diagrams to illustrate your answer.
3. Outline the growth of government regulation from the *Munn v. Illinois* case of 1877 to the deregulation days of the 1970s and 1980s.
4. What were the main events that led to the passage of the Sherman Act in 1890? What laws have been passed to augment and modify its powers since then?
5. What are the two basic philosophical rules for the application of antitrust? Which rule is easier to implement? Which rule is applicable today?
6. How does Japanese antitrust policy differ from U.S. antitrust policy? How do these differences affect the international competitiveness of each country?

PROBLEMS

1. Can you list several economic activities that are completely *free* from government regulation? Why have no regulations been applied to these activities? Do you think they should be regulated?
2. Regulations often set lower as well as upper limits on the prices that firms can charge. Explain and comment. Do regulated price floors fit the capture theory or the public interest theory?
3. Which one (if any) of the three price regulation formulas discussed in the chapter would you advocate for regulating utility prices? Cable television prices? Hospital prices? Why?
4. The FCC has regulations regarding what can be shown on television. For example, full-frontal nudity is illegal on broadcast programs (but is legal on restricted access cable television). It also regulates the number of minutes of advertising that can be shown during entertainment programs. Would you favor regulations that restricted the kind of advertisements that could be shown on Saturday morning cartoon shows? What about prime-time shows that air at 10:00 P.M.? Why or why not?
5. Does technological advance increase or decrease the need for antitrust laws? Explain and give examples.
6. In general, economists favor government regulations only reluctantly. In contrast, consumers frequently call for additional regulations to reduce the power of big business. What arguments could you make to help consumers understand the economist's point of view?
7. The chapter notes that OSHA was ridiculed when it established legal standards for the shape of toilet seats. Presumably, OSHA felt that incorrectly shaped toilet seats were a health hazard. If this is correct, why didn't the market automatically provide signals for comfy toilet seats? Why did OSHA believe it needed to intervene?

8. The Food and Drug Administration (FDA) is often criticized for taking too long to approve new drugs. Explain how advocates of both the public interest theory of regulation and the capture theory of regulation would react to this criticism of the FDA. Do you think the approval process should be modified for drugs designed to treat AIDS?

9. Suppose that you move to a small town in the Midwest, where, bankrolled by your granddaddy's money, you decide to bring in-line skating to the masses. Your store, Black & Blue In-Line, is a crashing success, so much so that a long-time resident decides to open up a competing shop. Not a problem—your granddaddy's money allows you to drop prices and keep them low long enough to force your new competitor out of business. Once your monopoly status is safe again, you proceed to raise prices to their former level. No one else threatens to enter the industry, and because there is little else for 14-year-old kids to do in town, business is good enough to expand your offerings. Your initial foray is into the refreshment area. Sodas and snacks go over well, but your best moneymaker turns out to be hassle-free cigarette sales to those 14-year-old in-line skaters. Unfortunately, your lawyer is now recommending that you hire additional legal staff to fend off pending antitrust and other problems. What problems do you think she is warning you about? What kind of defense should you mount?

CHAPTER 20

Poverty and Income Inequality

Some numbers to mull over:

• • • Nearly one in seven Americans lives in poverty.

• • • Almost one in five children lives in poverty.

• • • More than two in five African-American children live in poverty.

• • • The rich got richer and the poor got poorer in the 1980s.

• • • The less educated are becoming worse off relative to the highly educated.[1]

Are these facts something we should be concerned about? Are they an inevitable consequence of capitalism? Or are people poor simply because they are lazy? Is there really equal opportunity for all?

These are exceedingly difficult questions to answer. We have mounds of data on income distribution and poverty, but trying to discover cause and effect is difficult. And any attempt at objective, scientific inquiry is blunted by our passions: some ask how we can stand by and see children living in poverty. Others respond that it is not fair that anyone be taxed to take care of people who refuse to work.

This chapter will look at poverty and income inequality. Our main task will be to put the data in context and to maintain a semblance of objectivity in the process.

---

[1]The actual numbers are as follows: 14.5 percent of all persons were officially in poverty in 1992 (1994 *Economic Report of the President*, Table B-31). The remaining data come from Lawrence Mishel and Jared Bernstein, *The State of Working America, 1992–1993* (Armonk, N.Y.: M. E. Sharpe, 1993): 21.8 percent of children under age 18 were in poverty in 1991 (page 286); 45.9 percent of black children were in poverty in 1991 (page 286); between 1977 and 1989, the average money income of the richest fifth of the population rose from $63,546 to $81,399 while the average money income of the poorest 20 percent fell from $8,495 to $7,608 (page 102); in 1973, the hourly wage of a high school graduate was 68 percent as high as a college graduate; in 1991, this had fallen to 64 percent (page 162).

AFTER READING AND STUDYING THIS CHAPTER, YOU SHOULD BE ABLE TO:

••• Discuss the demographic characteristics of poverty, and explain how income distribution has changed over the past 50 years

••• Consider alternative explanations for the existence of income inequality

••• Present different philosophical arguments for the ideal distribution of income

••• Outline recent antipoverty programs used in the United States

•••••••• DATA AND DEFINITIONS

Topics like income distribution are sure to raise tempers. Some people say the poor are just lazy; others argue that the rich exploit the downtrodden. Some say that income inequality serves as a powerful incentive motivating people to work hard to get ahead; others believe that a more equitable income distribution would instill a sense of fairness and community. Whatever your feelings about these issues, you cannot begin to discuss them intelligently without first looking at the actual data.

••••••••

Income Distribution Data

Table 20.1 presents income distribution data for the United States by decade since 1950. The data are presented in *quintiles* or fifths of the population. A quick glance seems to suggest that income distribution has been roughly constant since 1950: the poorest quintile earns about 5 percent of total income, and the richest quintile earns about 40 percent of total income. A slight shift occurred in the 1980s—the income of the bottom quintile fell from 5.1 percent to 4.6 percent while the income of the top quintile rose from 41.6 percent to 44.3 percent—but most people would say that income distribution has been remarkably constant.

A closer examination of the data reveals that the shift toward upper incomes has been a bit more pronounced. In particular, if the data are examined by *decile* (tenths of the population), the poor appear to have been especially hard hit in the 1980s. According to one study, real income before taxes rose 21 percent for the top decile

••••• TABLE 20.1 INCOME DISTRIBUTION

Income Class	1950	1960	1970	1980	1990
Lowest 20%	4.5%	4.8%	5.4%	5.1%	4.6%
Second 20%	12.0	12.2	12.2	11.6	10.8
Middle 20%	17.4	17.8	17.6	17.5	16.6
Fourth 20%	23.4	24.0	23.8	24.3	23.8
Top 20%	42.7	41.3	40.9	41.6	44.3
Top 5%	17.3	15.9	15.6	15.3	17.4

SOURCE: *Statistical Abstract of the United States,* various issues.

and fell 12 percent for the bottom decile between 1979 and 1987.[2] And because tax rates for the rich fell while noncash benefits given to the poor (welfare, food stamps, and so on) were reduced, the after-tax gap between the rich and the poor grew even wider. Another study found that the after-tax income of the bottom decile fell 10.5 percent between 1977 and 1988 while the after-tax income of the top decile rose 24.4 percent.[3]

. . . .

The Lorenz Curve

Income distribution can be shown with the **Lorenz curve,** a graphical tool invented by a German statistician in the nineteenth century. As shown in Figure 20.1, the vertical axis of a Lorenz curve diagram shows cumulative family income. It is plotted in percentages, so its range is from 0 to 100 percent. The horizontal axis plots the cumulative percentage of families ranked by income, so it too has a range from 0 to 100 percent. The straight 45° line is the Lorenz curve of perfect income equality. For example, point *a* indicates that the poorest 20 percent of families earn 20 percent of the income, point *b* indicates that the poorest 60 percent of families earn 60 percent of the income, and so on. The curved line is the approximate Lorenz curve for the

Lorenz curve Curve used to show income distribution.

[2]Paul Krugman, *The Age of Diminished Expectations* (Cambridge, Mass.: MIT Press, 1990), p. 20.
[3]Kevin Phillips (interview), "Is the GOP's Capitalist Heyday About to End?" *Challenge* (September/October 1990): 25.

. . . . . **FIGURE 20.1 THE LORENZ CURVE**

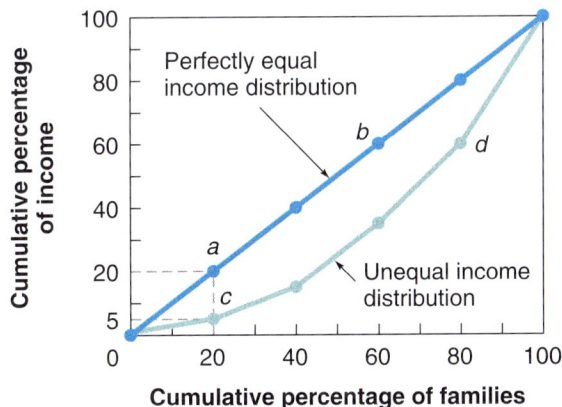

The Lorenz curve is used to give a graphical picture of income distribution. The straight 45° line is a plot of perfectly equal income distribution. Notice that at point *a*, 20 percent of the income is earned by 20 percent of the families; likewise, at point *b*, 60 percent of the income is earned by 60 percent of the families. The curved line is a plot of the 1990 data from Table 20.1. Point *c* indicates that the poorest 20 percent of the families earned (approximately) 5 percent of income, and point *d* shows that the four poorest quintiles (80 percent of families) earned about 55 percent of all income.

data in the 1990 column of Table 20.1. For example, point *c* shows that in 1990, the poorest quintile of the population earned (approximately) 5 percent of total income. The fact that this line lies to the right of the perfect income equality Lorenz curve indicates that income is distributed unequally. A line farther to the right would mean that income distribution is less equal; a line closer to the 45° line would indicate more equal income distribution.[4]

Comparing Lorenz Curves. One way to examine income distribution over time or between countries is to plot different Lorenz curves. For example, the Lorenz curves for every year in Table 20.1 would virtually overlap—an indication that there has been little change in income distribution in the past 50 years. Plotting Lorenz curves for the United States and the countries of Western Europe would show that the French Lorenz curve lies slightly to the right of the U.S. Lorenz curve, while the Lorenz curves for all other countries are to the left of the United States. This indicates that of the countries in Western Europe, only France has a less equal income distribution than the United States.

Policy can affect income distribution and shift the Lorenz curve. For example, making the income tax system more progressive—taxing the rich more heavily than the poor—should shift the Lorenz curve to the left. Income subsidies for the poor should also shift the Lorenz curve to the left. The policy initiatives of the 1960s—the War on Poverty, the Great Society, and other programs—seem to have had little appreciable effect on income distribution. One reason for this lack of apparent change is that many of these programs provided noncash benefits to the poor—food stamps, medical care, housing subsidies, and the like—which are not reflected in a plot of *income* distribution. We will have more to say about these programs shortly. Figure 20.2 illustrates how tax policy can shift the Lorenz curve.

Poverty

No matter how you look at it, there is a great deal of poverty in the United States—almost 37 million people in 1992. Furthermore, many of these people—almost 14 million—are children. Of particular concern in recent years is the dramatic rise in illegitimacy rates and the "children having children" phenomenon. Between 1970 and 1988, the birthrate for unmarried teenage girls between ages 15 and 19 rose from 22.4 per 1,000 girls to 36.8 per 1,000; the birthrate for unmarried 18 and 19 year olds reached 57.4 per 1,000 in 1989.[5] The rise in illegitimacy is especially distressing because evidence shows that states with higher teen birthrates have higher unemployment rates, higher divorce rates, lower rates of school completion—and higher

[4]A numerical measure of inequality is the *Gini coefficient*. It is calculated as the ratio of the area between the Lorenz curve and the 45° line divided by the area under the 45° line. A Gini coefficient of zero indicates perfect income equality; a coefficient of one indicates perfect income inequality—one family has all the money!

[5]Data are from the National Center for Health Statistics and were reported in Shirley L. Zimmerman, "Family Trends: What Implications for Family Policy?" *Family Relations* (October 1992). Reprinted in Susan F. Feiner, *Race and Gender in the American Economy* (Englewood Cliffs, N.J.: Prentice-Hall, 1994), pp. 39–53.

···· **FIGURE 20.2** DIFFERENT LORENZ CURVES

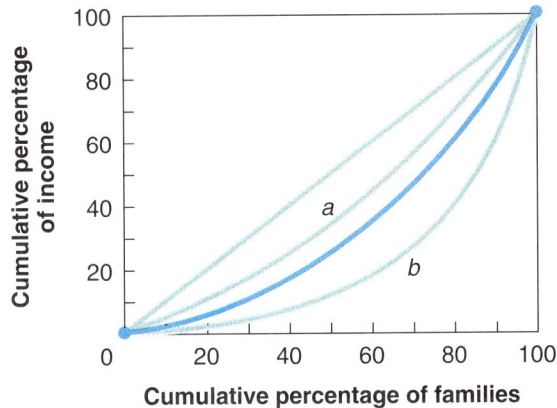

The location of the Lorenz curve depends on income distribution, and as policy affects income distribution, the Lorenz curve will shift. Suppose that the initial Lorenz curve is the dark line and that progressive taxes and antipoverty programs make income distribution more equal. This would shift the Lorenz curve to the left toward *a*. Regressive taxes and less equitable income distribution would shift the Lorenz curve to the right toward *b*. U.S. income distribution has become slightly less equal since World War II, so the Lorenz curve has shifted toward the right.

overall poverty rates.[6] What can or should be done about poverty is one of the most difficult issues of our times.

Economists identify two kinds of poverty, **absolute poverty** and **relative poverty.** People are said to be in absolute poverty if they do not have the basic essentials—food, shelter, medical attention—to sustain good health. Official poverty levels—$13,924 for a nonfarm family of four and $6,932 for a single individual in 1991—are based on the concept of absolute poverty.[7] People in relative poverty may have enough food and clothing to sustain their health, but are poor relative to other people in society. Relative poverty is often defined as a percentage of median income.[8] For example, relative poverty might be defined as having less than 40 percent of median income. Median income for a family of four in 1991 was $40,995, so a family with an income of less than $16,398 would be considered to be in "relative poverty" by this criterion. It may be possible to abolish all absolute poverty, but relative poverty will always be with us.

Several demographic groups are more likely to live in poverty:[9]

Absolute poverty A person in absolute poverty cannot afford the basic necessities of life.

Relative poverty A person in relative poverty is poor compared to other people, but does not necessarily lack basic necessities.

[6]Zimmerman (1992): 47.

[7]Data in this paragraph are all from the *Statistical Abstract of the United States,* 1993.

[8]We defined median income in Chapter 5. Median family income is the income such that half of all families make more than the median and half make less than the median.

[9]Data for this section come from Chapter 6, "Poverty: High Rates of Poverty Unresponsive to Economic Expansion," of Mishel and Bernstein (1993); U.S. Department of Commerce, *Statistical Abstract of the United States,* 1992, Section 14; and Chapter 6, "Poverty: Falling Wages, Torn Safety Net," of Lawrence Mishel and David M. Frankel, *The State of Working America, 1991–1992* (Armonk, N.Y.: M. E. Sharpe, 1992).

- In 1991, 14.2 percent of the population was officially living in poverty. Blacks are three times as likely to live in poverty as whites (32.7 percent versus 11.3 percent), but more whites live in poverty than blacks (22.3 million versus 9.8 million in 1990) because whites outnumber blacks in the general population.
- Women are only slightly more likely to live in poverty than men (14.4 percent versus 11.2 percent in 1988), but female-headed households are nearly five times more likely to be in poverty than male-headed households (32.4 percent versus 7.8 percent in 1990) because female-headed households typically have only one earner.
- Children are more likely to live in poverty than the elderly (21.8 percent versus 12.1 percent in 1990). Additionally, poverty among the elderly has been declining in the past 20 years while child poverty has been increasing.
- Most people in poverty do work: almost 60 percent held full- or part-time jobs in 1990; barely a quarter of poor persons over age 15 are employable but do not work.
- Poverty exists in both urban and rural settings; about half of all people in poverty live outside one of the 100 largest cities in the country. It also varies significantly across states. Mississippi had the highest poverty rate in 1990 (25.7 percent); Connecticut had the lowest poverty rate (6.0 percent).
- Poverty rates are higher in the United States than in most other industrialized countries. International comparisons are notoriously difficult, but the average national poverty rate in six Western European countries in the mid-1980s was 5.7 percent; it was 13.3 percent in the United States. The difference is even wider for child poverty: 6.4 percent in Western Europe versus 17.1 percent in the United States.[10]

Taken at face value, these data are distressing, but two qualifications improve the situation somewhat. First, these numbers provide only a *static* glimpse of the poverty story in recent years; the *dynamic* circumstances can be quite different. Consider a prospective medical doctor. When Andi and Brock finish their undergraduate degrees, they marry, and Brock agrees to work full-time while Andi attends medical school. For several years, they are tied to a geographical location where Brock can find only a low-paying job. Their income—under $10,000 per year—is barely enough to make ends meet. When Andi finishes medical school, she accepts a job with a starting salary of $120,000. She and Brock are clearly no longer even close to poverty.

The point is that both income distribution and poverty should be thought of as dynamic concepts. For many, poverty is a relatively short-term situation, but some people do seem to get stuck in poverty; about one-quarter of the people who receive welfare stay on it for 10 or more years. Perhaps the biggest problem of long-term poverty involves children who grow up in poverty. If the children's parents are not highly educated, there is less chance that they will offer positive enforcement with schoolwork; and if the parents are unemployed, it may be difficult for kids to learn good work habits. The data are depressing: of the people age 18 to 23 in the bottom fifth of basic skills distribution, 46 percent come from poor households, 53 percent

---

[10]Calculated from data in Table 9.9 of Mishel and Frankel (1992).

are welfare dependent, and 37 percent have been arrested.[11] The link between parental poverty and children's poverty has been called the *vicious circle of poverty*.

A second qualification to the data relates to the measurement of income. Many people living in poverty qualify for various kinds of transfer payments, both cash and *in-kind*. In-kind transfers consist of noncash assistance—food stamps, rent subsidies, Medicare, Medicaid, and so on. When this kind of assistance is included, the number of people in poverty falls. For example, the percentage of people below the poverty line in 1990 falls from 13.5 percent to 11.8 percent when noncash assistance is included.

FACTORS THAT AFFECT INCOME DISTRIBUTION

Even with the two qualifications we just mentioned, few could argue that poverty is not an issue of concern in the United States. But before we can do anything about poverty, we need to know why it exists. Unfortunately, there is no simple answer. The best we can offer is a series of partial explanations. One factor that obviously influences income distribution is ability. If you happen to have been born with a beautiful soprano singing voice, the Metropolitan Opera may have a job for you, and a pretty well-paying job at that. If your voice sounds more like a moose in rut, don't bother to audition at the Met. Clearly, differences in ability—physical as well as mental—can have a bearing on lifetime earnings. Economists recognize that ability is not the only thing that affects income distribution, however. In fact, it may not even be the main factor.

Worker Productivity

In Chapters 15–17 we showed that wages reflect marginal productivity—a suggestion that people who are more productive will be paid higher wages than people who are less productive. Still, we need to remember that there are numerous qualifications to **marginal productivity theory.** In particular, if monopoly power exists, wages deviate from marginal product. This can help workers when the monopoly power is on the workers' side—union power—or help management when there is little competition for sales or workers.

What determines worker productivity? Again there are several factors, but one of the most important is the level of **human capital.** Human capital consists of the education, training, and experience that increase worker productivity and add to future income. People who live in poverty typically have considerably less human capital than other people. The question then becomes why some people have more human capital than others. Educational opportunity is only part of the answer; just as significant is a home environment conducive to learning. It should come as no surprise that the parents of many college students are college graduates. Nor should it be surprising that in 1991, twice as high a percentage of whites as African Americans had completed four years of college (22.2 versus 11.5 percent). White/black high

Marginal productivity theory Theory of factor pricing and income distribution based on the premise that factors are paid in accordance with their contribution to output.

Human capital An individual's total knowledge, skills, and education. People with more human capital generally command higher wages.

[11]Data are from 1979–1985 and come from results of the Armed Forces Qualification test. Isabel V. Sawhill, "What about America's Underclass?" *Challenge* (May/June 1988): 27–36.

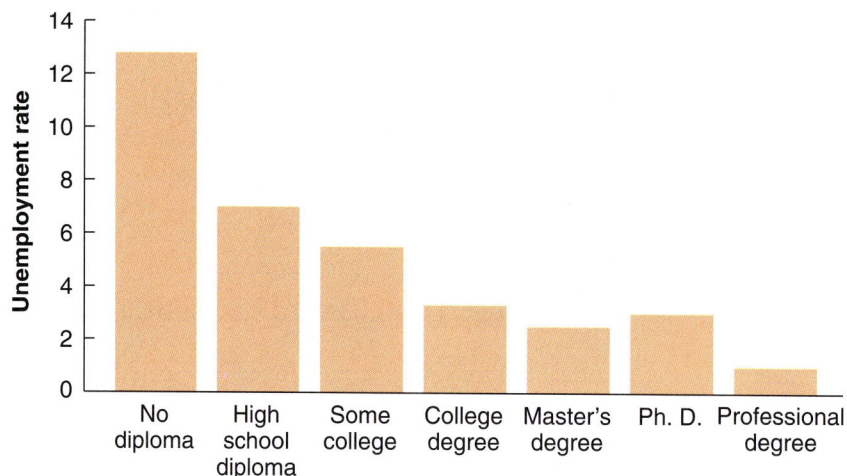

> ·····FIGURE 20.3 EDUCATION AND UNEMPLOYMENT
>
> People with less education have a greater chance of being unemployed than people with more education, and because employment is the main source of income for most people, education is closely linked to income distribution.

SOURCE: Data are for March 1993 and are from the 1994 *Economic Report of the President,* p. 108.

school graduation rates are quite close (39.1 versus 37.7 percent), but in a world requiring more and more education all the time, this figure offers little solace. There is evidence too that schools located in predominantly African-American neighborhoods may be inferior to schools located in predominantly white neighborhoods.[12] Education is not the only source of human capital, but as Figure 20.3 shows, people with more education are less likely to be unemployed than people with less education, so the connection between education and income is quite significant.

It is important to note that not all human capital is equally valuable and that the value of human capital changes and evolves over time. A person who is highly trained and experienced in a field for which there is little social need may earn less than a person who has less human capital but is in a field that is in high demand. For example, in the 1960s as the baby boom generation went off to college, the demand for college sociology teachers was high, and most sociologists with Ph.D.'s easily found college teaching jobs. Today college enrollments are declining and sociology courses are less popular. As a result, many sociology Ph.D.'s earn less than dental hygienists or temporary workers who have word processing and spreadsheet skills.

---

[12]In fact, it may not matter whether schools located in African-American neighborhoods are actually inferior; the issue may be only that these schools are *considered* inferior by prospective employers. This point is made by George Akerlof in his classic article, "The Market for Lemons: Quality Uncertainty and the Market Mechanism," *Quarterly Journal of Economics* 84 (August 1970): 488–500. Reprinted in George A. Akerlof, *An Economic Theorist's Book of Tales* (New York: Cambridge University Press, 1984). An Our Economic Heritage biography of George Akerlof appears in Chapter 32.

....

International Competition

In recent years, the foreign trade sector of the United States and most other countries in the world has expanded significantly. As a result, U.S. consumers have a wider selection of goods from which to choose, but U.S. workers must now face more serious competition from foreign workers. Over the past 20 years, rising international competition has affected different sectors of the economy in different ways and has had an impact on income distribution. Many economists believe that low-wage, low-skill workers have been hurt by international competition while high-skill, high-wage workers have benefited. For example, high school dropouts saw their real wages fall 20 percent between 1979 and 1992 while professional workers experienced a modest rise of 9 percent between 1972 and 1985.[13]

What has caused these trends? The issue is complex—and still unsettled—but early explanations are based largely on marginal productivity theory. Many workers in the United States produce the same products that low-paid workers produce abroad. For example, manufacturing workers in Mexico have productivity rates that approach 80 percent of the U.S. level, but earn wages only a sixth as high as U.S. workers.[14] Free trade means that these U.S. workers must compete directly with foreign workers who are nearly as productive but work for lower wages. The result is lower wages or unemployment for U.S. workers. High-wage, high-skill workers in the United States face less competition from abroad for a couple of reasons. First, many high-skill workers are in service industries that face little international competition. (How often do you use imported legal services or hire a CPA from Japan?) Second, many high-skill workers in the United States do not face direct competition from abroad because they possess skills that foreign workers simply do not have. As a result, high-skill U.S. workers benefit from increasing demand and receive higher wages, while low-skill U.S. workers experience decreasing demand and lower wages.[15]

What can be done about adverse income distribution consequences of free trade? In the absence of additional restraints on trade—an issue we will examine in some detail in Part VII—training, education, and apprenticeship programs for low-skilled workers seem to be the only solutions. The only catch is that training and education are expensive and take time.

....

Inheritances and Marriage

Inheritances or bequests as well as marriage can also have a significant impact on income distribution. Bequests are gifts from one generation to another. When your grandfather dies, you may inherit his pocket watch or maybe his stock portfolio, but you cannot be held legally responsible for any debts he may have owed when he

---

[13]Data are from "The Global Economy: Who Gets Hurt?" August 10, 1992, *Business Week,* pp. 48–53.

[14]These data are from Stephen Baker, Geri Smith, and Elizabeth Weiner, "The Mexican Worker," *Business Week,* April 19, 1993, pp. 84–92. For more details on Mexican autoworkers vis-à-vis U.S. autoworkers, see Stephen Baker, David Woodruff, and Elizabeth Weiner, "Detroit South," *Business Week*, March 16, 1992, pp. 98–103.

[15]An alternative explanation for the decline of low-skill wages relative to high-skill wages was offered in the Focus box on changing wage differentials in Chapter 16.

died.[16] Rich people have more wealth to bequeath than do poor people, so inheritances tend to preserve wealth and income distribution patterns. The fact that debts cannot be bequeathed amplifies the income distribution effects of inheritances.

Marriage also affects income distribution. If you are lucky enough to marry a movie star, you can rise from your humble background. But odds are that you will marry someone from the same socioeconomic background. Poor people usually marry poor people and rich people usually marry rich people, a phenomenon known to sociologists as *assortative mating*. Assortative mating tends to perpetuate the prevailing income distribution and amplify the income distribution effects of bequests. When two rich people marry, they stand to inherit the fortunes of two sets of parents; when two poor people marry, their chances of inheriting wealth are quite slim.

· · · · · · · ·

Luck and Discrimination

Finally, luck and discrimination can have a lot to do with your chances of falling into poverty. If you are unlucky enough to move to town just before the largest employer goes bankrupt, you may find yourself unemployed for no reason of your own. If you are an African-American college graduate, you can expect to earn 15.5 percent less than a white college graduate.[17] It must be recognized, however, that this is an aggregate figure that includes the graduates from all colleges—an African-American business graduate from State U. and a white business graduate from State U. will earn comparable salaries. Luck and discrimination obviously affect income distribution and the incidence of poverty; the important question is how *much* they matter. If your lot in life is determined mainly by luck, why put out any effort? Why not just play the lottery? If people believe that income distribution depends on luck and/or discrimination more than effort, the incentive to work is diminished considerably. This may explain why so many people living in poverty seem to have given up hope. If the incentive to work depends on the expectation of reward, then it is important that people not think that income distribution is largely determined by luck or discrimination.

RECAP   Basic Facts on Income Distribution

1. Income distribution has been roughly constant since World War II, although a slight shift toward upper incomes appears to have occurred in the past decade. The poorest quintile of the population earns under 5 percent of total income; the richest quintile earns about 40 percent of all income.
2. The Lorenz curve plots cumulative families and cumulative family income to present a graphical depiction of income distribution. A straight 45° Lorenz curve indicates perfectly equal income distribution; the farther the Lorenz curve is to the right, the less equal the income distribution is.
3. People are in absolute poverty if they lack the basic essentials for good health; relative poverty is calculated as a fraction of median income. In 1991, 14.2

[16]Actually, the estate may have to pay off existing debts before you can inherit that pocket watch, but you are not legally responsible for paying those debts out of your own money.
[17]This figure is for 1989 and comes from Mishel and Bernstein (1993), p. 206.

percent of the population was officially classified as being in poverty. Female-headed households, ethnic minorities, and children have the highest probability of being in poverty.

4. Ability and work effort are not the only factors affecting income. Other factors include human capital, exposure to international competition, inheritances, luck, and discrimination.

PHILOSOPHIES OF INCOME DISTRIBUTION

Economists and social philosophers have long debated the correct distribution of income. Some have argued for an equal distribution of income. Others advocate a more needs-based distribution—something along the lines of the Marxist maxim "from each according to his ability, to each according to his needs." Both of these arguments are directed at the needs side of income distribution. Needs are important, but just as important is effort: if people do not work, no one's needs will be met. The relationship between needs and effort is captured in a key tradeoff in economic analysis: the tradeoff between efficiency and equity.

Efficiency and Equity

Economists and social philosophers of the nineteenth century believed that money exhibited diminishing marginal utility. In other words, the last dollar earned by a millionaire provides less utility than the last dollar earned by a poor person. Now think for a minute: if the government takes one dollar away from the millionaire and gives it to the person in poverty, society will be better off; the millionaire will hardly notice the loss, while the poor person might be able to buy lunch. Take another dollar away from the millionaire, and society is even better off. Extending this logic forces the conclusion that social utility is maximized with a perfectly equal distribution of income. The only problem is that there would be little to divide equally because people would have little incentive to work.

The idea of income equality was rejected by J. B. Clark and his theory of marginal productivity. Clark inserted morality into his analysis when he said that if people were paid their marginal product, they were earning what they "deserved." Many economists have questioned the moral overtones in Clark's analysis, but the idea that wages correspond to the worker's contribution to society is a key component of marginal productivity theory: people earning high wages are contributing more to society than people earning low wages, assuming, of course, that the assumptions underlying marginal productivity theory hold. Further, marginal productivity theorists contend that wages act as an incentive to work—that is, to contribute to society.

These theorists suggest that attempts to equalize income distribution will reduce production because people will have little incentive to work; everyone may be getting a "fair" share, but no one gets very much. Wouldn't it be better to maintain some income inequality if that would lead to a great deal more output to share? This is the tradeoff that must be kept in mind when analyzing income distribution and poverty. Too much equity will cause inefficiency in the sense that the economy will be producing at less than potential. But too little equity—if the poor are genuinely miserable—will also result in inefficiency in the sense that more police, courts, and prisons will be necessary to suppress social discontent, not to mention the potential waste of human resources.

We are a long way from reaching a consensus on what is meant by a just distribution of income, but two popular views have formed the basis for much recent discussion. The work of Harvard philosopher John Rawls has formed the basis for the new liberal perspective; the work of another Harvard philosopher, Robert Nozick, is more popular among conservatives.

Rawlsian Justice

John Rawls first offered his ideas on justice in his classic *A Theory of Justice* published in 1971.[18] The Rawlsian theory of justice begins with a thought experiment: suppose you were born into the world behind a **veil of ignorance;** that is, suppose that you did not know your parents' income or occupations, your opportunities for education, and other information that might indicate where your family is in the income distribution. How would you want income to be distributed in this world? Would you prefer a world where income is distributed as in Table 20.1? Would you prefer a world where rich kids have better life chances—opportunities for education, for example—than poor kids? Or would you prefer a world where everyone has an equal opportunity for success in life? Rawls believes that most people would opt for equal opportunity. Being born with privilege is great—but only if you are lucky in the parent selection raffle. Rawls believes that most people prefer not to take risks and would choose to be born into a world of equal opportunity. Equal opportunity makes it possible for each of us to rise to upper-income brackets, as long as we are willing to put in the effort.

Rawls's veil of ignorance is only a thought experiment; it obviously cannot be implemented in the real world. Some people will always start out with advantages over other people. Still, the idea that equal opportunity is "just" is the basis for many social policies. It must be emphasized, however, that equal opportunity does *not* imply equal incomes. Rawls believes that the "just" distribution of income is the one that maximizes the income of the least advantaged. Rawls is in favor of taxing the rich to give to the poor, but he is aware that when tax rates get so high that they reduce the incentive to work, total income will fall, and both the rich and the poor will be worse off. Therefore, any income redistribution plan must preserve work incentives.

A simple example can illustrate the criterion for a Rawlsian income redistribution plan. Suppose that there are two people in society and that the initial income distribution is Person 1 = $100 and Person 2 = $500. Now consider two plans, Plan A and Plan B. Under Plan A, Person 2 is taxed to subsidize Person 1, and the resulting incomes are Person 1 = $200, Person 2 = $250. Notice that some of the income is lost in the redistribution process—Person 1 loses $250 but Person 2 gains only $100—because of the work disincentives of the income tax. Under Plan B, taxes and subsidies are higher, and the resulting incomes are Person 1 = $150 and Person 2 =

John Rawls Harvard philosopher best known for his theory of justice. Popular among liberals.

Veil of ignorance Thought construct of Rawls's theory of justice. If people were put behind a "veil of ignorance," they would choose to have equal opportunity.

[18]John Rawls, *A Theory of Justice* (Cambridge, Mass.: Harvard University Press, 1971).

$150. Plan B could be considered "fair" in the sense that it has equal incomes, but the least advantaged person is not as well off as under Plan A. Plan A fits Rawls's criterion because it maximizes the income of the least advantaged person; Plan B does not.

• • • • • • • •

Robert Nozick: Justice as Process

Conservatives find more comfort in the process theory of justice of **Robert Nozick.**[19] Nozick's process theory stresses the importance of the mechanism that distributes income and brings about justice. In contrast, Rawls's theory of justice is a "results" theory because it focuses on the end state. Nozick believes that justice should be based on a system of property rights and that property should be transferred only through voluntary exchange. Voluntary exchange does not include government appropriation of earned income.

Robert Nozick Harvard philosopher known for his process theory of justice. Popular among conservatives.

To understand Nozick's theory of justice, start by assuming that the existing distribution of income is just, and then consider the following scenario. Suppose that a particular economics professor writes an excellent introductory text, which sells 50,000 copies the first year it is in print. Our unnamed professor earns about $6 per copy, and you, the student, willingly buy the book. No one coerced you to buy the book—you could have taken a different course or opted against college—so you must think that the book is worth the money you paid for it. And the author *certainly* believes that he is entitled to the $300,000 in royalties that he earns. But these transactions have changed the distribution of income: the author is markedly better off, thank you. Can anyone argue that this distribution of income is not fair? No, says Nozick, because all of the transactions were voluntary. If the original distribution of income was fair, so is the new distribution of income.

Therein lies the rub. Nozick's process theory of distribution requires that the initial distribution of income be fair—and that subsequent changes in the distribution of income be brought about by voluntary processes. If the original distribution of income was not fair, the subsequent distributions may not be fair even if all transactions were voluntary. Like Rawls's theory, Nozick's theory cannot be applied directly to the real world, but does provide a philosophical underpinning: voluntary transactions and private property are "fair"; appropriation of private property and involuntary transactions are "unfair."

It is impossible to prove whether Nozick's definition of fairness is better or worse than Rawls's definition. The debate over what is a truly just distribution of income will continue forever because it is a normative issue.

> **RECAP**   Philosophies of Income Distribution
>
> 1. The key issue that must be addressed in all discussions of income distribution is the tradeoff between efficiency and equity. An equal distribution of income may seem "fair," but it may be inefficient because people will have little incentive to work.

[19]Robert Nozick, *Anarchy, State, and Utopia* (New York: Basic Books, 1974).

2. Rawlsian justice contends that people should have equal opportunity. Income should be redistributed to the poor, but only as long as redistribution makes the poor better off.

3. Robert Nozick believes that justice is a process and that only voluntary transactions and private property are "fair." Government plans to redistribute income are unfair because they involve involuntary transactions.

PROGRAMS TO FIGHT POVERTY

The government has had a variety of antipoverty programs in place for many years. The government helps low-income people with two main kinds of programs: progressive income taxes and various kinds of welfare programs. This section will examine some of those programs and look at alternative plans that economists have recommended.

Taxes and Income Distribution

Federal income taxes are progressive because upper-income taxpayers pay a higher proportion of their income in taxes than do lower-income taxpayers.[20] Progressive taxation shifts income from the rich to the poor and thus makes income distribution more equal. However, income distribution is affected by all taxes, not just the federal income tax. In addition to federal income taxes, most people pay state and local sales taxes, property taxes, state income taxes, and Social Security taxes. The combined effect of all taxes is to make the tax system only slightly progressive because most state and local taxes as well as Social Security taxes are proportional or regressive. Policy changes can and do affect the progressivity of the tax system. For example, in the 1980s, the Reagan administration reduced the number of income tax brackets from 14 to 3—and made the federal tax system significantly less progressive in the process. The Clinton administration reversed this trend by adding two additional tax brackets and increasing tax rates on upper-income individuals.

Progressive income taxes may seem like a relatively painless way to change the distribution of income and help those in need. However, many economists are concerned that progressive income taxes can result in a **disincentive to work.** Why? Suppose that your weekly paycheck is $500 and that your tax rate is 20 percent, so you take home $400. You are considering working next weekend to earn a little extra money. If you do, you will earn $200 but will take home only $120 because that extra income will be taxed at a 40 percent rate. Is $120 enough to give up a weekend at the beach? Perhaps not. The point is that progressive income taxes reduce take-home pay and thus reduce the incentive to work. Statistical studies indicate that work disincentives are strongest for families with two earners and for people who are considering overtime work.

Disincentive to work High marginal income tax rates reduce take-home pay and may thus reduce work effort.

[20]We defined progressive taxes in Chapter 6. If you are unsure about the difference between progressive, proportional, and regressive taxes, now might be a good time to look back at that chapter.

Traditional Welfare Programs

Social welfare spending by federal, state, and local governments has grown substantially in the past 30 years. Not only does government devote a higher fraction of its budget to social programs than ever before, but the budget itself is significantly larger than it was in the 1960s. Not everyone agrees that this money is well spent, but most would agree that past programs have changed the incidence of poverty. In particular, the incidence of poverty among the aged was twice as high as among the nonaged in the 1960s; today, the elderly have a much lower chance of being in poverty than the young. This is due in part to substantial increases in Social Security benefits. Another change is the narrowing black/white income gap. Educational subsidies and affirmative action programs are at least partially responsible for this shift. Unfortunately, these successes are countered with failures: poverty rates among youths (especially minority youths), people in single-parent families, and single, elderly people have increased substantially in recent years.[21] The success or failure of our current welfare system will depend on how well it can deal with the changing face of poverty.

People with limited incomes are aided by both cash and noncash benefits from all levels of government. In the United States, the four main federal welfare programs are Aid to Families with Dependent Children (AFDC), Supplementary Security Income (SSI), Medicaid, and the Food Stamp program:[22]

- AFDC is what most people mean when they talk about "welfare." Families with a single parent or two parents, one of whom is disabled, and no other sources of income qualify for AFDC payments.
- SSI assistance goes to blind and disabled individuals and to the elderly.
- Medicaid is medical care for people in the AFDC and SSI programs. In contrast, Medicare is subsidized medical care for the elderly.
- Almost 20 percent of the public qualified for food stamps in 1992. Administered by the Agriculture Department, the aim of the Food Stamp program is to assure that every American has an adequate diet.

Table 20.2 presents recent data on government programs and expenditure categories designed to aid people with limited incomes. A glance at the data reveals several important facts:

- Contrary to popular belief, AFDC benefits are actually quite small, only about 10 percent of total aid to low-income people.

---

[21]For more details on this new poverty, see Robert H. Haveman, "New Policy for the New Poverty," *Challenge* (September/October 1988): 27–36.

[22]The Social Security system is not included here because it does not involve a means test, so, strictly speaking, it is not a welfare program. As we discuss later, a means test is used to determine whether recipients qualify for a particular program. Clearly, generous Social Security benefits have helped many retired people rise out of poverty; this may have been a major reason for the decline in poverty among the elderly since the mid-1960s. Since 1985, retirees who have other sources of income are required to pay taxes on a portion of their Social Security benefits.

• • • • **TABLE 20.2 CASH AND NONCASH BENEFITS FOR PEOPLE WITH LIMITED INCOME**

	Total: Federal, State, Local			Federal Only	
Program:	1985	1988	1990	1985	1990
AFDC	$ 16,736	$ 19,019	$ 21,196	$ 8,909	$ 11,505
SSI	11,857	14,684	17,232	9,603	13,606
Food Stamps	13,470	14,369	17,702	12,599	16,517
Medicaid	41,258	54,304	72,228	22,844	41,195
Expenditure Category:					
Medical	$ 49,752	$ 66,644	$ 86,197	$ 27,880	$ 50,211
Cash	37,636	45,707	55,136	24,486	37,044
Food	20,391	21,355	25,257	19,362	24,011
Housing	14,113	14,701	17,544	14,113	17,544
Education	9,970	11,691	14,375	9,516	13,746
Services	5,476	5,659	5,801	3,551	3,661
Jobs and training	3,976	3,820	4,215	3,895	3,966
Energy assistance	2,292	2,001	1,802	2,261	1,680
Other	NA	930	303	NA	303
Total	$143,606	$172,508	$210,630	$105,064	$152,166

SOURCE: *Statistical Abstract of the United States,* 1993, Table No. 583. Data are in millions of current dollars.

- Medical expenditures are the largest single category of spending (about 41 percent) and the fastest growing (by almost 73 percent between 1980 and 1990).
- Finally, aid for low-income people, while significant, is only a relatively small fraction of government spending (approximately 12 percent of federal government spending and 11 percent of total government spending). This suggests, among other things, that the popular cry to "slash welfare" to eliminate the deficit is not feasible.

Problems with Existing Programs. Government spending to help low-income people may be less than you suspected, but it is still significant. Many of us would probably say that this is money well spent—*if* it reduces poverty and helps people become contributing members of society. Unfortunately, whether welfare programs work or not can be extremely difficult to determine. Several criticisms have been leveled at existing welfare programs.

By far the most often-heard criticism is that welfare programs create a disincentive to work. Put yourself in the position of an unmarried mother receiving AFDC: If you go out and get a job, odds are that the job will be low paying. Further, once you begin working, you will lose your AFDC benefits; you may also lose Medicaid and food stamps. You will also have to find a way to pay for day care. Would you work under those conditions? Another criticism of AFDC is that it breaks up the family structure because most two-adult families do not qualify for AFDC. Others believe that AFDC encourages illegitimate children because AFDC payments depend on the number of children in the household.[23]

Another problem with existing programs is that they are inefficient and cost too much. Under current programs, most recipients must pass a **means test**—a test to prove that they are truly needy. A rather elaborate bureaucratic structure is required to make certain that stated needs actually exist. Further, once people qualify for assistance, they are typically assigned a social worker who checks up on them. Together, the various social agencies in the United States employ more than 500,000 social workers, which means that a large fraction of the money spent on social programs goes to social workers, not welfare recipients.

Many economists believe that incentive effects make the cost of delivering welfare considerably higher than the published figures seem to imply. We already know that income taxes can adversely affect the incentive to work. Corporate taxes may reduce investment by lowering the after-tax rate of return. Further, some studies suggest that Social Security taxes may reduce savings: Why save for the future if you know you will get Social Security from the government? When Edgar Browning and William Johnson accounted for these and other inefficiencies, they concluded that the cost of delivering $100 in benefits to the poor could be as high as $350![24] It is easy to question the precision of this number, but the point is unassailable: the cost of delivering benefits to the poor is almost certainly greater than the benefits the poor receive. This is sometimes called the "administrative burden" of a social program.

Finally, specific criticisms have been levied at almost every program, even programs like Head Start that have been widely heralded as successful. Begun in the 1960s, Head Start is designed to help preschool kids from low-income families. It is now under fire because some studies have suggested that its benefits last only through about the third grade. Other investigators are concerned that Head Start may rob African-American children of their cultural heritage because class work is often designed and implemented by white teachers.

Means test An eligibility test. Some social programs are available only to people below a certain income; the income requirement is a means test.

. . . .

Alternative Poverty Programs

Economists come in several varieties—conservative, liberal, radical, and reactionary. Some want to increase spending to help the poor. Others believe that poverty programs reduce the incentive to work so much that they actually cause poverty. We cannot begin to settle disagreements this fundamental, but we can outline three reform programs that have received wide acclaim from economists of most persuasions. These programs are the negative income tax, the earned income tax credit, and workfare.

---

[23]Whether welfare creates an incentive for welfare mothers to have more children is hotly debated, but recent evidence seems to suggest that it does not. A study conducted by the Urban Institute in 1993 found that education, family, race, and income have a much greater effect on women's childbearing decisions than the size of the welfare check. For example, a monthly increase in welfare by $100— almost a 30 percent increase—would increase the probability of having additional children by only 0.1 percent. Further, single mothers on welfare are no more likely to have a second child before age 23 than are other young mothers. Gene Koretz, "Do Bigger Welfare Checks Mean More Kids? Not Really," *Business Week,* January 31, 1994, p. 22.

[24]Cited in Haveman (1988): 32.

Negative income tax (NIT) Social program designed to reduce work disincentives and bureaucratic costs of current poverty programs. People with incomes under a designated level would receive income subsidies.

Negative Income Tax. Different versions of the **negative income tax (NIT)** have been around since the early 1960s and are associated with people as diverse as Milton Friedman, Richard Nixon, and George McGovern. The main aims of an NIT program would be to reduce work disincentives and welfare bureaucracy while still providing for the basic needs of poor people. An NIT program would reduce welfare bureaucracy because it could be administered by an existing agency, the Internal Revenue Service, and it would reduce work disincentives because recipients would be able to take home most of their earned income without losing all of their negative income tax payments.

The best way to see how an NIT program would work is with two simple equations. The first equation is a linear NIT tax equation:[25]

$$T = -\$5,000 + 0.25Q \tag{1}$$

where T is total tax liability and Q is earned income. The second equation is the definition of disposable income (take-home pay):

$$Q_d = Q - T \tag{2}$$

Notice that if earned income is zero, the total tax liability is a negative $5,000; in other words, the tax "payer" would receive an income subsidy of $5,000:

$$T = -\$5,000 + 0.25(0) = -\$5,000$$

so disposable income is:

$$Q_d = 0 - (-\$5,000) = +5,000$$

Now look what happens if earned income is $4,000. Tax liability is:

$$T = -\$5,000 + 0.25(4,000) = -\$4,000$$

so disposable income is:

$$Q_d = \$4,000 - (-\$4,000) = \$8,000$$

In other words, working reduces the income subsidy by only a small amount. As a result, every additional dollar of income earned results in a higher after-tax income, so there is only a small work disincentive. Many economists believe this is the main advantage of the NIT. Figure 20.4 uses graphical analysis to illustrate the NIT.

An NIT program also has several other potential advantages. First, the bureaucratic costs would be reduced significantly because an NIT program could be administered by the Internal Revenue Service instead of the Health and Human Services Department. Second, an NIT program would preserve more self-respect and pride than conventional welfare programs because people would not be required to stand in line at the welfare office. Finally, some economists argue that reliance upon cash subsidies is preferable to in-kind transfers because individuals know best how to spend their money.

Though experimental NIT programs have met mixed success, economists generally favor the NIT as a replacement for the current welfare system. Public acceptance, on the other hand, has been lukewarm, at best. Many people think that an

[25]This very simple equation is used as an illustration only. A real NIT tax equation would be more complex to reflect progressivity, deductions, and other factors.

FIGURE 20.4 THE NEGATIVE INCOME TAX

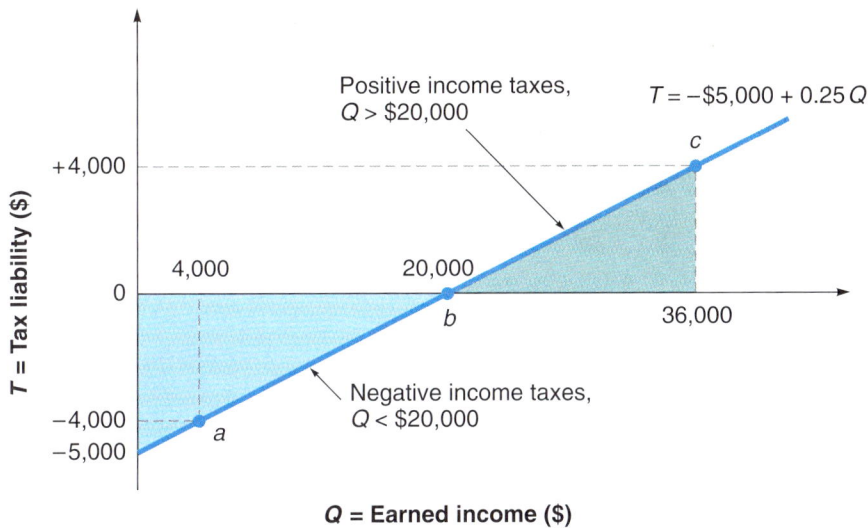

The negative income tax (NIT) provides an income subsidy at low incomes and an income tax at high incomes. In this example, the tax function is $T = -\$5,000 + 0.25Q$. If earned income is zero, the income subsidy is $5,000. If earned income is $4,000 (point a), the income tax is $-\$4,000$ so disposable income is $8,000. If earned income is $20,000 (point b), the tax liability is zero and disposable income is $20,000. Incomes above $20,000 result in positive income taxes. For example, if earned income is $36,000 (point c), the tax liability is $4,000 so disposable income is $32,000.

NIT just amounts to more "giveaways"; the fact that it reduces work disincentives is lost on many people. Further, many people believe that food stamps, housing subsidies, and other forms of in-kind welfare are preferable to cash assistance because they believe welfare recipients will spend their money on liquor and drugs instead of food and shelter. However, it is also true that food stamps are sold (illegally) for cash, which is then used to buy drugs, liquor, or whatever.

The Earned Income Tax Credit. A new program that is closely related to the negative income tax is the **earned income tax credit (EITC)**. The EITC provides a variable income subsidy to low-income workers and is designed to reduce work disincentives.

The current EITC has three stages: a "credit range" where it operates like a wage subsidy; a "plateau range" where it has no marginal effect; and a "phaseout range" where the credit is paid back as earnings rise. Here's how it will work in 1996 when it is fully implemented. As the earnings of a family with two or more children rise from $0 to $8,425 (in 1994 dollars), the family receives a 40 percent wage subsidy; families of other sizes get different subsidies. This means that if the family earns $6,000, it will take home $8,400 (= $6,000 × 1.4). The maximum wage subsidy is 40 percent of $8,425 or $3,370. As earned income rises from $8,425 to $11,000, the wage subsidy remains at $3,370; this is the plateau range. When income rises above

Earned Income Tax Credit Modern variant of NIT that provides variable income subsidy to low-income workers.

••••FIGURE 20.5 THE EARNED INCOME TAX CREDIT

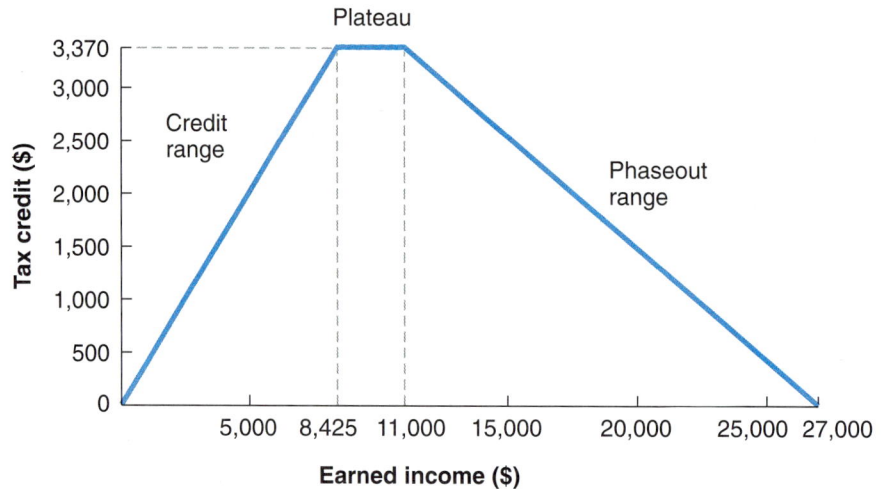

When the Earned Income Tax Credit is completely phased in in 1996, families with two children will receive a 40 percent wage subsidy on incomes from $0 to $8,425. The maximum subsidy, $3,370, will be received in the plateau range of incomes between $8,425 and $11,000. The EITC will be phased out on incomes over $11,000 at a rate of 21¢ per dollar earned. When earned income reaches $27,000, the family will earn no EITC payments.

$11,000 the family's tax credit is reduced 21¢ for each extra dollar earned. EITC benefits are exhausted when earned income reaches $27,000.

The advantage of the EITC rests in its effects on work incentives. It provides a strong work incentive in the credit range because people have to earn income to qualify for the wage subsidy. There is no incentive effect in the plateau range because wage subsidies are unaffected by income changes. It does generate a work disincentive in the phaseout range; this disincentive may be small, however, if the work decision is whether or not to work, rather than how many hours to work. Figure 20.5 illustrates the EITC for a family with two children in 1996.

Workfare. Many states have been experimenting with *work*fare as a substitute for *wel*fare. President Clinton has announced that **workfare** will be a key part of his program to eliminate "welfare as a way of life." Workfare is an attempt to do two things at once: reduce poverty and provide a means for self-support. Workfare recipients are required to work for their assistance checks. The advantage of workfare is that by requiring able-bodied welfare recipients to accept a job, any work disincentives are eliminated. It also has at least two disadvantages: First, the government could be forced to provide jobs for welfare recipients if none are available in the private sector. Second, some argue that requiring people to accept jobs they do not wish to take is akin to slavery—not a pleasant thought.

Workfare Alternative to welfare that attempts to reduce poverty and provide a means for self-support. Workfare recipients are required to work for their assistance checks.

There have been several workfare experiments in recent years.[26] For example, between 1975 and 1980, the National Supported Work Demonstration was tested in 15 sites around the United States. Under this program, welfare recipients were offered structured, paid work. The initial cost of the program was high, but within 19 to 27 months after enrollment, the income of program participants was nearly twice as high as that of a control group—a suggestion that voluntary employment strategies could be cost-effective as well as a means of reducing welfare dependency. In 1981, Congress created the Work Incentive (WIN) program and gave the states the option to use workfare as a component of their own welfare systems. By 1986, 37 states (including President Clinton's home state of Arkansas) had implemented some form of workfare. Unfortunately, state data are not consistent, so it is not clear what portion of the AFDC caseload is covered by workfare.

The results of these early experiments with workfare have been mixed. Most studies show that workfare has resulted in increases in employment and earnings of welfare recipients, and that these effects continued at least three years. Additionally, most workfare programs reduced welfare expenses. One of the unsuccessful workfare experiments was in West Virginia, where the program did not lead to increased earnings or employment. This failure was probably due to the fact that West Virginia is a largely rural state with exceptionaly high unemployment. Other studies have shown that workfare programs help some kinds of people more than others. In particular, first-time AFDC mothers stand to gain the most from workfare; long-time AFDC recipients and women with little or no past employment experience seem to gain very little.

· · · · · · · ·

The Need for a Broad-Based and Adaptable Program

Perhaps the most discouraging aspect of the poverty discussion is that the policies implemented in the 1960s appear to have changed the demographic composition of poverty. The demographic groups that were most likely to be poverty-stricken in the 1950s and 1960s—the elderly and ethnic minorities—have made remarkable progress. However, other groups—female-headed households and children—have replaced them on the welfare rolls. If we adopt a set of policies aimed at this "new" poverty, will other groups fall through the cracks? No one can say for sure, but there are some clues that might help us. One reason the elderly are better off today than in 1950 is the increasing expenditures on Social Security. Likewise, one reason why the black/white income differential has fallen is Affirmative Action. This evidence might tempt us to conclude that specific, targeted programs are more successful than general programs like AFDC. This may or may not be true, but even if it is, we need to recognize that society is changing rapidly. Targeting specific demographic groups may be efficient, but it may also leave out the next group ready to fall between the cracks. As the nature of poverty evolves, so must poverty policy. Over the long run, antipoverty policy must be broad enough to cover these people and must be adaptable to our ever changing society. A program that does this and also provides equal opportunity work incentives stands a chance of being successful—a chance.

---

[26]These results are summarized in Judith M. Gueron, "Work and Welfare: Lessons on Employment Programs," *Journal of Economic Perspectives* 4 (Winter 1990): 79–98.

WELFARE AS INVESTMENT SPENDING: THE COST OF HUNGRY CHILDREN

The main reason some economists favor workfare is the hope that it will reduce people's dependence on welfare and, in so doing, reduce the need for welfare spending in the future. As we have just discovered, workfare shows promise, but establishing a workfare program for children is obviously impractical. The aim of child welfare programs is to provide the essentials for a productive adult life. This means satisfying physical needs for food and medical care as well as education. Unfortunately, the United States has not been doing very well in this regard. According to a 1989 study by the Community Childhood Hunger Identification Project, one out of eight children in the United States suffers from malnutrition, and nearly one in four has experienced hunger over the past year. In some states—Alabama and Arkansas—nearly 40 percent of all children are hungry. This is distressing because by most accounts, child hunger appeared to have been virtually abolished by the 1970s. And hunger is not the only problem facing our children: the United States ranks nineteenth in both infant mortality and the number of teachers per 100 school-age children. We trail even such countries as Libya and Malta.

How did things get so bad in the richest country in the world? There are three reasons according to Larry Brown, director of the Center for Hunger, Poverty, and Nutritional Policy at Tufts University. First, eligibility requirements for school breakfast and lunch programs were stiffened significantly in the early 1980s. As a result, more than a million children were dropped from these programs. The recessions of the early 1980s and 1990s were the second cause. When unemployment soars, children are hit at least as hard as their parents. Finally, inflation has eroded the real value of welfare benefits. For example, in 1970, monthly AFDC benefits for a family of three in New York State were $279; in 1989, a family of three received $539, which was $325 less than what would have been necessary to cover inflation over the 1970–1989 period.

In recognition of these problems, the chief executive officers (CEOs) of five major corporations testified before the House Budget Committee in March 1991 and urged an expansion of the Women, Infants, and Children (WIC) program, which feeds 4.5 million people annually. These CEOs argued that the long-run competitiveness of the United States is linked to issues related to child care, cognition, and health. Said James Reiner, CEO of Honeywell, Inc.: "Unless children are given improved chances to develop adequately, the U.S. will face a serious shortage of responsible, employable adults."

SOURCE: The material for this box comes from Shlomo Maital and Kim I. Morgan, "Hungry Children Are Bad Business," *Challenge* (July/August 1992): 54–59.

> **RECAP**   **Programs to Combat Poverty**
>
> 1. Progressive income taxes tend to make income distribution more equal; however, only the federal income tax is significantly progressive. Most state and local taxes as well as the Social Security tax are proportional or regressive.
> 2. The main contemporary antipoverty programs include AFDC, SSI, Medicaid, and food stamps. About 12 percent of the total federal budget is spent on these and related antipoverty programs. The main criticisms of these programs are that they are inefficient and that they generate work disincentives.
> 3. Many economists advocate a negative income tax as a replacement for or a supplement to existing antipoverty programs. The NIT would be more efficient and generate fewer work disincentives. The earned income tax credit is a contemporary variation of the NIT.
> 4. Workfare would require able-bodied welfare recipients to accept jobs. Experiments with workfare have met mixed results, but the Clinton administration has advocated workfare as part of its poverty program overhaul.

·······SUMMARY

Poverty is not easy to think about. Most of us are disturbed by the thought of homelessness and hungry children. But poverty exists, and as social scientists, the only way we can hope to do anything about it is by first trying to understand the problem. That is easier said than done, but there are a number of key ideas that will help us put our thoughts in order:

1. Income distribution has been roughly constant over the past 50 years. The bottom quintile makes just under 5 percent of all income; the top quintile makes a little over 40 percent of all income. Income appears to have shifted slightly from the poor to the rich in the past 15 years.
2. About a seventh of the American public lives in poverty. Female-headed households, children, and ethnic minorities have the highest chance of living in poverty.
3. Several factors affect income distribution. Income is *not* dependent solely on abilities. Work effort, inheritance, luck, and discrimination all matter. It appears that increasing international competition is hurting low-skill, low-wage workers but helping high-skill, high-income workers.
4. Philosophers disagree on the ideal distribution of income. Perfectly equal income distribution will reduce work incentives and production. Rawls believes that the ideal income distribution should maximize the income of the poorest person and provide equal opportunity for all. Nozick believes that justice is a process and that any income distribution that results from voluntary transactions is just, assuming the original distribution is fair.
5. Together, federal, state, and local governments spend over $200 billion annually to fight poverty. The most important programs are AFDC, SSI, Medicaid, and the Food Stamp program.
6. Many people criticize existing programs because they are costly and generate work disincentives. The negative income tax program and workfare are often suggested

as more efficient alternatives to current programs. Experiments with these programs have shown mixed results.

KEY TERMS AND CONCEPTS

quintile	progressive tax
Lorenz curve	disincentive to work
absolute poverty	AFDC
relative poverty	SSI
vicious circle of poverty	Medicaid
marginal productivity theory	food stamps
human capital	means test
efficiency versus equity	negative income tax
John Rawls	workfare
veil of ignorance	Earned Income Tax Credit
Robert Nozick	

REVIEW QUESTIONS

1. What are the basic facts regarding income distribution in the United States? How has income distribution changed over the past 50 years? Over the past 15 years?
2. Draw a Lorenz curve to illustrate perfect income equality, income distribution in the United States, and income distribution after passage of a progressive income tax.
3. Which demographic groups are most likely to be in poverty? How have the demographics of poverty changed over the past 50 years? Why have these changes taken place?
4. Why do most economists believe that factors other than ability must affect income distribution? What are the main factors that affect income distribution?
5. What is the main question that must be answered in any discussion of income redistribution? Compare and contrast Rawls's and Nozick's philosophies of justice.
6. What are the main welfare programs in the United States? Approximately how much money is spent annually on these programs? What are some of the main criticisms economists have levied at these programs?
7. What are the potential advantages and disadvantages of workfare and a negative income tax?

PROBLEMS

1. Refer to Equations 1 and 2.
   a. Show that people pay zero taxes if their earned income is $20,000.
   b. Recall that the official poverty rate for a single nonelderly individual was $6,932 in 1991. Suppose that you want the NIT to guarantee that individuals receive at least that amount of money. How would you have to modify Equation 1?
2. Indicate whether the following are true, false, or uncertain, and explain why:
   a. Income distribution was less equal in 1990 than in 1980.

b. Income distribution was less equal in 1990 than in 1950.

c. If successful, AFDC should shift the Lorenz curve away from the 45° line.

d. Assume real GDP is $6 trillion and population is 250 million. Absolute poverty could be abolished with a perfectly equal distribution of income.

e. People living in poverty would be better off with in-kind assistance than cash assistance.

f. Being lucky is more important than being educated.

3. Do you think there should be a 100 percent tax on all inheritances? Why or why not? Would Rawls agree with your answer? Would Nozick?

4. Some economists believe that if all poverty programs were eliminated, people would not only look harder for jobs, but private charities would step in to aid the truly needy. Do you agree or disagree? Why? (*Hint:* Refer back to the "Privately Provided Public Goods" Focus box in Chapter 18.)

5. Most college students come from middle-class families. Further, public colleges are subsidized so that tuition is much less than the cost of college. How do college subsidies affect income distribution? Would you recommend any changes in college pricing?

6. Some people have recommended sterilization for AFDC mothers who continue to have children they cannot support. Do you agree or disagree with this policy? Why?

7. The reason people are poor is that they do not value money enough to go to work; therefore, the well-to-do have no obligation to help the poor. Comment.

8. Figure 20.3 shows that the unemployment rate for people with Ph.D.'s is higher than the rate for people with Master's degrees. Can you suggest an explanation for this apparent contradiction to the idea that unemployment declines as education increases?

CHAPTER 21

Economics and the Environment

You hear it on the news everyday: We have a hole in the ozone. The rain forests are being cut down. Nuclear waste is piling up. The spotted owl is on the verge of extinction. So are jobs in the logging industry. The list goes on and on. Are these fears justified? And more to the point: Can economists help us understand and solve these problems?

Like everyone else, economists care about these issues and occasionally get into rather heated debates over the importance of, say, the spotted owl relative to jobs in the logging industry. But economists have an advantage over many people when discussing the environment: they bring a measure of scientific objectivity to the analysis. This does not mean that they always find simple or single solutions to environmental problems. But it does mean that they are ready to compare costs and benefits and can often offer solutions that may not be obvious to noneconomists.

This chapter will survey several topics in environmental economics. We cannot look at every environmental issue, of course; population growth, air pollution, water pollution, solid waste disposal, deforestation, and holes in the ozone are just too much for a single chapter. All we can hope to do is look at some general principles and apply them to some specific cases. Our first task will be a brief tour into physics, specifically, the laws of thermodynamics. This will help us put the relationship between the economy and the environment in perspective. Next, we will look at the issue of common property rights, the situation that occurs when resources are available "free" to everyone. We will then examine some of the key issues involved with pollution control. Finally, we will look at population growth before we turn to the rather sticky issue of global cooperation on environmental policy.

AFTER READING AND STUDYING THIS CHAPTER, YOU SHOULD BE ABLE TO:

• • • State the two laws of thermodynamics and explain how they relate to the economy and the environment

• • • Define common property resources, and explain why policy is necessary for optimal allocation of common property resources

• • • Explain why economists usually prefer taxes to direct controls as a solution to pollution problems

• • • Outline recent trends in population growth, and discuss the interaction between population growth and the economy

• • • Explain why global cooperation is difficult but may be necessary to solve many environmental problems

THE LAWS OF THERMODYNAMICS

One of the aphorisms in economics is "everything depends on everything else." This is especially true in environmental economics: production decisions made today always affect the environment of tomorrow. Even if there is no pollution, current production means that fewer nonrenewable resources will be available for posterity. The environment provides materials and energy for use by the economic system. Some of the resources provided by the environment are used directly—for example, people breathe air—but most are transformed by the economic system.

Most scientists and economists believe that the environment and the economic system together form a *closed system*. A closed system is one in which all inputs and outputs are contained within the system. In contrast, an *open system* can import and export inputs and outputs. Individual economies are obviously open systems, but the relationship between the global economy and the global environment is best considered as a closed system.[1] Once we recognize that the system is closed, we can apply the two laws of thermodynamics to help understand the constraints on the system:

- The *first law of thermodynamics* states that energy and matter can be neither created nor destroyed. Matter-energy conversion is possible—burning wood produces heat energy, and nuclear fission converts matter into nuclear energy—but the total amount of energy and matter available to the economy is limited to what is present in the environment.

- The *second law of thermodynamics*, also known as the *entropy* law, states that the amount of energy not available for use ("entropy") will increase whenever energy conversion takes place. For example, large coal-fired electric power plants inevitably waste about 67 percent of the energy content of the coal. The implication of the second law is that even though energy cannot be destroyed, the amount of available energy will decrease over time.

---

[1]Obvious exceptions to the closed system assumption are solar energy and the disposal of waste into outer space. The sun is necessary for food production, but solar energy currently plays little role in the generation of other forms of energy. Waste disposal into outer space is impractical with current technology. Until solar energy and outer space play a significant role in the world economy, the closed system assumption is reasonable.

Taken together, the two laws of thermodynamics make an important statement about the relationship between the economic system and the environment: not only do we face rigid constraints on the basic inputs into the economy, but increasing entropy means that we will have less useful energy in the future. Some might respond that we have just made the case for space travel; others might argue that our closed system can be opened by making better use of solar power. But while few would doubt the advantages of either solution, fewer still would argue that space travel and solar power represent simple solutions to our current problems. Until we can move into space or develop efficient solar power converters, we must regard the system as closed. And with ever increasing global energy usage, problems will mount.

What can economists say about these problems? Something very important: Economists know the criteria for efficient use of energy and matter, and efficiency is the first step toward conservation. One caveat: In the area of environmental economics—perhaps more than in most areas of economic analysis—economic analysis must be interdisciplinary. It must incorporate technical advice from biologists, chemists, and physicists, as well as the ethical considerations of philosophers and religious leaders, and more besides. Many economists who have worked in environmental economics have taken this kind of interdisciplinary approach, but none more so than Kenneth Boulding, the subject of the Economic Heritage box on page 530.

RECAP   The Laws of Thermodynamics

The global economy is a closed system because all inputs and outputs are contained within the system. Economic analysis is important because it can help determine the most efficient ways to use resources. The two laws of thermodynamics apply to closed systems:

1. The first law of thermodynamics states that the total amount of matter and energy cannot be changed. This means that the amount of energy and matter available as inputs is fixed.
2. The second law of thermodynamics, the entropy law, states that matter-energy conversion can never be 100 percent efficient. This means that the amount of energy available for use will decline over time.

COMMON PROPERTY RIGHTS

We found out in Chapter 18 that some market failures can be solved by applying the Coase theorem: simply define property rights adequately, and things will take care of themselves. As a practical matter, however, it is often difficult to establish well-defined property rights. Not only are there potentially serious income-distribution effects, but in many cases the property rights assignments would be arbitrary, at best. A particularly vexing problem with property rights occurs when a resource is "owned" by everyone instead of a single individual. This is the case of **common property rights.** Examples of resources subject to common property rights include fish in the sea, the ocean itself, and public pasture lands. Such resources are called *common property resources.*

Common property rights Property interests that are held by everyone in a society rather than by individuals.

OUR ECONOMIC HERITAGE

KENNETH E. BOULDING:
HUMAN VALUES ON SPACESHIP EARTH

Not many economists can claim to have published three volumes of poetry, sung entire Gilbert and Sullivan musicals from memory, or written a one-man play on Adam Smith for PBS. In fact, only one economist can claim these accomplishments—and still have been nominated for Nobel Prizes in both economics and peace. That economist was Kenneth E. Boulding.

Born in Liverpool, England, in 1910, Kenneth Boulding studied chemistry at Oxford as an undergraduate and soon became interested in economics. He was raised a strict Methodist, but became a Quaker as a young man and was well-known for his pacifist views. His opposition to World War II led to his dismissal as an economist at the League of Nations. He also read Buddhist literature and often retreated to his Zen meditation garden in the hills overlooking his home in Boulder, Colorado. His wife, Elise, is a well-known sociologist. Professor Boulding never earned a Ph.D.: when told what he would have to do to earn the degree, he replied, "If I do that, I'll be a broken man!" He taught at several institutions including Harvard, the University of Chicago, and the University of Edinburgh before he accepted a position at the University of Colorado where he stayed until his death in 1993. Despite a heavy stammer, Boulding was an outstanding speaker and an inspiring teacher.

Boulding began his career as an economic theorist—he was the first to use indifference curves to show the trade-off between income and leisure—and his text, *Economic Theory,* is still considered a classic. In 1949, he was awarded the John Bates Clark Medal, an award given every two years to the economist under age 40 considered to have made an important contribution to economics. At times, he was associated with radical economics, but late in his career he claimed to want to "shake his stick at the Marxians." In his later years, Boulding's interdisciplinary work received the most attention. His 1956 book, *The Image,* is still regarded as the paragon of interdisciplinary scholarship, and his *Meaning of the Twentieth Century* (1964) preceded the popular futurist literature of the next two decades. These books presented an ethical, humanist approach to the economy and society. Boulding is also credited with the creation of entirely new areas of economics. For example, his 1949 book, *The Economics of Peace,* is still read in Peace Studies programs. It was this kind of work that led Nobel laureate Wassily Leontief to remark the Boulding had left economics to become a "universal philosopher."

Boulding's metaphor "spaceship earth" was to become something of a rallying cry for the environmental movement. The only way for humanity to survive, argued Boulding, was to adopt the same ethics that would be necessary for life in the closed system of a spaceship. Waste must be minimized and recycled; renewable energy sources must be emphasized; and population must be controlled. Boulding's solution to the population problem was to give every person the right to have one child—and allow people to trade these rights in an open market! Boulding's "green stamp" population program, as he liked to call it, was not universally acclaimed, but few could argue that he did not have a point. The same could be said for nearly everything he wrote.

Common property rights create a difficult problem because there is no incentive for individual conservation. Consider the fish in the sea. If property rights are "common," then everyone "owns" the fish so everyone will be free to try to catch them. Further, because so many people harvest the fish, the act of any single individual will have little if any noticeable impact on the entire fish stock. Therefore, individuals have no incentive to limit their catch to assure that fish stocks are not depleted. In fact, each individual has an incentive to catch fish while they are still plentiful. If *everyone* acts this way, however, fish stocks almost certainly will be depleted. On the other hand, if the right to harvest fish were given to one individual, that person would realize that overharvesting would deplete fish stocks and reduce future catches. Private ownership would automatically generate an incentive to preserve the fish stock. Fishing would continue only until the marginal revenue of the last fish caught is equal to the marginal cost of catching the last fish.

· · · · · · · ·

Analytics of Common Property Resources

The problem of overfishing and common property rights is shown in Figure 21.1. Suppose there is a lake where the total number of fish caught increases as the number of boats on the lake increases, but less than proportionately with the number of boats

FIGURE 21.1 OVERFISHING AND COMMON PROPERTY RIGHTS

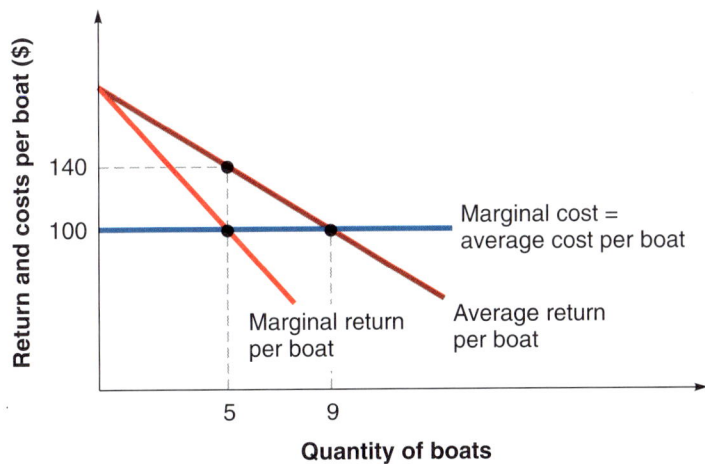

In the absence of government intervention, common property resources will be overexploited. If there were private fishing rights, the owner would recognize that the marginal return of more than five boats would be less than the marginal cost per boat so only five boats would be used to fish the lake. The monopoly fisher would make economic rent of $40 per boat and would have an incentive to conserve the fish stock to preserve economic rents over the long run. If there are common fishing rights, people will fish as long as the total cost of fishing is less than the total return from fishing. This occurs at the intersection of the average return curve and the average cost curve. This is inefficient because the marginal benefit of the last fish boat is less than the marginal cost of that boat.

on the lake. The average return per boat curve gives the average number of fish caught per boat. It is found by dividing the total number of fish caught by the number of boats on the lake. The average return curve is downward sloping because as more fishing effort is exerted, the fish population shrinks, and the average number of fish caught per boat declines. The marginal return per boat curve gives the number of fish caught by the next boat on the lake. The marginal return curve slopes down faster than the average return curve for the same reason all marginal curves slope down faster than their respective average curves: the output from each additional boat is less than the previous boat, so marginal return is less than average return. The marginal return curve can be thought of as the marginal social benefit curve because the number of fish caught on the next boat is the marginal social benefit of fishing in one more boat. To simplify the diagram, the marginal cost curve is assumed to be flat and equal to average cost. This indicates that each additional boat costs the same amount, $100 per day in this example.

Now, if the property rights to the fish are assigned to a single monopoly fisher, the monopolist would use five boats on the lake—the point where the marginal return of the next boat equals the marginal cost of the next boat. Notice that the monopoly fisher can command economic rent by putting only five boats on the lake because the average return per boat ($140) is greater than the cost per boat.

What happens if there are common property rights to the fish? Fishers will keep fishing until the total cost of fishing is equal to the total return earned from selling the fish. (Remember that total costs include normal profits.) This occurs when there are nine boats on the lake. Does fishing by nine boats threaten the viability of the fish population? It well could, but whether it actually would depends on several specifics of the particular species. What we do know is this: having nine fishing boats on the lake is inefficient because the marginal return from boats 6, 7, 8, and 9 is less than the marginal cost of putting those boats in the fishing fleet. The problem is that there is no incentive to limit the catch because no one can be sure of capturing economic rents. People will limit their catch today only if they know that they will benefit in the future. A monopoly fisher would want to limit the catch to capture economic rents and preserve the fish stock to assure a stream of income over time. Overuse of a common property resource is often referred to as the **tragedy of the commons** after a classic paper by Garrett Hardin.[2]

Tragedy of the commons Over-utilization of a common property resource; people will use the resource even when marginal revenue is less than the marginal cost of the last unit.

• • • • • • • •

Species Extinction?

But the existence of common property rights does *not* necessarily imply extinction: fishing will continue only until the profits are exhausted. On Figure 21.1, this occurs at Q = 9, the intersection of the average return and average cost curves. In a more normal situation, there are two reasons to suspect that the marginal cost of catching fish would rise as more fish are caught: First, fishing pressure will reduce the number of available fish so that more time is spent catching each fish. Second, catching fish today reduces the breeding stock and thus reduces the amount of fish available tomorrow. This means that the total marginal cost of catching fish has a *marginal user cost*

---

[2]Garrett Hardin, "Tragedy of the Commons," *Science* (December 1968): 1245–48.

as well as the *marginal extraction cost*.[3] In theory, with well-defined property rights, the owners of the fish would include both marginal costs in their profit calculations and would limit their catch to make sure that there are fish in the future. Marginal user costs would be ignored under common property rights because the actions of individual fishers would have no noticeable effect on the future supply of fish. Therefore, too many fish would be caught and the stocks could be depleted.

Species-specific factors also affect the likelihood of extinction. For example, consider salmon and halibut, two of the most important commercial fish caught in Alaska. Halibut are large, bottom-dwelling flat fish that are caught at depths up to and exceeding 400 feet. As more halibut are caught, they become scarcer, catches decline, and the marginal cost rises. Thus, the marginal cost of catching that last halibut would be exceedingly high, certainly too high to support a fleet of commercial halibut fishers. Salmon, on the other hand, have an interesting life story. They are born in fresh water, spend from two to five years in the open ocean, then return to the same stream where they were born to spawn and die. All that would be necessary to catch the last salmon would be to run a net across the river and catch the fish before they have a chance to spawn. The marginal cost of catching that last salmon is quite low, so low that several runs of salmon have already been eliminated.[4]

• • • • • • • •

Biodiversity

Is there a reason to be concerned about extinction? Isn't one fish pretty much like another? Perhaps, but most scientists would argue that there is a benefit to **biodiversity.** Biodiversity refers to two related concepts: (1) the genetic variability within a particular species and (2) the number of different species. Genetic diversity within a species is necessary for survival; without genetic diversity there is inbreeding and the species loses its vigor. Genetic diversity is also necessary for hybridization and breeding experiments. Such experiments have resulted in new crop strains, for example, disease-resistant barley and tomatoes that tolerate low temperatures. Species diversity is important not only for aesthetic reasons—it is not pleasant to think about the extinct passenger pigeon or Labrador duck—but because so many plants and animals have been shown to play important roles in science and medicine. Almost one-fourth of all prescription drugs are based on tropical plants, yet tropical deforestation is proceeding at an unprecedented rate. It *may* be that we can get along without any particular plant or animal, but we never know—and extinction is forever. Finally, the right to "enjoy" the environment may be just as important as the right to "use" the environment, a point suggested by the Focus box on page 534.

But can't we rely on the economist's notion that market forces will prevent extinc-

Biodiversity The genetic variability within a particular species and the number of different species.

---

[3]These terms were defined in Chapter 17.

[4]A number of salmon runs have been eliminated in the Northwest, California, and Alaska; most salmon runs on the East Coast are extinct or on the verge of extinction. Overfishing—commercial, sport, and subsistence—is only one reason for the loss of salmon. Another reason is development: as rivers are dammed to generate electricity, salmon are prevented from returning to their spawning beds. Salmon hatchery programs have been able to restore salmon in some places, but the gene stock has been altered permanently. In 1994, all open-water salmon fishing in Oregon and Washington was banned to protect the dwindling supply of salmon.

FOCUS ON

MEADOWLARK ECONOMICS

When economists do cost-benefit analysis, they tend to overlook something very important: the value of nature for nature's sake. In a fascinating collection of essays, *Meadowlark Economics,* James Eggert, an economics professor at the University of Wisconsin—Stout, offers his views on the value of meadowlarks, his favorite pastime, high jumping, recycling, craftsmanship, and other topics. The following is an excerpt from the title article:

"Ecology." Note that the words "economics" and "ecology" have the same prefix "eco," from the Greek *oikos,* which literally means "household." Thus the original definition of economics implied an understanding, a caring for, and the management of human households, whereas ecology implied an understanding and appreciation of the interrelationships within nature's "household." I believe these two households are becoming more in-

terdependent and their futures more and more intimately linked. When we fail to calculate ecological values or to see the connections, it paves the way for losses that are both unintended and unwanted. One example (on a small scale to be sure) is now occurring in our area, a dairy farming region of the upper Midwest. We are losing our meadowlarks!

Indeed, the people who walk or jog along our rural roads enjoy the few meadowlarks that are left. . . . The complete disappearance of meadowlarks would, plain and simple, be wrong ethically, and also would diminish the quality of our lives.

Why are we losing the meadowlarks? Most likely it is a result of a modern method of haying—"hayage." . . .

Despite their sweet song, these birds have no voice economically or politically. They represent zero within our conventional economic

accounting system (we do not even buy birdseed or build birdhouses for meadowlarks). Their disappearance would not create even the tiniest ripple in the Commerce Department's spreadsheets that are supposed to measure our standard of living.

SOURCE: James Eggert, *Meadowlark Economics* (Armonk, N.Y.: M. E. Sharpe, 1992), pp. 5–6. Used with permission.

Maximum sustainable yield The maximum harvest rate that permits a viable population of the species.

tion because the cost of catching that last fish is greater than the revenue that can be earned from catching it? Sometimes, but not always: Though it is rarely profitable to catch the very last fish, it may be profitable to catch so many fish that the population falls below a sustainable level. Enough individuals must be left alive to preserve genetic diversity. Biologists can help determine the **maximum sustainable yield—** the maximum harvest rate that permits a sustainable population of the species—but their calculations always contain an element of uncertainty. Some scientists, for example, note that it is virtually impossible to reach a consensus on the maximum sustainable yield because of the difficulty of conducting controlled experiments in the

ECONOMICS AND THE ENVIRONMENT   CHAPTER 21

wild. They conclude that we should interpret all claims of sustainability carefully.[5]

The question for economists, of course, is whether biological diversity is worth the cost. Ask the loggers in the Pacific Northwest whether preservation of the spotted owl is worth lost jobs and you will get an emphatic "No!" for an answer. Ask an avid backpacker the same question and you will get an answer that is just as emphatic—but quite different. It is not the economist's place to answer these or similar questions, only to supply pertinent information and note that *all* environmental actions involve both costs and benefits. The fact that it is exceedingly difficult to measure the costs and benefits of biodiversity means that we will always be debating these issues.

RECAP   **Common Property Rights**

Resources that are owned by everyone instead of individuals are subject to common property rights. In the absence of government policy, there is no incentive to conserve common property resources, and overutilization can take place.

1. When property is privately owned, there is an incentive to conserve, and resources will be utilized until the marginal cost is equal to marginal revenue. Common property resources will be used until the total cost is equal to total revenue. This is inefficient because the marginal benefit of the last unit is less than the marginal cost.
2. Overutilization of resources can lead to species extinction if utilization is carried beyond the maximum sustainable yield. Biologists admit that it is often difficult to determine maximum sustainable yield for particular species.
3. The genetic variability within a species and the number of species are called biodiversity. Biodiversity is important for scientific as well as aesthetic reasons.

POLLUTION POLICY: TAXES OR DIRECT CONTROLS?

We discovered in Chapter 18 that pollution is a negative externality to the production process. We also discussed two ways to deal with pollution: impose taxes to internalize the externality, or apply the Coase theorem and assign property rights. We are not about to dismiss that analysis, but we do need to extend it a bit. In particular, we need to explain why economists generally prefer taxes to direct controls as a solution to pollution problems.

Pollution Taxes

At first glance, it may seem that there is really no difference between pollution taxes and direct controls that require firms to adopt pollution-free production methods. In

---

[5]Donald Ludwig, Ray Hilborn, and Carl Walters, "Uncertainty, Resource Exploitation, and Conservation: Lessons from History," *Science* 260 (April 2, 1993): 17–18.

FIGURE 21.2 THE OPTIMAL QUANTITY OF POLLUTION

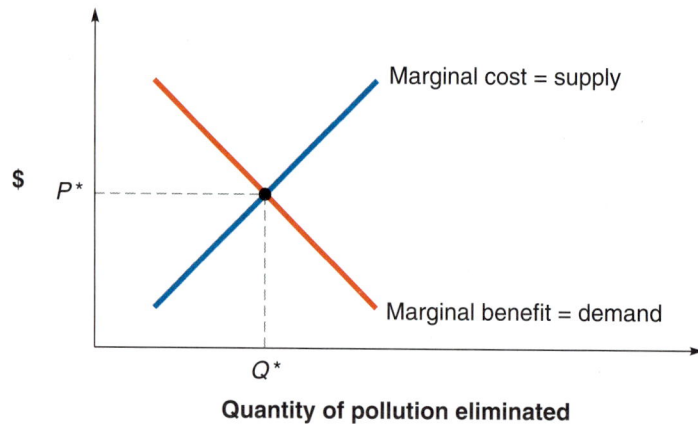

The demand curve for reducing pollution is the marginal benefit curve. It is downward sloping because marginal benefits decline as additional pollution is eliminated. The supply curve for pollution reduction is upward sloping because the marginal cost of pollution reduction rises as additional units of pollution are eliminated. The intersection between marginal benefit and marginal cost determine the optimal quantity of pollution reduction, $Q^\star$, and the price that should be paid to reduce pollution, $P^\star$. Note that the optimal quantity of pollution is not zero. This is because the cost of eliminating that last unit of pollution is greater than the benefit.

Optimal level of pollution The amount of pollution such that the marginal benefit of having less pollution is equal to the marginal cost of cleaning up the pollution. The optimal level is not zero.

fact, the differences can be significant, and economists almost always opt for taxes rather than direct controls. Here's why.

In Figure 21.2, suppose that the pollution authorities recognize that a particular paper mill is producing both air and water pollution. After studying the situation, they estimate the marginal benefit of reducing pollution to be the downward-sloping curve shown on the diagram. The benefit associated with getting rid of the first few units of pollution is higher than the benefit from getting rid of the last, almost unnoticeable, units of pollution. They also discover that the marginal cost of eliminating pollution rises as more pollution is eliminated. The first few units of pollution can be eliminated with simple plant maintenance, but to eliminate additional units of pollution would incur increasing costs, and complete elimination would require a complete new production technology. The intersection between the marginal benefit and marginal cost curves gives the optimal level of emissions reduction and the price of eliminating that amount of pollution. Notice that the **optimal level of pollution** *is not zero* because the cost of eliminating that last unit of pollution is greater than the benefit.

Two common methods are used to reduce pollution, pollution taxes and direct controls. To see their effects, it is convenient to look at pollution from the perspective of the firm as is done in Figure 21.3. Paper mills "demand" pollution in the sense that they receive benefits from it; the right to pollute gives them the right to produce paper. As they produce more paper, they produce more pollution. They will continue

····**FIGURE 21.3** THE DEMAND FOR POLLUTION

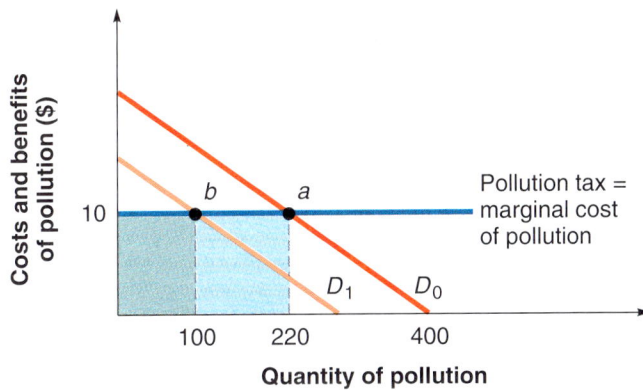

Pollution taxes can act as an incentive for firms to find cost-efficient ways to reduce pollution. The curve D_0 represents the firm's demand for pollution, given current production technologies and the firm's expected sales. If no cost is associated with pollution, the firm will "demand" (= produce) 400 units of pollution. Once a pollution tax of $10 is imposed, the firm will cut back on pollution to 220 units and be required to pay $2,200 in pollution taxes. To avoid these taxes, the firm will look for pollution-reducing technologies. This will lower the demand for pollution. If the pollution demand curve shifts to D_1, the amount of pollution will fall to 100 units, and the firm's pollution tax liability will be $1,000.

to "demand" pollution as long as the benefits of pollution (additional paper production) exceed the costs of pollution. In the absence of government regulation, the cost of pollution is zero. Once a pollution tax is implemented, the cost of pollution is positive, so firms will pollute only as long as the benefit of pollution exceeds the cost (which includes the tax).

The effect of pollution taxes is also shown in Figure 21.3. The original pollution demand curve, D_0, is downward sloping like most demand curves. If there are no pollution taxes, the firm will pollute until the marginal benefit of an extra unit of pollution is zero. This occurs at 400 units of pollution, the point where the pollution demand curve crosses the horizontal axis. On the typical supply and demand diagram (with the quantity of paper on the horizontal axis), this point corresponds to the point where the marginal revenue from selling paper is equal to the marginal private cost of producing paper. Now look what happens when the pollution agency imposes a pollution tax: the cost of pollution is no longer zero, so the quantity of pollution demanded is no longer 400. If the pollution tax is set at $10, the quantity of pollution will fall to 220. If the pollution tax is set at the right level (equal to the marginal external cost of pollution), this will be the optimal level of pollution. To reduce pollution to this level, the firm will have to reduce output or develop less polluting production methods.

The main reason economists generally favor pollution taxes over direct controls as a solution to pollution is that they act as an incentive to reduce pollution even further. For example, when the original emissions tax was imposed in Figure 21.3, the firm had to pay \$2,200 in pollution taxes (the entire shaded area); however, if it adopts more environmentally sound production methods, it can reduce its tax liability. Such measures would shift the pollution demand curve in to D_1 and reduce pollution tax liabilities to \$1,000 (the green area only).

The result we have just demonstrated is important: firms have an incentive to find less polluting production methods because it reduces their pollution tax liability. On the other hand, if the pollution authorities adopt direct controls that require firms to use a particular technology, they will have no incentive to reduce pollution below the mandated limits. In fact, a good bit of evidence suggests that this is exactly what firms do. When faced with regulated pollution standards, firms often adopt the specific standard established by the Environmental Protection Agency and then stop their search for alternative methods to reduce pollution. The price signals inherent in pollution taxes provide an incentive for firms to continue to search for methods to reduce pollution; direct controls do not supply these kinds of incentives. Nevertheless, direct controls sometimes have an advantage over pollution taxes because it can be quite difficult to determine the tax rate that will result in the optimal level of pollution. Consider what occurred along the Rhine River in Germany in the early 1990s. The giant chemical company BASF continued to pollute because the pollution taxes were too low to provide an incentive to reduce pollution, and given the bureaucratic structure of the European Economic Community, it has proven difficult to change the pollution tax rates. Had direct controls been instituted originally, this pollution would not have been a problem.

· · · · · · · ·

The Importance of Price Signals

The aim of pollution taxes is to establish the correct price signals so that markets can operate efficiently. When firms are forced to pay for their pollution, they pass on this cost as higher selling prices—a process we called "internalizing externalities" in Chapter 18. In many states, the same authorities responsible for establishing pollution taxes are also responsible for setting the price of utilities, water, and other resources. Unfortunately, these prices are often set without any concept of economic efficiency in mind. For example, many cities charge a flat fee for home garbage pickup. This reduces the incentive to recycle and reduce waste; fee schedules based on the number of cans of garbage encourage recycling and reduce waste. Seattle and other cities have used per-can garbage pricing to reduce solid waste by as much as 30 percent.

Perhaps the worst case of pricing inefficiency is water pricing in California. Farmers pay \$10 per acre foot of water—only a *tenth* of the cost of pumping that water—while cities pay over \$200 per acre foot of water. Farmers also receive subsidies to grow cotton and rice, crops more often associated with rainy climates than with the deserts of California. Further, agriculture produces 3 percent of the state's economic output yet consumes 85 percent of California's water; clearly, the farm lobby in California has a significant influence on water prices. Setting the price of water closer to the cost of providing water would undoubtedly result in fewer cotton and rice farmers in the state—but California's drought might almost magically disappear.[6]

_____

[6]These data are from "There's Another Desert War," *The Economist*, February 16, 1991, pp. 24–25.

Some Qualifications

We must add two important qualifications to this discussion. First, when pollution is so toxic or life-threatening that even a tiny amount can be deadly, the optimal level of pollution is zero, and direct controls may be preferable to taxes. The nuclear power industry is one such example: not only is there the potential of a core meltdown, but disposal of nuclear waste is critical. In the case of a meltdown—as occurred at Chernobyl in the Soviet Union in 1986—nuclear radiation can contaminate the countryside for miles around. There is evidence, for example, that reindeer milk in Lapland, over 1,000 miles from Chernobyl, was contaminated. Disposal of nuclear waste may be less dramatic, but it is just as serious because the waste remains radioactive for, literally, thousands of years. Costly and complicated regulations are among the reasons why no new nuclear power generators have been built in the United States in more than 20 years.[7]

The second qualification is that stringent environmental regulations can sometimes lead to dynamic competitive effects and increased exports. For example, Germany has some of the strictest environmental controls in the world: car companies are required to produce cars with recyclable parts, an Environmental Label jury puts the Blue Angel mark on some 3,500 environmentally friendly products, and regulations are in place to reduce harmful air pollution by 90 percent. Nevertheless, many firms have found that they can cut costs with recycling and measures designed to reduce pollution. Germany's environmental regulations have also given rise to the development of new industry in Germany—the export of environmentally friendly products. Says Harvard professor Michael Porter in his best-selling *The Competitive Advantage of Nations:* "Nations with the most rigorous requirements often lead in exports of affected products."[8] Vice-President Al Gore echoed a similar view in his book *Earth in the Balance* when he noted that Japan is ". . . already implementing an ambitious plan to cultivate what it believes to be a massive global market for new technologies for renewable energy and environmentally benign processes."[9]

A Market for Pollution Rights?

As we discovered in Chapter 18, the Coase theorem suggests an interesting and increasingly important solution to pollution problems: assign property rights to pollution and allow people to sell their **pollution rights** in the open market. For example, to reduce air pollution in California, New Jersey, and a few other states, firms

Pollution rights Market-based approach to environmental problems. Involves assigning the right to pollute to potential polluters and allowing firms and environmental groups to sell these rights.

---

[7]We can't leave this very brief discussion of nuclear power without noting that the industry has had a very good safety record in the United States. The most serious crisis occurred at the Three Mile Island nuclear plant in Pennsylvania in 1979. Unlike Chernobyl, there were no fatalities and only a small release of radiation. Stringent government regulations were one reason the emergency was contained. For a brief discussion of the problems of the nuclear power industry, see "Losing Its Charm," *The Economist,* November 21, 1992, pp. 21–24.

[8]For more discussion of environmental policies in Germany, see Curtis A. Moore, "Down Germany's Road to a Clean Tomorrow," *International Wildlife* (September/October 1992): 24–28. The Porter quotation comes from this article.

[9]Al Gore, *Earth in the Balance* (New York: Houghton Mifflin, 1992), p. 196.

are given the right to pollute a certain amount. If they pollute more than their allotment, they are fined unless they purchase a pollution right from a firm that has polluted less than allowed. Pollution rights for sale are occasionally advertised in the *Wall Street Journal* and other newspapers, and a small secondary market for pollution permits has existed on the Chicago Board of Trade since March 1993. Perhaps the most ambitious pollution market—the Regional Clean Air Incentive Market (RECLAIM)—was established in southern California in January 1994.[10]

Establishing a market for the right to pollute can be an efficient mechanism to reduce pollution because all firms have an incentive to reduce their pollution and will pollute only when the benefits outweigh the costs. Nevertheless, there are a number of potential problems with this policy. First, the public must be educated: people who do not understand economics are bothered (to say the least!) at the thought of "big business" buying or selling the right to pollute. Second, it is still necessary to establish the optimal level of pollution, and this is no easier to do with a market than with direct controls or taxes—though it would be possible for environmental groups (such as the Sierra Club) to buy pollution permits and thus reduce the amount of legal pollution. Finally, the market for pollution rights has to have some constraints on it. For example, when a pollution rights market was established in southern California in the late 1980s, some firms tried to sell their pollution rights and close their plants—not a popular move in a state with already high unemployment.

RECAP   Pollution Policy

Pollution represents a negative externality that is not counted in the firm's costs unless there is government intervention. There are three basic ways to deal with pollution: taxes, direct controls, and the establishment of a market for pollution rights.

1. Pollution taxes raise the private costs of production so that selling prices reflect all costs. Economists generally prefer pollution taxes to direct controls because they generate an incentive for firms to adopt technologies that reduce pollution.
2. Direct controls are government regulations that mandate specific production technologies or limit the quantity of pollution. As a general rule, economists dislike direct controls because they do not generate incentives to reduce pollution beyond the mandated limits.
3. In some instances it is possible to establish a market for pollution and use the market process to reduce pollution. This entails assigning pollution rights and allowing firms to trade these rights.
4. The optimal level of pollution is almost never zero because the cost of cleaning up the last unit of pollution is greater than the benefit. Finding the pollution tax to generate the optimal level of pollution can be difficult.

[10]"Right to Pollute," *The Economist,* October 30, 1993, pp. 77–78.

····· POPULATION

Some facts to ponder: the world population stood at 2.5 billion in 1950. In 1990 it was 5.3 billion. The United Nations estimates that it will be 11.5 billion in the year 2015. Population growth in the rich countries of Europe and North America is slowing; it is accelerating in the poor countries of Africa, Asia, and Central and South America. The population of the United States, around 260 million, represents about 5 percent of the world population.

Is population something we should be worried about? Perhaps—but a better answer is "It depends." We will not be overrun with masses of starving people next year or five years from now. But unless something is done to check population growth in the less-developed nations, our grandchildren may live in a much less pleasant world as the demand for resources and the production of waste increase worldwide. The problem is becoming acute even in advanced nations like the United States and Germany where immigration is pressing the limits of social services. Few analysts believe that the population will soon outstrip the food production capabilities of the planet, but without changes in global food distribution networks, there will continue to be pockets of starvation. Just as importantly, as the populations of the less-developed nations grow, there will be increasing demands for energy and resources and the inevitable by-products of waste. These are serious problems, but they are not insoluble. The first step to solving this problem is to understand it.

Population Trends in the United States

Figure 21.4 presents U.S. population by decade since 1790. The average annual growth rate of the U.S. population has been about 2.1 percent since 1790; the rate over the past decade has been about 1 percent per year, with about a third of that

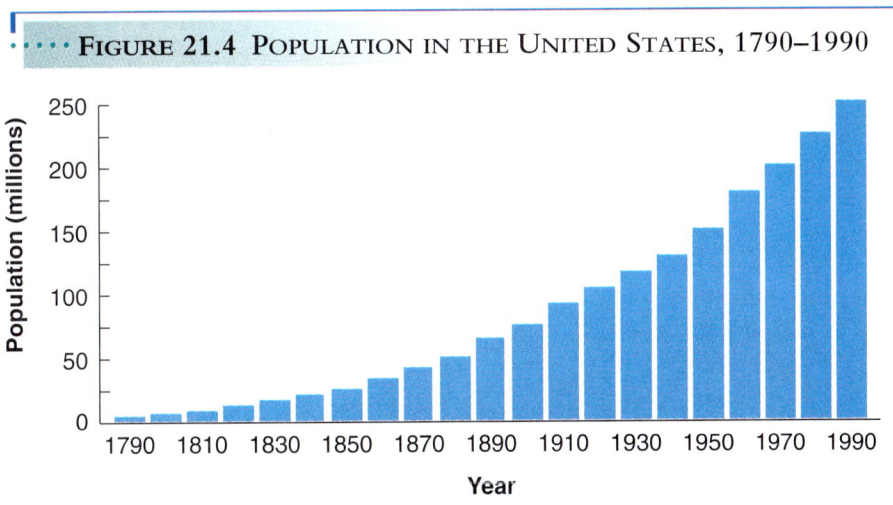

····· FIGURE 21.4 POPULATION IN THE UNITED STATES, 1790–1990

SOURCE: *Statistical Abstract of the United States,* 1993, Table 1, p. 8.

growth representing immigration. While the declining rate of population growth may be encouraging, we need to look beyond the numbers in the figure. Demographers and economists studying population focus on some important characteristics of the data to gauge future trends in population growth. Some of the most important concepts necessary for understanding the future path of population are the fertility rate, the replacement rate, and the age distribution:

• The *fertility rate* gives the average number of live births a typical women has in her lifetime. The fertility rate in the United States has been about 1.84 since the early 1970s.
• The *replacement rate* is the number of children that the average woman must bear to keep the population stationary. The replacement rate in the United States is 2.11—each woman must have 2 children to replace herself and her mate plus 0.11 to account for women who do not live to childbearing age and those who do not have children.
• Currently, only about 30 percent of the U.S. population is under age 14; the comparable figure in Mexico is about 45 percent.

What can we make of these facts? First, because the fertility rate is below the replacement rate, the population of the United States will begin to decline by about 5 percent per year (net of immigration and emigration). That decline will not begin for about 25 years, however, because of the current age distribution of the population. Over the next 25 years, the average age in the United States will increase, as will the population. This increase in average age will not be paralleled in Mexico and many other less-developed nations. In Mexico the large number of people under age 14 will make it very difficult to reduce population growth in the next 25 years. The situation is even more severe in most African nations.

Population and Economic Growth

There is two-way causality between population growth and economic growth.[11] Economic growth requires factor inputs, and labor is a factor of production. But economic growth also affects population growth: nations on the verge of industrialization tend to have higher population growth rates than nations with more developed economies.

Other things being equal, population growth leads to economic growth because labor is a factor of production. Nevertheless, there are at least two reasons to suspect that rapid population growth will result in a decline in the income per head or *per capita income*. First, rapid population growth usually means that the population is getting younger. In most cultures, the young do not work until age 16 or 18. This means that a smaller portion of the population is available for work, and thus that there is less output per person.[12] In 1990, for example, barely 50 percent of the

[11]Much of this section is based on Chapter 5 of Tom Tietenberg, *Environmental and Natural Resource Economics* (New York: Harper-Collins, 1992).
[12]It is also possible for population growth to be so slow that the population ages and retirement takes people out of the workforce. This has occurred in some developing countries because of increasing longevity; however, most of these nations still exhibit high birth rates.

population of Africa was of working age; the European nations averaged almost 70 percent.

A second reason to suspect that high population growth can lower living standards is based on the law of diminishing returns. Unless there are increases in technology or the capital stock, the marginal product of labor will fall as population grows. This has been the case in the developed nations; it is not true for all less-developed nations.

The Effects of Economic Growth on Population Growth

Economic historians have suggested that most nations go through three stages of demographic transition: Stage I occurs before industrialization. In this stage, birth rates are only slightly higher than death rates, so population growth is relatively slow. Industrialization ushers in Stage II. In this stage, death rates fall significantly and population growth accelerates. Rapid population growth is necessary to supply labor for the newly industrializing economy. Stage III is the period of *demographic transition*. During this stage, the birth rate declines significantly and population growth slows. Economic growth continues, so the growth in per capita income accelerates.

The theory of demographic transition is important because it introduces the idea that slower population growth is consistent with economic growth. In fact, we have seen this pattern almost everywhere in the world. As economies reach a certain level of industrialization, population growth comes under control. This suggests that one solution to the population problem is to raise living standards. However, the theory does not offer anything to help us speed up the process of population control. Just knowing that a solution to the population problem is a higher standard of living does not tell us how to raise the living standard in the places where it is most necessary.

Economics and Population Choice

Part of the reason why population growth has slowed in the developed nations is economic evolution: as the economy evolves from agriculture to industry, it is less important for families to have children to take over the farm. Culture can also have an important effect on population. In some cultures, large families are still considered a status symbol.

Some economists believe that as people become more educated and birth control becomes more widely available, economic reasoning and rational decision making will lower the average family size. According to this view, children are consumer goods, and economic evolution reduces the value of chidren in several ways. For example, in an agricultural society, children were needed to work the farm; this is not the case in an industrial economy. In less-developed societies without social security systems, large families were necessary for old-age security. Finally, children reduce the family income when both parents work outside the home because they must pay for day care. All of these factors reduce the value of children and increase the attractiveness of smaller families.[13]

---

[13]This view was developed most fully by Nobel laureate Gary Becker in *Treatise on the Family* (Cambridge, Mass.: Harvard University Press, 1981).

But even assuming that individuals use economic logic and choose to have small families, there are externalities associated with children that suggest that government involvement in family planning may be necessary. First, rapid population growth tends to increase income inequality: the poor have large families and get poorer; the rich have small families and get richer. Second, most nations subsidize education, and although parents pay some of the cost of education, there is little connection between tax liability and the number of children attending school. Because parents recognize neither the externality of income inequality nor the extra education subsidies, private choice will tend to result in families that are too big—at least from the economist's standpoint of efficiency.[14]

For these—and other—reasons, many nations have programs designed to make it easy to choose small families. Many clinics in the United States dispense free condoms and other forms of birth control to low-income people. Both men and women in India are paid to accept voluntary sterilization.[15] Some countries have gone even farther: the Chinese are given tax breaks for only one child, and abortions are "encouraged" for subsequent pregnancies. Singapore has perhaps the most interesting birth control program: income tax breaks decline as the number of children increases—except for families where both parents are college educated.

RECAP   Population

Few economists believe that we are on the brink of a massive worldwide population problem, but unchecked population growth does place increasing pressure on world resources and leads to increasing amounts of waste and pollution.

1. World population has more than doubled since 1950 and will probably double again in 20 years. The U.S. population is approximately 260 million and represents about 5 percent of the world population. Population growth in the United States has slowed in recent years; this is not the case in most less-developed nations.

2. Population is a factor of production, so population growth can generate economic growth. However, rapid population growth can increase the number of people too young to work relative to working-age people. This can cause per capita income to fall.

3. Some economists believe that family size is largely an economic choice. Large families are less necessary in industrial economies than in agricultural economies. Children also reduce the income of working parents. This may explain why population growth is lower in the advanced nations than in the less-developed nations.

---

[14]Economic factors probably do have an effect on the population choice of many people, but they are not the only factors and may not even be the main factors. Many noneconomic factors—religion, customs, love, and so on—also affect population choice and birth control. There is also a counterargument to the desirability of small families: low population growth can make it difficult to sustain social security systems.

[15]But it should be noted that Indira Gandhi lost an election in the late 1970s, at least partially because of her strong stand in favor of birth control.

POLICY IN THE GLOBAL SETTING

Air and water pollution share a common attribute: they can cross international boundaries. For example, factory smoke—especially smoke containing sulfur oxide and nitrogen oxide—produced in one country often travels to another country where it can result in what is called *acid rain*. When sulfur and nitrogen oxide particles fall to earth—either as dry particles or in rainfall—they can damage plant and animal life and can also change the pH balance of lake water. We cannot taste the difference, but acid rain allegedly has been responsible for killing fish in many lakes in Canada, the United States, and much of Western Europe.

Another kind of air pollution that crosses international boundaries comes from chlorofluorocarbons (CFCs). CFCs have been used as propellants in aerosol cans, air conditioners, and certain other products. There is evidence that CFCs collect in the upper atmosphere and are responsible for a hole in the ozone layer of the atmosphere above Antarctica.[16] The ozone layer offers protection from ultraviolet rays from the sun that have been shown to be responsible for skin cancer. Skin cancer rates have increased worldwide, but especially in the southern hemisphere. Plants and animals are also affected by high doses of ultraviolet rays. The use of CFCs in aerosol cans produced in the United States has been outlawed since 1988, and most other chemicals harmful to the ozone layer will be outlawed by 1995. But until CFCs are banned worldwide, destruction of the ozone layer may continue—and create potential harm for people regardless of whether CFCs are banned in their home countries or not.

The international scope of water pollution should be obvious. Rivers run across international boundaries, so any water pollution upstream becomes a problem downstream. What may be less well-known is that ocean pollution has become severe in recent decades. Solid waste from the United States shows up frequently in Central and South America; oil spills in international waters damage beaches and fisheries around the globe; the list goes on.

Solving these problems requires an international effort, but global cooperation on the environment is easier said than done for several reasons. For one thing, nations with different income levels place a different value on the environment. Low-income nations often feel that they cannot afford environmental protection because it might cause unemployment and slow economic growth. For example, one of the key sticking points in the North American Free Trade Agreement (NAFTA) was that environmental rules were more lax in Mexico than in the United States. Many people in the United States felt that this gave Mexico an unfair advantage in trade, but Mexico was hesitant to adopt stiffer environmental standards because it felt it could not afford to. Numerous examples occurred after the breakup of the former Soviet Union. For example, Sweden and Finland were concerned about air and water pollution coming from the Baltic nations—Estonia, Latvia, and Lithuania—yet these nations could hardly afford the measures necessary to clean up their environment, much less convert to modern, nonpolluting production methods. The Focus box on page 546 looks at this issue in more detail.

---

[16]We need to add that while many scientists find this evidence persuasive, some scientists scoff at the idea of a hole in the ozone layer as well as the linkage to CFCs.

ENVIRONMENTAL PROBLEMS IN THE FORMER SOVIET UNION

Why did the Soviet Union collapse? The standard economic argument goes like this: Centralized planning is inherently inefficient, so it was impossible for Soviet planners to produce the quantity and quality of goods that consumers wanted. The resulting shortages caused long waiting lines. Consumers grudgingly tolerated the lines, but only as long as the success of Western capitalism could be hidden from them. As news from the West leaked into the Soviet Union, discontent rose until the socialist system came to a screeching halt.

This is a good story with more than a little truth to it, but some authors have argued that the collapse of the Soviet system was caused, in large part at least, by the utter lack of concern for the environment or public health. Soviet citizens did not need to understand economics or know of a better life in the West to realize that their

health and environment were deteriorating. Environmental and ecological activists spearheaded the political movements in the Baltic Republics in 1988 and 1989, and similar movements appeared throughout the Soviet Union soon after. By early 1991, KGB officials conceded that the Soviet Union was on the verge of ecological crisis, but by then it was too late. When the Greens broadened their focus and expanded their influence, the collapse of the system became imminent.

Just how bad were public health and the Soviet environment? In a district of Turkmenistan, bacteria in the drinking water were blamed for the 1989 *official* infant mortality rate of 66.1 per thousand live births. A neighboring district reported that just over half of the population was sick with respiratory, circulatory, and other illnesses. To irrigate cotton fields, so much water has been taken from the

Aral Sea in Central Asia that the sea is evaporating, causing one of the greatest ecological catastrophes in history. In the factory city of Magnitogorsk, 90 percent of all children have pollution-related illnesses, and a clinic has been established to give "oxygen cocktails" to children and older citizens.

The ecological crisis in the Soviet Union was interesting in several ways. In theory at least, market capitalism generated efficiency while socialism, though inefficient, is supposed to establish equity. But the totalitarian socialist regime in the Soviet Union ignored public health and the environment even more than did the market-oriented United States. For example, although DDT was outlawed in 1970 in the Soviet Union, it was still being used in the late 1980s "by special permission." This is not a problem of socialist planning; it is a problem of a corrupt political system.

. . . .

The 1992 Earth Summit

The need for global cooperation on the environment has led to a number of international conferences and a series of international accords. One of the most recent was the United Nations Commission on Environment and Development Conference—popularly known as the Earth Summit—that took place in Rio de Janeiro in the summer of 1992. Two of the main topics at the conference were biodiversity and climate change, issues that clearly transcend international boundaries. Also discussed was the particularly thorny problem of rich countries imposing their environmental standards on poor countries. Finally, the conference discussed the relationship

In Nava, Estonia, a power station spews smoke from burning old shale.

In many other cases, socialist economics complicated the regulatory process. Soviet economic theory did not put a real price on resources held by the state, so trying to come up with a viable system of regulations and fees was difficult or impossible. In 1990, 70 factory directors were fined for discharging polluted water. Their fine was 50 rubles—almost enough to buy two packs of imported cigarettes.

Things have not improved very much since the breakup. Many of the new nations, starved for hard currency to buy much-needed imported goods, are accepting Western garbage for a fee. In the summer of 1992, for example, the German company ATG paid a former official of the Estonian government to accept 5,000 tons of used tires, ostensibly for use in Estonia's electricity generating plants. Soon after Estonian officials found out that there were no plans to modify the plants so they could use tires as fuel, the tires "mysteriously" erupted in flames. There have also been reports of organic waste, plastic, and other products being imported—for a fee—with labels reading "humanitarian aid."

What can be done about the environment in the former Soviet Union? Unfortunately, we cannot expect the countries to do much for themselves. Taking care of the environment is a luxury that the rich can afford, not the poor. Without massive aid from the West, we are likely to see continued environmental degradation.

SOURCES: Murray Feshbach and Alfred Friendly, Jr., *Ecocide in the USSR* (New York: Basic Books, 1992); William S. Brown, "Economic Transition in Estonia," *Journal of Economic Issues* (June 1993).

between the rules of international trade and environmental policy. The issue was a hot one because according to the General Agreement on Tariffs and Trade (GATT) policy, nations are not supposed to use trade sanctions to pressure for environmental reform. The United States, for example, violated GATT protocol when it limited tuna imports from Mexico because Mexican tuna fishers use nets that kill dolphins.

The Earth Summit concluded with over 800 pages of "green" guidelines and two treaties, one on the climate and one on biodiversity. President Bush chose not to sign the biodiversity treaty arguing that it was not well conceived. President Clinton did sign the treaty in 1993, but with some reservations. Other accomplishments of the Earth Summit included the establishment of the Sustainable Development Com-

FOCUS ON

THE PROBLEMS OF INTERNATIONAL COOPERATION: A GAME-THEORETIC APPROACH

Finding solutions to environmental problems in one country is hard enough, but trying to reach international agreements is even more difficult. Just how difficult was studied by Iowa State University economist Todd Sandler when he applied game theory to global environmental problems. As we learned in Chapter 14, game theory is a method for studying strategic interaction between different groups. Games involve players, payoffs, and strategies. By understanding the consequences of different strategies, it is often possible to find the most likely outcome to a given situation.

Suppose the world is composed of two countries, Nation A and Nation B, both of which pollute the environment. Further, the pollution crosses international boundaries. The cost of cleaning up pollution in each country is 12, but *both* countries benefit by 10 if either country curbs its pollution. The first payoff matrix represents the possible outcomes to this pollution game. The entries in the cell in the northwest corner indicate that if both countries curb pollution, they will each have a net gain of 8. This represents 20 in benefits (10 + 10) minus 12 for the cost of the cleanup. The

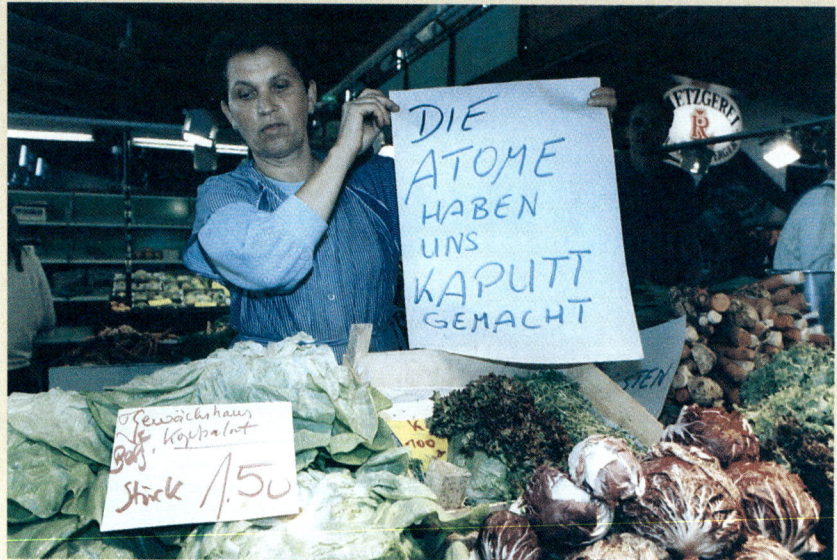

The atoms have destroyed us. A Frankfurt grocer has difficulty selling leafy green vegetables in May of 1986, weeks after the Chernobyl accident.

cells in the off-diagonal indicate what will happen if one country cleans up but the other does not: the country that cleans up will lose 2 (10 − 12) while the country that does not curb pollution will gain 10 and incur zero costs. The cell in the southeast corner indicates that if neither country curbs pollution, the gains will be zero.

What is the most likely outcome of this game? We can answer this question by applying the principles of game

theory and looking at the situation from either country's perspective. Look at the game from the perspective of Nation A: if Nation B curbs pollution, Nation A will gain 10 by doing nothing, but have a net gain of only 8 by spending 12 to curb pollution. The best choice is to do nothing. On the other hand, if Nation B decides not to curb pollution, Nation A will lose 2 if it cuts pollution but will lose nothing if it continues to pollute. Again the best choice is to not curb pollution. The result is that the game will end up in the southeast corner with neither country curbing its pollution. In the terminology of game theory, this game is a prisoner's dilemma, and the solution is a dominant strategy equilibrium.

The solution to game theory problems depends on the payoffs available to the players, and different payoff structures will result in different solutions. For example, if the cost of curbing emissions is only 8 but each country gains 10, the outcome will be for both countries to curb pollution. (This situation is analyzed in Problem 8 at the end of the chapter.) It is also possible to have a situation where *both* countries must curb pollution before either country gains. Such a situation is illustrated in the second payoff matrix. Notice that if both countries curb pollution, each gains 8; if neither cuts pollution, the gains are zero. However, if just one country curbs pollution, it will lose 12. This game has two possible outcomes—either both will curb pollution or neither will. These two equilibria are called Nash equilibria. The best outcome from society's standpoint—curb/curb—can be assured only if the countries establish treaties or agreements to cooperate

Nation A

Actions →	Curb	Don't Curb
Nation B Curb	A:8 B:8	A:10 B:−2
Don't Curb	A:−2 B:10	A:0 B:0

Nation A

Actions →	Curb	Don't Curb
Nation B Curb	A:8 B:8	A:0 B:−12
Don't Curb	A:−12 B:0	A:0 B:0

and have the ability to monitor each other's actions.

Which scenario best describes the problem of international pollution? We cannot really generalize. Professor Sandler believes that all of these cases have applications to the real world. The prisoner's dilemma, he believes, is a good model of global warming; deforestation may be an example of a Nash equilibrium as in the second matrix. Still, we can reach some important conclusions: First, various kinds of

strategies are associated with different environmental problems, so different solutions will be necessary. Second, unilateral actions can often be counterproductive. Finally, precisely because multilateral actions are necessary, forums like the Earth Summit must be ongoing and must focus on finding interdependent solutions to global environmental problems.

SOURCE: Todd Sandler, "After the Cold War, Secure the Global Commons," *Challenge* (July/August 1992): 16–23.

mission and increased aid for the Global Environment Facility. The Sustainable Development Commission develops guidelines to support reduced production of global-warming gases. The Global Environment Facility provides funds to support the two treaties.

It remains to be seen whether the treaties of the Earth Summit will have much of an effect on the global environment, but that a conference of this scope was held at all is significant. More than 20 years had passed since the last international conference on the environment. The wide attention directed toward the Earth Summit suggests that it will not be 20 years before another conference on the global environment is held. Nevertheless, as the international cooperation Focus box on page 548 shows, international cooperation on environmental matters will always be difficult.

RECAP   The Global Environment and Cooperation

Many environmental issues are transnational because they affect more than one country. This is especially true of air and water pollution. Transnational environmental problems may require international cooperation and meetings like the 1992 Earth Summit. Such cooperation can be difficult because nations with different incomes value the environment differently.

SUMMARY

Activists complain that the environment is being degraded, that we are running out of resources, and that population is exploding. Few would deny that there is some truth to these claims, but some significant environmental successes have also been achieved: the air in many cities is cleaner than it was a decade ago, the waters of the Great Lakes are less polluted than they used to be, and population growth is slowing, if only in the developed nations. Still, it is far too soon to become complacent. Scientists warn that our estimates of optimal harvest rates are imprecise, so we must be forever on guard against crossing the sustainable yield threshold. Nor do we know the long-run and possibly carcinogenic effects of the pollution we breathe, drink, and eat everyday. Finally, we must recognize that the earth is a closed system; the resources available to us are in fixed supply. And one of those resources is storage space for the millions of tons of waste produced daily.

The problems of the environment are serious and will not go away by themselves, but public awareness does appear to be increasing. Combine that with technological advance and the fact that economists have a great deal to say about the problem, and we may be able to make it to the next century after all.

The main points from this chapter are:

1. The earth can be considered a closed system where the two laws of thermodynamics hold: (1) The amount of energy and matter is fixed and cannot be increased or decreased, and (2) entropy increases over time.
2. Many resources are common property resources in the sense that they can be used by everyone. In the absence of government intervention, common

property resources will be overutilized. This can result in species extinction and destruction of the environment.

3. Most scientists believe that it is important to maintain biodiversity—the genetic variability within a species and among different species. Biodiversity is necessary to maintain species vigor. Additionally, scientific research often requires a wide variety of species, and there can be aesthetic reasons for species preservation as well.

4. The optimal quantity of pollution is not zero. Pollution should be reduced only until the marginal benefit of pollution reduction is equal to the marginal cost. Economists generally prefer to reduce pollution with taxes rather than direct controls. When the pollution is very toxic, however, the optimal quantity of pollution may be zero, and direct controls may be preferable to taxes. When possible, assigning property rights to pollution and allowing free-market transaction for the right to pollute may be desirable.

5. Population growth has slowed in the United States but is still rapid elsewhere, especially in the less-developed nations. Population growth often falls as the standard of living increases.

6. Many environmental problems cross international boundaries and require international solutions. This is especially true of air and water pollution. The 1992 Earth Summit sought to arrive at multilateral environmental standards, but it is proving difficult to establish policies that are acceptable to countries with different incomes and living standards.

KEY TERMS AND CONCEPTS

closed system
open system
first law of thermodynamics
second law of thermodynamics
entropy
common property rights
tragedy of the commons
biodiversity
maximum sustainable yield
optimal level of pollution

taxes versus direct controls
pollution rights
age distribution
fertility rate
replacement rate
per capita income
demographic transition
acid rain
Earth Summit

REVIEW QUESTIONS

1. State the two laws of thermodynamics. Explain how these laws place limits on economic activity.
2. What are common property rights? Explain why common property resources are overutilized in the absence of government intervention. Draw a diagram to illustrate your answer. How does the concept of maximum sustainable yield relate to this issue?
3. Why do economists generally favor pollution taxes to direct controls? Under what conditions might direct controls be preferred? When is it best to establish a market for pollution?

4. How does population growth in the United States compare to population growth in the developing nations? What are some of the possible implications of unchecked population growth?

5. When does pollution become an international problem? Why is international cooperation on pollution policy so difficult?

PROBLEMS

1. Refer back to the definition of a public good in Chapter 18, and explain how well biodiversity fits the definition. Give specific examples and comment.

2. In some countries, food prices are controlled to make it easier for poor people to eat. This policy tends to increase the population of the society at large, but decreases the population of farm children. Explain.

3. Does nuclear energy refute the laws of thermodynamics?

4. One of the reasons whales were hunted almost to extinction was that they were considered a common property resource. Today, strict regulations limit whale harvesting, but Norway and Japan continue to press for more lenient restrictions. Do you think it would be wise to "give" the entire whale population to Norway and Japan? Or would it be better to press for voluntary whaling limits by all nations?

5. Economists generally prefer taxes to direct controls; yet the public often seems to prefer direct pollution controls to pollution taxes. Why does this disagreement exist? What economic ideas would the public need to be taught to understand the economist's point of view?

6. Population growth seems to follow a predictable cycle of demographic transition as nations develop economically. Outline this cycle and explain why it exists. Also, explain why some economists believe that the best solution to the population problem is economic development.

7. Many environmental problems are transnational in scope—pollution is created in one nation but spreads to other nations. This suggests that environmental policy must be international, but achieving cooperation on environmental policy has proved to be very difficult. What are the main *economic* reasons for the difficulty in achieving global cooperation on environmental problems?

8. The following payoff matrix represents the outcomes from a global cooperation pollution control game. The cost of cleaning the environment is 8 to each country; the benefits are 10 to each country when either nation curbs pollution. Thus, if Nation A curbs pollution but Nation B does not, Nation A will gain 2 (= 10 − 8) while Nation B will gain 10 (= 10 − 0). The most likely outcome from this game is for both nations to curb pollution. Explain *why* this is the most likely outcome.

		Nation A	
	Actions →	*Curb*	*Don't Curb*
Nation B	*Curb*	A:12 B:12	A:10 B:2
	Don't Curb	A:2 B:10	A:0 B:0

PART V

MACROECONOMIC FUNDAMENTALS

CHAPTER 22

The Gross Domestic Product: Definitions, Trends, and Cycles

When you see economists on television, they are often making forecasts: Is the economy about to enter a recession? Is an acceleration of inflation around the corner? Forecasting is far from an exact science, but economists do look for certain regularities, events that occur time and again. For example, when gross domestic product (GDP) growth slows, unemployment almost always increases, and when GDP growth accelerates, inflation often increases at some point in the future. Much of the process of macroeconomic theorizing is an attempt to explain these and other "stylized facts" of the economy. This chapter presents an overview of the stylized facts of the U.S. economy in the twentieth century.

Much of our focus in this chapter will be on the GDP, so the first section will define GDP in some detail. After that, we will present some facts about U.S. economic performance and point out the regularities that all good theories must be able to explain. We will close this chapter with a brief look at some of the theories economists have used in the past to help them understand economic fluctuations. Although these theories are less popular today, they will help us appreciate the evolution of economic theory and put contemporary macroeconomics into historical perspective.

AFTER READING AND STUDYING THIS CHAPTER, YOU SHOULD BE ABLE TO:
- • • Define GDP and list its major components
- • • Know the recent behavior of and relationships between GDP growth, inflation, unemployment, and productivity growth
- • • Discuss and explain the modern relevance of early theories of the business cycle

WHAT IS THE GDP?

In the midst of the Great Depression of the 1930s, it became apparent that economists needed better ways to measure economic activity: How could we tell the magnitude of the depression if we had no way to measure it? This became a chief concern of Wesley Claire Mitchell (1874–1948), who, as director of the National Bureau of Economic Research, had been involved in the study of business cycles since early in the century. In the 1930s, Mitchell began working with Simon Kuznets (1901–1985) on the development of the system of national income accounting that is still used today.[1] Kuznets continued research in this area throughout his career and, along with the British economist Richard Stone (1913–), was awarded the 1971 Nobel Prize in economics for his work.

Modern national income accountants use several measures to describe aggregate economic activity, but none are more important than the gross domestic product:

> **Gross Domestic Product (GDP). GDP is the market value of all final goods and services produced within the nation in a year.**

There are several important points to remember about GDP:

- *GDP measures only legal market transactions.* Illegal transactions—prostitution, illicit drugs, illegal gambling, and so on—are omitted from the GDP. These transactions take place in what is often called the **underground economy** and are omitted from GDP calculations. The underground economy also includes transactions that are hidden from the government to avoid taxes. By some estimates, GDP is underestimated by as much as 15 percent because of the omission of underground transactions. The underground economy is discussed in more detail in the Focus box on page 558. Most nonmarket activities, for example, nonpaid work of housekeepers, are also omitted from GDP calculations.
- *GDP counts only final products.* If intermediate products as well as final products were counted, the estimate of GDP would be too high. An intermediate product is one that goes into the production of another product. For example, if you spend $10,000 for a new automobile, GDP will increase by $10,000. It would be incorrect to count intermediate products that went into the production of the car—tires, motor, windshield, and so on—separately because this would result in double counting and an overestimate of GDP. If you buy a new stereo for your car, however, GDP will increase because the stereo is a final product sold to the end consumer. Does the sale of a used car add to GDP? Only sometimes, and then only part of the selling price: when a used car dealer repairs or fixes your old clunker before selling it, the dealer's "value added" is counted toward GDP.
- *GDP is a flow variable.* GDP is a rate of production over time, not a stock of goods

Underground economy Transactions not counted in GDP; includes barter, illegal activities, and transactions that are not reported in order to avoid taxes.

[1]Both Mitchell and Kuznets are usually associated with the institutionalist school of thought, the same school associated with Thorstein Veblen (see Chapter 3). They are associated with this school because both aimed to study the real economy and neither stressed abstract theorizing. A collection of Mitchell's essays, *The Backward Act of Spending Money* (1937) may be the most accessible introduction to his work.

and services that have been produced. The phrase "annual GDP is running at $6 trillion" means that at the current rate of production, $6 trillion worth of final goods and services will be produced this year. As we pointed out in Chapter 5, flow variables have a time dimension; stock variables do not. The amount of money you have in your checking account is a stock variable; the amount of income you earn every week is a flow variable.

• *GDP is a measure of production, not well-being.* An increase in GDP means more jobs, but it can also mean more pollution, traffic congestion, and other negative by-products. Some environmentalists wonder whether society can afford ever growing GDP and even question whether society is better off with more GDP. Economists recognize the costs of pollution, but also note that cleaning up the environment would add to GDP. Social scientists are at work trying to generate a measure of economic welfare, but as yet have not been able to develop a good one.

One attempt to calculate economic welfare is the **measure of economic welfare (MEW)** developed by William Nordhaus and James Tobin. MEW is constructed by deducting from GDP certain items that do not add to economic welfare and adding those that do but are not counted in GDP. Among the most important deletions are the cost of national defense and police protection and losses associated with pollution. Why are these deleted? National defense and police protection do not provide benefits directly; they only reduce the chance of getting "negative benefits" from war or crime. Similarly, pollution reduces our quality of life, and if we pay to clean it up, we are using up resources that could have been used to produce goods. Additions include leisure time—people value leisure time, but it is not calculated in GDP unless income is spent enjoying leisure—and the value of goods and services that are not sold through the market.[2] The largest nonmarket service is that of spouses who work at home for no pay. MEW estimates are imprecise (at best), but Nordhaus and Tobin believe that our well-being has grown less rapidly than GDP.

Measure of economic welfare (MEW) An estimate of national economic well-being calculated by deducting from GDP items that do not contribute to economic welfare (e.g., the cost of national defense) and adding items that do contribute to well-being (e.g., leisure time).

CALCULATING GDP

There are three main ways to calculate GDP: the value-added approach, the income-received approach, and the expenditure approach. The Commerce Department uses the value-added approach when it generates its quarterly estimates of GDP based on data collected primarily from tax returns and manufacturing surveys. The other two approaches are usually more useful for theoretical economics.

GDP Is the Sum of Value Added

The value-added approach to GDP accounting is used to reduce the chance of double counting intermediate and final products. Figure 22.1 illustrates the value-added

---

[2]The issue of leisure time is especially important. As Juliet B. Schor documents, American workers have been spending more hours on the job every year for the past 20 years. See her best-selling book, *The Overworked American* (New York: Basic Books, 1992).

FOCUS ON

THE UNDERGROUND ECONOMY

The underground economy consists of three major kinds of activities: (1) illegal activities, such as prostitution, drugs, and other criminal activities; (2) working "off the books" to avoid taxes, and (3) working without necessary permits, as in the case of illegal aliens. By some estimates, GDP may be understated by as much as 15 percent due to the underground economy. Everyone knows the underground economy exists, but it is exceedingly difficult to estimate its size—precisely because it is underground.

We need to be concerned about the underground economy for several reasons. First, the existence of the underground economy means that GDP is higher and unemployment is lower than published figures indicate. Policy-makers cannot design effective policies without reliable information. Second, people working in the underground economy do not pay taxes. In this era of massive government deficits, this may be especially important.

WHY DO PEOPLE ENGAGE IN UNDERGROUND ACTIVITY?

One of the biggest reasons people participate in the underground economy

FIGURE 22.1 GDP IS THE SUM OF VALUE ADDED

The Commerce Department calculates GDP by summing the value added at each stage of production in order to avoid double counting. In this example, GDP is found by adding the contribution of the farmer ($50), the miller ($100), and the baker ($200): $50 + $100 + $200 = $350, which is the value of the final product, bread. This assumes that the baker sold the bread directly to the consumer and not to a restaurant.

is to evade taxes. When a doctor "trades" his services to the plumber, both have earned income, and neither is likely to be caught if they choose not to report the transaction to the Internal Revenue Service. Drug dealers and prostitutes may work simply to make the high incomes that come from illegal activities—incomes that, ironically, would be lower if these activities were made legal. Finally, some people may engage in underground activity simply as a rebellion against society.

HOW IS THE SIZE OF THE UNDERGROUND ECONOMY ESTIMATED?

Since these activities are illegal, any estimate of the underground economy is a "guesstimate," at best. Several methods have been used to estimate its size. One of the most popular methods is based on the idea that most underground activity involves cash. Thus, any deviation from the trend of the ra-

tio between cash and economic activity is seen as an indication of underground activity. In 1979, Edward Feige used such a method and estimated that the underground economy equaled 27 percent of GDP, but several people have criticized this estimate as being far too high. For example, Vito Tanzi used an elaborate statistical model relating currency demand to a number of economic variables and concluded that the underground economy was between 4.5 percent and 6 percent of GDP.

THE UNDERGROUND ECONOMY IN OTHER COUNTRIES

The size of the underground economy is influenced by differences in culture and attitudes toward government. Italy is generally thought to have the largest underground economy, perhaps 25 percent of measured GDP. Italian shopkeepers routinely keep two sets of books and often use two

cash registers. The underground economy in Russia could be even larger—but the data are so poor that no one really knows. Despite high taxes, the underground in Britain is probably fairly small—under 5 percent of GDP. The underground economy in Switzerland is smaller yet, almost certainly less than 3 percent of reported GDP.

POLICY IMPLICATIONS

Recognition of the underground economy was an important element in the 1982–1984 tax cuts. The Reagan administration felt that lower tax *rates* would reduce the incentive for tax evasion, cause people to exit the underground, and thus increase tax *revenues*. However, tax revenues fell significantly when tax rates were cut. It may be one thing to say that people will not cheat to avoid low taxes, but it is quite another to say that they will stop cheating once they have figured out how to do so.

approach. Suppose that the total final production of a nation consists entirely of bread. Finding the value of bread production (= GDP) using the value-added technique involves summing the value added at each stage of production. First, take the $50 worth of wheat the farmer produced and sold to the miller. The miller added $100 of value when he converted the $50 of wheat into $150 worth of flour. Likewise, the baker converted $150 worth of flour into $350 worth of bread by adding $200 of baking value. The total GDP of our bread-only-producing nation is thus $50 + $100 + $200 = $350. Notice what would happen if we summed the selling prices instead of the value added at each stage of production: $50 + $150 + $350 = $550. In other words, GDP would be greater than final value because of double counting.

Though conceptually simple, distinguishing between final and intermediate products can sometimes be difficult. For example, here we assumed that the bread was a final product because it was bought for home consumption. If the baker sold the bread to a restaurant, however, it would be an intermediate product ultimately destined to be sold to a restaurant customer. In this case, the $350 would be increased by the value added by the restaurant.

The Income-Received Approach

The income-received approach to GDP accounting calls attention to an important fact that we will need to use time and again in the next few chapters; *GDP is equal to the total income paid out in the economy*. The reasoning is straightforward. There are four sources of income in the economy: wages and salaries, rents, interest, and profits. Wages and salaries are earned by labor; rents are paid to land owners; interest is paid to the owners of capital; and profits are earned by entrepreneurs. Income payments depend on the productive contributions of the factor owners, so total factor payments equal the value of production. As a result, the sum of all income paid out in the economy is equal to GDP. This can be expressed as an equation:

$$\text{GDP} = \text{domestic income} = \text{wages} + \text{rents} + \text{interest} + \text{profits} \qquad [1]$$

There are some complications with using this method to calculate GDP,[3] but conceptually, this method would generate the same answer as the value-added approach. For much macroeconomic analysis, however, we will find that the expenditure approach is more useful.

The Expenditure Approach

The basis of the expenditure approach is that GDP is purchased by four groups: consumers, firms, government, and foreigners. This allows us to divide GDP into four major components: personal consumption expenditures, business investment expenditures, government purchases, and net exports. The equation for this method is:

$$\text{GDP} = E = C + I + G + (X - Z) \qquad [2]$$

Where:

$$\text{GDP} = E = \text{total expenditures on final goods and services}$$
$$C = \text{consumption spending}$$
$$I = \text{investment spending}$$
$$G = \text{government purchases}$$
$$X = \text{exports}$$
$$Z = \text{imports}[4]$$
$$(X - Z) = \text{net exports}$$

Equation 2 is quite important, so we need to elaborate on it here.

---

[3]The most important complications involve depreciation and indirect business taxes. These are treated in more detail in the appendix to this chapter.

[4]The letter "*Z*" is used for imports because we are reserving the letter "*M*" for money in later chapters.

FOCUS ON

IS THERE A VALUE-ADDED TAX IN THE FUTURE?

The United States has considered adopting a value-added tax (VAT) for several years now, at least partially in response to the record government deficits of the 1980s and 1990s. Value-added taxes are common throughout the world; in fact, all countries in Western Europe have them.

A VAT would be implemented by taxing the value added at each stage of production. In the example illustrated in Figure 22.1, a 10 percent VAT would cost the farmer $5, and since she would pass this tax on to the miller, wheat would sell for $55. Assuming every intermediate producer passed the VAT on the next level of production, a 10 percent VAT would raise the selling price by 10 percent. Thus, bread would now sell for $385.[1]

Three main objections have been raised to VATs. First, a VAT affects the economy just like a sales tax, which means that it falls most heavily on the poor who spend most of their income. The rich can avoid sales and value-added taxes by saving their

money. Second, many people are hesitant to give the government another power to tax: a 5 percent VAT this year could mean a 7 percent VAT next year, 10 percent the next, and so on. Finally, some have argued that a VAT would reduce investment because it raises the cost of investment goods.

Some economists believe that a careful design could minimize a VAT's negative impact on the economy. For example, allowing VAT deductions for exported goods might encourage exports. This is already being done in Europe. Second, some economists believe that the income tax should be reduced (or even eliminated) and replaced with a VAT. The hope is that such a move would encourage saving: a VAT taxes only spending, not saving; an income tax taxes both.

[1]This assumes that all sellers can pass on the entire amount of the VAT. In general, they cannot—a point we illustrated in Chapter 4.

VAT REFUNDS FOR VISITORS TO THE UNITED KINGDOM

Most countries which have a VAT provide foreign visitors with an opportunity for refunds.

Consumption. **Consumption** expenditures constitute the largest portion of GDP, approximately 65 percent in 1993 (see Table 22.1). In most recent years, consumers have spent about 95 percent of their after-tax income (termed *disposable personal income*) on consumption. The remainder is treated as saving by national income accountants. The biggest and fastest-growing component of consumer spending is on consumer services. Consumer services include rent and the rental value of owner-occupied housing, medical care, transportation, entertainment, and other items. Consumption spending on goods is divided into consumer *durables* and *nondurables*. Dura-

Consumption Household spending on consumer goods and services.

TABLE 22.1 THE EXPENDITURE COMPONENTS OF GDP, 1960–1993

Year	GDP	C	I	G	X	Z	(X − Z)
1960	$1,971	$1,211	$291	$477	$ 88	$ 96	$ −8
1970	2,874	1,814	430	666	161	196	−35
1980	3,776	2,447	594	704	321	290	+31
1985	4,280	2,866	746	813	309	455	−146
1988	4,719	3,162	773	887	422	526	−104
1989	4,838	3,223	784	904	472	545	−54
1990	4,897	3,273	747	933	511	565	−55
1991	4,861	3,259	676	946	543	563	−19
1992	4,986	3,342	733	945	578	612	−34
1993p	5,133	3,353	821	939	596	676	−79
Average annual growth rate, 1960–1993:	2.94%	3.13%	3.19%	2.07%	5.97%	6.09%	—
Average % of GDP:		66%	16%	20%	8%	10%	—
Range		61–67%	14–18%	19–24%	5–11%	5–12%	—

Consumption is the most stable component of GDP; it has averaged about two-thirds of GDP in recent years. The most volatile component of GDP is investment; business cycle fluctuations are often associated with investment volatility. Government spending is the component of GDP that can be most easily controlled. Exports and imports have grown more rapidly than any other components of GDP.

SOURCE: 1994 *Economic Report of the President,* Table B-2. Data are in billions of 1987 dollars; 1993 data are preliminary.

ble goods include furniture, autos, and other goods expected to last one year or more. Nondurables are used immediately or for only a short period; food and clothing are nondurable goods. An important attribute of consumer spending is that it is relatively stable. What volatility there is can usually be traced to the durable goods component.

Investment. Investment refers to business expenditure on plant and equipment (termed *business fixed investment*), residential construction (housing), and changes in inventories. Inventory changes are classified as investment because current inventories represent future sales. Also, GDP is a measure of this year's production, so anything a firm produces—whether sold or not—must be counted as current GDP. We will discover in the next chapter that there is an important distinction between intended and unintended inventory changes. Both count as part of current GDP, but their effect on the future path of GDP is quite different.

The sum of existing investment goods is called the *capital stock*. **Gross private domestic investment (GPDI)** is a measure of all investment spending. It includes the purchase of machines to replace those worn out as well as those purchased to expand capacity. The cost of worn-out machinery is called *depreciation* or **capital consumption allowances.** Subtracting depreciation from GPDI gives **net private domestic investment** (NPDI):

$$\text{GPDI} - \text{depreciation} = \text{NPDI} \qquad [3]$$

In most cases, NPDI is a better measure of investment because it represents the growth in the capital stock—an important factor for determining economic growth.

Gross private domestic investment (GPDI) The sum of all investment spending, including plant and equipment, residential structures, and inventory changes.

Capital consumption allowance The money set aside for depreciation of plant and equipment.

Net private domestic investment (NPDI) GPDI minus capital consumption allowances; measure of the increase in the capital stock.

For example, suppose that $1,000,000 is spent on gross investment and that each machine costs $100,000. This means that 10 machines are bought. However, if one existing machine must be replaced, then net investment is only $900,000 (= $1,000,000 − $100,000), and productive capacity has expanded by just 9 machines. If 3 machines must be replaced, then net investment is only $700,000, and productive capacity has increased by only 7 machines. The point is that gross investment is the same in each case, but net investment differs, and it is net investment that determines the productive capacity of the economy.

Investment is the most volatile component of GDP. Business cycle fluctuations can frequently be traced to changes in investment, and recent evidence seems to indicate that inventory fluctuations account for the bulk of investment fluctuations.[5] As a percentage of GDP, GPDI has been as low as 2.5 percent in 1933 and as high as 20 percent in some peak years. The 1983–1984 recovery was characterized by an investment boom: GPDI increased from $471.6 billion to $637.3 billion or nearly 17 percent of GDP. In 1993, GPDI was about 16 percent of GDP.

Government Purchases. **Government purchases** must be distinguished from government spending. Government purchases of goods and services represent the production of new products and thus add to GDP. The remainder of government spending (about 40 percent of the federal government's budget) consists largely of **transfer payments**—welfare, Social Security, interest payments on the national debt, and other payments made by the government to households. GDP accountants subtract transfer payments from total government spending because they show up as consumption spending when recipients spend their transfer payments. Transfer payments have been the fastest-growing component of government spending since 1980—and are predicted to continue to grow at close to 4 percent per year between 1994 and 1998.[6]

Like investment, government purchases exhibit some volatility. Nevertheless, there is a fundamental difference between the two: many large changes in government purchases are deliberate and are designed to offset undesirable changes in private sector spending. We will find out why and how changes in the level of government spending (and taxes) affect the economy in later chapters.

Net Exports. **Net exports** is the remaining major component of GDP. Net exports represent the difference between goods and services sold by the United States to foreigners (exports) and goods and services purchased by U.S. residents from foreign countries (imports). Exports from the United States stimulate our economy because income flows into the economy and provides jobs. Why do we subtract imports from exports? Consumption, investment, and government purchases include the amount spent on imported goods as well as those produced domestically, so we must subtract imports to get the amount spent on domestically produced goods. Imports slow the domestic economy because income flows abroad to buy foreign goods. This means

Government purchases Goods and services purchased by the government; accounts for about 60 percent of government spending.

Transfer payments Payments from one party to another without compensation. Government transfer payments include welfare, Social Security benefits, and interest on the national debt.

Net exports The difference between exports and imports.

[5]Alan S. Blinder and Louis S. Maccini, ''Taking Stock: A Critical Assessment of Recent Research in Inventories,'' *Journal of Economic Perspectives* 5 (Winter 1991): 73–96.
[6]This figure is calculated from Chart 1.10 with weights from Table B-78 of the 1994 *Economic Report of the President.*

that the impact of the foreign sector on GDP depends on net exports—the difference between imports and exports. When exports exceed imports, the United States has a trade surplus, and the foreign sector stimulates GDP; when imports exceed exports, the United States has a trade deficit, and the foreign sector exerts a contractionary effect on GDP.

Two important facts should be noted about the foreign sector of the United States. First, both imports and exports have grown significantly since World War II from barely 5 percent of GDP to over 12 percent in 1993. Second, net exports have been consistently negative for more than a decade. The worst years occurred in the mid-1980s when imports exceeded exports by about $150 billion annually, but this shrank to under $20 billion by 1991 before expanding to about $80 billion in 1993.

RECAP   Behavior of the Major Spending Components of GDP

1. Consumption is the largest and most stable component of GDP. Consumer services are the fastest-growing component of consumption; consumer durables are the most unstable component of personal consumption spending.
2. Investment includes plant and equipment expenditures, residential construction, and inventory changes. It is the most volatile component of GDP. Business cycle fluctuations are frequently caused by swings in investment, particularly inventory investment.
3. Government purchases average about 20 percent of GDP. Transfer payments have been the fastest-growing component of government spending for several years.
4. The export sector has been growing rapidly since World War II. The United States has run trade deficits every year since 1980, but the size of these deficits has shrunk from the highs of the mid-1980s.

THE RECORD: U.S. GDP FLUCTUATIONS IN THE TWENTIETH CENTURY

The reason we have spent so much time on GDP is that movements in GDP are closely related to movements in other important macroeconomic aggregates. For example, when GDP growth accelerates, unemployment usually falls and inflation often increases. The overriding characteristic of the U.S. economy has been economic growth. The average annual rate of growth since 1929 has been a little over 3 percent, and real GDP is about three times the size it was in 1950. Growth has not been steady—there have been significant economic fluctuations—but growing GDP has increased our standard of living appreciably. But before we can begin to explain *why* GDP growth has occurred and why there is a relationship between GDP and other economic variables, we need to look at the facts carefully.

GDP Fluctuations

Economic growth has not been steady. Periods of rapid growth seem inevitably to be followed by slower or declining GDP growth. This is shown in panel (a) of Figure

THE GROSS DOMESTIC PRODUCT: DEFINITIONS, TRENDS, AND CYCLES   CHAPTER 22

·····FIGURE 22.2 REAL GDP GROWTH IN THE UNITED STATES, 1929–1993

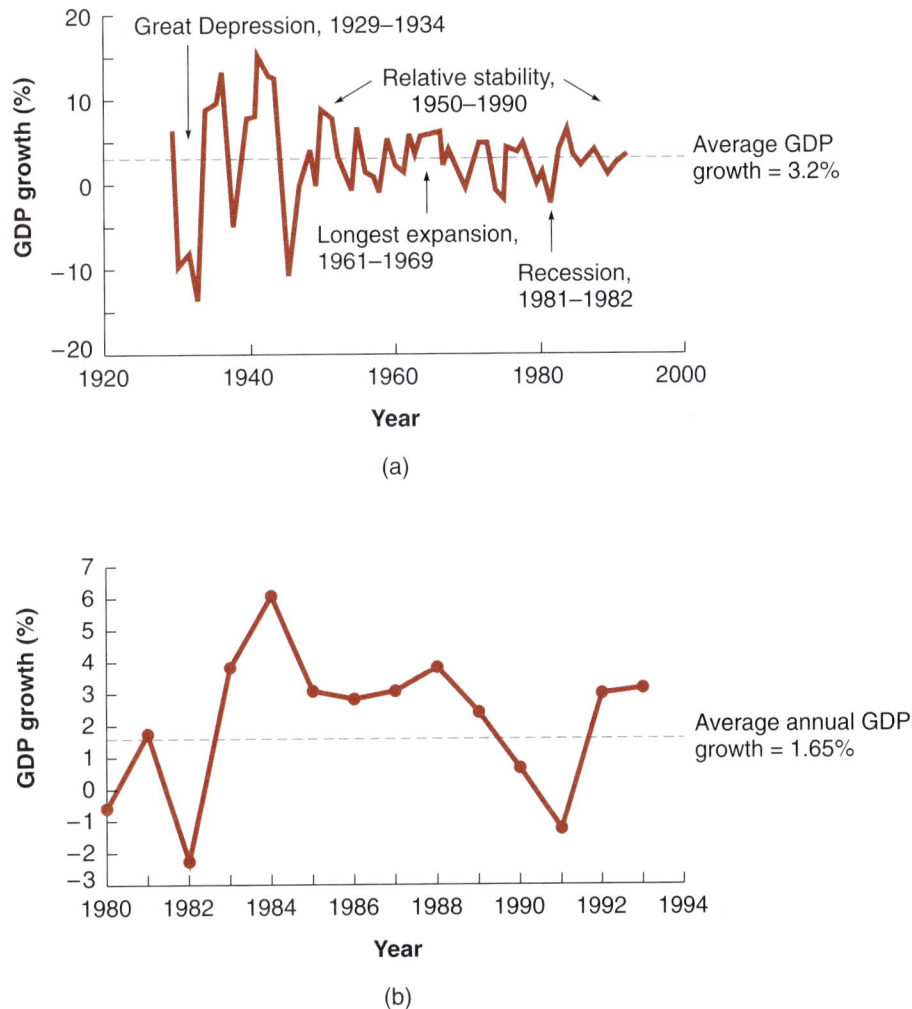

(a)

(b)

GDP growth has averaged about 3.2 percent per year since 1929. The most severe fluctuation, the Great Depression, occurred after the stock market crash in 1929. Fluctuations in the rate of growth appear to have diminished since World War II.

SOURCE: 1929–1960 data, *Historical Statistics of the United States, Colonial Times to 1970,* Series F-31; 1961–1993 data, 1994 *Economic Report of the President,* Table B-2.

22.2, which plots real GDP growth rates from 1929 to 1993. Panel (b) examines real GDP growth since 1980 in more detail.[7]

[7]If you have forgotten the difference between *real* and *nominal* variables, now would be a good time to refresh your memory by turning back to Chapter 5. There we noted that real variables were nominal variables that had been adjusted for inflation. This is usually accomplished by dividing the nominal value by the appropriate price index. Real GDP is equal to nominal GDP divided by the appropriate GDP deflator. Unless otherwise explicitly noted, all data in this chapter are real.

The graphs in Figure 22.2 bring to light several interesting points:

- The average rate of real economic growth since 1929 has been about 3.2 percent. Most economists believe that long-term growth is brought about by three main factors: more workers, a larger stock of capital machines, and increasing labor productivity. We will examine the relative importance of these and other factors in accounting for long-term GDP growth in Chapter 33.

- A severe economic downturn occurred in the 1930s, a period known as the Great Depression. The Great Depression is typically dated from the stock market crash of October 1929, but few economists today believe that the stock market crash was the only cause of the depression. Most economists believe that poor bank lending practices, policy mistakes, and a number of other factors were also important contributors to the Great Depression. Real GDP plunged almost 30 percent between 1929 and 1933 and did not return to its 1929 level until 1939.

- GDP fluctuations appear to have become less severe since about 1950. Economists are not certain why this has occurred. Possibly, economic policy has become more effective, or the economy may have undergone structural changes that have made it more stable.[8]

- Real GDP growth has been slow since 1980, only 1.65 percent per year. This figure improves considerably (to 2.82 percent) if the years of 1980–1983 are omitted, but many economists remain concerned about the recent growth performance of the U.S. economy.

Fluctuations in GDP growth are known as *business cycles*. The term "cycle" is probably inappropriate because it implies a certain regularity. Fluctuations are far from regular—they can vary from 1 to 10 or 12 years in duration—but the history of capitalism has been marked by general expansions followed by general contractions in economic activity. It is useful to think of business cycles as having two phases, expansion and contraction, and two turning points, peak and trough. These phases are illustrated in Figure 22.3. Business cycles are officially dated by the National Bureau of Economic Research or NBER as it is usually called. Whether the economy has entered a new phase of the cycle is always something of a judgment call. Economists at the NBER look at hundreds of different indicators; GDP growth is only one of the more important indicators. It should be noted too that the definition of a recession often heard in the media—two consecutive quarters of negative GDP growth—is *not* the definition used by the NBER. In fact, the NBER has been careful not to issue a formal definition of recession because every recession differs from the previous one. Generally speaking, a recession exists when there is an overall downturn in many economic indicators—GDP, employment, industrial production, and so on. Recessions are costly in human as well as strictly economic terms. People without jobs lose dignity as well as income, and idle machinery does no one any good.

Table 22.2 presents data on the 12 business cycles that have occurred since 1929. While it is apparent that each cycle differs from the previous cycle, we can make some broad generalizations about post–World War II economic fluctuations. The

---

[8]But as we point out in Chapter 33, some economists believe that the economy has *not* become appreciably more stable since 1950.

····**FIGURE 22.3 PHASES OF THE BUSINESS CYCLE**

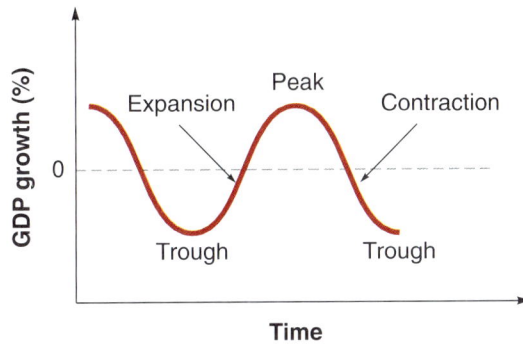

Though every cycle is different, all go through two distinct phases, an expansion and a contraction, and two turning points between phases, the peak and the trough. The NBER dates cycles from trough to trough. The typical post–World War II recession has lasted about one year; the typical expansion has lasted a little less than four years.

····**TABLE 22.2 BUSINESS CYCLES IN THE UNITED STATES, 1929–1991**

Peak	Trough	Unemployment at Peak	Unemployment at Trough	Percentage Change in Real GDP from Peak to Trough
8/29	3/33	3.2%	24.9%	−32.6%
5/37	6/38	11.0	20.0	−18.2
2/45	10/45	0.9	4.3	NA
11/48	10/49	3.8	7.9	−1.5
7/53	5/54	2.5	6.1	−3.2
8/57	4/58	3.7	7.5	−3.3
4/60	2/61	5.0	7.1	−1.2
12/69	11/70	3.4	6.1	−1.0
11/73	3/75	4.6	9.0	−4.9
1/80	7/80	5.7	7.8	−2.5
7/81	12/82	7.2	10.8	−2.6
7/90	3/91	5.5	6.8	−1.6

Post–World War II Averages

Average recession: 11 months
Average expansion: 44 months
Average rise in unemployment in recession: 2.76 percentage points
Average decline in GDP in recession: 1.23%

SOURCES: Geoffrey H. Moore, *Business Cycles, Inflation, and Forecasting,* 2d ed. (Cambridge, Mass.: Ballinger, 1983), Appendix A: 456–57; and *Federal Reserve Bulletin,* various issues.

average recession has been just under a year in length, and the typical expansion has lasted a little under four years. The longest recession occurred in 1981–1982 and lasted 17 months; the longest expansion occurred in the 1960s and lasted 106 months, though the expansion of the 1980s was almost as long. The expansion of the 1980s has been correctly labeled the longest *peacetime* expansion since World War II.

· · · · · · · ·

Unemployment Fluctuations

Table 22.2 also shows how the **unemployment rate** varied over the business cycle. The unemployment rate is calculated monthly by the Bureau of Labor Statistics as the ratio of the number of job seekers to the total labor force, defined as the number of workers plus seekers:

$$\text{Unemployment rate} = U = \frac{\text{job seekers}}{\text{workers + job seekers}} \qquad [4]$$

People are classified as unemployed only if they are actively looking for a job; people who have given up looking for a job are considered *discouraged workers* and not part of the labor force. The economy is operating at **full employment** when everyone who is willing and able to work can find a job, but full employment does *not* mean that the unemployment rate is zero. Most economists believe that the full employment rate of unemployment has risen from about 4 percent to around 6 percent over the past 40 years. This may seem strange: Why isn't the full employment rate of unemployment zero? To answer this question, we need to define three different kinds of unemployment.

Most of the variation in unemployment that occurs over the business cycle is **cyclical unemployment.** If the economy falls into a recession and you lose your job because your factory closes down, you will be classified as cyclically unemployed. People who have the wrong skills or live in the wrong location are said to be **structurally unemployed.** For example, a typist who has not acquired word processing skills will be structurally unemployed in short order in today's economy—whether the economy is in recession or not. The structurally unemployed have difficulty finding jobs even when the economy is booming. Finally, there will always be some people who deliberately quit their old jobs to look for better jobs. These people are said to be **frictionally unemployed.** Now we can answer the question we posed a moment ago: the full employment rate of unemployment is not zero because there will always be some people who are structurally or frictionally unemployed.

There are three main sources of error in unemployment statistics. First, at any point in time there can be a large number of discouraged workers who have given up looking for jobs and are no longer considered part of the workforce. The number of discouraged workers is difficult to estimate with accuracy—recent estimates have exceeded one million—but it is clear that this number rises when the measured rate of unemployment increases. The existence of discouraged workers means that published unemployment statistics underestimate the magnitude of the problem because these people are not counted in the unemployment calculations.

Second, a significant number of people are working in the underground economy; that is, supporting themselves with criminal activities or being paid in cash to avoid taxes. These people are not only omitted in the employment figures, but they frequently are counted as unemployed. The existence of underground work probably means that the measured unemployment rate overstates the "true" unemployment

Unemployment rate The ratio of job seekers to the total labor force (workers plus job seekers).

Full employment The maximum level of employment that can be achieved given the existence of frictional and structural unemployment.

Cyclical unemployment Unemployment caused by recession.

Structural unemployment Unemployment that exists because of lack of skills or being in the wrong location.

Frictional unemployment Unemployment that occurs when people are changing jobs.

rate by a percentage point or two. It must be recognized, however, that more people turn to underground employment when the prospects for "above ground" employment are poor. For example, bootlegging and moonshining have historically increased when the coal mines of Appalachia close down, and marijuana cultivation may have become more popular when the California state economy was in the doldrums in the 1980s and early 1990s.

Another source of error in the unemployment statistics stems from the immigration of illegal aliens. No one knows how many illegals enter the United States each year, but the Bureau of the Census estimated the annual figure to be between 100,000 and 300,000 during the 1980s; others think the number is much higher. Since many illegal aliens do find jobs, they represent an increase in the working population. If they were added to the official unemployment calculations, this would reduce the unemployment rate. Illegal aliens frequently take jobs that pay the minimum wage or lower and probably exert some downward pressure on low wages.

Two final factors that are not accounted for in the measured rate of unemployment are involuntary part-time work and underemployment. About 18 percent of all workers held part-time jobs in the early 1990s, but only two-thirds of these people did so by choice. Those working part-time involuntarily are officially counted as being employed. Workers are underemployed if they are working at a job for which they are overqualified—perhaps a Ph.D. engineer driving a taxi cab, or a college graduate working as a clerk. Determining the extent of underemployment is difficult, but many people think it has increased in recent years.

Many economists believe that the full employment rate of unemployment has risen since the 1950s. One explanation is based on structural changes in the economy. As technology evolves and the workplace changes, some people find that their job skills are no longer needed. This would suggest that the rise in unemployment is due to increases in structural unemployment. Another explanation attributes the rise in the full employment rate of unemployment to demographic changes in the labor force. One demographic change is the rise in the number of two-worker families. If both partners are in the labor force, the other can afford to look longer for just the right job. As a result, the full employment rate of unemployment will increase because longer search times increase the number of people out of work at a point in time. Finally, the upward trend in the unemployment rate is a global phenomenon, though it has affected the United States less than many advanced nations. Between 1980 and 1992, the average unemployment rate was 7 percent in the United States, 8.2 percent in Europe, and 9.4 percent in Canada.[9] Figure 22.4 plots the U.S. unemployment rate since World War II. We will explore the causes and consequences of unemployment in more depth in Chapter 27.

Table 22.2 presented data on unemployment rates at the peaks and troughs of business cycles, but it did not point out that changes in the unemployment rate typically occur a few months after business cycle turning points. Why is this true? Suppose you are running a business and find that you must cut production because of declining sales. If at all possible, you will try to keep your employees because if

[9]Data are from John Cornwall, "Full Employment in the 1990s," *Challenge* (November/December 1993): 4–11.

•••• **FIGURE 22.4 ANNUAL UNEMPLOYMENT, 1948–1993**

The unemployment rate tends to rise during recessions (indicated by the shaded bars) and fall during expansions. The upward trend in the unemployment rate may be due to changes in the composition of the labor force, structural factors, or other events.

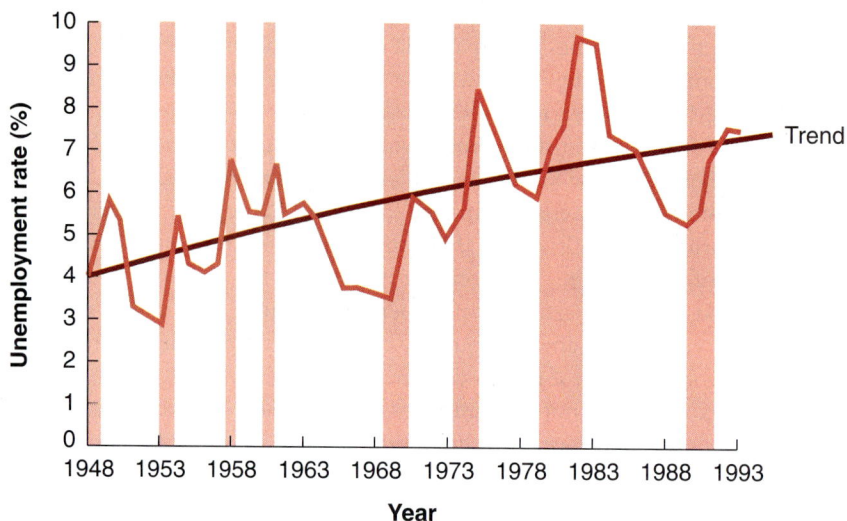

SOURCE: 1994 *Economic Report of the President,* Table B-40.

you lay them off, your best workers will find other jobs and be unavailable for a recall when business picks up. To avoid this problem, firms often ask their employees to work fewer hours and hope that the sales decline is only temporary. Firms are also slow to rehire workers they have laid off until they are certain that the economic expansion will continue. Until then, many firms hire only part-time workers. By doing so, the firms avoid the need to pay benefits. This is why the unemployment rate is considered a *lagging indicator* of economic activity. The Focus box on page 572 describes the leading as well as lagging indicators in more detail.

••••••••

Inflation

Inflation rate Continuing rise in the aggregate price level.

As we learned in Chapter 5, **inflation** is a continuing change in the price index. The percentage change in the price index is:

$$\text{Inflation rate} = p = \frac{\Delta P}{P} \qquad [5]$$

where the lowercase p is the inflation rate and the uppercase P is a price index. If a percentage change in the price index is positive and continuing, it is classified as inflation. Three price indices, and thus three measures of inflation, are commonly used in the United States. These are the consumer price index (CPI), the producer price index (PPI), and the GDP deflator. The GDP deflator gives the broadest measure of inflation because it includes the prices of more goods and services than either the CPI or the PPI.

Figure 22.5 plots the annual inflation rate (percentage change in the GDP deflator) between 1960 and 1993. The inflation rate often declines during recessions (indicated by the shaded areas) and accelerates during expansions, but this relationship is not

· · · · **FIGURE 22.5 RECENT INFLATION IN THE UNITED STATES**

Inflation trended upward in the 1960s and 1970s but has declined significantly in recent years. The average annual inflation rate over this period was 4.8 percent; however, inflation has been quite volatile. The worst inflationary experience in this period occurred in the 1970s. The inflation rate often rises during expansions and falls during contractions (indicated by the shaded area).

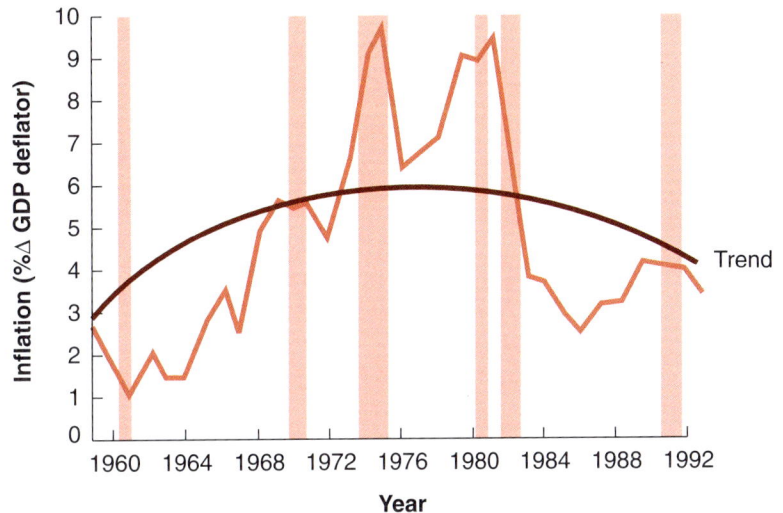

SOURCE: 1994 *Economic Report of the President,* Table B-3. Data are the percentage change in the GDP deflator.

nearly as reliable as the relationship between GDP growth and unemployment. Indeed, there have been several episodes of *stagflation*—the simultaneous occurrence of accelerating inflation and rising unemployment. The annual inflation rate in the United States has averaged about 4.8 percent since 1960, a rate comparable to Western Europe and Japan, and *much* lower than in many nations of the developing world, where prices often double every month. As we will find out in Chapter 27, rapid inflation can have adverse economic consequences including a disincentive to save, undesirable income redistribution, and economic inefficiency. The worst inflationary episode in the United States since World War II occurred in the 1970s when external events—including oil price hikes and rising farm prices—combined with rising wages to generate "double-digit" inflation. Inflation was brought down in the first half of the 1980s, partially at least, as a by-product of the 1981–1982 recession.

· · · · · · · ·

Productivity Growth

In the long run, our standard of living is affected most by **productivity growth.** Productivity measures the increase in output per unit of input. It increases when workers have more machines or knowledge and when they work more efficiently. When workers are more productive, they produce more goods and services and earn higher wages. Productivity growth can also lower the cost of production because each worker is able to produce more goods and services. Finally, productivity growth is also related to international competitiveness. Rapid productivity growth indicates that U.S. firms are adopting new technologies and can better compete with foreign producers. Unfortunately, productivity growth has been the most serious blemish on the U.S. economic record since 1970.

Productivity growth Growth in output per unit of input.

FOCUS ON

INDICATOR ANALYSIS

One of the most useful methods for forecasting business cycle turning points is economic indicator analysis. The economic indicators were developed almost 60 years ago by Wesley Mitchell and Arthur Burns. Burns and Mitchell found a set of economic data series that had a consistent relationship with business cycle turning points. Since their original development, the National Bureau of Economic Research (NBER) has continued to study and revise the economic indicators. Today, the NBER publishes three indicator series—the leading, lagging, and coincident indicators. A careful study of these series is often the best way to forecast cycle turning points.

THE LEADING INDICATORS

The Department of Commerce compiles a list of 11 leading indicators. These series were selected because of their stable statistical relationship with past economic activity, not necessarily any theoretical relationship. Nevertheless, the economic rationale for the

---

UNITED STATES DEPARTMENT OF

COMMERCE

NEWS

WASHINGTON, D.C. 20230

ECONOMICS
AND
STATISTICS
ADMINISTRATION

Bureau of
Economic Analysis

FOR WIRE TRANSMISSION: 8:30 A.M. EDT, TUESDAY, APRIL 5, 1994

Larry Moran: (202) 606-9691   BEA 94-13
Recorded Message: 606-5361

**COMPOSITE INDEXES OF LEADING, COINCIDENT, AND LAGGING
INDICATORS: FEBRUARY 1994**

The composite index of leading indicators decreased 0.1 percent in

February to 100.4 (1987=100), according to preliminary estimates released

---

inclusion of particular series is usually clear. For example, one of the leading indicators is the hours worked in manufacturing. Because firms can more easily adjust hours than employment, changes in the hours worked generally precede employment changes. The index also includes financial variables, variables that reflect delivery speed, inflation, and new business formation.

The 11 leading indicators are (1) stock market prices, (2) the real money supply, (3) an index of consumer expectations, (4) the percentage change in sensitive materials prices, (5) the average workweek of manufacturing production workers, (6) initial claims for unemployment insurance, (7) new building permits, (8) new orders for consumer goods, (9) contracts and orders for investment goods, (10) the change in manufacturers' unfilled or-

---

As Figure 22.6 shows, the trend in productivity growth is clearly downward. Over the period 1948–1970, annual labor productivity growth averaged 3.1 percent; between 1971 and 1990, it averaged only 1.3 percent per year, and between 1980 and 1990, it was only 1.1 percent per year. Productivity growth turned upward in 1992, but it is too early to determine whether this trend will continue. These seemingly small changes in productivity growth are especially important because of compounding effects. For example, at 3.1 percent per year, output per worker—and thus real income and the standard of living—will double approximately every 23 years.

ders for durable goods, and (11) vendor performance (how easy it is to get delivery of inputs).

The most common use of the leading indicators is the *index of leading indicators*—a mathematical combination of the 11 indicators into a single series. The index of leading indicators is published monthly and usually receives widespread attention in the popular media. It is usually announced on the last day of the following month (for example, September's index is announced on the last day of October) because it takes this long to process and prepare for publication. The index of leading indicators generally precedes cycle turning points by about six months. Like most economic data series, preliminary estimates of the economic indicators are first announced and then revised. These revisions can be quite large, so care must be taken in interpreting the preliminary announcement.

THE COINCIDENT INDICATORS

The coincident indicators are a set of data series that are thought to turn at the same time as the general economy. The coincident indicators include industrial production and personal income, but not GDP. GDP is not included because GDP data are available only quarterly, and the indicators are published monthly.

THE LAGGING INDICATORS

There are also lagging indicators. These series typically lag behind overall economic activity by about six months. Among the important lagging indicators are bank prime interest rates, the average duration of unemployment, and the unemployment rate.

HOW ACCURATE ARE INDICATOR FORECASTS?

The indicators can be fairly accurate if you are careful to interpret them correctly. The biggest problem with the economic indicators is that they frequently give *false signals*—they rise or fall without a corresponding change in aggregate economic activity. For this reason, economists look for trends in the economic indicators and usually dismiss evidence from a single month.

A three-month trend in the series reduces false signals dramatically. But note what the three-month lag does to the forecasting ability: if three months are needed to compile revised figures, and a three-month trend is necessary before interpretation, it may take six months to see a cycle turning point—very close to the average lead time. And even if investigators are willing to base forecasts on the first month's figures, a six-month lead time may not be sufficient time for planning.

When the indicators are watched carefully and interpreted correctly, they can be very accurate. In fact, every business cycle turning point since World War II has been preceded by a change in the leading indicators. Even the "false signals" are not entirely without meaning: if dips in the index do not result in full-fledged recessions, they almost always warn of *growth recessions*—declines in the rate of economic growth, which are not severe enough to be classified as recessions.

The typical worker will see his or her living standard double twice in a working lifetime. But at a productivity growth rate of 1.3 percent per year, output takes more than 53 years to double—so a typical worker's standard of living would double only with a working career lasting 53 years. The number of years required for productivity to double may seem outlandish, but it is merely a consequence of the workings of compound interest. The Focus box on the Rule of 72 presents a simple rule for calculating the length of time required for principal to double at compound interest rates.

•••• **FIGURE 22.6 DECLINING PRODUCTIVITY GROWTH**

Productivity growth has shown a downward trend since World War II. The average annual increase between 1948 and 1970 was 3.2 percent; between 1971 and 1990, it was only 1.26 percent. The downward trend may have been reversed in the 1990s.

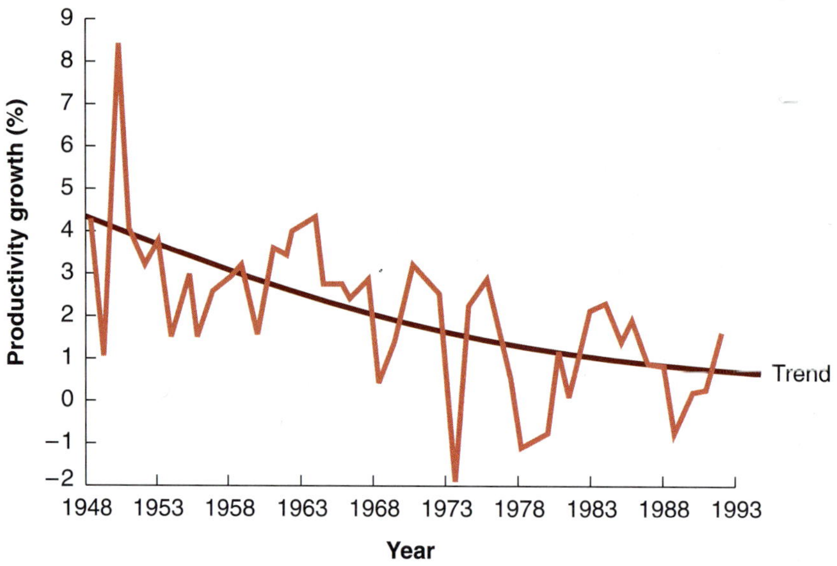

SOURCE: 1994 *Economic Report of the President,* Table B-48; pre-1960 data are from the 1991 *Economic Report of the President,* Table B-47. Data are output per hour, all persons, business sector.

Economists are still at work trying to understand the decline in productivity. Some of the decline in the 1970s may have been due to demographics. When millions of baby boomers finished school and went to work, the average experience level in the workplace fell, and with it, perhaps, productivity growth. The United States may also have been making the wrong kind of research and development decisions—devoting too much to "Nobel Prize" research and too little to process technology easily adopted by business—though this issue is hotly debated. We will explore productivity growth in more detail in Chapter 33.

RECAP   GDP Fluctuations in the Twentieth Century

1. There have been 12 business cycles since 1929. The most severe recession was the Great Depression of 1929–1933. The longest expansions took place in the 1960s and the 1980s.
2. Unemployment rises during contractions, falls during expansions, and has shown an upward trend since the 1950s. The full employment rate of unemployment is usually estimated to be between 5 and 6 percent of the workforce.
3. Inflation accelerated in the 1970s partially because of a series of external shocks. It declined in the 1980s and appears to be stabilizing in the 1990s.
4. Productivity growth is the most important determinant of our standard of living. It has declined significantly since the 1960s but may be improving in the 1990s.

FOCUS ON

THE RULE OF 72

How long it takes for output per hour to double at different productivity growth rates can be calculated quite easily on a financial calculator, but it can also be approximated with a mathematical trick, the Rule of 72. The Rule of 72 can be used to approximate the number of years it takes any sum to double if the growth rate compounds once a year.

As an example, suppose you deposit $1,000 in the bank at a 10 percent interest rate, compounded once a year. After one year, you would have $1,000 + 0.10($1,000) = $1,100. After two years, it would be $1,100 +

0.10($1,100) = $1,210; after three years, you would have $1,210 + 0.10($1,210) = $1,331; and so on. To figure out how long it would take to reach $2,000, you could continue the arithmetic, or you could apply the Rule of 72 to get an approximation: Simply divide 72 by the interest rate to get the number of years it takes a sum to double. In this case the calculations would be 72/10 = 7.2, so it takes 7.2 years for a sum to double at 10 percent interest. If the interest rate is 12 percent, it would take 72/12 = 6 years. These answers are approximate—it actually takes 7.27 and 6.12

years—but if you need that much precision, you are better off with a calculator or present value table.

How does the Rule of 72 relate to productivity growth and income? Suppose a typical worker in 1990 earns $30,000 and labor productivity grows at a 2 percent annual rate. Worker productivity would double in 36 years (72/2 = 36) so the typical worker would be earning $60,000 in the year 2026. On the other hand, if productivity growth were 3 percent per year, the typical worker would be earning $60,000 by the year 2014.

EARLY THEORIES OF THE BUSINESS CYCLE

The main purpose of macroeconomic theory is to explain the kind of data we have just discussed. Today, most macroeconomic theorists rely upon rather elaborate statistical models that attempt to separate the trends from random fluctuations. We will look at modern theories of the business cycle in later chapters, but before we do, a brief digression on three older theories may be instructive. Not only do these theories still have some relevance today, but they serve to emphasize that economic theory is always evolving. Just as theories that were popular in the nineteenth century have been supplanted today, modern economic theories are likely to be modified in the twenty-first century.

Malthus's Theories of Population and Recession

One of the early interpreters of Adam Smith was a minister, **Thomas Robert Malthus** (1766–1834). Malthus had an extremely dismal view of capitalist evolution. He believed that poverty and starvation were the inevitable result of a conflict between the laws of nature and human behavior. Malthus also believed that recessions were a logical consequence of population pressure.

Thomas Robert Malthus (1776–1834) British economist and minister who believed that population would inevitably grow faster than the food supply, leading to poverty and starvation.

FIGURE 22.7 THE MALTHUSIAN DILEMMA

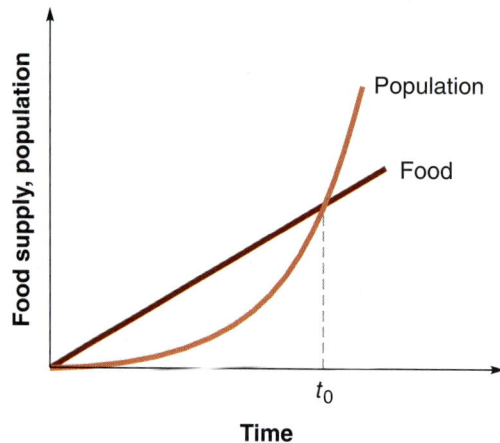

Malthus argued that the food supply could grow at only an arithmetic rate while the population would grow at a geometric rate. Unless there were preventative checks, the population would outstrip the food supply at time t_0, and the result would be poverty and starvation.

Malthus's dire predictions, developed in his *Essay on the Principle of Population* (1798), rested on three main ideas. First, population was limited by the availability of food. Second, when food is cheap and plentiful, population would grow at a geometric rate—2, 4, 8, 16, 32, and so on. Third, the food supply would grow at only an arithmetic rate—1, 2, 3, 4, and so on. The result: Unless there were preventative checks on population growth, population would outstrip the food supply. Malthus cited delayed marriage and "moral restraint" as possible checks, though he admitted that he had little faith that either would be successful.[10] But without a check on population, the consequence would be misery and starvation—unless war or plague intervened. The only conclusion that Malthus could reach from his analysis was that welfare and social programs for the poor did more harm than good. Such programs would give only temporary help and would allow the poor to have even more children. Figure 22.7 presents the fundamental problem posed by Malthus.

Malthus's Business Cycles. An extension of Malthus's theory of population was a theory of the business cycle. Malthus believed that the growing population would increase the supply of workers so much that wages would fall to (or below) the subsistence level. Low wages would mean that workers would not have enough money to buy everything that was produced in the economy. Additionally, thought Malthus, the capitalists were so intent on pursuing profits that they did not have time to spend all of their money. As a result, there would be a business cycle recession

[10]Malthus himself married late, but he did have four children; apparently, he didn't practice "moral restraint" any better than the rest of the nineteenth-century populace.

due to *underconsumption*. Malthus's underconsumption theory of recession foreshadowed important macroeconomic ideas of the mid-twentieth century we will discuss in the next few chapters.

Assessing Malthus. Was Malthus's theory of population correct? Like so many questions in economics, there is more than one answer. The mass starvation and misery Malthus predicted did not come about in his lifetime, at least not in his native England.[11] And later in the nineteenth and twentieth centuries, agricultural yields increased and effective birth control reduced the rate of population growth. Without these advances, Malthus may have been prophetic for parts of the world—poverty and starvation are appalling even today in Latin American, Asia, and Africa. Many observers believe, however, that this is the result of ineffective food distribution systems, not Malthusian excessive population growth.

● ● ● ● ● ● ●

The Long Cycles of Kondratiev and Schumpeter

In the 1920s the Russian economist **Nicholai Kondratiev** (1892–1938) did a statistical study on over a hundred years of price data in France, Britain, and the United States. Kondratiev noticed a pattern of *long waves* that seemed to appear and reappear. Prices rose sharply, fell sharply, then rose again with amazing regularity.[12] Kondratiev believed he found two and a half cycles—a 60-year cycle from 1789 to 1849, a 47-year cycle between 1849 and 1896, and a third cycle that began in 1896 and peaked in 1920. Extension of Kondratiev's analysis would suggest that his third wave would have ended in the late 1940s or early 1950s. A few modern observers saw evidence of a fourth wave. If the upswing began in the early 1950s, the peak would be reached around the mid-1970s—just the time of the recession of 1973–1975—and a 20- or 30-year contraction would follow. It was not merely coincidence that interest in Kondratiev revived in the 1970s and 1980s.

Kondratiev never explained why the long cycle existed. This was left to **Joseph Schumpeter** (1883–1950), an Austrian who taught at Harvard. Schumpeter felt that the long waves were due to *innovations*. To Schumpeter, innovations were not simply inventions; they were significant breakthroughs that changed the structure of the economy. Schumpeter felt that innovations would come at certain points in time—at periods he called *neighborhoods of equilibrium*—when entrepreneurial perceptions of risk would encourage a wave of innovations. One innovation mentioned by Schumpeter was the railroad. When track was laid to connect the East and West Coasts of the United States, whole towns sprang up and numerous supply industries were

Nicholai Kondratiev (1892–1938)
Russian economist and statistician who is credited with discovering the long-wave business cycle of 40–60 years.

Joseph Schumpeter (1883–1950)
Austrian-born economist who developed the innovation theory of the business cycle.

---

[11]His prediction of mass starvation may have been applicable to the potato famine of Ireland. The failure of the potato crop for several successive years in the 1840s produced a devastating famine. Starvation, disease, and emigration—especially to the United States—caused Ireland's population to decline from 8.2 million in 1841 to 6.6 million in 1851.

[12]Kondratiev began his research trying to discover the laws of motion of capitalism. He discovered that business cycles appeared to serve as a cleansing process that rid capitalism of the weaker firms, so that the system was stronger after the cycle than before. Unfortunately, discovering that capitalism was strengthening was not smart politics in the early days of the Soviet Union. Kondratiev was soon banished to Siberia and was shot in 1938.

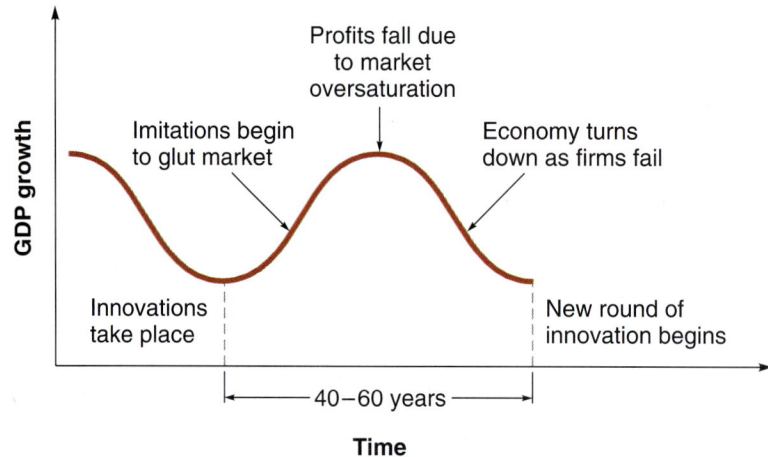

FIGURE 22.8 THE SCHUMPETER-KONDRATIEV LONG CYCLE

Both Schumpeter and Kondratiev thought they found evidence of a 40–60-year long cycle, though only Schumpeter provided an explanation for the cycle. Innovations would cluster around neighborhoods of equilibrium—typically cycle recessions—and spur the economy upward. As imitators entered the market, profits would fall due to saturation, and the economy would turn down.

created. The automobile could be considered an innovation that drove the economy in the 1920s.

According to Schumpeter, a new innovation would start the economy on an upward path. As subsidiary industries developed, the economy would begin a long cycle expansion. But within the expansion would be the seeds of contraction. Anxious to reap some of the innovators' profits, imitators would eventually glut the market and reduce profit opportunities. A contraction would occur due to this excess capacity. The next upturn would occur when another innovation was introduced. Why would the innovation be introduced at the cycle trough? Some investigators have suggested that innovations are "saved" during good times—why take an innovative risk when you're already making good profits?—and adopted when times turn bad. Figure 22.8 illustrates the timing of the innovation cycle.

Assessing Long Cycle Theory. The reasoning behind the Schumpeter-Kondratiev cycle may be persuasive, and long-wave theory seems to be enjoying something of a renaissance today.[13] But whether the theory is operative is another matter. Modern economists who have tried to date significant innovations have run into several problems. For example, Edwin Mansfield notes that the introduction of the diesel locomotive can be dated as either 1934, when the General Motors locomotive appeared,

[13]One of the most important recent works on the long wave is Andrew Tylecote, *The Long Wave in the World Economy: The Present Crisis in Historical Perspective* (New York and London: Routledge, 1993).

The most severe recession occurred in the 1930s; the longest expansions occurred in the 1960s and 1980s.

5. The unemployment rate tends to rise during contractions and fall during expansions and has shown an upward trend since World War II. Inflation reached its 30-year high in the United States in the 1970s; average inflation rates declined in the 1980s and appear to have stabilized so far in the 1990s. Productivity growth has shown a downward trend since the 1960s, but may be improving so far in the 1990s.

6. Early business cycle theories include Malthus's underconsumption theory, Kondratiev's long-wave theory, Schumpeter's innovation theory, and Jevons's sun spot theory.

KEY TERMS AND CONCEPTS

gross domestic product (GDP)
underground economy
flow variable
stock variable
measure of economic welfare (MEW)
value-added approach
value-added tax
income-received approach
expenditure approach
consumption
gross private domestic investment (GPDI)
capital consumption allowance
net private domestic investment (NPDI)
government purchases
transfer payments
net exports
Great Depression

business cycle
recession
unemployment rate
full employment
cyclical unemployment
structural unemployment
frictional unemployment
inflation
productivity growth
Malthus
underconsumption
Kondratiev
Schumpeter
innovations
overinvestment
Jevons
sun spot theory

REVIEW QUESTIONS

1. Which of the following would add to GDP?

Buying a used car
Getting a root canal
A homemaker cooking dinner

Painting an old house
Giving home-canned goods to a neighbor
Your professor producing enlightenment

2. Explain how to use each of the three methods for calculating GDP.

3. The expenditure approach to GDP accounting begins with the equation:

$$E = C + I + G + (X - Z)$$

Define each term in the equation and discuss how each has behaved in the post–World War II era.

4. What are the phases of a typical post–World War II business cycle in the United States? How long does each phase usually last?
5. What have been the trends in inflation, unemployment, and productivity growth since World War II?
6. Outline the major components of the cycle theories of Malthus, Jevons, Kondratiev, and Schumpeter. Are these theories viable today? In what ways?

······PROBLEMS

1. When you buy a pack of cigarettes, you may be adding to GDP twice. Explain. (*Hint:* Cigarettes come with a Surgeon's General warning label.)
2. Figure 22.5 presents annual inflation as well as a nonlinear trend line. Sketch in a linear trend line through the data. Which trend gives a better idea of the actual history of inflation? Why?
3. Suppose that per capita income in Country A is $6,000 while in Country B it is $12,000. If productivity growth is 4 percent per year in Country A and 2 percent in Country B, how long will it take before per capita income in Country A equals per capita income in Country B? (*Hint:* If you do not have a financial calculator, you can approximate the answer with the Rule of 72.)
4. Refer back to Figure 22.7. Two of the issues that Malthus failed to foresee were the advent of effective birth control and better farming practices. How would these two factors affect the graph? Would the intersection point differ from t_0?
5. Software piracy is illegal and immoral. As a mental exercise, however, consider the following: You buy Alien Invaders, a new computer game, for your 12-year-old brother. The price is $39.95. He proceeds to offer free copies to all of his friends, and 10 accept copies. Explain how much GDP would increase if (*a*) your brother's friends were planning to buy Alien Invaders anyway but did not because they got an illegal copy; (*b*) your brother's friends were planning to buy Alien Attack (also priced at $39.95) but did not because they got a free copy of Alien Invaders; and (*c*) your brother's friends were not planning to buy any computer games but took this one anyway.
6. Indicate whether the following are true, false, or uncertain, and explain why:
   a. The sale of used goods does not add to GDP.
   b. The existence of the underground economy means that unemployment figures overestimate the magnitude of unemployment.
   c. Malthus believed that recessions were caused by overinvestment.
   d. Productivity growth has shown an erratic but upward trend in the past 30 years.
   e. Value-added taxes affect the economy much like sales taxes.
   f. The unemployment rate is considered a leading indicator of economic activity.
   g. The equation of the expenditure approach is $E = C + I + G + X + Z$.
   h. Spending on consumer durables tends to be more stable than spending on consumer nondurables.
   i. Inflation and unemployment have moved together over the past 30 years.
7. Explain whether the following statement is true or false: Elimination of marriage licenses will increase GDP.

National Income Accounting

GDP is by far the most popular measure of aggregate economic activity, but it is not the only one. In fact, national income accountants use six measures. Following the movements of these six accounts can give a better idea of macroeconomic activity, because each provides a slightly different picture of the macroeconomy. All data in this appendix come from the 1994 *Economic Report of the President,* Tables B-23, B-24, and B-27. The data are in billions of current dollars for fiscal year 1992.

1. *Gross domestic product.* GDP is the value of all final goods and services produced in the United States and sold or added to inventory during a year. GDP includes production by both U.S. and foreign-owned firms.

   Gross domestic product: $6,038.5

2. *Gross national product.* Gross national product (GNP) is the value of all final goods and services produced by U.S.-owned firms anywhere in the world and sold or added to inventory during a year. GNP adds receipts of factor income from the rest of the world and subtracts payments of factor income to the rest of the world. For example, the income a U.S. citizen earns working for Texaco in the oil fields of Saudi Arabia is part of the U.S. GNP, but it is not counted as part of U.S. GDP because the production did not take place within the United States. That same income is part of the Saudi Arabian GDP because the money was earned in the domestic Saudi Arabian economy, but it is not counted toward the Saudi GNP.

   U.S. national income accountants relied upon GNP as their primary measure of aggregate economic activity until 1992 when it was replaced with GDP. This change was made to make it easier to compare U.S. economic performance with other nations that use GDP instead of GNP as their primary measure of aggregate economic activity. The difference between GDP and GNP is tiny in the United States:

GDP:	$6,038.5
+ receipts of factor income from the rest of world	+129.2
− payments of factor income from the rest of the world	−121.9
Gross national product:	$6,045.8

3. *Net national product.* Among the problems with the GNP (and GDP) is that it includes gross investment instead of net investment. It is possible for *gross* investment to be positive while *net* investment is negative. For example, if a firm acquires 10 machines over the course of a year but 15 machines wear out in the same year, gross investment would be the money spent on the 10

machines, but the capital stock would have shrunk by 5 machines. In this case, gross investment would be positive, but net investment would be negative. Gross investment is part of GNP, so GNP would increase by the amount of gross investment even though the productive capacity of the economy would decline. Net national product gets around this problem. It is defined as GNP minus capital consumption allowances. As a rough rule of thumb, capital consumption allowances are around 10 percent of GNP.

In theory, the net national product should be a much better measure of economic activity than GNP. Unfortunately, what gets reported as capital consumption allowances is a financial figure, not an actual real measure of worn-out machinery. For this reason, it is used much less frequently than GNP or GDP.

GNP	$6,045.8
− capital consumption allowances	−657.9
Net national product:	$5,387.9

4. *National income.* It is unfortunate that the GDP and GNP are frequently referred to as the "national income" because this term should be reserved for a specific measure that differs from either measure. The Commerce Department defines national income as the total earnings of labor and property that come from the production of goods and services. It can also be thought of as the factor cost of net national product. To calculate national income from net national product, we subtract payments that do not go to the factors of production. The most important payments include indirect business taxes (largely sales taxes) and business transfer payments (primarily retirement). The return for government-owned enterprises is accounted for by adding subsidies less current surpluses of government enterprises. An adjustment is usually made for statistical discrepancy.

Net national product:	$5,387.9
− indirect business taxes	−502.8
− business transfer payments	−27.6
− statistical discrepancy	−23.6
+ subsidies − surplus of government firms	+2.7
National income:	$4,836.6

5. *Personal income.* People receive income from sources other than working, and some income that is earned is not paid out. When we adjust national income for these factors, we get personal income:

National income:	$4,836.6
− corporate profits	−407.2
− net interest	−442.0
− social insurance contributions	−555.6
− wage accruals less disbursements	+20
+ government transfers to persons	+836.6
+ personal interest income	+694.3

+ personal dividend income	+140.4
+ business transfer payments	+21.6
Personal income:	$5,144.9

6. *Disposable personal income.* People's decisions to spend and save are based on their take-home pay, not their gross pay. Disposable personal income is aggregate personal income less personal tax and nontax payments. In recent years, disposable personal income has been about 70 percent of GDP. Personal taxes have been approximately 14 percent of personal income.

Personal income:	$5,144.9
− personal tax and nontax payments	−644.8
Disposable personal income:	$4,500.2

CHAPTER 23

The Beginnings of Macroeconomics: Say's Law, Inventory Adjustment, and the Multiplier

The Great Depression of the 1930s surprised economists as much as anyone. The human costs of 25 percent unemployment were tremendous—and remember there was no unemployment insurance and few families had two wage earners. Even many of the people who kept their jobs lost their life savings if they had deposits in one of the thousands of banks that failed—there was no deposit insurance either. As the depression deepened, policymakers and the public appealed to the economics profession for answers: What caused the collapse? And more importantly, what should be done about it?

Some economists said the solution was a dose of fiscal austerity. These economists called for a reduction in government spending and higher taxes to bring down government deficits. Others called for the Federal Reserve to reduce the money supply, arguing that less economic activity required fewer dollars in circulation. But many economists kept quiet or said very little about the depression. This may seem rather strange given the tendency of contemporary economists to speak up. Why were so many economists so quiet? The answer is simple: most economic models said that depressions like the 1930s could not exist. Consequently, no one had developed a set of policies to guide the economy out of such depressions. It was this environment that spawned the development of modern macroeconomics.

This chapter is a transitional chapter that will set the stage for a model-building process that will take the next several chapters to complete. The aim is to provide an intuitive feeling for the rather technical material in those chapters. Try to keep the ideas from this chapter in the back of your mind as you read the next few chapters; it will help you remember that there really is economics behind all those graphs!

Our analysis begins with Say's law of markets, one of the key ideas that economists used to reason that severe depressions could not occur. We then look at inventory adjustment and the spending multiplier, two of the main elements of the macroeconomic models that were developed during the Great Depression. Although updated considerably today, these ideas are still the basis for much contemporary macroeconomic research.

AFTER READING AND STUDYING THIS CHAPTER, YOU SHOULD BE ABLE TO:

• • • State Say's law, and explain how it relates to full employment and recessions

• • • Understand the criticisms of Say's law, and explain how these criticisms led to the development of Keynesian economics

• • • Explain the relationship between inventory adjustment, recessions, and expansions

• • • Describe the operation of the spending multiplier

SAY'S LAW OF MARKETS

Say's law "Supply creates its own demand."

About the same time that Malthus was writing his *Essay on Population,* a Frenchman by the name of Jean-Baptiste Say (1767–1832) began the task of translating and popularizing Adam Smith's *Wealth of Nations* for Continental Europe. Say had read *The Wealth of Nations* by the time he was 21, but it was another 15 years before he would publish his most important book, *Treatise on Political Economy* (1803), an interpretation of Adam Smith. The *Treatise* earned Say well-deserved respect in Europe and the United States where it was used as a text at Harvard and Dartmouth as late as 1870. Say's *Treatise* discussed many ideas, but the most important was a concept that came to be known as **Say's law of markets.** In its simplest version, Say's law states that "supply creates its own demand." This seemingly innocuous statement has had profound implications for the development of economics for almost two centuries. In its strictest interpretation, Say's law implies that a market economy can never be stuck in a prolonged recession.

The most important implication of Say's law is this: As long as everything that is produced is offered for exchange, there can never be overproduction and recession. At first glance, this does not seem to make sense. How can it happen that everything produced (supplied) in the economy is purchased (demanded)? What if the shoemaker produces too many brown shoes and not enough black shoes? Wouldn't there be excess brown shoes in inventory and a shortage of black shoes? No, at least not if prices are flexible. Say and his followers believed that flexible prices would assure that everything that was produced and offered on the market would find a buyer. For example, suppose that a pair of brown shoes normally sells for $10, but brown shoes suddenly fall out of fashion. The shoemakers would be stuck with unsold shoes—unless they were willing to lower the price to, say, $8 per pair. Lower prices would encourage people to buy brown shoes. The lower selling price would also be a signal to the shoemakers to produce fewer brown shoes in the next production period.

The richness of Say's law is that **price flexibility** and market adjustments carry over to all sectors of the economy; they do not stop with the shoe market. Because consumers are able to buy brown shoes for only $8 per pair, they have extra money left over for something else, say, green shirts. When the demand for green shirts increases, the price of green shirts rises. This acts as a signal for green shirt producers to increase production. It was this insight that led León Walras (see Chapter 3) to view the entire economy as a system of interrelated supply and demand equations—with excess demand in any market spilling over to the demand and supply in every other market.

> **Price flexibility** The ability of prices to adjust as market conditions change.

Economists of the late nineteenth century also believed that **wage flexibility** was necessary to assure full employment. Wage flexibility was thought to clear the labor market just as price flexibility cleared the goods markets. For example, if the demand for brown shoes fell, not only would brown shoe prices fall, but so would the demand for workers who make brown shoes. This decline in the demand for labor would lower the price of labor—the wage rate—and thus act as a signal for the workers to begin looking for better paying jobs. Nineteenth-century economists felt that wage flexibility was such a powerful allocative mechanism that they often accused unemployed workers of being **voluntarily unemployed** if they were not working. All that was necessary to find a job, they argued, was for the unemployed worker to take a wage cut. In the nineteenth century, many job skills were interchangeable, so it may have been reasonable to assume that many workers could move between jobs in response to wage changes. Whether this is true today is not quite so clear.

> **Wage flexibility** The ability of wages to adjust as market conditions change, thereby assuring full employment according to Say's law.

> **Voluntary unemployment** Unemployment caused by workers refusing to work at the market wage.

Unfortunately, there was a potential kink in the analysis: there was the chance that people would not spend all of their income. In fact, most people do save some of their income. Workers are paid income equivalent to the amount of goods they have produced, so if they decide to save a portion of their income, they will buy fewer goods than they produced. Does this imply a recession and a flaw in Say's law? Not necessarily. Early economists believed that **flexible interest rates** would assure that all savings were channeled into investment, so that everything that was produced would be purchased. The only reason people saved, it was argued, was to earn interest, so higher interest rates were necessary to increase saving. However, borrowers would be willing to pay interest only if they wanted the money to invest. Thus, if interest rates rose and saving increased, it was a signal that borrowers wanted more money so they could use it for investment. In other words, any of that income that "leaked out" as savings would be spent by someone else in the economy.

> **Interest rate flexibility** The ability of interest rates to adjust as market conditions change, thereby equalizing savings and investment according to Say's law.

Criticisms of Say's Law

Say's law became almost a sacred truth among economists—and is still important today—but it created a problem for economists trying to explain the Great Depression of the 1930s. As long as prices, wages, and interest rates were flexible, protracted recessions were not supposed to occur. What happened? Economists are still not sure why the Great Depression dragged on as long as it did, but the ensuing debate did cause some economists to begin to question Say's law. The main criticisms came from the English economist John Maynard Keynes (1883–1946). His early insights were to become the basis for modern macroeconomics and what has been called the Keynesian Revolution.

OUR ECONOMIC HERITAGE

JOHN MAYNARD KEYNES, THE FOUNDER OF MACROECONOMICS

Perhaps no name in economics elicits as much controversy as that of John Maynard Keynes (1883–1946). Keynes's 1936 book, *The General Theory of Employment, Interest and Money,* revolutionized the way economists looked at the economy and advocated a hands-on approach to solving economic problems. Although some economists ridicule Keynes and Keynesian economics today, no one can deny that Keynes provided the impetus for a marked turn in the evolution of economic theory.

John Maynard Keynes was the son of John Neville Keynes, a renowned economist and statistician. He was raised in relative affluence and showed signs of brilliance from his early days in school. He was one of Alfred Marshall's favorite students at Cambridge. In the years before World War I, Keynes wrote numerous popular pieces on economic issues and became something of a celebrity; his close friends included the literary intellectuals Virginia Woolf and E. M. Forster. He married a ballerina and frequently hosted rather wild parties.

Keynes's major field of expertise was monetary economics, and his book, *Treatise on Money* (1930), is still considered a classic. Another work, *The Economic Consequences of Peace* (1919), was prophetic in its prediction that the post–World War I agreements would break down and lead to World War II. But it was *The General Theory* that started the Keynesian Revolution and is the book for which Keynes will be longest remembered.

More than anything else, *The General Theory* was an attempt to show that the views of his contemporary economists were flawed by the assumption that the economy always operated at full employment. Keynes showed that, under quite plausible circumstances, the economy could get stuck in a recession. Coming as it did during the Great Depression, the most severe recession of the twentieth century, Keynes's message was widely accepted—at least initially—and economists began searching for policies to guide the economy on the path toward full employment. Today, the debates over what Keynes really meant and whether he steered the profession down the correct path are really beside the point. The Keynesian Revolution opened the door to activist government intervention in the economy, a door that is unlikely ever to close completely.

With the possible exception of *The General Theory,* Keynes wrote extremely well and is often quoted. A few quotations may give an idea of the kind of thinker he was:

- Perhaps the most widely quoted passage from Keynes is the following:★

  The ideas of economists and political philosophers, both when they are right and when they are wrong, are more powerful than is commonly understood. Indeed, the world is ruled by little else. Practical men, who believe themselves to be quite exempt from any intellectual influences, are usually the slaves of some defunct economist.

- In something of a self-criticism, Keynes wrote:

★The first three quotations are from a collection of essays, *Essays in Persuasion,* which is reprinted as vol. 9 of *The Collected Works of John Maynard Keynes. Essays* is a good place to begin a study of Keynes. The last quotation is quoted by E. Johnson in E. Johnson and H. Johnson, *The Shadow of Keynes* (Chicago: University of Chicago Press, 1978), p. 16.

Unlike some of his contemporaries, Keynes did not use wage and price rigidity in his attack on Say's law.[1] Nor did he believe that interest rate inflexibility was the

[1]We should note, however, that much current Keynesian macroeconomics is based on the assumption that prices and wages are not perfectly flexible.

John Maynard Keynes and his wife, Lydia Lopokova, 1923.

ble. But they fall into two classes—those needs which are absolute in the sense that we feel them whatever the situation of our fellow human beings may be, and those which are relative in the sense that we feel them only if their satisfaction lifts us above, makes us feel superior to, our fellows. Needs of the second class, those which gratify our desire for superiority, may indeed be insatiable; for the higher the general level, the higher still are they. But this is not so true of the absolute needs—a point may soon be reached, much sooner than we are all aware of, when these needs are satisfied in the sense that we prefer to devote our further energies to non-economic purposes.

Though never accused of being humble, Keynes is quoted by a biographer as saying:

I do not hope to be right; I hope to make progress.

Even Keynes critics must admit that he sparked controversy and, ultimately, economic progress.

If economists could manage to get themselves thought of as humble, competent people, on the level with dentists, that would be splendid!

Keynes was both an optimist and an idealist, as is apparent in the following passage:

Now it is true that the needs of human beings may seem to be insatia-

likely culprit. Instead, Keynes argued that savers and investors were different people with different motives, and that flexible interest rates were not sufficient to equate saving and investment. Look what could happen as the economy falls into a recession: the prospects for profit would diminish so firms would be reluctant to borrow money for investment and would be unwilling to pay high interest rates on any money they

Liquidity preference The desire for safe financial assets. According to Keynes, people want to hold liquid assets when they are uncertain about the future.

Liquidity The ease and safety of converting financial assets into other assets.

Inventory adjustment Process that moves economy to equilibrium; i.e., when production exceeds purchases, inventories will accumulate and firms will respond by cutting production and laying off workers.

did borrow. But at the same time, people would be increasing their savings in fear that they would be the next ones to be laid off. In such a scenario, saving increases at the same time investment decreases, and saving does not automatically become investment and spending. Keynes believed that the most important factor influencing saving is the level of household income, not the interest rate. If you earn barely enough to support your family, you will not save very much regardless of the interest rate. And if you have no dependents but earn $500,000 per year, you will probably save quite a lot even if interest rates are very low.[2]

Another part of Keynes's argument was his theory of **liquidity preference**. **Liquidity** refers to the ease and safety of converting financial assets into other assets. Money is the most liquid of all financial assets because it is most easily converted into goods or other financial assets. Stocks and bonds are less liquid than money; your broker will sell ("liquidate") your stock portfolio with just a phone call, but a sudden sale might mean a substantial loss if the market is down. Real estate is even less liquid: buying a house might be a great investment, but housing prices fluctuate, and it can take months to sell a house, so you should not tie up all of your wealth in housing.

Keynes believed that people often hold money as a refuge against uncertainty: when people are afraid the economy will fall into a recession, they tend to hold money, not lend it or deposit it in the bank.[3] If you are afraid of losing your job, you would probably rather have liquid cash than illiquid financial assets that you might have to sell at a loss. In fact, Keynes felt that confidence in the economy could reach such a low point that people would be unwilling to lend their money or buy interest-earning financial assets regardless of the return. And if the economic outlook was so uncertain that people chose to hold their money, there is little chance that firms would want to borrow it for investment and expansion.

Keynes accepted the idea that interest rates have an important influence on the level of investment; however, he believed that interest rates have only a secondary influence on the level of saving. The significance of Keynes's insight is this: if people prefer liquidity so much that they hold more money (that is, save) than they are willing or able to lend, production will exceed purchases. When firms find their inventories building up because they cannot sell all that they have produced, they cut production and lay off workers—a recession by any other words. It was this insight that led Keynes to write *The General Theory* and to change forever the way economists viewed the world. A brief biography of Keynes can be found in the Economic Heritage box.

THE INVENTORY ADJUSTMENT PROCESS

The ramifications of Keynes's argument regarding the importance of the savings-investment linkage can be shown with a numerical example of the **inventory adjustment** process. Remember what happens if firms find that they are producing

[2]Remember that saving in this context refers to putting money in the bank as well as buying financial assets like stocks and bonds.
[3]This may have been especially true in the Great Depression when bank accounts were not insured. Today, the Federal Deposit Insurance Corporation (FDIC) insures most bank accounts in the United States.

···· **TABLE 23.1** PLANS OF BUSINESSES AND HOUSEHOLDS

Firms' Production Plans	Households' Spending Plans
$Q = 100$	$Q = 100$
$C_e = 80$	$C = 70$
$I_p = 20$	$S = 30$

Definitions:

Q = production = income
C = consumption spending by households
S = household saving
C_e = production and expected sale of consumption goods by firms
I_p = production and planned sale of investment goods.

more than they can sell: their inventories begin to accumulate so they are forced to cut production and lay off workers. This example illustrates how inventories respond to different levels of income and spending assuming that prices and interest rates are fixed.[4] This example is simplified considerably; nevertheless, it is quite important because it emphasizes the *economics* behind the rather technical models we are about to develop. The key idea we are about ready to discover is that unintended changes in inventories can cause firms to hire or fire workers.

First, suppose that households have only two things they can do with their income: spend it on consumption goods or save it. Further, firms can produce only two kinds of goods: consumption goods, which are sold to households, and investment goods, which are sold to other firms. Finally, we know from the last chapter that the level of production is equal to the level of income because factor payments depend on the level of production. Now, let's suppose that the households are paid income (Q) equal to $100 and decide to spend $70 on consumption goods (C) and save (S) the remaining $30. Firms produce $100 worth of goods and services (because they have paid out $100 in income) and anticipate selling $80 of consumption goods to households and $20 of investment goods to other firms.

This scenario is shown in Table 23.1. The notation in this table is important. The letter Q represents both income and production, C is consumption spending by households, while C_e is the firms' production and expected sale of consumption goods. S is household saving. Finally, I_p stands for the production and planned sale of investment goods—machinery and the like.

A glance at Table 23.1 reveals that the spending and production plans do not quite mesh: firms plan to produce and sell $10 more of consumption goods than households want to buy, and household saving is greater than planned investment. What will happen to these extra consumption goods the firms have produced? They will

---

[4]Of course, prices and interest rates are not fixed in the real world, but this exercise still has a ring of truth to it unless price and interest rates adjust instantaneously. We will allow prices to change in Chapter 26, and financial markets and interest rates will be incorporated in Chapter 28.

•••• **TABLE 23.2** ACTIONS OF BUSINESSES AND HOUSEHOLDS

Firms' Actions	Households' Actions
$Q = 100$	$Q = 100$
$C = 70$	$C = 70$
$I_p = 20$	$S = 30$
$I_u = 10$	

NOTE: $S > I_p$ and $I_u > 0$ so production will fall in the next period.

•••• **TABLE 23.3** ACTIONS OF BUSINESSES AND HOUSEHOLDS

Firms' Actions	Households' Actions
$Q = 100$	$Q = 100$
$C_e = 80$	$C = 90$
$I_p = 20$	$S = 10$
$I_u = -10$	

NOTE: $S < I_p$ and $I_u < 0$ so production will rise in the next period.

become *unintended inventory* accumulation, which we designate as I_u. What will the firms do with the excess inventory? Sell it in the future, they hope. But holding inventories is costly—money tied up in inventory does not earn interest, and warehouse space is costly—so firms will cut production in the next period. This usually entails laying off workers and paying out less income. This is illustrated in Table 23.2, which shows the *actions* of firms and households based upon the *plans* we assumed in Table 23.1.

Table 23.3 presents the opposite situation. Here households want to buy more consumption goods than firms are planning to produce, so current spending exceeds current production. How can people buy more than is being produced? By drawing down existing inventories; that is, $I_u < 0$. When firms find that their inventories are shrinking, they will hire new workers to increase production. This will raise income in the next production period.

•••••••••

Equilibrium

You should be able to extend this analysis to another case. When saving equals planned investment and spending equals current production, there is no tendency for inventories to change. The economy is at rest in "equilibrium." The word "equilibrium" is in quotation marks because this concept of equilibrium is imprecise at best or misleading at worse. Equilibrium usually implies that the quantity supplied equals the quantity demanded. In the macroeconomy, this must mean equilibrium in all markets, including the labor market. However, Keynes felt that it was quite possible—even likely—that the economy would come to rest at equilibrium with a high level of unemployment. In the next chapter we will show that this is possible, but only under a particular set of assumptions.

As we mentioned in Chapter 22, the change in inventories is counted as investment because it represents action today that should bring sales and profits tomorrow. This means that *actual* saving always equals *actual* investment because we have defined investment to include the change in inventories. The key is whether *planned* saving and *planned* investment are equal. If they are, the economy is at rest in equilibrium; if they are not, unintended inventory changes will set in motion growth or recession. Business economists frequently monitor inventories to help them forecast future trends in the economy, a point examined in more detail in the Focus box on page 596.

RECAP   **The Inventory Adjustment Process**

The inventory adjustment process is the first and one of the most important adjustment processes behind the macroeconomic models we will be developing in the next few chapters, so it is important to make sure you understand the ideas carefully. Remember that:

1. If saving is greater than planned investment, production will exceed spending, and there will be an unintended increase in inventories. GDP will decline as firms lay off workers, cut production, and pay out less income in the next period.
2. If saving is less than planned investment, production will be less than spending, and there will be an unintended decline in inventories. GDP will increase as firms hire additional workers, pay out more income, and increase production in the next period.
3. When saving equals planned investment, there is no unintended change in inventories and no incentive for firms to increase or decrease production. The economy is said to be in equilibrium because there is no tendency for GDP to change.

THE SPENDING MULTIPLIER, k_e

Another important element in Keynesian macroeconomics is the **spending multiplier.** The spending multiplier is based on a very simple idea—that one person's spending is another person's income—but it carries an important message: a small change in spending can bring about a much larger change in income. The multiplier is important for understanding the causes of economic fluctuations and the potential effectiveness of policy. This section provides only an intuitive explanation of the multiplier based on the inventory adjustment process. We will discuss the spending multiplier more carefully in the next few chapters.

Spending multiplier Dynamic adjustment process in Keynesian model; an increase in autonomous spending will cause income to increase by a larger amount.

INVENTORY ADJUSTMENT AND ECONOMIC FORECASTING

Firms pick the optimal level of inventories by considering several factors. They obviously want to keep enough goods on hand to meet expected orders, but warehouse space and interest costs can be considerable, so firms try to minimize inventory. Inventory policy is important to well-run businesses, and analysis of changes in inventories can often provide important clues about the future path of the economy.

Economic forecasters analyze inventories in several contexts. Two of the most important are the *change in inventories* and the *inventory/sales ratio*. The change in inventories is a leading indicator of economic activity and often leads GDP turning points by about two quarters (six months). As we suggested earlier, an increase in inventories often leads to production cutbacks a few months later. The value of inventories divided by the value of sales gives the inventory/sales ratio. A low or declining ratio is regarded as a sign of future economic growth because

firms will eventually need to restock depleted inventories. A high and rising ratio frequently signals a downturn.

High inventories are costly because they tie up the firm's funds, and low inventory costs are often cited as a key to cost competitiveness. For example, low inventories were one reason the Japanese could produce automobiles more cheaply than U.S. automakers in

the 1970s and early 1980s. Japanese auto plants coordinate production so carefully that they use what is called a "just-in-time" inventory strategy. Auto parts are often kept on the shelves for only minutes. In contrast, many U.S. factories used what might be called a "just-in-case" strategy, which necessitated holding larger—and more costly—inventories. Parts

• • • • • • • •

Mechanics of the Spending Multiplier

Suppose that you fall for the temptation to buy a $1 ticket for the state lottery. You should be more than a little surprised if you win anything,[5] but let us suppose you win $100. Let us further suppose that you win your money in a mythical kingdom

---

[5]Why should you be more than a little surprised? Because the odds against winning anything in most state lotteries are *extremely* small. So small, in fact, that most state lotteries would be illegal in Las Vegas where gambling is regulated so that the players have a reasonable chance of winning. If you play the lottery, do so for fun, not with the expectation of ever getting your money back, much less "winning"!

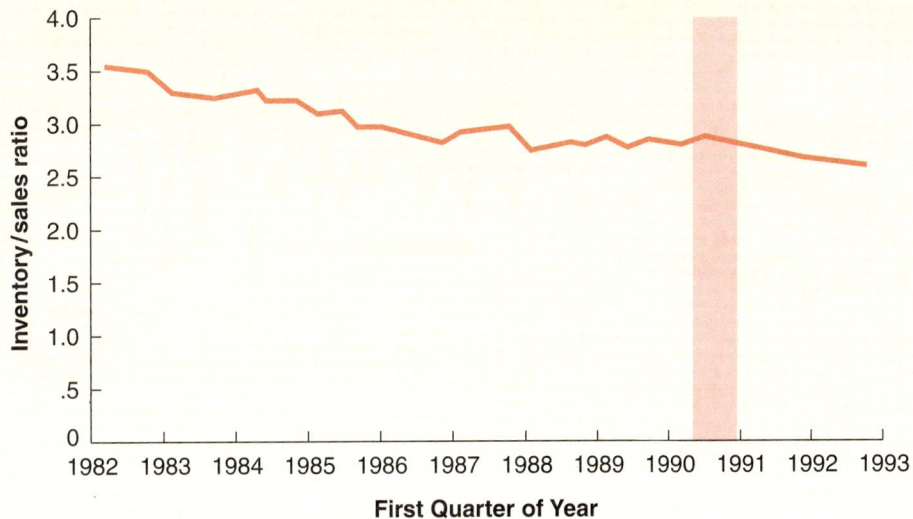

First Quarter of Year

were often kept for weeks in U.S. plants. One study indicated that barely 15 percent of U.S. auto parts were delivered just-in-time; the comparable figure for Japan was 45 percent.[1]

The chart above suggests that U.S. firms may be learning from the Japanese. The inventory/sales ratio fell steadily throughout the 1980s. The fact that U.S. firms began the 1990–

1991 recession (marked by the shaded area on the chart) with low inventories and thus had to resort to smaller production cutbacks may have prevented the recession from becoming more severe than it was. According to a 1993 study by the Federal Reserve Bank of Boston, much of the recent decline in inventories can be attributed to new inventory-management systems made possible by computers. As the number of computers in business increases, we can probably expect lower invento-

ries. This is probably a good sign for long-run productivity. At the same time, some have suggested that the desire to maintain low inventories was a reason for the sluggishness of the 1992–1993 recovery: in an effort to keep inventories low, firms kept production levels low and placed fewer orders for intermediate goods.

[1]These data were cited in William Abernathy, *Industrial Renaissance* (New York: Basic Books, 1983).

SOURCE: Data are from *Economic Report of the President,* various issues. The shaded area marks the July 1990–March 1991 recession.

without any taxes. To celebrate your luck, you take your best friend out to dinner and blow the entire $100.

Now, the restaurateur is pleasantly surprised to have a little extra business and decides to spend 90 percent of the extra income and save 10 percent. That means he will spend $90—which happens to be just the amount he needed for some dental work he had been putting off. Like most people, the dentist also spends a portion, say, 90 percent, and saves the rest of her income. Ninety percent of the $90 she received from the restaurateur is just enough to buy that $81 graphite fishing rod she has wanted for a while now. The fishing tackle shop owner is not only grateful to finally sell the rod, but can also use the money. Like everyone else in our mythical kingdom, he too spends 90 percent of his new income—$72.90 on books for his continuing education economics class—and saves the remaining 10 percent.

We could carry on the process, but you should be seeing the point: that initial $100 increase in spending has generated a multiple increase in income—$100 to the restaurateur, $90 to the dentist, $81 for the tackle shop owner, $72.90 to the bookstore, and so on. This is how the multiplier works: a small increase in spending generates a multiple increase in income. How much of an increase in income? We will show in Chapter 24 that in this case, the $100 increase in spending would result in an increase in income of $1,000, making a multiplier of $k_e = 1,000/100 = 10$. Table 23.4 illustrates the multiplier process.

The multiplier process is so important for two main reasons. First, it is critical to the process of adjustment to equilibrium. For example, in the inventory adjustment example illustrated in Table 23.2, production exceeded spending and unintended inventories accumulated by $10. We discovered that firms would lay off workers and cut back production in the next period—but we were not able to say *how much* they would cut production. The multiplier will help us answer that question. Second, the multiplier will be critical when we begin to analyze fiscal policy in Chapter 25. There we will use the multiplier to determine how much to cut taxes or increase government spending to boost the economy out of recession.

· · · · · · · · ·

Qualifications

At this point, we need to make some important qualifications. First, a technical point: the multiplier process must begin with a change in spending that is not associated with an increase in income; in this case, it began when you won $100 in the lottery. Subsequent rounds of spending are determined by changes in income—$100 to the restaurateur, $90 to the dentist, and so on. Second, the value of the multiplier depends on the portion of income that is spent in every round. In the example we have just worked through, we assumed everyone spent 90 percent of their new income so that only 10 percent "leaked out" of the spending stream in each round. If a smaller portion of income were spent every round—say, only 80 percent—the multiplier

· · · · · **TABLE 23.4 MECHANICS OF THE SPENDING MULTIPLIER**

Round	Change in Income	Change in Spending	Change in Saving
1	$100.00	$90.00	$10.00
2	90.00	81.00	9.00
3	81.00	72.90	8.10
4	72.90	65.61	7.29
5	65.61	59.05	6.56
⋮	⋮	⋮	⋮
∞	0.00	0.00	0.00
	$1,000.00	$900.00	$100.00

and resulting change in income would be smaller; if a larger portion of income were spent, the multiplier would be larger. Third, it takes an infinite number of spending rounds for the multiplier to work itself out. The practical implications of this are that the multiplier never works itself out completely. In fact, most economists *truncate* the multiplier after about two years. Finally, several other factors including actions in the financial markets and price changes reduce the real-world value of the spending multiplier significantly. Most estimates show spending multipliers on the order of something between 2 and 3.

SUMMARY

More than a few students begin wondering just what they have gotten themselves into when they reach this chapter. Not only is the material becoming more theoretical, but there seems to be a fair amount of disagreement among economists. Some economists think the economy tends to self-correct, but others think it is prone to crisis. Who is correct? Both are. Remember that we are developing *models* to help us understand the real economy. Say's law places most emphasis on wage, price, and interest rate flexibility and does a good job describing conditions that reduce the chance the economy will fall into recession. Keynes's attack on Say's law focused on different ideas to present the conditions that might lead to recession.

What is the key difference between the two approaches? Advocates of Say's law have faith that wage, price, and interest rate flexibility will cause all markets to clear; strict Keynesians deny the curative powers of these flexibilities. As we will see later, contemporary economists generally fall somewhere in between. Most economists recognize that price, wage, and interest rate flexibility help the economy recover from recession, but there is debate over the speed of adjustment. If prices, wages, and interest rates are so flexible that recessions are unlikely, there is little role for deliberate macroeconomic policy. But if price, wage, and interest adjustments are sluggish, the door is opened for activist macroeconomic policies. This is the real debate among most contemporary macroeconomists. The key points from the chapter are:

1. Say's law of markets holds that "supply creates its own demand." Price, wage, and interest rate flexibility are critical to Say's law.
2. Keynes criticized Say's law by arguing that savers and investors are different people with different motives. He did not believe that interest rate flexibility was sufficient to assure equality between saving and planned investment.
3. The macroeconomy is in equilibrium when saving equals planned investment or, equivalently, when planned spending equals production and income. When planned spending is less than production, there is an increase in unintended inventories. A rise in unintended inventories causes firms to cut production and lay off workers. When planned spending is greater than production, there is an unintended decrease in inventories. This causes firms to increase production and hire workers.
4. The spending multiplier is based on the fact that one person's spending is another person's income. A small change in spending will bring about a large change in income.

KEY TERMS AND CONCEPTS

Say's law

price flexibility

wage flexibility

voluntary unemployment

interest rate flexibility

wage rigidity

liquidity preference

liquidity

inventory adjustment

spending multiplier

REVIEW QUESTIONS

1. Explain how price, wage, and interest rate flexibility help the economy recover from recession.
2. What arguments did Keynes use in his attack on Say's law?
3. Explain the relationship between planned saving and planned investment, and between planned spending and income.
4. What is the spending multiplier? How is it affected by the spending and saving behavior of households?

PROBLEMS

1. The discussion in the chapter indicated that rising inventories signal a pending recession. Can you think of a situation when rising inventories are a signal of economic expansion?
2. Suppose that everyone spent all of their income. How would this affect the spending multiplier? Explain with an example.
3. Suppose that the economy enters a recession and wages and prices adjust as predicted by Say's law. However, interest rates are set by government decree and cannot change. Do you think Keynes would advocate eliminating interest rate controls as a means to help the economy recover? Why or why not?
4. Do you think that Malthus would have agreed with Say's law of markets? Why or why not? (You may need to refer back to Chapter 22 to review Malthus's ideas on macroeconomics.)
5. Suppose that a White House scandal resulted in widespread speculation that the president was on the verge of resigning. Suppose further that the vice-president is a virtual unknown. Use the theory of liquidity preference to explain why the economy might fall into a recession.

CHAPTER 24

The Income-Expenditure Model I: A Closed Economy with No Government

Economists use models because the world is too complex to understand without them. You can't just look out the window and understand what causes recessions or inflation. Some simplification is necessary, but not too much. The result from the last chapter—that the economy can fall into a recession if planned spending is less than production—only begins to provide an explanation for recession. We need to know *why* planned spending is less than production. This chapter is a first step in trying to understand why this condition might arise. Our approach is to look at the theories of consumption and investment and then combine these theories into an aggregate expenditure function, a key component of the income-expenditure model.

Before we begin, a word of caution is in order: the maxim "a little knowledge can be dangerous" is especially appropriate just now. The model we develop here will give us a glimpse at the causes of recession, but it is far from complete. Only after we have completed several more chapters will we be ready to diagnose recessions and cyclical fluctuations with any confidence. And even then, a bit of humility will be in order: economists have a long way to go before they can say, with conviction, that they understand the nature of business cycle fluctuations.

AFTER READING AND STUDYING THIS CHAPTER, YOU SHOULD BE ABLE TO:

• • • Write out the aggregate expenditure function, and explain its relationship to production and equilibrium

• • • State Keynes's fundamental law of consumption and the simple consumption function

• • • Explain the relationship between investment, interest rates, and income

• • • Find equilibrium income and the spending multiplier

ASSUMPTIONS AND DEFINITIONS

Before we begin to build the income-expenditure model, we need to state our assumptions and define two terms that we will be using in this and the next few chapters:

- *Simplifying assumptions.* All models involve assumptions, and the income-expenditure model is no exception. This model assumes that prices and all financial variables including the interest rate are constant. Do these assumptions mean the model is useless? Not in the least. Making these assumptions makes it easier to focus on the factors in which we are most interested—primarily the conditions that exist in equilibrium and the value of the spending multiplier. Once these pieces of the puzzle are in place, it is easy to explore the implications of price and interest rate flexibility.

  We are also assuming in this chapter that the economy has no government, taxes, or foreign sector. These assumptions will make the analysis less cumbersome, and later we can adjust the analysis to remove these restrictive assumptions. The no-taxes assumption does require one clarification, however: the absence of taxes means that there is no difference between income and disposable income. This means that household consumption is a function of income, not disposable income. When we consider taxes in the next chapter, consumption will be a function of disposable income.

- *Induced variables.* The income-expenditure model incorporates both autonomous and **induced variables.** An induced variable is one whose value depends on the level of national income. A portion of household consumption expenditure is induced because an increase in income permits people to buy more food, clothing, and other items. For the time being, consumption will be the only variable we treat as induced.

- *Autonomous variables.* **Autonomous variables** do not vary with income although they may be affected by other factors. In this chapter, we will be assuming that all investment spending and a portion of consumption spending are autonomous. All autonomous variables have a subscript zero; that is, the statement $I = I_0$ indicates that investment is entirely autonomous. It is read, "investment spending is autonomous," or "investment spending is assumed constant at the level I_0." But doesn't investment actually vary with income? It certainly can. As GDP rises, many firms expand production in an attempt to increase sales. This often requires an increase in investment. Assuming that investment is autonomous simplifies the analysis considerably, however, and we will relax this assumption when necessary.

Induced variable A variable that is influenced by the level of income.

Autonomous variable A variable that does not depend on income.

THE CONSUMPTION FUNCTION

The biggest portion of aggregate spending is personal consumption, which accounts for about 66 percent of all spending in the U.S. economy. If we can develop a model that adequately captures consumer behavior, we will be a long way toward understanding the macroeconomy. This is just the approach that Keynes followed

•••• TABLE 24.1 CONSUMPTION FUNCTION DATA

Line	Q	C	S	ΔQ	ΔC	APC	MPC
a	0	50	−50	—	—	—	—
b	100	130	−30	100	80	1.30	0.80
c	200	210	−10	100	80	1.05	0.80
d	300	290	+10	100	80	0.97	0.80
e	400	370	+30	100	80	0.93	0.80
f	500	450	+50	100	80	0.90	0.80
.							
.							
.							
g	1,000	850	+150	500	400	0.85	0.80

Key:

Q = income, C = consumption, S = saving, ΔQ = change in income, ΔC = change in consumption, APC = average propensity to consume, MPC = marginal propensity to consume

when he offered his "fundamental psychological" law of consumption. Keynes's theory will be the starting place for our development of the spending equation.

••••••••

Keynes's Fundamental Psychological Law

All good economic theories make sense—which is only logical given that economics is an attempt to understand predictable human behavior. Keynes's theory of consumption is no exception. It states simply that as people's income goes up, so does their consumption, but by a smaller amount. For example, if you get a $100 per month raise, you will probably increase your consumption spending by an amount less than $100, say, $80.[1] What do you do with the remaining $20? It goes into saving. Of course, some people might spend all of the $100 and others might spend nothing, but most people—and thus the economy as a whole—tend to do pretty much as Keynes suggested, spend some and save some. The amazing thing about this simple idea is that it can yield important results regarding the economy and economic policy.

A simple Keynesian **consumption function** is illustrated in Table 24.1. First, look at line *d*: income (Q) is 300, consumption (C) is 290, and saving (S) is 10. When income increases by 100 to 400 in line *e*, consumption rises by only 80 to 370. This is consistent with Keynes's law because the change in consumption, $\Delta C = 80$, is less than the change in income, $\Delta Q = 100$.[2] All of the entries in the table are derived from this simple fact.

Consumption function The relationship between consumption expenditure and disposable income.

[1] We need to recall the difference between *income* and *money* before proceeding. Income is a flow variable so it must have a time dimension. It makes a difference whether you earn $10 per hour or $10 per week. Money is a stock variable with no time dimension.
[2] Remember that the Greek letter "Δ" (delta) represents change. In this case, $\Delta C = C_2 - C_1$. Likewise, $\Delta Q = Q_2 - Q_1$.

Let's look at another line in the table, line *a*. Here, income is zero, but consumption is positive at 50. How is that possible? It is not possible in the long run. It may be possible to draw down existing savings ("dissave") in the short run, but eventually savings will be exhausted unless additional income is earned. Consumption is greater than income in lines *b* and *c* so saving must be negative at these income levels as well. The possibility of negative saving is an indication that the model we are developing is a short-run model. The point where $Q = 0$ is the intercept of the consumption function, 50 in this example. The intercept of the consumption function is *autonomous consumption,* the portion of consumption that does not depend on the level of income.

Another glance at the data in Table 24.1 reveals that the change in consumption column has the same entry for every line, $\Delta C = 80$. Income also increases by a constant amount, $\Delta Q = 100$, so the relationship between the change in consumption and the change in income is constant: $\Delta C/\Delta Q = 80/100 = 0.8$. This relationship has a special name, the **marginal propensity to consume** or **MPC** for short. The MPC tells what fraction of a change in income people generally spend; in this case, it means that people will spend 80¢ of each new dollar of income that they take home. It also means that if they take home $1 less, their consumption spending will fall by just 80¢. The MPC must fall between 0 and 1. It would be 0 if people did not spend any of their new income and 1 if they spent it all, but most people probably save a fraction of their new income.

The remaining column in the table is the **APC** or **average propensity to consume** column. The APC gives the ratio of total consumption to total income, C/Q. The APC differs from the MPC because it is the fraction of your total income that you spend—a number like 95 percent for many people—instead of the fraction of the *change* in income that you spend. The APC declines as income increases. For example, when income equals 300, consumption equals 290. This gives an APC of $290/300 = 0.97$. When income rises to 400, consumption rises to 370, but the APC falls to $370/400 = 0.93$.

A glance down the APC and MPC columns shows that the APC is greater than the MPC but approaches the MPC as income increases. Does this make sense? It does if we assume that these are short-run data. For example, an income change from $400 to $500 might be the result of earning a bonus or working overtime. In this case, you will probably spend some of your $100 bonus (say, $80), but you recognize that your income may fall back to the more normal $400 soon so it would be unwise to lock yourself into a higher car payment or move to a bigger apartment. Or suppose that you had a bad week and made only $300 instead of your usual $400. You would cut your consumption spending as little as possible (say, from $370 to $290) because you still have to pay bills and want to maintain the consumption level to which you are accustomed. The situation would be different if the data represented long-run or permanent changes in income. If you got a $100 raise and could count on that raise lasting indefinitely, you might lock yourself into a continuing payment obligation—perhaps buying a new car or moving into a larger (and more expensive) apartment. We are focusing on the short run here because we are most interested in understanding business cycles. A brief survey of consumption theories that are better suited to long-run analysis is presented in the Focus box on page 606.

Marginal propensity to consume (MPC) The change in consumption induced by one more unit of income.

Average propensity to consume (APC) Total consumption divided by disposable income.

Graphing the Consumption Function

The simple Keynesian consumption function is linear and has both autonomous and induced elements as shown in Figure 24.1. The vertical axis of the figure measures consumption spending, C, and the horizontal axis measures real income or GDP, Q. The intercept of the consumption function is the level of autonomous consumption, C_0. In this example, autonomous consumption is 50. The slope of the consumption function is the marginal propensity to consume, which will be indicated with a lowercase b. The MPC is 0.8 in this example. This is all the information we need to write the equation of the consumption function:

Keynesian consumption function:
consumption = autonomous consumption + MPC(income)

$$C = C_0 + bQ \qquad [1]$$

In this case, the consumption function is:

$$C = 50 + 0.8Q$$

Figure 24.1 also includes a **45° line** to help us understand the relationship between consumer spending and income. There is no "economics" behind the 45° line; it is

45° line A straight line that bisects the right angle formed by the horizontal and vertical axes. Any point on the line is equidistant from both axes, so the values will be equal.

FIGURE 24.1 THE KEYNESIAN CONSUMPTION FUNCTION

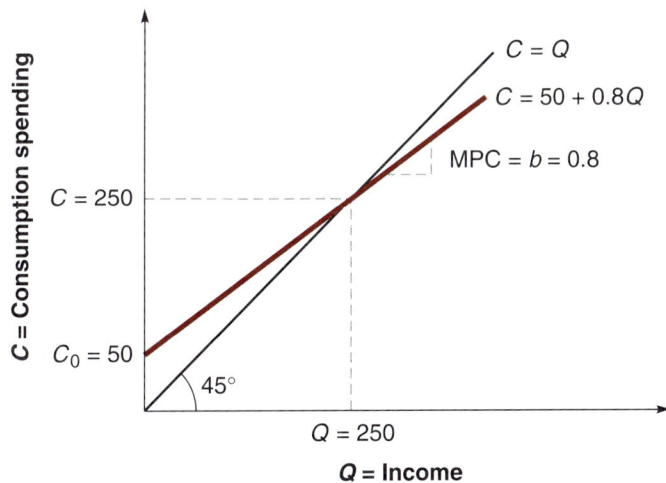

The Keynesian consumption function is based on Keynes's proposition that as income increases, so does consumption, but by a smaller amount. The intercept of the consumption function is autonomous consumption, $C_0 = 50$ in this example. The slope of the consumption function is the marginal propensity to consume, $b = 0.8$ in this example. The 45° line plots all points where $C = Q$. The intersection between the 45° line and the consumption function gives the value of Q where saving is zero and the APC = 1.

MODERN THEORIES OF CONSUMPTION

The Keynesian theory of consumption says little more than "as income increases, so does consumption, but less." Economists have long recognized that the consumption decision is more complex. Most contemporary theories of consumption hypothesize that people base their current consumption decisions on their income over several years and that they try to maximize utility over time. This Focus box will introduce you to some current thinking in the theory of consumption.

THE LIFE-CYCLE HYPOTHESIS

The life-cycle theory hypothesizes that people base current consumption on a prediction of their lifetime expected income. For example, a certain economics professor, who shall remain nameless, attended graduate school at the University of Colorado—Boulder. Like most graduate students, his teaching assistantship brought in barely

enough money to allow him to scrape out a meager existence—and much less than enough to permit him to indulge his passion for skiing. However, our graduate student realized that his current poverty would be alleviated as soon as he completed his Ph.D. and entered the high-paying field of college teaching. His response: Borrow as much as possible and hit the slopes. It would be easy to pay off the debt within a few years of graduation. Today, that onetime graduate student is well into middle age and, having paid off the debts he incurred in his early years, is in the process of saving for a comfortable retirement.

Sound reasonable? It should. Many people behave this way because they expect their income to follow a similar pattern: low income at early stages of their career, high income in the middle earning years, and low income when they retire. Further, because people know this, it is rational to bor-

row against middle-age income when young—to buy a house, furniture, and so on—and save some middle-age income for future retirement.

THE PERMANENT INCOME HYPOTHESIS

The permanent income theory holds that people must spread their income and consumption over time in order to maximize utility. An example will illustrate the basic idea. Suppose you graduate from college and take a job as a traveling encyclopedia salesperson. After a few months on the job, you begin to generate a stable income, say, $1,000 per month. One day, however, you happen to knock on the door of the Commissioner of Education, who, as it happens, is in the mood to buy new encyclopedias for every school in the entire state. Your commission turns out to be $20,000 this month. Now, if your consumption function is the same one illustrated in Table 24.1,

merely a plot of the points where the value on the vertical axis (consumption) is equal to the value on the horizontal axis (income). The intersection between the consumption function—which *is* based upon economic theory—and the 45° line gives the point where all income is spent on consumption; that is, where consumer behavior is such that $Q = C$. This occurs at an income level of 250—a value we derive in the appendix to this chapter. At income levels below 250, consumption is greater than income because the consumption function is above the 45° line; this indicates that saving is negative. At income levels above 250, income is greater than consumption because the 45° line is above the consumption function; this indicates that saving is positive.

you will spend $16,050. That is enough for a down payment on that BMW you have always wanted, plus a Concorde flight to Paris for lunch at Maxim's with a few of your nearest and dearest personal friends. You all have a grand time. The problem comes next month, when your income returns to the $1,000 average: you don't have enough money to buy groceries, pay the rent, and make the payment on your BMW. The BMW gets repossessed and your credit record is shot. Wouldn't it have been better to base your spending on average or permanent income and spread consumption over time? If you had put the bonus in the bank, you could count on the interest return every year.

IMPLICATIONS

Both the life-cycle hypothesis and the permanent income hypothesis hold that people base current consumption on several years of income. This implies that small changes in current income—say, a Christmas bonus—should not affect consumption very

much because people will spread that bonus over several years. It would, however, make sense to spend that Christmas bonus on a durable good—say a new stereo—because you would be spreading the bonus over several years by purchasing a good that will last several years. In fact, there is strong evidence that the demand for consumer durables is closely related to temporary income changes. The same kind of reasoning applies to short-term cycle fluctuations. People know that the income losses from cyclical downturns are temporary, so they reduce their saving—and thus increase their average propensity to consume—until the good times return. This explains why the short-run APC rises during recessions and falls during expansions. This fact cannot easily be explained with simple Keynesian theory. On the other hand, a permanent change in income—say, a promotion and raise—will change consumption significantly.

The small response to temporary changes in income has an important

implication for fiscal policy: if consumers perceive tax changes to be temporary—for example, a temporary income tax rebate—there is likely to be little change in consumption behavior. On the other hand, tax changes that are regarded as permanent should result in a significant change in consumption behavior.

THE SIMPLE KEYNESIAN CONSUMPTION, REPRISE

Modern work in consumption theory is ongoing and important, but this does not negate the insights from the simple Keynesian model. For short-run changes in income, all of these theories establish quite similar results: consumption will change less than income, and the MPC is between 0 and 1. Most important for our purposes, however, is the fact that it is easy to combine the simple Keynesian model with other elements of aggregate spending. This is an important step in our construction of the basic macroeconomic model we will use to determine equilibrium GDP.

. . . .

Shifting, Rotating, and Moving along the Consumption Function

A change in the level of income will result in movement *along* the consumption function; anything that affects the level of autonomous consumption will shift the consumption function, as shown in Figure 24.2. Three of the most important factors that can shift the consumption function are wealth, consumer confidence, and autonomous taxes. Other things being equal, an increase in wealth—remember that wealth is a stock while income is a flow—will reduce the need for saving. This causes the consumption function to shift upward and thus reduces autonomous saving; a decline in wealth will tend to shift the consumption function downward.

Expectations can affect the consumption function in several ways. For example,

···· **FIGURE 24.2 SHIFTING THE CONSUMPTION FUNCTION**

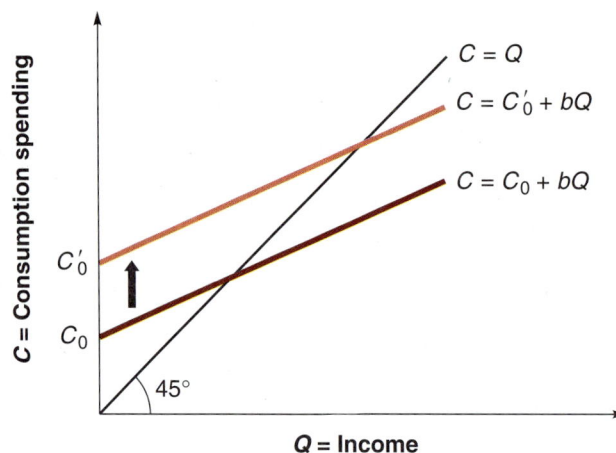

The consumption function will shift when the level of autonomous consumption changes. Three factors that will increase the level of autonomous consumption are an increase in consumer wealth, an increase in consumer confidence or positive expectations, and a cut in autonomous taxes. A decrease in wealth, or decline in consumer confidence, or an increase in autonomous taxes would shift the consumption function downward.

if consumers are confident of rapid economic growth in the future, they will not be very concerned about layoffs so consumption might increase for all levels of income. On the other hand, concern about an impending recession might cause consumers to cut back on their spending and would shift the consumption function downward. We will discover in the next chapter that taxes and transfers can also shift the consumption function: a decrease in autonomous taxes or an increase in transfers shifts the consumption function upward; an increase in autonomous taxes or a decrease in transfers shifts it downward.

The consumption function will rotate and change slope if there is a change in the MPC. If consumers start spending a higher fraction of their income, the MPC will increase, and the consumption function will become steeper. This might be caused by changing perceptions on the permanence of income fluctuations. For example, if you notice that your boss gives you a raise every time you volunteer to work over-time, you might start treating "temporary" overtime pay as a permanent raise and move into a new apartment. In this case, your MPC would rise because you would be spending a higher fraction of your overtime pay on a nicer (and more expensive) apartment. The graphical result, shown in Figure 24.3, is an increase in the slope of the consumption function. A sudden desire to use your new income to finance future graduate studies would reduce the MPC and make the consumption function flatter.

········

Consumption and Saving

You may have wondered why we said so little about the saving column in Table 24.1. This is not because saving is unimportant. In fact, saving can play a very impor-

···· **FIGURE 24.3** ROTATING THE CONSUMPTION FUNCTION

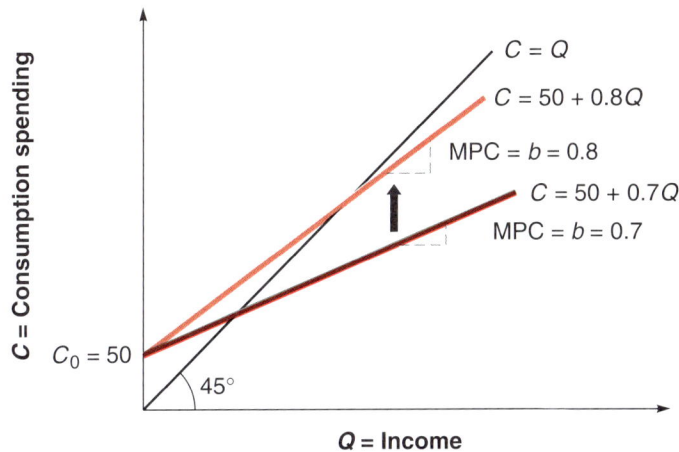

Anything that changes the MPC will change the slope of the consumption function. In this case the MPC has increased from 0.7 to 0.8 so the consumption function is steeper. Notice that autonomous consumption does not change.

tant role in the macroeconomy—but not in the simple model we are developing in this chapter. The appendix to this chapter shows that the saving function provides the same information as the consumption function and presents an alternative way to find equilibrium GDP that makes use of the relationship between saving and investment. Using saving instead of consumption does not really show anything new, however, so we can omit most discussion of saving until we examine the long run in later chapters. For the time being, we need to know only one additional bit of information about saving: the relationship between the **marginal propensity to save (MPS)** and the marginal propensity to consume. The marginal propensity to save gives the proportion of a change in income that people save. It is defined:

Marginal propensity to save (MPS) The change in saving induced by one more unit of income.

$$\text{Marginal propensity to save: MPS} = \frac{\Delta S}{\Delta Q}$$

In Table 24.1, saving changes by \$20 every time income changes by \$100, so the MPS is equal to 0.2. Notice that the MPC = 0.8 and the MPS = 0.2, so they add up to 1:

$$\text{MPC} + \text{MPS} = 1 \qquad [2]$$

The relationship between the MPC and the MPS will be important when we calculate spending multipliers later in this chapter.[3]

---

[3]When we add income taxes and imports in the next chapter, we will have to modify Equation 2 slightly. It is true as written because of the assumptions we made at the beginning of this chapter.

> **RECAP**   Facts about the Keynesian Consumption Function
>
> 1. Keynes's fundamental psychological law states that as income increases, consumption increases, but by a smaller amount.
> 2. The MPC is the ratio of a change in consumption to a change in income, $\Delta C/\Delta Q$. The MPC is usually assumed to be constant and is a fraction between 0 and 1.
> 3. The slope of the consumption function is the MPC. A higher MPC will make the consumption function steeper; a lower MPC will make it flatter. The intercept of the consumption function is autonomous consumption.
> 4. The APC is the ratio of total consumption to total income, C/Q. The APC is greater than the MPC but declines as income increases.
> 5. The MPS is the ratio of the change in saving to the change in income. The MPS plus the MPC is equal to 1.

INVESTMENT

Investment is a smaller component of aggregate spending than consumption; the ratio of gross private domestic investment to GDP averages about 15 percent in the United States. Unlike consumption, however, investment is extremely erratic; the investment/GDP ratio can fluctuate substantially from year to year. Business cycles can often be traced to fluctuations in investment. Economists know that many factors influence investment—interest rates, expectations, taxes, and so on—but they have not yet been able to formulate a model that can explain or predict investment with much accuracy.

Why is investment so difficult to forecast? One possible reason is that investment decisions are successful only if business executives can accurately forecast the future, which is extremely difficult to do. As a result, investment decisions are often based on intuition and on what Keynes called "animal spirits"—concepts difficult or impossible to model. For the time being, however, we are only concerned with how changes in the level of investment affect aggregate spending and GDP, so we will simplify things immensely by focusing on just two factors, interest rates and the state of business confidence.

Interest Rates and Investment

Investment is primarily a financial decision—the hope for monetary gain—but the act itself is one of spending by firms to acquire capital goods. Before investing, entrepreneurs must decide whether the return on investment will cover all costs and leave a profit. Economists express this return as a percentage. Suppose the cost of a new piece of machinery is $1,000,000 and that the expected return is $200,000 per year after paying all additional costs associated with using the new machine. The **expected return (R^e)** on this machine is then $200,000/1,000,000 = 20$ percent. If the firm has to borrow the $1,000,000, the investment project makes sense only if money can be borrowed at an interest rate less than 20 percent. What if the firm does not need to

Expected return (R^e) All investment decisions are based on imperfect knowledge of the future. Firms will acquire capital if the expected return is greater than the interest rate.

borrow the money? It should still buy the machine only if the interest rate is less than 20 percent. If the market rate is 20 percent or higher, the firm would be better off depositing the money in a bank at the higher interest rate.

The expected return on investment usually declines as the number of investment projects increases. The main reason for this is that at any point in time, the firm can undertake only a few investment projects, and some projects are better than others. The rational producer will engage in the most profitable project first, the second most profitable project next, and so on. At an interest rate of 10 percent, a project with a 20 percent expected return should be carried out. So should a project with an expected return of 15 percent. But a third plan, one with an expected return of only 10 percent, does not make sense because of the uncertainty surrounding the project. Firms need an expected rate of return above the market rate of interest to account for risk. In fact, even the project with the expected return of 15 percent may not be a good investment if you are not confident about your forecast of a 15 percent return.

The relationship between investment and expected return is called the **marginal efficiency of investment** or **MEI** for short. For any one firm, the MEI is likely to be "lumpy" because investment projects cannot be broken down into small units, but for the economy as a whole, it is probably fairly smooth as shown in Figure 24.4.

Marginal efficiency of investment (MEI) The relationship between expected return and investment.

FIGURE 24.4 THE MARGINAL EFFICIENCY OF INVESTMENT (MEI)

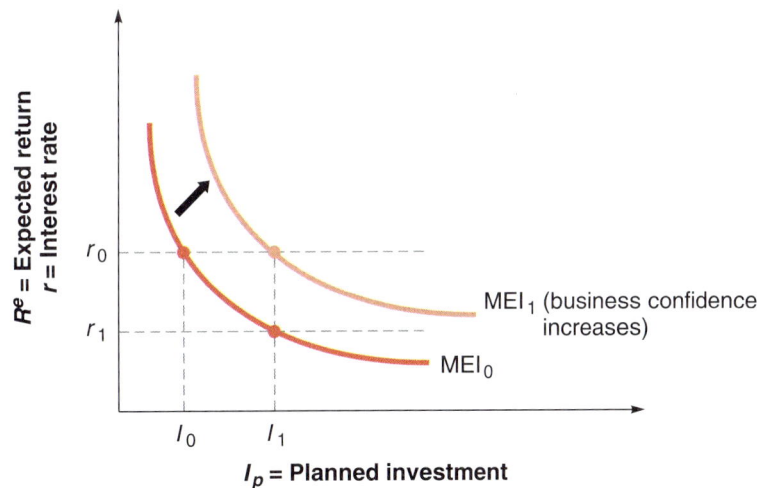

The marginal efficiency of investment (MEI) plots the relationship between the expected return (R^e) and planned investment (I_p). Expected return declines as investment increases, so lower interest rates are necessary to increase investment along a given MEI curve. Firms will invest only if the expected return exceeds the interest rate that could be earned on financial assets, and the expected return on risky projects must be greater than the interest rate that could be earned on risk-free financial assets. The MEI curve shifts when there is a change in business confidence. A more optimistic outlook would result in a shift from MEI_0 to MEI_1. The result is a higher level of investment for every interest rate. For example, if the interest rate is r_0, an increase in business confidence will raise investment from I_0 to I_1. A decline in business confidence would shift the MEI curve from MEI_1 to MEI_0, and there would be less investment for every interest rate. Notice that without the increase in business confidence, the interest rate would have to fall to r_1 before investment would increase to I_1.

· · · · · · · ·

Business Confidence and Investment

The MEI plots the relationship between the *expected* return on investment and the level of investment. Why did we emphasize the word "expected"? Investment projects typically last for several years, and the future cannot be known with certainty, so investment decisions are always subject to error. This is why many businesspeople seem to rely on intuition and rules of thumb as much as analytical methods when deciding whether to engage in an investment project. In fact, the state of **business confidence** is one of the most important factors influencing the level of investment.

Business confidence Firms' outlook on the future. When the outlook is optimistic, investment will increase at all interest rates; when the outlook is pessimistic, investment will decline at all interest rates.

The state of business confidence is an important shift factor for the MEI curve. If businesspeople begin to expect a stable and growing economy in the future, the MEI will shift away from the vertical axis so that a higher level of investment is associated with every interest rate. A more pessimistic outlook will shift the MEI toward the vertical axis and cause a decline in investment at every interest rate. This is shown in Figure 24.4.

Risk versus Uncertainty. Business confidence plays such an important role in the investment decision because all investment projects are risky. Firms try to rank the expected return and risks associated with various projects, but the real issue is whether firms have confidence in their ranking criteria. Many firms use statistical theory to assign an expected average return on each project, plus or minus a few percentage points to account for risk. While this approach is popular, it glosses over a key problem: investment is inherently *uncertain,* and uncertainty is a different concept from risk. Playing cards is a risky endeavor: the chances of getting a royal flush are very small, but it is possible to figure out the chances with precision and bet accordingly. The profitability of a new project is both risky and uncertain; you may have no idea whether the consumers will buy your product, or whether a competitor is ready to bring out a new model. You may use historical information to estimate the risk, but you cannot estimate the uncertainty.

Most investment decisions face uncertainty because the future cannot be known—until it becomes the present and cannot be changed. Thus, while the shape of the MEI is important, perhaps more important are the expectations and intuition of businesspeople. A low interest rate will encourage investment only if the future "feels" good.

· · · · · · · ·

Other Factors That Affect Investment

The interest rate and business confidence may be the most important factors affecting investment, but they are not the only ones. Expected inflation, plant capacity utilization, technology, and GDP growth can also affect the pace of investment.

- *Expected inflation.* If selling prices rise faster than costs, the firm's profits will increase, and this can stimulate investment expenditures. It should be noted, however, that a high rate of inflation often means volatile inflation, and this can generate future uncertainty and reduce investment.
- *Plant capacity.* Firms with extensive unused plant capacity are less likely to acquire new capital goods than firms that are running at maximum capacity.

····· **FIGURE 24.5** THE INVESTMENT FUNCTION

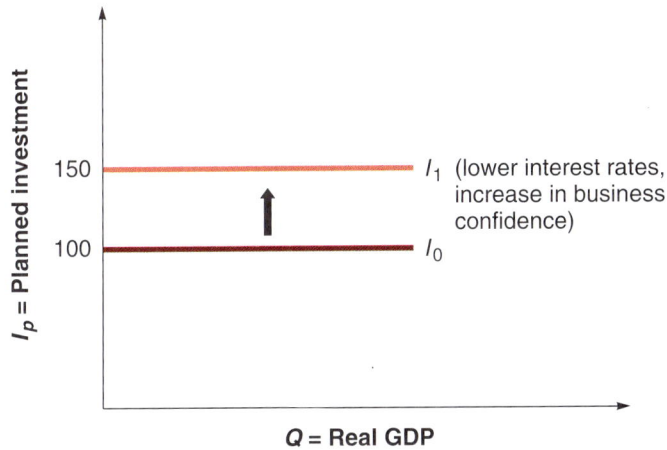

Investment is treated as autonomous with respect to income, so its graph is a horizontal line. The intercept of the investment function is the level of autonomous investment, I_0. The slope of the investment function is zero because there is no induced investment. Autonomous investment will shift upward from I_0 to I_1 if business confidence increases or if the interest rate falls.

· *Technology.* If a new production method becomes available, the first firm to adopt it is likely to have a cost advantage—and earn profits.
· *GDP growth.* A growing economy means increased sales that may require increased production and plant capacity.

········

The Investment Function

In the income-expenditure model, investment is treated as an autonomous variable because it is not assumed to be a function of income. Interest rates, business confidence, and other variables are shift factors. This means that the level of investment is assumed fixed for all levels of real GDP and the slope of the investment function is zero. The investment function is shown in Figure 24.5.

For our purposes, the two most important shift factors are interest rates and the level of business confidence. An increase in business confidence or a decline in interest rates will shift the investment function upward so that more investment takes place at all levels of income. A decrease in business confidence or an increase in interest rates will shift the investment function downward.

RECAP   Investment in the Income-Expenditure Model

1. The marginal efficiency of investment (MEI) is downward sloping because the expected return declines as additional investment projects are carried out. Firms invest if they believe that the expected return is greater than the inter-

est rate. Investment decisions are complicated because the future is fundamentally uncertain.

2. Investment is considered autonomous in the income-expenditure model. Other things being equal, lower interest rates or an increase in business confidence will increase investment and shift the investment line upward while higher interest rates or a decline in business confidence will shift it downward.

EQUILIBRIUM GDP

We are now ready to put some of the pieces together and solve for equilibrium GDP—the level of GDP at which the economy will tend to rest in the short run. As we learned in the last chapter, equilibrium exists when planned spending equals income and unintended inventory changes are zero. We need to combine this result with what we have just learned about the consumption and investment functions.

Graphing the Planned Spending Equation

In this chapter we are assuming that there is no government or foreign sector, so planned expenditure has just two terms, consumption and planned investment. Consumption, C, is the amount of consumption spending by households. Planned investment, I_p, is the amount of spending on investment goods plus *planned* inventory changes by firms. The planned spending equation is:

$$E_p = C + I_p \qquad [3]$$

Let's suppose that planned investment is 100:

$$I_p = 100$$

and that the consumption function is the same one we used in Table 24.1:

$$C = 50 + 0.8Q$$

Now we are ready for the first step in solving for equilibrium GDP, graphing the planned spending equation. Remember that GDP is the same thing as income because people are paid income when they produce goods and services. This means that finding equilibrium income is equivalent to finding equilibrium GDP.

The planned spending equation in Figure 24.6 has been constructed with vertical addition: the consumption and investment functions have been added vertically to find total planned spending at every level of income. For example, notice that when income (Q) is 500, consumption is 450 (we know this from Table 24.1), and we have just said that planned investment is 100, so planned spending equals 550 when $Q = 500$.

Likewise, when $Q = 0$, autonomous consumption is 50, and autonomous investment is 100, so planned spending is 150.

····· **FIGURE 24.6 THE PLANNED SPENDING FUNCTION**

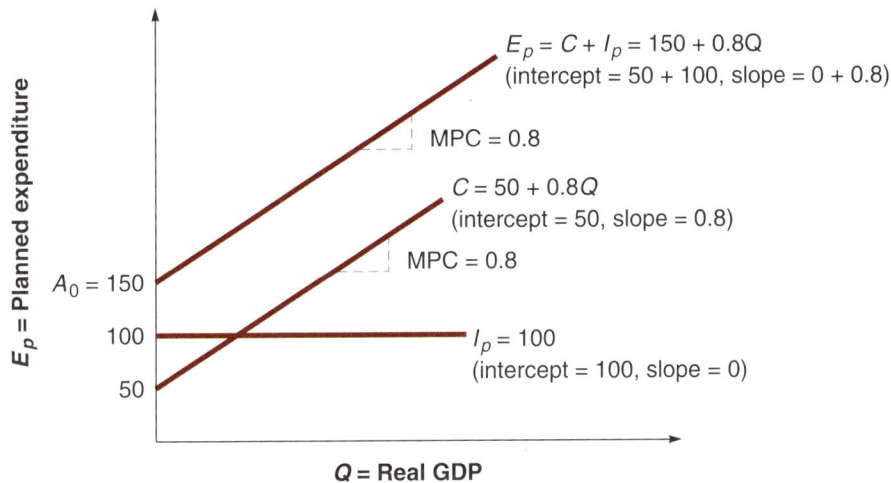

The planned spending function is found by adding together the different components of spending, consumption and investment in this example. The intercept of the planned spending function is total autonomous spending, A_0. In this case, autonomous consumption is 50, and autonomous investment is 100, so total autonomous spending is 150. The slope of the planned spending equation is called the marginal propensity to spend (MPE). Only the consumption function has an induced component in this model, so the slope of the spending function is the same as the slope of the consumption function, 0.8.

In essence, vertical addition amounts to summing the intercepts (50 + 100) and slopes (0 + 0.8) to get the equation of the planned spending line. The intercept of the planned spending function is called *total autonomous spending* (A_0). In this case, total planned autonomous spending equals autonomous consumption plus autonomous investment, but in a more elaborate model—including those we develop in the next chapter—total planned autonomous spending has additional components. The slope of the spending equation is called the **marginal propensity to spend (MPE)**. Notice that, in this case, the slope of the spending equation is the same as the slope of the consumption function so MPC = MPE. This is because only the consumption function has an induced component. This will also change in the next chapter when we add additional kinds of induced spending.

Marginal propensity to spend (MPE) The change in spending induced by one more unit of income.

········

Shifting and Rotating the Spending Function

Anything that shifts or rotates the consumption or investment functions will also shift or rotate the planned spending investment function, and in the same way. Thus, an increase in business confidence will shift both the investment function and the spending line upward; an increase in the interest rate or a decline in business confidence will shift the planned spending line downward. An increase in the MPC will rotate both the consumption function and the planned spending function upward making them steeper; a decrease in the MPC will make both functions less steep.

• • • • • • • •

Solving for Equilibrium

Recall from Chapter 23 that equilibrium exists when planned spending equals income because unintended inventory accumulation is zero. Table 24.2 presents several values for income, spending, and inventory changes based on the consumption function in Table 24.1 and autonomous investment of 100. We need to recall some key points about these data. First, income, Q, is the same thing as production because people earn income from producing goods and services. Second, the unintended change in inventories, I_u, is the difference between production (Q) and planned spending (E_p). Finally, notice that unintended inventories are zero when income is equal to 750. This is the level of equilibrium income. Once the economy gets to this level of income, it will stay there—until it is shocked by a change in business or consumer confidence, inflationary expectations, or any other factor that affects consumption or investment.

Fortunately, we do not have to fill out a complete table every time we need to find the level of equilibrium GDP. It can be done graphically. To do so, we use a 45° line just as we did with the consumption function in Figure 24.1. The 45° line gives all of the values where planned spending equals income; that is, the points where $E_p = Q$. There is no real "economics" in the 45° line, but it does provide an important point of reference: the intersection between the planned spending function (which *does* contain economics) and the 45° line is the point of equilibrium GDP. At this point, economic behavior—as described by the theories of consumption and

• • • • **TABLE 24.2 SOLVING FOR EQUILIBRIUM INCOME**

Q	C	I_p	E_p	I_u
0	50	100	150	−150
100	130	100	230	−130
200	210	100	310	−110
300	290	100	390	−90
400	370	100	470	−70
500	450	100	550	−50
600	530	100	630	−30
700	610	100	710	−10
750	**650**	**100**	**750**	**0**
800	690	100	790	+10
900	770	100	870	+30
1000	850	100	950	+50

Key relationships:

$$E_p = C + I_p \qquad C = 50 + 0.8Q$$
$$I_u = Q - E_p \qquad I_p = 100$$

Key:

Q = income = production, C = consumption, I_p = investment, E_p = planned spending, I_u = unintended inventory change.

····· **FIGURE 24.7** EQUILIBRIUM INCOME

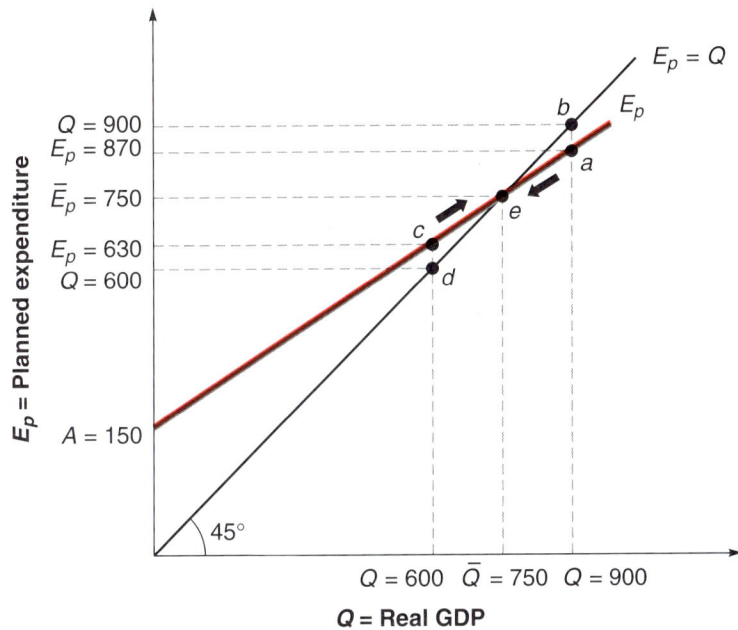

Equilibrium exists when planned spending is equal to income, $E_p = Q$. This occurs where the planned spending function crosses the 45° line. In this case, equilibrium exists when $\overline{Q} = 750$. At income values higher than 750, income is greater than planned spending so inventories pile up. As a result, firms lay off workers and pay out less income, and income declines toward $\overline{Q}$. This situation is illustrated by point a where $Q = 900 > 870 = E_p$. When income is less than $\overline{Q}$, planned spending is greater than income, and firms find their inventories shrinking. The response is to increase production and thus pay out more income. The economy will move toward a higher level of income and production. This situation is illustrated by point c: $Q = 600 < 630 = E_p$.

investment embodied in the planned spending function—is such that all production is purchased, so there is no unintended inventory change.

Figure 24.7 illustrates equilibrium GDP and two other levels of income and planned spending from Table 24.2.[4] The 45° line and the planned spending function intersect at $\overline{Q} = 750$, the level of equilibrium income, where the overbar indicates an equilibrium value. At income levels above $\overline{Q}$, planned spending is less than income so unintended inventories pile up, and firms are forced to cut production, lay off workers, and pay out less income. To see this, first extend a vertical line from $Q = 900$ to the planned spending function at point a. A horizontal line over to the vertical axis gives the level of planned spending, $E_p = 870$, that occurs when $Q = 900$. Now, if we extend a vertical line up from $Q = 900$ to point b on the 45° line, we can

---

[4]The graph in Figure 24.7 is sometimes called the *Keynesian cross* because it is central to the simple Keynesian macroeconomic model. You may see this notation in an Intermediate Macroeconomics or Money and Banking course.

transfer the income value from the horizontal axis to the vertical axis. This allows us to compare income and spending on the same axis. Because income is greater than planned spending ($Q > E_p$), we know that inventories will accumulate ($I_u > 0$) so the economy will slow down and move toward $\overline{Q}$.

The same technique can be used to show that the economy will expand from a level of income less than equilibrium. Begin at $Q = 600$, and extend a line up to point c, which shows the corresponding level of planned spending to be $E_p = 630$. Because planned spending is greater than income ($E_p > Q$), inventories will begin to fall ($I_u < 0$). Firms will respond by hiring workers and increasing production. As they pay out more income, the economy will move toward $\overline{Q}$. Only at $\overline{Q} = E_p$ is there no tendency for unintended inventory change and thus no tendency for the levels of production and income to change. Notice that we have said nothing to imply that equilibrium GDP is the level of GDP that would exist at full employment. In fact, one of the key implications of this model is that it is quite possible for the economy to come to rest in a recession.

THE SPENDING MULTIPLIER

You may have noticed something interesting in Figure 24.7: at points a and c, the difference between planned spending and income was only 30, but the economy was 150 away from its equilibrium value of $\overline{Q} = 750$. This is because equilibrium income changes by a larger amount than autonomous spending—a result we called the spending multiplier in the last chapter. Graphically, the relationship between the change in autonomous spending and the change in equilibrium income is the result of the relative slopes of the 45° line and the planned spending function: a vertical shift of the spending function will cause its intersection with the 45° line to move horizontally by a larger amount. This is a graphical interpretation of a point we made in the last chapter, "one person's spending becomes several people's income."

The economics behind the spending multiplier is shown in Figure 24.8, which is a blowup (not drawn to scale) of Figure 24.7 showing the effects of an increase in autonomous spending from 150 to 200, which shifts the planned spending line from E_{p1} to E_{p2}. This could be brought about by an increase in either autonomous investment or autonomous consumption. The intersection between the new spending line and the 45° line, point e_2, occurs at $Q_2 = 1,000$. Thus, the small change in autonomous spending, $\Delta A = 50$, has resulted in a larger change in equilibrium income, $\Delta Q = 250$, as in our multiplier analysis of the last chapter.

Here's what happens as the economy moves from one equilibrium point, e_1, to another, e_2. The initial $50 increase in autonomous spending is indicated by a move between spending lines from point e_1 to point m. As a result, income increases by $50 this first round of spending, as indicated by point n. Now, because income has increased by 50, spending will increase by a fraction of that amount. That fraction happens to be 0.8—the marginal propensity to consume. The level of spending in the second round is indicated by point o on the planned spending line E_{p2}. The diagram may be out of scale, but we can find the actual level of spending at point o by adding 0.8($50) to $800, the level of spending that occurred in the first round, to get $840. Notice that point o cannot be an equilibrium value because spending

····· FIGURE 24.8 THE OPERATION OF THE SPENDING MULTIPLIER

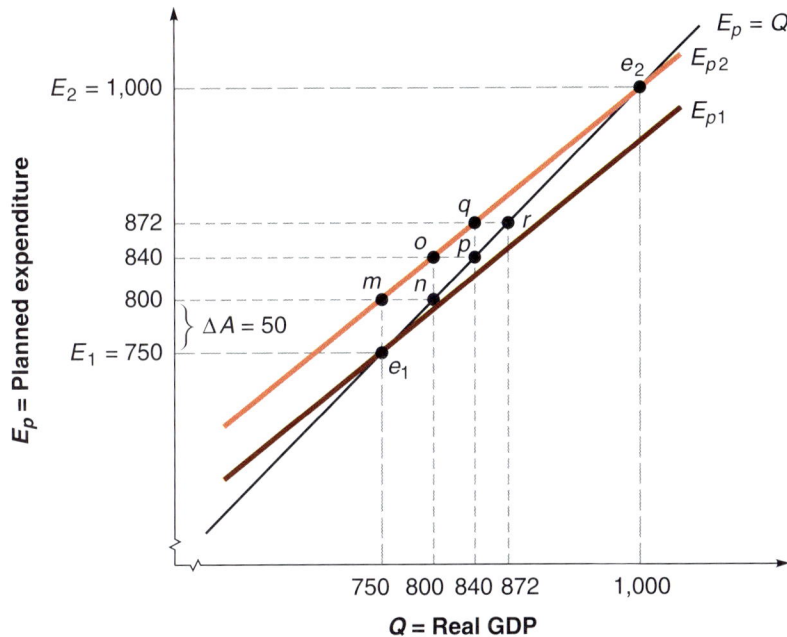

A small change in autonomous spending will result in a larger change in equilibrium GDP. An increase of $50 in autonomous spending will raise income from $750 to $800 in the first round. Because the MPC is assumed to be 0.8, spending will increase by 0.8($50) = $40 in the second round and move the economy to point o. In subsequent rounds, spending will increase by the MPC times the change in income. The economy will come to rest when planned spending is equal to income at point e_2. The spending multiplier is defined as the change in income, ΔQ, divided by the change in autonomous spending, ΔA. In this case, $\Delta Q =$ is $250 and $\Delta A =$ $50, so the spending multiplier, $k_e = \Delta Q/\Delta A$, is equal to 5.

(= 840) is greater than income (= 800) so there will be unintended inventory declines. The $840 that is spent in the second round represents a $40 increase in spending over the first round. People will spend 80 percent of their change in income or $32 [= 0.8(40)]. This means $872 will be spent in the third round. The process will continue indefinitely until point e_2 is reached and planned spending is equal to income.

········

Calculating the Spending Multiplier

Figure 24.8 showed that a small increase in autonomous spending ($\Delta A = 50$) resulted in a larger equilibrium income ($\Delta Q = 250$). The ratio of the change in equilibrium income to the change in autonomous spending is important because it is the definition of the spending multiplier.

$$\text{Spending multiplier, } k_e: \quad k_e \equiv \frac{\Delta Q}{\Delta A} \qquad\qquad [4]$$

In this case the multiplier is 5:

$$k_e = \frac{\Delta Q}{\Delta A} = \frac{250}{50} = 5$$

The multiplier is not an immutable constant. As we mentioned in the last chapter, the value of the multiplier depends on the portion of income that is spent in every round of spending. The portion of new income that is spent is the marginal propensity to spend (MPE), which, as we have seen, is the slope of the planned spending line. With a higher MPE, more spending takes place out of every change in income, so the spending multiplier is higher. With a lower MPE, less spending takes place out of every change in income, so the multiplier is lower. In the simple model we are developing in this chapter, the MPE is equal to the MPC, but this will be not true when we add income taxes and imports in the next chapter.

•••••FIGURE 24.9 THE SPENDING MULTIPLIER

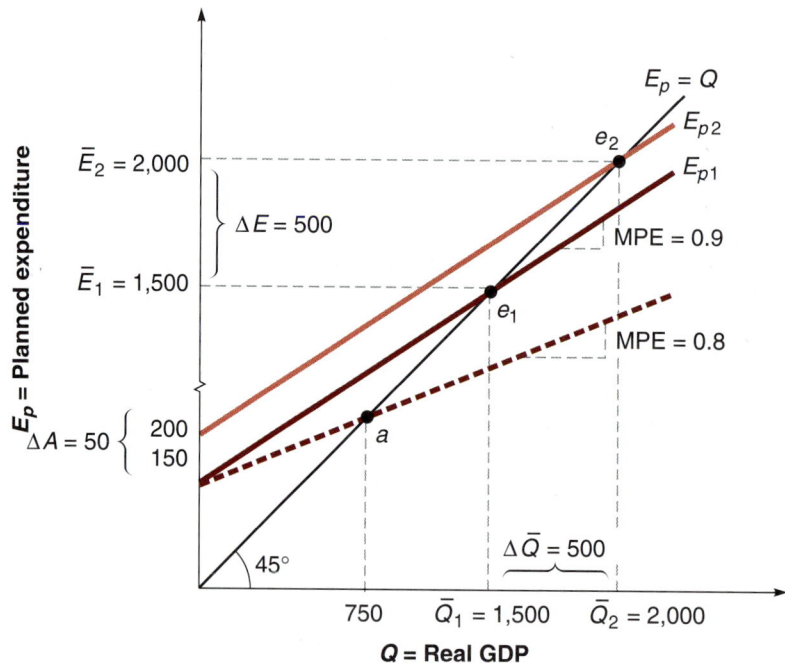

The MPE determines the value of the spending multiplier and the level of equilibrium GDP. The dotted spending line through point a shows that if autonomous spending is 150 and the MPE is 0.8, equilibrium GDP is 750. If the MPE rises to 0.9 as on spending line E_{p1}, equilibrium GDP rises to 1,500. A higher MPE also raises the multiplier. An increase of 50 in autonomous spending shifts the planned spending line up by 50 but raises equilibrium GDP by 500, so the multiplier is $k_e = 500/50 = 10$.

This relationship between the MPE and the spending multiplier is illustrated in Figure 24.9. The initial spending function, E_{p1}, has the same intercept ($A_0 = 150$) as the spending function from Figure 24.7 (indicated by the dotted spending line through point a) but a steeper slope because the MPE is equal to 0.9 instead of 0.8. The steeper slope of the planned spending function means that it intersects the 45° line at a higher level of income, 1,500 instead of 750. This is an important result: the higher the MPE, the higher the level of equilibrium income for a given level of autonomous spending. This should make sense: if all the people who receive $100 in additional income spend $90, income will rise more than if they spent only $80 of the additional $100 in income.

The second spending function in Figure 24.9, E_{p2}, has the same MPE as E_{p1} but a higher level of autonomous spending—200 instead of 150. Now look what has happened: the 50 increase in autonomous spending has increased equilibrium income by 500, not by 250 as it did in Figure 24.7. This is another important result: a higher MPE increases the spending multiplier so that a larger change in equilibrium income is associated with a given change in autonomous spending. What is the spending multiplier in this case? Once again, it is found by taking the ratio of the change in equilibrium income to the change in autonomous spending:

$$k_e = \frac{\Delta Q}{\Delta A} = \frac{500}{50} = 10$$

RECAP   Equilibrium Income and the Spending Multiplier

Understanding what we have just gone through is essential, so it is a good idea to recap the main points:

1. Equilibrium exists where planned spending equals income. Graphically, this occurs where the spending function crosses the 45° line.
2. The intercept of the spending line is total autonomous spending, A_0; the slope of the spending line is the marginal propensity to spend, MPE.
3. When spending is less than income, inventories will accumulate, firms will reduce production, and equilibrium income will fall.
4. When spending is greater than income, inventories will shrink, firms will increase production, and equilibrium income will rise.
5. The spending multiplier is the ratio of the change in equilibrium income to the change in autonomous spending.
6. A higher MPE will increase the spending multiplier and equilibrium income; a lower MPE will decrease the spending multiplier and equilibrium income.

Some Important Formulas

You may have already detected a simple way to calculate the spending multiplier. Notice that when MPE = 0.8, $k_e = 5$, and when MPE = 0.9, $k_e = 10$; that is, the spending multiplier is just the reciprocal of 1 minus the MPE:

$$k_e = \frac{1}{1 - \text{MPE}} \qquad [5]$$

Marginal leakage rate (MLR) In the income-expenditure model, the fraction of new spending that is not spent; the reciprocal of the spending multiplier.

A quick glance back at Table 23.4 in Chapter 23 verifies this formula. In that table the MPE (= MPC) was 0.9, and the initial $100 increase in spending resulted in an increase in income of $1,000. Remember that a higher MPE results in a higher spending multiplier.

The term in the denominator of Equation 5 is called the **marginal leakage rate (MLR)**. It represents all of the induced "leakages" out of the spending stream. In the current model, the only leakage is private saving—the marginal propensity to save—but we will add other leakages in the next chapter. Because MLR = 1 − MPE, Equation 5 can be written as:

$$k_e = \frac{1}{\text{MLR}} \qquad [6]$$

Another look at Figures 24.7 and 24.8 reveals an additional important relationship: equilibrium income is equal to autonomous spending times the spending multiplier. That is:

$$\overline{Q} = k_e(A_0) \qquad [7]$$

For example, in Figure 24.7, autonomous spending was $150 and the MPE was 0.8 so the multiplier was 5. Substituting these values into Equation 7 gives:

$$\overline{Q} = k_e(A_0) = 5(150) = 750$$

Finally, we can rewrite the definition of the spending multiplier to get another important formula: the relationship between the change in equilibrium income and the change in autonomous spending:

$$\Delta Q = k_e(\Delta A) \qquad [8]$$

This formula can be illustrated by the example in Figure 24.8. Autonomous spending rose by $50 and the spending multiplier was 5 so:

$$\Delta Q = k_e(\Delta A) = 5(50) = 250$$

These formulas will become especially important in the next chapter when we begin to look at fiscal policy.

······ SUMMARY

This chapter is important because the material we have just developed will be the foundation for the next few chapters where we look at economic policy. We need to understand what conditions hold at equilibrium before we are ready to use policies to change the level of equilibrium. The key points from this chapter are:

1. Keynes's theory of consumption states that as income increases, so does consumption, but by less. The slope of the Keynesian consumption function is the MPC; the intercept is autonomous consumption. An increase in the MPC means that people are spending a higher portion of their change in income. This increases equilibrium GDP and the spending multiplier.

2. The relationship between investment and expected return is called the marginal efficiency of investment. The MEI slopes downward because expected return declines as additional investment takes place. An increase in business confidence shifts the MEI curve away from the vertical axis. Firms will invest only if the expected return, adjusted for risk, is greater than the interest rate that could be earned on financial assets. Investment is assumed to be entirely autonomous in the income-expenditure model, and its graph is a horizontal line.

3. Equilibrium GDP exists when planned spending equals income or, alternatively, when planned investment equals saving.

4. The spending multiplier is defined as the ratio of a change in equilibrium income to a change in autonomous spending, $k_e = \Delta Q/\Delta A$. The formula for the spending multiplier is $k_e = 1/(1 - \text{MPE})$ or $k_e = 1/\text{MLR}$. An increase in the MLR will decrease the spending multiplier; a decrease in the MLR will increase the spending multiplier.

KEY TERMS AND CONCEPTS

induced variable
autonomous variable
consumption function
marginal propensity to consume (MPC)
average propensity to consume (APC)
45° line
marginal propensity to save (MPS)

expected return (R^e)
marginal efficiency of investment (MEI)
business confidence
equilibrium
marginal leakage rate (MLR)
spending multiplier
marginal propensity to spend (MPE)

REVIEW QUESTIONS

1. State Keynes's fundamental psychological law, and explain how it corresponds to the equation $C = C_0 + bQ$.
2. What factors shift the consumption function? What factors change the slope of the consumption function?
3. What is the MEI? What factors cause it to shift? How is it related to the interest rate?
4. What conditions must hold for the income-expenditure model to be in equilibrium? Draw a graph to illustrate your result.
5. Define the spending multiplier both verbally and mathematically, and illustrate it graphically.

PROBLEMS

1. Suppose that investment has an induced component and thus an upward slope on the income-expenditure diagram. How would this affect the value of the spending multiplier? How would it affect the level of equilibrium GDP? Finally, do you think it is reasonable for the investment function to be upward sloping? Why?

2. Explain whether, how, and why each of the following factors would shift the MEI curve:

   an increase in the interest rate   lower business taxes
   an increase in worker productivity   the removal of export barriers
   a decline in expected inflation   a stock market boom

3. Let $C = 100 + 0.9Q$ and $I = 300$ and answer the following questions. You can use algebra (see the chapter appendix for some help with the algebra), but also draw and label a diagram to illustrate your answers.
   a. Solve for equilibrium income, $\overline{Q}$.
   b. Find the spending multiplier, k_e.
   c. Suppose the MPC falls to 0.75. What happens to $\overline{Q}$? What happens to k_e?
   d. Now suppose that autonomous investment falls to 250. How much will this change $\overline{Q}$ using the initial MPC = 0.9? How much will it change $\overline{Q}$ using MPC = 0.75?
   e. Change the investment function to $I = 300 + 0.05Q$ and answer parts (*a*) and (*b*). Can you explain your results?

4. Suppose that the consumption function had no autonomous component. How would this affect the relationship between the MPC and the APC? You will probably need to draw a graph to answer this question.

5. As an investor, would you rather be faced with risk or uncertainty? Why?

6. Indicate whether the following are true, false, or uncertain, and explain why:
   a. The APC approaches the MPC as Q approaches infinity.
   b. The MPC is assumed to be greater than 0 and equal to or less than 1.
   c. An increase in income will shift the consumption function and the expenditure line upward.
   d. MPC + MPS = 1.
   e. The slope of the spending line is equal to the slope of the consumption function.
   f. If $E_p > Q$, GDP will fall in the next period.

Extending the Income-Expenditure Model: The Saving-Investment Approach and Some Algebra

The income-expenditure model can be extended in several ways. This appendix offers two extensions. First, we look at the saving function and show how to use the relationship between planned investment and saving to solve for equilibrium GDP. We then show how the main results from the income-expenditure model can be derived with simple algebra.

THE SIMPLE KEYNESIAN SAVING FUNCTION

Table 24A.1 adds saving data to the consumption data in Table 24.1. The columns labeled ΔS, APS, and MPS are the change in saving (ΔS), the average propensity to save *(APS)*, and the marginal propensity to save *(MPS)*. This terminology borrows directly from our discussion of the consumption function. The MPS gives the portion of the change in income that is saved ($\Delta S/\Delta Q$), and the APS gives the ratio of total saving to total income (S/Q).

Adding across the first three columns in Table 24A.1 reveals an important relationship we demonstrated in Chapter 24: in an economy with no government or foreign sector, income equals consumption plus saving; that is:

TABLE 24A.1 CONSUMPTION FUNCTION DATA

Line	Q	C	S	ΔQ	ΔC	ΔS	APC	MPC	APS	MPS
a	0	50	−50	—	—	—	—	—	—	—
b	100	130	−30	100	80	20	1.30	0.80	−0.30	0.20
c	200	210	−10	100	80	20	1.05	0.80	−0.05	0.20
d	300	290	+10	100	80	20	0.97	0.80	+0.03	0.20
e	400	370	+30	100	80	20	0.93	0.80	+0.07	0.20
f	500	450	+50	100	80	20	0.90	0.80	+0.10	0.20
g	1000	850	+150	500	400	100	0.85	0.80	+0.15	0.20

Key:

Q = income, C = consumption, S = saving, ΔQ = change in income, ΔC = change in consumption, ΔS = change in saving, APC = average propensity to consume, MPC = marginal propensity to consume, APS = average propensity to save, MPS = marginal propensity to save

$$Q = C + S \qquad\qquad\qquad \text{[A.1]}$$

There is also an important relationship between the APS and the APC and between the MPS and the MPC: both sum to unity. If you can do only two things with your income, spend it or save it, then the entire change in your income must be divided between your change in consumption and your change in saving. This means that the MPC plus the MPS must equal 1:

$$\text{MPS} + \text{MPC} = 1 \qquad\qquad\qquad \text{[A.2]}$$

Or:

$$\text{MPS} = 1 - \text{MPC} = 1 - b$$

where b is the MPC.

Likewise, a portion of your entire income is consumed (the APC), and a portion is saved (the APS). Since you cannot do anything else with your income, these portions must add up to 1, the whole income:

$$\text{APS} + \text{APC} = 1 \qquad\qquad\qquad \text{[A.3]}$$

. . . .

Graphing the Saving Function

The data in Table 24A.1 can also be used to graph the saving function. The intercept of the saving function, *autonomous saving,* is found in line *a* of the table, which gives the amount of saving when $Q = 0$; autonomous saving is -50 in this example. Notice that autonomous consumption is negative, which makes sense. If you have no income, consumption spending ($+50$) is possible only by drawing down past saving (-50). The slope of the saving function is the MPS. It gives the change in saving associated with a change in income, $\Delta S/\Delta Q$. Because saving rises 20 for every 100 increase in income, the MPS is 0.2. Again, a relationship exists between saving and consumption: if you can either spend or save your income and you spend 80¢ of each new dollar in income, then you must save the remaining 20¢. Putting this together gives us the equation of the Keynesian saving function:

> Keynesian saving function:
> saving = −autonomous consumption + MPS(income)
>
> $$S = -C_0 + (1 - b)Q \qquad\qquad\qquad \text{[A.4]}$$

In this case, the saving function is:

$$S = -50 + 0.2Q$$

The saving function is plotted in Figure 24A.1. As expected, its intercept is negative to reflect the fact that saving is negative at low levels of income. The upward slope means that people save a small fraction of every new dollar of income. Finally, the saving function crosses the income axis so that $S = 0$ at $Q = 250$—the same

• • • • **FIGURE 24A.1** THE SAVING FUNCTION

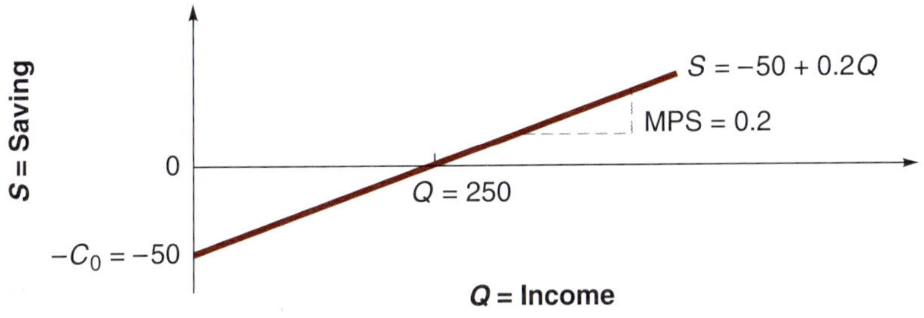

The saving function is derived directly from the consumption function. The intercept of the saving function is minus autonomous consumption, $-C_0$, and the slope of the saving function, the MPS, is equal to $1 - MPC$. The saving function crosses the Q axis where $S = 0$. This is the level of income such that $C = Q$.

value where the consumption function crossed the 45° line in Figure 24.1. There can be no saving when income = consumption because all income is spent on consumption.

• • • • • • • •

Shifting and Rotating the Saving Function

The saving function is just a mirror image of the consumption function, so it will shift or rotate whenever the consumption function shifts or rotates. The direction the saving function shifts can be a bit confusing, however. For example, an increase in autonomous saving from −50 to −20 causes the saving function to shift *upward,* not outward, because more saving is taken from a given level of income. This is shown in panel (a) of Figure 24A.2. Likewise, an increase in the MPS from 0.2 to 0.3 swivels the saving function counterclockwise so that more is saved out of every additional dollar of income. This is shown in panel (b). These changes are just the opposite of what would happen to the consumption function: an increase in autonomous saving causes the consumption function to shift down, and an increase in the MPS reduces the MPC and makes the consumption function flatter.

USING SAVING AND INVESTMENT TO SOLVE FOR EQUILIBRIUM

When we illustrated the inventory adjustment process in Chapter 23, we pointed out that two conditions hold in equilibrium: (1) planned spending equals income and (2) planned investment equals saving. In Chapter 24 we used only the first condition to derive equilibrium GDP, but the second condition can also be used. In fact, some things can be shown more easily by looking at the relationship between planned investment and saving than between planned spending and income.

•••• **FIGURE 24A.2** SHIFTING AND ROTATING THE SAVINGS FUNCTION

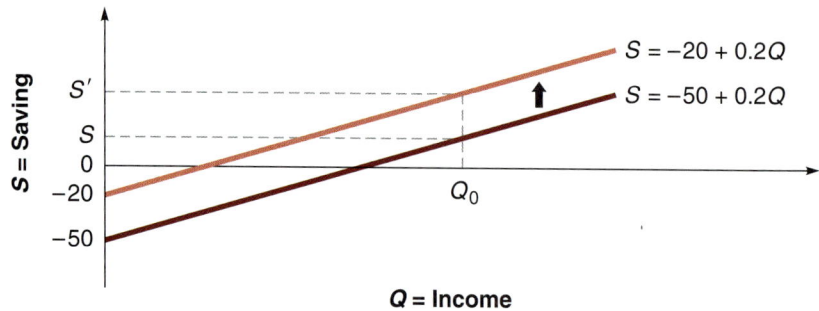

(a)

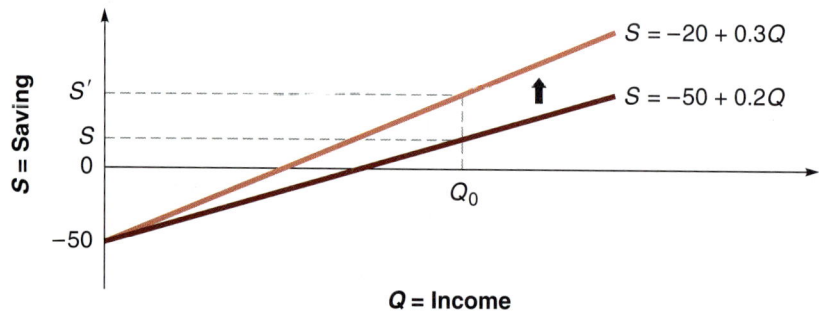

(b)

A change in the level of autonomous saving will result in a parallel shift in the saving function. In panel (a), autonomous saving rose from −50 to −20. As a result, total saving rises for every level of income. When $Q = Q_0$, saving is S when autonomous saving is −50, but S' when autonomous saving is −20. A change in the MPS will rotate the saving function. In panel (b), the MPS has risen from 0.2 to 0.3 so the saving function rotates counterclockwise with no change in the level of autonomous saving. When $Q = Q_0$, saving is S when the MPS is 0.2, but rises to S' when the MPS is 0.3.

••••••••

Saving Equals Planned Investment in Equilibrium

To solve for equilibrium GDP with the saving-investment approach, all that is necessary is to set planned investment equal to saving. This is done in Figure 24A.3, which uses the same planned investment function that was used in Figure 24.6, $I_p = 100$, as well as the saving function that corresponds to the consumption function we used in that figure. The consumption function was:

$$C = +50 + 0.8Q$$

so the corresponding saving function is:

FIGURE 24A.3 SAVING EQUALS PLANNED INVESTMENT IN EQUILIBRIUM

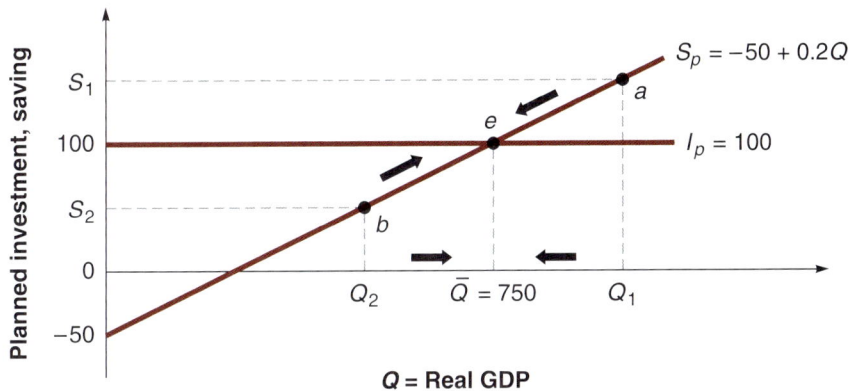

Equilibrium exists when planned investment equals saving. This occurs at point *e* where the autonomous investment function, $I_0 = 100$, crosses the saving function, $S = -50 + 0.2Q$. At income levels above $\overline{Q}$ like Q_1, saving is greater than investment, so spending "leaks out" of the spending stream and the economy slows down. When income is less than $\overline{Q}$ as it is at Q_2, saving is less than investment, and injections are greater than leakages. This causes the economy to accelerate toward $\overline{Q}$.

$$S = -50 + (1 - 0.8)Q$$

Notice that (1) the intercept of the saving function is the negative of the intercept of the consumption function, and (2) the slope of the saving function is equal to 1 minus the slope of the consumption function.

The planned investment and saving functions intersect at $\overline{Q} = 750$, the same equilibrium value we calculated in Figure 24.7. This is what we should expect: planned investment equals saving at the same level of equilibrium GDP as planned spending equals income. Notice that investment is less than saving when income is greater than equilibrium, that is, at $Q_1 > \overline{Q}$. Because less investment is being "injected" into the economy than "leaks out" as saving, inventories will pile up, firms will cut production, and GDP will move toward equilibrium. The opposite occurs when income is less than equilibrium as it is at Q_2: saving is less than investment, so injections exceed leakages and the economy expands toward equilibrium at $\overline{Q}$.

The Paradox of Thrift

The saving-investment diagram makes it easy to illustrate a rather remarkable result: the attempt to increase saving may not lead to an increase in aggregate saving and may result in a decline in GDP. This result is known as the *paradox of thrift*.

Figure 24A.4 illustrates one version of the paradox of thrift. Suppose that thriftiness suddenly breaks out and people decide to increase their saving such that, on average,

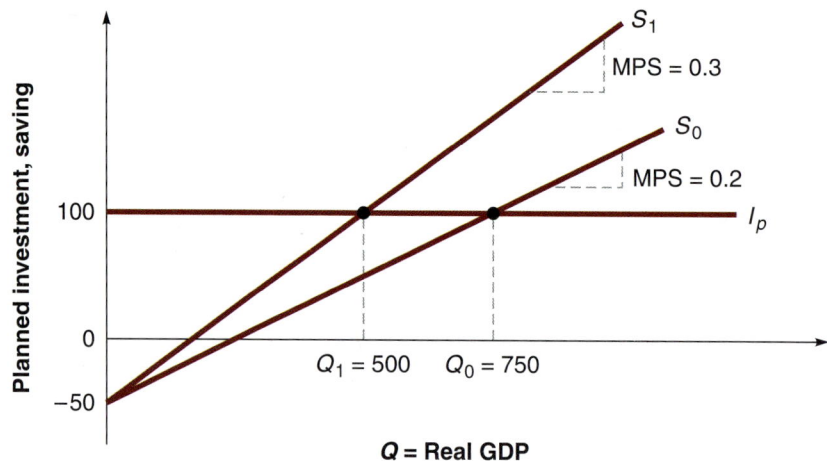

FIGURE 24A.4 THE PARADOX OF THRIFT

An increase in the desire to save may not result in more being saved. In this case, the marginal propensity to save has increased from 0.2 to 0.3. However, the lower level of spending means that less GDP is generated. As a result, people save a higher portion of a lower income: $S = 100$ in both cases.

the marginal propensity to save rises from 0.2 to 0.3. This would rotate the saving function from S_0 to S_1. Now, because equilibrium exists where saving equals planned investment, the higher MPS will cause the economy to slow down, and equilibrium GDP will fall from 750 to 500. But notice what happened to the levels of saving and investment: both stayed at 100. Investment stayed at 100 because we have assumed that it is entirely autonomous. This makes sense—or at least fits with our assumptions. But shouldn't saving increase? Not necessarily. People were initially saving a low portion of a high GDP; after the MPS increased, people saved a higher portion of a lower GDP.

Does the paradox of thrift mean that increased saving is a bad thing for the economy? Not necessarily. As we will find out later, increased saving may be good for the economy because it represents additional funds available for firms to borrow for capital expansion. However, this is a long-run result. In the short run, an increase in the desire to save does mean a decrease in the desire to spend. And a reduction in spending can mean a reduction in equilibrium GDP.

THE ALGEBRA OF THE INCOME-EXPENDITURE MODEL

We were not able to avoid the use of a few equations and a little algebra in our discussion of the income-expenditure model, but most of the analysis was verbal and graphical. The graphical approach may be less precise than algebra, but it often provides a better feel for the analysis. Algebra is by far the quickest way to solve for equilibrium, however. It can also handle many situations where graphical analysis is too cumbersome. This appendix carries the algebra from the chapter a few steps farther.

· · · · · · · · ·

The Algebra of the Consumption Function

The Keynesian consumption function is linear, so it has the same form as the linear functions we described in Chapter 2. The general form of the Keynesian consumption function is:

$$C = C_0 + bQ \qquad \text{[A.5]}$$

Where:

C = real aggregate personal consumption spending

C_0 = autonomous consumption spending

$b = \Delta C/\Delta Q$ = MPC

Q = real income (= disposable income because $T = 0$)

The specific consumption function we used in much of the chapter was:

$$C = 50 + 0.8Q \qquad \text{[A.6]}$$

· · · · · · · · ·

Solving for Q = C

Figure 24.1 showed that $Q = C$ when $Q = 250$. This can be demonstrated quite easily. Because we are looking for the value where $Q = C$, all that is necessary is to substitute Q for C and solve the equation for Q. Thus, Equation A.6 becomes:

$$Q = 50 + 0.8Q \qquad \text{[A.7]}$$

Now, subtract $0.8Q$ from each side of the equation:

$$0.2Q = 50 \qquad \text{[A.8]}$$

and divide by 0.2 to get:

$$Q = 250 \qquad \text{[A.9]}$$

which is what we wanted to show.

· · · · · · · · ·

Algebra of the Saving Function

A saving function can be derived directly from the consumption function. The intercept is negative autonomous consumption, and the slope is 1 minus the MPC. To see this, first recall that households can only do two things with their income, spend it on consumption or save it; that is:

$$Q = C + S \qquad \text{[A.10]}$$

which we can rewrite as:

$$S = Q - C \qquad \text{[A.11]}$$

Now, if we substitute the general form of the consumption function into Equation A.11, we have:

$$S = Q - (C_0 + bQ) \qquad \text{[A.12]}$$

which we can rearrange to get:

$$S = -C_0 + (1 - b)Q \qquad \text{[A.13]}$$

The specific saving function associated with the consumption function in Equation A.6 is:

$$S = -50 + 0.2Q \qquad \text{[A.14]}$$

· · · · · · · ·

Solving for Equilibrium

To solve for equilibrium GDP with the income-spending approach, first write the spending equation as:

$$E_p = C + I_p \qquad \text{[A.15]}$$

and note that income must equal planned spending in equilibrium; that is:

$$Q = C + I_p \qquad \text{[A.16]}$$

All that is necessary now is to substitute for I_p and C and solve. To follow the example in the chapter, let $I_p = 100$ and use the consumption function in Equation A.6. This gives:

$$Q = 50 + 0.8Q + 100 \qquad \text{[A.17]}$$

which is simply one equation with one unknown. To solve, isolate the Q's on one side of the equation by subtracting $0.8Q$ from each side:

$$0.2Q = 150 \qquad \text{[A.18]}$$

and divide by 0.2 for a solution:

$$\overline{Q} = \frac{150}{0.2} = 750 \qquad \text{[A.19]}$$

where the overbar indicates equilibrium.

What happens if $Q \neq E_p$? Consider a point like a from Figure 24.7. Let $Q = 900$ and solve for E_p:

$$E_p = 50 + 0.8(900) + 100 = 870 \qquad \text{[A.20]}$$

Because $E_p = 870 < Q = 900$, we know that inventories will rise; that is, $I_u > 0$. Firms will respond by cutting production and paying out less income. The economy will fall toward $\overline{Q} = 750$.

· · · · · · · ·

Finding the Spending Multiplier

The best way find the spending multiplier is to solve for equilibrium income as we have just done in Equation A.19, then back up one step to Equation A.18. Notice that the fraction on the left side of the equation, 0.2, is the marginal leakage rate, which in this simple model is just the marginal propensity to save. As we know from Equation 6 in Chapter 24, the spending multiplier is the reciprocal of the MLR:

$$k_e = \frac{1}{MLR} = \frac{1}{MPS} = \frac{1}{0.2} \qquad [A.21]$$

While memory of Equation A.21 and inspection of the consumption function would be sufficient to find the spending multiplier in this case, they will not be adequate in more complicated situations—like those encountered in the next chapter. You can, however, *always* find the multiplier by setting up the system to solve for equilibrium GDP and reducing the equation to the general form in Equation A.22:

$$[\text{fraction}] \times Q = \text{autonomous spending} \qquad [A.22]$$

The fraction on the left is always the marginal leakage rate, and its reciprocal is always the spending multiplier, so a better way to write this is:

$$[MLR] \times Q = A \qquad [A.23]$$

· · · · · · · · ·

Algebra of the Saving-Investment Approach

To find equilibrium income from the saving-investment approach, set the investment function equal to the saving function:

$$I_p = -C_0 + (1 - b)Q \qquad [A.24]$$

and solve for equilibrium. For the example in the chapter, this is:

$$100 = -50 + (1 - 0.8)Q \qquad [A.25]$$

Adding 50 to each side gives:

$$150 = 0.2Q \qquad [A.26]$$

and after dividing by 0.2 we again find:

$$\overline{Q} = 750 \qquad [A.27]$$

· · · · · · · · **PROBLEMS**

1. Let $C = 50 + 0.75Q$ and $I = 200$ and answer the following questions both graphically and algebraically.
   a. Find the saving function associated with the consumption function.
   b. Solve for equilibrium income using the equality between income and expenditure.
   c. Solve for equilibrium income using the relationships between planned investment and saving.
   d. Find the spending multiplier, k_e.
   e. Suppose the MPC rises to 0.8. What happens to $\overline{Q}$? What happens to k_e?
   f. Now suppose that autonomous investment rises to 250. How much will this change $\overline{Q}$ using the initial MPC = 0.75? How much will it change $\overline{Q}$ if the MPC = 0.8?

2. Suppose $\overline{Q} = 1,500$ and you know that $A = 300$. What is the MPC? What is the MPS? What is the MLR?

3. Suppose that $\overline{Q} = 1,000$ but potential GDP ($Q\star$) = 1,200. How much would autonomous spending have to increase to move the economy to $Q\star$ if the MLR is 0.2? If it is 0.3?

4. Suppose that $I_p = 250$ and the saving function is $S = -100 + 0.1Q$.
   a. Find equilibrium income.
   b. Show what happens to equilibrium income if the MPS rises to 0.2.
   c. Suppose that the investment function changes to $I_p = 250 + 0.01Q$ and answer parts (a) and (b) both graphically and algebraically.

CHAPTER 25

The Income-Expenditure Model II: Adding the Government and Foreign Sectors

The 1960 presidential debates were historic in at least two important ways. They were the first debates to be held on television before a national audience. Among other things, this meant that the charismatic and photogenic John Kennedy had an edge on the seemingly nervous Richard Nixon. Perhaps more significantly, they were the first presidential debates to focus so much attention on economic issues. No one will ever know whether Vice-President Nixon lost the debates because he appeared so nervous on camera or because the voters preferred the oratory of the junior senator from Massachusetts. We do know, however, that Kennedy was the first president since Franklin D. Roosevelt to advocate activist fiscal policies in an effort to boost the economy from recession. This chapter will provide the basic tools needed for understanding why and how Keynesian fiscal policies are supposed to work.

The policies that the Kennedy-Johnson administration pursued might be considered naive today—perhaps even inappropriate—given the changes the U.S. and the world economy have undergone in the past 30 years. Today, many economists prefer to leave the economy to its own devices and wait for it to self-correct, arguing, with some justification, that activist policies do more harm than good. Other economists would pursue a complex mix of fiscal and monetary policies. But in a serious recession, all but a very few economists would begin their analysis with a model quite similar to the one we will develop in this chapter.

AFTER READING AND STUDYING THIS CHAPTER, YOU SHOULD BE ABLE TO:
- ••• Define and illustrate recessionary and inflationary gaps, and explain how to use fiscal policy to close these gaps

$\cdots$ Explain how autonomous taxes and income taxes affect consumption, investment, equilibrium income, and the spending multiplier

$\cdots$ Understand how the foreign sector affects equilibrium GDP and the spending multiplier

$\cdots$ Know the relationship between the fiscal deficit and the foreign deficit, and why economists are concerned about them

ASSUMPTIONS AND DEFINITIONS

This chapter extends the material from the last chapter, and makes two changes to move the model a little closer to the real world. The first change will be to add the government sector; the second is to add the foreign sector.

In mixed economies like the United States, the government plays several roles: it taxes households and businesses, buys goods and services, and regulates certain activities. It is also actively involved with economic stabilization, the main focus of this chapter. When the government collects taxes, it tends to slow the economy because people have less money to spend on goods and services. When government spending increases, it tends to have a stimulative effect as spending and incomes multiply through the economy. The task at hand will be to explore how and why taxes and government spending are used to fight recession and inflation.

The foreign sector has two components, imports and exports. Domestic employment and GDP growth increase when American producers export goods and services to foreigners. Imports have just the opposite effect: when U.S. citizens buy foreign products, income flows out of the country. Consumers benefit from lower prices and a wide selection of goods to choose from, but imports can cost jobs at home. The difference between exports and imports is called net exports.

POTENTIAL GDP, ACTUAL GDP, AND THE GDP GAP

In the last chapter we found that the intersection between the aggregate planned spending line and the 45° line gives equilibrium GDP, but we said nothing about whether equilibrium occurred at full employment. We have already defined full employment as the amount of employment that occurs when everyone willing and able to work at the prevailing wage can find a job. In the short run, employment can exceed the full employment level, but this is likely to generate inflation as firms compete for scarce workers by offering higher wages. Most economists believe that the unemployment rate at full employment is between 5 and 6 percent, although this figure is the subject of considerable disagreement. The level of GDP that exists when the economy is fully employed is called **potential GDP (Q★)**. A main goal of macroeconomic policy is to move the economy toward potential GDP. The difference between actual GDP and potential GDP is called the **GDP gap**.

One of Keynes's chief contentions was that the economy could get stuck at a position of high unemployment with output less than potential GDP. It was this idea

Potential gross domestic product The amount of aggregate production that will take place when all firms are operating at optimal capacity and there is full employment.

GDP gap The difference between actual GDP and potential GDP; it is measured as the horizontal distance between equilibrium GDP and potential GDP on the income-expenditure diagram.

that led Keynes to call for government policies to deal with depression. He advocated public works projects, such as road building and park maintenance, to put people back to work, but there has never been widespread agreement that this strategy is best. During mild contractions, some economists believe that it is better to leave the economy alone and wait for self-correcting forces to restore potential GDP. Other economists prefer to use policies to reduce the length and severity of recessions.

Price Flexibility and the GDP Gap

You may have noticed in the last chapter that we said nothing about prices when we developed the income-expenditure model. The reason for this omission is that the income-expenditure model was originally developed to help understand depressions, and an analysis of price changes was considered unimportant in depressions. Today, most economists disagree and believe that price flexibility is always important—even during recessions. We will have to wait until the next chapter to examine the causes and consequences of price changes in detail, but we will need to refer to prices occasionally in this chapter. One easy way to add the effects of price changes to the income-expenditure model is by making three assumptions:

$$\bullet \text{ If } Q > Q^\star \text{ then } P\uparrow$$
$$\bullet \text{ If } Q < Q^\star, \text{ then } P\downarrow \qquad [1]$$
$$\bullet \text{ If } Q = Q^\star, \text{ then } \overline{P}$$

Where:
$P\uparrow$ indicates that there is a tendency for the price level to rise.
$P\downarrow$ indicates that there is a tendency for the price level to decline.
$\overline{P}$ indicates that there is a tendency for the price level to remain constant.

Though these are just assumptions, not predictions, of the income-expenditure model, they do make economic sense. When GDP is greater than potential GDP, the employment level is "over full" so there are few workers looking for jobs. Many workers put in overtime, and because there are few unemployed workers, about the only way firms can hire additional workers is by "bribing" them to quit their current jobs with higher wages. This will lead to higher selling prices because wages are a major cost of production. On the other hand, when actual GDP is less than potential GDP, the economy is in a recession. After a period of looking for jobs at their old wages, unemployed workers will eventually offer to work at a lower wage rate. If the recession is protracted and severe, such wage declines will often be reflected in a lower price level.

Before proceeding, we need to emphasize that the statements in Equation 1 are just working assumptions that are sometimes violated. On several occasions in recent U.S. history, the price level rose during recessions, but typically, this has been the result of external factors. For example, rising oil prices and other external supply shocks were partially responsible for the inflation of the 1970s that occurred during recession. There have also been many instances when prices and wages did not fall even though GDP was less than potential GDP. These situations are often attributed to the existence of price or wage contracts. For the time being, we need to accept the assumptions in Equation 1 so that we can explore the implications of recessionary and inflationary gaps; later we will explore what happens when the assumptions do not hold.

• • • • • • • •

Recessionary Gaps

A GDP gap is measured as the horizontal distance between equilibrium GDP and potential GDP on the income-expenditure diagram. Figure 25.1 illustrates one kind of GDP gap. In this case, equilibrium GDP ($\overline{Q}_1 = \overline{E}_1 = 750$) is less than potential GDP ($Q^\star = 1,000$) because there is too little autonomous spending on the initial planned spending line, E_{p1}. If autonomous spending were to increase, the aggregate spending line would shift up to E_{p2}, and the GDP gap would be closed. The vertical distance between E_{p1} and E_{p2} is called a **recessionary gap**. A recessionary gap can be closed by increasing autonomous spending enough to close the GDP gap. A main task of this chapter will be to show how recessionary gaps can be closed with fiscal policy.

Recessionary gap Exists when potential GDP is greater than equilibrium GDP.

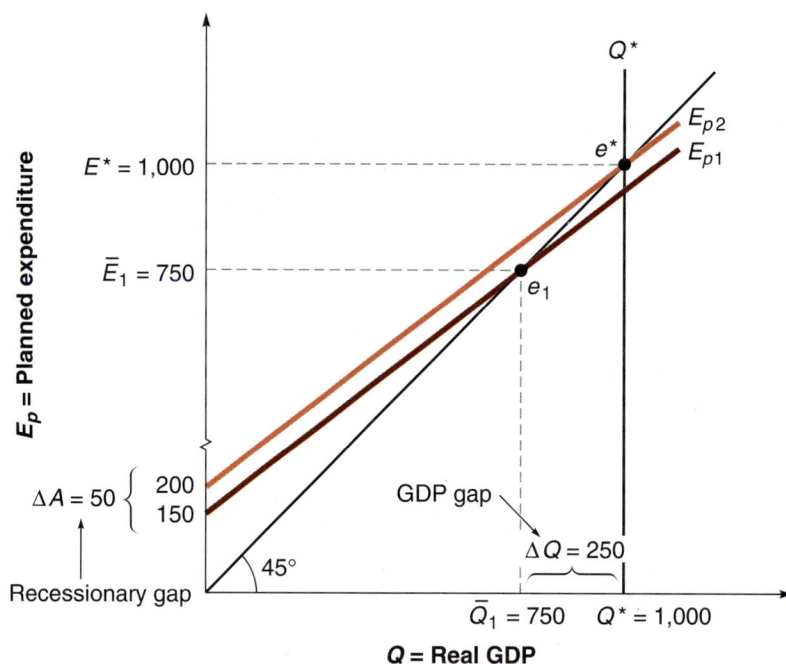

• • • • **FIGURE 25.1 RECESSIONARY GAP**

The GDP gap is the horizontal distance between equilibrium GDP and potential GDP, $\Delta Q = Q^\star - \overline{Q}$. In this case the GDP gap is +250. The amount of autonomous spending needed to move the economy from equilibrium to potential GDP is called the recessionary gap, ΔA, and is measured on the vertical axis. The relationship between the GDP gap and the recessionary gap can be found with the spending multiplier, $\Delta Q = k_e \Delta A$. In this case, an increase in autonomous spending of 50 would be necessary to close the GDP gap. Policymakers can either enact policies designed to shift the spending line upward or wait for self-correcting forces to bring about wage and price declines.

Notice that Figure 25.1 is essentially the same as Figure 24.8, the figure that we used to illustrate the spending multiplier. The only real difference is that we have now drawn a vertical line up through potential GDP, at $Q^\star = 1,000$. Why did the economy come to rest below potential GDP? There are several possible reasons, such as pessimistic business confidence or too little consumer spending, but in terms of the income-expenditure model, all of these factors amount to the same thing: too little autonomous spending. Given that, the questions become (1) how to shift the aggregate spending line from E_{p1} to E_{p2}, and (2) how much to shift it.

Closing a Recessionary Gap. If we are willing to wait, price declines will eventually close the recessionary gap—a result we should expect if the assumptions in Equation 1 are correct. Lower prices mean that the dollars people already hold have more purchasing power, so people can buy more real goods and services. This will shift the planned spending line upward and help the economy recover from recession. Few economists deny that this would *eventually* take place, but whether these self-correcting forces take place very quickly is another matter. Some economists believe that government policies are needed to speed up the process. Other economists believe that government intervention usually does more harm than good and would prefer to leave well enough alone except in the most severe recessions.

If the decision is made to use policy to help the economy recover, we need to know how much to shift the planned spending line. The answer depends on the value of the spending multiplier—the larger the multiplier, the smaller the necessary increase in autonomous spending. Equation 2 (the same as Equation 8 from Chapter 24) is a reformulation of the definition of the spending multiplier and gives all the information we need to close the GDP gap:

$$\Delta Q = k_e(\Delta A) \qquad [2]$$

In this case, the spending multiplier is 5, so shifting the spending line up by 50 will close the recessionary gap and the GDP gap. Of course, we have not said *how* to shift the aggregate spending line, but we will get to that detail in a moment.

Inflationary Gaps

While the formula in Equation 2 seems to imply that policymakers can shift the aggregate spending line with precision, this is far from the case. All of the numbers in Equation 2 are estimates, so it is possible that policies will not shift the aggregate spending line up far enough, or that they will overshoot potential GDP. When equilibrium GDP is higher than potential GDP, the economy is said to be operating with an **inflationary gap**. How can equilibrium GDP be higher than potential GDP? Just as full employment is not an immutable constant, neither is potential GDP a technological limit. It is an estimate of the amount of production that takes place when the economy is fully employed, and it depends on cultural and behavioral factors as well as physical limits. If the typical worker is putting in overtime, or if a large number of students, housekeepers, and other people not usually part of the labor force take jobs, equilibrium GDP will exceed potential GDP. As we know from the assumptions in Equation 1, this situation usually leads to rising prices, which is why

Inflationary gap Exists when equilibrium GDP is greater than potential GDP.

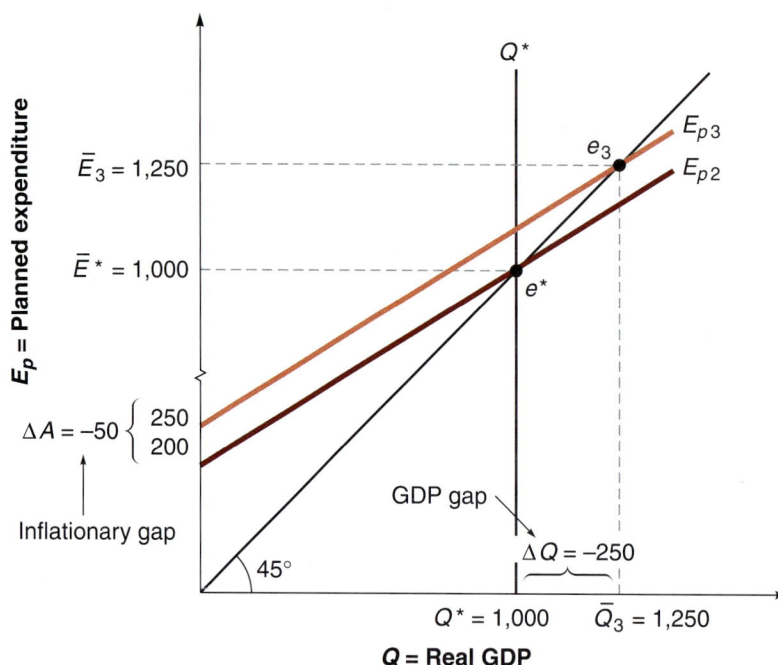

FIGURE 25.2 INFLATIONARY GAP

The economy is in an inflationary gap when planned spending exceeds the level necessary to generate potential GDP. The vertical distance between E_{p3} and E_{p2} is the inflationary gap; the horizontal distance between $\overline{Q}_3$ and $Q^\star$ is the GDP gap. In this case, lowering autonomous spending by 50 will close the inflationary gap and move the economy to potential GDP.

the vertical distance between E_{p3} and E_{p2} in Figure 25.2 is called an inflationary gap. In this figure, potential GDP is again assumed to be 1,000, but now equilibrium GDP is 1,250—perhaps the result of overly expansionary policy in the previous period. (The horizontal distance between $Q^\star$ and $\overline{Q}$ is always called a GDP gap.) Because the spending multiplier is still assumed to be 5, reducing autonomous spending by just 50 will restore potential GDP.

Closing an Inflationary Gap. Prices often begin to rise when actual GDP exceeds potential GDP. This reduces real purchasing power because the dollars that people currently hold can buy fewer goods at high prices, and this decline in purchasing power shifts the planned spending line downward. In terms of Figure 25.2, the economy moves from point e_3 to $e^\star$. As it does, the price level rises and GDP falls toward $Q^\star$. However, policymakers may want to speed up the adjustment process by shifting the aggregate spending line downward with contractionary policies like tax increases.[1]

---

[1]We cannot leave this section without noting that the income–expenditure model is really better suited for explaining recessions than inflation. Inflation is treated much more satisfactorily in Chapters 26, 27, and 29.

> **RECAP**   Inflationary and Recessionary Gaps
>
> 1. A GDP gap exists whenever equilibrium GDP, $\overline{Q}$, differs from potential GDP, $Q^\star$. Graphically, the GDP gap, ΔQ, is measured on the horizontal axis of the income-expenditure diagram.
> 2. When potential GDP is greater than equilibrium GDP, the economy is in a recessionary gap. To close the recessionary gap, it is necessary to increase autonomous spending by the amount $\Delta A = \Delta Q/k_c$, where k_c is the spending multiplier.
> 3. When potential GDP is less than equilibrium GDP, the economy is in an inflationary gap. To close the inflationary gap, autonomous spending must decrease by the amount $\Delta A = \Delta Q/k_c$.
> 4. Most economists believe that GDP gaps close automatically via the operation of self-correcting forces; however, these forces may take several years to operate, especially in the case of recessionary gaps. Therefore, many economists believe that policies should be implemented to move the economy toward potential GDP.

GOVERNMENT SPENDING AND TAXES

The government has two basic ways it can try to shift the aggregate spending line to restore potential GDP, fiscal and monetary policy. Fiscal policy involves changes in government spending and taxes, and monetary policy involves changes in the money supply. We will not be ready to look at monetary policy until Chapter 30, but we can examine some simple fiscal policies here. A more detailed discussion of fiscal policy appears in Chapter 31.

Government Purchases

As we pointed out in Chapter 22, we need to make a distinction between government *spending* and government *purchases* when analyzing the effects of government on the macroeconomy. Government spending includes the purchase of goods and services—military, roads, teachers' salaries, and the like—plus transfer payments like unemployment compensation, welfare, and interest on the national debt. Transfer payments are reflected in consumption spending because they show up as disposable income. They also have important effects on the economy and constitute over 40 percent of the government budget. Most of our focus in this chapter will be on changes in government purchases, however, because those changes are most often used with the intent of helping the economy recover from recession. Most large changes in government purchases come from legislation, so we will treat government purchases as being autonomous. This means that the government purchases function is a horizontal line as shown in Figure 25.3. An increase in government purchases shifts the line up; a decrease in government purchases shifts it down.

Adding government purchases to the income-expenditure model adds a term to the planned spending equation and to the corresponding planned spending line. The revised planned spending equation is now:

FIGURE 25.3 THE GOVERNMENT PURCHASES FUNCTION

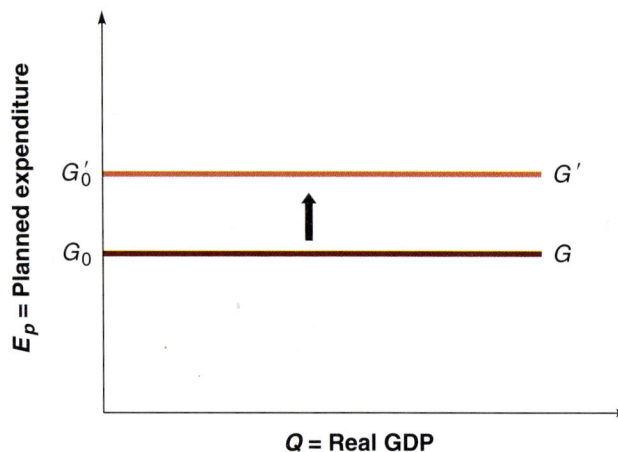

Government purchases are assumed to be entirely autonomous, so the graph is a horizontal line. An increase in government spending shifts the line upward; a decrease shifts it downward.

$$E_p = C + I_p + G \qquad [3]$$

The planned spending line is formed by vertical addition of the various components of aggregate spending—consumption, planned investment, and now government purchases—and will shift with a change in any kind of autonomous spending. This is significant: it means that GDP gaps like the ones in Figures 25.1 and 25.2 can be closed with policy—a change in the level of government purchases. All that is necessary is to determine the value of the spending multiplier and the level of potential GDP, and then substitute the change in autonomous government purchases (ΔG_0) for ΔA in Equation 2:

$$\Delta Q = k_e(\Delta G_0) \qquad [4]$$

In Figure 25.1, the GDP gap is 250 and the spending multiplier is 5, so the recessionary gap can be closed by increasing government purchases by 50.

The classic example of closing a recessionary gap with government purchases occurred in the Great Depression. With unemployment approaching 25 percent and GDP barely half the level it was in 1929, President Roosevelt enacted the New Deal, a series of government spending programs—the Works Progress Administration, the Civilian Conservation Corps, and others—to get the economy on its feet. The Great Depression did not end overnight, but most observers believe that Roosevelt's New

---

[2]Roosevelt's New Deal was based on pragmatism more than economic theory, but by the late 1930s, President Roosevelt had appointed an economic adviser, Lauchlin Currie, who had Keynesian leanings. Currie was the first person with a Ph.D. in economics to serve as an official economic adviser to the president. You can read more about the influence of early Keynesian economists on the policies of the New Deal in Anthony S. Campagna, *U.S. National Economic Policy, 1917–1985* (New York: Praeger, 1987).

Deal did start the economy on the road to recovery.[2] Still, it took the massive increases in defense spending—more government purchases—during World War II to move the economy beyond its predepression levels of output and employment.

The inflationary gap shown in Figure 25.2 could be closed by decreasing government purchases by 50. In the past, however, the government has more commonly used tax increases or monetary policy to close inflationary gaps, so the next topic on our agenda is the addition of taxes to the income-expenditure model.

Autonomous Taxes

There are two basic kinds of taxes: autonomous taxes and induced taxes. **Autonomous taxes** do not vary with the level of income; marriage licenses and various user fees are examples of autonomous taxes. Induced taxes do vary with income, so they are perhaps more appropriately called income taxes. Most federal and some state tax revenues come from various kinds of income taxes. Autonomous taxes and income taxes affect the economy differently so we need to look at them separately.

We can see how changes in autonomous taxes affect aggregate spending by adding an autonomous tax to the Keynesian consumption function. This is shown in Figure 25.4. Suppose that the initial consumption function is C and that there are no autonomous taxes. If there are no taxes, disposable income (Q_d) equals income (Q). The slope of the consumption function is the marginal propensity to consume (MPC) and is assumed to be 0.8. This means that people will spend 80 percent of the change in their disposable income on consumption and save 20 percent. The intercept, autonomous consumption (C_0), is set initially at 50.

Autonomous tax A tax that is levied on an autonomous variable and does not vary with income. In the income-expenditure model, autonomous taxes shift the planned spending line.

FIGURE 25.4 AUTONOMOUS TAXES AND CONSUMPTION

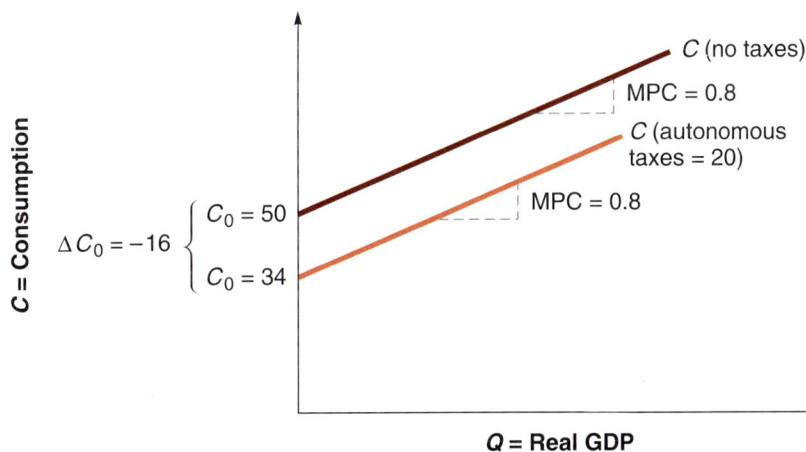

Autonomous taxes affect the intercept of the consumption function. An increase in autonomous taxes shifts the consumption function downward; a decrease in autonomous taxes shifts it upward. However, the consumption function does not shift by the entire amount of the autonomous tax. The amount of the shift is equal to the MPC times the change in autonomous taxes. In this case, the autonomous tax of 20 causes the intercept to shift down by 16 = 0.8(20).

Now suppose that autonomous taxes, T_0, rise from 0 to 20. Higher taxes cause the consumption function to shift down. *The consumption function will not shift down by the entire amount of the tax,* however, because people reduce both consumption and saving in response to the tax. We know how much autonomous consumption falls by looking at the marginal propensity to consume. When people realize they have to pay $20 in taxes, they reduce their consumption by an amount equal to the marginal propensity to consume times the tax. In this case, autonomous consumption falls by $0.8(20) = \$16$ so the new consumption function has an intercept of $34. But if consumption falls by only $16, where does the remaining $4 come from? It comes from reduced saving: saving falls by an amount equal to the marginal propensity to save times the tax increase or $0.2(20) = \$4$.

. . . .

Closing the GDP Gap with Autonomous Taxes

The consumption function is a component of the spending line, so the planned spending line will shift in the same direction and by the same amount as the consumption function. For example, if autonomous taxes increase by $50 and the marginal propensity to consume is 0.8, both the consumption function and the planned spending line will shift downward by $0.8(50) = \$40$. Remember that an *in*crease in taxes results in a *down*ward shift in the spending line. In general, this means that the change in autonomous spending is equal to minus the marginal propensity to consume times the change in autonomous taxes. This information allows us to rewrite Equation 2 as:

$$\Delta Q = k_e(\Delta A) = k_e(-b\Delta T_0) \qquad [5]$$

where b is the MPC.

Returning to the problem posed in Figure 25.1, if policymakers decide to close the recessionary gap by lowering autonomous taxes, how big a tax cut should they recommend? We know that we need to increase GDP by 250 because actual GDP is at 750 and potential GDP is 1,000. We also know that the spending multiplier is 5 and that the MPC is 0.8. Substituting this information into Equation 5 gives:

$$250 = 5(-0.8)(\Delta T_0)$$

This simplifies to:

$$250 = -4(\Delta T_0)$$

After dividing by -4 we find:

$$\Delta T_0 = -62.5$$

The result: If autonomous taxes are cut by 62.5, people will increase spending by 50—just the amount necessary to close the recessionary gap. What happens to the remaining 12.5 in disposable income available to consumers? It goes into saving.

. . . .

Income tax A tax imposed on income. In the income-expenditure model, income taxes change the slope of the planned spending line and the spending multiplier.

Income Taxes

Income taxes affect the slope of the consumption function and thus the slope of the planned spending line. This is shown in Figure 25.5. Suppose again that the pretax

FIGURE 25.5 INCOME TAXES AND CONSUMPTION

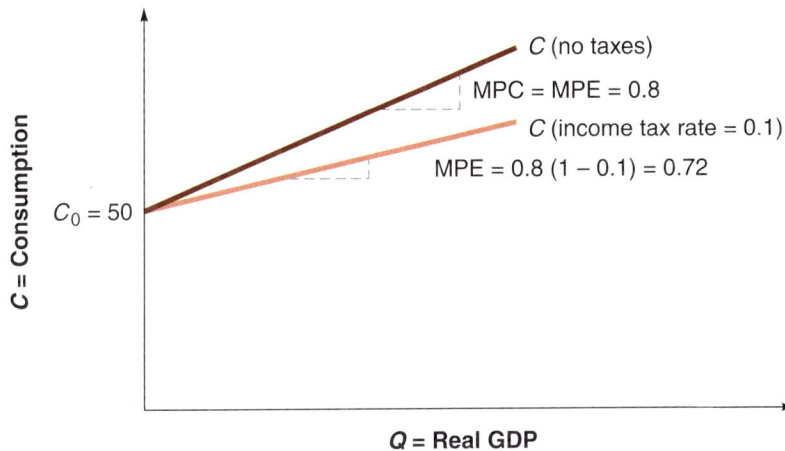

Income taxes affect the slope of the consumption function. An increase in income taxes makes the consumption function flatter; a decrease in income taxes makes it steeper. To find how much the slope changes, multiply the MPC times the income tax rate. In this case, the MPC = 0.8 and the income tax rate is 0.1 so the consumption function swivels downward by the amount 0.8(0.1). The new slope of the consumption function is $0.8(1 - 0.1) = 0.72$. In general, this is $b(1 - t)$ where b is the MPC and t is the income tax rate.

consumption function has an intercept of 50 and a slope of 0.8. Now, let the government impose a proportional income tax of 10 percent.[3] With a tax like this, if you make $100 per week, you would take home only $90. Would you cut your consumption by $10? Almost certainly not. If you are like most people, you will reduce both your consumption and your saving. How much will you cut consumption? Remember that the MPC tells us the fraction that is consumed out of a change in disposable income. The 10 percent income tax means that disposable income (income minus taxes) has declined by 10 percent, so disposable income is equal to nine-tenths of pretax income:

$$Q_d = Q - T = Q - 0.1Q = 0.9Q$$

Income taxes make the marginal propensity to spend lower than the marginal propensity to consume. If you still spend 80 percent of your disposable income, the marginal propensity to spend out of your pretax income is only 0.72 because 0.8(0.9) = 0.72. The general formula for finding the marginal propensity to spend in the presence of income taxes is:

$$MPE = b(1 - t) = b - bt \qquad [6]$$

[3]As we found out in Chapter 6, the federal income tax is slightly progressive, but proportional income taxes are much easier to analyze and, for our present purposes, illustrate the important ideas just as well.

Where:

b = MPC out of disposable income

t = income tax rate

Higher income taxes make the consumption function flatter, so they also make the planned spending line flatter. As shown in Figure 25.6, this means that the spending line crosses the 45° line at a lower level of GDP. To see how much lower, we need to make two calculations. First, we need to recalculate the spending multiplier. Instead of:

$$k_e = \frac{1}{1 - b} = \frac{1}{1 - 0.8} = 5$$

it is now:

$$k_e = \frac{1}{1 - b(1 - t)} = \frac{1}{1 - 0.72} = 3.57$$

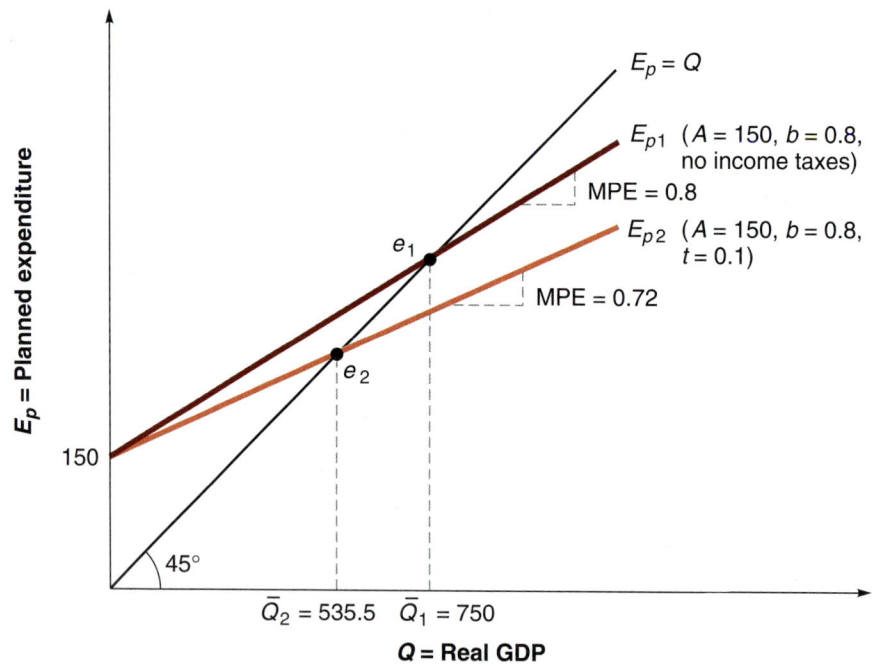

·····FIGURE 25.6 INCOME TAXES, THE SPENDING LINE, AND EQUILIBRIUM GDP

Income taxes change the slope of the spending line, the multiplier, and the level of equilibrium GDP. Along E_{p1}, there are no income taxes. Given an MPC = 0.8 and autonomous spending of 150, equilibrium GDP is at $\overline{Q}_1 = 750$. When an income tax of 10 percent is imposed, the slope of the spending line changes to $0.72 = 0.8(1 - 0.1)$, and the new spending line, E_{p2}, intersects the 45° line at a lower level, $\overline{Q}_2 = 535.5$.

because income taxes, an additional "leakage" from the spending stream, reduce the value of the spending multiplier.

The second calculation is to substitute this new multiplier into Equation 7 (a restatement of Equation 7 in Chapter 24):

$$\overline{Q} = k_e(A) \qquad [7]$$

If total autonomous spending is 150, this gives:

$$\overline{Q} = 3.57(150) = 535.5$$

This result is shown in Figure 25.6: the 10 percent income tax has lowered equilibrium GDP from $\overline{Q}_1 = 750$ to $\overline{Q}_2 = 535.5$.

· · · · · · · ·

Closing GDP Gaps with Income Taxes

It is possible to close the GDP gap with income tax changes.[4] When equilibrium GDP is less than potential GDP, an income tax cut can close the gap. As an example, suppose that potential GDP is 900 but that equilibrium GDP is only 834. Suppose further that the MPC is 0.8 and the income tax rate is 0.2; this gives a spending multiplier of $2.78 = 1/[1 - 0.8(1 - 0.2)]$. Substitution into Equation 7 reveals that autonomous spending must equal 300 given this multiplier and equilibrium GDP of 834. To find out how much to cut income taxes to move the economy to potential GDP, rewrite Equation 7 as:

$$\overline{Q} = \frac{1}{1 - b(1 - t)}(A)$$

and substitute potential GDP for $\overline{Q}$, 0.8 for b, and 300 for A, leaving t as an unknown:

$$900 = \frac{1}{1 - 0.8(1 - t)}(300)$$

All that is necessary now is to solve the expression for the income tax rate, t. The calculations reveal an income tax rate of 0.17.[5] Thus, a cut in income taxes from 20 percent to 17 percent would stimulate growth and move the economy to potential GDP.

RECAP   **Fiscal Policy and the Income-Expenditure Model**

1. Government purchases shift the planned spending line. An increase in government purchases shifts the planned spending line upward and increases equilibrium GDP; a decrease in government purchases shifts the planned spending line downward and lowers equilibrium GDP.

---

[4]This section can be omitted without loss of continuity.

[5]To work this problem, first multiply each side of the equation by $[1 - 0.8(1 - t)]$ to get $180 + 720t = 300$. Solving for t gives $t = 0.167 \approx 0.17$.

2. Autonomous consumption taxes shift the planned spending line by an amount equal to the MPC times the autonomous tax. An increase in autonomous taxes shifts the spending line downward and lowers equilibrium GDP; a decrease in autonomous taxes shifts the planned spending line upward and increases equilibrium GDP.

3. Income taxes change the slope of the planned spending line and the spending multiplier. An increase in income taxes makes the planned spending line flatter and lowers both equilibrium GDP and the spending multiplier. A decrease in income taxes makes the planned spending line steeper and increases both equilibrium GDP and the spending multiplier.

THE FOREIGN SECTOR

We have just one more component to add to the income-expenditure model, the foreign sector. Fortunately, adding the foreign sector is a simple task now that we have seen how taxes and government purchases affect the model.

Exports Goods and services produced in the domestic economy and sold abroad.

Imports Goods and services produced abroad and sold in the domestic economy.

The foreign sector has two components, exports (X) and imports (Z). **Exports** are goods and services produced at home and sold abroad; **imports** are goods and services produced in foreign nations but sold here. When Boeing sells airplanes in China or Apple Computer sells computers in Russia, income flows into the United States and generates jobs. This explains why the X term in the planned spending equation is entered with a plus sign. On the other hand, when we buy French wine or Australian wool, income flows out of the United States, and the economy slows down, so the Z term has a negative sign in the spending equation. The difference between exports and imports is called *net exports* and is indicated by the term ($X - Z$). The final planned spending equation of the income-expenditure model is:

$$E_p = C + I_p + G + (X - Z) \qquad [8]$$

Factors That Influence Net Exports

Several factors influence the level of net exports, but we are most concerned with three factors: the exchange rate, international price differentials, and GDP growth.

The exchange rate gives the price of one currency in terms of another. To see why the exchange rate affects net exports, assume that the dollar/yen (¥) exchange rate is currently $1 = ¥105. This means that a Toyota with a price of ¥1,050,000 in Japan would carry a price of $10,000 in the United States (¥1,050,000/105 = $10,000). If the dollar is "weak" and buys only 100 yen, that same Toyota would cost $10,500 in the United States. The result would be that fewer Toyotas would be imported into the United States. Look at the situation from Japan's perspective. When the dollar is "strong" ($1 = ¥105), the yen is weak because each yen buys only 1/105 dollars. This would make imports from the United States expensive in Japan. But if the dollar is weak ($1 = ¥100), the yen is strong because each yen buys 1/100 dollars, and U.S. goods are inexpensive in Japan. For another example, an Apple Macintosh computer that sells for $2,000 in the United States will cost £1,000 in England when the exchange rate is $1 = £0.5. If the dollar strengthened so that each dollar bought £0.6, the Macintosh would cost $2,000(0.6) = £1,200 in England, and Apple Computer would sell fewer computers in England. On the other hand, if the dollar weakened so that each dollar only bought £0.4, the price of Macintoshes in England would fall to $2,000(0.4) = £800, and Apple Computer sales in England would increase. The result: A stronger dollar increases U.S. imports and decreases U.S. exports; a weaker dollar decreases U.S. imports and increases U.S. exports.

Other factors that can affect net exports include the price level and GDP growth in both the domestic economy and foreign economies. When the price level in the United States rises relative to the price level abroad, U.S. citizens increase their imports of relatively cheap foreign goods. When the price level in the United States falls relative to the price level abroad, U.S. exports increase. Thus, as the price level in the United States rises relative to the rest of the world, imports into the United States increase, and exports from the United States decrease. A lower price level in the United States has just the opposite effect.

Finally, GDP growth can affect net exports as well. When the U.S. economy is growing rapidly, U.S. citizens buy more goods, including imports; when foreign economies are in recession, foreigners buy fewer U.S. exports. This is the main reason why the U.S. merchandise trade deficit increased from under $85 billion in 1992 to almost $130 billion in 1993. The U.S. economy was in the midst of a strong recovery while many of our trading partners were mired in recession. Unlike the exchange rate and international price-level differentials, domestic GDP growth is determined within the income-expenditure model. Holding foreign GDP growth constant, as GDP growth in the United States accelerates, net exports fall; as GDP growth slows, net exports increase.

We need to convert this information into graphical form so that we can combine it with the rest of the income-expenditure model. To do so, we need to look at exports and imports a little closer. The main results we are looking for are that (1) exports shift the planned spending line, and (2) imports change both the slope of the planned spending line and the spending multiplier.

The Export Function

Most of the important factors that influence the level of exports—the exchange rate, the price level, and foreign GDP growth—are external to the income-expenditure model, so we can treat exports as being autonomous. Consequently, exports change the intercept of the aggregate planned spending line. An increase in exports shifts the spending upward; a decrease shifts it downward. Factors that would shift the export line upward include a weaker domestic currency, higher prices abroad, and more rapid foreign GDP growth. Figure 25.7 illustrates the effect of autonomous exports on the planned spending line.

The Import Function

In contrast to exports, imports are best regarded as an induced variable. When the domestic economy is booming, people buy more goods, including more imports; when the domestic economy is sluggish, people buy fewer goods, including imports.

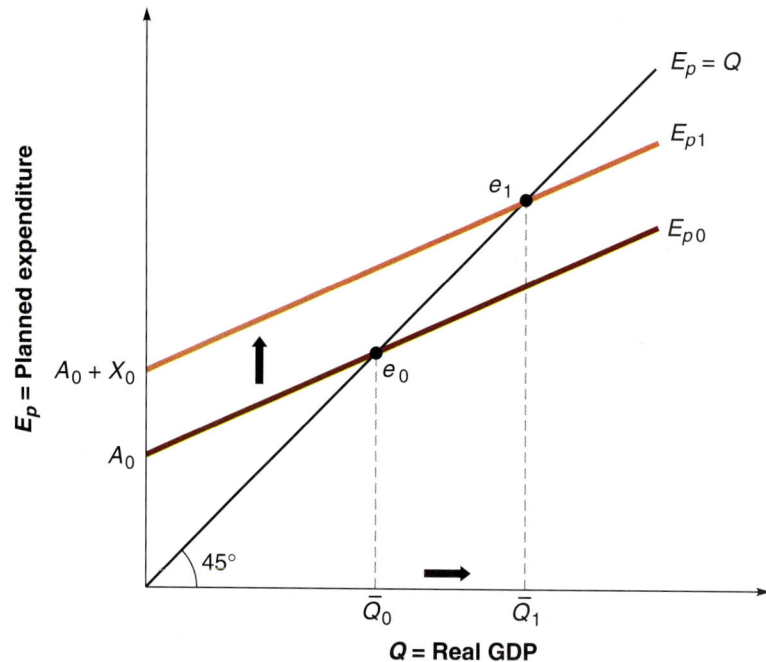

····· FIGURE 25.7 EXPORTS SHIFT THE SPENDING LINE

Other things being equal, an increase in exports will shift the planned spending line upward and increase equilibrium GDP. In this case, an increase in autonomous exports from 0 to X_0 has caused equilibrium GDP to rise from $\overline{Q}_0$ to $\overline{Q}_1$. The slope of the spending line does not change because exports are assumed to be entirely autonomous.

The slope of the import function is called the *marginal propensity to import,* or MPZ for short, and will be indicated by the lowercase letter z. The MPZ must be between 0 and 1 to indicate that people spend more than 0 percent but less than 100 percent of any change in their income on imports. Remember that the import term in the spending equation has a negative sign, so the marginal propensity to import represents a leakage from the spending stream and a *decrease* in the marginal propensity to spend on domestic goods and services. This means that, other things being equal, imports reduce the size of the spending multiplier and the level of equilibrium GDP. This is shown in Figure 25.8.

Imports reduce the spending multiplier because they reduce the marginal propensity to spend on domestic goods and services. The new formula for the MPE is:

$$\text{MPE} = b(1 - t) - z = b - bt - z \qquad [9]$$

Where:

    b = marginal propensity to consume (MPC)

    t = income tax rate

    z = marginal propensity to import (MPZ)

·····**FIGURE 25.8** IMPORTS CHANGE THE SLOPE
OF THE SPENDING LINE

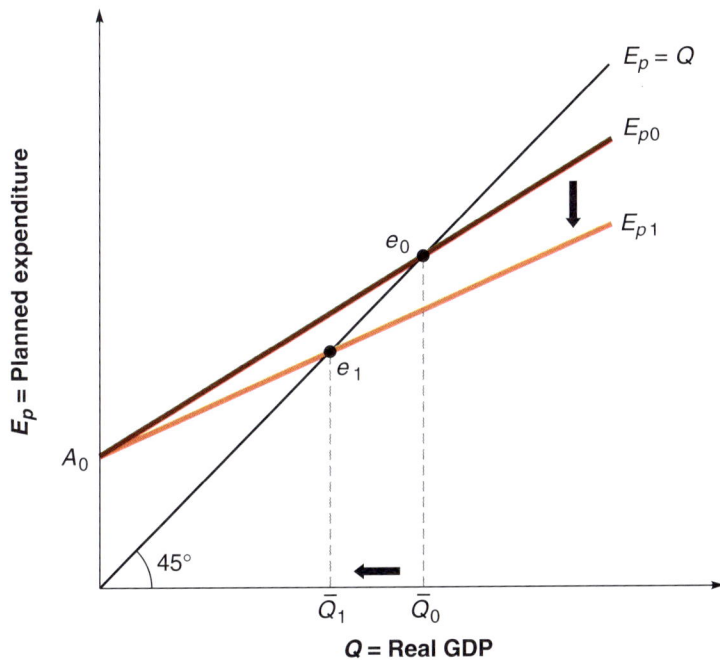

Other things being equal, an increase in the marginal propensity to import will make the planned spending line flatter and reduce both the spending multiplier and equilibrium GDP. The intercept of the spending line does not change because imports are assumed to be entirely induced.

Notice that the z shows up with a negative sign because income spent on imports "leaks out" of the domestic spending stream. As always, the spending multiplier is the reciprocal of $1 - \text{MPE}$, so the new spending multiplier is:

$$k_e = \frac{1}{1 - b + bt + z} \qquad [10]$$

As an example, if $b = 0.8$, $t = 0.1$, and $z = 0.05$, the spending multiplier would be:

$$k_e = \frac{1}{1 - 0.8 + 0.08 + 0.05} = \frac{1}{0.33} = 3.03$$

········

The Net Export Function

The combined effect of imports and exports—net exports—depends on the relative magnitudes of imports and exports. If imports exceed exports, net exports will exert a contractionary effect on the economy. If exports are greater than imports, there will be a stimulative effect on the economy. It is important to realize, however, that there can be two-way causality between net exports and the economy. Even though an increase in net exports will tend to raise equilibrium GDP, an increase in GDP will tend to decrease net exports because imports are an induced variable. As a result, net exports may be negative when the economy is doing quite well at the peak of a business cycle, but the deficit may shrink when the economy is mired in a severe recession—not quite what the average person on the street would think, but exactly what happened to the U.S. merchandise trade deficit between 1992 and 1993.

RECAP   The Foreign Sector and the Income-Expenditure Model

1. Exports stimulate the economy and imports slow the economy, so the effect of the foreign sector depends on net exports, the difference between exports and imports.
2. Exports are assumed to be autonomous. This means that an increase in exports shifts the planned spending line upward; a decrease in exports shifts the planned spending line downward.
3. Imports are a function of GDP growth and are treated as being entirely induced. An increase in the marginal propensity to import makes the planned spending line flatter and reduces both the spending multiplier and equilibrium GDP. A decrease in the marginal propensity to import makes the planned spending line steeper and increases both equilibrium GDP and the spending multiplier.

THE SPENDING MULTIPLIER IN THE REAL WORLD

With the inclusion of income taxes and the foreign sector, we have gone about as far as we can in the derivation of the spending multiplier in the income-expenditure model. Nevertheless, our model is still several iterations away from the real world. At least three modifications are necessary before we can arrive at a reasonably accurate estimate of the real-world spending multiplier:

1. Mathematically, the multiplier takes forever to work itself out. Spending induced by the multiplier goes on (literally) forever, but gets very small after a few spending periods. This is why most economists *truncate* the multiplier and examine its effects for only two years or so.
2. The multiplier usually has *price effects*. When spending increases, the prices of some goods will rise and reduce the amount that real GDP can increase. We will look at this issue in the next chapter.
3. Any change in autonomous spending is likely to affect *financial markets*. An increase in autonomous spending can cause interest rates to rise and choke off some investment, thus reducing the spending multiplier. This is known as *crowding out,* an issue we take up in Chapter 31.

Taking these (and other) considerations into account, economists typically arrive at real-world estimates of the spending multiplier that are between 2 and 3—meaning that a $100 increase in autonomous spending will generate between $200 and $300 in additional income. In actuality, however, there is not a single multiplier but several different multipliers associated with different kinds of spending. For example, the multipliers associated with defense spending are probably lower than the multipliers associated with education and public investment spending. Table 25.1 summarizes the various spending multipliers we have developed in the chapter.

• • • • TABLE 25.1 VARIOUS MULTIPLIERS

The spending multiplier is always defined as:

$$k_e = \frac{1}{1 - \text{MPE}}$$

but because the MPE changes as the model changes, so does the multiplier. This changes the level of equilibrium income as well as the amount of spending necessary to close any GDP gap.

- **Case I: Induced consumption only.** In the simplest case, the only kind of induced spending is induced consumption. In this case, the spending multiplier depends only on the marginal propensity to consume, the MPC, which is represented by the letter b:

$$k_1 = \frac{1}{1 - \text{MPC}} = \frac{1}{1 - b}$$

If the MPC is 0.9, the multiplier would be 10:

$$k = \frac{1}{1 - 0.9} = \frac{1}{0.1} = 10$$

- **Case II: Induced consumption and income taxes.** Income taxes represent a "leakage" from the spending stream, so when income taxes are added to the model, both the MPE and multiplier fall. The formula for this multiplier is:

$$k_2 = \frac{1}{1 - b + bt}$$

where t is the income tax rate. If the income tax rate is 0.2, the spending multiplier falls to:

$$k = \frac{1}{1 - 0.9 + 0.9(0.2)} = \frac{1}{0.28} = 3.57$$

- **Case III: Induced consumption, income taxes, and imports.** Adding induced imports reduces the spending multiplier even more. The new formula is:

$$k_3 = \frac{1}{1 - b + bt + z}$$

where z is the propensity to import. If $z = 0.1$, the spending multiplier falls to:

$$k = \frac{1}{1 - 0.9 + 0.9(0.2) + 0.1} = \frac{1}{0.38} = 2.63$$

- **Case IV: The real world.** Most real-world estimates of the multiplier are probably between 2 and 3. Real-world multipliers are lower than "textbook" multipliers because of price changes, activity in the financial markets, and the need to truncate multiplier effects.

Twin deficits Name coined by the media in the 1980s to refer to the simultaneous existence of the fiscal deficit and the trade deficit.

THE TWIN DEFICITS

The income-expenditure model can help us understand why and how the **twin deficits**—the fiscal and trade deficits—are related.[6] We discovered in Chapter 23 (and in the appendix to Chapter 24 as well) that equilibrium exists when saving equals planned investment. Saving represents a "leakage" from the spending stream and investment is an "injection." This chapter has expanded the income-expenditure model so we now have three kinds of leakages—savings, taxes and imports. We also have three kinds of injections—investment, government purchases, and exports. It follows that equilibrium exists when:

$$S + T + Z = I + G + X \qquad [11]$$

Some rearrangement gives:

$$(X - Z) + (G - T) = (S - I) \qquad [12]$$

In words, Equation 12 means that the trade balance $(X - Z)$[7] plus the fiscal deficit $(G - T)$ must equal the excess of saving over investment $(S - I)$. For example, if $Z = 700$, $X = 600$, $T = 900$, $G = 1,100$, and $S = 100$, there would be no funds available for private investment:

$$(600 - 700) + (1,100 - 900) = (100 - 0)$$

On the other hand, if $Z = X$ and $T = G$, the same $S = 100$ would support 100 worth of investment. This point is important: the twin deficits must be paid for by an excess of saving over investment, and using savings to pay for these deficits means that fewer funds are available for investment.

At first glance, the data seem to refute Equation 12. For example, in 1990, the trade balance was negative $90.4 billion, and the combined federal, state, and local government deficits totaled $136.1 billion, but private domestic investment was approximately equal to private domestic saving. Does this means that the identity in Equation 12 is incorrect? No. **Foreign financial capital inflows**—treated as saving by national income accountants—made up most of the difference. Why did so much foreign financial capital flow into the United States? Some was used to buy corporate stocks and bonds, but much of it was used to purchase government debt. The Treasury finances government deficits by borrowing money—most often by selling treasury bills and other government securities. In the 1980s, much of this debt was sold to foreigners who were attracted to high interest rates and the relative stability of U.S. financial markets. The willingness of foreigners to buy U.S. Treasury debt made it possible for the government to run record deficits and the public to go on an import binge simultaneously.

Foreign capital flows Movements of financial capital from one country to another. In the 1980s, much of the U.S. government debt was funded by foreign capital inflows.

[6]This section can be omitted without loss of continuity.

[7]Strictly speaking, what we are calling the "trade balance" in this and the next paragraph is the balance on the *current account* of the balance of payments. The current account balance equals the merchandise trade balance plus the balance on services and net transfers. Balance of payments accounting is discussed in more detail in Chapter 36.

• • • • • • • •

Potential Concerns over the Twin Deficits

It is hard to pick up a newspaper these days without reading something about the evils of the government deficit. In fact, deficits may not be nearly as bad as the person on the street seems to think, but there probably are some causes for concern. Many economists feel that the biggest potential problem associated with fiscal deficits is that they rob savings from the private sector. When the government borrows $200 billion per year, less money may be available for corporate borrowing and expansion. There is some evidence too that government borrowing may cause interest rates to rise, and high interest rates act as a further deterrent to investment. This will be addressed in more detail when we look at fiscal policy in Chapter 31.

Financial capital moves across international boundaries looking for the highest rate of return. Foreign financial capital inflows have provided funding for U.S. deficits, but they may also be a source of potential problems. Capital inflows to one country are capital outflows from another country, and capital outflows reduce the funds available for investment and growth. To keep financial capital at home, nations experiencing capital outflows are forced to maintain high interest rates. This reduces economic growth and investment even more. Second, large capital inflows raise the specter of an equally large and sudden capital flight. Foreign investors can withdraw their funds as quickly as they deposited them. A sudden withdrawal of foreign financial capital could drive up interest rates and wreck havoc on financial markets. These issues should not be overstated: to outlaw international capital flows would be folly, but some economists have argued for regulations to ensure orderly international capital markets.

• • • • • • • SUMMARY

This chapter has completed our three-chapter odyssey with the income-expenditure model. We have shown the important role of inventories in economic equilibrium, explained what can cause the economy to enter a recession, and shown how it may be possible to use policies to help the economy recover. The main points to remember from this chapter are:

1. A GDP gap exists when equilibrium GDP differs from potential GDP. To close a GDP gap, it is necessary to shift the expenditure function, either through a deliberate act of policy, such as change in government spending or taxes, or through an automatic price change.

2. When autonomous spending is less than the amount necessary to generate potential GDP, the economy is in a recessionary gap. Recessionary gaps can be closed by decreasing taxes or increasing government spending or by a decrease in the price level. When autonomous spending is greater than the amount necessary to generate potential GDP, the economy is in an inflationary gap. Inflationary gaps can be closed by increasing taxes or decreasing government spending or by an increase in the price level.

3. Autonomous taxes and government spending affect the intercept of the aggregate spending line; income taxes affect the slope of the spending line and the spending multiplier.

4. The difference between imports and exports is called the net export balance. Exports provide domestic jobs and employment; imports slow down the domestic economy. Exports are treated as being autonomous and shift the spending line; imports are a function of income and reduce the spending multiplier.

5. The government deficit and the trade deficit are related because both must be paid for by an excess of saving over investment. In recent years, much of the difference has been made up by foreign capital inflows into the United States.

KEY TERMS AND CONCEPTS

potential gross domestic product (Q⋆)   income tax
GDP gap   exports
price flexibility   imports
recessionary gap   net exports
inflationary gap   twin deficits
autonomous tax   foreign capital flows

REVIEW QUESTIONS

1. Explain how and why prices are assumed to adjust when GDP differs from potential GDP in the income-expenditure model.
2. Explain, with reference to both income taxes and autonomous taxes, why an increase in personal taxes reduces consumption less than the amount of the tax.
3. How does a decrease in government purchases affect the level of equilibrium GDP? How does an increase in autonomous taxes affect the level of equilibrium GDP? How does an increase in the income tax rate affect the spending multiplier and the level of equilibrium GDP? Answer both verbally and graphically.
4. What factors influence the level of exports? What factors influence the level of imports? How do net exports affect the slope and intercept of the spending line and the level of equilibrium GDP?
5. What are the "twin deficits"? How are they related?

PROBLEMS

1. The government can impose autonomous taxes on investment. For example, many firms must pay licensing fees. How do you think an increase in autonomous investment taxes would affect the level of equilibrium income? Draw a diagram to illustrate your result.
2. Figure 25.8 was drawn on the assumption that there were no autonomous imports. Is this reasonable? Explain. How would the existence of autonomous imports affect the level of equilibrium GDP? Draw a figure to illustrate your answer.
3. Suppose the government raises income taxes in an effort to close an inflationary gap. Is it possible for this policy to reduce $Q^\star$ as well as Q? Why or why not?
4. Given the following model:

$$C = 50 + 0.8Q_d \qquad T = 10 + 0.1Q \qquad G = 200 \qquad I = 150$$

a. Find equilibrium GDP, $\overline{Q}$. Draw a diagram to illustrate your result.
b. Find the spending multiplier, k_e.
c. Suppose that $Q^\star = 1,600$. How much should G be changed to restore $Q^\star$?
d. Suppose that $Q^\star = 1,600$. How much should T_0 be changed to restore $Q^\star$?
5. Given the following model:

$$C = 50 + 0.8Q_d \qquad T = 10 + 0.1Q \qquad G = 200$$
$$I = 150 \qquad Z = 0.05Q \qquad X = 100$$

a. Construct the private saving function and find equilibrium GDP using the "injection-leakage" approach. Draw a graph to illustrate your result.
b. Find the spending multiplier.
c. Is the government budget balanced at equilibrium GDP?
d. Is the nation running a trade deficit or surplus at equilibrium GDP?
6. Indicate whether and how each of the following shocks would affect the level of equilibrium GDP:
a. an increase in inflation in foreign countries
b. higher interest rates in the United States
c. an increase in the incentive to save
d. tax increases that balance the budget
e. a decrease in the MPC
f. a tariff (tax) on imported goods
7. Suppose that the government cuts business taxes in an effort to increase investment and close a recessionary gap. Is it possible for this policy to increase $Q^\star$ as well as Q? Why or why not?
8. In 1993, the Japanese government was concerned about the *endaka,* or rapid appreciation of the yen. How did the *endaka* affect Japanese exports and imports?
9. The income-expenditure model is the standard starting place for macroeconomic analysis, but many economists are hesitant to use it because it omits so many important aspects of the economy. What are some of these aspects? Do you think the model is still useful despite these simplifications?

CHAPTER 26

Aggregate Demand and Supply

Almost as soon as economists began to think that they might have figured out how to end recessions, they encountered another problem and it was a big one: inflation. Unfortunately, the income-expenditure model says very little about inflation. In fact, the income-expenditure model seems to imply that inflation can occur only when output exceeds potential GDP. The events of the 1970s provided a rather graphic counterexample: inflation accelerated to "double-digit" levels, and at the same time the unemployment rate approached 10 percent—then the post–World War II high.

One problem with the income-expenditure model is that it says nothing about the supply side of the economy. This is why it cannot provide an adequate analysis of the effects of rising oil prices, wage hikes, or cost-of-living adjustment clauses—events that have complicated economic matters for the past two decades. In this chapter we will take what we learned with the income-expenditure model and extend it to the aggregate demand–aggregate supply model, one of the most popular and useful macroeconomic models available.

AFTER READING AND STUDYING THIS CHAPTER, YOU SHOULD BE ABLE TO:
- • • Explain why the aggregate demand and aggregate supply curves are shaped as they are, and explain what causes them to shift.
- • • Use the aggregate demand–aggregate supply model to illustrate business fluctuations—inflation, recession, and stagflation
- • • Use the aggregate demand–aggregate supply model to help interpret U.S. economic history

ASSUMPTIONS AND DEFINITIONS

We need to define only a couple of new terms before developing the aggregate demand–aggregate supply model. This model provides a good framework for analyzing changes in the *price index,* but only an indirect method for analyzing *inflation*. What is the difference? The price index, P, is a measure of the average price level. We learned how to claculate and use price indices in Chapter 5. Inflation is the percentage increase in the price index, $\Delta P/P$. Further, economists generally consider changes in the price index to be inflation only if they are ongoing. For example, a one-time increase in the price index from 100 to 110 would be a shift in the price index, not inflation. On the other hand, an increase in the price index from 100 to 110 to 121 to 133 over a three-year period would represent a 10 percent rate of inflation. The aggregate demand–aggregate supply model is best suited for analyzing changes in the price index, but we can make some inferences about inflation by looking at the conditions that lead to continuing upward movement of the price index.

Deflation The opposite of inflation; a continuing decrease in the aggregate price level.

The opposite of inflation is **deflation**, a continuing decrease in the average price level. Deflation occurred in the 1930s but has been rare in the modern economy; nevertheless, the concept will play an important role in the self-correcting process analyzed by the aggregate demand–aggregate supply model. More common than deflation is **disinflation**, a reduction in the rate of inflation. Disinflation is often the product of deliberate anti-inflation policies. Disinflation occurred during much of the 1980s.

Disinflation A reduction in the rate of inflation.

We will also need to distinguish between *money* and *income* in this chapter because money is an important shift parameter for the aggregate demand curve. The money supply consists primarily of coins, currency, and checking account deposits. Money is a stock variable with no time dimension. In contrast, income is a flow variable with a time dimension; it makes a difference whether you are paid $10 per hour or $10 per week. The central bank of the United States, the Federal Reserve system, can influence the amount of money circulating in the economy, and these changes can have an important impact on the economy. When the money supply is increased, lenders are often willing to make loans at lower interest rates. This tends to increase investment and other kinds of spending, but it can also result in higher inflation. A lower money supply usually has the opposite effect: interest rates rise, the economy slows down, and inflation moderates. We will have a great deal more to say about monetary theory and policy in Chapters 29 and 30.

A main assumption that we will be making in this chapter is that gradual price and wage adjustments tend to move the economy toward potential GDP. This is not to say that the economy always gets to potential GDP because many factors can prevent this from happening. For the time being at least, we will also be assuming that wages and prices are "sticky" because they are tied to contracts; once you agree to work for a particular wage, it is often a year before you can look forward to a raise. The assumption of sticky wages and prices means that the economy will move to potential GDP only after contracts have been renegotiated and wages and prices have completely adjusted. As we are about to see, this process can take several years.

THE AGGREGATE DEMAND CURVE

The aggregate demand curve (*AD*) gives the various levels of real GDP that will be demanded at various price levels, *ceteris paribus*. Like most demand curves, it slopes downward as shown in panel (b) of Figure 26.1. Even though the aggregate demand curve may seem like a simple concept—after all it *looks* just like an individual demand curve—it is really fairly complex.

Deriving the Aggregate Demand Curve

One way to derive the aggregate demand curve is to allow changes in the price index to shift the planned spending line in the income-expenditure model and plot the resulting changes in equilibrium GDP. This is done in Figure 26.1.

Begin at point *a* in panel (a), and assume that the price level increases from P_0 to P_1. The higher price level makes any money or savings you have less valuable. You are less "wealthy" in the sense that you can now buy fewer goods and services with your dollars. A reasonable response to the price-level increase—for you as well as

FIGURE 26.1 DERIVING THE AGGREGATE DEMAND (*AD*) CURVE

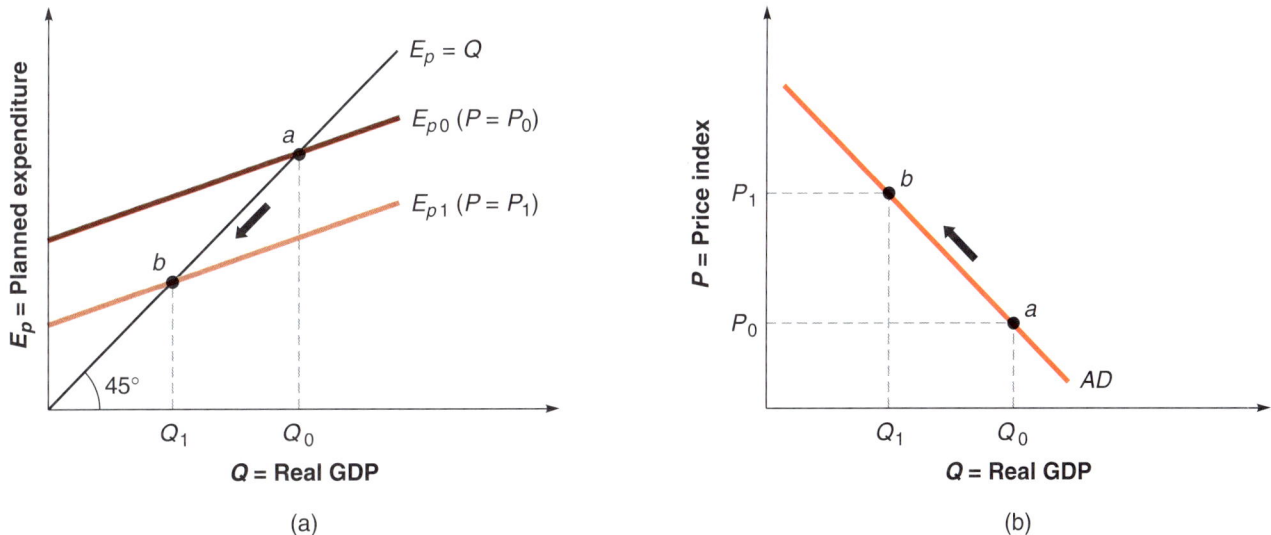

One way to derive the aggregate demand (*AD*) curve is to allow the price level to change in the income-expenditure model. An increase in the price index from P_0 to P_1 reduces real wealth and causes the planned spending line to shift from E_{p0} to E_{p1}. Equilibrium occurs at the intersection between the planned spending line and the 45° line, so real equilibrium GDP falls from Q_0 to Q_1. The aggregate demand curve in panel (b) plots the price indices, P_0 and P_1, and the GDP levels, Q_0 and Q_1, from the income-expenditure model in panel (a). Price-level changes also set in motion intertemporal and international substitution effects that cause GDP to change.

other consumers, business, and government—is a reduction in autonomous spending. In other words, *an increase in the price index will cause the planned spending line to shift down*. The result: The price-level increase causes equilibrium real GDP to fall from Q_0 to Q_1. The effect of price-level changes on real wealth is called a *wealth effect*.

The aggregate demand curve is derived in panel (b). It is just the plot of the various price levels and real GDP values consistent with equilibrium. Points *a* and *b* in panel (a) correspond to points *a* and *b* in panel (b). Notice that the higher price level is consistent with a lower level of real GDP. Note too that shifts in the planned spending lines in panel (a) correspond to movement along the aggregate demand curve in panel (b).

· · · · · · · ·

Other Explanations for the Shape of the Aggregate Demand Curve

The graphical exercise we have just completed is correct, but rather mechanical. As the price level changes, other events take place that affect the level of equilibrium GDP and give rise to the downward-sloping aggregate demand curve. In fact, there are actually several reasons why the aggregate demand curve slopes downward. Two of the most important are **intertemporal substitution** and **international substitution**.

Intertemporal substitution The process by which changes in the price index change interest rates and thereby affect the level of spending and equilibrium GDP. Higher rates act as an incentive to save and a disincentive to consume. Lower rates act as a stimulus to consumption and investment.

Intertemporal Substitution. Changes in the price index tend to change interest rates. Why? Suppose that banks have only a fixed amount of money available for lending and that the price index rises. The price hike will mean that prospective borrowers need larger loans to buy the goods they intend to purchase. When they ask for larger loans, banks will ration their loan money by charging higher interest rates. As interest rates rise, people begin to rethink their spending plans, and some people will postpone borrowing money. Further, some consumers will increase their savings because of the higher interest rate; this will allow them to consume more in the future. High interest rates will also cause firms to cut back on investment. All of these factors— less borrowing, higher saving, and less investment—will tend to shift the planned spending line downward and generate a downward-sloping aggregate demand curve.

The opposite would happen if the price level fell. Borrowers would need less money, and banks would be willing to make loans at lower interest rates. As the interest rate fell, autonomous spending would increase and cause the planned spending line to shift up. The result: Price declines increase equilibrium GDP.

International substitution The process by which international relative price differences affect the level of spending and equilibrium GDP. With a higher relative price level, foreign goods become relatively cheap, so imports increase and exports decline. With a lower relative price level, exports increase and imports decline.

International Substitution. International relative price differences can also affect the level of spending and equilibrium GDP. For example, suppose that the price level increases in the United States but does not change in the rest of the world. This would tend to decrease U.S. exports because U.S. goods would be more expensive to foreigners. At the same time, imports into the United States would increase because foreign goods would be inexpensive relative to U.S.-made goods. These two effects—an increase in imports and a decrease in exports—would combine to reduce net exports. The result would be a downward shift of the planned spending line and a movement up the aggregate demand curve. If the price level in the United States fell relative to the rest of the world, U.S. exports would rise while imports would fall, and there would be downward movement along the aggregate demand curve.

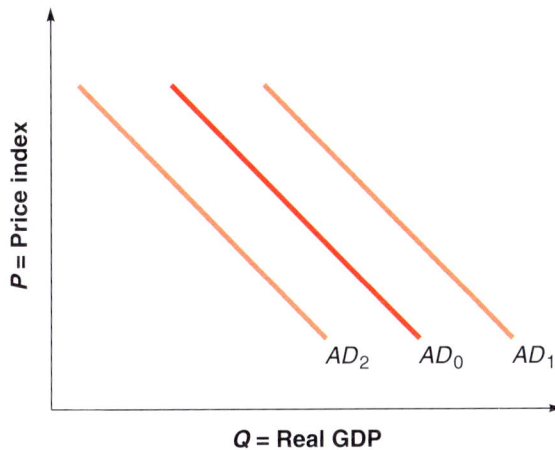

FIGURE 26.2 SHIFTING THE AGGREGATE DEMAND CURVE

Anything that shifts the aggregate spending line except a change in the price level will also cause the aggregate demand curve to shift. A shift in the AD curve from AD_0 to AD_1 represents an increase in aggregate demand; a shift from AD_0 to AD_2 represents a decrease in aggregate demand.

Factors That Shift the Aggregate Demand Curve

Several factors can cause the aggregate demand curve to shift. Graphically, anything that shifts the aggregate spending line *except a change in the price index* will also cause the aggregate demand curve to shift. Figure 26.2 illustrates shifts of the demand curve. An outward shift in the aggregate demand curve from AD_0 to AD_1 represents an increase in aggregate demand and indicates that more is demanded at every price level. A shift toward the price-level axis from AD_0 to AD_2 represents a decrease in aggregate demand and indicates that less is demanded at every price level. Some of the most important factors that shift the aggregate demand curve are fiscal and monetary policy, consumer and business confidence, exchange rates, and expected inflation.

Fiscal Policy. We found out in the last chapter that expansionary fiscal policy—either an increase in government spending or a decrease in taxes—will shift the planned spending line upward. Contractionary fiscal policies—a decrease in government spending or an increase in taxes—will shift the planned spending line downward. Fiscal policy has similar effects on the aggregate demand curve: An increase in government spending or a decrease in taxes will shift the aggregate demand curve from AD_0 to AD_1 in Figure 26.2, while a decrease in government spending or an increase in taxes would shift the aggregate demand curve from AD_0 to AD_2.[1]

---

[1] We will discover in Chapter 31 that under certain conditions an increase in government spending has little or no effect on the aggregate demand curve because government spending can lead to a reduction in the level of private spending. This phenomenon, known as *crowding out,* is thought to be more common when the economy is very close to potential GDP.

Monetary Policy. When the Federal Reserve increases the money supply, interest rates usually fall. We will analyze this in more detail in our discussion of monetary policy in Chapter 29, but the simple explanation is that the interest rate is the price of borrowing money, and if the supply of money increases, the price will fall. Falling interest rates increase business investment spending and purchases of consumer durables. This causes the aggregate demand curve to shift outward from AD_0 to AD_1 in Figure 26.2. A decrease in the money supply tends to raise interest rates and shifts the aggregate demand curve inward from AD_0 to AD_2.

Consumer and Business Confidence. Firms' decisions to invest and consumers' decisions to buy durable goods depend at least as much on their confidence in the future as on the interest rate. If the business community believes that a recession is imminent, investment will fall regardless of the interest rate. Likewise, consumers postpone durable goods purchases when they fear unemployment and recession. In this sense, recessions can be self-fulfilling prophecies: if people expect a recession, spending will fall and cause the aggregate demand curve to shift inward from AD_0 to AD_2. On the other hand, when people become more confident of the future, the aggregate demand curve will shift out toward AD_1, and the economy will grow.

Exchange Rates. One of the factors that influences our imports and exports is the exchange rate. The dollar exchange rate gives the amount of foreign currency that

• • • • • TABLE 26.1 FACTORS THAT SHIFT THE AGGREGATE DEMAND CURVE

Event	Result and Explanation
Increase in government spending	$AD \uparrow$: Government employment and purchases increase aggregate spending.
Lower personal taxes	$AD \uparrow$: Increased take-home pay causes spending to increase.
Decline in business confidence	$AD \downarrow$: Firms decrease investment, lay off workers, and pay out less income.
Increase in money supply	$AD \uparrow$: Increased availability of credit lowers interest rates and thus increases business investment.
U.S. dollar strengthens	$AD \downarrow$: Imported goods are cheaper so U.S. citizens increase imports; U.S. goods are more expensive to foreigners, so U.S. exports fall.
Foreign GDP growth accelerates	$AD \uparrow$: Foreign citizens have more income so they buy more goods, including U.S. exports.
Expectations of inflation increase	$AD \uparrow$: People buy now to avoid higher prices in the future.

NOTE: $\uparrow$ means rightward shift, $\downarrow$ means leftward shift. Also, the *AD* curve will shift in the opposite direction if the opposite event takes place. For example, a decrease in government spending will reduce aggregate demand; higher personal taxes will decrease aggregate demand, and so on.

can be purchased with one dollar. A "stronger" dollar means that each dollar can buy more foreign currency; a "weaker" dollar means that each dollar buys fewer units of foreign currency. A weaker dollar increases net exports because it raises the price of foreign goods in the United States and lowers the price of U.S. goods abroad. The result is an increase in aggregate demand and an outward shift of the aggregate demand curve from AD_0 to AD_1. A stronger dollar does just the opposite: foreign goods become less expensive in the United States so imports increase; U.S. goods become more expensive abroad so exports from the United States decline. The result is a decrease in aggregate demand and a shift from AD_0 to AD_2.

Expected Inflation. The best way to beat inflation is to buy goods before they go up in price. If people expect inflation to accelerate in the future, they will increase their current purchases. This will shift the aggregate demand curve to the right from AD_0 to AD_1. If people expect prices to fall in the future, they may postpone purchases today and wait for the lower prices tomorrow. This would cause the aggregate demand curve to shift toward the price-level axis, from AD_0 to AD_2. It is important to recognize that these shifts are brought about by *expectations* of price changes in the future. If the *current* price level changes, there is movement along the *AD* curve.

Other Factors. Many other factors can also shift the aggregate demand curve, so many, in fact, that it is impractical to list them all. Table 26.1 lists several of the important factors that can shift the aggregate demand curve. It would not hurt to memorize this table, but it is much more important that you understand *why* these events affect the aggregate demand curve as they do.

RECAP   The Aggregate Demand Curve

The aggregate demand curve (*AD*) looks like any other demand curve, but it is something else entirely. It gives the level of equilibrium GDP for various price indices. It is important to distinguish between shifts in and movements along the *AD* curve.

1. The aggregate demand curve is downward sloping because lower prices permit more purchases from a given amount of wealth. The downward slope is also explained by intertemporal and international substitution. A change in the domestic price level or GDP will result in movement along a given aggregate demand curve.
2. The main factors that shift the aggregate demand curve include fiscal and monetary policy, consumer and business expectations, the exchange rate, and economic growth abroad.

THE AGGREGATE SUPPLY CURVE

The short-run aggregate supply (*AS*) curve gives the amount of aggregate production that takes place at all price levels, *ceteris paribus*. As shown in Figure 26.3, the aggregate supply curve slopes upward because higher prices are needed to induce

• • • • **FIGURE 26.3 THE SHORT-RUN AGGREGATE SUPPLY (AS) CURVE**

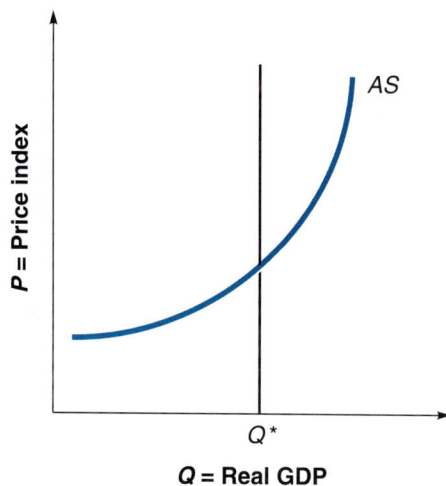

The short-run aggregate supply (*AS*) gives the different levels of aggregate production that will take place at different price levels, *ceteris paribus*. It slopes upward because as additional workers are added to a fixed stock of capital, the amount of capital per worker falls, and the output per worker diminishes. To maintain profits, firms must raise the selling price. At low levels of GDP, the aggregate supply curve is virtually horizontal because many firms are operating with unused capacity and can increase output without incurring increasing per unit costs of production. The aggregate supply curve becomes steeper as potential GDP is approached and is vertical at some point beyond potential GDP. This indicates that no additional production is possible in the short run regardless of the price level.

firms to produce more. Like the aggregate demand curve, the apparent simplicity of the aggregate supply curve is deceptive, so we will need to examine its shape and shift factors closely.

• • • • • • • •

The Shape of the Short-Run Aggregate Supply Curve

Like most short-run supply curves, the short-run aggregate supply curve slopes upward. There are two reasons for the upward slope. First, as with individual short-run supply curves, at least one factor of production—usually the stock of capital—is assumed to be fixed; therefore, to increase output, firms must add additional workers. As more workers are added to the fixed stock of capital, the amount of capital per worker declines. This causes the output per worker to decline (that is, to be subject to diminishing returns) and means that unit production costs rise for the firm. If nominal wages are fixed—as they are assumed to be along a given supply curve—firms will have to raise the selling price to cover their costs as output increases.

Notice that the aggregate supply curve in Figure 26.3 is virtually flat at levels of GDP considerably less than potential GDP, $Q^\star$. This shape is based on the assumption that at low levels of GDP there is so much unused plant capacity that workers can be added to previously idle capital without putting pressure on per unit costs of production. As the economy approaches potential GDP, there is less unused capital, per unit costs begin to rise, and firms are forced to raise selling prices. At very high levels of output, firms reach their physical limits, and the short-run aggregate supply curve becomes vertical. This indicates that, regardless of the selling price, no more output can be offered. Notice that the vertical part of the aggregate supply does not correspond to potential GDP; potential GDP is culturally determined by the length of the workweek, child labor laws, and the like. The economy can operate beyond potential GDP only temporarily. The vertical portion of the aggregate supply curve is determined by resource and technological constraints.

The Expectations Assumption

The short-run aggregate supply curve is drawn with the assumption that the wage rate is fixed, so any time wages change, the aggregate supply curve shifts. These changes are determined largely by expectations of the price level, which can also affect the slope of the aggregate supply curve.

Most economists believe that workers are more concerned with their **real wages** than with their **nominal** or **money wages**. The nominal or money wage is the wage you are paid in units of currency—say, $10 per hour. The real wage measures the purchasing power of nominal wages—how much you can buy with your wages. As we found out in Chapter 5, nominal values can be converted to real values by dividing by the price index. This means that the real wage is:

Real wage The nominal wage adjusted for the price index.

Nominal wage Wage rate in current or nominal terms; not adjusted for inflation.

$$\text{Real wage} = \frac{W}{P} \qquad [1]$$

Where:
  W = nominal or money wage
  P = the price index.

If the price index is at 1.00, $10 might be a pretty good wage: $10.00/1.00 = $10.00. But if the price index is higher, say, 1.50, that same nominal wage does not look too good: $10.00/1.50 = $6.67.

There are two basic theories about how nominal wages respond to changes in the price index. The **flexible wage** theory assumes that wages respond quickly to changes in the price index. When the price index rises, workers immediately ask for—and receive—nominal wage increases to cover the higher prices so that real wages are not affected. The **sticky wage** model assumes that nominal wages are based on long-term contracts and that nominal wages do not always adjust when the price level changes.

Flexible wage Wages that adjust quickly to market forces and help the economy move quickly to full employment and potential GDP.

Sticky wage Wages that do not respond quickly to market forces, perhaps because of the existence of long-term contracts.

The implications of these two models are important. If wages are perfectly flexible, nominal wages change and the aggregate supply curve shifts every time and as soon as the price level changes. (But notice that the shifts in the aggregate supply curve are not caused by the price level, but by the wage changes that are caused by the price change.) This would mean that the level of employment and real output are unaffected by fully expected changes in the price level. On the other hand, if nominal wages are sticky, an increase in the price level causes the real wage to fall so that

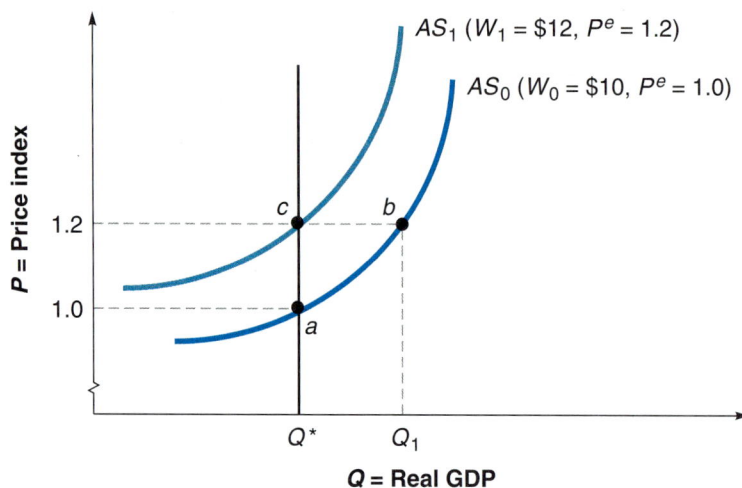

···· **FIGURE 26.4 EXPECTATIONS AND THE AGGREGATE SUPPLY CURVE**

Along a given short-run aggregate supply curve, the nominal wage is fixed, but the real wage will change as the price level changes. From point a, an increase in the price index from 1.0 to 1.2 will lower the real wage from \$10.00 to \$8.33. The lower real wage will induce firms to hire more workers and increase output from $Q^\star$ to Q_1 at point b. Under the sticky wage assumption, the economy will stay at point b until contracts expire and wages adjust; then the higher nominal wages will move the economy toward point c. Under the flexible wage assumption, the increase in prices from 1.0 to 1.2 will be immediately met by an increase in nominal wages, so the economy will move directly from point a to point c.

some workers end up working for less than they bargained for. The two assumptions are illustrated in Figure 26.4.

Suppose that the price index is initially 1.0 and that workers expect it will stay at that level for the foreseeable future. They agree to work for a nominal wage of \$10 per hour. Because the price index is 1.0, the real wage is also \$10 (= \$10.00/1.0). This is shown as point a on the figure. Now, if the price index rises to 1.2 and the nominal wage does not change, the real wage will fall to \$8.33 (= \$10.00/1.2). The result will be a move up the initial aggregate supply curve to point b because firms can afford to hire more workers at the lower real wage. However, point b can be maintained only until workers are able to negotiate higher nominal wages to restore their real wages. Once nominal wages increase, the aggregate supply curve will shift toward the price axis, and the economy will move toward point c.

The key, of course, is how quickly wages respond to the higher price level. The sticky wage model assumes that workers may have to settle for lower real wages (point b) for quite a while—a year or more in the case of many union contracts—with the result that output expands as firms hire workers at the lower real wage. The flexible wage model presents the polar case: the moment the price level starts to rise, workers immediately increase their nominal wages. This occurs so quickly that the economy never gets to point *b*; the price-level increase moves the economy directly from point *a* to point *c*. We will have more to say about the speed of adjustment later in this chapter as well as in the next chapter.

• • • • • • • •

Other Factors That Shift the Short-Run Aggregate Supply Curve

Price-level expectations and the nominal wage are not the only factors that shift the aggregate supply curve. Like any supply curve, the short-run aggregate supply curve shifts any time the costs of production change. One of the most difficult problems for policymakers since the 1970s has been **supply shocks**—rising oil and farm prices have been the most prominent. Oil and agricultural products are production inputs into many goods, so these supply shocks increase the cost of production and shift the short-run aggregate supply curve toward the price-level axis. There have also been beneficial supply shocks that have shifted the short-run aggregate supply curve to the right. The plunging oil prices of the mid-1980s and early 1990s are one example of beneficial supply shocks.[2]

Government regulations also shift the aggregate supply curve. Environmental and workplace safety rules provide important benefits to society, but they can also raise the costs of production. This often forces firms to raise their selling prices—and shifts the short-run aggregate supply curve to the left. The 1980s saw a wave of government *deregulation*—the relaxation of many environmental, worker safety, and other regulations. The effort was designed to lower the costs of production and shift the short-run aggregate supply curve to the right. Figure 26.5 illustrates how these factors shift the aggregate supply curve.

The aggregate supply curve will also shift when there is a change in the work effort. If workers put in more effort, the aggregate supply curve will shift away from the price axis; if workers work fewer hours or put in less effort, the aggregate supply curve will shift toward the price axis. Some economists believe that income taxes adversely affect the incentive to work. For example, the current income tax rate for most people is about 30 percent. This means that if you work an extra four hours on Saturday at $10 per hour, you will take home only $28 (= $40 × 0.7). If the income tax rate were increased to 40 percent, you would take home $24. The higher tax makes working on Saturday less enticing—maybe so much so that you will choose not to work. To the extent that income taxes do reduce the incentive to work, an increase in income taxes will shift the short-run aggregate supply curve toward the price-level axis, while cutting income taxes will shift it away from the price axis. However, most evidence suggests that current U.S. income tax rates have only a small effect on work effort.

Supply shock A dramatic increase or decrease in the price of an important production input. Such changes raise or lower production costs and shift the aggregate supply curve.

[2]Unless you happen to live in an oil-producing state like Alaska, Texas, Oklahoma, and Louisiana. These states were damaged by falling oil prices. Alaska, for example, receives over 85 percent of its state government budget from oil revenues.

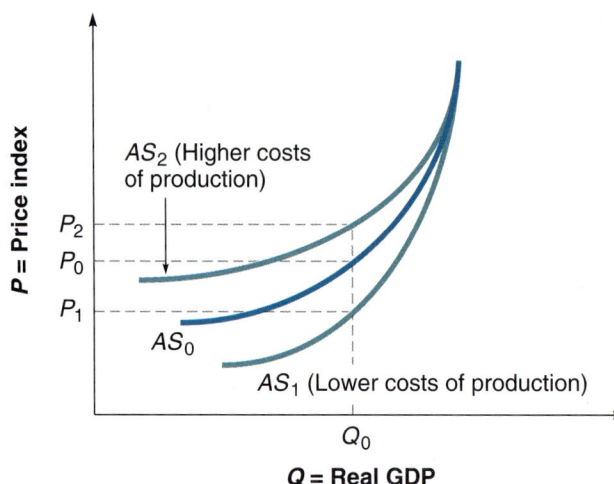

•••• FIGURE 26.5 SHIFTING THE SHORT-RUN AGGREGATE SUPPLY
CURVE

The short-run aggregate supply curve shows the different amounts of aggregate production that will take place for various price levels, and anything that affects the costs of
production will cause it to shift. Factors that lower the costs of production, including
wage cuts, government deregulation, and technological advances, will shift the aggregate
supply curve away from the price-level axis, as in the shift from AS_0 to AS_1 on the diagram. Notice that firms are willing to supply the same quantity, Q_0, at a lower price
level along AS_1. Factors that increase the cost of production—higher oil or agricultural
prices or wage increases—will shift the aggregate supply curve toward the price axis, as
in the shift from AS_0 to AS_2. Firms need a higher selling price to supply the same quantity along AS_2 as on AS_0. Other factors that can shift the aggregate supply curve include
work effort and income taxes. Notice that the vertical portions of the three short-run
aggregate supply curves merge, indicating that there is a technical limit to production in
the short run.

••••••••

The Long-Run Aggregate Supply Curve

Points *a* and *c* in Figure 26.4 are of special importance: at these points, expectations
conform to reality. Notice too that these points lie directly above potential GDP,
$Q^\star$. The vertical line through potential GDP is the *long-run aggregate supply curve (LS)*.
It is the long-run aggregate supply curve because it shows the amount of production
that will take place in the long run after all price adjustments have taken place. Points
like *b* to the right of $Q^\star$ cannot be maintained indefinitely because workers will
adjust their wages in response to higher prices. Likewise, points to the left of $Q^\star$ will
not exist in the long run because $Q < Q^\star$ implies high unemployment. These unemployed workers will eventually—although perhaps reluctantly—take wage cuts to
find jobs. Such cuts will lower the cost of production, shift the short-run aggregate
supply curve to the right, and increase employment and output.

If the flexible-price version of the labor market holds, the short-run aggregate supply curve moves so quickly that equilibrium GDP is always quite close to potential GDP. Does this imply that GDP never changes? Not at all—only that any sustained movements in GDP must be due to factors that affect potential GDP. Factors that affect potential GDP include the size of the labor force, technology, the resource base, and so on. The view that fluctuations in GDP are caused only by these kinds of events is called *real business cycle theory,* which we will explore in more detail in Chapter 32. Figure 26.6 shows how these events affect the long-run aggregate supply curve.

Factors That Shift the *LS* Curve

As we have just mentioned, changes in the size of the labor force, technology, and the resource base can shift the long-run aggregate supply curve, but so can several other factors. Most factors that shift the long-run aggregate supply curve also shift the short-run aggregate supply curve. Table 26.2 lists several factors that shift the long-run aggregate supply curve, but three of the more important are:

FIGURE 26.6 SHIFTING THE LONG-RUN AGGREGATE SUPPLY CURVE

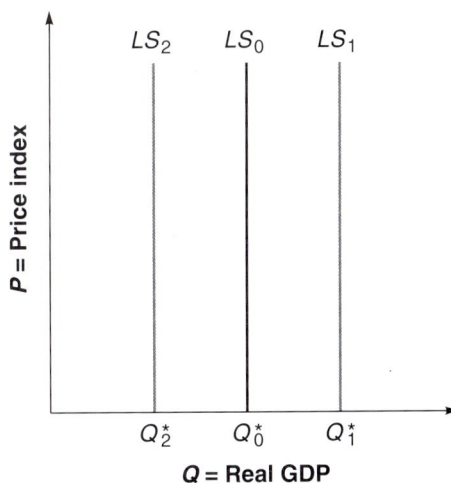

The long-run aggregate supply curve (*LS*) is vertical and located above potential GDP, $Q\star$. The long-run aggregate supply curve shows the level of production after all price adjustments have taken place. It will shift when there is a change in the potential productive capacity of the economy. For example, a technological change or an increase in the workforce will increase productive capacity and shift the long-run aggregate supply curve from LS_0 to LS_1. Factors that reduce the productive capacity of the economy such as higher oil prices and government regulations shift the long-run aggregate supply curve from LS_0 to LS_2.

> **TABLE 26.2** FACTORS THAT SHIFT THE SHORT-
> AND LONG-RUN AGGREGATE SUPPLY CURVES

Event	Result and Explanation
• *Factors that shift only the* AS *curve:*	
Wage increases	$AS\downarrow$: Wages are a cost of production. As costs rise, supply shifts left.
Higher business taxes	$AS\downarrow$: Taxes are a cost of production. Firms must raise prices to cover higher costs.
Workers expect future inflation	$AS\downarrow$: Wage demands will increase to cover the higher cost of living in the future.
• *Factors that shift both the* AS *and the* LS *curves:*	
Increase in the price of oil	$AS\downarrow$: Oil is an input into nearly every production process. More expensive oil increases the cost of production.
	$LS\downarrow$: As firms economize on the use of oil, energy input into productive processes declines so potential output falls.
Labor force increases	$AS\uparrow$: Wages fall because of more competition for available jobs.
	$LS\uparrow$: Larger workforce increases potential output.
Stock of physical capital increases	$AS\uparrow$: Workers have more machinery to work with and are thus more productive.
	$LS\uparrow$: Larger capital stock increases output potential.
Stock of human capital increases	$AS\uparrow$: Workers are more productive because they have more skills.
	$LS\uparrow$: Increased worker productivity raises potential output.
Technology advances	$AS\uparrow$: Workers are more productive because they have more efficient machinery.
	$LS\uparrow$: Increased productivity raises potential output.
Reduced government regulation	$AS\uparrow$: Regulations entail compliance costs. Fewer regulations lower costs.
	$LS\uparrow$: Firms can devote more resources to output.

NOTE: $\uparrow$ means rightward shift, $\downarrow$ means leftward shift. Also, the curves will shift in the opposite direction if the opposite event takes place. For example, a wage decrease will lower costs and shift the short-run aggregate supply curve to the right ($AS\uparrow$), and a decrease in the price of oil will shift both the short-run and the long-run aggregate supply curves to the right ($AS\uparrow$, $LS\uparrow$).

• *Stock of capital.* An important factor that can shift the long-run aggregate supply curve is the stock of capital. An increase in the number of machines—termed physical capital—will increase potential GDP and thus shift the long-run aggregate supply curve to the right in much the same way as an increase in the number of workers.

- *Human capital.* An increase in human capital can also shift the long-run aggregate supply curve outward. Human capital is the education and skills that workers acquire. As a society becomes more skilled and educated, the output of its workers increases. Some observers believe that a major reason why the U.S. standard of living is growing slower than that of many other countries is the slow growth of our human capital.
- *Population.* Population growth can also shift the long-run aggregate supply curve. A growing population means a growing labor force and thus a higher level of potential GDP, although not necessarily a higher level of potential GDP per person.

RECAP   The Aggregate Supply Curve

We are ready to combine the aggregate supply and aggregate demand curves and solve for equilibrium, but before doing so, it might help to summarize what we have just learned about the aggregate supply curve:

1. The short-run aggregate supply curve tends to be "flat" at low levels of production; it is upward sloping at higher levels of production because of diminishing returns; and it becomes very steep at $Q > Q^\star$.
2. The location of the short-run aggregate supply curve depends upon the wage rate and other factor costs, the expected price level, the stock of capital, technology, and other factors. It will shift whenever any of these variables change. Anything that raises (lowers) production costs will shift the short-run aggregate supply curve to the left (right).
3. When price expectations are incorrect, workers will change their wage demands, and the short-run aggregate supply curve will shift. When prices are higher than expected, wages will increase as soon as any contracts expire, and the short-run aggregate supply curve will shift upward.
4. When price-level expectations are correct, the economy operates at full employment and potential GDP along the long-run aggregate supply curve.
5. The long-run aggregate supply curve will shift when potential productive capacity of the economy changes. Factors that shift the long-run aggregate supply curve include technology, population, and work effort.

APPLICATIONS OF THE AGGREGATE DEMAND–AGGREGATE SUPPLY MODEL

The triple intersection of the aggregate demand curve, the short-run aggregate supply curve, and the long-run aggregate supply curve is the only point of long-run equilibrium. Three conditions must exist for long-run equilibrium: (1) The economy must be on the aggregate demand curve to assure that there is no unintended inventory change. (2) The economy must be on the short-run aggregate supply curve because this curve gives the amount of production that firms are willing to produce at all price levels. (3) The economy must be on the long-run aggregate supply curve for full employment to exist with no pressure for wage adjustment. The only place all three conditions hold is at the triple intersection of the curves. However, external events that shift any of the curves will set in motion changes that move the economy through cycles. In fact, the most valuable use of the aggregate demand–aggregate supply model is to trace out these cycles and help understand real-world economic events.

This section will use the aggregate demand–aggregate supply model to help explain the economics behind several important episodes in U.S. history. To keep the graphs as simple as possible, all of the curves will be drawn as straight lines. This does not alter the results in any significant way but does make the diagrams easier for you to draw as we go along—which, by the way, is an excellent way to make sure you understand the material.

Demand-Side Contraction

Economists since Adam Smith have marveled at the ability of market economies to self-correct from recession, at least theoretically. This process can be illustrated quite well with the aggregate demand–aggregate supply model. For example, suppose that business confidence collapses causing investment to fall. This would lead to a reduction in aggregate demand and shift the aggregate demand curve toward the price-level axis. In Figure 26.7, the aggregate demand curve shifts from AD_0 to AD_1, and the economy moves from point a to point b. At point b, both the price level and real

FIGURE 26.7 DEMAND-SIDE CONTRACTION

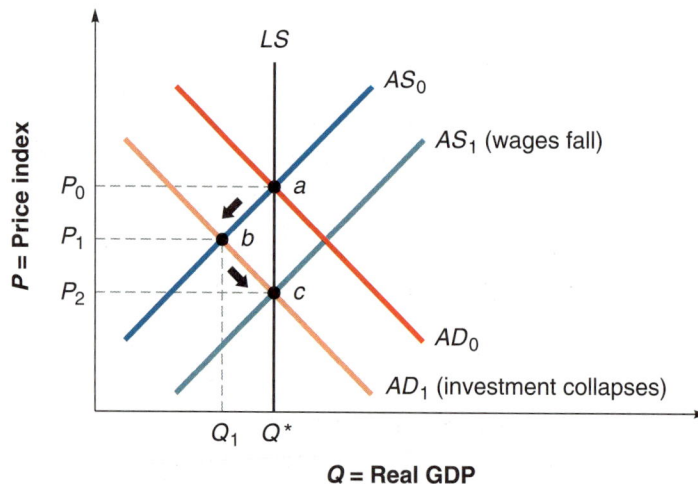

Flexible prices and wages act as self-correcting forces and help the economy recover from recessions. In this example, a decline in business confidence shifts the aggregate demand curve from AD_0 to AD_1 and moves the economy from point a to point b. At real GDP level Q_1, unemployed workers begin looking for new jobs. If they cannot find jobs at their old wage rates, they offer to work for lower wages. This causes the aggregate supply curve to shift from AS_0 toward AS_1. Wages keep falling as long as GDP is less than potential until the economy returns to full employment and potential GDP.

GDP have fallen. If all goes well, the aggregate demand–aggregate supply model predicts that the economy will return to potential GDP at point *c*. What causes this to occur? The key element is wage and price flexibility.

When workers find themselves unemployed, they will search for new jobs at their old wage rate. If they cannot find new jobs—a likely prospect given that the economy is in recession—they will offer to work at lower wages. As wages begin to fall, the aggregate supply curve will shift from AS_0 toward AS_1. Theoretically, wages will continue to fall as long as GDP is less than potential, and the short-run aggregate supply curve will keep shifting until potential GDP and full employment are restored at the intersection of AD_1, AS_1, and *LS*. Or so the story goes. Will workers really take a wage cut? There will obviously be strong resistance to doing so—among other things, workers will try to maintain wages high enough to cover their fixed obligations like their car and house payments—but once unemployment benefits run out, any job looks better than no job.

Price and Wage Flexibility in the Great Depression

Can we expect wage and price declines to restore full employment in the real world? There have been numerous cases of demand-side contraction in U.S. history, and many were characterized by falling wages and prices. If falling prices could ever generate recovery forces, they should have done so during the Great Depression of the 1930s.

From 1930 until 1933, prices and wages did fall, yet there was no sign of recovery. Why not? Several explanations have been offered. Some economists believe that falling prices generated so much pessimism that the aggregate demand curve shifted to the left as rapidly as falling wages shifted the short-run aggregate supply curve to the right. Other economists have suggested that wage declines did not increase hiring because employers were waiting for wages to fall even more. It is possible too that wages fell less than prices so that the real wage actually rose. The fact is, no one is certain why the Great Depression was as severe as it was. The Great Depression creates another problem for economic theorists: between 1934 and 1940, GDP was less than potential, but prices and wages stopped falling. Why this happened has never been answered satisfactorily.

Does the episode of the Great Depression mean that the aggregate demand–aggregate supply model is inapplicable to the real world? Not at all. It only means that the model must be used carefully. Today, many economists believe that there is an **asymmetry** in price and wage flexibility—prices and wages rise faster than they fall—but most economists agree that workers will eventually take wage cuts during severe recessions. In the relatively severe 1981–1982 recession, for example, many union workers negotiated contracts with lower wages but more employment guarantees.

Wage and price asymmetry
Wages and prices rise faster than they fall in response to market forces.

Demand-Side Expansion

The 1960s saw the United States fighting two wars—the war in Vietnam and the war at home against poverty. Both of these wars were costly and required substantial increases in government spending. Politically, these wars were less than successful: after losing over 50,000 lives, the United States withdrew from Vietnam, and little progress was made against poverty until late in the decade. Economically, the results may have been even worse: the two wars created a legacy that was to cripple the U.S. economy for more than a decade. The aggregate demand–aggregate supply model can help us understand what happened.

An idealized demand-side expansion is illustrated on Figure 26.8. Begin at point a where the economy is operating at potential GDP and the price level is 1.0. An increase in aggregate demand—higher government spending, lower taxes, or expansionary monetary policy—will shift the aggregate demand curve from AD_0 to AD_1. Now, because wages are assumed fixed along a given short-run aggregate supply curve, the increase in aggregate demand causes prices to begin to rise; thus, the real wage falls inducing firms to hire more workers. This increases output from $Q^\star$ to Q_1 as the economy moves to point b—a point of only short-run equilibrium. This point cannot be maintained indefinitely because the real wage has fallen. When their contracts expire, workers will ask for higher nominal wages, and the short-run aggregate supply curve will shift toward the price-level axis from AS_0 to AS_1. The short-run aggregate supply curve will continue shifting until real wages have been restored.

Demand-side expansions can be divided into two distinct periods. The path between points a and b indicates a rising price level and rising GDP. This is the typical situation in periods of what is called **demand-pull inflation**. The path between points b and c indicates a rising price level and falling production, as the economy self-corrects to the demand stimulus.

Demand-pull inflation Inflation that originates on the demand side of the economy, typically caused by excess money growth or expansionary fiscal policy.

FIGURE 26.8 DEMAND-SIDE EXPANSION

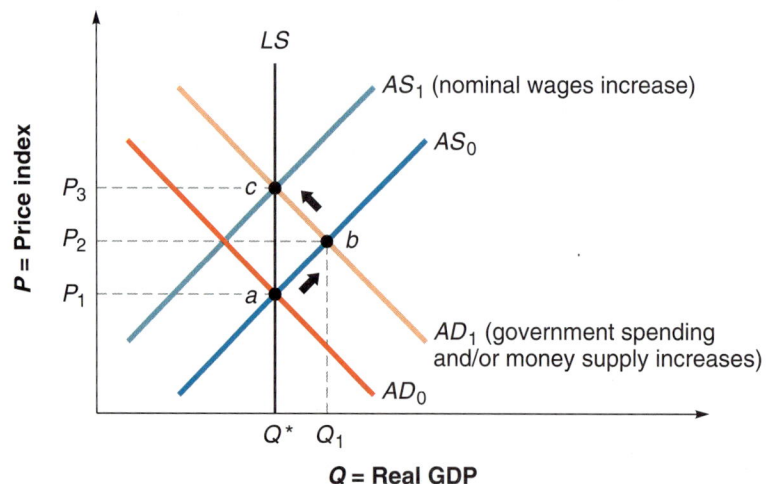

An increase in aggregate demand will shift the aggregate demand curve from AD_0 to AD_1 and move the economy to point b. Wages are fixed along the initial short-run aggregate supply curve, so the higher price level means that real wages have fallen and firms can hire more workers. Notice that the employment level is "over full" employment at point b because real GDP is greater than potential GDP. When workers revise their wages in response to the higher price level, the short-run aggregate supply curve will shift back toward point c. The time required for the move from b to c depends on the length of wage contracts and the way workers revise their price expectations.

····**TABLE 26.3** INFLATION AND OUTPUT DATA, 1964–1971

Year	Q	$\Delta Q/Q$	P	$\Delta P/P$	U	W	$\Delta W/W$
1964	$2,340.6	5.6%	27.7	1.8%	5.0%	$2.36	3.5%
1965	2,470.5	5.5	28.4	2.5	4.4	2.46	4.2
1966	2,616.2	5.9	29.4	3.5	3.7	2.56	4.1
1967	2,685.2	2.6	30.3	3.1	3.7	2.68	4.7
1968	2,796.9	4.2	31.8	5.0	3.5	2.85	6.3
1969	2,873.0	2.7	33.4	5.0	3.4	3.04	6.7
1970	2,873.9	0.0	35.2	5.4	4.8	3.23	6.3
1971	2,955.9	2.9	37.1	5.4	5.8	3.45	6.8

Key:

Q = real GDP in billions at 1987 dollars; P = GDP deflator, 1987 = 100; U = civilian unemployment rate; W = nominal hourly wage for nonagricultural workers, current dollars

SOURCE: 1994 *Economic Report of the President,* Tables B-2, B-3, B-40, and B-45.

Rising nominal wages are not the only response to the increase in aggregate demand. The higher level of production indicates that firms are using machinery more intensively, so it wears out more quickly—a costly proposition. Also, many of the new workers hired during the expansion period will be less experienced and less productive than old employees—and therefore most costly. All of these actions—an increase in wages, machinery depreciating more quickly, and the addition of less experienced workers—will serve to shift the short-run aggregate supply curve.

Application to the 1964–1971 Period. How closely does this scenario fit the actual data for the period 1964–1971 in Table 26.3? It fits pretty well if we interpret the facts carefully and make two modifications to allow for the dynamic nature of the economy. First, because the path from *a* to *c* can take several years, we need to adjust for the increase in potential GDP that occurs because of investment and the growing labor force. This means that we should consider the economy to be on a path like *a* → *b* only if actual GDP is growing faster than potential GDP. Likewise, the economy is doing poorly when GDP is growing less rapidly than potential GDP. Most economists believe the growth rate of potential GDP is a little over 3 percent per year.

The second modification relates to wages. In the 1960s, many workers were accustomed to annual wage increases regardless of the rate of inflation or productivity advances; such increases were often written into multiyear labor contracts so wages tended to grow every year, at least in nominal terms. An increase in the inflation rate would affect the negotiated wage in the next labor contract. Graphically, this would mean that the short-run aggregate supply curve was always shifting upward, but it would shift more in response to a higher rate of inflation.

Point *a* is a reasonable description of the U.S. economy in 1964. As Table 26.3 shows, the unemployment rate was 5 percent, and the GDP deflator rose less than 2 percent from the previous year. The path from *a* to *b* corresponds roughly to the

FOCUS ON

CAN WE HAVE ANOTHER GREAT DEPRESSION?

In one day, the stock market crash of October 1987 reduced the value of the public's stock holdings by almost $500 billion—half a *trillion* dollars. Many economists predicted that consumer expenditures would drop significantly in the months ahead because of the decline in wealth, and more than a few people wondered whether we were on the brink of another Great Depression. After all, the Great Depression had been preceded by a similar stock market crash in October 1929. This was not the only similarity. The 1920s and the 1980s both saw the financial markets rise seemingly without limit on a speculative fervor that made many people rich overnight. Both eras saw a tremendous number of corporate mergers and acquisitions, too often accomplished with shady dealing. Large tax cuts for the wealthy also preceded both crashes: in the 1920s, financier turned Treasury Secretary Andrew Mellon persuaded President Calvin Coolidge that a tax cut for the wealthy would spur economic growth; the economic advisers to the first Reagan administration could not have said it better. About the only dif-

ference was the one that mattered most: the crash of 1987 did not lead to a decade-long depression. Why not? And does this mean the modern economy is immune to a 1930s-type depression? The economy of 1987 was able to avoid a depression for several reasons.

INFUSION OF LIQUIDITY

When the stock market crashed in October 1987, Federal Reserve Chair Alan Greenspan went on television to assure the world financial markets that he would inject enough liquidity into the system to avoid a panic. He did this by increasing the money supply. This assured people that banks would have enough money on hand to meet the needs of borrowers who might find themselves unable to repay loans after losing millions on the stock market. This did not happen after the 1929 crash.

DEPOSIT INSURANCE

Bank deposits were not insured in the 1930s as they are today. When the stock market crashed, people who had

borrowed money to buy stocks found that they could not repay their loans. This meant that the banks that had made the loans were in trouble. When word of this got out, depositors ran to their banks to withdraw their money. Some people did not get all of their money back, and banks did not have enough funds to lend to firms to cover what might have been temporary losses on the market. By the fall of 1930, when the first of many banks was forced to close its doors, the economy was in the midst of a full-fledged financial panic. Nothing even remotely similar happened after the 1987 crash. A record number of bank and savings and loan failures occurred throughout the 1980s, but these were unrelated to the stock market crash, and very few depositors lost money. The only people running to their banks to withdraw their deposits were exceedingly paranoid, ignorant, or unwise enough to have kept their money in one of the very few uninsured financial institutions left in the United States.

years 1964–1967. Real GDP was growing rapidly and there was only moderate wage and price inflation. In 1968, however, wage growth spurted to 6.3 percent, and the GDP deflator advanced at a 5 percent clip—conditions consistent with an upward shift of the short-run aggregate supply curve and the path $b \rightarrow c$ in Figure 26.8. Real GDP growth declined from the 4.2 percent rate of 1968 to under 3 percent for the next three years.

It is worth noting that the economy might have settled down and come to rest at

Lines of anxious depositors, such as these in Newark, NJ, were a frequent occurrence in the 1930s.

made conditions ripe for a serious recession.

BUT THAT DOES NOT MEAN THAT THERE WILL NEVER BE ANOTHER DEPRESSION . . .

Most economists believe that economic theory and policy have progressed enough since the 1930s to significantly reduce the chance of another great depression, but few would bet that one will never happen. In the early years of the Great Depression, policymakers reduced government spending and the money supply—exactly the opposite of what would be prescribed today. The existence of deposit insurance reduces the likelihood of a run on the banking system. And the social safety net—unemployment compensation, welfare, and other programs—means that spending power does not decline nearly as much during economic slowdowns as before. But the economy could still fall off the cliff. If foreign investors fear the dollar is overvalued and decide to sell dollar-denominated assets *en masse,* or if Congress decides to balance the budget *now,* or if a major trade war breaks out, who knows what might happen?

CAUSALITY RUNS THE OTHER DIRECTION!

The connection between the stock market and the real sector of the economy is tenuous at best. Movements in the stock market often precede movements in the real economy, but whether they *cause* movements in the real economy is quite a different matter. The stock market does affect the level of wealth in the economy—if the value of your stock portfolio falls 20 percent overnight, you are worse off—but it does not mean that people are less productive or that firms are no longer competitive. The economy of 1987 was performing well enough to continue growing for another three years—so the stock market crash had little effect. The economy of 1929 was not in good shape. Evidence of a downturn had already appeared in the summer of 1929, and combined with particularly inept policies—slow money growth and trade policies that virtually eliminated exports—this

a point like *c* had it been left to its own devices. But there was no guarantee this would happen and elections do not wait. On August 15, 1971, President Richard Nixon imposed wage and price controls to artificially suppress inflation long enough to allow economic stimulus without the risk of further inflation. In the opinion of many, however, the main goal of this unorthodox policy was Nixon's reelection. We will see momentarily, however, that this short-run victory was to have long-run consequences.

Stagflation The simultaneous occurrence of inflation and stagnant GDP growth and unemployment.

Supply Shocks and Stagflation

The 1970s saw an entirely new kind of economic phenomena—a series of external supply shocks that hit the economy and confounded policymakers. Supply shocks create **stagflation**, the simultaneous occurrence of rising inflation and stagnant GDP growth. Stagflation creates more serious problems than demand-pull inflation because both inflation and unemployment rise; at least unemployment is low during demand-pull inflation. To make matters worse, stagflation has no obvious policy solutions.

Figure 26.9 illustrates the effects of a supply shock. Begin at point *a* and suppose that the price of oil rises from $10 per barrel to $20 per barrel. Oil is used in the production of almost everything, so the cost of production rises and firms are forced to raise their selling prices. As a result, the short-run aggregate supply curve shifts from AS_0 to AS_1, and the economy moves to point *b*. The decline in GDP from $Q\star$ to Q_1 indicates that unemployment has risen. The higher price level means that real wages have also declined. Nominal wages are the same on AS_0 and AS_1, so the higher price level reduces the real wage.

What is the appropriate policy response to a supply shock? There is no clear answer. If policymakers try to "extinguish" inflation by reducing aggregate demand, the economy will move to a point like *c*, which will make the recession worse. The other option is to "ratify" the inflation by increasing aggregate demand to fight the

FIGURE 26.9 SUPPLY SHOCKS AND STAGFLATION

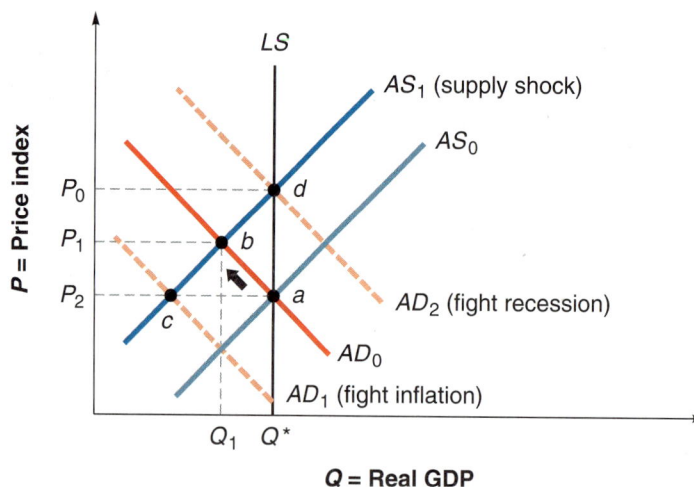

A supply shock shifts the short-run aggregate supply curve from AS_0 to AS_1, moves the economy from point *a* to point *b*, and causes the price level to rise and real GDP to fall. If policymakers try to extinguish the inflation by reducing aggregate demand, the result will be a more severe recession, point *c*. If they try to fight the recession by increasing aggregate demand, the result will be even higher prices, point *d*. A further complication arises when the supply shock also reduces the level of potential GDP and shifts the long-run aggregate supply curve to the left (not shown). If this happens, measures designed to eliminate the recession will cause even more inflation.

recession. This will move the economy to a point like *d* with even higher prices. Politics probably matters more than economics in these situations, but one bit of information may help in the decision: if the economy is heavily *indexed,* it may be best to fight inflation. Indexation is a method of adjusting for inflation. Many wage contracts, for example, contain **cost-of-living adjustment (COLA) clauses** that adjust wages automatically to the inflation rate. Because wages automatically increase in response to price increases, COLA clauses can turn a small, temporary price hike into severe inflation—especially if policymakers ratify the supply shock with expansionary aggregate demand policies. COLA clauses became popular in the United States after inflation accelerated in the late 1960s and early 1970s.

Supply shocks can also have long-run consequences by possibly reducing potential GDP. For example, when oil prices rise, firms will try to economize on the use of oil. This can lower productivity and potential output. Thus, the long-run aggregate supply curve may also shift to the left in response to a supply shock. If policies are later aimed at restoring the preshock level of GDP, inflation will accelerate even more because that level of GDP is now greater than the new level of potential GDP.

The best solution to a supply shock would be to shift the short-run aggregate supply curve back to where it was originally. Policymakers attempted to do this in the early 1980s with a series of supply-side measures—certain environmental rules and other government regulations were loosened to reduce the costs of production, and income tax rates were cut in an attempt to increase the incentive to work—but there is little evidence that they shifted the short-run aggregate supply curve sufficiently. The other option is to do nothing and hope that unemployed workers will take wage cuts, but because the real wage has already fallen, this becomes a more difficult choice for workers.

Application to the 1973–1979 Period. President Jimmy Carter may have lost the election in 1980 because he seemed to be saying that there was nothing that he or anyone else could do to solve the nation's economic problems. During the year, unemployment rose to over 7 percent, inflation was 9.2 percent, and the prime interest rate approached 20 percent.[3] Politically, Carter may have made a mistake by not promising a miracle economic cure, but he was not entirely wrong in blaming the poor economic performance on events beyond his control. For the entire decade of the 1970s, the U.S. economy was buffeted by external supply shocks, a new phenomenon for our economy and one that did not have any obvious policy solution.

The major supply shocks to hit the U.S. economy were rising food and energy prices. Figure 26.10 shows how closely the consumer price index (CPI) and supply shocks correlated between 1970 and 1992. Most economists estimate that food and energy shocks accounted for about a fourth of the 1970s inflation. Falling energy prices *reduced* CPI inflation in the mid-1980s.

Other events also contributed to this supply-side inflation. The removal of wage and price controls in 1974 caused wages and prices to "bounce" and may have added 2 percent to the inflation rate that year. A weakening dollar and low productivity growth also contributed. Along with these external events were what Arthur Okun

COLA (cost-of-living adjustment) clauses Contractual provisions that call for wages to be adjusted automatically to the inflation rate.

---

[3]The prime interest rate is the interest rate that big banks charge their best corporate customers for short-term loans. Banks often make loans below the prime rate, so the prime rate is best considered a reference rate for loan contracts today.

682

···· **FIGURE 26.10** FOOD AND ENERGY SHOCKS, 1970–1992

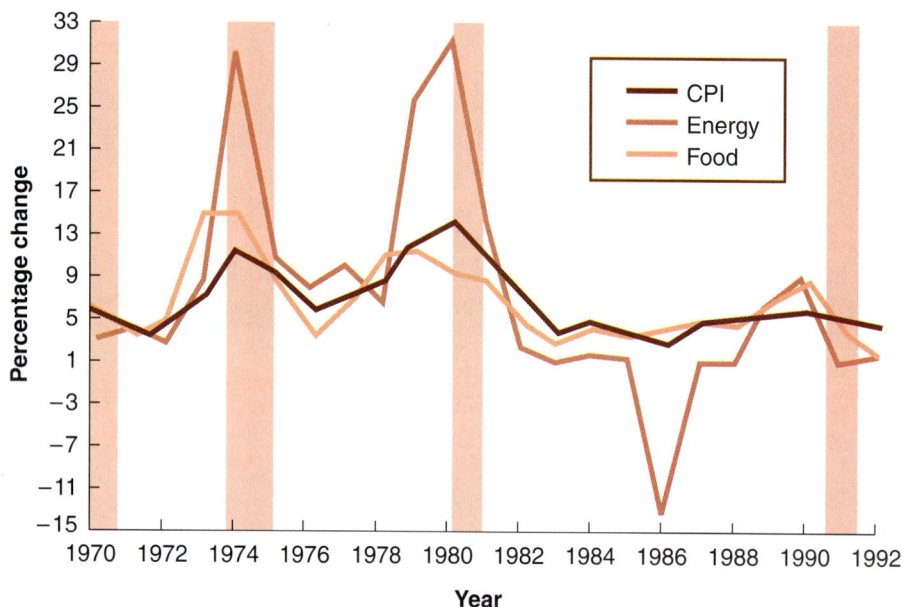

Food and energy shocks were substantial contributors to the overall inflation rate in the early 1970s, and energy shocks between 1978 and 1980 also had a significant impact on consumer price inflation. Falling energy prices were one factor that kept inflation low in the mid-1980s. NBER recessions are marked by the shaded areas.

SOURCE: *Statistical Abstract of the United States,* 1993, Table 757. Base year 1982–1984 = 100.

called "self-inflicted wounds"—policies that unintentionally contributed to the inflation rate. Two such self-inflicted wounds were the increases in the minimum wage and in Social Security taxes. Both increased the cost of labor and may have resulted in higher prices.

Supply shocks can also affect the rate of real GDP growth. As Figure 26.11 shows, fluctuations in real GDP growth during the 1970s correspond extremely well with the supply shock bombardment. It should be noted, however, that it is often difficult to separate the influence of supply shocks from other factors, such as policy changes, that occur at the same time and also affect the rate of GDP growth. For example, economic performance in the mid-1980s was sluggish despite falling energy prices. And the energy price shock that occurred in 1990 had only a negligible effect on a world economy that was already in a slow-growth mode.

Several policies were adopted to deal with the supply shocks of the 1970s, but none was very successful. When the first oil shock caused the price level to jump in 1974, President Gerald Ford reacted with a tax hike, and the Federal Reserve reduced the rate of growth of the money supply.[4] The result was a more severe economic

[4]President Ford had another anti-inflation policy, the ill-fated WIN program. "WIN" was an acronym for "whip inflation now." WIN was administered through a series of media advertisements cajoling consumers to shop for low prices and avoid being "piggy." WIN buttons were given out at supermarkets and malls in the apparent belief that wearing these buttons would cause inflation to go away.

···· FIGURE 26.11 REAL GDP FLUCTUATIONS AND ENERGY PRICES, 1970–1993

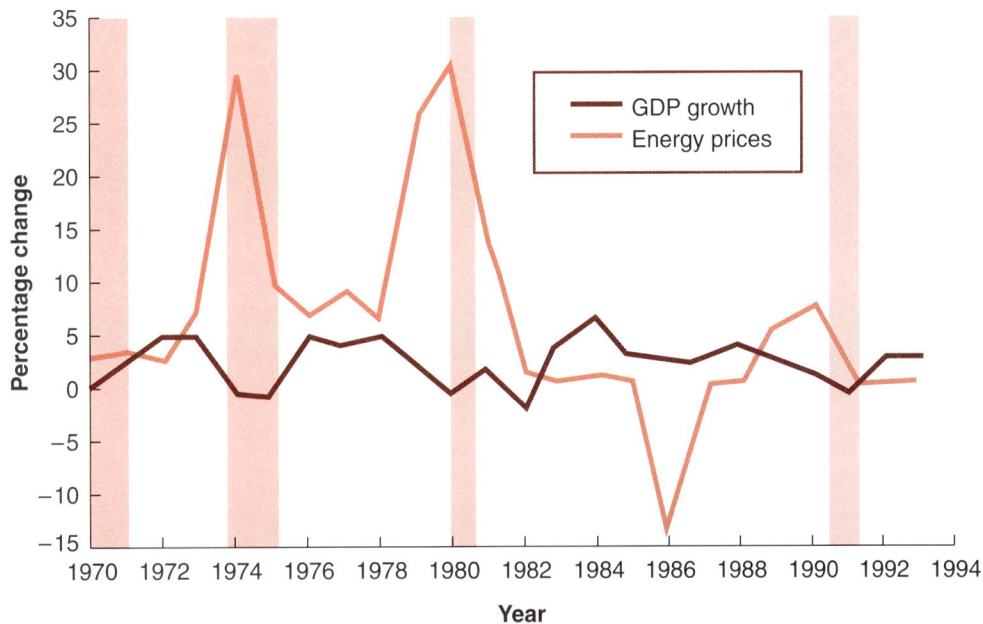

Energy price shocks were one reason for GDP fluctuations in the 1970s and 1980s. The first two oil price shocks—1973–1974 and 1979–1980—both contributed to economic downturns. In contrast, falling energy prices in the mid-1980s did not stimulate the economy. In fact, energy prices may have been falling because slow economic growth worldwide reduced the demand for oil. The last energy price spike on the graph was largely the result of the Iraqi invasion of Kuwait in 1990. Like the two previous oil price shocks, this shock was a factor in the subsequent economic downturn. NBER recessions are indicated by the shaded areas.

SOURCE: *Statistical Abstract of the United States,* 1993, Table 739, and 1994 *Economic Report of the President,* Tables B-2 and B-59.

slowdown—just as would be expected from Figure 26.9—and an increase in the unemployment rate to more than 9 percent. Jimmy Carter reversed these policies in 1977, just in time for the second oil shock. Again the result was just as would be predicted by the model: GDP growth accelerated while unemployment fell to under 6 percent, but inflation and interest rates zoomed into the double-digit range. In response to the second oil price shock in 1979, President Carter's new appointee, Federal Reserve Chair Paul Volcker, reversed policy again, this time clamping down on the money supply to get a handle on inflation. This plan was successful—by 1982 inflation was down to the low single-digit range—but by then unemployment was over 10 percent, and Ronald Reagan had been elected president.

If there is a moral to the supply shock story, it is probably this: external events can and do have profound effects on the economy. And, while the self-correcting forces inherent to market economies may be powerful, several years may pass before complete adjustment can take place. Finally, even when we know the causes of economic disturbances, it does not always follow that we know the solution.

FIGURE 26.12 DEMAND-SIDE CONTRACTION AND DISINFLATION

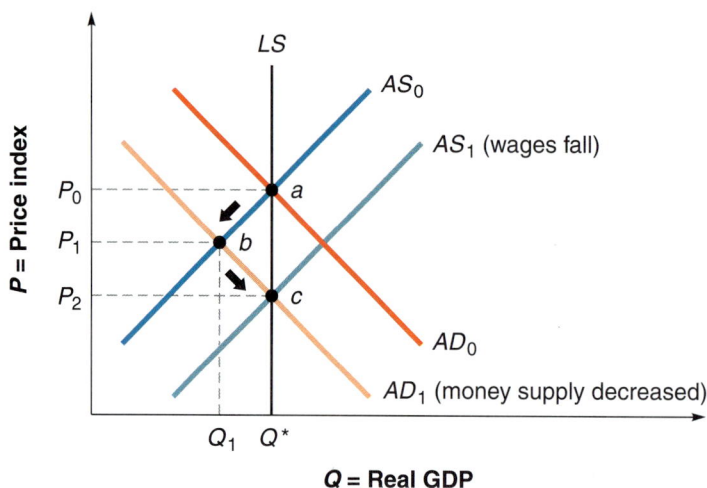

If inflation or the price index is too high, policymakers can reduce aggregate demand to slow the economy and lower prices. In this case, a reduction in the supply of money shifts the aggregate demand curve from AD_0 to AD_1 and moves the economy from point a to point b. At point b, real GDP has fallen, and the unemployment rate has risen. Unemployed workers, after searching for a job at their old wage rate, will reluctantly offer their services at a lower wage rate. This will cause the short-run aggregate supply curve to shift out from AS_0 to AS_1 and eventually restore potential GDP.

Disinflation

The policy reversal in 1979 was a signal that inflation had gotten so bad that policymakers were willing to deliberately trade jobs for price stability—but few people expected things to get as bad as they did. The hope was that slower growth in aggregate demand would moderate wage demands and bring about disinflation, a scenario pictured in Figure 26.12.[5]

Suppose the economy begins at point a where GDP is close to potential but the price level, P_0, is considered too high. If policymakers reduce aggregate demand—tax hikes, spending cuts, or slower growth in the money supply would all work—the aggregate demand curve will shift from AD_0 to AD_1 and move the economy to point b. Because GDP has fallen below potential, unemployment increases. The unemployed workers will presumably search for new jobs at their old wage rate, but after coming up empty will be forced to offer their services at lower wages. This will shift the short-run aggregate supply curve outward and eventually to AS_1 where potential GDP and full employment are restored.

---

[5]Actually, Figure 26.12 describes deflation, not disinflation; illustrating disinflation with the aggregate demand–aggregate supply model is difficult, so we must confine our analysis to deflation. This is not a serious problem, however, because the causes of deflation and disinflation are quite similar.

TABLE 26.4 INFLATION, UNEMPLOYMENT, AND OUTPUT DATA, 1979–1993

Year	Q	ΔQ/Q	P	ΔP/P	U	W	ΔW/W
1979	$3,796.8	2.5%	65.5	8.6%	5.8%	$ 6.16	8.3%
1980	3,776.3	−0.5	71.7	9.5	7.1	6.66	8.1
1981	3,843.1	1.8	78.9	10.0	7.6	7.25	8.9
1982	3,760.3	−2.2	83.8	6.2	9.7	7.68	5.9
1983	3,906.6	3.9	87.2	4.1	9.6	8.02	4.4
1984	4,148.5	6.2	91.0	4.4	7.5	8.32	3.7
1985	4,279.8	3.2	94.4	3.7	7.2	8.57	3.0
1986	4,404.5	2.9	96.9	2.6	7.0	8.76	2.2
1987	4,539.9	3.1	100.0	3.2	6.2	8.98	2.5
1988	4,718.6	3.9	103.9	3.9	5.5	9.28	3.3
1989	4,838.0	2.5	108.5	4.4	5.3	9.66	4.1
1990	4,897.3	0.8	113.3	4.3	5.5	10.01	3.8
1991	4,861.4	−0.7	117.7	4.1	6.7	10.32	3.2
1992	4,896.3	0.7	121.1	2.9	7.4	10.58	2.5
1993p	5,132.7	4.8	124.2	2.6	6.8	10.83	2.4

Key:

Q = real GDP in billions of 1987 dollars; P = GDP deflator, 1987 = 100; U = civilian unemployment rate; W = average hourly wage in nonagricultural industries, current dollars. 1993 data are preliminary.

SOURCE: 1994 *Economic Report of the President,* Tables B-2, B-3, B-40, and B-45.

Application to the 1981–1988 Period. The policies of slow growth in the money supply pursued by the Federal Reserve between 1979 and 1981 brought down inflation but also caused unemployment to rise to the highest level in over 40 years. As Table 26.4 shows, GDP growth was a negative 0.5 percent in 1980, only 1.8 percent in 1981, and a horrendous negative 2.2 percent in 1982. Progress against inflation was apparent by 1982, but by then unemployment was high enough to be a political liability. President Reagan was reelected in 1984 but the Republican Party lost seats in the House and Senate in 1982 and 1984, at least partially because of the ailing economy.

By most measures, GDP remained less than potential until 1987 or 1988 when the unemployment rate fell below 6 percent. The sluggish economy was one reason—large tax cuts were the other—for the massive growth in the government deficit. People without jobs pay few taxes and are entitled to welfare and unemployment compensation. The tax cuts helped stimulate the economy out of recession, but the persistent deficits throughout the expansion were to create problems later on. When the economy fell into another recession in 1990, policymakers were hesitant to apply fiscal stimulus for fear of making the deficit worse.

The experience of the 1980s suggests that disinflation is a long, drawn-out process, but such a conclusion is not always warranted for at least two reasons. First, because disinflation is likely to take several years, other things will always be happening concurrently. For example, the dollar strengthened significantly between 1981 and 1985, and oil prices fell dramatically over the 1982–1986 period. Both events helped to bring down inflation. Second, the speed of adjustment depends critically upon the credibility of policy and how expectations are formed. As we will see in the next chapter, a very credible anti-inflation policy combined with forward-looking inflationary expectations can shorten periods of disinflation drastically.

• • • • • • • •

The 1990s

Growth recession "Mini-recession" characterized by significant slowing of GDP growth, though not negative GDP growth, and high or rising unemployment.

The National Bureau of Economic Research identified a cycle peak in July 1990, and the economy continued in recession until March 1991. These data add up to a short recession—only eight months—and the official statistics show a rather mild downturn: GDP fell only 1.6 percent and unemployment never topped 7 percent. However, these figures probably understate the severity of this recession. Some economists believe that a **growth recession** began as early as the second quarter of 1989. A growth recession is a period of sluggish economic growth—generally 2 percent or less—typically marked by high or even rising unemployment. Other economists contend that the recession did not end in March 1991 because the unemployment rate continued to rise until June 1992 when it reached a peak of 7.7 percent. The growth recession plus the period of rising unemployment add up to about 35 months— roughly three times the length of a typical recession. This may go a long way toward explaining President Bush's loss in the 1992 election.

Economists have suggested several reasons for this economic downturn. Sluggish money growth beginning in 1987 may have contributed to the growth recession. Also, consumption spending began to contract in the late 1980s, at least partially because consumer debt was approaching record levels and people were hesitant to borrow. Events in the Middle East were also a contributing factor, in particular, the Iraqi invasion of Kuwait in 1990 and the subsequent war in early 1991; the invasion disrupted oil shipments through the Persian Gulf and caused oil prices to rise. In retrospect, it is apparent that the supply shock from the oil price hike was less severe than either of the two previous oil price shocks (see Figure 26.10), but consumers were now well aware of the adverse consequences of oil supply shocks. As a result, consumer confidence dwindled, and many consumers cut back on spending in fear of losing their jobs. Finally, responding to pressure to do something about the deficit, President Bush and Congress enacted a tax increase in 1990. All of these factors tended to shift the aggregate demand curve to the left and contributed to the recession.

Expansionary monetary policy, falling oil prices, and increased consumption all helped the economy turn the corner in the second half of 1991, but the recovery that followed could be called lackluster at best. Economists are still trying to understand why economic growth during this expansion was slower than in most expansions. One possibility is that consumers were still worried about their debt burdens and thus hesitant to purchase consumer durables and other big ticket items. Economists at the Brookings Institution have suggested that there may be an unemployment rate "threshold effect" that can explain why consumer confidence and consumer spending remained low.[6] According to this line of reasoning, consumers are

---

[6]George L. Perry and Charles L. Schultze, "Was This Recession Different? Are They All Different?" *Brookings Papers* 1 (1993): 145–212.

hesitant to increase spending as long as the unemployment rate remains high because they are afraid that they will be the next to lose their jobs. If correct, this idea suggests that improving employment expectations are a self-fulfilling prophecy. The key, of course, is how to improve employment expectations. Finally, the 1990s saw many firms restructuring to become more competitive in the global economy. For many of these firms, restructuring has meant layoffs and downsizing. But hopefully, it will also mean a more competitive posture in the future.

SUMMARY

Practicing economists use models more elaborate than the aggregate demand–aggregate supply model we have just developed, but they often formulate their initial ideas within this framework. The basic aggregate demand–aggregate supply model has several variations: Some economists reject the assumption that wages are tied to contracts and prefer to assume perfect price flexibility; others reject the notion that the economy tends to move toward potential GDP. When the aggregate demand–aggregate supply model is used with different sets of assumptions, we arrive at alternative explanations of economic history and different policy recommendations, but incorporating these assumptions into the basic model is a simple task. This is testimony to the power of the aggregate demand–aggregate supply model.

The main points to remember from this chapter are:

1. The aggregate demand curve (*AD*) gives the different levels of real GDP that will be purchased at various price levels, *ceteris paribus*. The aggregate demand curve slopes downward because higher prices reduce the purchasing power of money and lower the amount of goods and services that can be purchased. Other explanations for the downward slope of the aggregate demand curve include intertemporal and international substitution effects. The main factors that shift the aggregate demand curve are fiscal and monetary policy, business and consumer confidence, and exchange rates.

2. The short-run aggregate supply curve (*AS*) gives the different levels of real GDP that firms will offer at various price levels, *ceteris paribus*. The short-run aggregate supply curve slopes upward because of diminishing returns: as more workers are added to a fixed stock of capital, output per worker declines. The main factors that shift the short-run aggregate supply curve are changes in price expectations, wages and other factor prices, government regulations, and work incentives.

3. The long-run aggregate supply curve (*LS*) is a vertical line at the level of potential GDP. Expectations are correct when the economy is on the long-run aggregate supply curve. Factors that shift the long-run aggregate supply curve include changes in technology, the size of the capital stock, and the size of the labor force.

4. A demand-side contraction occurs when the aggregate demand curve shifts left toward the price-level axis. When this occurs, wages start to fall, shifting the short-run aggregate supply curve to the right and helping the economy recover to potential GDP. Alternatively, the government could increase aggregate demand with fiscal or monetary policy stimulus.

5. Demand-pull inflation occurs when aggregate demand increases and moves GDP beyond potential GDP. Price expectations and wages adjust to return the economy to potential GDP.

6. Supply shocks cause stagflation and create problems for policymakers. If policymakers choose to fight inflation, the recession will worsen; if they choose to fight unemployment, inflation will accelerate.

7. Policymakers use reductions in aggregate demand to bring about disinflation, the winding down of the inflation rate. Unfortunately, the process of disinflation may result in a protracted period of high unemployment.

•••••••• KEY TERMS AND CONCEPTS

price index	diminishing returns
inflation	real wage
deflation	nominal wage
disinflation	flexible wage
money	sticky wage
income	supply shock
stock/flow	deregulation
intertemporal substitution	wage and price asymmetry
international substitution	demand-pull inflation
fiscal policy	stagflation
monetary policy	COLA (cost-of-living adjustment) clause
consumer and business confidence	growth recession
exchange rate	

•••••••• REVIEW QUESTIONS

1. What is the difference between the price index and inflation, and between inflation, disinflation, and deflation? Is the aggregate demand–aggregate supply model very well suited for analyzing inflation and disinflation? Why or why not?

2. Using graphs, carefully explain why the aggregate demand curve is downward sloping. What are the main factors that cause the aggregate demand curve to shift?

3. Why is the short-run aggregate supply curve upward sloping? Why is it relatively flat at low levels of GDP? Why is it relatively steep at high levels of GDP? What are the main factors that shift the short-run aggregate supply curve?

4. What is the long-run aggregate supply curve? What factors cause it to shift?

5. Carefully explain why and how flexible wages and prices act to move the economy toward potential GDP. Why does the economy end up at the triple intersection of the aggregate demand curve, the short-run aggregate supply curve, and the long-run aggregate supply curve?

6. Use the aggregate demand–aggregate supply model to illustrate a demand-side contraction, demand-pull inflation, and an external supply shock. Comment on the best policy responses in each situation.

7. Using the aggregate demand–aggregate supply model, illustrate U.S. economic performance in the 1930s, the 1970s, and the 1980s.

········PROBLEMS

1. Suppose that the aggregate demand curve shifts outward but productivity growth is causing the long-run aggregate supply curve to shift out even faster. Does this mean that the economy will be going through a period of deflation? Why or why not? Draw a diagram to illustrate your answer.

2. If wages adjust instantaneously to changes in the price index, are all of the curves in the aggregate demand–aggregate supply model necessary for explaining how the economy responds to aggregate demand and aggregate supply shocks?

3. Although the OPEC oil price shocks of the 1970s caused prices to rise, some economists argued that they did not cause *inflation*. Explain and comment.

4. Suppose that aggregate demand falls and the economy is thrown into a recession. After looking for jobs at their old wages, workers reluctantly take wage cuts. Suppose, however, that the price level falls even more than nominal wages fall. How would this affect the ability of the economy to self-correct? Do you think this scenario is a likely one?

5. COLA clauses are against the law in Germany and Japan. Do you think they should be outlawed in the United States? Why or why not?

6. Use the aggregate demand–aggregate supply model to illustrate U.S. economic performance in the 1990s based on the analysis in this chapter.

7. Explain how each of the following will affect the shape or location of the aggregate demand curve:
   a. an increase in the spending multiplier   b. a vertical MEI curve
   c. an increase in thriftiness   d. lower personal income taxes
   e. higher interest rates

8. Explain how each of the following will affect the shape or location of the short-run aggregate supply curve:
   a. a union strike for higher wages   b. lower personal income taxes
   c. the discovery of new oil fields in   d. strict antipollution legislation
      Nebraska
   e. higher interest rates

CHAPTER 27

Expectations and the Tradeoff between Inflation and Unemployment

The world is always changing! What used to be an exorbitant price now looks like a good deal. What used to be a good starting salary is now an insult. When you make decisions to take a job or buy a car, you need to form an expectation about the economy in the future. You need to predict whether your salary is going to grow as fast as the price level. You need to predict whether your savings will be enough in the future. How do people form their expectations of the future? How do expectations affect the economy and policy effectiveness? These are among the most important topics in contemporary macroeconomics—and the questions we begin to deal with in this chapter.

We had to talk about expectations in the last chapter when we discussed the short-run aggregate supply curve. When the actual price index was higher than the expected price index, workers asked for wage increases. This caused the short-run aggregate supply curve to shift upward, reduced GDP, and put some people out of work. But think for a minute: Do you know what the price index is right now? Probably not. But you very well may have an idea of what the rate of inflation has been over the past year. When you decide to take a job, you agree to work for the same wage for several months or even a year before you are eligible for a raise. You need to estimate the rate of change of the price level—the inflation rate—over the period of your wage agreement. If you guess the rate of inflation correctly, you will be OK; but if you underestimate inflation, you may find that you cannot buy what you want and cannot live the lifestyle you anticipated. And if your guess of inflation turns out to be too high, your excessive wage demands may put you out of work.

Economists have studied this tradeoff between inflation and unemployment for more than 30 years. Through much of the 1960s, the prevailing view was that higher unemployment was necessary to reduce inflation and that lower unemployment meant higher inflation. In the 1970s, many economists began to question whether this tradeoff really existed. Today there appears to be a consensus that *if* a tradeoff does exist between inflation and unemployment, it exists only in the short run, not the long run.

In this chapter we will try to sort out the theory and evidence regarding the tradeoff between inflation and unemployment. Our first task will be to look at unemployment and inflation in some detail. Our focus in this section will be on the social and economic costs of inflation and unemployment—important information given that policymakers often tolerate an increase in one in order to reduce the other. Next we will show how the aggregate demand–aggregate supply model can be used to illustrate inflation (as opposed to a change in the price index). Finally, we will look at the role of expectations to see how they affect the tradeoff between inflation and unemployment.

AFTER READING AND STUDYING THIS CHAPTER, YOU SHOULD BE ABLE TO:
- Discuss the economic and social costs of unemployment and inflation
- Explain why the full employment rate of unemployment is different today than it was in the 1950s
- Understand why anticipated inflation imposes fewer costs on society than unanticipated inflation
- Use the aggregate demand–aggregate supply model to illustrate the conditions for continuing inflation
- Compare adaptive expectations and rational expectations, and show how they affect the tradeoff between inflation and unemployment

UNEMPLOYMENT: DEFINITIONS AND DATA

The Bureau of Labor Statistics conducts monthly telephone surveys of approximately 60,000 households to estimate the unemployment rate. People who worked in the past week, either full-time or part-time, are classified as employed. People are classified as unemployed if (1) they did not work in the past week, (2) they looked for a job in the past four weeks, and (3) they are currently available for work. People waiting to start a new job within 30 days are also considered unemployed. All others—students, homemakers, and people who have given up looking for jobs—are considered nonworkers and do not count as part of the labor force. The data are usually *seasonally adjusted* to account for the normal variation in employment due to Christmas hiring, school vacations, and so on. The unemployment rate is then calculated by dividing the number of unemployed workers by the number of

····· TABLE 27.1 UNEMPLOYMENT CALCULATIONS, DECEMBER 1993

Civilian employment:	120,661,000
+ Total unemployed:	8,237,000
= Labor force:	128,898,000
Unemployment rate:	8,237,000/128,898,000 = 6.4%

SOURCE: 1994 *Economic Report of the President,* Table B-33.

····· TABLE 27.2 THE DEMOGRAPHICS OF UNEMPLOYMENT

Year	U	Adult Males	Adult Females	Persons Aged, 16–19	Women HH	Nonwhites
1960	5.5%	4.7%	5.1%	14.7%	NA%	10.2%
1965	4.5	3.2	4.5	14.8	NA	8.1
1970	4.9	3.5	4.8	15.3	5.4	8.1
1975	8.5	6.8	8.0	19.9	10.0	13.8
1980	7.1	5.9	6.4	17.8	9.2	13.1
1985	7.2	6.2	6.6	18.6	10.4	13.7
1990	5.5	4.9	4.8	15.5	8.2	10.1
1991	6.7	6.3	5.7	18.6	9.1	11.1
1992	7.4	7.0	6.3	20.0	9.9	12.7
1993	6.8	6.4	5.9	19.0	9.5	11.7

U is the unemployment rate. Adults are age 20 and above. Women HH stands for women who are head of household.
SOURCE: 1994 *Economic Report of the President,* Table B-40.

workers plus the number of unemployed workers. The numbers for December 1993 are shown in Table 27.1.[1]

The Demographics of Unemployment

Not everyone is equally likely to face unemployment. As Table 27.2 shows, young people and racial minorities have higher unemployment rates than adult white males. There are several possible explanations for the higher unemployment rates among minorities and young people. One possibility is that employers practice what economists call **pure discrimination** and simply choose not to hire young people, old people, women, or minorities. Though outlawed in the United States, some discrimination of this sort undoubtedly still goes on. It should be noted, however, that any kind of discrimination can be costly to the firm. By arbitrarily choosing not to hire

Pure discrimination Wage or employment discrimination based on irrational dislike for certain ethnic or cultural groups.

[1]Beginning in January 1994, the Current Population Survey was changed to reflect different labor force participation rates. Before this change was made, some women who were working at home but still looking for jobs outside the home were incorrectly counted as being not part of the labor force. This change will raise the unemployment rate as much as half a percentage point. See the 1994 *Economic Report of the President,* page 104. All data in this chapter were compiled with the old survey methods.

Statistical discrimination The elimination of certain people from consideration for hiring because they belong to groups who tend to have poor work habits or work histories.

people from certain demographic groups, the employer limits the candidate pool and may pass up exceptionally talented individuals.

Pure discrimination is not the only cause of demographic differences in unemployment rates. There is also what economists call **statistical discrimination**. Statistical discrimination can lower recruiting costs by eliminating people from the candidate pool who *as a group* tend to have unstable work histories and/or poor work habits. Single people, African Americans, and young people change jobs more often than do adult, married, white males. Likewise, these groups tend to have fewer years of education and work experience. Thus, the firm may be able to reduce recruiting costs by limiting its search to adult, married, white males. Like pure discrimination, statistical discrimination reduces the size of the labor pool and can thus deprive the firm of good workers. It is also illegal—but extremely difficult to detect.

Women faced higher unemployment rates than men until recently. Now, however, as Table 27.2 shows, women have lower unemployment rates than men. Several explanations have been offered for the declining unemployment rates among women. One possibility is that women are concentrated in the service sector of the economy while most recent job losses have been in the manufacturing sector, which is largely male dominated.

Reasons for Unemployment

The Bureau of Labor Statistics classifies the unemployed into four groups by reason for unemployment: new entrants into the labor force, reentrants, people who have quit their jobs (job leavers), and people who have lost their jobs (job losers). Table 27.3 provides this breakdown along with some demographic data. Data like these can help explain why different demographic groups have different unemployment rates. For example, notice that all groups have higher reentry rates than adult men. People who have just reentered the labor force will be unemployed until they find a job, so this may help explain why adult men tend to have lower unemployment rates. In the past, the quit rate—the proportion of people who voluntarily leave their jobs—also seemed to explain differential unemployment rates by demographic groups. People who quit more often will show up in the unemployment statistics more often, and women, minorities, and young people had the highest quit rates. One explanation for these higher quit rates is that these groups are frequently paid lower wages and hold jobs with fewer advancement opportunities than adult white

••••• TABLE 27.3   UNEMPLOYMENT BY REASON, 1993

	Adult Men	Adult Women	Both Sexes, Aged 16–19	Whites	Blacks	Percentage of Total Labor Force
Job losers	68.7%	49.7%	14.9%	54.7%	49.6%	3.3%
Job leavers	11.4	13.1	14.8	13.0	10.7	0.8
Reentrants	17.7	32.5	27.1	23.7	28.6	1.5
New entrants	2.2	4.8	43.1	8.6	11.1	0.6

NOTE: Data are for November 1993. The unemployment rate in November 1993 was 6.3 percent.
SOURCE: *Employment and Earnings,* January, Table A-14.

males, and it is much easier to quit a low-paying job than a good one. As the data in Table 27.3 show, however, blacks had lower quit rates than adult men in November 1993, implying that higher unemployment among blacks was caused by factors other than high quit rates.

Unemployment Duration

The length of time people remain unemployed is called the *duration* of unemployment. The duration of unemployment usually increases during recessions and falls during expansions. For example, in the recession year of 1975, the average duration was more than four weeks longer than in the previous year. This relationship does not hold with precision, however. In the wake of the 1981–1982 recession, the economy began a relatively strong recovery, but the duration of unemployment increased by almost five weeks in 1983. This increase may have occurred because the recession was harsh enough to cause severe labor imbalances. Workers who lost manufacturing jobs in the Midwest and Northeast were forced to move or switch careers, something they did only after exhausting all possibilities in their home communities or chosen field.

We can deduce another bit of information by comparing the mean and median duration of unemployment. The mean duration is found the same way you calculate any simple average: add together all of the observations and divide by the number of observations. In the case of unemployment duration, just add together the duration of every person in the sample and divide by the number of people in the sample. The median gives the midpoint of a distribution. A median of 12 weeks means that half of all unemployed workers were out of work more than 12 weeks and half were out of work less than 12 weeks. Now, notice that the median duration is always much lower than the mean, often half as much. This means that most of the observations are in the lower end of the sample. In 1993, for example, half of all unemployed workers found jobs in 8.4 weeks or less (or quit looking), even though the average (mean) duration was over 18 weeks. Unemployment duration data are shown in Table 27.4.

TABLE 27.4 THE DURATION OF UNEMPLOYMENT IN THE UNITED STATES

Year	Total Unemployed	Under 5 Weeks	5–14 Weeks	15–26 Weeks	Over 27 Weeks	Mean	Median
1970	4,093	2,139	1,290	428	235	8.6	4.9
1975	7,929	2,940	2,484	1,303	1,203	14.2	8.4
1980	7,637	3,295	2,470	1,052	820	11.9	6.5
1985	8,312	3,350	2,451	1,104	1,280	15.6	6.8
1989	6,528	3,174	1,978	730	646	11.9	4.8
1990	6,874	3,169	2,201	809	695	12.1	5.4
1991	8,426	3,380	2,724	1,225	1,098	13.8	6.9
1992	9,384	3,270	2,760	1,424	1,930	17.9	8.8
1993	8,734	3,160	2,522	1,274	1,778	18.1	8.4

NOTE: Data are in thousands of people.
SOURCE: 1994 *Economic Report of the President,* Table B-42.

Be careful not to misinterpret these facts. Even though most people do find jobs rather quickly, many people have several spells of unemployment each year. There is also a substantial group of "hard-core" unemployed workers who are out of work many weeks during the year. Finally, after several weeks of unemployment, some workers become discouraged and quit looking for a job. This reduces the unemployment rate because discouraged workers are not counted as part of the workforce.

WHY IS THE UNEMPLOYMENT RATE SO HIGH AT FULL EMPLOYMENT?

The full employment rate of unemployment is almost certainly higher today than it was in the 1960s or earlier, but just how much higher or whether it has fallen since the 1970s remains unsettled. In the 1960s, many economists estimated full employment to be about 4 percent of the labor force; today, the consensus estimate is probably between 5 and 6 percent. Several popular theories offer explanations of why the full employment rate of unemployment has risen. The most important theories deal with changes in the labor force participation rate, the search process, unemployment compensation, and structural factors. Before we are ready to look at these theories, however, we need to examine just what we mean by full employment.

Several terms are frequently used to refer to full employment. Many economists prefer the term **natural rate of employment** because the term "full" has connotations that may be inappropriate. Like full employment, the natural rate of employment cannot be observed, only estimated. It is usually defined as the minimum level of unemployment consistent with nonaccelerating inflation. This is sometimes abbreviated with the acronym **NAIRU**—for *Non-Accelerating Inflationary Rate of Unemployment*. The key idea behind NAIRU and the natural rate of unemployment is that conditions in the job market can influence the inflation rate. As we will find out momentarily, when unemployment is high, workers are hesitant to ask for wage increases. This tends to moderate inflationary pressures in the economy. The opposite occurs when employment is high: both wages and inflation tend to rise. Some economists distinguish between full employment and the NAIRU, but for our purposes they are equivalent.

Labor Force Participation Rates

The composition of the labor force is much different today than it was 40 years ago. The overall unemployment rate will change when the labor force participation rate of different demographic groups changes. In the 1950s, few women worked outside the home, and the proportion of teenagers looking for work was smaller as well. As we found out in the previous section, teenagers tend to have higher unemployment rates than adult men, and until recently, so did women. Most economists believe that increased labor force participation rates of these groups tended to raise the unemployment rate in the 1970s. Now, however, the fact that the unemployment rate for women is often lower than it is for adult men has probably lowered the unemployment rate somewhat.

Natural rate of employment The rate of employment that exists when the economy is operating at the potential or natural rate of GDP.

NAIRU (non-accelerating inflationary rate of unemployment) The minimum level of unemployment that can be sustained without an acceleration in the rate of inflation.

Search Theory

If you got fired from your job today, you could probably find a new job on the way home—Burger World, your local fast-food eating emporium, always seems to have a "Now Hiring" sign out front. Should you take it? That depends on the possibility of finding a better job and how long you would have to search for it. According to the **search theory** of unemployment, you should keep looking for a new job as long as the benefit derived from the extra day's search is equal to or greater than the cost of another day's search. The more it costs to search, the less time you should spend searching; the less it costs to search, the more time you should spend searching. While people are searching, they are unemployed, so long searches increase the measured unemployment rate. However, searching may result in a better match between workers and job openings; it would be a waste of your newly acquired economics skills to flip burgers all day! This suggests that the search process helps the labor market better allocate resources.

The benefits of a job search should not be overestimated. During mild recessions, there is likely to be a *congestion effect*. When workers hear of a "good" job, they may pass up "acceptable" jobs and congest the market looking for the few good jobs. If enough people do this, the economic benefits of searching can be lost. Perhaps more significant, during severe recessions, evidence indicates that long job searches are long not because workers are obtaining more information and raising their wage demands, but because of the prevalence of "Not Hiring" signs.

Search theory People will search for new jobs as long as the cost of searching is less than the expected return from the search; therefore, people may not accept the first job that is offered.

Unemployment Compensation

The availability of unemployment insurance allows people to search longer and thus remain unemployed for a longer period. How much longer? One study showed that **unemployment compensation** increases the duration of unemployment in the United States between 16 and 31 percent.[2] High unemployment rates in Europe—approaching 9 and 10 percent for much of the 1980s and 1990s—may be the result of liberal unemployment benefits as well.[3] Some economists have used this evidence to argue that taxes on unemployment compensation should be increased or that unemployment compensation should be reduced or even eliminated. Others feel that the humanitarian benefits of unemployment compensation far outweigh the economic costs. In addition, a number of studies have suggested that the level of unemployment compensation has little if any impact on the duration of unemployment.[4]

The relationship between unemployment compensation and the unemployment rate may seem persuasive, but must be considered carefully. Unemployment benefits have not risen relative to real spendable earnings over the past 30 years, so trying to attribute the secular increase in unemployment to unemployment compensation is

Unemployment compensation Transfer payment given to people who have lost their jobs.

[2]Stephen T. Marston, "The Impact of Unemployment Insurance on Job Search," *Brookings Papers on Economic Activity* 1 (1975): 13–46; some researchers feel that the increase could be larger.

[3]These and other elements of contemporary European economies are discussed in more detail in Chapter 34.

[4]See, for example, John Schmidt and Jonathan Wadsworth, "Unemployment Benefit Levels and Search Activity," *Oxford Bulletin of Economics and Statistics* 55 (February 1993): 1–24; and R. Gritz and Thomas MaCurdy, "Unemployment Compensation and Episodes of Nonemployment," *Empirical Economics* 17 (1992): 183–204.

THE UNEMPLOYMENT INSURANCE SYSTEM

The unemployment insurance system began as part of the Social Security Act of 1935. Most unemployment benefits are provided by the states and funded with taxes levied on employers. The federal government pays benefits only when states run out of money and during prolonged recessions when supplemental benefits are usually provided. How much does unemployment cost the taxpayer? Not much. In the recession year of 1982, unemployment benefits totaled just under $24 billion, of which only $3 billion was paid by the federal government. When unemployment insurance was extended for an additional 26 weeks during the 1990–1992 recession, the cost to the federal government was just $5 billion, or under one-half percent of the total federal budget.

Funds for the system are provided by a tax on employers; three states also tax employees. This tax is levied in two parts, a fixed rate and a variable rate. The fixed rate averages a little under 3 percent of wage income. The variable rate is experience rated: firms with a history of frequent layoffs pay a higher tax than firms that rarely lay off workers.

Eligibility requirements vary somewhat from state to state, but most requirements are similar. To receive unemployment benefits, applicants must demonstrate that they were employed full-time for six months and must be on temporary or permanent layoff.

In line for benefits at the unemployment office.

People who quit with "just cause" may also collect unemployment insurance. People who were fired for misconduct cannot collect benefits.

The level of benefits also varies from state to state, but averages about 50 percent of earnings; in 1990 the average weekly unemployment check was about $160. Generally, benefits are provided for 26 weeks, starting one week after unemployment begins, but coverage is often extended when the state unemployment rate reaches a certain "trigger level." Supplemental federal assistance is sometimes available after extended state benefits have been exhausted.

Since 1980, eligibility requirements for unemployment insurance have been tightened in three ways. First, the trigger levels for extended and supplemental benefits have been raised. During the 1981–1982 recession, this significantly reduced the number of unemployed people who received benefits. Second, all states now reduce unemployment payments to workers who are receiving private pensions or Social Security retirement benefits. Finally, unemployment compensation is taxed when total income is more than $18,000 for couples or more than $12,000 for individuals.

difficult. Further, while the percentage of workers covered by unemployment compensation rose between 1970 and 1980, it has fallen quite substantially since then: 68 percent of all unemployed workers were eligible for benefits during the 1975 recession; in June 1983, the figure was below 40 percent; and the number was even lower in the early 1990s. The low percentage of people receiving unemployment benefits may be attributable to several things. Among the most important are stiffer eligibility requirements and the tendency of many service and part-time workers to change jobs frequently, which prevents them from qualifying for unemployment compensation.

Structural Factors

Another reason for the rise in the full employment rate of unemployment may be an increase in structural unemployment. People are said to be structurally unemployed if they lack the right skills or are in the wrong location to find jobs. One of the biggest changes in the U.S. economy over the past 20 years has been the shift of workers out of manufacturing and into the service sector of the economy. In the 1970s, almost a third of total employment was in the manufacturing sector; today less than a fourth is in that sector. The proportion of employment in the service sector rose from about 60 percent to almost 70 percent over the same period. The fact that many displaced manufacturing workers have been able to find jobs in the service sector is an indication that the U.S. workforce is flexible and mobile. Unfortunately, many service sector jobs pay lower wages than manufacturing jobs.

Some economists believe that the increase in structural unemployment has been caused by **deindustrialization**—the long-term decline of basic industries. Labor Secretary Robert Reich, for example, has noted that low-wage, less-developed nations can now produce steel, autos, and other standardized mass-produced goods as efficiently as the United States. One way to compete with these nations is with comparably low wages. A better solution, contends Reich, is for workers to develop more flexible skills so that factories can concentrate on short production runs of specialized products. This would help reduce structural unemployment.

Deindustrialization The long-term decline of basic manufacturing industries in the United States.

Other observers have pointed to industrial relocation as a major cause of structural unemployment. In the 1970s and 1980s, many firms relocated from the Northeast to the Sunbelt or established plants abroad. Relocation in the Sunbelt reduced costs in several ways—warmer winters require less energy for heating bills, and the South's nonunion workers receive lower wages—but it also left masses of workers unemployed in the Northeast. Many firms also moved their production facilities abroad to reap even greater cost advantages.

THE COSTS OF UNEMPLOYMENT

Why did we spend so much time discussing unemployment? The economic, social, and human costs of unemployment can be immense. The unemployed are more likely to commit suicide or engage in criminal activities, and evidence indicates that spouse and child abuse are associated with unemployment. The precise relationship between these activities and unemployment is difficult to measure, but we know one exists. More easily measurable costs of unemployment include lost output, an increase in involuntary part-time work, less upward mobility, and underemployment.

Lost Output

Okun's law A rule of thumb that shows the connection between unemployment and GDP by giving a measure of the lost output due to cyclical unemployment.

The relationship between unemployment and lost GDP has been captured in a rough rule of thumb known as **Okun's law**, named after the economist Arthur Okun (1929–1979). Okun's law is written as:

$$\text{Okun's law: } \frac{Q^\star - Q}{Q} = \frac{\Delta Q}{Q} \approx 2.5(U - U^\star) \qquad [1]$$

In words, Equation 1 says that the percentage change in real output is approximately two and half times the difference between the existing level of unemployment and the full employment rate of unemployment. The calculations in Equation 1 are based on the difference between U and $U^\star$, so Okun's law gives a measure of the lost output due to cyclical unemployment.

As an example, consider the lost output in 1991, the year the economy began recovering from the 1990–1991 recession. The average unemployment rate in 1991 was 6.7 percent (= 0.067) and real GDP was \$4,821 billion. If we assume that the full employment rate of unemployment is 5.5 percent (= 0.055), then the amount of lost GDP in 1991 was:

$$\frac{\Delta Q}{\$4,821} = 2.5(0.067 - 0.055) = 0.03$$

$$\Delta Q = 0.03(\$4,821) = \$144.6 \text{ billion}$$

In other words, the lost output from 1.2 percentage points in unemployment above the full employment rate was just over \$144 billion; the amount would be higher if we used a lower estimate of $U^\star$. While these numbers seem large, they pale beside the output losses of the 1980s. Even conservative estimates suggest that lost output between 1980 and 1986 amounted to more than a trillion dollars. It is important to stress that estimates based on Okun's law are crude—the number 2.5 is approximate at best—but they do provide a rough measure of the output losses associated with cyclical unemployment.

Additional Costs of Unemployment

Involuntary part-time work varies over the business cycle, increasing during recessions and decreasing during expansions. Part-time employees represent several cost advantages to the employer—rarely do they qualify for health or retirement benefits, and they frequently are paid lower wages than full-time workers. Involuntary part-time work has increased significantly in recent years.[5]

[5]It is significant that the largest employer in the United States in 1992 was Manpower, Inc. Manpower supplies part-time and temporary employees to firms that need workers but are unwilling or unable to hire full-time, permanent workers. The average wage paid to Manpower workers was about \$15 per hour. The annual salary of someone making \$15 per hour (and working full-time) is about \$30,000—but very few Manpower employees receive health or retirement benefits.

High unemployment can reduce your prospects for a raise or promotion and tends to generate **underemployment**. Underemployment occurs when people are forced to take jobs that do not fully use their skills or experience. College graduates who drive taxis would be classified as underemployed. Underemployment is a detriment to both the individual and society because low wages mean a low standard of living and lower productivity. Some economists worry that underemployment may be showing a secular increase. If correct, this is discouraging news for college students.

Finally, there is evidence that high unemployment can lead to sluggish productivity growth. When unemployment is high, firms are reluctant to acquire new machinery or train workers. Productivity growth is the single most important factor determining living standards and will be analyzed in some detail in Chapter 33.

Underemployment Working at a job that does not require the skills of the worker.

> **RECAP**   Unemployment
>
> Unemployment is defined as the ratio of the number of people looking for jobs divided by the number of people working plus the number of people looking for jobs. The full employment rate of unemployment appears to have risen from about 4 percent in the 1950s to between 5 and 6 percent today. This increase may be due to changing labor force participation rates, structural changes in the labor force, increased employment search time, or other factors. High unemployment results in lost output and human dignity, involuntary part-time work, and underemployment.

ANTICIPATED AND UNANTICIPATED INFLATION

Although unemployment permits search time and thus may help the labor market better allocate resources, few economists would argue that there is a net gain from high unemployment. Still, policymakers frequently enact programs that they know will cause unemployment to rise. Why? They do so because high unemployment is thought to reduce wage demands and inflation. Before we can decide whether price stability is worth the cost in high unemployment, we need to examine the costs associated with inflation.

As in many areas of macroeconomics, anticipations and expectations are vitally important in determining the effects of inflation. In fact, when inflation is perfectly anticipated, it imposes few costs on society—almost certainly less than the cost of getting rid of inflation with a deliberate recession. Unfortunately, inflation often comes as a surprise and cannot be accurately predicted. Further, even when inflation is accurately anticipated, the institutional structure of the modern economy prevents complete or immediate adaptation to rising prices. Without the necessary adjustments, inflation affects income distribution, the saving-consumption tradeoff, and economic efficiency. Even perfectly **anticipated inflation** generates inefficiency and wastes economic resources.

Anticipated inflation Inflation that is expected. Indexing wages and taxes and using variable interest rates for loans are methods of coping with anticipated inflation.

Perfectly Anticipated Inflation

If people knew in advance that inflation would occur in the future, they would try to make several adaptations. Workers would demand that their wages automatically rise with prices. Taxpayers would insist that their taxes be *indexed* or adjusted for the rate of inflation. With indexing, the income tax brackets are based on real income, not nominal income, and the standard deduction rises by the inflation rate each year. Corporations would want their taxes to be levied on real profits, not nominal profits, and would adjust their inventory and depreciation valuations for inflation. These adjustments are relatively simple to accomplish—so simple that Congress actually began indexing personal income taxes and certain business taxes on January 1, 1985, and has indexed Social Security payments since 1972.

Real and Nominal Interest Rates. Adjusting interest rates for inflation is more complicated. When financial institutions loan money, they have a **real interest rate** they desire to make on the loan. The real interest rate is the difference in purchasing power between the money lent and the money repaid. For example, suppose you borrow $500 to buy a mountain bike and are charged a **nominal interest rate** of 10 percent. You agree to repay $550 at the end of a year. If prices rise 10 percent during the year, the same mountain bike will cost $550 a year later. When you pay back $550, you will be paying back the same amount of purchasing power that you borrowed—just enough to buy one mountain bike. In this case, the real interest rate is zero. When the real interest rate is zero, the lender gives up liquidity and takes a risk for no return. For the real interest rate to be positive, the nominal interest rate must exceed the inflation rate. If the inflation rate is higher than the nominal interest rate, the real interest rate is negative. More formally, the real interest rate (r) is defined as the nominal interest rate (i) minus the inflation rate (p), or:

$$r = i - p \qquad [2]$$

Real interest rate The nominal interest rate adjusted for inflation.

Nominal interest rate The interest rate charged by the lending institution; not corrected for inflation.

If the nominal interest rate is 6 percent and the inflation rate is 4 percent, the real interest rate is 2 percent.

One problem with Equation 2 is that many loan contracts are written for several years and have fixed interest rates. For example, suppose you are shopping for a 10-year loan at a time when the inflation rate is expected to stay at the current rate of 4 percent. The nominal rate of interest would probably be about 7 percent. This would make the real interest rate 3 percent, which is well within the normal range of 2 to 4 percent.[6] If the inflation rate rose to 8 percent as soon as you signed your loan contract, however, the real interest rate would be negative. This would be great for you because you would be paying back less purchasing power than you borrowed, but your friendly loan officer would be a bit upset because she would be getting back less purchasing power than she lent out.

To avoid this kind of loss, many loans written in the 1980s had variable interest rates. This was especially true of long-term loans like home mortgages. Most variable interest rate contracts put a cap on the maximum interest rate that can be charged,

[6]The real interest rate normally hovers around 2 to 4 percent, but it can fluctuate considerably. For example, in the early 1980s, rapid disinflation brought inflation down much faster than nominal interest rates. The result was an increase in the real interest rate from under 2 percent to over 8 percent between 1980 and 1982. High real interest rates were a contributing factor to the recession of 1981–1982.

and many limit how often the interest rate can be adjusted each year. Such restrictions prevent interest rates from fully adjusting to inflation but do reduce the chance that borrowers will be hit by ballooning payments if inflation accelerates. The record low interest rates of the early 1990s reduced the popularity of adjustable rate loans, but we will undoubtedly see them again if inflation accelerates in the future.

Efficiency or "Welfare" Costs. Even if wages, taxes, and interest rates kept pace with inflation, society would still incur what economists call welfare costs. In this context, the term "welfare" refers to economic efficiency, not transfer payments or aid for the needy. At least two welfare costs are associated with even perfectly anticipated inflation. The first involves **cash management**. When inflation is high, the purchasing power of cash depreciates rapidly. To maintain the value of their financial wealth, people engage in active cash management; that is, they make more frequent trips to the bank to minimize their cash holdings and maximize the amount of money kept in interest-earning accounts.[7] Corporations find themselves devoting extra effort to financial matters instead of productive activities. From society's perspective, such efforts are inefficient and wasteful because little tangible is produced.

Cash management When inflation is anticipated, people and firms devote extra effort to managing their finances; this may prevent erosion of savings, but it produces nothing for society.

 Menu costs are a second welfare cost of perfectly anticipated inflation. Inflation forces firms to spend extra time and effort changing prices on menus, catalogs, and other lists. There is no good way to estimate the menu costs of inflation, but they are probably a major source of the frustration that consumers feel from inflation: it is no fun to see higher prices every time you go into your favorite store!

Menu costs Transaction costs associated with changing prices.

Unanticipated Inflation

It is very difficult to forecast future inflation accurately so inflationary "surprises" are common. When inflation is not perfectly anticipated, it imposes several additional costs on society. The costs of **unanticipated inflation** include income redistribution, the disincentive to save, tax distortions, and market inefficiency.

Unanticipated inflation Inflation that is not expected and is therefore not built into wage contracts; interest rates, and tax brackets.

Income Redistribution. Unanticipated inflation can lead to a redistribution of income. When nominal interest rates are not indexed, inflation that is higher than anticipated causes the real interest rate to fall below the rate that is desired. This results in a redistribution of purchasing power from lenders to borrowers because loans are repaid with less valuable dollars than were borrowed. Corporations and the government gain from inflation too. Inflation allows corporations to pay dividends and redeem bonds with less valuable dollars. The government retires the national debt with cheaper dollars. In fact, some people have argued that the government prints money and uses inflation to reduce the real value of its existing debt instead of raising taxes; this practice is often called an **inflation tax**. Because lenders tend to be from upper-income brackets and borrowers are often from the middle class, inflation may redis-

Inflation tax Occurs when the government uses inflation to reduce the real value of the national debt instead of raising taxes.

---

[7]When interest rates are high, it is a good idea to use a bank card for most of your day-to-day purchases—as long as you pay off the total balance every month. This practice will allow you to keep more money in interest-earning accounts and still buy what you want to buy. Of course, if you don't pay off the entire balance every month, bank cards can be very expensive.

704

PART V   MACROECONOMIC FUNDAMENTALS

tribute income toward the middle class. Groups in the very lowest income brackets—welfare and Social Security recipients—may not be hurt by inflation if their entitlement checks are indexed to consumer price inflation, though only some welfare checks are indexed to the inflation rate.

Disincentive to Save. Low real interest rates can act as a disincentive to save. Economists believe that people save more at high interest rates than at low interest rates because high interest rates make savings grow faster. The key is the real interest rate. It makes more sense to save when the nominal interest rate is 6 percent and the inflation rate is 2 percent than when the nominal interest rate is 10 percent and the inflation rate is 9 percent. In the first case, the value of your savings will grow 4 percent faster than prices, so you will have 4 percent more purchasing power in the future. In the second case, you will have 10 percent more dollars in the future, but only 1 percent more purchasing power. Is 1 percent enough for you to postpone current consumption for the future? Many people would say no. Periods of low real interest rates are the best times to borrow for that new car or home—and borrowing is an act of *dissaving,* not saving.

The real interest rate is not the only linkage between inflation and saving. For example, unanticipated, double-digit inflation caused home prices to rise extremely rapidly in the 1970s. The housing wealth held by many home owners more than doubled. Many people responded to their new wealth by reducing their savings: Why save if we are already rich? Another effect was an unprecedented boom in the housing market, an issue discussed in the Focus box on page 705.

Tax Distortions. Bracket creep has been eliminated now that most personal taxes are indexed. Nevertheless, inflation still adversely affects business taxes. Under current law, depreciation deductions are based on historical values. For example, if a firm purchases a machine for $1,000 and is allowed to depreciate 10 percent of the machine's value after one year of use, then the firm can deduct $100 from its tax liability. If inflation is 20 percent, however, the replacement cost of the machine will be $1,200, so a tax deduction of $120 would be needed to account for 10 percent depreciation. Thus, basing depreciation deductions on historical values reduces the amount of allowable deductions and thus inhibits investment. If depreciation were based on inflation-adjusted replacement values, more could be depreciated and corporate tax liability would fall.

Taxes are also levied against nominal instead of real capital gains. For example, if a firm acquires an asset for $100 and later sells it for $110, the firm has a nominal capital gain of $10 that is subject to tax. But if there has been 10 percent inflation, the firm's real capital gain is zero; nevertheless, it still owes tax on the $10. Adjusting capital gains for inflation would lower tax liability and could stimulate investment. Taxes are also levied against the nominal interest return on savings instead of the real interest return. Taxing the real return on savings would reduce tax liability and thus encourage saving.

Tax distortions due to inflation have received less public attention lately—the Tax Reform Act of 1986 did not address tax distortions directly—but if inflation returns to the double-digit levels of the 1970s, it will be necessary develop new tax laws as well as new accounting methods.

FOCUS ON

INFLATION AND THE HOUSING MARKET

People buy houses not only for the stream of consumption benefits and tax advantages, but also as an investment. In the double-digit inflation years of the 1970s, people who could get loan money often made enormous capital gains on housing. And unlike most other forms of investment, housing speculation during the inflation years of the 1970s did not take any special expertise.

Buyers gain from housing purchases because small down payments generate tremendous leverage. Suppose you expect inflation to accelerate to 15 percent but market expectations are for less than 10 percent. This means you can borrow 30-year mortgage money at only 10 percent interest. You secure the loan and put down $10,000 to buy a $100,000 home. House payments (less taxes and fees) will be $789.81 per month, and only $500 will go toward principal in the entire first year. (These figures can be calculated on a financial calculator.) The day you sign the papers, your housing balance sheet looks like this:

Down payment:	$10,000
Mortgage liability:	$90,000
Home value:	$100,000
Net worth:	$10,000

If we ignore closing costs, brokerage fees, taxes, and so on, you would break even if you sold the house for $100,000 the next day.

At the end of a year, 15 percent inflation will make the house worth $115,000, and you have the prospect of a healthy capital gain. The balance sheet will look like this:

Total payments:	$19,478	($10,000 down + $789.81/month)
Mortgage liability:	$89,500	($90,000 − $500)
Home value:	$115,000	
Net worth:	$25,500	($115,000 − $89,500)

That $25,500 represents a 31 percent nominal return on the $19,478 you have paid into the house ($6,022/ $19,478 ≈ 31%). That is still close to a 27 percent real rate of return even after adjusting for 15 percent inflation. And if we include the tax deductibility of the $8,978 paid in interest, the rate of return increases even more.

What would have happened if the market (and the loan officer) had anticipated 15 percent inflation? Your loan probably would have been closer to 18 percent than 10 percent. This would have several effects. First, your monthly payments would be higher— $1,356—so you might not have been able to qualify for the loan in the first place. Also, much less of your payment would go toward principal—only $83 in the first year—so the mortgage liability would decline considerably less in the first year. In short, the real rate of return would drop quite a bit.

Efficiency Effects. Another potentially serious cost of inflation is that it can distort price signals and interfere with the market's ability to transmit information. During a period of inflation, the firm's receipts can look higher than they actually are. As a result, the firm may invest in increased capacity that is unwarranted—and will ultimately be unprofitable. Inflation may also cause private citizens to overestimate their income, spend too much on consumption, and thus save too little. Finally, there is evidence that high inflation leads to more variable inflation and thus increases economic uncertainty. All of these factors will cause the market economy to operate less efficiently than it should.

> **RECAP**   Inflation
>
> Inflation is a continuing increase in the average price level. The main costs of perfectly anticipated inflation are welfare costs including menu costs and cash management. Unanticipated inflation redistributes income from lenders to borrowers, acts as a disincentive to save, generates tax distortions, and clouds the information content of prices.

THE PHILLIPS CURVE

In 1958, a New Zealand–born economist, A. W. Phillips, published a statistical study on the relationship between unemployment and wage growth in the United Kingdom.[8] Phillips found that there was a tradeoff between wage growth and unemployment—higher unemployment typically corresponded to lower wage growth, and vice versa. Phillips's work immediately attracted a great deal of attention. When Nobel laureates Paul Samuelson and Robert Solow extended Phillips's work to an analysis of the relationship between inflation and unemployment, they believed they had found a "missing equation" that completed the standard Keynesian income-expenditure model. It was not long before the term **"Phillips curve"**—a plot of the tradeoff between inflation and unemployment—became part of every economist's lexicon. Figure 27.1 presents a hypothetical short-run Phillips curve.

Policymakers began to exploit the Phillips curve tradeoff almost as quickly as economists had coined the term. The solution to unemployment was a bit more inflation; the solution to inflation was a little bit more unemployment. The only catch was that it was not quite clear *why* a tradeoff existed between inflation and unemployment. Most early explanations of the tradeoff focused on the labor market: when unemployment is low, the demand for labor must be high relative to supply. This high demand causes wages to rise, and because wages are a cost of production, it causes prices to rise as well. The reverse would occur when unemployment was high: there would be little pressure for wage hikes and thus little inflation.

Phillips curve A plot of the tradeoff between inflation and unemployment.

[8]A. W. Phillips, "The Relationship between the Unemployment Rate and the Rate of Change of Money Wage Rates in the United Kingdom, 1861–1957," *Economica* 25 (November 1958): 283–99.

·····**FIGURE 27.1** THE PHILLIPS CURVE

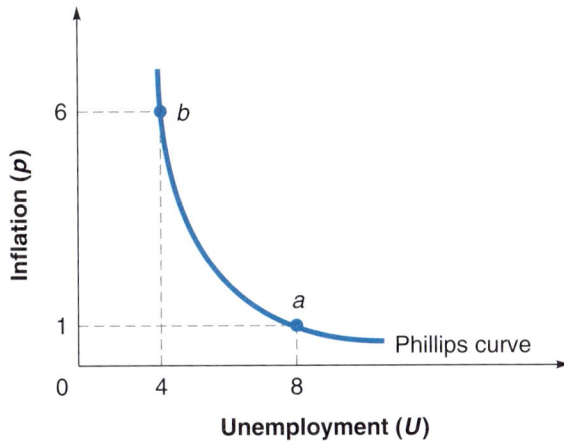

The short-run Phillips curve gives the tradeoff between inflation and unemployment. When the relationship was initially discovered, economists thought the tradeoff was stable. If so, policymakers would be able to choose between a point such as *a*, with low inflation but high unemployment, and *b*, with high inflation and low unemployment. Unfortunately, it was soon discovered that the Phillips curve can shift and that the tradeoff is not stable.

The idea of a tradeoff between inflation and unemployment became entrenched in the minds of many policymakers, and by the 1960s, they were beginning to talk about "fine-tuning" the economy to achieve the proper balance of inflation and unemployment. Unfortunately, things started to act up shortly thereafter. When the Nixon administration tried to combat inflation by slowing the economy in 1970, unemployment rose, but inflation hardly budged. And four years later, inflation and unemployment began to move in the same direction, a development that seemed to negate the idea of a tradeoff. Over the next 20 years, quite a bit of imagination was needed to fit Phillips curves to the data. Figure 27.2 is a plot of the unemployment and inflation data for the period 1970–1993.

Data like those in Figure 27.2 prompted some economists to claim that the Phillips curve tradeoff was dead. Others said no, at least not in the short run. The problem was that the Phillips curve was shifting—inflation and unemployment would move in the same direction if the Phillips curve shifted outward. But this sidestepped the real issue: *Why* did the Phillips curve shift? Milton Friedman[9] and Edmund Phelps[10] were addressing this question when they developed the expectations-augmented Phillips curve.

[9]Milton Friedman, "The Role of Monetary Policy," *American Economic Review* 58 (March 1968): 1–17.
[10]Edmund S. Phelps, "Phillips Curves, Expectations of Inflation, and Optimal Unemployment over Time," *Economica* 34 (1967): 245–81.

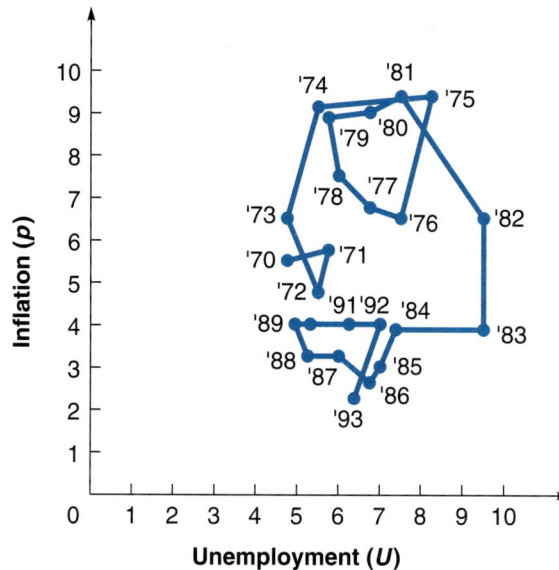

FIGURE 27.2 THE PHILLIPS CURVE, 1970–1993

A plot of unemployment and inflation rates over the period 1970–1993 reveals that the tradeoff was anything but stable. This is an indication that the Phillips curve shifted.

SOURCE: Data are from the 1994 *Economic Report of the President,* Tables B-3 and B-40. Inflation is measured as the percentage change in the GDP deflator.

Natural rate hypothesis Theory that the economy, if left alone, will automatically return to the natural rate of unemployment and the potential or natural rate of GDP.

THE EXPECTATIONS-AUGMENTED PHILLIPS CURVE

The expectations-augmented Phillips curve incorporates the natural rate hypothesis, includes short-run and long-run Phillips curves, and emphasizes the importance of inflationary expectations. The **natural rate hypothesis** is essentially a modern version of the invisible hand metaphor of Adam Smith. According to the natural rate hypothesis, self-correcting forces move the economy to the full or "natural" rate of employment in the long run. This implies that there is no tradeoff between unemployment and inflation in the long run. Graphically, the natural rate hypothesis implies the existence of a vertical long-run Phillips curve located at the natural rate of unemployment. Expectations are important to Phillips curve analysis because they determine how much and how quickly wages adjust and shift the short-run Phillips curve.

Though it is possible to construct elaborate Phillips curve models that contain all of these elements, the analysis gets rather unwieldy pretty quickly. Fortunately, the same sort of story can be told more simply with the aggregate demand–aggregate supply model we developed in the last chapter. To do so, however, we first need to show how the aggregate demand–aggregate supply model can be used to illustrate inflation as opposed to a shift in the price index. This involves a multiperiod version of the basic aggregate demand–aggregate supply model.

····· **FIGURE 27.3** INFLATION AND THE MULTIPERIOD AGGREGATE DEMAND–AGGREGATE SUPPLY MODEL

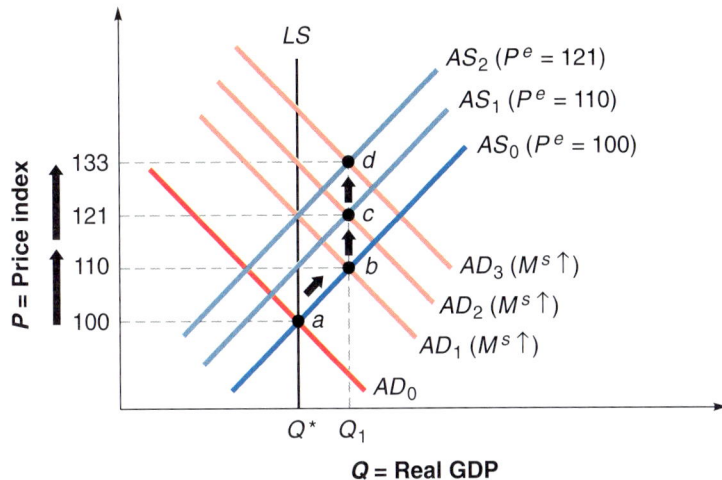

To illustrate inflation—that is, a continuing increase in the price index—with the aggregate demand–aggregate supply model, it is necessary to assume that aggregate demand is continually growing. In this example, the economy begins at point *a*. When the Federal Reserve increases the money supply, the aggregate demand curve shifts from AD_0 to AD_1, and the price index rises from 100 to 110. As wages adjust to the higher price index, the Federal Reserve again increases the money supply. As a result, the economy moves to point *c*, and the price index rises by another 10 percent to 121. As soon as workers respond to the higher price index, the Federal Reserve again increases the money supply, and the economy moves to point *d* with a price index of 133. The path *a→d* indicates a continuing increase in the price index—the definition of inflation. The path from *a* to *b* illustrates the tradeoff between inflation and unemployment—inflation has accelerated while unemployment has fallen.

········

Multiperiod Aggregate Demand–Aggregate Supply Analysis

Figure 27.3 illustrates the tradeoff between inflation and unemployment with a multiperiod aggregate demand–aggregate supply model. The economy begins at point *a*, the triple intersection between the aggregate demand curve (AD_0), the short-run aggregate supply curve (AS_0), and the long-run aggregate supply curve (*LS*). Notice that we have labeled the intersection of the long-run aggregate supply curve as potential GDP ($Q^\star$), not the natural rate of output as would be standard with most Phillips curve models. This doesn't create any special difficulties because the two concepts are quite similar, as we noted previously.

The inflationary process begins with an increase in the rate of growth of the money supply (M^s). This shifts the aggregate demand curve outward from AD_0 to AD_1, and the economy rests momentarily at point *b*. At point *b*, the price index has risen from 100 to 110, but this is *not* inflation: Remember that inflation is a continuing increase in the price index, not a one-time shift. When workers realize that the price index is higher than anticipated, they will ask for higher wages, and the aggregate supply curve will shift from AS_0 to AS_1. A key assumption that we are making in this example is that workers expect the price index to remain at 110. This means that the new short-run aggregate supply curve will intersect the long-run aggregate supply curve at the price index 110. As soon as wages begin to adjust, the Federal Reserve increases the money supply again. Consequently, the economy moves to point c, and the price index rises another 10 percent to 121. At point c, workers again respond to higher prices by adjusting their wage demands, and the Federal Reserve again increases the money supply so the economy moves to point d where the price index is 133. The path from a to d illustrates inflation because there is a continuing rise in the price index. Note too that at points b, c, and d, GDP is greater than potential GDP. This means that there is "over full" employment so the unemployment rate is less than the full employment rate of unemployment.

Four important points should be noted from the analysis in Figure 27.3:

- First, inflation is the result of a continuing expansion of aggregate demand. Had there not been a continuing increase in the money supply, all we would have observed would have been a change in the price index, not inflation, because after the short-run aggregate supply curve shifted back, prices would have stopped rising. According to this model, inflation can *only* be caused by a continuing increase in aggregate demand.

- Second, the economy is producing beyond potential GDP while it is on the path between points b and d, so the unemployment rate is below the full or natural rate, $U^\star$. The path between a and b illustrates the tradeoff between inflation and unemployment: inflation is accelerating from 0 to 10 percent while unemployment is falling below $U^\star$. (Falling inflation and rising unemployment could be illustrated on the multiperiod aggregate demand–aggregate supply model with series of decreases in aggregate demand and declines in wage demands.)

- Third, this model implies that the *only* way for the economy to operate above $Q^\star$ (and thus below $U^\star$) for any protracted period is for aggregate demand to shift out more rapidly than wages and price expectations adjust to higher prices. When workers catch on that inflation is continually increasing, they will ask for wage increases higher than those illustrated by the figure. If this occurs, the short-run aggregate supply curve will shift up more rapidly than the aggregate demand curve shifts out, so inflation will accelerate more rapidly than illustrated and GDP will return to $Q^\star$.

- Fourth, as we found out in the last chapter, long-run equilibrium can occur only at those points on the long-run aggregate supply curve where price expectations are correct and there is full employment. In the multiperiod situation where aggregate demand is continually expanding, long-run equilibrium requires that the rate of wage growth be equal to the inflation rate. How workers form their expectations of future inflation is a key to understanding the relationship between inflation and unemployment.

A Caveat

The Phillips curve model and its multiperiod aggregate demand–aggregate supply variant provide an interesting and important explanation for the tradeoff between inflation and unemployment. When inflation is faster than anticipated, unemployment is less than the natural rate; likewise, when inflation is slower than anticipated, unemployment is higher than the natural rate. However, it would be a mistake to believe that these models can account for all of the variation in inflation and unemployment observed in the real world. Some inflationary episodes simply do not fit the Phillips curve framework, and unemployment sometimes refuses to budge despite rising inflation. The best that we can say is this: the Phillips curve model is one of several models that economists use to help understand the relationship between inflation and unemployment and the way that relationship has evolved over time. On occasion the Phillips curve seems to fit the facts quite well; at other times it does not. The task of the economist is to use the right model at the right time and to be willing to entertain alternative explanations as necessary. For the time being, we cannot stress enough that our analysis of inflation and unemployment is incomplete until we have studied monetary theory and policy in some detail—the topic of the next few chapters.

RATIONAL AND ADAPTIVE EXPECTATIONS

The most important factor influencing wage demands—and hence inflation and unemployment—may be expectations of the price index and inflation. For example, suppose you are working under a contract that calls for a 6 percent annual wage increase to keep pace with 6 percent anticipated inflation, but inflation unexpectedly accelerates to a 10 percent annual rate. You would be pretty upset. With prices rising 4 percent faster than your wages, you will be losing 4 percent of your purchasing power every year. The obvious solution is to ask for a new wage contract based on a higher rate of inflation. How much of a wage increase should you ask for? If you expect inflation to stay at 10 percent, a new contract calling for a 10 percent annual wage increase may be appropriate. But by applying the multiperiod aggregate demand–aggregate supply analysis we just developed, you realize that inflation will rise above 10 percent if you (and other workers) ask for a 10 percent annual raise. Accordingly, you ask for a wage contract calling for more than a 10 percent annual raise. Clearly, workers' expectations of future inflation have an important effect on the economy.

Economists encountered several problems when they began to incorporate expectations into their macroeconomic models. One problem was that expectations cannot be observed. The best that can be done is to survey people, but surveys are expensive and not always reliable. As a result, most contemporary expectations models are based primarily on reason and logic. Another problem was that expectations are a link between today and the future, yet the future is fundamentally unknowable. This is why some economists argue that many people use "rules of thumb" and other noneconomic criteria when forming their expectations of the future. We will explore some of the implications of this view at the end of the chapter.

Despite these problems, economists have settled on only a small number of basic expectations hypotheses. Two of the most popular are **adaptive expectations** and **rational expectations**, which we will examine in this section. The examples we will use involve expectations of the price index, not the inflation rate. This will simplify

Adaptive expectations Model of expectation formation that assumes people are backward looking and make consistent mistakes.

Rational expectations Theory of expectation formation based on the idea that people are forward looking, use all available information, and make no consistent mistakes.

the analysis considerably, but in no way changes the basic results: if expectations are adaptive, business cycle swings tend to be wider and last longer than if expectations are rational.

Adaptive Expectations

The adaptive expectations hypothesis holds that people form their expectations of the future by looking at the past. Compared to rational expectations, economic adjustment is slow when people form their expectations adaptively. In the case of price-level (or inflationary) expectations, the adaptive expectations hypothesis means that people base their prediction of tomorrow's price level on current and past price levels. While this may seem reasonable at first glance, it can lead to consistently biased forecast errors—the primary reason so many economists are uncomfortable with this model.

In Figure 27.4, suppose the economy begins at point a at the intersection of the long-run aggregate supply curve, the short-run aggregate supply curve, and the aggregate demand curve. The expected price index is 100, so the short-run aggregate supply curve intersects the long-run aggregate supply curve at $P = 100$. Now suppose that policymakers raise aggregate demand. Some of the increase in demand will result in higher production, and some will result in higher prices, so the economy moves to point b with a price index of 105 and GDP at Q_1. How workers will respond to the price increase depends on the way they form their expectations. If workers believe that the price index of 105 will persist, they will demand 5 percent wage increases. This will shift the short-run aggregate supply curve to the left so that it intersects the long-run aggregate supply curve at the price index 105. But look what happens: the wage hike has not only lowered GDP from Q_1 to Q_2, but expectations have turned out to be incorrect because prices have risen above the level expected by workers to $P = 107$.

Expectations are incorrect at point b so the economy cannot stay at this point. The price level has risen more than expected so workers are not earning the real wage that they anticipated. As soon as their contracts expire, workers will again demand higher wages. If they expect the current price level ($P = 107$) to continue, their wage demands will shift the short-run aggregate supply curve upward so that it intersects the long-run aggregate supply curve at $P = 107$. But workers are again frustrated: the economy could have operated with price level 107 only at the old wage rate; once workers demand higher wages, both GDP and the price index must rise. This process continues for several contract periods until the economy winds up in its long-run resting point at the intersection between the long-run aggregate supply curve and the aggregate demand curve. This occurs at point z.

This process of adjustment can go on quite some time if expectations are adaptive.[11] Several econometric studies conducted in the 1960s and 1970s seemed to verify that the adjustment path of the economy was consistent with the adaptive expectations hypothesis. Nevertheless, many economists have become disenchanted with the

---

[11]It is likely that the economy will temporarily "overshoot" point z because workers will raise their wages once point z is reached. However, this will cause GDP to fall below potential GDP, putting downward pressure on wages and moving the economy back to point z.

•••• FIGURE 27.4 SLOW ADJUSTMENT AND ADAPTIVE
EXPECTATIONS

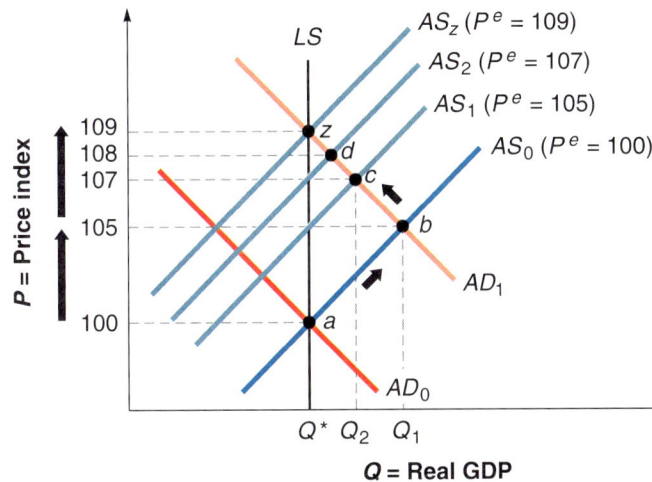

Under the adaptive expectations hypothesis, economic adjustment is slow because workers base expectations on current and past information. As a result, workers make consistent mistakes. In this example, the economy begins at point a where the expected price
index ($P^e = 100$) is equal to the actual price index. An increase in aggregate demand
raises the price index to 105 while GDP rises to Q_1. If workers believe the price index
will remain at 105, they will ask for a 5 percent wage increase. This will shift the short-
run aggregate supply curve from AS_0 to AS_1 so that it intersects the long-run aggregate
supply curve at $P = 105$. The economy cannot maintain a price index of 105, however,
because wages have increased. The economy will then move to point c with a price
index of 107. When contracts expire, workers will again ask for an increase in wages,
and the short-run aggregate supply curve will shift to AS_2. This will cause prices to rise
again. The process will continue until the economy arrives at point z, the intersection of
the long-run aggregate supply curve, the short-run aggregate supply curve, and the
aggregate demand curve.

adaptive expectations hypothesis because it seems to imply that workers make consistent mistakes and do not use information efficiently. This was the main reason why
many economists came to prefer the rational expectations hypothesis in the 1970s.

•••••••

Rational Expectations

The theory of rational expectations dates back to an important 1961 paper by John
Muth,[12] but more than a decade elapsed before the rational expectations revolution
took the economic profession by storm. The rational expectations hypothesis differs
from the adaptive expectations hypothesis in that it assumes that workers look at the
long-run consequences of economic events and act accordingly. More specifically,
the rational expectations hypothesis assumes that:

[12]John Muth, "Rational Expectations and the Theory of Price Movements," *Econometrica* 29 (1960):
315–35.

····**FIGURE 27.5 FAST ADJUSTMENT AND RATIONAL EXPECTATIONS**

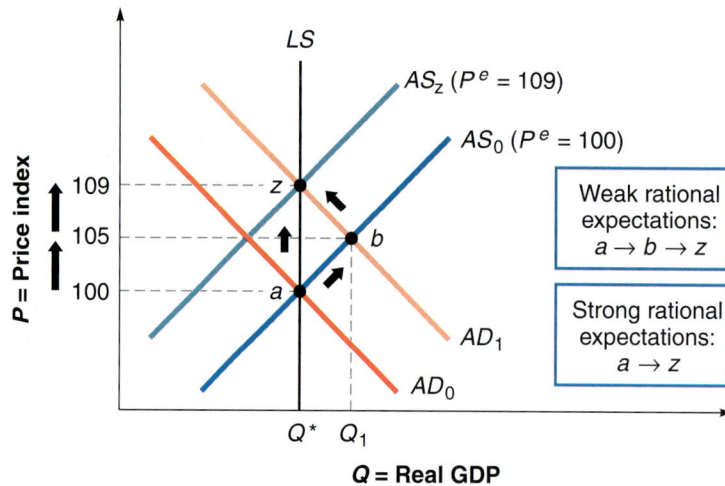

Adjustment is faster under rational expectations because workers use all available information and respond to the long-run consequences of economic events. In this case, the economy begins at point a with the expected price level equal to the actual price level of 100. An increase in aggregate demand shifts the aggregate demand curve out to AD_1, which intersects the short-run aggregate supply curve at point b and the long-run aggregate supply curve at $P = 109$. How the economy responds depends on whether weak or strong rational expectations apply. Under the weak rational expectations hypothesis, workers have contracts and cannot immediately adjust to the aggregate demand increase. This means the economy will move to point b until contracts expire, when it will move directly to point z. Under the strong rational expectations hypothesis, there are no contracts so workers immediately adjust their wages in response to the price-level increase. Workers know that the price level will rest at 109 in the long run, so the short-run aggregate supply curve immediately shifts to AS_z.

- People use all available and relevant information.
- People are forward looking and understand the long-run consequences of policy changes.

These assumptions lead to a model where people do not make consistent mistakes and where economic adjustment is much faster.

The rational expectations scenario is illustrated in Figure 27.5. As in Figure 27.4, the economy begins in long-run equilibrium with both the actual and the expected price index at 100. Aggregate demand again shifts outward and intersects the short-run aggregate supply curve at point b—but the economy may not move to this point. Remember that people use all available information and are forward looking. This means that they will know that the economy will end up at point z and will adjust their wages accordingly. Instead of a series of price and wage adjustments, the aggregate supply curve will shift directly from AS_0 to AS_z as quickly as possible.

The rational expectations hypothesis has two versions, the **strong model** and the **weak model**. The strong model assumes perfectly flexible wages and prices. Under this assumption, the economy would never pass through point b. The instant the aggregate demand curve shifts outward, wages will increase and shift the short-run aggregate supply curve to AS_z, moving the economy directly to point z. Does the strong rational expectations hypothesis imply that the economy can never be off the long-run aggregate supply curve? No. When the economy is hit by unanticipated shocks—perhaps an increase in oil prices or a sudden technology breakthrough—workers' expectations will turn out to be incorrect, and the economy will move off the long-run aggregate supply curve. Because such shocks are random, however, any deviation will also be random and only temporary.

The weak rational expectations model assumes that wages and prices are "sticky" so that workers cannot immediately respond to external shocks. In this case, the economy will stay at a point like b in Figure 27.5 until contracts expire and are renegotiated. Workers then demand a wage based on the price level expected to prevail in the long run, $P = 109$ in this example. This shifts the short-run aggregate supply curve directly to AS_z. Notice that the adjustment path that results from the weak rational expectations hypothesis ($a{\rightarrow}b{\rightarrow}z$) is similar to the path predicted by the adaptive expectations hypothesis ($a{\rightarrow}b{\rightarrow}c{\rightarrow}d{\rightarrow}\ldots z$), so for all practical purposes, it makes little difference which model is used.

Criticisms of the Rational Expectations Model. Though useful in theoretical exercises, the strong version of rational expectations has few advocates today. The weak version of rational expectations, however, is a popular theory in contemporary macroeconomics. Still, several criticisms have been levied at the rational expectations hypothesis. First, many people reject rational expectations as a reasonable description of the way people actually behave. Ask yourself this question: When a policy change is announced, do you calculate the long-run consequences and change your behavior accordingly? Do you even *know* the long-run consequences? Probably not—and by virtue of the fact that you are studying this course, you know more economics than many people on the street! In reality, few economists argue that people actually behave like the textbook model of rational expectations, but many do believe that it provides a reasonable "as if" model for predicting behavior.

A second criticism is that economic events are not always consistent with the rational expectations hypothesis. In particular, the rational expectations hypothesis holds that unemployment should remain close to the natural rate. When the unemployment rate rose above 10 percent during the 1981–1982 recession, many economists began to question the usefulness of the rational expectations hypothesis.

Third, even if the rational expectations hypothesis is correct, it may be irrelevant in a world with contracts. Many labor and raw materials prices are tied to contracts for as long as three years. When these contracts are written up, they may be "rational," but if events change significantly during the period of the contract, the outcome will be quite different from the rational expectations prediction. For example, contracts written in 1980 were based on the expectation of continuing high inflation. When inflation fell dramatically in the next three years, real wages rose and workers lost their jobs.

Finally, some economists believe that the future is so fundamentally unknowable

Strong rational expectations Rational expectations assumption combined with perfect wage and price flexibility.

Weak rational expectations Rational expectations assumption combined with sticky wages and prices.

that people cannot and do not even try to form "rational" expectations. Instead, they use rules of thumb and hunches when they try to anticipate the future; such behavior may be more consistent with adaptive expectations than rational expectations. Using hunches and rules of thumb is the antithesis of what rational expectations predicts—but it may be an accurate description of the way many people behave.

The verdict is still out on rational expectations. Many economists accept its logic, but just how to apply it remains unsettled. It is probably safe to say that most economists reject the strong rational expectations model for short-run analysis, but the weak version has dominated empirical macroeconomic research for almost two decades. Most popular contemporary models used to predict how the economy responds to policy changes and other events have some version of the rational expectations hypothesis embedded in them. We will discover in Chapters 30, 31, and 32 that an understanding of different expectations models is critical for understanding current monetary and fiscal policy debates.

RECAP   Expectations in the Inflation-Unemployment Tradeoff

1. The adaptive expectations hypothesis holds that people form expectations of the future by looking at current and past information. It results in slow adjustment to external shocks and policy. The main criticism of the adaptive expectations model is that it implies that people consistently over- or under-estimate inflation and never learn from their past mistakes.

2. The rational expectations hypothesis holds that people use all available and relevant information, know the long-run consequences of economic events and policies, and do not make consistent mistakes. It results in quicker adjustment than adaptive expectations.

3. The weak version of rational expectations assumes sticky wages and prices; the strong version assumes perfectly flexible wages and prices. Economic adjustment under the weak version is similar to adaptive expectations. Under the strong rational expectations model, the economy can be off the long-run aggregate supply curve only temporarily, and only in response to unforeseen events.

········ SUMMARY

It would be much easier for policymakers to deal with unemployment if they did not have to worry about inflation. Unfortunately, inflation often accelerates when unemployment falls. Is higher inflation a good trade for lower unemployment? Is lower inflation worth the cost of higher unemployment? These are the central questions in many policy debates, but they have no easy answers. The main points to remember from this chapter are:

1. The full or natural rate of unemployment has probably risen over the past 30 years. Changing labor force participation rates, unemployment compensation, and longer employment searches may explain why the rate of unemployment is so high at full employment. The main costs of high unemployment include output

and human dignity losses, underemployment, and involuntary part-time employment.

2. Unanticipated inflation imposes more costs on society than does anticipated inflation. The main costs of unanticipated inflation are saving disincentives, income redistribution, and market inefficiencies. The main costs of anticipated inflation are efficiency losses including menu costs and cash management.

3. The Phillips curve plots the tradeoff between inflation and unemployment. Since its discovery in the 1960s, many economists have come to question whether the tradeoff between inflation and unemployment is stable or whether it even exists.

4. How people form expectations of future prices affects the adjustment path of the economy and the tradeoff between inflation and unemployment. The adaptive expectations hypothesis assumes that people form expectations of the future by looking at current and past events. This model is less popular today because it implies that people make consistent errors. The rational expectations model assumes that people use all available and relevant information when forecasting the future. If expectations are rational, people understand the long-run consequences of external shocks and policy, adjust their wage demands accordingly, and do not make consistent errors. The rational expectations model has been criticized because it may imply that people understand the economy better than they actually do.

KEY TERMS AND CONCEPTS

seasonal adjustment
pure discrimination
statistical discrimination
duration of unemployment
full employment
natural rate of employment
NAIRU
labor force participation rate
search theory
congestion effect
unemployment compensation
structural unemployment
deindustrialization
Okun's law
cyclical unemployment
underemployment
anticipated inflation

real interest rate
nominal interest rate
welfare costs
cash management
menu costs
unanticipated inflation
income redistribution
inflation tax
disincentive to save
tax distortions
Phillips curve
natural rate hypothesis
adaptive expectations
rational expectations
strong rational expectations
weak rational expectations

REVIEW QUESTIONS

1. Why are young people and minorities more likely to be unemployed than other demographic groups? What has happened to the unemployment rate among women in the past 40 years? Why?

2. Explain how labor force participation rates, job searches, unemployment compensation, and structural factors affect the full employment rate of unemployment.

3. What are the main social and economic costs of high unemployment?

4. Distinguish between anticipated inflation and unanticipated inflation. What are the main social and economic costs of each type of inflation?

5. Use the aggregate demand–aggregate supply model to illustrate the conditions necessary for continuing inflation.

6. Define adaptive and rational expectations. What are the main criticisms of adaptive expectations? What are the main criticisms of rational expectations?

7. Using graphs, illustrate the adjustment path as the economy responds to an increase in aggregate demand assuming (a) adaptive expectations, (b) strong rational expectations, and (c) weak rational expectations.

PROBLEMS

1. Using the aggregate demand–aggregate supply model, show how the economy responds to a negative external supply shock (for example, an increase in the price of imported oil) assuming that expectations are (a) adaptive and (b) rational.

2. Explain and comment on the following statement: The Phillips curve is little more than a dynamic version of the short-run aggregate supply curve.

3. Many studies show that the economy follows a similar adjustment path under weak rational expectations and adaptive expectations. Assuming this is correct, does it make any difference whether economists use models based on one theory of expectations formation or the other?

4. Indicate whether the following statement is true or false and explain why: If policymakers want to keep the unemployment rate below $U^\star$, they will have to generate accelerating inflation. Draw a graph to illustrate your answer.

5. Okun's law states that $\Delta Q/Q = 2.5(U - U^\star)$; that is, the percentage change in GDP is two and a half times as large as the percentage change in unemployment. Why is it two and a half times as large? Shouldn't a one percentage point change in unemployment result in a one percentage point change in output? Do you think Okun's law will remain viable in the future as more workers move into the service sector?

6. Suppose that $U^\star = 5$ percent. Using data from the current *Economic Report of the President,* calculate the estimated output losses for the period 1993–1995.

7. How much real return would you earn if $i = 18$ percent and $p = 15$ percent and you bought the house described in the Focus box on page 705?

8. Suppose you were the president and had just instructed your economics team to reduce aggregate demand in order to halt inflation. Do you think your reelection chances would be greater or less if expectations were rational? Why?

PART VI

MONEY AND MACROECONOMIC POLICIES

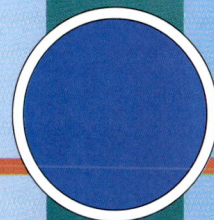

CHAPTER 28

Money, Banking, and the Federal Reserve

We have talked about money several times already; it is almost impossible to discuss economics without doing so. But we have not defined money or made more than passing remarks about how it affects the economy. Money is vitally important. We work for money incomes, entrepreneurs take risks to make money profits, and debts are written in terms of money contracts. We cannot understand economic behavior without understanding money.

An economy without money is almost unthinkable, but it really should not be. Money is a relatively recent invention in human history. Until the Middle Ages, most economic transactions were barter transactions—the exchange of goods for goods. Farmers traded their crops to the blacksmith for tools or to the cobbler for shoes. But the problem with barter exchange is that it requires a *double coincidence* of wants: if the blacksmith has enough food, he has no reason to do business with the farmer; if the cobbler needs no grain, how can the farmer get shoes? Money solved these problems because it enabled producers to exchange their wares for money and then use the money to buy what they needed.

Money was also instrumental in the breakdown of the social structures of the Middle Ages. As trade between Europe and the Far East grew, so did a new class of people—the merchant-traders—and with them, the universal acceptance of money as a medium of exchange. People transacted with gold bullion and later coins and currency instead of goods. The effects were immediate and far-reaching. Not only did money eliminate the need for a double coincidence of wants, but when people realized that money could serve as a store of value, the desire to acquire and accumulate money became a primary motivating force in society.

The effects of the monetization of life even extended to religion. Some scholars believe that the Protestant Reformation was, in part at least, an effort to rationalize the acquisitive goals of the new money-using society. Before the Reformation, it was the humble who went to heaven; after the Reformation, it was the wealthy who found salvation. Money and economic success were thought to be indications of spiritual well-being. By the fifteenth century, economists had discovered that the amount of money in circulation affected business cycles and inflation. It was not long before economists began debates over the conduct of monetary policy and the role of the central bank.

But we digress. We know today that money is important and that it has profound effects on the economy. Before we can look into these issues, however, we need to define money, discuss how it is created by the banking system, and explain how the central bank of the United States, the Federal Reserve system, controls the amount of money in circulation.

AFTER READING AND STUDYING THIS CHAPTER, YOU SHOULD BE ABLE TO:
· · · Define money and the monetary aggregates
· · · Explain how fractional reserve banking systems operate
· · · Know the functions, structure, and history of the Federal Reserve
· · · Explain how the Federal Reserve controls the supply of money and the money multiplier

· · · · · · · · FUNCTIONS AND DEFINITIONS OF MONEY

Money Anything that serves as a medium of exchange, a store of value, a unit of account, or a standard of deferred payment.

Money can be anything that serves as a medium of exchange, a store of value, a unit of account, or a standard of deferred payment. The earliest forms of money were specific commodities that societies agreed would be accepted as money. Native Americans used sea shells, prisoners used cigarettes, and the Yap Islanders of the South Pacific still use huge stones as commodity money. Almost anything that is accepted as money can serve as money, but by the nineteenth century, most developed nations had settled on gold and silver. Today, coins, currency, and checking account deposits have replaced commodity monies.

· · · · · · · ·

The Evolution of Money

Precious metals are rarely used as money today. Why not? Like all commodity monies, precious metals have disadvantages as money. Commodity monies have an *intrinsic value*; that is, they have value for nonmonetary uses. While intrinsic value may negate the need for the government to regulate the value of money, scarce resources must be devoted to the production of commodity monies, and commodities used as money are not available for alternate uses in the economy. For example, the high conductivity properties of gold make it especially valuable in electronics and the space program.

Fiat money Money that has value only by government decree or "fiat."

Money without intrinsic value that is not backed by a commodity is called **fiat money**. Fiat money is declared legal tender by government decree ("fiat"). Paper money is the most common form of fiat money today. A dollar bill is fiat money; it has no value except to serve as money. You wouldn't want to write a letter on a dollar bill, would you? Paper money has the advantage that it can be produced cheaply, but because it has no intrinsic value, its value depends on its acceptance and economic conditions. To limit the supply of money and preserve its value, private individuals are not allowed to print or mint fiat monies.

But isn't paper money backed by gold? Not any more—and it has not been for the better part of the twentieth century. In the nineteenth century, the United States and most other industrial countries backed their currencies with gold—meaning that people could take paper currency to the bank and exchange it for gold. Gold backing broke down in the 1930s when nations realized that it was important for them to be able to control the amount of money in circulation. Doing so is easier with fiat money. Still, there are periodic calls for a return to the gold standard, usually by people who are concerned that the government lacks the discipline to control the money supply effectively. The Focus box on page 724 provides a brief discussion of the history of the gold standard and new gold standard proposals.

Although paper money is still in use, almost 90 percent of all transactions today are made by **bank money**. Bank money is checking account money. As we will find out shortly, banks "create" checking account money through the process of fractional reserve banking, a main topic of this chapter. Bank money differs from fiat money: fiat money—currency and coin issued by the government—has value by government decree; bank money—checking account money—has value only when the issuing bank is solvent. Checking account money issued on failed banks has no value unless it has been insured.

> **Bank money** Checking accounts.

Money and the monetary system are still evolving. For example, until the 1980s, it was illegal for banks to offer checking account facilities on savings accounts or pay interest on most checking accounts. And only recently have people had access to Automatic Teller Machines (ATMs) or been able to use credit cards for such a wide range of purchases. Credit cards and ATMs are *not* forms of money, but they do represent new ways to use money. Credit cards provide instant approval for short-term loans and a "float" period between the time you make the purchase and the time you pay off your credit card balance. ATMs give instant access to cash—but only if you have money in your checking account. The legalization of interest-bearing checking accounts was only one component of a policy of widespread financial deregulation that took place in the 1980s. As we point out in the Focus box on page 746, financial deregulation had costs as well as benefits.

Functions of Money

Money has four main functions. The most important function of money is as a *medium of exchange*. Other financial assets can serve as a medium of exchange, but not as efficiently as money. For example, it is sometimes possible to exchange stocks, bonds, or other financial assets for goods, but you usually must convert them into cash before you can exchange them for what you want. This typically entails a brokerage fee and could mean a loss if you are forced to sell your stock when the market is down. Assets that can be easily and cheaply converted into money are said to be very *liquid*. Money is the most liquid of all financial assets; less liquid financial assets are often called *near monies*.

FOCUS ON

SHOULD WE RETURN TO THE GOLD STANDARD?

When President Reagan appointed a commission to consider a return to the gold standard, there were both cheers and jeers. Most economists were on the jeering side, but a few economists, some politicians, and a number of other people favored a return to gold. In the end, President Reagan's Gold Commission did not recommend a return to gold, but the issue is still worth a closer look. We will undoubtedly hear calls for a return to gold again.

The major countries of the world operated on the gold standard between the 1870s and 1914 and then briefly between the two world wars. People who think the gold standard will automatically result in price stability and strong self-correcting forces may be remembering a past that never was. In both the United States and the United Kingdom, real per capita income growth was lower and unemployment was higher during the gold standard than after. Average annual inflation was a few points lower, but the variability of the inflation rate was about the same under both systems.

One reason why prices were not stable under the gold standard is that the stock of monetary gold grew at a very variable rate due to fluctuations in gold production and the nonmonetary demand for gold. This variability would be one of the biggest problems with a return to the gold standard: the money supply would depend upon the luck of the miners. Many observers doubt that gold discoveries would keep up with the monetary needs of the economy.

GOLD STANDARD PROPOSALS

Several different gold standards have been proposed. The purest form calls for 100 percent gold backing of all currency in circulation and would permit free convertibility of all currency into gold. Such a rule would force extreme monetary discipline on the Federal Reserve because the money supply would be limited by the stock of gold. It would also put an end to fractional reserve banking (discussed later in the chapter). A more moderate proposal would back only a fraction of the stock of currency with gold. This would permit fractional reserve bank-

ing, and it would also allow the Fed to pursue discretionary monetary policies because the fraction could presumably be varied just like reserve requirements. But this proposal would defeat one of the chief advantages of a gold standard—monetary discipline.

Different gold standards might also have different convertibility rules instead of allowing unlimited currency-gold conversion. Under one suggestion, only foreign governments would be permitted to trade dollars for gold. The international gold standard operated in this way between the world wars. This might be appropriate if the gold standard was intended primarily as a mechanism to establish fixed exchange rates. Some observers have even suggested that no conversion be allowed—apparently believing that mere knowledge of gold backing would be enough to assure monetary discipline and stabilize the economy.

PROBLEMS WITH IMPLEMENTATION

Adopting the gold standard would involve several difficulties, at least at first. The most immediate problem would

The second function of money is as a *unit of account*; that is, goods are priced in terms of units of money. This reduces the number of calculations you need to make when shopping. For example, if the price of a new car is $20,000, the price of a half gallon of milk is $1.50, and the price of a movie ticket is $7.50, you know their prices in relation to each other. This information is necessary for you to make the right purchase decision. Without a unit of account, you would need to calculate a

Assay marked gold ingots.

be setting the dollar price of gold. If the price is too high, people would trade gold for dollars, increase the money supply, and cause inflation. If the price is too low, people would trade dollars for gold and exhaust the stock of gold. The obvious choice is the market price, but even this presents difficulties because of price fluctuations. Another option would be to set the official price equal to the cost of mining gold.

There is another problem with the gold standard. While it might impose monetary discipline on the Federal Reserve, similar discipline could not be applied to other countries. South Africa may hold as much as 50 percent of the world's monetary gold (in gold bars and the like), and no one really knows how much is held in the republics of the former Soviet Union. If any of these countries decided to dump their gold on the world market,

U.S. monetary policy could be damaged considerably. There are also approximately 1,500 million ounces of nonmonetary gold (in jewelry and the like) in the world that might be exchanged for currency under the gold standard.

The chances of the United States returning to the gold standard seem remote today, but the gold standard may be appropriate for nations trying to gain international acceptance for their currencies. For example, the Baltic nation of Estonia was the first of the former Soviet nations to implement its own currency after the breakup of the Soviet Union in 1991. Estonia backed its new currency, the *kroon*, with gold that was repatriated after the Soviet breakup. It also tied its currency to the German mark. To date, this plan has been successful: the Estonian *kroon* is one of the most stable currencies in Europe, and foreign investors have flocked to Estonia. How long Estonia will remain on the gold standard is anybody's guess, but it is reasonable to think that gold backing will be suspended when the Estonian economy has overcome the initial shock of economic transition.

huge number of exchange ratios before you could make the correct purchase decision. If there are only three goods, there are six ratios: the car costs 13,333.33 times as much as the milk and 2,666.67 times as much as the movie ticket; the milk costs only 0.000075 as much as the car and 0.20 times as much as the movie ticket; the movie ticket costs 0.000375 as much as the car and 5 times as much as the milk. Isn't it easier just to set the price in terms of a unit of account?

The third main function of money is as a *store of value*. Paper and bank money do not spoil, so they can keep their nominal value over time. If you have a little money saved up, you can pay the rent and buy food even if you lose your job. Holding other financial assets can be risky because their selling prices might fall in the future—probably at just the time you would want to cash in! Money is not a completely risk-free store of value, however, because money loses its value during periods of inflation. This is one reason why most people keep some of their wealth in money and some in other financial assets—stocks, bonds, real estate, and so on. An investment portfolio that includes several different kinds of financial assets is said to be *diversified*. Financial analysts have shown that diversification reduces risk because all of your financial assets are unlikely to lose value at the same time.

A fourth function of money is as a *standard of deferred payment*. Many transactions involve promises of future delivery at an agreed-upon price. By establishing a money contract, both the buyer and seller reduce the amount of risk. For example, farmers typically borrow money at the beginning of the growing year and agree to pay back a certain amount of money when their crops come in—perhaps the loan amount plus 10 percent interest. But suppose the contract was written for payment in goods and the farmer agreed to pay 10 percent of his wheat harvest to the lender. In this case, the lender would lose if the price of wheat was low because she could not sell the wheat for very much. The farmer would lose if the price of wheat was high because the loan would have cost too much. Money contracts reduce the chance of these kinds of losses.

Finally, it should be mentioned that money is *unique*. Not only is it the most liquid of all financial assets, but it is different from other financial assets. Most of us have a confidence in money that we do not have in other financial assets. Money is the asset we turn to when times are bad; some people also turn to gold. The uniqueness of money stems partially from the fact that the private sector is not allowed to produce fiat currency. Banks can create bank money with fractional reserve banking, but how much they can create is strictly regulated. Controlling the amount of money in circulation is important because it helps maintain the store of value function of money. Most other financial assets can be produced by private firms, so there is always the chance that too much will be produced and that their value will fall. The private sector cannot depreciate money, but the government can—and has done so frequently in the past by printing too much money. The phrase "printing money" is often misused, however, a point we develop in the Focus box on page 742.

. . . .

Measures of the Money Supply

We still have not gotten around to defining money, which is not as simple as it might seem. The key property of that stuff we call "money" is that it serves as a medium of exchange, but several other assets also serve this function, so we need to look at the issue more closely. A simple working definition of money is "currency outside banks plus checking accounts." Unfortunately, the financial system has undergone numerous changes over the past 20 years, so more detailed definitions are necessary. The central bank of the United States, the Federal Reserve, keeps track of several measures of the *monetary aggregates* because different measures tell different things about the economy. The following are the five most important monetary aggregates:

- **M1** is the *narrowest* measure of the money supply. It includes only those assets that are intended to be used for immediate transactions; thus, it includes the most liquid components of the money supply. The main components of M1 are currency outside banks, demand deposits and other checkable deposits, and traveler's checks.[1]

We need to make three comments about this definition. First, only currency "outside banks" held by the public is considered money because, by law, banks must hold a certain fraction of their deposits at all times in their vaults or on deposit at the Federal Reserve. These holdings are known as **bank reserves**. Bank reserves are not available for immediate transactions, so they are not considered part of the money supply. Second, the term "demand deposits" refers to checkable accounts or checking account deposits at commercial banks. These deposits represent money that can be withdrawn "on demand." Checking account deposits at savings and loan institutions and accounts that have restrictions on the size or number of checks that can be written are called *other checkable deposits (OCDs)*. One popular kind of OCD is the negotiable order of withdrawal or NOW account. The distinction between demand deposits and OCDs is necessary because OCDs frequently have certain restrictions that make them slightly less liquid than demand deposits at commercial banks; however, many depositors probably see no distinction between demand deposits and OCDs. The media frequently refer to M1 as "the basic money supply." In December 1993, M1 totaled $1,131.2 billion.

- **M2** is *broader* than M1 because it includes everything in M1 plus financial assets that can be used for current transactions but are frequently held for longer periods. The main components of M2 are M1, overnight repurchase agreements (RPs) and Eurodollars, money market mutual fund (MMMF) balances, money market deposit accounts (MMDAs), savings deposits, and small (under $100,000) time deposits. In December 1993, M2 amounted to $3,551.7 billion.

We need to define the individual components. An overnight repurchase agreement is an overnight loan between two financial institutions. It is called a repurchase agreement because one financial institution sells an asset to another financial institution with the agreement to buy it back the next day. This provides the first financial institution with needed cash reserves for one day.[2] The Eurodollar market represents U.S. dollars held abroad, both in Europe and the rest of the world. Eurodollar accounts often pay higher interest rates than similar U.S. accounts because they are regulated differently. Money market mutual funds and money market deposit accounts are relatively new kinds of financial assets. MMMFs pool the funds of many small investors, thereby allowing them to invest in a diversified portfolio of short-term securities. MMDAs use a pool of funds from many small investors to buy high interest–earning, large-denomination financial assets. MMMFs and MMDAs typically have restrictive check-writing privileges. Savings

M1 The narrowest measure of money. It includes only those assets that are intended to be used for immediate transactions; currency held outside banks, demand deposits, other checkable deposits, and traveler's checks.

Bank reserves Currency held in bank vaults or on deposit at the Federal Reserve.

M2 Includes all assets in M1 plus financial assets that can be used for current transactions but are frequently held for longer periods.

---

[1]The precise definitions of the various monetary aggregates can be found in any issue of the *Federal Reserve Bulletin*, in footnotes to Table 1.10. All data in this section are from Table 1.21 of the March 1994 *Federal Reserve Bulletin*.

[2]The immediacy of repurchase transactions might suggest that repos should be included in M1 instead of M2; however, repos are merely shifts of investment assets between institutions, not transaction accounts.

M3 Includes all assets in M2 plus deposits that are usually held for substantial periods of time.

L The broadest definition of money in common use.

Debt Corporate bonds, mortgages, consumer credit, and other bank loans.

deposits earn interest but have no check-writing privileges. Time deposits earn somewhat higher interest than savings accounts, but must be left in the financial institution for a fixed period. Early withdrawals are charged a penalty.

- **M3** is even broader than M2. It includes deposits that are usually held for substantial periods of time. The main components of M3 are M2, large (over $100,000) time deposits, term RPs and Eurodollars, and institutional-only MMMF balances. "Term" RPs and Eurodollars must be held for a fixed period of time before they can be converted into cash. This means that they are less liquid than overnight assets. Likewise, institutional-only MMMF balances are typically very large and are used for transactions much less frequently than individually owned MMMFs. In December 1993, M3 equaled $4,207.7 billion.

- **L** is the broadest monetary aggregate in common use. It consists of M3 plus many other liquid assets including nonbank holdings of U.S. treasury bills and savings bonds, and Eurodollar deposits held by U.S. citizens. In November 1993, this total was $5,093.4 billion.

- The Federal Reserve also compiles a measure of total **Debt**. This consists of corporate bonds, mortgages, consumer credit, and other bank loans. How is debt related to the supply of money? As we will see shortly, bank money is created whenever financial institutions make loans, so a measure of total debt gives the broadest possible measure of money and money-like financial assets. In Chapter 30, we will note that some policymakers believe that it is more important to control total debt than a particular money aggregate. In November 1993, the Federal Reserve calculated Debt to be $12,241.8 billion.

Which monetary aggregate is most important? Many economists would say M2 because it seems to be more highly correlated with nominal GDP than the other definitions. However, the relationship between M2 and the economy has not held up very well in the last few years, so most monetary economists look at several money supply aggregates—as well as credit demand, interest rates, exchange rates, and other factors—before making their forecasts or policy recommendations. It is important to follow all of the monetary aggregates because they frequently move at different rates.

Data for the monetary aggregates are shown in Figure 28.1 and Table 28.1. Several things are worth noting about these data. First, all of the monetary aggregates have grown substantially over the past 25 years. Second, the legalization of NOW accounts and other OCDs shows up in Table 28.1 as the increase in OCDs from $28 billion in 1980 to $179 billion in 1985; this is also reflected in the steeper slopes of the M2, M3, and L lines over the 1980–1985 period on Figure 28.1. Third, M1 has grown more rapidly than the other monetary aggregates since 1990. Part of the reason for this is that falling interest rates reduced the incentive for people to keep money in non-M1 accounts like MMMFs, MMDAs, and small time and savings deposits.

One final point: The official definitions of the monetary aggregates are constantly changing! Changes in the way financial institutions can operate mean that people have more options in the ways they can hold money. This has created quite a few problems in interpreting monetary statistics: what used to be called M1A is no longer calculated; what used to be called M1B is now M1, and this M1 is not the same as the old M1! Make sure you read the footnotes before interpreting any data. Further, new kinds of accounts, and hence new definitions of money, are being created all of

•••• **FIGURE 28.1** THE MONETARY AGGREGATES, 1970–1993

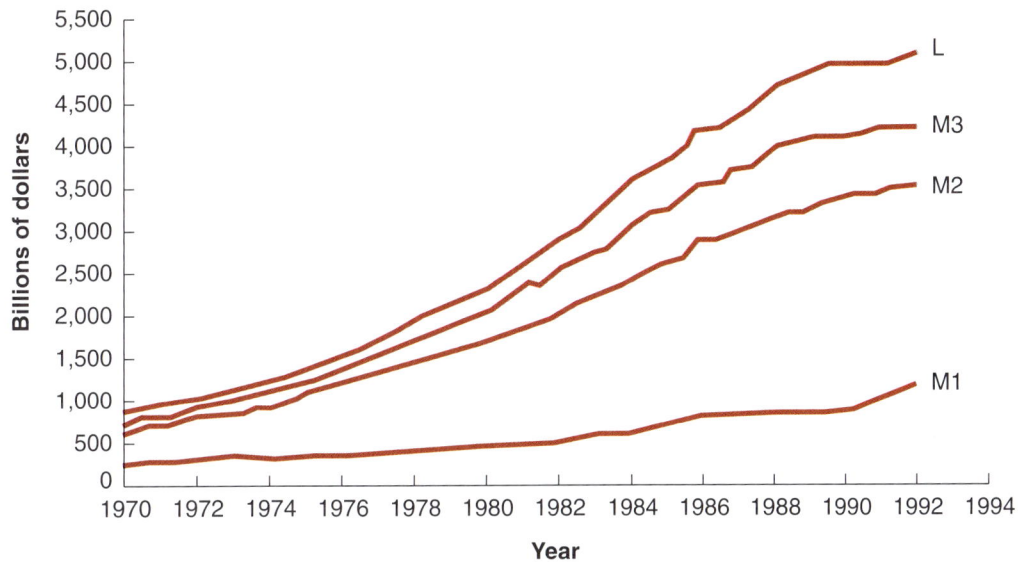

The monetary aggregates have grown substantially over the past 25 years. From the 1980s on, the broad aggregates grew more rapidly than the narrow M1 in most years due to the increasing importance of other checkable accounts, money market mutual funds, and money market deposit accounts. This trend seems to have been reversed since 1990 as M1 has grown faster than the other monetary aggregates.

SOURCE: 1994 *Economic Report of the President*, Table B-68.

••••• **TABLE 28.1** THE CHANGING COMPOSITION OF THE MONETARY AGGREGATES

Year	Currency	Traveler's Checks	Demand Deposits	OCDs	RPs	MMMFs	S + MMDAs	Small Time Deposits
1960	$ 28.7	$0.4	$111.6	$ 0.0	$ 0.0	$ 0.0	$ 159.1	$ 12.5
1970	48.6	1.0	164.7	0.1	1.3	0.0	260.9	151.1
1975	72.8	2.3	211.6	0.9	5.9	1.7	388.8	337.9
1980	115.3	4.2	261.4	28.0	28.8	61.6	400.1	728.7
1985	167.8	5.9	266.8	179.6	73.5	177.2	815.1	885.5
1990	245.9	8.4	277.5	293.8	73.7	350.5	920.8	1,172.3
1991	267.3	8.2	289.5	333.2	76.2	363.9	1,042.5	1,064.7
1992	292.3	8.1	340.8	385.2	74.9	342.3	1,186.0	867.3
1993	321.5	8.0	386.1	415.7	84.7	336.4	1,218.6	783.5

Key:

OCDs = other checkable deposits, RPs = repurchase certificates, MMMFs = money market mutual funds, S + MMDAs = savings deposits plus money market deposit accounts

NOTE: All data are in billions of current dollars and are for year-end except the 1993 data, which are for November.

SOURCE: 1994 *Economic Report of the President*, Table B-69.

the time. To really understand the financial situation of the economy, one must continually revise the data and definitions. The changing relationship between money and the economy is summed up in Goodhart's law, named after Charles Goodhart, former chief monetary adviser to the Bank of England: Whenever the central bank tries to control a given measure of money, that measure will lose its previous significance.

RECAP   The Monetary Aggregates

1. M1 is the narrowest measure of the money supply. It consists of monies intended for immediate transactions. The main components of M1 are currency outside banks and checkable deposits, both of which are highly liquid.
2. M2 is broader than M1 because it includes noncheckable savings deposits and small time deposits. Many economists believe that M2 is more closely related to economic activity than the other monetary aggregates.
3. M3 is broader yet. It is defined as M2 plus large time deposits and other less liquid near monies.
4. L and Debt are the broadest definitions of money financial measures in common use.
5. Since 1990, M1 has grown more rapidly than the other monetary aggregates, primarily because of the increasing importance of MMDAs and MMMFs.

FRACTIONAL RESERVE BANKING

We found out in Chapter 5 that the main role of banks and other financial institutions is *financial intermediation*—the process of linking borrowers and lenders. One way banks make profits is by paying lower interest rates on deposits than they charge on loans. Bank lending creates money. When you borrow money to buy a new car, the bank will give you a bank check. You then give this check to the car dealer, who will deposit it into his checking account. Checking account deposits are part of the money supply, so the loan process has "created money." This section explains the process of money creation.

The Origins of Fractional Reserve Banking

Fractional reserve banking Banks accept deposits but keep only a fraction as bank reserves and lend out the rest; this process "creates" money.

Fractional reserve banking started almost by accident. By the Middle Ages, gold had become the most commonly accepted form of money. Fearful of robbers, many people paid goldsmiths to store and protect their gold. Goldsmiths were the obvious choice for safekeeping because they already had vaults for their own gold. When depositors left their gold with the goldsmith, they were issued paper receipts. Eventually, depositors began to use these receipts to pay for goods and services. Gold receipts were easy to carry and conceal and, as long as the goldsmith was known, were just as widely accepted as gold itself. For all practical purposes, gold deposit slips had become gold-backed paper currency.

The goldsmiths soon realized that they almost always had more gold on hand than people wanted to withdraw. They also realized that they could profit from these extra gold deposits by making loans. This practice was safe as long as the goldsmith was careful to keep the amount of lending small relative to the deposits and to make sure that there was always enough gold on hand to meet the demands of depositors. Eventually, many of the goldsmiths realized that lending was more profitable than safekeeping, so they began to accept deposits for free. It was not too long before depositors were being paid interest on their deposits.

How does the goldsmith story differ from modern commercial banking? Very little. The banking industry is highly regulated today, but banks make profits pretty much the same way goldsmiths did five hundred years ago—by paying a lower rate of interest on deposits than they charge on loans. And if the banks make sure that there is always enough money on hand to meet the day-to-day withdrawals, depositors need never be aware that "their" money is being lent to someone else.

Fractional Reserve Banking Today

What may not have been apparent from the goldsmith story is that the process of making loans actually "creates" money. If you deposit $100 worth of gold with the goldsmith, then you have a $100 gold note to spend when you need it. But when the goldsmith uses $50 of your deposit to make a loan to someone else, that person has $50 and you still have your $100. The amount of money in circulation has just increased by $50. What happens if you go to the smith tomorrow to withdraw your $100? The smith will give you $100—but it may actually be gold that was deposited by a third person.

To see how banks and other financial institutions create money, we need to look at commercial bank balance sheets. To do so, let's first examine how a bank, call it First Bank, is established. The first step is to secure a state or national bank charter. In the United States, all banks are required to have a charter. Any person or group can get a charter as long as they can show that they are trustworthy and have a minimum amount of *bank capital*. Bank capital is often raised by selling shares of stock, either to the founders of the bank or to outside individuals. Bank capital is then used to buy buildings, office equipment, and so on. How bank capital is raised and how it is spent are important to bank operations—we will see just how important when we look at the Focus box on Reforming the Financial System at the end of the chapter—but let's ignore this issue for now and focus our attention on the way banks create money through fractional reserve banking.

Let's suppose customers deposit $1,000,000 cash in checking accounts in First Bank. First Bank issues checking accounts for the amount of $1,000,000 to the depositors and puts the cash in its vault. This transaction represents both *assets* and *liabilities* to the bank. Cash is a valuable asset because the bank can use it to make profits. Vault cash is a component of the bank's total reserves, so the $1,000,000 deposit is listed as total reserves on the balance sheet. A liability is an obligation that the bank owes to someone. The demand deposits are a liability because the bank owes that amount to its checking account customers. Bank books are kept with double entry accounting procedures, so most bank transactions entail both assets and liabilities. The $1,000,000 deposit will make the balance sheet look like Balance Sheet I:

BALANCE SHEET I: FIRST BANK			
Assets		Liabilities	
Total reserves	$1,000,000	Demand deposits	$1,000,000
Total	$1,000,000	Total	$1,000,000

Before we examine how First Bank uses its new assets to make profits, we need to pause to determine what has happened to the money supply. Bank money (checking account deposits) has increased by $1,000,000, but currency in circulation has decreased by the same amount, so the money supply has not changed. What about the additional $1,000,000 cash held in reserves? Vault cash, part of bank reserves, is not considered part of the money supply because it is not available for immediate transactions. Reserves, including vault cash, are the basis for bank lending, and once such loans are made, the money supply will increase.

By law, commercial banks must keep a fraction of their deposits either in their vaults or on deposit at the district branch of the Federal Reserve. The amount that commercial banks are required to keep is called *required reserves* and is not available for lending. Any deposits exceeding the legal reserve requirement can be lent out. Most of that money usually is lent out, but commercial banks typically do keep a small amount of *excess reserves* on hand to make sure they have enough cash to meet unforeseen circumstances.

The **required reserve ratio** is the ratio of legal required reserves to total demand deposit liabilities. It is defined as:

Required reserve ratio Ratio of required reserves to demand deposits.

$$rr = \text{required reserve ratio} = \frac{\text{required reserves}}{\text{demand deposit liabilities}} \quad [1]$$

For this example, let's suppose that the required reserve ratio is 10 percent. This means that First Bank must hold $100,000 in required reserves. It can legally lend out the remaining $900,000 or 90 percent of its demand deposits. This means that the balance sheet would look like Balance Sheet II:

BALANCE SHEET II: FIRST BANK			
Assets		Liabilities	
Total reserves	$1,000,000	Demand deposits	$1,000,000
Required reserves	100,000		
Excess reserves	900,000		
Total	$1,000,000	Total	$1,000,000

The initial bank deposit is $1,000,000. The required reserve ratio is 10 percent, so the bank must keep $100,000 of the demand deposits as required reserves (vault cash or on deposit at the Federal Reserve). The remaining $900,000 is available for lending.

Notice the format we are using on Balance Sheet II: the indented entries (Required reserves and Excess reserves) are the subcomponents of the entry immediately above (Total reserves), so required reserves plus excess reserves equal total reserves. This explains why total assets are $1,000,000, not $2,000,000.

Banks rarely keep very many excess reserves on hand because they do not earn profit. If we assume that the bank desires zero excess reserves and is able to find a loan customer for the entire $900,000, the new balance sheet will look like Balance Sheet III:

Balance Sheet III: First Bank

Assets		Liabilities	
Total reserves	$1,000,000	Demand deposits	$1,900,000
Required reserves	190,000		
Excess reserves	810,000		
Loan	900,000		
Total	$1,900,000	Total	$1,900,000

The loan of $900,000 increases liabilities by $900,000 because demand deposits have increased by this amount. Assets also increase by $900,000 because First Bank now has an interest-earning loan of $900,000. Required reserves are 10 percent of liabilities. Excess reserves are total reserves minus required reserves. The $900,000 increase in demand deposits represents an increase in the money supply.

First Bank lent the $900,000 by creating a demand deposit for its loan customer. This increases both the bank's liabilities (demand deposits) and its assets (loans) by $900,000. Now the money supply *has* increased: the initial deposit of $1,000,000 has resulted in the creation of an additional $900,000 in checking account deposits.

Presumably, the reason the loan customer needed that $900,000 loan is to spend the money. To make things simple, let's suppose that our borrower immediately turns around and spends all $900,000 on a work of art, say, an undiscovered painting by Miro. The seller takes the $900,000 check and deposits it in Second Bank. Second Bank graciously accepts the $900,000 deposit, keeps the required $90,000 reserves, and finds a borrower for the remaining $810,000 that can legally be lent out.

This transaction changes the balance sheets of both First Bank and Second Bank. When the seller cashes the $900,000 check drawn on First Bank, both demand deposits and cash reserves at First Bank fall by $900,000. Demand deposits fall by $900,000 because the borrower has spent all of the loan to buy the painting, and cash reserves fall when Second Bank presents the check at First Bank and asks for cash. First Bank still has the $900,000 loan, so assets equal $1,000,000—the required reserves of $100,000 plus the loan. Liabilities return to $1,000,000, the original deposit that set this process in motion. First Bank now has zero excess reserves. First Bank's new balance sheet is shown on Balance Sheet IV:

Balance Sheet IV: First Bank

Assets		Liabilities	
Total reserves	$100,000	Demand deposits	$1,000,000
Required reserves	100,000		
Excess reserves	0		
Loan	900,000		
Total	$1,000,000	Total	$1,000,000

When the $900,000 loan is spent, the borrower's demand deposit account falls by $900,000. When that check is cashed by Second Bank, cash reserves at First Bank fall by the same $900,000. First Bank has zero excess reserves because total reserves are exactly 10 percent of liabilities.

When the $900,000 check is deposited at Second Bank, its demand deposit liabilities rise by $900,000. Reserve regulations require Second Bank to keep 10 percent of this deposit as reserves, but it can legally lend out the remaining $810,000. Until this money is lent out, it is considered excess reserves. Second Bank's initial balance sheet is as shown in Balance Sheet V. To keep things simple, we are assuming that Second Bank had zero deposits and reserves until this transaction.

BALANCE SHEET V: SECOND BANK

Assets		Liabilities	
Total reserves	$900,000	Demand deposits	$900,000
Required reserves	90,000		
Excess reserves	810,000		
Total	$900,000	Total	$900,000

The $900,000 deposit at Second Bank is treated as a liability because Second Bank owes that money to its customer. Second Bank's reserves increase by $900,000, 10 percent of which it is required to keep as vault cash or on deposit at the Federal Reserve. Excess reserves totaling $810,000 may be lent out.

As soon as Second Bank can find a creditworthy loan customer, it lends out its excess reserves of $810,000 by creating a checking account deposit for the customer. This means that Second Bank's demand deposits will increase to $1,710,000—$900,000 plus $810,000 once the loan is made. The loan also represents an increase on the asset side of the balance sheet, so assets also equal $1,710,000—$810,000 in loans plus $900,000 in cash reserves. Once these transactions are completed, Second Bank's balance sheet will look like Balance Sheet VI:

BALANCE SHEET VI: SECOND BANK

Assets		Liabilities	
Total reserves	$900,000	Demand deposits	$1,710,000
Required reserves	171,000		
Excess reserves	729,000		
Loan	810,000		
Total	$1,710,000	Total	$1,710,000

When Second Bank finds a borrower for its $810,000 excess reserves, it makes a loan of that amount. This will increase Second Bank's demand deposits by an additional $810,000; the loan also appears as an increase on the asset side of Second Bank's balance sheet. The $810,000 increase in demand deposits represents an increase in the money supply.

The chain of events repeats itself when the $810,000 loan is spent: Third Bank receives a deposit of $810,000, keeps the required 10 percent, $81,000, and lends out the remaining 90 percent, $729,000. That $729,000 is deposited into another bank, and the process continues. To this point, that initial deposit of $1,000,000 has caused the money supply to increase by:

$$\$900,000 + \$810,000 + \$729,000 = \$2,439,000$$

but we are not finished. Eventually, the money supply will increase by $9,000,000, or 10 times the original loan amount of $900,000. How do we know that the money supply will increase by this amount? The money supply expansion process is an example of an infinite series—it takes literally forever for the money creation process to work itself out. Mathematicians can tell us how to find the sum of an infinite series,[3] but it is much simpler to use the money multiplier. But a warning before we go on: the *money* multiplier is not the same thing as the *spending* multiplier we developed in Chapter 24! Income and money are distinct concepts, and so are their associated multipliers.

· · · · · · · ·

The Money Multiplier

The **potential money multiplier (*mm★*)** gives the maximum amount of money that can be generated from an initial increase in excess reserves. The formula for the potential money multiplier is:

$$mm^\star = \frac{1}{rr} \qquad [2]$$

Potential money multiplier (*mm★*) The maximum value of the money multiplier; reciprocal of required reserve ratio.

where *rr* is the required reserve ratio. In the example we have been developing, the potential money multiplier is 10 because $1/0.1 = 10$. Notice that an increase in the required reserve ratio will cause the money multiplier to fall; a decrease in the required reserve ratio will increase the money multiplier.

The money multiplier that exists in the real world, the **actual money multiplier (*mm*)**, is lower than the potential money multiplier for two main reasons: cash leakages and excess reserves. When depositors withdraw cash from their checking accounts, bank reserves fall. This reduces the amount of lending that can take place and thus lowers the money multiplier. Banks typically hold very few excess reserves because reserves do not earn interest. However, any excess reserves that banks do hold will reduce the money multiplier because the denominator of Equation 2 would increase.

Actual money multiplier (*mm*) The ratio of the money supply to the monetary base; smaller than the potential money multiplier.

While it is possible to modify the formula in Equation 2 for cash leakages and excess reserves, the result is rather unwieldy. Equation 3 presents a different expression that shows that the actual money multiplier (*mm*) is the ratio of the money supply (M^s) to the **monetary base (MB)**. The monetary base consists of currency

Monetary base (MB) Currency held by the nonbank public plus bank reserves; also called high-powered money.

---

[3]Finding an infinite sum looks harder than it really is. Let S be the sum, rr the required reserve ratio, and ΔER the initial amount of excess reserves; then:

$$S = \Delta ER + (1 - rr)\, \Delta ER + (1 - rr)^2(\Delta ER) + (1 - rr)^3(\Delta ER) + \cdots$$

and recognize that because $(1 - rr)$ is less than 1, it becomes very small as it is raised to higher exponents. This allows us to ignore terms far out in the series. Now, multiply each side by $-(1 - rr)$:

$$-(1 - rr)S = -(1 - rr)\, \Delta ER - (1 - rr)^2(\Delta ER) - (1 - rr)^3(\Delta ER) - (1 - rr)^4(\Delta ER) + \cdots$$

and subtract the two expressions to get:

$$S[1 - (1 - rr)] = \Delta ER$$

which can be written as

$$S = \frac{\Delta ER}{rr} = \left(\frac{1}{rr}\right) \Delta ER$$

held by the public plus bank reserves. The monetary base is sometimes called *high-powered money* because it is the source of monetary expansion. A larger monetary base means that more lending can take place and thus that the money supply will increase; a smaller monetary base reduces lending and the money supply.

$$mm = \frac{M^s}{MB} \qquad\qquad [3]$$

Equation 3 can be rewritten as:

$$M^s = mm(MB) \qquad\qquad [4]$$

Equations 3 and 4 will be especially important in the next section when we look at the tools available to the Federal Reserve for controlling the money supply.[4]

RECAP   Fractional Reserve Banking and the Money Multiplier

Ninety percent of the money we use consists of bank money—checking account deposits—so it is important to understand where this money comes from and how it is "created."

1. Banks create money every time they make a loan. Banks are required to keep a small fraction of their deposits on hand or on deposit with the Federal Reserve system. This fraction is called the required reserve ratio.
2. The potential money multiplier is the reciprocal of the required reserve ratio. The actual money multiplier is smaller than the potential money multiplier because of cash leakages and excess reserves.
3. The total money supply is equal to the actual money multiplier times the monetary base.

THE CENTRAL BANK OF THE UNITED STATES: THE FEDERAL RESERVE SYSTEM

The purpose of a central bank is to control the supply of money and regulate the banking system in the best interests of the public. In the United States, these duties are carried out by the Federal Reserve system, a network of 12 regional banks. The Federal Reserve banks are privately owned but are operated in the public interest. Most profits earned by the Federal Reserve banks are turned over to the Treasury. Many people prefer to think of the Federal Reserve system as a "quasi-public" institution because it is so highly regulated by the government.

---

[4]Notice that we are not distinguishing between the multipliers associated with the various money aggregates—the M1 money multiplier, the M2 money multiplier, and so on. For actual policy purposes, these distinctions are important, but because there are no theoretical differences among them, we are omitting this detail.

History of the Federal Reserve

The first central bank of the United States, the Bank of the United States, was chartered in 1791. Most nations had had central banks for some time, but opposition to the Bank of the United States was fierce from the outset. The main criticisms were that a central bank (1) would be unfair competition to private commercial banks and (2) would siphon funds away from rural banks for industrial development in urban areas. Congress chose not to renew the charter of the Bank of the United States in 1811, charging that it was unconstitutional, that it encouraged the use of paper money, and that much of its stock was foreign owned.

The United States was without a central bank for only five years. In 1816, the Second Bank of the United States was chartered, at least partially in response to the high inflation of the previous four years. Almost as soon as the charter was granted, inflation began to accelerate, however, and depressions occurred in 1818 and 1820. Opposition to the bank grew, and in 1832 President Andrew Jackson vetoed a bill to renew its charter.

The United States did not have another central bank until the Federal Reserve system was established in 1913. The Federal Reserve (commonly referred to as the "Fed") was established to fulfill four functions:

1. A *lender of last resort* to furnish currency to banks in times of financial crisis.
2. A monetary authority to adjust the nation's money supply according to the needs of the economy.
3. A payment system for clearing and collecting checks.
4. A supervisor and regulator of the banking system.

There are several reasons why the Fed has succeeded where the previous central banks failed. Two of the more important ones are the right to issue currency and the regional structure. When it was established in 1913, the Fed was authorized to issue a new kind of bank note, the Federal Reserve note. Federal Reserve notes now constitute the predominant form of paper money in the United States. Previous central banks were not given this right and had to manage the money supply by controlling the number of bank notes issued by state banks, not always a simple task. The regional structure of the Fed—12 banks scattered across the nation—helped diffuse the opposition that plagued the first two central banks. With authority spread throughout the nation, there was less concern that money would be siphoned from one area of the country to another.

Finally, like virtually everything in the economy, the financial system and the role of the Fed are constantly evolving. The Focus box on page 746 addresses some of the important issues that will be of concern to the Fed and other agencies involved with regulating the financial system in the years to come.

Structure of the Federal Reserve

The Federal Reserve system is composed of the 12 regional banks and their branches, as well as thousands of member banks. Each regional bank is responsible for controlling banking operations and supervising banks in its own region, but the policies of the various branches are tightly coordinated. Figure 28.2 shows the location of the 12 regional Federal Reserve banks.

• • • • FIGURE 28.2 THE 12 DISTRICT BANKS OF THE FEDERAL RESERVE SYSTEM

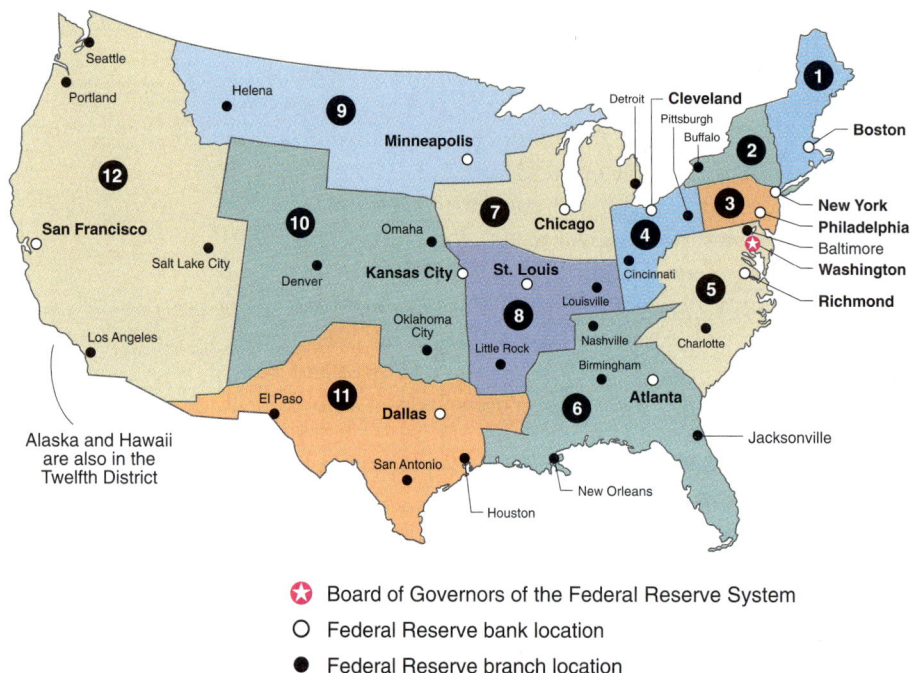

Board of Governors of the Federal Reserve System

Federal Reserve bank location

Federal Reserve branch location

The 12 regional banks of the Federal Reserve system are located in New York, Chicago, Richmond, Dallas, San Francisco, Cleveland, Philadelphia, Minneapolis, St. Louis, Boston, Kansas City, and Atlanta.

Board of Governors The seven-member Federal Reserve Board, which serves as the main governing body of the Federal Reserve system.

The Board of Governors. The main governing body of the Federal Reserve system is the **Board of Governors**, often called the Federal Reserve Board or FRB for short. The Board has seven members, each of whom is nominated by the president and confirmed by the U.S. Senate. No nominee to the Board has ever failed to receive confirmation. Terms last 14 years and are staggered so that one member is nominated every other year. Members of the Board are usually bankers or economists with Ph.D.'s. Some observers have criticized the makeup of the Board because it has been overwhelming white and male.[5]

The most powerful member of the Board of Governors—some people say the second most powerful person in the United States—is the chair. The chair is appointed to a four-year, renewable term by the president and approved by the Senate. The term of office for the FRB chair is not concurrent with the president's term in office. The current chair is Alan Greenspan, who was appointed by President Reagan and reappointed by President Bush. Like most previous Fed chairs, Greenspan wields an enormous amount of influence on the Board of Governors.

[5]The Federal Reserve is not the only central bank in the world that is predominantly male. The German central bank, the *Bundesbank,* has had only one female member since 1948. Julia Dingwort-Nusseck, an aggressive television journalist from Lower Saxony who served from 1976 through 1988, holds that distinction. A ladies' toilet had to be specially built for her on the thirteenth floor, site of Central Bank Council policy meetings. I am grateful to Ann Metcalfe for pointing this out to me. See David Marsh, *The Most Powerful Bank: Inside Germany's Bundesbank* (New York: Times Books, 1993), pp. 53–54. In 1994, President Clinton appointed Janet Yellen, an economics professor from Berkeley to the FRB. Dr. Yellen is the fourth woman to serve on the Board of Governors.

Federal Open Market Committee (FOMC). The main policy-making body of the Fed is the **Federal Open Market Committee (FOMC)**. The FOMC conducts the day-to-day buying and selling of government securities, which is the chief method used to control the money supply (described later in the chapter). The FOMC consists of 12 members, including the Board of Governors, the president of the New York Federal Reserve bank, and four other reserve bank presidents who are appointed on a rotating basis.

Federal Open Market Committee (FOMC) The chief policy arm of the Federal Reserve system; buys and sells government securities to control the money supply.

The Independence of the Fed

The central bank of the United States is different from the central banks of most other industrialized nations in that it is not a branch of government and its activities are subject to few formal governmental controls.[6] The Fed is required to report periodically to Congress, however, and proposals to bring the Fed under the control of Congress or the Treasury surface regularly.

There are both advantages and disadvantages to the Fed's independence. The main advantage is that monetary policy is somewhat removed from the vagaries of politics so that the Fed has less incentive to try to manipulate the economy before an election. On the other hand, the independence of the Fed can make it difficult to coordinate monetary and fiscal policy. The independence of the Fed also makes it easy for the president or Congress to blame the Fed for economic troubles; if the Fed were a branch of the government, this might be harder to do.

The independence of the Fed is a perennial issue. Some economists have argued that the Fed should be independent but that the president should be allowed to appoint the chair upon assuming office. Others have argued that the Fed should remain independent but be required by law to engage in monetary policies consistent with goals set out by Congress. The Focus box on page 740 addresses the issue of Fed independence in more detail.

TOOLS OF THE FEDERAL RESERVE

The Federal Reserve has three main tools that can be used to change the money supply: open market operations, the required reserve ratio, and the discount rate. The Fed also has a variety of minor tools at its disposal that can be used to change credit and financial conditions.

Open Market Operations

Like all banks, the Fed has an investment portfolio, much of which consists of U.S. Treasury bills and other government securities.[7] The government sells securities when it needs to borrow money to finance its deficits. The Fed carries out most day-to-day control of the money supply by buying and selling government securities from its portfolio. These transactions are carried out on the open market, so these operations are called open market operations.

---

[6]Two other countries that also have independent central banks are Germany and Japan.
[7]We discussed different kinds of government debt instruments in Chapter 6.

FOCUS ON

DOES THE FED RESPOND TO POLITICAL PRESSURE?

Public opinion polls consistently show that economic concerns are among the most important issues to voters, and many investigators believe that politicians use fiscal policy to fight unemployment as elections approach. Then, once the election is over, they must turn around and fight inflation. Though not definitive, the evidence suggests that this has been done on numerous occasions and in several countries.

In the eyes of some people, the strongest argument for an independent Federal Reserve is that it would be free from partisan politics. Is it possible that even the independent Fed can be swayed by the political process? Perhaps, but the data do not reveal anything systematic. Robert Auerbach of the University of California—Riverside contends that the Federal Reserve preserves its independence precisely by carrying out the president's wishes —most of the time. Acting any other way would result in calls for institutional reform to limit the Fed's independence. Robert Hetzel of the Federal Reserve Bank of Richmond, carries this analysis a step further. To fend off congressional controls, the Fed is forced to pursue politically safe short-term goals instead of possibly more appropriate long-term goals.

Some people, including writers at the British news magazine, *The Economist*, approach the subject from a different angle. They believe that infla-

Economics Professors Janet Yellen of Berkeley (second from left) and Alan Blinder of Princeton (far right) meet the press upon their nomination to the Federal Reserve Board in the spring of 1994. Making the presentations are (left-right) White House Economics Advisor Robert Rubin, Secretary of the Treasury Lloyd Bentsen, and Counsel of Economic Advisors Chief Laura Tyson.

tion has been too high in the United States largely because the Fed has refused to attack inflation head-on. Doing so would require a policy of slow growth of the money supply. The catch is that such a policy might cause unemployment to rise to politically intolerable levels. The suggestion is that the Fed is not so independent after all. Nevertheless, it is also easy to demonstrate (as we do in Chapter 30) that if the Fed is as concerned about unemployment as it is about inflation, it has a strong incentive to adopt a high inflation policy—regardless of the

presence or absence of political pressure.

Perhaps we do have the best of all worlds: a central bank that can be independent when it needs to be, but one where the omnipresent threat of institutional reform keeps activities in line with the wishes of our elected representatives.

SOURCES: Robert D. Auerbach, "Institutional Preservation and the Federal Reserve," *Contemporary Policy Issues* 9 (July 1991): 45–58; Robert Hetzel, "Central Banks Independence in Historical Perspective," *Journal of Monetary Economics* 25 (January 1990): 165–76.

Open market operations affect the level of bank reserves, and thus the amount of money in circulation. If the Fed wants to decrease the money supply, it sells more securities than it buys. When banks and securities dealers buy securities from the Fed, they write checks payable to the Fed. This reduces the amount of cash and bank reserves in the economy, so both the monetary base and the money supply fall. The reverse happens when the Fed buys more securities than it sells: the Fed gives banks and securities dealers checks in exchange for the securities. If these checks are deposited in commercial banks, the level of bank reserves increases; if these checks are cashed, the amount of currency in circulation increases so the monetary base and the money supply increase.

OPEN MARKET OPERATIONS

- If the Fed buys securities:
$$MB \uparrow \text{ and } M^s \uparrow$$
- If the Fed sells securities:
$$MB \downarrow \text{ and } M^s \downarrow$$

The Required Reserve Ratio

The most powerful, but least often used tool the Fed has, is its ability to change the reserve ratio. A decrease in the required reserve ratio means that banks can lend out a higher multiple of their reserves. This increases both the money multiplier and the money supply. An increase in the reserve ratio does just the opposite: banks can lend out only a smaller multiple of their reserves so both the money multiplier and the money supply fall.

CHANGING THE REQUIRED RESERVE RATIO

- If the Fed raises the required reserve ratio:
$$rr \uparrow \rightarrow mm \downarrow \text{ and } M^s \downarrow$$
- If the Fed lowers the required reserve ratio:
$$rr \downarrow \rightarrow mm \uparrow \text{ and } M^s \uparrow$$

The Fed rarely raises the reserve ratio because such changes can have too much of an impact on the economy. If a bank had no excess reserves—a condition known as being "loaned up"—an increase in the required reserve ratio would force the bank to borrow or call in outstanding loans. This could lead to a financial panic. In recent years, most changes in reserve requirements have been for technical reasons, though the reduction of the reserve requirement on demand deposits from 12 to 10 percent in early 1992 seems to have been part of a monetary policy stimulus program. It may have also been an effort to increase the profitability of the banking system by reducing the percentage of non-interest-earning assets in banks' portfolios.

Reserve requirements differ depending on the kind of deposits; in general, they are higher for accounts with frequent transactions and lower for accounts that stay in the bank for long periods of time. For example, the reserve requirement on Individual Retirement Accounts is zero because these are long-term accounts with infrequent transactions. As the financial system evolves and new kinds of accounts are introduced, the Fed responds by changing reserve requirements.

FOCUS ON

PRINTING MONEY, INFLATION, AND THE DEFICIT

If you read the editorial pages even occasionally, you have inevitably come across an essay by a so-called expert stating that the government is paying for the deficit by "printing money" and that this was causing inflation. There is some truth to the idea that excessive money growth can cause inflation; we will develop that idea in the next chapter. But it is *not* true that the government has been "printing money" to pay for the deficit—at least not for about hundred years. When the Treasury runs a deficit—as it has for most of the past 50 years—it must borrow the money to pay for it. It does this by selling treasury bills, savings bonds, and other kinds of government securities. These securities are usually sold to members of the public who pay for them by writing checks to the Treasury. The deficit is financed—*and no money has been printed*!

The only time it is correct to say that the deficit has been financed by "printing money" is when the Fed buys new-issue government securities. The Fed cannot normally buy securities directly from the Treasury; they must be bought in the open market. When the Fed does buy these securities, however, it pays for them by writing a check to the seller—one of

the few securities dealers licensed to sell new-issue government securities. The Fed's act of writing a check to pay for the newly issued securities does increase the money supply—just as if the Fed had turned on the printing presses. This process is known as "monetizing the deficit."

How much of the debt does the Fed monetize? Very little in recent years. For example, during the high-deficit years of the 1980s, less than 0.1 percent of the annual deficit was mone-

tized. No economist would say that this was enough to cause inflation. Things have not always been this way, however. During the Civil War, a large portion of the war debt was monetized—enough to generate rapid inflation. And many of the developing countries—Brazil, Mexico, and Venezuela, to name just three—have frequently resorted to printing money to take care of government debt. The result has been what one would expect: rapid inflation.

••••**TABLE 28.2 RESERVE REQUIREMENTS**
OF DEPOSITORY INSTITUTIONS

Type of Deposit:	Requirements	
	Percentage of Deposits	Effective Date
Net Transaction Accounts		
$0–$51.9 million	3%	12/21/93
More than $51.9 million	10	12/21/93
Nonpersonal time deposits	0	12/27/90
Eurocurrency liabilities	0	12/27/90

NOTE: Net Transactions Accounts include all deposits against which the depositor is permitted to make withdrawals by negotiable or transferable instrument or telephone for the purpose of making payments to third persons; this essentially means checkable accounts. MMDAs and similar accounts are excluded.
SOURCE: *Federal Reserve Bulletin,* March 1994, Table 1.15.

Table 28.2 presents official reserve requirements as of December 1993. Notice that small banks—those with less than $51.9 million in transactions accounts—have lower reserve requirements than larger banks. However, because most deposits are held in banks with more than $51.9 million in deposits, the legal reserve requirement for transaction accounts is, in effect, 10 percent.[8]

••••••••

The Discount Rate

All financial institutions that issue checking accounts are now required to be members of the Federal Reserve system. This gives the institutions the right to borrow reserves from the Fed—and thus fulfills the Fed's role as a lender of last resort. However, most recent lending by the Fed has not been of the "lender of last resort" variety but rather has occurred because banks had a temporary need for reserves. The interest rate financial institutions pay when they borrow from the Fed is called the *discount rate (d)*. If the Fed lowers the discount rate, banks will be more inclined to borrow reserves from the Fed than other sources; this will give them reserves with which to expand the monetary base and increase the money supply. An increase in the discount rate does the opposite: the monetary base falls and the money supply shrinks.

CHANGING THE DISCOUNT RATE

• If the Fed raises the discount rate:
$$d \uparrow \rightarrow MB \downarrow \text{ and } M^s \downarrow$$
• If the Fed lowers the discount rate:
$$d \downarrow \rightarrow MB \uparrow \text{ and } M^s \uparrow$$

Banks have other sources of funds, so a change in the discount rate may not have an immediate or appreciable effect on bank borrowing. In fact, some observers feel

[8]It should be mentioned that the footnotes accompanying the table in the *Federal Reserve Bulletin* complicate the picture somewhat. For example, financial institutions that report reserves to the Fed quarterly have different reserve requirements than institutions that report weekly.

FOCUS ON

THE SAVINGS AND LOAN ASSOCIATION CRISIS

For most of the 1980s, it was hard to pick up a newspaper without reading something about the savings and loan crisis. Hundreds of savings and loan associations (S&Ls) went bankrupt in the 1980s, and in 1989, the Bush administration estimated that another 700 would have to be closed over the next 10 years. Although not a single depositor has yet to lose any money, the cost to the taxpayers may exceed $180 billion. It is hard to pin the collapse of the S&Ls on any particular event. Several things, taken together, were responsible.

BACKGROUND

Savings banks and savings and loan associations, or "thrifts" as they are often called, have been around since the early nineteenth century, and for most of that time, they concentrated primarily on home mortgages. To encourage mortgage lending, Congress gave the thrifts special tax breaks and interest rate regulations. These regulations assured that S&Ls could pay slightly higher interest rates on savings

account deposits than could commercial banks, and because it was illegal to pay interest on checking account deposits, the thrifts were assured a steady flow of low-interest deposits. This allowed them to offer home mortgages at low rates.

Things went well until the 1970s. With both inflation and interest rates rising to double digits, depositors took their money out of the regulated low-interest accounts at S&Ls, often putting it in money market accounts at brokerage houses or commercial banks. The act of taking money out of low interest–earning accounts in commercial banks, S&Ls, and other financial intermediaries and putting it into higher interest–earning assets such as treasury securities is called *disintermediation*. It soon became apparent that a policy change was necessary if the thrift industry was to survive.

DEREGULATION

Congress passed two important pieces of financial legislation in the 1980s, the Depository Institutions Deregulation

and Monetary Control Act of 1980 (DIDMCA) and the Depository Institutions Act of 1982 (Garn–St. Germain Bill). These two acts removed interest rate ceilings and permitted thrifts to invest in a wider variety of assets.

While many economists applauded DIDMCA and Garn–St. Germain, problems arose almost immediately. One problem was that many of the newly deregulated thrifts found that they soon had a serious *maturity gap* on their hands: they were now able to attract funds by paying high interest rates on their deposits, but almost all of their existing assets were in long-term mortgages that paid much lower interest rates. Liabilities (deposits) were short term and assets (primarily mortgages) were long term, so rising interest rates raised costs more than revenues—not a healthy prospect for business. This maturity gap was perhaps the most fundamental problem the thrifts faced in the 1980s, but fraud and scandals contributed to their difficulties as well.

that in the past 20 years or so the discount rate has been used more to signal pending changes in Federal Reserve policy than to change monetary policy directly. The most important alternate source of bank borrowing is the *federal funds market*, which consists of very short-term interbank reserve borrowing. The interest rate on these loans, the *federal funds rate*, is determined by market forces, and only indirectly influenced by Fed policy. Nevertheless, the Fed monitors the federal funds rate closely as a barometer for credit conditions and uses the rate as information in its conduct of monetary

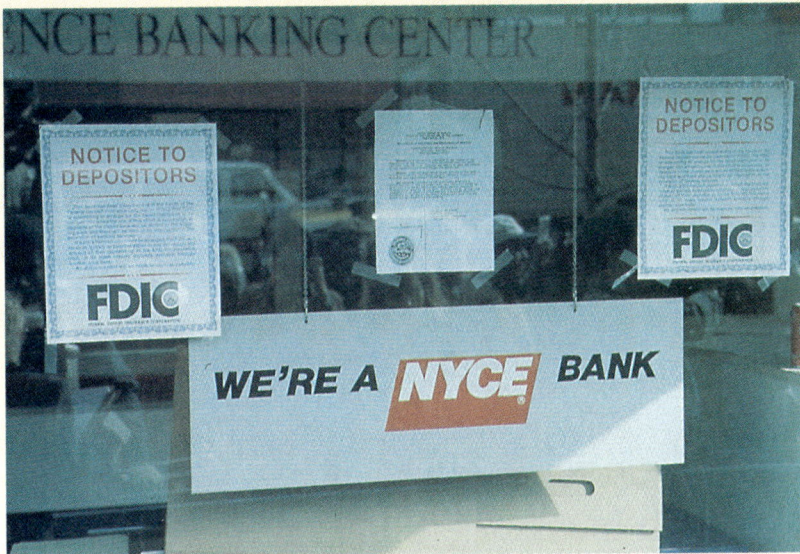

Bank closing by FDIC

over by the Federal Deposit Insurance Corporation (FDIC), which had formerly insured only commercial banks.

THE FIRRE ACT OF 1989

In 1989, Congress passed the Financial Institutions Reform, Recovery, and Enforcement (FIRRE) Act to bail out the insolvent thrifts. Initially, $50 billion in government bonds were sold to raise money to pay off depositors. The FIRRE Act authorized the formation of the Resolution Trust Corporation (RTC) to assume responsibility for the failing thrifts. Depending on the circumstances, the RTC sold, merged, or shut down insolvent thrifts.

The problems of the 1980s have led to a new series of regulations to reduce the amount of risk. More attention is also being paid to fraud and corruption, but the problems of the thrift industry will be with us for some years to come. If it is any consolation, some economists believe that once the current problems are behind us, the financial system of the future will be stronger than it was in the past—precisely because of the elimination of costly and inefficient regulations. Other economists are not so sanguine.

RISKY INVESTMENTS

The new regulations also allowed the thrifts to invest in more risky assets—commercial real estate and oil were two of the more popular investments in the early 1980s. By investing in high-risk, high-return assets, the thrifts were able to offer very high rates of return on their deposits. Further, because the thrifts were insured by the Federal Savings and Loan Insurance Corporation (FSLIC), depositors did not have to worry about the risk associated with such investments. If the thrift folded, you would get your money (up to $100,000) back from the government. But when the commercial real estate market collapsed and oil prices plummeted, thrifts all over the country—but especially in Texas, Oklahoma, and California—began to fold overnight. The industry collapse was so severe that the FSLIC ran out of funds in 1989 and had to be taken

policy. Many economists believe that the federal funds rate is a good indicator of future Fed policies.[9]

[9]This view is held by Alan Blinder, who was appointed to the Board of Governors of the Fed in 1994 by President Clinton after serving on the president's Council of Economic Advisers, and was reported in Ben S. Bernanke and Alan S. Blinder, "The Federal Funds Rate and the Channels of Monetary Transmission," *American Economic Review* 82 (September 1992): 901–21.

FOCUS ON

REFORMING THE FINANCIAL SYSTEM

In the opinion of some economists, the thrifts are not the only financial institutions in trouble. The entire financial system may have almost as many problems. Commercial bank failures have not, to date, been as severe as those in the thrift industry, but hundreds of commercial banks failed in the last half of the 1980s, and the trend has improved little so far in the 1990s. In 1991, the FDIC counted over 1,000 commercial banks on its problem list. This is not the time to run to your bank and take out your money—remember that all deposits up to $100,000 are insured—but it is a time to rethink the philosophy of bank and thrift regulation. Several issues are being considered by economists and policymakers.

RISK-BASED CAPITAL STANDARDS

All businesses must have capital—shareholder stock or other assets that provide a financial cushion in the

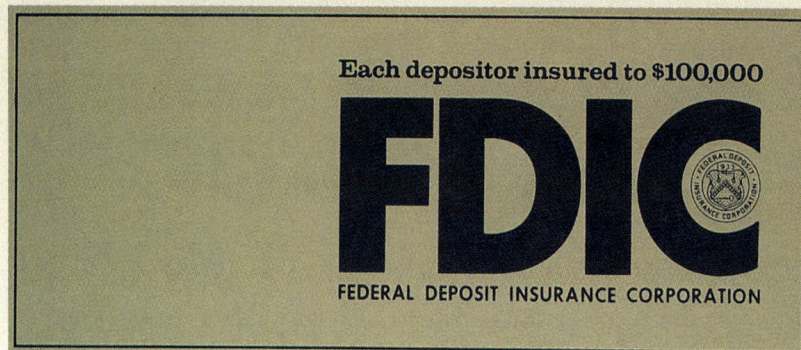

Each depositor insured to $100,000

FDIC

FEDERAL DEPOSIT INSURANCE CORPORATION

event of short-term losses. Bank capital is no different, except for one thing: bank capital is often an *extremely* small fraction—only 3 or 4 percent—of total assets. Low capital ratios mean not only thinner cushions for temporary losses, but they may also encourage bankers to take excessive risks because there is so little to lose.

Low capital ratios were not a serious problem until the 1980s when deregulation allowed banks and thrifts to invest deposits in more risky assets. Partially in response to the record number

of bank and thrift failures, the Bank of International Settlements—an international organization that coordinates and regulates international banking practices—implemented *risk-based capital standards*. Risk-based capital standards require banks that make risky investments to hold higher levels of capital. For example, bank capital must be at least 8 percent of risky investments like commercial and industrial loans but only 4 percent of less risky investments like home mortgages. The new capital standards will

· · · · · · · ·

The Fed's Minor Tools

In addition to the three major tools, the Fed has an array of minor tools. Two of the most important are the ability to set margin requirements on stock market purchases and the power to enact selective credit controls.

People can buy stock by making only a small down payment. This is called buying on the *margin*. Margin purchases can result in a large percentage return if the stock rises before it is sold, but can be devastating if the stock price falls. This is how buying on the margin works: Suppose you were able to buy a share of $100 stock with a

make the banking industry less profitable—but less risky as well.

INTERNATIONAL COMPETITION

The domestic banking industry is facing increased competition from international banks. Large international banks are establishing branches in the United States; for example, almost 25 percent of the bank deposits in California are held in nondomestic banks. There is nothing inherently wrong with foreign branch banks in the United States; the fact that so many depositors choose to use their services is a clear indication that they are beneficial to the consumer. However, foreign banks often have a competitive advantage over domestic banks because they are regulated less stringently—although foreign banks with operations in the United States are subject to Federal Reserve regulations.

One difference between U.S. commercial banks and foreign commercial banks is that, with few exceptions, U.S. banks cannot underwrite corporate securities. This business is reserved for investment banks because it is considered too risky for commercial banks. Precisely because it is risky, however, security underwriting can have a high return. Foreign banks that can make this return can offer better service to their depositors. Allowing commercial banks to underwrite securities would require overturning the Glass-Steagall Act of 1933, which specified the legal activities of commercial and industrial banks. Some economists favor elimination of the Glass-Steagall Act, but whether this can or should be done at a time of massive bank failures is questionable.

MORAL HAZARD AND DEPOSIT INSURANCE

The rash of thrift and bank failures in the 1980s and 1990s bankrupted the FSLIC and has forced the FDIC to ask Congress for billions of dollars. Perhaps surprisingly, many economists responded by saying that deposit insurance should be reduced or even eliminated. Their reasoning went like this: If you know that your deposits are insured, you are less likely to study the investments being made by your depository institution. You will put your money in the bank that offers the highest interest rate and ignore the risk because you know your deposits are insured. In other words, insurance may cause you to take more risks than you would normally take without insurance. This behavior is sometimes called *moral hazard*. Bank managers may be subject to moral hazard as well: knowing that they can attract funds only by offering the highest interest rates, they may be inclined to take more risks than if depositors were concerned about losing their money. The only way to prevent this kind of risk taking is to eliminate deposit insurance, or so the argument goes.

Despite the validity of the economic argument favoring an elimination of deposit insurance, its political prospects are just about nil. As more and more tax dollars are used to fund the FDIC, however, we may see lower liability limits and higher insurance fees charged to banks that make risky investments.

down payment of only $50. If the stock rises to $110, you can sell it, pay the lender (usually your stockbroker) the remaining $50 you owe from your purchase, and keep the $10 profit. The $10 profit, only 10 percent of the initial $100 stock price, represents a 20 percent return on your $50 investment. But look what happens if the stock falls to $90: when you sell it and pay your broker the $50 you owe, you will find that you lost 20 percent of your investment. Just a few losses like that can lead to bankruptcy pretty quickly—just as it did in the stock market crash of October 29, 1929. More stringent eligibility requirements for margin purchases today reduce the chance of a repeat of 1929.

The Fed has used its power to control credit on a limited number of occasions. During the Korean War, minimum down payments on home and auto loans were enacted to reduce spending and dampen inflation. The Fed also imposed credit controls in 1980 to reduce consumer credit card purchases. The result was so disastrous—a reduction in credit card purchases led to a "free-fall" economy when retail sales collapsed—that this power has been severely limited.

RECAP   Tools of the Fed

The Fed has three major and several minor tools it can use to affect the monetary base (*MB*), the money multiplier (*mm*), and the money supply (*M^s*):

1. Day-to-day control of the money supply is carried out through *open market operations*:

   • If the Fed sells securities in the open market, *MB* ↓ and *M^s* ↓ .
   • If the Fed buys securities in the open market, *MB* ↑ and *M^s* ↑ .

2. The Fed's most powerful tool is its ability to change *required reserve ratio*. This tool is so powerful that it is rarely used.

   • If the Fed raises the reserve requirement, *mm* ↓ and *M^s* ↓ .
   • If the Fed lowers the reserve requirement, *mm* ↑ and *M^s* ↑ .

3. When financial institutions borrow from the Fed, they pay an interest rate called the *discount rate:*

   • If the Fed raises the discount rate, *MB* ↓ and *M^s* ↓ .
   • If the Fed lowers the discount rate, *MB* ↑ and *M^s* ↑ .

4. The Fed also has the right to control stock market margin requirements and credit availability

---

SUMMARY

This chapter is a necessary prerequisite for the next two chapters on monetary theory and policy. It should also have helped you understand some of the more pressing economic issues of the day. The main points to remember from this chapter are:

1. Checking account deposits or bank money is the most common kind of money in use in modern economies. Money is backed by government fiat, not gold.

2. Money serves four main functions: medium of exchange, unit of account, store of value, and standard of deferred payment. Money is the most liquid of all financial assets.

3. The main monetary aggregates are M1, M2, M3, L, and Debt. M1 is the most liquid because it is used almost exclusively for immediate transactions; M2 may correlate best with nominal GDP; M3, L, and Debt are broader monetary aggregates.

4. Banks and other financial institutions create money through the process of frac-

tional reserve banking. Banks accept deposits, hold only a small fraction in reserve, and lend out the rest.

5. The reciprocal of the required reserve ratio is the potential money multiplier. The actual money multiplier is less than the potential money multiplier because of cash leakages and excess reserves.

6. The Federal Reserve system manages the money supply and regulates the financial system. The three main tools it uses to control the money supply are open market operations, changing the reserve requirement, and changing the discount rate.

·······KEY TERMS AND CONCEPTS

money
fiat money
paper money
bank money
medium of exchange
liquidity
unit of account
store of value
standard of deferred payment
currency
M1
bank reserves
checkable account
other checkable deposits (OCDs)
M2
overnight repurchase agreement
Eurodollars

money market mutual fund (MMMF)
money market deposit account (MMDA)
M3
L
Debt
fractional reserve banking
required reserve ratio
potential money multiplier ($mm\star$)
actual money multiplier (mm)
monetary base
high-powered money
Board of Governors
Federal Open Market Committee
  (FOMC)
margin requirements
credit controls

·······REVIEW QUESTIONS

1. What are the four main functions of money?
2. Define M1, M2, M3, L, and Debt. Which monetary aggregate is the most liquid? Why? Why have the broader monetary aggregates grown faster than M1 in most years since 1980?
3. Explain how banks create money with fractional reserve banking.
4. What is the money multiplier? What are the differences between the potential money multiplier and the actual money multiplier? How is the money multiplier related to the money supply?
5. What are the main functions of the Fed? How is the Fed structured?
6. What are the main policy tools of the Fed? Explain how each is related to the money multiplier, the monetary base, and the money supply.

PROBLEMS

1. Rank the following according to their liquidity:
   a. Real estate
   b. M3
   c. Rare coins
   d. An automobile factory
   e. Long-term U.S. government bonds
   f. Long-term Polish government bonds

2. Should the Fed be independent of the federal government? Would you favor or oppose a law aligning the terms of the chair of the Fed and the president? What problems do you foresee with requiring the Fed to implement policies designed to achieve goals spelled out by Congress?

3. In many countries of the world, U.S. travelers get a better exchange rate on traveler's checks than they do for cash. Can you think of any reasons for this?

4. Suppose that Individual Retirement Accounts (IRAs) were outlawed, and people were required to shift their wealth into other financial assets. How would this affect the various monetary aggregates? Would M1 grow faster or slower than M3? Why?

5. Only the government can print money in the United States; however, commercial banks can issue traveler's checks. How does this differ from printing money? What if banks gave loans in the form of traveler's checks?

6. State whether and how each of the following affects the money multiplier and the monetary base:
   a. The Treasury sells securities to the public.
   b. The Fed lowers the discount rate in the midst of a severe recession.
   c. The Fed raises the required reserve ratio.
   d. The Fed buys securities from the Treasury.
   e. Financial uncertainty causes people to withdraw money from banks.

7. When the stock market crashed in October 1987, Fed Chair Greenspan announced on television that he would supply liquidity to the market. What did he mean by this statement? Which of the four roles of the Fed was he playing?

CHAPTER 29

Monetary Theory

Try this thought experiment: Suppose a fleet of helicopters flies over the United States and drops a billion $20 bills. Would the economy be any better off? Would factories produce any more goods and services? Would workers be any more productive than they were the day before? It is hard to imagine that they would be. If you were lucky enough to grab a few of those twenties, would you be better off? Could you take that vacation you have always wanted or pay off that nagging debt? Maybe, but only if you jumped pretty quickly. Most economists believe that the long-run effect of an increase in the money supply—even if it comes about in a more standard fashion!—is an increase in the price level. Just increasing the amount of paper in people's hands does not make them more productive workers, and if no more goods and services are available in the economy, the added money will cause prices to rise as people bid against each other. On the other hand, some economists believe that an increase in the money supply can have a positive effect on the levels of production and income in the short run.

This chapter examines the effects of money on the economy. In particular, we need to look at alternative views on the linkage between money, prices, and the real sector of the economy. As with so many aspects of economics, we will find that there is some disagreement, but also a large body of commonly accepted theory.

AFTER READING AND STUDYING THIS CHAPTER, YOU SHOULD BE ABLE TO:

• • • Understand the equation of exchange and its relationship to the quantity theory of money

• • • Know the determinants of money demand

••• Explain how interest rates are determined in the money market
••• Discuss alternative linkages between money, prices, and real economic activity

THE QUANTITY THEORY OF MONEY

One of the earliest efforts to explore the linkage between money and the economy was the *quantity theory of money*. This theory dates back as far as the fourteenth century, and while it has been updated considerably since then, the modern versions are clear descendants of the original insight. In its crudest and simplest form, the quantity theory holds that an increase in the rate of growth of the money supply will cause inflation to accelerate, but have no impact on the level of real GDP. More complex versions allow changes in the money supply to affect real GDP, but only in the short run. To understand these assertions, we first need to develop the equation of exchange, the basis for the quantity theory.

The Equation of Exchange

Equation of exchange The basic building block of the quantity theory of money: $MV = PQ$.

The **equation of exchange** is written as:

$$MV \equiv PQ \qquad [1]$$

Where:
M = money supply
V = velocity of money circulation
P = price index
Q = real GDP

Velocity (V) As in the income velocity of money, the number of times a dollar changes hands in the course of a year.

You should be familiar with all of the terms in the equation of exchange except V, the **velocity** of circulation. Velocity measures how often, on average, each dollar is spent on goods and services in a year. Though velocity is conceptually simple, we will find out momentarily that fluctuations in velocity complicate monetary theory and policy considerably.

Notice the triple equals sign ($\equiv$) in the equation of exchange. This is to indicate that the equation of exchange is really an *identity*. An identity is a relationship that is always true by definition. As stated in [1], the equation of exchange is always true: It takes money (M) to buy goods and services, money changes hands when purchases are made (V), and you pay a price (P) for all of the real goods and services that you buy (Q); therefore, it must hold that $MV = PQ$.[1]

The Crude Quantity Theory of Money

Crude quantity theory of money Early version of the quantity theory of money that assumed both velocity and real GDP were fixed. The theory held that an increase in the rate of growth of the money supply will cause inflation to accelerate.

No one quibbles with the equation of exchange. What did—and still does—generate controversy are the assumptions about V and Q, which change the equation of

---

[1]We should note too that it is impossible to observe all money changing hands over the course of a year, so velocity is estimated empirically by dividing nominal GDP (PQ) by the money supply (M).

···· **FIGURE 29.1** VELOCITY AND PAY SCHEDULES

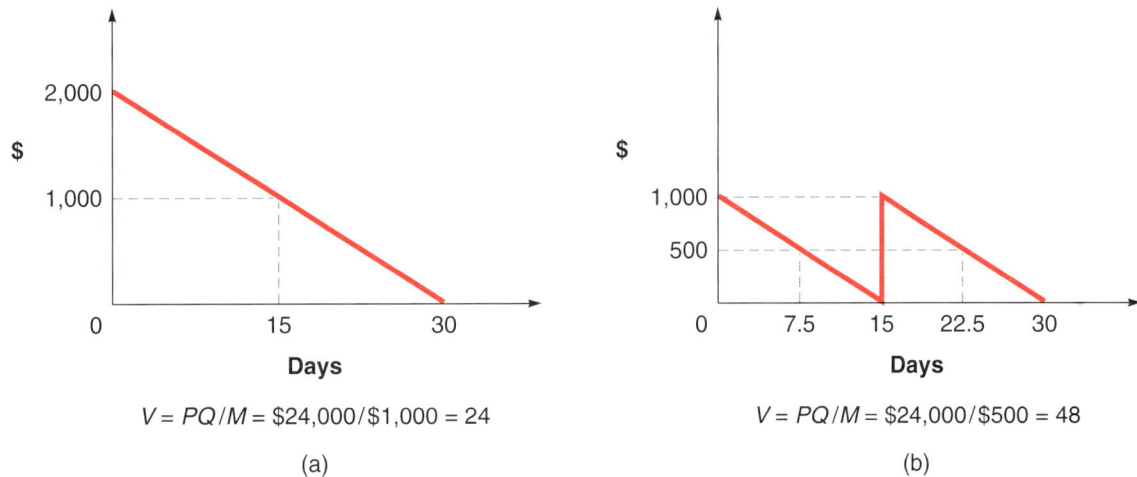

$V = PQ/M = \$24{,}000/\$1{,}000 = 24$

(a)

$V = PQ/M = \$24{,}000/\$500 = 48$

(b)

One of the determinants of velocity is the frequency of pay periods. In panel (a), a $24,000 annual income is paid in monthly checks of $2,000. If all of this money is spent during the month, the average cash balance will be $1,000. In panel (b), the same $24,000 annual income is paid bimonthly with 24 checks of $1,000 each. In this case, the average cash balance falls to $500. Velocity can be calculated as the ratio of annual income (PQ) to average cash balance (M): $V = PQ/M$. The more frequent the pay period, the lower the average cash balance and the higher the velocity.

exchange into different versions of the quantity theory of money. To convert the equation of exchange into the quantity theory, nineteenth-century economists assumed that both V and Q were fixed, at least in the short run. Why did they make these assumptions? They believed that self-correcting forces were strong enough to keep real GDP at its potential level, that is, $\overline{Q} = Q^\star$, where the overbar indicates that Q is fixed. The assumption of a constant velocity requires a bit more elaboration.

Velocity was assumed to be constant because of institutional factors, specifically, the frequency of pay periods. Suppose that you earn a salary of $24,000 per year and receive monthly checks of $2,000. If you spend the same amount of money every day and all of your paycheck every month, you will hold, on average, $1,000. How do we know? You will hold more than $1,000 for the first two weeks of the month and less than $1,000 for the last two weeks of the month; this works out to an average cash balance of $1,000. On the other hand, if you were paid the same $24,000 per year, but received paychecks twice a month, your average cash balance would be only $500. The key is that you can make the same number of purchases regardless of how often you are paid; the frequency of pay periods affects only the amount of cash you hold on average.[2] This is illustrated in Figure 29.1.

How do pay periods and average cash balance relate to the assumption of a constant velocity? Divide each side of the equation of exchange, Equation 1, by M to get:

[2]This is a simplified discussion of velocity; more advanced discussions are best suited for upper-level courses. One complication is whether people buy new or used goods. If you spend your money on new goods, each transaction will increase GDP; if you spend it on used goods, transactions do not increase GDP.

$$V = \frac{PQ}{M} \qquad\qquad [2]$$

Now, if we interpret PQ as your annual income and M as your average cash balance, then velocity is just the ratio of annual income to average cash balance.[3] In the example we have just considered, with monthly paychecks, velocity turns out to be 24:

$$V = \frac{PQ}{M} = \frac{\$24{,}000}{\$1{,}000} = 24$$

while bimonthly paychecks result in a higher velocity:

$$V = \frac{PQ}{M} = \frac{\$24{,}000}{\$500} = 48$$

The general result is that velocity varies inversely with the average cash balance. Some people are paid weekly and some are paid monthly, so the velocity for the entire economy is an average of all individual velocities. Further, pay periods are stable—few people get one paycheck this month and four paychecks next month unless they change jobs—so it seemed reasonable for nineteenth-century economists to assume that velocity was constant.

To see the implications of these assumptions, we need to write the equation of exchange in percentage change form:[4]

$$\frac{\Delta M}{M} + \frac{\Delta V}{V} \cong \frac{\Delta P}{P} + \frac{\Delta Q}{Q} \qquad\qquad [3]$$

Where:

$\dfrac{\Delta M}{M}$ = percentage change in the money supply

$\dfrac{\Delta V}{V}$ = percentage change in velocity

$\dfrac{\Delta P}{P}$ = percentage change in the price index; that is, the inflation rate

$\dfrac{\Delta Q}{Q}$ = percentage change in real GDP

$\cong$ = approximately equal

[3]In fact, this is essentially the way monetary economists find velocity in the real world. They calculate nominal GDP (PQ) and divide it by the monetary aggregate they are interested in—M1, M2, or whatever. The result is an estimate of the velocity associated with the particular monetary aggregate used as the divisor. V1 and V2 are calculated this way in the Focus box on monetary policy in the early 1980s in Chapter 30.
[4]Students with calculus will recognize that Equation 3 can be found by totally differentiating Equation 1. Without calculus, it is best to remember this rule: The percentage change in the product of two variables is (approximately) equal to the sum of the percentage changes in the variables.

In words, Equation 3 says that the percentage change in the money supply plus the percentage change in velocity is approximately equal to the inflation rate plus the percentage change in real GDP. For example, suppose that the initial values are $M = \$1,000$, $V = 5$, $P = 1.0$, and $Q = \$5,000$. Substituting these values into Equation 1 would give:

$$(\$1,000)(5) = (1.0)(\$5,000)$$

Now, if the money supply increases by 10 percent to $1,100, velocity falls by 5 percent to 4.75, and the price level does not change, then Equation 3 requires that GDP rise by approximately 5 percent:

$$0.10 + (-0.05) \cong 0 + (0.05)$$

The corresponding values in Equation 1 are:

$$\$1,100(4.75) = 1.0(\$5,225)$$

Notice that the new value for Q, $5,225, is only approximately equal to 5 percent more than the original value of $5,000—as is required by Equation 3.

But remember that early economists assumed that both Q and V were fixed. In terms of Equation 3, this means that $\Delta V = \Delta Q = 0$. Equation 3 becomes:

$$\frac{\Delta M}{M} \cong \frac{\Delta P}{P} \qquad \text{[4]}$$

This is the result we have been looking for: If velocity and real output cannot change, *any increase in the growth rate of the money supply automatically becomes an increase in the inflation rate*. This line of reasoning led many economists to say that money was a *veil* that hid the real sector of the economy, and that inflation was a simple and not very interesting problem. All that was necessary to restrain inflation was to limit the growth rate of the money supply.

A Modern Version of the Quantity Theory of Money

Few economists today accept the assumptions that GDP and velocity are fixed. However, many economists do believe that they are stable enough to make the equation of exchange usable. The assumption of a stable growth rate of real GDP is derived from the kind of analysis we presented in Chapters 26 and 27; that is, the natural rate hypothesis. Recall that this hypothesis holds that self-correcting forces are strong enough to keep the economy moving toward the potential or natural rate of output. Many economists interpret the natural rate hypothesis to mean that GDP fluctuations tend to be small on average.

Economists rejected the assumption of a constant velocity not because they felt that payment schedules had started to fluctuate, but because they realized that money is used both for transactions—to buy goods and services—and as an asset. If money is an asset, the decision to hold or spend money must depend partially upon the interest rate paid on money and other financial assets. Think of it this way: If you have the choice between holding an asset (money) that pays little or no interest or another asset that pays a higher rate of interest, what will you do? Hold the high

Modern quantity theory of money New version of the quantity theory that does not assume fixed velocity and real GDP.

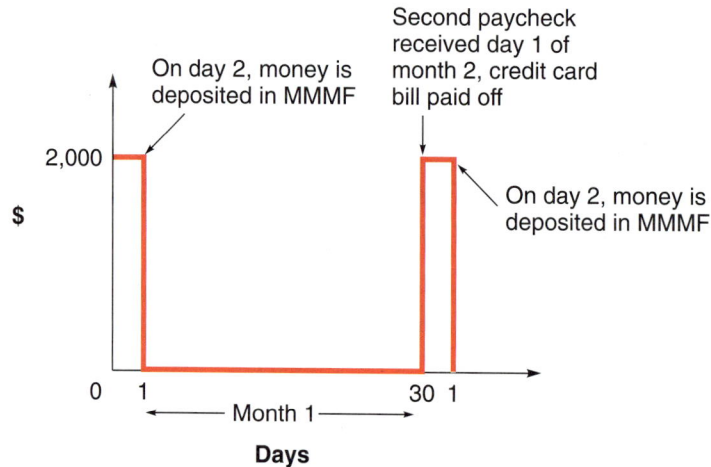

····FIGURE 29.2 VELOCITY AND INTEREST RATES

$$acb = \$2{,}000\,/\,30 = \$66.67;$$
$$V = \$24{,}000\,/\,\$66.67 = 359.98$$

It is possible to deposit money in interest-earning accounts and use credit cards for current transactions. On day 2 of the month, the $2,000 received on day 1 is deposited in a money market mutual fund, and a bank card is used for monthly transactions. At the end of the month, the money is withdrawn and used to pay off credit card debt. The result: Cash balance is $2,000 for one day and 0 for 29 days, so average cash balance (acb) is $2,000/30 = $66.67. Velocity ($V$) is $24,000/$66.67 = 359.98.

interest–earning asset, of course. The only catch is that money provides liquidity benefits that other financial assets do not, so you must trade off the advantages of liquidity versus the opportunity cost of lost interest.

Now, suppose you have the option of paying for your purchases with cash, check, or a credit card like Visa or Master Card. When interest rates are high, you should put your money in an interest-earning asset—perhaps a money market mutual fund—and make as many purchases as possible with your credit card. This would allow you to earn interest on your money until the Visa bill comes due. Further, if you are careful to pay off the entire balance on the bank card every month, you will have no interest payments. In effect, you would be able to use your money for two things: to carry out transactions and to earn interest. When interest rates rose to double-digit levels in the 1970s, this is exactly what many people did.

Figure 29.2 illustrates what happens to velocity when people put their money in short-term deposit accounts and use credit cards to carry out their transactions. Suppose that, as in the example illustrated in Figure 29.1a, you are paid $2,000 per month and that you spend the entire amount every month. On day 2 of the month, however, you take the entire $2,000 to your broker for deposit in a money market mutual fund (MMMF). This reduces your cash balance to zero. You then use your Visa card to make all purchases over the course of the month. On the last day of the month, day 30, you take the money out of the MMMF and use it to pay off your credit card balance. No interest has been charged on the loan, but you have earned some interest on your MMMF. What has happened to your average cash balance and velocity? You held $2,000 for one day and nothing for the remaining 29 days of the month. This makes your average cash balance equal to $2,000/30 = $66.67. Velocity jumps all the way to $24,000/$66.67 = 359.98![5]

The example we just went through is a bit extreme; few people use credit cards for *all* of their transactions. Everyone needs a little cash for incidentals, and if interest rates are not too high, making frequent trips to your friendly broker or the ATM is not worth the hassle. But it should be clear what happens if bank cards are available and interest rates are high: Active cash management becomes worthwhile, average cash balance falls, and velocity increases. More generally:

- In the long run, velocity depends on the technology of transactions; that is, credit card usage and other institutional factors. Velocity has risen over time because of increased use of credit cards and other transactions technologies.
- In the short run, velocity responds to changes in the interest rate. An increase in interest rates will reduce average cash balances and increase velocity; a decrease in interest rates will increase average cash balances and decrease velocity.

Before going on, we need to call attention to a simplification we will be using throughout most of this chapter: most of the discussion refers to "the" interest rate, when, in fact, there are many different interest rates in the real world. The assumption of a single interest rate will simplify the analysis considerably and usually does not alter the important results. The Focus box on page 764 defines and discusses some of the different interest rates in the real world, and the Focus box on page 769, "Forecasting with the Yield Curve," describes one case when it is crucial to examine more than one interest rate.

Applying the Modern Quantity Theory

The possibility that velocity and real GDP can change does not make the quantity theory useless, but it does mean that the theory must be interpreted more carefully and that more information is necessary before using it. For example, if GDP growth is projected to be 2 percent in the coming year, and falling interest rates indicate that velocity will decline by 1 percent, a 6 percent rate of growth of the money supply would result in approximately 3 percent inflation. How do we know this? Substitution into Equation 3 gives:

$$\frac{\Delta M}{M} + \frac{\Delta V}{V} = \frac{\Delta P}{P} + \frac{\Delta Q}{Q}$$
$$6 + (-1) = p + (2)$$
$$p = 3$$

Don't get carried away just yet. The arithmetic we just went through can be valuable, but only as a first approximation. The prediction of 3 percent inflation is only as accurate as the forecasts of real GDP and velocity, and any inference about

[5]But notice that this is referring to M1 velocity because MMMF balances are included in M2.

•••• FIGURE 29.3 THE HISTORICAL RELATIONSHIP BETWEEN MONEY AND INFLATION

There does appear to be a long-term relationship between M2 money growth ($\Delta M/M$) and inflation ($\Delta P/P$), although this relationship does not always hold over the short run. Inflation is measured as the percentage change in the GNP deflator, base year 1958.

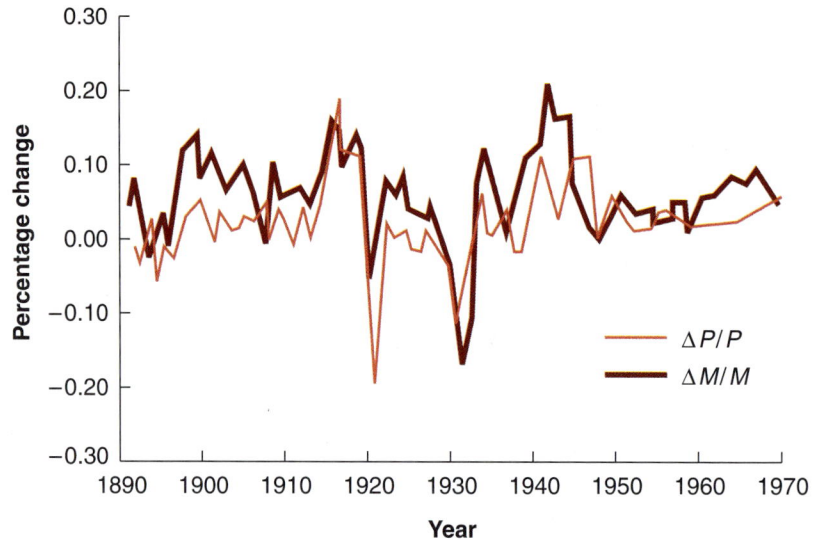

SOURCE: Bureau of the Census, *Historical Statistics of the United States, Colonial Times to 1970* (Kraus International Publications, 1989), Series X 410–419 and F 1–5.

the short run derived from the quantity theory must be drawn very carefully. Figure 29.3, a plot of inflation and the percentage change in the M2 money supply over the period 1890–1970, should make this point clear: Although there does appear to be a strong long-term relationship between money growth and inflation, there are numerous short-term deviations—deviations that would make any forecast based on the quantity theory suspect. Finally, the relationship between money, inflation, and the GDP may have weakened significantly recently—a possibility that, as we will see in the next chapter, complicates the conduct of monetary policy enormously.[6]

Despite such reservations, the quantity theory remains a valuable tool for many economists. In fact, economists at the Federal Reserve have recently been using an updated version of the quantity theory—the $P\star$ model—to make short-term predictions. The $P\star$ model is the subject of the Focus box on page 760.

•••••• SUPPLY AND DEMAND IN THE MONEY MARKET

The quantity theory of money says very little about *how* money affects the economy, only that it does and that it can result in inflation and/or changes in real GDP. As we demonstrated in the application of the modern quantity theory, this is often enough information to be quite useful. However, some economists question whether the direct link between money and the economy is very strong. More

---

[6]It was undoubtedly belief in the relationship between money growth and inflation that led the CIA to flood Iraq with counterfeit currency in the early 1990s. The hope was that inflation would destabilize the economy and result in an overthrow of Saddam Hussein's regime. Iraq complained of the CIA's monetary warfare in a letter to the United Nations dated May 6, 1992. See "Fake Money Used to Destabilize Iraq," *Lincoln Journal* (May 28, 1992): 1+.

···· **FIGURE 29.4 THE MONEY SUPPLY CURVE**

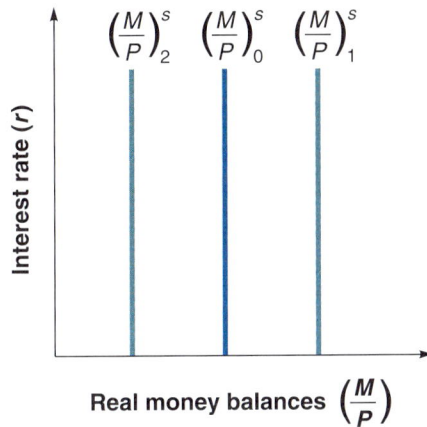

The money supply curve is vertical in interest rate/real money balance space. If we begin on $(M/P)^s_0$, an increase in the money supply will shift the money supply curve to the right, away from the interest rate axis toward $(M/P)^s_1$. A decrease in the money supply will shift the money supply curve to the left toward $(M/P)^s_2$.

important, they argue, is the connection between money and interest rates. The interest rate is just a price—the price of borrowing money—so we can determine how money affects interest rates with a supply and demand model.

·······

The Money Supply Curve

The **money supply curve** gives the amount of real money balances (M/P) available in the economy for various real interest rates (r). The money supply curve is shown in Figure 29.4. Three important facts about Figure 29.4 need to be noted. First, notice that the vertical axis is labeled as the real interest rate. As we found out in Chapter 27, the real interest rate is the nominal interest rate minus the inflation rate: $r = i - p$. Second, we have plotted the real money supply, not the nominal money supply, on the horizontal axis. The value of money depends on the price level so any analysis of the effect of money on the economy must consider the price level as well as the number of dollars in circulation. A rise in the price level will reduce the real money supply; a decline in the price level will increase the real money supply. Finally, the money supply curve is typically drawn as a straight vertical line on the assumption that the Federal Reserve has complete control over the amount of money in circulation.[7]

Money supply curve A graphic depiction of the amount of real money balances available in the economy at various real interest rates; typically drawn as a straight vertical line.

[7]Actually, not all economists are comfortable with the assumption that the money supply curve is vertical. Problems 1 and 2 at the end of the chapter consider two of the reasons why. Banks keep more excess reserves at low interest rates than at high interest rates, so the money supply curve will have a slight upward slope. Also, when loan demand is strong—and thus interest rates are high—banks tend to create new kinds of accounts and find ways to increase loans. This too would tend to result in an upward-sloping money supply curve. The debate over the shape of the money supply curve is ongoing. This issue will come up again in the next chapter.

FOCUS ON

$P\star$: A MODERN APPLICATION OF THE QUANTITY THEORY

In the summer of 1988, the Board of Governors of the Federal Reserve announced a new method for forecasting inflation, the *P-Star*, or $P\star$, model. The new model attracted immediate attention in the media, not only because it was sold as an effective method for forecasting inflation, but because it was extremely simple.

Like the quantity theory, the $P\star$ model begins with the equation of exchange, $MV = PQ$, where M stands for M2 and the rest of the terms are as defined in Equation 1. The equation is most useful when written as:

$$P = M \left(\frac{V}{Q} \right)$$

To use the model to forecast inflation, assumptions about V and Q are nec-essary. The assumptions are that (1) the average value of V is 2.65 and its growth rate is close to zero in the short run, and (2) the growth rate of Q will average 2.5 percent per year. It is then a simple matter to substitute the expected value of monetary growth and solve for $P\star$. This is the price level implied by money growth and the assumed values for V and Q. $P\star$ is then compared to the current actual price level, P. If the current price level is below $P\star$, the forecast is for inflation to accelerate over the next two to three years as prices catch up to their long-run values. If the current rate is above $P\star$, the forecast is for inflation to decelerate over the next two to three years.

The accompanying figure illustrates how the $P\star$ model would be applied. The center line represents the long-run forecast of the price index calculated by substituting money growth into the forecast equation. If the current price level is above the long-run price index, the forecast is for the price level to fall toward the long-run index within a couple of years.

At first glance, the $P\star$ model seems to be nothing more than an application of the venerable quantity theory. It is actually much more than that. Most people use the quantity theory to predict inflation over the long run—say, 5 or 10 years—not over a period as short as two years. If the $P\star$ model is successful for short-term inflation forecasts, it represents quite an advance over the traditional quantity

Shifting the Money Supply Curve. Monetary policy shifts the money supply curve. An increase in the money supply shifts the money supply curve to the right and away from the interest rate axis; this is illustrated by the shift from $(M/P)_0^s$ to $(M/P)_1^s$ in Figure 29.4. A decrease shifts the money supply curve to the left toward the interest rate axis; this is illustrated by the shift from $(M/P)_0^s$ to $(M/P)_2^s$ in the figure. Most changes in the money supply are the result of Federal Reserve policy, so the money supply will increase if the Fed buys securities on the open market, lowers the discount rate, or lowers the required reserve ratio. The money supply will decrease if the Fed sells securities on the open market, raises the discount rate, or raises the required reserve ratio.

. . . .

The Money Demand Curve

Why do people hold money instead of other financial assets? The main reason, of course, is to make purchases, but this is not the only reason. As we found out in the

theory. Unfortunately, it probably does not. It is only as reliable as the estimates of $V^\star$ and $Q^\star$, and both of these variables may be subject to significant change. For example, following the introduction of Super-NOW and other money market instruments, velocity dropped—perhaps because of a decline in the opportunity cost of holding money in M2 accounts. The trend rate of growth of real GDP has also shifted noticeably on several oc-

casions: it was 3.5 percent in the early 1970s and fell to 2.8 percent following the oil shocks—but averaged 2.5 percent over the 1982–1989 period. Clearly, the average values chosen for $V^\star$ and $Q^\star$ are somewhat arbitrary—and the choice will affect the inflation forecast.

This does not mean that the $P^\star$ model is without its uses. It does provide a quick and simple forecast of inflation—and a good starting place for

a more elaborate model. As an example, suppose that $V^\star = 2.65$, $Q = \$6$ trillion, and $M = \$3$ trillion and substitute these values into the $P^\star$ equation:

$$P^\star = 3\left(\frac{2.65}{6}\right) = \frac{7.95}{6} = 1.325$$

If the current price index is 1.2, this means that the price level must rise about 10 percent: $(1.325 - 1.2)/1.2 = 0.10$. Now, if velocity is constant, money growth is 5 percent, and real GDP grows at 2.5 percent over the next few years, we can get a rough estimate of the inflation rate:

$$\frac{\Delta M}{M} + \frac{\Delta V}{V} = \frac{\Delta P}{P} + \frac{\Delta Q}{Q}$$
$$5 + 0 = 2.5 + 2.5$$

At a 2.5 percent annual rate, it will take about four years for the price index to reach its $P^\star$ value.

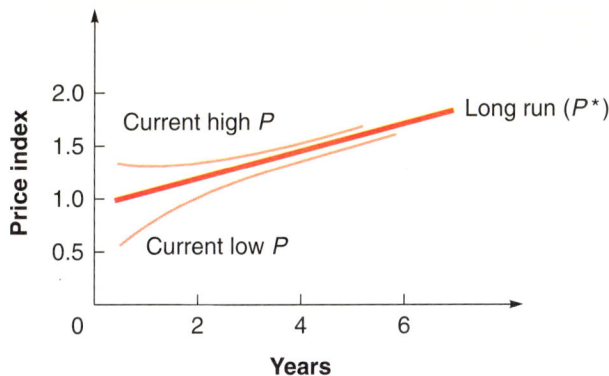

last chapter, money is the most liquid of all financial assets. It is also a refuge against uncertainty. If you are afraid of losing your job, you would rather have your wealth stored in liquid money than illiquid real estate or rare coins; if you are afraid the economy is on the brink of depression, you would probably prefer money to stocks and bonds because the issuing companies may go out of business. Unfortunately, holding money means earning little or no interest because the interest rate on checkable accounts is always lower than the return on other financial assets. The lower interest return on money represents an **opportunity cost of holding money**.

The opportunity cost of holding money provides one explanation for the downward slope of the **money demand curve** as shown in Figure 29.5. People decide how much money to hold by comparing the need for liquidity with the opportunity cost of forgone interest. When interest rates are high, people will spend their money to buy interest-bearing financial assets; this represents a decrease in the quantity of money demanded (a movement *along* a given money demand curve). When interest

Opportunity cost of money Holding money entails earning a lower interest rate than could be obtained on other financial assets.

Money demand curve A graphic depiction of the quantity of money demanded at various interest rates; typically downward sloping.

FIGURE 29.5 THE MONEY DEMAND CURVE

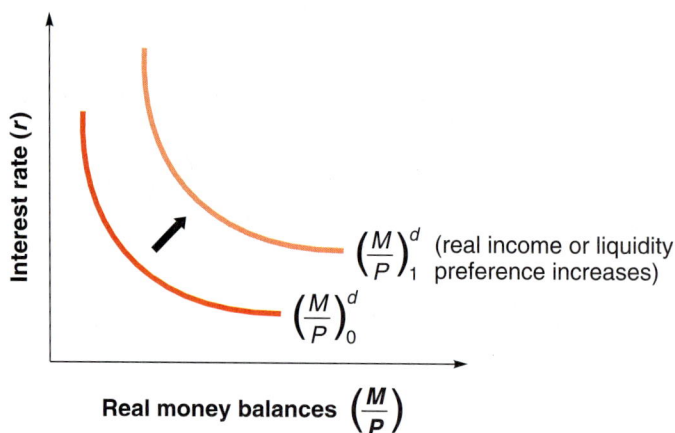

The money demand curve slopes downward with respect to the real interest rate (r) because higher interest rates represent a higher opportunity cost of holding money. At low real interest rates, people will hold money and benefit from its liquidity; at high interest rates, they will hold less money and more interest-earning financial assets. Higher income will lead to more transactions, so people will need to hold more money at every interest rate. This will cause the money demand curve to shift away from the interest axis, as indicated by the shift from $(M/P)_0^d$ to $(M/P)_1^d$. An increase in liquidity preference can also shift the money demand curve outward. Lower income or a decline in liquidity preference will shift the money demand curve toward the interest rate axis.

rates are low, the liquidity benefits of money outweigh the return on financial assets, so the quantity of money demanded will be high.

An alternative explanation for the downward slope of the money demand curve is Keynes's theory of **speculative demand**. In the simplest version of this theory, people must choose between holding money that pays zero interest and holding bonds that pay a fixed return. The decision of which to hold depends on the expectation of future changes in the interest rate. If people expect interest rates to rise, they will be reluctant to tie up their money in bonds. Instead, they should hold their money, wait for the interest rate to rise, and then buy bonds. On the other hand, if people expect interest rates to fall, they should buy bonds so they can lock in the high interest return. This reasoning accounts for the shape of the money demand curve because, on average, more people will expect interest rates to fall if they are currently high than if rates are low; therefore, people will hold less money and more bonds at high interest rates than at low interest rates.

Shifting the Money Demand Curve. Several factors can shift the money demand curve, but the two most important are probably real income and the state of liquidity preference. Higher incomes allow people to make more transactions, and to do so, they need to hold more money. For example, when you were working part-time in high school and your income was only $50 a week, you typically held (demanded) only a few dollars at any point in time. Once you graduate with your economics

Speculative demand People hold money if they expect interest rates to rise; they hold bonds if they expect interest rates to fall.

degree and start earning $600 per week, you will probably keep (demand) more money in your wallet and checking account. In other words, people with higher incomes will desire to hold more real money balances at every interest rate. Graphically, an increase in real income will shift the money demand curve away from the interest rate axis. This is illustrated by a shift from $(M/P)_0^d$ to $(M/P)_1^d$ in Figure 29.5. A decrease in income will shift the money demand curve toward the interest rate axis; that is, from $(M/P)_1^d$ toward $(M/P)_0^d$.

Another important factor that affects money demand is the *state of liquidity preference*. When people fear a pending financial crisis—say, a crash of the stock market or rising unemployment—they often shift out of relatively risky financial assets and into money because money is considered the safest and most liquid financial asset. This means that an increase in liquidity preference will increase the demand for money and cause the money demand curve to shift away from the interest rate axis. A decline in liquidity preference—people are more willing to hold relatively risky financial assets—will cause the money demand curve to shift toward the interest rate axis.

Equilibrium in the Money Market

As Figure 29.6 shows, the intersection between the money demand and money supply curves determines the interest rate, and as money demand or money supply changes, so does the interest rate. How does the intersection between money demand and money supply determine the equilibrium interest rate in the **money market**?

Money market The financial market that trades financial assets with maturities under one year; intersection between money demand and money supply determines the equilibrium interest rate.

• • • • FIGURE 29.6 EQUILIBRIUM IN THE MONEY MARKET

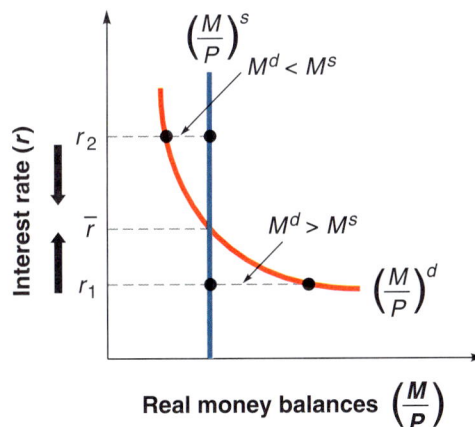

The intersection between the money demand curve and the money supply curve determines the equilibrium interest rate, $\bar{r}$. When the interest rate is above the equilibrium rate, $r_2 > \bar{r}$, the quantity of money demanded is less than the quantity of money supplied. As people use their excess money to buy bonds, the price of bonds will rise, and interest rates will fall. When the interest rate is below the equilibrium rate, $r_1 < \bar{r}$, the quantity of money demanded is greater than the quantity of money supplied. As people sell bonds to obtain money, the price of bonds will fall, and interest rates will rise.

FOCUS ON

INTEREST RATES IN THE REAL WORLD

We have been speaking about *the* interest rate when we should really be talking about interest rate*s*. There are hundreds, perhaps thousands, of different interest rates in the economy. Many different rates are cited by the media, so it is important to understand their differences. The following are some of the more important interest rates you are likely to encounter:

- *Prime rate.* The base rate on short-term loans to large corporations from large U.S. commercial banks. Banks occasionally lend at below the prime rate to their best customers. Movements in the prime are an important indicator of short-term credit conditions.
- *Discount rate.* The rate on loans from the Federal Reserve to member banks to cover temporary bank reserve needs. It is often set at

slightly below the federal funds rate.
- *Commercial paper rate.* High-quality unsecured short-term notes sold by major corporations through securities dealers. Commercial paper rates are typically slightly below the prime rate. Large corporations often issue commercial paper instead of borrowing at the prime rate.
- *Federal funds rate.* The rate on very short-term—often overnight—interbank loans. Banks often borrow in the federal funds market instead of at the Fed's discount window; a good indicator of short-term credit conditions.
- *London interbank offered rates (LIBOR).* The average rate on interbank rates for dollar deposits in London banks; similar to federal funds market in the United States.

- *Treasury bills.* The interest rate on government debt with maturity less than a year. Many money market deposit accounts invest in T-bills; low risk but low return.
- *Treasury bonds.* Also government debt, but longer maturity than bills. Financial analysts use the term "bill" to refer to debt with a maturity of less than a year, "note" for debt that matures in one to three years, and "bond" for longer debt. The longest government bonds have a 30-year maturity.
- *Corporate bonds.* Typically have interest rates somewhat higher than government bonds of the same maturity because they are considered more risky; corporations may default, but the U.S. government almost certainly will not.

Given a fixed money supply, the interest rate must adjust as people trade off the opportunity cost of holding money with the amount of money needed for transactions. For example, when the interest rate, r_2, is higher than the equilibrium rate, $\bar{r}$, the quantity of money demanded will be less than the available money supply. This means that people will be holding more of their wealth in money than they desire. What will they do with this extra money? Some of it will undoubtedly be used to purchase bonds. As the demand for bonds increases, so will the price of bonds. The opposite happens when interest rates are below the equilibrium rate: the quantity of money demanded will be greater than the quantity of money supplied, so people will sell financial assets to acquire money balances. As they do, the supply of bonds on the market will increase, and their prices will decline. How do **bond prices** relate to the interest rate? In a simple but very important way: *Bond prices and interest rates vary inversely*. If we know what is happening on the bond market, we know what is

Bond prices The price of bonds varies inversely with interest rates.

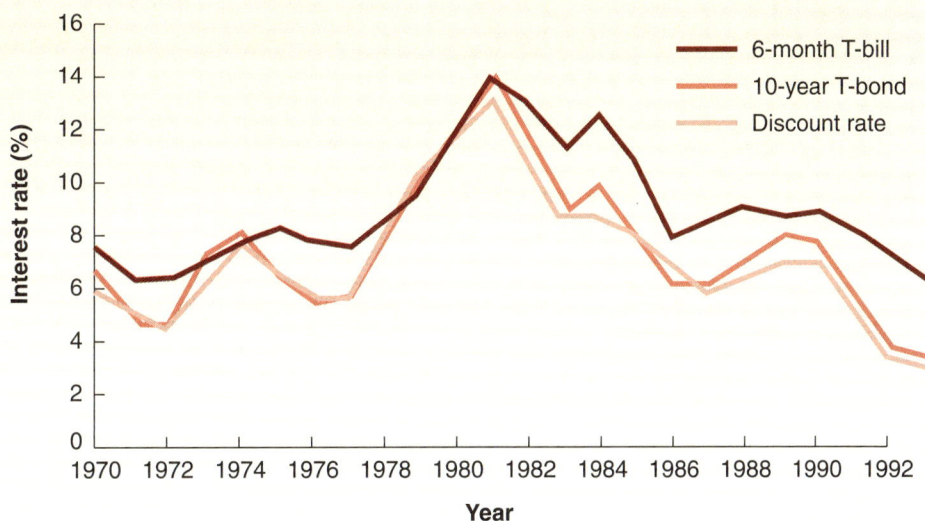

SOURCE: Data are from Table B-72 of the 1994 *Economic Report of the President*.

The figure plots annual average rates for three interest rates: a short-term market rate (the six-month treasury bill rate), a long-term market rate (the 10-year treasury bond rate), and the discount rate, an administered policy variable over the period 1970–1993. As expected, all interest rates tend to move together, but a few points should be noted. First, the long-term rate is usually a little higher than the short-term rates; it also shows less variation. Long-term rates are usually higher than short-term rates because lenders need a higher rate of return to induce them to part with funds for the long period. Second, the discount rate generally moves quite closely with the rate on six-month *T*-bills; when the economy began to falter in the late 1980s, however, the Fed lowered the discount rate in an effort to stimulate the economy. Finally, all interest rates began to fall dramatically in the early 1990s. This brought interest rates to the lowest levels since the late 1950s.

happening to interest rates. To explain why this relationship exists, we need to take a detour into the bond market.

Bond Prices and Interest Rates. Suppose you are offered a bond for $1,000 and the issuing corporation agrees to pay you $100 per year forever. (In fact, most bonds have a fixed maturity date, but the mathematics are simpler with a bond that lasts forever.) You do the calculations and figure out that you are getting paid 10 percent interest on your $1,000 ($100/1,000 = 10\%$). Should you buy the bond? That depends on the alternative uses for your money. If you can invest[8] the $1,000 at more than 10 percent, do so, and do not buy the bond; but if 10 percent is your best financial investment, you should buy the bond.

[8]A caution is in order: The word "invest" refers to *financial*, not *real* investment.

Capital gain Profit made from buying an asset at a low price and selling it at a high price.

Now, suppose that the day after you make the purchase, interest rates fall to 5 percent. Great! You stand to make a substantial **capital gain**. Why? Your bond promises to pay $100 per year, so it is worth as much as any financial asset with the same return. To earn $100 per year on a bank deposit at 5 percent interest, you would have to deposit $2,000—which is also the price you could get for your bond in the secondary market. Of course, had the interest rate risen soon after you bought the bond, you would have had a *capital loss* because the selling price of your bond would be less than the original $1,000 purchase price. Important result: *Bond prices and interest rates vary inversely.* Bondholders make capital gains if interest rates fall; they incur capital losses if interest rates rise.

• • • • • • • •

Shifting the Money Supply Curve

When the Federal Reserve conducts monetary policy, the aim is often to change interest rates. Generally speaking, an increase in the money supply tends to lower interest rates, and a decrease in the money supply tends to raise interest rates. This is shown graphically in Figure 29.7. What is the process that brings about these results? When the Fed increases the money supply, some of that money is typically used to buy bonds. As the demand for bonds increases, the price of bonds rises and as it does, interest rates decline. Alternatively, the money supply increases when banks and other financial institutions have more excess reserves to lend out. Additional lending usually means lower lending rates. The reverse happens when the money supply shrinks: people demand fewer bonds, and banks have reserves to lend, so interest rates rise.

At least two qualifications to the foregoing are necessary. First, if the Fed's actions cause a significant change in inflationary expectations, interest rates may move in the opposite direction than we have just suggested. For example, if the money supply increases so much that people expect inflation to accelerate substantially, the nominal interest rate may rise as lenders add an inflationary premium to loan rates.[9] Second,

[9]This phenomenon is known as the Fisher effect and is discussed in the next chapter.

FIGURE 29.7   SHIFTING THE MONEY SUPPLY CURVE

An increase in the money supply shifts the money supply curve outward toward $(M/P)^s_1$ and lowers interest rates from r_0 to r_1; a decrease in the money supply shifts the money supply curve inward toward $(M/P)^s_2$ and raises interest rates from r_0 to r_2.

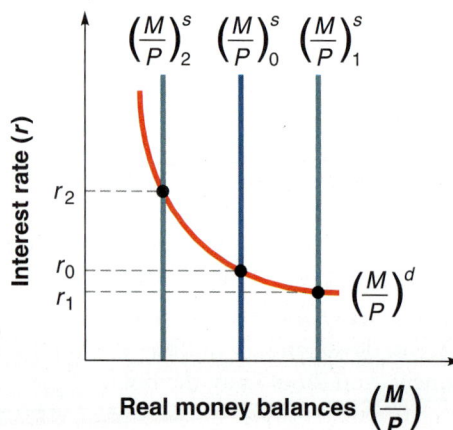

···· **FIGURE 29.8 SHIFTING THE MONEY DEMAND CURVE**

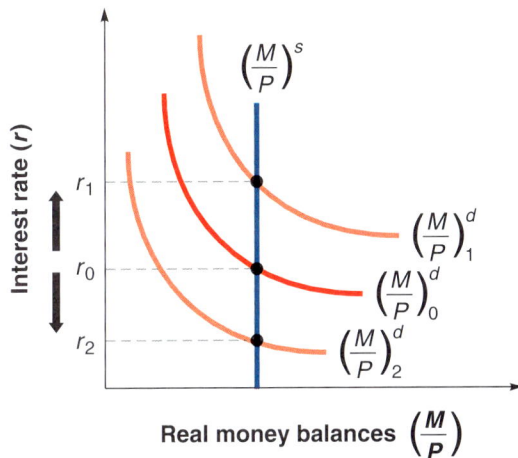

An increase in money demand will shift the money demand curve outward toward $(M/P)_1^d$ and raise the interest rate from r_0 to r_1; a decrease in money demand will shift the money demand curve inward toward $(M/P)_2^d$ and lower the interest rate from r_0 to r_2.

if the economy is in a severe recession, an increase in the money supply may not have a noticeable effect on interest rates. Why not? Interest rates often fall to very low levels in severe recessions—under 2 percent in the Great Depression of the 1930s—and when rates are this low, people have little incentive to buy bonds and other interest-bearing financial assets. If people do not buy bonds, there will be no change in the price of bonds, and thus no change in interest rates.[10]

········

Shifting the Money Demand Curve

Changes in money demand can affect interest rates as well. An increase in liquidity preference or real income will cause the money demand curve to shift outward and increase interest rates; a decrease in money demand will cause interest rates to fall. This is clearly what the graph in Figure 29.8 indicates, but again, what is the *process* that generates these results? Because the money supply is assumed to be fixed, a shift in money demand cannot change the amount of money in the economy. It can, however, change the velocity of money in active circulation. For example, when interest rates are low, some people hold "extra" money waiting for good financial opportunities. When the demand for money increases, interest rates rise, and some of that "idle" money is lent out and enters the spending stream.

[10]This situation is known as the *liquidity trap* and is generally discounted as being highly unlikely by most economists. However, there is at least a shred of truth to it: When the economy is in a *severe* recession, interest rates fall so low that monetary policy may be unable to force them lower and stimulate the economy.

THE MONETARY TRANSMISSION MECHANISM

Our discussion of the money market focused on how changes in money demand and money supply affect the interest rate, which is one of the key linkages between money and the economy. The interest rate is not the only linkage between money and the economy, however. This section looks at different views of the monetary transmission mechanism, or the linkage between money and the economy.

Interest Rate Linkages

When interest rates change, they have a primary effect on interest-sensitive components of spending and secondary effects on many other sectors of the economy. The main kinds of interest-sensitive spending are business investment in new capital, consumer durables, and residential construction.

Investment. We explored the relationship between investment and interest rates in Chapter 24 when we developed the marginal efficiency of investment (MEI) curve. The MEI curve is downward sloping with respect to the interest rate—an indication that higher interest rates tend to depress investment while lower interest rates tend to stimulate investment. Note that we qualified this statement with the word "tend." The MEI curve shifts when business expectations, tax rates, and many other factors change, so it is possible for a higher level of investment to be associated with higher, not lower, interest rates. Still, when the ubiquitous *ceteris paribus* assumption holds, higher interest rates do cause firms to postpone or cut back on investment plans.

Consumer Durables. Consumer durables are goods that last more than a year and include such items as automobiles, televisions, and other "big-ticket" goods. Why are consumer durables more sensitive to interest rate changes than consumer non-durables? Durables last a long time, so consumers can often use discretion in deciding when and whether to purchase these goods. Also, many durables are bought on installment plans so part of the price includes financing costs. A graph of the relationship between consumer durables and interest rates would look just like an MEI curve: high interest rates tend to reduce consumer durables purchases while low interest rates tend to increase them. Factors that can cause the consumer durables curve to shift include a change in consumer confidence and a change in consumer taxes.

Residential Construction. Housing and residential construction are treated as investment in the national income accounts, and both are extremely sensitive to interest rates. It is easy to see why: on a typical 30-year, $100,000 home loan, the monthly payment (not including taxes and mortgage insurance) is $878 at an interest rate of 10 percent, but only $665 at a 7 percent interest rate. Credit agencies determine who qualifies for loans by looking at housing payments as a percentage of monthly income, and many more people would qualify for the 7 percent loan than the 10 percent

FOCUS ON

FORECASTING WITH THE YIELD CURVE

Financial economists are concerned about different interest rates because the spread between long- and short-run interest rates is an important leading indicator of economic activity. Under normal circumstances, short-term interest rates should be lower than long-term interest rates for two reasons: (1) lenders need a higher return to induce them to part with money for a long time, and (2) long-term loans are typically more risky than short-term loans because there is a greater chance of incurring a capital loss. This suggests that the *yield curve*, or the plot of interest rate versus maturity, should be upward sloping as in figure (a).

When long-term interest rates fall below short-term interest rates, the yield curve is said to be *inverted*, and the economy almost always falls into a recession within six to nine months. Why does an inverted yield curve lead to a recession? That's a good question, and one that economists cannot answer definitively. According to one explanation, if the financial markets expect inflation in the future, long-term nominal interest rates must rise to cover this inflation. Inflation often accompanies business cycle expansions, so an upward-sloping yield curve may indicate expansion. Thus, an inverted yield curve may be an indication that the financial markets ex-

pect less inflation in the future and thus a cyclical downturn.

How accurate are forecasts based on the yield curve? Since World War II, *every* business cycle downturn has been preceded by an inverted yield curve. But there have also been some false signals in that the yield curve has sometimes inverted without a corresponding recession. It should be noted too that while the yield curve inverted prior to the 1991–1992 recession, the inversion was brief and corrected before the economy actually turned down. The lesson is simple: like all forecasting tools, the yield curve indicator should be used cautiously and in conjunction with other indicators.

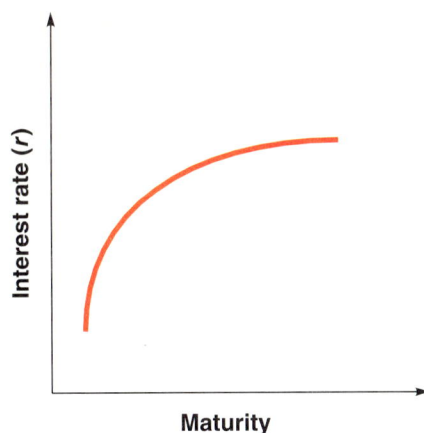

(a) Normal yield curve

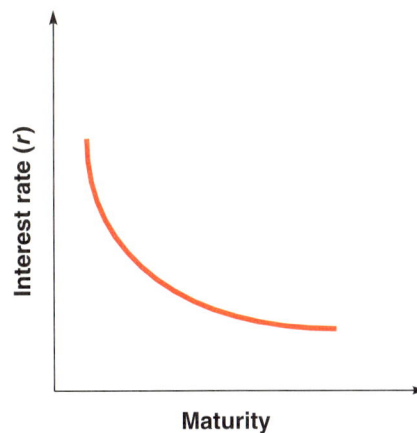

(b) Inverted yield curve

loan. This explains why the housing market responds so violently to interest rate changes. Note, however, that changes in the money supply have a more immediate effect on short-term rates than on long-term rates such as mortgages.

· · · · · · · ·

Graphical Analysis

Figure 29.9 shows the interest rate linkage between changes in the money supply and economic activity. To simplify matters, the diagram illustrates only the link between investment and GDP, but the same results would hold if we were looking at consumer durables, residential construction, or any other interest-sensitive component of spending. The general result is that an increase in the money supply will lower interest rates and raise both real GDP and the price index. A decrease in the money supply will do the opposite: raise interest rates, and lower both real GDP and the price index.

Panel (a) illustrates the effects of an increase in the money supply. As expected, this causes the interest rate to fall from r_0 to r_1. Other things being equal, lower interest rates tend to increase the level of investment, so investment rises from I_0 to I_1 along the MEI curve in panel (b). Investment is a component of autonomous spending, so a higher level of investment will increase autonomous spending from A_0 to A_1 in panel (c). A higher level of autonomous spending will shift the planned spending line upward from E_{p0} to E_{p1} so the economy will move toward a higher level of real GDP, Q_1. But the economy will get to Q_1 only if there is no change in the price level, and as panel (d) shows, this is not the case. Anything that shifts the planned spending line except a change in the price index also shifts the aggregate demand curve. Given the upward slope of the aggregate supply curve, both prices and the level of real GDP rise, and the economy ends up with GDP Q_2, price level P_1, and interest rate r_1.

· · · · · · · ·

Milton Friedman's Theory of Money Demand

Many economists believe that money affects the economy through several linkages other than the interest rate. In fact, Milton Friedman, the dean of monetary economics (see the Economic Heritage box in Chapter 30), believes that the link between money and the economy is so strong that policymakers should refrain from activist monetary management. The key to understanding **Friedman's theory** is to think of the linkage between money and the economy as a theory of money demand: only when people decide to spend their money can changes in the money supply affect the economy; if people decide to hold money, changes in the money supply will have no effect.

Friedman believes that the decision to hold or spend money is a portfolio choice that involves physical goods as well as financial assets. This contrasts with the interest rate linkage we just discussed, which sees money demand as a choice of which financial assets to hold—"risky" bonds or "safe" money. Friedman argues that whenever the money supply increases, some people will end up with too much money in their portfolios. To reach portfolio equilibrium, they will use their excess money to buy goods or financial assets. This will set in motion economic changes—and establish a link between money and economic activity.

Friedman believes that the rate of inflation also affects the demand for money. When inflation is high, people will reduce their money holdings by purchasing goods in order to avoid having to pay the high prices that will prevail in the future. This point is significant: The decision to hold or spend money represents a choice between holding different kinds of financial assets and buying physical goods, so a change in

Friedman's theory of money demand Economist Milton Friedman's theory that the money supply affects the economy through several linkages because money demand is a portfolio choice that involves physical goods and services as well as financial assets. The theory suggests that money has such a powerful effect on the economy that policymakers should refrain from actively managing the money supply.

•••• FIGURE 29.9 INTEREST RATE LINKAGE BETWEEN MONEY AND ECONOMIC ACTIVITY

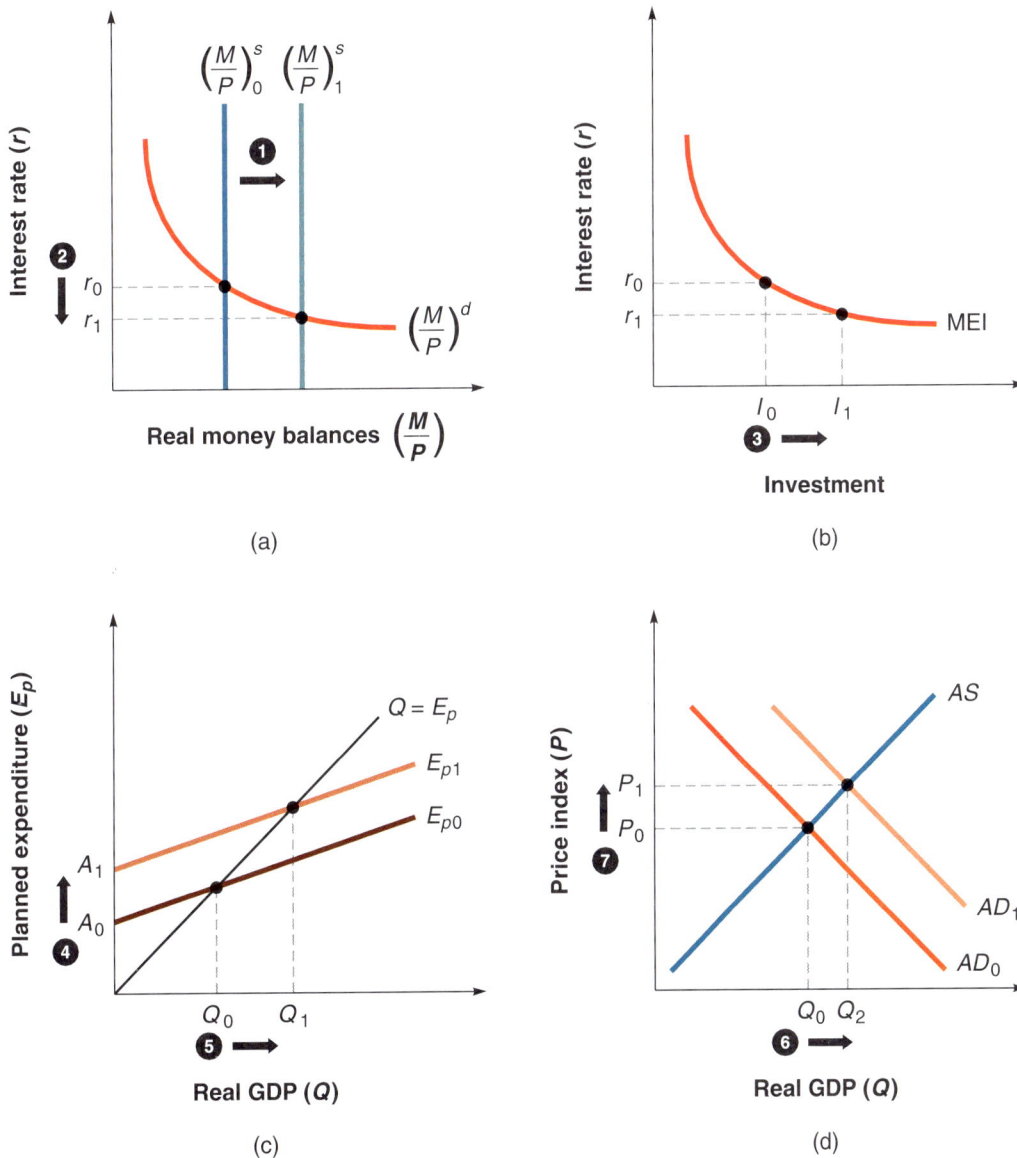

(a)

(b)

(c)

(d)

An increase in the money supply will tend to lower interest rates and raise both real GDP and the price level. In this example, the money supply increases (1) causing interest rates to fall (2). This results in an increase in investment as the economy moves down the MEI curve (3). Higher investment shifts the planned spending line up because investment is a component of autonomous spending (4). This tends to raise equilibrium real GDP (5). Because the aggregate supply curve is upward sloping, however, the increase in planned spending results in both an increase in real GDP (6) and an increase in the price index (7).

the money supply has a potential effect on all kinds of spending, not just interest-sensitive components of spending. This is why Friedman believes that money has such a powerful impact on the economy.

Friedman believes that as a result of these numerous links, money can affect the economy with potentially "long and variable lags." In the short run, the impact will be on both prices and output, but in the tradition of the quantity theory, Friedman contends that changes in the money supply impact primarily on the price level in the long run.

RECAP   The Linkage between Money and the Economy

There are several competing theories on the linkage between money and the economy. Many economists believe that money growth affects the rate of inflation in the long run; the real question is how much it affects real economic activity in the short run. As we discovered in Chapter 26, when the economy is close to potential GDP, the short-run aggregate supply curve is relatively steep so money affects prices more than real GDP, but when the economy is in a recession, the short-run aggregate supply curve is relatively flat so money has more effect on real GDP than on prices.

- "Crude" quantity theory:

  - *Assumptions:* Velocity and real GDP are fixed; that is, $\Delta V = \Delta Q = 0$.
  - *Linkage:* Inflation depends solely on the rate of money growth; that is:

  $$\frac{\Delta M}{M} = \frac{\Delta P}{P}$$

  - *Notes:* Inflation can be controlled by tight money. The theory is generally dismissed for short-run analysis.

- Modern quantity theory:

  - *Assumptions:* Velocity and real GDP can vary, but are predictable. Velocity depends on the interest rate in the short run and institutional factors in the long run.
  - *Linkage:* Changing the money supply affects both the price index and real GDP in the short run, but only the price index in the long run.
  - *Notes:* The percentage change formulation of the equation of exchange:

  $$\frac{\Delta M}{M} + \frac{\Delta V}{V} = \frac{\Delta P}{P} + \frac{\Delta Q}{Q}$$

  is useful for quick predictions of inflation and economic growth.

- Money supply and demand model:

  - *Assumptions:* The money demand curve is downward sloping because of the opportunity cost of holding money; liquidity preference and real income are the main shift factors. The money supply curve is assumed to be vertical and controllable by the Fed. The Fed can shift the money supply curve with policy.

- *Linkage:* The intersection between the money demand and money supply curves determines the interest rate. Changes in the interest rate affect interest-sensitive components of spending, primarily investment, consumer durables, and residential construction.

- *Notes:* Activity in the bond market is especially important because changes in the money supply affect the demand for bonds. Bond prices and interest rates vary inversely.

- Friedman's model:

  - *Assumptions:* The decision to hold or spend money is a portfolio choice. People choose between holding money or spending it on goods, services, or financial assets.

  - *Linkage:* A change in the money supply can affect all kinds of spending, even spending on non–interest-sensitive goods, as buyers respond to the anticipation of changing future prices.

  - *Notes:* Money has an extremely powerful effect on the economy, although perhaps with "long and variable lags."

COMPLICATIONS: UNSTABLE MONEY DEMAND

If the crude quantity theory held, monetary theory would be simple and not very interesting: inflation would depend only on the rate of growth of the money supply, severe contractions could not exist, and the study of macroeconomics would not be so vitally important. Unfortunately, things are not that simple. Friedman's theory is much closer to the truth than the crude quantity theory, but it too has a rather serious shortcoming: there is nothing in Friedman's theory to suggest that the demand for money or velocity is *stable*. This was not a problem until a series of studies revealed that the historical relationship between money and economic activity apparently changed in the 1970s. For reasons that are still not well understood, the relationship between money and economic activity underwent a significant change around the middle of the 1970s.

What does it mean to say that money demand is unstable? If money demand were stable, it would be possible to predict how much money people would hold, how much they would spend on goods and services, and how much they would spend on various financial assets for a given income, rate of inflation, and interest rate. And that would mean that policymakers would know precisely how much to increase or decrease the money supply. But if the demand for money is unstable, the response to a change in the money supply is uncertain. For example, suppose the economy is in recession and the Fed decides that monetary stimulus is necessary to bring down interest rates. If people hold more money than is predicted, the increase in the money supply may be insufficient to bring interest rates down to the desired level. But if people hold less money than is predicted, the monetary stimulus may cause the economy to overheat and result in inflation. The problems associated with unstable money demand are illustrated in Figure 29.10. The economy begins at point *a* with interest rate r_0, and the Fed decides that it must increase the money supply to bring interest rates down to r_1. However, the demand for money increases at the same time the

···· FIGURE 29.10 UNSTABLE MONEY DEMAND COMPLICATES POLICY

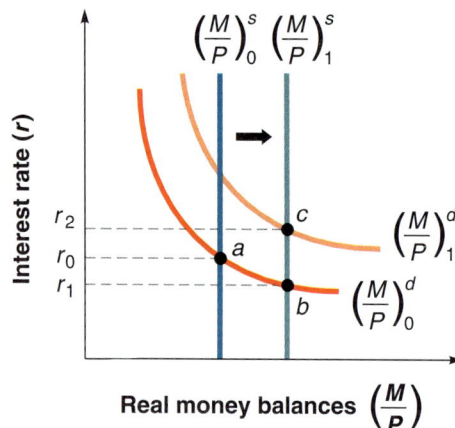

For reasons still not well understood, money demand became unstable in the mid-1970s. This complicates monetary policy considerably. Suppose the Fed wants to bring interest rates down from the current level of r_0 to r_1. Increasing the money supply from $(M/P)_0^s$ to $(M/P)_1^s$ would be sufficient unless the money demand curve shifts outward toward $(M/P)_1^d$. An additional increase in the money supply could bring interest rates down to the desired level, but would also lead to inflation if the money demand curve shifted back to $(M/P)_0^d$.

money supply is increased so interest rates rise to r_2 instead of falling to r_1. If the Fed *knew* that the money demand curve would stay where it is, it might be appropriate to increase the money supply again to get to the desired interest rate. However, increasing the money supply by this amount will be inflationary if the money demand curve shifts back toward its original location.

The question, of course, is *why* money demand is unstable. Several explanations have been offered, but none has proven conclusive. Part of the answer is undoubtedly the pace of financial innovation. People now have many more ways to hold and keep their money than they used to, and the ability to transfer funds between accounts with a phone call or an automatic teller machine makes it hard to determine whether money is being kept in M1 or M2 accounts. Another possible explanation is the internationalization of financial markets. With billions of dollar-denominated accounts in Europe and Asia—it has been estimated that as much as 70 percent of all U.S. currency is held abroad[11]—even small changes in interest rates are likely to open the floodgates for international money movements. Other explanations have been suggested, but the instability of money demand remains a mystery almost 20 years after it was detected. We will have more to say about this issue in the next chapter.

[11]This estimate is from Richard D. Porter, "Foreign Holdings of U.S. Currency," *International Economic Insights* (November/December 1993): 5. Porter is deputy associate director, division of monetary affairs, Board of Governors of the Federal Reserve system. Note that this is an estimate of *currency*, not money; it is doubtful that 70 percent of all U.S. dollar-denominated *money* is held abroad.

SUMMARY

This chapter has surveyed some of the theories on the linkage between money, inflation, and real economic activity. You will find that a thorough understanding of this material will make the next chapter quite a bit easier, but you should still be prepared to be confronted with a bit of disagreement over important policy issues. Monetary theory and policy are two of the most hotly debated issues in contemporary macroeconomics. They are also among the most important. Good monetary theory will lead to good monetary policy. And good policies will have a significant effect on your employment after graduation as well as the value of your savings in retirement. The main points from this chapter are:

1. The crude quantity theory of money holds that if velocity and real GDP are fixed, a change in the money supply can affect only the price level.
2. The modern quantity theory allows velocity and real GDP to change. Velocity is a function of interest rates in the short run and institutional factors in the long run; GDP fluctuates as the economy goes through business cycles. This implies that a change in the money supply affects both real GDP and the price level in the short run, but affects only inflation in the long run.
3. Some economists believe that the linkage between money and the economy is through interest rates. An increase in the money supply usually causes interest rates to fall; a decrease in the money supply usually causes interest rates to rise. Interest-sensitive components of spending, primarily investment, consumer durables, and residential construction, are affected by changes in the money supply.
4. Milton Friedman and others believe that the money supply affects the economy through several linkages because money demand is a portfolio choice that involves real goods and services as well as financial assets. This suggests that money can have an extremely powerful impact on the economy.
5. In recent years, the demand for money has appeared to be unstable. This may have been caused by financial innovations or the internationalization of financial markets. Unstable money demand complicates monetary policy significantly.

KEY TERMS AND CONCEPTS

crude quantity theory of money
equation of exchange
velocity
average cash balance
modern quantity theory of money
interest rate
money supply curve
opportunity cost of money
money demand curve
speculative demand

liquidity preference
money market
bond prices
capital gain
monetary transmission mechanism
marginal efficiency of investment (MEI)
consumer durables
yield curve
Friedman's theory of money demand

REVIEW QUESTIONS

1. Write out the equation of exchange, define each term, and explain why the equation is an identity, not a theory.
2. What assumptions were made to convert the equation of exchange into the crude quantity theory of money? Into the modern quantity theory of money?
3. What factors affect velocity in the short run? The long run?
4. Why is the money supply curve assumed to be vertical? What causes the money supply curve to shift? Why does the money demand curve slope downward? What causes the money demand curve to shift? Draw a diagram to illustrate your answers.
5. What is the relationship between bond prices, interest rates, and capital gains? How is the bond market related to the money market?
6. Carefully explain the linkages between the money market, interest rates, and aggregate demand. How do these linkages compare with the views of Milton Friedman?

PROBLEMS

1. Suppose that banks are able to create new kinds of accounts and do so when they perceive loan demand to be strong. Would this affect the shape of the money supply curve? Would it affect the location of the money supply curve?
2. Banks typically hold very few excess reserves; however, there is some evidence that the level of excess reserves is affected by interest rates. How do you think interest rates would affect excess reserves? How would this affect the shape and/or location of the money supply curve?
3. The text noted that the purchase of consumer durables is interest sensitive. However, suppose you have enough cash to buy a needed consumer durable and thus do not have to borrow money to finance your purchase. Should you be concerned about the interest rate? Why or why not?
4. The chapter listed only two factors that can shift the money demand curve, real income and the state of liquidity preference. These are probably the most important factors, but several other factors can shift the money demand curve as well. Explain whether, how, and why each of the following would shift the money demand curve:
   a. An increase in the price index
   b. An increase in the interest rate
   c. An increase in expected inflation
   d. A stock market crash
   e. Falling bond prices
   f. An increase in wealth
5. Suppose that all wages were tied to contracts that called for wages to rise at 5 percent per year. Would this affect the usefulness of the quantity theory of money?
6. a. Use the $P\star$ model described in the Focus box to forecast inflation over the near term. Assume $Q = \$5$ trillion, $\Delta Q/Q = 2.5$ percent; $V = 3$, $\Delta V/V = 0$; $M = \$2$ trillion, $\Delta M/M = 8$ percent.

    b. Now assume that $\Delta V/V = -1$ percent but that the rest of the information is the same. How does this change your forecast?

    c. Suppose that your GDP growth rate forecast from part (*a*) turns out to be incorrect such that $\Delta Q/Q = 1.5$ percent. If all of the other data in part (*a*) remain correct, what will happen to your new forecast of inflation? Does your answer make sense?

7. Suppose that external supply shocks are estimated to generate 8 percent inflation for the next year. Suppose further that the money supply is growing at 8 percent as well. Forecast what will happen to the economy over the next year. Would you recommend a monetary policy change? Why?

8. Suppose the government passed a law making it illegal for the Federal Reserve to increase the money supply. What would this do to the economy? Would your answer change if there were no wage contracts?

9. How do you think the Christmas season affects the demand for money? Explain using diagrams.

10. Refer back to Figure 29.9. Illustrate a situation where increasing the money supply has (*a*) no effect on the price level and (*b*) no effect on real GDP.

11. The money demand curve is sometimes drawn as follows:
    When do you think such a situation might arise? Why might the money demand curve be horizontal? (*Hint:* See footnote 10.)

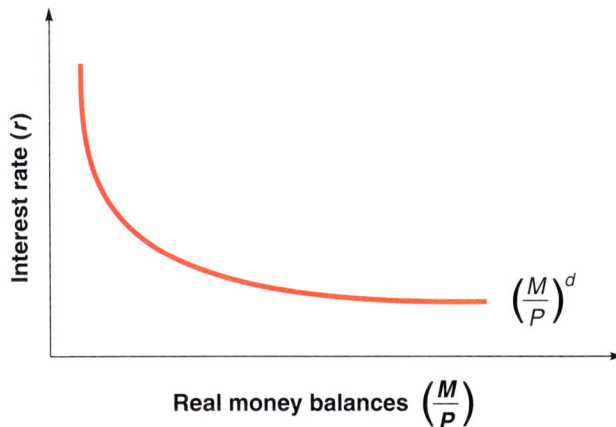

CHAPTER 30

Monetary Policy

Monetary policy involves quite a bit more than just shifting the money supply curve around. It should be coordinated with fiscal policy. The trade-off between inflation and unemployment must be considered. Policies must lead to a feeling of confidence in the financial markets. And in today's economy, no policies can operate in isolation: the monetary policies pursued by Germany and Japan will affect financial conditions and economic activity in the United States and the rest of the world. But perhaps most importantly, monetary policy is complicated because there is only an indirect and often unreliable linkage between the instruments of monetary policy (bank reserves and the money supply) and the ultimate policy targets—employment, inflation, GDP growth, and so on.

This chapter will sort out some of the complications surrounding monetary policy. The operative word is "some." Though the material in this chapter will allow us to better appreciate the importance of the Federal Reserve and monetary policy, we will not be ready to reach any final conclusions concerning the proper conduct of monetary policy until we look at fiscal policy in more detail in the next chapter and examine some policy debates in the following chapter.

AFTER READING AND STUDYING THIS CHAPTER, YOU SHOULD BE ABLE TO:
- • • Distinguish between monetary policy instruments, intermediate targets, and policy goals
- • • Understand how policy lags and credibility influence policy effectiveness
- • • Know the advantages and disadvantages of a constant growth rate monetary policy
- • • Know the advantages and difficulties of interest rate targeting

INSTRUMENTS, INTERMEDIATE TARGETS, AND POLICY GOALS

The Federal Reserve does not have the power to manipulate the economy directly. The connection between the Fed's actions and the real economy is indirect and sometimes tenuous. That connection has three components. First, the Fed has a variety of **policy instruments** that it can use in its conduct of monetary policy. The most important policy instruments are open market operations, the discount rate, and the required reserve ratio—the same policy instruments we discussed in the last chapter. The role of policy instruments is to influence one or more of the Fed's **intermediate targets**. The most important intermediate targets are interest rates and the rate of growth of the money supply. Intermediate targets are important because they can influence the Fed's **policy goals**. These goals include price stability, employment, the balance of payments, and so on. Stated this way, it may appear that the Fed's task is straightforward: manipulate a policy instrument, hit an intermediate target, and achieve a policy goal. Nothing could be further from the truth! The Fed frequently misses intermediate targets, and the connection between intermediate targets and policy goals is imprecise at best.

In and of themselves, intermediate targets are not very important. You care less about the rate of money growth than about what the rate of money growth means for inflation or your prospects for getting a job. Still, the selection of intermediate targets is vitally important because of the connection between intermediate targets and policy goals. The Federal Reserve uses three main criteria in selecting optimal intermediate targets: measurability, linkage, and control.

- **Measurability.** This refers to the ability of policymakers to actually measure the intermediate targets they wish to control. If the Federal Reserve is unable to measure its targets precisely, it cannot be sure of the effects of its policy changes. The two most important intermediate targets, real interest rates and money growth, are both weak in this area. It is difficult to measure real interest rates accurately; further, what might be considered a "low" interest rate in 1990 may be different from what was considered "low" in 1980. As deregulation of the financial system proceeds, the definitions of money must constantly be revised. If you are not even sure how to define an intermediate target, how can you measure it?

- **Linkage.** Even if intermediate targets could be accurately measured, they would be of little value if they were not reliably linked to the ultimate policy goals. This issue has been the source of much of the frustration with recent monetary policy. As we pointed out in Chapter 29, financial innovations, deregulation, and other factors have upset the historical relationships among the money supply, the price level, and nominal GDP. For example, the 1983–1985 recovery in the midst of record high real interest rates and the protracted 1990–1991 recession despite low nominal interest rates caused many economists to question the connection between interest rates and economic activity. This is one reason why some economists advocate a "hands-off" approach to monetary policy.

- **Control.** The Federal Reserve also needs to be able to control the chosen intermediate targets. Can the Federal Reserve control the money supply and interest

Policy instruments The tools available to the Fed in its conduct of monetary policy. The most important are open market operations, the discount rate, and the required reserve ratio.

Intermediate targets Monetary policy officials use policy instruments to control intermediate targets that are thought to have a strong linkage to policy goals. Important intermediate targets include the money supply and interest rates.

Policy goals The ultimate aims of monetary policy; for instance, full employment, stable prices, and economic growth.

Measurability The ability of policymakers to calculate the value of the intermediate targets they wish to control.

Linkage The intermediate target should be reliably connected to the monetary policy goals.

Control The ability of policymakers to manage intermediate targets with monetary policy instruments.

rates? Not directly. The Federal Reserve must use its instruments to affect intermediate targets, and unfortunately, the connection between the instruments and the intermediate targets is often weak. For example, the policy instrument most often used to change the money supply is the level of bank reserves. By buying and selling securities on the open market, the Federal Reserve can change the level of bank reserves. But whether banks lend out their reserves or keep them in their vaults will determine what happens to the money supply.

The problems we have just raised do not mean that effective monetary policy is impossible—but they do mean that the public should not expect miracles from the Fed. The simple fact is that the Fed does not have a "magic bullet" to cure what ails the economy. But economic theory does progress, and policymakers do learn from past mistakes. With any luck, our understanding of the relationships among instruments, intermediate targets, and policy goals will improve with time.

MONETARY POLICY COMPLICATIONS: LAGS, EXPECTATIONS, AND CREDIBILITY

When we used the supply and demand diagrams to illustrate monetary policy in Chapter 29, we conveniently ignored several important ideas including lags, expectations, and credibility. As we are about to see, these issues create another set of complications in the conduct of monetary policy.

Monetary Policy Lags

Monetary policy does not occur instantaneously. It takes time to recognize that a policy change is necessary, time to actually implement the policy change, and time before any impacts are felt. Consequently, three lags are associated with monetary policy actions:

- **Recognition lag.** Before any policy change can take place, data must be collected and trends detected. The time required for this is the recognition lag. The recognition lag takes at least a few months and often longer because policymakers should not act at the first sign of trouble. For example, suppose the Federal Reserve is concerned about inflation. A one-month blip in the consumer price index may be the result of a bad harvest, an oil price shock, or an increase in taxes on commodities like cigarettes. In this situation, the economy is experiencing a one-time increase in the price index, not continuing inflation, and restrictive monetary policy is probably unnecessary. Most economists believe that the Federal Reserve should consider changing policy only when inflation or stagnation is expected to continue for several months.

- **Implementation lag.** The time between the decision to change policy and the actual policy action is called the implementation lag. The chief policymaking body of the Federal Reserve, the Federal Open Market Committee (FOMC), meets every five to eight weeks, so the implementation lag is only three to four weeks, on average. The short implementation lag represents a major advantage of monetary policy over fiscal policy for short-run stabilization. As you may realize, Con-

Recognition lag The time it takes for policymakers to realize that a policy change is necessary.

Implementation lag Once the need for a policy change is recognized, it takes time before policy changes can be enacted. This time is the implementation lag.

Impact lag The time it takes before the economy responds to a policy change.

gress often requires months—or even years—to enact specific changes in the tax law or federal spending.

- **Impact lag.** The impact lag is where most of the disagreement arises. Pioneering work by Milton Friedman and others in the 1950s and 1960s led to the belief that money affected the economy with "long and variable lags." This research implied that monetary policy could have uncertain effects on the economy well into the future. More recent work has raised some questions about these results. It now appears that the lag between monetary policy changes and economic activity is relatively short, but still variable. Many studies show that it usually takes between six months and a year before the economy feels the brunt of a policy change.[1]

Together, the three lags add up to something close to a year. The time required may be the most serious criticism of monetary policy activism—but fiscal policy often involves even longer lags. To be effective, forecasters must be able to predict the path of the economy at least a year in the future. Computer models and economic theory are advancing rapidly, but few forecasters would bet the ranch on their ability to forecast that far into the future.

• • • • • • •

Expectations and Monetary Policy Effectiveness

Expectation formation poses a further complication for the effectiveness of monetary policy and may require modification of what we have just said about lags. Recall that under the rational expectations hypothesis, individuals are forward looking and make optimal use of all relevant information, including probable policy actions by the government. This means that only unanticipated changes in the money supply can have an effect on the real sector of the economy; anticipated money growth affects only nominal variables. For example, consider what happens when a producer learns about faster money growth. Realizing that both her selling price and her input costs will rise in the long run—a prediction of the quantity theory of money—she does not anticipate a change in long-run profits. Consequently, her rational response is to refrain from increasing plant capacity and production. On the other hand, what if she notices that selling prices are rising but is unaware that the rate of inflation has accelerated due to faster money growth? In this case, she might interpret the higher selling price as being due to an increase in demand with no cost increase to follow. Her rational response would be to increase production.

Policy ineffectiveness rule Argues that anticipated aggregate demand policies affect only inflation and have no lasting effect on real output or employment. The rule assumes rational expectations, wage and price flexibility, and the quantity theory.

Such behavior relates to monetary policy in a simple but a very important way. If (1) the rational expectations assumption holds, (2) wages and prices are flexible, and (3) the quantity theory correctly describes the long-run relationship between money and the economy, then *anticipated monetary policy has no effect on the real sector of the economy*! This result, known as the **policy ineffectiveness rule**, means that the Federal Reserve has no influence over the level of GDP or unemployment unless it can "surprise" the economy with unanticipated policy changes.

The policy ineffectiveness rule is illustrated with aggregate demand–aggregate sup-

[1]For example, a recent paper by Christina D. Romer and David H. Romer, "New Evidence on the Monetary Transmission Mechanism," *Brookings Papers* 1 (1990): 149–213 estimated that the impact of money on output peaks eight months after the policy change and declines slowly over the next two years.

·····**FIGURE 30.1** EXPECTATIONS AND MONETARY POLICY

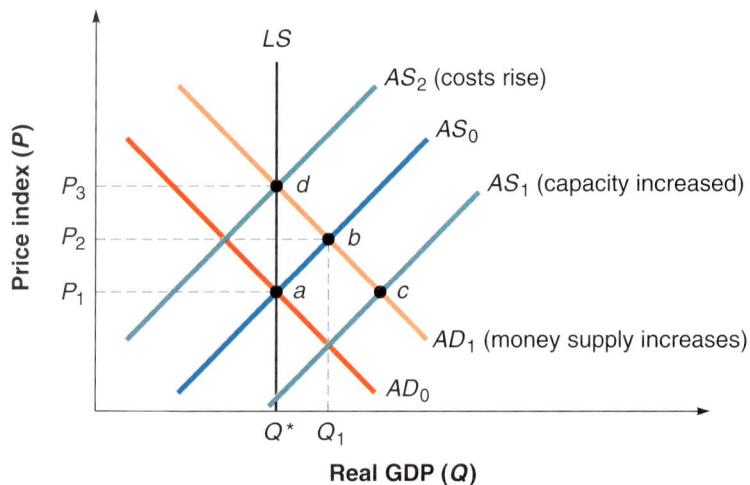

The economy begins at point *a*, and the Fed increases the money supply. The path of the economy depends on how expectations are formed. If producers observe higher prices at point *b*, but do not realize there has been a monetary expansion, they may respond by increasing plant capacity and production. This would shift the short-run aggregate supply curve to AS_1 and move the economy to point *c*. Rational expectations advocates believe this scenario is unlikely because it assumes that people are misinformed and learn slowly. If producers do realize that price increases are due to expansionary monetary policy, they will understand that their costs will rise. As a result, the monetary expansion will move the economy from point *a* to point *b* only temporarily. When costs adjust, the short-run aggregate supply curve will shift to the left, and the economy will move to point *d*. This result illustrates the policy ineffectiveness rule because the monetary expansion has raised prices but had no long-run impact on the level of real GDP.

ply analysis in Figure 30.1. Suppose that the economy begins at point *a* and that the Fed increases the money supply. This will initially raise both output and prices and move the economy to point *b*. What happens next depends on expectations: if firms interpret the higher prices as an increase in profits, they will expand production, the short-run aggregate supply curve will shift to AS_1, and the economy will move to point *c*. But if firms recognize that the higher prices are the result of expansionary monetary policy, they will realize that their costs will soon rise and negate any temporary profit increase. As a result, the aggregate supply curve will shift to AS_2, and the economy will move to point *d*. This result illustrates the policy ineffectiveness rule because expansionary monetary policy has affected only the price index, not real GDP.

Does this mean that the Fed should advocate policy secrecy? Almost certainly not. Unpredictable money growth makes it difficult to distinguish between temporary and permanent price changes and removes some of the information content from price signals. Few economists argue that the best monetary policy is a sequence of policy surprises.

The foregoing comments must be qualified. The policy ineffectiveness rule depends crucially upon the three assumptions we made—rational expectations, wage and price flexibility, and the quantity theory. In the real world, many prices are tied to contracts, so even anticipated money growth can have short-run real effects. If our producer knew that her unionized workers' wages were fixed for the next three years, an increase in selling prices—for any reason—would mean higher profits, and she should hire more workers and increase production as the real wage fell.

· · · · · · · ·

The Credibility Effect

Many economists have stressed that policy credibility is an important determinant of policy effectiveness. The basic idea is that if people believe that policymakers will follow through with their intentions, the economy will respond more quickly. For example, just the *announcement* of an anti-inflation policy should cause workers to revise their wage demands downward to ensure that they will not lose their jobs— but only if the policy announcement is perceived as being credible. If workers do not believe that policymakers will stick to their anti-inflation guns, people will hesitate to take wage and price cuts, and the economy will fall into a recession.

Just how credible has monetary policy been in the past? The answer is not clear. An announced and inviolate monetary policy would eventually be believed—but we have never had such a thing! Policymakers have frequently *said* that they were going to keep money tight until inflation was eliminated, but they have almost always recanted when the recession began to be politically difficult. The problem is that there is no way to measure credibility, so any investigation of the **credibility effect** will always be subject to alternative interpretations. A modern application of the credibility hypothesis is presented in the inflation game in the Focus box on page 786.

Credibility effect If people believe that policymakers will follow through on their announced intentions, the economy will respond more quickly.

> ### RECAP   Intermediate Targeting and Monetary Policy Complications
>
> The Federal Reserve cannot control the economy directly; the best it can do is to use policy instruments to manipulate intermediate targets that affect the actual economy. Monetary policy is complicated by the existence of lags, credibility, and expectations.
>
> 1. The main intermediate targets of the Fed are interest rates and the money supply. The Fed uses its policy tools—reserve requirements, the discount rate, and open market operations—to change bank reserves and interest rates.
> 2. Desirable properties of intermediate targets include measurability, control, and reliable linkage to policy goals.
> 3. Monetary policy lags include the recognition lag, the implementation lag, and the impact lag. These lags add up to a minimum of about one year. Credible policy announcements can speed up the response of the economy to policy changes, but if expectations are rational, monetary policy may affect only prices and inflation, not the real sector of the economy.

NONDISCRETIONARY MONETARY POLICY: THE CONSTANT GROWTH RATE RULE

Many economists feel that the best approach to monetary policy is to follow a *monetary rule*; that is, to set the money supply to grow at a constant rate. Economists who advocate this policy are often called **monetarists**. The monetary rule is based on several considerations, the most important of which is probably the belief that the economy has strong self-correcting forces—so strong that activist policy intervention is rarely necessary. Economists who reject the monetary rule usually argue that the Fed should have more flexibility to manipulate the money supply in order to move interest rates to a level consistent with policy goals. This section looks at the monetary rule; the next section looks at interest rate targeting.

Monetarist Macroeconomists who follow the views of Milton Friedman. Basic views include belief in self-correcting nature of markets, *laissez faire*, and the constant growth rate rule for the money supply.

Assumptions of the Constant Growth Rate Rule

In the eyes of most monetarists, it is almost always best to leave the economy alone, even when it appears to be falling into a recession. This view is based on four main assumptions:

1. The lags associated with policy intervention are so long that monetary policy changes are likely to be ill-timed.
2. Money affects the economy through so many linkages that attempts to "fine-tune" the economy are likely to be met with uncertain results.
3. A stable financial environment is more easily achieved with stable money growth. This permits interest rates to respond to market forces and thus allocate credit to the uses that yield the greatest return.
4. Even though the Federal Reserve is nominally independent, politicians wield enormous influence—enough to sway monetary policy toward political rather than economic ends.

There are actually several varieties of the **constant growth rate rule**. In its purest form, this policy would set money growth at a fixed rate of perhaps 6 percent per year and leave it there, regardless of the rate of inflation or unemployment. Other versions would establish a range of monetary growth—say, between 4 and 8 percent per year. Still others would establish a fixed rate but allow for policy discretion in the event of raging inflation or serious recession. Although there are obvious technical differences between these versions of the constant growth rate rule, all stem from a belief in the four assumptions stated above.

Constant growth rate rule Any of several versions of a monetary rule that call for the money supply to grow at a fixed rate or within a fixed range.

Implementing the Monetary Rule

To implement the monetary rule, the Fed must announce and stick to a narrow band for the growth of the monetary aggregates. For example, the Fed's target might be for M2 to grow between 6 and 8 percent per year. The announcement is important because it provides information to the financial markets. Once the Fed has announced a money growth target, it must not deviate from it. This means, for example, that if

FOCUS ON

AN INFLATION GAME

The importance of the credibility hypothesis can be seen with a simple application of game theory to monetary policy. As we discussed in detail in Chapter 14, game theory is a mathematical technique that can be used to model strategic behavior. This application of game theory follows Cukierman[1] as interpreted by Sheffrin.[2]

The key idea behind this model is that workers choose expected inflation, and the Fed chooses actual inflation. More precisely, the model assumes:

- Workers must decide on their nominal wage demands before the Fed picks money growth.
- Workers are interested in their real wages, so they must form an expectation of inflation before deciding on their nominal wage demands.
- Firms will hire more workers at lower real wages than at high real wages.
- The Fed prefers full employment and low inflation.

Combining these four simple assumptions into a game theory *payoff matrix* yields some interesting results.

For simplicity, we assume that there are two possible rates of inflation, "low" (L) and "high" (H). These are entered in the boxes bordering the payoff matrix. The cells within the matrix give the "payoffs" for the Fed and the workers; the workers' payoffs are shown in the upper half of each cell, and the Fed's payoffs are shown in the lower half. Positive numbers represent positive gains—lower inflation or higher employment for the Fed, or higher real wages for the workers—while negative numbers represent losses, and a zero indicates no change.

Workers prefer outcomes along the diagonal running from upper left to lower right (the *principal diagonal*) because their expectations would be correct. To see why, suppose that the workers expect low inflation ($p^e = L$) and thus ask for only modest nominal wages. If their expectation of low inflation is correct ($p = L$), the workers will have no extra gain; this is represented by the 0 in the upper corner of the northwest cell. On the other hand, if the workers expect low inflation, but the Fed inflates the economy ($p = H$), real wages will fall and the workers

will be worse off. This is indicated by the −1 in the upper corner of the southwest cell. If the workers correctly expect inflation to be high, they will again gain nothing because their nominal wages will have been eroded by inflation. This is indicated by the 0 in the top corner of the southeast cell. The worst situation for the workers is if they expect high inflation but the Fed does not inflate the economy: many workers will lose their jobs because the real wage will be too high. As a result, the unemployed workers might offer to work for firms at very low wages and negate any past wage gains. This is indicated by the 1 in the northeast cell.

The Fed's preferences are a bit more complex. Its most preferred outcome is when workers expect low inflation but the Fed inflates the economy, $p^e = L, p = H$. This would generate economic growth because low real wages stimulate employment. This payoff is designated by a +1 in the lower half of the southwest cell. The Fed's second choice is for both parties to agree upon low inflation, $p^e = L, p = L$. This is represented by the 0 in the lower half of the northwest cell. The

the economy falls into a severe recession, the Fed must resist the temptation to increase the money supply.

It is interesting to note that although some economists claim that it is possible to compute an "optimal quantity of money" and an optimal money growth rate, many monetarists argue that having a constant and predictable money growth rate is more

	Actions →	L	H
Fed Chooses Actual Inflation (*p*)	*L*	W: 0 F: 0	W: −1 F: −2
	H	W: −1 F: +1	W: 0 F: −1

Workers Choose Expected Inflation (*p^e*)

third choice for the Fed would be for both parties to expect high inflation, $p^e = H$, $p = H$. The economy experiences inflation, but at least real wages do not rise enough to cause a recession. This scenario is represented by the −1 in the lower half of the southeast cell. Finally, the worst scenario from the Fed's perspective is for workers to demand high wages in expectation of inflation, but for the Fed to adopt low-inflation policies, $p^e = H$, $p = L$. This situation results in both inflation and unemployment and is represented by the −2 in the lower half of the northeast cell.

Now, by using the principles of game theory, we can find the *dominant strategy*. The dominant strategy provides the most likely reasoning for both players and can help determine the most likely outcome of the game. Look at the game from the Fed's

standpoint. No matter what wages the workers demand, the Fed must inflate the economy. If workers demand low-inflation wages and the Fed inflates, the economy booms as low real wages cause employment to rise (W: −1, F: +1). If workers demand high-inflation wages, the economy falls into recession, and the Fed loses more by not inflating (W: −1, F: −2) than if it does inflate the economy to keep up with the wages (W: 0, F: −1). The only possible gain for the Fed is with high-inflation policies. We reach the same conclusion if we look at the problem from the workers' perspective: workers cannot gain from a low wage contract regardless of how the Fed responds. If they ask for low wages, the Fed is better off by inflating the economy so their payoff will be −1. If the workers opt for high wages, the Fed will lose less by inflating the economy

(F: −1 compared to F: −2). The result: Workers will demand high wages.

This model has three important implications: First, inflation is too high in equilibrium in the sense that if the Fed and the workers could cooperate, they would be able to agree upon the low-inflation outcome in the northwest corner of the payoff matrix. The second point is relevant to the credibility hypothesis: all low-inflation policy announcements from the Fed are likely to be met with suspicion. If this game fits the real world, the correct strategy for the Fed is to inflate the economy regardless of the workers' wage demands. Finally, the outcome of this game may depend on how often it is repeated: if the Fed continually reneges on its promise to fight inflation, no one would ever expect workers to believe the Fed. On the other hand, the cooperative low-inflation outcome may be possible after a few episodes of protracted anti-inflation policies.

[1]Alex Cukierman, "Central Bank Behavior and Credibility: Some Recent Theoretical Developments," *Review of the Federal Reserve Bank of St. Louis* 68 (May 1986): 5–17.
[2]Steven Sheffrin, *The Making of Economic Policy* (Cambridge, Mass.: Basil Blackwell, 1989).

important than the rate of growth per se. As a rule of thumb, the rate of growth of the money supply should be equal to the long-run rate of growth of real output—perhaps 3.5 percent—plus the targeted rate of inflation. For example, if the long-run inflation target is 3 percent, this would suggest money growth should be around 6.5 percent.

• • • • • • • •

Problems with the Monetary Rule

At one time, the idea of a monetary rule had wide acceptance among economists; however, several recent events have caused many economists to question whether a monetary rule is the best policy. The two main problems with the monetary rule are (1) the apparent instability of money demand and the resulting breakdown of the relationship between nominal GDP and the monetary aggregates, and (2) difficulties in targeting money growth. Also, as pointed out in the Focus box on monetary policy in the early 1980s, a recent attempt to implement the monetary rule did not work out quite as planned.

Instability of Money Demand. There is increasing evidence that the demand for money is unstable.[2] That is, people may not hold or spend a constant fraction of their money. If this is correct, then a given money supply can have varying effects on the economy. In this situation, it may be preferable to change the money supply in response to changes in money demand. Why the demand for money may be unstable—if, in fact, it really is—has not been determined. Some economists believe that the instability is due to rapid financial innovations and the confusion that ensues as people learn how to use new kinds of deposit accounts. If this is the main source of money demand instability, we might expect a return to stability once the pace of financial innovation subsides.

Figure 30.2 plots GDP, M1, and M2 over the period 1960–1993. Until the late 1970s, increases in the rate of money growth generally corresponded to increases in the rate of nominal GDP growth, and decreases in the rate of money growth were generally associated with decreases in the rate of nominal GDP growth. However, this relationship apparently broke down in the 1980s. The instability of money demand is one reason why the long-run relationship between the monetary aggregates and GDP appears to be breaking down, but there may be other reasons as well.

Inability of the Fed to Hit Its Targets. Another potential problem with the monetary rule is that it may not be possible for the Fed to control the money supply accurately enough to achieve its targets. There are two main reasons to believe this. First, an enormous number of U.S. dollars are held abroad in the *Eurodollar market*.[3] These dollars can enter and leave U.S. financial markets literally in an instant in response to changes in U.S. interest rates. If Fed policy raises U.S. interest rates, Eurodollars will enter U.S. markets in search of higher interest returns. This will increase the amount of money in circulation—perhaps contrary to the aims of the Fed. Second, some economists believe that the money supply is *endogenous*; that is, that the amount of money in circulation is controlled by the level of economic activity, not the Fed. What is the reasoning behind this position? Remember that most of the money in

[2]The evidence comes from a number of sources, but there is still debate on this issue. One recent study that found money demand instability was Benjamin M. Friedman and Kenneth N. Kuttner, "Money, Income, Prices, and Interest Rates," *American Economic Review* 82 (June 1992): 472–92. Notice that money demand instability implies velocity instability because the reciprocal of money demand is velocity.

[3]The Eurodollar market was discussed in Chapter 28.

···· FIGURE 30.2 MONEY AND NOMINAL GDP, 1960–1993

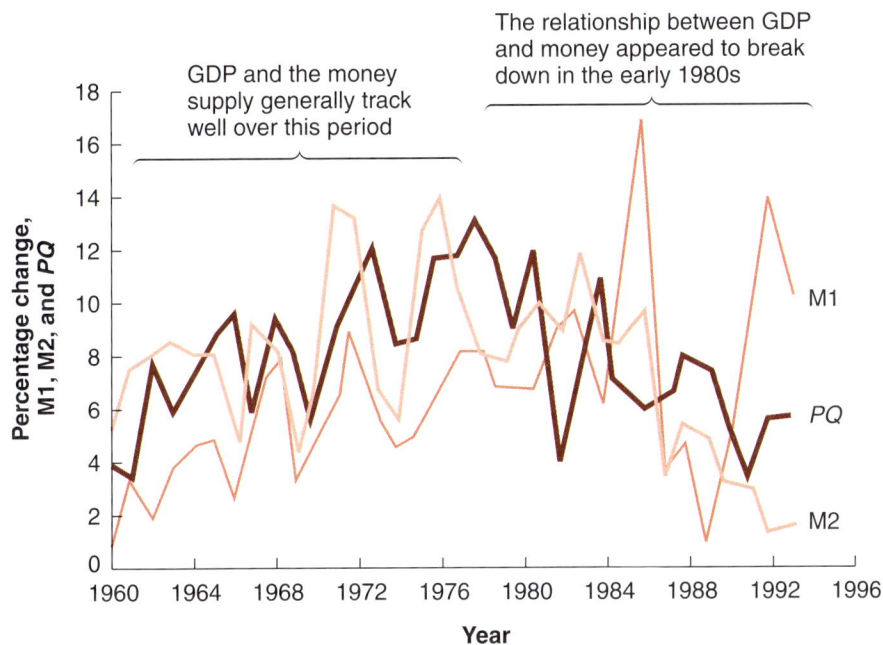

Until the late 1970s, the growth rates of M1 and M2 tracked fairly well with the growth rate of nominal GDP (*PQ*). An increase in money growth tended to be associated with an increase in nominal GDP while a decrease in money growth usually led to a decrease in the rate of growth of nominal GDP. Why this relationship apparently broke down in the 1980s is still a mystery.

SOURCE: 1994 *Economic Report of the President*, Tables B-1 and B-68.

the economy consists of bank deposits and loans. When the economy is booming, banks make more loans and thus increase the amount of money in circulation. The endogeneity of the money supply may be especially significant in this era of financial deregulation. As banks develop new and creative financing techniques, they expand their loan possibilities—and the money supply.

RECAP   Monetarism and Nondiscretionary Monetary Policy

1. Monetarists feel that the economy has strong self-correcting forces and that forecasting errors, lags, and credibility make policy activism difficult. The best policy is for the Fed to set money growth at a constant rate and resist further intervention into the economy.
2. Problems with the constant growth rate monetary rule include the potential for wide swings in interest rates, the inability to control the money supply accurately, and money demand instability.

MONETARY POLICY IN THE EARLY 1980s: VOLCKER'S EXPERIMENT WITH A MONETARY RULE

The monetarists' long-standing calls for a monetary rule finally made headway when the Federal Reserve changed its operating procedures in 1979. Instead of changing the money supply to target interest rates, the Federal Reserve decided to target bank reserves directly and ignore interest rates. The money aggregate initially chosen as a target in 1979 was M1, the narrowest monetary aggregate.

The growth rate of M1 had averaged just over 8 percent for 1977, 1978, and the first nine months of 1979. To bring inflation under control, Fed Chair Paul Volcker put the brakes on the money supply in October 1979. Inflation came down, and by 1982 consumer prices were rising at less than 4 percent per year. Unfortunately, there were two adverse side effects: high unemployment and high interest rates. The unemployment rate, only 5.8 percent in 1979, shot up to almost 11 percent by the end of 1982 while real, inflation-adjusted interest rates nearly doubled. The success against inflation cannot be underestimated; inflation declined dramatically, setting the stage for the long expansion of the 1980s. However, the side effects were much more severe than anticipated. By October 1982, Volcker's experiment was over, and the Fed returned to a more activist policy of manipulating bank reserves to target interest rates.

We can see why interest rates and unemployment rose so much in the early 1980s by using the quantity theory of money, specifically Equation 3 from Chapter 29:

$$\frac{\Delta M}{M} + \frac{\Delta V}{V} \cong \frac{\Delta P}{P} + \frac{\Delta Q}{Q}$$

In other words, the percentage change in the money supply plus the percentage change in velocity must approximately equal the inflation rate plus the percentage change in real GDP. As we mentioned in the last chapter, few economists would debate the validity of this equation; however, there is nothing in the equation itself to determine how a change in the money supply is broken down into changes in V, P, and Q. Much of the inflation the U.S. economy experienced in the 1970s was caused by supply-side factors—long-term wage contracts, external oil prices, and so on—and was so built in to the economy that the disinflation process took several years to complete. This meant that unless velocity accelerated significantly, real GDP was bound to fall—as indeed it did.

The accompanying table presents the data for the period 1978–1983 to show the effects of Volcker's monetary experiment. All of the data were taken from the 1994 *Economic Report of the President* with the exception of the velocity columns, which were calculated as the ratio of nominal GDP (*PQ*) to M1 and M2. A quick glance shows that, as expected, the quantity theory equation holds up pretty well in most years. For example, in 1980, the percentage change in M1 (column 5 = 6.8) plus the percentage change in M1 velocity (column 10 = 2.0) summed to 8.8. This is quite close to 9.0—the sum of real GDP growth (column 12 = −0.5) and the inflation rate (column 7 = 9.5). We get a similar story in 1981: M1 growth was 6.8 percent—not nearly enough to pay for the 10 percent inflation without a big jump in velocity. Unfortunately, M1 velocity increased by only 4.7 percent. This means that only 1.5 percent points were left over for real GDP growth (6.8 + 4.7 − 10.0 = 1.5). This was approximately equal to the slow 1.8 percent growth in real GDP for 1981.

With the economy stagnating in 1981, Volcker abandoned the monetary rule in October and pumped up the money supply to stimulate the economy. By some accounts, his policy reversal was too late: M1 money growth rose to 8.7 percent in 1982, but velocity fell 4.6 percent. The result: Despite some progress against inflation—it was only 6.2 percent for the year—real GDP fell 2.2 percent.

Perhaps the biggest public outcry against Volcker's monetary rule experiment concerned the rising nominal interest rates; ironically, one of the main reasons for his policy change was to combat high interest rates. The three-month treasury bill rate had risen from 7.2 percent in 1978 to over 10 percent in 1979, and long-term

Paul Volcker, Chairman of the Federal Reserve Board (1979–1987).

rates were at similar lofty levels. As expected, the slower money growth of the Volcker experiment caused interest rates to rise even more in the short run—the T-bill rate topped 14 percent in 1982. What was not expected was that real interest rates would continue to climb even after monetary policy was eased in 1982. What happened? Simple: Nominal interest rates came down between 1982 and 1987, but inflation declined faster and more.

Real interest rates rose from under 2 percent through most of the 1970s to almost 6 percent in 1984.[1] Even a dec-

[1] Let $r = i - p$ where i = the three-month treasury bill rate and p = the percentage change in the GDP deflator. In 1984 the calculations were 5.7 = 9.6 − 3.9. Of course, for most investment decisions, the long-run real interest rate is what matters most. Unfortunately, calculation of long-run real rates is more complicated. Most studies estimate that long-run real rates rose in the first half of the 1980s, but not as much as short-run rates.

ade later, economists still debate whether the rise in real interest rates in the first half of the 1980s was caused primarily by tight money or the record fiscal deficits. Most economists would probably agree that both events had some effect on interest rates.

Did this episode spell the end of the monetary rule? That depends upon whom you ask. Some economists answer a definitive, "Yes." Other economists contend that Volcker never really implemented a monetary rule because his policy "rules" were discretionary, not fixed. The Fed does seem to practice a monetary rule today, albeit one that contains considerable built-in flexibility. The Fed announces its money growth targets with rather wide bands—for example, M1 growth was targeted to grow between 4 and 8 percent—and stands ready to move outside these bands when necessary. Rigid monetarists would prefer that the Fed adopt and maintain narrower bands, but others feel that growth announcements can accomplish a main function of the monetary rule—stable financial markets.

THE VOLCKER MONETARY EXPERIMENT

(1) Year	(2) PQ	(3) M1	(4) M2	(5) %ΔM1	(6) %M2	(7) %ΔP	(8) V1	(9) V2	(10) %ΔV1	(11) %ΔV2	(12). %ΔQ
1978	$2,232.7	$358.4	$1,388.7	8.2%	7.9%	7.9%	6.28	1.62	—	—	—
1979	2,488.6	382.7	1,496.7	6.8	7.8	8.6	6.55	1.68	4.4%	3.4%	2.5%
1980	2,708.0	408.8	1,629.5	6.8	8.9	9.5	6.68	1.68	2.0	0.0	−0.5
1981	3,030.6	436.5	1,792.9	6.8	10.0	10.0	6.99	1.70	4.7	1.5	1.8
1982	3,149.6	474.6	1,951.9	8.7	8.9	6.2	6.67	1.62	−4.6	−4.8	−2.2
1983	3,405.0	521.4	2,186.1	9.9	12.0	4.1	6.54	1.56	−2.1	−3.9	3.9
			Average	7.9	9.2	7.7			0.9	−0.8	1.1

KEY:

PQ = nominal GDP; M1, M2 = monetary aggregates as defined in Chapter 28; %Δ = percentage change; P = GDP deflator; V1 = M1 velocity = $PQ/M1$; V2 = M2 velocity = $PQ/M2$; Q = real GDP

SOURCE: 1994 *Economic Report of the President*, Tables B–1, B–2, B–3, B–68.

OUR ECONOMIC HERITAGE

MILTON FRIEDMAN: THE FOUNDER OF MONETARISM

The father of modern monetarism is undoubtedly Milton Friedman (b. 1912). Friedman's lifework has been dedicated to showing the advantages of *laissez faire* and that government intervention most often leads to inefficiency. In 1977 he was awarded the Nobel Prize for his lifetime accomplishments.

Friedman studied with some of the best economists of his era. His undergraduate professor, Arthur Burns, was later to become the chair of the Council of Economic Advisers and the Federal Reserve Board. In graduate school, Friedman took courses from Frank Knight, known for his work in risk and uncertainty, and Wesley Mitchell, head of the National Bureau of Economic Research and the leading empirical researcher of the time.

Friedman's work has been controversial from the start. His doctoral dissertation was a study of the American Medical Association. Among other things, he showed that artificially high training requirements imposed by the AMA restricted the number of doctors and raised the price of medical care—but increased physicians' salaries. Friedman was forced to tone down his arguments to get the study published, then a requirement for completion of the Ph.D. at Columbia.

After school, Friedman had stints in government before he took up permanent residence in academia. Most of his professional career was spent at the University of Chicago where his followers have come to be known as the "Chicago School" to some and "Friedmaniacs" to others. To his fellow economists, Friedman is best known for his work in monetary and consumption theory and his frequent involvement in public policy debates. He is one of the few contemporary economists who has been able to publish popular economics as well as scholarly pieces. He is well-known for the *Newsweek* column he wrote during the 1970s and the popular book and PBS television series *Free to Choose,* which he coauthored with his wife Rose. His best-selling collection of essays, *Capitalism and Freedom* (Chicago: University of Chicago Press, 1962), presents well-reasoned, nontechnical arguments for *laissez faire.*

Friedman never decided to lend his talents to the policymaking circles in Washington, though he was frequently rumored to be the next Federal Reserve or CEA chair. He retired from the University of Chicago in 1977, but his work will undoubtedly influence students and policymakers for years to come. He is currently affiliated with the Hoover Institute, a conservative think tank associated with Stanford University.

ACTIVIST MONETARY POLICY: TARGETING INTEREST RATES

Economists who oppose the monetary rule favor adopting **activist monetary policies** to manipulate interest rates and the supply of credit as necessary. These economists feel that the economy is so unstable that leaving it on automatic pilot will lead to problems. Economists who are comfortable with such a hands-on approach to policy are usually called **Keynesians** of one sort or another.[4]

Assumptions of the Monetary Activisits

Most Keynesian economists make three key assumptions:

1. The self-correcting forces in the economy tend to be weak and slow, and the economy is prone to wide cyclical fluctuations.
2. Economic theory and forecasting techniques have progressed sufficiently to make policy activism effective.
3. The primary linkage between money and economic activity is through interest rates.

The implication of these assumptions is that the Fed should continuously monitor the economy and be ready to steer it with activist policies. Instead of following a monetary rule, the money supply should be adjusted as necessary to move interest rates in the desired direction. This usually means increasing the rate of growth of the money supply during recessions and decreasing the rate of growth during periods of inflation.

Implementation

The Federal Reserve often uses the federal funds rate as its primary interest rate target.[5] When the federal funds rate rises above the desired level, the Federal Reserve buys government securities to increase bank reserves and the money supply; this tends to lower interest rates. When the federal funds rate falls below the target level, the Federal Reserve sells government securities to reduce the money supply and raise interest rates. The media often refer to these actions as "setting the federal funds rate"; however, it must be stressed that the federal funds rate is a market rate. Consequently, the Federal Reserve can only influence the federal funds rate; it cannot arbitrarily set it at a particular level.

Activist monetary policy The idea that the Fed should continuously monitor the economy and adjust the money supply as needed to move interest rates in the desired direction.

Keynesians Economists who favor an activist monetary policy that manipulates interest rates and the supply of credit to guide the economy.

---

[4]There are several varieties of Keynesians. The more moderate are usually called Neo-Keynesians. Most of the discussion that follows is consistent with a generic Neo-Keynesian view. The post-Keynesians are a more radical branch of Keynesians. This school focuses on income distribution and believes that self-correcting forces (point 1 in the list) are so weak that the government must guide investment and other aspects of the economy. The newest branch of Keynesians is the New Keynesian school. We will have more to say about the New Keynesians and other schools of thought in Chapter 32, and we will touch on the post-Keynesians in Chapter 33.

[5]Recall from Chapter 29 that the federal funds rate is a very short-term interest rate, the interest rate banks charge each other for overnight loans.

INTEREST RATE TARGETING IN THE 1990S

The recession of 1990–1991 was special in several ways. It was not especially severe—unemployment never rose above 7.5 percent—but at least until the fourth quarter of 1993, the subsequent recovery was sluggish, at best. It was also, by some accounts, the only recession since World War II that was not brought on by tight money, though monetary policy did tighten somewhat in the late 1980s. But perhaps most importantly, the recession *began* with a huge fiscal deficit, so large that it was politically difficult to use fiscal stimulus—tax cuts or spending increases—to get the economy back on its feet.

With fiscal policy ruled out, the only way to get the economy moving again was to use monetary policy. Beginning in the fall of 1990, Fed Chair Alan Greenspan did everything in his control to pump up the money supply and bring down interest rates. The discount rate was lowered eight times between the end of 1990 and early 1992

and reached 3.5 percent, its lowest level in almost 20 years. (The discount rate fell to 3 percent in 1993 before it was raised in early 1994.) The lower discount rate and more rapid money growth—M1 grew at an annual rate of 8.7 percent in 1991, though neither M2 nor M3 budged from their growth rates of a year earlier—combined to bring the federal funds rate down to its lowest level in two decades as well. Even the reserve requirements on demand deposits were lowered from 12 percent to 10 percent in early 1992. All to no avail—or so it seemed. The recession dragged on long enough to become a serious political liability to the Bush administration. What was wrong? Why didn't the record low interest rates jump-start the economy?

There are several possible explanations. First, as shown in the accompanying chart, short-term interest rates did come down dramatically, but long-term rates remained stubbornly high, too high for investment to take

Federal Reserve Board Chairman Alan Greenspan.

off; not until mid-1993 did the return on Aaa bonds fall below 7 percent. Long-term rates may have remained high because the financial markets believed that the Fed's expansionary pol-

The Federal Reserve also uses the discount rate to maneuver interest rates. Banks decide whether to borrow needed reserves at the discount window or in the federal funds market by looking at the interest rate differential, so changes in the discount rate frequently result in similar moves in the federal funds rate. The discount rate is often set slightly below the federal funds rate, but banks are frequently willing to pay the higher federal funds rate to avoid the publicity of having to borrow at the discount window to cover reserve shortages.

Interest rate targeting The practice of manipulating interest rates by adjusting the money supply. Increasing the money supply tends to lower interest rates, and reducing the money supply tends to raise interest rates.

Problems with Interest Rate Targeting

Monetarists have long been critical of **interest rate targeting** because it requires the Federal Reserve to give up control of the money supply. If interest rates are consid-

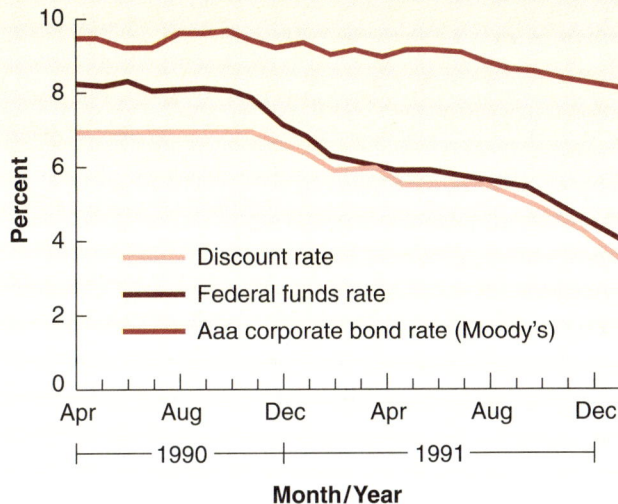

Percent (y-axis)

- Discount rate
- Federal funds rate
- Aaa corporate bond rate (Moody's)

Apr   Aug   Dec   Apr   Aug   Dec

├──── 1990 ────┼──── 1991 ────┤

Month/Year

icies would cause inflation. Second, the economy entered the recession with a record level of consumer debt and the banking system in crisis. Many analysts believed that consumers were hesitant to take on new debt, even at the lower interest rates, because of this existing debt. Third, expectations may

have been so depressed that no monetary policy would have been adequate to yank the economy out of recession. Finally, maybe the interest rate reductions *did* work, but only after a longer lag than expected. The summer recovery, though weak, was certainly aided somewhat by lower rates.

It is interesting to speculate what would have happened had a monetary rule been in place throughout the recession. Slower M1 growth might have dampened inflationary expectations enough to bring down long-term rates, though possibly at the expense of higher short-term rates. A monetary rule might also have calmed the financial markets; in fact, some people suggested that the Fed's actions to bring down interest rates were so extreme that they caused people to think the economy was in worse shape than it really was. But this is just speculation. Even if a monetary rule is applied successfully during the next business cycle, it will be impossible to say whether a monetary rule would have worked better during the 1990–1991 recession because all recessions are different.

SOURCE: *Federal Reserve Bulletin*, various issues, Table A-26.

ered too high, the appropriate response by the Fed is to increase the money supply—an act that can move money supply growth beyond the target range. This problem is illustrated in Figure 30.3. Suppose that the Fed has decided that the money supply indicated by the money supply curve $(M/P)_0^s$ is correct and that the initial interest rate, r_0, is also correct. Now suppose that there is an increase in GDP growth. This will shift the money demand curve from $(M/P)_0^d$ to $(M/P)_1^d$ and raise the interest rate above the desired level. The problem is that if the Fed wants to bring interest rates back down to r_0, it will be necessary to increase the money supply beyond the desired $(M/P)_0^s$—and that might generate inflation.

Another problem with interest rate targeting is that it is not sufficient to pick a particular interest rate. It is also necessary to calculate the appropriate interest rates for different stages of the business cycle. For example, suppose that the Fed tries to

796

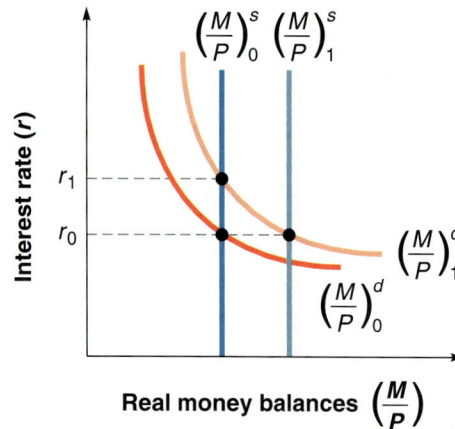

FIGURE 30.3 PROBLEMS WITH INTEREST RATE TARGETS

The basic problem with interest rate targeting is that it forces the Fed to give up its money supply targets. Suppose that the money market begins at the intersection of $(M/P)_0^d$ and $(M/P)_0^s$, and that the Fed feels that both the money supply and the interest rate are correct. An increase in GDP growth will shift the money demand curve out from $(M/P)_0^d$ to $(M/P)_1^d$ and cause the interest rate to rise to r_1. To bring the interest rate back to the target level of r_0, the Fed would have to increase the money supply to $(M/P)_1^s$. This would move the money supply outside the target level and could lead to inflation.

peg interest rates at level $\bar{r}$. If the economy enters a recession, the demand for money will tend to fall as income declines. The result will be lower interest rates as the money demand curve shifts toward the left. If the Fed is intent on keeping rates at $\bar{r}$, the correct response is to decrease the money supply—which will tend to make the recession worse.

Finally, for interest rate targeting to be successful, some kind of coordination between the fiscal and monetary authorities is needed. As we discuss in the next chapter, the ballooning government deficits of the 1980s and 1990s are often mentioned as a reason why long-term interest rates remained so high during the 1990–1991 recession despite expansionary monetary policies.

Real Interest Rate Targeting: The Fisher Effect

Perhaps the most serious problem with interest rate targets is that the Fed may be able to target only nominal interest rates, not real interest rates. As we found out in Chapter 27, the real interest rate cannot be directly observed. To target the real interest rate the Federal Reserve would have to estimate future inflation and subtract this estimate from the nominal interest rate. Some economists believe that this is such a formidable problem that using real interest rates as intermediate targets may be impossible. However, advocates argue that measuring the real interest rate involves no more guesswork than trying to measure the money supply in a world of financial innovation.

···· **FIGURE 30.4 THE FISHER EFFECT**

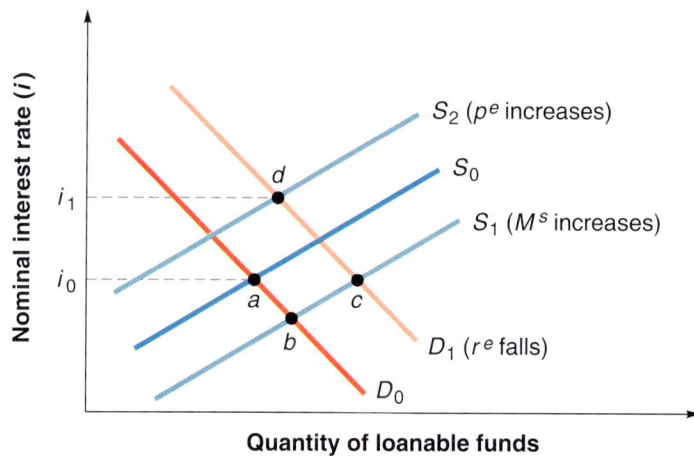

When the Federal Reserve tries to lower the real interest rate by increasing the supply of money, the supply of loanable funds shifts out from S_0 toward S_1. If the increase in the money supply results in an increase in expected inflation, the demand for loanable funds will increase from D_0 toward D_1. Higher expected inflation will reduce the amount of funds lenders are willing to lend at every nominal interest rate, so the supply curve will shift from S_1 toward S_2. After all adjustments have taken place, the nominal interest rate will rise enough to cover expected inflation and return the real interest rate to its "natural" level.

The difficulty of targeting real interest rates can be explained by an application of the **Fisher effect**, named after the American economist Irving Fisher.[6] The Fisher effect shows the connection between nominal interest rates and the inflationary consequences of monetary policy. This effect is illustrated in Figure 30.4, which presents the supply and demand for loanable funds. Loanable funds represent the amount of funds available in the loan market. The demand for loanable funds is downward sloping because people will borrow less money at high interest rates. The supply of loanable funds is upward sloping because lenders are willing to part with more funds if they receive a high interest return. Notice that the vertical axis in the figure measures the nominal interest rate; this allows us to see how inflationary expectations affect interest rates and complicate the Fed's task of real interest rate targeting.

To see why the Federal Reserve may have little control over the real interest rate, consider what happens if it tries to lower the real interest rate by increasing the money supply. The supply of loanable funds will shift out from S_0 to S_1 as more money becomes available for lending. However, increasing the money supply may also raise the expected rate of inflation, which will do two things. First, borrowers will increase their demand for loans thinking they will be able to repay debts with less valuable dollars. This will shift the demand curve outward to D_1. Second, higher expected inflation will reduce the amount of funds lenders are willing to lend at any given

Fisher effect If a monetary expansion increases the expected rate of inflation, nominal interest rates may rise, not fall.

[6]Irving Fisher, *The Theory of Interest* (New York: Macmillan, 1930).

nominal interest rate. This will shift the supply curve to S_2. The result: Depending on the relative shifts of the supply and demand curves, nominal interest rates can *rise* in response to an increase in the money supply. After all adjustments have been completed, the real interest rate may return to its "natural" level—the rate of return on physical capital—but the short-run fluctuations could be destabilizing.

RECAP   **Keynesian Activist Monetary Policy**

1. Keynesian economists believe that the Fed should intervene as necessary to target interest rates and move the economy toward potential GDP. These economists feel that the economy is prone to wide swings, that self-correcting forces are weak, and that it is possible to forecast the economy sufficiently well for policy purposes.
2. A main focus of activist monetary policy is interest rate targeting because interest rates are thought to be the primary linkage between money and the economy. Problems with interest rate targeting include the inability to observe or control real interest rates, the need for fiscal and monetary policy coordination, and the requirement that the Fed relinquish control of the money supply.

ADDITIONAL MONETARY TARGETS

The Fed is not limited to two targets. In 1983 the Fed announced that it would be monitoring several "informational variables" in addition to interest rates and the monetary aggregates. Two of the more important informational variables are total credit and exchange rates. The Fed adopted this new eclectic view in part because of the problems of relying upon the two main targets, but also because times had changed: the contemporary financial environment is increasingly complex and constantly changing.

Total Credit

Harvard economist Benjamin Friedman (no relation to Milton Friedman) has argued for several years that the Federal Reserve should adopt a multitarget framework and specify target ranges for the level of total credit and the money supply. Friedman contends that using total credit as a policy target offers several advantages. Total credit can be accurately measured and easily controlled. It has also had a very stable link with nonfinancial economic activity—at least until the mid-1980s. Perhaps most importantly, Friedman has shown that causality flows from credit to real income and prices whereas the link between money and economic activity has frequently been shown to be two-way. Thus, a **credit target** provides important information about future movements in the ultimate policy goal variables.

The relationship between total credit and nominal GDP is shown in Figure 30.5, which plots the percentage change in nominal GDP and the percentage change in total debt for the period 1970–1993. (Total debt and total credit are different sides

Credit targets Alternative intermediate target of monetary policy. Advocated by Benjamin Friedman who believes credit can be easily measured and controlled.

·····FIGURE 30.5 TOTAL DEBT AND NOMINAL GDP GROWTH, 1970–1993

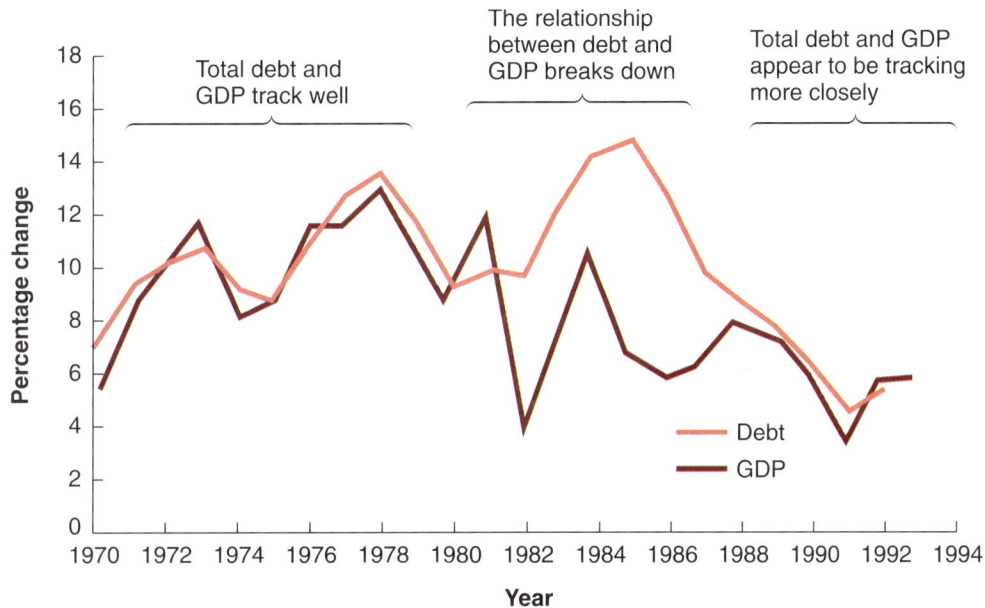

The relationship between the percentage change in total debt and the percentage change in nominal GDP appeared to break down in the early 1980s. This may have been because of the record federal government deficits of the times. The two series appear to be tracking more closely again in recent years.

NOTE: Total debt consists of outstanding credit market debt of the U.S. government, state and local governments, and private nonfinancial sectors.
SOURCE: 1994 *Economic Report of the President*, Tables B-1 and B-68.

of the same thing; an increase in credit means that someone has gone into debt.) Notice that the relationship between total debt and GDP appears to break down in the 1980s. Why? One explanation is that total debt expanded much more rapidly than GDP because of the unprecedented rise in government debt and foreign capital inflows. The ratio of private debt to income increased rapidly as well. If it turns out that these were extraordinary events, the historical relationship between credit and the economy may return in the future.

········

Exchange Rates

The Federal Reserve also includes the **exchange rate**—the price of foreign currency in terms of dollars—as one of its "informational variables," though not as an explicit target. Should exchange rates be watched more closely; that is, should there be an explicit exchange rate target? There are several reasons to consider this option. A stable exchange rate would tend to foster international trade, and the "correct" exchange rate would prevent much of the balance of payments disequilibria that have plagued the United States since the 1980s. Unfortunately, pegging the exchange rate would not be easy. A major complication would be trying to peg the real as opposed

Exchange rate The price of a foreign currency in terms of the dollar. Exchange rates are used as an informational variable by the Federal Reserve.

to the nominal exchange rate. The real exchange rate is the nominal exchange rate adjusted for country differences in price levels. The Federal Reserve *may* be able to keep the dollar exchange rate within a target region by adjusting monetary growth to keep U.S. inflation in line with world inflation. But this would mean that U.S. domestic policies would be subservient to foreign economic policies unless there was a large degree of international economic cooperation. Exchange rates and international policy coordination are treated in depth in Chapters 36 and 37.

Nominal Income

Nominal income target The use of the growth in nominal GDP as a target by the Federal Reserve. Reducing (increasing) the rate of money supply growth could slow (accelerate) the rate of nominal GDP growth.

Finally, some economists believe that the Fed should adopt a **nominal income growth target**. For example, the Fed might pick a target of 6 percent nominal income growth. This would permit 3 percent real GDP growth and 3 percent inflation. If nominal GDP began to grow at a faster rate, money supply growth would be slowed; if nominal GDP grew at a slower rate, money growth would be accelerated. Advocates of this policy believe that it would result in fewer fluctuations in output; critics believe that the Fed would pick too high a target and cause inflation to accelerate.

FOREIGN COMPLICATIONS

Reserve currency A currency that is used so widely in international markets that many nations and people worldwide keep large stocks of it. The U.S. dollar is a reserve currency.

The U.S. dollar plays a special role in the world economy today: it serves as a **reserve currency**; that is, because the dollar is so widely used on international markets, many people and nations keep large stocks of dollars on hand. These foreign-owned dollars are used for both international trade and the purchase of dollar-denominated financial assets. What this means is that almost every time the Fed enacts a domestic policy change, dollars flow out of or into the United States. For example, suppose that the Fed tightens the money supply to dampen inflation. This will usually cause U.S. interest rates to rise—and attract foreign financial capital into the United States. Likewise, when the money supply is expanded to stimulate the economy, some of this money will flow abroad in search of higher interest rates. In both cases, the flow of funds complicates Federal Reserve policy.

International financial capital flows affect not only the United States, but any country whose currency is actively traded on international markets; Japan, Germany, and Great Britain are affected at least as much as the United States. The flow of currencies across borders may explain why the historical relationship between money and the economy seemed to break down in the 1970s and 1980s. This point has been made by Ronald McKinnon of Stanford University and the International Monetary Fund. McKinnon, who calls himself a "world monetarist," notes that the inflation of the 1970s and the worldwide recession of 1981–1983 could have been predicted by looking at the combined money growth of the large industrialized countries. **World money supply** growth increased during the inflation episodes and decreased prior to the recession.

World money supply The stock of money of all trading nations in the world; or more practically, the stock of money in the major industrial nations.

It is hard to criticize world monetarism. If money matters, the whole money supply must be considered, not just the portion that happens to be most easily controlled by the Federal Reserve. This obviously complicates Fed policy, but perhaps not as much as you might think because the number of currencies that are easily substitutable is fairly small. In the 1980s, McKinnon argued that monetary policy cooperation among Germany, Japan, and the United States would have been sufficient to bring order to the world monetary system. Today, the mix would probably be modified to include the European Union, Japan, and the United States.

Such cooperation was infrequent in the past. Can we expect to see this kind of economic cooperation in the future? Several developments since the 1980s suggest that cooperation may increase in the future. The G-7 countries—the United States, Japan, Germany, France, Great Britain, Canada, and Italy—met several times in the 1980s to discuss common policy goals, and if economic unification ever takes place in Europe, the number of parties that need to cooperate will be even lower. However, both Japan and the European Union have maintained that the huge U.S. fiscal deficits make interest rate and exchange rate management difficult. Thus, the prospects for meaningful economic cooperation appear dim at present.

SUMMARY

Ultimately, most economic policy debates boil down to a discussion of rules versus discretion and whether you believe the economy is fundamentally stable or not. Monetarists think it is stable and therefore generally favor a hands-off approach to monetary policy. Keynesians believe the economy is prone to fluctuations and are more inclined to favor policy activism. As we will find out in the next two chapters, there are other schools of thought and more facets to the rules versus discretion debate. For the time being, however, it is important to distinguish between these two idealized positions.

Monetarists and others who favor policy rules generally believe:

1. The self-correcting powers of the market system tend to make fluctuations mild and brief.
2. Monetary policy is subject to lags of varying length. This means that activist policy changes are likely to do more harm than good. Further, economic forecasters are not able to predict the economy accurately enough for policy purposes.
3. Anticipated money changes will affect only inflation; unanticipated money changes can affect output in the short run, but only inflation in the long run. However, unannounced changes in the rate of growth of the money supply are likely to generate uncertainty in the financial markets.

Keynesians reject most policy rules and instead prefer to give the Fed discretion to change policy as necessary. They reach this conclusion because they believe:

1. The economy is prone to wide fluctuations because the self-correcting powers of the market are weak and slow.
2. Lags are associated with all policies, but economic forecasts are accurate enough for policy purposes.
3. Keynesians generally favor using monetary policy to target interest rates. Some activists also favor exchange rate, credit, or nominal GDP targeting.

•••••••• KEY TERMS AND CONCEPTS

policy instruments	constant growth rate rule
intermediate targets	real interest rates
policy goals	nominal interest rates
measurability	activist monetary policy
linkage	Keynesians
control	interest rate targeting
recognition lag	Fisher effect
implementation lag	credit targets
impact lag	exchange rate
rational expectations	nominal income target
policy ineffectiveness rule	reserve currency
credibility effect	world money supply
monetarist	

•••••••• REVIEW QUESTIONS

1. What is the relationship between the Fed's policy goals, intermediate targets, and policy instruments? Give examples of each and discuss the desirable qualities of intermediate targets.
2. What are the three lags associated with monetary policy? Explain how lags, expectations, and credibility influence the effectiveness of monetary policy.
3. What four assumptions form the basis for the monetarists' advocacy of the constant growth rate rule? How would the constant growth rate rule be implemented? How does money demand instability complicate the use of a monetary rule?
4. Why do Keynesians advocate activist monetary policies? What factors make interest rate targeting so difficult? Use a diagram to illustrate your answer.
5. What are the potential advantages and disadvantages of using credit, nominal GDP, and exchange rates as intermediate targets of monetary policy?
6. How does the flow of funds across international boundaries affect monetary policy?

•••••••• PROBLEMS

1. Suppose the Fed adopts an anti-inflationary stance and reduces the rate of growth of the money supply. Explain what will happen to inflation, interest rates, and unemployment assuming (a) the Fisher effect does not exist and (b) the Fisher effect does exist.
2. Another problem with interest rate targeting is that it can lead to wide fluctuations in GDP if aggregate expenditure is unstable. For example, suppose that business confidence booms, causing investment spending to accelerate. We know from Chapter 29 that this will result in an increase in money demand, shift the money demand curve outward, and raise interest rates. Explain why a policy of targeting interest rates will tend to make GDP fluctuations wider than if the Fed ignored interest rate fluctuations.

3. Suppose that economic theory advances so much that economists are able to accurately predict turning points in the business cycle one year in advance. Do you think this would influence the monetary policy views of a Keynesian? A monetarist? Why?

4. Suppose the government were to (miraculously!) balance the budget. How would this affect the Federal Reserve? Do you think its policy options would be expanded? Why?

5. The currency ratio—the ratio of currency to the money supply—increases during the Christmas holiday season because people hold additional cash to make shopping easier. Explain how the Fed should react if it (*a*) follows a constant growth rate policy and if it (*b*) is attempting to target interest rates.

6. Figure 30.4 illustrated the case where an increase in the money supply resulted in an increase in nominal interest rates. Assume that the Fisher effect does not exist and show how the same increase in the money supply can result in a decrease or no change in the nominal interest rate.

7. A number of economists advocate nominal income targets for monetary policy, but very few seem to favor real income targets. Why do you think this is so?

8. Use the aggregate demand–aggregate supply model from Chapter 26 to illustrate the following scenarios, and comment on the implications of your diagram:
   a. Credible anti-inflation monetary policy
   b. Not credible anti-inflation monetary policy
   c. Expansionary monetary policy assuming rational expectations
   d. Supply shocks in an economy characterized by the monetary rule

CHAPTER 31

Fiscal Policy, Deficits, and the Debt

Probably no economic issue is more discussed than the government budget deficit. How much harm will the ballooning deficit cause? Why don't we balance the budget? Does the deficit rob our children? Does it cause inflation? Raise interest rates and reduce investment? Will the nation go bankrupt? These are just some of the questions that we hear every day. No matter how hard you try, you cannot avoid the deficit. And, unfortunately, as we are about to find out, the deficit may be subject to more misconceptions than any other issue in economics. This chapter should help you separate fact from fiction.

Deficits are not the only important topic in the analysis of fiscal policies. As we know from Part V fiscal policies can be used to manipulate the economy—tax cuts and government spending increases have been the classic remedies for recession—but they also affect the incentives to work and save. Some economists believe that the incentive effects of fiscal policy are so important that they are hesitant to use activist fiscal policies at all. Other economists dismiss these incentive effects. We need to find out why. Finally, unlike monetary policy, fiscal policy is rarely enacted without extended political debates—and political outcomes.

AFTER READING AND STUDYING THIS CHAPTER, YOU SHOULD BE ABLE TO:

••• Understand the difference between discretionary and nondiscretionary fiscal policies

••• Explain how fiscal policies can affect the incentives to work, save, and invest

••• Distinguish between structural and cyclical deficits

• • • Differentiate between the deficit and the national debt

• • • Explain the relationship between the fiscal deficit and the foreign trade deficit

• • • Outline the fiscal policy aspects of the rules versus discretion debate

DISCRETIONARY AND NONDISCRETIONARY FISCAL POLICIES

Ask the person on the street about fiscal policy, and you will probably hear something about the need to balance the budget. This is certainly an important issue—and one that we will be addressing in some detail soon—but in the past at least, most fiscal policy changes were intended primarily to manipulate the macroeconomy.

Discretionary fiscal policies require congressional action. When Congress votes to cut taxes or close a military base, it has engaged in discretionary fiscal policies. Political motives may be behind many discretionary fiscal policies, but the economic impacts cannot be dismissed. We cannot deny the political aspects of fiscal policy, but most of our attention will focus on its economic effect.

Not all fiscal policies require deliberate acts of Congress. In fact, government spending and tax revenues both vary over the course of the business cycle. For example, when the economy enters a recession, income tax revenues automatically fall because fewer people have jobs and pay taxes. The reverse happens during expansions: more people find jobs, and people get raises so tax revenues rise. This tends to dampen any inflationary pressures that may be building in the expanding economy. For this reason, income taxes are called **automatic stabilizers**. Similarly, some government spending programs—unemployment compensation and welfare, for example—rise during cyclical contractions and fall during cyclical expansions so they too act as automatic stabilizers. Automatic stabilizers represent *nondiscretionary fiscal policies* because they do not require an act of Congress (after the initial legislation establishing the tax or program).

Automatic stabilizers can result in both a **fiscal dividend** and a **fiscal drag**. A fiscal dividend is the automatic increase in tax revenue that the government collects because of economic growth. In the past, fiscal dividends have provided a ready excuse for periodic tax cuts and, in the process, usually tax reforms; they have also been used to expand old programs or fund new programs. If the government does not cut taxes or spend the proceeds from the fiscal dividend, there can be contractionary pressure on the economy—a fiscal drag.

The implementation of income tax *indexation* in 1984 all but eliminated the fiscal dividend from inflation and reduced the stabilization properties of the income tax as well. Indexation was considered necessary because of **bracket creep**. Bracket creep occurs when nominal income rises, forcing people into higher income tax brackets, even though their real income has remained the same or fallen. For example, suppose that the tax system is progressive such that people pay 10 percent on all income up to $20,000 and 20 percent on income over $20,000.[1] If you earn $20,000 in Year 1,

Discretionary fiscal policies Deliberate changes in government spending and taxes that require congressional action.

Automatic stabilizers Nondiscretionary fiscal policies that tend to reduce the amplitude of business cycle fluctuations.

Fiscal dividend In the absence of tax indexation, economic growth and inflation puts people in higher tax brackets and thus raises government tax revenues automatically.

Fiscal drag Higher tax revenues due to the fiscal dividend may act as a "drag" on economic growth.

Bracket creep The effect of inflation on nonindexed progressive income taxes. Inflation causes nominal income to rise and shifts people into higher tax brackets even though their real income has not risen.

[1]We defined progressive, regressive, and proportional taxes in Chapter 6.

your tax liability will be 10 percent of $20,000 or $2,000. Now, suppose that in Year 2, your income doubles to $40,000, but all prices also double. This means that your nominal income has increased, but your real income has remained constant. After taxes, however, you are worse off because you have just "crept" into a higher income bracket: your tax liability has increased to 15 percent of your income: 0.1($20,000) + 0.2($20,000) = $6,000. Some people would say that this is not "fair," which is the main reason income tax indexation was instituted in 1984. Under the current indexation system, tax brackets and deductions are adjusted each year to reflect the previous year's inflation. In the example here, the tax rate on $40,000 would remain 10 percent.

FISCAL POLICY LAGS

Discretionary fiscal policies are subject to the same kinds of lags that affect monetary policy—recognition, implementation, and impact. Only the recognition lag is the same length for the two policies, however. The implementation lag is likely to be much longer for fiscal policy than it is for monetary policy, and the impact lag can be quite variable.

Why is the implementation lag so long for fiscal policy? Politics is only part of the answer. Politicians have vested interests in fiscal policies. If a tax cut is to be enacted, they want to make sure their constituents benefit. Tax increases are never popular, so Congress will enact them only after an appropriately lengthy period of reasoned debate. Spending policies are just as political: Whose military base should be closed? In which state should the new nuclear energy research plant be built? Such decisions are frequently based on political seniority or similar factors; economic criteria are too often dismissed.[2] Still, it is too simplistic to say that fiscal policy implementation lags are entirely "political." Many more people are involved in the fiscal policy process than just the 535 members of Congress—there are lobbyists, interest groups, and so on—and the federal budget is established on an annual basis. In contrast, the 12 members of the Federal Open Market Committee meet almost every month, so monetary policy changes can be instituted quite quickly.

The impact lag of fiscal policies depends on the particular policy. For example, an individual income tax cut could begin to affect the economy within weeks of its passage by Congress. All that would be needed would be a change in the withholding tables, and you would take home more money in your next paycheck. How soon spending programs affect the economy depends not only on when the funds are authorized, but also when they are actually spent. For example, an increase in the defense budget will affect the economy immediately if the authorization is to raise military salaries, but the effect might take several years if the authorization is for a new battleship.

---

[2]Political scientists have noted a connection between defense spending per state and the seniority of the congressional delegation. For example, Jesse Helms, a U.S. senator for 30 years, has been able to attract billions of defense dollars to his state of North Carolina. Of course, it is not clear whether Helms's seniority and ranking membership on the Senate Armed Forces Committee were responsible for the defense dollars being spent in North Carolina, or whether Helms was reelected because he was able to get the dollars for his state.

The potentially lengthy implementation lag and the uncertain impact lag are the main reasons why few economists advocate discretionary fiscal policies for short-run macroeconomic stabilization. There is some agreement that fiscal policy can be used to provide incentives for long-run growth, but even this issue is not clear. We will look at long-run policy issues in Chapter 33.

TAXES AND INCENTIVES

The deficit has only recently become a preoccupation of economists. Until the last 15 years or so, most analysis of fiscal policy issues revolved around the incentive effects of various kinds of taxes. Taxes affect several kinds of incentives including the incentives to work and save.

Taxes and the Incentive to Work

What is the best way to avoid income taxes? *Don't work!* Few people would opt for that rather drastic exercise in tax avoidance, but you have to admit it would be effective.

Incentive to work The motivation to work. Marginal income tax rates may have an adverse effect on the incentive to work.

The real issue is not whether taxes will cause people to exit the labor force, but how much income taxes affect the **incentive to work**. Here's an example: Many college professors have the opportunity to teach summer school classes for extra pay. Unfortunately, the extra pay is typically quite small—around $3,000 per class at many schools. Still, $3,000 for six weeks of part-time work might be enough for your professor to shorten her vacation a bit—except that she will not take home anything close to $3,000. At current tax rates of 28 percent, you have to subtract $840 from the $3,000. Then subtract 7.65 percent for Social Security, plus state income taxes, medical benefits, and so on. Your professor would be lucky to take home $2,000 of the $3,000 salary.

The story is not completely hypothetical. Several studies have shown that marginal income tax rates do have an effect on the incentive to work, but that most of the impact falls on overtime work and spousal employment.[3] In other words, if you are single and work only 40 hours a week, a tax increase might cause you to grumble, but odds are that you will still put in your 40 hours. On the other hand, if you occasionally put in a few hours of overtime or your spouse has a part-time job, higher taxes *might* cause you to rethink working overtime or your spouse to rethink that part-time job. In the aggregate, these effects might be important. For example, in 1981, economists at the Council of Economic Advisers estimated that a 10 percent cut in the marginal income tax rate would increase the labor supply enough to increase potential GDP by about 0.6 percent. It must be mentioned, however, that many people, especially people with low incomes, may respond to higher marginal tax rates by working more, not less. If the tax increase reduces their take-home pay so much that they cannot pay the bills, they will respond by working more hours.

---

[3]Remember that the marginal income tax rate is the rate paid on the next unit of income. The formula for the marginal tax rate is $\Delta T/\Delta Q$ where T is tax liability and Q is income. This contrasts with the average income tax rate. The formula for the average tax rate is T/Q.

The fact that income taxes can both increase and decrease work effort may explain why the incentive effects of income taxes are typically estimated to be small in the aggregate.

· · · · · · · ·

The Laffer Curve

One of the most celebrated models of the effect of taxes on incentives is the **Laffer curve**, named after its originator, Arthur Laffer, who is now at Pepperdine University. The Laffer curve is based on the idea that the tax *rate* can affect the tax *base* so much that an increase in the tax rate can result in either an increase or a decrease in tax revenues. The Laffer curve was used as justification for the 1981–1983 tax cuts of the Reagan administration.

A Laffer curve is drawn in Figure 31.1. The vertical axis measures the average of all marginal income tax rates in the economy (t). If there are two people in the economy and one pays a 50 percent marginal tax rate and the other pays a 20 percent marginal tax rate, the average marginal tax rate would be 35 (= 70/2) percent, and this figure would be plotted on the diagram. The horizontal axis plots tax revenues (T). The two end points are easy to explain. If the tax rate is zero, tax revenue must be zero as well. Likewise, if the tax rate is 100 percent, no one would work, so tax revenue would also be zero. The interesting situations occur when the tax rate is

Laffer curve This curve shows the relationship between marginal income tax rates and tax revenues; key idea behind 1981–1983 tax cuts.

FIGURE 31.1 THE LAFFER CURVE

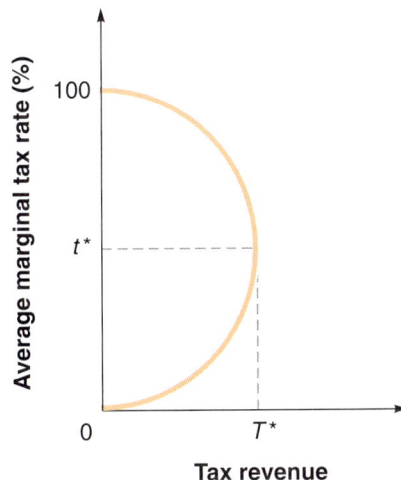

The Laffer curve illustrates the effect of tax rates on the incentive to work and tax revenues. If the average marginal tax rate is zero, tax revenues are zero; if the average marginal tax rate is 100 percent, tax revenues are also zero because no one would work. As the average marginal tax rate rises from 0 toward $t^\star$, tax revenues rise. Maximum tax revenue, $T^\star$, occurs at a tax rate of $t^\star$. If the tax rate is raised above $t^\star$, tax revenues will fall as people reduce their work effort by a larger percentage than the increase in the tax rate.

Economic Recovery Tax Act (ERTA) Major piece of economic legislation of the Reagan administration. Called for, among other things, significant income tax cuts over a three-year period.

Incentive to save The motivation to save. Some argue that by such measures as taxing interest from saving and allowing a deduction for mortgage interest, the U.S. tax system creates disincentives to save.

between 0 and 100 percent. Notice that as the marginal tax rate is raised from 0 toward $t^\star$, tax revenue increases. This is because tax rates are not high enough to generate significant work disincentives. As the tax rate rises above $t^\star$, however, more people decide that working is not worth the trouble. As people exit the labor force and/or decide to illegally hide income, the tax base shrinks and, with it, tax revenue.[4]

Is Laffer curve theory plausible? Certainly: No one can deny that at $t = 0$ or $t = 100$ tax revenues are zero. Likewise, as t rises from zero, tax revenues rise to a point where they begin to fall. However, the practical applicability of the theory is quite another matter. When the Reagan advisers said that the tax cuts of the **Economic Recovery Tax Act** would help to balance the budget (see the Focus box on page 812), they were assuming that the economy was on the upper portion of the Laffer curve. Had they been correct, it *might* have been possible to cut taxes and reduce the budget deficit. It now appears that the economy was on the lower portion of the curve, which meant that the tax cuts reduced tax revenues and the deficit ballooned. Unfortunately, economists know of no simple way to determine exactly where on the Laffer curve the economy is operating at any point in time.

. . . .

Taxes and the Incentive to Save

Saving is important because it is a source of funds for investment, and some economists believe that people in the United States save and invest too little. Taxes can affect the **incentive to save** in several ways. First, most of the interest from saving is taxed in the United States. For example, the interest you earn on a savings account must be declared to the IRS when you file taxes in April. This acts as a disincentive to save. Certain kinds of savings instruments—Individual Retirement Accounts (IRAs) and municipal bonds, for example—are not taxed, but they account for only a small portion of total saving. Many economists believe that a simple way to increase personal saving would be to eliminate the tax on interest earnings from small savings accounts.

One of the most important saving disincentives is caused by the tax deduction for home mortgage interest. Home owners in the United States can deduct home mortgage interest—the largest tax "loophole" in the U.S. tax code. Just how large? Interest often represents as much as $800 of a typical home mortgage payment of $1,000. This translates into a $248 tax cut *per month* for someone in the 31 percent tax bracket. How does this deduction act as a disincentive to save? The tax deduction encourages people to go into debt—which is precisely the opposite of saving. Without the tax deduction, people would demand smaller houses and save a greater portion of their income. Over time, the United States would invest fewer resources in housing, and more funds would be available for lending to other industries. Some economists believe that the ability to deduct home mortgage interest is a major reason why the saving rate in the United States is so low; few other countries allow the deduction of home mortgage interest.

---

[4]Students who have completed microeconomics will note that the substitution effect is larger on the upward-sloping portion of the Laffer curve while the income effect is larger on the backward-bending portion of the curve.

A National Consumption Tax? You can always avoid paying taxes on savings by spending your money instead. The problem, of course, is that would result in lower saving—and potentially have adverse effects on investment as well. Some economists who believe that it is important to increase the amount of saving in the United States have recommended that the income tax be reduced and revenue losses made up with a national consumption tax.[5] Implementation of a consumption tax would be relatively easy. Consumption spending could be calculated as the difference between annual income and annual saving; providing this information to the IRS would be no more difficult than filling out a 1040A form. Theoretically, at least, when people realized that the way to avoid the consumption tax was to save, the national saving rate would increase. Three objections have been raised to the idea of a national consumption tax. First, it would be regressive because it would be difficult for the poor to avoid it; this problem might be reduced by exempting certain necessities like food and clothing from the consumption tax. Second, many people are hesitant to give the government another power to tax. Finally, if a consumption tax did reduce current spending, it could be contractionary.

. . . .

Business Taxes and Investment

Corporate profits are subject to the corporate income tax. The only catch is that no one really knows who pays corporate taxes! At first glance, it may appear that the corporation pays the tax in the form of lower after-tax returns. However, corporations may try to shift the tax to the consumer in the form of higher prices or to the shareholder in the form of lower dividends. This is one reason why some economists now believe that corporate taxes should be reduced or even eliminated.

Several kinds of tax policies have been designed to stimulate business investment, but the **investment tax credit (ITC)** and **accelerated depreciation allowances** have been the most important in recent years. The ITC was first instituted in the 1960s and has been used on and off several times since then. The ITC allows firms to reduce the tax liability on their profits by a portion of the cost of new investment expenditures. This reduces the cost of investment and thus stimulates investment. Accelerated depreciation allowances permit firms to write off capital goods more quickly. When a firm can deduct a larger amount of depreciation from its gross sales, its net taxable income falls. This increases the firm's cash flow and thus increases money available for investment expenditures.

Another tax that can have an effect on investment is the **capital gains tax**.[6] Until the **Tax Reform Act of 1986**, capital gains were afforded preferential treatment; that is, income from capital gains was taxed at lower rates than labor income. Why should capital gains be given preferential treatment? Some economists believe that lower taxes on capital gains encourage people to invest in real and financial assets because the gains they make from selling these assets are taxed at a lower rate. A lower capital

Investment tax credit (ITC) Fiscal policy designed to stimulate business investment. Firms receive a tax credit for money spent on new investments.

Accelerated depreciation allowance Firms are allowed to depreciate capital goods more rapidly than they actually wear out; this reduces tax liability and leaves the firm with additional after-tax profits to be used for investment.

Capital gains tax Tax on profits from buying an asset at a low price and selling it at a high price.

Tax Reform Act of 1986 Revenue-neutral tax act that simplified the personal income tax system by reducing the number of tax brackets from 14 to 3 and shifted burden from individuals to business.

---

[5]An alternative would be a value-added tax. See the Focus box in Chapter 22 for a discussion of value-added taxes.

[6]Remember the definition of a capital gain in Chapter 29: If you buy a financial asset at a low price and sell it at a high price, you have made a capital gain. Bond holders make capital gains when interest rates fall; stockholders make capital gains when improving profit expectations (or other factors) increase the price of stock.

A Brief Look at Recent Tax Policies

The 1980s and 1990s were a period of significant fiscal policy changes; some would say a fiscal revolution. The most important fiscal policies were the Economic Recovery Tax Act of 1981, the Tax Reform Act of 1986, and President Clinton's 1993 tax package.

The Economic Recovery Tax Act

The 1980 presidential election, like most elections in recent memory, centered on economic issues. The key idea behind candidate Reagan's economic platform was *supply-side economics*—the idea that the best way to boost the economy from recession was to provide incentives for saving and investment that would stimulate capital expansion, technology, and productivity growth. Supply-side economics was based on the premise that old-fashioned Keynesian aggregate demand policies and high marginal tax rates did more harm than good because of adverse economic incentives. One of the key components of supply-side economics was a tax cut proposal that was to become the Economic Recovery Tax Act of 1981 (ERTA). ERTA capitalized on this idea by calling for 10 percent cuts in the marginal income tax rate each year for three years in a row. Congress did not complete the legislation until October, so the final cuts were 5 percent in the first year and 10 percent for the next two years. Additionally, income tax rates were indexed to inflation beginning in the fourth year.

How did ERTA affect the economy? The assumption made in the 1981 *Economic Report of the President* was that a 10 percent cut in income taxes would increase work effort and thus potential output by as much as 0.6 percent. Was this correct? Perhaps, but a definitive answer is next to impossible because ERTA was not enacted in isolation. For example, transfer payment cuts accompanied the tax cuts. What is clear is that the economy enjoyed almost eight years of uninterrupted expansion beginning in December 1982—a fact that ERTA advocates do not fail to mention. ERTA advocates call less attention to the largest peacetime fiscal deficits in U.S. history that followed in the wake of the tax cuts.

ERTA also had an impact on income distribution. According to a Congressional Budget Office study that compared the average net gain after taxes and transfer changes between 1982 and 1984, people with incomes under $10,000 lost $440 while people with incomes over $80,000 gained $8,930. This issue was brought up repeatedly by the Democrats and was to be a factor in the passage of the Tax Reform Act of 1986.

The Tax Reform Act of 1986

After more than a year of debate, Congress passed the Tax Reform Act of 1986. The act accomplished three main things. First, it simplified the tax system by reducing the number of income brackets from 14 to 3 (15, 28, and 31 percent) and eliminating many deductions and preferences. Second, it lowered income taxes for many middle- and lower-income families. Third, it shifted almost $120 billion of the tax burden from individuals to business. Finally, it was advertised as being *revenue-neutral*, a buzz word meaning that it would not affect the deficit.

The Tax Reform Act was the result of genuine compromise—compromise between the Senate and the House, between Democrats and Republicans, and between Congress and the president. The compromise was possible because the tax system had become horrendously complex and was widely perceived to be unfair. Like any compromise, it involved winners and losers. Many people had to give up their IRAs. Individuals can no longer deduct state and local sales taxes or consumer interest, although mortgage interest on primary and secondary residences may still be deducted. Many tax shelters, especially in

real estate, were restricted or eliminated completely. Business had to accept a minimum tax and give up accelerated depreciation. Private universities were no longer allowed to issue tax-free bonds. The biggest winners were lower- and middle-income families who could not take advantage of deductions and loopholes under the old tax plan. Preferential treatment for capital gains was also eliminated.

What have been the economic effects of the new law? The biggest initial concern was that the elimination of the investment tax credit and the introduction of less-accelerated depreciation allowances would reduce the incentive to invest. However, there is also hope that the new business tax structure will increase the quality of investment. Many investments previously were profitable only because of the tax advantages.

Lower personal tax rates may increase the incentive to save, although most empirical evidence suggests that this effect will be fairly small, and new restrictions on IRAs will offset much of any savings increase. A 1992 study by the Federal Reserve Bank of St. Louis showed that the elimination of the deductibility of consumer interest led to a small reduction in consumer borrowing and thus to a like increase in personal saving. Lower personal marginal tax rates may also increase the incentive to work, though again the effects are likely to be small. Finally, tax compliance may improve if people perceive the new law as more fair than the old system.

THE CLINTON TAX PACKAGE OF 1993

Candidate Clinton campaigned on the promise of a middle-class tax cut but was forced to raise taxes in an attempt to bring the deficit under control. Most of the tax hikes were levied at upper-income individuals: The highest tax bracket under the Tax Reform Act of 1986 was 31 percent; the new law added two higher tax brackets. Couples now pay 36 percent on taxable income over $140,000, and the highest tax bracket calls for a 39.6 percent rate on taxable incomes over $250,000. The plan also called for increased taxes on upper-income retirees who pay taxes on Social Security benefits. The biggest hit to middle-income taxpayers was probably the 4.3 cent per gallon tax increase on gasoline. It is safe to say that no one likes higher taxes, but it should also be noted that U.S. citizens remain the lowest-taxed people in the industrial world. The following table provides the tax rates and tax brackets established by the 1993 tax plan. These data are meant only as a rough guide; the Tax Code allows for numerous exceptions and qualifications.

Unlike ERTA or the Tax Reform Act of 1986, the main purpose of the Clinton tax package was to deal with the deficit, not to stimulate the economy or reform the tax system. The hope, of course, was that a policy that made credible progress against the deficit would stimulate business. However, many people expressed concern that small businesses will bear too much of the burden because many small business owners are taxed as individuals and therefore are liable for the 39.6 percent maximum income tax rate. The maximum tax rate on corporate incomes over $10 million is only 36 percent. It remains to be seen how this tax plan will affect the economy.

1993 INCOME TAX RATES

		Single		
$0–22,100	$22,101–53,500	$53,501–115,000	$115,001–250,000	Over $250,001
15%	28%	31%	36%	39.6%
		Married		
$0–36,900	$36,901–89,150	$89,151–140,000	$140,001–250,000	Over $250,001
15%	28%	31%	36%	39.6%

gains tax could also encourage firms to retain earnings instead of paying out dividends because stockholders would be taxed less on capital gains than on dividend income. However, other economists believe that preferential treatment for capital gains primarily encourages paper investment—stock trading, not physical capital accumulation—and represents an unfair benefit for the rich.

THE FISCAL DEFICIT: DEFINITIONS AND DATA

Fiscal deficit The difference between annual government spending and annual government tax revenues.

That ogre, the **fiscal deficit**, is just the difference between government spending and tax revenues. Nothing could be simpler: if you have a budget deficit, just raise taxes or cut spending. Right? Hardly! Not only will special interest groups fight tooth and nail to prevent their special spending program from being cut, but almost *everyone* will resist a tax hike. And finally, we economists know that raising taxes or cutting spending can slow the economy and bring on recession. That simple accounting entity called a fiscal deficit can be an insurmountable political obstacle.

The Actual Budget Deficit

The deficit problem has not always been so severe. Politicians and some economists moaned about deficits even in the 1950s, but in retrospect, those deficits were tiny—something a quick look back at Figure 6.1 in Chapter 6 will reveal. Still, even that glimpse misses a key point: most economists think that the impact of the deficit depends not on its absolute size, but on its size relative to the amount of saving in the economy. It is also important to understand the cause of the deficit and consider when it occurs. To understand these issues, we need first to distinguish between cyclical and structural deficits.

The government cannot forecast the deficit precisely because both tax revenues and government spending depend on the state of the economy. All the government can do is estimate the size of the deficit for different states of the economy. This means that a budget that would have been balanced at full employment will become a deficit if the economy falls into a recession. For example, suppose the government budget is $200 and it estimates potential GDP to be $1,000; then, a tax rate of 20 percent will result in a balanced budget if the economy is operating at potential GDP. If the economy falls into a recession, however, actual GDP will fall below $1,000 and tax revenues will fall below $200. The resulting deficit is called a **cyclical deficit**: the economy went through a business cycle contraction, and the government deficit automatically increased. On the other hand, if projected government spending is greater than projected tax revenues even at potential GDP, the deficit is said to be **structural**. It is important to note that while the government can enact a budget with a zero structural deficit, it cannot enact a budget with a zero cyclical deficit because it is impossible to forecast GDP growth precisely.

Cyclical deficit A deficit caused by recession. Cyclical deficits tend to reduce the severity of recessions.

Structural deficit The fiscal deficit that exists when the economy is operating at potential GDP and full employment; often thought to cause "crowding out."

These definitions can be made more precise with a bit of algebra. If we assume that government spending is entirely autonomous but that tax revenues are entirely induced,[7] the actual budget deficit can be written as:

---

[7]Recall the definitions of *autonomous* and *induced* from Chapter 24: an autonomous variable does not vary with income; an induced variable does vary with income.

$$\text{Actual budget deficit: } D = G_0 - T = G_0 - tPQ \qquad [1]$$

Where:

D = actual deficit

G_0 = level of government expenditure, assumed autonomous[8]

T = tax revenue

t = income tax rate, $0 < t < 1$

PQ = nominal GDP; P = price index, Q = real GDP

Now, there are four variables in Equation 1—G_0, t, P, and Q—so the actual budget deficit will change if any of these variables change. Most importantly, because policymakers can directly control only government spending and the tax rate, not the price level or real GDP, it may not be possible to set the level of the deficit precisely.

Cyclical and Structural Deficits

To gauge the effect of the deficit on the economy, economists compare the actual budget deficit to the structural deficit. The structural deficit can be written as:

$$\text{Structural budget deficit: } D^\star = G_0 - tPQ^\star \qquad [2]$$

Where:

$D^\star$ = structural deficit

$Q^\star$ = potential GDP

G_0, t, and P are defined as before.

The problem with Equation 2, of course, is that it is impossible to observe potential GDP, so any estimate of the structural deficit is just that, an estimate. Some economists estimated that about half of the deficits of the 1980s were structural, but there was little consensus about these estimates. The difference between the actual deficit and the structural deficit is the cyclical deficit. The cyclical deficit—also an estimate because it can be calculated only for a given estimate of potential GDP—is an automatic stabilizer because it acts to dampen economic fluctuations. When the economy falls into a recession, cyclical unemployment rises. The result is an automatic increase in the cyclical deficit because income tax revenue falls while government spending for unemployment compensation, welfare, and other entitlement programs increases. When the economy expands, the reverse occurs and the cyclical deficit shrinks. This acts to slow the economic expansion and reduce the chances of demand-pull inflation.[9] Not all economists agree with this analysis or accept the relationship between the cyclical deficits and economic activity. For example, Robert Eisner (see the Focus box on page 818) questions whether we are measuring the deficit correctly and recommends an alternate method of measurement.

[8]The assumption that government spending is autonomous means that we are ignoring unemployment insurance and other kinds of government spending that vary with economic activity. This does not alter the essential results because we are assuming that taxes are induced.

[9]We discussed demand-pull inflation in Chapters 26 and 27. Demand-pull inflation occurs when a continuing increase in aggregate demand causes the price index to spiral upward. In the early stages of demand-pull inflation, real GDP also increases.

····FIGURE 31.2 THE CYCLICAL AND STRUCTURAL DEFICITS

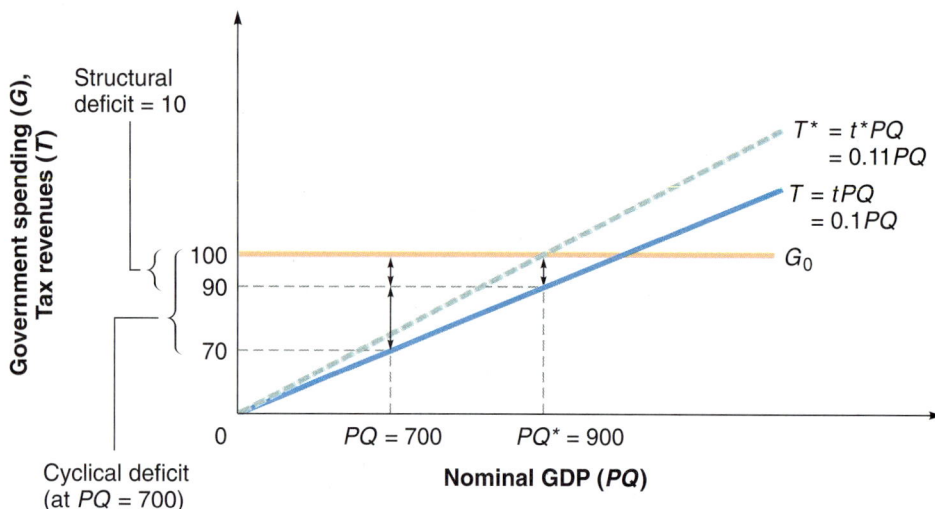

The cyclical deficit varies over the business cycle; the structural deficit does not. In this example, the structural deficit is equal to the distance between the government spending function and the tax function above potential GDP, which is assumed to be $900. The tax function takes 10 percent of nominal GDP, and government spending is $100, so the structural deficit is $10 for all levels of GDP. The magnitude of the cyclical deficit depends on the state of the economy. If the economy is operating at $PQ = 700$, tax revenues will be $70 and government spending is $100, so the actual deficit is $30. The cyclical deficit is $20—the difference between the actual deficit and the structural deficit. The structural deficit could be eliminated by reducing government spending so that the government line intersects the tax function above $PQ^{\star}$ (not shown) or by increasing taxes. An increase in the tax rate to 11 percent would approximately eliminate the structural deficit. $0.11(900) = \$99 \approx \$100$.

Figure 31.2 illustrates the cyclical and structural deficits graphically. Nominal GDP is on the horizontal axis, and both government spending and tax revenues are measured on the vertical axis. We are assuming that government spending is all autonomous, so it is graphed as a horizontal line equal to $100. The tax function is upward sloping to reflect the fact that the income tax rate is a positive fraction of nominal GDP. In this case, the tax rate is 10 percent. Now, if potential GDP is estimated to be $900, there will be a structural deficit of $10—government spending will be $100 but tax revenues will be only $0.1(900) = \$90$. The structural deficit exists regardless of the level of actual GDP. If actual GDP is $700, tax revenues will be only $70, so the actual deficit will rise to $30 (= $100 − $70), of which $20 is cyclical and $10 is structural. The cyclical deficit could be eliminated with economic growth that raised GDP to $900. Elimination of the structural deficit would require a policy change. One option would be to increase the tax rate to 11 percent. This is shown as the dotted line in the figure. Another option would be to reduce government spending, which would cause the government line to shift down to intersect the tax function at $PQ^{\star}$. Note, however, that either policy will tend to slow economic growth and thus increase the cyclical deficit.

••••• **FIGURE 31.3** DEFICIT/SAVING RATIO, 1960–1992

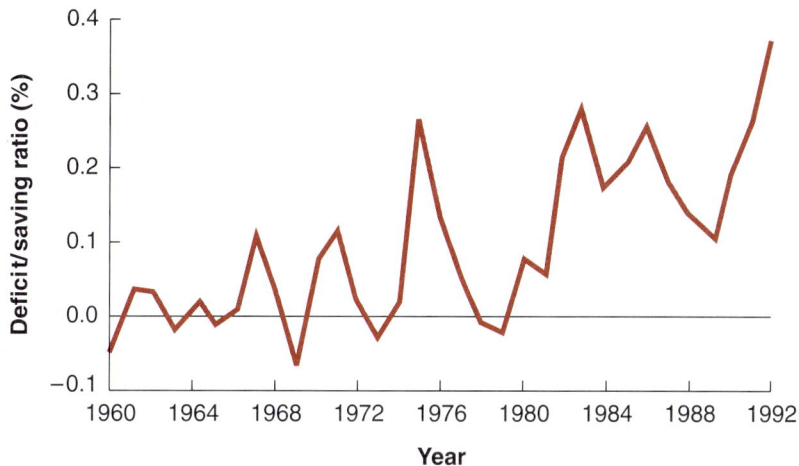

Saving is gross saving by individuals and corporations; deficits are from total government—the combined deficits of all levels of government.

SOURCE: 1994 *Economic Report of the President*, Tables B-27 and B-80.

••••••••

The Deficit/Saving Ratio

When the government runs a deficit, it must be financed by borrowing money. Government borrowing constitutes a major part of the demand for loanable funds. For a given supply of loanable funds, increased government borrowing can result in higher interest rates and, possibly, a decline in private investment because less funds are available for private borrowing. This is the problem of **crowding out**, potentially one of the most serious problems of government deficits. To gauge whether government borrowing represents a significant drain on the supply of loanable funds available for private investment, economists look at the deficit/saving ratio, with a higher ratio indicating more likely crowding out.

Crowding out The decline in private investment due to government borrowing, which drains the supply of loanable funds and leads to higher interest rates.

The deficit/saving ratio is plotted in Figure 31.3. Notice that while the ratio has had ups and downs, it also appears to have been drifting upward since the late 1970s. The chart invites three questions. First, why is the series so erratic? The answer is simple: because of economic fluctuations and the resulting cyclical deficits. The sharp spikes correspond to recessions; the valleys correspond to cyclical peaks. Second, what explains the ratio's upward drift? This question is a little tougher. Many economists contend that, at least from the 1980s onward, the upward trend represents growing structural deficits brought on by excessive spending and overzealous tax cutting in the 1980s. This issue is far from resolved, however.

Finally, how does the U.S. experience compare to that of other countries? The answer is not very well. Some countries run larger deficits (as a fraction of GDP) than the United States—but almost every country saves a much higher fraction of GDP as well. For example, over the period 1980–1988, total gross private saving was 18.7 percent of GDP in the United States while the deficit was 2.1 percent. Things

FOCUS ON

WILL THE REAL DEFICIT PLEASE STAND UP?
ROBERT EISNER'S ADJUSTED DEFICIT

Separating the structural deficit from the actual deficit gives an important insight into the effect of fiscal policy on the economy. But, even the structural deficit does not track very well with GDP fluctuations and thus may not give a very good indication of the stance of fiscal policy. The problem, says Robert Eisner of Northwestern University, is that we have been measuring the deficit incorrectly. Many of Eisner's ideas on the deficit can be found in his recent book, *The Misunderstood Economy* (Cambridge, Mass.: Harvard Business School Press, 1994).

Eisner makes two basic points. First, he believes that the government should follow accounting practices similar to those used by business and distinguish between current and capital expenditures. Capital expenditures, such as education and social infrastructure, yield future returns whereas current expenditures, such as defense and current maintenance of parks, do not. This difference is important in assessing the burden of the deficit. Second, Eisner believes that the deficit must be adjusted for inflation and changes in the real interest rate. Current inflation lowers the real value of existing debt and thus reduces the true cost of current deficits. Falling real interest rates, which frequently accompany inflation, also lower the real value of existing government debt.

When the federal deficit is adjusted for price and interest rate effects, the fiscal history of the United States changes remarkably. Though both the actual and the structural budget have

Robert Eisner

are quite different in the other advanced democracies of the world: total gross private savings averaged 22.4 percent, while the average government budget was in *surplus* to the tune of 0.9 percent of GDP.[10] Things may improve in the future because of demographic changes. In the 1970s and 1980s, the high-saving proportion of the population—those between ages 45 and 64—was lower in the United States than in either Japan and Germany. During the next 20 years, this group will grow faster in the United States than in either country. If the past is any guide, the level of saving should increase somewhat as a result.[11]

[10]The "advanced democracies" are the Organization for Economic Cooperation and Development (OECD) countries. The OECD countries include Western Europe, the United States, Canada, and Japan as well as Australia and New Zealand. The data come from OECD *National Accounts*.

[11]This conclusion is offered by Stephen A. Meyer, "Saving and Demographics: Some International Comparisons," *Business Review*, Federal Reserve Bank of Philadelphia (March/April 1992): 13–22.

been in deficit every year since 1970—an indication of fiscal stimulus—Eisner's adjusted deficit showed a surplus during the recession years. Eisner uses this as evidence that his adjusted deficit is a better indicator of the impact of fiscal policy, and that the large adjusted deficit was a major contributing cause for the 1981–1982 recession. The accompanying figure plots GDP growth and changes in the adjusted deficit, lagged one year. Note how closely the two series track—evidence in support of Eisner's position.

Eisner's adjusted deficit has received quite a bit of attention lately, but not all economists are convinced that it is the deficit measure we should concentrate on. Many believe that the standard structural deficit has not tracked well with economic activity because of conflicting monetary policy: the fiscal stimulus from the structural deficits of the 1970s and the 1980s was not apparent because money was tight at the same time. Further, to the extent that expectations matter in economic affairs, it is the published deficit that will elicit responses from economic agents, not a deficit calculated by an academic economist, even one who happens to be a past president of the American Economic Association.

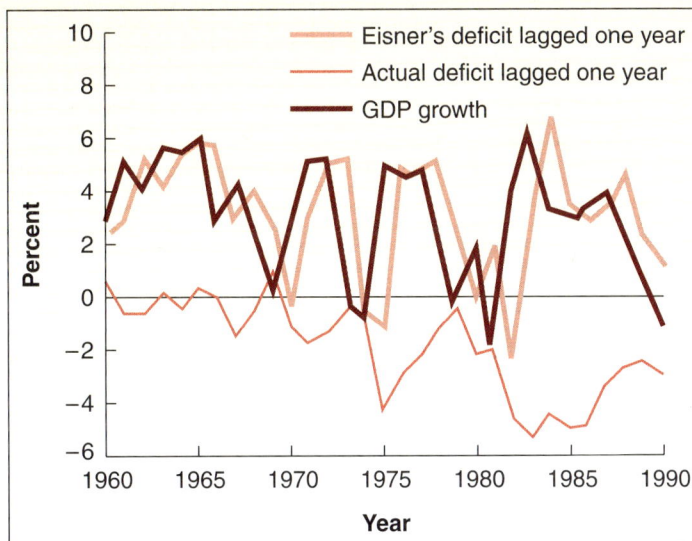

SOURCE: Deficit calculations by Robert Eisner; real GDP growth from 1994 *Economic Report of the President,* Table B-2. All data are in percentage change.

PROBLEMS WITH THE FISCAL DEFICIT

As we have already mentioned, one potential effect of the deficit is crowding out, a problem that needs further elaboration because the extent depends on the stage of the business cycle and consumer expectations. Also, many people contend that deficits cause inflation. Finally, the fiscal deficit can have an adverse effect on the trade deficit.

Crowding Out over the Business Cycle

We know that government borrowing can put pressure on the financial markets and may cause interest rates to rise. If rates do rise, private investment will be "crowded out"; in effect, government spending will replace private spending. Does this *always* occur? Almost certainly not. Most economists feel that crowding out is a problem only if the economy is expanding and close to potential GDP. If the economy is in a recession, the government deficit can actually *crowd in* private spending by stimulating the economy and improving business confidence.

Much of the recent discussion on the crowding out issue centered around analysis of the fiscal deficits of the 1980s. As we already know, deficits ballooned in the early 1980s and stayed large despite the growing real GDP during the 1983–1990 expansion. If ever there was a case of crowding out, this should have been one. In reality, however, although the rate of investment spending was quite low, it actually increased over this period. Is this evidence that the crowding out hypothesis is incorrect? Perhaps, but another factor was also involved: foreign capital inflows. The combination of high deficits and tight money did cause real interest rates to rise during the period. In a closed economy, the effects could have been disastrous, but the economy is not closed. High interest rates in the United States attracted foreign investors to U.S. capital markets. Foreign demand for U.S. financial assets—both corporate and government—tended to moderate interest rates and the potential for crowding out.[12] Most economists feel that foreign participation in U.S. financial markets was a stabilizing influence on the U.S. economy. Some people and politicians disagreed, however. While it may be good for foreigners to lend us money now, it may not be quite so good when we have to pay off our loans in the future. We will look at this issue in more detail in Chapter 36.

• • • • • • • •

Ricardian Equivalence

Ricardian equivalence theorem
Holds that government deficits do not affect real interest rates because expectations of future tax increases cause people to increase saving today.

Perhaps the biggest controversy surrounding the crowding out debate concerns an idea known as the **Ricardian equivalence theorem**, a key implication of the rational expectations hypothesis. In short, this theorem states that deficits have no effect on real interest rates and thus cannot result in crowding out. What is the reasoning behind this assertion? Fiscal deficits, it is argued, are a signal to households that the government must raise taxes in the future. In anticipation of this future tax increase, consumers increase their current saving to make sure they have enough money to pay the expected higher future taxes. As a result, the pool of savings increases enough to offset the pressure on interest rates caused by government borrowing. In theory at least, private saving increases so much that the deficit has no impact on interest rates at all.

Ricardian equivalence is illustrated with a loanable funds diagram in Figure 31.4. The vertical axis measures the real interest rate, and the horizontal axis measures the quantity of loanable funds—funds that borrowers desire and savers are willing to lend. The loanable funds supply curve is upward sloping to reflect the fact that people are more willing to lend at higher interest rates than at low interest rates. The loanable funds demand curve is downward sloping because less is borrowed at high interest rates than at low interest rates, *ceteris paribus*. The equilibrium interest rate occurs at

---

[12]What is the mechanism that causes foreign demand for U.S. financial assets to reduce interest rates? Recall that bond prices and interest rates are inversely related. As the number of buyers increased, the price of bonds rose. This caused interest rates to fall.

···· FIGURE 31.4 CROWDING OUT AND RICARDIAN EQUIVALENCE

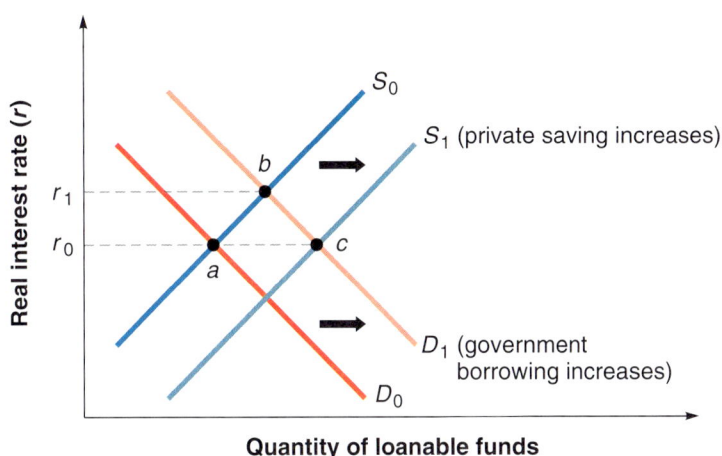

Government borrowing will tend to raise interest rates unless Ricardian equivalence applies. In this case, the government borrows to finance its deficit. Government borrowing represents an increase in the demand for loanable funds so the demand curve shifts out from D_0 to D_1. If the supply of loanable funds does not change, the interest rate will rise from r_0 to r_1 and result in crowding out. Ricardian equivalence assumes that people will increase current saving in anticipation of higher taxes in the future. This will shift the supply curve out from S_0 to S_1, prevent interest rates from rising, and eliminate crowding out.

the intersection of the demand and supply curves at point a. Now suppose that the government borrows to finance a fiscal deficit. This will shift the loanable funds demand curve outward from D_0 to D_1 and move the economy to point b. The result will be higher interest rates and crowding out—unless Ricardian equivalence applies. If people increase current saving in anticipation of higher taxes in the future, the loanable funds supply curve will also shift outward from S_0 to S_1. The economy will end up at point c with no increase in interest rates and thus no crowding out.

Is there evidence to support Ricardian equivalence? Yes. Studies by Robert Barro of Harvard, Paul Evans of Ohio State, and others have found what they believe to be clear evidence in support of the theory. However, Alan Blinder of Princeton, Paul Samuelson of MIT, and others have found evidence to refute Ricardian equivalence.[13] The verdict is obviously still out. Most economists accept that savings decisions are made with an eye toward the future, but precisely how much people adjust their current saving in response to current deficits is hard to say. Credibility also matters. In the 1980s, the Reagan administration argued that it was possible to grow out of the deficit, and in 1988 George Bush campaigned with a "No new taxes"

[13]The theory is also something of a litmus test for rational expectations theorists. When Nobel laureate Paul Samuelson asked Robert Barro if he really believed Ricardian equivalence, Barro reportedly responded, "Yes, and so does every other good economist under age 40."

FOCUS ON

A BAD IDEA WHOSE TIME HAD COME:
THE GRAMM-RUDMAN DEFICIT REDUCTION ACT

The budget proposal submitted by President Reagan in early 1985 called for the elimination of some social programs in order to increase defense spending and lower the deficit from more than $200 billion to "only" $180 billion without having to raise taxes. After unsuccessful attempts to reach a compromise budget, Congress came up with the Gramm-Rudman Act, which President Reagan signed into law in December. No one really liked the act. Even Phil Gramm, one of the principal authors, called it a "bad idea whose time had come," but it seemed to be the only measure likely to come out of Congress with any hope of reducing the deficit.

The intent of the Gramm-Rudman Act was to force Congress to balance the budget by reducing the deficit by $36 billion each year until 1991. The Office of Management and Budget (OMB) and the Congressional Budget Office (CBO) were required to review the annual budget proposal from Congress to determine whether it came within $10 billion of the deficit target. If not, half of the excess spending would be cut from defense spending, and half from social spending, with certain programs—Social Security and some antipoverty programs—exempt. The need to cut spending would be reported to the comptroller general who would then instruct the president to hold back or *sequester* the required amount of money. This aspect of the law was declared unconstitutional in the summer of 1986 because it gave executive powers to the comptroller general. But since the rest of the act was upheld, this ruling meant only that Congress had to find other ways to cut spending. When the first deadline for deficit reductions arrived on October 10, 1986, Congress acted characteristically: it ignored the law. The deficit for fiscal year 1986 was $221 billion, $77 billion more than the Gramm-Rudman mandate.

Several concerns have been expressed about the law. The most immediate question was whether it would cause a recession by mandating too rapid a reduction in the deficit. Gramm-Rudman did recognize the role of automatic stabilizers to some extent because sequestration was to be suspended when GDP growth fell below a 1 percent annual rate for two successive quarters. However, no provision was made for the *level* of GDP. When GDP is still considerably below potential, the economy may need additional stimulation even though GDP growth exceeds 1 percent.

The biggest problem with Gramm-Rudman was its provision for auto-

pledge. For Ricardian equivalence to hold, savers must have believed that Reagan and Bush were mistaken—or less than honest.

· · · · · · · ·

Does the Deficit Cause Inflation?

As we found out in Chapter 28, deficits can be inflationary. The reasoning is based on an application of the quantity theory of money: if the Federal Reserve "monetizes" the deficit by purchasing newly issued government debt, the money supply increases and this can cause inflation. However, deficits are usually financed by selling securities to commercial banks and the public. In this case, there is little change in

Co-sponsors of a bill to balance the budget, left to right, Senator Warren Rudman, R-NH; Senator Phil Gramm, R-TX; and Senator Ernest Hollings, D-SC.

matic and *arbitrary* sequestration. For example, would it be appropriate to cut defense and the national zoo budget equally? When cuts are necessary, it is undoubtedly better to decide rationally which programs can be cut and which should not be. Ironically, this provision could be the reason the act was passed by Congress and signed by the president. Congress probably thought it would be a way to achieve cuts in Reagan's defense buildup. President Reagan may have thought it would be a way to force Congress to accept some of his cuts in nondefense spending.

Gramm-Rudman is inflexible because it requires all adjustments to the deficit to come from the spending side. Most—but not all—economists believe that if something must be done about the deficit, a better solution would be to combine spending cuts with tax increases. Given that deficit reduction targets do have a certain political appeal, a more flexible and preferable plan would be to target reductions in the structural budget deficit.

In retrospect, the concerns over the act were really moot because Congress chose to ignore its mandates. The deficit fell below $150 billion in 1988 and 1989, but topped $200 billion in 1991—the year the act had mandated a balanced budget. As the economy limped through 1992, the deficit topped $300 billion—not only the highest absolute figure in U.S. history, but close to the highest as a percentage of GDP as well. And no one had repealed the Gramm-Rudman Act in the meantime . . .

the money supply, and presumably little inflation. Further, the largest deficits in U.S. history occurred in the 1980s and early 1990s—a period marked by remarkable price stability. Does this mean that deficits are not inflationary? Not exactly.

Potentially, deficits can lead to inflation through at least two mechanisms. First, deficits represent an increase in aggregate demand, so if they occur when the economy is close to potential GDP, they can lead to demand-pull inflation. Second, to the extent that deficits represent a shift of resources from "productive" uses by the private sector to "nonproductive" uses by the government, they represent increases in spending and income without a corresponding increase in output. This too can be inflationary.

· · · · · · · ·

The Twin Deficits

Many economists feel that there is a connection between the fiscal deficit and the trade deficit—the so-called twin deficit problem. During the 1980s, for example, both rose to record highs. There are two reasons why the twin deficits may be related. First, as we found out in Chapter 25, the income-expenditure model holds that leakages (saving, imports, and taxes) and injections (investment, exports, and government) will be equal when the economy is in equilibrium. This suggests that a fiscal deficit ($G > T$) is related to the trade deficit ($Z > X$). It does *not* necessarily follow, however, that a larger fiscal deficit always leads to a larger trade deficit, because the difference could be made up by an excess of saving over investment.

The other possible linkage between the twin deficits is through interest rates and exchange rates. If government deficits affect interest rates, they also affect exchange rates. To see why, suppose that interest rates are higher in the United States than in the rest of the world. High interest rates act as an incentive for foreigners to buy interest-earning assets in the United States. Because these assets are denominated in U.S. dollars, foreign citizens must first exchange their currencies for dollars. This increases the demand for dollars. An increase in demand causes price to rise, and the price of dollars is the exchange rate. We will spend more time on exchange rates and international finance in Chapters 36 and 37.

Many economists believe that this scenario occurred in the first half of the 1980s. Fiscal deficits caused real interest rates to rise, and this caused the dollar to strengthen against most major currencies. For example, in 1980, the dollar bought only 1.85 German marks; by mid-1985 it bought 2.78. What was the effect of the stronger dollar? Each dollar bought more foreign currency so imported goods became cheaper. U.S. citizens responded by increasing their purchase of foreign products. The reverse was true for our trading partners: the stronger dollar meant weaker foreign currencies. This raised the price of imports from the United States and reduced U.S. exports.

Evidence from the 1980s is not sufficient to prove that the twin deficits have a cause and effect relationship. The consensus view appears to be that the twin deficits are related, but some economists have used statistical models to show that they are unrelated. Part of the reason for the disagreement may be that it is probably the structural deficit that affects interest rates, but the structural deficit can only be estimated, not observed directly.

THE NATIONAL DEBT

National debt The sum of all annual fiscal deficits and surpluses since the United States became a sovereign state.

The fiscal deficit is an annual figure; the **national debt** is the sum of all past outstanding fiscal deficits and surpluses. Like the deficit, the national debt is the subject of frequent newspaper editorials and political debate. Some of these concerns are undoubtedly justified, but just as with the deficit, public hysteria probably overstates the problem.

· · · · · · · ·

Data and Definitions

We plotted the rise of the national debt in Figure 6.2 of Chapter 6. There it was apparent that the national debt had increased dramatically in the past decade—not surprising given that the deficit increased so rapidly in the 1980s. Most economists analyze the effects of the national debt by looking at its ratio to GDP. This ratio is useful because it helps to put the national debt in perspective. For example, the national debt in 1993—about $4.5 trillion—was more than 50 percent greater than the 1983 GDP, but it was only about 75 percent as large as the 1993 GDP.

The national debt/GDP ratio for the years 1940–1993 is shown in Figure 31.5. Notice that the debt/GDP ratio rose significantly in the 1940s when the government went into debt to finance World War II. At its peak in 1945, the ratio was almost 1.3, meaning that the national debt was about 30 percent larger than annual GDP. After the war, the debt/GDP ratio fell steadily because GDP grew faster than the national debt. This trend reversed in the 1980s because GDP growth slowed and the deficit jumped to record highs.

· · · · · · · ·

Capital versus Consumption Expenditures

The pattern revealed in Figure 31.5 highlights an important issue in understanding the potential problems associated with the national debt. The seriousness of the problem depends, in part, on what caused the debt. The big jump in the debt/GDP ratio in the 1940s was caused by the need to finance World War II. Would anyone seriously argue that the United States was worse off having incurred the debt? Almost certainly not. World War II expenditures represented "investment" in the sense that future generations—the people paying back the debts of the 1940s with higher taxes—receive benefits from the war victory. There is a sense of equity in the idea that the people benefiting from a program help pay for it.

· · · · · **FIGURE 31.5 DEBT/GDP RATIO, 1940–1993**

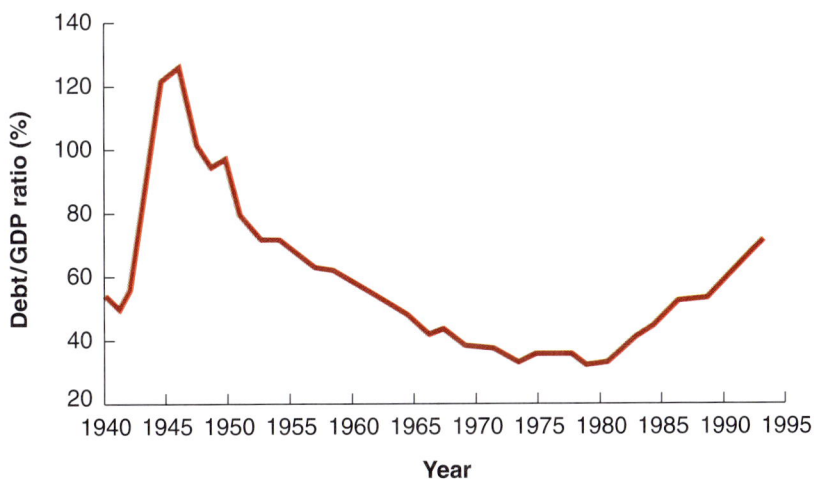

The debt/GDP ratio rose dramatically in the 1940s due to the expenditures necessary to fight World War II. The ratio fell steadily until 1980 because GDP grew faster than the national debt. The deficits of the 1980s reversed that trend.

SOURCE: 1994 *Economic Report of the President*, Table B-79.

The situation is different when the national debt rises because of current expenditures that do not generate benefits for future generations. This is why some people were concerned about the rising debt levels of the 1980s. Very little was invested in social infrastructure—roads, schools, and the like—or other goods that would benefit future taxpayers. Debt caused by these kinds of expenditures can impose a burden on future generations who will be making tax payments without receiving any benefits.

. . . .

Income Distribution

One of the problems with the fiscal deficit is that it may raise interest rates; one of the problems with the national debt is that it results in interest costs to the government. In fact, interest on the national debt has been the fastest-growing component of government spending in the 1980s and 1990s. In 1993, interest on the debt was almost 14 percent of total government spending, or roughly 3.1 percent of GDP. These interest payments can be a problem because they represent a transfer from all taxpayers to the people who were wealthy enough to buy government debt when it was issued. Nevertheless, this problem may not be as significant as it seems at first because some government debt is bought by middle-income taxpayers and very low-income individuals pay few taxes, so the income redistribution effects of the government debt are probably small.

A related problem is that much U.S. government debt is purchased by foreign citizens. Consequently, interest payments will flow out of the United States in the years ahead. Should we be worried about this? Probably not—remember that these transactions are voluntary: foreign citizens purchase U.S. debt because they want future interest payments more than they want the money they use to buy the debt; U.S. citizens sell the debt because they want to borrow the money today. Had there been a prohibition on the sale of U.S. debt to foreigners in the 1980s, interest rates would have risen more than they did, and domestic investment might have collapsed completely. In the future, interest payments will flow out of the United States, but in the meantime, foreign funds are being used to invest in the U.S. economy.

Table 31.1 shows the ownership of the national debt in recent years. The proportion held by foreigners has remained roughly constant at about one-sixth of total national debt. The biggest changes have involved commercial banks, private citizens, and state and local treasuries: Commercial banks and private citizens have decreased their holdings while state and local treasuries have increased their holdings.

. . . .

But Won't We Go Bankrupt?

More than a few "experts" will tell you that the United States is on the brink of bankruptcy because of the ballooning national debt. Nothing could be farther from the truth! As we have just discovered, there are legitimate reasons to be concerned about the national debt—especially if it is growing faster than GDP, and perhaps if a large portion of it is held externally. But the government will never go bankrupt for a simple reason: it has the power to print money. It could turn on the printing presses and churn out 50 billion new $100 bills and pay off the debt tomorrow. Not a good idea—there might be a tad bit of inflation!—but this does mean that the

TABLE 31.1 OWNERSHIP SHARES OF MAJOR HOLDINGS OF NET NATIONAL DEBT

Holder of Net Federal Debt	1981	1986	1991
Federal Reserve banks	15.6%	11.2%	9.7%
Private investors	84.4	89.2	90.7
Commercial banks	14.6	11.4	7.6
Insurance companies	3.4	5.4	5.8
State and local treasuries	12.0	18.9	18.1
Individuals	13.7	9.3	8.9
Foreign	17.2	14.7	16.6

SOURCE: Federal Reserve Bank of St. Louis, *National Economic Trends*, June 1992. Figures do not add up because only major holders are included.

government will never go bankrupt. The real issue is whether a continuing debt will present long-term problems. Most economists would say no—and let's hope they are correct because the *national debt will not be paid off in your lifetime*! The federal government may run a surplus from time to time in the future, but making a dent in the $5 trillion plus national debt is quite another matter. The best solution to the national debt is simple and obvious: make sure that government spending is for goods and services that actually benefit the economy, and make sure that taxes are levied in an efficient and equitable way. If these two criteria are fulfilled, the national debt can be rolled over and over forever. And it will be.

FISCAL POLICY RULES VERSUS DISCRETION

As we learned in the last chapter, one of the key debates in monetary policy concerns whether the Federal Reserve should adopt a constant growth rate rule or use a "hands-on" approach and change the money supply as necessary. A similar debate surrounds fiscal policy: Should the government follow a rule requiring a balanced budget? Or is policy activism preferred? The question is a simple one for politicians: Publicly at least, they must worship at the shrine of a balanced budget. Just when and how they plan to balance the budget is not always clear, but they all seem to have good budget-balancing rhetoric.

Economists think the issue is more complex. As we have seen, budget deficits present numerous potential problems, but requiring that government receipts exactly equal government spending every time the earth circles the sun seems rather silly—and, indeed, only a very few economists argue for an annually balanced budget. Requiring that the budget balance over the business cycle is another thing entirely. Doing this would allow automatic stabilizers to operate and would reduce crowding out at the same time. Deficits would be tolerated during recessions as a means to speed recovery; surpluses would help prevent inflation when the economy moved past potential GDP.

Does a rule requiring a zero structural deficit make sense? It certainly does to monetarists and other economists who believe that the economy is so stable that government intervention is unnecessary. But Keynesians and others who view the economy as going through periodic—and wasteful—fluctuations have about as much use for a cyclically balanced budget rule as they do for the monetary growth rule. These economists believe that crowding out is rare because the economy is frequently operating far from potential GDP; instead, they emphasize the benefits of crowding in. Most Keynesians also believe that the adverse incentive effects of fiscal policies— less work and less saving—are so small that they can be safely ignored. Keynesians conclude that fiscal policy activism is just as necessary as monetary policy activism: Policymakers should continually monitor and forecast the economy and adopt fiscal policies to keep the economy moving toward potential GDP.

········

Policy Coordination

Finally, we need to mention one other issue: no policy exists in isolation, and fiscal policy is no exception. The success of a policy program depends on the monetary environment as much as the fiscal environment. For example, a plan to stimulate the economy with tax cuts might be successful if accompanied by easy monetary policy; it might not be successful if money growth is so slow that interest rates rise. This need for coordination is one reason why the central bank in many countries is a branch of the government. This is not the case in the United States and may explain the numerous clashes between our fiscal and monetary authorities. Are clashes between the fiscal and monetary authorities inevitable? Not necessarily. One way to minimize future clashes would be for either the monetary or the fiscal authorities to adopt and announce a policy rule. This would permit policy activism by the other. If it is true that fiscal policy is less efficient for short-run stabilization, a fiscal policy rule combined with monetary policy activism may be the best solution.

········ SUMMARY

The deficits of the 1980s moved fiscal policy to the front page, and the magnitude of the problem means that it is likely to stay there until the end of the century. You need a thorough understanding of fiscal policy to help you separate fact from fiction: the national debt will not bankrupt the nation, and the annual deficit does not spell the end of life as we know it. But fiscal policy, deficits, and the national debt can and do affect the economy; it is prudent to know why and how.

1. The government employs both discretionary and nondiscretionary fiscal policies. Discretionary policies require deliberate acts of Congress; nondiscretionary policies do not. Nondiscretionary policies act as automatic stabilizers and are largely responsible for changes in the cyclical deficit. The structural deficit is the deficit that exists at potential GDP. Most economists are more concerned about structural deficits than cyclical deficits.

2. Many economists believe that high marginal income tax rates can adversely affect the incentives to work and save. High income taxes reduce the incentive to work, while taxes on saving and the deductibility of home mortgage interest reduce the incentive to save. Most empirical evidence suggests that the incentive effects of taxes are relatively small.

3. Many economists believe that deficits, especially structural deficits, cause interest rates to rise and crowd out private investment. The Ricardian equivalence theorem rejects this idea with the argument that current deficits are a signal for future tax increases and result in increased current saving. The applicability of the Ricardian equivalence theorem to the real world is a hotly debated issue.

4. The national debt is the sum total of all past annual fiscal deficits and surpluses. It increased almost fivefold over the 1980–1993 period. Most economists worry about the national debt only when it is growing faster than GDP—as it has done for the past decade. The main problems associated with the national debt are that interest payments constitute a significant and growing portion of government expenditure, and that it results in a transfer of income to upper-income individuals. There is also some concern that much of the debt is owned by foreigners; interest payments to foreigners represent future income flows out of the United States.

5. Most economists maintain that it is inappropriate to use fiscal policy as a short-run stabilization tool. However, some fiscal policies, including accelerated depreciation and the investment tax credit, have been shown to have positive long-run effects on business investment. There is less agreement on the effect of preferential treatment for capital gains.

········ KEY TERMS AND CONCEPTS

discretionary fiscal policies

automatic stabilizers

nondiscretionary fiscal policies

fiscal dividend

fiscal drag

bracket creep

incentive to work

Laffer curve

Economic Recovery Tax Act (ERTA)

incentive to save

investment tax credit (ITC)

accelerated depreciation allowance

capital gains tax

Tax Reform Act of 1986

fiscal deficit

cyclical deficit

structural deficit

crowding out

deficit/saving ratio

Ricardian equivalence theorem

foreign trade deficit

twin deficits

Gramm-Rudman Act

national debt

········ REVIEW QUESTIONS

1. What is the difference between discretionary and nondiscretionary fiscal policies? Why are nondiscretionary fiscal policies called automatic stabilizers?

2. Why do many economists believe that fiscal policy is an inappropriate tool for short-run stabilization?

3. Explain how income taxes can affect the incentive to save and the incentive to work. Under what conditions can a tax decrease result in higher tax revenues? When would a tax decrease cause government revenues to fall?

4. What is the difference between the actual deficit and the structural deficit? Why are most economists more concerned about the structural deficit than the actual deficit?

Why do some economists dismiss fiscal deficits as being unimportant?

5. What has happened to the deficit/saving ratio in recent years? Why is this ratio so important to economists?

6. What is the difference between the fiscal deficit and the national debt? What are the potential consequences if the national debt rises faster than GDP?

·······PROBLEMS

1. Determine whether each of the following acts as an automatic stabilizer:
    a. Corporate income taxes
    b. Farm subsidies
    c. Student loans
    d. Social Security taxes
    e. Social Security benefits
    f. A proportional income tax
    g. A national sales tax

2. a. The Economic Recovery Tax Act called for indexing personal income taxes starting in the fourth year after the act was passed. How does this affect the automatic stabilization role of the personal income tax?
    b. ERTA did not call for indexation of the corporate income tax. How would indexation of the corporate income tax affect investment?

3. Suppose that a law is passed making it illegal to work more than 40 hours per week. How would this influence the incentive effects of income tax hikes? Of income tax cuts?

4. Refer back to the Laffer curve diagram in Figure 31.1. Suppose that the marginal income tax rate is equal to $t^\star$, but the government decides it needs to raise additional revenues. What kind of policies would you recommend? Why?

5. Many countries do not allow the deduction of home mortgage interest. Explain how this would likely affect the (a) average size of housing, (b) price of housing, (c) average rental rate, (d) amount of business investment, and (e) amount of nonhousing investment in the economy.

6. Economists usually argue that permanent consumption taxes are more effective than temporary taxes on consumption. Why? (*Hint:* Refer back to Friedman's theory of the consumption function in Chapter 24.) However, it is frequently argued that a temporary investment tax credit would be more effective than a permanent investment tax credit. Explain.

7. Suppose the government deficit is $400 billion. Would someone who estimates full employment to be 5 percent or someone who estimates it to be 7 percent be more likely to be concerned about the deficit? Why?

8. Some people argue that the current income tax system should be replaced with a flat tax—a proportional income tax of perhaps 15 percent. How would such a tax affect the incentive to work? The incentive to save? Do you think it would be a fair tax?

9. Monetarists favor policy rules and Keynesians favor policy discretion; however, many economists lie somewhere between these polar cases. Which of the following do you think would make more sense: fiscal rules combined with monetary activism, or monetary rules combined with fiscal activism. Why?

TABLE 6.7 STATE AND LOCAL GOVERNMENT SPENDING, 1990–91

Category	Amount	Percent of Total
Total	$908.1	100.0%
Education	309.3	34.1
Public Welfare	130.4	14.4
Highways	64.9	7.1
All Other	403.5	44.4

SOURCE: 1994 *Economic Report of the President,* Table B-84. Data are in billions of current dollars.

government deficits of the 1980s is that spending has been shifted from the federal to the state and local governments. Many states have been forced to cut back on services or raise taxes.

The data in Table 6.7 lump state and local government expenditures together, but there are some important differences in how they spend their monies: The two largest categories of local government spending are education (40 percent) and welfare, health, and hospitals (15 percent). The two largest categories of state government spending are welfare, health, and hospitals (40 percent) and education (25 percent). Even these data may be somewhat misleading, however, because spending percentages vary widely by state.

SUMMARY

We have covered more than just data in this chapter; we have also looked at the reasons why the government intervenes in market economies, how it raises taxes, and how this tax money is spent. The main points to remember from this chapter are:

1. The main functions of the government in modern mixed economies are to protect property rights, provide public goods, and stabilize economic fluctuations. The government also regulates business and redistributes income.
2. Government spending has increased significantly over the past 30 years. Increased spending on social programs was the reason for most of the increase until the 1980s. Since then, interest on the national debt has increased faster than any other component of federal government spending.
3. The federal government receives most of its revenues from personal income and Social Security taxes. State and local revenues are derived primarily from sales, property, and personal income taxes. The federal tax structure is probably more progressive than the tax system of most state and local governments.
4. The largest components of federal government spending are Social Security, national defense, and interest on the national debt. The largest components of state and local government spending are education, welfare, and highways.
5. Most economists feel that deficits that occur when the economy is at full employment pose more of a problem than deficits that occur during recessions. The federal government finances deficits by selling government securities.

KEY TERMS AND CONCEPTS

property rights   regressive tax
public good   sales tax
private good   progressive tax
free rider   income tax
market failure   savings bond
Employment Act of 1946   treasury debt
deficit   property tax
national debt   municipal bond
proportional tax   entitlement programs

REVIEW QUESTIONS

1. What are the main functions of government? Give examples to illustrate each function.
2. Why has the federal government grown so much in the past 40 years? What are the main sources and uses of federal government funds?
3. Why has state and local government grown so much in the past 40 years? What are the main sources and uses of state and local government funds?
4. What is the difference between the government deficit and the national debt? Why are many economists concerned about growing deficits and debt?
5. Define and give examples of progressive, regressive, and proportional taxes. Explain how each kind of tax can affect work incentives.

PROBLEMS

1. a. Refer back to footnote 6 on page 137. The implicit price deflator for government purchases in 1960 was 24.7. What was real government spending in 1960?
   b. Refer back to footnote number 2 on page 128. The GDP deflator was used to convert the nominal figures to the real figures. Can you figure out what the GDP deflator was for 1940 and 1993?
2. What is wrong with this story? Suppose you get a summer job, and by mid-summer you are doing so well that you get a raise. When you pick up your paycheck, however, your boss tells you that your raise put you in a higher tax bracket so that you now are taking home less money.
3. Would you favor a constitutional amendment requiring a balanced federal budget every year? Why or why not?
4. Suppose that the federal government cut taxes and spending by 50 percent so that the states were forced to pay for many of the services that had previously been covered by the federal government. This would require the states to increase taxes. How would this affect the progressivity of the U.S. tax system? Explain.
5. Many states exempt food and medicine from sales taxes. How does this affect the progressivity of the sales tax?

6. Suppose that the income tax rate has three brackets: 10 percent for the first $10,000, 15 percent for the second $10,000, and 25 percent for anything over $20,000. Calculate the amount of taxes and the average tax rate that would be paid on incomes of $15,000, $20,000, and $100,000. Show your work.

7. Some economists contend that the corporate income tax is progressive; others argue that it is regressive. Explain why this disagreement exists. (*Hint:* Who actually pays the corporate income tax?)

8. The text states, "The interest on municipal bonds is tax-free, so state and local governments can often raise money at interest rates below prevailing market rates." Explain. Also, do you think it would be a good idea to make the interest on treasury notes and savings bonds tax-free? Why or why not?

CHAPTER 32

The Business Cycle and Contemporary Policy Debates

You have heard the joke: . . . and so the president says, "What I really want is a one-armed economist, one who won't say the economy looks great, but, on the other hand, a depression is just around the corner." Unfortunately, jokes like this are all too true. Economists agree on more things than many people realize, but no one can deny that economists disagree on some important policy matters, especially when they are invited to do so in public. We have already touched on some of these debates—whether the Fed should adopt a constant money growth policy, whether deficits cause crowding out, and so on—but there are other important disagreements that we need to look at in this chapter.

Most of these disagreements involve the fundamental visions that economists hold about the ability of the economy to self-correct. Many economists believe that market forces are always moving the economy toward full employment and potential GDP; others feel that sticky prices make this unlikely. Some economists contend that all business cycle fluctuations are caused by technological shocks and that policy can have no effect; others counter that policy activism since World War II has been a major reason for the reduction in cycle fluctuations. Still others suggest that the business cycle has not stabilized significantly in the postwar period. Trying to make sense of these disparate views may be a little daunting, but it is certainly possible. And it is vitally important for understanding contemporary macroeconomic policy debates.

AFTER READING AND STUDYING THIS CHAPTER, YOU SHOULD BE ABLE TO:

• • • Compare and contrast the new classical, real business cycle, and new Keynesian theories of the business cycle

··· Outline policy proposals consistent with these three schools of thought
··· Interpret recent economic events in light of the theories of the business cycle

········ A REVISED ECONOMIC HISTORY

The study of business cycles has always been at the forefront of economic analysis. Everyone knows that the economy goes through ups and downs and that these fluctuations can be costly to society. When the economy booms, firms buy machinery and hire workers; when the economy falls into a recession, both people and machines lie idle in a tremendous waste of resources. If macroeconomic analysis has a single goal, it is to explain the nature of these cycles. The early theories of the cycle presented in Chapter 22—Malthus's theory of population growth, Jevons's sunspot theory, and the Kondratiev-Schumpeter long-cycle theory—were just a sampling of a long list of theories. Many of these theories are now largely discredited.

Chapter 22 also presented data that showed that GDP fluctuations have become less severe since World War II. While this interpretation of the record is widely accepted, a challenge was raised by Christina Romer in the 1980s.[1] Using new statistical techniques, Romer has concluded that the pre–World War II fluctuations were not as severe as is commonly thought and thus that the postwar economy has not been appreciably more stable than the prewar economy. The precise methods that Romer used to reach her conclusions need not detain us here—among other things she noted that early data were imprecise, so she had to reconstruct several data series—but the implications of her work are important. If Romer's analysis is correct, then postwar macroeconomic stabilization policies may have had little effect. Not everyone agrees with Romer's revisionist history, but this body of work is one of the key reasons why economists continue the search for new macroeconomic models. We need new models to explain the new data. The three schools of thought discussed in this chapter represent various directions this search has taken.

········

The New Schools: An Overview

Different economists have taken various paths in their search for new explanations of economic events. One problem with the older models—especially the Keynesian income-expenditure model—is that they were incapable of adequately dealing with the external supply shocks that bombarded the economy in the 1970s. When economists began to develop models to deal with this problem, they had to pay more explicit attention to the real sector of the economy, specifically technology and resource shocks. This line of work lead to the *real business cycle theory,* a school of thought that advocates an extreme version of *laissez faire.* Why should the government bother with trying to manipulate the economy if firms and people are already behaving optimally and random external shocks are the primary source of fluctuations?

---

[1]Christina Romer, "Spurious Volatility in Historical Unemployment Data," *Journal of Political Economy* 94 (February 1986): 1–37, and "Is the Stabilization of the Post War Economy a Figment of the Data?" *American Economic Review* 76 (June 1986): 314–34.

Several economists also recognized that many of the traditional models implied that people did not use all of the information available to them. This was the major impetus behind the development of the rational expectations hypothesis we discussed in Chapter 27. The rational expectations assumption is a key element of the *new classical school* of thought, and different versions of the expectations assumption have been incorporated into many contemporary macroeconomic models.

The *laissez faire* economics of the new classical and real business cycle schools is contrary to the traditional activist Keynesian position. The Keynesian policies of the 1970s may have been unsuccessful at dealing with inflation and stagflation, but this did not mean policy activism should be abandoned altogether—at least not according to the *new Keynesian school,* the third school of thought we address in this chapter. The new Keynesians have developed several reasons for believing that the market may be incapable of automatically moving to full employment.

REVIEW: TRADITIONAL MODELS OF THE BUSINESS CYCLE

Before proceeding, we need to clarify the terminology, specifically what we mean by the terms "business cycle" and "business fluctuation." We also need to review the standard cycle theories we developed in Chapters 27 and 28.

Terminology

Economists use the term **"business cycle"** somewhat differently today than they did 50 or 100 years ago. The grand cycle theorists of the past were searching for explanations of the great crashes and inflations that characterized the economy of their day. Today, the term "business cycle" is used to refer to fluctuations of GDP around its potential rate and to the movement of prices over time, not necessarily to great crashes or periods of hyperinflation. This sort of business cycle analysis may be less grandiose than the older analysis, but it is probably more scientific. More importantly, perhaps, it also lends itself more readily to policy prescriptions. Finally, modern economists do not suggest business cycles are regular or periodic. For this reason, some economists prefer the term "business fluctuation" to "business cycle," although the latter term is probably more popular.

Business cycles/fluctuations The movements of GDP around its potential rate and the movements of prices over time. Fluctuations is the more appropriate term in that the movements are not regular or periodic.

Business Cycles under the Adaptive Expectations Assumption

According to the adaptive expectations assumption, people form their expectations of the future by naively looking only at the past. The implication is that people can make consistent mistakes. If prices are rising but people base their wage demands on last period's price level, their expectations will be incorrect because prices will rise above the expected level. This slows down adjustment as the economy responds to external shocks and policy, and if prices and wages are tied to long-term contracts, the adjustment process will be even slower. The policy implications of the adaptive expectations assumption are that (1) fighting inflation by reducing aggregate demand

••••• FIGURE 32.1 BUSINESS CYCLES UNDER ADAPTIVE AND RATIONAL EXPECTATIONS

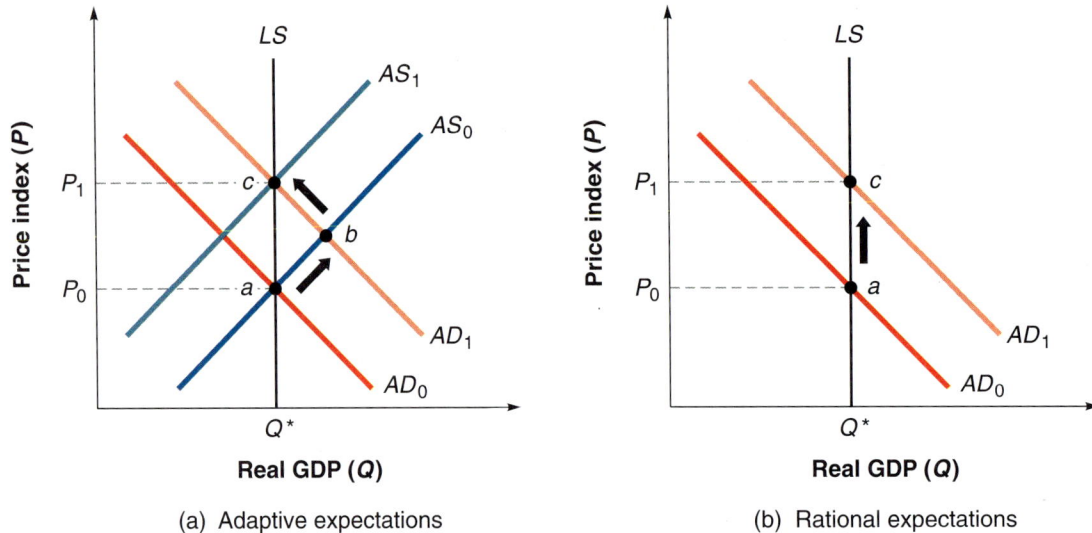

(a) Adaptive expectations

(b) Rational expectations

When expectations are adaptive, the economy responds to policy and external shocks slowly as both prices and output change. This is illustrated in panel (a). An increase in aggregate demand initially raises output and prices as the economy moves from point *a* to point *b*. As expectations adjust, the supply curve shifts back, and the economy moves to $Q^\star$ with a higher price index at point *c*. Under the strong rational expectations assumption, illustrated in panel (b), people respond to an increase in aggregate demand by immediately raising wages enough to cover the higher price index that will exist in the future. As a result, the economy moves directly from point *a* to point *c*. Output does not change, so the short-run aggregate supply curve is the same as the long-run aggregate supply curve. Under the weak rational expectations assumption, prices are assumed to be sticky, and the economy follows a path similar to the adaptive expectations model.

can be costly in terms of lost output and high unemployment, but that (2) policymakers can engineer an expansion by increasing aggregate demand growth. Panel (a) of Figure 32.1 illustrates how the economy responds to an aggregate demand stimulus under the adaptive expectations assumption.

••••••••

Business Cycles under the Rational Expectations Assumption

The rational expectations assumption holds that people are forward looking, use all available information, and do not make consistent mistakes. Under the rational expectations assumption, people would base their wage demands on the long-run rate of inflation, not the past or current inflation rate as is assumed under adaptive expectations. If prices are also perfectly flexible, the rational expectations assumption implies that the economy can never move away from potential GDP and full employment—unless there are economic surprises or imperfect information. In theory, the economy adjusts very quickly under the rational expectations assumption, and inflation can be eliminated without significant output losses. However, the strong rational expectations assumption also means that the *policy ineffectiveness rule* applies; in other words, attempts by policymakers to stimulate the economy cause inflation but do not change output. Under the weak rational expectations assumption, people are forward looking, but inflexible wages and prices prevent the economy from adjusting quickly. As a result, the economy can go through business cycles much like those described by the adaptive expectations model. Most rational expectations advocates favor nondiscretionary policy including constant money growth and a small government sector. Panel (b) of Figure 32.1 illustrates how the economy responds to an aggregate demand stimulus under the rational expectations assumption.

The rational expectations hypothesis has been criticized as being unrealistic—not everyone is quite so calculating—and because it does not always accurately predict economic events. Still, few economists are willing to reject the rational expectations hypothesis entirely; reasonable people *must* use all available information, but just how they use it may not be well understood.

THE NEW CLASSICAL SCHOOL

We have already developed the main idea behind the **new classical school**—the rational expectations hypothesis. New classical economists combine the rational expectations assumption with another key assumption, the **efficient markets hypothesis**, to develop a theory suggesting that the only causes of business cycles are unanticipated shocks and imperfect information. This leads them to conclude that government intervention is both ineffective and unnecessary. The main planks of the new classical position can be summarized as follows:

New classical school Contemporary school of macroeconomics that emphasizes self-correcting markets, the policy ineffectiveness rule, rational expectations, and the Lucas critique.

Efficient markets hypothesis Argues that markets quickly digest information and move prices to equilibrium.

PLANKS OF THE NEW CLASSICAL SCHOOL

1. The assumption of flexible prices and wages provides a good description of the economy.
2. Money growth affects only the inflation rate in the long run. In the short run, only unanticipated changes in the money supply can affect the real sector of the economy.
3. Most business cycles are the result of imperfect or asymmetric information.
4. Policymakers should not attempt to use activist policies for short-run stabilization.

The Efficient Markets Hypothesis

We already know what it means to say that expectations are rational, but what does it mean to say that markets are efficient? A market is efficient if it quickly digests information and moves prices to equilibrium in order to clear the market. The best example of an efficient market is probably the stock market. Have you ever gotten a hot stock tip from someone? Unless your tipster had illegal inside information, odds are that by the time you called your broker, the price had risen so much that the stock was not such a bargain after all; other people acted on the same information, bought the stock, and bid up the price. The difficulty of outguessing the stock market is an indication of its efficiency.

FIGURE 32.2   THE EFFICIENT MARKETS HYPOTHESIS

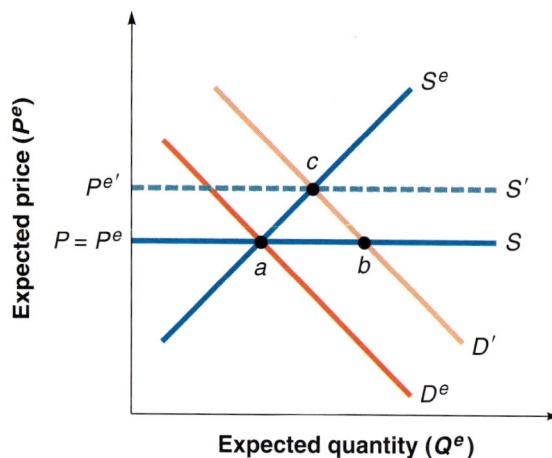

According to the efficient markets hypothesis, people hold inventories and form expectations of supply, demand, and price. Any deviation from the expected price will result in buying or selling and move the actual price to the expected price. For example, suppose the market begins at point a on the intersection of D^e and S^e. Now, suppose that actual demand increases as shown by the line D'. As the price begins to rise above P^e, people will sell from their inventories to force the price back to the long-run equilibrium rate, $P = P^e$, and the market will move to point b along the actual supply curve, S. If the increase in demand is perceived as being permanent, however, the long-run expected price will rise, and the actual supply curve S will shift upward to the dotted line, S'. The actual demand curve, D', then becomes a new expected demand curve, and the market clears at the expected price of $P^{e'}$.

Figure 32.2 illustrates the efficient markets hypothesis. The horizontal axis measures the *expected* quantity of stock, and the vertical axis measures the *expected* stock price. Similarly, the demand and supply curves are labeled D^e and S^e, for expected demand and expected supply. The intersection of D^e and S^e gives the expected stock price, P^e. The horizontal line through P^e turns out to be the *actual* supply curve for stocks. Just why this is so is the key to understanding the efficient markets hypothesis.

At any point in time, stock market investors hold an inventory of stock that they are ready to sell if the actual price exceeds the expected price. Likewise, people will buy if the actual price is less than the expected price. Now, suppose that the actual price is greater than the expected price. People holding stock will immediately sell. This will lower the actual price and bring it down toward P^e. The reverse happens if the actual price is less than the expected price: people will buy stocks and force the price up toward P^e. The catch is that price changes also depend on whether the expected price changes. As long as the expected price is constant, the actual price will always be moving toward P^e; this explains why the *actual* supply curve (S) is horizontal in Figure 32.2. The horizontal supply curve will shift, however, if the expected price changes—for example, due to an increase in demand that is perceived to be permanent.

Does this mean that people can accurately predict stock prices? Not at all. The efficient markets hypothesis says only that if price deviates from the expected price, the act of buying or selling brings the market price in line with expectations. However, perceptions of the expected price may be incorrect in any particular instance, and as price expectations change, the supply curve will shift. The result can be significant price volatility.[2]

Implications. The efficient markets hypothesis has two important implications. First, actual market prices equal expected future prices and thus embody all information relevant to determining price. This means that studying the history of the stock before deciding whether to buy or sell is futile. Why waste your time trying to learn something that the current price is already telling you? Second, the efficient markets hypothesis implies that no one can consistently "beat the market"; the very act of trying to make an extraordinary profit reduces the chance of doing so. For example, when everyone hears that stock prices are about to rise, they rush out to buy stocks— which causes the price to rise so much before they buy that they can't make a profit. Remember that the next time you get a hot tip. In the context of the new classical school, the efficient markets hypothesis bolsters the rational expectations hypothesis and the case for the self-correcting economy. If the current price is equal to the expected future price, and the expected future price is equal to the *actual* future price, how can expectations be anything other than rational? To forecast the future, all that is necessary is to observe the present.

The efficient markets hypothesis is so well established in modern finance theory that many stockbrokers do not even pretend to have hot tips any more. (Some brokers do trade on rumors, but that is a separate issue.) Instead, most brokers help their clients diversify their portfolios to produce the desired trade-off between risk and return. The efficient markets hypothesis has received less acclaim in other areas of economics, however. In particular, the hypothesis holds well only in markets characterized by extreme price flexibility and inventories. The labor market may be the most important counterexample to the efficient markets hypothesis. In many markets, wages are tied to contracts and cultural factors and do not adjust quickly in response to supply and demand; this is a far cry from the economist's conception of an efficient market.[3]

• • • • • • • •

New Classical Business Cycles

Can the economy ever deviate from full employment and potential output if expectations are rational and markets are efficient? Yes. Both internal and external events

---

[2]We should point out that the study of efficient markets is considerably more sophisticated than this single example and diagram may indicate. Many financial theorists distinguish between three degrees of market efficiency, weak, semistrong, and strong, depending on the amount of information actually embodied in current prices. You can find more about the efficient markets hypothesis in any text on financial management; one of the more popular is Eugene F. Brigham, *Fundamentals of Financial Management,* 5th ed. (Chicago: Dryden Press, 1989).
[3]Chapter 16 examined several "alternative" theories of the labor market that conflict with the efficient markets hypothesis.

OUR ECONOMIC HERITAGE

ROBERT E. LUCAS AND THOMAS J. SARGENT: FOUNDERS OF THE NEW CLASSICAL SCHOOL

The two economists most closely associated with new classical economics are probably Robert Lucas and Thomas Sargent. Lucas is generally credited as being the first to emphasize the importance of rational expectations to macroeconomics. Sargent is perhaps best known for helping to develop what is now called the Sargent-Wallace proposition—the idea that only unanticipated monetary shocks can have any real effects on the economy.

Robert Lucas (b. 1937) majored in history as an undergraduate and became interested in economics as a solution to social problems. He studied with Milton Friedman in graduate school at the University of Chicago. Lucas was drawn to the new classical position when he and his collaborators tried to incorporate more realistic versions of the labor market into the standard macroeconomic models. The consummate new classical, Lucas even sees the cause of the Great Depression as imperfect information and economic mistakes. Though he claims that he was never able to understand Keynes's *General Theory,* Lucas is well versed in most aspects of modern macroeconomics and the mathematics used by economists. He is critical of the fine-tuning often practiced by policymakers, but believes that market forces will ultimately prevail: "I think this economy is going to grow at 3 percent a year no matter what happens. Forever. One administration,

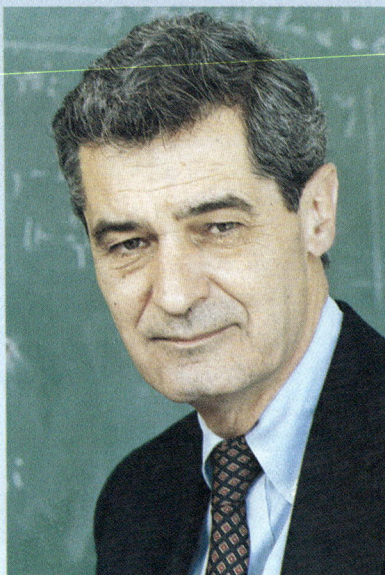

Robert E. Lucas

Thomas J. Sargent

like the current one [Reagan's first term], can mess things up, but that's all transient. . . ." Lucas teaches at the University of Chicago.

Thomas Sargent received his Ph.D. from Harvard and met Lucas while at Carnegie Mellon University. Early in his career, Sargent decided that something was wrong with the standard Keynesian approach to macroeconomics. In particular, Sargent noted that the Keynesians analyzed economic behavior in the context of certainty, but treated economic data as probabilistic. This amounted to adding randomness as an afterthought. Not only that, but most economic models were static while economic

behavior is inevitably dynamic. Sargent overcame these problems in a series of papers that are central to the new classical school. Sargent has always been highly mathematical and is considered a top-notch econometrician. Sargent, Christopher Simms, and other new classical economists have recently been working on methods that allow estimation and forecasts without any *a priori* theoretical assumptions—an approach consistent with the Lucas critique. Sargent currently teaches at Stanford and is affiliated with the Hoover Institution. He served as an adviser for the Minneapolis Federal Reserve Bank for several years.

can cause the economy to go through cycles. The internal event is incomplete information. Remember that the rational expectations assumption does not mean people have complete information, only that they optimally use all of the relevant information they have available. Robert Lucas, Thomas Sargent, and other new classical theorists believe that imperfect information is the principal cause of business cycles. Lucas and Sargent are the subject of the Economic Heritage box on page 838. The external events that can cause cycles are unexpected random shocks that frustrate expectations. In either case, the resulting cycles are likely to be mild because of the assumed efficacy of self-correcting forces.

To understand how imperfect information can generate cycles, suppose that you are a businessperson and suspect that the demand for your product has risen. You respond by raising your selling price. If your costs do not rise, the price increase represents an increase in profit and a signal to increase production so that you can grab a larger share of the apparently growing market. If other producers also increase production in response to rising prices, the economy will move into the expansion phase of a business cycle. But what if your information was imperfect? That is, what if your costs did rise along with your selling price? You would experience no increase in profits so the expansion would have been unwarranted. If you had had cost as well as price information, there would have been no business cycle expansion.

A particular kind of imperfect information is **asymmetric information**. This is information that is known to one group but not another. For example, if firms know that their selling price will rise, but workers do not, workers might settle for a lower nominal wage than they otherwise would. The higher expected prices will lower the expected real wage—and thus increase the quantity of labor the firms are willing to hire. Thus, asymmetric information can affect the level of employment and output—which is another way of saying that it can cause business cycles.

Asymmetric information Information that is known to one group but not to another; can result in business cycles.

New Classical Policy Proscriptions

The policy ineffectiveness rule is a key element of new classical economics: people adjust wages and prices to anticipated changes in aggregate demand and thus eliminate the effects of policy on real output. Not only is government intervention incapable of generating recovery, but it can actually do harm if it is applied inconsistently. Whenever the government intervenes with fiscal or monetary policy, prices change. This can make it difficult for people to determine the difference between absolute and relative prices—and generate informational asymmetries.

New classicals are not especially concerned about the fiscal deficit. Assuming Ricardian equivalence—as do most new classicals—government deficits do not, in themselves, affect interest rates or crowd out private investment. However, government spending does use scarce resources, so they are not available for private uses. This is why most new classicals favor a small role for the government and a strict *laissez faire* approach to policy.

New classicals are strong advocates of fixed policy rules because of a proposition known as **time inconsistency**. Time inconsistency refers to the idea that policymakers have an incentive to change their policies once they have been announced

Time inconsistency There are incentives for policymakers to change their policies once they have been announced. As a result, people are less likely to respond to policy changes.

and people have acted accordingly. For example, suppose that the Fed announces a low-inflation policy and then proceeds to reduce money growth. After people respond with low wage demands, the Fed could increase money growth to stimulate the economy without inflation. But people know that the Fed can do this, so they are less likely to respond to the initial low-inflation policy actions. The only way to get people to believe that the Fed is serious about low inflation is to remove discretion from monetary policy—legislate a monetary rule.

. . . .

Assessment

New classicals argue that their models were able to explain the stagflation of the 1970s and early 1980s better than the standard Keynesian models we developed in Chapters 23–26. Both monetary and fiscal policy were stimulative throughout most of the period between 1973 and 1984, yet the unemployment rate averaged 7.3 percent—perhaps two percentage points above what is usually regarded as the full employment rate. New classicals feel that this episode provides evidence of the policy ineffectiveness rule: if there is a systematic relationship between anticipated policy changes and economic activity, the rapid money growth and high deficits should have brought down unemployment. Instead, the fiscal and monetary stimuli showed up almost entirely as inflation.

The new classicals have also claimed another kind of success: a theoretical explanation for the consistent failure of economic forecasters. The argument, called the **Lucas critique** after its developer Robert Lucas, goes like this. Every time an economic forecast is made, people digest this information and act accordingly. For example, if the "consensus" forecast is for 10 percent inflation, people will adjust their wage demands to that level—and cause inflation to rise above the forecast level. If people respond to forecasts, none of the values built into econometric forecasting models—the marginal propensity to consume, the relationship between interest rates and investment, the demand for money, and so on—should be regarded as stable. Forecasts *have* to be wrong so policies based on forecasts are as likely to hurt things as to help them. Many new classicals use this as further evidence that policymakers should leave the economy alone.

When new classical models were developed in the late 1970s and early 1980s, they generated immediate attention. Unlike the orthodox Keynesian models they were replacing, the new models were based on a firm microeconomic foundation and on the assumptions that people are rational and that markets move toward equilibrium. A number of economists were concerned about several issues, however. First, it was unclear how to distinguish between real and monetary shocks. For example, will the economy respond differently to an external supply shock than to an unanticipated reduction in monetary growth? If so, how? The new classical model did not adequately address this question. Second, it was not clear why imperfect information could persist. Why would some people know things that others did not? In the modern economy, information is disseminated almost instantaneously through numerous sources. To suggest that firms would know about price hikes while workers would not just does not make sense—especially if markets are efficient. Finally, some economists were leery of new classical models because they did not appear to fit some

Lucas critique Suggests that economic forecasts tend to be incorrect because forecasts cause people to change their behavior.

important real-world data. In particular, new classical models seemed to suggest that business cycles should be shorter than they actually are.[4]

· · · · · · REAL BUSINESS CYCLE THEORY

As we found out in Chapter 26, supply shocks can have short-run as well as long-run effects on the economy. For example, when the price of oil quadrupled between 1973 and 1975, all firms had to find ways to economize on their use of oil. This often meant a decline in output, and for firms that were not able to adjust, it meant shutting down. The result, as shown in Figure 32.3, was an upward shift of the short-run aggregate supply curve (AS_0) and a leftward shift of the long-run aggregate supply curve (LS). The analysis of supply shocks led some economists to suggest that potential GDP and the natural rate of unemployment varied in response to structural change. The reasoning went like this: During periods of significant structural change—say, the economy is moving from cheap oil to expensive oil—labor must be reallocated among different sectors of the economy. As the pace of structural change accelerates, both frictional and structural unemployment rise, and with them, the natural rate of unemployment.

[4]A number of other empirical issues have been raised with new classical models as well. One of the most important is that the models imply that the real wage should be countercyclical—rising during contractions and falling during expansions. This is rarely the case; real wages typically move pro-cyclically. Many of the contemporary models used to explain pro-cyclical movements in real wages are based on monopolistic competition.

· · · · FIGURE 32.3 SUPPLY SHOCKS AND POTENTIAL GDP

Supply shocks can have both short-run and long-run consequences. In this case, a negative supply shock (an increase in the price of oil) raises the cost of production of most goods and shifts the short-run aggregate supply curve from AS_0 to AS_1. Firms restructure in response to higher oil prices, and as they do, potential GDP may decline. This would shift the long-run aggregate supply cuve (LS) to the left. Real business cycle theorists focus attention on the effects of technology and other real shocks to the economy.

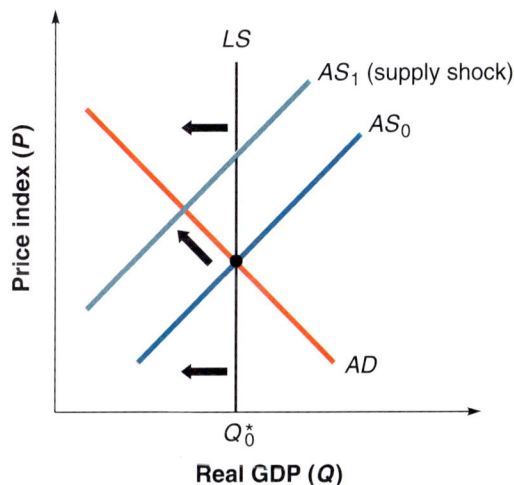

Real business cycle theory Contemporary school of macroeconomic thought emphasizing the importance of intertemporal substitution and technology shocks.

An outgrowth of this line of reasoning is the **real business cycle** school.[5] The work of Edward Prescott, a leading member of this school, is examined in the Economic Heritage box on page 845. Some economists consider the real business cycle school to be a branch of the new classical school because it too assumes rational expectations and reaches many of the same policy recommendations. However, there are enough differences to make a separate classification worthwhile. The following are the main planks of the real business cycle school:

> • • • • ⬦ **PLANKS OF THE REAL BUSINESS CYCLE THEORY**
>
> 1. The assumption of flexible prices and wages provides a good description of the economy.
> 2. Business cycles are primarily the result of fiscal policy and technology shocks.
> 3. Money affects only the rate of inflation in both the long run and the short run.
> 4. *Laissez faire* policies should be followed to allow the private economy to work efficiently.

• • • • • • • •

The Real Business Cycle Model

Intertemporal substitution decision Interest rates affect the labor supply in that at higher interest rates, workers have an incentive to save and will therefore work more hours.

A key assumption of real business cycle theory is that workers decide how many hours to work by making an **intertemporal substitution decision**. This implies that interest rates are an important determinant of the labor supply decision. For example, if interest rates rise, money earned today can be invested for a higher return, so workers have an incentive to work more hours. This suggests that for a given real wage, people will be more willing to work at high interest rates than at low interest rates.

The influence of the interest rate on the intertemporal work/leisure decision is shown in Figure 32.4. The vertical axis measures the real interest rate (r), and the horizontal axis measures real GDP (Q). The **real aggregate supply curve**, **RS**, is upward sloping to reflect the fact that, other things being equal, workers will offer more hours at higher interest rates than at lower interest rates. The **real aggregate demand curve**, **RD**, is downward sloping in recognition of the fact that fewer purchases will be made at higher interest rates than at lower interest rates, *ceteris paribus*.[6] The intersection of the *RD* and *RS* curves gives the equilibrium levels of real GDP and the real interest rate.

Real aggregate supply curve (RS) Graphical depiction of the relationship between real GDP produced and the interest rate; upward sloping because workers will offer to work more at higher interest rates.

Real aggregate demand curve (RD) Graphical depiction of the relationship between real GDP demanded and the interest rate; downward sloping because less will be purchased at higher interest rates than at lower interest rates.

---

[5]A good nontechnical introduction to the real business cycle school can be found in Charles I. Plosser, "Understanding Real Business Cycles," *Journal of Economic Perspectives* 3 (Summer 1989): 51–78. Much of this section draws on this article.

[6]Notice that these are *not* the same aggregate demand and aggregate supply curves that we developed in Chapter 26. Our focus here is on intertemporal substitution so we need to place the interest rate on the vertical axis. In Chapter 26, we were concerned about a different issue, self-correcting forces associated with flexible prices and the use of fiscal and monetary policy, so the price index was on the vertical axis.

· · · · **FIGURE 32.4** REAL BUSINESS CYCLE *RS* AND *RD* CURVES

The real aggregate demand curve (*RD*) is downward sloping because higher interest rates reduce the demand for interest-sensitive components of spending—investment, consumer durables, and the like. The real aggregate supply curve (*RS*) is upward sloping because higher interest rates will increase the supply of labor and output. The intersection between the *RS* and *RD* curves gives the equilibrium interest rate and level of GDP.

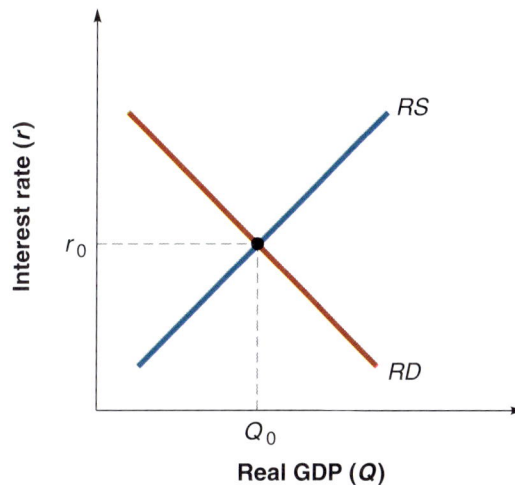

Real business cycle theorists believe that most cycles are caused by real shocks to the economy, in particular, **technology shocks**. To see why, look at Figure 32.5. Suppose that there is a technological innovation, say, the introduction of low-cost RISC-based personal computers.[7] Technology shocks typically shift both the *RS* and the *RD* curves. The favorable technology shock will shift the *RS* curve outward because the innovation allows the production of more and better goods and services. The *RD* curve will also shift outward because people will want these new, technologically sophisticated goods. The effect of the favorable technology shock on interest rates will depend on whether the *RD* curve shifts more or less than the *RS* curve. If the *RD* curve shifts more than the *RS* curve, interest rates will rise; if the *RD* curve shifts less than the *RS* curve, interest rates will fall.

Even temporary shocks can affect intertemporal substitution. To illustrate, suppose that you fish for a living and have unusually good luck one season. One response would be to use all of your extra earnings for extra consumption—perhaps a three-month vacation in Hawaii. Another response would be to use the extra money to buy a new boat. Which should you choose? That depends on the value you place on current consumption versus future consumption. If you value future consumption highly, the second response may be more reasonable. If you do use some of your temporary earnings to buy the new boat, your fishing success should increase over the long run. In the aggregate economy, this means that temporary shocks to the economy can affect potential GDP and thus long-run production possibilities in the economy.

Technology shock A change in technology that reduces costs and/or results in quality improvement; primary cause of cycle fluctuations in real business cycle theory.

[7]The acronym RISC stands for *reduced instruction set computer*. RISC computers can process magnitudes more information in a fraction of the time that the more common CISC (*complex instruction set computer*) computers require. The PowerPC chip, jointly developed by Motorola, Apple, and IBM and introduced in 1994, was the first RISC processor to be widely available in personal computers.

····· FIGURE 32.5 TECHNOLOGY-INDUCED REAL BUSINESS CYCLE

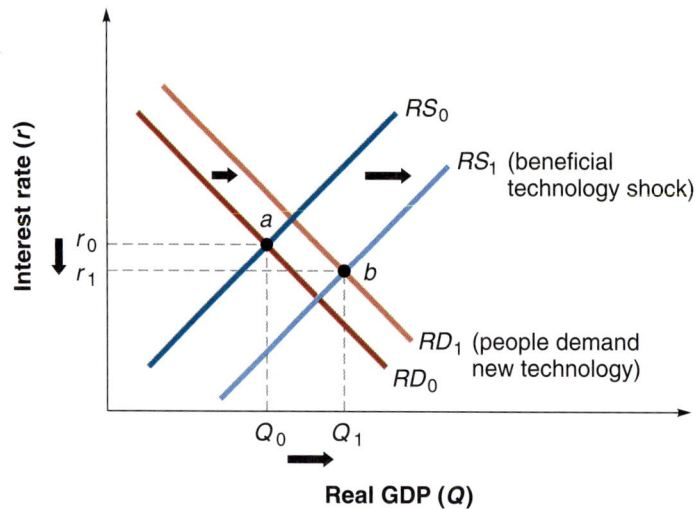

A favorable technology shock will shift both the RD and the RS curves. The RS curve will shift because firms can offer more goods at lower cost. The RD curve will shift because people will desire the new products. The effect of the shock on interest rates depends on the relative magnitudes of the RD and RS shifts. If RS shifts more than RD, interest rates will fall; if RS shifts less than RD, interest rates will rise.

········

Real Business Cycle Policies

Most real business cycle theorists believe that fiscal policies can affect the economy. Their reasoning is as follows: An increase in government spending (or a cut in taxes) will cause the RD curve to shift outward and thus increase interest rates. Higher interest rates will increase the level of production because people will be willing to offer more hours of labor. The result is an expansion of output and higher prices—a business cycle expansion—in response to what may have been a temporary fiscal policy stimulus. Fiscal policy may also shift the RS curve. An income tax cut that increases the after-tax return on working will shift the RS curve outward. The RS curve would also shift outward if government spending was devoted to social infrastructure or other programs that increased labor productivity. These views are subject to debate among real business cycle theorists.

The role of money and monetary policy in real business cycle theory is far from settled. Real business cycle theory holds that money affects only nominal variables so it cannot affect real output or employment in either the long run or the short run. In fact, many real business cycle theorists argue that the money supply is *endogenous*. The word "endogenous" means "determined within the system." If the money supply is endogenous, it can change in response to economic activity. For example, if a technology shock increases GDP, the demand for money will rise. If the Fed increases

OUR ECONOMIC HERITAGE

EDWARD C. PRESCOTT: A LEADING FIGURE IN REAL BUSINESS CYCLE THEORY

The study of contemporary macro-economics would not be the same had Edward C. Prescott (b. 1940) not changed his major from interdisciplinary studies to economics while in graduate school at Carnegie Mellon University. Prescott attributes his change of heart to the teaching skill of his thesis adviser, Michael Lovell, who convinced him of the importance of economics and sparked his interest in business cycles. Prescott also took courses from Robert Lucas, a leading figure in new classical economics, while at Carnegie Mellon. When he received his Ph.D. in 1967, Prescott took a post at the University of Pennsylvania where he taught from 1967 to 1971. He then returned to Carnegie Mellon where he stayed until 1980. He has been at the University of Minnesota since 1980. He has also been an adviser to the Minneapolis Federal Reserve Bank for several years.

Many of Prescott's important papers have been coauthored with Finn Kydland, with whom he has been working since the early 1970s. When Prescott and Kydland began their work, they expected to find that fluctuations caused by technology shocks were small and of a different variety than most business cycle fluctuations. Their intuition was that business cycle shocks were due to monetary surprises—an idea that might have been expected given Prescott's training with Lucas and other new classicals. Prescott and Kydland were astonished when they discovered that persistent random shocks induced fluctuations of the business cycle type.

The key contribution of Kydland and Prescott was their analysis of the importance of technological disturbances. They discovered that changes in total factor productivity varied substantially over time, especially in the short run. Total factor productivity—defined as the percentage change in real output minus the percentage change in total inputs and discussed in more detail in the next chapter—is a measure of technological change. When Kydland and Prescott discovered that total factor productivity fell in every year in which real GDP fell, the theory of real business cycles was born. Kydland and Prescott were surprised to find that technology shocks accounted for fully 70 percent of the volatility of post–World War II business cycles in the United States.

Other important members of the real business cycle school include Charles Plosser of the University of Washington and Robert G. King of the University of Rochester.

Edward Prescott

the money supply to meet this increase in money demand—as it frequently appears to do—then the money supply depends on the state of the economy; that is, it is endogenous. In contrast, most traditional economists feel that the money supply is essentially *exogenous* and that the Fed uses its control of the money supply to guide the economy.

• • • • • • • •

Assessment

Real business cycle theory is not without its critics. Many people argue that it is unreasonable to believe that technology shocks have been the major cause of cyclical fluctuations. For example, a key paper by Edward Prescott showing that technology shocks were highly correlated with output fluctuations over the 1948–1980 period has been criticized for measuring technology shocks incorrectly. Other economists have argued that fluctuations in employment are the result of changes in the demand for labor, not changes in intertemporal substitution.[8]

Perhaps the strongest vote of confidence for real business cycle theory comes from statistical analysis of economic time series. Using statistical methods that have only recently been developed, econometricians have shown that temporary economic fluctuations and fiscal policies can have permanent effects. For example, what appears to be only a temporary 1 percent decline in GDP today can cause GDP to be at least 1 percent lower 20 years from today. If this is correct—and we will not know until the econometricians settle their mathematical battles—the case for real business cycle theory may be strengthened considerably.

NEW KEYNESIAN THEORY

New classical and real business cycle theorists agree on several points, the most important being their belief that the assumption of flexible prices and wages is a good descriptor of the economy. In contrast, the **new Keynesians** believe that it is much more reasonable to assume inflexible or "sticky" wages and prices. This difference is profound, because it is the central reason why new Keynesians believe that the economy may not always move toward potential GDP and full employment. A great deal of new Keynesian research has been directed toward finding rational explanations for sticky prices and wages.[9]

The following are the chief planks of the new Keynesians:

New Keynesian school Contemporary school of macroeconomics based on the assumption of imperfect information and sticky wages and prices.

PLANKS OF THE NEW KEYNESIANS

1. Menu costs and staggering cause wages and prices to adjust slowly; actual wages and prices may deviate from equilibrium.
2. Fluctuations in aggregate demand can have a lasting influence on potential GDP and full employment.
3. The government must stand ready to use activist monetary and fiscal policies.

[8]See Edward C. Prescott, "Theory Ahead of Business Cycle Measurement," and Larry H. Summers, "Some Skeptical Observations on Real Business Cycles." Both appeared in the Fall 1986 issue of the *Quarterly Review* of the Federal Reserve Bank of Minneapolis.

[9]Much of this section is based on the articles by Akerlof and Yellen, Blanchard and Kiyotaki, and Mankiw, in N. Gregory Mankiw and David Romer, eds., *New Keynesian Economics* (Cambridge, Mass.: MIT Press, 1991). A good and largely nontechnical introduction to the new Keynesian school can be found in the symposium, "Keynesian Economics Today," *Journal of Economic Perspectives* 7 (Winter 1993): 3–82. This is a collection of several articles by new Keynesians and "old" Keynesians, with a new classical theorist thrown in for good measure.

Sources of Price Stickiness

New Keynesians have suggested several reasons why prices may not be flexible in the real world, even if there are no contracts. Two of the more important reasons are **menu costs** and **staggering**.

Much traditional economic theory overlooks the fact that in the real world, the process of setting prices can be costly. For example, a restaurant may have to print a new menu, a mail-order store may have to publish a new catalog, or a manager may have to hold a meeting to inform the sales staff about price changes. Such costs—termed menu costs—force firms to compare the benefits of new prices with the costs of actually changing prices. If menu costs are high enough, prices may become sticky and deviate from equilibrium. This generates economic inefficiencies.

Some new Keynesians have noted that price flexibility imposes a positive *aggregate demand externality* on other firms in the economy and that menu costs may interfere with this positive externality. Externalities are costs or benefits that are not reflected in market prices.[10] For example, if Firm A decides to lower its price, firms that do business with Firm A will benefit from lower costs. So will firms that do not do business directly with Firm A because the aggregate price level will fall a small amount. This decline in the aggregate price level is the external benefit from price flexibility. But if menu costs are so high that Firm A chooses not to lower its price, this external benefit of lower prices will be lost. The key point is that the individual firm will look at only its individual benefit, not the benefits that would accrue to society at large from lowering price. When economic decisions do not take account of all costs, they are said to be inefficient.

Staggering generates a different kind of price stickiness; it makes aggregate wages and prices adjust slowly, even if individual wages and prices adjust quickly. To see this, suppose that half of the firms in society adjust their prices in the middle of the month and half make their adjustments at the end of the month. Now, let the Fed increase the money supply on January 1. Firms that make adjustments mid-month will raise their prices and wages—but not very much. If they raise their prices too much, they will lose sales to the firms that will not be raising their prices until the end of the month. At the end of the month, those firms will raise their prices, but again not by very much, because of the relatively low prices of firms that raised their prices mid-month. Prices will eventually adjust completely to the money growth, but the process will probably take several periods. In the meantime, output will fluctuate as relative prices change.

Staggered wages can have another important effect on the economy. Suppose that the Fed decreases money growth in an attempt to bring down inflation. If workers accept a wage cut, they will be less likely to lose their jobs; however, no one wants to be the first to take the wage cut. If you are the first to accept lower wages, you will be worse off than your neighbor because your relative wage will decline. When you do decide to take the wage cut, you will probably accept only a small decrease

Menu costs The transaction costs associated with changing prices on menus and other price lists; they contribute to price stickiness.

Staggering Another reason for price stickiness; aggregate prices and wages adjust slowly because firms and workers do not raise or lower their prices or wage demands all at once.

---

[10]Externalities were introduced in Chapter 4 and discussed in more detail in Chapters 18 and 21. The most common negative externality is pollution. It imposes a cost on society that is not reflected in the firm's cost of production in the absence of government intervention.

to preserve as much of your relative wage as possible. The result: Staggered wages, like staggered prices, result in slow responses to changes in aggregate demand. Further, at any point in time, wages and prices are likely to be "incorrect" in the sense that they diverge from their equilibrium values.

• • • • • • • •

Hysteresis

Some new Keynesian economists reject the natural rate hypothesis—the idea that self-correcting forces always move the economy back to full employment and potential GDP—because they believe that economic shocks can have permanent effects on the natural rate of unemployment and potential GDP. There are two reasons for this position. First, when the economy falls into recession, workers lose job skills from being unemployed for extended periods. As a result, they have a harder time finding jobs once the economy recovers. Second, if the recession lasts very long, some workers will become discouraged and lose their incentive to work. When the economy recovers, these workers may not even look for new jobs. This suggests that the long-run aggregate supply curve shifts in response to shifts in aggregate demand, a process known as **hysteresis**.[11]

Hysteresis The theory that economic shocks can permanently affect the economy and prevent unemployment from returning to its natural rate.

Hysteresis is illustrated in Figure 32.6. Suppose the economy begins at point a at the intersection of AD_0 and AS_0. Now, let the Fed decrease money growth in an effort to fight inflation. As always, this will shift the aggregate demand curve inward toward AD_1. Sticky wages and prices imply that the short-run effect is a reduction in output as well as some decline in the price level. Hysteresis occurs if unemployment persists long enough to affect the behavior of workers or cause their skills to deteriorate. If so, the long-run aggregate supply curve, LS_0, will shift inward toward LS_1. This will reduce potential GDP and raise the "natural" rate of unemployment. Is there any way to reduce the natural rate of unemployment and raise potential GDP? Perhaps. A sustained increase in aggregate demand might raise the demand for workers so much that firms would offer both higher wages and on-the-job training. But while that is happening, inflation may accelerate to politically intolerable levels; consequently, adopting such policies may be difficult.

Evidence on Hysteresis. Interest in hysteresis developed in the United Kingdom following the anti-inflation policies of the Thatcher government in the 1980s. Tight money combined with the public sector borrowing requirement—a policy that prevented the fiscal deficit from growing—brought down inflation, but also caused unemployment to rise to post–World War II highs. That high unemployment accompanied disinflation was not surprising, but economists were confounded when the high unemployment persisted even after the economy recovered later in the decade. The theory of hysteresis grew out of an attempt to explain this situation.

Is hysteresis applicable to the United States? Perhaps, but the evidence is not yet in. Hysteresis may partially explain the rise in the natural rate of unemployment from under 4 percent in the 1950s to around 6 percent in the 1980s because several episodes of tight money designed to restrain inflation occurred during those decades. How-

---

[11]Notice that hysteresis provides an alternative explanation for the permanence of aggregate demand shocks to the one suggested by real business cycle theory on page 843.

····· **FIGURE 32.6** HYSTERESIS AND DEMAND SHOCKS

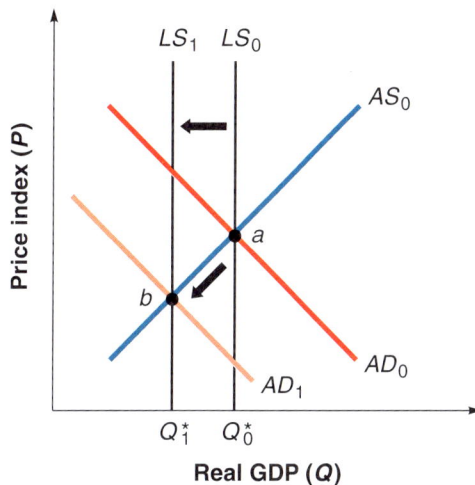

A decrease in aggregate demand can cause a permanent decrease in potential GDP and raise the "natural" rate of unemployment. In this example, suppose the Fed decreases the money supply to reduce inflation. This shifts the aggregate demand curve from AD_0 to AD_1 and reduces inflationary pressure. If the reduction in aggregate demand persists long enough, workers' skills and incentive to work will deteriorate. This will cause the long-run aggregate supply curve to shift inward from LS_0 to LS_1. If policymakers later attempt to return the economy to the old level of potential GDP, $Q_0^\star$, inflation will accelerate to politically intolerable levels.

ever, the fact that the unemployment rate fell below 5.5 percent in 1990 suggests that U.S. labor markets may differ from those in the United Kingdom.

········

Other Elements of the New Keynesian Model

Like the real business cycle school, the new Keynesian school is still in its formative stages. Nevertheless, one theme runs through the entire theory: the inability of the market mechanism to consistently move the economy to potential GDP and full employment. Two ideas that support this view are the efficiency wage theory developed by George Akerlof and the Tobin-Mundell effect. George Akerlof is the subject of the Economic Heritage box on page 853, and the Focus box on page 852 uses a game-theoretic model to illustrate another key theme in new Keynesian economics—that prices may be sticky even in the absence of long-term contracts.

Efficiency Wage Theory. **Efficiency wage theory** suggests that businesses may find it in their long-term interest to pay wages above the market level. Why? Higher wages may increase worker morale and productivity and thus lower turnover and training costs. Above-market wages might keep individual businesses competitive, but they may also increase unemployment. If a firm grants a high-wage "gift" to its employees, workers have more to lose by quitting and looking for another job; odds

Efficiency wage theory Holds that firms may pay above-market wages to increase worker productivity, reduce turnover, and lower recruiting costs.

FOCUS ON

HENRY FORD'S GAMBLE

An early example of efficiency wage theory occurred in 1914. In the midst of a recession, Ford Motor Company *raised* the wage it paid industrial workers from $2–$3 a day to $5 a day and shortened the workday from 10 to 8 hours. Conventional economic theory suggested then—just as it does today—that such a move would be disastrous. Henry Ford apparently had not studied economics. He said the raise was ". . . neither charity nor wages, but profit sharing and efficiency engineering."[1] Ford's move was not really profit sharing, at least not as we know it today. The higher wages were tied to the company's current profits so it was easier to lower wages in bad times, and there was no expectation that wages would continue to rise as long as profits did. Instead, Ford's policy was much closer to what we call efficiency wage theory today.

Like most industrial firms of the era, Ford had experienced rapid employee turnover. Factory work was so miserable that young men would frequently work just long enough to save some money and then move on. (Ford expected "the young ladies to get married" and thus was not too worried about their turnover.) Did the higher wage reduce employee turnover as ef-

ficiency wage theory would predict? Perhaps, but most of these problems had been solved in 1913 when working conditions were improved. Monthly turnover fell from 48 percent in December 1912 to 6.4 percent in October 1913.

Efficiency wage theory also predicts that higher wages will increase the quality of job applicants. Did this happen? Again it is hard to say, but we do know that most jobs were unskilled and could be met with illiterate or even child labor. The few skilled positions were easy to fill because Ford already paid wages higher than most competitors.

But the five-dollar day did accomplish something important: it temporarily ended any labor problems at Ford. In many ways, Henry Ford was a progressive on labor issues—he supported workplace safety programs, was interested in worker's compensation, and opposed piecework—but he was also very concerned about the union movement, especially the Industrial Workers of the World (IWW). The "Wobblies," as the IWW members were called, were among the most radical elements in the union movement; in fact, they were so radical that American Federation of Labor members were threatened with expulsion if caught associating with the IWW. Henry Ford is reputed to have remarked that he would ". . . lick the

Henry Ford

IWW by paying the men $5.00 a day."

In retrospect, it appears that Henry Ford did practice efficiency wage theory, but long before the celebrated five-dollar day.[2] The five-dollar day may have been an attempt at union bashing, but it was unnecessary: the IWW was on its way out before 1914, but the AFL-CIO was just around the corner.

[1]Quoted in Alan Nevins, *Ford: The Times, the Man, the Company* (New York: Charles Scribner's Sons, 1954), p. 534. Much of this discussion comes from Chapter 5, "The Five-Dollar Day."

[2]Some authors contend that the five-dollar day was the best example of efficiency wage theory. See Daniel M. G. Raff and Lawrence H. Summers, "Did Henry Ford Pay Efficiency Wages?" *Journal of Labor Economics* 5(4) Part 2 (October 1987): S57–86.

are that they will only find jobs at the lower market rate. The high-wage offer should also increase the number of qualified people applying for employment. If firms are truly interested in worker morale, however, they will be hesitant to lay off workers, even unproductive workers. But keeping unproductive workers could eliminate the productivity gains derived from the efficiency wage. Labor costs above the market level reduce employment, just as the minimum wage causes unemployment. Notice that this sort of unemployment is involuntary in the sense that workers cannot increase their attractiveness to employers by offering to work for lower wages.

Though efficiency wage theory has generated a great deal of interest in recent years, it is certainly not a panacea. It offers a partial explanation for persistent high unemployment, but it is not a good explanation for wide swings in unemployment over the business cycle. Another problem with efficiency wage theory may be its unorthodox policy recommendations. Since unemployment can be involuntary, more generous unemployment compensation may be appropriate. Since management keeps wages above the market level, the minimum wage need not be repealed. Finally, if effort and productivity increase with the wage rate, government subsidies for high-wage industries may be beneficial. Interventionist policies such as these are not too fashionable with most orthodox economists. The Focus box on Henry Ford presents an application of efficiency wage theory to U.S. economic history.

The Tobin-Mundell Effect. Economists have applauded the self-correcting power of price flexibility almost as long as economics has been a discipline, but Keynesians have always wondered about the ability of price flexibility to achieve full employment and potential GDP. For example, suppose that autonomous spending falls and the economy is thrown into a recession. As we found out in Chapter 26, falling prices increase real wealth. This allows real purchases to increase and helps the economy recover. But what happens if the deflation is anticipated? Things could get worse, not better, because people might hold off on spending until prices fall even more. This will cause the *AD* curve to shift even farther to the left. The perverse response of the economy to falling prices is known as the **Tobin-Mundell effect**.

The general implication of the Tobin-Mundell effect is that price flexibility can be destabilizing. In fact, some new Keynesians believe that the chief cause for the relative stability of the U.S. economy in the post–World War II era is wage and price rigidity caused by unions and contracts. If true, this has important implications for government policy toward labor unions: Should union membership be encouraged to help stabilize the economy? It is worth noting that union membership in Germany and Japan is higher than in the United States and that both countries have enjoyed more economic stability than the United States in the post–World War II period.[12] However, it must be mentioned too that German and Japanese unions are different from U.S. unions. For example, labor-management relations have always been better in Germany and Japan than in the United States, and the number of days lost to strikes has been much smaller. Possibly, then, union behavior affects economic stability more than the mere existence of unions.

Tobin-Mundell effect A perverse response to falling prices that can prevent the economy from self-correcting from a recession.

[12]About 16 percent of all workers in the United States belong to unions in the 1990s, compared to about 35 percent in Japan and almost 39 percent in West Germany.

RECESSIONS AS COORDINATION FAILURES

Good theories of the business cycle must be able to explain recessions. New classicals contend that recessions result from imperfect information that causes workers to demand excessive wages; real business cycle theorists hold that they are the result of negative technology shocks; orthodox Keynesians maintain that they are caused by declines in confidence, and so on. Another theory is that recessions are caused by *coordination failures*. This theory fits best with the new Keynesian model, but the methodology used to present the theory—game theory—has been used by economists of all persuasions. For example, Edward Prescott, a leading figure in the real business cycle school, has done important work in game theory.

To illustrate, suppose the economy is composed of only two firms, Firm A and Firm B and that the Fed has just cut money growth to reduce inflation.[1] The question is how the firms will respond. If neither firm cuts its price, the economy will go into a recession because there is not enough money in circulation to support the still high prices. Both firms will be better off if they cut their selling prices. The recession will be avoided, and both firms will be able to maintain their sales. But what happens if only one firm cuts its price? There could still be a moderate recession, but the firm that maintains high prices might

[1]This example is drawn from N. Gregory Mankiw, *Macroeconomics* (New York: Worth, 1992), pp. 315–16.

make more profits than the firm that cuts its price. The question posed by the game theorist is, What is the most likely outcome to this scenario?

The possible outcomes are shown in the following payoff matrix. If both firms cut prices, they will each make $50. This is shown in the northwest cell. If both firms maintain high prices, they will make only $25 because their sales will decline. This outcome is shown in the southeast cell. The outcomes when one firm cuts its price but the other does not are shown in the off-diagonal cells. In each case, the firm that cuts its price is assumed to make $10, and the firm that maintains its high price is assumed to make $30. The low-price firm makes $10 because of its low profit margin, and the high-price firm makes only $30 because it loses market share to the low-price firm.

Firm A

Firm B	Actions → ↓	Price Cut	No Price Cut
	Price Cut	A:50 / B:50	A:30 / B:10
	No Price Cut	A:10 / B:30	A:25 / B:25

Which outcome is most likely? The answer depends on what each firm expects the other to do. Look at the situation from Firm A's perspective. If Firm B cuts its price, Firm A is better off by following the price cut; both firms will make $50. But if Firm B does not cut its price, Firm A should

maintain high prices as well: it will make only $10 if it cuts prices but $25 if it does not. Firm B would reach the same conclusions as to the correct response to Firm A's behavior. In general, then, if firms expect their competitor to cut prices, both will cut prices and the result will be optimal—there is no recession and inflation has been eliminated. But if firms do not expect their competitor to cut prices, prices will stay high, and the economy will end up in a recession with high prices. The result is a suboptimal outcome because of a coordination failure. Either case is possible, so the solution to this game is said to have *multiple equilibria*.

In the case we have just illustrated, the firms probably would coordinate and move to the high-profit outcome of price cuts. But notice that this outcome is not automatic; it requires coordination on the part of the two firms. In the real world, such coordination is much less likely because there are so many firms; antitrust laws also make this sort of coordination illegal. The conclusion: Prices can be sticky simply because people expect them to be sticky—even if the sticky prices do not benefit anyone, and even if there are no contracts. New Keynesians feel that such coordination failures are common enough in the economy that some activist policy intervention is needed.

GEORGE A. AKERLOF: A LEADING NEW KEYNESIAN ECONOMIST

A number of economists have contributed to the development of the new Keynesian school of thought, but few have made more important contributions than George A. Akerlof (b. 1940). Akerlof received his Ph.D. in 1966 from MIT and took a post at the University of California-Berkeley where he continues to teach today.

Akerlof became interested in economics as a child and showed remarkable economic intuition very early on. When he was 10 or 11, his father lost his job, and Akerlof remembers wondering what would happen next: if his family stopped spending, would some other father lose his job? Would the entire economy collapse into recession? Akerlof was to discover in his first economics class at Yale that spending multipliers were not that large and that families with low incomes spend out of savings.

Akerlof has always been known for his unorthodox research. Early in graduate school, he became convinced that there were problems with standard neoclassical economics. In particular, it was hazy about details. Part of the reason for this, of course, was that economists wanted to think very generally about economic issues and often had to gloss over details to do so. But Akerlof was convinced that the commitment to generality obscured the important specifics of many situations. From this idea came a key insight that contributed to the development of efficiency wage theory: the specific nature of workers' willingness to work may lead to firms voluntarily paying above-market wages. Much of the rest of Akerlof's work has been devoted to the examination of how special considerations alter simple economic generalizations.

Akerlof's approach to economic theorizing differs from orthodox analysis in another important way: he believes that economic theory must make use of assumptions derived from psychology, anthropology, sociology, and the other social sciences. His collection of essays, *An Economist's Book of Tales* (New York: Cambridge University Press, 1984, 1990), includes a number of articles that examine the implications of alternative assumptions for economic analysis. Many are a bit difficult for undergraduates, but a quick survey of the titles shows the wide scope of Akerlof's thinking. What other economist can claim to have authored papers with such titles as "The Economics of Caste and of the Rat Race and Other Woeful Tales," "The Economic Consequences of Cognitive Dissonance," and "A Theory of Social Custom, of Which Unemployment May Be One Consequence"?

In recent years, much of Akerlof's work has focused on the important and difficult problems of the economic transition of the former socialist economies. In a 1991 paper for the Brookings Institution,[1] Akerlof and his colleagues recommended that wage subsidies be given to the workers of the former East Germany until their productivity catches up with the productivity of workers in the former West Germany. They even suggested that such wage subsidies would reduce budget deficits. The idea of wage subsidies clearly has roots in Akerlof's theory of efficiency wages, and, like the theory of efficiency wages, it is controversial: some surveys suggest that barely one-eighth of the firms in former East Germany complain of high wage costs; if this is correct, the case for widespread wage subsidies is questionable.

Many of Akerlof's important papers have been coauthored with his wife Janet Yellen. Yellen is a respected new Keynesian economist in her own right and was nominated to the Federal Reserve Bank in 1994. Other important new Keynesian economists include Olivier Blanchard of MIT, N. Gregory Mankiw of Harvard, and David Romer of Berkeley.

[1] George A. Akerlof, Andrew K. Rose, Janet L. Yellen, and Helga Hessenius, "East Germany in from the Cold: The Economic Aftermath of Currency Union," *Brookings Papers* 1 (1991): 1–106.

·······SUMMARY

The schools of thought we have explored in this chapter—new classical, real business cycle, and new Keynesian—all have the same policy tools available to them. And while they reach some rather different policy recommendations, the issue boils down to the same question we asked in the last two chapters: Should the government adopt a set of policy rules, or should it engage in activist discretionary policies? A comparison of the different policy prescriptions serves as a useful summary to this chapter.

1. *New classical policy.* The new classicals' belief in rational expectations and efficient markets leads them to conclude that the government should play as small a role in the economy as possible. They favor a constant money growth rule to restrain inflation; some new classicals even advocate a policy of zero inflation. While the Ricardian equivalence theorem holds that government deficits do not affect interest rates, new classicals do not dismiss the deficit. The aim of the fiscal authorities should be to reduce the size of the government sector as much as possible to free resources for the private sector.

   According to the new classicals, activist policy is doomed to failure because of two main problems. First, economists are unable to accurately forecast the effects of a policy change. Once a forecast is made, people act on the forecast and change their behavior. Consequently, it is impossible for forecasters to know the future state of the economy and thus implement the appropriate policy change. Second, people know that policymakers have an incentive to change their policies once they have been enacted. If people do not believe that policies will persist, economic adjustment will be slow. Both problems can be eliminated by requiring that policymakers adopt a set of rules—a constant growth rate for the money supply and a cyclically balanced budget with as small a government sector as possible.

2. *Real business cycle policy.* Real business cycle theorists feel that most aggregate demand policies are irrelevant. Monetary policy affects only inflation, in both the short run and the long run. Fiscal policy can affect the real economy, but most cycle fluctuations are caused by external shocks to the system, primarily technology shocks. The decision to work involves a trade-off between current and future consumption, so interest rates affect the supply of labor and out-put. Policymakers have little—if any—influence on the evolution of technology, so the best approach may be to leave the economy alone. The same set of policies advocated by the new classicals—constant money growth and fiscal policy rules—are preferable to policy activism. These policies permit the private economy to operate efficiently.

3. *New Keynesian policy.* New Keynesians believe that the price mechanism does not always move the economy toward potential GDP and full employment. This view is based on several theories that explain why prices and wages tend to be sticky—menu costs, staggering, efficiency wage theory, and so on. Sticky wages and prices provide a rationale for policy activism: changing the money supply as necessary to target interest rates and credit, and using fiscal policy as necessary to prevent recessions. Just as importantly, some new Keynesians stand ready to use targeted policies—investment incentives aimed at particular industries, tax breaks for cer-

tain groups, and so on. Finally, new Keynesians are hesitant to fight inflation with sustained tight money because of the possibility of hysteresis—long-run damage to the economy in the form of an increase in the natural rate of unemployment.

KEY TERMS AND CONCEPTS

real business cycle theory

new classical school

new Keynesian school

business cycles/fluctuations

adaptive/rational expectations

policy ineffectiveness rule

efficient markets hypothesis

asymmetric information

time inconsistency

Lucas critique

intertemporal substitution decision

real aggregate supply curve (RS)

real aggregate demand curve (RD)

technology shock

endogenous money

exogenous money

menu costs

staggering

hysteresis

efficiency wage theory

Tobin-Mundell effect

coordination failure

REVIEW QUESTION

1. For each of the three schools of thought discussed in this chapter:
   a. List and compare the main planks.
   b. List and compare the assumptions regarding price flexibility.
   c. Identify key distinguishing elements, such as the role of technology shocks or the existence of hysteresis.
   d. List and compare the monetary and fiscal policy prescriptions.

PROBLEMS

1. The new classical idea of time inconsistency is applicable to many areas of analysis. Explain how time inconsistency relates to each of the following:
   a. A proposal for a temporary tax cut on capital expenditures
   b. An announcement that the government will never negotiate with terrorists
   c. A stepped-up program to catch tax evaders
2. Illustrate the Tobin-Mundell effect with the aggregate demand–aggregate supply model. What assumption do you have to make about expectations? How does the Tobin-Mundell effect fit with Christina Romer's revisionist economic history?
3. Refer back to the derivation of the aggregate supply curve in Chapter 26. This particular derivation is often called a *Lucas supply curve* after the new classical economist Robert Lucas. Explain why this curve is consistent with the new classical school.
4. Computers are on nearly every desk today. How do you think the advent of personal computers has affected the menu costs of price changes in the airline industry? The grocery store industry? The doctor's office? Your professor's grading system?

5. Many apartment rent contracts call for a six-month lease followed by a month-to-month contract. Suppose that in month 7 you are given the option to sign a new six-month lease or continue with the month-to-month option. Which option would you prefer? Why? Would your answer have been different in the 1970s than today? Why?

6. The efficient markets example used in the text was the stock market; the counterexample was the labor market.
   a. List three examples of markets that can be regarded as relatively efficient.
   b. Suggest changes that could make the labor market more efficient.

7. In December 1982, the unemployment rate rose to 10.8 percent—the highest level since World War II. How would this be explained by a new classical? By a real business cycle economist? By a new Keynesian? What policies would each school recommend to reduce unemployment?

8. Which school of thought do you think is most consistent with the economic policies of the current administration? Which school of thought best describes the policies conducted by the Fed?

9. The entries in the Recessions as Coordination Failures payoff matrix in the text are not the only possible outcomes. Suppose that the same two firms calculate their responses to Fed policy such that the payoff matrix is like the following:

Firm A

Actions → ↓	Price Cut	No Price Cut
Firm B Price Cut	A:50 B:50	A:25 B:20
No Price Cut	A:20 B:25	A:25 B:25

   a. Determine the most likely outcome(s) to this game.
   b. Do you think this payoff matrix is more or less reasonable than the one in the Focus box? Why?

10. Explain and comment on the following statement: Emergency medical care uses scarce resources, so they are not available for the manufacture of bubble gum. This is why most new classicals prefer little government spending on emergency medical care.

11. This chapter began by stating that economists probably agree more than they disagree. Based on the information in the chapter, does it appear that rational expectations is one of the points of general agreement? Does rational expectations appear to violate the new Keynesian perspective?

CHAPTER 33

The Long Run:
Growth and Productivity

In the first two decades after World War II, the U.S. economy and our rising standard of living were the envy of the rest of the world. Things changed significantly in the 1970s and 1980s, however. Real income growth slowed to a snail's pace, and people started to wonder—perhaps for the first time in U.S. history—whether children would be better off than their parents. What happened? More importantly, *why* did it happen? In this chapter, we will turn our focus to the long run and try to answer these questions.

On one level, the causes of economic growth are simple to understand: the rate of economic growth must depend on the rate of capital accumulation—both human and physical—and the pace of technological advance. Nothing could be simpler. The only catch is that we do not know *why* technology and capital accumulation proceed as they do. Economists have looked at these issues since the dawn of modern economics, but not until the 1950s were models developed that were capable of measuring the contributions of different factors to economic growth. Those models—particularly, the neoclassical model—showed great promise at first, but lost favor when economists discovered that they excluded some of the main factors affecting economic growth. That discovery led to a period of inactivity in growth economics before a renaissance of sorts occurred in the 1980s with the publication of several papers that emphasized the role of information, education, and technology. The new growth theory was born.

In this chapter, we will review the facts of economic growth and productivity and then look at some growth models and a variety of policies designed to improve the long-run prospects of the economy.

AFTER READING AND STUDYING THIS CHAPTER, YOU SHOULD BE ABLE TO:

··· Describe recent productivity data for the United States and other countries, and explain why productivity growth is so important

··· Outline the structure and predictions of the neoclassical growth model, and explain why it has lost favor

··· Explain how the new economic growth theory differs from traditional growth theory

··· Offer policy recommendations for increasing productivity growth

THE PRODUCTIVITY CRISIS

Economists are always asked to make forecasts: Will the recovery start next quarter? How fast will GDP grow next year? Our ability to answer these questions is not perfect, but we are good enough to be taken seriously by policymakers and business leaders. All forecasters have their own special techniques—some combination of statistics, intuition, and guesswork—but most short-term forecasts are really just a prediction of how the economy will move around its long-run trend over the next quarter or two. If your data say the economy will be below its trend rate of growth, you predict bad times ahead; if my forecast says the economy will be above its long-run trend, I predict good times. Whoever is correct more often can charge higher fees—and stay in business.

Economists are *much* less successful at predicting long-term trends. When the U.S. economy fell into a decade-long funk in the 1970s, more than a few economists were surprised, and almost no one predicted the downturn before it occurred. Why did economists miss the long-term trends of the 1970s? There were several reasons, but one of the most important is that they were unable to forecast productivity growth, one of the key determinants of long-term economic growth. Before we can understand economic growth, we need to understand productivity.

········

Definitions and Data

Until now we have been loosely defining productivity as simply the output per worker. The concept is much more complex. One way to calculate productivity is to divide output by inputs, with both measured in money terms. The problem with measurement in money terms is that productivity automatically increases when wages are cut. This result is hardly what we would expect if wages affect work effort, and it is certainly not the key to long-run productivity growth. A better method would be to calculate a physical measure of output per unit of input, but this raises another set of problems. It is difficult to determine the output associated with particular inputs, and it does not always make sense to speak of "automobiles per worker" since workers cannot produce cars without machinery. Measuring different kinds of workers and different kinds of products produced within the same firm can also be difficult. Despite these problems, economists have attempted to come up with useful measures of productivity.

Two kinds of productivity are frequently calculated. The most common measure of productivity, **labor productivity**, is calculated as the total value of output divided

Labor productivity Output per unit of labor input.

by either the number of workers or the number of hours worked. The broader **total factor productivity** is a measure of the output contributions of all inputs—plant and equipment, managers, workers, energy, and any other factors. As a nation we are most concerned with total factor productivity, because this is the source of long-term real aggregate income growth. It is also closely related to international competitiveness. But workers are more concerned with labor productivity because real wages track it closely. It is important to look at both measures of productivity because they do not always move together. For example, if a firm increases capital investment, labor productivity will rise since workers have more machinery to work with. But if machinery costs rise more than the value of output, total factor productivity will decline.

Over the long run, we are concerned with productivity growth as much as with the level of productivity. Two kinds of productivity growth are important. **Cyclical productivity growth** refers to productivity changes over the business cycle. When the economy turns down, firms usually cut production before they lay off workers. As a result, measured productivity declines because the same amount of machinery is being used to produce less output. As the economy recovers from recession, workers work more hours, and firms add workers to the fixed stock of capital. This causes cyclical productivity to increase. It is important to distinguish between cyclical and long-run or **secular productivity growth**. Secular productivity growth is a measure of the increase in productivity due to changes in the capital stock, technology, and other factors. It is secular productivity growth that is most closely related to our standard of living.

Table 33.1 presents data on the recent productivity performance of the United States and seven other advanced industrial countries. The left column shows that secular productivity growth in the United States averaged only 1.0 percent per year between 1979 and 1988. (This is an aggregate figure. Certain sectors—manufacturing exports, for example—enjoyed much higher rates of productivity growth over this period.) This rate was considerably below the U.S. rate in the 1960s and only about half the average rate for other Western industrialized nations in the 1980s. Still,

Total factor productivity A measure of the output contributions of all inputs, computed by dividing total output by total inputs.

Cyclical productivity growth Productivity growth caused by ups and downs of the business cycle.

Secular productivity growth Long-run productivity growth that is due to changes in capital stock, technological advances and the like and is not related to the business cycle.

•••• **TABLE 33.1 COMPARATIVE PRODUCTIVITY GROWTH RATES, 1979–1988**

Country	Secular Productivity Growth		Investment Share	
	Percent	Rank	Percent	Rank
Canada	1.2	7	15.1	2
France	2.0	2	14.3	5
Italy	1.9	3	15.1	2
Japan	3.0	1	23.3	1
Sweden	1.4	6	13.7	6
United Kingdom	1.8	4	13.0	7
United States	1.0	8	12.7	8
West Germany	1.6	5	14.8	4

SOURCE: S. Bowles, D. Gordon, and T. Weisskopf, *After the Wasteland* (Armonk, N.Y.: M. E. Sharpe, 1990), Table 1.2, p. 6.

productivity growth averaged only 0.9 percent per year in the 1970s, so the 1980s represented a slight improvement for the United States. Especially discouraging is the fact that productivity growth in the 1970s was less than half of the rate for the depression years of the 1930s.

The right column in the table lists the average share of investment as a percentage of GDP. A comparison of the two columns shows that, while not perfect, a correlation appears to exist between productivity growth and the share of investment; notice that Japan was number 1 in both categories while the United States was number 8 in both. This suggests that one way to increase productivity growth is to increase investment. As discouraging as the relative growth rate of the United States compared to the advanced industrial countries has been, we have lagged even further behind some of the newly industrialized countries, a point made in the Focus box on page 862. It is important to emphasize that the data in Table 33.1 refer to the *growth* in productivity, not the *level* of productivity. By most accounts, productivity remains higher in the United States than any place else in the world.

So far in the 1990s, things may be looking up for U.S. productivity growth, although it is too early to be certain. The recovery that began in March 1991 differed from other recoveries in an important way: employment grew very little until the last half of 1993, and the unemployment rate continued to increase for 15 months after the recession was officially over. The only way it is possible for real output to increase without a corresponding rise in employment is for productivity to advance. Cyclical productivity typically increases at about a 3 percent annual rate in the first year and a half following a recession; this is about twice the rate of secular productivity increase over the past three decades. In the first year and a half following the 1990–1991 recession, productivity increased at only a 2.5 percent annual rate. On the surface, this would seem to indicate that the productivity problem remains. However, very little of this productivity advance appears to have been caused by cyclical factors because labor hours increased very little. This suggests that most of the productivity advance was the result of secular factors including added capital and worker skills. This trend can be expected to continue over the next decade for at least two reasons: (1) the average age of the workforce is increasing, so less effort will have to be devoted to training young workers, and (2) lower real interest rates will reduce the cost of capital. Figure 33.1 provides recent productivity data.

• • • • • • • •

Productivity and Economic Growth

You could probably guess that technology, capital accumulation, and economic growth are related. Increasing any of these factors will tend to stimulate productivity growth. Unfortunately, we do not have very good theories about how these factors advance. What causes technological advance? Why do firms increase investment? Lower taxes and interest rates are certainly important, but uncertainty and expectations are important as well.

We do know that there is an important connection between productivity growth and economic growth, a connection known as **Verdoorn's law**. According to Verdoorn's law, labor productivity increases as aggregate output grows. There are three reasons to expect this to be true. First, as output expands, there is likely to be some **learning by doing**—workers often discover techniques that increase efficiency with-

Verdoorn's law Labor productivity increases as aggregate output grows. This occurs because of learning by doing, worker transference to high-productivity industries, and investment in new machinery and new technology.

Learning by doing As workers gain experience, reduce defects, and increase efficiency, productivity increases.

• • • • FIGURE 33.1 LABOR PRODUCTIVITY GROWTH, 1990–1993

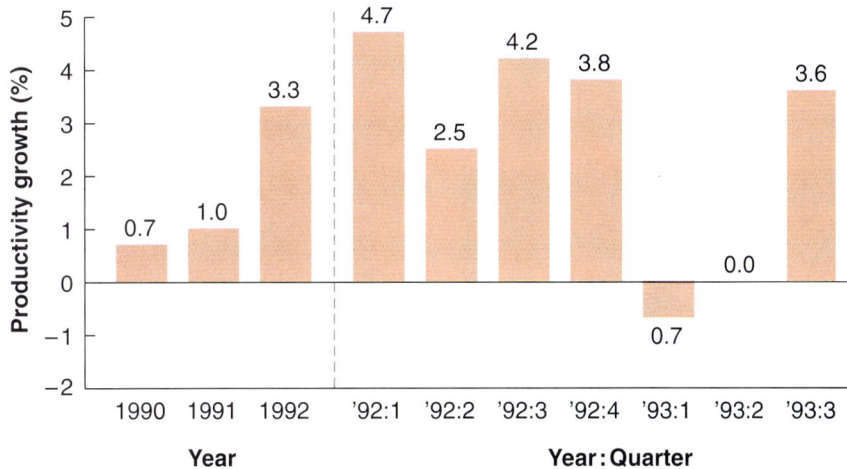

Cyclical productivity growth rebounded following the 1990–1991 recession, and productivity growth has been good so far in the 1990s.

SOURCE: 1994 *Economic Report of the President,* Table B-48. All data are annual rates of growth in output per hour, nonfarm business sector.

out new investment or technology. Second, the faster output expands, the faster the rate of transference of workers from low-productivity industries to high-productivity industries. This tends to raise the average rate of productivity. Finally, as growth accelerates and the economy moves toward full employment, expansion is possible only by investing in new machinery and new technology. All of these events tend to increase productivity.

RECAP   Productivity and Economic Growth

Productivity measures output per unit of input, and productivity growth is the most important variable determining long-run changes in the standard of living. Productivity depends on many factors including worker skill and capital investment; productivity growth also tends to increase with GDP growth. For reasons not well understood, U.S. productivity growth declined significantly in the 1970s and 1980s. It may be improving in the 1990s.

• • • • • • • NEOCLASSICAL GROWTH MODELS

Until the 1980s, the most popular theory of economic growth was the **neoclassical growth model**. Early versions of this model date back to work by Robert Solow, Paul Samuelson, and others in the 1950s. Though the neoclassical model is less popular today, we need to see where it went wrong before we examine more modern theories of growth.

Neoclassical growth model A model of economic growth that assumes an aggregate production function, constant returns to scale, and diminishing marginal productivity.

FOCUS ON

ECONOMIC GROWTH IN THE ASIAN TIGERS

If the United States had a tough time in the economic race of the 1970s and 1980s, the so-called Asian Tigers had a great time. The Asian Tigers—the Republic of (South) Korea, Singapore, Hong Kong, and Taiwan—earned their name from their aggressive economic policies. These policies involved several things. First, as Table 1 shows, the tigers devoted a much higher percentage of GDP to investment than did the United States, and even a little more than Japan. The results are shown in Table 2: rapid economic growth and rising standards of living at a time when many of the industrialized nations were struggling.

Higher investment was not the only thing that affected economic growth in the Asian Tigers. Their governments also applied a considerable amount of less-than-subtle social and cultural pressure to work habits and family planning. For example, in an attempt to increase the intelligence of the population, Singapore offered free ocean cruises for single college graduates—with the hope that the young vacation-

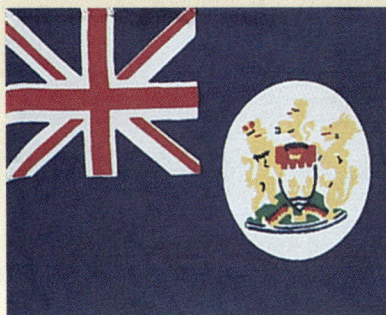

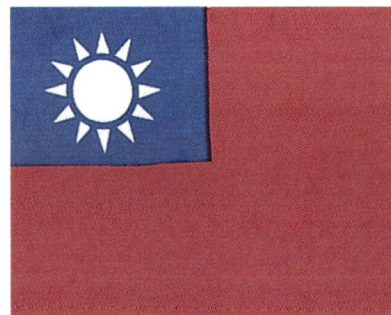

ers would fall in love, get married, and have children! Hong Kong helped increase labor productivity by eliminating almost all government controls on the marketplace—a move to efficiency to be sure, but also one that has been

criticized because it may encourage child labor. And all of the tigers have enacted rather stringent drug laws—death for possession in many cases—at least partially to make sure that workers are alert and hard working.

Predictions of the Neoclassical Growth Model

The standard neoclassical growth model begins with an aggregate production function stating that output (GDP) is a function of the amount of labor and capital employed. The neoclassical production function is assumed to obey two restrictions: **constant returns to scale** and **diminishing marginal productivity**. The assumption

Constant returns to scale Occur when a given percentage increase in all inputs causes output to increase by the same percentage.

····· **TABLE 1 INVESTMENT/GDP RATIO (SELECTED YEARS)**

Country	1970	1975	1980	1985	1989
Korea	24.7%	27.1%	31.7%	29.3%	37.3%
Singapore	38.7	40.0	46.3	42.5	35.4
Hong Kong	21.4	24.2	36.0	21.7	26.8
Japan	37.6	33.3	32.3	28.5	32.9
United States	12.0	13.3	16.0	16.3	15.1

····· **TABLE 2 REAL GDP GROWTH (AVERAGE RATE, PRECEDING FIVE YEARS)**★

Country	1975	1980	1985	1989
Korea	9.5%	7.9%	8.5%	10.2%
Singapore	8.6	7.0	7.1	6.8
Hong Kong	6.1	10.9	5.2	8.0
Japan	4.5	5.0	3.9	4.3
United States	2.2	3.3	2.7	3.5

★The 1989 column is the average for the preceding four years.
SOURCE: Data are from *World Tables* (published for the World Bank by Johns Hopkins University Press, 1991).

What can we learn from the Asian Tiger experience? At least three points stand out: First, there does appear to be a connection between investment and the rate of long-term economic growth. The Japanese experience is additional evidence in support of this point. Second, the Asian Tigers had access to a huge export market—Japan and the Western industrialized nations—so much of their growth was driven by exports. Finally, we must not jump to the conclusion that a higher investment/GDP ratio alone is sufficient to stimulate economic growth. The Asian Tigers also implemented a variety of economic incentives. Whether similar measures would work in the United States—or even whether they are desirable or politically feasible—is a difficult question.

The story behind the phenomenal success of the Asian Tigers is more complex—and interesting—than we can show here. For example, the savings rates of the Asian Tigers are considerably higher than the savings rate in the United States, and many economists believe that this is a major reason for their high rates of growth. But this merely begs the issue: *Why* are their savings rates so high? For a very readable and nontechnical account of these economies, see Jon Woronoff, *Asia's "Miracle" Economies,* 2d ed. (Armonk, N.Y.: M. E. Sharpe, 1992).

of constant returns to scale means that output will double if all inputs are doubled.[1] The assumption of diminishing marginal product means that if one factor of production is fixed, say, the stock of capital, adding more labor will result in smaller and smaller increases in output.

Diminishing marginal productivity If at least one factor of production is fixed, adding additional units of other factors will cause the output per unit of input to diminish.

[1]Returns to scale and diminishing marginal product were the main topics of Chapter 9.

Neither of these assumptions seems unreasonable; nevertheless, economists soon found that the growth models based on these assumptions led to predictions that did not fit the real world very well. There were three main problems. First, the assumption of diminishing marginal returns implies that if the stock of capital is growing faster than the labor force (i.e., the capital/labor ratio is rising), the marginal product of capital should be falling. This in turn implies that the return on new investment should decline over time. It has not. The return on new investment in the past few decades has been higher than in the nineteenth and early twentieth centuries.

The second problem with the neoclassical growth model is that it cannot explain divergent growth rates between rich and poor nations. The assumption of diminishing returns implies that the return on investment should be higher in a poor country with a low capital stock than in a rich country with a high capital stock. This does not hold worldwide: the rich, high-capital nations have tended to have higher rates of return and higher economic growth rates than the poor, low-capital nations. The growth rate differential between the developed nations and the Asian Tigers is an exception: the tigers did start with a smaller capital stock but have grown more rapidly than the United States and most other industrialized nations.

Finally, the neoclassical growth model makes a prediction about the relationship between investment and economic growth that seems unsatisfactory to some economists. According to the model, an increase in the rate of investment—say, from 10 percent of GDP to 15 percent of GDP—will raise the *level* of GDP but not the *rate* of long-term GDP growth. Why not? The higher rate of investment will result in a larger stock of capital; however, unless the rate of growth of the labor supply also increases, the marginal product of capital will decline. The mathematics behind the neoclassical model shows that the decrease in the marginal product of capital will exactly offset the increase in the capital stock so that the rate of GDP growth is independent of the rate of investment. This is illustrated in Figure 33.2.

The Role of Technological Progress

There is a way out of these problems: technological progress. An increase in the amount of capital per worker will not depress the return on capital if technological advances make the new capital more productive than the old capital. Technology may also explain why the return on investment in less-developed, capital-poor countries is lower than the return in the capital-rich, developed nations: the rich nations are more likely to invest in capital with cutting-edge technology. Even the neoclassical prediction that higher rates of investment cannot increase the rate of long-term economic growth can be reversed if the new capital is more technologically sophisticated than existing capital.

Unfortunately, rescuing the model with technology creates another problem because we do not have a good theory of technological progress. Most of the statistical studies conducted to test the neoclassical growth model treated technological change as a statistical "residual" that appeared randomly. Even this would not be so bad if the residual was small, but it is not. Many studies found the residual accounted for as much as half of long-term economic growth. And when trying to explain the productivity crisis of the 1970s, Edward Denison and other investigators found that

•••• FIGURE 33.2 INVESTMENT AND ECONOMIC GROWTH

The neoclassical growth model predicts that a change in the level of investment will affect the *level* of GDP, but not the *rate* of long-term GDP growth. An increase in the level of investment at time t_0 will cause the level of GDP to increase as the economy moves from path A to path B, but the rate of GDP growth will increase only temporarily. Once the economy arrives at its new long-term growth path at time t_1, the rate of economic growth will stabilize at the old rate. The reasoning behind this assertion is that an increase in the rate of investment will reduce the marginal product of capital unless the rate of growth of the labor supply increases correspondingly.

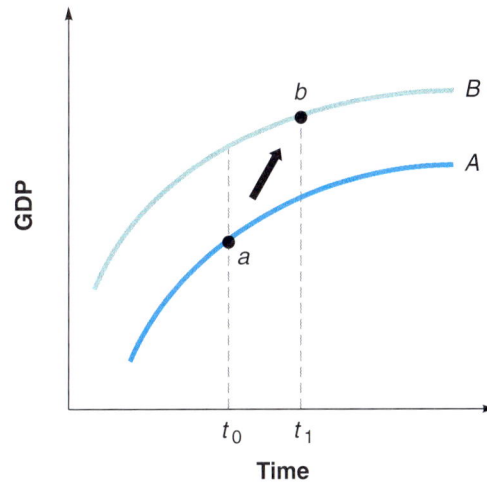

the residual may have accounted for 80 percent of the slowdown.[2] A theory that explains only 20 percent of what it is supposed to be explaining must be modified significantly, if not discarded—which is what happened in the 1980s.

THE NEW ECONOMIC GROWTH THEORY

In 1982, Robert Solow, one of the founders of neoclassical growth theory wrote:

> I think there are definite signs that [growth theory] is just about played out, at least in its familiar form. Anyone working inside economic theory these days knows in his or her bones that growth theory is now an unpromising pond for an enterprising theorist to fish in. I do not mean to say confidently that this state of affairs will last. A good new idea can transform the subject.[3]

That new idea came from the doctoral dissertation and a series of papers by Paul

[2]The leading figure in "growth accounting" is undoubtedly Edward F. Denison. His book, *Trends in American Economic Growth, 1929–1982* (Washington, D.C.: Brookings, 1985), provides the methodology he used to compute the contribution of various factors to economic growth.
[3]From Robert M. Solow, "Some Lessons from Growth Theory," in W. F. Sharpe and C. M. Cootner, eds., *Financial Economics: Essays in Honor of Paul Cootner* (Englewood Cliffs, N.J.: Prentice-Hall, 1982), pp. 246–59. Quoted in Robert M. Solow, "Growth Theory," in David Greenaway, Michael Bleaney, and Ian M. T. Stewart, *Companion to Contemporary Economic Thought* (London: Routledge, 1991), p. 393.

Romer, now a professor of economics at the University of California at Berkeley.[4] Romer began with the neoclassical model but made one seemingly innocuous modification: he added knowledge and information to the production function. This simple change was to revolutionize the way economists looked at the problems of growth and productivity.

• • • • • • • •

Information, the Capital Stock, and Competition

How did Romer add knowledge and information to the production function? He recognized that knowledge is costly just like any economic good; to acquire knowledge, people have to forgo current consumption. For example, you go to college to acquire knowledge—and by going to college, you incur an opportunity cost of lost income and leisure. The same thing holds for societies: to acquire knowledge, current consumption must be sacrificed.

Romer also recognized that a larger existing stock of capital may make the acquisition of new knowledge and technology more profitable. For example, although most of the initial breakthroughs in high-definition television (HDTV) were made in the United States, U.S. firms could have difficulty profitably manufacturing HDTVs because the stock of consumer electronics capital—the consumer electronics industry—in the United States is so small. The special incentives given to the Japanese consumer electronics industry in the 1950s helped establish the consumer electronics capital stock and may explain why Japan has been so successful in this industry for the past 30 years.

New economic growth theory A contemporary theory of economic growth that differs from the neoclassical growth model by adding knowledge to the production function and allowing for increasing returns to scale.

Increasing returns to scale Occur when a given percentage increase in all inputs causes output to increase by a larger percentage.

Finally, the **new growth theory** implies that production can exhibit **increasing returns to scale**, instead of constant returns to scale as assumed by the neoclassical model. Increasing returns to scale mean that if all inputs double, output more than doubles. Increasing returns are a consequence of including information and knowledge in the production function: If information—as well as the capital stock and labor force—doubles, efficiency will improve because productivity will increase. This will cause the cost of output to fall. As a result, firms can lower prices as they expand output. This point has important implications for international competition: if established firms have a cost advantage over entering firms, then the first firms to enter the industry may have a permanent advantage over new entrants. Is it any wonder that not a single VCR has ever been commercially produced in the United States—even though VCR technology was developed here?

• • • • • • • •

Capital Measurement Problems

Paul Romer's work has become the standard framework for the analysis of growth and productivity and is leading to new kinds of policy recommendations. Nevertheless, Romer's work is not without its critics. They include the English economist Maurice Scott of Oxford University, who feels that the neoclassical production func-

---

[4] A symposium on the new growth theory was published in the *Journal of Economic Perspectives* 8 (Winter 1994): 3–72. Paul Romer's paper, "The Origins of Endogenous Growth," provides a good introduction to the theory and a substantial bibliography on the subject. Paul Romer is not related to Christina Romer.

tion must be abandoned altogether because it does not measure capital accurately. Neoclassical economists measure the net stock of capital—gross investment minus depreciation. The problem with this measurement is that it implies that depreciation is a physical process, the wearing down of machinery, when it is actually an accounting concept useful only for tax purposes. In the real world, machines are discarded or sold as scrap when they are no longer profitable to operate—and this may occur before they have worn out. The solution, says Scott, is to modify the production function to include gross investment instead of net investment.

Like Romer, Scott feels that technological progress is vitally important for explaining economic growth. Unlike Romer, however, Scott believes that gross investment and technology are essentially the same thing. Does this make sense? Perhaps not at first glance, but several studies have suggested that inventions are almost always stimulated by industrial needs—just as investment is. In fact, it is difficult to find actual cases where an invention was the result of a pure scientific discovery without industrial motivations.[5] Technology is also "embedded" in capital goods so firms usually must acquire new capital in order to acquire new technology. How could a manufacturing plant enjoy the benefits of industrial robot technology without buying robots?

What are the implications of this view of investment? First, like Romer, Scott disagrees with the neoclassicals who believe that information and technology are random events. Given the linkage between investment and technology, policies that stimulate investment can also stimulate technology. However, Romer criticizes Scott because he cannot explain the differences between growth in countries like India and Taiwan. Levels of investment have been similar in the two countries, but India's return has been small compared to Taiwan's. Part of the growth differential is attributable to cultural differences, but information flows may also be important: India's relatively closed economy prevents some foreign technology and information from flowing into the country, whereas Taiwan's open economy encourages the inflow of new ideas as well as foreign investment.

THE SOCIAL MODEL OF PRODUCTIVITY GROWTH

Another challenge to the new growth theory comes from Samuel Bowles, David Gordon, and Thomas Weisskopf (BGW).[6] In their opinion, production is not simply a mechanical process of combining machines, labor, and technology. The key to understanding the production process, and hence productivity, is understanding how people interact with machines and technology. Why did productivity increase so much during World War II? Not because the number of machines or technology

[5]The laser is sometimes cited as an example of an invention that was not stimulated by industrial needs, but Alexander Graham Bell, the inventor of the telephone, anticipated an important industrial application of communication by light waves long before the first laser was demonstrated in 1960. Further, the use of lasers for communication had to wait development of fiber optic technology—which was motivated by industrial needs.

[6]The original work was Samuel Bowles, David Gordon, and Thomas Weisskopf, *Beyond the Wasteland* (New York: Anchor Press/Doubleday, 1983). In 1990, this book was updated with the publication of *After the Wasteland* (Armonk, N.Y.: M. E. Sharpe, 1990).

Social model An economic model
that suggests that productivity growth
is dependent on work effort and
other social factors as well as labor,
capital, and technology inputs.

increased overnight. Productivity increased largely because patriotism caused people
to work harder. Thus, to understand the causes of the productivity decline, work
effort, business innovation, and other social factors must be included in the analysis.
The **social model** developed by BGW includes these factors and was reputedly able
to account for *all* of the productivity decline in the 1970s.

· · · · · · · ·

Proxy Variables

The BGW theory holds that work effort and other social factors accounted for a large
portion of the decline in productivity. Unfortunately, these variables are hard to
measure. The solution was to find substitute or *proxy variables* that are observable and
that capture the social factors that influence productivity growth.

To capture work effort and intensity, BGW chose two kinds of proxy variables,
one set to capture worker motivation and another to reflect management control.
For example, some of the variables used to measure worker motivation were the
growth in real after-tax hourly earnings, the number of industrial accidents, and the
incidence of strikes. The growth in real after-tax income was assumed to result in an
increase in work effort; a decrease in income would reduce effort. The number of
industrial accidents and the incidence of strikes were chosen as indicators of worker
unrest; workers afraid of an industrial accident are less likely to work efficiently. One
of the variables used to measure management control was the intensity of supervision,
defined as the ratio of supervisors to production workers; the higher the ratio, the
greater the degree of supervision. An elaborate statistical model containing both social
variables and "traditional" variables—capital investment and capital utilization rates,
energy inputs, and so on—was then constructed to test the hypothesis that social
factors influence productivity growth.

· · · · · · · ·

Results of the Social Model

BGW began their study trying to explain the productivity crisis of the 1970s, specifically, why productivity growth had fallen from an average rate of 2.96 percent
per year between 1948 and 1966 to 2.07 percent between 1966 and 1973, and then
to a miserable 0.83 percent rate between 1973 and 1979. As Figure 33.3 shows, the
proxies for work intensity accounted for over 80 percent of the productivity slowdown in the periods 1948–1966 and 1966–1973. These results can be viewed as
being consistent with Denison's conclusion that the residual was largely responsible
for the productivity slowdown. The residual captures the effects of omitted variables,
and Denison did not include social variables in his model.

The BGW model yields slightly different results for the post-1973 productivity
slowdown. Declining work intensity accounted for only 30 percent of that slowdown. Most of the rest of the decline was due to the more traditional causes of capital
utilization and capital intensity. The other two variables listed in Figure 33.3, innovative pressure and citizen protest, represent the combined effects of proxies designed
to measure technical innovation and worker resistance to corporate power. Technical
innovation increases productivity growth as firms adopt new and more effective technologies. Resistance to corporate power is often expressed as demands for workplace
safety, consumer protection, or a pollution-free environment. Although these

····**FIGURE 33.3** **THE SOCIAL MODEL AND THE PRODUCTIVITY DECLINE**

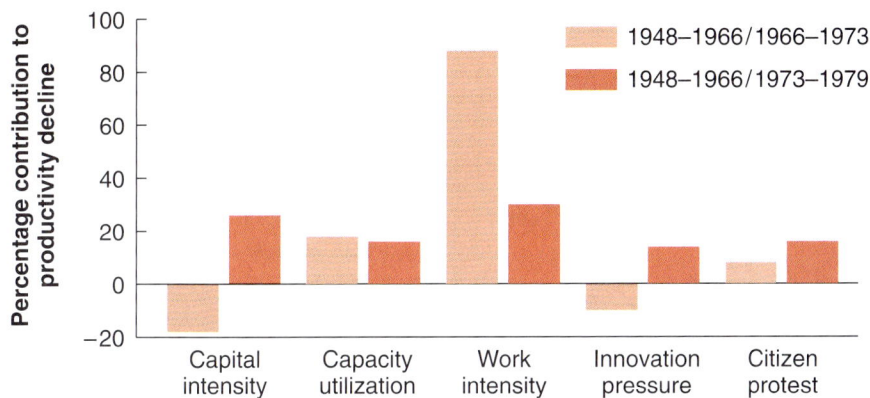

The social model explains the productivity decline as a function of social factors. Average productivity growth in the United States fell by 0.89 percentage points from the 1948–1966 average of 2.96 percent per year to 2.07 percent per year in the period 1966–1973. The causes of the productivity decline over this period are shown by the light bars. The main cause of the decline was reduced worker intensity, which accounted for about 80 percent of the decline; decreased capacity utilization and citizen protest were also contributing factors. Innovative pressure and capital intensity worked to increase productivity over the period. The average annual productivity growth over the period 1973–1979 was 2.13 percentage points below the 1948–1966 average. The causes of the productivity decline over this period are shown by the dark bars. Work intensity accounted for about 30 percent of this decline; much of the rest of the decline was due to traditional factors of declining capital utilization and capital intensity.

demands may have social benefits, they lower measured productivity because implementing these changes is costly.

········

A Final Answer?

The apparent ability of the BGW model to account for all of the causes of the productivity decline is quite an accomplishment—if it is correct. The model is still the subject of ongoing research, and no definitive assessment has been reached. The most common criticism of the model is that the proxy variables are subject to different interpretations. For this reason, many analysts have suggested that the results of the BGW model should be regarded as preliminary until it can be applied to cross-cultural data.

There is another and perhaps more serious problem with the BGW model. Even if it does have the "final answer," it does not suggest any unique or novel policy recommendations. Simply being able to say that attitudinal variables are important causes of productivity growth does nothing to increase productivity. The real question is how to change attitudes in the workplace. The BGW model provides no way to choose between union busting—which might reduce strikes—and planning boards that combine business, labor, and the government. The authors recommend wage-led growth and workplace democracy as productivity stimulants—higher wages to reduce the relative cost of capital and increase motivation, and democracy to increase job identification and effort. These are important goals and may be implemented as the population becomes more educated.

RECAP   Economic Growth Models

1. Neoclassical growth models assume constant returns to scale and diminishing marginal product. Neoclassical models predict that an increase in investment will increase the level of GDP, but not the rate of GDP growth. When used to test for the causes of the productivity decline, these models typically showed that most of the decline was due to the residual. These models have become less popular in recent years.

2. The new economic growth models emphasize the role of information and technology. New economic growth models allow for increasing returns to scale and can explain why advanced nations typically grow faster than less-developed nations. These models are quite popular but have been criticized for their inability to measure capital and technology adequately.

3. The social model explains growth as a consequence of social factors including work effort, business innovation, and other factors. This model attributes virtually all of the productivity growth decline of the 1970s to social factors. The main criticism of the social model is that it is difficult to interpret its proxy variables.

·······•· POLICY AND THE PRODUCTIVITY PROBLEM

In April 1992, 100 economists—including six Nobel Prize winners—wrote an open letter to President Bush and the Congress calling for two measures to help the economy recover from the recession; lower interest rates and a $50 billion grant to the states from the federal government.[7] The call for lower interest rates was not too surprising; inflation was close to zero so there was little risk on that front. But the call for $50 billion more in federal spending was surprising given that the deficit was approaching $400 billion. Why would responsible economists make such a call? The key was that the money was to be spent on things that would help the economy in the long run: education, transportation, and other elements of the social infrastructure. Such policies are also consistent with modern views on the policies necessary to stimulate economic growth and productivity.

---

[7]The Nobel Prize winners were Kenneth Arrow, Lawrence Klein, Franco Modigliani, William Sharpe, Robert Solow, and James Tobin. Not all economists agreed with the call, of course. For example, Martin Feldstein, president of the NBER and past chair of the Council of Economic Advisers under President Reagan, said that the increased spending would send a bad message to the financial markets. The text of the letter can be found in the April/May 1992 issue of *Challenge*.

· · · · · · · ·

Education and Economic Growth

In 1988 candidate George Bush said he wanted to be known as the "education president" and suggested that better education would help the United States compete in the world economy. Economists could not agree more. Educated workers learn new tasks more quickly and thus reduce training costs. Many investigators have noted that declining scores on college entrance exams are correlated with sluggish productivity growth. Cognitive skills are especially important in modern technological societies. Workers with the ability to learn quickly can easily switch from the production of one sophisticated, high-technology product to another; countries with less-skilled workers often inherit the production of standardized products.[8]

Education provides indirect benefits as well. Highly educated people are much less likely to commit crimes—and thus reduce the need to use scarce resources for police protection.[9] Education also helps integrate immigrants into the economic mainstream so that they can enter the workforce more rapidly. Finally, public education is egalitarian. The best chance for poor children to rise out of poverty is to acquire a good education, the same education that is available to middle-class children. Many people believe that a more egalitarian society is a more productive society because there is a stronger sense of social identity.

Just how bad is education in the United States? Our high school students ranked ninth in the world in math abilities in the 1980s. Given that U.S. students spend less time in the classroom than their counterparts in Japan and much of Europe, things do not look to improve any time soon. Nearly 15 percent of American adolescents fail to complete high school—and the rate is considerably higher in many areas. Even worse, perhaps 20 percent of the adult population is functionally illiterate.

What can be done to improve education? Different people have different answers, but it is generally agreed that improving early education is vital. This is why many observers believe that more effort should be spent trying to help preschoolers learn the value of education and how to learn. Effective preschool programs may reduce the dropout rate. There is also general agreement on the need for more and better programs to train teachers, especially mathematics teachers. Finally, more people must be attracted to the teaching profession. This requires not only higher salaries, but changes in the value society puts on teaching; in too many circles, teaching is considered a less-than-prestigious occupation.

Most public money for education comes from state and local governments; the federal government contributes less than 10 percent of all public funds spent on education. Using state and local funds for schools permits more local control of school systems, but it also makes it more difficult to mount a national strategy to improve the system. Further, because most states have constitutions requiring them to run balanced budgets, spending more money on education usually means raising taxes, never a popular move.

---

[8]A good discussion of the relationship between education and productivity growth can be found in Richard J. Murnane, "Education and the Productivity of the Work Force: Looking Ahead," in Robert E. Litan, Robert Z. Lawrence, and Charles L. Schultze, *American Living Standards* (Washington, D.C.: Brookings Institution, 1988), pp. 215–45.
[9]According to the April 14, 1992 issue of *U.S. News and World Report,* police protection cost U.S. taxpayers an amount equal to 2.3 percent of GDP in 1991—approximately $120 billion.

....

Social Infrastructure and Productivity Growth

A number of recent studies by David Alan Aschauer and others have shown that public nonmilitary investment is positively related to productivity growth.[10] Nonmilitary public investment—roads, airports, mass transit, and so on—is called **social infrastructure**.

Social infrastructure Roads, sewage, and other systems that make social and economic activities possible.

Public investment has both direct and indirect benefits for productivity growth. The direct effects include increased availability of public capital that supports production in the private sector. For example, more and better roads make it easier for firms to distribute their goods and services. The indirect effects result from the fact that public and private capital are complementary; that is, an increase in public investment will tend to increase the rate of return on private investment. Aschauer has estimated that for every dollar increase in public nonmilitary investment, private investment rises by 45 cents.

Aschauer reached his conclusions by studying public nonmilitary investment and productivity growth in the G-7 countries.[11] The relationship between public investment and productivity growth is apparent in all of the G-7 countries, but it has been most striking in the United States. Over the period 1967–1985, public nonmilitary investment in the United States fell from 1.7 percent of GDP to 0.3 percent of GDP.[12] These figures are especially important because Aschauer estimates that a one percentage point increase in the share of GDP devoted to public capital will increase labor productivity by 0.73 percentage points. Such an increase would amount to a nearly 25 percent improvement in average annual productivity growth.

Aschauer's studies have received wide attention and seem to be generally accepted, though there are some critics including Robert Barro of Harvard. Barro believes that Aschauer has reversed the causality: during periods of rising productivity, tax revenues increase, and with them, funds for public investment. Others have suggested that Aschauer's policies are simply not politically viable in this era of massive federal deficits.

INDUSTRIAL POLICY

Industrial policy A system of taxes, subsidies, and targeted investment incentives designed to move the economy along a prearranged path.

Use the term "**industrial policy**" in a group of mild-mannered economists, and you will almost certainly elicit a less-than-mild response. Many will start screaming about the propriety of interfering with the market process, but at least a few will say that the United States needs an industrial policy if it ever hopes to compete in the international economy. Just what is industrial policy? The term means different things to different people, but it is definitely *not* a system of centralized planning and

---

[10]Two nontechnical pieces by Aschauer include "Public Investment and Productivity Growth in the Group of Seven," *Economic Perspectives* 13 Federal Reserve Bank of Chicago (September/October 1989): 17–25 and "Infrastructure: America's Third Deficit," *Challenge* (March/April 1991): 39–45.

[11]The G-7 countries are the seven largest industrialized democracies: the United States, the United Kingdom, France, Japan, Canada, Germany, and Italy.

[12]West Germany, France, the United Kingdom, and Canada followed patterns similar to the United States. Public nonmilitary investment in Japan rose from 3.8 percent of GDP in 1967 to 5.8 percent in 1979 before falling back to 3.1 percent in 1985. Public nonmilitary investment hovered around 3 percent of GDP in Italy.

socialist ownership. Most industrial policy programs involve a system of taxes and subsidies designed to move the economy along a prearranged path. The most important goals of industrial policies are to ease the transition of resources from declining industries to growing industries and to increase aggregate productivity growth. A major difference between industrial policy and standard fiscal and monetary policies is that industrial policies involve targeted incentives for specific industries. Most developed countries have industrial policies. Japan has probably received the most attention in the media, but Germany, France, and other countries have industrial policies as well.

· · · · · · · ·

Industrial Policy in Japan

U.S. investigators have focused most of their attention on the Japanese model of industrial policy. The primary agency responsible for Japanese industrial policy is the Ministry of International Trade and Industry, more often known by its acronym MITI.[13] MITI serves several functions. It selects industries and products for development, eases adjustment due to industrial dislocation, assists in regional development, and is involved in many other areas. MITI is not autonomous; its actions are reviewed by the Diet, the prime minister, and the Ministry of Finance. The Japan Development Bank and Long Term Credit Bank complement MITI by providing preferential loans, and the Bank of Japan rations credit to selected industries. It must be emphasized that MITI only *aids* private industry; it does not replace the market. Rarely does MITI finance 100 percent of a project. For example, only 50 percent of the financing for Japan's fifth-generation computer project has been funded by MITI; the remaining 50 percent is coming from the private sector. Contrast this approach to what has occurred in the United States and Europe: Boeing tried but failed to convince the U.S. government to finance all of the costs of building a supersonic transport (SST). The Concorde SST was entirely government financed in France and Great Britain but has been a money loser since its inception.

Perhaps the most important function of MITI is to provide visions of future Japanese industrial development. In the past, these visions have apparently been at odds with the law of comparative advantage. For example, in the 1950s Japan had a great deal of labor relative to capital. This would suggest that Japanese exports should have focused on labor-intensive products. Instead of fostering the growth of labor-intensive production, however, MITI encouraged steel, autos, and other areas of high-value-added, capital-intensive production. MITI chose these industries because it believed that future world income growth would generate high demand for these products. MITI's visions serve as a focus for public discussion about the future of the Japanese economy. MITI has occasionally erred—it opposed Honda's entry into the auto business and Sony's move into consumer electronics—but these mistakes appear to be exceptions to a generally successful record.

Economists are divided on how important MITI has been in Japan's industrial development. Some people believe that the Japanese miracle has occurred in spite of

[13]This section draws upon Robert S. Ozaki, "How Japanese Industrial Policy Works," in Chalmers Johnson, ed., *The Industrial Policy Debate* (San Francisco: ICS Press, 1984), pp. 47–70, Toshimasa Tsuruta, "Japan's Industrial Policy," in Lester Thurow, ed., *The Management Challenge* (Cambridge, Mass.: MIT Press, 1985), pp. 160–88, and Robert Reich, *The Next American Frontier* (New York, Penguin Books, 1983).

MITI, and note that Japan's high savings rate and small government sector help the market more than any industrial policy agency possibly could. The savings rate in Japan is about three times that of the U.S. rate. Only 10 percent of GDP flows through the government sector in Japan; the comparable figure in the United States is over 20 percent. Further, critics note that most Japanese development funds go to social programs, environmental protection, and industrial "losers," not the Japanese firms that have conquered the world economy. Others counter that it is difficult to assess MITI's impact accurately because most industrial loans are from private banks—but banks are more willing to give industrial loans after MITI has given its stamp of approval.[14]

• • • • • • • •

Industrial Policies in Other Countries

The United States is the only country where the term "industrial policy" generates so much heated debate. Most other advanced nations use various kinds of industrial policies to supplement fiscal and monetary policies.

Germany. Germany's free-market industrial policy combines aid to targeted industries with measures that encourage labor-management cooperation and provide extensive worker training and retraining programs. The German economy is much more reliant upon manufacturing than is the U.S. economy. Nearly half of German GDP comes from manufacturing, compared to only a quarter in the United States. This partially explains why so much aid is given to heavy industry, about 9 percent of total federal government expenditures in the pre-unification days. Historically, almost half of all industrial aid has gone to industries known to be in decline—coal, shipping, and steel—but the German people apparently feel that allowing these industries to die would have undesirable social consequences.

Another key element of German industrial policy is *co-determination*—the integration of labor and management in the firm's decision-making operations. Labor representation on the supervisory boards of large companies is required by law. This prevents much labor-management friction and seems to reduce the incidence of labor strife.

It will be interesting to see if the industrial policies that West Germany used so successfully before reunification will be successful when they are applied to the former East Germany. By 1992, over $100 billion in aid had gone to the former East Germany. Much of that money was spent retraining workers and revamping the aging Soviet-era factories. Whether the unified Germany will be as productive as the old West Germany will not be known for several years.

---

[14]Any "victory" that Japan has won in the arena of international competition has come with a price. The price was not only long hours at work and school, but the alienation of many of its trading partners. Japan bashing has been common in the United States—both in parking lots and in Congress—and Europeans have begun to resent not only Japanese imports, but production in Japanese-owned factories in Europe. Recognizing that too much success might be a bad thing, MITI has asked some industries to reduce working hours and has advocated *kyosei*—"living together"—to reduce international trade friction. A more effective solution might be an easing of the trade barriers that make entry into the Japanese market so difficult. See "Couldn't We All Do a Little Bit Worse?" *The Economist* (April 14, 1992): 19.

France. The main idea behind French industrial policy is *indicative planning,* which has been practiced since World War II. Each year, leaders from management, labor, and government meet to discuss and coordinate their production plans for the coming year. For example, if automakers announce a higher production target, steel producers know to increase output to meet the needs of the auto industry without having to pay overtime shifts. Indicative planning is entirely voluntary, but the benefits are obvious: if your firm ignores the plan, you may find it difficult to find suppliers or buyers.

The French system has undergone significant changes since François Mitterrand, a socialist, was elected president in 1981. Mitterrand's original plan was to use macroeconomic policies to reduce unemployment in the short run and to restructure the economy over the long run. He also made the tax system more progressive in order to redistribute French income, the most unevenly distributed in Europe. The most controversial aspect of the Mitterrand plan was the nationalization of dominant companies in certain key industries. The aim was to use selective nationalization to lead the development of other industries. Unfortunately, the results were not what Mitterrand had hoped. The franc began to fall as soon as the election results were announced, financial capital fled the country, and inflation began to accelerate.

The Socialist Party began losing power in the mid-1980s and entered the 1990s with only a tenuous hold on a coalition government. In recent years, conservatives have sponsored a number of privatization plans, and new financial capital issued by state-owned enterprises is no longer guaranteed by the government. Additionally, several laws have been enacted to reduce immigration, ostensibly to protect the jobs of French-born citizens.

Sweden. Contrary to popular belief, Sweden is not really a "socialist" country; only a small component of industry is owned by the public sector. Sweden does have an extensive social welfare system with essentially free education and medical care, as well as a very liberal welfare network. Some observers feel that the success of the Swedish economy is due in part to this social system. Workers who do not have to worry about their basic material needs may be more confident and productive at work.

All economic policies in Sweden have two constraints: full employment must be preserved, and the trade balance must be maintained to permit the importation of needed products that cannot be produced at home. To achieve these goals, Sweden has relied on a variety of incentives and subsidies. For example, in the 1950s Sweden realized that its textile industry could not compete with textile imports from the low-wage, less-developed nations. The solution was a "humane" acceleration of market forces: textile workers were given training subsidies to help them find new jobs as the industry declined. Today, the Swedish textile industry still exists, but operates in only a very small niche providing the world with upscale designer clothing. A less successful attempt at industrial policy occurred in the 1960s when Swedish policymakers tried to defy market forces and prop up the country's ailing shipbuilding industry. The result was a costly mistake that is often held up as an indictment of Swedish industrial policy. Today, Swedish economic policy relies upon the market and rarely offers industrial aid unless private business is willing to join in the risk. In

FOCUS ON

THE CONTRARIAN VIEW: CRISIS? WHAT CRISIS?

Not everyone agrees that productivity growth is a problem in the United States. Though we may have problems in certain industries, U.S. workers remain the most productive in the world. By many measures, the United States has the highest standard of living in the world. So what is the problem? Why are so many people concerned about the productivity crisis? Perhaps they shouldn't be. Some economists believe that the so-called productivity crisis is just a case of mistaken identity. Points made by these economists include the following:

- *The industrial structure has changed.* Part of the reason things look so bad is that the economy is undergoing a natural evolution from manufacturing to services. In 1963, about 30 percent of all jobs were in manufacturing; today, the number is about 17 percent. Why does this matter? Productivity growth in services has been much slower than

in manufacturing, so when the weights of the two sectors change, the aggregate productivity growth rate falls. Over the period 1963–1986, productivity growth in manufacturing averaged 2.6 percent; it was only 0.2 percent in the services. Further, because measuring productivity growth in service industries is extremely difficult, it is possible that productivity growth in the service sector is actually higher than we think.

- *The United States has not lost its competitive edge.* When the trade balance declined from a $7 billion surplus in 1981 to a $160 billion deficit in 1987, many people worried that the United States had lost its competitive edge. What actually happened was that the fiscal deficit resulted in misaligned exchange rates. As the dollar began to fall, the trade deficit also started to decline and fell below $40 billion in 1992.

True, the U.S. recession and reduced imports were part of the reason for the decline, but increased exports also played a big part: exports rose 86 percent between 1986 and 1991. The United States now has 18 percent of the world's manufactured exports; Japan has only 15 percent. Countries that cannot compete internationally do not hold a fifth of the world's export market.

- *We idealize an aberrant past.* The American public is fascinated by the "good old days" of the 1950s, but our enthusiasm for the past may distort our view of the present. The United States was the only industrial country that was not bombed during World War II, so it was easy for us to dominate international trade following the war. Strong demand for U.S. goods and a sizable trade surplus resulted in rapidly rising productivity and living stan-

---

1991, the newly elected conservative coalition government announced the sale of 35 government-owned companies. The government does impose strict environmental regulations and, in recent years, has aided the environmental cleanup in the Baltic republics and elsewhere in Eastern Europe.

• • • • • • • •

The Pros and Cons of Industrial Policy

Even if industrial policy has been responsible for the Japanese and German economic miracles, this achievement is not, in itself, enough to warrant a call for industrial policy elsewhere. Industrial policy may have succeeded in Japan—or in Germany, France, or Sweden—because of specific cultural conditions that are not present in other economies. A serious industrial policy proposal must isolate the arguments for

The Andersons from "Father Knows Best," a 1950s TV show.

was before World War II. Today's concern over foreigners buying up America seems justified compared to the 1950s, but foreign investment in the United States today is about on par with what it was in 1914. Viewed in this context, the 1970s and 1980s do not look so bad; they seem to be in line with the previous 150 years of U.S. history. If we could just forget the aberrant 1950s, we might be able to get on with things.

Is the so-called productivity crisis much ado about nothing? Perhaps. But if you ask people on the street about the future, they will likely tell you that their kids will not be as well off as their parents. Or perhaps they will point out that both parents *have* to work, something that was not the case when they were growing up. Rightly or wrongly, our collective expectation of the future has diminished. This is a first in U.S. history, and something that economists cannot ignore.

dards. Why do we remember those days so vividly? It could be because of television: reruns of "Leave it to Beaver" and "Ozzie and Harriet" are still with us.

When compared to earlier periods in U.S. history, the 1950s were far from typical. The U.S. share of world GDP has fallen since the 1950s—to about the same level it

and against industrial policy to see whether they are applicable to the specific economy in question.

Pro–industrial Policy. Industrial policy advocates have made four main arguments. First, many advocates contend that supply and demand no longer rule the international economy. All nations use a variety of subsidies, tariffs, and other measures to help particular industries and interest groups. To counter these nonmarket measures, the United States must engage in a variety of activities such as strategic industrial targeting and negotiation for international market shares.[15] Second, capitalism never

[15]Strategic industrial targeting involves special incentives for industries that exhibit decreasing costs or are thought to have significant external benefits. This topic is discussed in some detail in Chapter 37.

has been very good at *disinvestment*—the process of replacing old capital with new capital. When firms or industries lose their competitive advantage, industrial policy may help to cushion the social costs of the phaseout. Third, industrial change can cause regional cycles of boom and bust. The availability of cheap labor and favorable tax laws elsewhere has resulted in industrial emigration between regions and nations. One result for the United States has been the emergence of areas like the "rust belt" and the growing competition between regions for scarce jobs. Industrial policy advocates say that a national policy is necessary to structure tax incentives to prevent the creation of ghost towns. Finally, many economists contend that an industrial policy is necessary because the United States already has one, albeit an inefficient, disorganized program that protects certain industries and special interest groups with no social goal in mind. One way to dismantle a bad program, perhaps the only way, is to establish a new program.

Anti–industrial Policy. At least three anti–industrial policy arguments can be made. First, economists frequently argue that the market is the most efficient allocator of resources. If the economy is in trouble, less government intervention should improve economic performance; additional interference through an industrial policy would only make things worse. Second, although the market may not always allocate resources optimally, there is nothing to say the government could do a better job. How could the government possibly know the ideal path of industrial development? A much better strategy would be to pursue traditional fiscal and monetary policies to promote economic growth. Finally, many argue that the economy is simply not in trouble. In their view, bad figures on productivity growth are simply the result of the move to a service economy; unemployment increases are due to an increase in the natural rate, and so on. Any remaining problems with international competitiveness are the result of a temporarily overvalued dollar. The Focus box on page 876 elaborates on some of these points.

RECAP   Productivity Policies

A number of policies have been recommended to stimulate productivity growth. Many economists believe that the educational system must be improved so that workers can be more easily trained for complex tasks. Others recommend additional spending on social infrastructure, noting that private sector productivity is stimulated by social infrastructure. Finally, some economists recommend that the United States adopt an industrial policy to guide the economy and encourage investment in targeted industries.

SUMMARY

Economists have always been concerned about the long run, but only recently have they begun to develop models that may lead to policies that will help solve the productivity crisis of the last 20 years.

1. Productivity measures the change in output per unit of input. It is the most important factor in determining long-run changes in the standard of living. Productivity growth in the United States slowed in the 1970s and 1980s. It is too

early to be certain, but some investigators are encouraged by the productivity performance following the 1990–1991 recession. Productivity growth depends on several factors; one of the most important is economic growth.

2. The neoclassical growth model assumes constant returns to scale and diminishing returns. Most empirical studies using the neoclassical model showed that the "residual" is an important factor determining economic growth and productivity. The residual is often interpreted as technology; however, the neoclassical model does not have a good theory of technological advance.

3. The new growth theory, which includes information in the production function, has been used to explain why economic growth rates differ between nations. The theory implies that production will exhibit increasing returns to scale. This means that nations with established industries may enjoy a long-term advantage over other nations.

4. The social model of productivity holds that the key to productivity is work effort, which in turn depends on a variety of social factors. Social factors are difficult to quantify, so proxy variables are used in empirical studies of this model. Interpreting proxy variables can be difficult, however. Advocates of the social model believe that productivity will increase with the implementation of workplace democracy.

5. Many economists believe that the best way to stimulate long-term economic and productivity growth is to improve education and increase public investment in the social infrastructure. With a better educated labor force, firms' training costs are reduced, and workers are able to learn new tasks more readily. Social infrastructure increases the return on private investment.

6. Most nations use industrial policies as well as fiscal and monetary policies to guide their economies. Industrial policy consists of taxes and subsidies designed to aid preselected industries. MITI, an industrial policy agency of Japan, is often cited as the prototypical industrial policy agency. Critics argue that an industrial policy will tend to pick the wrong industries and that the market is the most efficient way of allocating resources.

KEY TERMS AND CONCEPTS

labor productivity
total factor productivity
cyclical productivity growth
secular productivity growth
Verdoorn's law
learning by doing
neoclassical growth model
constant returns to scale
diminishing marginal productivity

technological progress residual
new economic growth theory
increasing returns to scale
social model
proxy variable
education
social infrastructure
industrial policy

REVIEW QUESTIONS

1. What is the difference between cyclical productivity growth and secular productivity growth? What factors determine productivity? What has happened to

U.S. productivity growth over the past 25 years? Why is this so important?

2. What are the key assumptions and predictions of the neoclassical growth model? What were the main reasons why economists began to look for alternatives to the neoclassical model?

3. Explain how the addition of information to the neoclassical production function can lead to increasing returns to scale. Why is this so important?

4. Why were BGW forced to use proxy variables in their social model of productivity growth? What are the main conclusions of their work?

5. How do education and investment in social infrastructure affect productivity growth?

6. What are the main aims of industrial policy? How is it practiced in Japan? What are some of the key elements of the industrial policies of other nations? Should the United States implement an industrial policy?

PROBLEMS

1. One proxy that BGW used to capture business innovation was the business failure rate. Explain why this might be a reasonable proxy for innovation.

2. U.S. productivity growth was negative in 1985. Does this mean that the typical worker lost skills over the course of the year? Why or why not?

3. Do you think Paul Romer would favor the adoption of an industrial policy for the United States? Why or why not?

4. It is possible for labor productivity to rise even though the firm's cost of output increases. Explain.

5. Suppose that unions were outlawed and that the average wage rate fell. Explain why this could either increase or decrease the rate of growth. (*Hint:* Look at the policy proposals of BGW.)

6. A European executive has been quoted as saying, "The Japanese should stop trying single-mindedly to produce the best goods at the cheapest prices to win the biggest market share."[16] Comment on this statement and explain how it relates to the Contrarian View Focus box.

7. When soldiers returned from World War II, many enrolled in college at the expense of the government, courtesy of the GI Bill. It is often stated that the GI Bill was the most efficient program ever enacted by Congress. Explain, comment, and relate to the current educational system.

8. Aschauer's statistical studies show that social investment can increase the corporate profits rate. Explain why this is true.

9. What components of the industrial policies of Japan, Germany, France, and Sweden do you think are most applicable to the United States? Why?

10. In the 1980s, the French government subsidized the development of a domestic VCR industry, even though there was little expectation that the VCR industry would ever turn a profit. Was this sheer stupidity? Or was there a method to the government's madness?

[16]Quoted in "Couldn't We All Do a Little Bit Worse?" *The Economist* (April 14, 1992): 19.

PART VII

THE INTERNATIONAL ECONOMY

CHAPTER 34

Evolving Economic Systems

Estonia, the most northerly of the Baltic republics, was one of the first Soviet republics to break away from the former Soviet Union. It had good reason to seek independence. Southern Estonia, long known as the "Baltic Switzerland" for its beauty, was a virtual wasteland, the product of Soviet bombing practice. The north coast of Estonia, once known for its beautiful rivers and salmon fisheries, reeked with smoke from oil shale processing. Slaughterhouse waste polluted the rivers, and well water was a fire hazard. But perhaps more importantly, 50 years of Soviet domination had affected the character of the Estonian people. Too many people seemed to have given up hope, and the idea of a national culture was fast slipping away. It was time for a revolution. The Green Party's revolt against the environmental devastation by the Soviets quickly became a rallying cry for national independence, and in November 1988, the Estonian Supreme Soviet declared independence. Initial reaction from Moscow was harsh, but talks proceeded quickly, and economic independence for the three Baltic states—Estonia, Latvia, and Lithuania—was granted on January 1, 1990. On August 20, 1991, one day after the coup in Moscow, Estonia declared complete independence. Three weeks later, on September 9, 1991, Estonia applied for membership in the International Monetary Fund and shortly thereafter applied to the World Bank and European Bank for Reconstruction and Development. On September 17, 1991, Estonia was admitted to the United Nations.

The case of Estonia is especially instructive for the study of comparative economics. Before World War II, Estonia had a higher standard of living than Sweden. When the Soviet Union collapsed, it had the highest standard of living of the Soviet republics—but that was orders of magnitude lower than Sweden. What had happened in 50 years? Why did Estonia decline relative to

Sweden? The quick answer is that Western market economies worked better than Soviet central planning, but the issue is much more complex. The collapse of the Soviet Union may have signaled the victory of capitalism over socialism, but it should not be interpreted as the victory of any particular brand of capitalism. The U.S. version of capitalism performed better than Soviet-style central planning, but so did the Japanese variety of capitalism, the German variety, and even the Swedish variety. The study of comparative economics today is not so much the analysis of "capitalism versus socialism" as the analysis of the different varieties of capitalism and the study of economic evolution.

This chapter will examine comparative economic systems and try to put the process of economic evolution in some perspective. Social and economic systems are always changing. Capitalism is far different today than it was just 50 years ago, and it will continue to evolve in the future.

AFTER READING AND STUDYING THIS CHAPTER, YOU SHOULD BE ABLE TO:
• • • Outline the evolution of Western capitalism from its roots in European feudalism
• • • Discuss the Marxian critique of capitalism, and explain how capitalism differs from socialism
• • • Explain why the Soviet Union collapsed and analyze the policies that have been implemented to establish market capitalism in the former Soviet Union
• • • Discuss some of the key features of Japanese and European capitalism

THE RISE OF CAPITALISM

Capitalist economies are characterized by private ownership of the means of production; socialist economies rely upon public ownership of the means of production. All economic systems, however, are really a mix of public and private ownership. Even before the Soviet Union's collapse, private enterprise existed there, although most was confined to small businesses and farms. Many utility companies in the United States and other capitalist economies are owned by state and local governments. In addition, some capitalist governments direct long-term economic development and subsidize loans for selected industries. Still, the fundamental philosophies of **capitalism** and **socialism** differ substantially: proponents of capitalism claim that private property and market forces are more efficient; socialists argue that public ownership and planning are just as efficient and more equitable.

The Heritage of Feudalism

Capitalism has not been with us forever. It is the product of cultural factors, history, and social evolution, and in the West at least, it descended from **feudalism**. The basic social and economic unit in feudal society was the manor, a largely self-sufficient

Capitalism An economic system characterized by private ownership of the factors of production and market allocation of resources.

Socialism An economic system characterized by public ownership of the factors of production and planning.

Feudalism The social and economic system of the Middle Ages; characterized by a largely agrarian economy and rather rigid social classes.

farming community ruled by the nobility and the church, protected by knights, and tilled by serfs. Under feudalism, one's social role was also one's economic role: the serfs worked, the knights fought, the clergy prayed, and the nobility ruled. The socioeconomic classes were rigid. If your father was a serf, you would almost certainly be a serf too, although some serfs did manage to join the clergy. The upper classes were much better off than the lower classes, but there was little social strife. People accepted that their lives were determined by birth, and the belief in original sin was so ingrained that few people thought that a better or more equitable society was possible. All that began to change with the rise of the mercantile economy around the end of the tenth century.[1]

The Mercantile Economy

Two important factors led to the rise of the **mercantile economy**. First, technical innovations, including crop rotation and better plows, resulted in agricultural surpluses. This released labor from agriculture to produce goods for the new merchant class to trade. Second, towns began to spring up in more densely populated areas. Travel between towns often required protection against marauding bandits, yet the quest for profit was strong and the rise of commerce was rapid. By the twelfth century, many towns were virtual city-states independent of the feudal lords. Many cities developed their own governments and armies. From the twelfth century on, the growth of European commerce accelerated; French champagne, Flemish wool, and other products became available over virtually the entire continent.

Ultimately, the rise of regional commerce doomed feudalism. Under the manorial system, most transactions were conducted by barter; for example, serfs received the knights' protection in exchange for crops. The church's opposition to the accumulation of wealth discouraged trade, but the desire for profit and wealth proved to be stronger than the feudal status quo.[2] With the rise of commerce, a more efficient means of payment was needed, and money—often gold coins—filled the bill. With money came the development of banks and a financial system. The rigid class distinctions began to break down as serfs realized that only a few successful trading expeditions would make them as rich as their lords. Soon social philosophers were debating the existence of stabilizing forces under the new economic system, which came to be called capitalism.

Urbanization and the Industrial Revolution

Another important development that contributed to the downfall of the feudal system was the **enclosure movement**. The enclosure movement began in twelfth-century England and had spread throughout Europe by the nineteenth century. Prior to the enclosure movement, much land was open and available for peasants to use for grazing

Mercantile economy Emerged with the breakdown of feudal society and the rise of a merchant class, beginning around the twelfth century.

Enclosure movement The process by which large landowners fenced in formerly public lands; peasants who had used the open fields for grazing were forced off the land and moved into the cities.

[1]Much of this section comes from E. Ray Canterbery, *The Making of Economics* (Belmont, Calif.: Wadsworth, 1976), especially Chapters 1–4.
[2]Actually, the church was opposed to worldly wealth only when it was acquired through trade; in general, the church did not oppose wealth per se. This made life for the feudal lords a bit less uncomfortable.

Industrial Revolution The rapid increase in industrialization that occurred during the eighteenth and nineteenth centuries; accompanied by technical innovations, more efficient production methods, urbanization, and a growing middle class.

livestock. But as the population grew and the demand for wool increased, landowners realized that they could fence the land, employ only a few sheepherders, and make a substantial profit. As a result, small farmers lost their chance for a livelihood and had to move to the city. The city was where the action was in seventeenth-century England.

Seventeenth-century England was already on the threshold of the **Industrial Revolution**. It had coal to fire steel mills and thus the ability to produce the materials necessary for large-scale manufacturing. It had concentrations of labor in the cities, thanks in part to the enclosure movement. Finally, money was flowing into England from the slave and tobacco trades. All of these developments had taken place before 1750, the date often given as the beginning of the Industrial Revolution.

The economic effects of the Industrial Revolution were amazing. More than 1,300 patents were registered between 1780 and 1800 in England. James Watt's rotary steam engine, which provided power for manufacturing, was far more efficient than the old Newcomen engine. James Hargreaves's spinning jenny increased spinners' output 800 percent. The invention of the lathe, which was used for making other machines, rapidly accelerated the pace of capital accumulation. These and other inventions caused real per capita income to rise at a rate of 1.0 to 1.5 percent per year between 1780 and 1850. When we consider that per capita income had been stagnant for the previous two centuries, this figure is remarkable. The economic impact of the Industrial Revolution was nothing short of amazing.

The social effects were no less profound. Traditional ways changed beyond recognition. Life was better for most, but worse for some. Political power still rested in the hands of the nobility, but economic power was shifting to the expanding merchant class, the predecessors of today's middle class. The merchant class was not constrained by the traditions of feudalism because there had been no middle class under feudalism. Merchants were motivated by a desire to increase the output of machines—and profits. Hard work and saving were virtues. The merchant economy had evolved into capitalism.

> **RECAP**   The Rise of Capitalism
>
> Western capitalism evolved from the feudalism of Western Europe in the Middle Ages. Under feudalism, social and economic roles were determined by birth. Technological innovations in the tenth century led to a labor surplus, monetary transactions replaced barter, and the merchant class evolved. The desire for profit became a prime motivation. The enclosure movement began in twelfth-century England and spread throughout Europe over the next 500 years. This movement displaced small farmers and forced them to move to cities to find work in the factories of the Industrial Revolution. The Industrial Revolution (about 1750–1850) resulted in dramatic increases in economic growth, but entailed social costs as well.

Karl Marx (1818–1883) German economist and philosopher who prophesied the collapse of capitalism and the succession of socialism.

MARX AND THE COLLAPSE OF CAPITALISM

The achievements of early capitalism were not lost on **Karl Marx** (1818–1883), but most of his attention was directed to its social costs. In his view, capitalism had led to miserable conditions for the working classes; child labor, the squalid living conditions in the cities, and the growing disparity in incomes were all by-products of capitalism. The problem, said Marx, was that the workers or **proletariat** were slaves of machinery. The owners of the machinery, the capitalists or **bourgeoisie**, exploited the workers by paying them wages that were less than the value of their output. But what were the workers to do? Without capital, they could not be productive, and only the bourgeoisie owned the capital. The solution, thought Marx, was a proletariat revolution that would replace capitalism with socialism. Like capitalism, socialism would be only a transitory economic system. The success of socialism—abundance and the end of poverty—would usher in the utopian state of **communism**. Marx's concept of communism differed considerably from what we might think of as communism today. According to Marx, communism would evolve only after years of abundance had changed human motivations: people would work for the enjoyment of working; greed would cease to exist; and people would be inquisitive, not acquisitive.

Proletariat Marxian term for the working class.

Bourgeoisie In Marxian analysis, the capitalists.

Communism In Marxian analysis, a utopian state that would evolve out of socialism after years of abundance had changed human motivations.

Marx felt that capitalism would collapse through its own internal contradictions. He predicted that socialism would rise from the ashes of capitalism, but he actually provided very little in the way of a framework for the establishment of a socialist economy. Most of his work was an attempt to discover the capitalist laws of motion. We do not have time to go into Marxian analysis in detail, but we do need to make one key point: the Bolshevik Revolution that led to the birth of the Soviet Union in 1917 was not the kind of revolution that Marx had predicted.

• • • • • • • •

Marxian Terms and Definitions

Before we can outline the Marxian theory of the collapse of capitalism, we need to present some basic building blocks of Marxian analysis.

First, Marx believed in the **labor theory of value**. According to this theory, the value of any good is determined by the amount of labor embodied in the productive process. For example, if a chair takes 1 hour to produce and a table takes 2 hours to produce, then 1 table could be traded for 2 chairs on the market. Few economists today have much use for the labor theory of value because it looks only at the supply side of the market and ignores the demand side. However, firms must charge prices high enough to cover their costs of production, and in industries where wages are the biggest cost of production, pricing may approximate the labor theory of value—although firms must still produce the products that consumers want.[3]

Labor theory of value The value of any good is equal to the value of the labor used in producing it.

A second component of Marxian analysis is the **exploitation of labor**. Marx felt that the capitalists would pay the workers only a subsistence wage even though the workers produced output that was worth much more than their wages. The difference between the value of labor and the wage rate was called *surplus value*. Surplus value was the main source of the firm's profits.

Exploitation of labor The idea that workers are paid wages less than the value of their output.

---

[3]The labor theory of value was fundamental to economic thought from 1750 until 1870, when it was replaced with supply and demand analysis. Today, it is still used to illustrate certain ideas in the classroom—we will use it in our discussion of comparative advantage in the next chapter—and some economists, for example, Nobel Prize winner Arthur Lewis (1915–1991), continue to use it in their study of economic development and other topics.

Organic composition of capital
The ratio between capital and labor used in the production process.

Industrial reserve army of the unemployed Name given to the rising numbers of workers displaced by the acquisition of capital.

A third component of Marxism is the **organic composition of capital**, or the ratio between capital (machinery) and labor used in the production process. An increase in the organic composition of capital meant that the firm was displacing workers with machines. In order for firms to compete in the market, they had to invest in new, sophisticated machinery. But doing so often meant displacing workers with machines. The resulting high unemployment would keep wages down, but it also meant that the number of workers firms could exploit would decline. As a result, surplus value and thus profits would fall.

Finally, Marx predicted that business cycles would become more severe and that capitalism would eventually collapse. His reasoning went like this: Firms make profits by exploiting labor; however, competition forces firms to acquire modern capital goods. This competition drives some firms out of business and results in increasing industrial concentration and rising unemployment, which Marx called the **industrial reserve army of the unemployed**. Over time, business cycles would become more severe because the growing industrial concentration meant that each business failure took with it larger firms and more jobs. At some point, the system would collapse, and the industrial reserve army would rise up to establish a socialist system.

• • • • • • • •

Assessing Marx

Was Marx correct about the collapse of capitalism? Hardly. Marx thought the revolution would occur first in the most advanced countries because it depended on the displacement of workers by capital. Marx thought that his adopted home of England was the most likely prospect. That did not happen—although some scholars have argued that the Great Depression of the 1930s was the manifestation of Marx's prediction. More to the point for our analysis just now, *none* of the communist revolutions of the twentieth century took place in a highly advanced country: Russia was the most backward country in Europe; China was one of the most backward countries in Asia; and Cuba was not much more advanced than its Latin American neighbors when Fidel Castro overthrew Fulgencio Batista's regime in 1959.

It is perhaps significant that following the Great Depression—which, incidentally, had little effect on the Soviet Union—capitalism underwent significant changes in most countries. For example, many elements of the "social safety net"—Social Security, unemployment compensation, deposit insurance, activist macroeconomic stabilization policies, and the like—were implemented in the United States during or immediately after the Great Depression. Thus, capitalism after the Great Depression was much different than before. We will never know whether Marx would have predicted that this new kind of capitalism would collapse.

> **RECAP**   Marx and the Collapse of Capitalism
>
> Marx saw capitalism as a battle between the classes, the proletariat and the bourgeoisie, and thought that capitalism would collapse from its internal inconsistencies. Firms exploit workers by paying wages less than the value of labor. This exploitation is the source of the firm's surplus value or profits. Competition between firms results in workers being displaced by machines; however, machines cannot be exploited.

Born in Germany in 1818, Karl Marx enrolled at the University of Bonn at age 17 intending to study law and follow his father into the legal profession. At Bonn, he fell under the influence of the radical Hegelian philosophy that was to form the basis of his theory of *dialectical materialism*—the theory that social evolution was the history of the class struggle, and that social classes were determined by economic factors. After only a year at Bonn, Marx left for the University of Berlin to study art, history, and philosophy. He continued his studies at the University of Jena where he received a doctorate in 1841.

Marx's radical views and association with the Young Hegelians made it impossible for him to secure an academic post, so he did free-lance writing and became more active with radical reformers. In 1841 he married and moved to Paris, then a center for European radicalism. In 1843 he met Friedrich Engels, who was to become his lifelong collaborator. Marx was expelled from France in 1845 and went to Brussels. There he published a newspaper and joined the Communist League, an international workers' society. It was here that Marx and Engels wrote their *Communist Manifesto* (1848), which, according to Engels, was "to do for history what Darwin's theory has done for biology." The *Communist Manifesto* concluded with the call: "The workers have nothing to lose in this [revolution] but their chains. They have the world to gain. Workers of the world, unite!"

Radical rhetoric like this got Marx expelled from Belgium. He returned to France and Germany to work in those countries' revolutionary movements, but was expelled again. In 1849 Marx went to London where he was to live until his death. Although Engels assisted him financially—Engels worked for his father in the textile industry—Marx spent the rest of his life in virtual poverty. He read voluminously; a letter to his daughter said, "I am a machine condemned to devour books and then hurl them transformed on to the dunghill of history."[1] For a time he was London correspondent for the *New York Tribune*. In 1867, he published the first volume of his monumental *Das Kapital;* the second (1885) and third volumes (1894) were edited by Engels and published after Marx's death. *Kapital* offered a systematic criticism of the exploitative and self-destructive tendencies of capitalism and was to become the "bible of the working class."

[1]Cited in Phyllis Deane, *The Evolution of Economic Ideas* (New York: Cambridge University Press, 1978), p. 126.

Marx did not confine his radicalism to his pen. In 1864 he cofounded the First International, an association of labor, reform, and radical movements. The First International dissolved in 1874, but Marx continued to be consulted by many as the leading socialist figure of the day. During the years of the First International, Marx adopted a hard-line stance and vitriolic rhetoric that precluded any collaboration with the bourgeoisie. This kind of attitude has limited the appeal of socialist reformers to the present day.

As workers are displaced by capital, profits decline, and some firms go out of business. Over time, industrial concentration increases, and business cycles become more severe until the system collapses. The collapse occurs first in the most technologically advanced nations. Capitalism is replaced by socialism, then communism.

······ THE RISE AND FALL OF THE SOVIET UNION

The Russia of 1991 was much like the Russian Empire of 1917: people were cold and hungry, soldiers were demoralized, and the government seemed to be on the verge of collapse. In the first Russian Revolution, war losses, political skepticism, and riots in Moscow forced Tsar Nicholas II to abdicate his throne on March 2, 1917. When his brother refused to accept the crown, a provisional government was formed by liberals in the legislative assembly. The provisional government did not last. It was indecisive and had to contend with the growing influence of the workers' and soldiers' councils ("soviets"). Promised land reform was not forthcoming, and continuing losses in World War I eroded confidence.

The Bolsheviks (Russian communists) tried to seize control in July, but lacked the support of the soviets. In October 1917, their second attempt to overthrow the provisional government proved successful. The **Bolshevik Revolution** was led by **Vladimir Ilyich Lenin** (1870–1924), a longtime revolutionary who returned from exile in Western Europe. In January 1918, the Bolsheviks disbanded the assembly, and in July they executed the royal family. Three years of civil war ensued, but by 1921 Lenin was in firm control of Russia. Lenin was reclusive, disciplined, and energetic. He founded a tactical kind of Marxism where theory and policy adapted to circumstances. He had grand visions for his new socialist state: there would be no injustice and no private property; wealth would be distributed equally; and workers would run the factories.

Lenin embarked on an ambitious plan to industrialize the largely agricultural Russian economy, but not all of his measures were successful or well thought out. Between 1918 and 1920, his War Communism plan attempted to virtually abolish money and private trade; farm output was requisitioned, and workers were paid equal in-kind wages. War Communism was an unmitigated disaster: industrial output fell by almost a quarter, agricultural output fell by more than a third, and inflation was rampant.

Lenin's second blueprint, the New Economic Policy, fared better. Some private markets were reestablished, and agricultural taxes replaced requisitioning. A state planning commission, *Gosplan,* was established in 1921 to develop the outlines for a national economic plan for the next decade. Eventually, most industries were nationalized, and agriculture was reorganized into huge state-owned farms or "collectives." The New Economic Policy was successful, at least initially. By 1926, both industrial and agricultural output exceeded their pre-revolution levels. A convertible, stable currency was established and began to be quoted on international currency exchanges. But signs of future problems were beginning to appear: planning errors resulted in severe shortages of capital goods throughout the 1920s.

Lenin died in 1924 and was replaced by Joseph Stalin (1879–1953) who ruled with absolute and ruthless authority until his death in 1953. Stalin continued the move toward the collectivization of agriculture and rapid industrialization, but shortages of consumer goods became apparent by 1927. Known as the "man of steel," Stalin quashed peasant uprisings and purged political opponents and by 1929 had assumed complete dictatorial power. Nevertheless, the Soviet planning system resulted in an economy that grew ten-fold between 1917 and its collapse in 1991—

Bolshevik Revolution (1917) The revolution that replaced the tsarist government of Russia with the communist government of the Soviet Union.

V. I. Lenin (1870–1924) Leader of the Bolshevik Revolution (1917), first president, and chief architect of the Soviet Union.

a growth rate significantly faster than that achieved by any of the capitalist economies over the same period.

. . . .

The Collapse of the Soviet Union

News commentators often cite social resentment arising from corrupt politics as a reason for the collapse of the Soviet Union. There is certainly a measure of truth to this assertion—many politicians did own *dachas* (summer houses) while most people had only tiny apartments in the city—but few economists would agree that political corruption was the main reason for the collapse. Most economists would argue that the collapse of the Soviet Union was caused by economic factors related to the absence of a system of rational market prices. The socialist planning authorities tried to fulfill their goals of full employment and industrialization in the context of a costly arms race with the West without the benefit of a market pricing mechanism. As a result, many consumer goods were in perpetually short supply, and people often waited hours in line to buy low-quality merchandise. The absence of market signals also resulted in a workplace that was inherently inefficient. There was little connection between work effort and incomes so workers had little incentive to work; they frequently called in sick and did low-quality work when on the job. The importance of worker motivation was perhaps most apparent in Soviet agriculture: small, private plots, consisting of barely 3 percent of arable land, produced 25 percent of all agricultural output; the huge, state-owned, collective farms, which covered 97 percent of the arable land, produced only 75 percent of farm output.[4]

A firm's survival did not depend on market criteria either. Poorly run firms were often given additional funding from the government to cover losses; that is, they operated with what has been called a **soft budget constraint**. And which firms qualified for soft budget constraints too often depended on the personal relationship between the managers and the politicians, not on the strategic importance of the firm. In short, the socialism of the former Soviet Union collapsed because it was utterly inefficient.

These conditions festered until 1991.[5] President Mikhail Gorbachev had instituted a series of reforms in the previous few years—*glasnost* to open up Soviet society and remove communist terror and **perestroika** to restructure the economy—but corruption was still widespread in government and the workplace, and the economy remained weak. When Boris Yeltsin replaced Gorbachev after the coup of August 1991, he inherited a budget deficit that amounted to almost 20 percent of GDP, a virtually worthless currency (the ruble), and declining exports. As the Soviet economy began to crumble, foreign lenders withdrew credit. The G-7—the seven largest industrial nations, Japan, Germany, Canada, Great Britain, France, Italy and the

Soft budget constraint Instead of being required to make profits, poorly run firms in the former socialist economies were often given additional funding from the government to cover their losses. They operated with a soft budget constraint.

Perestroika A Russian term meaning "restructuring"; used by Gorbachev to signify the economic changes he hoped to implement.

[4]Marshall I. Goldman, *USSR in Crisis: The Failure of an Economic System* (New York: W. W. Norton, 1983), p. 2, and *Gorbachev's Challenge* (New York: W. W. Norton, 1987), pp. 33–37. Cited in Walter Adams and James Brock, *Adam Smith Goes to Moscow* (Princeton, N.J.: Princeton University Press, 1993), p. 22. *Adam Smith Goes to Moscow* is an excellent introduction to the problems of transforming the former socialist economies. Written as a play, it is humorous as well as scholarly and informative.
[5]The immediate conditions that led to the collapse of the Soviet Union can be found in Jeffrey Sachs, "Goodwill Is Not Enough," *The Economist* (December 21, 1991/January 3, 1992): 101–4.

FOCUS ON

THE ROLE OF ECONOMISTS IN THE FORMER SOVIET UNION

Until Mikhail Gorbachev assumed power in the mid-1980s, the role of economists in the former Soviet Union was hardly scientific: their usual task was to show that existing state policies were optimal. Granted, government economists in the United States are occasionally encouraged to make unjustifiably rosy forecasts, but most U.S. economists have at least a modicum of objectivity. Even if Soviet economists had been allowed to be objective, however, they would have had great difficulty arriving at accurate predictions because of the serious distortions caused by price controls.

Economic training in the former Soviet Union differed substantially from what is taught in the West. No

courses dealt with the theory of the firm, industrial organization, public finance, or consumer theory. Instead, students were required to study Marxism and the history of the Communist Party. Paul Samuelson's leading principles text, *Economics,* was translated into Russian in 1964, but was not widely available. Few people had access to professional journals. Economics students could choose between two tracks of study: political economy and mathematical economics. Political economy was largely descriptive with strong Marxist-Leninist tendencies; mathematical economics was technical and a separate discipline. Almost 90 percent of the people with advanced degrees in economics held nonacademic positions.

Despite an appreciation for mathematics in general in the Soviet Union, mathematical economics developed slowly because it was perceived as a threat to Marxism. Most early mathematical economics models were inconsistent with the labor theory of value, the basic tenet of Marxism. Additionally, early pioneers in Soviet mathematical economics were regarded as irrelevant. This situation changed somewhat, however, as mathematical economists began to develop models useful for natural resource pricing and state planning. This work led to the development of input/output analysis and other mathematical programming techniques used by Western economists today. Still, state control of economic research resulted

United States—issued warnings about the creditworthiness of the Soviet Union and did not extend loans. The Soviet republics recognized disorder in Moscow and refused to pay taxes. The breakup was complete.

But simply stating that the Soviet Union collapsed because it was inefficient or could not pay its foreign debts does not provide a road map for restructuring the former socialist economies. To do that, we need to compare the behavior of firms and workers under capitalism and socialism. To many scholars in comparative economics, the key issue is supply and demand, specifically, the demand constraints of capitalism and the supply constraints of socialism.[6]

[6]Among the authors who have analyzed capitalism and socialism with the demand-constraint/supply-constraint approach are the Hungarian economist Janos Kornai, *The Socialist System: The Political Economy of Communism* (Princeton, N.J.: Princeton University Press, 1992) and Edward Nell, "The Failure of Demand Management in Socialism," in Mark Knell and Christine Rider, eds., *Socialist Economies in Transition* (Brookfield, Vt.: Edward Elgar, 1992), pp. 83–116.

An economics doctoral student defending her thesis at Moscow University in 1985.

Soviet economics is in disarray today. Political economy has lost its ideological foundations, and the forte of mathematical economics—state planning models—is less important. Today, the economics profession in the former Soviet Union thirsts for knowledge. Western economics texts are being translated as rapidly as possible, and a steady stream of Western economics professors are traveling to the former Soviet Union to offer advice and encouragement. Two things suggest that the economics profession in the former Soviet Union will make rapid progress: Soviet economists are already trained in mathematics, so they can speak the language of Western economics. And they know how badly they need help.

in an economics that was largely divorced from Soviet reality. This is probably one reason why Soviet economists were held in low esteem by the Soviet public; the other reason was that the most visible Soviet economists were merely mouthpieces for the increasingly unpopular government.

SOURCE: Michael Alexeev, Clifford Gaddy, and Jim Leitzel, "Economics in the Former Soviet Union," *Journal of Economic Perspectives* 62 (Spring 1992): 137–48.

· · · · · · · ·

Demand-Constrained Economies

Capitalist economies typically face demand constraints: lack of demand for workers is a reason for unemployment, and lack of demand for goods means that firms cannot always sell everything they produce. Demand constraints have several important implications for the operations of capitalist economies. First, high unemployment acts to keep wages low. This reduces production costs and keeps profits high; however, it also means that workers' incomes may not be sufficient to buy everything that is produced. Further, when firms find that they cannot sell everything they have produced, they offer goods at discounts. Firms may also build plants with excess capacity for strategic purposes. During periods of rapid demand growth, firms must be able to meet the demand for their products so they will not lose market share to competitors. Putting in overtime shifts or producing beyond optimal capacity can increase costs.

Demand-constrained economies
A name given to capitalist economies because they are typically characterized by an excess of supply.

What is the nature of competition in **demand-constrained economies**? Some economists believe that demand constraints provide a crucial incentive for innovation and cost-consciousness. Lack of demand forces firms to compete on the both price and quality. Firms cannot assume that they can sell everything they produce, so they are always looking for ways to lower production costs and produce better products. Firms that are able to do so are successful; firms that cannot face the *hard* budget constraint of bankruptcy.

Supply-Constrained Economies

The two most important goals of the socialist planners of the former Soviet Union were rapid industrialization and full employment. They achieved both objectives. Until the breakup in 1991, unemployment had been counted in the hundreds of persons, not in percentages of the entire workforce, and the economic growth rate of the Soviet Union surpassed that of the Western economies in most years until the 1980s. However, a by-product of fulfilling these two goals was a perverse set of incentives that was to have lasting and, ultimately, terminal effects on the former Soviet Union.

The twin goals of industrialization and full employment resulted in chronic supply constraints. To accomplish rapid industrialization (and the Cold War military buildup), planners maintained an investment bias: too many resources were devoted to investment so too few resources were available for consumer goods. Maintenance of full employment when too few consumer goods are being produced is a sure route to shortages—especially when prices are set below equilibrium. Producers and shopkeepers realized that they could sell everything they put on the shelves, so they had no incentive to look for more efficient production methods or to develop better products. Neither was there an incentive to be courteous to customers—after all, where else could they go?[7] After a few decades of excess demand and chronic shortages, firms no longer understood the importance of costs in their production calculations. In fact, when the former Soviet Union collapsed, the production value of many firms—perhaps a quarter—was *negative;* the cost of inputs exceeded the value of output.[8]

Supply-constrained economies A name given to socialist economies because they are typically characterized by an excess of demand.

The simple solution to **supply-constrained economies** appears to be the removal of price controls to allow prices to rise to their equilibrium levels. Once people realize that they do not have enough money to buy the goods in the store, they stop waiting in line, and the supply constraint appears to vanish. But unless higher prices also result in an increase in the quantity supplied, consumers will suffer. Further, to succeed in the world of demand-constrained capitalist economies, managers and workers must cut costs and create new products. How long it will take to accomplish these changes is the key question behind transition policies.

---

[7]An editorial in the November 13–19, 1992 *Baltic Independent,* "Welcome to the Big Mac," expresses this view quite well. Admitting that McDonald's food may be "rather boring and characterless," the editor argues that McDonald's clean, friendly environment will raise standards above the ". . . dirty kiosks which charge Stockholm prices for a Smolensk level of service which will have to improve."
[8]"Russia's Value Gap," *The Economist* (October 24, 1992): 75.

RECAP   The Rise and Fall of the Soviet Union

The Soviet Union came into existence following the Bolshevik Revolution in 1917. The first premier of the Soviet Union, V. I. Lenin, sought to establish a socialist state where there would be neither injustice nor private property, and where wealth would be distributed equally. Not all programs of the Soviet Union were successful, but economic growth was faster than in most Western economies. By the 1980s, however, it became apparent that Soviet-style socialism was not working. Planning failures resulted in massive shortages of many consumer goods, and too many resources were being diverted to the military. Workers were inefficient, at least partially because there was little connection between work effort and wages. Ineffective managers were often rewarded with government loans—the soft budget constraint.

Mikhail Gorbachev instituted a series of economic reforms in the 1980s, but they were only partially successful. When Gorbachev was replaced by Boris Yeltsin in 1991, there were massive government deficits and foreign debt. When foreign banks and governments refused to extend loans, and the Soviet republics refused to pay taxes to Moscow, the Soviet Union collapsed.

Socialist economies like the Soviet Union are typically characterized by a supply constraint—an excess of demand over supply. There is little incentive to cut costs or increase quality in supply-constrained economies because producers know they can sell everything they make. In contrast, capitalist economies are typically characterized by a demand constraint—an excess of supply over demand. This acts as an incentive for producers to cut costs and increase quality in order to expand market share.

THE TRANSITION FROM SOCIALISM TO CAPITALISM

Even before the Soviet Union collapsed, economists were exploring the best way to establish capitalism in the formerly socialist economies. The inevitable debates took place, but it soon became apparent that the favorite approach was shock therapy or the *big bang* championed by Harvard economist Jeffrey Sachs, the International Monetary Fund (IMF), and others. Simply put, the goal of shock therapy is to make the move from authoritarian socialism to democratic capitalism as quickly as possible.[9] Variations of the basic shock therapy model have been applied to most of the formerly socialist economies in Eastern Europe and the countries of the former Soviet Union. Other economists have argued that the costs of shock therapy will inevitably outweigh the benefits and that a gradualist approach is preferable.

[9]It is true that the Western advisers assisting with the economic transition of the former socialist economies are intent on establishing *democratic* capitalism, but we should emphasize that democracy (a political system) and capitalism (an economic system) do not necessarily go hand in hand. This point is not lost on the people of Afghanistan, Romania, and elsewhere, where the transition to capitalism has been accompanied by calls for the return of monarchy. See "The Craving for Kings," *The Economist* (April 25, 1992): 52. Further, Karen Smith, et al., "Is Democracy Bad for Growth," *Business Week,* June 7, 1993, pp. 84–88, suggest that it is not democracy that is good for the economy, but decentralization. See also Adam Przeworski and Fernando Limongi, "Political Regimes and Economic Growth," *Journal of Economic Perspectives* 7 (Summer 1993): 51–69.

Shock therapy The approach advocated by Sachs and others for converting the formerly socialist economies to capitalism; involves moving to capitalism as quickly as possible.

Privatization Selling government-owned firms to private citizens.

Marketization Removal of price controls and central planning to allow markets to allocate goods and services.

Shock Therapy

Shock therapy advocates believe that the transition process from socialism to capitalism is a "seamless web" that must be implemented all at once because of the political instability of the former socialist economies. A rapid transition to capitalism will reveal the benefits of the transition more quickly and thus tend to stabilize the political situation; a gradual approach would sustain shortages and weaken an already weak government.[10]

Shock therapy has two main components: **privatization** and **marketization**. Privatization involves selling off government-owned enterprises. Marketization is the process of allowing market prices to allocate goods and services instead of government planners; in other words, marketization involves the removal of price controls and central planning. Additionally, shock therapy advocates believe it important for economies in transition to adopt anti-inflationary fiscal and monetary policies.

Several approaches have been used to bring about privatization. In most of the formerly socialist economies, privatization vouchers were given to citizens who were then allowed to buy and sell ownership shares in factories. Privatization on this scale—the former Czechoslovakia alone privatized more than 1,200 firms between the end of communist rule in 1989 and 1993—had never been attempted before and met with mixed success. One problem was that many citizens simply did not understand what they were supposed to do with their vouchers; another problem was that firms with outdated technology found no bidders. Some countries experimented with giving factories to the workers—a good idea for workers in the few firms that could compete in the capitalist world, but a bad idea for the many firms that no one wanted. Some countries put factories up for sale, with certain restrictions on foreign ownership.

Assessing Shock Therapy. How well has shock therapy worked? The results in the first few years have not been good. Most countries experienced inflation; in some countries, it was as high as 2,000 percent in 1991–1992, but rates of 50 or 80 percent per year were closer to the norm by 1993. Unemployment averaged almost 15 percent in the former socialist economies as late as 1993. And in few countries was GDP as high in 1993 as in 1989. Social problems were just as serious: crime and homelessness increased dramatically, while social spending and employment programs were cut back. Most shock therapy advocates now admit they expected effects of this sort. Capitalism took centuries to emerge in the West, and as it did, it developed institutions necessary for capitalist integrity—property rights, fractional reserve banking, financial markets, public controls for macroeconomic stability, among others.[11] None

---

[10]David Lipton and Jeffrey Sachs, "Privatization in Eastern Europe: The Case of Poland," *Brookings Papers on Economic Activity* 2 (1990): 293–333.

[11]It may be surprising to discover that personal checking accounts were almost unknown in the former Soviet Union. Virtually all transactions between individuals were in cash, although checks were used for some interfirm transactions. Today, many interfirm transactions are in the nature of *pseudocredit*. Firms purchase intermediate products from suppliers and then refuse to pay their bills, or they ship products at high prices, recognizing that they will never receive payment, and list the shipments as income to inflate profits. In 1992 perhaps 40 percent of all enterprise credit in Russia was pseudocredit. See Adams and Brock (1993): 98.

of these institutions existed in the former Soviet Union at the moment shock therapy was imposed.

This is not to say that shock therapy was completely unsuccessful. In Russia, Poland, and most of the former socialist economies, entrepreneurial spirit is flourishing in the form of "street capitalism." Vendors and kiosks are everywhere and sell everything from plastic dolls to beluga caviar. Most of the goods sold in these street bazaars have been purchased at state-owned stores and are sold with a significant markup; many consumers apparently either do not know what is available or are willing to pay to avoid waiting in line. But some goods are imported or produced and sold by a new class of home-grown *biznezmen*. These goods represent a supply response to price liberalization, a key factor in the transition to capitalism. These small producers and importers may be the best sign that capitalism is beginning to emerge in the formerly socialist economies.[12]

But kiosks and street vendors are a far cry from the kind of modern, competitive economy that will be necessary before the transition economies can compete in international markets. At least two additional changes are necessary: the attitudes of workers and managers must change, and massive industrial restructuring is required. Changing worker and manager attitudes is not impossible, but it will not happen overnight. Supply constraints and nearly a century of communist rule have all but eliminated worker incentives and managerial efficiency—qualities needed in modern capitalist firms.[13] And the amount of restructuring that is necessary is almost too massive to contemplate; the former Soviet Union has been called "an open air museum of industrial technology."[14] The former East Germany was one of the strongest economies in the Soviet bloc, but even there 8,000 firms had to be scrapped or restructured. The cost was $35 billion in 1991—fully 2 percent of all-German GDP—and somewhat higher in 1992.[15] The situation is worse in the other former socialist economies; by one estimate, at least $500 billion will be needed for the restructuring effort.[16] Where will that money come from? Foreign investment is one option, but who is willing to invest in an economy with a shaky government and

---

[12]For an optimistic commentary on the prospects for reform in Russia by the Moscow correspondent to *Business Week,* see Rose Brady, "Four Years That Shook My World," *Business Week,* July 26, 1993, pp. 48–49.

[13]Some writers believe that there is very little difference between the attitudes of people under capitalism and socialism. In a 1992 study by the Brookings Institution, "Hunting for *Homo Sovietus:* Situational versus Attitudinal Factors in Economic Behavior," *Brookings Papers* 1 (1992): 127–94, authors Robert J. Shiller, Maxim Boycko, and Vladimir Korobov concluded that situational variables are more important than attitudinal variables. If correct, this suggests that there is no inherent timidity or lack of ambition in *homo sovietus* that would preclude a market economy. The authors contend that once privatization and marketization have taken hold, citizens of the former socialist economies will act much like their Western counterparts.

[14]V. A. Naishul, "Problems of Creating a Market in the USSR," *Communist Economies* 2 (1990): 34. Quoted in Adams and Brock (1993): 85. On the same page, Adams and Brock also note that the only revenue reported by a textile mill in 1991 was from the sale of a spinning machine to a museum in Munich!

[15]Data are from "Cheer Up, It's Working," *The Economist* (August 10, 1991): 16.

[16]Robert H. Wessel, "Privatization in the Former Soviet Union—One Year Later," *Business Economics* 28 (January 1993): 31–34.

the ever present threat of backpedaling toward socialism?[17] Government lending by the industrialized nations is another prospect, but when wealthy countries like the United States spend weeks debating a loan of just $1 billion, the prospect of raising $500 billion seems remote.

No one would deny that there have been transition costs, but the costs may not be as high as they appear at first glance. For example, Poland's inflation rate in 1992 remained a stubborn 5 percent per month, but this was down from the 2,000 percent rise between 1989 and 1990. Further, because people no longer waited in lines, the real inflation rate was even lower. The decline in aggregate production may not be as severe as the data indicate either because the socialist production figures were almost certainly inflated. Unemployment data are similarly suspect. Though the unemployment rate under socialism was close to zero, that figure included massive amounts of *disguised unemployment*—people who were paid to punch the clock but produced nothing. Disguised unemployment is possible under the soft budget constraints of socialism.

· · · · · · · ·

The Gradualist Approach

The jury is still out on shock therapy. It may well be the best way to minimize the inevitable pain of economic transition. However, the United Nations has advocated a more gradual approach, one that first establishes a "clear set of rules for the distribution of economic returns from property" and creates a set of incentives for "property owners to put their assets to the most productive use."[18] Advocates of the **gradualist** approach argue that the shock therapists err when they focus on the equilibrium end states ("market capitalism") instead of the processes and mechanisms that give rise to economic evolution.[19] Real-world economies are exceedingly complex and are characterized by uncertainty and the lack of information. The only way to coordinate the activities of producers, consumers, and the government under these circumstances is by relying upon a set of regular routines and behavioral patterns. The key point for economic transition is that existing routines and behavioral patterns are the product of the *preexisting* economic structure. This means that even if shock therapy results in the best long-run structure of the economy, it will cause severe short-run dislocations because routines and behavioral patterns are based on the preexisting socialist economy.

The Hungarian Experience. Hungary and China have both adopted a more gradualist approach to economic transition. Economic transition in Hungary differs from the

Gradualism An alternative to shock therapy as a means for restructuring the socialist economies. Involves phased-in institutional changes, privatization, and marketization.

---

[17]The possibility that the people will vote for a return to the old ways is very real. In November 1992, Lithuanians voted the Communist Party back into power; the voters apparently believed that the Communists could improve on the 50 percent decline in industrial production in 1991 and the over 2,000 percent inflation between 1990 and 1992.

[18]United Nations, *Economic Survey of Europe, 1990–1991*. Cited in Christian Gehrke and Mark Knell "Transitions from Centrally Planned to Market Economies," in Mark Knell and Christine Rider, eds., *Socialist Economies in Transition* (Brookfield, Vt.: Edward Elgar, 1992), pp. 43–64.

[19]This paragraph is based on Peter Murrell, "Evolution in Economics and in the Economic Reform of the Centrally Planned Economies," in Christopher Clague and Gordon C. Rausser, *The Emergence of Market Economies in Eastern Europe* (Cambridge, Mass.: Blackwell, 1992), pp. 35–54.

shock therapy approach in several ways. First, Hungary had a head start on the other former socialist economies because it began market reforms as far back as 1968. This may partially explain why Hungary had the second (after Czechoslovakia) highest standard of living in Eastern Europe under socialism. Second, much of the privatization is being initiated by the firms themselves, not by the government, although the State Property Agency is required to approve all privatizations. The intent behind this law is to prevent the *nomenklatura* (the old management bureaucracy) from acquiring the assets of former state-owned firms. Third, instead of giving away privatization vouchers, the Hungarian government has sold the vouchers. The argument behind this approach was that people do not treat freely acquired property seriously. Note, however, that this approach was possible only because Hungarians already enjoyed a relatively high standard of living; few people in the other former socialist economies had enough wealth to buy privatization vouchers.[20] Finally, Hungary's relatively high standard of living made it possible to establish a social safety net—welfare, unemployment compensation, pensions, and the like—to assure that few people would fall through the transition cracks.

Hungary's gradualist approach seems to be working so far. Economic restructuring resulted in only a 4 percent decline in GDP in 1990 and a 10 percent decline in 1991. Exports are almost 30 percent of GDP and rising. Inflation was only 20 percent in 1992. These successes have not gone unnoticed in the West. In 1992, the United States lifted its strict controls on exports to Hungary, the first time it had done so for a former Warsaw Pact nation, and the International Expositions Office in Paris awarded a World's Fair to Budapest for 1996. In 1991, Suzuki announced a joint venture to build cars in Hungary, thereby becoming the first Japanese automaker to open business in Eastern Europe.

Gradualism in China. After World War II, China adopted a central planning model and instituted numerous measures designed to control population growth and other facets of Chinese life. As the massacre at Tiananmen Square in 1989 demonstrated, these controls have often led to human rights violations. From a purely *economic* standpoint, however, the gradualist approach to economic transition in China may offer important lessons.

China was caught up in the same kind of supply-constrained, investment-biased economy as the Soviet Union, at least until the Third Plenary Session of the Thirteenth Congress of the Communist Party in 1978.[21] At that meeting, the decision was made to decentralize power. The objective of the Chinese government became ". . . not to privatize existing state enterprises, but to create a socialist commodity market with a variety of ownership forms." Individual production managers were given the authority to offer increased incentives for economic performance, and profit-sharing programs were established. Managers of state-owned firms were allowed to sign profit contracts that specified performance goals in return for salary

---

[20]For example, in 1992 the average person in Estonia had enough savings to buy two tanks of gasoline—not quite enough to buy a factory.

[21]This and the next paragraph are based on Mark Knell and Wenyan Yang, "Lessons from China on a Strategy for the Socialist Economies in Transition," in Mark Knell and Christine Rider, eds., *Socialist Economies in Transition* (Brookfield, Vt.: Edward Elgar, 1992), pp. 216–35.

FOCUS ON

THE TWO JAPANESE ECONOMIC MIRACLES: A *VERY* BRIEF ECONOMIC HISTORY OF JAPAN

Japan has actually experienced two economic miracles: its rise from feudalism in the nineteenth century, and its revival after defeat in World War II. In both cases, significant social and institutional changes were instrumental in the economic success. This point is important because it suggests that Japan's economic success was not the product of a long history or country-specific cultural heritage. And this suggests that other nations may be able to implement the kind of social changes necessary for economic miracles.

Until Commodore Perry's Black Ships arrived in 1853 to "open" Japan, Japan was a feudal society with few resources or material riches. Society was divided into several castes (rigid social classes) with little opportunity for advancement between the castes. Initially, resistance to Western influence was strong, but the Japanese eventually accepted a policy of combining West-

ern technology with Japanese spirit. In 1868, the Emperor Meiji formed a strong oligarchy intent on establishing a "rich nation and strong army." The emperor sought to break down the social classes and adopted Western legal and educational systems. Foreign knowledge was encouraged, but the Meiji government was extremely wary of accepting foreign loans. The government began a program to build infrastructure and increase agricultural productivity. The bulk of tax revenues came from agriculture. The state subsidized selected industries and established a few government-owned firms. Most government projects were financial failures, however, and had to be turned over to private ownership. By the end of the nineteenth century, few state-owned enterprises remained, with the major exception being iron and steel.

As a result of the emperor's involvement in the economy, close ties were established between politicians and the business leaders who took over failing government firms. Production and the standard of living grew steadily, and Japan was able to export the surplus, a necessary requirement in a resource-poor country. Business leaders formed business groups—*zaibatsu,* the forerunners of today's *keiretsu*—and began to pay less and less attention to the government.

Japan made military as well as economic progress. The Japanese conquered Okinawa and Formosa and then turned their attention to Korea in 1910 and Manchuria in 1931. These successes led to Japan's entry into and ultimate defeat in World War II. Ironically, the measures instituted by the United States after World War II may have been largely responsible for Japan's economic miracle. Among the

and bonuses. By 1991, fully 85 percent of all state-owned enterprises were operating under such contracts.

China did not decontrol all prices immediately, but instead used prices as signals to encourage regional competition and privatization. Prices were set high enough to allow private firms to compete with state-owned enterprises. The results have been impressive: in 1980, state enterprises accounted for 76 percent of all production; by 1990, the figure was down to 55 percent. This achievement is significant. As we noted earlier, much of the "street capitalism" in the former Soviet Union consists largely of people who buy goods at the state-controlled prices and resell them at higher prices in the street bazaars. These dealers serve a needed function because they eliminate waiting lines at state-owned shops, but China's regional competition may be more important because it results in increased output.

Perry's expedition being received in Japan.

management strife that had plagued Japanese business before the war.

- Finally, the Japanese military machine was shut down, freeing resources for economic growth.

As Japan began to rebuild its economy following World War II, its own unique brand of capitalism unfolded. A complex web of relationships between business leaders and government bureaucrats developed, but comprehensive central planning was discouraged, at least partially because of the memory of government failures during the Meiji regime. The government did favor firms that had the support of the Ministry of International Trade and Industry (MITI), but the fear of a "second coming of the Black Ships" acted as an extra incentive for economic progress.

more important features were the following:

- An egalitarian constitution was established. This put an end to the caste system and may have instilled work incentives because incomes and wealth now depended on hard work.

- The *zaibatsu* was disbanded. This measure removed the influence of unethical politicians and old business leaders. In doing so, it opened positions for younger, more energetic managers.

- Labor unions were encouraged. This eliminated much of the labor-

Source: Jon Woronoff, *Asia's "Miracle" Economies,* 2d ed. (Armonk, N.Y.: M. E. Sharpe, 1992).

China's gradual transition to decentralized socialism and privatization differs from any economic system ever envisioned by Western economists, but it seems to be working. Economic growth was 12 percent in 1992 and is forecast to average 7 percent per year over the next decade; this rate of growth is more than double the rate forecast for the United States. According to a recent study by the World Bank, in 1992 China accounted for about 23 percent of world population, produced about 5 percent of world GDP, and had a per capita GDP of $2,460, a figure slightly higher than the Philippines.[22] The success of China's gradualist approach—and the prospect of 1.2 billion consumers—has attracted multinationals from all over the globe includ-

[22]Data were reported in "Chinese Puzzles," *The Economist* (May 15, 1993): 83. In contrast, the U.S. share of world GDP was 22.5 percent, and the Japanese share was 7.6 percent.

ing Eastman Kodak, Motorola, Heinz, NEC, and Samsung. One problem on the horizon for the near term is inflation. Despite economic reforms, state banks still hold over 85 percent of all financial assets and have been guilty of funneling credit to money-losing state-owned firms; perhaps a quarter of these loans will never be repaid. Combining these loans with an official government deficit equal to 4 percent of GDP means that the real deficit is nearly 10 percent of GDP.[23] Until something is done about lending practices and the deficit, prospects for monetary stability in China seem remote.

RECAP   Shock Therapy versus Gradualism

Two basic approaches have been suggested for dealing with the economic transition of the former socialist economies, shock therapy and gradualism.

Shock therapy relies on immediate privatization and marketization. The advantage of shock therapy is that the end results may be visible quickly, and a rapid transition to capitalism is thought to stabilize the government. The disadvantages are output losses, unemployment, and inflation in the short run. Shock therapy has been applied in Poland, Russia, and other countries in Eastern Europe and the former Soviet Union.

Gradualism is based on the idea that economic behavior is a product of the existing economic system. The immediate transition from socialism to capitalism will be inefficient because many people will continue to behave as they did under socialism. As a result, the short-run costs of shock therapy may be even larger than supposed. At this point, the gradualist approach in Hungary and China seems to be working.

THE VARIETIES OF CAPITALISM

The revival of the former socialist economies has not proceeded as rapidly or as smoothly as had been hoped. But it may be proceeding as well as could be expected. The complete overhaul of an economic system is difficult and, as we are discovering, time-consuming. As these former socialist economies get over the initial shock of transition, they will evolve their own brands of capitalism. In some countries, it may resemble the mixed capitalism of the United States and the United Kingdom; other countries may model their new economies after the more interventionist capitalism of Japan or the economies of Western Europe; still others may evolve into an entirely new brand of capitalism. To understand the possible evolutionary paths of the former socialist economies—as well as that of the United States and the advanced capitalist economies—we need to examine some of the more important aspects of the different varieties of capitalism in the world today. Two cases that are especially instructive are Japan and Western Europe.

[23]Data were reported in "China's Financial Fix," *The Economist* (July 10, 1993): 69–70.

. . . .

Labor Relations in Japan

In contrast to industrial policy—a topic we covered in Chapter 33—the role of labor relations in Japan has aroused little debate. Nearly all Japanese scholars believe that the Japanese system of labor relations has been instrumental in that country's high rate of economic growth. Contrary to popular belief, however, the system of labor relations in Japan is *not* the product of centuries of cultural evolution; it developed only after World War II.[24] A brief economic history of Japan is provided in the Focus box on page 900.

Labor relations in Japan and the United States differ in several key respects. First, until quite recently, most male workers in large Japanese firms (about 30 percent of all workers) had essentially *lifetime employment* contracts. Workers with lifetime employment contracts rarely change jobs, so firms are willing to invest in worker training. In the West, many firms are reluctant to invest in workers who may change jobs. Second, promotions and salaries in Japan are based largely on seniority. This augments the incentive to stay with one firm. Third, blue-collar workers are treated much like white-collar workers. For example, most blue-collar workers receive salaries, not hourly wages. This reduces labor-management dissension. Finally, most Japanese unions are enterprise unions, not trade unions as in the United States. An enterprise union covers all workers in a particular firm; a trade union represents a particular type of labor in various firms and industries. Many economists believe that enterprise unions make labor-management cooperation easier.

No one can deny Japan's economic success over the past 30 years, but whether this success can continue is a matter of debate. There is already evidence that young people in Japan are starting to question the work ethics of their elders; not everyone wants to work long hours and devote his or her life to the corporation.[25] Corporate layoffs during the severe recession of the early 1990s may have marked the beginning of the end of lifetime employment; how this will affect work incentives is anybody's guess. There is evidence too that parents are beginning to pamper their children to a fault; Japanese kids are less physically fit than their parents and are devoting less time to their schoolwork.[26]

. . . .

The European Social Market Economy

The economies of Western Europe and the United States differ in several ways, although many of these differences may be fading in the 1990s. To the casual observer, the most significant contrast has been in the amount of money spent on social welfare and worker training programs. For decades, Europeans have enjoyed

[24]This discussion of labor relations in Japan is based on Takatoshi Ito, *The Japanese Economy* (Cambridge, Mass.: MIT Press, 1992). See especially Chapter 8, "The Labor Market."
[25]In 1989, Japanese industrial workers averaged 2,088 hours per year versus 1,989 in the United States and only 1,638 in West Germany. In 1987, partially because of pressure from the United States, Japan lowered the legal number of hours that could be worked per week from 48 to 46. The hope was that more leisure time would translate into more consumption—and more imported U.S. goods. See "Free, Young, and Japanese," *The Economist* (December 21, 1991): 38.
[26]"Japan's Pampered Children," *The Economist* (February 9, 1991): 51.

Eurosclerosis Term coined to refer to the sluggish European growth during the 1980s, thought to be caused by excessive spending on welfare, worker benefits, and other social programs.

liberal social programs including worker training, generous job pensions, long paid vacations, child care, free health care, and various other subsidies. The reasoning behind these programs was not simply humanitarian: Europeans argued that such programs would increase worker morale and productivity while reducing crime and other social costs. For a time at least, this argument seemed correct: European economic growth rates exceeded U.S. economic growth in most years in the 1950s, 1960s, and 1970s. When growth soured in the 1980s, however, some observers began to speak of **eurosclerosis**—a newly coined word meaning a "disease" brought on by costly and rigid labor markets and social programs. When Europe fell into a severe recession in the early 1990s, there were cries for a move toward free markets and the dismantling of the social welfare system. What happened, and why?

First, it is not clear that Europe's only problem in the 1980s was eurosclerosis. The European economy of the mid-1980s did perform poorly, but things seemed to turn around late in the decade as prospects for increased European economic cooperation improved. For example, employment in Germany grew by 8.6 percent between 1987 and 1991.[27] Many of Germany's problems can be traced to the difficult and costly process of German reunification following the collapse of the Soviet Union. No economy can spend the billions necessary to annex a backward nation without some adverse effects, but Germany's commitment to worker training and retraining has made reunification especially difficult and costly. When reunification was announced, East German wages were converted into Deutsche marks at a ratio of 1:1. The immediate result was that East Germans saw their wages rise almost 400 percent in terms of purchasing power. This allowed them to buy Western goods, but the higher wages also meant that East German industries were woefully noncompetitive. More than a third of all East German firms have proven to be noncompetitive. As a result, the government of unified Germany has had to invest billions of Deutsche marks to revamp East German industries and train East German workers. Much of this money had to be borrowed from abroad. Not only did this mean capital outflows from other nations, but borrowing of this magnitude raised interest rates. These factors combined to set the stage for a continentwide recession with unemployment approaching 10 percent in 1993 and 1994.

Nevertheless, the eurosclerosis argument cannot be dismissed outright. European unit labor costs have been rising faster than anywhere else since the 1970s—largely because of rising benefits.[28] Today, labor costs as much as 50 percent more in Europe than in other industrialized nations. For example, in 1992 the average German manufacturing worker received wages and benefits totaling $26.89 per hour, of which $12.47 was health and pension funding benefits. The comparable figure for the United States was $15.89, of which $4.44 was benefits. Europeans also work fewer hours and take longer paid vacations than U.S. workers: the average worker in Germany worked 1,519 hours in 1992 and took 40 days of paid vacation; workers in the

[27]Analysis of the decline of the German economy can be found in Rudiger Dornbusch, "The End of the German Miracle," *Journal of Economic Literature* 31 (June 1993): 881–85. This article is a review of Herbert Giersch, Karl-Heinz Paqué, and Knut Borchardt, *The Fading Miracle: Four Decades of Market Economy in Germany* (New York: Cambridge University Press, 1992).
[28]These data are from Terence Roth, "Europe's Safety Nets Begin to Tear," *Wall Street Journal,* July 1, 1993, p. A10.

United States put in 1,857 hours and took about two weeks of vacation. Most European nations also have rules that ban or discourage part-time and weekend work.

To regain competitiveness, most European nations are reducing government intervention in the economy and cutting social programs—moves that some interpret as emulation of the U.S. free-market system. These reforms may have desirable long-run consequences, but the short-run costs have been significant. When Britain began dismantling its social welfare system in the 1980s, a severe recession ensued. When the Dutch government announced in 1993 that they would eliminate automatic unemployment compensation for students upon graduation, more than 20,000 students rioted at The Hague. Spain's decision to reduce unemployment benefits in 1992 resulted in a nationwide general strike. Decisions by Sweden, France, and Italy to sell off government-owned businesses have sparked less criticism.

The European experience contrasts with the U.S. experience in some important ways. Both Europe and the United States have significant employment problems largely because in today's high-tech world, unskilled workers compete with cheap labor in Asia, Eastern Europe, and elsewhere. In Europe the ranks of the long-term unemployed have increased steadily, at least partially because of rigid wages for low-skilled workers. Long-term unemployment is less of a problem in the United States, perhaps because real wages for low-skilled workers have declined 20 percent in the past decade. It is important to note, however, that unemployment is less of a problem for skilled workers in Europe. This suggests that wage flexibility combined with European-style job training, efforts to match workers to available jobs, and programs to move young people from school to work could be successful at reducing long-term unemployment in the United States.

SUMMARY

Economic evolution is a fact of life: feudalism evolved into capitalism, capitalism became socialism (in some countries), and now socialism is being transformed into capitalism in many countries. Few economists could have forecast these changes. Even Marx, who predicted that capitalism would be replaced by socialism, missed the point because his model called for a different kind of transformation and for different reasons. If a single point should be remembered from this chapter, it is this: economic systems are always changing. The capitalism of today will be different from the capitalism of tomorrow. The main points from this chapter are:

1. Capitalism is an economic system characterized by private ownership of the means of production. Socialism is an economic system characterized by public ownership of the means of production. The roots of capitalism can be traced to feudalism, the enclosure movement, and the Industrial Revolution.

2. Marx felt that capitalism would collapse because of its internal inconsistencies. The bourgeoisie exploited the proletariat, but as machines replaced workers, profits would fall. Industrial concentration would increase, business cycles would become more severe, and the system would collapse in the most technologically advanced countries first. Most people believe that Marx's prediction of the collapse of capitalism was incorrect.

3. The Soviet Union was established following the Bolshevik Revolution in 1917. The central planning system of the Soviet Union resulted in generally high economic growth, but severe shortages and an investment bias. The resulting supply constraint on the economy generated few incentives to work, to control costs, or to innovate. The Soviet Union collapsed into several independent states in 1991.

4. Many economists believe that the best way to transform the former socialist economies to capitalism is with shock therapy. This involves immediate privatization and marketization. Critics note that shock therapy imposes severe social and economic costs; advocates contend that immediate transition is necessary so that people can see the results of restructuring. The gradualist approach to economic transition has been used in only a few countries but appears to be somewhat successful.

5. There are many varieties of capitalism in the world. Japanese capitalism relies upon industrial policies and a system of labor relations that encourages long-term employment, worker training, and labor-management cooperation. Capitalism in Western Europe has been characterized by liberal benefit programs; however, many of these programs have been cut back in recent years. U.S. capitalism relies upon relatively free markets.

KEY TERMS AND CONCEPTS

capitalism
socialism
feudalism
mercantile economy
enclosure movement
Industrial Revolution
Karl Marx
proletariat
bourgeoisie
communism
labor theory of value
exploitation of labor
organic composition of capital
industrial reserve army of the unemployed

Bolshevik Revolution
V. I. Lenin
Gosplan
soft budget constraint
perestroika
demand-constrained economies
supply-constrained economies
shock therapy
privatization
marketization
gradualism
eurosclerosis

REVIEW QUESTIONS

1. What factors led to the demise of feudalism and the rise of capitalism?
2. Outline the Marxian theory of the collapse of capitalism and explain why the Bolshevik Revolution does *not* fit the Marxian model.
3. What is a soft budget constraint? Can they ever exist in capitalist economies?
4. Discuss the pros and cons of shock therapy.

5. In what ways do the gradualist transitions in Hungary and China differ from shock therapy?

6. Why did the Soviet Union collapse? Do you think the collapse could have been averted if the socialist planners had understood supply and demand analysis?

7. In what ways do the economies of Japan and Western Europe seem to be moving toward the U.S. system? What aspects of the Japanese and Western European economies do you think can be best applied to the U.S. economy?

·······PROBLEMS

1. What role does the middle class play in Marxian theory?

2. Unemployment is necessary for capitalism to survive. Explain and comment.

3. Indicate whether the following are true, false, or uncertain. Explain your answers.
   a. According to the labor theory of value, demand has no effect on value.
   b. The short-run costs are higher, but the long-run costs are lower in shock therapy than in gradualism.
   c. Money was used in most transactions under feudalism.
   d. Firms increase profits by acquiring technologically sophisticated machinery.
   e. War Communism was more successful than the New Economic Policy.
   f. Shock therapy has proven more successful than gradualism.
   g. The main problem with China's transition program is that China has not been able to attract foreign investors.

4. Suppose that prices had been decontrolled in the Soviet Union in 1988. Do you think this would have been sufficient to avert the collapse of socialism?

5. Compare and contrast the economic role of the state in contemporary China and contemporary Russia.

6. The text notes that one of the strengths of the U.S. system of labor relations is flexibility; however, it also notes that many workers in Japan have what amount to lifetime employment contracts. Does this mean that worker flexibility is unimportant in Japan? Explain and comment.

7. The text notes that the soft budget constraint was instrumental in socialist firms' ability to survive despite inherent inefficiencies, whereas competitive firms face a hard budget constraint. Do all firms in capitalist economies face hard budget constraints? What about monopolies and large corporations?

8. The two main components of shock therapy are privatization and marketization. Do you think that both are necessary? Would it be possible to have a system with marketization but not private enterprise? Explain and comment.

9. Many universities are run much like the former Soviet Union in the sense that there is no merit pay for faculty. Further, once faculty get tenure, they have lifetime employment, much like the Japanese (and former Soviet) system. Do you think this system generates efficiency? Can you recommend a better system? Can you explain why the current system exists?

10. A large number of the jobs added in the United States so far in the 1990s have been part-time and without benefits. How does this affect the potential competitiveness of the U.S. economy? Explain with reference to both the European and Japanese systems.

CHAPTER 35

International Trade: Comparative Advantage and the Gains from Trade

You have heard it time and again: high-wage U.S. workers just cannot compete with low-wage workers in Asia and Latin America. The argument must contain more than a little truth: there are more imported goods on the shelves, and unemployment at home seems to be on the rise. The story in Asia and Latin America is a little different. They say that they cannot compete with technological giants like the United States. Obviously, someone is wrong: If we are hurt by low-wage foreign workers, how can they be hurt by high-wage U.S. workers? The economist's usual retort is that the United States can compete with low-wage workers abroad, and less-developed countries have little to fear from technological giants. In fact, both countries stand to gain from free and open trade; measures to keep out imported goods may help some groups, but inevitably hurt society as a whole. This contention is due to the law of comparative advantage, one of the most important ideas in economics.

This chapter will analyze the growing importance of the trade sector in the United States and explain how and why nations benefit from international trade. We will also look at some of the many arguments that have been and continue to be used to restrain free trade.

AFTER READING AND STUDYING THIS CHAPTER, YOU SHOULD BE ABLE TO:

- ··· Understand the importance of the growing international sector in the U.S. economy
- ··· Discuss the law of comparative advantage, and use it to show how all countries can gain from free trade
- ··· Use the production possibilities curve to illustrate the terms of trade and the expansion of consumption possibilities due to international trade

· · · Use supply and demand analysis to illustrate the effects of trade on production, consumption, and prices

· · · Show how tariffs and quotas affect prices and the volume of trade

· · · Analyze the arguments that have been used for trade restrictions

· · · · · · · THE GROWING INTERNATIONAL SECTOR

One of the most important trends in recent U.S. economic history is the growing magnitude of international trade and investment. As Table 35.1 shows, the international component of the U.S. economy grew dramatically between 1960 and 1993. This is perhaps most apparent in column 8, which gives the ratio of imports plus exports to annual GDP. This ratio rose from 9 percent to 25 percent, meaning that fully a quarter of the goods and services that we buy or sell involve the international economy. These numbers are as impressive as they are important. Few U.S. firms do not face stiff competition—either actual or potential—from foreign firms. Consumers appreciate the price competition and wide selection offered by foreign products, but workers fear they will lose their jobs to imports. It is this trade-off between consumer benefits and fear of foreign competition that forms the basis for political debates on trade sanctions.

Columns 6 and 7 of the table show that U.S. earnings on foreign investments also grew substantially between the 1960s and the 1990s. In constant 1987 dollars, U.S. receipts were barely $16 billion in 1960 but more than $130 billion in 1990. Foreign earnings in the United States grew as well, from $5 billion to more than $100 billion in 1990. Foreign investment has grown so rapidly for several reasons. For one thing, wages are lower in the United States. When the German automakers BMW and Mercedes decided to build factories in the United States, they had an eye toward

· · · · TABLE 35.1 THE GROWING INTERNATIONAL SECTOR

(1) Year	(2) GDP	(3) Exports	(4) Imports	(5) Net Exports	(6) Receipts	(7) Payments	(8) (Exports + Imports)/GDP
1960	$1,970.8	$ 88.4	$ 96.1	$ −7.6	$ 16.1	$ 5.0	9%
1965	2,470.5	118.1	124.5	−6.4	24.7	8.3	10
1970	2,873.9	161.3	196.4	−35.2	33.4	19.4	12
1975	3,221.7	232.9	209.8	23.1	43.4	21.5	14
1980	3,776.3	320.5	289.9	30.7	83.4	41.9	16
1985	4,279.8	309.2	454.6	−145.3	91.6	74.3	18
1990	4,897.3	510.5	565.1	−54.7	138.6	117.6	22
1991	4,861.4	543.4	562.5	−19.1	115.0	94.6	23
1992	4,986.3	578.0	611.6	−33.6	99.8	86.9	24
1993p	5,132.7	596.4	675.7	−79.3	NA	NA	25

KEY: Net exports = exports − imports; Receipts = earnings on U.S. investments abroad; Payments = foreign earnings on investments in the United States. Data are in billions of 1987 dollars. 1993 data are preliminary.

SOURCE: 1994 *Economic Report of the President*, Tables B-2, B-3, and B-103.

reducing labor costs from over $25 per hour in Germany to about $16 in the United States. The United States has also seen a great deal of what has been called **defensive foreign investment** in recent years. Fearing import restrictions, many foreign companies built factories in the United States. Japanese automobile plants in the United States are often cited as examples of defensive foreign investment. Finally, much foreign investment is of the financial variety. High interest rates and a booming stock market in the United States attracted a great deal of foreign financial capital in the 1980s, but capital inflows tapered off significantly in the 1990s.

· · · · · · · ·

Why Do Nations Trade?

International trade is more complicated than intranational or domestic trade for several reasons. It often entails significant transportation costs, customs duties, licensing fees, and other complications. Further, most international transactions require payment in foreign currency. If French citizens want to buy Italian sports cars, they must first exchange French francs for Italian lira—and as we will find out in the next chapter, trading foreign currencies can be risky as well as complicated. The fact that the volume of international trade is so large and growing despite these complications indicates that it must offer significant gains. Among the most important motivations for trade are:

- *Mutual benefit*. When people engage in voluntary market transactions, both the buyer and the seller benefit. The buyer would rather have the good, and the seller would rather have the money—or the transaction would not have taken place. This is the principle of **mutual benefit**. It forms the basis for all market transactions, including international trade: the importer prefers the product and the exporter prefers the money, and both are better off after completing the transaction. The principle of mutual benefit may be the strongest argument for free trade.
- *Price differentials*. Most countries could produce many of the goods they import, but do not because of the **price differential**—the goods are cheaper when imported. For example, the United States could grow bananas in hothouses, but the cost would be much higher than the cost of importing bananas from Central America. The sensible thing to do is to import bananas. Not only do consumers get bananas for a lower price, but the resources that would have been devoted to hothouse bananas are available for more productive uses. The real world is never quite this simple, however. Once we begin to import bananas from Central America, any hothouse banana producers in the United States stand to lose their jobs. This potential for job losses is one reason why many groups call for restrictions on free trade.
- *Resource endowments*. The source of price differentials is often found in a country's **resource endowments**. Imported bananas are inexpensive because Central America has land and climate—the resource base—that are ideally suited for growing bananas. A country's resource base includes its climate and geography, as well as its labor and capital stocks. In theory, countries with abundant labor and low wages export goods that are produced with labor-intensive production methods and import goods that are produced with capital-intensive production meth-

Defensive foreign investment Foreign investment intended to stave off tariff barriers or other import restrictions.

Mutual benefit The fundamental reason for exchange; both parties must benefit or the trade would not take place.

Price differentials Production costs vary from country to country. Consequently, it is sometimes cheaper to import goods than to produce them domestically.

Resource endowments Countries have different resource bases (climate, geography, labor and capital stocks) and therefore can produce goods at different costs. Resource endowments are often the reason for price differentials.

ods.[1] For example, textiles are an important export from labor-abundant Mexico, and aircraft are an important export of the capital-abundant United States.

Resource endowment differentials highlight another key reason nations trade: factor immobility. If the factors of production—land, labor, and capital—were perfectly mobile across international boundaries, there would be little incentive to trade goods and services because the factors of production would move instead. In fact, capital is quite mobile in the modern world, but there are cultural and often legal restrictions against labor migration, and it is obviously impossible to move land. Most of the analysis in this and the next chapter will be based on the assumption that factors cannot move across international boundaries. The significance of this assumption will be apparent when we look at regional trading blocs and the North American Free Trade Agreement in Chapter 37.

- *Product variety.* Mutual benefit, resource endowments, and price differentials are not the only reasons for trade. Much trade in the world today is between countries that have roughly similar standards of living and technologies. This suggests that trade often takes place between countries with similar resource endowments and prices. How can these countries benefit from trade? One explanation is that consumers desire **product variety**. French wines and German cars may not be superior to their American counterparts, but it is nice to serve a *pouilly fuisse* on occasion and I would love to drive a Porsche.

Product variety Consumers' desire for different, though not necessarily superior, products is one reason for international trade.

Tables 35.2 and 35.3 present data that can be interpreted in light of this discussion. Table 35.2 lists the major merchandise imports and exports to and from the United States in 1992. Notice that the bulk of this merchandise trade involved manufactured goods. Part of this trade can be explained by price differentials and resource endowments, but some was undoubtedly caused by a desire for product variety. Mineral fuel imports (primarily oil) accounted for 10 percent of all imports. Price differentials are the main reason we import so much oil. On the other hand, vehicle and vehicle parts imports—14 percent of imports—may be motivated primarily by the desire for product variety and quality; most current studies show that production costs at U.S. automobile plants are quite competitive. About 9 percent of U.S. exports are agricultural products; the United States is the world's leading agricultural exporter.

Table 35.3 lists the major trading partners of the United States. Notice that trade with Canada, Japan, and Western Europe constitutes more than half of the volume of trade. Note too that the merchandise trade deficit with Japan (about $51 billion) plus the deficit with OPEC (about $13 billion) amounted to about two-thirds of the $96 billion merchandise trade deficit. Why should we be concerned about trade deficits? Trade deficits represent an outflow of income and spending from the United States and can mean lost jobs. Consumers enjoy the wide selection of imported goods, but workers fearful of losing their jobs have other things on their minds. This explains why there is so much rhetoric about asking Japan to buy more U.S. exports and taxing oil imports. After Canada and Japan, the third largest trading partner of the United States is Mexico. In 1992, U.S. exports to Mexico totaled about $40.6 billion

---

[1]That relative factor endowments determine the pattern of trade is the major result of one of the most important theorems in international economics, the Heckscher-Ohlin theorem, named after its codevelopers, the Swedish economists E. F. Heckscher (1879–1952) and Bertil Ohlin (1899–1979). Ohlin won the Nobel Prize in economics in 1977.

· · · · **Table 35.2** Major Merchandise Imports and Exports of the United States, 1992

Exports	Value	Percentage	Imports	Value	Percentage
Total	**$448.2**	100%	**Total**	**$532.5**	100%
Manufactured goods	347.5	78	Manufactured goods	434.3	82
Electrical machinery	32.0	7	Vehicles and parts	72.0	14
Office machinery	26.9	6	Electrical machinery	39.7	8
Airplanes	26.4	6	Office machinery	36.4	7
Industrial machinery	18.4	4	Clothing	31.2	6
Agricultural	42.1	9	Agricultural	23.4	4
Corn	4.9	1	Vegetables and fruit	5.7	1
Vegetable and fruit	5.7	1	Meat	2.7	1
Wheat	4.5	1	Coffee	1.6	<1
Mineral fuel	11.1	2	Mineral fuel	55.0	10
Other	47.5	11	Other	19.8	4

Source: *Statistical Abstract of the United States,* 1993, Table 1350. Data are in billions of current dollars.

· · · · **Table 35.3** Merchandise Imports and Exports by Area, 1992

Exports		Imports		Balance
Total	**$440.1**	**Total**	**$536**	**−$96.2**
Industrial countries	264.9	Industrial countries	316.2	−51.3
Canada	91.1	Canada	100.9	−9.8
Japan	46.9	Japan	97.4	−50.5
Western Europe	114.5	Western Europe	111.3	+3.2
Australia, New Zealand, South Africa	12.4	Australia, New Zealand, South Africa	6.6	+5.8
Other countries	175.1	Other countries	220.1	−45.0
OPEC	20.7	OPEC	33.7	−13.0
Eastern Europe	5.6	Eastern Europe	2.0	+3.6
Latin America, Asia, Africa	148.8	Latin America, Asia, Africa	184.4	−35.6

Source: 1994 *Economic Report of the President,* Table B-1052. Data are in billions of current dollars.

while imports were $35.2 billion. Trade between the United States and Mexico will undoubtedly increase in the future as the North American Free Trade Agreement is implemented.

RECAP   The Growing International Sector

International trade has played an increasing role in the U.S. economy and will undoubtedly continue to do so in the future. Nations trade for mutual benefit, to take advantage of price differentials, and for product variety. Most U.S. trade involves manufactured goods. Additionally, about 10 percent of our exports are agricultural products, and oil constitutes about 10 percent of our imports. The major trading partners of the United States are Canada, Japan, Mexico, and Western Europe. The United States has run persistent trade deficits with Japan for two decades.

ABSOLUTE AND COMPARATIVE ADVANTAGE

Until David Ricardo discovered the law of comparative advantage in the early 19th century, many economists believed that international trade was a zero sum game—that the exporter's gains exactly offset the importer's losses. (Ricardo was the subject of an *Economic Heritage* focus in Chapter 9.) This reasoning was the prime motivation behind the early mercantilist doctrine that trade policies should be designed to encourage exports and discourage imports. That all changed—in the eyes of economists, if not politicians or the public—with Ricardo. Ricardo showed that both parties gained from free trade, even if one was a "technological giant" and the other a less-developed nation. Here is a classic story that economics professors have used for years to explain the law of comparative advantage.

Suppose that you are the most highly paid lawyer in the city and charge a fee of $2,000 per hour. Suppose further that you are also the world's best typist and can type 400 words per minute. Should you do your own typing? Certainly not if you have enough legal work to keep you busy full time. Every hour you spend typing incurs an opportunity cost of $2,000 in forgone legal fees. That makes typing pretty expensive. What you might do is hire eight 50-words-per-minute typists, pay them each $10 per hour, and thus pay only $80 per hour to type 400 words per minute. The opportunity cost of practicing law (and earning $2,000 per hour) is only $80 per hour. The best way to spend your time is to do what you do at the lowest opportunity cost.

How does this example relate to trade between nations? Comparative advantage is one of the main bases for trade among nations. The lawyer is the technological giant able to produce everything more efficiently than any other country in the world. But resources are scarce even for technological giants, so resources should be used to produce goods that can be produced at the lowest opportunity cost. Goods that incur high opportunity costs of production (typing) should be imported.

The Law of Comparative Advantage

Like Adam Smith and Karl Marx, Ricardo believed in the *labor theory of value,* a theory we introduced in the previous chapter. According to this theory, value depends on the amount of labor embodied in the productive process, and goods exchange on the market based on the amount of labor required to produce them. For example, if a textile worker could make two shirts or one coat per day, the price of a coat would be twice as high as the price of a shirt. The labor theory of value has been dismissed by most contemporary economists in part because it says nothing about the demand side of the market, but it is still useful for illustrating the basic concepts of comparative advantage.

Table 35.4 shows the amount of wine (*W*) and cheese (*C*) that can be produced with one hour of labor in the United States (US) and the United Kingdom (UK). Notice that more wine and cheese can be produced per hour in the US than in the UK: an hour of labor produces 3 units of wine or 4 units of cheese in the US versus only 1 unit of wine or 2 units of cheese in the UK. This means that the US has an **absolute advantage** in the production of both goods. (In this case, the US would

Absolute advantage A nation has an absolute advantage in the production of good *X* if fewer resources are required in the production process.

····· **TABLE 35.4 COMPARATIVE ADVANTAGE MATRIX**

	UK	US
Wine (*W*)	1	3
Cheese (*C*)	2	4

The entries in the table represent the output from one hour of labor input. In the US, one unit of labor can produce either 3 units of wine or 4 units of cheese. This means that the opportunity cost of a unit of wine is 1.33 units of cheese ($3W = 4C$ or $1W = 1.33C$). In the UK, one unit of labor can produce either 1 unit of wine or 2 units of cheese, so the opportunity cost of a unit of wine is 2 units of cheese ($1W = 2C$). The opportunity cost of wine is lower in the US than in the UK so the US has a comparative advantage in wine production. The UK has a comparative advantage in cheese production: $1C = 0.5W$ versus $1C = 0.75W$. The US has an absolute advantage in both products.

be classified as the "technological giant" compared to the UK.) This might seem to indicate that the US stands to gain nothing from trade with the UK: Why import goods if you can produce everything with more absolute efficiency than the other nation? However, it is **comparative advantage**, not absolute advantage, that forms the basis for trade. Countries should produce and export those goods in which they have a comparative advantage, and they should import goods in which they have a comparative disadvantage. To find out which goods will be imported and exported, we first need to determine comparative advantage.

Comparative advantage is found by calculating the relative opportunity costs of production. In the US, each hour of labor can produce 3 units of wine or 4 units of cheese. This can be written as:

$$US: 3W = 4C$$

But if we solve for $1W$ (divide both sides by 3) or $1C$ (divide both sides by 4), we can better see the opportunity costs of wine and cheese:

$$US: 1W = 1.33C \quad or \quad 1C = 0.75W$$

In other words, each unit of wine that is produced means giving up 1.33 units of cheese, and each unit of cheese represents the lost production of 0.75 units of wine.

The opportunity costs of production differ in the UK. Using data from the first column in Table 35.4, it is apparent that each unit of wine produced in the UK involves giving up 2 units of cheese, while each unit of cheese incurs an opportunity cost of 0.5 units of wine:

$$UK: 1W = 2C \quad or \quad 1C = 0.5W$$

Now we have enough information to determine comparative advantage. Notice that each unit of wine costs 2 units of cheese in the UK but only 1.33 units of cheese in the US. This means that the relative opportunity cost of wine is lower in the US,

Comparative advantage The situation where a country can produce a good at a lower opportunity cost than another country.

so the US has a comparative advantage in wine production. The UK has a comparative advantage in cheese production: each unit of cheese costs only 0.5 units of wine in the UK but 0.75 units of wine in the US. The US should produce and export wine in exchange for cheese; the UK should produce and export cheese in exchange for wine.

. . . .

The Gains from Trade

The remarkable implication of the law of comparative advantage is that *world output can rise without additional factor inputs* when countries specialize in the production of the goods in which they have a comparative advantage. To see this, suppose that the UK and the US are the only countries in the world, and that they each have 100 workers. Suppose further that survival mandates that each worker have one unit of cheese. This means that the UK must devote at least 50 workers to cheese production $(50 \times 2 = 100)$ and the US must employ at least 25 workers in the cheese industry $(25 \times 4 = 100)$. This leaves 50 workers for the wine industry in the UK and 75 workers for the wine industry in the US. Pretrade production is:

	Cheese	Wine
UK:	50(2) = 100	50(1) = 50
US:	25(4) = 100	75(3) = 225
World:	200	275

Now, suppose that once trade commences, there is complete specialization; that is, the US produces only wine and the UK produces only cheese. World output would be:

	Cheese	Wine
UK:	100(2) = 200	0
US:	0	100(3) = 300
World:	200	300

This is a remarkable result: world output has increased—there is the same amount of cheese but more wine—so the consumers of the world are better off. Further, because wages are related to productivity, wages have risen in both countries. All that is necessary to realize these **gains from trade** is for the US to trade some of its wine for cheese.

The result we have just demonstrated holds even if we relax the seemingly restrictive assumptions of two countries, two goods, zero transportation costs, and so on. The only qualification of note is that in the real world complete specialization does not take place. It did in this example only because we assumed constant costs—no matter how much wine was produced in the US, the opportunity cost was 1.33 units of cheese. In most situations, costs begin to rise before complete specialization occurs, but the general (and important!) result holds: if countries produce goods with low opportunity costs and import goods with high opportunity costs, world output increases and *every* nation gains. However, it must be stressed that while the nation as a whole clearly gains from free trade, some individuals within the nation may not

Gains from trade Benefits derived from free trade; world output can rise without additional factor inputs if all countries specialize in products in which they have a comparative advantage.

gain. For example, free trade will mean that the dairy farmers in the United States will find that their dairy farms have suddenly fallen in value; dairy farmers may also find it difficult to acquire the skills necessary to enter the wine industry. This is one reason why there are always groups opposed to free trade, an issue we develop later in the chapter.

. . . .

The Terms of Trade

World output has indeed risen, but unless the US is able to trade some wine for cheese, workers in the US will not get much work done. Likewise, the British certainly do not need the cholesterol of all that cheese—and might wish to imbibe on occasion. So trade takes place. The question we need to answer now, is what are the **terms of trade**? That is, how much wine must the US give in exchange for each unit of cheese?

Terms of trade The price ratio between imported and exported goods.

Before trade takes place, each unit of cheese costs 0.75 units of forgone wine in the US. Thus, the US has no incentive to trade unless it can get cheese for less than 0.75 units of wine. Likewise, before trade takes place, each unit of cheese trades for 0.50 units of wine in the UK. The British will not be willing to trade cheese for wine unless they can get more than 0.50 units of wine in exchange for a unit of cheese. Putting these facts together, we get a *terms of trade inequality*:

Terms of trade inequality:
$$0.50W < 1C < 0.75W \qquad\qquad [1]$$

UK benefits if it gets more than 0.50 units of W per C	US benefits if it gives less than 0.75 units of W per C

Let's look at the terms of trade from another perspective. Before trade, each unit of wine carries an opportunity cost of 1.33 units of cheese in the US and 2.00 units of cheese in the UK. The US is going to import cheese, so it wants more than 1.33 units of cheese per unit of wine. The UK is going to export cheese, so it wants to give less than 2.00 units of cheese per unit of wine. The corresponding terms of trade inequality is:

Terms of trade inequality: $1.33C < 1W < 2.00C \qquad\qquad [2]$

which is mathematically identical to the previous inequality in [1].[2]

Without more information, we cannot determine precisely where within the inequality the terms of trade will rest.[3] The US is clearly better off getting more

---

[2]To see this, merely take the reciprocal of either inequality to get the other, and remember to reverse the inequality signs when you take the reciprocal.

[3]Some of the additional information that is required is the elasticity of demand for the two goods, the size of the countries, and the volume of trade.

cheese per unit of wine, and the UK would prefer to give as little cheese as possible per unit of wine. In the example that follows, we will assume some specific terms of trade to keep things simple.

RECAP   Comparative Advantage and the Gains from Trade

The law of comparative advantage states that all countries can gain from trade as long as pretrade relative opportunity costs differ. It explains why developed nations do not need to fear imports from low-wage underdeveloped nations and vice versa. Nations should produce and export only those goods that can be produced with low relative opportunity costs; they should import goods that have a high relative opportunity cost of production. Free trade will result in increased specialization and higher output as resources are allocated to production methods with low opportunity costs of production. Free trade benefits society as a whole, but some groups may be hurt because specialization will reduce the demand for their services.

TRADE AND THE PPC

Everything we have just been through can be illustrated graphically with the production possibilities curve we introduced in Chapter 2. To make the example simple, we will continue to assume that production exhibits the constant costs of Table 35.4 and that each country has 100 units of labor. This information is enough to derive the production possibilities curves for the two countries.

Table 35.5 gives the wine and cheese production possibilities for the US and the UK. Point *a* shows how much cheese is produced if all workers are assigned to the wine industry; points *b* through *f* are found by successive movements of 20 workers from wine production into cheese production in the US. Points *g* through *l* give the wine and cheese production as workers are moved out of the wine industry in the UK.

The data from Table 35.5 are plotted in Figure 35.1. Panel (a) shows the production and consumption possibilities for the US, and panel (b) shows the same

TABLE 35.5 WINE AND CHEESE PRODUCTION POSSIBILITIES FOR THE US AND THE UK

	a	b	c	d	e	f
US Wine	300	240	180	120	60	0
US Cheese	0	80	160	240	320	400

	g	h	i	j	k	l
UK Wine	100	80	60	40	20	0
UK Cheese	0	40	80	120	160	200

····· FIGURE 35.1 THE GAINS FROM TRADE

Panel (a) presents the production and consumption possibilities for the US. The opportunity cost of wine in the US is 1.33 units of cheese so the slope of the production possibilities curve (PPC) is −1.33. Panel (b) gives the production and consumption possibilities for the UK. The opportunity cost of wine in the UK is 2 units of cheese, so the slope of its production possibilities curve is −2.0. This means that the US has a comparative advantage in wine production and will export wine because the opportunity cost of wine is lower in the US than in the UK.

If the terms of trade are $1W = 1.6C$ or $1C = 0.625W$, the consumption possibilities curve (CPC) will intersect at $480C$ for the US and $125W$ for the UK. The consumption possibilities curves for the two countries are parallel and represent the terms of trade. The area between the consumption possibilities curves and the production possibilities curves represents the expanded consumption choices due to trade. If the UK exports $100C$ to the US, it will earn $62.5W$. Posttrade consumption in the UK will be $100C + 62.5W$. Posttrade consumption in the US will be $100C + 237.5W$. *Note:* For clarity the axis of the two graphs have not been drawn to scale.

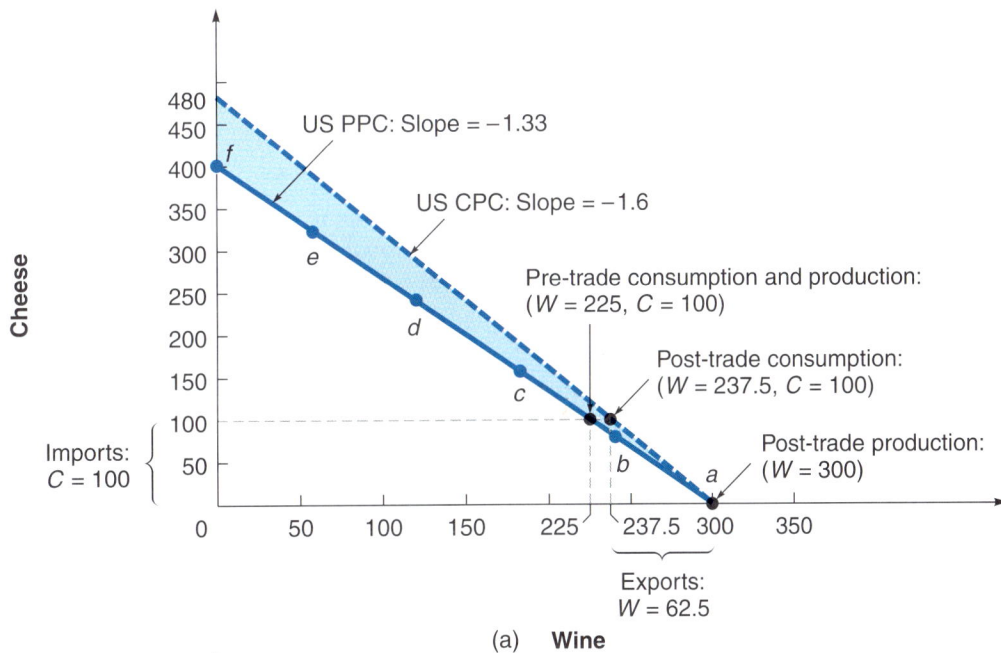

(a) Wine

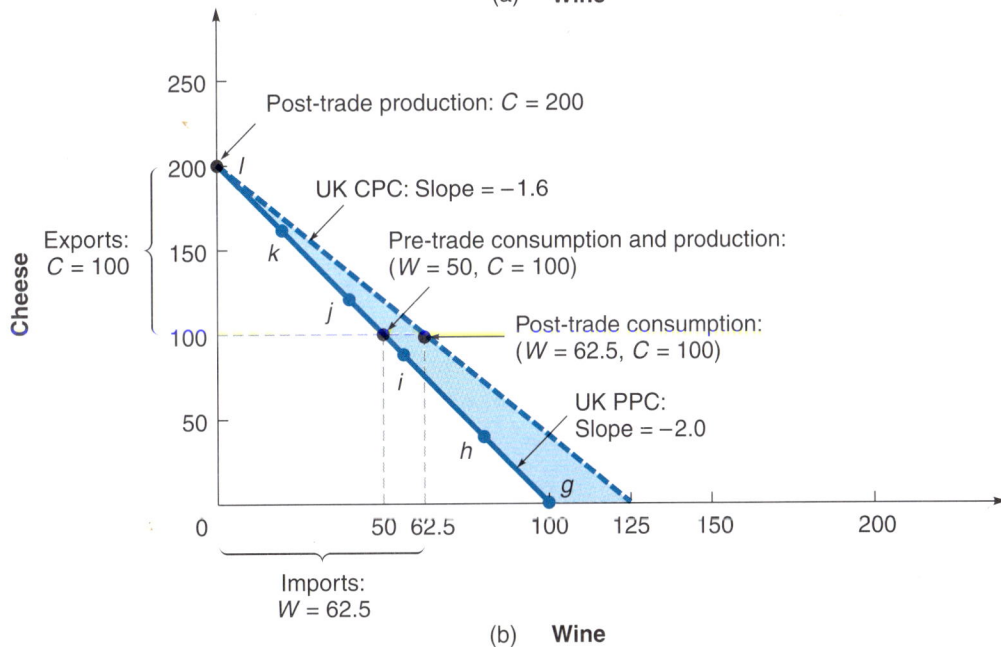

(b) Wine

information for the UK. The solid lines are the production possibilities curves (PPC) for each country. Notice that the production possibilities curves are linear, an indication of the constant opportunity costs assumption. The slope of the production possibilities curve is the opportunity cost of wine production. The opportunity cost per unit of wine is 1.33 units of cheese in the US, so the slope of the US production possibilities curve is -1.33; the opportunity cost of wine is 2 units of cheese in the UK, so the slope of the UK production possibilities curve is -2.00.

In the absence of trade—a situation denoted as "autarky" in economic terminology—consumption is constrained by domestic production, so the production possibilities curve is also the **consumption possibilities curve (CPC)**. Once trade commences and specialization takes place, however, consumption possibilities expand beyond the production possibilities. How much consumption possibilities exceed production possibilities depends on the terms of trade. To illustrate, let's assume that the terms of trade are:

$$1W = 1.6C \quad \text{or} \quad 1C = 0.625W$$

This means that the US can earn 1.6 units of cheese from each unit of wine that it exports. This represents a gain because each unit of wine forgone earned only 1.33 units of cheese before trade. The UK gets 0.625 units of wine for each unit of cheese it exports. This too is a gain over the pretrade value of 0.5 units of wine per unit of cheese.

Finding the slope of the consumption possibilities curve is simple. The US will continue to produce wine, so the horizontal intercept remains at 300. Now if all wine were traded for cheese at the rate of $1W = 1.6C$, then the 300 units of wine could earn $300(1.6) = 480$ units of cheese. This is the vertical intercept of the consumption possibilities curve for the US. For the UK, the cheese (vertical) intercept is 200. If 200 units of cheese were traded for wine at a rate of $1C = 0.625W$, the UK could import $200(0.625) = 125W$. This is the horizontal intercept of the UK consumption possibilities curve. The shaded area between the consumption possibilities curve and the production possibilities curve represents the expanded consumption choices available from trade.

Without knowing the specific preferences of the two countries, we cannot determine just how much trade will take place, but let's suppose that each country decides that it requires 100 units of cheese. If there were no trade, this requirement would mean that the US would produce 100 units of cheese and 225 units of wine, while the UK would produce 100 units of cheese and 50 units of wine. If we allow for specialization and free trade, however, each will be better off because they can consume the same amount of cheese but more wine. With complete specialization, the UK can produce 200 units of cheese. If it exports 100 units, it will be able to consume 100 units of domestic cheese and 62.5 units of imported wine—a gain of 12.5 units of wine. If the US specializes and produces 300 units of wine and exports 62.5 units for 100 units of cheese, it will be able to consume 100 units of imported cheese and 237.5 units of domestic wine—also a gain of 12.5 units of wine. Both points are on the countries' respective consumption possibilities curves—and beyond their production possibilities curves. Free trade has increased world output and consumption, so both countries are better off.

Consumption possibilities curve (CPC) The choices available for national consumption; consumption possibilities exceed production possibilities under free trade.

Before going on, we should note that the gains from trade depend on the terms of trade. For example, compared to the terms of trade discussed above, if the terms of trade were $1C = 0.56W$, the US would be better off and the UK would be worse off. The US would have to trade only 56 units of wine to get 100 units of cheese; US consumption would be $244W$ plus $100C$. UK consumption would be $100C$ plus $56W$.

RECAP   Graphical Analysis of Trade and Comparative Advantage

The production possibilities curve plots the various output combinations possible with full utilization of a given supply of resources and technology. Assuming costs are constant, the production possibilities curve is linear, and its slope is the pretrade opportunity costs of production. Once trade commences, consumption possibilities expand beyond production possibilities. The slope of the consumption possibilities curve represents the terms of trade. The area between the production possibilities curve and the consumption possibilities curve represents the expanded consumption choices due to trade.

SUPPLY AND DEMAND ANALYSIS OF TRADE

Costs are rarely constant in the real world. Generally, costs rise as production increases so complete specialization does not take place. Countries import only as long as the price of imported goods is less than the price of domestically produced goods. This can be illustrated with concave production possibility curves like the ones we used in Chapter 2, but we can get the same effect by working with familiar supply and demand curves. An advantage of using supply and demand curves is that they provide a simplified framework for the analysis of tariffs and quotas.

Pretrade Price Differentials

Figure 35.2 shows the market for a rare cognac in Arcadia and Benistan, the only countries in the world assumed to produce and consume this particular cognac. The pretrade price of cognac in Arcadia, $5, is lower than the pretrade price of cognac in Benistan, $8. Before trade commences, Arcadia produces and consumes 90 units of cognac, and Benistan produces and consumes 75 units. The price differential acts as an inducement for trade. Arcadia, the low-cost producer, will export cognac, and Benistan, the high-cost producer, will import cognac. Once trade takes place, the price of cognac will be $6 in both countries after adjustment for transportation costs. This is the "world price." The price will rise in the exporting country and fall in the importing country, but the price *change* is not necessarily the same in both countries. How much it rises or falls depends on the shapes of the demand and supply curves. In this case, the price fell $2 in Benistan and rose only $1 in Arcadia.

The new price will affect production and consumption in both countries. Higher prices in Arcadia will increase the quantity supplied from 90 to 100. It will also reduce domestic consumption from 90 to 80. The difference between production and consumption, $100 - 80 = 20$, is the amount that is exported. The opposite will happen

•••• **FIGURE 35.2 PRICE DIFFERENTIALS AND THE DIRECTION OF TRADE**

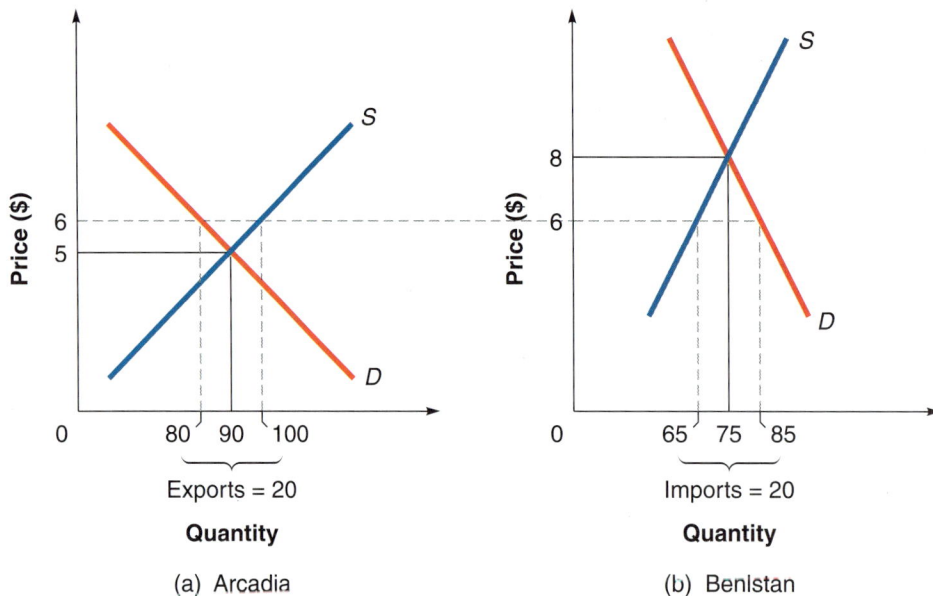

(a) Arcadia   (b) Benistan

Before trade begins, Arcadia produces and consumes 90 units of cognac while Benistan produces and consumes 75 units of cognac. The pretrade price of cognac is lower in Arcadia than in Benistan, $5 < $8. The price differential acts as an inducement for trade. Benistan, the high-cost producer, is the importer. When additional cognac is put on the market in Benistan, the price will fall from $8 to the world price of $6. Increased production for exports will cause the price to rise in Arcadia from $5 to $6. The price will be the same in both countries after adjustment for transportation costs, assumed to be zero in the diagram. Arcadia will export 100 − 80 = 20 units of cognac; this is also the quantity that Benistan will import, 85 − 65 = 20. Notice that consumers in the exporting country now pay higher prices and producers benefit. In the importing country, consumers pay lower prices and producers lose sales.

in Benistan: price will fall so domestic production will decrease from 75 to 65 while consumption will rise from 75 to 85. The difference between consumption and production, 85 − 65 = 20, is the quantity that is imported. We are assuming that only Arcadia and Benistan trade in cognac, so exports must equal imports.

••••••••

The Gains from Trade—Reprise

Does everybody gain from trade? No, but economic theory shows how society can benefit. Free trade raises prices and helps producers in the exporting country, but higher prices do not exactly please consumers in the exporting country. Further, although lower prices in the importing country benefit consumers, they also mean that some domestic producers lose market share or go out of business. On the surface, it is not obvious that the gains outweigh the losses: Who is to say that the benefits to the consumers in the importing country outweigh the losses to the producers? Or that the benefits to the producers in the exporting country are greater than the losses to the consumers? The economist's retort is simple and straightforward: We know that benefits outweigh the losses because of the law of comparative advantage. Free trade will increase output, real wages, and the standard of living for the entire trading world.

923

INTERNATIONAL TRADE: COMPARATIVE ADVANTAGE AND THE GAINS FROM TRADE   CHAPTER 35

But there is a catch. Once trade commences, some people will lose their jobs in the importing country, and some consumers in the exporting country will find that they cannot buy all that they used to at the old price. In order for the benefits of trade to be realized, resource reallocation must take place. Some workers in the cognac industry of Benistan will have to find jobs elsewhere; some consumers in Arcadia will have to find substitutes for cognac. In the real world, such adjustments can be quite costly, at least in the short run, and are often the basis for calls for trade restrictions.

The Impact of Tariffs

Figure 35.3 illustrates the general effects of an import tariff when the importing country is "small" relative to the market. A "small" country imports such a small portion of the world market that it cannot influence the world price of traded goods.[4] In this case, the importing country has imposed a 50¢ tax or **tariff** on each bushel of wheat that is imported. Tariffs raise the price of imported goods and reduce the volume of trade. In this case, the price rises from $4.00 to $4.50. The higher price reduces the quantity demanded so imports fall from 40 bushels (indicated by the dotted lines) to 20 units (indicated by the solid lines). The tariff also increases the domestic quantity supplied from 50 to 60 bushels. The shaded area in Figure 35.3 represents the tariff revenue collected by the government: 20 bushels of wheat are imported and each carries a tariff of 50¢, so total tariff revenue is $10.

Tariff A tax on imported goods.

The Impact of Quotas

Figure 35.3 can also be used to show the effects of quantity restrictions on imports, commonly known as **quotas**. Suppose that the government of the importing country decides that the domestic wheat farmers each tolerate only a certain amount of wheat imports, say, 20 bushels. To see how this would affect prices and the volume of trade, all we would need to do would be to find the quota distance between the demand and supply curves. In fact, we have already found this distance: it occurs where the $4.50 price line intersects the demand and supply curves. In other words, we could reduce the volume of imports by either instituting a quota or imposing a tariff of the right size.

Quota A restriction on the quantity of goods that can be imported.

Tariffs versus Quotas

But just because the same figure can be used to illustrate tariffs and quotas does *not* mean that they have the same effects on trade. Two important differences must be noted. First, tariffs only interfere with market incentives; quotas virtually eliminate market incentives. If the foreign wheat farmers could figure out a way to reduce the costs of production, they could lower prices and increase exports despite the tariff. Quotas allow no such activities; no matter how cost-efficient the foreign wheat

[4]This is obviously not the case in the Arcadia/Benistan example illustrated in Figure 35.2 because Arcadia and Benistan are the only countries in the world that consume this particular rare liquor. When tariffs are imposed in the "large country" case, the export price will fall by less than the tariff in the exporting country, and price will rise less than the tariff in the importing country.

FIGURE 35.3 THE EFFECT OF TARIFFS ON TRADE AND PRICES

Tariffs raise the price in the importing country and reduce the volume of trade. In this case, a 50¢ tariff is imposed on imports. This causes price to rise from the world price of $4.00 to $4.50. Higher prices cause consumption and imports to fall. The new level of consumption is 80, and imports fall from 40 to 20.

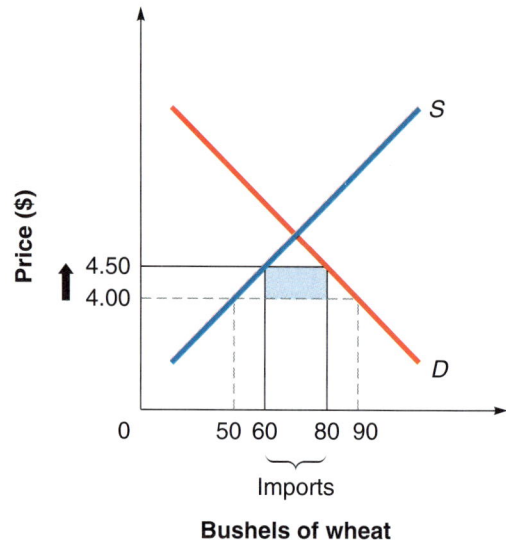

General Agreement on Tariffs and Trade (GATT) International body formed in 1947 to reduce tariff barriers and establish the rules for international trade.

farmers become, there is no way to increase exports to nations with quotas—and no way for the people in the importing countries to benefit from foreign production efficiencies. This is the main reason why the **General Agreement on Tariffs and Trade (GATT)**, an international body formed in 1947 to establish the rules of the game for international trade, is opposed to quotas under most circumstances. The Focus box on page 926 outlines some of GATT's more important accomplishments.

The other difference between tariffs and quotas relates to income distribution effects. When the government imposed the 50¢ tariff on each bushel of wheat that is imported, it collected tariff revenues in the amount indicated by the shaded rectangle. Presumably, this revenue could be used to retrain workers displaced by imports, provide for national defense, subsidize college professors' salaries, or even retire the national debt.[5] On the other hand, under a quota system, the rectangle would represent monopoly profits that went to the fortunate firms holding import licenses. The goods could be bought at the world price of $4.00 and, because of the quota, sold at a price of $4.50, thus earning the importer a monopoly profit.

It is not at all clear that the government could find a better use for the tariff revenues than the private sector, but neither is it clear that the monopoly profits should be given arbitrarily to businesses that happen to have import licenses. If quotas are used, the best option may be to auction off the import licenses to the highest bidder. Prospective importers should be willing to bid an amount equal to the economic profits they expected to make, and the government would then be free to spend the money in the public interest.

[5]Tariff revenues are less than 2 percent of the federal government's revenue, approximately $17 billion in 1992. This was not the case in the eighteenth and nineteenth centuries when tariffs were a major source of government revenue.

Nontariff Barriers

Quotas are just one kind of **nontariff barrier**; there are many other types, and in recent years, they have been used with increasing frequency to restrict imports and protect domestic industries. Government procurement policies that favor domestic producers are a common type of nontariff barrier. For example, the U.S. government's "Buy American" program is a nontariff barrier because it makes it difficult for foreign producers to sell to U.S. government agencies. Another example of a nontariff barrier is a French embargo on chickens that have been fed certain growth hormones. This restriction certainly protects French chicken farmers as much as public health. The United States used to have restrictions that prohibited importing Mexican tomatoes that were less than a certain diameter. This helped U.S. tomato farmers without violating GATT guidelines because no tomato-size guidelines existed. Other kinds of nontariff barriers include licensing fees that discriminate against foreign firms, restrictions on foreign investment, local content requirements that mandate the percentage of domestically made parts in certain goods, and voluntary export restrictions.[6] The wide variety of nontariff barriers should not disguise their impact on the economy. Like any trade restrictions, they reduce the volume of trade and raise the price of imported goods. They can also have secondary effects. For example, when Japanese auto producers agreed to a system of voluntary export restrictions in the early 1980s, they did not simply reduce the volume of autos exported to the United States; they also began shipping higher-quality, higher-priced automobiles. As a result, consumers had fewer low-price cars to choose from, and U.S. auto producers began to experience more competition in the upscale segment of the auto market. GATT has had difficulty developing general policies for dealing with nontariff barriers because they come in so many varieties.

Nontariff barriers Trade restrictions other than taxes on imports.

RECAP **Supply and Demand Analysis of Trade**

Complete specialization will not take place under increasing costs. Countries will import goods only as long as the price of imported goods is less than the price of domestically produced goods. Consumers in importing countries will gain but producers will lose; the reverse happens in exporting countries. As long as trade is voluntary, however, there will be mutual benefit, and world gains will outweigh world losses.

1. Tariffs reduce the volume of trade, raise prices in importing countries, and lower prices in exporting countries. Economists generally dislike trade restrictions but feel that tariffs are preferable to other trade restrictions because they do not completely suppress market forces.
2. Like tariffs, quotas affect prices and the volume of trade, but unlike tariffs, they completely suppress market incentives. Additionally, they guarantee a monopoly profit for the importer.
3. Nontariff barriers, including government procurement practices, licensing fees, and investment discrimination, have been used with increasing frequency in recent years. Like all trade restrictions, nontariff barriers reduce the volume of trade and lead to higher prices.

---

[6]You can find an extensive list of the foreign goods that American consumers are protected from in James Bovard, *The Free Trade Fraud* (New York: St. Martin's Press, 1991). Among the items Bovard lists are the dangers from foreign tomatoes, ice cream, women's underwear, roofing shingles, and motorcycle batteries.

FOCUS ON

THE GENERAL AGREEMENT ON TARIFFS AND TRADE

Soon after World War II, the United States and some of its trading partners met to set the postwar rules for international trade. The result, the General Agreement on Tariffs and Trade (GATT), was signed by 23 countries. GATT has more than 100 members today.

GATT is based on three basic principles: (1) unconditional most favored nation treatment, meaning that tariffs and tariff reductions should be applied in a nondiscriminatory fashion to all GATT members; (2) the reduction of tariffs through multilateral negotiations; and (3) the elimination of import quotas, with exceptions for agriculture and balance of payments considerations. Today, GATT's most important function is to provide a forum for settling trade disputes between member nations. Few would deny that GATT has been instrumental in reducing tariffs, but it has not been uncontroversial. For example, many developing nations have refused to join GATT because they believe that trade

rules favor the industrial nations and make it difficult for developing nations to become competitive in manufacturing and services.

GATT negotiations are referred to as "rounds." Some of the most important GATT rounds have been:

1964–1967, the Kennedy Round. President Kennedy pressed Congress for passage of the Trade Expansion Act in 1962. His concern was that the newly formed European Economic Community (EC) would erect a common external tariff to keep out imports from nonmember nations including the United States. The Trade Expansion Act gave the United States authority to enter into GATT-sponsored multilateral negotiations to reduce tariffs. Significant tariff reductions were achieved—on the order of 35 percent—and trade with the EC expanded. Partially because of trade liberalization following the Kennedy Round, Con-

gress passed the Trade Act of 1974. This act includes the now-infamous Section 301, which gives authority to the U.S. Trade Representative to retaliate with import restrictions when foreign nations are found to be engaging in unfair trade practices. In the spring of 1994, President Clinton threatened to reinstate Section 301 to force Japan to open its markets to U.S. cellular telephones.

1974–1979, the Tokyo Round. This round focused on nontariff barriers as well as tariffs. In the United States, tariffs on industrial products were reduced an average of 31 percent while tariffs on agricultural products fell 17 percent; similar cuts were approved by the EC, Japan, and Canada. Nontariff barrier reductions proved to be especially difficult for trade negotiations to deal with because they come in so many varieties—customs duties, government procurement practices, licensing fees, and so on. Still,

Japanese farmers protesting imported U.S. rice.

many nontariff barriers were reduced or eliminated following the Tokyo Round.

- *1986–1993, the Uruguay Round.* The Uruguay Round was the most ambitious round to date because it dealt with the tough issues of agriculture, services, and nontariff barriers. This may explain why the negotiations broke off in 1990, although they resumed the following year. The goal of free trade in agriculture is especially difficult to achieve because no nation wants to rely on imports for food. Perhaps the most noticeable accomplishment of the Uruguay Round related to agriculture was Japan's agreement to allow limited rice imports; previously, *all* rice imports were banned even though Japanese domestic rice prices are several times higher than the world price. Achieving free trade in services will be almost as difficult. Service industries are a sign of industrial development. Nearly everyone wants to develop their domestic service industries; few want to rely on imported services. The Uruguay Round was especially important for the United States because it leads the world in food and service exports.

GATT remains the major force in world trade policy, but it suffers from a serious weakness. Unlike the International Monetary Fund, which has the power to withhold loans, or the United Nations, which has military might, GATT has no power to enforce its recommendations. GATT will be successful only as long as its recommendations are fair and beneficial. Unfortunately, many GATT rules are routinely violated, and its inability to resolve sticky issues has led many to predict the death of GATT in the near future. The World Trade Organization will replace GATT when the Uruguay Round revisions are implemented in 1995.

THE POLITICS AND ECONOMICS OF TRADE RESTRICTIONS

The benefits of free trade may be obvious to most economists, but calls for tariffs and other restraints on trade are common among politicians and the public. Why is there so much disagreement? One answer is simply ignorance. Without an understanding of the law of comparative advantage, it seems "obvious" that rich nations must keep out products made with cheap foreign labor and that poor nations must guard against goods from the technological giants. Most economists reject these arguments, but there are other justifications for trade restraints that are more subtle.

The Costs of Trade Restrictions

Numerous studies have been conducted to estimate the costs of trade restrictions. The numbers are often startling. For example, the Reagan administration implemented voluntary export restraints (VERs) to protect the steel industry from foreign competition.[7] Under this program, traders agreed to "voluntarily" limit their steel exports to the United States. Notice, however, that fewer steel imports mean more expensive steel and higher costs for firms that use steel in their products but do not produce it themselves. Consequently, products made with steel became more expensive. A study by the U.S. Trade Commission concluded that consumers would have gained about $850 million had the steel VERs been eliminated in 1988.[8]

Voluntary export restraints were also applied to Japanese auto imports. In 1981, President Reagan asked the Japanese to "voluntarily" limit auto exports to the United States (the implicit threat that mandatory restrictions would be forthcoming if traders did not "voluntarily" restrict exports may have encouraged the spirit of voluntarism). Auto shipments for 1981 were set at 7.7 percent below the 1980 level and then allowed to grow by an amount equal to 16.5 percent of the increase in U.S. auto sales. In 1984, the United States released Japan from its informal agreement to limit exports, but Japan chose to continue the limits, believing that it would be impolitic to suddenly flood the weak U.S. economy with Japanese autos. It was estimated that the Japanese auto VERs raised the price of U.S. cars an average of $660; Japanese car prices rose an average of $1,300. Some 44,000 jobs were saved in the U.S. auto industry, but the cost of saving each job was estimated at nearly $80,000.[9] Most of this money went into the pockets of Japanese auto dealers and manufacturers.

---

[7]Steel VERs were only one step in a long history of trade protection for the steel industry. For example, the Carter administration used a system of trigger prices to initiate a Treasury Department investigation to determine whether foreigners were dumping steel on the U.S. market at unfair prices. While the investigation was in process, no steel could be imported.

[8]Data are from U.S. International Trade Commission, *The Economic Effects of Significant U.S. Import Restraints, Phase I: Manufacturing* (Washington, D.C.: U.S. Government Printing Office, 1989).

[9]Data are from U.S. International Trade Commission, *A Review of Recent Developments in the U.S. Automobile Industry Including an Assessment of the Japanese Voluntary Restraint Agreements* (Washington, D.C.: U.S. Government Printing Office, 1985).

With the cost of trade protection so high, why do politicians support such policies? One reason lies in the politics of interest groups. For example, automobile import quotas may help the auto industry, but they hurt society as a whole because they raise the price of automobiles and reduce consumer choice. However, the costs to society, while large, are spread so thinly that voters may not even recognize that they are hurt by import restrictions. At the same time, the benefits to individual workers are so large that they become active in the political process. Still, policymakers cannot say that they want to help one group at the expense of another; they need to rationalize that trade protection serves the public interest.

. . . .

Tariffs to Protect Infant Industries

One common argument for trade restrictions is the **infant industry** argument. According to this argument, "infant" industries need temporary trade restrictions to protect them from foreign competition until they can work out the early kinks inevitable to new business. Once the infant has grown up, protection is no longer needed, so the tariff is removed, or so the story goes.

Infant industry argument An argument justifying tariffs on the ground that new industries need protection during their early years.

There are several problems with the infant industry argument. First, it is never clear just which industry should be protected. Critics of the infant industry argument contend that only industries that can develop without government help will be successful. For example, in 1971 the Greek government made it illegal to import bananas on the mistaken belief that a little protection was all that was necessary to jump-start a tropical fruit industry on Crete, one of the Greek isles. The banana industry never took off because the climate on Crete is much too dry to support banana plantations. Another problem with tariff protection for infant industries is that the "temporary" assistance often becomes a permanent industrial subsidy. For example, even after it was clear that a banana industry could not survive on Crete, there was resistance to removing the import ban because Greek apple farmers argued that imported bananas would depress apple prices. Not until Greece joined the European Economic Community in 1981 was it possible to buy imported bananas legally in Greece—by that time a flourishing illegal market in bananas had been established.

A modern twist on the infant industry argument has been suggested by Lester Thurow and some other economists.[10] Consider the following: Every videocassette recorder (VCR) ever bought in the United States has been produced abroad. Given the foreign head start in VCR production, it is unlikely that any level of tariffs or industry subsidies could make a U.S. VCR industry competitive on international markets. So why should we even consider protection and subsidies for VCR makers? The answer is industrial learning. If U.S. firms learn how to make VCRs, they may be ready to produce the next round of consumer electronics—high-definition television, personal digital assistants, or whatever. If they do not learn how to make

---

[10]Thurow makes this and other (quite controversial!) arguments in his best-selling books, *The Zero-Sum Solution* (New York: Simon & Schuster, 1985) and *Head to Head* (New York: Morrow, 1992). Both books are well within the reach of introductory economics students and are highly recommended.

VCRs, the United States may lose out on future consumer electronics products. In this sense, it is not an infant VCR industry that is being protected, but an infant consumer electronics industry.

· · · · · · · ·

Decreasing-Cost Industries

Strategic trade policies Policies designed to protect decreasing-cost industries (often high-tech industries) until they are able to develop scale economies.

Another argument that has recently been used as an underpinning for trade policy is based on the economics of decreasing-cost industries. The average cost of production in some industries—especially high-tech industries—tends to decline as production expands. This suggests that nations may benefit from policies that prevent foreign competition long enough to allow the industry to enjoy scale economies. Trade policies designed to benefit decreasing-cost industries are often called **strategic trade policies**. Many nations have adopted strategic trade policies for their high-technology industries.

The decreasing-cost argument differs from the infant industry argument in an important way: policymakers do not have to search for infant industries that might develop comparative advantage in the future; all they have to do is to target industries shown to exhibit significant decreasing costs. The presence of decreasing costs may explain why most nations have some sort of protection for their high-tech industries. The catch is that not everyone can play this game; the first nation to establish a foothold in the decreasing-cost industry will have a leg up on everyone that follows. Further, there may be too many decreasing-cost industries to target. If so, deciding which industry to target is every bit as complicated as finding genuine "infant" industries. In addition, as with infant industries, it is difficult to remove protection from decreasing-cost industries once it is in place. Strategic trade policies are discussed in more detail in Chapter 37.

· · · · · · · ·

National Security

National security argument An argument justifying trade restrictions on the ground that certain industries are critical to the nation's defense and that the nation must maintain the capability to produce key products in case of war.

National security is often used as an argument for trade restrictions. In this view, certain industries are of such national importance that they must be protected, even if it is costly to do so. The steel industry is one such industry. In the years following World War II, world steel capacity increased, and many of the steel plants in the United States became obsolete. Had there been no restrictions on imported steel, many—perhaps most—U.S. steel firms would have gone out of business. Consumers would have enjoyed cheaper steel, but it would have been necessary to import steel for the defense industry—not a comforting thought in the event of war. The Focus box on software export restrictions provides another example of trade restrictions in the interest of national security. Another example of the national security argument is found in the "Counterproductive Energy Policies" Focus box in Chapter 17.

Economists cannot use cost-benefit analysis to refute the national security argument because it is impossible to measure the benefits of national security. This idea does have an interesting corollary, however: in a world of completely free trade, war would be less likely than it is today. With free trade, the volume of trade would expand and more specialization would take place. And as countries came to rely upon imports for needed goods and services, they would hesitate to go to war. It does not make sense to go to war against your market.

FOCUS ON

UNINTENDED CONSEQUENCES FROM TRADE RESTRICTIONS: SOFTWARE EXPORT RESTRICTIONS

Computer software is one of the growth areas in U.S. exports. U.S. corporations are the world leaders in software exports with many producers deriving a large portion of their revenues from international sales. Microsoft, the industry leader, earned 55 percent of its revenue from international sales in 1992. The potential export market is huge: the European software market is expected to be nearly $42 billion in 1995 compared to only $34 billion in the United States; the Japanese market should top $10 billion by 1995. Despite the difficulties of developing software in foreign languages, the prospect for continued U.S. domination in this important industry is bright—with one notable exception: software developers must deal with the National Security Agency almost every time they try to export a new product.[1]

The National Security Agency is most concerned about software encryption programs. Encryption programs are used to "scramble" data and make it difficult for unwanted eyes to

read confidential files. For example, if a firm is planning to introduce a new product, it may want to keep this information confidential until the introduction actually takes place. Encryption is standard procedure at many firms and is also a growth area in business software. The National Security Agency, however, is concerned that if encryption algorithms get out, foreign interests will use them to crack confidential U.S. government files. According to a Los Angeles attorney, "As far as the government is concerned, [encryption] is the same thing as bringing a nuclear bomb in a suitcase." Let's hope not because National Security Agency rules designed to prevent foreign access to U.S.-developed encryption software are simply not working. Encryption programs are sold on the street in Asia, can be purchased through the mail, and can be transferred across electronic mail networks. The only ones being hurt are the honest software exporters who must deal with National Security Agency red tape. Red tape costs money as firms jump through paperwork hoops and cripple encryption programs for export.

There is a certain irony to the National Security Agency rules on en-

cryption. Rules designed to protect national security may be sacrificing corporate security because U.S. corporate offices abroad are not permitted to use the same encryption programs they can use in their U.S. offices. If a U.S. corporation uses a computer network abroad without the security of an encryption program, it is open to corporate espionage from the host country. To avoid possible security leaks, many U.S. corporate offices abroad are buying foreign encryption software—software widely regarded as being inferior to U.S. software.

SOURCE: Gigi Bisson, "Global Software Expansion Is Hampered by Strict U.S. Laws," *MacWeek*, June 14, 1993, pp. 38–42.

[1]Hardware dealers must also apply for an export license when exporting computers that run faster than 50 MHz. The 50 MHz rule may have been reasonable in the past but hardly makes sense today, given that many off-the-shelf systems now run at 66 MHz and faster.

• • • • • • • •

Fair Trade versus Free Trade

Fair trade Term used by people who advocate tariffs or other measures as an incentive to get other nations to open their markets to our imports.

Dumping Selling goods abroad for less than the price they are sold for at home, after adjustment for transportation costs.

Persistent trade deficits with Japan and a few other countries have led to calls for **fair trade** instead of free trade. The basic argument is twofold: (1) foreign nations sell exports at unreasonably low prices, and (2) they refuse to buy our products.

Selling goods abroad at unreasonably low prices is called **dumping**. Technically, dumping occurs when foreign buyers are charged less than domestic buyers after adjustment for transportation costs and tariffs. While this sounds straightforward, actually detecting dumping can be difficult. For example, in industries with declining costs or excess capacity, it may make good sense to reduce prices as output expands into international markets. But even if price cuts really do cause a loss, they may make sense by providing an inexpensive employment program for the exporting nation. When the Department of Commerce determines that foreign goods are being sold in the United States at less than fair value, it levies an antidumping duty in addition to any normal tariffs. The United States has been both the dumpee and the dumper. Between 1980 and 1986, for example, GATT cited the United States for dumping 350 times; foreign nations were cited for dumping in the United States 112 times.

Why do foreigners refuse to buy our products? Sometimes our products are too expensive or of low quality. But we often have difficulty selling them for very different reasons, especially in the case of Japan. There is little doubt that Japan does play the international trade game differently than other nations. As we discussed in Chapters 19 and 34, Japanese *keiretsus* are cartel-like structures that link numerous firms. The *keiretsu* ethic is to buy from your friends—which obviously makes it difficult for foreign firms to enter the Japanese market. *Keiretsus* may be partially responsible for Japan's "economic miracle," but when loyalty means paying premium prices instead of buying imports, it is often called unfair trade. The key point is that the *keiretsu* ethic is a product of the Japanese *culture,* and trying to change a culture with economic arguments may be difficult.[11]

Some people—including officials within the Clinton administration who have argued for what they call "managed trade"—have advocated quantity restrictions on imports from Japan. For example, if the Japanese want to sell us $90 billion worth of goods, then they must buy at least $70 (or $80 or $90) billion worth of our goods. While this may be a short-term solution to trade difficulties, this kind of managed trade tends to stifle competitive pressure and can slow innovation.[12] Others have argued that we should threaten to impose substantial tariffs or quotas on Japanese imports unless they open their markets to specific U.S. exports. Calls to allow rice

---

[11]However, the disastrous 1993 growing season and resulting anemic rice crop show that economic incentives can be powerful. Japanese rice costs 7 times as much as U.S. rice, but rigid import restrictions have kept out U.S. rice, ostensibly to protect Japanese rice farmers but also to prevent reliance upon imported food. The Japanese government allowed what was meant to be one-time U.S. rice imports in 1993 when domestic stocks became dangerously low. Later that year, the Japanese agreed to a small amount of imported rice as part of the Uruguay Round of the GATT negotiations.
[12]This point is made by, among others, Michael E. Porter in his best-selling *The Competitive Advantage of Nations* (New York: Free Press, 1990). Porter is a Professor of Business at Harvard. *The Competitive Advantage of Nations* was listed by *Business Week* as one of the best business books of 1990; it is well-written and thought-provoking enough to be considered a classic.

and other U.S. agricultural exports and to permit U.S. construction firms to bid on building projects have been heard frequently. Unfortunately, the prospect for free trade in agriculture is especially remote: Would *you* want to rely on the vagaries of international politics for your next meal? This is distressing for the leading agricultural exporter in the world, the United States.

Income Distribution Effects

Still another argument for trade restrictions rests on the impact of trade liberalization on income distribution. There is growing evidence that recent moves toward free trade have tended to widen the income gap between the rich and the poor. As Figure 35.4 shows, trade affects people with lower education and skill levels much more than people with more education and skills. The result has been an increase in the real wages of professional workers and a decrease in real wages for nonprofessional workers. Income distribution effects were one of the main sticking points in the passage of the North American Free Trade Agreement, a topic discussed in more detail in Chapter 37.

Income distribution may be at the basis of trade policies in the textile industry. The U.S. textile industry has faced stiff competition since the 1950s when Japan accounted for over half of all textile imports. Beginning in 1957, a series of voluntary export restraints and multilateral agreements were signed to stabilize the textile market. In 1974, 50 nations agreed to the **Multifiber Arrangement**. The Multifiber Arrangement set the standards for bilateral agreements between textile trading countries. In 1990, the United States had bilateral agreements with Hong Kong, Taiwan, and South Korea, three countries that accounted for over 80 percent of all textile

Multifiber Arrangement Agreement signed in 1974 by 50 nations that set the standards for bilateral arrangements between textile trading countries.

•••• FIGURE 35.4 EDUCATION AND EMPLOYMENT IN TRADE-SENSITIVE INDUSTRIES

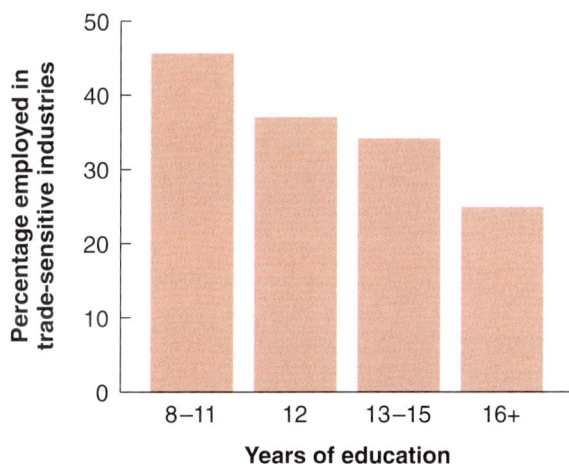

SOURCE: Aaron Bernstein, Walecia Konrad, and Lois Therrien, "The Global Economy: Who Gets Hurt?" *Business Week,* August 10, 1992, pp. 48–53.

imports. There is little doubt that in the absence of trade restrictions, foreign producers could supply most of the textile needs of U.S. consumers, and at considerably lower prices. Under terms of the Uruguay Round, the Multifiber Arrangement will be phased out by the year 2005.

How does the Multifiber Arrangement relate to income distribution? Many of the people working in the textile and apparel industries in the United States have little education and job skills that are not readily transferable to other jobs. Some of these workers are immigrants who speak little English. Without import restrictions, many of these people would lose their jobs and require welfare and/or job training. Limiting textile imports may be an inexpensive way to help these people.

RECAP   Trade Restraints

Many economists favor free trade, but politicians, the public, and some economists often call for tariffs or restraints on trade. Some of the main arguments for trade restrictions include:

1. Trade restrictions often hurt members of the whole society only a small amount but help members of special interest groups a large amount. These groups often lobby for trade restrictions.
2. Some people feel that tariffs are necessary to help infant industries. Doing so can present two problems: deciding which industries to protect can be difficult, and the temporary protection is often not removed and becomes a permanent subsidy.
3. Some industries receive trade protection for national security purposes. Protection of the steel and petroleum industries is often justified on national security grounds.
4. In the United States, there have been recent calls for "fair trade" as opposed to "free trade." This call is based on the argument that foreign countries dump their products on U.S. markets and refuse to buy U.S. exports.
5. There is some evidence that free trade results in adverse effects on income distribution. This has been used as a rationale for calls to protect certain low-wage industries.

SUMMARY

International trade is probably subject to more misunderstanding than any other area in economics. The person on the street may fear foreign competition for lack of understanding; others contend that international trade increases world output and raises everyone's standard of living. Most economists are opposed to trade restrictions, though some have argued that tariff protection may be necessary to enforce fair trade practices or to encourage production in decreasing-cost industries. The main points to remember from this chapter are:

1. The international sector of the U.S. economy has grown substantially over the past 30 years. Major trading partners of the United States include Canada, Japan,

Mexico, and Western Europe. About 80 percent of our trade involves manufactured goods.

2. All nations gain from free trade. World output increases and incomes rise due to specialization. Most criticisms of free trade derive from the fact that resources are reallocated as trade commences so some people are forced to change jobs. The main inducements for trade include price differentials and the demand for product variety.

3. The gains from trade can be analyzed with production possibility curve (PPC) analysis. Countries should produce and export goods that can be produced with low relative opportunity costs; they should import goods that can be produced only with high relative opportunity costs. The slope of the PPC gives the pretrade relative opportunity costs of production. When two nations have PPCs with different slopes, there are possibilities of gains from trade. The slope of the consumption possibilities curve (CPC) gives the terms of trade.

4. When costs are increasing, complete specialization will not take place. Price will rise in exporting countries and fall in importing countries. Producers in importing countries and consumers in exporting countries are hurt by trade; producers in exporting countries and consumers in importing countries gain from trade. However, economic theory suggests that the gains from free trade outweigh the losses.

5. Many economists dislike most trade restrictions, but do favor tariffs over quotas because tariffs preserve some elements of competition while quotas eliminate most market incentives. Tariffs also raise revenue for the government while quotas generate monopoly profits for people holding import licenses. Nontariff barriers include licensing fees, procurement practices, and voluntary export restrictions. Nontariff barriers have been used with increasing frequency in recent years.

6. Trade restrictions reduce the volume of trade and raise prices in the importing country. Trade restrictions are often the product of lobbying by special interest groups. Some arguments for trade restrictions include the infant industry argument, the presence of decreasing costs, national security, the plea for "fair" trade, and the effect of trade on income distribution.

KEY TERMS AND CONCEPTS

defensive foreign investment
mutual benefit
price differentials
resource endowments
product variety
labor theory of value
absolute advantage
comparative advantage
specialization
gains from trade
terms of trade
production possibilities curve (PPC)
consumption possibilities curve (CPC)

tariff
quota
General Agreement on Tariffs and Trade (GATT)
income distribution
nontariff barriers
voluntary export restrictions
infant industry argument
strategic trade policies
national security argument
fair trade
dumping
Multifiber Arrangement

REVIEW QUESTIONS

1. Why do nations trade? Explain how price differentials, resource endowments, and the demand for product variety give rise to international trade.
2. Who are the major trading partners of the United States? What are the main kinds of goods that are imported and exported? How has the trade sector of the U.S. economy grown over the past 50 years?
3. State the law of comparative advantage and use it to explain why all nations can gain from free trade.
4. Using supply and demand analysis, explain why trade will commence between two nations and why complete specialization is unlikely.
5. Using supply and demand analysis, illustrate how tariffs and quotas affect the volume of trade, domestic prices, and world prices. Why do economists generally prefer tariffs to nontariff barriers?
6. Policymakers have frequently advocated tariffs based on the infant industry argument, the existence of decreasing costs, national security, and the belief that "fair" trade may not be synonymous with "free" trade. Analyze these arguments from both a political and an economic perspective.

PROBLEMS

1. The North American Free Trade Agreement will phase in free trade between the United States, Canada, and Mexico. Do you think an automobile worker should be fearful of this agreement? Why or why not? Should a college professor be concerned about the agreement? Why or why not?
2. In 1991, almost 90 percent of the merchandise imports into the United States were from Canada, Japan, and Western Europe, nations with comparable standards of living. Do you think most of this trade was induced by price differentials or the demand for product variety? Explain.
3. The following table shows the output from one unit of labor in Armenia and Belorussia. Answer the following questions using this information:

	Armenia	Belorussia
Xylophones	1	2
Yo-yos	2	3

   a. Which country has an absolute advantage in xylophone production? In yo-yo production?
   b. Which country has a comparative advantage in xylophone production? In yo-yo production?
   c. Once trade commences, which country will export xylophones? Yo-yos?
   d. Suppose that before trade commences, each country devotes 50 workers to each industry. What is world output?
   e. Now, suppose that complete specialization takes place, and assume that each country has 100 workers. What is world output?
   f. Draw the PPC curves for both nations.
   g. What are the terms of trade inequalities?

    h. Using words, explain why the terms of trade $1.8Y = 1X$ would be attractive to both Armenia and Belorussia.

    i. Draw the CPC curves and indicate the potential gains from trade based on the terms of trade $1.8Y = 1X$.

4. Using supply and demand curves, illustrate:

    a. why free trade causes the price of automobiles to fall in the United States.

    b. why U.S. auto producers and U.S. auto consumers have different perspectives on the advantages of free trade.

    c. the revenue collected by the U.S. government from a tariff on imported automobiles.

    d. the amount of monopoly profits earned by importers under a system of quotas.

5. What is the difference between the infant industry argument for tariffs and strategic trade policy?

6. Consumers would seem to benefit when other nations dump their goods at artificially low prices. So why don't we just ignore nations stupid enough to dump their goods at a loss?

7. Refer back to Figure 35.1 and the accompanying information. Assume that the terms of trade are $1W = 1.6C$ and U.S. preferences are such that only 80 units of cheese are needed, then:

    a. determine the pretrade and posttrade production and consumption in the US.

    b. determine the pretrade and posttrade production and consumption in the UK.

    c. write out the equation for the US and UK PPC and CPC and show how this equation can be used to solve for the answers in parts (*a*) and (*b*).

8. Footnote 4 stated that in the "large country" case, the selling price in the exporting country will fall if a tariff is imposed in the importing country. Illustrate this result using graphs like those in Figure 35.2. Explain your result and why it might apply to the Arcadia/Benistan example.

9. The United States has laws to prop up the price of imported sugar, most of which comes from small countries in Central America and the Caribbean. Part of the reason for these laws is to protect U.S. sugar producers, but another reason is national security. Sugar is obviously not a strategic good like oil or certain metals used in weapons. Can you explain why interference in the free trade in sugar might be related to national security?

10. Explain and comment: Free trade would be more viable politically if the nation were more highly educated. (*Hint:* The answer is not just that educated people would understand economics!)

CHAPTER 36

International Finance: The Balance of Payments and Exchange Rates

The volume of international financial capital flows swamps the volume of international trade: nearly $200 billion in foreign capital flows across international boundaries *every day*. As you might expect, more than a few people make it their business to profit from international capital flows. Many investment houses keep their offices open around the clock so they can buy and sell currencies in markets around the world. A number of traders became millionaires in the 1980s—but at least as many lost their shirts too!

What caused the financial capital movement? Much of it was the result of increasing investment by multinational corporations as they looked for the most profitable locations for setting up shop. Another source was the fiscal deficit of the United States: with the government running deficits in excess of $200 billion per year, it had to borrow money, and much of this money came from abroad. The trade deficit was also a source of the capital flows: the only way the United States could import more goods and services than it exported was by borrowing money from abroad—which it did to the tune of some $100 billion per year during some years in the 1980s.

Finally, much of the capital flow was pure speculation: with exchange rates fluctuating widely, there were ample opportunities for speculative gains. For example, if speculators had a hunch that the dollar would increase ("appreciate") in value, they would buy dollars with foreign currencies. Later, when the dollar had appreciated, they would sell the dollars for more currency than they had used to buy the dollars originally. Of course, if the dollar lost value ("depreciated"), such transactions resulted in a loss. Exchange rate fluctuations may provide jobs for currency speculators, but they also increase the risks associated with international trade. In fact, the extreme volatility of exchange rates over the past 20 years has been one of the chief puzzles international economists have sought to explain.

What causes exchange rate fluctuations? Are capital flows a cause for concern? Should we be concerned about persistent trade deficits? These are the main issues we will look at in this chapter.

AFTER READING AND STUDYING THIS CHAPTER, YOU SHOULD BE ABLE TO:
- • • • Discuss balance of payments accounting, and distinguish between current account and capital account transactions
- • • • Outline the Bretton Woods system and explain why it collapsed
- • • • Use supply and demand analysis to show how market forces influence exchange rates
- • • • Illustrate why and how governments intervene to support their currencies
- • • • Explain how the exchange rate regime affects fiscal and monetary policies

BALANCE OF PAYMENTS ACCOUNTING

Balance of payments A record of transactions between one nation and the rest of the world.

The **balance of payments** is a record of international transactions between one country and the rest of the world. A *credit* is recorded on the balance of payments when money flows into the domestic economy. Important credit items for the United States include exports of goods and services, foreign tourism in the United States, the returns from past foreign investments, and the purchase of U.S. assets by foreigners. Transactions that result in money outflows are recorded as *debits* on the balance of payments. Major debit items are imports of goods and services, U.S. tourism abroad, and the purchase of foreign assets by U.S. citizens.

Double-Entry Accounting

The balance of payments is recorded as a double-entry accounting system so it is always in balance. This system is sometimes confusing, so a few examples might be helpful:

- Suppose that Apple Computer sells a computer to Japan for $5,000. The computer export is recorded as a merchandise trade credit because the United States will receive the $5,000 payment. The actual payment to Apple Computer is called a short-term capital flow because the United States has "imported" a claim against a Japanese bank.
- Suppose that a U.S. citizen owns stock in a German company and receives a dividend check of $1,000. The dividend payment is treated as a credit on the balance of payments because the $1,000 flows into the United States. It is also considered a debit because the German company no longer owes that $1,000 to the United States; in other words, the United States has "imported" a $1,000 short-term capital asset.
- Finally, suppose that a U.S. tourist travels to Scotland and spends $20,000 in search of the Loch Ness monster. This would generate a $20,000 debit because the U.S. tourist has purchased the joy of travel and adventure from Scotland; it would also

generate a credit because $20,000 worth of checks would have been "exported" to Scotland to pay for that adventure.

• • • • • • • •

Structure of the Balance of Payments

The balance of payments is always in balance so it does not really make sense to talk about a "deficit on the balance of payments"—despite what you may hear on the radio or read in the newspaper. However, the balance of payments is divided into subaccounts, and these accounts can have a deficit or surplus.

The **current account** is a record of the monetary value of the flows associated with the trade in goods, services, and unilateral transfers. Within the current account, the **merchandise trade account** records the physical goods that are imported and exported. The *services account* covers several kinds of items including money spent at foreign restaurants and hotels, transportation, legal services, and computer software. Dividends and interest payments on foreign investments are also included in the services account. Finally, the unilateral transfers account records one-sided transactions, primarily private gifts and government grants.

Table 36.1 presents recent data for the U.S. current account. Most of these data should make sense—the United States imported more goods and services than it exported, earned more investment income than it paid out, and so on. But what about the $60 billion in foreign cash grants that the United States received between 1990 and 1991? These grants were payments from allies for the U.S. costs of fighting the Gulf War. Notice that these grants make the current account deficit less than it would have been otherwise. Figure 36.1 plots the U.S. current account balance over the period 1960–1992. As is readily apparent, the current account balance showed a slight surplus until the 1980s when the United States began to experience large deficits. In 1987, the current account deficit topped $160 billion.

The **capital account** measures the purchase and sale of assets—stocks and bonds, government securities, and bank deposits, as well as titles to real estate and factories. It includes transactions by both the private and the public sector: official capital

Current account A subaccount of the balance of payments that records the monetary value of the flows associated with the movement of goods and services, as well as transfer payments, across international boundaries.

Merchandise trade account A subaccount of the current account of the balance of payments that records imports and exports of goods.

Capital account A subaccount of the balance of payments that records the flow of financial capital across international boundaries.

• • • • **TABLE 36.1** U.S. CURRENT ACCOUNT, 1987–1992

	1987	1988	1989	1990	1991	1992
Goods and services, net	−151	−114	−90	−77	−28	−41
Merchandise trade balance	−160	−127	−116	−109	−73	−96
Service transactions, net	8	13	26	32	45	55
Investment income, net	11	12	14	19	16	10
Direct investment, net	31	39	48	54	53	49
Portfolio investment, net	−20	−26	−34	−35	−37	−39
Unilateral transfers, net	−23	−25	−26	−33	8	−31
Foreign cash grants to United States	0	0	0	17	43	1
Other transfers	−23	−25	−26	−50	−35	−33
Current account balance	−163	−127	−101	−90	−4	−62

SOURCE: *Federal Reserve Bulletin* (May 1993): 380. Data are in billions of current dollars.

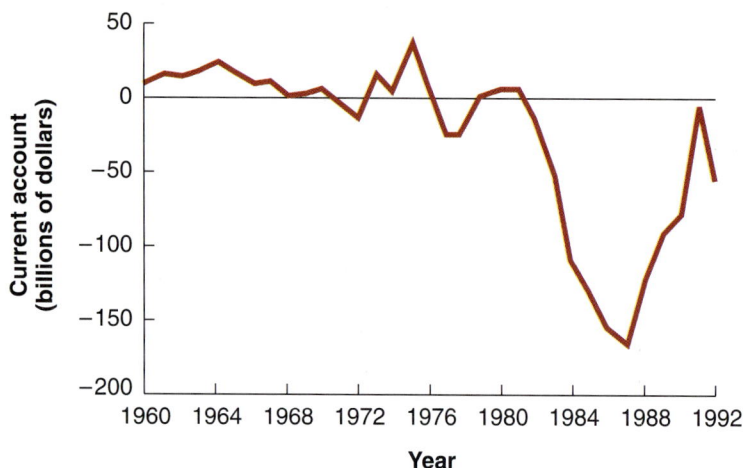

•••• FIGURE 36.1 THE U.S. CURRENT ACCOUNT, 1960–1992

The U.S. current account was in rough balance in the 1960s and 1970s but fell into significant deficits in the 1980s. Double-entry bookkeeping of the balance of payments means that the capital account plus the current account is approximately zero. Thus, a time series graph of the capital account balance would be a mirror image of this figure.

SOURCE: 1994 *Economic Report of the President,* Tables B-3, and B-103. Data are in billions of constant 1987 dollars.

transactions are carried out by governments; private capital transactions are conducted by private business. Capital transactions are recorded as a credit when they result in money inflows and a debit when they result in outflows. This means that the purchase of a foreign factory by a U.S. corporation is a debit on the capital account. If the purchase is a profitable one, however, the future profits paid to the U.S. corporation will be treated as credits on the current account. Recent data for the U.S. capital account are presented in Table 36.2.

A subaccount of the capital account is the **official settlements account** or official reserve assets account. The main components of the official settlements account are official reserve assets and liabilities to foreign agencies. Transactions on this account are often designed to influence the exchange rate, an issue we will discuss later in the chapter.

A quick comparison of Lines 1 and 4 of Table 36.2 shows that the current capital accounts almost balance out—deficits on the current account correspond to surpluses on the capital account. This is not just coincidence: double-entry bookkeeping requires that the balance of payments be in balance, so a surplus on one account must be countered by a deficit on another account. If the two accounts do not balance, there must be a statistical discrepancy. Economists cannot say with certainty what kind of transactions account for the statistical discrepancy (otherwise, they would not be discrepancies!), but they generally agree that much of the statistical discrepancy consists of short-term capital flows because these flows are the hardest to detect.[1] A

Official settlements account A subaccount of the capital account that records official reserve assets and liabilities to foreign agencies.

---

[1] The especially large statistical discrepancy in 1990 is probably due to erratic interest rates and fluctuating exchange rates that resulted in large short-term international capital flows. Such flows are often difficult to detect.

•••• **Table 36.2 U.S. Capital Account, 1988–1992**

	1988	1989	1990	1991	1992
1. Current account balance	−127	−101	−90	−4	−62
2. Official capital, net	39	−16	34	28	43
Foreign official assets in United States	40	9	34	18	40
U.S. official reserve assets	−4	−25	−2	6	4
Other U.S. government assets	3	1	2	3	−1
3. Private capital, net	88	114	9	−23	32
Net inflows reported by U.S. banks	14	12	24	−18	47
Securities transactions, net	35	42	−35	7	14
U.S. Treasury securities	20	30	−3	16	35
U.S. corporate bonds	23	27	11	27	32
U.S. corporate stocks	−1	7	−15	9	−5
Direct investment, net	45	43	17	−17	−37
Foreign direct investment in United States	57	68	45	12	−4
U.S. direct investment abroad	−12	−25	−28	−28	−33
Other	−7	17	2	5	8
4. Capital account balance	127	99	43	5	75
Statistical discrepancy	0	2	47	−1	−13

NOTE: The balance on the capital account is found by summing Lines 2 and 3. The difference between the current account and the capital account may differ from the statistical discrepancy due to rounding.

SOURCE: *Federal Reserve Bulletin* (May 1993): 387. Data are in billions of current dollars.

time series plot of the capital account balance would look like a mirror image of the current account time series plot in Figure 36.1.

Should We Worry about Surpluses and Deficits?

The persistent deficit on the current account has been a cause for concern in recent years. Two basic arguments have been advanced regarding this deficit. First, many economists believe that the current account deficit is the result of misguided macroeconomic policies—specifically, the fiscal deficit—that have inflated the value of the dollar relative to foreign currencies and made imports cheap for U.S. citizens. This leads to increased imports and a deficit on the merchandise trade balance. If fiscal policies are the cause of the current account deficit, the solution is simple: put the fiscal house in order. The other argument is that U.S. industry is becoming less competitive in international markets so that foreigners do not demand U.S. goods. This would suggest that simply putting the fiscal house in order is an insufficient solution. Many people, however, believe that the problem is not the current account deficit, but its mirror image, the capital account surplus.

Should we be concerned about the capital account surplus? Again there are multiple arguments. Some economists believe that a capital account surplus is an indication of the strength of the domestic economy: Why would anyone lend us money or invest in our economy if they did not believe that our economy was fundamentally strong? Foreign capital inflows provide funds for corporate expansion. Other economists are not so sanguine. Large international capital inflows into the United States represent equally large capital outflows from other nations. Capital outflows reduce the liquidity available for investment and growth abroad. To prevent capital outflows, nations are forced to maintain high interest rates, which reduce economic growth in the world economy. Second, although foreign capital inflows have certainly been helpful in financing large government deficits and private investment, the only reason to invest in the U.S. economy is to earn profits and interest returns. Capital inflows today will mean capital outflows tomorrow; how these outflows will affect the U.S. economy in the future is not clear. Finally, large capital inflows raise the specter of an equally large and sudden capital flight. Fear of recession or depreciation of the dollar could cause foreign investors to withdraw their funds as quickly as they deposited them. A sudden withdrawal of foreign capital could drive up interest rates and destabilize financial markets. Such concerns were voiced throughout the 1980s, but the feared destabilizing capital flight did not occur.

RECAP   Balance of Payments Accounting

The balance of payments is a record of the international transactions between one country and the rest of the world. It is based on double-entry bookkeeping, so it is always in balance. Deficits and surpluses can exist in subaccounts of the balance of payments, however. Transactions that result in funds flowing into the country are treated as credits; transactions that result in funds flowing out of the country are counted as debits.

1. The current account records imports and exports of goods and services, as well as the flow from past investments. The United States has had persistent current account deficits for more than a decade.
2. The merchandise trade balance records only the import and export of goods; it does not include the flow from past investments. Most of the deficit on the current account has been due to the merchandise trade balance.
3. The capital account is a record of international capital flows. Foreign investment in the United States counts as a credit on the capital account; U.S. investment abroad is a debit on the capital account. The United States has had a surplus on the capital account for over a decade. The current account deficits of recent years have been mirrored by capital account surpluses.
4. Some people are concerned about the current account deficit and capital account surpluses. The current account deficit may indicate an increasing reliance upon foreign goods and declining international competitiveness; however, it may also be the result of inappropriate macroeconomic policies. Foreign investment in the United States can create jobs and help finance the government deficit, but it also means that there will be outflows in the future.

A BRIEF HISTORY OF EXCHANGE RATE POLICY

One of the reasons international finance is in the news so much these days is that the dollar exchange rate has been quite volatile. For example, between 1990 and 1993, the dollar depreciated nearly 30 percent against the Japanese yen as the exchange rate fell from about 145 yen to the dollar to about 110. This is a tremendous decline. Think how you would feel if you were an automobile importer: after signing a contract to buy 1,000 Japanese automobiles for ¥1,450,000 each (= $10,000), you suddenly discover that you are obligated to pay $13,181 (= 1,450,000/110) per car. You are paying the same yen price, but a much higher dollar price. Can you still sell those cars at a profit? Perhaps, but maybe not. You have just experienced one of the major risks of international trade, something economists call **exchange rate risk**. Exchange rate risk is reduced under a system of fixed exchange rates. The gold standard and the Bretton Woods system were both fixed exchange rate systems.

Exchange rate risk The risk associated with exchange rate fluctuations.

The Gold Standard

The major countries of the world operated on the **gold standard** between the 1870s and 1914 and then briefly again between the two world wars. Trading nations agreed to exchange their currencies for gold at a fixed rate. That way, traders had the option of using either gold or currencies for international transactions and could avoid exchange rate risk. Fixed exchange rates may eliminate exchange rate risk, but they do something just as bad: they remove the influence of market forces on exchange rates. This can result in serious balance of payments difficulties. One of the worst cases occurred in Great Britain following World War I. During the war, international trade had ground to a virtual halt, and the trading nations suspended gold conversions. After the war, Great Britain (and many other nations) reestablished the gold standard with the exchange rates that prevailed before the war. During and immediately after the war, however, Great Britain had experienced so much inflation that British goods were no longer competitive on international markets. In a system of flexible exchange rates, the British pound would have depreciated. This would have lowered the price of British goods on international markets and raised the price of British imports. However, the prewar exchange rate meant that imports were cheap to British citizens—so cheap that Great Britain experienced a massive trade imbalance and fell into recession. The opposite occurred in the United States: relatively low inflation during World War I meant that the dollar was undervalued when the gold standard was restored. As a result, the United States experienced an export boom and cyclical expansion—a major cause of the Roaring Twenties.

Gold standard A monetary system in which currency is backed by a fixed amount of gold and exchange rates are fixed.

The Bretton Woods System

Modern exchange rate history—and the basis for the current system of international finance—began in the waning months of World War II at Bretton Woods, New Hampshire. Leaders from the Allied powers of World War II met at Bretton Woods in 1944 to establish the rules of the game for international finance after the war.[2] The result was a program that contained elements of prewar fixed exchange rates with some flexibility designed to eliminate the rigidities that had led to periodic crises under the gold standard.

The **Bretton Woods** system had three major elements. First, the dollar was

Bretton Woods System International monetary system based on a dollar exchange standard and the maintenance of exchange rates within a narrow range; also established the International Monetary Fund and the World Bank.

[2]The Soviet Union attended the Bretton Woods Conference but did not sign the Bretton Woods Agreement.

Dollar exchange standard Name given to the exchange rate system established by the Bretton Woods Agreement: the dollar was tied to gold, and all member currencies were tied to the dollar.

International Monetary Fund (IMF) Organization created under the Bretton Woods system. Lends money to member nations in the event of short-term balance of payments difficulties.

World Bank International bank established following the Bretton Woods conference. Its primary role is to provide low-interest development loans to less-developed nations.

Devaluation bias The main reason for the failure of the Bretton Woods system. Nations experiencing trade deficits were willing to devalue their currencies, but nations with trade surpluses were unwilling to revalue their currencies because it would cause an economic slowdown at home.

Dollar shortage Period in the 1950s when the dollar was undervalued under the Bretton Woods system.

assigned the role of key currency and tied to gold at a rate of $35 per ounce of gold. The other currencies were tied to the dollar, not gold, at a fixed or *par value*. Because the United States agreed to exchange dollars for gold, however, other currencies were tied to gold via what came to be known as the **dollar exchange standard**.

The second element of the Bretton Woods system was the agreement that nations would attempt to maintain fixed exchange rates by using their reserves of international currencies to finance temporary international deficits. Only in the case of fundamental disequilibrium were nations allowed to adjust their exchange rates more than 10 percent. A fundamental disequilibrium was defined as a long-run, continuous trade deficit that could not be reversed by domestic policies.

Finally, two important international institutions grew out of the Bretton Woods Conference, the **International Monetary Fund (IMF)** and the International Bank of Reconstruction and Development, often referred to as the **World Bank**. The main purpose of the IMF was to provide short-term balance of payments loans. Most of these loans were intended to be used to prevent currency depreciation. The World Bank was set up to provide long-term loans for economic development. Both institutions still exist today and wield considerable influence over the global economy. They have also been the subject of controversy: IMF loans have been subject to *conditionality* since the 1970s. This typically means that money is lent to a nation experiencing balance of payments difficulties only on the condition that the nation enact *austerity measures*—deficit reductions or other measures that often lead to domestic recession. In recent years, World Bank and IMF loans to the formerly socialist nations have often been granted only after the nation shows evidence of making a rapid transition to capitalism.[3]

The End of Bretton Woods

The Bretton Woods system performed reasonably well—for about 20 years. The volume of international trade grew dramatically, and the war-ravaged nations were able to recover. Inherent in the system, however, was a serious **devaluation bias** because nations were willing to devalue their currencies, but not to revalue them. Why? If a country was experiencing a current account deficit, devaluation would reduce imports, increase exports, and stimulate the domestic economy. Countries experiencing persistent trade surpluses were supposed to revalue their currencies. The problem was that revaluation could be painful because a stronger currency would result in fewer exports, more imports, and recession at home. Few politicians were willing to enact such measures. As a result, some nations—particularly Japan and West Germany—experienced persistent surpluses while the United States began to experience persistent deficits in the 1960s. Why didn't the United States simply devalue the dollar? It couldn't. The Bretton Woods system was based on a fixed dollar/gold price, and any deviation would spell the end of the system.

The existence of a devaluation bias was not apparent until the 1960s. The dollar was undervalued in the 1950s. This resulted in what has come to be known as the **dollar shortage** era. Europe and Japan needed dollars to buy American capital goods so they could rebuild their economies. The United States maintained a persistent

---

[3]This is the "shock therapy" approach to economic transition discussed in Chapter 34.

trade surplus while West Germany, Japan, and many other nations had trade deficits. By the early 1960s, however, the situation had changed. Most nations had recovered from the war and no longer needed to import as many American goods. As demand for dollars and U.S. goods fell, the dollar shortage became a **dollar glut**. The dollar was now overvalued. Foreigners did not want or need dollars, so they did what they were permitted to do under the Bretton Woods Agreement: they exchanged their dollars for gold, and gold began to flow out of the United States. Cries to "Stop the gold flow" began to be heard in the United States.

Dollar glut Period in the 1960s and early 1970s when the dollar was overvalued under the Bretton Woods system.

The Smithsonian Agreement

The disequilibria of the Bretton Woods system came to a head in 1971: holding dollars it did not want, France threatened to exchange all of its dollars for gold, knowing full well that the United States did not have enough gold to cover such a transaction. Other nations appeared to be ready to follow suit, but President Nixon made a speech on Friday, August 13, stating that the Bretton Woods system was fundamentally sound. Two days later, after the world financial markets had closed, President Nixon made another speech that was to mark the beginning of the end of Bretton Woods: he announced that he was suspending gold payments and allowing the dollar to float on international currency markets. Three months later, the Group 10 nations—the 10 largest noncommunist industrial nations in the world—met in Washington, D.C., and signed the **Smithsonian Agreement**. This agreement devalued the dollar about 9 percent by raising the dollar price of gold from $35 to $38 per ounce. Some nations—including West Germany and Japan—agreed to supplemental revaluations of their currencies so the average devaluation of the dollar against the Group 10 was about 12 percent.

Smithsonian Agreement Agreement signed in 1971 that devalued the dollar in an effort to salvage the Bretton Woods system. The effort failed, however, and in 1973 currencies were allowed to float, ending the Bretton Woods system of fixed exchange rates.

The initial optimism aroused by the Smithsonian Agreement proved to be misplaced. The United States experienced a large trade deficit in 1972, and the dollar was devalued another 10 percent in February 1973, but uncertainty persisted in the international financial markets. A month later exchange rates were allowed to float, and the Bretton Woods system was history.

RECAP **The Bretton Woods System**

The Bretton Woods system was established in 1944 to set the rules of the game for international finance. The main components of the system were:

1. *Fixed exchange rates.* All member nations agreed to tie their currencies to the dollar and resist significant changes except in the case of "fundamental disequilibrium."
2. *Dollar exchange standard.* Only the dollar was tied to gold, but all nations could trade their currencies for dollars and then buy gold at a rate of $35 per ounce from the United States.
3. *Devaluation bias.* The intent of the system was for nations to revalue in the event of a persistent trade surplus or devalue in the event of a persistent trade deficit. However, the surplus nations resisted revaluation. This led to balance of payments problems for the United States in the late 1960s and early 1970s.
4. *Smithsonian Agreement.* After attempts to devalue the dollar and revalue the

currencies of the surplus nations in 1971 and 1972, the Bretton Woods system was abandoned in 1973, and currencies were allowed to float.

FLEXIBLE EXCHANGE RATES

The problem with fixed exchange rates was simple: exchange rates are prices, and prices must reflect market conditions. If not, shortages or surpluses will occur. The Bretton Woods system recognized this problem by building in a mechanism for adjusting exchange rates, but the devaluation bias made this mechanism ineffective. As we are about to see, when exchange rates are allowed to adjust to market forces, the tendency for persistent balance of payments disequilibria is reduced, but not always eliminated.

The Market for Foreign Exchange

In the absence of government intervention, exchange rates are determined by the forces of supply and demand, just like most prices. As shown in Figure 36.2, the demand curve for foreign currency is downward sloping, and the supply curve is upward sloping. The intersection between the supply and demand curves gives the equilibrium exchange rate. Changes in demand and supply will cause the exchange rate to rise or fall.

What is the reasoning behind the curves drawn in the figure? In panel (a), the demand for dollars represents the demand for dollar-denominated goods, services, and financial assets by the British. When dollars are expensive—say, each dollar costs one pound sterling ($1.00 = £1.00)—then dollar-priced goods are expensive as well. For example, a car that costs $10,000 in the United States would cost a British citizen £10,000. Therefore, the quantity of dollars demanded is small, say, Q_1. On the other hand, when dollars are cheap—say, each dollar costs only one-fourth pound ($1.00 = £0.25)—so too are dollar-priced goods; the same car that costs $10,000 in the United States would cost only £2,500 in Britain. As a result, a larger quantity of dollars is demanded, say, Q_3 on the diagram. This explains why the dollar demand curve slopes downward.

The shape of the dollar supply curve can be justified with similar reasoning. American citizens offer dollars in exchange for pounds sterling when they want to buy goods, services, and financial assets priced in British pounds sterling. When only a few pounds are received in exchange for each dollar ($1.00 = £0.25), British goods are expensive so only a few dollars (Q_1) will be offered in exchange for pounds. But when the dollar is strong ($1.00 = £1.00), many dollars will be offered in exchange for pounds (Q_3).

Panel (b) of Figure 36.2 depicts the market for sterling instead of dollars; yet it presents exactly the same information as panel (a). How can this be? When British citizens demand dollars, they supply pounds; when Americans demand pounds, they supply dollars. This means that the demand curve for dollars is the same as the supply curve for pounds, and the supply curve for pounds is the same as the demand curve for dollars. Notice that the price of dollars in terms of pounds in panel (a) is the reciprocal of the price of pounds in terms of dollars in panel (b). For example, at

···· **FIGURE 36.2** THE MARKET FOR FOREIGN EXCHANGE

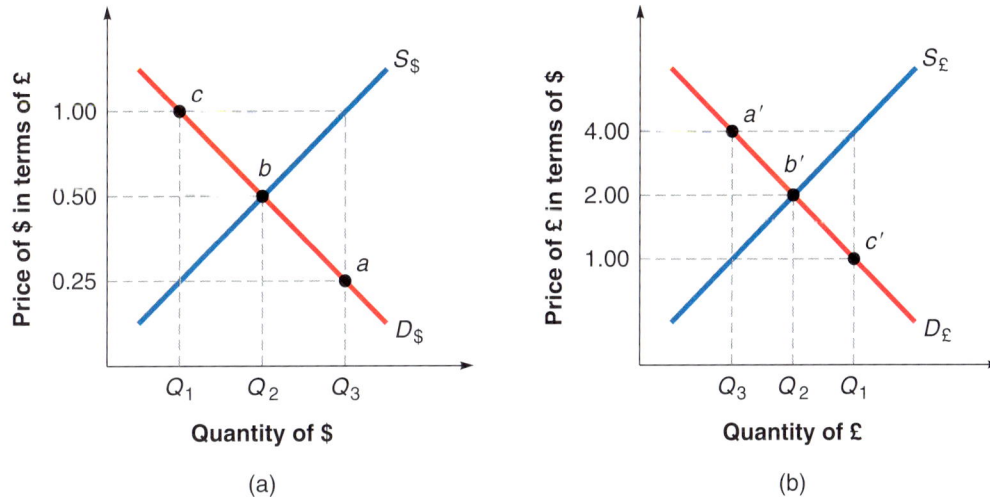

Exchange rates are just prices and, as such, are determined by the forces of supply and demand. Panel (a) shows the market for dollars. The demand for dollars represents the demand for dollar-priced goods, services, and financial assets. It is downward sloping because when dollars are expensive, $1.00 = £1.00, goods priced in dollars are also expensive so the demand for such goods is low. The supply curve for dollars represents the dollars that are offered in exchange for British pounds. When each dollar can be exchanged for many pounds, pound-priced goods are inexpensive so many dollars will be offered. The intersection between the supply and demand curves gives the equilibrium exchange rate. Panel (b) is a mirror image of panel (a). The demand for pounds is the same thing as the supply of dollars because dollars must be offered (supplied) in exchange for pounds, and the supply of pounds gives the same information as the demand for dollars. The price of dollars in terms of pounds is the reciprocal of the price of pounds in terms of dollars. In equilibrium, $1.00 = £0.50 and £1.00 = $2.00.

point *a* on the demand curve in panel (a), the exchange rate on the dollar demand curve is £0.25 = $1.00. The corresponding point in panel (b) is point *a′* on the supply curve where the exchange rate is £1.00 = $4.00. To show that these two exchange rates are equivalent, simply take the reciprocal of either one to get the other.[4] By the same reasoning, points *b* and *c* in panel (a) correspond to points *b′* and *c′* in panel (b) ($2.00 = £1.00 or £1.00 = $0.50 and $1.00 = £1.00).

Equilibrium Exchange Rates. When exchange rates are free to fluctuate, they will move to the intersection of the supply and demand curves. In Figure 36.2, this occurs at a price of £0.50 = $1.00 in panel (a) and £1.00 = $2.00 in panel (b). Balance of payments equilibrium occurs at the equilibrium exchange rate: currency outflow, as represented by the quantity of dollars supplied, is equal to currency inflow, as represented by the quantity of dollars demanded. Note, however, that this does not mean that individual subaccounts of the balance of payments are in balance. It is

[4]The elasticity of the dollar demand curve will affect the shape of the pound supply curve. The supply curve is upward sloping only for exchange rates that correspond to the elastic portion of the dollar demand curve; it is backward bending at exchange rates that correspond to the inelastic portion of the dollar demand curve. We have omitted the inelastic portion to simplify the analysis.

> •••• **FIGURE 36.3** FIXED EXCHANGE RATES AND BALANCE OF PAYMENTS DISEQUILIBRIUM
>
>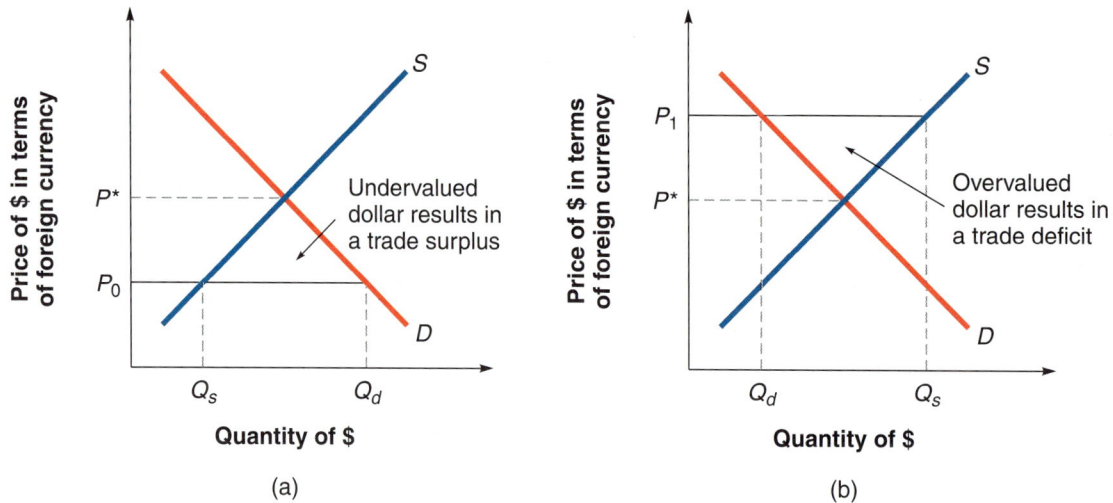
>
> (a)   (b)
>
> Fixed exchange rates can lead to disequilibrium in the balance of trade. In panel (a), the dollar is held at an artificially low value as it was during the dollar shortage era of the 1950s. The result was a persistent balance of trade surplus for the United States because imports were too expensive and the quantity of dollars demanded was greater than the quantity of dollars supplied.
>
> In panel (b), the dollar is held at an artificially high value as it was in the 1960s when there was a "dollar glut." The result was a persistent trade deficit. Imports were cheap, and the quantity of dollars demanded was less than the quantity of dollars supplied.

possible to have a deficit (or surplus) on the current account and a surplus (or deficit) on the capital account.

Fixed Exchange Rates and Balance of Payments Disequilibria. Figure 36.3 shows that fixed exchange rates can lead to balance of payments disequilibrium as occurred during the Bretton Woods era. Panel (a) shows what happens when the dollar is undervalued: the quantity of dollars demanded exceeds the quantity of dollars supplied. The quantity of dollars demanded represents the demand for U.S. goods, so an excess demand for dollars would mean that the United States experienced a persistent surplus. This is what occurred during the dollar shortage era of the 1950s when the United States enjoyed persistent surpluses on the current account. Panel (b) shows what happened when the demand for dollars fell in the 1960s: the dollar became overvalued and there was a dollar glut. As a result, the United States began to experience persistent deficits on the current account. Persistent balance of payments disequilibrium was the ultimate cause of the collapse of Bretton Woods and the move to flexible exchange rates.

• • • • • • • •

Factors That Affect Equilibrium Exchange Rates

The supply and demand apparatus we have just developed is useful for illustrating how different events can affect equilibrium exchange rates under a system of flexible exchange rates. Several factors can be important. In the short run, interest rate differentials are the predominant determinant of exchange rates; GDP growth has an

important influence in the medium term; and relative inflation rates dominate over the long run. Expectations can also affect exchange rates.

Interest Rate Differentials. The combined foreign exchange transactions in the three largest trading centers in the world—New York, Tokyo, and London—total nearly $200 billion *every day.* [5] Much of this money (often called "hot money") is traded for very short periods—often only a few hours or days—in search of higher interest rates. Many economists believe that these flows are responsible for most day-to-day fluctuations in exchange rates. When there are no impediments to the flow of financial capital across international borders—a condition economists characterize as "capital mobility"—interest rate differentials are eliminated. As funds flow out of the low–interest rate economies, interest rates tend to rise; the flow of funds into the high–interest rate economies tends to lower interest rates. [6]

Figure 36.4 shows how interest rate differentials affect exchange rates. Suppose that initially the dollar is priced at £0.50 but U.S. interest rates rise relative to British interest rates. The prospect of earning a higher return on dollar-denominated financial assets can have two effects. First, British investors will demand additional dollars in order to buy more dollar-denominated financial assets. This will shift the dollar demand curve from D_0 to D_1. Second, U.S. investors will offer fewer dollars in exchange for pounds sterling because they will want to make fewer investments in pound-denominated financial assets. This will shift the dollar supply curve toward the exchange rate axis. The result: The dollar will appreciate from £0.50 to £0.52. The opposite would occur if interest rates in the United States were low relative to Great Britain: the demand for dollars would drop, and the supply of dollars would increase so the dollar would depreciate.

International financial capital flows tend to equalize world interest rates. In this case, high interest rates in the United States attract funds, which will tend to lower U.S. interest rates, and the outflow of funds from Great Britain will tend to raise rates there. Financial capital flows will stop when interest rate differentials have been eliminated.

Interest Rates and Exchange Rates

Other things being equal, if:

$$r\$ \uparrow \quad \text{then} \quad E\$ \uparrow$$
$$r\$ \downarrow \quad \text{then} \quad E\$ \downarrow$$

where:

$$r\$ = \text{U.S. interest rate}$$
$$E\$ = \text{dollar exchange rate}$$

---

[5] Richard M. Levich, "Financial Innovations in International Financial Markets," in Martin Feldstein, ed., *The United States in the World Economy* (Chicago: University of Chicago Press, 1988), p. 220.
[6] This statement must be qualified to take account of risk. As we discussed in Chapter 17, people require a risk premium to invest in risky assets. This means that a higher interest rate must be paid on a risky asset than a "safe" asset. In relation to international finance, interest rate differentials will equalize only up to the risk premium, so interest rates in unstable economies will remain higher than the interest rates in more stable economies.

···· **FIGURE 36.4** THE EFFECT OF INTEREST RATES
ON EXCHANGE RATES

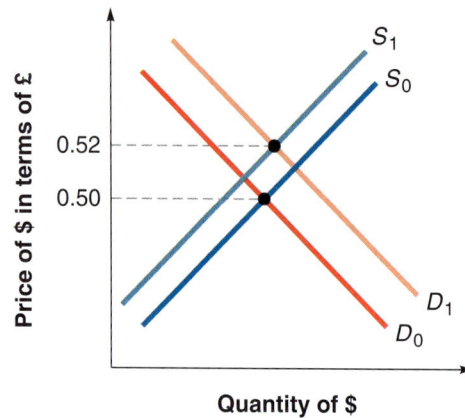

When interest rates in the United States rise relative to the rest of the world, the demand for dollars and dollar-denominated financial assets rises. British demand for high interest–earning U.S. assets results in an outward shift of the dollar demand curve from D_0 to D_1. At the same time, U.S. investors will demand fewer British assets and thus need fewer British pounds. This will cause the dollar supply curve to shift from S_0 to S_1. As a result, the dollar will appreciate from $1.00 = £0.50 to $1.00 = £0.52. Had interest rates in the United States fallen relative to the rest of the world, the dollar would have depreciated. This could be represented by a shift from D_1 to D_0 and from S_1 to S_0.

GDP Growth. Relative GDP growth can also affect exchange rates. For example, if the U.S. economy slips into a recession while its trading partners experience an economic boom, the U.S. demand for goods—including imports—will fall. As Americans cut back on their demand for imports, they will have less need for foreign currencies. Therefore, fewer dollars will be offered on international markets in exchange for foreign currencies. The result, as shown in Figure 36.5, will be a shift of the dollar supply curve toward the price axis from S_0 to S_1 and appreciation of the dollar from £0.50 to £0.52. Had the U.S. economy boomed while our trading partners fell into recession, the opposite would have happened: an outward shift in the dollar supply curve would have resulted in a depreciation of the dollar.

GDP Growth and Exchange Rates

Other things being equal, if:

$$Q\$ \uparrow \text{ then } E\$ \downarrow$$
$$Q\$ \downarrow \text{ then } E\$ \uparrow$$

where:

$$Q\$ = \text{U.S. GDP growth}$$
$$E\$ = \text{dollar exchange rate}$$

···· **FIGURE 36.5** THE EFFECT OF GDP GROWTH
 ON EXCHANGE RATES

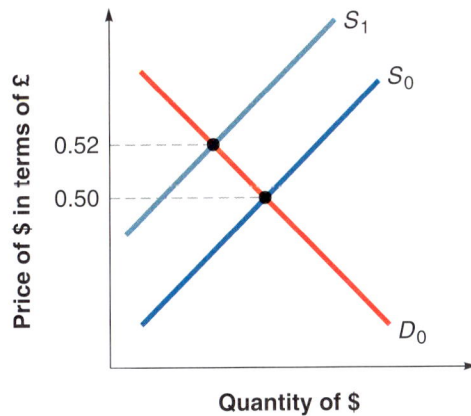

If the U.S. economy falls into a recession, the demand for all goods, including imported goods, will decline. Therefore, fewer dollars will be offered on international markets in exchange for foreign currencies. This will shift the dollar supply curve from S_0 to S_1 and cause the dollar to appreciate. If GDP growth in the United States accelerates, the dollar supply curve will shift outward, and the dollar will depreciate.

Relative Inflation Rates: The Theory of Purchasing Power Parity. In the long run, the theory of **purchasing power parity** holds that a dollar spent in the United States should buy as much as a dollar spent anywhere in the world (after adjustment for transportation costs). The reasoning is straightforward. Suppose that a personal computer costs $2,000 in the United States and 4,000 deutsche marks (DM) in Germany. At an exchange rate of $1.00 = DM2.00, it would make no difference where you bought the computer. But what if the exchange rate were $1.00 = DM3.00? Instead of paying $2,000 for the computer in the United States, the smart thing to do would be to exchange $1,333.33 (= 4,000/3) for DM4,000 and buy the machine in Germany. As long as the transportation costs are less than $666.67, you would save money.

According to the theory of purchasing power parity, such opportunities cannot persist. Here's why: If you did notice that computers were cheaper in Germany than in the United States, chances are that more than a few people would notice the same thing. And as they took advantage of the savings, two things would happen. First, the demand for deutsche marks would increase, causing the mark to appreciate. Second, as more computers were purchased in Germany, there is a good chance that German computer prices would start to rise. Theoretically, these adjustments would continue until purchasing power parity existed; that is, until a dollar spent on a computer in the United States bought the same amount as a dollar spent on a computer in Germany—and everywhere else in the world.

The theory of purchasing power parity actually links relative inflation rates to exchange rates. For example, if inflation is 6 percent in the United States and 3

Purchasing power parity Theory of exchange rate determination that says that a dollar should purchase as much in the United States as anywhere else in the world, after adjustment for transportation costs. According to the theory, in the long run, changes in exchange rates reflect relative inflation rates.

FOCUS ON

PURCHASING POWER PARITY IN THE REAL(?) WORLD

Despite some recent problems, the theory of purchasing power parity remains a key component of international economic analysis. Actual application of the theory has only one key requirement: It is necessary to find identical products in different nations. The British news magazine *The Economist* found such an item and has been using it to check on purchasing power parity since 1986. That product is McDonald's Big Mac hamburger.

The accompanying table, a condensation of one in *The Economist*, shows the price in local currency, implied purchasing power parity of the dollar, actual exchange rate, and percentage of over- or underevaluation of the dollar as of October 1992. The implied purchasing power parity of the dollar was calculated by taking the ratio of the local price to the dollar price. Notice that the dollar appears to be undervalued relative to the currencies of most industrialized nations but overvalued relative to the currencies of most less-developed nations. The

Country	Price in Local Currency	Implied Purchasing Power Parity of the Dollar	Actual Exchange Rate (10/4/92)	Percentage Over(+) or Under(−) Valuation of the Dollar
Argentina	Peso 3.30	1.51	0.99	−34
Australia	A$2.54	1.16	1.31	+13
Belgium	BFr108	49.32	33.55	−32
Brazil	Cr3,800	1,735	2,153	+24
Britain	£1.74	0.79	0.57	−28
Canada	C$2.76	1.26	1.19	−6
China	Yuan 6.30	2.88	5.44	+89
Denmark	DKr27.25	12.44	6.32	−49
France	FF218.10	8.26	5.55	−33
Germany	DM4.50	2.05	1.64	−20
Hong Kong	HK$8.90	4.06	7.73	+91
Italy	Lire 4,100	1,872	1,233	−34
Japan	¥380	174	133	−24
Russia	Ruble 58	26.48	98.95	+273
United States	$2.19	—	—	—

percent in Germany, the dollar should depreciate 3 percent relative to the deutsche mark. This is shown in Figure 36.6. Suppose that the market for dollars begins at the intersection of D_0 and S_0 with each dollar selling for DM2.00 but inflation in the United States accelerates relative to inflation in Germany. Two things will occur. First, Americans will want to buy the less expensive German goods, and to do so, they will need to exchange dollars for deutsche marks. This will shift the dollar supply

implication is that the dollar should have risen in the succeeding months. It did—but only against some currencies. For example, by April 1993, the dollar had weakened against the yen ($1.00 = ¥112) and deutsche mark ($1.00 = DM1.59) but strengthened against the Canadian dollar ($1.00 = C$1.26) and Italian lira ($1.00 = lire 1,536).

The Big Mac purchasing power parity index should be taken with a grain of salt (and perhaps catsup) because local conditions and habits can influence prices. It is likely, for example, that less competition allows higher profit margins on Big Macs sold abroad than in the United States. Further, the Big Mac price differential may persist because it is not possible for people to buy cheap Big Macs in one nation and sell them for a profit in nations where Big Macs are expensive. Such a process—called *arbitrage*—tends to eliminate price differentials rather quickly. Remember too that purchasing power parity theory is a theory of *long-run* adjustment so it may be too much to ask for short-run verification of the theory.

Finally, we cannot let our discussion of two all-beef patties, special sauce, lettuce, cheese, pickles, and onions on a sesame seed bun go without a comment on the growing popularity of *The Economist*'s annual Big Mac purchasing power index. Each time the index is published, it elicits a number of thoughtful and often humorous letters to the editor. The May 8, 1993 issue of *The Economist,* for example, contained a letter from Tokyo noting that when General MacArthur was told that the Japanese yen symbol (¥) also means "circle" in the kanji alphabet, he decided to set the postwar dollar/yen exchange rate at ¥360 = $1.00. Rarely have economic policies been based on such poetic reasoning. The same letter surmised that few of the millions of Japanese who regularly enjoy Big Macs realize that they are dining on the namesake of their late military governor, "Big Mac."

SOURCE: "Big Mac Currencies," *The Economist* (April 18, 1992). 1993 data are from the *Federal Reserve Bulletin.*

curve out from S_0 to S_1. Second, Germans will want to buy fewer of the expensive American goods. This will shift the dollar demand curve from D_0 to D_1. The result will be a depreciation of the dollar relative to the mark from $1.00 = DM2.00 to $1.00 = DM1.94. If U.S. inflation had fallen relative to Germany, the opposite would have occurred: the demand for dollars would have increased, the supply of dollars would have decreased, and the dollar would have appreciated.

····• FIGURE 36.6 EXCHANGE RATES AND PURCHASING
POWER PARITY

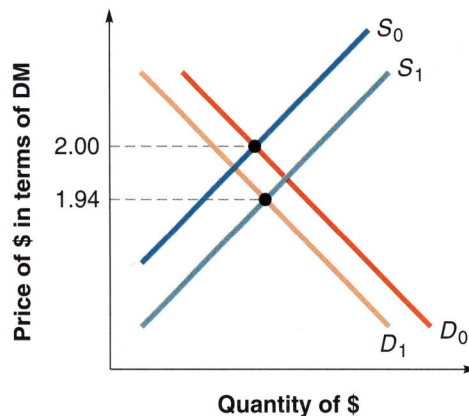

The theory of purchasing power parity explains how relative inflation rates affect exchange rates. If inflation in the United States rises 3 percent relative to inflation in Germany, U.S. citizens will increase their demand for low-priced German goods. As a result, the supply of dollars offered in exchange for deutsche marks will increase, and the dollar supply curve will shift from S_0 to S_1. At the same time, Germans will decrease their demand for high-priced American goods. This will cause the dollar demand curve to shift in from D_0 to D_1. The result will be a depreciation of the dollar from DM2.00 to DM1.94. Had U.S. inflation fallen relative to Germany, the dollar would have appreciated.

Inflation and Exchange Rates

Other things being equal, if:

$$p\$ \uparrow \quad \text{then } E\$ \downarrow$$
$$p\$ \downarrow \quad \text{then } E\$ \uparrow$$

where:

$$p\$ = \text{U.S. inflation rate}$$
$$E\$ = \text{dollar exchange rate}$$

The theory of purchasing power parity has come under attack in recent years for several reasons. Many economists—especially the new Keynesians[7]—contend that wages and prices are "sticky" so that changes in the exchange rate are not always reflected in changes in prices. This is especially true when exchange rates are volatile; firms seem to take a "wait and see" attitude to make sure that any fluctuations in the exchange rate are permanent before changing prices. Sticky wages and prices weaken the linkage between inflation and exchange rates, the key component of purchasing power parity theory, although it must be stressed that purchasing power parity is a

[7]Keynesian economists generally advocate a "hands-on" aproach to economic policy.

long-run theory and price stickiness usually exists only in the short run. A second criticism of purchasing power parity theory is based on the fact that most trade in the world today is between the developed nations and consists of manufactured goods. Unlike grain and raw materials, manufactured goods are not uniform. Consequently, some pricing discretion exists, further weakening the connection between exchange rates and domestic inflation rates. Finally, some studies have shown that noneconomic factors can influence exchange rates as much as economic factors like purchasing power parity. For example, one study showed that in wartime Vietnam, 20 to 25 percent of the value of the Vietnamese piaster depended on the presence of U.S. troops; the suggestion is that American troop presence provided a measure of economic stability. Other studies have found that war news had a similar effect on the value of greenbacks during the American Civil War.[8]

Confidence and Expectations. The foregoing discussion may have left you thinking that exchange rate prediction is a simple matter. Nothing could be further from the truth. At any point in time, *all* of these factors simultaneously affect exchange rates, and it can be quite difficult to determine which factor is exerting the most influence. Additionally, recent experience seems to indicate that confidence and expectations may be just as important as other factors in determining exchange rate movements.

How do expectations affect exchange rates? Consider the following scenario. Suppose that you are a financial investor and notice that one-year interest rates in Germany are 9 percent, nearly double the rate obtainable on comparable-risk, one-year U.S. securities. The current dollar/mark exchange rate is DM2.00 = $1.00, and you decide to spend $50,000 to buy DM100,000 worth of German securities. Unfortunately, once you tie up your money in the securities, the German mark depreciates to a rate of DM2.20 = $1.00. That does not affect the 9 percent interest you are earning on the securities, but it does affect what happens when you cash in your investment. At the end of a year, your DM100,000 investment is worth DM109,000—but when you exchange the marks for dollars at the new rate of DM2.20 = $1.00, you have only DM109,000/2.20 = $49,545.45! This kind of loss can be avoided by purchasing a forward contract (a kind of insurance premium offered on international currency markets), but forward contracts are not free.[9] The point is that if a sufficiently large number of people expect a currency to depreciate, it probably will because speculators and currency traders will want to sell their currencies before they get caught with a loss.

The perception of economic stability can also affect exchange rates. For example, after the collapse of the Soviet Union, many of the newly independent nations issued their own currencies. Despite attractive interest rates, foreign investors were

---

[8]Ronnie J. Phillips, "'War News' and Black Market Exchange Rate Deviations from Purchasing Power Parity," *Journal of International Economics* 25 (November 1988): 373–78.

[9]Forward and futures contracts are properly the subject of courses in international finance, but they should be briefly mentioned here. When a buyer agrees to purchase goods from a foreign supplier, the buyer often purchases a forward contract at the same time. The forward contract will lock in a particular exchange rate. When it comes time to complete the transaction, the buyer will first sell the forward contract for foreign currency and then use that foreign currency to purchase goods. Forward contracts eliminate exchange rate risk but are costly because a brokerage commission must be paid for the contract.

extremely reluctant to hold assets denominated in these new currencies. The reason for their reluctance was simple: No one knew whether the governments that issued the new currencies would be around next year—or even next month.[10] Finally, while the dollar does not play the key role it did during the Bretton Woods era, it is still quite important and is often used as a refuge during periods of uncertainty. For example, war and the rumor of war often cause investors to shift into dollars. This can cause the dollar to appreciate—despite any economic fundamentals to the contrary.

An interesting way that expectations can affect exchange rates is illustrated by the so-called *peso problem*.[11] The peso problem refers to the fact that potential events—even when they do not occur—can affect expectations and exchange rates. For example, Mexico is an oil-producing nation, so anticipation of rising oil prices typically causes the Mexican peso to appreciate. But, if the anticipated oil price rise never occurs, the peso exchange rate will be incorrect, and Mexico will experience a trade deficit. The problem is that there is no way to determine how often peso problems occur because anticipations and expectations cannot be observed. To the extent that peso problems do take place, however, exchange rates are disconnected from real economic events. This is an indication of market inefficiency.

Exchange Rate Volatility: Overshooting. But even after adjusting for confidence and expectations, predicting exchange rates is a daunting task because of a phenomenon known as **exchange rate overshooting**. The theory of overshooting may explain why exchange rates have been so volatile in the post–Bretton Woods era. The theory of overshooting was developed by MIT economist Rudiger Dornbusch.[12]

Exchange rate overshooting A theory that holds that exchange rates can fluctuate in wide bands around their long-run equilibrium values. It assumes purchasing power parity, capital mobility, rational expectations, and wage-price stickiness. The theory may explain the extreme volatility of exchange rates since the end of the Bretton Woods system.

Overshooting theory makes four key assumptions: purchasing power parity, capital mobility, rational expectations,[13] and wage-price stickiness. Here is how it works: Suppose that the Fed suddenly expands the money supply in an effort to stimulate the economy. With any luck, the Fed will be successful, but its policy will almost certainly have some long-run inflationary impact as well. The catch is that with sticky wages and prices, only some of the inflationary impact will show up in the short run. This means that interest rates will fall in the short run as the real money supply (M^s/P) expands. In the long run, prices will rise and reduce the real money supply.

It is the short-run effect on the exchange rate that is of interest to us. If investors

[10]This explains why some of the nations chose to tie their currencies to gold or foreign currencies. Estonia, for example, was the first of the newly independent countries to issue its own currency, the *kroon*. To assure convertibility, Estonia tied the kroon to the deutsche mark and backed it with gold that was returned from Western banks following independence.

[11]The name "peso problem" derives from the fact that the Mexican peso underwent numerous and large fluctuations in the late 1970s and early 1980s without any corresponding real causal events ever occurring.

[12]Rudiger Dornbusch, "Expectations and Exchange Rate Dynamics," *Journal of Political Economy* 84 (December 1976): 1161–76. This article is a bit daunting for introductory students. A better place to read about overshooting is an intermediate-level international economics text. See, for example, Chapter 17 of Paul Krugman and Maurice Obstfeld, *International Economics* (New York: Harper-Collins, 1994). You can also look for Dornbusch's monthly columns in *Business Week*. These columns are frequently devoted to international issues.

[13]The rational expectations approach to economics was discussed in Chapters 27 and 32.

have rational expectations, they will know that higher prices in the future will generate inflation and cause the dollar to depreciate via purchasing power parity. This means that they will hold dollar-denominated assets only if they earn higher interest rates; otherwise, the expected future depreciation will result in losses. However, remember that the short-run rise in the real money supply has caused interest rates to fall temporarily. Therefore, to restore short-run equilibrium, the dollar will depreciate below or "overshoot" its long-run equilibrium value. Had the process begun with a contraction of the money supply, the exchange rate would have temporarily moved to a higher level than its long-run equilibrium value. In sum, the theory of overshooting states that if expectations are rational and wages and prices are sticky, exchange rates can fluctuate in wide bands around their long-run equilibrium values.

How much validity is there to the overshooting argument? Apparently quite a bit. The best example of overshooting may have taken place between 1980 and 1985 when the dollar rose 30 percent against the yen and 76 percent against the mark even though inflation was much higher in the United States than in either Japan or Germany. The 30 percent decline of the dollar relative to the yen between 1990 and 1993 may have been another example.

RECAP   Factors That Influence Exchange Rates

Exchange rates are the prices of currencies and are determined by the forces of supply and demand. The main factors that affect exchange rates are:

1. *Interest rate differentials.* High interest rates relative to the rest of the world will cause a currency to appreciate; low interest rates relative to the rest of the world will cause a currency to depreciate. Interest rate differentials are often responsible for short-run fluctuations in exchange rates.
2. *GDP growth rates.* Economic growth increases the demand for imported goods and thus increases the supply of currency on international markets. This weakens the currency. Recession reduces the demand for imported goods and causes currency to strengthen.
3. *Inflation rates.* In the long run, the theory of purchasing power parity holds that currencies will adjust to inflation rate differentials. High inflation results in currency depreciation; low inflation causes appreciation. The theory of purchasing power parity has been under attack in recent years.
4. *Expectations and confidence.* International financial investors are more willing to hold foreign currencies when they are confident of political and economic stability. Further, fear of currency depreciation can cause investors to sell currencies and accelerate a currency decline.
5. *Overshooting.* If expectations are rational and prices are sticky, exchange rates tend to be quite volatile because they overshoot their long-run equilibrium values.

MANAGED EXCHANGE RATES

The Smithsonian Agreement may have spelled the end of fixed exchange rates, but it did not mean that exchange rates were perfectly free to float. Instead,

FOCUS ON

EXCHANGE RATE FLUCTUATIONS IN THE REAL WORLD: AN EMPIRICAL ANALYSIS

The extreme volatility of exchange rates over the past 20 years has caused some economists to conclude that exchange rates follow a *random walk*—meaning that the best predictor of exchange rates is to simply assume that they will not change because any other forecast will miss by an even wider mark. Many economists, however, believe that economic fundamentals—relative interest rates, inflation, and so on—are responsible for exchange rate fluctuations and contend that statistical models can be effective exchange rate predictors. One such economist is Adrian Throop of the San Francisco Federal Reserve Bank. Throop's work leads him to believe that four factors—productivity, the real price of oil, the U.S. budget deficit, and real long-term interest rates—are responsible for most changes in the trade-weighted value of the dollar over the past 20 years. The *trade-weighted exchange rate* is an "average" exchange rate that incorporates the values of all of the ma-

jor currencies with which the United States trades. Throop's work represents a refinement, not a replacement, of the analysis we have just been through: productivity growth and the real price of oil are related to inflation and purchasing power parity, while the government deficit affects exchange rates though its impact on interest rates:

- *Productivity.* Exchange rates tend to equalize the prices of traded goods at home and abroad. However, the trade-weighted dollar is computed for overall price levels, which include the price of traded as well as nontraded goods. Throop adjusted for the productivity in traded goods to improve his forecast of exchange rates.

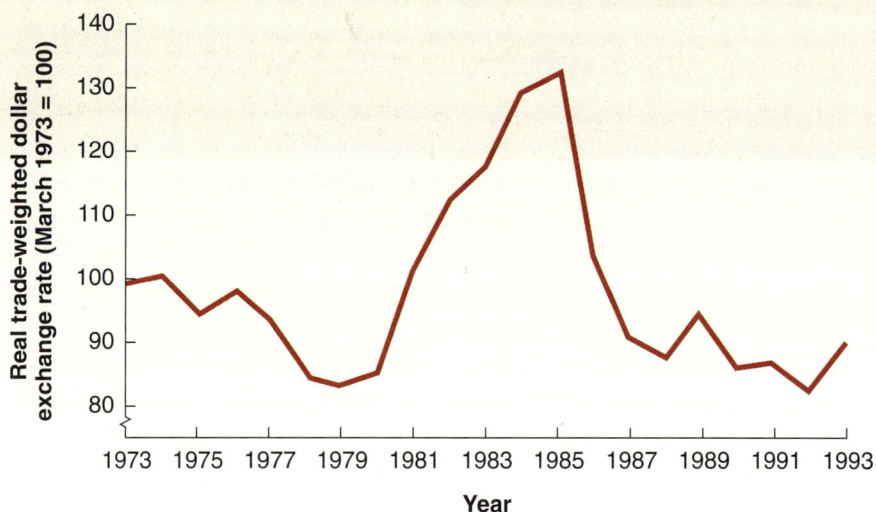

exchange rates have been managed by the central banks and treasuries of the world. Just how successful governments are at managing exchange rates is highly debated, but no one would deny that they have tried to control exchange rates. The question is *why* governments would want to intervene in international financial markets. Some economists would say that any interference with market processes is wrong, but politicians and policymakers may think differently: letting the currency appreciate can make imports too attractive and cost jobs at home—but letting the currency depreciate will raise the price of imported goods and cause inflation. Neither prospect bodes well for a politician on the eve of an election.

The real price of oil. The United States imports about 40 percent of its oil, but this is a smaller fraction than most of its trading partners. Thus, the sharp rise in the real price of oil in the late 1970s and early 1980s actually strengthened the dollar. Likewise, the sharp decline in the real price of oil after 1986 was instrumental in the decline in the dollar. It is also significant that most oil sold on the world market is priced in dollars, so other countries must hold dollars to buy oil. This is why the term "petrodollar" was coined in the 1970s.

The U.S. budget deficit. Higher deficits tend to raise interest rates and attract foreign capital, and foreign capital inflows tend to strengthen the dollar. Perhaps most significantly, Throop believes that the capital inflows and stronger dollar persist even after foreign interest rates have adjusted to U.S. levels.

Real long-term interest rates. The dollar's value will adjust as long as a real long-term interest rate differential exists between dollar-denominated assets and foreign assets, adjusted for a risk premium. The higher the interest rate in the United States, the stronger the dollar.

Throop's analysis reveals that 80 percent of the variation of the dollar can be explained by his four main factors. He accounts for all of the major swings in the dollar but misses some of the minor swings. Throop's policy implication may be especially important: If real factors are responsible for most variation in exchange rates, then monetary policy can have relatively little effect on real exchange rates because monetary policy affects only nominal values.

SOURCE: Adrian Throop, "The Dollar: Short-Run Volatility and Long-Run Adjustment," *FRBSF Weekly Letter* (October 9, 1992). Exchange rate data are from the 1994 *Economic Report of the President,* Table B-110.

Exchange Rate Intervention

On paper at least, changing the value of a currency seems like a simple proposition: all that is necessary is for the policymakers to buy or sell currency on international markets. For example, suppose that the United States is experiencing a persistent trade deficit with Japan. To reduce imports and increase exports, the Federal Reserve could use dollars to buy yen (¥) on international markets. As Figure 36.7 shows, this would shift the dollar supply curve outward from S_0 to S_1 and cause the dollar to depreciate against the yen from ¥120 = $1 to ¥110 = $1. The weaker dollar would

FIGURE 36.7 MANAGING EXCHANGE RATES

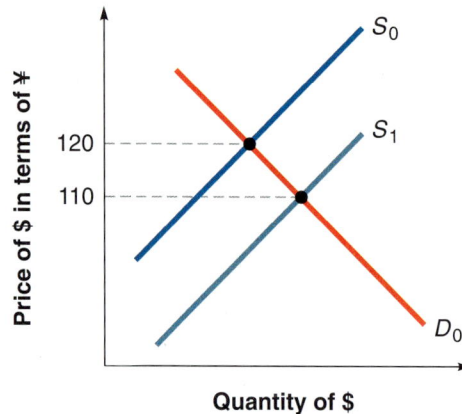

If the Fed feels that the dollar is too strong, it can sell dollars to bring about depreciation. In this case, the exchange rate begins at ¥120 = $1. Selling dollars for yen will
cause the dollar supply curve to shift from S_0 to S_1, and the dollar to depreciate to
¥110 = $1. A weaker dollar will cause some inflation at home but reduce imports and
raise exports. If the Fed is worried about inflation at home, it can buy dollars on international markets. This would shift the dollar demand curve outward and cause the dollar
to appreciate. Most recent studies show that it is difficult for a single nation to affect its
exchange rate because of the sheer volume of international financial transactions.

raise the price of Japanese imports, lower the price of U.S. exports to Japan, and
reduce the trade imbalance. A disadvantage of the weaker dollar is that Japanese goods
would now cost more in the United States so the inflation rate would edge upward.
The opposite policy would be indicated if the goal was to decrease domestic inflation:
the Fed could buy dollars on international markets with foreign currencies. This
would cause the dollar to appreciate, lower the price of imports, and reduce inflationary pressures. The disadvantage of a stronger dollar is slower domestic economic
growth and a larger trade deficit.

The United States, Japan, Germany, and many other nations frequently intervene
to support their currencies, but government intervention represents little more than
the proverbial "drop in the bucket" of international capital movements. Given the
nearly $200 billion in daily currency transactions, even the United States does not
have adequate currency reserves to stem market forces. It is possible, however, that
the combined efforts of several governments may be able to affect market rates. For
example, in 1985 the dollar appeared to be overvalued, at least partially because of
high U.S. interest rates caused by the fiscal deficit. With the United States running
a trade deficit of nearly $200 billion, the finance ministers of the seven largest indus-
trial nations (the G-7) met at the Plaza Hotel in New York to sign the *Plaza Accord*.
The Plaza Accord acknowledged that the dollar was overvalued and set up a framework for monetary policy coordination to bring down the dollar. The plan apparently
worked because the dollar did come down from its lofty heights. Two years later,

another meeting was held at the Louvre in Paris. The resulting *Louvre Agreement* recognized that the dollar was valued approximately correctly and called for continued loose coordination of monetary policies to maintain stable exchange rates. However, the dollar began to rise and appreciated by over 10 percent in 1988–1989.

It is unclear what we can learn from the 1985–1989 experience with policy coordination, and economists remain undecided about the effectiveness of international policy coordination. It seemed to work in 1985–1987 but not in 1988–1989. Whether the dollar would have fallen in the absence of the Plaza Accord will never be known; it is entirely possible that policy had no effect whatsoever, and that the dollar would have fallen in the absence of intervention. But even if policy coordination can be successful, it cannot be counted on to solve a nation's balance of payments troubles because it can be quite difficult to achieve cooperation in the first place. The Plaza Accord and Louvre Agreement were relatively easy to negotiate because Japan and the European nations feared that the United States would impose restrictive tariffs if policy coordination was not forthcoming. The U.S. promise to adopt fiscal discipline at home undoubtedly helped as well.[14]

The *j*-Curve

Finally, even when exchange intervention is successful, a lag of several months or longer may occur before there is any appreciable effect on the balance of trade. This lag is called the **j-curve** and is illustrated in Figure 36.8. The vertical axis measures the merchandise trade balance, and the horizontal axis measures time in months. Suppose the balance of trade begins with a $50 billion deficit and that policymakers decide to devalue the currency to eliminate the trade deficit. The devaluation takes place in Month 1. Notice that the trade deficit increases to $60 billion by Month 3 before gradually declining over the next four months. The trade deficit is finally eliminated in Month 7. This is a reasonable example; many empirical estimates suggest that the *j*-curve is typically between six months and a year in duration though some studies indicate that it might be much longer.

Why does it take so long for a devaluation to reduce a balance of trade deficit? There are two reasons. First, import orders may be in the pipeline at the time of the devaluation, and they instantly become more expensive. Importing the same quantity of goods but paying a higher price—caused by the weaker currency—will increase the trade deficit. Second, people normally take several months to find domestic substitutes for the now more expensive imports. Until substitutes are available, there will be little change in the quantity of goods that are imported, despite the higher price.[15] Finally, it must be added that devaluation cannot cure every economy's ills even after

j-curve Graphical representation illustrating that a devaluation may make a trade deficit worse before it gets better.

---

[14]You can find an excellent, nontechnical discussion of 1980s exchange rate policy cooperation (and discord) in Paul Volcker and Toyoo Gyohten, *Changing Fortunes* (New York: Times Books, 1992). Volcker was Federal Reserve chair during the Carter and Reagan administrations and Gyohten was vice minister for international affairs of the Ministry of Finance of Japan.

[15]The time response of the *j*-curve depends on the price elasticity of demand. The term "elasticity pessimism" was coined in the 1980s to call attention to the long time it seemed to take before devaluations would affect the trade balance.

FIGURE 36.8 THE *j*-CURVE

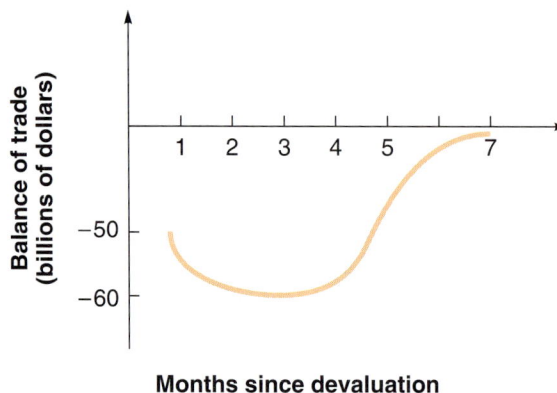

Months since devaluation

Currency devaluation is likely to make the trade deficit worse in the short run because of the *j*-curve effect. In Month 1, the economy is experiencing a $50 billion trade deficit so the currency is devalued. Because people cannot immediately find substitutes for imported goods, they import the same quantity but pay a higher price. This causes the trade deficit to increase to $60 billion by Month 3. As people find domestic substitutes, imports decline, and the trade deficit falls. The trade deficit is eliminated in Month 7. Empirical estimates reveal that the *j*-curve may be a year or longer in duration.

the *j*-curve has worked itself out. Many firms in the former Soviet Union, for example, are so inefficient that the value of their output is actually less than the value of their inputs. No exchange rate will make these firms competitive; the only solution will be massive restructuring.[16] To a lesser extent, the same may be true for some industries in the West.

POLICY UNDER FIXED AND FLEXIBLE EXCHANGE RATE REGIMES

The effectiveness of fiscal and monetary policy depends crucially upon the exchange rate regime and the extent of capital mobility.[17] Monetary policy is more effective when exchange rates are flexible while fiscal policy is more effective when exchange rates are fixed.

• • • • • • • •

Policy under Fixed Exchange Rates

Suppose that exchange rates are fixed and the government decides to use expansionary fiscal policy—either tax cuts or increased government spending—to revive the slug-

---

[16]"The Value-Subtracters," *The Economist,* (January 5, 1991).

[17]A quick review of Chapters 30 and 31 on monetary and fiscal policy may be helpful before reading this section.

gish economy. Unless the economy begins in a severe recession, the fiscal stimulus will cause interest rates to rise. If there is no international sector, the effect of the fiscal stimulus stops there. In an open economy, however, there is an additional effect because the higher interest rates attract foreign financial capital. The foreign capital tends to stem the rise in interest rates and thus makes the fiscal policy multiplier larger than it would be if there were no international sector.

In contrast, monetary policy is weakened when exchange rates are fixed. For example, if monetary policy is used to stimulate the economy, interest rates will tend to fall in the short run. Lower interest rates will cause financial capital to leave the domestic economy as investors look for higher yields elsewhere. This will reduce the stimulative impact of expansionary monetary policy.

Policy under Flexible Exchange Rates

If exchange rates are flexible, fiscal policy becomes impotent while monetary policy is strengthened. As before, a fiscal stimulus tends to raise interest rates, and higher interest rates cause the currency to appreciate. The stronger currency raises imports and lowers exports. The resulting balance of trade deficit weakens the domestic economy and counters much of the fiscal stimulus. The opposite occurs with monetary policy: increasing the money supply causes interest rates to fall and weakens the currency. This leads to an increase in exports and further economic stimulus.

While it is hard to criticize the theory behind the foregoing discussion, real-world lags may seem to reverse the relative effectiveness of monetary and fiscal policy. Fiscal policy often affects the domestic economy within just a few months after a tax cut or spending increase is implemented, while it may take a year before the full effects of monetary policy are felt. Since the trade balance may not respond to a change in the exchange rate for nearly a year, it may appear that fiscal policy is more effective than monetary policy even under flexible exchange rates—at least in the short run.

The Policy Mix

Neither fiscal policy nor monetary policy is ever enacted in isolation. If government deficits increase interest rates, the Fed may be forced to expand the money supply to head off crowding out; likewise, if expansionary monetary policy generates inflation, the cost of government programs—and the size of the government budget—will increase. In other words, it is the policy mix, not fiscal or monetary policy per se that is important.

Many economists believe that the best policy mix is one that combines relatively tight fiscal policy (small deficits) with relatively easy (expansionary) monetary policy because this mix will tend to keep interest rates low. However, some economists have argued that the opposite policy mix—easy fiscal and tight monetary—is preferable when exchange rates are flexible and capital is mobile. The experience of the U.S. economy in 1980s can help us sort out this debate.

In mid-1980, the United States began to feel the effects of a half year of tight money. Declining inflation caused the dollar to appreciate, and the economy fell into a recession. Exports declined almost 5 percent between 1980 and 1982 as the dollar rose to record levels. Over the same period, fiscal policy was essentially neutral because the structural deficit was close to zero. In early 1983, money growth was increased, and fiscal policy became expansionary as the Reagan tax cuts took effect. Easy fiscal policy apparently had more effect than the relatively easy monetary policy because real interest rates began to climb. Traditional macroeconomic theory would have suggested that such high interest rates would stop the economy in its tracks, but quite the opposite happened. The economy began a recovery that lasted almost to the end of the decade. The recovery was made possible by foreign financial capital inflows—high interest rates attracted enough foreign capital to prevent the fiscal deficit from crowding out domestic investment. The appreciating dollar also helped to keep inflation below 4 percent. One blemish on the record was the current account deficit in excess of $100 billion each year between 1984 and 1986.

In retrospect, it appears that the tight money suppressed inflation while the fiscal expansion generated growth, eased the pain of disinflation, and attracted enough foreign capital to pay for the budget deficits. Unfortunately, the situation was not quite so simple. Not only did capital inflows necessitate future profit and dividend outflows, but the huge fiscal deficits sustained by the United States raised the ire of our economic allies. The coordinated actions of European central banks to bring down the dollar in the spring of 1985 were indicative of just how upset they became. And when Germany and Japan refused U.S. requests to stimulate their economies in 1986, they cited U.S. fiscal irresponsibility as the reason. This suggests that the combination of tight fiscal policy with easy money may be preferable because it allows room for international economic policy cooperation, but the verdict is still out on the optimal policy mix.

PROS AND CONS OF FIXED AND FLEXIBLE EXCHANGE RATES

Almost as soon as the Bretton Woods Agreement was signed, many economists began to predict its demise by arguing that fixed exchange rates could not suppress market forces forever. We know now that they were right—Bretton Woods did collapse—but we also know that flexible exchange rates have been far from a panacea. This section reviews the advantages and disadvantages of fixed versus flexible exchange rates. The debate over fixed versus flexible exchange rates is likely to remain one of the central policy debates in the years to come. The following are some of the points that will be addressed in these debates:

- *Flexible exchange rates automatically assure balance of payments equilibrium.* Flexible exchange rates reflect market forces and adjust as productivity, inflation, interest rates, and other factors vary. As a result, there can be no persistent balance of payments disequilibrium. Under fixed exchange rates, the balance of payments can get stuck in "fundamental disequilibrium," which results in capital outflows and necessitates exchange devaluation by deficit countries.

- *Flexible exchange rates insulate the domestic economy from foreign shocks.* For example, suppose that Canada, the largest trading partner of the United States, falls into a severe recession. This will reduce the demand for U.S. exports and hurt the U.S. economy. If exchange rates are flexible, however, the U.S. dollar will depreciate relative to the Canadian dollar and reduce the effect of the Canadian recession on the U.S. economy. However, exchange rate overshooting tends to weaken the insulating properties of flexible exchange rates.

- *Flexible exchange rates require little international policy cooperation.* The ultimate failure of the Bretton Woods system was the refusal of the surplus countries to revalue. Until international economic cooperation is more likely, flexible exchange rates may be the best exchange rate regime.
- *But fixed exchange rates may provide more stability.* The problem with flexible exchange rates is their volatility. Exchange rates have fluctuated wildly since flexibility was instituted in 1973. The resulting exchange rate risk has caused serious problems for the world economy. Despite floating rates, there have also been balance of payments disequilibria; these may be explained by price stickiness and the failure of purchasing power parity to hold. Finally, governments have not been able to resist the temptation to intervene in the "free" market for foreign exchange.

SUMMARY

There is a simple reason why much of the economic and financial news today concerns international finance: international trade is hampered in the absence of a stable system of international finance, and international trade is vital to all modern economies. Understanding the basics of international finance is important for all informed citizens, not just introductory economics students and businesspeople. The main points from this chapter are:

1. The balance of payments is a record of the international transactions between one country and the rest of the world. It is always in balance. The current account is a subaccount of the balance of payments that records imports and exports of goods and services. The United States has had deficits on the current account for the past decade and a half. The capital account records international capital flows. A surplus on the capital account indicates that foreign capital inflows exceed domestic capital outflows. The U.S. capital account surplus has been necessary to balance the current account deficit. It is unclear whether current account deficits or capital account surpluses should be cause for concern.
2. Following World War II, the Bretton Woods Agreement established fixed exchange rates with the dollar playing the role of reserve currency. The dollar carried a fixed gold price, and foreign nations were allowed to exchange their currencies for dollars and buy gold with dollars. The dollar shortage era of the 1950s suggests that the dollar was initially undervalued; in the 1960s, however, the glut of dollars on international markets made it apparent that the dollar had become overvalued. Surplus nations refused to revalue their currencies, and the Bretton Woods system collapsed in 1973.
3. In the absence of government intervention, exchange rates are determined by market forces. Among the most important influences on exchange rates are interest rates, GDP growth, inflation, and expectations. Other things being equal, high interest rates, low GDP growth, and low inflation tend to strengthen a currency. Flexible exchange rates have been quite volatile since their inception in 1973; this volatility may be explained by the theory of overshooting.
4. Nations attempt to manage their exchange rates by buying and selling currencies

on world financial markets. To strengthen the dollar, the United States would buy dollars on international markets; to weaken the dollar, it would sell dollars on international markets. Most evidence suggests that managing exchange rates is quite difficult; however, the coordinated actions of many nations may be more successful.

5. The exchange rate regime affects the effectiveness of fiscal and monetary policy. Fiscal policy is more effective when exchange rates are fixed; monetary policy is more effective when exchange rates are flexible. When exchange rates are free to float, most economists believe that the best policy mix combines tight fiscal policy with easy monetary policy.

• • • • • • • KEY TERMS AND CONCEPTS

balance of payments	World Bank
short-term capital flow	austerity measures
current account	devaluation bias
merchandise trade account	dollar shortage
unilateral transfers	dollar glut
capital account	Smithsonian Agreement
official settlements account	flexible exchange rates
statistical discrepancy	interest rate differentials
exchange rate risk	GDP growth
gold standard	purchasing power parity
Bretton Woods	overshooting
par value	Plaza Accord
dollar exchange standard	Louvre Agreement
fundamental disequilibrium	j-curve
International Monetary Fund (IMF)	policy mix

• • • • • • • REVIEW QUESTIONS

1. What are the major subaccounts of the balance of payments? Are there reasons to be concerned about deficits on these subaccounts?
2. What were the main elements of the Bretton Woods system? How did it perform? Why did it collapse in 1973?
3. Using supply and demand analysis, explain and illustrate how interest rates, GDP growth, inflation, and expectations affect exchange rates.
4. Why are exchange rate fluctuations so volatile?
5. Using supply and demand analysis, illustrate how actions by the central bank and/or treasury can bring about a currency depreciation and a currency appreciation. Also, explain why nations may want to influence the value of their currencies, and comment on the effectiveness of exchange rate intervention.

·········· PROBLEMS

1. Determine whether each of the following would show up as a debit or credit, and indicate on which subaccount of the balance of payments it would appear:
   a. A U.S. citizen takes a vacation in France.
   b. Ford builds a plant in Russia but incurs losses for the first three years.
   c. A Japanese consortium buys golf courses in California.
   d. Idaho farmers export potatoes to Germany.
   e. The U.S. government sells dollars in an effort to stem the rise of the dollar.
   f. The United States gives Croatia military weapons to be used for self-defense.
   g. Marijuana is illegally smuggled into the United States from Colombia.

2. As a U.S. citizen, would you be better off if the dollar were "strong" or "weak"? Why? (*Hint:* There are both advantages and disadvantages to a strong dollar!)

3. Would a better performance by the U.S. economy in the 1960s have made the survival of Bretton Woods more likely? Why or why not?

4. Suppose that exchange rates are fixed and the dollar is undervalued.
   a. What evidence would you look for to be sure that the dollar is actually undervalued?
   b. Other than revaluation, what measures could be taken to restore balance of payments equilibrium?
   c. What incentives would there be to maintain an undervalued dollar?

5. Suppose that exchange rates are perfectly flexible. Using supply and demand analysis, explain how each of the following would affect the value of the dollar:
   a. Inflation accelerates in the United States.
   b. The United States falls into a severe recession.
   c. Fiscal austerity results in falling U.S. interest rates.
   d. Rumors of an impending U.S. stock market crash run wild.
   e. The United States reports a larger than expected deficit on the merchandise trade balance.
   f. War breaks out in the Persian Gulf and investors flee to the dollar.

6. Suppose that the Fed is concerned about inflation and therefore reduces monetary growth. Explain how this could result in the exchange rate overshooting its long-run equilibrium value.

7. Suppose that there were no international capital flows. Would it make any difference whether a nation had a mix of tight fiscal/easy monetary policy or easy fiscal/tight monetary policy? Explain.

8. Why do many economists prefer flexible exchange rates to fixed exchange rates? How has recent experience dampened the enthusiasm for flexible exchange rates?

CHAPTER 37

Policy in the Open Economy

When the United States began to run record deficits on the current account in the 1980s, there were calls for policy changes in many circles. Many people said that the real problem was the fiscal deficit, which raised real interest rates and caused the dollar to become overvalued. The solution, of course, was a strong dose of fiscal responsibility. Others noted the decline in manufacturing employment and said that the United States was becoming less competitive in international markets. In this case, the solution was government assistance for targeted industries—which, of course, flew in the face of the fiscal responsibility advocated by the deficit hawks. Still others blamed the Japanese for not playing fair: these people insisted that unless and until the Japanese open their markets to our goods, we should raise tariff barriers to keep out their goods. And some economists argued that there was really no problem at all because the current account deficit implied a capital account surplus of nearly the same magnitude. How could there be a problem if foreigners were so willing to invest in our economy?

These debates began more than a decade ago, but they are still raging loudly today. Economic debates do not play well in the media, but they frequently do lead to new ideas and progress in economic theory and policy. This chapter will examine some of the contemporary debates on global economics and global economic policies.

AFTER READING AND STUDYING THIS CHAPTER, YOU SHOULD BE ABLE TO:
- • • Understand the relationship between the twin deficits, national saving, and competitiveness
- • • Outline the main components of the new international economics and strategic trade policies
- • • Explain the potential benefits of regional economic integration, and analyze the European Economic Community and North American Free Trade Agreement
- • • Explain the rationale behind exchange rate target zones

THE TWIN DEFICITS

The United States has been running twin deficits for almost 15 years: a deficit on the current account of the balance of payments, and a fiscal deficit, the difference between government spending and tax revenues. The term "twin deficits" is not a misnomer: macroeconomists know that the two deficits are related by an important accounting identity that requires leakages to equal withdrawals. In the context of the open economy income-expenditure model,[1] this identity states that imports plus savings and taxes must equal exports plus investment and government purchases, or:

$$Z + S + T = X + I + G \qquad [1]$$

Where:
Z = imports
S = private saving
T = tax revenues
X = exports
I = investment
G = government purchases

Some rearrangement of Equation 1 gives:

$$(X - Z) + (G - T) = (S - I) \qquad [2]$$

Equation 2 shows that the balance on the current account, $(X - Z)$, plus the budget deficit, $(G - T)$, must be financed by an excess of saving over investment.[2] Many economists interpret this to mean that the twin deficits can exhaust the supply of savings and lead to slow investment and economic growth.

Economists do not debate the validity of Equations 1 or 2. They are true by definition and (thankfully!) fit the facts. So where is the debate? We are just playing with accounting identities. The debate is over the assumed causality behind the identity. To see this, it is convenient to write Equation 1 as:

[1] The theory behind this identity was developed in the discussion of the income-expenditure model in Chapters 23–25.

[2] In Chapter 24 the term $(X - Z)$ was called "net exports" in order to avoid having to detour into balance of payments accounting, a main topic of Chapter 36. The term "balance on the current account" is preferable and easily identifiable from the national income and product accounts.

$$(X - Z) = S + (T - G) - I \qquad [3]$$

Or simply:

$$\frac{\text{Current account}}{\text{balance}} = \frac{\text{private}}{\text{saving}} + \frac{\text{budget}}{\text{surplus}} - \frac{\text{domestic}}{\text{investment}} \qquad [4]$$

Alternatively, we could write:

$$\text{Current account balance} = \text{national saving} - \text{domestic investment} \qquad [5]$$

because the government surplus represents public saving (and the government deficit represents public dissaving).

Now we can see the problem: many economists believe that the real problem with the U.S. economy is not the twin deficits per se, but the shortage of national saving. For example, suppose that the current account balance is −$100, that private saving is +$100, and that the government is running a deficit of $200 (meaning that the government "surplus" is −$200). Substituting these values into Equation 4 shows that there can be no investment: −$100 = +$100 − $200 − 0. If private saving increases to +$200, investment can rise to $100: −$100 = $200 − $200 − (+$100).

This sort of analysis has caused some economists to suggest that the U.S. economy has been saving too little in recent years. In the 1960s and 1970s, gross national saving was roughly equal to investment at about 15 percent of GDP, but the saving rate fell by three percentage points in the early 1980s. A main reason for the decline in national saving has been the fiscal deficit—"dissaving" by the government. Not only does the fiscal deficit mean that the government is spending money that it does not have, but government borrowing has a tendency to raise interest rates. Higher interest rates can have two negative consequences for the economy: First, as we pointed out in Chapter 31, they can "crowd out" investment, at least when the economy is close to full employment. Second, they cause the dollar to appreciate. This lowers the price of imports and can worsen the trade balance.

But even admitting that the United States saves too little does not necessarily imply that this is the source of the twin deficits problem. In fact, some economists believe that the real problem is declining industrial competitiveness; that is, that U.S. firms have somehow lost their ability to compete effectively in the world marketplace.[3] To understand this view, consider what would happen if our competitiveness suddenly improved due to a technological advance that reduced production costs or raised quality, or both. The result would be, *ceteris paribus,* an increase in exports and a reduction in the current account deficit. Further, increased exports would raise employment and national income. Both private saving and tax revenues would rise because higher income would allow people to save more and pay more in taxes. In terms of Equation 4, the current account balance would shrink, and the government surplus would rise, while both private saving and investment increased. In sum, improved competitiveness would reduce the twin deficits and increase saving in one fell swoop.

[3]This discussion is based on Robert A. Blecker, *Beyond the Twin Deficits* (Armonk, N.Y.: M. E. Sharpe, 1992).

There is only one catch to the competitiveness argument: even if it is correct, designing policies to improve national competitiveness is difficult, if not impossible. Further, many economists have suggested that any competitiveness problem that may have existed in the 1970s and early 1980s had all but vanished by the late 1980s: not only was there significant improvement in the trade deficit, but U.S. productivity growth equaled or exceeded that of most other industrial countries.[4]

A Case for Depreciation?

Another proposed solution to the twin deficits problem is currency depreciation. A currency depreciation would work like this: Once the value of the dollar is brought down—via the sale of dollars or tight fiscal policies that lowered interest rates—the deficit on the current account would shrink as imports fell and exports rose. As exports rose and domestic production picked up to replace imports, unemployment would fall. This would raise the tax base and shrink the fiscal deficit. Reduced government borrowing would free private savings for investment.

But a currency depreciation would present problems as well. First, a weaker dollar means higher inflation at home because imported goods are now more expensive. More importantly, a weaker currency represents a decline in the standard of living because consumers are not able to buy as many imported goods as before the devaluation. This problem may not be significant with a one-time depreciation, but frequent depreciations would mean a continuing decline in living standards.

The second problem is subject to more controversy. According to Paul Krugman and others,[5] the linkage between exchange rates and the price of traded goods has become so weak that currency depreciation may have little effect on trade. His reasoning is based on several ideas, the most important of which is a theory of international price stickiness that he calls his **sunk cost model**.[6] According to Krugman, establishing a foreign market can be so difficult and costly that firms are reluctant to exit foreign markets even when they become less profitable. For example, suppose a German brewery studied the U.S. market and decided that it could profitably sell beer at an exchange rate of DM2.00 = $1.00. The beer, which costs DM10 in Germany, is priced at $5.00 (= DM10/2) in the United States. If the dollar weakens to DM1.80 = $1.00, the U.S. price of the imported beer should rise to $5.55 (= DM10/1.8). But, if the German firm has already incurred significant sunk costs in studying the U.S. market and opening up distributorships, it will be reluctant to raise prices and lose market share. This may be especially true in an era of exchange rate volatility because the exchange rate could soon return to the initial rate. In fact, the German firm may have set up the distributorships planning for this kind of currency fluctuation and confident that it could turn a profit over a wide range of

Sunk cost model Theory developed by Paul Krugman to explain the weak connection between exchange rates and the price of traded goods; holds that once firms have incurred sunk costs in establishing a foreign market, they are reluctant to raise prices and lose market share, at least in the short run.

---

[4]Comparative productivity growth rates were presented in Chapter 33.

[5]Paul Krugman, *Exchange Rate Instability* (Cambridge, Mass.: MIT Press, 1989). This book, based on a series of three lectures given at the London School of Economics in 1988, is an excellent introduction to the work of one of the most important young international economists of our times. Most of the analysis is nontechnical enough for beginning students.

[6]Sunk costs were defined in Chapter 14 when we discussed contestable markets. A sunk cost is a cost that is not recoverable even if the firm shuts down and sells its assets.

exchange rates. There have been several cases when the sunk cost model appeared to apply. For example, Japanese auto prices hardly budged in the late 1980s despite a rapidly rising yen. This could indicate that Japanese auto producers were so concerned about losing market share that they accepted a reduction in profits. Nevertheless, the Japanese auto producers were able to hold down prices only in the short run; eventually, Japanese auto prices did rise to reflect the stronger yen.

. . . .

A Caveat

We should not overstate the case against depreciation or increased saving. Many economists believe that the twin deficits are a problem of macroeconomics, and that fiscal responsibility and a weaker dollar will reduce both deficits and free saving for investment. However, this view is not without its critics in the United States, and economists in Europe and elsewhere increasingly advocate measures designed to increase competitiveness as solutions to their twin deficit problems.

R E C A P   **The Twin Deficits**

The United States has run fiscal deficits and deficits on the current account for over a decade. Many economists believe that the twin deficits are related and a cause for concern.

1. *Savings shortage.* The macroeconomic identity, $Z + S + T = X + I + G$, holds that deficits must be financed by national saving. The simultaneous existence of the twin deficits requires that private saving exceed private investment. In this view, the best solution to the twin deficits is to increase national saving and reduce the government deficit. This would provide funds for investment and negate the adverse consequences of the deficits.
2. *Currency depreciation.* Currency depreciation could reduce both deficits. A weaker currency would make imports more expensive and exports cheaper for foreigners. However, depreciation causes domestic inflation. It also represents a decline in the standard of living so it cannot be used on a continuing basis. Further, the existence of international price stickiness has weakened the linkage between exchange rates and export prices.
3. *Competitiveness.* The macroeconomic identity does not imply cause and effect; therefore, it is possible that the twin deficits are the result of declining competitiveness. In this view, an increase in competitiveness would increase exports and national income. A higher national income would increase both private saving and tax revenues.

THE NEW INTERNATIONAL ECONOMICS AND STRATEGIC TRADE POLICIES

The model of international trade developed in Chapter 35 has an elegance that captured economists for almost two centuries. Unfortunately, the elegance of free trade does not always fit the real world. Nations not only use tariffs and nontariff

New international economics
Relaxes the assumptions of perfect competition, free trade, and the absence of externalities and raises the possibility that strategic trade policies may be an effective way to manage trade.

barriers to keep out imports, but they use subsidies and other measures to aid industries considered to be especially important. Although many—probably most—economists in the United States abhor such policies, an increasing number of economists are exploring the **new international economics**, which is defined (loosely) as the theory of international economics without the assumptions of free trade and perfect competition. Many economists in the Clinton administration, including Council of Economic Advisers chair Laura D'Andrea Tyson, advocate policies based on the new international economics.[7] Tyson is the subject of an Economic Heritage box on page 978, and Paul Krugman of MIT, who is perhaps the leading figure in the development of the new international economics, is featured in the Economic Heritage box on page 982.[8]

A few economists started to question the viability of free trade arguments when the United States began to run persistent trade deficits in the 1970s and 1980s. One of the sources of the trade deficit, of course, was oil. When petroleum imports jumped from $8.4 billion in 1973, to $26.6 billion in 1974, and then to $79.5 billion in 1979, it became apparent that OPEC had benefited from practicing a policy of non-free trade. This fact was not lost on economists and policymakers: if a nation (in this case, Saudi Arabia) had a large share of the market, it stood to benefit from restricting exports and raising export prices. The immediate extension was that nations could extract benefits from trade restrictions—at least as long as they held a large share of the world market and could prevent foreign competition.

· · · · · · · ·

Competitive versus Noncompetitive Markets

The theory of free trade assumes competitive markets. A market is considered competitive if it includes many firms selling similar products. Standardized commodities—agricultural products and sheet steel are two examples—often fit the competitive model well. Technologically sophisticated products—including supercomputers, aircraft, and many chemicals—often do not fit the competitive model. These industries are typically dominated by only a few firms with little significant competition. Producers are often able to charge prices in excess of their costs and thus earn what economists call *economic rents*[9]—at least until new firms enter the industry and drive

---

[7]In "Creating Advantage: How Government Policies Shape International Trade in the Semiconductor Industry," in Paul Krugman, ed., *Strategic Trade Policy and the New International Economics* (Cambridge, Mass.: MIT Press, 1986), Tyson, along with coauthors Michael Borrus and John Zysman, defined the new trade theory as, "The new trade theory examines the determinants and patterns of international trade under conditions that diverge from the stringent and unrealistic assumptions on which traditional comparative advantage theory is based. These assumptions, which include perfect competition, constant returns to scale, and the absence of externalities, are clearly at odds with conditions in the markets for many manufactured goods, especially the high-technology goods . . ." (p. 112).

[8]It must be noted that although Krugman developed many of the key ideas of the new international economics, he has become quite disenchanted with many of the policy proposals associated with this theory. See his paper, "What Do Undergraduates Need to Know about International Trade?" *American Economic Review* 83(2): May 1993, 22–26.

[9]Economic rent is a factor payment over and above the payment necessary to bring that factor into production; only factors that are limited or fixed in supply can command economic rents. Firms can earn economic rents only when there are few competitors.

down prices and profits. It is obviously to a firm's advantage to be in a noncompetitive market. Trade policies designed to help domestic firms extract economic rents from the world economy are often called **strategic trade policies**.

Three factors determine whether a firm can generate economic rents: economies of scale, learning curves, and the dynamics of innovation. Economies of scale depend on the size of the firm relative to the market and plant efficiency. For example, suppose the world market can absorb 1,000 widgets per year and that only two technologies are capable of producing widgets. One technology is capable of producing 100 widgets per year at a cost of $20 per widget. The other is capable of producing 800 widgets per year at a cost of $10 per widget. In this case, the firm that entered the industry first and adopted the 800-widget technology would have an advantage over later entrants into the industry. It could produce 800 widgets per year, charge $20 per widget, and reap economic rents. Small firms could not lower price below $20 without losing money, and if a new firm tried to build a factory capable of producing 800 widgets per year, the existing firm could lower price to $10.

But scale economies cannot last forever. As time passes, technology evolves and competitors learn to lower costs. To maintain economic rents, established firms have to innovate—offer new products, increase quality, or lower costs—faster than potential competitors can chip away their economic rents. No one can predict the path of innovation, so competitors will occasionally manage to steal market share from established firms. However, economic rents assure that established firms will have funds for research and development.

Externalities

Positive externalities (also called external economies) provide another justification for strategic trade policies. As we have seen, positive externalities exist whenever there are benefits to individuals or firms other than the producer. In the case of strategic trade policy, the externalities refer to the idea that the social returns in some industries can exceed the returns to the individual firm. This may be especially true in the high-technology industries. For example, basic research in computer technology can have spinoffs for consumer electronics and other areas. Another externality involves labor: if subsidies increase the profitability of the computer industry, more workers will be hired—and trained. The growing volume of trade in high-technology goods is making externalities increasingly important.

Strategic Trade Policies

Many nations have tried to secure economic rents with strategic trade policies designed to stimulate domestic industries and keep out foreign competition. The most common strategic trade policies have been subsidies for research and development, but measures to keep out foreign competition and increase market share have been used as well. Japanese strategic trade policies appear to have been especially successful. In semiconductors, for example, Japan was clearly behind the United States in the 1970s. Recognizing the strategic importance of the semiconductor industry—as well as the potential for scale economies and positive exter-

> **Strategic trade policies** Policies designed to extract economic rents; often applied to high-tech industries. May include subsidies for research and development, measures to keep out foreign competition, and stimulus to selected domestic industries.

OUR
ECONOMIC
HERITAGE

LAURA D'ANDREA TYSON: "CAUTIOUS ACTIVIST" AT THE COUNCIL OF ECONOMIC ADVISERS

The appointment of Laura D'Andrea Tyson to chair President Clinton's Council of Economic Advisers (CEA) was greeted with surprise in many circles, with disapproval in others—but with approval from people who believe that the government must be more actively involved in international trade. Laura Tyson may be an unorthodox economist, but she is also the closest thing to an economist among the top-level Clinton appointees. Clinton almost seemed to have gone out of his way to appoint non-economists to top economics positions in his administration: Labor Secretary Robert Reich is trained in law, not economics, and was a professor of public policy; Ira Magaziner, also a lawyer, was tapped to design the health care program; and the new Economic Security Council was staffed with politicians and *businesspeople* of all things, not academic economists. Why did Clinton select Tyson to chair his Council of Economic Advisers? Cynics hint that she was selected for one reason—her sex—but this cannot be the only reason. Clinton was frequently seen reading Tyson's latest book, *Who's Bashing Whom: Trade Conflict in the High Tech Industries,* during the campaign, and Tyson had long been an adviser to the Clinton campaign.

Laura D'Andrea Tyson was born in 1947 to a middle-class, second-generation Italian-American family and raised in New Jersey. Her father was a financial officer for a company in Manhattan. She graduated valedictorian from high school where she was both a cheerleader and selected Miss Scholastic at a local Junior Miss pageant. She did her undergraduate work in economics and math at Smith and was again valedictorian. When she graduated in 1969, she went straight to MIT to study economics. Her dissertation examined inflation in Yugoslavia. Comparative economics was

nalities—the Japanese government provided loans to domestic semiconductor firms and closed the market to imports. The Japanese government also adopted a policy of "controlled competition" to reduce risk and encourage long-term investment. The result: By the late 1970s, Japan was exporting semiconductors to the United States.

Successful implementation of strategic trade policies is complicated by the same problems that plague the infant industry argument discussed in Chapter 35. One problem is that there is no easy way to determine which industries are indeed strategic. The simple answer is the high-tech industries because of externalities and potential economic rents, but which high-tech industries? Should *all* industries that

not on the cutting edge of economic analysis in the mid-1970s, so Tyson took a professional risk by choosing this topic for her thesis—and she was to find out later that interest in Yugoslavia was the mark of a "dangerous leftist," at least in the eyes of the editors of the *Wall Street Journal*. After completing her degree in 1974, Tyson spent a short time as a staff economist at the World Bank before taking a three-year appointment at Princeton. She left for Berkeley in 1978.

It was at Berkeley that Tyson began the work that would later attract the attention of candidate Clinton. The Berkeley Roundtable on International Economics (BRIE) was doing work in technology and trade, strategic trade policies, and other international policy issues. Tyson wrote and edited a number of books and articles with other BRIE participants and was soon selected to be the director of research for BRIE. She was also appointed to the Board of Economists of the *Los Angeles Times*.

Tyson's work with BRIE led her to conclude that standard models of international trade are incomplete, if not flawed. A main thesis of *Who's Bashing Whom?* is that the high-technology industries are more important than other industries because they provide important external benefits and high-wage jobs. Further, international trade and competition in the high-tech industries are skewed, because our trading rivals intervene more heavily than we do. Tyson believes that appropriate responses include subsidies, trade retaliation, and managed trade. *None of these ideas fits within the confines of orthodox economic analysis.*

Does this mean that Tyson really is the "dangerous leftist" she was accused of being? No. Her description of herself as a ". . . liberal economist with a cautious, activist bent" is probably closer to the truth. Fred Bergsten of the Institute for International Economics has called her a "superbly trained neoclassical economist who understands both modern trade theory and the revisionist critique that free trade is irrelevant in a world of imperfect competition and government support. . . ." That sounds very much like the definition of a new international economist—and it has the advantage of avoiding the terms "leftist" and "activist" with all their built-in associations. If Tyson's stint at the CEA is successful, Bergsten's description will be heard more often than others.

SOURCES: Susan Dentzer, "A Woman of Influence," *Working Woman,* August 1993, pp. 31+; Laura D'Andrea Tyson, *Who's Bashing Whom?* (Washington, D.C.: Institute for International Economics, 1993); Jadish Bhagwati, "Rough Trade," *The New Republic,* May 31, 1993, pp. 35–40; Gene M. Grossman, Review of *Who's Bashing Whom, Journal of Economic Literature* 31 (December 1993): 1985–86.

use computers or microchips be protected? Another problem would arise if strategic trade policies were applied to industries thought to generate significant externalities. By definition, external benefits do not carry a market price, so there is no good way to measure externalities. How could policymakers compare the externalities generated by the computer industry to those generated by the aircraft industry? Finally, we have no way of predicting how our trading partners would respond to a set of U.S. strategic trade policies. The policies could lead to an enhanced bargaining position. The Japanese, for example, might be more inclined to open their markets to U.S. imports. Or the policies could undermine what little international cooperation exists today. There is just no way to know.

RECAP   The New International Economics and Strategic Trade Policies

The new international economics drops the assumptions of free trade and perfect competition. Economists comfortable with the new international economics frequently advocate the use of strategic trade policies.

1. *Noncompetitive markets.* Many technologically sophisticated products are produced in noncompetitive markets dominated by a few firms able to set prices above costs. The factors that determine whether firms can extract economic rents are economies of scale, learning curves, and the pace of innovation.

2. *Externalities.* Some industries, particularly high-tech industries, may generate positive externalities; that is, the benefits to society are greater than the benefits to the firm. High-tech industries generate externalities because their trained workers and research can be used in many industries.

3. *Strategic trade policies.* These policies are designed to extract economic rents from high-tech and other industries. Strategic trade policies include subsidies for research and development as well as measures to increase market share and keep out foreign competition. The Japanese have used strategic trade policies successfully in the past; there is ongoing debate as to whether the United States should adopt strategic trade policies.

REGIONAL INTEGRATION

European Union (EU) A regional trading bloc composed of 12 members: Belgium, Denmark, France, Germany, Great Britain, Greece, Ireland, Italy, Luxembourg, the Netherlands, Portugal, and Spain. Often referred to by its former name, the European Community or EC.

Most favored nation (MFN) Status given to trading partners under which low tariffs are imposed on their goods.

Rarely are tariffs and other import restrictions applied in a nondiscriminatory fashion. Most countries have different levels of protection designed to reward friends and punish others. For example, countries in the **European Union (EU)**, a regional trading bloc of 12 nations, tax goods traded within the EU at lower rates than goods coming from outside the EU.[10] Compared to most nations, the United States has a record of relatively free trade, but it too discriminates in its trade restrictions. Trade between the United States and some countries—Cuba and Libya—is embargoed. In other words, trade is illegal between the United States and these nations, though there are certain exceptions for humanitarian needs. At the other extreme are nations that receive **most favored nation** status. These nations pay low tariffs and automatically qualify for any tariff reductions that are negotiated with other most favored nations. For example, if the United States negotiates a tariff reduction on flat display computer screens with Japan, the same tariff reduction would be applied to flat display computer screen imports from Germany because both nations have most favored nation status.

Why do nations apply trade restrictions in a discriminatory fashion? Why do they form regional trading blocs? These questions are important because they will help us understand the likely effects of one of the most important pieces of international economic legislation in recent U.S. history, the North American Free Trade Agree-

---

[10]The EU was called the European Economic Community (ECC) when it was formed in 1958. That name was later changed to European Community (EC). In recognition of the changes associated with Europe 1992, the name was changed to EU. The media still frequently refer to the EU as the EC.

ment (NAFTA). They should also help us predict the outlines of the international economy of the next century—an economy that many people believe will be dominated by just three regional trading blocs, the European Union, North America, and Asia.

Trade Creation and Trade Diversion

Regional trading blocs typically lower or remove internal tariffs and thus represent a move toward free trade. In this sense, they generate economic efficiency. However, regional blocs can also reduce economic efficiency because they change previously established patterns of trade, which were presumably based on market signals and were thus efficient. These two effects are called **trade creation** and **trade diversion**.

Trade creation occurs because of lower tariffs within the trading bloc. Suppose a country is producing at home only because doing so is cheaper than paying the tariff on imported goods. A tariff reduction could lower the price of imports enough to allow the country to import goods from more efficient foreign firms. This would free domestic labor and capital for use in other—more efficient—home industries. The same event can also cause trade diversion, however. If the external tariff gives member countries an advantage over nonmember countries, the pattern of trade will no longer reflect true economic costs. Trade is thus diverted from efficient nonmember nations to less-efficient member nations. The result is a reduction in world efficiency.

Trade creation and trade diversion can be illustrated with some simple tables. Table 37.1 shows the trade creation effect of regional blocs. The cost of producing one bottle of wine in France, Italy, and the United States is shown on the first line of the table. Italy is the low-cost producer, but cannot export wine to France because of the $2 French tariff. The United States is the high-cost producer and is unable to export wine to either France or Italy. Notice what happens when Italy and France form a regional trading bloc and eliminate their internal tariff. Italy now has a cost advantage in France and begins to export wine to France. In this example, no trade diversion effect occurs because the United States is the high-cost producer. With or without tariffs, U.S. wine cannot compete in the French market.

Table 37.2 tells another story. Before the regional bloc is formed, the United States is the low-cost producer and exports wine to France despite the $2 tariff. However, once the regional bloc is formed and internal tariffs are eliminated, Italian wine has a cost advantage so the United States loses its export market. This is an

Trade creation Beneficial effect of regional trading blocs. Occurs because lower internal tariffs enable low-cost producers in member nations to expand exports to other members.

Trade diversion Detrimental effect of regional trading blocs. Can occur if low internal tariffs give an advantage to member nations over low-cost nonmember nations.

···· TABLE 37.1 THE FRENCH MARKET FOR WINE: TRADE CREATION

	Before Regional Integration			After Regional Integration		
	France	Italy	United States	France	Italy	United States
Manufacturer's cost	$5	$4	$6	$5	$4	$6
Tariff	0	2	2	0	0	2
French wholesale price	$5	$6	$8	$5	$4	$8

OUR ECONOMIC HERITAGE

PAUL KRUGMAN: A LEADING FIGURE IN THE NEW INTERNATIONAL ECONOMICS

No one has been more important in the development of the new international economics than Paul Krugman (b. 1953) of the Massachusetts Institute of Technology. Barely 40 years old, Krugman already has one of the most impressive résumés within the economics profession. Not only has he made seminal contributions in the new international economics and economic geography, but he has advised the World Bank and IMF, served on the Council of Economic Advisers during the Reagan administration, and advised the Clinton presidential campaign. Like few economists today, Krugman has been able to contribute to both technical economic analysis and popular economics: in 1991 he was awarded the John Bates Clark Medal by the American Economic Association, an award given every two years to "the American economist under forty who is adjudged to have made a significant contribution to

economic thought and knowledge," and his 1991 book, *The Age of Diminished Expectations,* was a huge popular success.

Krugman was born and raised in middle-class New York suburbs. He claims that his upbringing was quite ordinary and that his interest in economics grew out of love for science fiction as much as anything else. In his early teens, Krugman's secret fantasy was to become a "psychohistorian" like Hari Seldon, the hero in Isaac Asimov's classic *Foundation* trilogy who used social science mathematics to prevent the collapse of galactic civilization.

Krugman studied economics and history as an undergraduate at Yale. There he wrote a paper on the long-run elasticity of demand for gasoline that attracted the attention of William Nordhaus. Nordhaus asked him to be a research assistant, and from that point on, Krugman says, he was a "profes-

sional economist." In 1974, Krugman enrolled in the graduate economics program at MIT. After receiving his Ph.D. in 1977, he took a post at Yale where he stayed until 1979 when he returned to MIT.

····· **TABLE 37.2 THE FRENCH MARKET FOR WINE: TRADE DIVERSION**

	Before Regional Integration			After Regional Integration		
	France	Italy	United States	France	Italy	United States
Manufacturer's cost	$6	$4	$3	$6	$4	$3
Tariff	0	2	2	0	0	2
French wholesale price	$6	$6	$5	$6	$4	$5

Krugman's main professional contribution has been to show the importance of increasing returns to economics. The idea of increasing returns is not new to economics—Keynesian economists like Nicholas Kaldor stressed the importance of increasing returns in the 1960s and before—but Krugman convinced the economics profession that increasing returns is *interesting* because it gives rise to multiple equilibria: Which technology would evolve for high-definition TV? Which city will get the European financial center? The existence of multiple equilibria means that economic analysis must include history. Krugman notes, for example, that there has been no important commercial traffic on the Erie Canal since 1850, yet the head start that the canal gave to New York City has allowed New York to remain the largest city in the nation.

Krugman has written on a wide range of topics—including even a piece on the economics of interstellar trade—but most of his work follows a very definite methodology. Says Krugman ". . . [S]tart with an informal verbal story, often one drawn from casual empiricism or from non-mainstream economic literature. Then try to build the simplest possible model that will illustrate that story. In the course of the model-building the story tends to change along with your intuition, but at the end of the process you have a simple model that is a very special case, but that makes a lot of intuitive sense and effectively gives you a language to discuss things that previously were off limits. The intuition can then also serve as the basis for empirical work. . . ."

One has to wonder how Paul Krugman has time for a life given the sheer volume of his research output. Krugman says little publicly about his personal life—save that he has a mature and mutually supportive relationship with his cats!—but he is clear about his love for economics and the process of discovery:

But the honest truth is that what drives me as an economist is that economics is *fun*. I think I understand why so many people think that economics is a boring subject, but they are wrong. On the contrary, there is hardly anything I know that is as exciting as finding that the great events that move history, the forces that determine the destiny of empires and the fate of kings, can sometimes be explained, predicted, or even controlled by a few symbols on a printed page. We all want power, we all want success, but the ultimate reward is the simple joy of understanding.

SOURCES: Avinash Dixit, "In Honor of Paul Krugman: Winner of the 1991 John Bates Clark Medal," *Journal of Economic Perspectives* 7 (Spring 1993): 173–87; Paul Krugman, "Incidents from My Career," forthcoming in *Making of Modern Economics II;* Paul Krugman, "How I Work," *American Economist* 38 (Fall 1993): 25–31.

example of trade diversion—the regional trading bloc has shifted trade away from the efficient producer (the United States) to a less-efficient producer (Italy).

In general, regional trading blocs result in both trade creation and trade diversion so it is necessary to analyze each situation individually. Nevertheless, some general tendencies can be noted. Most importantly, trade creation tends to dominate when the regional bloc is composed of countries with similar resource endowments and industrial structures. This suggests that the EU generates more trade creation than trade diversion. Regional trading blocs composed of countries with quite different resource endowments and industrial structures may generate more trade diversion than trade creation. The North American free trade zone may fall into this category because the resource endowments of both Canada and the United States are very different from Mexico's.

· · · · · · · ·

Dynamic Effects of Regional Trading Blocs

Dynamic effects Improved efficiency and increased economic growth due to the economies of scale and increased competition made possible by regional trading blocs.

Regional trading blocs can have important **dynamic effects** over time. In fact, the hope that integration would generate economies of scale was one of the main motivations behind the formation of the European Economic Community in 1958. Many people argued that the national markets in the individual European nations were too small to support firms large enough to achieve the same economies of scale that U.S. firms enjoyed. There was certainly some truth to this assertion, at least in 1958. Many individual firms in the United States were larger than the entire industries in some European nations.

Individual firms in the EU have grown significantly over the past 40 years, and many are now as large or larger than their U.S. competitors. Some of this growth has been caused by mergers between firms in different European nations, but much simply represents a response to the rapidly growing European market. In 1958, the combined GDP of the original six members of the European Economic Community was only one-third of U.S. GDP; today, the GDP of those original six members is larger than U.S. GDP, and the combined GDP of the EU's 12 members is much larger than U.S. GDP.

A second dynamic effect of regional integration is increased competition. When protected by national tariffs, firms have a tendency to become less innovative and cost-conscious. The elimination of national tariffs and increased regional competition force firms to cut costs and innovate—or go out of business. Finally, successful regional integration should calm political tensions and increase the likelihood of peace. To the extent that it does, this should stimulate trade.

· · · · · · · ·

The European Economic Community

Treaty of Rome (1958) Treaty that established the European Economic Community.

The European Economic Community was formed in 1958 with the passage of the **Treaty of Rome**. The six original members of the European Economic Community were Belgium, France, Germany, Italy, Luxembourg, and the Netherlands; Denmark, Great Britain, and Ireland joined in 1973; Greece joined in 1981; and Portugal and Spain became members in 1986. The most difficult task in forming the European Economic Community was finding a way to phase in the common external tariff and eliminate internal tariffs. This process was complicated because high-tariff nations like France would experience lower tariffs while low-tariff nations like Germany would have higher tariffs.

It was apparent that the European Economic Community provided benefits to its membership from the very beginning; the trade creation effect was clearly larger than the trade diversion effect. Efficiency gains occurred as resources were reallocated according to national factor endowments, and scale economies increased. Multinational corporations from the United States and elsewhere were also attracted by the larger market of the European Economic Community.

One area where the European Economic Community did not increase economic efficiency was agriculture. The Common Agricultural Policy used a system of **variable import levies** to give maximum protection to farming interests. Under this system, tariffs on imported agricultural products changed according to domestic agricultural prices: When domestic prices were low, tariffs were increased; when domestic prices were high, tariffs were lowered. The proceeds from these tariffs were then used to subsidize the price of agricultural exports. Such complicated rules were applied to agricultural trade because countries fear that free trade in agricultural products may drive domestic farmers out of business. Without a domestic agricultural sector, a nation could experience severe problems in the event that the trade agreement ever breaks down. Agricultural policy remains a point of contention between the United States and the EU—not surprising given that the United States is the world's largest agricultural exporter—but the Uruguay Round of the GATT negotiations ironed out some of these problems in 1993.

The addition of Greece, Spain, and Portugal in the 1980s not only made the European Community the largest trading bloc in the world, but it also represented a significant change because these countries had lower incomes and wages than the older members of the community. Consequently, the other nations were concerned that jobs would "migrate south" and that low-wage workers from the south would move to high-wage countries in the north and bid down wages. The growing anti-foreigner sentiment in Germany, France and elsewhere is an indication that some of this has occurred.[11]

Europe 1992. The European Economic Community was successful at removing many external barriers and other restrictions on trade, but it never achieved complete economic integration. Negotiations in the late 1980s and early 1990s were aimed at the elimination of any remaining impediments to free trade within the community. The original intent was to have these reforms in place by 1992—hence the name **Europe 1992**—but it now appears that many of these reforms will not be implemented before 1995 at the earliest. Some of the remaining trade barriers to be removed include limitations on the movement of workers, especially professional workers; capital controls that have made it difficult to invest across borders; government procurement practices that favor domestic producers; and a number of legal and industrial standards that impose different regulations on business.

The main document outlining the structure of Europe 1992 is the **Maastricht Treaty**. The treaty goes further than merely modifying regional economic policies: it calls for common foreign and defense policy, common citizenship, a more powerful European parliament, and a common currency, the **ECU** (pronounced "a-que").[12] The ratification process for the Maastricht Treaty began in the summer of 1992. The debates were lively, to say the least, and it is not clear at this writing what form the

Variable import levies Agricultural tariffs that vary according to domestic prices. When domestic prices are low (high), higher (lower) tariffs are imposed on imports of those products.

Europe 1992 Term used to refer to the economic unification of Europe that was scheduled to begin in 1992.

Maastricht Treaty The main document outlining the structure of Europe 1992; calls for common foreign and defense policy, common citizenship, a more powerful European parliament, and a common currency.

ECU Acronym for European currency unit; a market basket of several European currencies used as a reserve currency to maintain exchange rates under the European monetary system.

---

[11]It must be mentioned that much of this sentiment is directed at immigrants from North Africa and the Balkans—areas that are not members of the EU.

[12]ECU stands for "European currency unit." International investors and multinational corporations have been using accounts denominated in ECUs for several years now; however, ECU accounts actually consist of a portfolio of international currencies weighted to minimize exchange rate risk. In 1992, the ECU was the third largest reserve currency, after the dollar and deutsche mark. The Maastricht Treaty does not call for coinage of actual ECU notes and coins until 1996 at the earliest.

treaty will take when it is finally implemented.[13] If the treaty is ratified in its current state, Europe will become, for all intents and purposes, a single economy—the largest economy in the world. Other countries considering application for membership are Sweden, Norway, and several members of the former Eastern Bloc.

· · · · · · · ·

The North American Free Trade Agreement

North American Free Trade Agreement (NAFTA) Trade agreement between Canada, Mexico, and the United States designed to create a free trade zone in North America.

In late 1992, the leaders of the United States, Canada, and Mexico signed the **North American Free Trade Agreement (NAFTA)** to create a North American free trade zone. The agreement was later approved by the Canadian Parliament, the Mexican Senate, and, after an extremely bitter debate, the U.S. Congress. Elements of NAFTA began phasing in on January 1, 1994. With a combined GDP of over $6 trillion and more than 360 million customers, the North American free trade area promises to be the largest free trade zone in the world when all trade restrictions are removed in the year 2009. Table 37.3 presents 1992 trade data for the NAFTA countries.

Some people believe that NAFTA represents just the kind of economic clout needed to counter Japan and unified Europe. Others worry that NAFTA will open the U.S. economy to unfair competition from low-wage Mexican workers and will lead to massive relocation of U.S. factories in Mexico. The main elements of NAFTA include the following:

- *Tariff elimination.* The tariffs on most goods will be eliminated or phased out over a period of 5 to 10 years. Some agricultural products will be protected for as long as 15 years.
- *Most favored nation treatment in services.* Service providers from all NAFTA countries will be treated equally. This provision is especially important for the United States, the world's largest service exporter.
- *Elimination of most discriminatory policies on investment.* In most cases, foreign investors must be treated the same as domestic investors.
- *Intellectual property rights.* NAFTA requires each country to provide both product and process patents for virtually all kinds of inventions. U.S. software producers have frequently complained about lost sales due to software piracy.
- *Banking reform.* U.S. and Canadian banks will be allowed to locate in Mexico, overturning a prohibition that has existed for over 50 years. The presence of U.S. and Canadian banks in Mexico should help stabilize Mexican financial markets.
- *Local content.* Despite its name, NAFTA does not establish perfectly free trade. One restriction is the "Rules of Origin" requirement, which requires a minimum level of local content in foreign-owned production facilities. This will require U.S.-owned automobile plants in Mexico to use local sources for at least 62 percent of the value of their production.

[13]The Danes turned the treaty down in June 1992 by a vote of 50.7 to 49.3 percent—then accepted it by a similar small majority in 1993. In France, the treaty was passed by less than 1 percent of the vote in September 1992. One reason for the closeness of the French vote could be the exchange rate crisis that happened to be occurring in Europe at the time. The best place to read about European politics and economics is *The Economist.* The December 14, 1991 issue contains an article "The Deal Is Done," that examines some of the political issues surrounding Maastricht. Six months later, the June 6, 1992 issue contains an article, "Why the Danes Wouldn't," that offers an explanation for the Danes' initial rejection of the treaty.

····**TABLE 37.3 TRADING SHARES AND NAFTA**

United States		Canada		Mexico	
Trading Partners	Percentage of Trade	Trading Partners	Percentage of Trade	Trading Partners	Percentage of Trade
Canada	17.1%	United States	69.2%	United States	72.9%
Japan	15.3	Japan	6.1	Japan	5.2
Mexico	7.0	Germany	2.1	Germany	3.6
Germany	4.7	France	1.4	Canada	3.1
Britain	4.4	South Korea	1.4	Spain	2.1

Combined NAFTA GDP: $6,450 billion
Intra-NAFTA trade: $245 billion
Extra-NAFTA trade: $801 billion
Population: 360 million

SOURCE: This table is based on the table, "A Lot at Stake," in "America Builds a Trade Bloc," *The Economist,* (August 15, 1992). Data are from the International Monetary Fund.

The NAFTA debate in the U.S. Congress was one of the most heated in recent memory. Most opposition came from politicians (especially Democrats) and organized labor. Many of NAFTA's opponents raised the possibility that free trade with Mexico would cost U.S. jobs. They pointed out that Mexican workers are paid 80 percent less than U.S. workers and argued that U.S. firms would move their plants to Mexico to capitalize on the lower wages.[14] More direct competition from low-wage Mexican workers could also exert downward pressure on U.S. wages. Such reasoning led the Manufacturing Policy Project to predict that some six million U.S. manufacturing jobs would be vulnerable to NAFTA.[15]

There are at least three reasons to believe that the Manufacturing Policy Project predictions are overly pessimistic. First, lower trade barriers will help the United States more than Mexico because Mexican trade barriers are already higher than U.S. barriers. Second, Mexico is expected to increase its imports of U.S.-made capital goods. Third, as wealth increases in Mexico, demand for imports will increase. These arguments were the basis for a study by the Institute for International Economics, which concluded that even though about 112,000 jobs would be lost as a result of NAFTA, more than 242,000 jobs would be created. This amounts to a net increase of about 130,000 jobs, or 0.1 percent of the U.S. workforce.

[14]In 1991, the average hourly manufacturing wage rate was $15.45 in the United States and $17.31 in Canada, but only $2.17 in Mexico. The annual growth rate for wages was 20.6 percent in Mexico versus 3.8 percent in the United States and 8.1 percent in Canada. U.S. Department of Labor, Bureau of Labor Statistics, *International Comparisons of Hourly Compensation Costs for Production Workers in Manufacturing,* 1991 (Report 825). Note, however, that whether low-wage producers have a cost advantage over high-wage producers depends on labor productivity.
[15]Data for this and the next paragraph come from Ramon Moreno, "NAFTA and U.S. Jobs," *FRBSF Weekly Letter* 93 (June 24, 1993): 1+.

A second concern about NAFTA was that Mexican environmental laws are often less stringent and frequently less rigidly enforced than U.S. environmental laws. This lowers production costs and provides another incentive for U.S. investment in Mexico. Clinton administration officials dealt with the environmental concerns by promising to encourage Mexico to adopt environmental policies similar to those of the United States. In addition, in the summer of 1993, a federal court ruled that an environmental impact study would be required before NAFTA could be implemented.[16]

Fewer objections were aimed at the prospect of free trade with Canada, at least in the United States. This is probably because the Canadian economy is so similar to the U.S. economy in terms of wages, government regulations, and so on. Many problems had also been resolved in 1988 when the similar but less comprehensive United States–Canada Free Trade Agreement was passed. Many Canadians opposed NAFTA, however, because they feared that it would lead to U.S. cultural domination of Canada. For example, there was concern that large chain bookstores from the United States would force smaller Canadian "boutique" bookstores out of business. And if they did, Canadians would find themselves reading trashy novels by U.S. writers instead of "good literature" by Canadian authors.

RECAP   **The Economics of Regional Trading Blocs**

Regional trading blocs typically have low (or zero) internal tariffs and common external tariffs. The European Economic Community and the North American Free Trade Zone are two examples.

1. *Trade creation and diversion.* Regional trading blocs both create and divert trade. Trade creation develops because of lower tariff barriers within the trading blocs; trade diversion can occur if low internal tariffs give an advantage to a member nation over a low-cost nonmember nation.

2. *Dynamic effects of regional trading blocs.* Internal competition and economies of scale can result in increased efficiency. This may explain why economic growth in the EU has exceeded economic growth in the United States since the community's formation.

3. *The European Union.* The EU grew out of the European Economic Community, which was formed in 1958. The EU now has 12 member nations. Most observers believe that the trade creation effect within the EU has been greater than the trade diversion effect. The exception may be agriculture where variable import levies have made it especially difficult for U.S. agricultural exporters. The current plan is to convert the EU into an economic union, complete with a common currency, but full implementation of these reforms is proving difficult.

4. *The North American Free Trade Zone.* NAFTA calls for the formation of a free trade zone comprising Canada, Mexico, and the United States. The North American Free Trade Zone will be the largest free trade zone in the world. Chief elements of the treaty include internal tariff elimination, most favored

---

[16]This court ruling was later overturned, but other environmental suits are likely in the future.

nation treatment of services, and the elimination of discriminatory investment policies. During the debate before congressional ratification of the treaty, concerns were raised regarding loss of jobs in the United States and weak environmental rules in Mexico.

EXCHANGE RATES: THE TIME FOR TARGET ZONES?

Unlike many debates in economics, the debate over fixed versus flexible exchange rates is not divided along liberal and conservative lines. Some conservatives prefer flexible exchange rates, while other conservatives advocate a return to the fixed exchange rates of the gold standard. Some liberals advocate fixed exchange rates as a solution to exchange rate volatility; other liberals believe flexible exchange rates are necessary to permit relative price changes. In fact, the chance of observing either extreme—rigidly fixed exchange rates or perfectly flexible exchange rates—is unlikely. Much more likely is something in between; that is, fixed exchange rates with a method for periodic adjustments or increased international cooperation at managing flexible exchange rates. One model for exchange rate coordination is the target zone approach advocated by Paul Krugman and others; the European Monetary System is an example of this system.

The European Monetary System

The **European Monetary System (EMS)** was formed in 1979 a few years after the breakdown of the Bretton Woods system of fixed exchange rates. The aim of the EMS was to have the currencies of the member nations float jointly and vary no more than ±2.25 percent of each other.[17] The hope was that this approach would reduce exchange rate risk and encourage trade within the system. The ECU was introduced by the EMS to help maintain exchange rate stability. Composed of a market basket of member currencies, ECUs are used as a reserve currency and bought and sold to manage exchange rates. In recent years, ECUs have also been used as a medium of exchange—tourists can even buy ECU-denominated traveler's checks—and some bond issues have been denominated in the ECU.

An important step in maintaining exchange rate stability is monetary and fiscal policy coordination. There is evidence that some monetary policy coordination has been achieved, but the nations of the EU have autonomous fiscal policies. The problem with policy coordination is that the economies of member nations do not always perform the same way so optimal policies will differ. For example, if Germany fell into a recession at the same time that France experienced high inflation, a stimulative policy would be indicated for Germany, but contractionary policies would be pre-

European Monetary System (EMS) A system of target bands for exchange rates established in 1979 after the breakdown of the Bretton Woods system.

[17]Until Britain and Italy dropped out in September 1992, the EMS had nine "full" members (Belgium, Britain, Denmark, France, Ireland, Italy, Germany, Luxembourg, and the Netherlands) and two other members (Greece and Spain). In the original agreement, the Italian lira was allowed to fluctuate 6 percent instead of 2.25 percent; the British pound was given the same wide bound when Britain joined the EMS in 1990.

ferred in France. If these policies were adopted, it would be difficult to maintain exchange rates within the target zone. The need for policy coordination is one reason why the Maastricht Treaty included an "excessive deficits procedure" that requires member nations to maintain small fiscal deficits.

The EMS faced a severe crisis in September 1992, ironically, at just the time when the citizens of France and Great Britain were voting on the Maastricht Treaty. Speculative runs were made against the British pound and Italian lira, causing both countries to drop out of the EMS and allow their currencies to float. Many observers believe that the runs against the pound and lira—as well as the Swedish krona and Finnish mark—were caused by the high cost of German reunification. Germany was forced to borrow heavily to finance reunification, and to do so, it had to pay high interest rates. High interest rates in Germany made the deutsche mark attractive relative to other European currencies, and as financial investors began trading for deutsche marks, there was pressure on other currencies to fall. France was able to defend its franc successfully and remain within the EMS; Britain and Italy were not so lucky.

The EMS currency crisis of 1992 came at an especially inauspicious time because it clearly influenced some votes on the Maastricht Treaty. To the extent that the crisis was caused by German reunification, however, it may be perceived as a one-time event. The goal of the EMS remains complete monetary unification and a common currency. If the Maastricht proposals are implemented as written, unification will occur in 1999 when a European Central Bank will be established. Like the Federal Reserve and the German central bank, the *Bundesbank,* the European Central Bank would be an autonomous agency independent of the member governments.

• • • • • • • •

Are Target Zones in the Future?

Paul Krugman,[18] John Williamson,[19] and other economists[20] have recently come to the conclusion that the present system of imperfectly managed flexible exchange rates must be replaced with a system of targeted exchange rate zones.

Most target zone proposals call for fairly wide target zones for exchange rates—perhaps 10 percent—and thus represent something of a halfway measure between fixed and flexible rates. Despite the wide target bands, the hope is that currency speculation will keep exchange rate movements quite small. For example, suppose that the dollar is near the top of its target zone. Currency speculators will believe that the dollar is more likely to depreciate than appreciate so they will sell dollars. This would cause the dollar to move downward—toward the midpoint of the target zone. The zones would not need to be adjusted unless there was clear evidence that economic fundamentals had changed.

---

[18]Paul Krugman, *Exchange Rate Instability* (Cambridge, Mass.: MIT Press, 1989). See especially Chapter 3.
[19]John Williamson, *The Exchange Rate System* (Washington, D.C.: Institute for International Economics, 1983).
[20]A good survey of recent work on exchange rate target zones can be found in Lars E. O. Svensson, "An Interpretation of Recent Research on Exchange Rate Target Zones," *Journal of Economic Perspectives* 6 (Fall 1992): 119–44.

There is considerable debate about the desirability of currency target zones. For example, Martin Feldstein agrees that the primary benefit would be to reduce exchange rate volatility, but he also notes that statistical studies show that volatile exchange rates have little effect on the volume of international trade.[21] Further, traders can buy futures contracts to lock in exchange rates. Feldstein is also concerned about the loss of autonomy in domestic monetary policy.

Another problem with targeted rates is that no one knows the "correct" exchange rate so it would be difficult to find initial par values. So many structural changes have occurred since the dollar enjoyed a period of stability that it is difficult to even guess the equilibrium value. Persistent trade deficits seem to indicate that the dollar is overvalued, but according to purchasing power parity theory, it may not be.

But any discussion of target zones for exchange rates begs the central issue: for target zones to have any chance of working, there will have to be more international economic cooperation than we have seen since World War II. The United States may be willing to use domestic policies to target exchange rates if Germany applies economic stimulus, Japan opens its markets, and free trade is allowed in agricultural products worldwide. Germany and Japan might insist that the United States get its fiscal deficit under control. Who goes first? Cynics will forever argue that the prospects for policy coordination are between slim and none, but there are some encouraging signs. For the past 20 years or so, leaders from the large industrial nations have held annual Economic Summit meetings to discuss domestic and international macroeconomic policies. In the 1970s, the Carter administration was able to persuade the large industrial nations to agree to stimulative policies; the Reagan administration had some success at currency stabilization; and the Clinton administration successfully pressed for cooperation to eliminate trade barriers in 1993. The forum for beginning the discussion appears to be in place. All we need is a little luck—and a touch of humility.

RECAP Exchange Rate Policy

The volatility of exchange rates since the end of Bretton Woods has led many economists to explore alternative systems of exchange rates. Some economists believe that flexible exchange rates are still preferable, while others favor a return to fixed exchange rates. Much attention, however, has focused on target zones for exchange rates, which represent something of an intermediate solution.

1. *The European monetary system.* The EMS, which was instituted in 1979, was designed to establish a target zone for European currencies. The aim was to keep member currencies from fluctuating more than 2.25 percent from par. The European currency unit (ECU) is used to help maintain exchange rate stability. The EMS faced a serious crisis in 1992, when both Italy and Britain were forced to drop out of the system.
2. *Target zones.* Some economists believe that a target zone with wide bands should be established worldwide. This would reduce exchange rate risk and

[21]Martin Feldstein, "Does One Market Require One Money?" *Policy Implications of Trade and Currency Zones* (Kansas City: Federal Reserve Bank of Kansas City, 1991): 77–84.

increase the volume of trade. To be effective, a target zone system would require monetary and fiscal policy coordination. Critics argue that exchange rate volatility has little effect on the volume of trade and that target zones remove too much domestic policy autonomy.

SUMMARY

This chapter has surveyed some of the economic problems and policies of the global economy of the 1990s and beyond. If any conclusion is to be reached, it is that increased policy cooperation may be necessary, but achieving this will be difficult.

1. The United States has been faced with budget and current account deficits for more than a decade. The macroeconomic identity assures that the two deficits are related to each other. However, it is not clear whether the problem lies in a shortage of national savings or declining international competitiveness.
2. The aim of the new international economics is to develop models and policies for the international economy without assuming perfect competition and free trade. Many new international economists advocate the use of strategic trade policies. Strategic trade policies are designed to help industries that produce economic rents and positive externalities. High-tech industries are often the target of strategic trade policies.
3. Nations often form regional trading blocs. Typically, these blocs have high common external tariffs and low internal tariffs. The hope is that trading blocs will increase trade and result in dynamic efficiency gains. The European Union and the North American Free Trade Zone are two examples.
4. Exchange rate volatility since the end of Bretton Woods has caused many economists to look for alternatives to flexible exchange rates. One common proposal is for wide-band target zones. The European Monetary System is an example of target zones. Target zones may reduce exchange rate volatility but they also require nations to sacrifice some domestic policy autonomy.

KEY TERMS AND CONCEPTS

twin deficits
depreciation
sunk cost model
new international economics
economic rent
strategic trade policies
positive externalities
European Union (EU)
most favored nation
trade creation
trade diversion

dynamic effects
regional integration
Treaty of Rome
variable import levies
Europe 1992
Maastricht Treaty
ECU
North American Free Trade Agreement (NAFTA)
European Monetary System (EMS)

······REVIEW QUESTIONS

1. What are the "twin deficits"? How are they related to each other? Is the U.S. saving rate related to the twin deficit problem?
2. What is the new international economics? How does it differ from traditional international economics?
3. What are strategic trade policies? Under what conditions might such policies be appropriate?
4. What are the potential advantages and disadvantages of regional trading blocs? Under what conditions will the advantages outweigh the disadvantages?
5. How are the economies of the EU nations integrated? How will this integration change if the Maastricht Treaty is implemented?
6. What are the main elements of NAFTA? Why was there so much debate before NAFTA was passed in 1993?
7. How would a system of exchange rate target zones operate? Why do some economists prefer such a system to the current system?

······PROBLEMS

1. Suppose that the United States suddenly balanced the budget but there was still a large deficit on the current account. What policies would you propose to eliminate the current account deficit? Or would you just ignore the deficit? Why?
2. Discuss the pros and cons of using currency depreciation as a solution to a trade deficit.
3. Perhaps the biggest problem with strategic trade policies is that it is difficult to pick the right industry for targeting. Explain why it may be more difficult to target an industry thought to have significant positive externalities than one that generates large economic rents.
4. One of the criteria for membership in the EU is that prospective members must have per capita GDP no less than half of the EU average per capita GDP. What is the economic rationale behind this membership criterion?
5. One of the chief potential advantages of trading blocs is that they generate dynamic efficiency gains. What specific efficiency gains do you think will result from NAFTA? Will everyone in the United States benefit from these efficiency gains?
6. Which elements of NAFTA do you think are most acceptable to U.S. workers? To U.S. business interests? To U.S. consumers?
7. Explain why an exchange rate target zone with wide bands could result in virtually fixed exchange rates.
8. The ECU was introduced as a tool for managing exchange rates under the EMS. Using supply and demand diagrams (you may want to refer back to Figure 6 from Chapter 36) show how the ECU could be bought and sold to maintain EMS exchange rate targets.

PART VIII

THE ECONOMICS DEGREE

CHAPTER 38

The Economics Degree

Well, where do you go from here? If you are like most students, you found your first economic course a bit challenging, but also informative and even a bit interesting. You can stop here, or you can go on. What you do next is up to you—isn't it always? If you do choose to study economics, you'll find that there are many job options. Large and small firms employ economists; high schools and colleges need economics teachers; lawyers need economic advice; and even environmental groups and nonprofit agencies are hiring economists. This chapter should help you prepare for what's ahead in the world of economics.

THE ECONOMICS CAREER

Much of the introduction to economics provided in this text focused on two things: the doctrinal history of economics as told largely by academic economists, and the growing influence of economics on policy. However, it would be wrong to interpret this to mean that economics is confined to the ivory towers of academe and policymaking circles. Economists work in manufacturing, mining, banking, insurance, retailing, and many other fields, and an undergraduate degree in economics is a particularly useful general degree. Training in economics is useful for analytical reasoning and critical thinking—perhaps the most important attributes in business today and in the future.

Business Economists

Business began to hire economists in increasing numbers shortly after World War II, and the economics profession has grown rapidly since then. This growth has occurred for several reasons. One reason is that management has become aware of the need for planning and problem-solving assistance—just the sort of tasks that are well suited to economic logic. Another reason is the increasing complexity of the global economy and its implications for business: someone is needed to analyze and interpret the wealth of often confusing data. Both large and small firms need economists. Large firms often have separate economic research divisions; smaller firms may have just one trained economist who divides his or her time among planning, forecasting, and finance and other duties. Firms that do not employ in-house economists often hire outside economic consultants.

The role of the economist may differ from that of the manager. Economists analyze data and provide information; the manager uses this information to make decisions. Economists may not get as much publicity, but the power to provide information can be important: good information makes for good decisions—bad information means just the opposite. This may explain why so many corporate CEOs rose to their positions through the economics division.

TABLE 38.1 ECONOMISTS AT WORK

Job Task	Percentage of Time
Forecasting and analysis of U.S. economy	21%
Industry forecasting and analysis	24
International forecasting and analysis	14
Product forecasting, microeconomics	10
Domestic policy analysis	8
Other analytical areas (market research, client support, demographics, etc.)	14
Administration	9

SOURCE: Dennis K. Hoover, "Business Economists: Not Just Forecasters," *Business Economics* 27 (July 1992): 56–59.

Many people think that economists spend all of their time forecasting, but this is incorrect. Economists do forecast, but most economists today are likely to have many other duties as well. In fact, in many firms, economists are really generalists and problem solvers who know a little bit about everything. For example, economists are often called upon to interpret key economic variables as they apply to the business or analyze inventory policies, financial market conditions, and the prospects for expansion. Many economists are also actively involved with public relations—giving speeches to the community or providing analysis for company publications. Table 38.1 provides the results from a 1991 survey of 32 large nonfinancial corporations and shows that business economists spend only about 60 percent of their time forecasting; the remainder of their time at work is spent in policy analysis, administration, market research, and other tasks.

Economists in the Government and Academe

Many economists work for the government or in academe. Almost all government agencies employ economists. Economists at the Environmental Protection Agency do environmental impact studies and develop alternative policies to protect the environment. Economists at the Central Intelligence Agency assess the stability of foreign countries. Economists at the Forest Service study optimal harvest rates and determine the best ways to use natural resources. The Peace Corps is frequently looking for people with undergraduate economics degrees who are willing to spend two years in a less-developed nation. In recent years, Peace Corps volunteers have also been sent to countries in the former Soviet Union. Government jobs—federal as well as state and local—can be quite competitive and usually require a civil service examination.

No one should pretend that the academic job market in the second half of the 1990s is good. Many new Ph.D.'s in English, sociology, and other disciplines never find the teaching jobs they spent so much time working for, but there are still a few disciplines where well-qualified graduates can land a college teaching job. Ph.D.'s in computer science and finance are in high demand; graduates from top schools often receive several job offers. The academic market for economics is not as good as either of these fields, but well-qualified graduates can usually find academic posts if they are persistent. The starting salary for an assistant professor of economics with a new Ph.D. has been in the mid to upper $30,000 range in recent years. Liberal arts colleges and schools without graduate programs usually pay lower salaries than research universities with graduate programs.

The Job Market in the Future

Though the economics profession has shown an upward trend since World War II, the market for economists has undergone cycles like most professions. For example, the average size of economics divisions in large corporations shrank from 8.3 to 6.5 persons (about 22 percent) following the recession of the 1980s. About half of the companies surveyed said the decline was due to company-wide downsizing, and a third said it was because of increased productivity. It is perhaps significant that less than a quarter said that they had reduced the scope of operation of the economics division; this would suggest continuing opportunities for economists as the economy grows in the future.[1] On the other hand, a recent article in *Forbes* suggested that the demand for economists was shrinking, largely because of the dismal record of economic forecasts.[2] It is notable too that while the average economist's salary increased by 317 percent between 1964 and 1994, the consumer price index rose by 366 percent.[3] This represents a decline in the real income of the typical economist—not an encouraging statistic, but not unlike the experience of many other professions over the same period.

Most would probably agree that the "typical" career track for economists in the business world has changed in recent years. For example, in the years after World War II, most bank economists followed a direct track through the economic and financial management divisions of their banks. Today, people generally take a more circular route upward with stops in different areas of the bank.[4] Again this career path should not be surprising; it is the same in most occupations. As the world changes, everyone must change with it. People who are capable of performing only a specialized task will fall along the wayside. This explains why so many business schools and business school accrediting agencies have emphasized the need for students planning a career in business to take more courses in liberal arts and develop written and oral communication skills.

Many economists are employed in the legal profession, and this trend will undoubtedly accelerate in the future.[5] Typical projects for economists working in legal analysis include damage estimates for civil litigation and antitrust cases. Economists are often asked to provide both economic presentations and expert testimony. Some consulting economists specialize as "forensic economists" and hire themselves out to lawyers as expert witnesses at rates as high as $200 per hour. The influence of economic analysis on the law has become so important that some schools now offer joint degrees in law and economics. Some law firms hire economic consultants; others employ their own in-house economists. The demand for economic analysis by lawyers is so high that some large economics consulting firms, such as Charles River Associates in Cambridge, Massachusetts, now have a separate division devoted entirely to economic analysis of legal issues.

Economists are showing up in places few would have anticipated until very recently. One place is secondary education: more and more high schools are offering high school economics courses, and in some cases students are required to take a

[1]Data are from Dennis K. Hoover, "Business Economists: Not Just Forecasters," *Business Economics* 27 (July 1992): 59. *Business Economics* is an excellent source for information on careers in economics. Most issues contain a section, "The Business Economist at Work," which is devoted to this topic.

[2]Dana Wechsler, "Dreary Days in the Dismal Science," *Forbes*, January 21, 1991, pp. 68–71. Not pleasant reading for the aspiring economist, but the author does interview several business economists who have been able to use their economics skills to find other niches in business.

[3]Data are from *Salary Characteristics, 1994*, p. 8, compiled with survey data by the National Association of Business Economists.

[4]Albert E. DePrince, Jr., and William F. Ford, "The Changing Fortunes of Bank Economists," *Business Economics* 28 (January 1993): 50–55.

[5]For a more detailed picture of the role of the economist in the legal profession, see James A. Hurdle, "Economists Inside and Outside of the Law: Providing Economic Analysis to Attorneys," *Business Economics* (October 1992): 57–62.

TABLE 38.2 ECONOMISTS' STARTING SALARIES BY EDUCATION

Degree	Median Starting Salary
Bachelor's	$26,997
Master's	32,006
Ph.D.	44,998
Average	32,003

SOURCE: National Association of Business Economists, *Salary Characteristics, 1994,* Table 15.

course in economics. A degree in secondary education emphasizing math and economics is especially attractive to many school districts. Nonprofit agencies—the Sierra Club, Greenpeace, and the Nature Conservancy—are employing more economists as well. A main reason these organizations are hiring economists is that market-based solutions to environmental problems—which economists have been advocating for years—have finally been accepted by environmentalists. Finally, as the world economy becomes more integrated, even small firms need to be aware of import competition and the prospect for export markets. The global economy is fundamentally more complex than the local economy and thus requires more careful analysis and planning—just the sort of thing done best by economists.

Salary

Salary should not be the only factor that influences your career choice, but neither can it be ignored. Economists tend to do rather well as a series of annual surveys by the National Association of Business Economists has revealed.[6]

Several factors determine economists' salaries. As with most professions, economists with advanced degrees earn substantially more than those holding only a bachelor's degree. As Table 38.2 shows, the median starting salary for economists in 1994 was about $32,000, while economists with a bachelor's degree earned $27,000 and Ph.D. economists started out at $45,000. Perhaps more important than starting salary, however, is the fact that economists with only a bachelor's degree often have only limited advancement opportunities. As in many fields today, it almost always pays to get an advanced degree.

Economists' salaries increase with experience. In 1994, the median base salary for economists of all experience levels was $70,000. Additionally, more than half of all economists (58 percent) earned $10,000 in extra compensation (often overtime or bonus pay) from their jobs, and about a quarter of all full-time economists earned another $5,000 from "professional secondary income"—typically, consulting. This suggests that the "typical" experienced economist actually earned about $77,000 in 1994.

[6]All data in this section are from *Salary Characteristics, 1994,* compiled with survey data by the National Association of Business Economists. The survey is done annually. Large and small businesses as well as government, academic, and consulting economists were included.

TABLE 38.3 ECONOMISTS' SALARIES BY INDUSTRY

Industry	Median Salary	Industry	Median Salary
Durable manufacturing	$69,000	Nondurable manufacturing	$94,000
Retail/wholesale trade	60,000	Banking	85,000
Securities and investment	95,000	Insurance	77,000
Communication and utilities	66,000	Publishing	61,000
Transportation	75,000	Mining	76,000
Real estate	61,000	Consulting	73,000
Nonprofit research	58,000	Trade association	74,000
Government	60,000	Academic	58,000
All others	85,000		

SOURCE: National Association of Business Economists, *Salary Characteristics, 1994,* Table 4.

The industry you work in also has a lot to do with your salary. Economists employed in the securities industry had the highest median salary ($95,000) while economists in academe had the lowest median salaries ($58,000). Table 38.3 provides a breakdown of economists' salaries by industry.

Finally economists' salaries also depend on the particular job responsibilities. Perhaps surprisingly, economists whose primary responsibility is general administration reported the highest median salaries ($85,000) while the lowest salaries belonged to econometricians, market researchers, and teachers. These data are reported in Table 38.4.

COLLEGE COURSE WORK

Unlike great athletes, most great economists are made, not born. True, it takes quantitative skills and a certain knack to see the interrelationship among variables, but becoming an economist requires study. Unlike many degrees—accounting and physics, for example—an economics degree is a general degree intended to teach problem-solving techniques as well as basic economics principles. This is why economics majors are so successful in a variety of career paths.

Your school has a specific set of requirements you'll need to complete for a major or minor in economics, but you'll also have to choose a number of electives. The courses you pick as your electives can be just as important as your major course work. What criteria should you use? That's up to you, but consider the following: first, ask your classmates, professors, or adviser for recommendations on courses that complement your degree plan. This may mean courses in biology if you are interested in environmental economics or a foreign language if you find yourself drawn to international economics. Second, look at courses that you never would have thought of taking—perhaps art or eastern philosophy. The best skill to have in the economy of the future will be the ability to digest new information and act accordingly. Exposure to new and different ideas is the only way to train for that skill. Third, if you think you might want to go to graduate school in economics or business, you should take as much math as you can possibly fit into your schedule. Two courses in calculus

•••• **TABLE 38.4 ECONOMISTS' SALARIES BY JOB RESPONSIBILITY**

Job Responsibility	Median Salary	Job Responsibility	Median Salary
Corporate planning	$75,000	International economist	$76,000
Econometrician	60,400	Macro forecaster	73,732
Energy economist	66,000	Marketing research	58,300
Financial economist	80,000	Statistician	35,543
General administration	85,000	Teacher	55,000
General administration/economist	82,500	Micro/regional economist	61,300
Industrial economist	73,500	All others	64,750
Consulting	75,000		

SOURCE: National Association of Business Economists, *Salary Characteristics, 1994,* Table 7.

should be considered the bare minimum for graduate work in economics. Finally, pick courses that you like. If you find yourself taking many courses that you don't like, you're probably studying the wrong subject.

That said, the National Association of Business Economists (NABE) recommends that undergraduate economics students take courses in accounting, computers, finance, statistics, mathematics, and English, as well as their major courses in economics. Quantitative skills are important, but the NABE also recommends courses in the social sciences—history, political science, psychology, and sociology—and stresses:

> In fact, for the majority of business economists, the ability to write clear, correct and readable English is a more important asset than a highly technical knowledge of statistics and mathematics.[7]

This may explain why many prospective employers ask for a writing sample from applicants. A college term paper—especially one on a topical issue in economics with some data analysis—makes a good addition to any job application file.

•••••••

Graduate School in Economics

Most people whose job title includes the word "economist" have a graduate degree in economics. If you did well in your undergraduate course work and, most importantly, if you enjoyed your economics courses, you should consider graduate school. The admission requirements for economics graduate programs vary from school to school, but all schools require facility with calculus and statistics, as well as familiarity with economic theory at the intermediate level. Admission into master's degree programs may be easier than Ph.D. programs. Typical master's programs take two years to complete and may or may not require a thesis. Most Ph.D. programs require two

---

[7]This quotation and much of the material in this chapter comes from *Careers in Business Economics* (Cleveland: NABE, 1992). This valuable pamphlet is updated periodically and is available for $1 from NABE, 28790 Chagrin Blvd., Suite 300, Cleveland, OH 44122. Students may become members of NABE (which includes a subscription to *Business Economics*) for $20 by writing the same address.

to three years of course work and a doctoral dissertation. The dissertation is an original piece of scholarship that can take a year or more to write. Most Ph.D. programs do not require a master's degree for admission.

Financial aid for economics graduate studies is widely available, and most Ph.D. students receive aid of one sort or another. The most common financial aid for economics graduate students is the teaching assistantship. In the first year, most TAs assist a professor in an undergraduate class. This usually involves grading papers and teaching labs for 10 to 15 hours per week. In their second or third year, TAs are often given full responsibility for a class. Research assistantships are also available. RAs assist professors in their research. This work may involve data collection and data entry, statistical work, or library research. Most programs recognize that economics graduate study is a full-time job and pay TAs and RAs enough to live on—almost. Depending on the school, the pay can run about $10,000 per year.

Where should you apply for graduate school? That depends on several factors. First, graduate programs can be quite competitive, so you'll do well to talk to your adviser first to find out where you have a chance for admission and financial aid. Your adviser should have a pretty good idea based on your grades, math background, and Graduate Record Examination scores. GRE exams are offered several times a year, but you'll need to take them in December of your senior year—at the latest—to have a chance for admission in the following fall. Many, but not all, graduate programs require both the general portion and the advanced test in economics. You should also ask your adviser where you can study the branch of economics you want to pursue. For example, the University of Arizona is a great place to study experimental economics; economists at MIT are doing state-of-the-art work in new Keynesian economics; the University of Nebraska is one of the best places to study institutional economics; several top econometricians teach at the University of California at San Diego, and so on. Be sure to apply to several schools. The standard approach is to apply to a couple of "reach" schools that you hope but do not expect to be admitted to, several schools you expect to be admitted to, and a couple of "fall back" schools just in case you do poorly on the Graduate Record Exam or whatever. Make an on-campus visit if at all possible. Finally, there is a real hierarchy in economics graduate programs so it is almost always best to go to the most highly rated program that will admit you, *especially* if you plan an academic career. Unfortunately, schools are rated according to several different criteria, so there is always debate over which are the top schools. It can't hurt to look at a recent study ranking economics departments, but be sure to take these with a grain of salt.[8]

Should you work for a few years before going to graduate school? That too depends on several factors. First, unlike most graduate business programs, few economics graduate programs recommend that applicants spend a few years in the business world before beginning graduate school. Most course work in graduate school is so abstract that the experience you gain running a small business (or whatever) will have little effect on your success in school. In fact, enrolling immediately after undergraduate studies may be best because your quantitative and other skills won't have

[8]One recent study is David Colander, "Research on the Economics Profession," *Journal of Economic Perspectives* 3 (Fall 1989): 137–48. This paper ranks departments by field and includes a good bibliography of other studies ranking economics departments.

had time to slip away. The most important issue, however, is you. If you feel a bit burnt out after four or five years of undergraduate work, by all means take a few years off before applying graduate school. If you're not completely ready to dedicate the time and effort, you simply won't be successful in graduate school.

We can't leave this discussion of graduate programs in economics without reference to a book that all prospective economics graduate students should read, *The Making of an Economist,* by Arjo Klamer and David Colander (Boulder, Colorado: Westview Press, 1990).[9] This book consists of interviews with graduate students at several of the top Ph.D. programs in the United States. It's not fun reading—many of the students complain bitterly about the quality of the instruction, the irrelevance of the material, and the demands placed on their time. The encouraging thing about the book is that it sparked debate and reaction from the economics profession and, it is hoped, change in the standard graduate curriculum. Much of that debate can be found in a 1991 symposium published in the *Journal of Economic Literature.*[10]

Assistance for Minority and Foreign Students

The American Economic Association sponsors several programs that are aimed at making graduate studies more successful for foreign and minority students.

The Summer Minority Program at Stanford University is a two-month program intended primarily for juniors and qualified sophomores majoring in economics who are planning to pursue a Ph.D. in economics.[11] The curriculum consists of three honors courses in microeconomics, macroeconomics, and quantitative methods. Weekly seminars are conducted by prominent minority economists. Courses are offered for credit as part of the regular Stanford summer session. All students admitted to the program receive a stipend that covers tuition, room and board, books, and transportation. The application deadline is usually March 1.

The Economics Institute is located at the University of Colorado in Boulder, Colorado.[12] It is designed to give foreign students a taste of graduate studies in the United States before they start taking courses for grades. Courses are offered in English, mathematics, statistics and econometrics, and economic theory. Noted graduate professors from several U.S. graduate programs teach at the Economics Institute.

Finally, the Committee on the Status of Women in the Economics Profession (CSWEP) is an arm of the American Economic Association that provides information and encouragement to women considering graduate work or careers in economics.[13]

---

[9]A shorter version of this study appeared as "The Making of an Economist," *Journal of Economic Perspectives* 1 (Fall 1987):95–111.

[10]Anne O, Kruger, et al., "Report of the Commission on Graduate Education in Economics," W. Lee Hansen, "The Education and Training of Economics Doctorates: Major Findings of the American Economic Association's Commission on Graduate Education in Economics," and Hirchel Kasper et al., "The Education of Economists: From Undergraduate to Graduate Study," *Journal of Economic Literature* 29 (September 1991): 1035–1109.

[11]For information, contact Susan A. Maher, AEA Program Director, Food Research Institute, Stanford University, Stanford, CA 94305-6084. Telephone: (415) 723-3653.

[12]For information, write The Economics Institute, 1030 13th Street, Room 23, Boulder, CO 80302. Telephone: (303) 492-3000. Fax: (303) 492-3006.

[13]For information, write CSWEP c/o Joan G. Haworth, 4901 Tower Court, Tallahassee, FL 32303.

CSWEP publishes a thrice-yearly newsletter that provides information on job opportunities and scholarships as well as articles about women's progress in the economics profession. Membership dues in CSWEP are $20, but full-time students may join for free.

. . . .

Graduate School in Other Disciplines

A degree in economics can provide an excellent background for graduate studies in other disciplines. In fact, there are probably more undergraduate economics majors in law school and masters of business administration (MBA) programs than in economics graduate programs. Law school admission advisers are especially pleased to see economics graduates because economic logic extends so easily to the logic of the law. Economics students tend to do well in MBA programs as well. Part of the reason for this may be that undergraduate economics programs provide students with the kind of quantitative skills that are necessary for success in good MBA programs. Many economics majors also choose to pursue graduate degrees in the other social sciences.

You should *always* follow your heart when choosing a degree program; if you don't like your studies, you won't do well in school or on the job after graduation. At the same time, it is also important to look at job prospects in the field. This may be especially true when considering graduate school in law and business. These programs have been so popular for the last two decades that some people feel that a glut of MBAs and lawyers has developed in the United States. For this reason, many advisers tell students planning to pursue these degrees to do so only if they can get accepted at one of the top 10 or 20 programs in the country. *Business Week* publishes an annual rating of the top MBA programs in the country every spring. Recent issues have suggested that experience can be just as valuable as an MBA degree unless the degree is from one of the top schools. It is relatively difficult to obtain financial aid for law school and MBA programs.

····ECONOMICS IN THE FUTURE

Economics is a science, and sciences change. The quantitative nature of economics today stands in stark contrast to the moral philosophy approach of Adam Smith. The discipline of economics and the role of the economist have changed in the past and will continue to change in the future. How will that affect the economics profession in the future? We can only guess, but three things come to mind immediately.

. . . .

The Role of Forecasters

Much of the reason the demand for economists grew following World War II was that corporate managers realized the value of economic forecasts. They also believed that people trained in the black arts of econometrics were able to construct the best forecasts. Two things may be happening to reduce the demand for economic forecasters. First, the large econometric models developed since the 1950s do not always generate forecasts that are markedly better than simple techniques. Second, the development of powerful desktop computers and simple forecasting software have made it possible for nonspecialists to construct econometric forecasts. However, even nonspecialists need a good grasp of economic theory before they are ready to interpret the results they get from their easy-to-use forecasting software.

New and more sophisticated forecasting techniques may be just around the corner. One of the most promising approaches involves nonlinear models based on chaos theory and other new kinds of mathematics.[14] These models can capture situations where a small initial cause can result in a large effect. For example, a small increase in the interest rate may cause a large drop in the stock market—or a small drop. Standard economic theory has difficulty dealing with this kind of situation because the same cause appears to result in two quite different effects. One reason for the current interest in nonlinear models is computing power. Until very recently, personal computers were not capable of calculations at the speed necessary to compute solutions to nonlinear systems. Nonlinear models already have been used by "rocket scientists" on Wall Street—economists and financial theorists who used advanced mathematical techniques—to predict stock market fluctuations.

· · · · · · · ·

The Collapse of Socialism

The collapse of the Soviet Union not only freed millions from the yoke of communism, but it also ended one of the great ideological debates of our era. No longer is there much discussion of the efficiency of capitalism versus the equity of socialism. The concern now is how to design the best policies to work under the different varieties of capitalism. Economics Nobel laureate James Buchanan believes that this will result in less polarized debate within the profession and a willingness to recommend policies that have an explicit normative basis. While the capitalism/socialism ideological debate raged, economists were trapped into using "objective" models and resisted policy recommendations with any taint of state intervention, aka socialism. The result, according to Buchanan, was that policy recommendations were often sterile.

The collapse of socialism has also accomplished something much more mundane: it has opened up new markets for firms willing to invest the time and effort. Consumer products companies—McDonald's, Pepsico., Mars Candy, Pizza Hut, and others—have been among the first to jump into these markets, but manufacturing companies have been setting up plants as well. Foreign investment is always risky and difficult, and this is especially true in the former socialist economies. Nevertheless, this expansion has been a boon to economists and the economics profession. Many firms have found it necessary to expand their economics divisions or hire consulting firms to conduct studies. Even the government has gotten into the act: the Peace Corps now sends business and economics majors to teach market economics to people in the former socialist economies.

---

[14]A popular introduction to chaos theory can be found in James Gleick's best-selling *Chaos: Making a New Science* (New York: Viking, 1987).

• • • • • • • •

Economics and Moral Philosophy

Buchanan's belief that economists will be more willing to recommend policies with an explicit normative bent echoes the views of a number of other economists who believe that the economics of the future will return to its roots in moral philosophy.[15] Economics is too important to be confined to "objective" and "positive" analysis. It must tackle the issues of equality, well-being, and environmental regulation head-on. Economists need to be concerned with moral and ethical issues for at least four reasons:

1. The morality of economic agents often influences economic outcomes. For example, economists have noted that blood donations are more efficient than commercial arrangements that pay "donors" for blood. The reason is obvious: true donors have no incentive to lie about possible blood infections; people who are selling blood for money do. The economist who ignored ethical issues and suggested that more blood would be donated if donors were paid could be making a tragic mistake.

2. The economist's standard view on welfare economics already has a strong underpinning of morality. Consider the Pareto optimality criterion, the linchpin of modern welfare economics. According to this rule, any policy that makes one person worse off, even if everybody else is better off, fails because it is impossible to "scientifically" determine whether the gains of the group outweigh the losses of the single individual. In the real world, of course, *all* policies hurt some people and help others. If economists want to contribute in a meaningful way to real-world policy debate, they must be willing to relax the Pareto criterion—and make value judgments.

3. The conclusions of economics must be linked to moral commitments that drive policy. For example, from the economist's standpoint, it was irrational to spend the hundreds of thousands of dollars to dig Baby Jessica out of an abandoned well in Texas because the same amount of money would have saved the lives of more children had it been spent on neonatal care. Would it have been better to pump poison gas down the well to lessen Jessica's suffering? Certainly not, at least not according to most of the people who clung to their television sets to follow the ordeal—and later watched a TV movie that chronicled the affair. Economists must understand that there are strongly held moral values, and that these values are just as important as any conception of rationality economists may have.

4. Finally, even if economists wanted to ignore moral and normative issues, it would be impossible to do so. Positive and normative judgments interact. Normative concerns dictate the questions that positive economists will ask. To pretend to be positive is to refuse to analyze the normative content of your analysis—which is far from scientific.

What is the consequence of this new moralizing by economists? It means that econ-

---

[15]This section draws upon Daniel M. Hausman and Michael S. McPherson, "Taking Ethics Seriously: Economics and Contemporary Moral Philosophy," *Journal of Economic Literature* 31 (June 1993): 671–731.

omists will be forced to expand their purview and communicate with experts in other disciplines. It means that economists will have to take a stand on the *meaning* of their technical analysis. This will be a new challenge for a generation of technical economists, but it will also be a refreshing change for the policymakers who need real advice and counsel from the economics profession.

FOR FURTHER READING

If this course has whetted your appetite for economics, you should consider a few more courses in economics or even a major or minor in economics. And in the meantime, you should start reading economics. Don't despair! Not all economics is as dry as a textbook. There are a number of places to turn for lighter but still valuable economics. Here are a few things to look at as you bask on the beach this summer:

- The *Wall Street Journal*. If you aren't already reading the *Wall Street Journal,* it's time to start. The WSJ is not only a well-written business newspaper, but it also has articles on politics, sports, and the arts, as well as an occasional humorous piece. Keeping up with the news from the WSJ is one of the best ways to prepare for your first "real" job interview. Your professor should have student subscription forms. And carrying a copy of the WSJ with your own name printed on the mailing label looks quite chic.
- *Business Week*. Like the WSJ, *Business Week* is a national publication devoted to business news. As a weekly, it has a bit more room for analysis and in-depth coverage. Its editorial bias is also more moderate. Student subscription rates are available.
- *The Economist*. Published in England, *The Economist* is more of a news magazine than an economics publication per se. It is well-written, quite witty, and has a decidedly pro-market editorial stance. Unfortunately, it is somewhat expensive— $110 per year—though student subscriptions are available for $75 per year. *The Economist* has been publishing an annual edition since 1991 that should be available in your library; this is a great reference for term papers on international politics and economics.
- *Challenge Magazine*. This magazine, subtitled "The Magazine of Economic Affairs," is published six times a year. Unlike *Business Week* and *The Economist, Challenge* is not a news magazine but focuses on recent developments in economics and economic policy debates. Its editorial stance is clearly to the left of *Business Week,* but there are frequent contributions from conservative economists. *Challenge* also includes a "For Further Reading" section that is useful for building bibliographies for term papers. *Challenge* offers student rates. You should be able to find it in your school library.
- *Journal of Economic Perspectives*. Most economics journals are far too technical for introductory students. This is one of the reasons why the American Economic Association founded the *Journal of Economic Perspectives* in 1987. Many of the papers in JEP are commissioned surveys for nonspecialists, and most are written by well-known experts in the field. Like *Challenge,* JEP also includes a "Recommendations for Further Reading" section.

The American Economic Association also publishes two other journals, the *American Economic Review* and the *Journal of Economic Literature*. Few articles in the AER are accessible to beginning students, with one exception: the May issue consists primarily of articles presented at the annual meeting the preceding January. Some of these articles are nontechnical enough for beginning students. The *Journal of Economic Literature* is an invaluable reference publication. It includes current articles in economics, book reviews, and article abstracts, as well as one or two commissioned survey articles. It's a great place to begin research for a term paper.

. . . .

Best-Sellers and Classics

What about an economics tome or two for the plane ride home? Several well-known economists have written books for the general public—but you'll undoubtedly find that your newly acquired background in economics will make the reading much more worthwhile. One of the most successful popular economics writers is Lester Thurow, dean of the Sloan School of Management at MIT. Some of Thurow's books include *The Zero Sum Society* (New York: Penguin, 1980), which examined the problems societies face when income growth slows; *The Zero Sum Solution* (New York: Simon & Schuster, 1985), which offered recommendations for building a competitive, world-class economy for the United States; *Dangerous Currents* (New York: Random House, 1983), a collection of essays on the state of economics; and *Head to Head* (New York: Morrow, 1992), which warned of the coming economic battle between the United States, Japan, and Europe. Paul Krugman, also of MIT, is the author of *The Age of Diminished Expectations,* rev. ed. (Cambridge, Mass.: MIT Press, 1993), which analyzes contemporary U.S. economic problems and explains why people are now willing to settle for less. Labor Secretary Robert Reich has written widely on the need for government subsidies for industrial development and worker training. His most recent book, *The Work of Nations* (New York: Knopf, 1991), asked the question, "Who is 'us'?" to emphasize that the global nature of modern corporations means that our wealth is determined not by what we own, but by what we do. This explains Reich's emphasis on worker training and retraining. In an earlier book, *The Next American Frontier* (New York: Penguin Books, 1983), Reich made his case for industrial policy—an argument that did not endear him to many economists, but did catch the attention of his former classmate, Bill Clinton. Many of Reich's arguments from this book have been updated in *Who's Bashing Whom: Trade Conflict in High-Technology Industries* (Washington, D.C.: Institute for International Economics, 1992) by CEA chair, Laura D'Andrea Tyson. All of these books are available in paperback.

Economics Nobel laureate Milton Friedman's classics *Capitalism and Freedom* (Chicago: University of Chicago Press, 1962) and *Free to Choose* (New York: Harcourt Brace Jovanovich, 1980) provide well-written introductions to Friedman's libertarian philosophy and its applicability to market economies. Both are collections of articles; the second is a companion volume for a PBS documentary Friedman did with his wife Rose. You may not agree with everything that Friedman says, but you'll have to admit that he makes you think.

Liberal John Kenneth Galbraith may be the wittiest economist writing today and the most fun to read. His most recent book, *The Culture of Contentment* (Boston:

Houghton Mifflin, 1992), argues that a "greatly self-satisfied elite is now dominate in the electoral process." As a result, the nation has drifted into a "self-serving economic and social stasis." If you're interested in the history of economics and economic history, look at his PBS companion volume, *The Age of Uncertainty* (Boston: Houghton Mifflin, 1977), or perhaps *Economics in Perspective: A Critical History* (Boston: Houghton Mifflin, 1987). Like Friedman, Galbraith always generates controversy. You'll also find yourself chuckling from time to time at his keen observational powers.

If none of these books sparks your interest, *Business Week* runs two articles every year—typically one before the Christmas season and one before summer vacation—on the best current business books. Books reviewed by *Business Week* usually aren't available in paperback editions for a year or more, but you should be able to pick up the hardcover editions at your public library. Or try this: give one to your mom for Christmas, but read it before you wrap it.

Glossary of Key Terms and Symbols

A

A_0. Total autonomous spending.

Ability to Pay. Criterion for determining fairness of taxes; progressive income taxes fit this criterion because people in higher income brackets pay a higher portion of their income in taxes. Compare *benefits received*.

Absolute Advantage. A nation has an absolute advantage in the production of good X if fewer resources are required in the production process. However, *comparative advantage*, not absolute advantage, is the basis for international trade.

Absolute Income Hypothesis. Simple theory of consumption. In the simple Keynesian model, $(C = C_0 + cQ_d)$, as disposable income increases, consumption increases, but by a smaller amount. See also *life-cycle hypothesis* and *permanent income hypothesis*.

Absolute Poverty. People are in absolute poverty if they do not have the basic necessities of life. Compare *relative poverty*.

Accelerated Depreciation Allowance. Tax program designed to stimulate investment. Firms are allowed to depreciate capital goods more rapidly than they actually wear out; this reduces the firm's tax liability and leaves the firm with additional after-tax profits to be used for investment.

AD. Aggregate demand curve.

Ad Valorem **Tax.** Sales tax levied as a percentage of the value of the good being sold. *Value-added taxes* are *ad valorem* taxes. Compare *unit sales tax*.

Adaptive Expectations. Model of expectation formation that assumes people are backward looking and make mistakes. Results in slow adjustment. Compare *rational expectations*.

Adding Up Problem. In marginal productivity theory, the sum of all factor payments must "add up" to the value of the output. See also *Euler's theorem*.

AFL/CIO (American Federation of Labor/Congress of Industrial Organizations). Umbrella organization for most organized labor in the United States.

Agency Problem. Exists when an "agent" acts on behalf of a principal and the motivations of the agent differ from those of the principal. For example, the goals of corporate managers may differ from the goals of stockholders. Agency costs include the costs principals must pay to monitor the agent.

Aggregate Demand Curve (AD). Downward-sloping curve in (P, Q)-space. The downward slope is caused by the effect of higher prices on real spending and GDP, intertemporal substitution, and international substitution. Important shift factors include fiscal and monetary policy, consumer and business confidence, and expectations.

Aggregate Supply Curve (AS). Upward-sloping curve in (P, Q)-space. The upward slope is caused by diminishing returns; generally thought to be relatively flat at low levels of real GDP and steep at high levels of real GDP. Shift factors include wage adjustment, regulations, and work incentives. See also *long-run aggregate supply curve*.

Aid to Families with Dependent Children (AFDC). Basic welfare program of the United States. Often criticized for instilling work disincentives.

Allocative Efficiency. A welfare criterion holding that the marginal benefit of a good must equal the opportunity cost of producing that good; exists when $P = MC$. See also *technical efficiency*.

Analytical Time. Economists often divide time into periods useful for analysis; for example, the *short run* and the *long run*. Contrast *historical time*.

Anticipated Inflation. Inflation is anticipated if wages, interest rates, and taxes are indexed to inflation. Anticipated inflation imposes *welfare costs* on society. Compare *unanticipated inflation*.

Arbitrage. Investment strategy that involves the simultaneous purchase and sale of an asset. Can exist only when markets are imperfect.

Assumption. A postulate or premise used as a starting place for the development of a theory in order to isolate the issue of interest.

Asymmetric Information. Information held by only one side of the market. For example, firms may have a better idea of future inflation than workers.

Austerity Measures. When nations with balance of payments difficulties request loans from the IMF, they are often required to enact austerity measures to reduce their trade deficits. These measures often include deficit reductions and tight monetary policy.

Automatic Stabilizer. Nondiscretionary fiscal policies that tend to reduce the amplitude of business cycle fluctuations. Examples include personal and corporate income taxes and unemployment compensation.

Autonomous Spending. Spending that does not depend on the level of income; compare to *induced spending*.

Autonomous Tax (T_0). Tax levied on an *autonomous variable*. Autonomous taxes shift the spending line in the income-expenditure model.

Autonomous Variable. Variable that does not depend on income; i.e., investment (I_0), government spending (G_0), and autonomous consumption (C_0). The level of autonomous spending determines the intercept of the spending line in the income-expenditure model.

Average Fixed Cost (AFC). Total fixed cost divided by quantity. Declines as output increases.

Average Product (AP). Total product divided by output. The *AP* curve is crossed from above at its maximum value by the *marginal product* curve.

Average Propensity to Consume (APC). Total consumption divided by disposable income. Time series: roughly constant over the long run, but fluctuates *countercyclically* over the short run. Cross-sectional: declines as income increases.

Average Propensity to Save (APS). Total saving divided by disposable income; *APS* + *APC* = 1.

Average Revenue (AR). Total revenue divided by quantity; equivalent to the demand curve facing the firm.

Average Total Cost (ATC). Total cost divided by quantity; *ATC* = *AFC* + *AVC*. U-shaped; minimum exists at intersection with *marginal cost*.

Average Variable Cost (AVC). Variable cost divided by quantity. U-shaped; minimum exists at intersection with *marginal cost*.

B

Balance of Payments. Record of transactions between one nation and the rest of the world. Double-entry bookkeeping assures that there is always a balance; however, subaccounts of the balance of payments—see *capital account* and *current account*—can be in deficit or surplus.

Balance of Trade. Also called *merchandise trade balance.* Subaccount of the *current account* that includes exports and imports of goods but not services.

Bank Reserves. Currency held in bank vaults and on deposit at the Federal Reserve; basis for *fractional reserve banking*. Not counted as part of the money supply.

Barrier to Entry. Condition that precludes firms from entering an industry to compete for profits. The existence of substantial barriers to entry is necessary for *monopolies* and *oligopolies* to survive.

Barter. Nonmonetary transaction; trading goods for goods. For barter to take place, a double coincidence of wants must exist.

Base Year. The first year used in the calculation of a price index; assigned a value of 100 or 1.0.

Benefits Received. Criterion for determining fairness of taxes; property taxes may fit this criterion because people with more property may stand to benefit more from public services such as police protection. Compare *ability to pay*.

Biodiversity. The genetic variability within a particular species as well as the number of different species. Genetic diversity within a species is necessary for survival; species diversity is important for intrinsic reasons and because many plants and animals have been shown to play important roles in science and medicine.

Board of Governors. Main policymaking body of the Federal Reserve system. Consists of six members appointed for staggered 14-year terms and a chair appointed for a four-year term.

Bolshevik Revolution (1917). Revolution that replaced the tsarist government of Russia with the Soviet Union; V. I. *Lenin* was a leading figure in the revolution and the first leader of the new Soviet Union.

Bond. A financial asset; a promissory note. Corporations and the government borrow money by selling bonds. See also *capital gain*.

Bourgeoisie. In Marxian analysis, the bourgeoisie were the capitalists; the class that exploited labor.

Bracket Creep. The effect of inflation on nonindexed progressive income taxes. Higher inflation causes nominal incomes to rise and shifts people into higher tax brackets even though their real income has not risen. Eliminated by indexing the tax system.

Bretton Woods Agreement (1944). The Allied powers of World War II met at Bret-

ton Woods to establish the rules of the game for postwar international trade. The main features of the system were fixed exchange rates and the dollar exchange standard; it also established the *IMF* and the *World Bank*. The system collapsed in 1973. See also *devaluation bias* and *Smithsonian Agreement*.

Budget Constraint. In consumer theory, the maximum amount of income available to the consumer. Graphically, the budget constraint is a straight line with a slope equal to the negative of the price ratio of the two goods in the consumption bundle.

Business Cycle. Actually a misnomer; should be business fluctuation. The periodic ups and downs of economic activity over time; business cycles appear to be a natural process of capitalism. See also *Kondratiev*, *Malthus*, and *recession*.

C

c. The marginal propensity to consume; $\Delta C/\Delta Q_d$.

C_0. Autonomous consumption.

Capacity Utilization Rate. During *recessions*, firms cut back on production and leave plant and equipment idle; this means that they are not working up to capacity. By examining changes in the capacity utilization rate, economists can get an idea of the state of the economy. Most firms operate with excess capacity to ensure that they will have the ability to meet an unexpected large order.

Capital. Most often refers to machinery used in the production process; financial capital is money available to buy machinery or other financial assets.

Capital Account. Subaccount of the *balance of payments*. Records the flow of financial capital across international boundaries. The United States has been running a surplus on the capital account for several years.

Capital Consumption Allowances. In GDP accounting, the amount of money set aside for depreciation of plant and equipment. GDP − capital consumption allowances = NDP; GPDI − capital consumption allowances = NPDI.

Capital Gain. Profit made from buying an asset at a low price and selling it at a high price. See also *capital gains tax*.

Capital Gains Tax. Tax on profits from buying an asset at a low price and selling it at a high price. Some economists believe that capital gains should be given preferential treatment—lower taxes than wage income—as an incentive to increase investment.

Capital/Labor Ratio. The ratio of the amount of machinery used in a production process to the number of workers. Most production processes permit various capital/labor ratios, but some processes require a fixed proportion of labor to capital.

Capitalism. Economic system characterized by private ownership of the means of production. Compare to *socialism*.

Capital Market. Financial market where financial assets with maturities longer than one year are traded. See also *money market*.

Capitalization. The conversion of a payment into the value of a financial asset. For example, if the interest rate is 10 percent and the annual return is $100 per year forever, the capitalized value of this return stream is $100/0.10 = $1,000. Taxes on unimproved land are also capitalized into the value of the land; higher taxes lower the value of the land.

Capture Theory of Regulation. Theory of government regulation, advanced by Stigler, that asserts that the regulators will be "captured" by the regulatees and thus enact regulations that benefit the regulatees more than the public. Compare *public interest theory*.

Cardinal Utility. Idea that consumer satisfaction ("utility") can be measured in countable units called "utils." Rejected by most economists who favor theories based on the assumption of *ordinal utility*.

Cartel. Association of producers who agree to limit output and fix prices. OPEC is a cartel.

ceteris paribus. Latin phrase meaning "everything else held constant." Frequently applied to economic models to isolate the variable of interest. For example, high interest rates reduce investment, *ceteris paribus*.

Checkable Account. Any deposit account that has check-writing privileges. Most money in the United States is in checkable accounts.

Classical School. School of economic thought that dominated economics in the eighteenth and nineteenth century. Founded by *Adam Smith;* leading members included *Ricardo* and *Malthus*. Some scholars place *Marx* in this school.

Clayton Act (1914). Important amendment to the *Sherman Act* of 1890. Forbade price discrimination, tying arrangements, and exclusive dealing.

Closed Shop. Arrangement between union and management that restricts hiring to members of the union. Most closed shops were ruled illegal by the *Taft-Hartley Act* of 1947. See also *open shop* and *union shop*.

Closed System. In macroeconomic models, a system is closed if there is no foreign sector.

Coase Theorem. Formulated by Ronald Coase, this theorem holds that externalities do not lead to resource misallocation as long as there is a system of well-defined property rights.

COLA (Cost of Living Adjustment) Clause. Method of indexing wages to inflation. May lead to stagflation and make it difficult to control inflation. COLA clauses became popular in the high-inflation years of the 1970s; many union contracts omitted COLA clauses following the recession of the 1980s.

Command Economy. Economy where government planners decide what, how and for whom. The former Soviet Union was a command economy. Compare *traditional economy*.

Commercial Bank. "Full-service" financial institution that accepts deposits and offers checkable accounts. Due to the financial deregulation of the 1980s, there is now little difference between commercial banks and *savings and loan associations*.

Common Property Resource. Land, fish, or other resource that is jointly owned by all individuals. Common property resources are often overutilized. See *tragedy of the commons*.

Communism. In Marxian analysis, a utopian state that would evolve out of socialism after years of abundance had changed human motivations. People would work for the enjoyment of working. Greed would cease to exist.

Comparable Worth Legislation. Wages for "women's jobs" are typically lower than wages for "men's jobs"; therefore, some have argued for laws requiring that wages be based on comparable worth instead of the market or tradition. Jobs that require similar levels of skills and contribute the same amount to the economy would pay similar wages.

Comparative Advantage. Discovered by Ricardo, the basic principle underlying the doctrine of free trade. Nations should produce and export those goods that can be produced at the lowest relative opportunity cost. All nations will gain from free trade, and world output will increase. Compare *absolute advantage*.

Comparative Static Analysis. Economic methodology that involves analysis of different points of static equilibrium. Finding the new equilibrium point that results from an external supply shock is an exercise in comparative statics.

Compensating Wage Differential. Pay differences based on job attractiveness, danger, or similar factors. For example, workers on the Alaskan pipeline are paid extra wages to compensate for the severe winters.

Complementary Good. A good that is used in conjunction with another; for example, CDs and CD players, gasoline and automobiles. If the price of a good increases, the demand for a complementary good will decrease.

Concentration Ratio. Common measure of industrial concentration. 4-, 8-, and 20-firm concentration ratios are often calculated. The higher the concentration ratio, the greater the degree of monopoly power. Compare *Herfindahl index*.

Congeneric Merger. A merger between

related firms that do not produce the same product or have a producer-supplier relationship. Congeneric mergers allow a degree of diversification and may be somewhat safer than *conglomerate mergers* because management may better understand the ins and outs of the acquired firm's industry.

Congestion Effect. May occur during mild recessions. When workers hear of a "good" job, they may pass up "acceptable" jobs and congest the market looking for the few good jobs. If enough people do this, the economic benefits of the job search can be lost.

Conglomerate. A large firm with many subsidiaries producing unrelated products.

Conglomerate Merger. A merger between unrelated firms that leads to a conglomerate. Conglomerate mergers may help firms diversify risk; however, the difficulties involved with managing unrelated firms have led to a decline in popularity in recent years.

Conspicuous Consumption. Veblen's idea that people will sometimes choose to consume expensive goods to impress their neighbors. Most likely to occur in wealthy societies. Would result in a upward-sloping demand curve.

Constant Growth Rate Rule. The money supply should be allowed to grow at a constant rate regardless of the state of economic activity. This would eliminate inflation and generate economic and financial stability. Developed by *Milton Friedman;* basic premise of *monetarists;* also advocated by *new classicals.*

Constant Return to Scale. In production theory, if doubling inputs causes output to double, then the production function is said to exhibit constant returns to scale. Compare *decreasing returns to scale, diminishing marginal returns,* and *increasing returns to scale.*

Consumer Confidence Index (CCI). Index calculated by consumer survey; often leads turning points in the business cycle. Similar to *index of consumer sentiment.*

Consumer Equilibrium. Consumers are in equilibrium when their spending yields maximum satisfaction. This occurs when the last penny spent on each good yields the same utility, or when $MU_a/P_a = MU_b/P_b = \cdots MU_z/P_z$.

Consumer Price Index (CPI). Price index composed of a typical market basket purchased by typical urban consumer; used in many wage indexation plans. Probably overstates true inflation somewhat. See also *GDP deflator.*

Consumer Sovereignty. Idea that consumer wants originate within the individual; basic premise of consumer theory. Contrast *dependency effect* and *revised sequence.*

Consumer Surplus. The area under the demand curve but above the price line. This is the "bargain" that consumers get in competitive markets. Sales taxes can reduce the amount of consumer surplus. See also *producer surplus.*

Consumption Function. Relationship between consumption expenditure and disposable income. See also *absolute income hypothesis, life-cycle hypothesis,* and *permanent income hypothesis.*

Consumption Possibilities Curve (CPC). The choices available for national consumption. Free trade increases world output and allows nations to expand their consumption possibilities beyond their *production possibilities curve.*

Contestable Markets. Theory developed by Baumol and others. Even monopoly firms may act like competitive firms if they fear the potential entry of other firms. Contrast *structure-conducts performance model;* see also *sunk costs.*

Control. Desirable attribute of *intermediate target* for monetary policy; the ability of policymakers to manage intermediate targets with *policy instruments.* Unfortunately, the connection between instruments and intermediate targets is often weak. See also *linkage* and *measurability.*

Controlled Experiment. Basic scientific methodology used to determine cause and effect: all factors except X are held constant to determine whether X causes Y. It is very difficult to conduct controlled experiments in economics.

Cooperative Game. In *game theory,* a game where players agree to cooperate to determine the outcome. Less interesting than a *noncooperative game.*

Core Economy. From theory of the *dual economy,* the large, capital-intensive, technologically advanced firms that typically pay high wages and earn high profits. Contrast *periphery economy.*

Corporate Income Tax. Tax levied on corporate profits. Unclear whether this tax is paid by stockholders through lower dividends, workers through lower wages, or consumers through higher prices. May act as a disincentive to invest.

Corporation. Form of business characterized by limited liability, separation of ownership from control, and relatively easy access to financial markets. Subject to double taxation.

Correlation. Statistical property of association between two or more variables. Correlation does *not* imply causality.

Cost-Benefit Analysis. Basic methodology used to determine desirability of policy: the costs are compared to the benefits; if benefits exceed costs, the policy is implemented. Unfortunately, it is frequently difficult to measure costs and benefits.

Cost-of-Service Formula. Regulatory formula where companies provide the regulatory agency with cost information, and the agency sets a regulated price based on a "fair profit." This approach gives firms little incentive to reduce costs because there is no profit reward for a cost reduction. Currently used to regulate the price of natural gas in interstate natural gas pipelines. See also *price-cap formula* and *yardstick competition.*

Countercyclical. Varies in the opposite direction of the business cycle. For example, unemployment increases when the business cycle turns down; therefore, unemployment is said to be countercyclical.

Coupon Payment. Annual or biannual return on a bond.

CPI. See *consumer price index.*

Credibility Effect. If the resolve of policymakers is believable, macroeconomic adjustment may be quicker. For example, credible anti-inflation policies may reduce inflation with a less severe recession.

Credit Controls. Minor policy tool of the Fed; the right to place restrictions on credit. Last used in 1980.

Credit Targets. Alternative intermediate target of monetary policy. Advocated by Benjamin Friedman who believes credit can be easily measured and controlled.

Cross Elasticity. Measure of responsiveness in the quantity demanded of good X as the price of good Y changes: $E_{xy} = (\Delta Q_x / \overline{Q_x}) / (\Delta P_y / \overline{P_y})$.

Cross-Sectional Data. Data collected at a point in time; for example, family income by state for the year 1992. Compare *time series data*.

Crowding Out. Decline in private investment due to high interest rates caused by government borrowing. Most severe during cyclical expansions.

Crude Quantity Theory of Money. Early version of the quantity theory of money that assumed both velocity and real GDP were fixed. This implied that the rate of inflation equaled the rate of money growth.

Currency. Basic unit of the money supply; as used by economists, refers to both paper and metallic money (coins).

Current Account. Subaccount of the *balance of payments* that records the movement of goods and services plus transfer payments across international boundaries. The United States has run persistent deficits on the current account for the past 15 years. See also *capital account*.

Current Reserves. In resource economics, the amount of natural resources available at existing prices. Compare to *potential reserves* and *resource endowment*.

Cutthroat Competition. Pricing strategy designed to drive competitors out of the market; typically involves setting prices very low.

Cyclical Deficit. Deficit caused by recession; as the economy falls into recession, government spending automatically increases and tax revenues automatically fall. Often considered to be good because it stim-

ulates the economy. Compare *structural deficit*.

Cyclical Productivity Growth. Productivity growth caused by ups and downs of the business cycle. When the economy recovers from a recession, firms add workers to existing but idle machinery; this increases productivity. The opposite occurs during recessions. See also *secular productivity growth*.

Cyclical Unemployment. Unemployment caused by recession; unemployment greater than *full employment*. See also *frictional unemployment, natural rate of unemployment,* and *structural unemployment*.

D

d. The sales or demand curve facing the firm.

D. Demand curve.

Decreasing-Cost Firm. If average total costs fall as output expands, the firm is a decreasing-cost firm. Decreasing costs can lead to monopoly.

Decreasing Returns to Scale (DRS). If all inputs are increased by 10 percent and output increases by less than 10 percent, then the production process is DRS. May be caused by managerial inefficiency. See also *constant returns to scale* and *increasing returns to scale*.

Defensive Foreign Investment. Name given to foreign investment intended to stave off tariff barriers. Some have argued that Japanese automobile plants in the United States are defensive foreign investments.

Deficit/Saving Ratio. Ratio of fiscal deficit to private saving. Important because saving is necessary to finance the deficit. An increase in this ratio is an indication that the deficit may be crowding out private investment.

Deflation. The opposite of inflation; a decrease in the aggregate price level. Rare in recent years. Compare *disinflation*.

Deindustrialization. The decline of manufacturing industries. Some people believe that the United States has been deindustrializing since the 1970s; others note that de-

clining employment in manufacturing is the result of increased worker productivity.

Demand-Constrained Economy. A term applied to capitalist economies because most firms and labor markets suffer from a lack of demand. This acts as an incentive for innovation and cost cutting. Compare *supply-constrained economy*.

Demand Curve. Graphical representation of the relationship between own-price and the quantity that will be purchased. Slopes downward because of diminishing marginal utility and income and substitution effects. Important shift factors include income, tastes, other prices, and the number of buyers.

Demand-Pull Inflation. Inflation that originates on the demand side of the economy, typically caused by excess money growth or expansionary fiscal policy. Characterized initially by increasing employment and rising prices; later, employment falls as wages catch up with higher prices. See also *supply shock*.

Dependency Effect. Term used by J. K. Galbraith to argue that consumer wants depend on the goods that are offered and advertised by corporations; contradiction to *consumer sovereignty*. See also *revised sequence*.

Dependent Variable. The "effect" variable; if X causes Y, then Y is the dependent variable. In the theory of consumption, consumption depends on disposable income so consumption is the dependent variable. See also *independent variable*.

Depletable Resources. Natural resources that can be exhausted. Oil is a depletable and nonrecyclable resource; aluminum is a depletable but recyclable resource.

Depository Institutions Deregulation and Monetary Control Act (DIDMCA). Financial legislation passed in 1980 that increased competition in the banking industry, legalized NOW accounts, and phased out most interest rate ceilings.

Deregulation. Any number of measures designed to reduce government interference with business. In theory, deregulation lowers costs and increases output. Key component of Reagan's *supply-side economics*.

Derived Demand. In marginal productivity theory of factor pricing, the demand for the factors of production is "derived" from the output of the factors. That is, firms do not demand workers, they demand the productivity of labor.

Devaluation. Act by government to reduce the value of its currency; typically used to combat trade deficits.

Devaluation Bias. Main reason for failure of the Bretton Woods system. Nations experiencing trade deficits were willing to devalue their currencies, but nations with trade surpluses were unwilling to revalue their currencies because it would cause an economic slowdown at home.

DIDMCA. See *Depository Institutions Deregulation and Monetary Control Act.*

Differential Rent. Rent on land that depends on diminishing marginal productivity; competition for the best land will bid up rents and exhaust the economic profits that would have gone to the firms locating on the better land, and the least productive land earns no rent.

Diminishing Marginal Productivity. In production theory, if at least one factor of production is fixed, adding additional units of other factors will eventually cause the output per unit of input to diminish. See also *law of diminishing returns.*

Diminishing Marginal Rate of Factor Substitution. In every production process, combining additional units of one factor with a fixed amount of another factor causes the marginal product of the first factor to decline. Therefore, as firms consider different factor ratios, they are willing to trade a diminishing number of units of one factor for each unit of the other factor.

Diminishing Marginal Rate of Substitution. In utility theory, the consumption of each additional unit of a good yields less utility; therefore, as more units of good X are consumed, the consumer can give up fewer and fewer units of good Y and maintain the same level of satisfaction; explains why *indifference curves* are convex to the origin.

Diminishing Marginal Returns. Second stage of the production function. Exists when additional inputs cause output to increase, but at a diminishing rate. Production usually takes place in this stage. See also *negative marginal returns* and *increasing marginal returns.*

Diminishing Returns. Same as *diminishing marginal productivity.*

Direct Relationship. If Y increases (decreases) when X increases (decreases), then the relationship between X and Y is direct; an upward-sloping supply curve is a direct relationship between price and quantity supplied.

Directly Unproductive Activities. An alternative name for *rent-seeking behavior.* Often refers to the act of acquiring a monopoly license so the firm can earn lucrative monopoly returns. The process of acquiring the license is often costly and "unproductive" from society's standpoint.

Discount Rate. (*a*) One of the three main monetary policy tools of the Fed; the interest rate charged on loans to commercial banks. The Fed increases the discount rate to reduce the money supply and decreases the discount rate to increase the money supply. (*b*) The interest rate used in capital budgeting and *present value* computation. In the formula,

$$PV = \sum_{t=1}^{\infty} R_t/(1+r)^t,\ r \text{ is the discount}$$

rate.

Disincentive to Work. Typically refers to high marginal income tax rates that reduce take-home pay and thus may discourage work effort. Work disincentives shift both the labor supply curve and the aggregate supply curve to the left.

Disinflation. The gradual declining rate of inflation; occurred in the 1980s. Compare *deflation.*

Disintermediation. Taking money out of financial intermediaries; usually caused by interest rate ceilings that keep bank and savings and loan rates below market rates. The elimination of most interest rate ceilings with the passage of *DIDMCA* in 1980 eliminated most disintermediation.

Disposable Income (Q_d). Income minus taxes.

Dividend. The stockholder's share of corporate profits; rising dividend payments often cause stock prices to rise.

DJIA. See *Dow Jones Industrial Index.*

Dollar Exchange Standard. Name given to the exchange rate system established by the *Bretton Woods Agreement.* The dollar was tied to gold, and all member currencies were tied to the dollar. Foreign countries could exchange dollars for gold in the United States.

Dollar Glut. Period in the 1960s and early 1970s when the dollar was overvalued. This led to persistent balance of payments disequilibria in the United States. Failure of the surplus nations to revalue their currencies led to the collapse of *Bretton Woods.* See also *devaluation bias.*

Dollar Shortage. Period in the 1950s when the dollar was undervalued by *Bretton Woods* system. Foreign nations needed dollars to buy U.S. goods to rebuild their war-ravaged economies. See also *dollar glut.*

Dominant Strategy. Term from *game theory.* A dominant strategy is one that both players will pursue regardless of the expected acts of the other player. Occurs in *prisoner's dilemma* and other games.

Dominant Strategy Equilibrium. Outcome of *dominant strategy.*

Double Taxation. Refers to corporate taxation. Corporations are taxed twice: both corporate profits and the dividends paid to shareholders are taxed.

Dow Jones Industrial Index (DJIA). Index of 30 large "Blue Chip" stocks thought to signal overall performance of the stock market. Many people believe a more broad-based index like the Standard and Poor Index is a better indicator of stock market performance.

Dual Economy. A conception of the economy as being composed of large firms in the *core* and small firms in the *periphery.*

Duality. In production theory, duality refers to the idea that maximizing output subject to a cost constraint is equivalent to minimizing cost subject to an output constraint.

Dumping. Selling goods abroad for less

than the price they are sold for at home, after adjustment for transportation costs. May be used to stimulate the domestic economy. *GATT* allows tariffs to be imposed to punish nations found guilty of dumping.

DUP. See *directly unproductive activities*.

Durable Goods. Goods that last one year or more, such as automobiles and refrigerators. Important because consumers often postpone durable goods purchases when they lack confidence in the economic future. See also *nondurable goods*.

E

Earth Summit. Meeting held in Rio de Janeiro in 1992 to discuss world environmental problems. The main topics of the conference were biodiversity and climate change. The United States did not sign two major treaties that came out of the conference.

Econometrics. Application of statistics to economic analysis; often used in forecasting models.

Economic Growth. Typically refers to increasing *GDP*. All economies go through economic growth cycles over time. U.S. GDP growth has averaged about 3 percent per year since World War II.

Economic Profits. Profit greater than the rate necessary to maintain the established level of production; i.e., $P > ATC$. Perfectly competitive firms cannot make economic profits in the long run. Also called Abnormal profits.

Economic Recovery Tax Act (ERTA). Major piece of economic legislation of the Reagan administration. Called for, among other things, significant income tax cuts over a three-year period. Often blamed for record fiscal deficits of the 1980s.

Economic Rent. Factor payment exceeding payment necessary to bring the factor into production. All rent on unimproved land is economic rent; the economic profit accruing to a monopolist represents economic rent.

Economic Tax Incidence. Refers to who actually pays the tax, which often differs from the *legal tax incidence*. For example, if corporations are able to raise selling price to cover taxes, the economic incidence of the corporate tax falls on the consumer; the legal incidence falls on the corporation.

Economies of Scale. If a firm is able to lower per unit production costs by increasing the size of its plant, then it can enjoy economies of scale.

Economies of Scope. Reduction in average cost resulting from the joint production of two or more products; can result from the merger of firms producing similar products.

ECU. Acronym for European currency unit; a market basket of several European currencies used as a reserve currency to maintain exchange rates under the *European monetary system*. Could be the single European currency when (and if) economic unification takes place in Europe.

Efficiency. Important welfare criterion. Exists when output is maximized for a given amount of inputs.

Efficiency Wage Theory. *New Keynesian* theory of the labor market. Holds that firms may pay above-market wages to increase worker productivity, reduce turnover, and lower recruiting costs.

Efficient Markets Hypothesis. Theory that markets digest information quickly. Implies that it is impossible to outguess the market on a regular basis. Therefore, the best investment strategy is diversification because trying to pick individual winners is impossible. See also *new classical economics* and *rational expectations*.

Efficient Tax. A tax that can be levied with minimum cost and has a minimum effect on economic incentives.

Elasticity. The responsiveness of one variable to a change in another variable; used in several contexts in economics. See also *cross elasticity, elasticity of supply,* and *price elasticity of demand*.

Elasticity of Supply. Percentage change in the quantity supplied divided by the percentage change in price. $Es = (\Delta Qs/\overline{Qs})/(\Delta P/\overline{P})$.

Employment Act of 1946. One of the most important pieces of economic legislation of the twentieth century. Established the Council of Economic Advisers and required Congress to pursue policies for high employment, economic growth, and price stability.

EMS. See *European monetary system*.

Enclosure Movement. One of the key events that led to the collapse of feudalism and the rise of capitalism; began in twelfth-century England and spread throughout Europe through the nineteenth century. Peasants were no longer allowed to use public land for grazing when landowners realized that they could fence the land, raise sheep, and make a substantial profit. As a result, small farmers had to move to the city.

Endogeneity Question. Issue raised by new industrial economics in criticisms of SCP model: SCP advocates believe that industry structure is determined exogenously by outside factors; new industrial economists believe that industry structure can be determined endogenously by firm behavior.

Endogenous. A variable whose value is determined by the system under investigation. For example, the level of consumption is endogenous in the income-expenditure model because higher levels of GDP increase consumption. See also *exogenous*.

Endogenous Money Supply. Theory of some Keynesian economists that the money supply depends on the state of economic activity; that is, that the Fed cannot control the money supply. Rejected by many *monetarist* and *new classical* economists.

Entitlement Programs. Programs such as welfare, Social Security, and Medicare to which people are entitled by law. These programs have grown rapidly in recent years and are a major issue in budget-cutting debates.

Entrepreneur. A person who takes risks and combines the various factors of production into a business enterprise. Often thought to be the primary dynamic factor under capitalism.

Entropy. From physics, refers to energy that is not available for use. According to the *second law of thermodynamics,* entropy increases whenever matter or energy is converted from one use to another.

Equation of Exchange. Basic building block of the *quantity theory of money*: $MV = PQ$ where M = money supply, V = velocity, P = price index, and Q = real GDP.

Equilibrium. State of rest. A market is in equilibrium if the quantity supplied is equal to the quantity demanded. Most markets will stay in equilibrium until outside factors result in movement to a new point of equilibrium.

Equity. Fairness; a *normative* judgment. Many economic policies must trade off *efficiency* and equity.

ERTA. See *Economic Recovery Tax Act.*

Euler's Theorem. Key theorem in marginal productivity theory. Holds that factor payments will exhaust the selling price of output. See also *adding up problem.*

Eurodollars. U.S. dollars held outside the United States, in Europe as well as elsewhere. Eurodollars often move into and out of the United States in response to interest rate fluctuations. This can complicate domestic monetary policy.

Europe 1992. Term used to refer to the economic unification of Europe that was scheduled to begin in 1992. See also *Maastricht Treaty.*

European Economic Community. Regional trading bloc consisting of 12 nations in Europe, now known as the European Union (EU). Established by the *Treaty of Rome* in 1958. The EU nations have a common external tariff and low internal tariffs. Variable import levies on agricultural imports have been a major point of contention with the United States.

European Monetary System (EMS). System of target bands for exchange rates established in 1979 after the breakdown of the *Bretton Woods* system. Designed to reduce exchange rate risk and encourage trade within the system.

European Union (EU). See European Economic Community.

Eurosclerosis. Term coined to refer to the sluggish European growth of the 1980s; thought to be caused by excessive spending on welfare, worker benefits, and other social programs.

Excess Capacity Theorem. From the theory of *monopolistic competition:* the tangency between the *average revenue* curve must occur on the downward-sloping portion of the *average total cost* curve, so monopolistically competitive firms never operate at the minimum point on their average cost curves. The result is chronic excess capacity and inefficiency.

Excess Reserves. Reserves greater than *required reserves.* These reserves are available for lending and expansion of the money supply.

Exchange Rate. The price of a foreign currency. For example, $1.00 = ¥110.

Exchange Rate Risk. A risk associated with exchange rate fluctuations. Importers are hurt by depreciation of their domestic currency because it means that foreign currencies and thus foreign goods are more expensive. Advocates of fixed exchange rates believe that fixed rates reduce exchange rate risk and thus increase the volume of international trade.

Exclusion Principle. *Private goods* are subject to this principle, *public goods* are not. A person using a private good can exclude others from using it; a person using a public good cannot exclude others from using the same good. This is a reason why public goods cannot be sold in the market.

Exogenous. Determined outside the model. For example, interest rates are exogenous to the income-expenditure model. Compare *endogenous.*

Exogenous Money Supply. Assumption made by many economists that the Fed can control the money supply; that is, that economic activity does not influence the amount of money in circulation. Compare *endogenous money supply.*

Expectations-Augmented Phillips Curve. Model showing how expectations of wage and price inflation affect the tradeoff between inflation and unemployment.

Expected Return (R^e). All investment decisions are based on imperfect knowledge of the future. Firms will acquire capital if the expected return is greater than the interest rate.

Expenditure Approach. Method of national income accounting based on the identity, $Q = C + I + G + (X - Z)$, where Q = real GDP, C = consumption expenditure, I = investment expenditure, G = government expenditure on goods and services, and $(X - Z)$ = net exports.

Exports. Goods produced in the domestic economy and sold abroad; recorded as a credit on the balance of payments. Important exports of the United States include agricultural products, aircraft, computers, and services. See also *imports.*

Externality. The benefit or cost to society from a private action that is not included in price or cost calculations. For example, pollution is an externality because it represents a cost to society that is not included in the cost calculations of the firm nor is it paid for by the people who buy products produced by the firm.

Extreme Value. In graphical analysis, the maximum or minimum point on a curve. Economists are often concerned with extreme values of functions.

F

Factor Market. The market for inputs—land, labor, and capital. Contrast *output market.*

Fair Trade. Term used by people who advocate the use of tariffs or other measures as incentives to get other nations to open their markets to our imports. Japan is often the target of fair trade advocates.

Fallacy of Composition. Methodological error holding that what is correct for one is correct for all. For example, if one person tries to save more, he or she probably can, but if everyone tries to save more, the economy will fall into recession, and aggregate saving may fall.

FDIC. See *Federal Deposit Insurance Corporation.*

Feasible Region. Area of attainable outcomes. In consumer theory, the area between the axis and the budget constraint; in production possibilities curve analysis, the area between the axis and the PPC curve.

Featherbedding. Labor union tactic designed to increase the demand for union labor. When diesel locomotives replaced steam locomotives, unions forced railroads to keep workers who had loaded coal into the steam engines, even though coal was no longer used.

Federal Deposit Insurance Corporation (FDIC). Federal agency established in 1933 to insure deposits. Current limit is $100,000 per account. Reduces depositor losses and thus lessens the risk of a bank run.

Federal Open Market Committee (FOMC). The chief policy arm of the Federal Reserve system. Directs the buying and selling of government securities to control the money supply.

Federal Reserve System. Central bank of the United States established in 1913 and consisting of 12 regional Federal Reserve banks. Most policy decisions are made by the Board of Governors and the Federal Open Market Committee. Independent of the Treasury.

Fertility Rate. The average number of live births a woman has in her lifetime; about 1.84 in the United States.

Feudalism. Social and economic system of the Middle Ages; predecessor to capitalism. Characterized by rigid social classes and a largely agrarian economy. The rise of a merchant class, the quest for profit, and the *enclosure movement* were key events that spelled the end of feudalism around the seventeenth century.

Fiat Money. Money that has value only by government decree or "fiat." Paper money is fiat money.

Financial Intermediation. Process of linking savers and borrowers; banks and savings and loan associations are financial intermediaries. See also *disintermediation.*

Firm. The basic production unit in the economy. A firm may consist of one or more *plants.* All firms producing the same product comprise an industry.

First-Degree Price Discrimination. Monopolist strategy of charging the highest price each consumer is willing to pay; eliminates all consumer surplus. Compare *second-degree price discrimination* and *third-degree price discrimination.*

First Law of Thermodynamics. The total amount of energy and matter can be neither created nor destroyed. See also *second law of thermodynamics.*

Fiscal Deficit. The difference between annual government spending and annual government tax revenues. Large deficits may cause interest rates to rise and *crowd out* private investment. See also *national debt.*

Fiscal Dividend. The result of *bracket creep.* In the absence of tax indexation, inflation puts people in higher tax brackets and thus raises government tax revenues automatically.

Fiscal Drag. Higher tax revenues due to the *fiscal dividend* may act as a "drag" on economic growth.

Fiscal Policy. Tax and spending policies of the government. One of the two main tools for economic stabilization. See also *monetary policy.*

Fisher Effect. After Irving Fisher, the effect of monetary policy and inflation on interest rates. If a monetary expansion increases the expected rate of inflation, nominal interest rates will rise, not fall.

Fixed Coefficient Technology. Production process that requires a fixed number of workers per machine. When production exhibits fixed coefficients, changes in factor prices will not change factor proportions.

Fixed Costs. Costs that do not vary with output; i.e., insurance premiums. Fixed costs do not affect the decision to produce or shut down because they must be paid in either case. Compare *variable costs.*

Flow Variable. A variable that has a time dimension; income is a flow variable because it matters whether you earn $10 per hour or per day. Compare *stock variable.*

FOMC. See *Federal Open Market Committee.*

Food Stamps. A type of in-kind welfare payment in the form of coupons that can be exchanged for food.

Fractional Reserve Banking. Banks accept deposits but keep only a fraction (about 10 percent) as bank reserves and lend out the rest. The fraction that is kept is regulated by the Federal Reserve. See also *required reserves.*

Free Entry and Exit. Assumption of the competitive model. New firms are assumed to enter the industry when industry profits are high and to exit the industry when losses occur.

Free Rider. People can receive benefits from *public goods* whether they pay for them or not, so in the absence of mandatory taxes, some people would enjoy the benefits without paying. These people are called free riders.

Free Trade. Term used to describe the absence of tariffs and other trade restrictions. According to the *law of comparative advantage,* all nations gain from free trade.

Frictional Unemployment. The unemployment that occurs when people are changing jobs. May provide a benefit to the economy if people find jobs that better fit their job skills. Compare *cyclical unemployment* and *structural unemployment.*

Friedman, Milton (b. 1912). Nobel Prize–winning conservative economist known for his advocacy of the *constant growth rate rule* and *laissez faire* policies. Developed the *permanent income hypothesis.*

Full Employment. The maximum level of employment that can be achieved given the existence of *frictional* and *structural unemployment.* Generally thought to exist when between 5 and 6 percent of the labor force is unemployed.

Fundamental Disequilibrium. In the *Bretton Woods* system, the condition when a nation had persistent balance of payments problems brought on by a significantly over- (or under-) valued exchange rate. In cases of fundamental disequilibrium, nations were allowed large adjustments to their exchange rates.

G

G_0. Autonomous government purchases.

G-7. See *Group 7.*

Gains from Trade. Benefits derived from free trade. As nations specialize in the production of goods in which they have a *comparative advantage,* output and income rise; both nations benefit.

Galbraith, John Kenneth (b. 1910). Contemporary liberal economist best known for criticisms of conventional wisdom and corporate power.

Game Theory. Mathematical technique used to analyze strategic behavior among a small number of participants. Games involve players, strategies, and payoffs. See also *dominant strategy, Nash equilibrium,* and *prisoner's dilemma.*

GATT. See *General Agreement on Tariffs and Trade.*

GDP. See *gross domestic product.*

GDP deflator (*P*). Price index composed of a wide range of goods and services produced in the economy. Used to convert nominal GDP to real GDP.

GDP Gap. Difference between actual GDP (Q) and potential GDP ($Q^\star$). When $Q < Q^\star$, the economy is in recession; when $Q > Q^\star$, inflation is likely. Many macroeconomic policies are designed to close the GDP gap.

General Agreement on Tariffs and Trade (GATT). International body formed in 1947 to reduce tariff barriers and establish the rules for international trade. Basic principles are unconditional *most favored nation* treatment for all GATT members, multilateral negotiations to reduce tariffs, and the elimination of import quotas.

General Equilibrium. Condition where all markets within the economy are in simultaneous equilibrium and there is no tendency for change. First analyzed by Léon Walras.

Glasnost. Russian word meaning "opening"; used by Gorbachev to signify the relaxation of Soviet political oppression. See also *perestroika.*

Glass Steagall Act. Law passed in 1933 that separated commercial banks and investment banks. Also prohibited interest on checking deposits and gave the Fed the right to impose reserve requirements.

Gold Standard. Monetary system in which currency is backed by a fixed amount of gold and exchange rates are fixed. Most trading nations were on some form of gold standard until World War I. After World War II, the gold standard was replaced with the *dollar exchange standard.*

Gosplan. State planning commission established by *Lenin* in 1921 to develop a national economic plan for the next decade. Nationalized most industries and collectivized agriculture.

Government Failure. Term used by *public choice* theorists. Refers to the idea that governments are just as likely to make mistakes as markets; therefore, the smaller the role of government, the better.

GPDI. See *gross private domestic investment.*

Gradualism. Alternative to *shock therapy* as a means for restructuring the former socialist economies. Involves phased-in institutional changes, privatization, and marketization. Gradualism has apparently been used successfully in China and Hungary.

Gramm-Rudman Act. Law passed in 1985 that required the government to reduce the deficit each year by a fixed amount. Essentially ignored by Congress.

Great Depression. Worldwide depression that occurred in the 1930s. In the United States, unemployment approached 25 percent in 1933, the worst year of the depression. Election of Franklin D. Roosevelt in 1932 led to a series of stimulative policies that, combined with the stimulus from defense spending for World War II, led to recovery.

Grim Strategy. From *game theory*. Strategy where it pays to move second.

Gross Domestic Product (GDP). Final market value of all goods and services produced in a year. A *flow* variable, GDP is the basic measure of macroeconomic performance.

Gross Private Domestic Investment (GPDI). The sum of all spending on plant and equipment, residential structures, and inventory change in a year; includes spending to replace worn-out capital. Contrast *net private domestic investment.*

Group 7 (G-7). Loose organization of the seven largest industrial countries in the world—Canada, France, Great Britain, Germany, Japan, Italy, and the United States. Meet periodically to discuss issues in international economics. See also *Louvre Accord* and *Plaza Accord.*

Growth Recession. "Mini-recession" characterized by significant slowing of GDP growth but not negative GDP.

H

Herfindahl Index. Index of industrial concentration calculated by squaring the percentage shares of each firm. Generally considered superior to *concentration ratios.*

High-Powered Money. Currency and bank reserves available for multiple expansion of the money supply. See also *bank reserves, fractional reserve banking,* and *money multiplier.*

Historical Time. Also known as calendar time; time as measured by clocks and history. Contrast *analytical time.*

Homogeneous Products. Identical products; competitive firms are assumed to produce homogeneous products.

Horizontal Merger. Merger between firms in the same industry producing similar products. For example, a merger between General Motors and Ford would be a horizontal merger. Contrast *vertical merger.*

Household. Basic consuming unit in economic analysis. Households sell resources to firms, earn income, and purchase products.

Human Capital. Term first used by G. Becker. The sum total of all knowledge, skills, and education of an individual. People with more human capital usually command higher wages than people with less human capital.

Hypothesis. Guess or conjecture to be tested by scientific analysis.

Hysteresis. Theory applied to unemployment, which states that there is no tendency for unemployment to return to its *natural rate* after being disturbed. May explain the secular increase in unemployment in Great Britain and the United States in the 1980s.

I

I_0. Autonomous investment.

ICC. See *Interstate Commerce Commission*.

ICS. See *index of consumer sentiment*.

IMF. See *International Monetary Fund*.

Impact Lag. In fiscal and monetary policy analysis; the time it takes before the effect of a policy change is actually felt by the economy; often thought to be between six and nine months for monetary policy; can vary considerably for fiscal policy. See also *implementation lag* and *recognition lag*.

Imperfect Information. Lack of information on the part of firms or workers; may explain why economic adjustment is slow. See also *rational expectations*.

Implementation Lag. Once the need for a policy change is recognized, it takes time before policy changes can be enacted. This time is the implementation lag. See also *impact lag* and *recognition lag*.

Imports. Goods and services produced abroad and sold in the domestic economy. Important U.S. imports include oil and manufactured products, especially automobiles. See also *balance of trade* and *exports*.

Impossibility Theorem. Formulated by K. Arrow, a theorem from welfare economics stating that majority rule can lead to nonsensical (intransitive) results.

Income. A *flow variable;* the payment to factor owners. Contrast *money,* a *stock variable*.

Income Effect. Effect of a price change. A rise (fall) in price lowers (raises) real income and reduces the amount that can be purchased. See also *substitution effect*.

Income Elasticity. The ratio of the percentage change in quantity to the percentage change in income; $E_y = (\Delta Q/Q)/(\Delta Y/Y)$. Income elasticity is positive for *normal goods* and negative for *inferior goods*.

Income-Expenditure (Q/E) Model. Simple Keynesian model of national income determination. Equilibrium exists when national income = planned spending and there are no unintended inventory changes. See also *spending multiplier*.

Income-Received Approach. A method of national income accounting involving summation of all factor payments: wages, interest, rents, and profits.

Income Tax. Tax on personal income; the basic source of revenue for the federal government. The current system is slightly *progressive* because a higher fraction of income is taken from upper-income people than from lower-income people. Income taxes are often thought to generate *disincentives to work*.

Increasing-Cost Firm. Firm that is operating beyond optimal capacity on the upward-sloping portion of the *average total cost* curve.

Increasing Marginal Returns. First stage of the production function. If the capital stock is fixed, adding additional workers will result in more output per worker because of specialization. Competitive firms never operate in this stage. See also *negative marginal returns* and *negative marginal returns*.

Increasing Returns to Scale. If a firm increases all inputs by X percent and output increases by more than X percent, then the firm exhibits increasing returns to scale. Can result from increasing managerial efficiency.

Independent Variable. The cause variable in a multivariable relationship. For example, as price rises, the quantity demanded falls. Price is the independent variable; quantity demanded is the *dependent variable*.

Index of Consumer Sentiment (ICS). Index compiled from monthly survey data on consumer expectations by the University of Michigan. Considered a good *leading indicator* of aggregate economic activity.

Indifference Curve. Graphical device used to depict consumer theory; represented improvement over earlier theory because it eliminated the need to assume *cardinal utility*. The convex shape is caused by the assumption of a *diminishing marginal rate of substitution*.

Indifference Map. The hypothetical plot of all possible *indifference curves*.

Induced Variable. In the income-expenditure model, a variable that is influenced by the level of income. The term cQ_d from the function $C = C_0 + cQ_d$ is an induced variable. See also *autonomous variable*.

Industrial Army of the Unemployed. In Marxian analysis, the rising numbers of workers displaced by the acquisition of capital. *Marx* felt that the industrial army would rise up to overthrow the *bourgeoisie*.

Industrial Policy. System of taxes and subsidies designed to move the economy along a prearranged path. The most important goals are to ease the transition of resources from declining industries to growing industries and to increase aggregate productivity growth. Used extensively in Japan and some other countries; subject of intense debate in the United States.

Industrial Revolution. Social and economic upheaval in eighteenth- and nineteenth-century Europe that ushered in capitalism. Tremendous increases in industrial efficiency changed production methods as well as social organization.

Industry. The collection of *firms* competing with each other selling identical or similar products.

Industry Equilibrium. In perfect competition, the condition where all firms are operating with zero economic profits so there is no incentive for entry or exit from the industry.

Infant Industry. A new industry that has not yet developed scale economies and thus cannot compete on international markets. Tariff protection for infant industries is sometime advocated; however, it is difficult to decide whether the infant industry will be competitive in the future, and removing temporary protection can be hard.

Inferior Good. A good that people demand less of as their incomes increase. For example, most people consider hamburger inferior to steak. The *income elasticity* of inferior goods is negative.

Inflation. A continual rise in the price index, typically caused by excessive monetary growth. In the short run, fighting inflation often means higher unemployment. See also *deflation, disinflation,* and *Phillips curve.*

Inflation Tax. The effect of *bracket creep* on tax liability. Higher inflation raises income and shifts people into higher tax brackets. Cynics contend that the government engineers inflation to raise tax revenues without the public's knowledge.

Inflationary Gap. The difference between the level of *autonomous spending* necessary to generate potential GDP and the actual level of autonomous spending. Measured vertically on the income-expenditure diagram. Exists when actual GDP is greater than potential GDP; typically causes inflation. See also *GDP gap* and *recessionary gap.*

Informative Advertising. The "good" role of advertising; advertising that increases consumer knowledge about products and thus allows more informed choices. Contrast *persuasive advertising.*

Inframarginal Rent. Exists when suppliers vary in their willingness to offer their services; the difference between the factor payment and the minimum payment necessary to bring the factor into production is inframarginal rent. Also called *producer surplus.*

Innovations. Important inventions that drive economic development and give rise to business cycles. According to J. Schumpeter, innovations are the cause of 40- to 60-year cycles. See also *Kondratiev.*

Input Market. See *factor market.*

Intercept. In graphical analysis, the point where the function (line) crosses an axis. When plotted in (C, Q_d)-space, the vertical intercept of the consumption function $C = C_0 + cQ_d$ is C_0. This is found by setting $Q_d = 0$ and solving for C.

Interest Rate. The cost of borrowing money; also, the income paid to the owner of capital. Always expressed as a percentage. If you borrow $100 and agree to pay back $110 in a year, the interest rate is $10/100 = 10$ percent. See also *nominal interest rate* and *real interest rate.*

Intermediate Target. Monetary policy officials desire stable prices and economic growth, but they cannot control these variables directly. Instead, they use *policy instruments* to control intermediate targets that are thought to be strongly linked to policy goals. Important intermediate targets include the money supply and interest rates.

International Monetary Fund (IMF). Organization established in 1947 as part of the *Bretton Woods* system. Lends money to member nations in the event of short-term balance of payments difficulties. See also *austerity measures* and *World Bank.*

International Substitution. An explanation for the downward slope of the *aggregate demand curve.* An increase in the price level will cause people to search for low-price foreign substitutes. This will reduce the demand for domestic products and result in a lower level of real GDP. See also *intertemporal substitution.*

Interstate Commerce Commission (ICC). Government regulatory body established in 1887 to ensure fair prices and regulate rail traffic across state borders. Powers were expanded considerably during the Great Depression.

Intertemporal Allocation. Choice between use today and use at other time periods. Models of intertemporal allocation are often applied to the use of finite resources.

Intertemporal Substitution. An explanation for the downward slope of the *aggregate demand curve.* An increase in the price level will reduce the real money supply and thus raise interest rates. This will act as an incentive to save and thus as a disincentive to consume. The result will be a lower level of real GDP. See also *international substitution.*

Intransitivity. A transitive relationship exists when *a* is preferred to *b* and *b* is preferred to *c*. Therefore, *a* is preferred to *c*. If *a* is not preferred to *c*, the relationship is intransitive. See also *impossibility theorem.*

Inventory Adjustment. Key equilibrating process in the income-expenditure model. When production (income) exceeds purchases (expenditure), inventories will accu-

mulate, and firms will respond by cutting production and laying off workers; when production (income) is less than purchases (expenditure), inventories will decline, and firms will respond by increasing production and hiring workers. The economy is in equilibrium when there is no unintended inventory change.

Inventory/Sales Ratio. The value of inventories divided by the value of sales. A low or declining ratio is regarded as a sign of future economic growth; a high and rising ratio frequently signals a downturn.

Inverse Relationship. If Y increases when X decreases, then X and Y have an inverse relationship. Price and quantity demanded have an inverse relationship. See also *direct relationship.*

Investment Tax Credit. Fiscal policy designed to stimulate business investment. Firms are given a tax reduction—a "credit"—for money spent on new investment.

Invisible Hand. Metaphor used by Adam *Smith* to describe the workings of market economies. If all people were free to pursue their own self-interest, nature would guide the economy as if by an invisible hand. Many government programs are based on the implicit premise that the invisible hand does not always provide adequate guidance for the economy.

Involuntary Unemployment. Unemployment that is caused by a cylical downturn; not caused by the refusal of workers to accept market wages, so it cannot be easily eliminated by wage cuts. See also *voluntary unemployment.*

Isocost. Budget line for the firm's factor input decision. The slope is the negative ratio of factor prices. Tangency between an isocost curve and an *isoquant* curve gives the optimal input combination.

Isoquant. Plot of different factor combinations that give equal output. The convex shape is due to the *diminishing marginal rate of technical substitution.* Tangency between an isocost curve and isoquant curve gives the optimal input combination.

J

j-Curve. In international trade, a graphical representation of the fact that a devaluation may make the trade deficit worse before it gets better. The deficit worsens in the short run because it takes time to find substitutes for imported goods.

Job Competition. Model of the labor market developed by L. Thurow. Wages are tied to specific jobs, not individual productivity, and job applicants are ranked according to background credentials. Highly educated people find jobs associated with higher productivity and higher wages.

Joint Profit Maximization. Strategy used by cartels to maximize profits for all firms within the industry; typically involves output constraint. When oligopolies practice joint profit maximization, industry behavior is identical to a monopoly.

K

Key Job. In *wage contour* theory, the key job is a very visible job, perhaps the top of a promotion ladder or the job with the most workers.

Key Wage. The wage paid to the key job; wage differentials are based on the relationship to the key wage.

Keynes, John Maynard (1883–1946). British economist whose book *The General Theory* (1936) presented the framework for most modern macroeconomics.

Keynesian. Generic label often applied to economists willing to use activist government policies to guide the economy. See also *monetarist* and *new Keynesian*.

Kinked Demand Curve. Oligopoly model developed by P. Sweezy. The key assumptions are that price hikes will not be matched by rivals, whereas price cuts will be matched. The result is a kink in the demand (= average revenue) curve and a blank spot in the marginal revenue curve. Sweezy used the model to show that inflation was not caused by union wages.

Kondratiev, Nicholas (1892–1930). Russian economist and statistician who is cred-ited with discovering the long-wave business cycle of 40–60 years. Joseph *Schumpeter* based his *innovation* cycle theory on Kondratiev's work.

L

L. The broadest definition of money in common use. Consists of *M3* plus many other liquid assets including nonbank holdings of U.S. treasury bills and savings bonds and Eurodollar deposits held by U.S. citizens.

Labor Exploitation. Idea that workers are paid wages amounting to less than the value of their output. Assumed by *Marx* to be common under capitalism; other economists believe it may occur under monopoly and oligopoly.

Labor Force Participation Rate. Percentage of the population in the workforce. The labor force participation rate for women rose significantly in the 1960s and 1970s. Some believe that this is a reason for the secular rise in unemployment over that period.

Labor Mobility. The ability of workers to change jobs. High-skilled workers generally have more mobility than low-skilled workers.

Labor Productivity. Output per unit of labor input. Real wages move in tandem with productivity in the long run. Factors that influence labor productivity include human capital, work incentives, and the capital/labor ratio.

Labor Theory of Value. Theory espoused by Adam *Smith* and *Marx* holding that the value of any product depended on the amount of labor embodied in the process of production. A key element in Marx's theory of *labor exploitation*. Dismissed by most economists today because it ignores the demand side.

Labor Union. Organization of workers that seeks to improve working conditions and wages. Most often occur in concentrated industries. The union movement in the United States has declined in recent years; under 20 percent of the workforce is unionized today.

Laffer Curve. Named after Pepperdine professor Arthur Laffer, this curve shows the relationship between marginal income tax rates and tax revenues. At some point, increases in the tax rate will cause tax revenues to decline because some people will stop working. A key idea behind the tax cuts of the Reagan administration.

Laissez Faire. French phrase meaning "leave us alone." Used by economists to express the view that markets work best in the absence of government intervention.

Law of Comparative Advantage. See *comparative advantage*.

Law of Demand. The quantity demanded varies inversely with price, *ceteris paribus*. Actually, a theory because there are numerous exceptions; for example, see *conspicuous consumption*.

Law of Diminishing Returns. Basic law of short-run production theory discovered by Ricardo. If at least one factor of production is fixed, adding additional factors will result in three stages of production: *increasing marginal returns, diminishing marginal returns,* and *negative marginal returns*.

Law of Increasing Costs. As the production of anything rises, the opportunity cost of forgone production will eventually increase. Applies to all production processes. Basis for concave shape of the *production possibilities curve*.

Law of Supply. The quantity supplied varies directly with price, *ceteris paribus*. Actually, a theory because there are numerous exceptions; for example, many production processes exhibit constant costs over wide regions of output.

Learning by Doing. Increase in productivity that is not associated with capital accumulation, technology, or other new factor inputs. Occurs as workers gain experience, reduce defects, and increase efficiency.

Legal Tax Incidence. Laws stating who is required to pay the tax to the government. May differ from the *economic tax incidence* if the tax is shifted to other groups. For example, property taxes may be reflected in higher rents so that renters, not property owners, pay the tax.

Lenin, V. I. (1870–1924). Leader of Bolshevik Revolution (1917), first president, and chief architect of the Soviet Union. Installed planning system and nationalized most industry.

Life-Cycle Hypothesis. Theory of aggregate consumption behavior developed by Modigliani. Holds that current consumption is based on lifetime expected income so that temporary changes in income have little effect on current consumption. See also *absolute income hypothesis* and *permanent income hypothesis*.

Limit Pricing. Oligopoly pricing strategy of charging low prices to deter entry into the industry.

Limited Liability. One of the chief advantages of the corporate form of business. The liability of the owners of the firm—the stockholders—is limited to the amount of money they have invested in stock.

Linear Function. A function that when graphed is a straight line. The consumption function from the *absolute income hypothesis* is a linear function.

Linkage. One of the desirable attributes of intermediate targets of monetary policy. The intermediate target should have a reliable link to the policy goals. Financial innovations, deregulation, and other factors appear to have weakened the historical linkage between the money supply, inflation, and nominal income.

Liquidity. The ability to convert assets from one form to another; e.g., the ability to sell stock. Assets are more liquid if they can be converted with low transactions costs and without risk. Money is the most liquid of all financial assets.

Liquidity Preference. The desire for safe financial assets. According to Keynes's theory of liquidity preference, people want to hold liquid financial (primarily money) assets when they fear the future.

Loanable Funds. Money that savers are willing to lend to borrowers. High interest rates will increase the quantity of loanable funds supplied but decrease the quantity of loanable funds demanded.

Long Run. Period of analytical time when there are no constants; everything can change. In production theory, firms can change the size of the plant in the long run; they cannot in the *short run*. In macroeconomics, all expectations are correct in the long run so there is no incentive to change.

Long Run Aggregate Supply Curve (LS). Vertical line in the aggregate demand/aggregate supply model illustrating that output will equal potential GDP in the long run. Compare to short run *aggregate supply curve*.

Long-Run Supply of Capital. Horizontal line in (r, K)-space at the $r\star$, the interest rate at which people are willing to lend money. Horizontal shape reflects the assumption of a perfectly elastic supply of capital in the long run. At interest rates above $r\star$, households will be willing to supply additional savings; at interest rates below $r\star$, no savings will be offered.

Lorenz Curve. Curve used to show income distribution. The vertical axis plots the cumulative percentage of income; the horizontal axis shows the cumulative percentage of families. The straight 45° line indicates perfectly equitable income distribution; curves to the right of 45° line indicate income inequality.

Louvre Agreement. Agreement signed by the *Group* 7 nations in 1987 recognizing that the value of the dollar was approximately correct and calling for continued monetary policy coordination to maintain stable exchange rates. Apparently unsuccessful; the dollar appreciated by over 10 percent in 1988–1989. See also *Plaza Accord*.

Lucas Critique. Critique developed by Robert Lucas; it suggests that economic forecasts tend to be incorrect because forecasts cause people to change their behavior. Central idea of *new classical economics*.

M

M1. The narrowest definition of money, M1 includes only those assets that are intended to be used for immediate transactions. Includes most checkable accounts, currency held by the nonbank public, and traveler's checks.

M2. Somewhat broader than M1, M2 includes financial assets that can be used for current transactions but are frequently held for longer periods. The main components of M2 are M1, overnight repurchase agreements and Eurodollars, money market mutual fund balances, money market deposit accounts, savings deposits, and small (under $100,000) time deposits. Often thought to track best with GDP.

M3. Broader than M2, M3 includes deposits that are usually held for substantial periods of time. The main components are M2, large time deposits, term repurchase agreements and Eurodollars, and institutional-only money market mutual fund balances.

Maastricht Treaty. The main document outlining the structure of Europe 1992; calls for common foreign and defense policy, common citizenship, a more powerful European parliament, and a common currency, the *ECU*. Ratification process began in the summer of 1992.

Macroeconomics. One of the two main branches of economic theory, macroeconomics deals with "large" economic issues such as inflation, unemployment, and GDP growth. See also *microeconomics*.

Malthus, Thomas Robert (1776–1834). British economist and minister who believed that poverty and starvation were the inevitable result of a conflict between the laws of nature and human behavior. In *Essay on Population* (1798), Malthus argued that population grew at a geometrical rate while food grew at only an arithmetical rate, thus leading to starvation and poverty.

Margin Requirements. The minimum down payment on stock purchases. The Federal Reserve has the authority to set margin requirements.

Marginal Cost. The change in costs associated with the production of one additional unit of output, $MC = \Delta TC/\Delta Q$. The marginal cost curve above the *average variable cost* curve is the supply curve for competitive firms.

Marginal Efficiency of Investment (MEI). The relationship between expected return and investment; the graph is downward sloping in (R^e, I)-space. Important shift factors include business confidence and GDP growth.

Marginal Extraction Cost. The cost of extracting one additional unit of a natural resource. See also *marginal user cost* and *total marginal cost.*

Marginal Leakage Rate. In the income-expenditure model, the fraction of new spending that is not spent; also the reciprocal of the *spending multiplier.*

Marginal Physical Product (MPP). The output, measured in physical units, not dollar values, of the next factor input. See also *marginal revenue product.*

Marginal Product. Same as marginal physical product; term is used when there is no confusion with *marginal revenue product.*

Marginal Productivity Rent. Rent that depends on the productivity of improvements to land; compare *economic rent.*

Marginal Productivity Theory. Theory of factor pricing and income distribution based on the premise that factors are paid in accordance with their contributions to output.

Marginal Propensity to Consume (MPC). The change in consumption induced by one more unit of disposable income; also the slope of the consumption function, $MPC = \Delta C / \Delta Q_d$.

Marginal Propensity to Save (MPS). The change in saving induced by one more unit of disposable income; also the slope of the saving function, $MPS = \Delta S / \Delta Q_d$.

Marginal Propensity to Spend (MPE). The change in spending induced by one more unit of income; also the slope of the expenditure function, $MPE = \Delta E / \Delta Q$.

Marginal Revenue (MR). The change in revenue from selling one more unit of output, $MR = \Delta TR / \Delta Q$.

Marginal Revenue Product (MRP). The additional revenue associated with employing one additional factor of production; for a competitive firm, marginal physical product times selling price, $MRP = MPP(P)$.

Marginal User Cost. Use of finite resources today means that less will be available tomorrow; this cost to future generations is called marginal user cost. See also *marginal extraction cost* and *total marginal cost.*

Marginal Utility. The change in satisfaction (utility) associated with consumption of one additional unit of a good. The principle of *diminishing marginal utility* holds that marginal utility will decline as additional units are consumed.

Marginal Utility/Price Ratio. Consumer equilibrium exists when the ratio of marginal utility to price is equal for all goods; i.e., $MU_a / P_a = MU_b / P_b = \cdots MU_z / P_z$.

Market. Interaction between buyer and seller; not necessarily a place. Economists believe that market pressures can efficiently allocate economic resources.

Market Economy. Economy where production and distribution are determined by the interplay of market forces.

Market Failure. Situation where market outcomes are not optimal; may be caused by *imperfect information, public goods,* or *externalities.* Market failures often indicate the need for government intervention.

Market Period. Period of analytical time where all production has taken place and goods are brought to the market. The supply curve is vertical. An example is a fish market. See also *long run* and *short run.*

Marketization. One of the steps of *shock therapy.* Removal of price controls and central planning to allow markets to allocate goods and services. See also *privatization.*

Marx, Karl (1818–1883). German economist and philosopher who prophesied the collapse of capitalism and the succession of socialism. His *Communist Manifesto* (1848) and *Das Kapital* (Vol. 1, 1867) continue to influence radical reformers.

Mass Production. Factory system involving large amounts of machinery and relatively unskilled labor. Main production method of the early twentieth century, it is now being replaced by more specialized methods using skilled labor.

Maturity Gap. A problem that was instrumental in the savings and loan crisis of the 1980s. Newly deregulated thrifts were able to attract funds by paying high interest rates on their deposits, but most existing assets were in long-term mortgages paying lower interest rates. Further, liabilities were short term and assets were long term, so rising interest rates raised costs more than revenues.

Maximum Sustainable Yield. The maximum harvest rate that permits a viable population of the species. This calculation always involves an element of uncertainty because of the difficulty of conducting controlled experiments in the wild.

Mean. Arithmetic average. Formula: $\text{mean} = (1/n) \sum_{n=1}^{n} x_i$ where there are n elements to be averaged. See also *median.*

Means Test. An eligibility test. Some social programs (i.e., AFDC) are available only to people below a certain income; the income requirement is a means test. Other social programs (i.e., Social Security) are available to all people regardless of income; these programs do not have a means test. See also *entitlement programs.*

Measurability. Desirable attribute of intermediate target for monetary policy; the ability of policymakers to calculate the value of the intermediate targets they wish to control. If the Federal Reserve is unable to measure its targets precisely, it cannot be sure of the effects of its policy changes. See also *control* and *linkage.*

Median. The middle observation; an observation such that half the values are higher and half are lower. Median income is often used as a summary measure of income. See also *mean.*

Medicaid. Social program that provides medical care for low-income people. See also *Medicare.*

Medicare. Social program that provides medical care for the elderly. No *means test.*

Medium of Exchange. One of the four main functions of money; an instrument to facilitate the exchange of goods and services between buyer and seller. See also *standard of deferred payment, store of value,* and *unit of account.*

MEI. See *marginal efficiency of investment.*

Menu Costs. Transactions cost associated with changing prices. Firms must physically change the prices on menus and other price lists. Prices will only be changed if the value of price changes exceeds the cost of changing them. Used by new Keynesians to explain sticky prices and wages.

Mercantile Economy. Intermediate stage of economic development between *feudalism* and *capitalism.* Occurred with the breakdown of feudal society and the rise of a merchant class around the sixteenth century.

Merchandise Trade Balance. Subaccount of the *current account* of the *balance of payments.* Records imports and exports of goods. Also called *balance of trade.*

Merger. Consolidation of two or more firms into a single larger firm. See also *horizontal merger* and *vertical merger.*

Merit Good. Good deemed by society to be so important that it must be provided free or at a subsidized price to all citizens. Examples include health care and school lunch programs. See also *public good.*

MES. See *minimum efficient scale.*

MFA. See *Multifiber Agreement.*

MFN. See *most favored nation.*

Microeconomics. One of the two main branches of economic theory, microeconomics deals with "small" economic issues including the behavior of individual households, firms, and industries. See also *macroeconomics.*

Minimum Efficient Scale (MES). The smallest-size plant that can use the most modern and technologically advanced production methods. Can lead to oligopoly. See also *economies of scale.*

Minimum Wage. Legal restriction on lowest wage that can be paid to workers. Many economists believe minimum wages cause unemployment, especially among young people and low-skilled workers.

Mixed Economy. Economy with elements of different economic systems; i.e., a market economy with some public ownership. The United States is a mixed economy as are all of the advanced industrial countries of the world.

MMDA. See *money market deposit account.*

MMMF. See *money market mutual fund.*

Model. A theory used to explain and/or predict behavior. In economics, models are often graphical.

Modern Quantity Theory of Money. New version of the *crude quantity theory* that does not assume fixed velocity and real GDP. Key component of monetarist and new classical theories.

Monetarist. Macroeconomist who follows the views of Milton Friedman. Basic views include belief in self-correcting nature of markets, *laissez faire,* and the *constant growth rate rule.* See also *new classical economics.*

Monetary Base. Currency held by the nonbank public plus bank reserves; money available for multiple expansion of the money supply. Also called *high-powered money.* See also *fractional reserve banking* and *money multiplier.*

Monetary Policy. Actions by the Federal Reserve to influence the amount of money and credit in circulation. Main tools of monetary policy include *discount rate, open market operations,* and *required reserves.*

Monetary Rule. See *constant growth rate rule.*

Money. Anything that serves as a medium of exchange can serve as money; in modern economies, however, money consists primarily of checkable accounts and currency held by the nonbank public. See also *L, M1, M2,* and *M3.*

Money Market. Financial market that trades financial assets with maturities under one year. See also *capital market.*

Money Market Deposit Account (MMDA). Recently developed financial instrument that uses a pool of funds from many small investors to buy high interest–earning, large-denomination financial assets; may have restrictive check-writing privileges. See also *money market mutual fund.*

Money Market Mutual Fund (MMMF). Recently developed financial instrument that pools the funds of many small investors to enable them to invest in diversified portfolios; may have restrictive check-writing privileges. See also *money market deposit account.*

Money Multiplier (mm). The ratio of the money supply to the monetary base; lower than the *potential money multiplier* because of cash leakages and excess reserves.

Monopolistic Competition. Industry composed of many sellers of slighty differentiated products with free entry and exit. Examples include ice cream makers and retail trade. Compare to *oligopoly* and *perfect competition.*

Monopoly. Industry composed of one firm selling a product for which there is no good substitute. See also *natural monopoly.*

Monopsony. Factor market in which there is only one buyer.

Moral Hazard. Behavior considered "immoral" that is associated with the existence of insurance. For example, depositors may invest their money just to receive the insurance benefit while bank managers may take more risks if deposits are insured.

Most Favored Nation (MFN). Status given to trading partners. If Nation *A* grants MFN status to Nation *B,* then any trade concession given by Nation *A* to Nation *C* automatically applies to Nation *B.*

MPC. See *marginal propensity to consume.*

MPE. See *marginal propensity to spend.*

MPP. See *marginal physical product.*

MPS. See *marginal propensity to save.*

Multifiber Agreement (MFA). Agreement signed in 1974 by 50 nations that set the standards for bilateral arrangements between textile trading countries.

Munn v. Illinois (1877). Important case in history of government regulation. The Supreme Court ruled that the state of Illinois could regulate prices at grain elevators because grain elevator operators had colluded to keep prices artificially high. The case was the legal basis for regulation of the railroad industry a decade later.

Mutual Benefit. The fundamental reason for exchange; both parties must benefit or the trade would not take place.

N

NAFTA. See *North American Free Trade Agreement*.

NAIRU. Acronym for *non-accelerating inflation rate of unemployment*. The minimum level of unemployment that can be sustained without an acceleration in the rate of inflation. Similar to *natural rate of unemployment*.

Nash Equilibrium. From *game theory*. Exists where there is no *dominant strategy* outcome, and both outcomes are equally plausible. Once the game gets to either cell, there is no incentive to change strategies. All dominant strategy equilibria are also Nash equilibria, but not all Nash equilibria are dominant strategy equilibria.

National Bureau of Economic Research (NBER). Quasi-public agency headquartered at Columbia University that is responsible for dating business cycles.

National Debt. The total of all annual fiscal deficits and surpluses since the United States became a sovereign state. More than doubled in the 1980s; currently exceeds $5 trillion.

National Labor Relations Act. See *Wagner Act*.

Natural Monopoly. A monopoly created because costs continue falling as output expands beyond the level demanded by the market, making it unprofitable for other firms to enter the industry. Many public utility firms are classified as natural monopolies.

Natural Rate Hypothesis. Theory that the economy, if left alone, will automatically return to the *natural rate of unemployment* and the *potential* or natural rate of *GDP*. Accepted by most monetarist and new classical economists; rejected by many new Keynesians. Compare *hysteresis*.

Natural Rate of Unemployment. Rate of unemployment that exists when the econ-

omy is operating at the *potential* or natural rate of *GDP*. See also *full employment* and *NAIRU*.

Negative Externality. The cost to society from a private action that is not included in market price or cost calculations. Sometimes called diseconomy. Pollution is a negative externality. See also *positive externality*.

Negative Income Tax. Social program designed to reduce work disincentives and bureaucratic costs of current poverty programs. People with income under a designated level would receive income subsidies (i.e., pay a "negative tax"). See also *Aid to Families with Dependent Children* and *workfare*.

Negative Marginal Returns. The third stage of the production function. Exists when additional inputs cause output to decline. Firms never willingly operate in this stage. See also *diminishing marginal returns* and *increasing marginal returns*.

Neoclassical Economics. Orthodox school of economic thought based on the work of Alfred Marshall, Léon Walras, and others. Neoclassical economists generally espouse *laissez faire*.

Neoclassical Growth Model. Standard macroeconomic growth model based on the work of Paul Samuelson, Robert Solow, and others. Assumes an aggregate production function, *constant returns to scale,* and *diminishing marginal productivity*. Inability to account for productivity slowdown in the 1970s has led to the search for new models of economic growth. See *new economic growth theory* and *social model*.

Net Exports ($X - Z$). The difference between exports (X) and imports (Z).

Net Marginal Revenue Product. The difference between marginal revenue product and marginal factor cost. The firm should employ additional factors of production as long as net marginal revenue product is positive.

Net Present Value. The difference between the present value of a return stream and the cost of acquiring that stream; i.e., $NPV = PV \quad C$.

Net Private Domestic Investment (NPDI). *Gross private domestic investment* mi-

nus capital consumption allowances; measure of the increase in size of the capital stock.

New Classical Economics. Relatively new school of macroeconomics. Major planks include a belief in self-correcting markets, the *policy ineffectiveness rule,* and the *Lucas critique*.

New Economic Growth Theory. Contemporary theory of economic growth based on the work of Paul Romer and others. Main differences with neoclassical growth theory include incorporation of knowledge into the production function and allowance for increasing returns to scale.

New Economic History. School of thought deriving from the work of Christina Romer and others that suggests that pre–World War II fluctuations were not as severe as is commonly thought. If correct, this implies that most postwar macroeconomic stabilization policies may have had little effect.

New Industrial Economics. Modern approach to industrial economics based on strategic behavior and game theory. Compare to *structure-conduct-performance*.

New International Economics. School of thought based on the work of Paul Krugman and others that relaxes the assumption of perfect competition and the absence of externalities. In doing so, it lays open the possibility that *strategic trade policies* may be an effective way to manage trade.

New Keynesian Economics. Contemporary school of macroeconomics based on the assumption of imperfect information and sticky wages and prices. New Keynesian economists believe that discretionary policies are appropriate.

Nominal Interest Rate (i). The interest rate charged by the lending institution; not corrected for inflation. See also *real interest rate*.

Nominal Variable. Variable measured in current terms; not adjusted for inflation or changes in the price level. See also *real variable*.

Nominal Wage (W). Wage rate in current or nominal terms; not adjusted for inflation. See also *real wage*.

Noncooperative Game. A game in which players are not allowed to make binding agreements; more interesting from the point of view of the game theoriest. See also *cooperative game*.

Nondurable Good. Good that is used soon after it is bought; most consumption spending is on nondurable goods. See also *durable goods*.

Nonlinear Function. Mathematical relationship that, when plotted, is not a straight line. The short run *Phillips curve* is a nonlinear function.

Nonrenewable Resources. Natural resources that are in fixed supply and cannot be replenished. Examples include oil and coal. See also *renewable resource*.

Nontariff Barrier (NTB). Trade restrictions other than taxes on imports. Quotas are often classified as NTBs. Other NTBs include procurement programs, licensing fees, and local content legislation.

Non-Zero Sum Game. Strategy game in which the winner's gain is not equal to the loser's loss. Voluntary exchange is a positive sum game because both parties gain.

Normal Good. Good that gives positive utility; more will be purchased at lower prices and higher incomes than at higher prices and lower incomes. See also *inferior good*.

Normal Profits. Profits just sufficient for the firm to stay in business but not expand. In the long run, free entry and exit assure that competitive firms make normal profits.

Normative Economics. Deals with value-laden questions. The question, "What should the unemployment rate be?" is a question of normative economics; the question, "What is the unemployment rate?" is a question of *positive economics*.

North American Free Trade Agreement (NAFTA). Trade agreement between Canada, Mexico, and the United States designed to phase out all trade restrictions among these three nations. Negotiated in 1992, finally signed in 1993.

Nozick, Robert. Harvard philosopher known for his process theory of justice. Pop-ular among conservatives. See also *John Rawls*.

O

Occupational Safety and Health Administration (OSHA). Government agency responsible for regulating safety in the workplace. Often criticized for raising business costs without producing significant benefits to consumers or workers.

Official Settlements Account. Subaccount of the *balance of payments* that records official reserve assets and liabilities to foreign agencies. Transactions on this account are often designed to influence the exchange rate.

Okun's Law. Rule of thumb that shows connection between unemployment and GDP: $\Delta Q/Q = 2.5(U - U\star)$, where $U\star$ is the full employment rate of unemployment and Q is real GDP.

Oligopoly. Market structure characterized by a small number of firms that must take explicit cognizance of the actions of their rivals. Often analyzed with *game theory*. See also *kinked demand curve*.

OPEC (Organization for Petroleum Exporting Companies). *Cartel* of oil producing nations that restricts world petroleum supplies and therefore influences world oil prices.

Open Market Operations. The basic monetary policy tool of the Federal Reserve; government securities are bought and sold on the open market to change the level of bank reserves. Selling securities reduces the money supply; buying securities increases the money supply. See also *discount rate, reserve requirements*.

Open Shop. Firm that hires both union and nonunion workers. Compare *closed shop* and *union shop*.

Open System. A model that includes a foreign sector.

Opportunity Cost. The value of the best forgone alternative; all economic choices involve opportunity costs.

Optimal Factor Inputs. The factor inputs that result in miminum inputs for a given level of output. Exists when the marginal product/factor price ratios are equal for all inputs.

Optimal Plant Size. Plant size that minimizes average total costs.

Optimal Production Technique. Production technique that utilizes optimal input combinations. Exists when the marginal product/factor price ratios are equal for all inputs.

Optimal Quantity of Pollution. Not zero; the amount of pollution such that the marginal benefit of having less pollution is equal to the marginal cost of cleaning up the pollution.

Ordinal Utility. From indifference curve analysis. Ordinal utility theory assumes only that consumers are able to rank consumption bundles, not to measure the quantity of utility with cardinal numbers. Considered methodologically superior to *cardinal utility* analysis.

Organic Composition of Capital. Term from Marxian analysis; the ratio between capital (machinery) and labor used in the production process. An increase in this ratio was an indication that the firm was displacing workers with machines.

OSHA. See *Occupational Safety and Health Administration*.

Output Market. Market for goods and services; compare *factor market* and *input market*.

Overinvestment. Theory that business cycles are caused by reaction to overinvestment in previous period; often associated with the work of J. Forrester and Joseph Schumpeter.

Overshooting. Theory of exchange rate volatility formulated by S. Fischer. Assumes purchasing power parity, capital mobility, rational expectations, and wage-price stickiness. May explain extreme volatility of exchange rates since the end of the Bretton Woods system.

P

p. Inflation rate; percentage change in the price index; $\Delta P/P$.

P. Price index. See also *consumer price index, GDP deflator,* and *producer price index.*

P★. Modern application of the quantity theory of money to economic forecasting used by the Federal Reserve.

Paper Entrepreneurialism. Name given by Robert Reich to financial investment as opposed to real investment. Reich and others argue that too much effort has been exerted on making profits from trading paper and that too little effort has been expended on investing in real capital.

Paradox of Thrift. An increase in the desire to save may result in a decrease in the amount saved. Unlikely to actually occur in the real world; however, a higher propensity to save will slow economic activity. This could reduce income and, potentially, lower the amount that is saved.

Partnership. Business ownership structure involving one or more individuals. May allow some managerial specialization. Unlimited liability. See also *corporation* and *sole proprietorship.*

Patent. The discoverer's legal right to an invention. Patent laws may act as an incentive for invention by assuring profits, but they also reduce competition.

Peak Load Pricing. Marginal cost pricing technique. Firms raise prices during periods of maximum use to reduce demand and thus reduce the optimal size of the plant.

Per Capita Income. Income divided by population.

Per Se Rule. Antitrust philosophy stating that the mere existence of monopoly is enough to warrant antitrust action. First invoked in 1940 in the *Socony-Vacuum* case. Still the main approach of antitrust.

Perestroika. Russian term meaning "restructuring"; was used by Gorbachev to signify the economic changes he hoped to implement. See also *glasnost.*

Perfect Competition. Term occasionally used in place of *pure competition;* sometimes used to indicate a market that is pure competition plus perfect information.

Periphery Economy. In the theory of *dual economy,* small, low-profit, nonunion firms that typically pay low wages with low benefits. See also *core economy.*

Permanent Income Hypothesis. Theory of consumption developed by Milton Friedman. Argues that current consumption is based on expected permanent income over a period of three to four years. Explains why current consumption may not respond to temporary tax changes. See also *absolute income hypothesis* and *life-cycle hypothesis.*

Persuasive Advertising. Advertising designed to convince people to buy things they might not otherwise buy. Rejected by economists who believe consumers are sovereign. Compare *informative advertising.*

Phillips Curve. Plot of the tradeoff between inflation and unemployment. Downward sloping and convex in (p, u)-space.

Plant. Establishment that produces or distributes goods and services; a factory, warehouse, or retail or wholesale store. See also *firm.*

Plaza Accord. Agreement signed in 1985 by the G-7 nations acknowledging that the dollar was overvalued and setting up a framework for monetary policy coordination to bring down the dollar. Apparently successful; the dollar did depreciate. See also *Louvre Agreement.*

Policy Goals. The ultimate aims of policy—full employment, stable prices, economic growth—as opposed to intermediate targets of low interest rates and stable money growth.

Policy Ineffectiveness Rule. Theory associated with *new classical economics.* Argues that aggregate demand policies affect only inflation and have no lasting effect on real output or employment. Therefore, extreme *laissez faire* is the best approach to macroeconomic policy.

Policy Instrument. Bank reserves and other tools available to the Fed to influence *intermediate targets* and *policy goals.* Good policy instruments have a reliable *linkage* to intermediate targets.

Policy Mix. Combination of *fiscal* and *monetary policy.* The independence of the Federal Reserve sometimes makes it difficult to coordinate monetary and fiscal policy.

Pollution Rights. Market-based approach to environmental problems. Involves assigning the right to pollute to potential polluters and allowing firms to sell these rights.

Portfolio Effects. In Milton Friedman's theory of money demand, a change in the money supply will cause people to adjust their holdings of many financial and real assets. These adjustments are called portfolio effects.

Positive Economics. Purports to deal with objective questions that have no value content. The question, "What is the unemployment rate?" is a question of positive economics; the question, "What should the unemployment rate be?" is a question of *normative economics.*

Positive Externality. External benefit not included in private cost or price calculations. For example, if a high-tech firm locates in a small community, the high wages it pays its workers will benefit many other businesses in the community. Positive externalities are often subsidized by the government. See also *negative externality.*

Post Hoc, Ergo Propter Hoc. Latin phrase that translates loosely to "after this, therefore because of this." Refers to a methodological problem of assuming causality because two events follow each other in time.

Potential GDP (Q★). The amount of aggregate production that will take place when all firms are operating at optimal capacity and there is full employment. Can be exceeded in the short run, but this will generally result in inflation.

Potential Money Multiplier (mm★). The maximum value of the money multiplier; the reciprocal of the required reserve ration, $1/rr$.

Potential Reserves. The amount of a resource that is available with current technology if we are willing to pay the cost of extraction. See also *resource endowment.*

PPC. See *production possibilities curve.*

PPI. See *producer price index.*

Predatory Pricing. Practice used by large firms to drive competitors out of the market; involves setting prices so low that less-well-financed firms fold first. Later, the large firms raise prices to make abnormal profits. Standard Oil was accused of predatory pricing in the 1800s; this led to the passage of antitrust legislation.

Present Value. The current value of having a stream of income over time. $PV = \sum_{t=1}^{\infty} R_t/(1 + r)^t$ where R_t is the return at year t and r is the appropriate *discount rate*.

Price and Wage Flexibility. The ability of prices and wages to adjust as market conditions change. Self-correcting forces rely upon price and wage flexibility. See also *sticky prices and wages*.

Price-Cap Formula. Regulation formula where the regulatory body establishes an initial level of prices and links the regulated company's future price increases to an aggregate price index minus expected productivity increases. As costs change over the long run, firms can earn abnormal profits or suffer losses. See also *cost-of-service formula* and *yardstick competition*.

Price Ceiling. Government regulation that limits prices; can cause shortages. See also *price floor*.

Price Discrimination. Ability to charge different prices to different customers. When successful, price discriminators can extract all *consumer surplus* from buyers. Price discriminators must be able to segregate different classes of buyers.

Price Elasticity of Demand (E_p). Most common application of elasticity concept. The percentage change in quantity demanded divided by the percentage change in price: $E_p = (\Delta Q/\overline{Q})/(\Delta P/\overline{P})$.

Price Floor. Regulation that prevents prices from falling below a certain level. Can create surpluses. The minimum wage is a price floor.

Price Index. A single number used to provide a measure of the aggregate price level. Found by constructing a weighted average with the weights consisting of quantities of goods in a typical bundle. See also *consumer price index, GDP deflator,* and *producer price index*.

Price Maker. Firm that has enough market power to set prices; oligopolies and monopolies are typically price makers. Contrast *price taker*.

Price Taker. Firm that has no market power and must charge the price set by the market. Firms in perfectly competitive markets are price takers. See also *price maker*.

Principle of Diminishing Marginal Utility. Theory developed in the late nineteenth century stating that the satisfaction ("utility") from consuming additional units of a good at a point in time declines; basis for the theory of demand.

Prisoner's Dilemma. Classic situation from *game theory*; the *dominant strategy* is for both prisoners to confess to the crime. Compare *Nash equilibrium*.

Private Good. Good subject to exclusion principle and rival consumption; can be efficiently allocated by market processes. Contrast *public good*.

Privatization. Selling government-owned firms to private citizens; one of the key steps of *shock therapy;* also occurred in Europe in the 1980s and 1990s. See also *marketization*.

Process Technology. Technology necessary for producing goods and services; firms with modern process technology are typically low-cost producers. Compare *product technology*.

Producer Price Index (PPI). Price index measuring the prices of wholesale goods; changes in the producer price index often precede changes in the *consumer price index*.

Producer Surplus. Area between the supply curve and the selling price; the difference between the price the firm would be willing to sell the product for and the price received; *economic rent*. See also *consumer surplus*.

Product Differentiation. Slight product variations; key distinction between *pure competition* and *monopolistic competition*. Product differentiation results in some inefficiency but provides consumer variety.

Product Technology. Technology for producing specific products, usually modern high-tech products. Some economists argue that the United States has been successful at

designing new products and product technology, but not at adopting efficient *process technology*.

Production Possibilities Curve (PPC). Curve showing production combinations available to an economy given finite factor inputs and technology. The concave shape is due to the *law of increasing costs*. Points on the curve assume efficient resource utilization; points inside the curve assume factor unemployment.

Productivity Growth. Growth rate in output per unit of input. Productivity growth is the most important factor in determining long-run growth in the standard of living.

Profit (π). The difference between total revenue and total cost, $\pi = TR - TC$. Also the factor payment to the entrepreneur, the "entrepreneurial wage." See also *economic profits* and *normal profits*.

Profit Maximization. Primary motivation of most firms and entrepreneurs. Profits are maximized by producing the quantity such that marginal revenue is equal to marginal cost.

Progressive Tax. Tax that takes a higher percentage of income from rich people than from poor people. Many income taxes are progressive taxes. See also *proportional tax* and *regressive tax*.

Proletariat. Marxian term for the working class; assumed to be exploited by the *bourgeoisie*. See also *industrial army of the unemployed*.

Property Rights. System of ownership; key attribute of capitalism. Without well-defined property rights, allocation is inefficient. See also *Coase theorem*.

Property Tax. Tax on personal property; most often applied to real estate. The *economic tax incidence* of property taxes is unclear because of various shifting possibilities.

Proportional Tax. Tax that takes the same fraction of income at all income levels. Many state income taxes are proportional taxes. See also *progressive tax* and *regressive tax*.

Proprietors' Income. In national income accounting, the income that is paid to sole proprietors.

Proxy Variable. Variable that is used when the desired variable is not available. Economic interpretation of proxy variables can be difficult. Several proxy variables were used in the *social model* of Bowles, et al.

Public Choice. Method of applying economic reasoning to the government decision-making process, voting, and collective choice. Many public choice theorists believe that the least government is the best government.

Public Good. Good that is not subject to *rival consumption* or the *exclusion principle;* cannot be allocated efficiently by the market. Examples include national defense and lighthouses. Contrast *private good.*

Public Interest Theory of Regulation. Theory that states that government regulations provide public benefits; assumes regulators are motivated solely by public interest. Contrast *capture theory of regulation.*

Purchasing Power Parity. Theory of exchange rate determination that says that a dollar should purchase as much in the United States as anywhere else in the world, after adjustment for transportation costs. Long-run determinant of exchange rates.

Pure Competition. Market structure characterized by many sellers of *homogeneous products* with free entry and exit. Results in both technical and allocative efficiency in the long run. See also *perfect competition.*

Pure Discrimination. Wage or employment discrimination based on irrational dislike for certain ethnic or cultural groups. Partial explanation for demographic differences in unemployment rates.

Pure Economic Rent. Factor payment in excess of the amount necessary to bring the factor into production. Exists when the factor supply curve is vertical as on unimproved land.

Q

Q/E Model. See *income-expenditure model.*

Quantity Theory of Money. See *crude quantity theory, modern quantity theory.*

Quasi-Public Good. Good that has both private good and public good attributes; education and parks are typical examples. Sometimes provided by the public sector, sometimes provided by the private sector.

Quintile. One-fifth of the population under study. Income distribution is often studied by breaking the population into quintiles.

Quota. A restriction on the quantity of goods that can be imported. Quotas are a violation of *GATT* principles. See also *nontariff barrier* and *tariff.*

R

r. See *real interest rate.*

R^e. See *expected return.*

Random Walk. Theory that says there is no trend between successive observations in an economic series. Applied to exchange rate behavior and many other areas of economics.

Rate of Return. The ratio of profits to the cost of an investment good; firms will invest in projects with higher expected rates of return before projects with lower expected rates of return. See also *marginal efficiency of investment.*

Rational Expectations. Popular theory of expectation formation based on the idea that people are forward looking, use all available information, and make no consistent mistakes. See also *adaptive expectations* and *new classical economics.*

Rawls, John. Harvard philosopher best known for his theory of justice; popular with liberals. See also *Robert Nozick* and *veil of ignorance.*

RD. See *real aggregate demand curve.*

Real Aggregate Demand Curve (RD). From *real business cycle theory,* the relationship between real GDP demanded and the interest rate; downward sloping because fewer purchases will be made at higher interest rates than at lower interest rates, *ceteris paribus.* Important shift parameters include technology shocks and fiscal policy.

Real Aggregate Supply Curve (RS). From *real business cycle theory,* the relationship between real GDP produced and the interest rate; upward sloping because workers will offer more hours at higher interest rates than at lower interest rates. Technology is an important shift parameter.

Real Business Cycle Theory. Contemporary school of macroeconomic thought emphasizing the importance of intertemporal substitution and technology shocks. Proponents believe that technology and fiscal policy can have permanent effects on the economy.

Real Interest Rate (r). The *nominal interest rate* adjusted for expected inflation; $r = i - p^e$.

Real Variable. Any economic variable adjusted for inflation or the price index. Generally, the real values of variables expressed in percentage terms are found by subtracting the inflation rate (see *real interest rate*) whereas variables expressed as levels are found by dividing by the price index (see *real wage*).

Real Wage (w). The nominal wage adjusted for the price index, $w = W/P$.

Recession. A general downturn in aggregate economic activity. A rule of thumb—not an official definition—is that two quarters of negative GDP growth constitute a recession.

Recessionary Gap. The difference between the level of *autonomous spending* necessary to generate potential GDP and the actual level of autonomous spending; exists when potential GDP is greater than actual GDP. Measured vertically on the income-expenditure diagram. See also *GDP gap* and *inflationary gap.*

Recognition Lag. The time it takes policymakers to realize that a policy change is necessary; at least a few months, perhaps as long as six. See also *impact lag* and *implementation lag.*

Recyclable Resources. Natural resources that can be used more than once, such as aluminum, other metals, and paper. It is impossible to achieve 100 percent recycling so the supply of even recyclable resources will diminish over time.

Regional Trading Bloc. Organization designed to increase trade between particular nations; can result in both *trade diversion* and *trade creation*. Often results in a common external tariff and zero or low internal tariffs. An example is the European Union.

Regressive Tax. Tax that takes a higher percentage of income from low-income people than from high-income people. The *sales tax* is a regressive tax.

Regulatory Lag. A problem with government regulatory changes; the time lag between enacting new regulations or changing old regulations. Firms may make excess profits or losses during the lag period.

Relative Property. Poverty compared to other people, but not necessarily poor health, housing, and so on. There will always be relative poverty because some people will always be less well off than others. Compare *absolute poverty*.

Renewable Resources. Natural resources that can be replenished and thus need not be exhausted if managed properly. Examples include trees and water.

Rent Control. Government policies designed to keep rents low so that people can afford housing. May cause shortages.

Rent-Seeking Behavior. Actions designed to limit competition and make economic profits. Firms that lobby the government for restrictions on imports are rent seeking.

Replacement Rate. The number of children that the average woman must bear to keep the population stationary; about 2.11 in the United States.

Reputation Building. A strategy in *game theory*. Players cultivate a reputation for cooperation or tough bargaining with consistent behavior for several rounds of the game.

Required Reserves. Minimum fraction of deposits that banks must hold; about 10 percent in the United States. Regulated by the Federal Reserve.

Reservation Wage. The minimum wage that a job seeker will accept; generally will accept jobs at this wage only after searching for jobs at higher wages. See also *search theory*.

Reserve Currency. Foreign currency which a nation holds as part of its foreign exchange reserves; used to finance international trade.

Reserve Ratio. Ratio of demand deposits to bank reserves; banks typically keep a small amount of *excess reserves* as well as *required reserves*. Reciprocal of the *money multiplier*.

Residual. In econometric models, the portion that cannot be explained by the data. In many growth models, as much as half of the explanation was attributed to the residual.

Resource Endowment. The amount of natural resources available to a nation. Affects comparative advantage and price differentials.

Revised Sequence. Term coined by John Kenneth Galbraith. The idea that consumer preferences are formed by mass advertising rather than firms responding to consumer preferences. This suggests that much production is wasteful. See also *dependency effect*.

Ricardo, David (1772–1823). Nineteenth century British economist credited with discovering the laws of *comparative advantage* and *diminishing returns*.

Ricardian Equivalence Theorem. Key theorem in *new classical economics*. Holds that government deficits do not affect interest rates because the expectation of future tax increases causes people to increase saving today.

Right-to-Work State. State with right-to-work laws; i.e., no one can be forced to join a union as a prerequisite for employment. See also *closed shop, open shop,* and *union shop*.

Risk. The chance of an event occurring with a known probability. An event is risky if it is possible to estimate the expected return plus or minus a variance. Compare *uncertainty*.

Risk-Based Capital Requirements. Require banks that make risky investments to hold higher levels of capital. Implemented in the 1980s to reduce bank risk; will also lower bank profits.

Rival Consumption. Consumption is rival if my consumption of a good makes it impossible for you to consume it as well. Applies to all *private goods;* does not apply to *public goods*.

Roundabout Production. Production process that uses capital; said to be roundabout because it is first necessary to make the machines.

RD. See *real aggregate demand curve*.

RS. See *real aggregate supply curve*.

Rule of Reason. Antitrust philosophy stating that trusts should be broken up only if there was intent to restrain trade; established with a series of court cases beginning with the famous Standard Oil case of 1911. Supplanted by the per se rule with the *Socony-Vacuum* case of 1940.

S

Sales Curve (d). The demand curve facing a firm; equivalent to the average revenue curve.

Sales Tax. Indirect business tax levied on final sales; legal incidence rests on business; most economic incidence on consumer. Regressive. See also *ad valorem tax* and *unit sales tax*.

Saving (S). The portion of income that is not spent on goods and services. Rising income and high interest rates generally cause savings to rise.

Saving Function. Relationship between saving and disposable income. The simple Keynesian saving function is $S = -C_0 + (1 - c)Q_d$ where $(1 - c)$ is the *marginal propensity to save,* $-C_0$ is negative autonomous consumption, Q_d is *disposable income,* and S is *saving*.

Savings and Loan Association (S&L). Financial institution originally involved almost exclusively with small savings and home mortgages. Financial deregulation in the 1980s has blurred the distinction between S&Ls and commercial banks.

Savings Bond. Small-denomination financial instrument issued by the federal government to finance government debt. Low return, extremely safe.

Savings Incentives. Catalysts that increase saving; i.e., consumption taxes instead of income taxes, higher interest rates, and lower taxes on interest income. Some economists believe that the current tax program has strong savings *dis*incentives.

Say's Law. "Supply creates its own demand." After J. B. Say; significant component of *neoclassical economics*. If correct, it is impossible to have a protracted recession.

Scarcity. The fundamental economic problem. Economic goods are scarce because wants are insatiable and resources are finite.

Scattergram. Statistical plot of two sets of data; often an economic series against time. Scattergrams are useful for detecting trends in the data.

Schumpeter, Joseph A. (1883–1950). Austrian-born economist who taught at Harvard. Developed innovation theory of the business cycle. Also emphasized the role of the entrepreneur as the driving force of capitalism.

SCP Model. See *structure-conduct-performance model*.

Search Theory. Theory of the labor market that says that people will search for new jobs as long as the cost of searching is less than the expected return from the search; therefore, people will not accept the first job that is offered. Search activity may explain the rise in the *natural rate of unemployment*.

Seasonal Adjustment. Statistical technique used to remove fluctuations that occur over the course of a year. For example, unemployment always rises in the summer when school is let out; retail sales always rise around Christmas. Economic data series are seasonally adjusted to make it easier to detect trends.

SEC. See *Securities and Exchange Commission*.

Second-Degree Price Discrimination. Monopolist price strategy that charges lower prices to volume buyers. See also *first-degree price discrimination* and *third-degree price discrimination*.

Second Law of Thermodynamics. The conversion of energy from one form to another can never be 100 percent efficient; therefore, the amount of energy not available for use ("entropy") will increase when energy conversion takes place. Also known as the *entropy* law.

Secular Productivity Growth. Productivity growth over time; a key factor in long run changes in the standard of living. See also *cyclical productivity*.

Securities and Exchange Commission (SEC). Government agency established in 1934 to monitor stock trading.

Securities Markets. Financial markets in which stocks and bonds are traded.

Self-Correcting Forces. Flexible wages, prices, and interest rates that help the economy recover from recession and move toward potential GDP and full employment. Neoclassical economists believe that self-correcting forces are strong; many Keynesians believe they are weak and slow.

Services. Nonphysical output; i.e., the work of an accountant, doctor, or chef. There has been a massive shift of resources from goods industries to the service sector in most advanced nations.

Sherman Act (1890). Key antitrust law that prohibits monopolies and conspiracies to restrain trade. However, imprecise wording necessitated several amendments including the *Clayton Act* of 1914.

Shock Therapy. Name given to the approach advocated by Jeffrey Sachs and others to convert the formerly socialist economies to capitalism. Involves *marketization* and *privatization* as quickly as possible. Compare *gradualism*.

Short Run. Period of *analytical time* where something is fixed and/or complete adjustment is not possible. In the theory of the firm, the short run is often defined as a period where the size of the plant is fixed. See also *long run* and *market period*.

Short-Term Capital Flows. In international finance, the flow of currencies across international boundaries often in response to interest rate differentials.

Shortage. A situation where the quantity demanded is greater than the quantity supplied; can only occur if price is fixed below equilibrium. See also *surplus*.

Shutdown Point. The price at which it pays the firm to cease operations because not all variable costs are being covered; the min-

imum point of the average variable cost curve.

"Sin" Tax. A tax on cigarettes, alcohol, and other "sins." Sin taxes have been used to raise money for health care and other programs.

Single Tax. From Henry George, a tax on unimproved land. George felt that this single tax would be adequate to fund all government operations. Further, it was a good tax because the landowners' income was unearned.

Slope. In graphical analysis, the ratio of the vertical change of a function to the horizontal change; "rise over run." For the function $C = C_0 + cQ_d$, c is the slope. See also *intercept*.

Smith, Adam (1723–1790). Scottish economist and moral philosopher often called the father of modern economics. In *The Wealth of Nations* (1776), Smith described the workings of market economies, the *invisible hand*, and the *specialization of labor* and provided a framework for modern economics.

Smithsonian Agreement. Agreement signed in 1971 that realigned exchange rates and led to the end of the Bretton Woods system of fixed exchange rates.

Social Infrastructure. Roads, communication networks, sewage systems, and other systems that make social and economic activities possible.

Social Model. Economic growth model developed by Bowles, et al., that suggests that productivity growth is dependent on work effort and other social factors as well as labor, capital, and technology inputs. Compare to *neoclassical growth model*.

Socialism. Economic system characterized by government ownership of the means of production. Compare to *capitalism*.

***Socony-Vacuum* (1940).** Antitrust case that spelled the end of the *rule of reason*.

Soft Budget Constraint. Instead of being required to make profits, poorly run firms in the former socialist economics were often given additional funding from the government to cover their losses; that is, they operated with a soft budget constraint.

Sole Proprietorship. Business organization owned and operated by a single individual. Often has difficulty raising financial capital and is subject to unlimited liability. Compare *corporation* and *partnership*.

Specialization of Labor. Dividing job tasks into small components so that workers can become proficient; increases worker productivity.

Speculative Demand. Keynesian conception of money demand. People hold money if they expect interest rates to rise; they hold bonds if they expect interest rates to fall. Possible explanation for downward relationship between interest rates and money demand.

Spending Multiplier (k_s). The reciprocal of the *marginal leakage rate*; key part of income-expenditure model. An increase in *autonomous spending* will cause income to increase by a larger amount, perhaps by a factor of two or three in the real world.

Stagflation. Simultaneous occurrence of rising inflation and unemployment. Can be caused by external *supply shocks*. Occurred during several years in the 1970s.

Standard of Deferred Payment. One of the four main functions of money. As long as money holds value, it can be used to settle debts in the future. See also *medium of exchange, store of value,* and *unit of account*.

Statistical Discrimination. Possible explanation for demographic differences between unemployment rates. Method used to lower recruiting costs by eliminating people from the candidate pool who as a group tend to have unstable work histories and/or poor work habits. Compare *pure discrimination*.

Sticky Wages and Prices. Wages and prices that do not respond quickly to market forces, perhaps because of the existence of long-term contracts. Sticky wages and prices impede the ability of the economy to self-correct. New Keynesian economists focus attention on the causes and consequences of sticky wages and prices.

Stock Market. Financial market where corporate ownership shares (stock) are traded. The New York Stock Exchange is the largest stock exchange in the world. See also *Dow Jones Industrial Index*.

Stock Variable. A variable that has no time dimension. For example, the amount of money in your wallet is a stock variable; the income you receive in your monthly paycheck is a *flow variable*.

Store of Value. One of the four main functions of money. Money held to be used at a later date. See also *medium of exchange, standard of deferred payment,* and *unit of account*.

Strategic Trade Policies. Policies designed to extract economic rents from high-tech and other industries; include subsidies for research and development and measures to keep out foreign competition. Key idea of the *new international economics*.

Strong Rational Expectations. *Rational expectations* assumption combined with perfect wage and price flexibility. See also *weak rational expectations*.

Structural Deficit. The fiscal deficit that exists when the economy is operating at potential GDP and full employment; often thought to cause *crowding out*. See also *cyclical deficit*.

Structural Unemployment. Unemployment that exists because people lack skills or are in the wrong location. Difficult to eliminate with aggregate demand policies. See also *cyclical unemployment* and *frictional unemployment*.

Structure-Conduct-Performance (SCP). Methodology of industrial economics based on the assumption that industry structure (the number of firms, entry conditions, etc.) determine conduct (pricing behavior, advertising, etc.) and performance (profitability, etc.) Contrast to the *new industrial economics*.

Substitute Good. A good that can be used in place of another. If goods *X* and *Y* are substitutes, a rise in the price of either good will increase the demand for the other. See also *complementary good*.

Substitution Effect. Effect of a price change. A rise in the price of good *X* raises the relative price of good *X* with respect to good *Y* and reduces the quantity demanded of good *X*. Key explanation for downward slope of demand curves. See also *income effect*.

Sunk Costs. Costs that cannot be recovered even after liquidation. A market is *contestable* if potential entrants would incur no sunk costs. See also *sunk cost model*.

Sunk Cost Model. Theory developed by Paul Krugman to explain the weak connection between exchange rates and the price of traded goods. Establishing a foreign market can be so costly that firms are reluctant to exit foreign markets even when they become less profitable.

Sunspot Theory. A nineteenth-century business cycle theory developed by W. S. Jevons. Held that sunspots affected earth weather and thus agriculture. Largely discounted today.

Supermajority Rule. Compromise voting rule that requires less than unanimous but more than 50 percent vote for passage. Advocated by some public choice theorists who recognize that unanimity voting is unworkable but that majority voting can result in *tyranny of the majority*.

Supply-Constrained Economy. Term describing socialist economies. The lack of production and work incentives combined with artificially low prices resulted in severe shortages—supply contraints—in many industries.

Supply Shock. Event, often caused by external factors, that raises production costs and shifts the *aggregate supply curve* toward the price index axis causing *stagflation*. The oil price hikes of the 1970s were supply shocks.

Supply-Side Economics. Name given to economic policies pursued by economists in the Reagan administration and others. Instead of using Keynesian aggregate demand stimuli, supply-side policies attempted to increase work and production incentives via tax cuts and deregulation.

Surplus. Situation that exists when the quantity supplied is greater than the quantity demanded. In a market economy, can only occur when prices are fixed and too high.

Sustainable Industrial Configuration. Term from theory of *contestable markets*. An industrial configuration is sustainable when no firms are making economic profits and there is no incentive for entry or exit.

Switch Point. Point where the transition from one resource to another is complete. The switch point is reached when the first resource rises to the cost of the new resource and will take place before the first resource is completely exhausted.

Synergy. A possible effect of mergers, synergy can come from several sources including economies of scale, improved managerial efficiency, and increased market power. Synergistic effects make the value of the new company greater than the value of the two individual companies.

T

Tacit Collusion. Unwritten complicity between firms to divide a market, fix prices, or otherwise act as a cartel; illegal, but difficult to detect.

Taft–Hartley Act (1947). Act that gave the government the right to impose a "cooling off" period to halt strikes that interfere with public health or safety; also made *closed shops* illegal and gave states the right to pass *right-to-work* legislation.

Tangent. In graphical analysis, one curve is tangent to another if they touch but do not intersect.

Tariff. A tax on imported goods, typically used to protect domestic industry; generally regarded as the least unsatisfactory kind of trade restraint. See also *nontariff barrier* and *quota.*

Tax Reform Act of 1986. Revenue-neutral tax act that simplified the personal income tax system by reducing the number of tax brackets from 14 to 2 and shifted the burden from individuals to business.

Tax Wedge. Term describing the difference between wages and after-tax income; may act as a work disincentive.

TC. See *total cost.*

Technical Efficiency. Welfare condition; exists when maximum output can be produced at minimum cost; $P = \min ATC$. See also *allocative efficiency.*

Technology Shock. A change in technology that reduces costs and/or results in quality improvement. According to *real business cycle theory,* technology shocks are responsible for most business cycle fluctuations.

Terms of Trade. In trade theory, the price ratio between imported and exported goods; a beneficial increase in the terms of trade indicates that more imports are earned per unit of exports.

Theory. A model or framework used for testing hypotheses. All theories rest on certain *assumptions;* most are used to both predict and explain behavior.

Third-Degree Price Discrimination. Monopolist pricing strategy whereby the monopolist charges different prices to different classes of customers; often practiced by movie theaters. See also *first-degree price discrimination* and *second-degree price discrimination.*

Time Inconsistency. Key idea of *new classical economics;* used as a rationale for a *constant growth rate rule.* Policymakers have incentives to change their policies once they have been announced. As a result, people are less likely to respond to policy changes.

Time Preference. The choice between acting today or in the future. Individuals with a high rate of time preference will choose to consume today and save little for tomorrow. High interest rates can act as an incentive to save and overcome some time preference.

Time Series Data. Data that are collected over a period of time; for example, quarterly observations on GDP or per capita income. See also *cross-sectional data.*

Tit-for-Tat Strategy. A strategy for repeated games in *game theory* models. Players respond to the action of the other players in the previous period only; a mild form of retaliation. See also *trigger strategy.*

Tobin–Mundell Effect. A perverse response to falling prices that can prevent the economy from self-correcting from a recession. If price declines are anticipated, people may reduce spending until prices fall even more. The result is a leftward shift of the aggregate demand curve and a more serious recession. Key idea of *new Keynesian economics.*

Total Cost (TC). Fixed plus variable costs; includes a normal profit for the entrepreneur.

Total Factor Productivity. Measure of the output contributions of all inputs; the source of long-term real aggregate income growth and international competitiveness. See also *labor productivity.*

Total Marginal Cost. In the analysis of intertemporal resource allocation, total marginal cost is the sum of *marginal extraction cost* plus *marginal user cost.*

Total Product (TP). The entire output from a production process. The total product curve is nonlinear because of the *law of diminishing returns.* See also *average product* and *marginal product.*

Total Revenue (TR). Complete earnings from the sale of output; selling price times quantity sold; $TR = PQ$. See also *average revenue* and *marginal revenue.*

TP. See *total product.*

TR. See *total revenue.*

Trade Creation. Beneficial effect of regional trading blocs. Occurs because of lower internal tariffs. See also *trade diversion.*

Trade Diversion. Detrimental effect of regional trading blocs. Can occur if low internal tariffs give an advantage to a member nation over a low-cost nonmember nation. See also *trade creation.*

Traditional Economy. An economic system is said to be traditional if it is guided by inherited customs and folkways instead of by the market or planning. All economies have some traditional elements.

Tragedy of the Commons. Overutilization of a common property resource; people will use the resource until marginal revenue is less than the marginal cost of the last unit. Government regulations are necessary to eliminate the tragedy of the commons.

Transfer Payments. Payments from one party to another without compensation. Examples include welfare and farm subsidies. Also called unilateral transfers.

Transmission Mechanism. Term referring to the linkage between money and the real economy.

Treaty of Rome (1958). Treaty that established the European Economic Community.

Trigger Strategy. A strategy for repeated games in *game theory* models. The strongest form of punishment; if one player breaks the agreement, the other punishes forever. Compare to *tit-for-tat strategy*.

Twin Deficits. Name used by the media in the 1980s to refer to both the fiscal deficit and the trade deficit.

Tyranny of the Majority. From *public choice* theory, the idea that a simple majority rule can result in actions that help the majority at the expense of the minority. Main justification for *supermajority rule* or *unanimity rule*.

U

Unanimity Rule. Voting rule that requires 100 percent approval before passage of any legislation. Recommended by *public choice* theorists to avoid *tyranny of the majority*. See also *supermajority rule*.

Unanticipated Inflation. Inflation is unanticipated if it is not built into wage contracts, interest rates, and tax brackets. Unanticipated inflation acts as a disincentive to save. See also *anticipated inflation*.

Uncertainty. Unknown; condition of being in doubt. In contrast to *risk*, an uncertain event is one where it is impossible to estimate the expected return. The future is fundamentally uncertain because it cannot be known.

Underconsumption. Early explanation for recessions developed by Malthus and others. Underconsumption resulted from two main factors: workers were paid such low wages that they didn't have enough money to buy everything that was produced in the economy, and capitalists were so busy pursuing profits that they didn't have time to spend all of their money.

Underemployment. Working at jobs that do not require the skills of the worker; i.e.,

a Ph.D. driving a taxi. Underemployment tends to rise when *unemployment* rises.

Underground Economy. Barter and illegal activities that are unreported to avoid taxes. The underground economy may be as large as 10 percent of GDP in the United States; many economists believe that underground activities are often a response to high taxes.

Unemployment. Exists when people willing and able to work cannot find jobs. The unemployment rate is calculated as the ratio of people seeking employment to the number of people working plus the number of people seeking employment.

Unemployment Compensation. Transfer payment given to people who have lost their jobs. Unemployment compensation allows people to search for jobs that fit their skills and abilities; however, it may also prolong the period of unemployment.

Unilateral Transfers. See *transfer payments*.

Unintended Inventory Changes. Changes in business inventories that result from sales forecast errors. Overly optimistic/ forecasts result in unintended inventory accumulation; pessimistic forecasts cause inventories to decline. Unintended inventory changes typically result in changes in the level of production in the next period. A key dynamic element in the income-expenditure model.

Union Shop. A shop that requires new employees to join a union within a specified period of time. Compare *closed shop* and *open shop*.

Unit of Account. One of the four main functions of money. Prices are set in terms of monetary units; this eliminates the need to calculate an almost infinite number or price ratios. See also *medium of exchange, standard of deferred payment,* and *store of value*.

Unit Sales Tax. Tax levied as a fixed amount for each unit sold; results in a parallel upward shift of the supply curve. The selling price typically rises less than the amount of the tax. See also *ad valorem tax*.

Utility. Satisfaction derived from consuming a good or service. Consumers try to maximize utility given their budgets.

V

V. See *velocity*.

Value-Added Approach. Method of national income accounting used to avoid double counting. National income is calculated by summing the value added at each stage of production.

Value-Added Tax. Tax levied on the incremental value added at each stage of production; affects economy much like a national sales tax. Most European nations have value-added taxes.

Variable Cost (VC). Cost that changes as output changes; i.e., labor costs rise as more employees are hired. Compare *fixed costs*.

Veil of Ignorance. Thought construct of John Rawls's theory of justice. According to Rawls, if people were put behind a "veil of ignorance," they would choose to have equal opportunity.

Velocity (V). In the income velocity of money, the number of times a dollar changes hands in the course of a year. See also *quantity theory of money*.

Verdoorn's Law. Labor productivity increases as aggregate output grows. This occurs because of learning by doing, worker transference to high-productivity industries, and investment in new machinery and new technology.

Vertical Merger. Merger between firms that have a producer/supplier, producer/distributor, or similar relationship. Contrast *horizontal merger*.

Vicious Circle of Poverty. Phrase referring to the difficulty children of poverty families have in rising out of poverty; therefore, they often raise their own children in poverty.

Vita Theory. Alternative theory of the labor market that recognizes that workers are not homogeneous and should be classified by location, skill, and skill level. Labor market disequilibrium will exist if there is an excess supply of a particular skill and skill level.

Voluntary Exchange. Trade between two parties that is not mandated by government decree. Voluntary exchange results in *mutual* *benefit* and thus makes both parties better off. A key reason why economists favor free markets.

Voluntary Unemployment. Unemployment caused by workers refusing to work at the market wage. Some economists believe that most unemployment could be eradicated if workers took wage cuts. See also *involuntary unemployment.*

Voting Paradox. Implication of Arrow's *impossibility theorem* stating that no voting rule can assure consistent and reasonable outcomes; therefore, all election outcomes are suspect.

Voucher System. Alternative school funding system that would give parents the option of sending their children to public school for free or using vouchers to partially pay for private school. An advantage is that it would provide choice and competition in schools; a disadvantage is that most benefits may go to middle- and upper-class families.

W

w. See *real wage.*

W. See *nominal wage.*

Wage Contour. Alternative theory of the labor market; the intra- and interfirm array of wage differentials. Wage contours affect workers' perception of fairness and labor productivity because the labor market allocates hours, not effort. See also *key job* and *key wage.*

Wage Flexibility. See *price and wage flexibility.*

Wage Staggering. New Keynesian idea that is used to explain sticky prices and wages. Firms raise wages and prices slowly over time to prevent losing market share or profits. As a result, demand shocks can affect output as well as prices.

Wagner Act (1935). Also called the the *National Labor Relations Act.* Perhaps the most important piece of pro-labor legislation in U.S. history, this act established the National Labor Relations Board to assure that employers do not engage in unfair labor practices and gave all workers the legal right to organize.

Weak Rational Expectations. *Rational expectations* assumption combined with sticky wages and prices. See also *strong rational expectations.*

Wealth. The stock of assets held by a person or firm. Compare *income.*

Welfare Costs. Generally refer to efficiency losses. For example, anticipated inflation causes people to devote energy to cash management; this may prevent their savings from eroding, but it produces nothing for society.

"Women's Jobs." Jobs that have been traditionally held by women—nurses, teachers, etc. Some people have recommended the adoption of *comparable worth legislation* to eliminate the differential between "women's jobs" and "men's jobs."

Workfare. An alternative to welfare that attempts to reduce poverty and provide a means for self-support. Workfare recipients are required to work for their assistance checks; this eliminates work disincentives.

World Bank. International bank established after the *Bretton Woods* conference. Its primary role is to provide low-interest development loans to less-developed nations. See also *International Monetary Fund.*

World Money Supply. The stock of money of all trading nations in the world; or more practically, the stock of money in the major industrial nations. R. McKinnon and others believe that monetary policy will be effective only when it is possible to coordinate monetary policy in the United States, Japan, and the European Union.

X

X_0. Autonomous exports.

Y

Yardstick Competition. Modern alternative to the *price-cap formula.* Under this approach, the regulated company is allowed price changes comparable to price changes in similar industries. Provides an incentive for firms to find ways to lower costs and thus increase profits, but it can be difficult to find "similar" industries. See also *cost-of-service formula.*

Yield Curve. Relationship between interest rates and length to maturity. Generally upward sloping because long-term interest rates are higher than short-term rates. Frequently inverts before recessions.

Z

z. The marginal propensity to import.

Z. Total imports.

Zero Sum Game. Game in which the winner's gains exactly offset the losses of the loser.

INDEX

The letter "n" after page numbers refers to footnotes or source notes.

WIC (Women, Infants, and Children) program, 522
Wicksell, Knut, 470
Williamson, John, 990
Willig, Robert, 334n
WIN (whip inflation now) program, 682n
WIN (Work Incentive) program, 521
Winston, Clifford, 484n
Wobblies (Industrial Workers of the World), 850
Women
    on central bank boards, 738n, 740
    discrimination against, 369–370, 376–377, 693, 694
    economics careers for, 1005–1006
    labor force participation rate of, 109–110, 693n, 696
    median income of, 107–108
    poverty among, 506
    unemployment rates among, 693, 694
    and welfare, 521
Women, Infants, and Children (WIC) program, 522
"Women's" jobs, 370, 376–377
Woodruff, David, 509n
Woolf, Virginia, 590
Work
    involuntary part-time, 569, 570
    versus leisure, 162–164, 364–367
Work disincentives
    defined, 164
    and earned income tax credit, 520
    and taxes, 514

income, 133–134, 163–164, 517, 669, 808–810, 812–813
    negative income, 518
    and welfare programs, 516
Work effort
    and efficiency, 297
    and income taxes, 669
    in productivity growth, 868
    in Soviet Union, 891
Work Incentive (WIN) program, 521
Work incentives
    defined, 808
    and income distribution, 511–512
    and interest rates, 842, 843
    in Japan, 903
    and labor supply, 366
    in productivity growth, 868–869
    in Soviet Union, 891
    and taxes. See Work disincentives, and taxes
Work/leisure decision, 162–164, 364–367
Work of Nations, The (Reich), 1010
Worker training programs in Europe, 904
Worker unrest indicators, 868
Workers. See also Labor entries
    attitudes of, 869–870, 897
    discouraged, 568, 696
    laying off, 592–597. See also Unemployment entries
    productivity of. See Labor productivity entries
    stability of, in dual economy, 411, 412
Workfare, 520–522
Workforce. See Labor force entries

Works Progress Administration, 642
World Bank, 946
World monetarism, 800–801
World money supply, 800–801
World Trade Organization, 927
Worldly Philosophers, The (Heilbroner), 11n
Woronoff, Jon, 863, 901n

X

X-efficiency, 297

Y

Yang, Wenyan, 899n
Yardstick competition, 482
Yellen, Janet I., 738n, 740, 846n, 853n
Yeltsin, Boris, 316, 891
Yield curves in forecasting, 769

Z

Zaibatsus in Japan, 900, 901
Zeller, Wendy, 398n
Zero-sum games, 337
Zero Sum Society, The (Thurow), 1010
Zero Sum Solution, The (Thurow), 1010
Zimmerman, Shirley L., 504n, 505n
Zinn, Laura, 319n
Zysman, John, 976n